ENCYCLOPEDIA
OF WITCH
CRAFT

Also by Judika Illes:

Encyclopedia of 5,000 Spells

Judika Illes

ENCYCLOPEDIA
OF WITCH
CRAFT

the complete a–z for
the entire magical world

HarperOne
An Imprint of HarperCollinsPublishers

Dedication

For Clara Fisher and Irma Illes, with love
In memory of Zsuzsanna and Margit Grosz

Definition of "Witch, Witchcraft" from:

The Witch Book by Raymond Buckland, Visible Ink Press 2002
Reprinted by permission of Visible Ink Press

Funk and Wagnalls Standard Dictionary of Folklore, Mythology and Legend by Maria Leach,
Copyright 1949, 1950, 1972 by Harper & Row Publishers Inc.
Reprinted by permission of HarperCollins Publishers, Inc.

HarperOne

ENCYCLOPEDIA OF WITCHCRAFT: *The A–Z of the Entire Magical World*. Copyright © 2005 by Judika Illes. All rights reserved. Printed in the United States of America. No part of this book may be used or reproduced in any manner whatsoever without written permission except in the case of brief quotations embodied in critical articles and reviews. For information address HarperCollins Publishers, 195 Broadway, New York, NY 10007.

HarperCollins books may be purchased for educational, business, or sales promotional use. For information please e-mail the Special Markets Department at SPsales@harpercollins.com.

HarperCollins website: http://www.harpercollins.com

HarperCollins®, 👐®, and HarperOne™ are trademarks of HarperCollins Publishers.

First published in the United Kingdom in 2005 by *HarperElement*.

FIRST U.S. EDITION PRINTED IN 2014

Library of Congress Cataloging-in-Publication Data is available on request.

ISBN 978–0–06–237201–7

Printed in China by South China Printing

14 15 16 17 18   10 9 8 7 6 5 4 3 2 1

Contents

Acknowledgments

My heartfelt thanks to the staff of HarperElement who labored so hard and meticulously on the *Encyclopedia of Witchcraft*, especially Steve Fischer, Chris Ahearn, Belinda Budge, Carole Tonkinson, Katy Carrington, Simon Gerratt, Neil Dowden, Kathy Dyke, Lizzie Hutchins, Charmian Parkin, Jacqui Caulton, Nicole Linhardt, and Graham Holmes. Special thanks to Greg Brandenburgh, once again present at the conception.

I am so blessed to work with Charlotte Ridings whose thoughtful insights, scrupulous editing, *amazing* memory, wit, and gentle touch have contributed immeasurably to this book and its predecessor, the *Encyclopedia of 5,000 Spells.*

Pamela Apkarian-Russell of Castle Halloween, Angela Villalba of the Mexican Sugar Skull Company, and Jim Balent and Holly Golightly of BroadSword Comics all showed extraordinary kindness and generosity. The NonWiccan Witches Group at Yahoogroups.com generously, fearlessly, and thoughtfully shared their opinions and insights.

Eric Bobek translated from the Dutch. Mia Makabuhay opened new doors, providing insight and interpretations. Deepest gratitude to Caitlin Doyle and Mary Thompson for their efforts and hard work on behalf of this new edition. Thanks once again to Graham Holmes. Special thanks to Hannah Willow and Adele Clough for teaching an American girl to distinguish between rabbits and hares.

Too often the history of witchcraft has been written by complete outsiders or by those inherently unsympathetic to the topic. Too much of the history of witchcraft is the history of anonymous suffering: *regardless* of the actual number of those killed during the Burning Times, *regardless* of whether those killed and brutalized during that era genuinely were or weren't witches, too many lives were destroyed, too many traditions lost, ultimately because of intolerance. Intolerance toward magical practitioners still exists. Historically, the witch's voice has been suppressed: I am honored, privileged, and humbled to be able to recount some of their stories and hope I have done them justice.

Foreword

Many things have changed since I wrote the original manuscript of the *Encyclopedia of Witchcraft*. Absinthe is no longer illegal. Death midwifery has been revived. Films long lost have since been found. Thanks to the success of the Marvel movie franchise, comic books and their characters are no longer obscure; in fact, quite the opposite. Hoodoo and the Fairy Faith have experienced a renaissance.

Unfortunately, some things have not changed. In 2004, I wrote: *Although the Witchcraze eventually burned itself out in Europe, today's newspapers periodically, with some frequency, report the brutal murders of people identified as witches in India and throughout Africa. Now, at the beginning of the twenty-first century, it is still not safe, depending where you're located, to be branded a witch.*

Ten years later, this statement remains true, the only difference being that the frequency has increased and the territory has expanded. According to Amnesty International, in 2009 approximately one-thousand accused witches in Gambia were locked in detention centers. Throughout Africa, thousands of children have been abandoned on suspicion of being witches. Also in 2009, a special anti-witchcraft task force was created by the government of Saudi Arabia, leading to numerous arrests and executions. This unit provides complete confidentiality to informants, just as the Inquisition once did in Europe. In December 2013, *The Times of India* reported that, despite laws introduced to combat the phenomenon, witch hunts continue unabated, especially in rural areas. Their study indicates that many of these cases are rooted in property disputes, just as so many witch hunts were centuries ago during Europe's Burning Times.

Dear readers, I am honored and delighted to be able to share my love of witchcraft and all things witchy with you: the spells, the spirits, the revelry, knowledge, and power. I fervently hope that, in years to come, witch hunting will only be remembered as a shameful and archaic thing of the past and that witches or those suspected or accused of being witches are safe, protected, and appreciated.

Judika Illes, Beltane 2014

Introduction

Most of my clothes are black. I have a black cat. My favorite holiday is Halloween. I have perpetually unruly hair. Given the right company, I will happily chatter on about astrology, magic, herbs, and divination. I write books of magic spells. So perhaps it's not surprising that periodically I'm asked whether I'm a witch.

Invariably, my response is to say that my answer depends upon the inquirer's definition of witchcraft. Inevitably this leads to frustration (and often to anger) on the part of the inquirer: they think they've asked a very simple, straightforward question because, of course, every child, any idiot so to speak, knows the definition of "*witch.*" Their perception is that I'm being snippy and evasive (stereotypical witch behavior, incidentally) when in fact I'm just wary. I've already experienced too many unpleasant encounters with those whose definitions of witchcraft did not correspond with my own—or with each other's for that matter. I've learned that, just like beauty, what constitutes witchcraft is dependent upon the eye of its beholder.

Don't believe me? Let's look in the dictionary.

The following definition is from *Webster's Seventh New Collegiate Dictionary*:

WITCH (n ME *wicche* fr. OE *wicca*, masc. wizard and *wicce* fem. witch; akin to MHG *wicken* to bewitch, OE *wigle* divination, OHG *wih* holy—more at victim)
1a. Wizard, Sorcerer
1b. a woman practicing the black arts: SORCERESS
1c. one supposed to possess supernatural powers esp. by compact with devil or familiar
1d. or *Witcher*: Dowser
2. an ugly old woman: HAG
3. a charming or alluring woman

Oh boy, we've got some contradictions right there. Which witch does my inquirer suppose me to be? Should I take the question as a compliment or as an insult? It's probably safe to presume that most women wouldn't strongly object to the insinuation that they're charming or alluring but what if the witch this particular questioner has in mind is actually that ugly old hag or Satan's minion?

Hags, wizards, compacts with the devil: these definitions, or at least the words used to express them, demonstrate an archaic tone. In all fairness, I grabbed the first dictionary at hand. The definition quoted above comes from a well-worn 1965 edition, not *that* long ago considering the entire scope of time, but still, perhaps a newer edition might offer a more modern definition. With the wonders of modern technology and automatic updates, *Merriam-Webster's Online Dictionary* is about as up-to-date as dictionaries get, yet its definition of the word *witch* is similar to the one from 1965 with but one significant addition:

WITCH

1: one that is credited with usually malignant supernatural powers; especially: a woman practicing usually black witchcraft often with the aid of a devil or familiar: SORCERESS—compare WARLOCK
2: an ugly old woman: HAG
3: a charming or alluring girl or woman
4: a practitioner of Wicca

Now in addition to *"practicing usually black witchcraft"* the witch may also be *"a practitioner of Wicca"* although whether Wicca and black witchcraft are different or synonymous is not addressed.

Both dictionary definitions link witches with women; at least that much seems clear. Or is it? The further one searches for a definitive definition of the witch the more elusive and labyrinthine the subject becomes.

Other references suggest a narrower definition of witchcraft, albeit with greater flexibility regarding gender. According to Dr Margaret Alice Murray, the controversial scholar who wrote a long-standing definition of witchcraft for the *Encyclopedia Britannica*, the word *"witch"*

has been used since the fifteenth century almost exclusively to describe persons, either male or female, who worked magic.

Funk and Wagnalls Standard Dictionary of Folklore, Mythology and Legend further clarifies this issue of gender. That book defines a witch as

> *a person who practices sorcery; a sorcerer or sorceress; one having supernatural powers in the natural world, especially to work evil and usually by association with evil spirits or the Devil: formerly applied to both men and women but now generally restricted to women. Belief in witches exists in all lands, from earliest times to the present day.*

Although Margaret Murray's definition is neutral in tone, the others possess, to varying degrees, an air of malevolency. So perhaps I should be insulted at the suggestion that I'm *"witchy."*

You want a really virulent definition of *"witch"*? Try this one:

"Witches are the devil's whores who steal milk, raise storms, ride on goats or broomsticks, lame or maim people, torture babies in their cradles, change things into different shapes so that a human being seems to be a cow or an ox and force people into love and immorality."

Martin Luther, 1522

Perhaps not. Maybe I should be flattered. Author Raymond Buckland, a pivotal figure in the evolution of modern Wicca and an authority on magic, divination, and witchcraft, acknowledges the very same etymology quoted in the dictionaries yet proposes a positive understanding of the word "*witch*":

> *The actual meaning of the word Witch is linked to "wisdom" and is the same root as "to have wit" and "to know." It comes from the Anglo-Saxon* wicce *(f) or* wicca *(m) meaning "wise one," witches being both female and male.*

On the other hand, many would advise me to absolutely *not* engage in discussion with anyone who wishes to know whether I'm a witch, not because of any potential insult but because the whole notion of witches and witchcraft is absurd. *Their* definition of "*witch*" doesn't extend to living, breathing human beings. I can't possibly be a witch; it's not even worth discussing, because witches are made up, fictional: they don't exist outside fairy tales, stories, and legends. Obviously anyone asking me this question is simple-minded, delusional, mentally ill or just teasing. Those adhering to this definition may in fact love witchcraft very much—in its place, which is fiction. Their witches exist in realms inhabited by trolls, ogres, fire-breathing dragons, and handsome princes who miraculously arrive on white horses at the very last second. They are integral to fairy and folk tales but are not perceived as belonging to "real life" except as a story-teller's device.

Sophisticated minds, especially those of a Jungian bent, might also dispute the reality of a living, breathing, practicing witch—although their objection is based on a completely different definition of "*witch*." For them, the witch is not an individual belonging either to real life or fairy tales but is an extremely powerful archetype, a reflection of human fears and desire. That the witch-figure is universally recognized and understood all over the globe is hardly surprising because, of course, human archetypes are universal and shared by all.

In true Jungian terminology—as defined by Carl Jung, a man not averse to metaphysical study—witches are projections of the dark side of the *anima*, the female side, of human nature.

Furthermore, that archetypal witch, the one so prominently featured in Halloween iconography, *is* recognizable as a "*witch*" virtually everywhere on Earth: the concept of the solitary person (depending upon culture it is *not* always a woman) in touch with the secret powers of nature and willing to put those powers into practical use resonates around the world, although the general attitude towards this person may differ greatly.

Have we exhausted all possible ways to define "*witch*"? Oh, no. Not yet, not hardly, not by a long shot. We've just begun to explore the many ways the word is understood by different people. Yet another definition's many adherents possess no consensus regarding whether witches really exist, but they do agree that, whether witches live and breathe or are merely fantasy figures, the witch is not truly human. *This* witch is defined as a supernatural being, living in our midst, who only *appears* to be human but is actually some sort of different species, possessing hereditary superpowers and performing feats impossible for a mere mortal. This type of witch is the kind most frequently seen on television and in movies. Often they're unhappy because they'd really like to be human: think *Bell, Book and Candle* or *Bewitched*. Sometimes, like Harry Potter, they've had miserable, unhappy existences as human beings, but are delighted to discover that they are really witches and whose lives are much happier spent in an alternative witch universe. Witchcraft is not learned or achieved through compact with either devil or angel but is hereditary, a matter of genetic destiny.

If my inquirer subscribes to this notion of witchcraft, mere verbal affirmation will not be a sufficient answer for him. He will want a demonstration of my powers because these witches can *do* things other people can't, such as fly or teleport. If he's *really* convinced I'm a witch, my protestations that I lack super-powers won't be believed; he'll think I'm just being coy or secretive, snippy and evasive once again.

Yet another definition also identifies witches as a product of biological destiny, although of a very different kind. This definition's witches *are* human, albeit perhaps only partially. The Book of Genesis recounts the tale of the Watchers: the rebel angels who fell in love with human women. They had children who then had more children. Some believe witches to be among the results of this forbidden miscegenation. Angelic ancestry created special "witch blood," which, even highly diluted, bestows magic power, metaphysical interests, and a rebellious, disobedient nature. There are those who hope that someday this theory can be proven, in the same manner that one's percentage of Neanderthal DNA can now be calculated via genetic testing.

Attempts to pin down a rigid definition of witchcraft, one shared by all, are something like entering a carnival fun-house, a hall of mirrors, where asking someone to define what is a witch reveals more about that person than about either witches or witchcraft. We look at the same image but see different things. We use one word but mean different things. So many people love, loathe, and are passionately fascinated by witchcraft, yet there are so many conflicting definitions of what constitutes a witch, each of which may be deeply, sincerely, and passionately held.

Although most people are absolutely sure that they can precisely define the word "*witch*," there is profound disagreement and contradic-tion amongst their definitions. For instance, although I recognize that every one of the preceding definitions possesses adherents, *not one* of them entirely satisfies my own personal perception of witches. And yet, had I not in recent years come into contact with so many whose definitions of the word differed so much from my own, I, too, would have been absolutely sure that I understood *exactly* what everyone else would understand to be a witch.

What isn't expressed in any of the definitions given above is a perception of the witch as a figure of female empowerment: in a world of good, polite, agreeable, well-behaved, passive girls, the witch is an independent, empowered, autonomous, frequently assertive, and defiant woman, beholden to no one. (Unless, of course, you subscribe to the notion of the witch as a minion of Satan, in which case she couldn't be more beholden.) Candace Savage, author of *Witch: The Wild Ride from Wicked to Wicca*, describes the witch as embodying "*bad girl power.*" Whether one admires, detests or fears powerful women will have a lot to do with how one defines and perceives the witch.

Of course, there is another significant reason, perhaps the most crucial of all, as to why one shouldn't casually identify oneself as a witch without first understanding what that word means to others: *safety*. Does the other party perceive witches as admirable beings to emulate, or as evil beings to avoid or even exterminate? If you identify yourself as a witch, are you a role model, a kindred spirit, or the enemy?

Despite definitions linking witches to evil and malfeasance, historically it has been the witch who has been victim rather than perpetrator, most notoriously in Europe during the era known alternately as the Burning Times, the Witch-hunts or the Witch-craze. This was quite a long period, spanning roughly from the fourteenth through the eighteenth centuries and affecting to varying degrees, with very few exceptions, virtually the entire European continent. During this period attempts were made to root out all facets of witchcraft and witchery. Those accused of witchcraft were arrested; brutal torture was used to obtain confessions as well as identification of still more witches. Estimates of the numbers killed as witches during the Burning Times range from the tens of thousands to millions, depending upon one's source.

This isn't just old history incidentally, cautionary tales of long ago. Although the Witchcraze eventually burned itself out in Europe, today's newspapers periodically, with some frequency, report the brutal murders of people identified as witches in India and throughout Africa. It is still not safe, depending where you're located, to be branded a witch.

Frankly, the more one discusses witches, the more confusing the matter becomes. Perhaps if one could accurately define "*witchcraft*," defining the witch would be easier. Think again. The only thing more elusive than a single, definitive definition of the witch is one precise explanation of the craft that she practices!

Let's take another look at the dictionary. How does that 1965 edition, for instance, define witchcraft? Three possibilities are offered:

WITCHCRAFT (n)

1a. the use of sorcery or magic
1b. intercourse with the devil or with a familiar
2. an irresistible influence or fascination: ENCHANTMENT

The definition suggesting that witchcraft is "*the use of sorcery or magic*" is widely accepted. Many people, including many self-professed witches, perceive it to be an obvious fact that witchcraft is synonymous with the magical arts. Where they differ is whether that practice is perceived as natural, and worthy of respect and admiration, or whether it is perceived as sinful, evil, and unhealthy.

Have we finally reached a consensus? Is a witch, then, someone who uses sorcery or magic? Not so fast. That definition leads to even more questions. For instance, exactly *how much* magic or sorcery does one have to use to be considered a witch? At what point are you a witch? Do you need a year and a day of study, as some believe, or does one single spell or experiment with divination define you as a witch? Teenagers playing with ouija boards: are they witches? Does dabbling in witchcraft make you a witch or is some dedication to the magical arts, some mastery, required? Do your spells have to be successful? What if you stop casting spells but retain the knowledge, are you still a witch? Are you a witch if you want to cast spells, or dream about spell-casting, but, for one reason or another, don't?

Of course, all this ignores the even bigger question at the root of this definition of witchcraft. These considerations presuppose that you accept the reality of magic power: a minority position in modern Western society. Most people don't believe in magic, or at least officially say they don't. If magic and sorcery don't exist, does witchcraft?

Well, yes, maybe it could, depending once again upon your definition. Another definition harks back to the original Anglo-Saxon meaning of the word. "*Witchcraft: the craft of the wise, the knowledgeable.*" This may be understood to refer to magical workings, however Raymond Buckland proposes a definition of witchcraft not included in the dictionary: witchcraft

is an ancient Pagan religion with a belief in both male and female deities, with a reverence for nature and all life, and recognition of a need for fertility among plants, animals and humans. In western Europe Witchcraft grew into a loosely formalized religion with its own priesthood.

Witchcraft, then, is no longer sorcery or magic but religion, with the witch, the wise one, a member of its priesthood.

Buckland's definition envisions witchcraft as a specific religious path with doctrines and practices as well defined as that of any other religious faith, even if loosely formalized. Others also perceive a religious root but differ on other aspects: according to these authorities the whole concept of *"witchcraft"* is a construct created by Christians who had hostile perceptions of Pagan spirituality. Pagan deities were degraded into demons and devils, their devotees maligned as witches: one person's god transformed into another person's devil, in other words. These spiritual traditions aren't one but many: what unifies them is the Christian perception of them as evil and devilish.

Witchcraft as religion? The scary old woman in the forest doesn't wish to harm you but only wants to practice her religion in peace? That concept would surprise—and perhaps disappoint—many people. Witchcraft as religion does offer the possibility of witchcraft without magic. If you accept the definition of witchcraft as being a suppressed Pagan religion, then it exists even if magic doesn't. One can celebrate the cycles of the year, the inherent sacredness of Earth, without recourse to magic.

Witchcraft as religion, witchcraft as magical art: Margaret Murray recognized that one single word was being used to express different concepts. She distinguished between what she termed *"operative witchcraft,"* defined as the casting of spells or charms, for either good or ill and common to every nation as part of shared human heritage, and *"ritual witchcraft,"* the ancient religion of Western Europe.

Various definitions of *"witch,"* including Carl Jung's, make frequent reference to the female sex. During the Burning Times, victims were overwhelmingly female. In fact, your greatest risk factor for being accused of witchcraft and killed during the Burning Times in most of Europe (exceptions: Finland, Estonia, and Iceland) was being a woman. Some would argue that this is because witchcraft is the surviving remnant of women's ancient shamanic arts. Once sacred and valued, over the centuries these shamanic arts became denigrated, diabolized, feared, and driven underground: surviving practitioners, the *"witches,"* would be regarded with fear or respect, depending upon the perspective of the beholder.

On the other hand, maybe there is no *"witchcraft,"* only misogyny. Maybe magic and spirituality are irrelevant to my questioner; what he's really trying to tell me is that I'm not *"nice."* The word *"witch"* is often used as a pejorative for women, a slur, a derogatory insult-word. As an example, a recent letter to the editor from a reader of *People* magazine described a particularly unpopular female participant in a reality-television show as *"a real witch."* It was emphatically not meant as a compliment. The letter-writer makes no assertions whatsoever regarding this woman's spiritual beliefs or magic power; instead it was intended as a description of character. A *"witch"* is understood to be disagreeable, deceitful, immoral or amoral, strident, defiant, arrogant, unpleasant, overly assertive, *"unfeminine,"* not *"nice"* or *"lady-like,"* in short, an uppity woman.

Within the metaphysical, magical community, *"witch"* may be a badge of pride and a title of respect, although even here, that's not consistently so. Outside that community, the use of the word *"witch"* is quite often intended as an insult—very often the insult-word of choice for those who prefer not to sully their lips with that other common slur-word for women with which witch rhymes. Used to describe a spiritual devotee or a magical practitioner, *"witch"* is most often a woman but may refer to a man; used as an insult, a *"witch"* is *always* female.

So does "*witch*" refer to a specific type of woman, to specific behaviors some perceive as unattractive or dangerous in women, or does it refer to *all* women, "*every woman a witch*" as the old saying goes? "*Witch*" as slur doesn't preclude a magical understanding. Some perceive that inherent in the female sex—going right back to that first woman Eve with her too familiar snake—every woman is a witch or at least potentially so, that latent witch in the making. This perspective is expressed most explicitly—and dangerously—in *The Malleus Maleficarum*, the most influential of witch-hunter's manuals, but it didn't disappear with the witch-hunts, making frequent modern appearances, as for instance in Fritz Leiber's novel, *Conjure Wife*, whose hero, a distinguished anthropology professor, an expert (or so he thinks!) on magical practices, is shocked to discover the truth about the female sex—including his own wife.

On the other hand—and when discussing witchcraft there seems *always* to be another hand—some would agree with that old statement "*every woman a witch*" yet understand it as a positive affirmation: every woman's potential for witchcraft perceived as every woman's personal connection with the divine Feminine; every woman a magical goddess on Earth, a living conduit to the sacred, something to be encouraged, cherished and protected, not discouraged and exterminated.

So when someone asks whether you are a witch, are they trying to determine whether you are a practitioner of the magical arts, a living goddess, a danger to society, a snippy, evasive woman, a follower of a specific spiritual path, or some or all of the above?

Maybe it's none of the above. We haven't run out of definitions yet. Another definition suggests that witchcraft derives from the healing arts, once largely the domain of women. Once upon a time, women held significant, prominent roles as community healers. As medicine became an exclusively male profession, legally enforced as such, women who attempted to maintain their former roles were branded as dangerous "*witches*." Women were forbidden to study medicine, forbidden to practice medicine—leading to a medieval definition of witchcraft: "*If a woman dare to cure without having studied, she is a witch and must die.*" Essentially these witches are practicing medicine without a license, a practice that remains illegal today, although with far less dire consequences.

Of course, one can argue that healing is (or was) a spiritual practice, that healing is (or was) a magical art and that some would define those law-breaking practitioners, those "*witches*" who continued to practice in secret, as uppity, defiant, arrogant women, although others might call them heroines.

We're going in circles. With all these contradictions and ambiguity one would imagine the witch to be some obscure figure. This couldn't be further from the truth. It would be extremely difficult to find anyone, from the smallest child to the most remote villager, who doesn't know what a witch is—or at least a witch as defined by *their* definition.

This passionate debate regarding the true identity of witches only underscores how deeply the witch resonates in each person's consciousness. Because one's own individual personal definition rings so clearly and profoundly, any other definition seems inadequate, misguided or just plain wrong. Witches evoke a passionate response, whether that passion resonates as fear or as love. People emulate witches. They long for witches in times of trouble. They run from witches as sources of trouble. Witches are held up as role models or as examples of exactly what not to be. Even those who fear, hate, and despise witches can't leave them alone, as history has too often tragically proved.

If one attempts to remove the witch-figure from worldwide folklore, you promptly eliminate the vast majority of fairy and folk tales. Think about the Western canon of fairy tales: if there's no witch, then there's no *Hansel and Gretel*, no *Beauty and the Beast*, no *Snow White* or *Rapunzel*. Witchcraft doesn't only figure in entertainment dating from days of yore; the witch continually reappears, evolving with the times. Need we even say *"Harry Potter"*? If there's no witch, count the movies, books, and television shows that no longer exist. Now some might protest that these works do not reflect the reality of witchcraft, but as we've seen, there is no single, simple reality of witchcraft. Witchcraft is important precisely because it's so fluid, so mysterious, so resistant to definition, so able to touch so many different buttons in so many souls.

Is there *any* common denominator that underlies or unifies all these differing theories of witchcraft? Maybe. There is yet another theory of witchcraft. This vision understands witchcraft to be the surviving vestiges of ancient Paleolithic culture originally shared by all human societies all over Earth: witchcraft as the original religion, the cult of Earth's powers, the mother of spirituality. As people spread out, migrated and diverged, variations emerged; however witchcraft's roots remain universal. As *Funk and Wagnalls* succinctly put it: *"Belief in witches exists in all lands, from earliest times to the present day."* This primal witch is our shared human heritage, although whether one reacts to her with love, awe, fear, and/or revulsion depends upon many factors.

Modern religions/spiritual paths as well as magical practices of all kinds, including the healing arts, may be understood as descending from this primal "witchcraft'"—or as reactions against it. Those who understand witches to be not flesh-and-blood reality but stories and archetypes can also trace the descent of *their* witch from this primal witchcraft.

Another way of understanding this primal witchcraft is as a worldview, a way of seeing, looking at and understanding the universe. Looking *at* the witch reveals more about the gazer then the witch. Instead, let's try looking through that primal witch's eyes. In witchcraft's worldview, Earth is a place of mystery and wonder, full of powers of which one can avail oneself, if one only knows how. The witch is the one who *knows*. A good majority of the words used around the world, in various languages, not just Anglo-Saxon, to identify the concept of the *"witch"* involve acquisition of wisdom. A Russian euphemism for witches and sorcerers translates as *"people with knowledge."* The witch isn't just a smart person, however; what the witch knows is more than just common knowledge. The witch knows Earth's secrets.

Whether you perceive the witch as powerful or evil may depend upon whether you perceive knowledge as desirable or dangerous; whether you perceive that human knowledge is something that should be limited. The witch doesn't think so. She, or he as the case may be, wants to *know*. This may be the heart of the matter.

> Saint Patrick's Breastplate, a famous Irish prayer attributed to that snake-banishing saint, begs God's protection against *"incantations of false prophets, against the black laws of Paganism, against spells of women, smiths and druids, against all knowledge that is forbidden the human soul."*

Although in Christian myth, Original Sin, triggered by the serpent's temptation of Eve, is often understood to be sex, a close reading of the Bible reveals that what the snake really offers Eve is *knowledge*. In fact, wherever snakes and people exist together, snakes are associated with wisdom—and with witchcraft. In various subversive retellings of that biblical tale, ancient Gnostic as well as neo-Pagan, the snake is attempting to assist Eve, to be her ally, not to entrap her.

Looking through the witch's eyes may offer a very different perspective than that which many modern people are accustomed. One sees a world of power and mystery, full of secrets, delights, and dangers to be uncovered. However it is not a black-and-white world; it is not a world with rigidly distinct boundaries but a *transformative* world, a world filled with *possibility*, not *what is* but *what could be*, a blending, fluid, shifting but rhythmically consistent landscape.

> ✴ *It is no accident that the heavenly body universally associated with witchcraft is the moon, whose shape changes continually, although her rhythm is constant*
>
> ✴ *It is no accident that the element universally associated with witchcraft is water, whose tides are ruled by the moon; water appears, disappears, changes shape, shifts continually, but remains rhythmically constant*
>
> ✴ *It is no accident that the human gender most associated with witchcraft is the female one: the female body, like lunar phases and ocean tides, changes continually, often to the despair of the individual woman herself, although the rhythms also possess consistency if we let ourselves feel them.*

Although this may resonate in the souls of witches it doesn't explain the allure witches hold for so many who do not identify themselves as witches. Why the almost universal fascination with witches? Maybe because they're *fun*. Yes, there are tragedies associated with witchcraft (just look at this book's section on the Burning Times), sorry days in the history of witchcraft, but those tragedies are not witchcraft's defining factor. So many in both the general public and the magical community are attracted to witches precisely because they are fun, and in fact that's a very serious point about witchcraft.

During a particularly dour era in Europe, between the fourteenth and eighteenth centuries, witches were consistently condemned for, among other things, having fun. Among the charges typically brought against witches was that instead of attending church and being solemn and serious, they were out partying, whether with each other, the devil, with fairies or the Wild Hunt. Among the crimes associated with witchcraft was having fun at a time when fun was suspect. What exactly were those witches accused of doing at their sabbats? Feasting, dancing, making love. So-called telltale signs of witchcraft are those stereotypes that automatically brand a woman as a witch: among the most common is loud, hearty laughter—the infamous witches' cackle.

While others mortified their flesh, the witches applied sensual unguents. While others deprived themselves, the witches indulged. It's not surprising that on Halloween, a night when repressions are set free, so many don the garb of the witch. In a time of repression, witches danced secretly in the forest. They were accused of flying away from their husbands and responsibilities to consort with the devil, portrayed by the witch-hunters as a being of tremendous, unflagging sexuality. The devil, at least as portrayed in trial transcripts, *never* gets tired and *never* demands that you do your housework.

Cards on the table. According to the tenets of French postmodernist literature, it is impossible for an author to remove themselves completely from the content of their work. In other words, no author is capable of writing a completely unbiased work and thus should address their personal beliefs and biases up front. This is probably particularly true when writing about a topic like witchcraft that inspires such passionate emotion. Therefore, I feel I should come clean about my own perceptions of witchcraft.

I confess: ever since I was old enough to toddle, I've dressed up as a witch on Halloween, never as anything else, even into adulthood. Even now, I own a "Morticia" dress. Once at a masquerade party a man who knew next to nothing about me commented how comfortable I seemed in that dress, my "costume." It's true: as a child, had I been this articulate, I would have said that Halloween was the only night of the year that I *wasn't* dressing up.

I love witches and have done ever since I can remember. I craved fairy tales as a child: the witch resonated in my soul (my version of her anyway) and I identified with her instead of fearing her as I knew, even then, was the expected response.

What is it that I loved about the witch? These are hard things to articulate because, as the Jungians write, the witch-figure touches such deep primal emotions that an exploration of what attracts or repels us about witchcraft becomes an exploration of one's deepest self. Certainly the magical aspect of witchcraft attracted me; I was simultaneously attracted to astrology, divination, and occult philosophy. But I also think that, as a child raised to be very "good," "well-behaved," and "obedient" the defiant quality inherent in witches was extremely attractive. Of course, the witch can afford to be defiant (at least in folk tales) because she has the power to back up her disobedience. As a child raised amid adults possessing many psychic wounds, a child raised to have a lot of fear, the witch's lack of fear, her knowledge of secret defenses, her willingness to have fun and break rules, as well as her ability to instill fear in others resonated deeply within me, as I think it does for so many regardless of spiritual affiliation or belief in the existence of magic, although that resonance may inspire either devotion or revulsion depending upon the individual.

If you read studies of witchcraft, especially older or more academic ones, it's clear that it never occurs to many authors that were the witch-hunts to resume they too might be accused, condemned by their very interest in the topic. However, it is not the victim with whom they identify, hence the focus on the witch-hunters, judges, and general public. For a variety of reasons, I have never had any doubt as to which end of the stake I'd find myself on.

I identify with the witch, always. As a child, my least favorite fairy tales were the ones where the witch is made to appear irredeemably grotesque—*Hansel and Gretel*, for instance. Even then, I understood this as defamation and distortion and perceived that in some way it was directed toward me. Frankly the French postmodernists are right: I can no more write neutrally about witch-hunters than I could about Nazi genocide, white supremacists or serial killers. (Although, as the French postmodernists would point out, neither can anyone else, whether they realize it or not.)

That said, I also appreciate that many who perceive the witch as evil, corrupt, and devilish do so from sincerity and religious conviction, not from foolishness and superstition. Witchcraft touches enormous chords within the human soul and not all perceive these chords as positive. Denying the reactions, making fun of those who perceive the witch as dangerous, further denies the complexity of the witch.

As a child, I loved pretty much anything featuring a witch: *Wendy Witch*, *Bewitched*, Baba Yaga, Andrew Lang's fairy tales. The only entertainment featuring a witch that I didn't enjoy—positively dreaded when it appeared on TV annually—was the film version of *The Wizard of Oz*. The winged monkeys did scare me, although the wicked witch didn't. I found Margaret Hamilton much more frightening in her guise as Miss Gulch. What really terrified me, though was Dorothy's family, her aunt and uncle, who would not defy Miss Gulch and save Toto, either openly and defiantly or sneakily and surreptitiously. I found their passivity terrifying. I thought Dorothy was an idiot for returning to Kansas and the people who, although she loved them, had already demonstrated their unwillingness to protect her and her interests.

My perspective may have been unique and probably reflects my experiences as a small child raised amid an immigrant community of adult survivors of concentration camps, extermination camps, labor camps, displaced persons camps and European prison camps. I was always aware of how crucial and vital it is to have people who will protect you, defend you, hide you, take risks for you and not deny you.

Thus, unlike to many scholars and witches alike, the Burning Times are not an abstraction to me. They are very real. It is not a coincidence to me that the extermination of witches occurred in the same areas of Europe that would but a few hundred years later exterminate Jews and Gypsies, my family among them. It is not a coincidence to me that the genocide associated with World War II began in the same areas of Europe where killing witches was most virulent. According to records, there were towns in Germany left without women, just as years later there would be towns left without Jews.

Except for studies specifically devoted to them, history books rarely discuss the witch-

hunts except as a footnote or as an aberration, as an example of how superstitious and ignorant people used to be. It's treated as an embarrassment to be rushed over (and of course, honest discussion of witches and witchcraft, as we've seen, introduces all sorts of sensitive issues); focus tends to be limited to the nature of the perpetrators (why were they so crazy about killing witches?) and of the victims: were they or were they not *really* witches? More sympathetic studies tend to emphasize that they were not, as if this somehow makes the killing more tragic.

Then the witch-hunts just go away. We mourn the many dead. There is little if any focus on the impact that this era, an era that lasted for centuries in some areas, not mere years or decades, had on the survivors, including those who narrowly escaped the clutches of the witch-hunters, those whose families were tragically affected, the many who profited from the witch-hunts as well as those who watched on the sidelines. Yet I can personally guarantee you that that impact must have been tremendous, having spent my life with similar survivors.

After the witch-craze was over, presumably the survivors, bystanders, and perpetrators all went back to a normal life together, side-by-side. And the impact? Women of the Victorian age and beyond, basically until the 1960s (coinciding *coincidentally* with the resurgence of public witchcraft), are frequently criticized for their passive, submissive, obedient natures. I suspect that this passivity is a survival skill, learned in the wake of the witch-hunts. Even today the word *"witch"* used as a pejorative holds an implicit threat: behave yourself or else …

It's fun to revel with the witches, but any honest examination of the history of witchcraft and perceptions toward witches reveals a lot more than fun and games. Among the topics concealed within the history of witchcraft are secret histories of spirituality, cultural attitudes toward women and parenthood, the evolution of modern medicine and agriculture, perceptions of race, gender, ethnicity, and the untold tales of many nations. Abortion wars didn't begin with Roe vs. Wade; their long roots are entwined amidst the history of witchcraft, as are those of other modern issues like animal rights, eating disorders, ecology, environmental practices and more.

Studies of witchcraft are somewhat like that old legend about the blind men examining the elephant: one attempts to define the creature solely by its tail, another by its trunk, still another by its foot. Most studies of witchcraft focus on one definition or aspect of witchcraft—modern Wicca for instance, or the witch trials—satisfying some readers but inevitably leaving others searching for the witch that resonates in their hearts.

The *Encyclopedia of Witchcraft* contains many visions and versions of witchcraft. The word *"witch"* historically has been used to encompass wise women, priestesses, sorcerers, wizards, magicians, healers, conjurers, shamans, and powerful women, as well as archetypal figures of fantasy. I haven't deliberately excluded any

Thirteen Clues That YOU Might Be A Witch

Witches, in my book anyway, come in all shapes, sizes, colors, and genders. Identification via wardrobe is unreliable: anyone can dress up. However, there are some true, telltale clues. If any one or more of these statements applies to you, then you might be a witch—or, at least, have the option of heading down that road, should you so choose.

1. You're fascinated by the magical arts, the occult sciences, and/or the hidden powers of Earth.
2. You perceive Earth as sacred, filled with mystery, worthy of awe.
3. You feel an affinity with wild weather, wild creatures, and Earth's wild places.
4. You perceive power, positive strength, and magic, maybe even the divine, in women.
5. You can maintain a relationship with an individual of another species, such as a bird or an animal. (Whether you define your opposing gender as another species is up to you.)
6. By nature, you're nocturnal.
7. Darkness doesn't scare you—not consistently anyway.
8. You have an independent nature; you like to make your own rules and you value your privacy and autonomy.
9. You possess curiosity and a thirst for knowledge.
10. Ancient stories (myths, legends, fairy tales) enthrall you.
11. You think the universe might hold undiscovered mysteries. Not everything can be explained by science; not everything can be controlled by people.
12. The mysteries of birth and death fascinate you.
13. You consider yourself a witch, or sometimes suspect that you are one, or think you might like to be one.

Encyclopedia of Witchcraft

of them. The focus is mainly on so-called *"operative witchcraft"*—witchcraft revolving around magical practice, witchcraft as an international community of magical practitioners, dedicated to varying traditions but all ultimately descended from and rooted in that first ancient shamanic tradition. Witchcraft as religion or spiritual tradition is incorporated into this larger vision.

Witchcraft has many faces: alluringly beautiful enchantresses but also hags, crones, queens, wizards, and even saints. (No, *not* Joan of Arc, whose jailors were never able to make a witchcraft accusation stick, although they tried hard.) Within these pages you'll discover a host of famous and infamous witches, an examination of the Burning Times, and a celebration of the sacred witch, the witch worshipped as goddess.

I hope that you will find the witch who resonates in your heart in these pages, or at least discover some clues to help you track her down. Can I offer one single definition of the witch guaranteed to satisfy every reader? No. No one can. The witch refuses to be pinned down and defined by mere words, of which she is the magical master. No one owns her. She is independent, defiant, and resists narrow definition.

So *finally*, what *do* I tell that person who wants to know if I'm a witch? Frankly, way too much time has been spent over the ages worrying about whether other people are witches. It seems inevitably to lead to trouble. The more important question is: Are y*ou* a witch?

Language

One of the first things any magical practitioner must learn is to pay serious attention to the critical power of words. Because so much of the confusion and misunderstanding regarding witchcraft derives from linguistic sources, it's important, for purposes of clarity, to be sure that we're all on the same page.

Even a cursory glance through this encyclopedia's **HALL OF FAME** demonstrates that powerful magical practitioners come in both male and female varieties. However, so that I don't have to keep saying *"he or she,"* and also because of the powerful associations between witchcraft and women—and *especially* because so many of the victims of witch-hunting were and remain female—unless specific reference is made to male practitioners, I've used female pronouns to refer to witches in general. No disrespect intended toward the many wonderful male workers of magic, powerful male witches, throughout history.

For purposes of clarity and to avoid confusion, within these pages the following words are defined as follows:

* ✳ *Wicca: a narrow definition—the modern religion deriving from the pre-Christian spiritual traditions of the British Isles, what some would call Gardnerian Wicca; Margaret Murray's* "ritual witchcraft." *Spelled with a capital "W"*
* ✳ *Wicca, wicce: the Anglo-Saxon root words, masculine and feminine respectively, from which the modern words* Wicca, witchcraft, witch, wit, wise, *and* wisdom *may derive. Spelled with a lower-case "w"*
* ✳ *Wiccan: a narrow definition: one who follows the path of Wicca; a practitioner of Margaret Murray's* "ritual witchcraft." *Spelled with a capital "W"*
* ✳ *Witch: a broad definition: a practitioner of witchcraft as defined below; also someone perceived and identified as a "witch." Spelled with a lower-case "w"*
* ✳ *Witchcraft: a broad definition: the magical arts, encompassing shamanism and traditional healing; Margaret Murray's* "operative witchcraft." *Spelled with a lower-case "w"*

⊛ Elements of Witchcraft

I wasn't being entirely sarcastic about my perpetually unruly hair being grounds for suspicion of witchcraft. J.K. Rowling's depiction of Harry Potter's messy, defiant hair isn't mere description and character development but a deep clue to his identity, based on centuries of tradition.

A fairly universal stereotype of the witch portrays her with unruly hair; perhaps a visual declaration that she is a person who will not be ruled. In fact, in Jewish and Slavic folklore, among others, to describe a woman as having *"disheveled hair"* is the telltale instant giveaway that she is some kind of witch, whether human, demonic or divine.

Hair also figures prominently in the myth of Sedna, Inuit ruler of the seas. Sedna sits on the ocean floor, her chief companion her familiar dog. (Visualize something like an Alaskan malamute.) She controls the balance between the sea creatures, who wish to live, and the people ashore, who wish to live, too, and thus must hunt, catch, and eat those sea creatures. Sedna, like the sea, is volatile and moody: she manifests anger and depression by withholding the ocean's bounty.

When food becomes scarce, the only way to restore balance is to soothe, comfort, and appease Sedna. An intrepid shaman must soul-journey to Sedna's watery abode, approach her and calmly, gently, comb out the painful knots and tangles from her long, thick matted hair. Only when this is accomplished will Sedna's anger, frustration, and deadly agitation pass.

Witchcraft, shamanism (more about this soon), magic, conjuring, herbalism, "traditional" healing, "traditional" spirituality, religion: like Sedna's locks these may all be too deeply entangled to ever completely separate. However, attempts to comb them out will hopefully soothe agitation and frustration, and will definitely reveal secrets and release hidden treasures.

Let's examine the primal roots of witchcraft and the various historical elements that have shaped witchcraft and influenced perceptions of it.

The Roots of Witchcraft: The Magical World

How far back do we have to go to find that primal witch? Well, how far back *can* we get? Because however far we can go, we will discover magical practices waiting for us.

Recognition of magic power and the accompanying urge to manipulate it exists from earliest creation. Folklorist and practitioner of magic Zora Neale Hurston identified God as the original hoodoo doctor, because he spoke the world into creation with a series of magical words. That's a concept that would have been familiar to the ancient Egyptians. Among their many creation stories is one where Ptah the craftsman god, the original mason, also brings the world into existence using magic words. Other creation stories from all over Earth posit a similar magical creation. The world and all inhabitants, including people, are created via incantation, song (charm), visualization, spell-casting or image-magic: figures molded from Earth, life magically breathed into them.

Other creation stories make the magical connection very explicit. In another Egyptian creation tale, the Creator, having contemplated creation, realizes that all will not be well and that people are potentially in for a lot of grief, heartache, and trouble. Feeling remorseful, the Creator quickly invents magic power (*heka*, to the ancient Egyptians) for people to use to ward off the harsh blows of fate. Magic is thus a crucial necessity of divine origin.

Another creation myth is both explicit about primordial witchcraft and ambivalent toward it. The Zuni are an indigenous nation of the North American south-west; according to their cosmology, shortly after Earth was populated, a sacred pair, male and female, commonly identified in English translation as *"witches,"* emerge

bearing gifts. While traveling around, examining Earth, this pair, these witches, meet some young women and ask them who they are. The girls say they are Corn Maidens but they have a problem: corn doesn't exist yet.

The witches immediately remedy the situation, distributing seven varieties of corn as well as squash and melon seeds, the staple diet of the indigenous farmers of the American south-west. This gift stimulates the Corn Maidens to form a pair of lines facing the sun and begin a dance in tribute: the birth of religion and agriculture, with full approval from the witches. This is a *nice* witch story. The witches, however, also bear another gift: death. They insist death is necessary to prevent Earth from becoming overcrowded. People, however, are horrified and behold witches, responsible for life-saving sustenance *and* the introduction of death, with suspicion ever after. It is an early acknowledgement of ambivalence toward witchcraft: the power to heal and preserve may also be wielded to harm and destroy.

You don't hold any stock with mythology and ancient creation tales? That's OK; let's take a look at what the archeologists and anthropologists have to say. Plenty of physical evidence documents the primordial origins of witchcraft and magical perspective.

Physical Evidence of Magical Thought

Much of what we know of Paleolithic (Old Stone Age) and Neolithic (New Stone Age) cultures derives from excavations of funerary sites. Survivors lovingly cared for their dead compatriots, preparing them, sometimes painstakingly, sometimes at great expense, for whatever was perceived as lying ahead. They cleansed and groomed the bodies, dressed them, ornamented them with flowers, beads, seashells, and amulets. They left grave goods: whatever was needed for pleasure, nourishment, and safety in the next realm as well as for the journey there. Sometimes payment and/or guides for that journey were magically provided too, as well as guardians to protect whatever was understood to be left behind.

"Life" to these ancient people, clearly didn't just terminate with death, as if the plug being pulled, everything was over. They had a broader, magical perspective of what constitutes "life" that didn't end with the last heartbeat or breath. Instead one existence passed into another, one road leading from one realm into another. The modern phenomenon known as the *one-way street*, however, had yet to be invented. Had it been, there would be far less discussion of shamanism today and maybe none of necromancy. All roads could be accessed from both directions. Mysteries of death and what comes after remain integral to witchcraft.

The mysteries of death were not our ancestors' only concerns, however; neither are they the main focus of witchcraft. Mysteries of birth and life were equally important—the flip side of the coin.

In 1908, a small statuette depicting a round, rotund female was discovered by the archeologist Josef Szombathy near Willendorf, Austria. The most famous of countless similar statuettes she was nicknamed the "Venus of Willendorf" and is now in Vienna's natural history museum.

Her nickname was meant ironically. To modern ears, the name "Venus" epitomizes female beauty and grace, which currently almost inevitably means thin, smooth, firm, and youthful. The Willendorf Venus amused the archeologists who discovered her. Like many other statuettes of her era, she is fat and corpu-

lent, displaying rolls of flesh and large, sagging breasts. She is not a figure of humor, however, nor was she intended to be grotesque. She is very carefully crafted. Her hair is beautifully coiffed in seven concentric rings—seven apparently already recognized as a magical number. She is an object of wonder.

How long ago was the Venus of Willendorf crafted? Whose eyes should we attempt to see her through? As the technology of establishing chronology improves, her age has been revised several times, consistently backwards. She was originally thought to date from 15,000 to 10,000 BCE, but the date now suggested is from 24,000 to 22,000 BCE, quite a few years ago. Today, in this era of super-sized meals and sedentary occupations, the Venus of Willendorf's figure is far from unique. People battle to avoid her shape, resorting to surgery and all sorts of drastic diets. Imagine, however the hard-scrabble existence of some 20,000 years ago. Through the eyes of those days, the Venus of Willendorf must have been regal, queenly, self-contained, divine. She is the image of woman as the source of life, plenty, peace, fertility, and prosperity. Today's ideal woman is squeezed into as little physical space as humanly possible. Not the Venus of Willendorf. She's expansive, comfortable, and takes up as much space as she needs.

The Venus of Willendorf is but the most renowned of countless other ancient surviving images of the sacred female. Not all share her figure; some are slender. Almost uniformly, however, those parts of the human anatomy that are uniquely female (breasts, vulva, pregnant belly) are emphasized and frequently exaggerated. Whoever created these images (and they are literally countless and crafted over millennia) made sure that no one could ignore or overlook the fact that they are resolutely, profoundly *female*.

What we can see is that the people who created and venerated these images were not afraid or repulsed by large women, powerful women, or sexual women. Some of these images seem remote. Some may be wearing masks, others lack facial features altogether, yet virtually all have vaginas, accentuated so that you can't miss them. Some cradle their breasts, offering them to viewers the way a nursing mother does with her child. Some point knowingly to genitals and swollen bellies. They are simultaneously maternal and sexual. Maternity and dynamic female sexuality were obviously not mutually exclusive to the eyes that carved and beheld these figures. Many are very beautiful even by modern conventional standards, with loving, mysterious faces. What is very clear is that our ancient ancestors perceived profound power and magic in the female form. In fact, many anthropologists and scholars of religion believe that the oldest cosmologies start with a mother. In other words, the very first god was a mother.

And of course, who is more godlike than a mother? It is difficult to remember in these days of modern conveniences like infant formula, hospitals, and nannies but once upon a time survival, happiness, and health depended entirely upon one's mother. If your mother was powerful, devoted, healthy, and focused on your well-being your future seemed assured. If your mother was vulnerable, unable or unwilling to care for you for any reason, your future was tenuous indeed.

Everyone's individual mother might be their own private goddess, but actual goddesses served as mothers of communities, tribes, and nations. Many of these simultaneously wonderful and terrible goddesses survive, as for instance India's Kali and Russia's Baba Yaga. *Kali Mata* (Mother Kali) remains an actively venerated Hindu goddess; her vast complexities and contradictions celebrated and wondered upon. By contrast Baba (*Grandma*) Yaga was banished to the forest and marginalized as a witch.

> Loads of wonderful images of the divine female, together with analyses, may be found in Buffie Johnson's *Lady of the Beasts* (HarperSanFrancisco, 1988), as well as in the many works of archeologist and historian Marija Gimbutas.

The image of the sacred female doesn't stand alone. Among the several dancing figures painted in the cave of Les Trois Frères in Ariège, France is one nicknamed the *"Dancing Sorcerer."* Dating from approximately 10,000 BCE, this two-and-a-half-foot high figure is a composite of many creatures. He possesses the antlers and torso of a stag and a wolf's tail. Interpreters argue as to whether his paws and phallus belong to a bear or a lion. The beard and dancing legs definitely belong to a man and there is something essentially human about the entire dancing figure. Many speculate that what we see depicted is a costumed, masked man.

This horned figure may be a dancing shaman or sorcerer, or both. He may be the "Master of the Beasts." He may be the ancestor of one or more of the wide variety of horned male deities: Cernunos, Herne, Faunus, or Pan, or he may be an early depiction of any or all of them. He will emerge from his hidden cave to haunt us during the Witch-hunts. (See **HORNED ONE**.)

Among the most historically revealing archeological excavations is that of the city of Çatal Hüyük, located in what is now modern Turkey. The city was rebuilt many times over thousands of years. There are 12 layers on the site; the age of the oldest has not yet been reliably determined but the most recent is from *c.* 5600 BCE. The entire area was forsaken in approximately 4900 BCE for reasons yet unknown. This was a large city; at its height it's believed to have supported

6,000 people (a huge population at that time), and it contained many shrines and temples. Among unearthed artifacts are those which are immediately recognizable and meaningful to modern witches and/or goddess devotees: bull's horns all over the place, images of birthing women strategically placed near these horns, plus a statue of a massive, enthroned woman, seated between a pair of lions or leopards (animals which both once inhabited Europe). The image is recognizable as that of the Magna Mater, the Mountain Mother, the Great Goddess Kybele, who, according to one version of her sacred myth, is a deified witch. (See **DIVINE WITCH**: Baba Yaga; Kybele.)

Animism

In the late nineteenth and early twentieth centuries, Charles Darwin's then-revolutionary theory of evolution was also applied to the social sciences: so-called social Darwinism. Although this has since fallen from fashion, at one time common anthropological wisdom was firmly convinced that human civilizations preceded orderly through Darwinian stages, with magical thought as the first, earliest stage. Some cultures advanced while others stopped, arrested at that early stage. Magical perspective, the witches' viewpoint, equaled primitive thought, with "*primitive*" implying something very negative, the antithesis of "*civilization.*"

Because contemporary magical thinkers were also perceived as primitive, backwards, and foolish, even when Western and well-educated, there was no thought of consulting with them when excavating sites or examining magical images. (This is changing; archeologists at Çatal Hüyük now engage in discussion with modern goddess devotees.) Instead attempts were made to define magical thinking from an outsider's point of view, an outsider who was proud of his distance from that perspective.

The word "animism" was coined by the English anthropologist Sir Edward Tylor (2 October 1832–2 January 1917), generally acknowledged as the "father of anthropology." Tylor gave this name to what was perceived as the earliest phase of magical and religious thinking, deriving it from the Greek "*anima*" meaning "soul." According to Tylor, prehistoric humans believed that every person, creature, and object—*everything*!—had a soul, was *animated*, and hence the name *animism*. That Sir Tylor did not identify or particularly empathize with the human subjects of his research is apparent by the words he chose to describe them: "*savages*" and "*rude races.*" (No need to pick on Tylor, this was fairly standard language for anthropologists and social scientists of his time and later.)

Animism was perceived as a backward, primitive, uncivilized, unenlightened belief: the lowest rung on the ladder to civilization. That said, if one can cut through the thicket of value judgments, Tylor came very close to defining what might be understood as magical perception: the vision of the world that makes shamanism, witchcraft, and magical practices possible and desirable.

It is an ecstatic vision. In this vision, *everything* is alive, continually interacts and can potentially communicate, if it so chooses, if it can be so compelled and, most crucially, if *you* can understand. There is no such thing as an inanimate object. Because you cannot hear or understand them doesn't mean that rocks, wind, trees, and objects are not communicating or cannot communicate. The shaman can hear, the shaman can understand and, maybe most importantly, the shaman can hold up her end in a dialogue.

The shaman, sorcerer or witch (and whether at this stage of the game there is any difference is subject largely to linguistics) is the person who desires this knowledge and/or shows personal aptitude for this type of communication. This aptitude is invaluable and may have been crucial to the survival, success, and proliferation of the human species. Creation stories tend to end with that magical act of creation. What happened next? Quite often, as in that Zuni tale, the witches show up bearing life-saving knowledge and skill.

Imagine the earliest people on Earth, our most remote ancestors, encountering new plants, strange animals, and substances never before seen. They have no pre-existing scientific context.

Science posits a lengthy trial-and-error period. Conventional shamanic wisdom suggests that those animated plants, animals, and substances identified themselves and explained their gifts and dangers in a manner comprehensible to the shaman, who served as their medium to the greater human community. Animals, humans' elder siblings, taught us healing, hunting, and basic living skills. This is not ancient history. This type of shamanism still exists, although it is as endangered as the rainforests in which it is now largely centered.

Shamanic Vision

According to many traditional understandings, there is no such thing as one monolithic world; that perception displays limited vision. Instead, the mundane world we live in, the world we experience only through our five senses, is but one among various realms or planes of existence. Although there may also be others, international conventional shamanic wisdom suggests that the following realms exist:

✳ *Earth: the tangible realm of mortal people and creatures*

✳ *Spirit World: the realm of deities and spiritual beings—angels, fairies, djinn, and so forth*

✳ *Dreamland: experiences in dreams really happen; just on a different plane of existence*

✳ *Realm of the Dead: the after-life*

These realms are not linear; instead they are simultaneous, parallel. They interconnect. You can communicate across realms; you can travel between them. Spirits go back and forth effortlessly; ghosts sometimes get stuck in the wrong realm and need a shaman to point them in the right direction, maybe giving them a little shove in the process.

Boundaries exist between these different realms, although precisely how permeable those boundaries are or aren't varies and is dependent on a number of factors, not least being something as simple as time of year. (Thus the time period known as Halloween/Samhain/*El Dia de Los Muertos* is acknowledged as the time when those borders are particularly permeable, from *all* directions.) There are portals of entry between realms, if you can find them, if you can survive them, if you have the skill and knowledge to navigate your return. This is the soul-journey of the expert shaman.

Greek and Roman myths tell of Odysseus' and Aeneas' journeys to Hades. Orpheus journeys to Hades attempting to escort his beloved Eurydice back from the realm of the dead. In Norse mythology, emissaries are sent to Hel to see whether beloved, deceased Balder could be released. Because these *"journeys"* are often understood only literally, as if one ventures to the Realm of the Dead in the exact same way one travels to Disneyland, they are too frequently understood as "mythic" only in the sense of being fictional.

Philip Pullman's *His Dark Materials* trilogy of novels envisions another way of accessing portals between realms via the use of a magical tool, the subtle knife.

Shamanic functions include:

✴ *Communication with other realms, including those of the spirits and the deceased*

✴ *Soul retrieval and other forms of healing*

✴ *Location of lost or stolen items, in particular buried treasure*

Despite jokes otherwise, shamanism may be the real first profession. (As for the alternative, many sacred prostitutes simultaneously served as shamans, not passive figures but dynamic ones, especially those engaged in ritual possession, channeling their goddess.) The shaman is a unique specialist although there are cultures that support large multi-person shamanic societies—with *"support"* frequently being the key word. Typically a community provides for a shaman's needs in exchange for shamanic services, in particular in hunting/gathering or farming communities.

Sounds like a good deal? Well, yes and no. Shamanism isn't easy; the experiences can be frightening, unpleasant, and dangerous, acquiring the skills painful, and simultaneously traumatic and exhilarating: typically the pivotal initiation experience is described as a spiritual *"death."* Some part of the spiritual anatomy, although not the physical body, dies—ripped apart or butchered by spirits, frequently cooked up in a cauldron, consumed by the spirits and then finally, hopefully, if one passes all tests, put

back together (re-membered) and resurrected. The shaman is able to journey into the after-life because she has "died" and returned. She is a liminal figure who exists in several realms simultaneously.

Because it's dangerous, because there may be a lengthy apprenticeship (despite modern advertising, one *cannot* become a shaman over a weekend, although certainly skills can be taught), and because skill comes from experience, the full-fledged shaman is often an older person, and very frequently a woman for a variety of reasons. (In some areas, China or Northern Europe for instance, shamanism was exclusively a female preserve for a very long time.)

✴ *Hard as it may be to believe today, once upon a time in many places, menopausal women were regarded with a reverence verging on awe; their wise blood retained, its power increased exponentially within*

✴ *If a woman survived childbearing, she was also more likely to survive into old age, a phenomenon that may still be witnessed if you calculate the percentage of women to men in virtually every retirement community*

✴ *On the other hand, a woman with no children to provide for her old age might have a strong incentive to develop psychic skills in order to remain a valued, cared-for member of society*

Although some enlist, many more are drafted. Very frequently the individual has little choice in the matter. The spirits choose you, their call manifesting through dreams, visions (not necessarily your own), illness, bad luck, and/or animal attack. Traditionally, in some places, surviving bear, snake, or jaguar attacks was interpreted as a shamanic call.

Sometimes the shaman's refusal to heed the call affects a whole community adversely: bad luck spreads around, as in the biblical tale of Jonah. (Read it again. He didn't just accidentally end up in that whale's belly; there was a reason Jonah found himself lost in the depths of the sea.) If the cause of misfortune is traced back to her recalcitrance, the community may insist that the shaman assume her role or risk ostracism, banishment, or worse—being sacrificed to appease the spirits.

On the other hand, if shamanic aptitude or a calling is recognized, a community may nurture the individual so that she may acquire her skills, providing her with the best material goods, and sometimes tolerating bad, erratic, unpredictable behavior because a powerful, consistently effective shaman is invaluable. The shaman is responsible for the community's well-being and survival, its life and death. Why? Because shamanic services were perceived as crucial and integral to a wide variety of dangerous pursuits, including:

🕊 *Childbirth, spiritual initiations, healing, and funerals: dangerous on the spiritual plane because of intense contact with other realms. On the physical plane, risk of physical contamination (infection) frequently exists. (Shamanically-speaking, these planes and dangers are not distinct.)*

🕊 *Hunting: eating meat involves killing a fellow creature, whose spirit guardians must be appeased to avoid disaster and maintain spiritual balance*

🕊 *Agriculture: digging holes or otherwise rooting around in Earth may be understood as rape if Earth hasn't expressly granted permission, which perhaps only the shaman can hear or interpret. Harvest may be understood as murder, as in* "John Barleycorn must die." *Plants are fellow living creatures, possessing their own spirit guardians who must be propitiated and appeased to maintain spiritual balance*

There is no need to accuse or ask whether someone is a shaman. Her results speak for themselves. If things consistently aren't going well, a more successful shaman will be found. It's a little bit like traditional Chinese medicine, where a physician is desirable and respected only provided her patients remain healthy.

The shaman provides a needed service that, although fraught with spiritual danger, is expected to be reliable and dependable. The shaman must perform functions as needed: like a modern physician, she may be "*on call*" at all times, 24/7. The popular vision of shamanism as the role primitive societies invented for those with seizure disorders or the mentally unbalanced is incorrect, simplistic, and based on the notion that all other realms and spirits are "*made up*," because if they don't exist then, of course, the shaman's journey is pure fantasy or fraud.

Shamanism is performed in various ways, through soul-journeying (going to the spirits), or through ritual possession (having them come to you.) The shaman summons spirits and ghosts and sends them packing—exorcism—as individual need arises. Her work may be enhanced by music, especially drums, chants, singing, dance, or silence. The entranced shaman may appear to be asleep or in a coma or even dead. For ancient people lacking scientific context, with no hospital monitoring equipment to measure life, the shaman who appears dead *is* dead, at least temporarily. She is a figure of tremendous power.

The shaman may develop profound individual ties with animals, plants, spirits, or other allies.

The ecstatic component of shamanism cannot be emphasized enough; the very word *"ecstasy"* derives from a Greek shamanic term *"existanai"* (*"to put out of place"* as in a soul out of body). At best, shamanism is an ecstatic, transcendent, rapturous experience, for the individual shaman and also for the community whom she leads in shamanic ritual. This intense, dynamic rapture can be experienced and witnessed through ecstatic music and dance, the best sex, ritual possession, some forms of divination, or *glosso-lalia* (speaking in tongues), all of which may be components of shamanism.

Let's be honest: the shaman can make people nervous, some people anyway, past as well as present. She knows a lot of stuff that you don't. She knows stuff you don't even know that you don't know. Through soul-journeying and clair-voyance, she may know stuff about you that you would prefer not be known.

The shaman is very likely also to be a solitary person, at least some of the time. The soul-journey, the psychic journey is an intensely pri-vate, individual experience. The shaman talks with animals; the shaman talks with dead people; the shaman talks with ghosts and spirits who scare other people (and not every spirit or ghost, ancestral or otherwise, is pleasant, attrac-tive, and nice); the shaman may even be able to assume the form of animals. Imagine today, when someone is observed muttering intensely to themselves, should a cell-phone or other simi-lar modern reassurance that all is well not be immediately apparent, most of us will automati-cally give the mutterer a wide berth. Some shamans mutter all the time. (A Slavic euphe-mism for witch is *"mutterer."*) Are they talking to their spirit allies, your long-dead ex-husband, or some other shaman across town who can magi-cally hear them? Or maybe they're just nuts. (Among the many telltale stereotypes resulting in an accusation of witchcraft during the Burn-ing Times was being observed muttering to yourself, particularly if you were a ragged, old beggar-woman.)

What if the shaman yields to temptation and puts her powers to personal, selfish use? What if, in a time of conflicting interests, the shaman is bribed to favor one party or another?

New Age people are often dismayed to hear those from traditional cultures speak negatively of witchcraft and witches. Tolerance of witches is expected from these seemingly magic-toler-ant societies. Of course, cultures that incorpo-rate magical practices have also been known to burn witches. In these cases, *"witch"* is often understood to mean a shaman gone bad, a breach of a sacred trust.

The shaman doesn't have to become corrupt to stop working full-time for the community. Eventually some suffer burn-out, at least tem-porarily, too tired or psychically drained. Maybe, for one reason or another, the spirits stop talking to you. Some shamans, perhaps fol-lowing bad experiences (the primordial "bad trip"), failure, emotional exhaustion, psychic torpor, or perhaps just as directed by the spirits, might retreat into privacy—a cave, a hut in the forest, a little home on a mountain top or in a swamp—to recuperate, replenish their energy and live a private, magical life. People would know the shaman was there, this person in the wilds. She might be frightening, they might leave her alone most of the time, warn their children not to bother her—who knows what she could do if provoked?—but in a moment of desperation, when a magical solution seems like the only option, particularly when a private secret magical solution is required, one would know exactly where to go to plead or pay for assistance.

The Fruitful Earth: "The Fertility Cult"

Anthropological discussions of witchcraft's origins almost inevitably refer to witchcraft as deriving from ancient *"fertility cults."* Little if any explanation is ever given as to exactly what constitutes a fertility cult, as if the meaning of the term should be self-evident. To a very large extent this is because old-school anthropologists—and society in general—were uncomfortable with explicit discussion of sexuality until recent decades (and not always even now).

The use of the word *"cult"* is the tip-off that we are outsiders looking in. Cult is a word used by outsiders to describe a phenomenon of which they are not part and toward which they bear either ambivalence or disapproval. "Cult" in modern usage carries a negative connotation: *we* have religion, strange other people have cults. At best, "fertility cult" has an archaic ring

evoking Orientalist images of sacred prostitution. At worst, "cult" carries sinister overtones: people must be rescued from "cults," deprogrammed from the brainwashing kind.

Those old-school anthropologists may have been looking with outsiders' eyes but they weren't completely off-base or wrong: witchcraft, from its primal roots to this year's Halloween paraphernalia, demonstrates a profound preoccupation with fertility, even if it isn't always blatant or easily recognized. So, in plain English, what is this fertility cult?

Now, first, stop rolling your eyes. Since the emergence of the women's rights movement, terms like "fertility cult" and the traditional preoccupation with maternity have fallen into disrepute and for good reason. Over the centuries reverence for women's reproductive abilities evolved into a trap with women only valued for potential fertility, like some prized chicken or cow.

Although obviously reproduction is crucial to survival as a species, it may not have been the literal output, the end-results, that were worshipped but instead a perception of women's fertility power, a female equivalent of something similar to *machismo*, for which (significantly) no word or name now exists—with the exception perhaps of certain understandings of *"witch."* Machismo, perceived as intense male virility, almost a hyper-masculinity, is a perceived power potentially projected by men regardless of whether they are engaged in sexual activity at that moment. The dynamic power, the capacity, is always there, regardless of whether it's used.

Likewise, women may have been understood to radiate *fertility-power*, for lack of a better name, whether or not they were actively engaged in reproduction. This is based on the very ancient use of contraception and abortion in areas that especially venerated sexy fertility goddesses, as well as on the image of specific female spirits of fertility, like Artemis, who emphatically and deliberately lack children. The *Artemisia* family of plants, which are intimately identified with witchcraft, were gifts from Artemis to humans, hence their name. They were used in ancient times as menstrual regulators: historically they have been used for either encouraging or terminating pregnancy.

To understand the ancient obsession with fertility one has to appreciate just how *hard* life was once upon a time. We in the modern industrialized world are buffered from so much of life's harshness. Human remains suggest that the average Paleolithic lifespan was only about 33 years. Death was a constant presence. Hunger, thirst, illness, the dangers of a harsh environment—remaining alive was not a passive act. Death, hunger, sterility must be consciously, vigilantly, consistently warded off.

The emphasis on fertility and rebirth that one sees in the most ancient human artwork and spiritual artifacts is an act of sheer defiance. It expresses the determination to survive, to bear children and see them survive, and to ecstatically celebrate and experience every possible moment of joy wrenched from potentially bitter experience: this is the birth of spirituality, religion, and witchcraft.

At its most primal and ancient, the fertility cult, for lack of anything better to call it, acknowledges that life is precious, sacred, potentially full of joy but all too often tenuous and fraught with danger. Earth is a wonderful place; there is no better place to be but life is short and continually threatened. Life and the forces that renew and regenerate it are sacred but must be constantly, carefully, enhanced, empowered, and preserved. To remain alive, to bring forth new life, one cannot be passive. Life emerges from a balancing act between male and female forces. The world can be divided into complementary energies. There are forces that bring forth life

(yin/female), there are forces that stimulate that process (yang/male). There are forces that generate fertility, understood as abundance of all kinds, as well as those that serve as obstacles and challenges.

When these forces are harmoniously balanced, life is preserved and continues to be generated. Times are good and living is comparatively easy. Earth, left alone, possesses her own balancing act but if one, whether individual or community, possesses a personal agenda with specific desired results, whether personal fertility, animal husbandry, hunting or agriculture, then the balancing act becomes more precarious. Those scales must be tipped in your favor.

The Chinese yin-yang pictogram provides a visual depiction for this philosophy. Black yin and white yang are nestled beside each other; each contains a spark of the other's essence. They are not mutually exclusive forces but require each other to exist. They do not war with each other. Their opposition may be understood as the opposing force that permits a vaulted ceiling to exist. Each needs the other: there is no perception of black without white, no perception of cold without knowledge of heat. Disharmony arises when there is imbalance between forces, when one side threatens to overwhelm the other.

Earth's complementary energies may be divided into affinities or affiliations. Thus women are affiliated with darkness, the moon, water, and certain kinds of magic powers. All are connected and share an essence:

❋ *If the moon's phases are consistent and reliable, all is well.*

❋ *If a woman's phases are consistent and reliable, all is well*

❋ *If a woman's phases are inconsistent or unreliable, they can be realigned by strengthening her affinity with the moon, the tides, and other lunar forces*

Women are sacred and powerful because they can give life, because their bodies reflect the lunar phases, because the emergence of womanhood and fertility is announced by the rhythmic shedding of magical blood (and in many tribal societies, just as in many offices or wherever women live closely together, menstruation becomes synchronized and frequently linked to a specific moon phase).

Women are sacred and powerful because they can magically provide nourishment from their own body in a godlike manner. Every woman thus is potentially a goddess; it is the image of the female divine brought down to life. Sparks of sacred life exist in every woman. It is no wonder that the most ancient depictions of divinity are modeled after females, whether human, animal, bird or fish.

So is this it? The fertility cult as a celebration of women? Yes and no.

Men are magic, too. It doesn't matter how magical and godlike the female is, there's no reproduction without men, as is clear from tales of the machinations that Amazons or other female-only societies go through in order to conceive. It couldn't be clearer than in the ancient tale of Isis, Mistress of Magic, who has enough power to stop the sun in the sky but can't conceive the child she is destined to bear without sexual intercourse. Isis can resurrect her dead husband long enough for a quickie, she can charm up a working gold penis because the original went missing during the resurrection

process, but with all that power she is unable to conceive a child without sperm.

It doesn't matter how fertile Earth is, if it doesn't rain or if irrigation isn't otherwise provided, there will be no harvest. No rain, no growth. No semen, no pregnancy. You don't have to be a rocket scientist to understand these simple facts.

Anthropologists debate as to whether the ancients understood the male role in reproduction. Although their understanding was certainly not as technical or analytical as the modern understanding of pregnancy and conception, based on a slew of ancient virile storm gods (Zeus, Baal, Thor, Chango) clearly some connection was made; some appreciation that men, too, are integral to conception.

Women bear but men activate the process. Sometimes the deity manifests in the form of a dancing shamanic man (Dionysus, Shiva, Bes), while in other cases he is a primordial source of fertility, the personified irrepressible procreative urge (Ogun, Faunus, and countless horned male spirits).

Other connections were made as well. Symbols radiate power. Basic magical fertility theory involves manipulation of various powers to generate a constant, steady, healthy, beneficial flow of fertility, not just of human beings but all living interconnected beings. The ultimate symbol, sacred shorthand transcending language, is the union of human genitalia. Each depicted separately radiates a magical, protective force. Put together they magically generate life.

Images of the human genitalia rank among the oldest religious artifacts; some images still linger on the outskirts of modern religious symbolism. Often the genitals are divorced from the rest of the body and venerated independently, such as Himalayan lingams and yonis. Sometimes the whole package is left intact, as with ithyphallic statues of gods. (In plain English, this means statues depicting deities with erect, prominent, sometimes *really big* penises.) You don't have to go back thousands of years; this imagery is recent too, as in the suppressed sacred genital imagery of traditional Japanese culture or that modern tourist souvenir, the Thai penis amulet.

Sometimes the imagery is more abstract, often geometric. Triangles are utilized to demonstrate the directions of genitals: upward for the male, downward for the female. The hexagram, the six-pointed Star of David, depicts their merger, the union of fire and water. The protective image of the triangle is ubiquitous in what belly-dancers call "tribal style." You'll see it on countless Oriental rugs and Middle Eastern amulets. It is also ubiquitous in the Western witch's wardrobe: she is rarely shown without her peaked, triangular hat.

Representations of this sacred merger of male and female may be observed elsewhere:

❈ *The pestle in the mortar*

❈ *The fire in the hearth*

❈ *The stick in the broom*

❈ *The broomstick between the legs*

❈ *The sword in its scabbard*

❈ *The foot in the shoe (think about the prominence of shoes in wedding rituals)*

Other fertility motifs may be harder for the modern eye to catch, mainly because our industrialized landscape is so vastly different from those of our ancestors who, as the cliché goes, lived much closer to nature. The most prominent of these are cattle horns, which in form symboli-

cally unite male and female generative forces. The phallic connection may seem obvious, but cattle horns are also potently linked to female generative power. Think of all those ancient cow goddesses: Hathor, Isis, Io. The very continent of Europe is named in honor of Europa who rode a bull across the sea and who is virtually always depicted holding onto one horn.

What ancient eyes were exposed to that we are missing, in addition to the ubiquitous presence of cattle, was the inside of the human body, viewed without any modern scientific context. When a body was opened up (whether because of murder, funeral or sacrificial procedure, Caesarian section, curiosity, or exploration), the resemblance of the female reproductive organs, from the ovaries, moving down the fallopian tubes into the vaginal canal, to a bull's skull with horns was noted. The connection is very explicitly portrayed in relief on Çatal Hüyük shrine walls. Images of the parturient (birthing) goddess are placed above bulls' skulls with enormous horns, or sometimes over just the horns alone. The female figure's belly may be marked with a circle, emphasizing the promise that lies within. Luckily, that promise is easily, consistently, observed in the horns and so it isn't necessary to look inside the body. Instead that promise, that symbol, may be observed on every sacred cow.

You can see those horns, that promise of generative power, in the sky too, depending upon the phase of the moon. The Egyptian goddesses Hathor and Isis are often depicted as beautiful, elegant, generous women wearing horned headdresses with a full moon held between the points. The horns within the female body are connected through essence and affinity with lunar horns in the sky, the cow's horns on Earth and the horns of powerful female deities.

Horns on a male deity invariably indicate that he's virile, sexually insatiable, always ready, willing and able, hot, *horny*. Horns on amulets, like those found amongst traditional Italian amulets, protect and generate male reproductive ability. They also ward off the Evil Eye, understood as the antithesis of fertility.

The image of the sacred cow is almost as universal as witchcraft. It's found in ancient statuary and in cave paintings. The sacred cow survives in modern India but once upon a time it was also common in Egypt, Greece, Ireland, Scandinavia, the Middle East and throughout Africa, not to mention the traditional Native American veneration of the buffalo, a form of wild cattle. This veneration hides in the Bible too: not only in the obvious golden calf, believed to represent Hathor or her son, but also in Leah, the only innately fertile biblical matriarch, whose name may be translated as "wild cow." Even today describing a woman as "cow-eyed," like the goddess Hera, is still considered a great compliment in Greece, a testament to female beauty, although it doesn't translate well into English.

It isn't the cow or bull that is worshipped in such fertility cults—it's the potential and promise that they so potently represent, symbolize, and epitomize that is viewed with such veneration. The fertility cult isn't limited to awe for cattle either. Other animals were recognized as radiating profound fertility power too:

✳ *Those perceived as resembling human reproductive organs (hedgehogs, snakes, weasels)*

✳ *Those perceived as being especially prolific (cats, rabbits, frogs, toads)*

✳ *Those able to reproduce in the most challenging environments (snakes again, scorpions)*

All of these animals will be encountered when we explore those animals most associated with witchcraft (see **ANIMALS**).

The basis of the "fertility cult" is that life is beautiful and precious. Earth is wonderful, sacred; there is no better place to be. Physical expression of life is sacred and worthy of regeneration and reproduction. The physical universe—Earth and her living waters, the moon, other animals, plants, spiritual entities, the very human body—all are linked in a holistic web. In the best of all possible worlds, all powers within this universe are in balance, with good health, the potential for new life as desired, happiness, and joy as the result.

It's not all positive, however. What of those who are barren, who can't or won't conceive? What if your individual goals are different than those of the community? What if your vision for your future, for whatever reason, doesn't involve reproduction? If involuntary infertility is linked to spiritual imbalance, what is the perceived impact of the individual on the community? The barren woman may be perceived as dangerous to the common good, particularly in societies where agriculture and individual fertility are intensely linked.

Because women are linked to the moon, to Earth, seeds, and growth, and because those affinities aren't perceived as only traveling one-way, an inability or unwillingness to conceive is often understood as adversely affecting the harvest, and hence everyone's ability to eat. A woman's infertility may be contagious or emblematic of some kind of dangerous imbalance or spiritual violation.

The healer/shaman/witch who can remedy this situation, producing miracles, stimulating conception whether through herbalism, negotiation with the spirits or any other magical process is a valued, priceless member of society. She is also feared: if she can increase odds of pregnancy, she probably has the power to decrease or eliminate it too. Maybe someone's infertility is her fault.

Of course, all of this postulates that fertility, sex, human bodies, existence on the Earthly plane is a good thing, and thus worthy and desirous of being reproduced. This, however, isn't a view shared by all.

Dualism

Of course, there's more than one way of making sense of the universe. The perspective of the "fertility cult" understands the world as filled with magical forces that must be balanced and carefully manipulated to achieve harmony. If any of these forces is pushed too far in any direction, balance is shattered and disharmony reigns; growth (fertility, prosperity, abundance) stagnates or stops.

But what if you're seeing it all wrong? What if those forces cannot be balanced but are diametrically opposed? What if these forces are really in mortal combat? What if the perception that making love is sacred is only an illusion and instead what is really being made is spiritual warfare? What if the magic unification of two *complementary* forces (male/female) is impossible and the only possible outcome of a meeting between these two *opposing* forces is victory for one side, submission for the other?

What if that yin-yang symbol depicting merger and complementary coexistence of opposing forces is incorrect? Maybe the true diagram that maps existence is linear: two columns arranged like a balance sheet, or like a chessboard with opposing pieces lined up on either end.

No longer a spectrum, the material word can be organized into oppositional pairs:

Sun	Moon
Light	Dark
Male	Female
Human	Animal
Solid	Fluid
Right	Left
White	Black
High	Low
Soul	Body
Spirit	Material

Contrasting powers are no longer understood as complementary forces arranged on a spectrum; instead they are oppositional and no spectrum exists. There are no gray areas. Boundaries between oppositional forces are clear, distinct, and absolute. (In other words, no little white dot inside the black side or black dot within the white as in the yin-yang symbol.) Each opposing force is mutually exclusive of the other.

Every item on one side of the balance sheet is linked to every other item on its side and opposed to all items on the other. Each item on one side shares an essence with the others on its side; they serve the same master. The categories on this world balance sheet not only include physical observations but perceived moral, value judgments as well:

Good	Bad/Evil
Strong	Weak
Clarity	Ambiguity
Order	Chaos
Safe	Dangerous
Tame	Wild
Manifest	Hidden
Masculine	Feminine
New	Old

Because "evil" is now understood as absolutely distinct from "good," serious theological concerns arise as to the origins of evil, where it comes from, who's responsible and how it may be eradicated, once and for all. Questions as to who is leading each side, exactly who's responsible and in charge, become crucial.

Those concerns aren't relevant to the old shamanic/fertility cult perspective. It doesn't figure value judgments into the equation, at least not on an abstract basis. Any power (light, dark, masculine, feminine) may be used for good or evil; it is *how* it is used that affects the outcome. The power in itself is neutral. This is absolutely not the case with what will become known as *"dualism."*

I've given a very, very, very simplistic explanation of a profound disagreement in perspective that ultimately had earth-shattering, world-altering consequences, not least on spirituality, witchcraft, and women's roles. How we treat women, children, the Earth, our natural environment, plants, and animals all derive from this dichotomy. At its most basic, the difference between the two perspectives stems from a very simple root: some people tolerate ambiguity (and may even enjoy it) while others do not.

The dualist perspective stems from very human emotions: fear and anxiety, a desire for security, clarity and order, firm unwavering boundaries, a need to categorize. Look at the balance sheet: *order* and *clarity* emerge on the same balance side as *good, safe*, and *light. Male* is on that side, too, as is *right, high*, and *white*. That old shamanic swirling world of invisible, merging, ambiguous powers is chaotic, fluid, and messy. It finds itself on the balance sheet on the same side as *evil, dark, dangerous, wild*, and *female*.

The word *"dualism"* is derived from the Latin *duo*, "two." In English, the name also contains a pun: the two sides on that eternal chessboard *duel* with each other. That's the most basic explanation of *"dualism"* although that word, like *"witchcraft"* has come to mean many things to many people. (In psychological and literary circles, as opposed to religious and historical ones, *"dualism"* is often used to discuss philosophers like Kant, Heidegger, and Descartes.) However, at its most basic, the term is used to denote a theological system that explains the universe as the outcome of two eternally opposed and conflicting principles, such as good and evil. There is no way to balance these forces because balance implies compromise and compromise strengthens evil. Everything in the universe can be classified on one side or the other. If classification isn't clear, if something is ambiguous, then it's quite obvious on which side of the balance sheet that something belongs.

In the dualist view, soul and body are distinct, and potentially in serious conflict. There's only one of each and by nature they are out of balance. Too much attention to the finite body (and for extreme dualists, *any* attention) only places the immortal soul in danger. To strengthen the side of good, the perishable physical body must be sublimated, perhaps even mortified, and the soul nourished. Immortality is achieved through the survival and salvation of the soul.

On the other hand, sometimes these perspectives of the world are two sides of a single coin, like seeing the same glass as either half-full or half-empty. For instance, because women bring forth new humans from their own bodies and can provide nourishment from those bodies, and because parallels are clearly observed between women's bodies and such physical phenomena as lunar phases and tides, in the shamanic/fertility cult perspective, women are perceived as embodying divine energy. This is because those lunar phases, nature, the whole physical world are all understood to be sacred.

From the dualist perspective, however, those very same observations of women, their reproductive ability, their associations with the dark depths of night and ocean, all indicate women's powerful affinity with the physical world, which is affiliated with the evil side of the universal balance sheet, hence turning her into a danger zone for men's immortal souls.

It is hard to conceive of a philosophy that has had greater worldwide impact than dualism. It has infiltrated virtually every corner of Earth, its roots so deep that they permeate our very languages. Without an understanding and awareness of dualism, you cannot understand the fear, revulsion, and/or ambivalence so many feel towards witchcraft. Because of this it is worth our while to take a brief tour through the history of dualism.

Its birthplace seems to have been in Persia, in what is now modern Iran, from whence it spread through the Middle East, the Mediterranean and beyond. Dates vary as to when Zoroaster (Zarathusra) was born in Iran. Conservative Zoroastrians, members of the religion founded on his teachings, suggest 6000 BCE. Historians generally suggest sometime between 1500 and 1000 BCE. Previously, Iranian religion had been similar to that of polytheistic Mesopotamia and the Pagan Middle East. Zoroaster preached a new faith with a new perspective. Initially he was attacked for his ideas, but eventually he found favor with the king. Zoroastrianism became the state religion and remained so until the Islamic *jihad* arrived in Persia in 650 CE. Many Zoroastrians fled to India where a community remains, as they do in Iran and elsewhere.

Although these facts may be unfamiliar to most Western readers, elements of Zoroastrian religion will be familiar to many:

✺ *Zoroastrianism envisions the universe as a battleground of two gods who existed from the beginning: the Lord of Light and Righteousness and the Lord of Darkness and Evil. The universe is divided between into their armies, including people, who must choose a side. Fence-sitting is not an option; there is no gray area, no middle-ground; it is a world of distinct, clear boundaries. One must actively, consciously enlist in the army of the Lord of Light because if one does not do so then one willingly or inadvertently supports the opposition, the Lord of Darkness*

✺ *Many Zoroastrians believe in a savior born from a virgin of the lineage of Zoroaster who will raise the dead and preside over the Final Judgment*

✺ *In the inevitable final show-down, the apocalyptic battle between the forces of good and evil, the Lord of Darkness and his forces will be destroyed. The dead will be resurrected and the world purged and cleansed via a flood of molten metal, although only the wicked are scalded. The righteous will wade through this fiery flood as if through warm milk*

✺ *There is a Final Judgment of souls. Sinners are punished (but ultimately forgiven) and then humans will be immortal, free from all Earthly ills: death, disease, old age, hunger, poverty*

This vision of a world struggling between forces of good and evil permeates the philosophies and spiritual traditions known as "*Gnosticism*" as well.

In the most literal sense, *gnosis* refers to the knowledge or understanding (divine comprehension) that produces, or at least supports spiritual salvation. The Gnostic is saved when he personally sees the light and experiences epiphany.

There was never one unified Gnostic movement. Instead the term refers to a series of schools and teachers, emerging in strength during the first century CE, centered mainly in Egypt and Judea. There's wide variety, a broad spectrum of beliefs held by the various Gnostic schools, and Pagan, Jewish, and Christian schools of Gnosticism exist. Eventually, Gnostic philosophy would exert a profound influence on mainstream Christianity.

Although there are many variations on the theme, a typical Gnostic vision goes something like this: despite religious propaganda to the contrary, the material world was not created by the highest, good God. A lower being formed the physical world but in the process, true divine sparks of light were trapped. Thus Earth is corrupt, tainted, or even possibly evil, but it contains sparks of godly, divine, trapped goodness that can potentially be nurtured, saved, freed, and redeemed. Human suffering derives from entrapment in this physical world, which is governed by an Evil Being who impersonates God and usurps His power.

Some ancient Gnostic Christians perceived that the creator of the physical world—the *demi-urge* in Gnostic-speak—was the God of the Old Testament. Christ was an emissary sent to bypass the demi-urge by the true God. Once the notion of the Trinity became established, incorporating the Father, Son, and Holy Ghost, however, this perception became problematic and was considered heretical.

To put it mildly, the early centuries of the Common Era were times of tremendous spiritual seeking. Back in Persia, dualist philosophy continued to evolve. In 216 CE, a man named Mani (Manes) was born near the Tigris River in Babylonia, modern Iraq but then part of the Persian Empire. He was an intensely restless spiritual pilgrim who traveled widely, seeking enlightenment. Born a Zoroastrian, he studied and experimented with Buddhism and Gnosticism and even converted to mainstream Christianity for a while.

No religion he encountered satisfied him, although he found truths in many. He perceived all of them as incomplete, so he decided to perfect them, proclaiming himself the messiah of a new faith, Manicheism, characterized by an intense dualist vision.

Mani was a prolific artist and writer, setting down his philosophy and vision in words and drawings that were preserved for centuries. His became an important faith, not only during his lifetime but also for many centuries afterwards, with communities of adherents from Persia to Spain to China. Manicheism, at one time, was considered to be among Christianity's chief competitors. The Church perceived Manicheism as a great threat and actively campaigned against it for centuries. None of Mani's drawings, and only fragments of his writings survive because they were systematically searched out and destroyed by the Roman Catholic Church.

Mani's luck changed when a new Persian ruler devoted to Zoroastrianism came to power. As the story goes (and to be fair, the story derives from those as opposed to the Zoroastrian magi as they were to Mani) the magi perceived Mani as a competitor and pressured the king, Bahram I, to arrest and condemn him. Various reports exist of his death, every one of them horrific. Either he was crucified, or flayed alive, or beheaded with his head stuck on a pole for extended public display. His martyrdom, however, only increased his popularity among some believers and made his faith, with its martyred, possibly crucified messiah, even more of an alternative path to Christianity.

The mission of Manicheism is to entirely separate spiritual light from material darkness. If and when this process is complete, then the Kingdom of Darkness will be for ever defeated. A microcosm of this war is fought within each human being as the soul struggles to break free from the corporal body, while simultaneously the corporal body, under the dominion of the Lord of Darkness, tempts and encourages backsliding. Each person must achieve individual salvation: each human is a battlefield for the forces of Light and Darkness. You must actively choose your side. Among the keys to achieving liberation of one's spiritual essence is an unwavering, complete obedience to the Manichean Church.

Some people are closer to that goal than others. Persons on the verge of spiritual liberation were known as the Elect. The Elect led highly disciplined, ascetic lives, abstaining from sex because indulgence in sensual pleasures (sex for its own sake) strengthens the body at the expense of the soul, and because babies, the result of sex for reproduction, are but fresh prisons for entrapped sparks of light. Furthermore, those precious sparks of light may be contained within sperm, which should thus be protected from the moist, darkness of the womb.

The Elect maintained a strict vegetarian diet, with one exception. Saint Augustine (13 November 354–28 August 430), a Manichean for nine years prior to his conversion to Christianity, reports that the Elect ritually consumed a concoction of dough and semen, the theory being that the trapped sparks of light might be liberated if consumed by those on the brink of salvation themselves.

Saint Augustine, pillar of the Christian Church, was a spiritual seeker, too, who explored Pagan paths and Manicheism before devoting himself to Christianity. Although he rejected much Manicheist doctrine, Augustine also introduced the Manichean worldview into conventional Christian thought. Among those doctrines rejected by Augustine is the notion that knowledge (*gnosis*) leads to liberation. In Augustine's view, humans are too tainted by Original Sin to accomplish salvation either through knowledge or other individual effort. It can only be achieved through obedience to Christian doctrine, the shepherd guiding the flock. However, he did retain the basic Manichean distrust of matter and the material—especially regarding sex.

Augustine taught that Adam's defiance of God (as stimulated by Eve) produced a state of unbalanced desire (concupiscence) which infects every sexual act with the possible exception of completely pleasure-free, mechanical intercourse solely for the purpose of reproduction within the clear, firm boundaries of lawful Christian marriage.

Dualism permeates world culture, human culture, and *especially* Western culture. Dualist influence so pervades the vocabulary of modern spirituality that we don't consider what common words literally mean: redemption, salvation, liberation—from what? They derive from the dualist worldview:

❋ *Redemption of the soul from the prison of the body*

❋ *Salvation of the soul from its Earthly trap*

Dualists are right: dualism and the fertility cult, shamanic or otherwise, are incompatible views. From the moment of its emergence, dualism has been on an intense, inevitable collision course with those celebrating the cult of fertility, who wish to revel in Earth rather than be saved from her. At their roots, they are genuinely two oppositional viewpoints, two ways of looking at, organizing, and understanding the world. On the dualist side, there is no room for tolerance because compromise means that you've assented to the power of the Lord of Darkness. Very frequently, dualists have categorized people they've encountered who have possessed a shamanic or fertility-cultish perspective as *"witches."* The results for those thus categorized, whether in Europe, North America, Africa or elsewhere, have consistently been disastrous.

It's very tempting to see the "fertility cult" as the ancestor of witchcraft and dualism as that of its opponents; that very temptation demonstrates why dualism can be so attractive. Real life, however, is rarely that black-and-white and that would be a simplistic vision that denies the complexity of witchcraft as well as world history.

There are very few places left on Earth that have not been influenced by *both* dualism and the more ancient shamanic/fertility cult. Most cultures blend these influences to varying degrees. Dualism even pervades the world of witchcraft. In those immortal words spoken by Glinda to Dorothy in *The Wizard of Oz*, "*Are you a good witch or a bad witch?*" Many, if asked whether they are a witch, answer affirmatively but stipulate that they are a "*good*" witch, as if whatever powers they possess can *only* be used for good, not possibly for ill. (This may make the self-identified witch more comfortable with her identity, however historically, this distinction has made no difference to dualist authority, who often perceive the "good" witch as even more dangerous than her evil sister. See **WITCH-CRAZE!**)

Witchcraft, defined as magical practices, is seemingly a crucial human need. Like the Egyptians' *heka*, it emerges whenever it is necessary to attempt to ward off those harsh blows of fate or maybe whenever there's just not enough joy and fun around. Witchcraft exists *everywhere* in various forms, and is thus found in all kinds of communities possessing all sorts of philosophies. What differs is how witchcraft is perceived (by the witches as well as outsiders) and whether it operates secretly or openly.

Animals

W*here would the witch* be without her cat? That black dog over there—is that a stray roaming loose, a disguised witch on the prowl or a messenger for the goddess Hecate? And those flies buzzing around? Do they merely indicate the presence of food or do they hold deeper significance?

Around the world, specific animals are associated with witchcraft. In some societies, certain animals are so intrinsically identified with witchcraft that should you have a close association with one (or in an era of witchcraft hysteria, even a brushing acquaintance will do), there'll be no need to ask whether you're a witch; that very relationship defines you as one.

There is no creature, living, extinct, or mythical, that does not have its place among the magical powers of witchcraft. Each creature possesses its own magical powers, to be drawn upon by the human practitioner as needed. Elks, for instance, are invoked for romance; dragons to guard wealth. However, certain animals are specifically identified with witchcraft, whether as teachers of the art or because of relationships with witches. These are the animals that are featured in this section.

Animals closely identified with witchcraft are invariably also closely identified with sex, birth, death, secret wisdom, wild nature, and/or intensely radiant male or female reproductive energy, the potential for creation, and hence magic. What is a magic spell, after all, but the act of bringing *something* into existence?

The various magical partnerships between animals and people, including such concepts as *familiars*, *allies*, and *nahuals* are also discussed in this section, as is *transformation*, which incorporates the various magical and spiritual traditions that blur the boundaries between species.

While outside observers may sometimes react to the witchcraft animals with fear, witches and other magical practitioners traditionally view their animals as partners and their relationships as alliances.

Allies

In magical theory, it's generally acknowledged that every individual possesses allies in the various realms: botanical, mineral, spirit, and animal. They share your essence and possess a loyalty and affinity toward you, and so are reliable magical partners. As an example, the Egyptian goddess Isis is affiliated with myrrh, bloodstone, a constellation of compatible fellow spirits, cows, scorpions, snakes, and crocodiles. She also has alliances with certain people, whom she protects but who are expected to offer devotion in exchange.

Alliances, as their name implies, are mutual relationships: obligations exist on both sides. These are not relationships to be exploited but are instead meant to be treasured and nurtured. It is a loving, caring relationship and as such cannot be forced or compelled on either side.

Because animals are closest in nature to humans, they are our most accessible allies. Different people possess different needs: some are fairly solitary, one or two allies may be sufficient, in the same manner that one or two human friends are sufficient. Social butterflies may require a crowd. Some alliances are life-long; others are transitory, ships passing in the night. It's believed that every individual is born with at least one ally from each realm. (They accompany you through incarnations.) Other alliances may be forged as needed during a lifetime.

A familiar is an ally but an ally may not be a familiar. Familiars are generally understood to be exactly what their name implies: familiar. These are animals with whom one can share your home and daily life: ferrets, cats, dogs, hedgehogs, birds, frogs, and snakes. Extended

contact need not be difficult or dangerous. Depending upon circumstances, a wild or potentially dangerous creature *may* become your familiar but they must choose you as, for instance, wild dolphins, which will occasionally form a friendship with a specific swimmer.

The possibility of familiars, then, is relatively limited whereas the world of animal allies is vast. What if domestic animals don't fulfill your magical needs—your magic requires a komodo dragon or a snow leopard? What if your magic requires a velociraptor, a dragon, or a unicorn?

Because these animals may be accessed on a spirit level, animals with whom one could not normally have true contact become possible allies. Whether one possesses a relationship with a specific spirit-animal or with the spirit presiding *over* that animal is subject to interpretation and may vary.

How do you discover the identities of your allies? Various methods exist:

Consciously or subconsciously, their identities may already be known to you. Intense passionate emotions, whether positive or not, may indicate an existing alliance. If you just adore lynxes, well, there you are. Conversely, passionate fear may also indicate alliance. (Where there's no relationship, there tends to be little emotion, one way or the other, just neutrality.) Arachnophobes, I hate to break the news …

Animals may reveal themselves to you. Magic scoffs at the concept of coincidence. If something reoccurs with frequency, pay attention: it may be a clue.

Alliances may be revealed through dreams. Do certain animals consistently appear in your dreams? These may be your allies. Animals that feature in nightmares may also be allies; the nightmares may be due to miscommunication. A fierce wolf lies in wait for you in Dreamland, consistently appearing in your dreams. Terrified, you run or hide. The wolf, who longs to assist you or at least travel by your side, pursues, unable to communicate with you in a manner that would soothe your fears. This is a stalemate, the consistently reappearing nightmare that makes sleep something to dread and avoid. Next time some creature or person pursues you in a dream, don't run. Stop, turn, face them, and ask them what they want. (This takes practice. Don't feel bad if you can't immediately accomplish something that sounds so simple. Before going to sleep, verbally affirm your plan of action and *eventually* it *will* work.) Because it's a dream, anything can happen; you may be very pleasantly surprised.

Allies are revealed through divination. Various divination systems, usually cards, are commercially available; many are wonderful and extremely effective. The one drawback to these systems is that they tend to emphasize animals from a specific locale (Celtic or indigenous American most typically) and by nature are limited to a finite number of choices. Remember that you do not have to be limited to a set number of allies and that one can incorporate various systems as well as other methods.

Alliances are revealed through shamanic vision. Traditionally visions have been incubated through ascetic practices such as fasting or extended solitude in a place of power such as a cave or mountain, although with the exception of the extremely experienced, these practices tend to be mentored and supervised. (Always make sure that you are safe and that someone knows where you are and when to look for you.)

Alliances are identified through visualization, of which various methods exist.

Allow yourself to be surprised. Although you may be sure you know your allies' identities, hidden allies may shock you when they reveal themselves. Also, do not be disappointed. We long for alliances with dramatic, romantic, wild, powerful creatures that bolster our self-image and are dismayed when instead our allies are revealed as ants, slugs, and bees. Every creature has power and gifts to share. Ants teach important lessons about persistence; rats are the ultimate survival artists, and in many places are perceived as incredibly lucky allies to have. Negative perceptions are often cultural. If you have negative perceptions of an animal, explore and research different perspectives and you may be pleasantly surprised. Spiders and bats for instance, while ominous in some cultures are incredibly auspicious in others.

Alliances may also be earned. If you crave a relationship with a particular animal, earn it by showing yourself to be a true ally. If you long for a hippopotamus ally, for instance, work to protect the species and preserve its natural environment. Investigate and see what needs to be done. On the spiritual level, erect an altar (or build a website) in the creature's honor or devote one to its presiding spirit or affiliated deity. Should your good works draw attention, the desired ally will signal to you by using one of the previously discussed methods.

See also: Familiars, Nahual.

Baboons

Baboons are the animals most especially identified with witchcraft throughout Africa, alongside bats, hyenas, and owls. Historically and currently, baboons are understood to serve as witches' familiars or mounts, or even to be witches themselves.

Although an accident of alphabetical order, for a variety of reasons, it is fitting that an encyclopedia of witchcraft's selection of featured animals should begin with the baboon:

✸ According to Egyptian myth, a baboon deity is responsible for the invention of magic

✸ Few other animals, perhaps only cats or wolves, can demonstrate so powerfully how a creature once beheld as sacred, powerful, valuable, and god-like can become diabolized and perceived as worthless, embarrassing pests

✸ Persecution of baboons because of their perceived identification with witchcraft didn't end thousands or even hundreds of years ago, but continues today

Baboons are descended from Old World monkeys. There are two sub-species, gelada and savanna, with the savanna baboons further divided into five sub-species: Chacma; Guinea; Olive; Yellow; Hamadryas (the sacred or dog-faced baboon).

Gelada baboons are found only in Ethiopia's Simien Mountains. However, on the whole, baboons are the most successful of all Africa's monkeys and are widely distributed throughout the continent. They are also found on the Arabian Peninsula.

Their very proliferation has caused them to be exterminated as vermin, with some communities offering a bounty on their heads. (Ironically, once upon a time baboons were sacred symbols of fecundity.) Biologists who specialize in baboons frequently spend considerable time convincing local farmers not to shoot baboons on sight.

Farmers very often dislike baboons, perceiving them as competition. Baboons are smart, aggressive, organized, and clannish—and they want to feed their families. They're wary, suspicious, and may take flight easily; however don't mistake that for being intimidated. As wild territory becomes scarce, rather than retreating baboons, unlike some other animals, will enter human territory looking for food, "stealing" fruit and produce as well as the occasional baby

goat. Associations with witchcraft do not increase their popularity.

Male baboons possess something of a reputation as belligerent brawlers, although recent studies indicate that this reputation may not be entirely deserved, or at least not as across-the-board as once perceived. They certainly look fierce, possessing huge, sharp canine teeth, which they display as a sign of aggression and dominance.

When it comes to discussing or observing baboons there's little avoiding the topic of sex, as their genitalia tend to be particularly prominent. No Viagra needed here: it apparently takes very little stimulus for the male baboon to display and maintain an impressive erection—particularly noticeable with the hamadryas, whose luxuriant mane doesn't cover his private parts or his vivid red behind. Baboons greet each other via genital presentation (inspection). Hans Kummer, author of *In Quest of the Sacred Baboon*, suggests that the animal's lunar associations derive from the females' round genital swellings, which fluctuate in monthly rhythms similar to those of the moon and, by extension, women's menstrual periods.

Baboons feature prominently in Egyptian mythology. Whenever Egyptian myth discusses baboons, the reference is *always* to hamadryas, which look different from other baboons, more canine, whereas the others appear more monkey-like. Hamadryas baboons are impressive, regal creatures possessing a square, very symmetrical head, often literally a *"blockhead."* Males have a flowing leonine mane. They resemble some kind of composite creature: part dog, part lion, part human and part monkey, which must have increased their appeal to the Egyptians. (*All* types of baboons are identified with witches, however, as are mandrills, once believed to be a baboon sub-species but now shown to be genetically distinct.)

Hamadryas baboons no longer exist in Egypt due to hunting and loss of habitat. It is believed that they were never indigenous to Egypt but were imported from the mysterious land of Punt, now understood to be somewhere in the Horn of Africa. However, the Egyptians must have been aware of hamadryas baboons from an extremely early historical stage, as two of Egypt's most ancient deities share their shape: Thoth and Babi.

Lord Thoth was understood to be the supreme god Ra's right-hand man. Ra is the sun; Thoth is affiliated with the moon. Thoth rides through the skies as protective escort for Ra's solar barq. Baboons share Thoth's solar *and* lunar associations. Similar to roosters and crows, baboons greet the sun with noisy chatter.

Living hamadryas baboons were perceived to be either potentially a manifestation of Lord Thoth or a member of his retinue, hence deserving of respect. Many baboons spent their lives housed in temple complexes. Allegedly, Egyptian priests tested male baboons by placing writing implements before them. If the baboon ignored them he was revealed to be nothing more than a baboon; if however he picked one up and began scribbling, perfectly feasible for this highly intelligent, manually dexterous creature, he was then consecrated to Thoth or Ra.

Thoth's nature is calm, rational, and sharply intellectual. He is what is known as a "cool" deity: he doesn't anger easily, thinks before reacting, argues rather than attacks, and can be depended upon to defuse volatile situations. For instance, during a mythological episode when Ra's daughter Sekhmet descended to Earth in an uncontrollable murderous rampage that none of the other gods could stop, it was Thoth who was ultimately successful in disarming her and leading her back home.

Whether Thoth is capable of cooling down his fellow baboon spirit (or perhaps alter ego)

Babi is unknown. Babi (a.k.a. Baba) is a similarly primordial god, from whose name the word "baboon" derives. Lord of the Night Sky, Babi is called the Bull of the Baboons, meaning he's the pre-eminent alpha male. Essentially he is the god of testosterone.

Babi is fierce, aggressive, and belligerent; no peacemaker, he steals offerings from other spirits. He's bloodthirsty, devouring human entrails as snacks. A terrible, fearsome deity, Babi was also a role model to which one might aspire. He was very specifically a role model for the pharaoh, who prayed to possess Babi's power, ferocity, instant reactions and, not least, his virility.

Babi controls the darkness. His phallus serves as the bolt on the gates of heaven. The boat that ferries souls to the next life uses Babi's phallus as its mast. Although Babi was recognized as a destructive force, allied with the equally volatile spirit Seth, his powers were also perceived as potentially beneficial. Various magic spells exist to protect oneself from Babi; others seek his aid. (Babi had no formal cult; his relationships with people derive entirely through magical action, including spells and amulets.) Babi wards off snakes, controls darkness and turbulent waters. An alliance with him offers safety and protection—provided you can stay safe from *him*.

Different Egyptian deities were affiliated with various parts of the human anatomy for purposes of healing; Babi, no surprise, heals afflictions of the penis. He is also Master of Sex in the afterlife. (Egyptians expected to enjoy all the pleasures of Earth in the next life, too, not least a healthy sex life.) Men were buried with magic spells identifying their sexuality with Babi's, so that they'd retain their virility after death.

Perceptions change. In medieval Europe, the hamadryas baboon became a symbol of lust as deadly sin. Baboons in general came to represent evil spirits. Perhaps most insulting, baboons, whose form once graced the Lord of

Wisdom, became identified with his opposite: today if you're called a big baboon, it's an insult, no ambiguity about it.

Associations of baboons with witchcraft are not only ancient or medieval but also current. South Africa has been plagued with witch-burnings in recent years. Various incidents featuring baboons are indicative not only of cruelty but of the negative passions still inspired by witchcraft. As an example, in March 1996 a baboon was spotted in a village in Mpumalanga Province. A woman announced loudly that this baboon was a witch. A crowd then chased the baboon into a tree, from whence a man grabbed it, swinging it around violently until the baboon became dizzy and disoriented. The baboon was flung to the ground and beaten with iron bars. Gasoline was poured over it and a rubber tire was placed around the baboon, which was set aflame. The woman who first identified the baboon as a witch claimed that it was a particularly huge baboon. When the flames burned out, the corpse was discovered to be small; this perceived transformation, combined with the lengthy time the baboon took to die, was recognized by some as sufficient proof of witchcraft.

See also: **DIVINE WITCH**: Seth; Thoth; **HALL OF FAME**: Hermes Trismegistus.

Bats

Familiar features of Halloween paraphernalia and old-style horror movies, virtually everywhere that bats are found they are identified with witchcraft, perceived as witches' familiars, mounts, and alter egos.

Bats are ancient creatures, having inhabited Earth for about 50 million years. There are nearly one thousand kinds of bats, who comprise nearly one quarter of all mammal species. They are unique as they are the only mammal who can truly fly. (Others, like the flying squirrel, merely glide.)

Bats inspired awe because their form was ambiguous: they resemble some kind of cross between an animal and a bird. In ancient Asian belief, bats were understood to be the most perfect bird because they nurse their young.

Most bats are nocturnal; they famously sleep through the day, hanging upside down in huge colonies, emerging at dusk from the caves they inhabit, sometimes in huge swarms. Animals that live in caves, grottoes or underground are metaphysically perceived as being especially close to Earth, and thus privy to her deepest secrets.

Medieval Europeans associated bats with dragons—magical winged creatures that live in caves and grottos. At first glance this may seem very flattering for a little bat, however this association proved unfortunate, as by the Middle Ages, the only role European dragons were left to play was as a target for questing knights. And small bats are much easier to kill than fire-breathing dragons.

Dragons were also associated with Satan; this association rubbed off on bats and they became closely associated with devils, demons and the anti-Christ. Medieval artwork frequently depicts Satan (as well as his demons and devotees) with bat's wings; angels, on the other hand, were consistently painted with wings of white birds. That bat you see flying around might really be a demon.

Unfortunately for bats *and* women, in medieval Europe the sight of a flying bat was often interpreted as really being a transformed witch up to no good. Witches were believed to transform into bats, to ride bats like horses, and also to smear their broomsticks with bat's blood so as to achieve lift-off. In 1322, Lady Jacaume of Bayonne, France was publicly burned at the stake as a witch. The evidence? Swarms of bats had been observed flying about her house and garden.

Today the concept of a person and bat exchanging shapes automatically brings Dracula to mind, and indeed the most common bat in modern Halloween imagery is the vampire. However, the bats that thrilled and chilled medieval Europeans were not vampires but "ordinary" bats; the original major fear regarding bats is that they would become entangled in a woman's hair, not that they'd suck her blood. (With the exception of a very few blood-consuming species, bats eat either fruit or insects.)

Vampire bats are indigenous *only* to the Western Hemisphere. (The three surviving blood-consuming bat species range from Argentina to Mexico.) They are not and were *never* found in Central Europe, where the concept of an undead creature who survives by sapping the vitality of the living has existed since time immemorial. In certain areas of Central Europe and the Balkans, "*vampire*" and "*werewolf*" are synonymous; vampire is also used to indicate a "*witch*," so vampire bat may also be understood to mean "*witch bat*." (See **DICTIONARY**: Vampire.)

Vampire bats received that name from the mythic vampire, not vice versa. After blood-consuming bats were "discovered" by Europeans, the name was bestowed upon them. Bram Stoker was intrigued by the concept of blood-consuming bats and so incorporated them into his novel *Dracula*, whose success forever changed perceptions of bats *and* mythical vampires, who were traditionally not always typecast as blood-suckers; many traditional vampires preferred consuming sexual fluids or more abstract life forces, such as the aura.

The concept of a mythic blood-consuming "vampiric" spirit was, however, well-known in Central and South America prior to European contact. Bats figure prominently in Central American myth. This is the area where blood-consuming bats *do* exist and so bats also have associations with death and blood sacrifice.

Not all associations with bats are negative, not even vampire bats. The Kogi people of northern Columbia associate the vampire with human fertility. Their euphemistic expression for a girl who begins to menstruate is that she has been "bitten by the bat." According to the Kogi, the bat was the very first animal to be created, emerging directly from the Creator's body.

Some tribes in New Guinea also perceive bats as fertility symbols, perhaps because of the prominent penis of some species located there.

In China, bats are regarded as especially auspicious, their very name a pun for luck. Bat images abound in art and ornamentation.

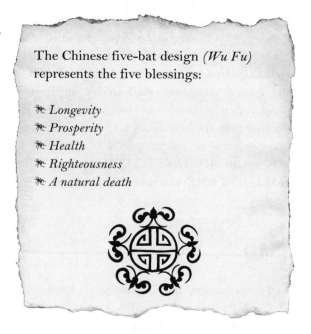

The Chinese five-bat design *(Wu Fu)* represents the five blessings:

* *Longevity*
* *Prosperity*
* *Health*
* *Righteousness*
* *A natural death*

Bats figure prominently in African folklore. In East Africa, bats are witches' mounts. In the Ivory Coast, bats represent souls of the departed, while in Madagascar, bats aren't just any old souls but those of criminals, sorcerers, and the unburied dead.

Bats have powerful associations with death and ghosts. A hoodoo charm to stop ghostly harassment displays African magical roots: Should you feel that ghost's unwanted presence, toss one single black cat hair, obtained without harming the cat, over your left shoulder saying, *"Skit, scat! Become a bat!"*

Rather than inspiring avoidance, associations of bats with witches and magic inspired the use of whole bat corpses and various anatomical parts (hearts, wings, blood) to be featured prominently in magic spells.

* *References to bat's wings in magic spells may refer to holly leaves, which may always be substituted*

* *Bat nuts (dried ling nuts), which if held from one angle resemble bats, may be substituted for bats in any spell*

* *Similar to bat's wings as code for holly leaves, "bat's blood" may have been a euphemism for another magical ingredient, perhaps a resin. At some point, people did use real bat's blood as ink. However, since the 1920s commercially marketed* Bat's Blood Ink *is scented red ink.*

Perhaps because bats were understood to be transformed witches they have also been used to protect from malevolent witchcraft. A particularly unpleasant English custom involved nailing a live bat above the doorway to ward off witches, perhaps akin to the American rancher's practice of posting dead coyotes or wolves to warn others away.

Negative associations have taken a deadly toll: many species of bats are extremely endangered due to loss of their habitat and because people have perceived them as vermin fit for extermination. This terribly upsets the balance of nature: bats are genuine fertility figures, responsible for the pollination of many plant species, particularly in the desert. Without the bat, these botanical species cannot multiply. Bats are also responsible for insect-control: one bat can gobble up as many as 600 mosquitoes in one hour.

Modern witchcraft practices suggest that maintaining a bat house (similar to a bird house) on your property will bring joy and good luck.

Bears

Bears are conspicuous in witchcraft lore by their very absence. They are the creatures so sacred that many fear to mention their name.

This is no exaggeration. Bears are the animals of shamanism par excellence. Throughout Northern lands, whether North America, Europe or Asia, bears are the original sacred animal, sponsors and symbols of shamanic healing societies. They are the teachers and perhaps originators of shamanism. Because bears dig in the Earth, they are also understood as the original root-workers and possess profound connections with healing, herbalism, and root magic. Bears are simultaneously sacred and dangerous creatures, benevolent and frightening, possessing powers too strong for the uninitiated to withstand.

Shamanic religion is often synonymous with bear religion. In traditional shamanic cultures, bears were worshipped and venerated. These bear cultures (some survive; there once were many, ranging across the entire far Northern hemisphere) typically never utter the name *"bear"*: that would be like taking the Lord's name in vain or maybe like not calling the devil so that he won't come. Euphemisms are substituted: *"Big Brother,"* *"Old Honey Thief,"* and the like. (In a similar manner, ancient Greeks never mentioned the name of the Lord of the Dead; Hades, which names his realm and Pluto, meaning *"The Rich One,"* are both euphemisms.)

Bear religion is among Earth's original religions. Fairly soon after people began worshipping mothers, they began worshipping bears, too. Sometimes both were worshipped simultaneously. Paleolithic goddess statuettes depict huge mother bears nursing petite human infants.

Bears possess a great resemblance to humans. They stand upright and eat a similar diet. In a Native American story, a boy abandoned in the woods far from other people discovers that out of all the forest animals, the only animal that he as a human can live with comfortably is the bear.

Ursus spelaeus, the cave bear, appeared on Earth approximately 300,000 years ago and was physically very similar to the modern brown (grizzly) bear. Other than slight anatomical differences, the major distinction was size: cave bears were *huge*, weighing up to one ton. They were perhaps 30 percent taller than brown bears.

Cave bears hibernated, unsurprisingly, in caves, where they also gave birth and frequently died, leaving their skeletons behind. Remains have been found throughout the European mountain chains (Alps, Ardennes, Carpathians and Urals). The bones of at least 30,000 cave bears formed a deep layer of bone in the Dragon Cave near Mixnitz, Austria.

Not all bones were left as they fell. Among the very first indications of human spiritual traditions are ancient cave bear shrines. In Alpine grottoes dating to *c.*100,000 BCE, cave bear skulls are marked with red ochre and then carefully arranged alongside ritual hearths. Bear skulls were also arranged on stone slabs and placed in wall niches. The caves contain altars, flagstone flooring, benches, and tables. This is literally Neanderthal religion; Neanderthal people built these shrines.

Bear religion didn't end with the Neanderthals; similar traditions still exist amongst some tribal peoples. Nor were these caves restricted to the Alps. In one bear cave discovered in south-western France, one crawls on hands and knees through a long, dark, narrow passage leading to a cul-de-sac where a bear's skeleton awaits.

Vestiges of the sacred nature of bears survive in place names, like Berne, Switzerland, city of the bears. Europe is now largely devoid of bears. They have lost virtually all of their former territory in North America as well. There is a mistaken belief that no bears ever existed in Africa. This is true south of the Sahara, however Atlas bears once ranged from Morocco to Libya; the last Atlas bear is believed to have been shot in 1840 in the Tetuan Mountains. Bears of one type or another are indigenous to all continents except Australia and Antarctica. (Koala bears are not true bears.) A healthy adult bear has no enemies other than people. Wherever bears survive, they are endangered because of loss of habitat and because they have been exterminated as a competitive species and for sport and museum collections. Because various parts of bears' bodies are valued in East Asian medicine, poachers place a high price on bears even though this hunting is largely illegal.

The ancient Norse associated bears with the shaman god Odin. Warriors who fought under his protection were known as *"berserkers"* (*berserk* means bear shirt). They fought naked but for bear skins, ritually channeling bear power—temporarily incorporating the bear's spirit—in order to become fierce, formidable, and virtually unbeatable, striking terror into their opponents as they went berserk. (In a sense, they become temporary were-bears; their comrades, also under Odin's protection, were wolf warriors.)

Bear-centered spirituality survives wherever traditional Northern shamanism survives, particularly among Native Americans. Native American bear doctors and bear societies still exist. Among the few explicit linkages of bears to witchcraft occurs in the Ojibwa tradition of bear-walking, a form of shape-shifting sorcery.

Bears were sacred in warmer climates, too. The Greek goddess Artemis's name may derive from her affiliation with bears, which were among her most sacred animals and sometime her alter-ego. Her young temple priestesses were known as "bears."

The few references to bears in European fairy tales usually tell of men doomed to wear the bear's form because of unhappy encounters with witches, as in *Snow White and Rose Red* and some versions of *East of the Sun, West of the Moon*. These stories read negatively *if* one assumes that transformation into a bear's shape is negative; reading between the lines, if one understands wearing the bear's skin as a secret reference to shamanism, different conclusions can be drawn.

See **DIVINE WITCH:** Artemis; Odin.

Caprimulgids: Nightjars, Nighthawks, and Frogmouths

The nocturnal birds known as nighthawks are neither hawks nor owls; instead they are *caprimulgids* or "goatsuckers." The *Caprimulgiformes* are an avian order numbering 91 species including nightjars, nighthawks, frogmouths, goatsuckers, and whippoorwills. They live in Africa, Australia, the Americas, Europe, and Asia. Alongside the better-known owls and corvids, these are the birds most intensely identified with witchcraft.

Owls are their nearest relatives and it's believed that owls and nightjars, the lay term most frequently used to encompass this avian family, share descent from a common ancestor, perhaps not more than 100 million years ago.

Long-winged, long-tailed birds with relatively big eyes, they are characterized by some unique features:

✻ *They possess enormous mouths fringed with bristles that prevent the escape of insects, their main food.*

✻ *They have proportionately short legs and weak feet, unsuitable for walking, unlike corvids which spend a lot of time hopping on the ground. Nightjars are adapted for a life spent mainly in the air.*

✻ *They have loud, distinctive voices.*

Nightjars roost motionless in trees or on the ground during day. As their plumage is dull brown or gray, they are easily camouflaged; thus their loud cry can come as a sudden surprise. They are rarely observed during the day but are more readily seen at twilight or night. Shadowy and mysterious, they have long been associated with witchcraft and magic. Nightjar blood is an ingredient in ancient Egyptian magic spells. Nightjars and their relatives are also associated with prophecy, death, and the devil.

Their gaping fringed mouths are unique for birds and lead to comparisons with the female genitalia, sometimes even with the dread *vagina dentata*. Whether these associations are perceived as affirmations of fertility power or as diabolical embarrassments depend upon the eye of the beholder.

Nightjar is an English word; in German they're known as *hexe* (witch). Considering that caprimulgids are harmless, insect-eating birds, they possess a fearsome reputation as vampires and are the subject of various superstitions. This vampiric reputation dates back at least to Aristotle. Nightjars are believed to suck blood or milk from animals—hence their family name, *"goatsuckers."* (They don't.) One theory suggests that because they forage for insects, nightjars often linger around livestock, especially goats. If for any reason an animal was bleeding, or a nanny goat's milk was dripping and a large-mouthed, eerie-voiced nightjar was discovered nearby, conclusions might be drawn and the nightjar blamed.

During the witch-hunt era, goats were identified as emblems of Satan who allegedly gave witches imps that they suckled on their own milk. With a name like "goatsucker," the inference is clear; how could these birds *not* be associated with witchcraft and the devil? As example of their reputation, a species of nightjar from Sulawesi is actually named the diabolical nightjar (*Eurostopodus diabolicus*).

Yoruba witches fly around at night in the form of nightjars, sucking victims' blood, while the Tukana Indians of South America believe that dead souls transform into nightjars and suck blood and vitality vampirically from the living.

Cats

Traditional depictions of the Roman goddess of Liberty show her holding a cup in one hand, a broken scepter in the other and with a cat lying at her feet. The cat, that animal which famously does *not* come when called, has long been an emblem of independence—and of free, independent, autonomous women.

Historically, attitudes toward cats parallel those toward women: when women have been respected and honored, their psychic gifts cherished, cats are beloved, sometimes deified; when women are perceived as dangerous and perverse, cats have been degraded and demonized. When women's knowledge is particularly respected, cats are venerated; when women's knowledge is particularly feared, cats are tortured and killed.

As we begin the twenty-first century, no other animal in the Western world is as identified with witchcraft as the domestic cat, particularly black cats. Black cats are sometimes used as shorthand to represent witches: a common Halloween image depicts a black kitten emerging from a cauldron or peaked hat. It's not even necessary to see the witch; the kitty's presence is sufficient for witchcraft to be evoked.

Cats are beautiful, intelligent creatures that cannot be ruled. It is not that they are intentionally disobedient (well, not usually; although as most cat owners will acknowledge, there *is* the occasional knowing spiteful act), but that the entire concept of obedience is foreign to their nature. Cats perform various services for humans, not least gracing us with their beauty, but only on their own terms; they can only be enticed, not commanded.

Cats epitomize the pleasure principle: sensuous creatures, they crave warmth, fine foods, soft fabrics, the choice seat in the house. Nocturnal, independent and mysterious, cats come and go as they please. Don't be fooled: although domestic creatures, cats are never entirely tame.

They have profound associations with sex. It's no coincidence that *"pussy,"* the common nickname for cats, is also a common nickname for the female genitalia. (The word *"puss"* may actually originally derive from *"lepus"* or rabbit, another animal profoundly associated with sex and witchcraft.)

Both male and female cats have reputations as lusty, prodigiously sexual creatures. Female cats will take one lover after another, as will the males. (To accuse a man of *"tom-catting around"* suggests he may not be a prime candidate for *"til death do us part."*)

Since at least the time of Aristotle, cats have been used to symbolize lasciviousness and sexual insatiability, in folklore as well as an artistic device. Cats are affiliated with sexually autonomous female deities like Bastet, Diana, Freya, Hathor, Hecate, Kybele, and Lilith.

During the Witchcraze, women were accused of being sexually insatiable. Because mortal men lacked the capacity to satisfy them, these women craved Satan's charms, taking demonic lovers who often manifested in the form of black tom cats—or at least that's the witch-hunter's version. By the eighteenth century, *"cat"* had become slang for a prostitute, hence the *"cat house."*

Cats' associations with sex have deeper implications: cats possess lush fertility. *Felis*, the scientific name for cats, derives its origin from the Latin root *fe, "to bear young."* Other words deriving from this source are *feline, fecund* and *fetus.* Cats, like frogs, are often considered weather harbingers, announcing the start of the fertilizing rain. Jewelry in the form of images of a mother cat surrounded by a large litter of kittens was a popular fertility charm in ancient Egypt.

The earliest indication of intimate relations between people and cats derives from a recently discovered (2004) burial in Cyprus, dating back approximately 9500 years ago. A carefully buried cat was discovered inches from a human burial, which also contained jewelry, polished stones, shells, and tools. The cat's bones were arranged to parallel that of the human and displayed no signs of butchering. It appears to have been a beloved companion animal. Cats are not native to Cyprus and so it is believed to have been imported (although cats are notorious stowaways on ships).

General wisdom suggests that cats were first domesticated in Egypt (although Libya or Nubia are alternative suggestions), where domestic cats were bred at least four thousand years ago. (However, because of that recently discovered burial, dates are being retabulated backwards.) Ancient Egypt certainly provides the first written records of cats, the clearest evidence of domestic cats and the closest identification with deification of cats.

As Egyptian culture became increasingly agrarian, stored grain attracted mice and other vermin, who, in their turn, attracted cats, who very quickly demonstrated their usefulness to people. Cats became sacred guardians of the grain. (See **ERGOT**.)

The most famous sacred Egyptian cat is Bastet, whose titles included *Mistress of the Oracle* and *Great Conjuress of the Casket.* She is depicted as a cat, often bejeweled, or as a woman with a cat's head, sometimes surrounded by kittens. Bastet has dominion over sex, fertility, marriage, magic, music, childbirth, prosperity, joy, dance, and healing—in short the pleasures of life. She provides humans with a range of protections: against infertility, the dangers of childbirth, evil spirits, illness and bodily injuries, especially those caused by venomous creatures. A tomb inscription says Bastet bestows *"life, prosperity and health every day and long life and beautiful old age."*

Bastet offers special protection to women and children and serves as matron of magicians and healers. Her cult originated in the swamps of the Nile Delta. The earliest known portrait of Bastet dates to *c.* 3000 BCE. She was a pervasive figure in Egypt from about 2000 BCE, and by about 950 BCE, her cult was found throughout Egypt; she was the most popular female deity in the kingdom. Worship of Bastet reached its zenith during the reign of Osorkon II (874–853) when a major temple was erected at her cult city Bubastis. Devotion to Bastet officially survived until 30 BCE and the Roman conquest.

Bastet's annual festival in Bubastis was Egypt's most popular festival. An ancestor of today's Mardi Gras, the festival was renowned for its parties, revelry, and drunkenness. Herodotus, the Greek traveler and historian writing in the fifth century BCE, claimed that more wine was consumed in Egypt during this festival than during the entire remainder of the year. Although many details have been lost, Bastet's festival celebrated female sexuality and generative power. Boats sailed up the Nile headed for Bubastis. As a barge approached towns and settlements on its way to the festival, it would halt and the mainly female celebrants on board would loudly hail the local women congregating on the riverbanks. They would shout sexual obscenities to each other, dance wildly, and perform *ana-suromai*, the ritual act of lifting up the skirts to expose the vulva, associated with laughter, healing, and defiance of grief.

Bastet, daughter of the sun, is a solar spirit, associated with the life-giving warmth of the sun. (Her sister Sekhmet, a lioness, represents the sun's scorching, destructive potential.) Bastet possesses lunar associations as well. She is the mother of the moon. Her son Khonsu was reputedly able to impregnate women with his moonbeams. (That belief survives in the superstition against single women sleeping exposed to moonlight.) The Greek biographer Plutarch, writing in the first century CE, suggested that one of the reasons Egyptians worshipped cats is that cats' nocturnal habits reveal powerful lunar affiliations. Cats' eyes also appear to grow in size and luminosity in harmony with the moon's waxing.

The ancient Egyptian cat was not exclusively a sacred temple animal but was also a family pet or domestic animal, a bit of holiness in one's own home. Although Egypt had many sacred animals, no others lived so intimately with so many people. (Compare and contrast other sacred creatures, like baboons or crocodiles, which by necessity were kept at a distance.) Familiarity didn't breed contempt, however: even a house cat maintained its mysterious, sacred nature. Herodotus reports that anyone convicted of intentionally killing a sacred animal was sentenced to death, and to varying extents *all* cats were sacred. Four hundred years later, the Sicilian historian Diodorus Siculus (born *c.* 100 BCE) witnessed an incident where a Roman official accidentally killed a cat and was promptly lynched by a mob. Although the fact that he was a Roman official suggests that the cat may have been the last straw in a deadly dynamic, Diodorus suggests that the situation wasn't uncommon and that most such deaths occurred as spontaneous lynchings by enraged mobs before the person could be legally tried and judged. When a pet cat died, it was customary for the human family with whom it lived to shave their eyebrows as a sign of mourning and respect.

Wide distribution of the domestic cat occurred only after the Egyptian kingdom lost its independence to Rome. Even then, for centuries, domestic cats remained rare throughout Europe. (Ferrets were used to eliminate vermin prior to introduction of cats.) Not until the fourth century of the Common Era were domestic cats widely distributed in Italy. As domestic cats gradually dispersed, their identification with the mysteries of ancient Egypt traveled with them, leading to associations with magic, witchcraft, and women's sexual, lunar and reproductive secrets.

Although domestic cats were rare in Europe, uncommon in the British Isles, for instance, even into the tenth century, wild forest cats were common. Although wild cats can cross-breed with domestic cats, they are larger and typically possess different natures: fierce, wary, and solitary rather than sweet and cuddly. Vestiges of wild, fierce Celtic cat goddesses may survive in the witch-hags who frequently transform into cats, as for instance, Black Annis.

Cats have potent associations with yet another powerful female deity—Freya—Norse Lady of love, romance, sex, fertility, childbirth, shamanism, enchantments, witchcraft, and death. An oracular, sexually autonomous spirit, Freya typically manifests as a breathtakingly beautiful, golden woman: her chariot is drawn by her familiars, two huge gray cats named Bee Gold (honey) and Tree Gold (amber), who embody Freya's twin qualities of ferociousness and fecundity. Cats are Freya's sacred animals; a traditional method of petitioning or pleasing the goddess was to offer pans of milk to cats, an old Norse country custom that survived. To be kind to a cat is to entreat Freya's blessings and to remain in her good graces.

Eventually cats would be tortured and killed specifically because of their associations with Freya. After the introduction of Christianity, Freya's devotees did not abandon her easily or willingly, and she became among the most demonized of spirits, coming to embody the stereotype of the seductive witch. Cats shared Freya's demonization. (See **DIVINE WITCH**: Freya.)

By the Middle Ages, cats had become so identified with witchcraft that in 1484, Pope Innocent VIII issued a decree, understood by many scholars as the official start of the Witchcraze, denouncing cats and their owners. Any cat in the company of a woman could be assumed to be a familiar. If one can assume the cat is a familiar, what might one assume about the woman?

Pope Innocent commanded that when a witch was burned, her cats were to be burned with her.

He decreed that all European cat-worshippers be burned as witches. (This was in response to a strong revival of devotion to Freya in fifteenth-century Germany.) He authorized the killing of cats even without an accompanying witch. A vicious cycle emerged: the destruction of European cats is believed to have encouraged the proliferation of rodents, which in turn encouraged the spread of deadly disease, blamed on witchcraft and heresy, which in turn led to fear, panic, and more killing of cats.

Folklorist Jacob Grimm, of the Brothers Grimm, suggests in his book *Teutonic Mythology* that the sinister aspect of the cat derives from Freya's dual role, not only as a spirit of love and fertility but also as a death-spirit. As leader of the Valkyries, female warrior spirits who helped select the dead, Freya had dibs on half the fallen on a battlefield, the other half belonging to Odin.

The degradation and destruction of cats parallels that of women and their increasing loss of autonomy. Women, however, might engage in subterfuge or adjust their personalities and lifestyles in attempts to be beyond suspicion; the inherent nature and habits of cats betrayed them. Their nocturnal lives, their desire to prowl free at night, "singing" at the moon, their passionate sexuality, all now doomed them to associations with the devil and/or witchcraft. Instead of worship and respect, cats were feared and avoided at best.

According to the witch-hunter's perceptions of witchcraft, cats played various roles:

※ *Cats were believed to be common familiars. Should a woman display a close relationship with a cat, this was considered a telltale sign of witchcraft and perhaps sufficient evidence to warrant death for woman and cat.*

※ *Cats provided witches with a mode of magical transportation. Reminiscent of Freya's air-borne cat-drawn chariot, witches rode to sabbats on cats' backs or traveled about in feline form. Shapeshifting witches were believed able to assume the form of cats.*

※ *Sometimes the cats* are *the witches. Does the woman transform into a cat or vice versa? Cats are traditionally Hungarian witches' alter egos, their doubles. Is the witch a cat or is the cat a witch? In this hall of mirrors, who can tell? In one Hungarian witch-trial transcript, the prosecution's witness recounts how upon encountering two cats at night, whom he perceived as nocturnal apparitions, he began to talk with them, informing them that he wasn't afraid of them because* "Lord Jesus Christ is with us." *The cats, he claimed, responded with peals of human laughter.*

In Slavic areas, cats may be vampires; hence the still-existing superstition that cats will suck a sleeping baby's life out. In North African communities, cats may be *djinn* in disguise and so one is cautioned against ever harming a cat for fear of spiritual retribution.

Witch-hunter Jean Bodin insisted that all cats are witches in disguise. Nicholas Remy, another famed witch-hunter, argued that they were demons instead. Hungarian witch-lore suggests that cats do indeed become witches, but only between the ages of 7 and 12, and even this may be prevented. The Hungarians, a grain-producing people, who perhaps didn't relish leaving their barns without feline protection, determined that shaving a cross into the cat's fur was sufficient to rescue it from this fate. According to Somerset folklore, cats born in May were especially inclined to be witches in disguise and hence were frequently killed.

Stories of women transforming into cats are common witchcraft tales. A husband from Scotland's Isle of Skye claimed to be perplexed by his wife's secretive nightly excursions. One night he followed her and witnessed her transformation into a black cat. The wife invoked Satan's name and sailed out to sea in a sieve with seven other cats. The husband invoked the Trinity and the sieve promptly overturned, drowning all the witches—or at least so said the husband, the only witness to his wife's disappearance. One wonders how many other women's disappearances were accounted for by those who swore that when last seen the women had transformed into cats or bats.

In a French variation on this theme, a woman was cooking an omelet when a black cat sauntered into her home and settled itself by her hearth. Apparently unfazed by her visitor, the woman did nothing but continue to cook. The cat stared at her for a few minutes then announced, *"It's done. Flip it over."*

In a traditional fairy tale, when a talking animal tells you something, it's worth paying attention. However, in this story, the woman, seemingly unsurprised, only claimed to be outraged at being bossed around by a cat. She flung the hot pan at the cat, hitting it. The cat fled. The next morning, a malicious, "catty" neighbor was observed with a great red burn on her cheek.

There are *millions* of these stories, which are not limited to European origin. In Japanese folklore, cats transform into women who are frequently identified as witches. (Japan has a witch-tradition but no history of European-style witch-hunts.) Sometimes these cats are saintly, if sexual. In the famous legend of Okesa the dancer, a devoted cat saves a human family from poverty by transforming into a prostitute and earning enough to support them.

Not all these legends are stories, at least not in the fictional sense; few of the documented tales have happy endings.

✳ *In 1586, Anna Winkelz Ipfel was burned as a witch in Bergtheim, Germany for allegedly disguising herself as a black cat.*

✳ *In 1607, Bartie Paterson was hanged as a witch in England. According to witnesses, Bartie transformed into a cat and, together with other witches disguised as cats, "sang" in the backyard of one of the witnesses.*

✳ *In March 1607, Isobel Grierson was brought to court in Scotland, charged with witchcraft. She allegedly invaded the Clarke household in the middle of the night in the form of a cat, accompanied by other cats, who together raised "a great and fearful noise." The sleeping Mr and Mrs Adam Clarke were woken by this racket, as was their servant woman who had been lying in another bed near theirs. Apparently the cats were only the welcoming crew; shortly after this feline invasion, the devil himself also allegedly arrived, in the form of a black man. Isobel was burned to death for this, as well as for various murders by magic. (See Transformation.)*

Cats were also identified with Satan, believed to favor the shape of a cat, inevitably a large black tom. In 1233 Pope Gregory IX declared that heretics worshiped the devil in the form of a black tom cat.

Of course one person's devil is another person's guardian spirit. In Slavic areas, especially Russia and Poland, the *ovinnik*, guardian spirit of the threshing barn takes the form of a huge disheveled black cat with glowing eyes. Offerings of blini or the last sheaves of grain are offered to him in exchanges for protection and divination services. The *ovinnik* is no cute, cuddly kitty; should he ever be seriously displeased, he'll burn the barn down (frequently with the owner or his children within).

Elements of degraded, corrupt, perverted sacrifice are apparent in the treatment meted out to European cats, as if rather than venerating and preserving what is powerful and holy, it's cruelly, wantonly destroyed instead.

The torture and killing of cats occurred in various contexts: in conjunction with human witch trials, as random acts of violence, but also as organized, documented ritual killings:

✳ *In Paris, it was customary to burn a sack or basket filled with cats in the Place de Greve on St John's Eve, a tradition also popular in other parts of France. (Although Louis XIV abolished the Parisian custom in 1648, it continued in the provinces until at least as late as 1796.)*

✳ *Various French towns built bonfires to burn masses of cats on the first Sunday in Lent.*

✳ *Cats were burned in Alsace at Easter.*

(See **CALENDAR:** Midsummer's; Ostara.)

Although all cats are associated with witchcraft, the black cat is most powerfully identified. Black cats' special identification with witchcraft is not limited to Western European or Christian perspectives. Chinese, Hindu, Japanese, Jewish, North African, and Romany witch-lore make the same connection, although whether it is understood to be a sacred or malevolent connection depends upon cultural and individual perceptions.

People tend to fear or love black cats, frequently revealing their attitudes toward witchcraft. The major superstition regarding black cats is that they bring bad luck should they cross your path and people will cross the street to avoid them. This isn't so ridiculous if one recalls that black cats were once commonly believed to be witches in disguise, out looking for fun and trouble. In Britain, however, black cats are lucky; white cats are identified with bad luck, as are many white animals, perhaps because of associations with ghosts and death.

Chickens

Because chickens were perceived as being twice born (once when the egg is laid, once when it hatches), they were regarded as sacred. Black is the color of night, fertility, and gestation and so black hens were considered the most sacred of all.

Many magic spells stipulate that feathers or eggs must come from a pure black hen. The very first egg laid by a black hen is considered extremely magically powerful and is coveted for love and fertility spells.

Black hens are identified with and sacred to the supreme witch goddess Hecate (see **DIVINE WITCH**: Hecate). This spiritual memory survives in the Mother Goose rhyme, "*Heckity peckity, my black hen …*" In some parts of Britain, witches were allegedly incapable of approaching black chicken feathers, and so on Halloween it was customary to kill a black hen. The hen was cooked but the feathers were artfully arranged: hung onto the door of the house, over the bed or onto children or horses. It sounds suspiciously like a surreptitious method of offering a sacrifice to Hecate.

In African-derived magic, black hen's feathers are used for magical cleansings. (Cleansing spells remove negative energy, spiritual debris, curses and malevolent spells.) Burn the feathers to a very, very fine ash, and then dust them on the person to be cleansed.

Black hens counter malevolent spells and allegedly remove jinxes. In the United States, frizzly (black and white speckled) hens are the substitute of choice and may even be preferable. Should the feathers be frizzly, it is immaterial whether the bird is a hen or rooster: in the hoodoo and conjure traditions of the Southern United States, frizzly hens or roosters were kept in the yard to scratch up any "tricks" (malevolent spells left on the property to fester and cause harm). Frizzled poultry was a valuable commodity: the bird might also be loaned or rented out to others in need. A renowned New Orleans root doctor went by the name of *The Frizzly Rooster*, his specialty lifting jinxes, hexes, and tricks. (See **BOTANICALS**: Roots; **DICTIONARY**: Root-worker.)

Chickens have served as oracles since ancient days. Various methods exist, however *alectromancy* is the standard method of divination by poultry. Individual letters of the alphabet are used to form a circle. An equal quantity of wheat is placed on each letter; the bird is placed in the center of the circle and carefully observed as it eats the grain. The corresponding letters should spell out a prophecy, which may then be interpreted. It is a primitive ancestor of the modern ouija board.

Ancient armies typically traveled with flocks of poultry, to lay eggs but also to perform grain divination. (In theory the greater the number of chickens and circles, the greater the possible complexity of the message.) A famous story describes a Roman general whose fleet was about to attack Carthage during the first Punic War. Before the attack was mounted, chickens were brought on deck and grain scattered for them. The seasick birds refused to eat. Rather than paying attention to the oracle, which clearly advised hesitation, the enraged, impatient (and perhaps queasy) general announced, *"If they won't eat, let them drink!"* and ordered the poultry thrown overboard. Needless to say, the Romans suffered a crushing defeat.

Corvids: Crows, Ravens, and Jackdaws

The corvids are a large, widely distributed family of birds including crows, ravens, and jackdaws, powerfully associated with witchcraft and magic. (Other members of the family include rooks and jays.)

Scientific knowledge and genetic research has altered the way humans classify living beings. Once upon a time, classification was based purely on powers of observation. Because crows, ravens, and jackdaws bear an obvious family resemblance, both physically and personality-wise, they have always been understood as related. Magpies, which have profound but different associations with witchcraft, are also corvids, but because they were understood to be a distinct, if similar, species, they have their own encyclopedia entry. See Magpies.

Crows and ravens are big, loud, noisy, black birds. Crows and ravens are often referred to interchangeably. Technically ravens may be slightly larger, with shaggy, disheveled-looking feathers, unlike shiny, sleek black crows. They also possess slightly different habits, being somewhat more solitary than crows, which may roost together in communities numbering hundreds. Ravens will also hunt more than crows, which are mainly scavengers.

When mythology distinguishes between the two, ravens are usually associated with transformative magic while crows are identified with healing. Both are teachers and sponsors of magic and shamanism.

Crows and ravens are characterized by their shiny black color and by their raucous, loud voices. Diurnal birds, like roosters, they noisily greet the sun. If you live in an area with many crows, they will be your daily alarm clock. Crows, like baboons and roosters, are strongly identified with solar power and may be understood to venerate or worship the sun themselves. In a Pacific Northwest myth, Earth is enshrouded in darkness; Crow is literally the one who hangs the sun in the sky.

Crows and ravens, like bears and humans, are omnivores; crows do not like to hunt, however, but prefer to scavenge and not only on road-kill. Historically corvids hover over battlefields waiting for an opportunity to feast on the dead. Crows thus have profound associations with spirits presiding over death, war, and disaster. In Irish Gaelic, *badbh* meaning *"crow"* is a synonym for *"witch."* It is also the name of a Celtic battle goddess, who may manifest in the shape of her namesake bird.

Crows are oracular birds; they evoke the spirit of prophecy and are also affiliated with oracular spirits. Among the deities with whom crows/ravens are associated are:

❋ *Amaterasu (Japanese)*

❋ *Apollo (Greek)*

* Badbh *(Irish)*

* Cathubodua *(Romano-Celtic Gaul, now France)*

* Epona *(Celtic)*

* Kali *(Indian)*

* Macha *(Irish)*

* The Morrigan *(Irish; known as the "battle raven" or "battle crow")*

* Nantosuelta *(Gaulish, now Germany)*

* Nephthys *(Egyptian)*

* Odin *(Norse, Aesir;* "God of the Ravens")

* Tlazolteotl *(Aztec)*

Trickster heroes, Crow and Raven play an *enormous* role in world mythology, including Celtic, Greek, Hungarian, Japanese, Jewish, Native American, Scandinavian, and Vietnamese traditions, but most especially in the indigenous traditions of Siberia and North America's Pacific Northwest.

Crows truly are tricksters and clowns; it isn't just mythological affectation. If you spend time with them, you will observe their games and tricks. They are assertive, unafraid of people and as willing to play a joke on a person as they are on a dog, cat or on each other. Shiny things appeal to them and they've been known to steal them. Crows coexist well with people and occasionally become companion animals. Crows will, on occasion, mimic human language or the sounds of other animals.

The associations of crow/raven with witchcraft, magic, and shamanism pre-date Christianity. What changes post-Christianity is the *perception* of those associations. Rather than positive associations with wise-women, shaman, and seers, crows were now associated with diabolism and sin. In the eyes of Christian Europe, crows and ravens were linked with witchcraft because of their color, their raucousness, harsh voices, sharp intelligence, and assertive nature. Legends emerged explaining *why* crows were black—typically involving punishment for some kind of sin. According to the standard story, once upon a time, crows were pure white but they did something very bad and so were punished by being painted permanently black. Because crows are black birds that daily herald the light, the Church identified them with Satan in his guise as Lucifer, the fallen angel and light bringer.

Jackdaws, which are quite similar to crows and ravens, are restricted to the Eastern Hemisphere, ranging from Eurasia to northwestern Africa. It derives its name from its call: *"jack!"* It resembles a smallish, grayish-black crow, but is as noisy, raucous and sociable as its larger relations. It eats insects, worms, fruits, and carrion. The world's most famous jackdaw may be Sybil Leek's companion, Hotfoot Jackson, the star of her 1966 book, *The Jackdaw and the Witch: A True Fable.*

Coyotes

Coyotes exemplify *"threshold animals"*: wild animals that exist, thrive, and stay wild amidst human society, even flourishing among us.

Coyotes are medium-sized North American canines, midway between wolves and dogs. Once upon a time, coyotes were restricted to a reasonably limited section of North America; however as other predators (wolves and cougars especially) have been exterminated, coyotes have filled the void. Unlike most other creatures, coyotes have a far wider range today than ever before, although this is against all odds—attempts have been made to exterminate coyotes, too. They have been poisoned, shot, and trapped; in many areas bounties still remain on their hides.

Coyotes are the trickster supreme, akin to crows and rabbits but more so. They are clever, wary, and adaptable, epitomizing humor, curiosity, and intelligence. Coyotes in my own Los Angeles hill neighborhood were observed looking both ways before they crossed the street, something my golden retriever could *never* learn.

Coyote is a central figure in Native North American mythology, playing a broad range of roles. Coyote alternately creates the universe (because he's lonely or curious or bored) creates people, creates death, darkness, and disaster and/or serves as human beings' primary teacher. Coyote introduces people to sex, magic, and witchcraft, in both the positive and negative sense of that word. He is the spirit of eternity, regeneration, endurance, and persistence. He gets people into lots of trouble but is frequently also the only one capable of getting them out of it. Coyote teaches sacred rituals, secret knowledge, and malevolent witchcraft.

North America is a vast continent and tremendous variety exists among Native American cultures, truly a veritable "*500 nations*" possessing varied philosophies, cosmologies, and perspectives. Coyote is sacred to many; malevolent to a few. Coyote is particularly prominent among tribes in California: for the Miwok,

Coyote is creator and supreme divinity, but for the Maidu, Coyote is a divine antagonist.

Navajo tradition understands Coyote as a malicious trickster responsible for the introduction of harmful magical practices. Coyote's name may be synonymous with malevolent witchcraft, making it an insult to be called a coyote—the equivalent of the pejorative use of the word "*witch*" although traditional Navajo belief understands men to be as likely to be witches as women.

Jackals (which bear a physical resemblance to coyotes but are smaller) play a similar, if more shadowy, role in Africa, Western Asia and India. Jackals are tricksters possessing strong associations with sex and death and are often funerary deities, the most prominent being Egypt's Anubis, credited with inventing the mummification process. Anubis manifests as either a full-fledged jackal or as a man with a jackal's head. He may have been Lord of the Dead prior to Osiris' rise to prominence. Funerary priests wore jackal masks, perhaps channeling the spirit of Anubis. Jackals are also powerfully affiliated with deities Kali and Lilith.

In a Tewa legend, Coyote marries Yellow Corn Girl and teaches her to transform into animal shape by jumping through hoops. He then teaches her methods of killing by witchcraft. She thus becomes the first witch, at least in the malevolent sense. Coyote is the source of witchcraft similar to the biblical angels who entangled themselves with the Daughters of Man, as recounted in Genesis 6:2-4.

Shape-shifters, skin-walkers and nahuals frequently take the form of coyotes—whether this is understood positively or negatively depends upon perceptions of the practice.

Dogs

The history of dogs' ancient alliance with humans is shrouded in the mysteries of time. They have been our steadfast companions and guardians since that proverbial time immemorial. Even cultures that historically do not domesticate animals, such as many of the indigenous cultures of North America, have maintained dogs as companion animals.

Because of this long alliance, it should come as no surprise that dogs have intense spiritual associations with protection and with healing and death, two sides of the same coin. In every one of these aspects dogs are understood to be guardian spirits:

* *Dogs protect people from spiritual and physical dangers in life.*

* *Ancient people perceived illness as both physical ailment and spiritual crisis: dogs battle on behalf of their human allies.*

* *Dogs protect dead human souls and accompany, guide, and assist them in their journey to the next realm.*

Perhaps because feral dogs were observed lurking in ancient cemeteries ready to devour offerings and dig up bodies, dogs achieved early identification with death and funerary rites. Dogs also lingered on battlefields where they competed with crows for their share of the dead.

Although everyone dies alone, it was once commonly believed that without a dog's assistance one would never be able to locate the realm of the dead. This was a widespread concept although how it was interpreted and acted upon varied. In some Central American beliefs, there's no need to do anything: when one's soul begins that journey, a dog will be found waiting by a riverbank ready to serve as your guide. Of course, should that spirit-dog not show up for any reason, your soul would wander for ever, never achieving peace. Some cultures refused to take chances: dogs were sacrificed and buried together with a person (or placed on the pyre) so that they might start the journey together. The Aztecs evolved a happier solution: they buried their dead with terracotta dogs who, through ritual and spell-casting, were able to perform this function just as well as flesh and blood dogs.

The ancient Egyptians may not have rigidly distinguished between jackals and dogs: Anubis, Lord of Embalming, Guide to the After-Life, may be understood as either species or both. His color is black, not because it is the color of death but because for the Egyptians it represented regeneration and rebirth. Anubis rules the Dog Star in conjunction with his adopted mother Isis, the first syllable of whose Egyptian name Au Set resembles a dog's bark: *ow, ow, ow!*

The Norse Queen of the After-Life, Hel (Christianity borrowed her name for the eternal realm of post-life punishment) has her own companion pack of wolves and dogs that nibble arriving corpses. (Vestiges of the ancient Indo-European custom of offering dogs a bite of the corpse may survive in this legend.) These may be the original hell-hounds who will survive to ride with the Wild Hunt.

Dogs are most profoundly identified with the Eurasian witch goddess Hecate, Queen of the Night, spirit of birth, death, magic, healing, witchcraft, travel, and victory. Hecate guards the threshold between life and death, serving as a psychopomp (one who guides the dead).

Hecate also serves as the personal handmaiden of Persephone, Queen of Hades.

Hades is famously guarded by Cerberus, the monstrous three-headed hound of hell. Hecate's sacred number is three; she is typically depicted with three heads and very frequently assumes the guise of a dog. Cerberus may be Hecate's pet dog or he may even be Hecate in disguise. Whether Hecate transforms into a dog or is in fact a dog spirit who transforms into other shapes (old crone, seductive beauty, occasionally even a black cat!) is a little like asking which came first, the chicken or the egg. See **DIVINE WITCH:** Hecate.

Dogs serve as sacred companion animals to many spirits, most having to do with healing, death, war, and protection:

* *Artemis (Greek)*
* *Asklepios (Greek)*
* *Babalu-Aye (West African)*
* *Epona (Celtic/Roman)*
* *Erinyes (Greek justice spirits who chase sinners like blood-hounds in pursuit)*
* *Hecate (Eurasian)*
* *Hel (Norse)*
* *Hermes (Greek)*
* *Nehalennia (Dutch/Germanic)*
* *Ogun (Yoruba)*
* *Sirona (Celtic)*

Hecate originated in what is now Turkey. In Sumer, another goddess was intensely linked to dogs: Bau, the daughter of Sirius the Dog Star. Sometimes depicted as dog-headed, it's tempting to associate her name with "bow-wow." In her later Babylonian incarnation, Gula Bau,

spirit of healing, walks Earth accompanied by her pack of hounds.

Hecate is not the only deity to transform into canine form. The Middle Eastern and North African spirits known as *djinn* have been known to lurk in the form of dogs, usually loitering in the marketplace just before dawn. In Jewish mystical folklore, Lilith and Asmodeus, respectively Queen and King of Demons, travel incognito disguised as large black hounds.

Black hound is the key: although to some extent all dogs have associations with funeral rites, magical healing, and protection, the dog most powerfully identified with magic, witches, and witchcraft is the black dog, the bigger and blacker the better. (Large black poodles have particularly strong associations, perhaps in honor of magician Cornelius Agrippa's beloved pet, *Monsieur.*)

In addition to serving as witches' familiars, black dogs may be transformed witches or witch goddesses. Nicholas Remy, the merciless witch-trial judge from Lorraine, alleged that women transformed into rabid dogs and wolves.

In witch-crazed Europe, dogs were understood as the devil's favored companion or maybe even his favorite disguise. According to witch-trial transcripts, Satan routinely appeared at the sabbats he hosted in the shape of a massive black dog.

Dogs are believed to venture out at night to do battle with evil spirits. This is not an untypical international belief: lone dogs at night, particularly large black ones, are understood to either be evil spirits or out battling evil spirits. British folklore is full of stories of spectral black hounds mysteriously appearing to guard, guide, and accompany lone travelers, particularly when venturing through forests. Once the journey is over or safety is reached, the dog vanishes as mysteriously as it arrived.

Donkeys

Once upon a time, as with so many witchcraft animals, the humble donkey was venerated and held sacred. It was no coincidence that Christ chose to ride a donkey on his fateful entry into Jerusalem but fulfillment of prophecy. Dionysus rode a donkey, too. The Greek goddess Hestia has a donkey for a companion (or her consort). The most famous donkey in the Old Testament belonged to the sorcerer-shaman Balaam; it spoke, protested when beaten and was able to see an angel when its master could not.

Donkeys were first domesticated in the Nile Valley in pre-dynastic Egypt. Among their early tasks was helping thresh grain, leading to their close identification with the Corn Mother. This practice would degenerate into base cruelty: donkeys were blindfolded or even blinded so they'd walk in endless circles, turning the mill wheel.

Donkeys were once synonymous with phallic energy and the phallic organ itself, particularly in ancient Egypt, where the phonetic elements for their word for donkey ("*a-a*"; "hee-haw"?) were represented by the ideogram for donkey and a phallus. The veneration today reserved for the stallion was once given to the donkey. Roman couples carved donkey heads on their beds in hopes of enhancing fertility. Donkeys had close associations with the summer solstice (Midsummer's Eve), as they were believed to ritually mate at that time, just like people celebrating that fertility festival. Shakespeare's audience would have understood the reference to the donkey's head in *A Midsummer Night's Dream*.

In medieval Europe, donkeys became identified with rampant, uncontrolled, sinful lust. They were prominently featured in the Feast of Fools; donkeys were understood to be among the devil's favorite guises.

The popular festival known as The Feast of the Ass was celebrated in Northern France during the Middle Ages. Held annually on January 14th, it allegedly commemorated the flight of the Holy Family into Egypt. A young girl holding a baby was seated astride a donkey and lead through the streets and into the church. It was a raucous, somewhat sacrilegious festival with many elements reminiscent of Pagan, fertility, and, specifically, Dionysian rites. The donkey was actually brought into the church where it was given food and drink on a table, similar to a sacrificial offering. The festival concluded with a midnight mass, which the officiating priest ended by braying three times. This feast was suppressed by the Church in the fifteenth century, although it lingered in places for a long time afterwards.

Unlike cats or crows, the donkey's disreputable and demonic associations pre-date Christianity. Their associations with sex, magic and dangerous, unpredictable deities already lead many to be ambivalent toward them. The donkey was among the Egyptian deity Set's sacred animals. Despite periods of popularity, Set, Lord of Magic, especially sex magic, was an ambiguous, volatile deity, a disreputable and dangerous god.

The associations between donkeys and Set were strong and images of Set with a donkey's head were engraved on magical talismanic gems. The Egyptians identified Set as the god of foreigners, most especially their Semitic neighbors. (The invading Hyksos kings, believed to be of Semitic origin, adored Set.) Set was also identified (by the Egyptians) with the god of the Jewish people who even then bore an ancient reputation as powerful magicians. (One of the Jewish god's names (*Yah*) sounds similar to *io*, the Coptic word for donkey.)

Dionysus, to whom donkeys are sacred, also became increasingly suspect and disregarded. As the Common Era loomed, there was little room or official sympathy for a wild shamanic god of intoxication, sex, and ecstasy, especially a god who encouraged women to dance wild, free and independent. King Midas was punished with donkey's ears when he dared to suggest that a satyr was a finer musician than that Hellenic golden boy, Apollo. Satyrs were worshippers of Dionysus and on one level the story may be understood as a rebuke towards Dionysus.

By the dawning of the Common Era, conventional society and religion regarded donkeys poorly. No longer sacred, they were associated with foreigners, practitioners of magic, lechery and uncontrolled sex, and heretical strange religions, symbolic of lust and immorality. To accuse someone of worshipping an ass was considered the ultimate insult. That insult was frequently made:

✳ *In Alexandria, Greek propaganda accused Jews of worshipping a donkey's head.*

✳ *Throughout their vast empire, Roman propaganda accused Christians of worshipping a donkey's head.*

✳ *To suggest someone "worshipped the donkey" was also an allusion to Dionysus and his suppressed Bacchanalia.*

Hidden within the intended insults, perhaps what authorities were using the donkey to symbolically express was that these varied spiritual traditions were stubbornly persistent and dangerously defiant.

These familiar accusations survived into the Christian era, although accusers and targets changed. Christians, once accused of worshipping donkeys themselves, now accused the Knights Templar of worshipping a mysterious idol named Baphomet. Among the forms suggested for Baphomet was that of a donkey's head. Witches were accused of adoring Satan in the form of a donkey with huge, erect phallus while engaged in orgies at bacchanalia-like sabbats.

According to folklore, the donkey is the animal into which victims of witchcraft are most likely to find themselves transformed, the most famous example being Lucius Apuleius who was turned into an ass when he tried to steal a sorceress' magic in the second-century CE book, *The Golden Ass.*

Familiars

Familiars are witches' animal friends, partners, and companions. The term "familiar" implies an actual, specific, living animal—unlike the larger term "ally" which is inclusive of spirit animals. In general, familiars are what their name says: *familiar.* These are the animal companions people keep as pets within their homes.

Do you have a familiar? If you have had an intense emotional bond with a living creature other than a human, then one might say you have had a familiar, whether you work magic with that animal in any capacity or not. The dog who won't leave your side, the cat who nightly sleeps on your feet, the bird who begins to sing as soon as it catches sight of you: these are all familiars, or at least potentially so. The dog who guards you with his life is as much a familiar as the cat who assists you in magic ritual. Mutual love, loyalty, and devotion define the relationship between familiars and humans. Whether that relationship is also part of a working magical partnership is up to you.

In terms of witchcraft, the familiar is the witch's partner, assisting her in various magical working including divination and spell-casting. Although any creature could be a familiar, certain animals are considered most likely to become familiars or to be most suitable or powerful, including cats, dogs, ferrets, crows, hedgehogs, toads, snakes, and other animals found within this section of the *Encyclopedia of Witchcraft*.

A very high percentage of the animal species considered most likely to be familiars have been identified with the moon, lunar deities, and fertility ever since Neolithic times including cats, frogs and toads, snakes, canines, hedgehogs, and birds.

That defines the identity of the familiar and its role in witchcraft as seen by witches, past and present. However, that definition presupposes that intense emotional and psychic bonds between humans and other living beings are possible and are something positive. That's a fairly modern viewpoint: one way of looking at familiar-keeping witches of the Middle Ages is that they were way ahead of their time, at least in terms of animals.

Today hardly anyone blinks an eye at people who talk of how much they love their cats, dogs, lizards or other pets. The pet industry is a hugely profitable business: people buy special food and toys for their animals. They spend fortunes to heal their ailing animals. Even today, however, many consider this crazy, and they were in the majority not that long ago.

There are still people who adamantly insist that they would never keep an animal in their house. No need to wonder why. Once upon a time, intense affection and familiarity with another species could get you arrested for witchcraft. Humans were not the only ones killed en masse during the Burning Times: most familiars of convicted witches were burned alive too.

During the Witchcraze, the witches' viewpoint was not the officially accepted definition of "*familiar.*" According to the inquisitors, familiars weren't just plain old animals of whom witches were very fond. Familiars were special gifts from Satan given to witches upon their initiation at sabbats to act as messengers and servants. The familiar's animal or bird form might only be a satanic illusion; the familiar really being an imp or demon in disguise. Some inquisitors perceived that the familiar wasn't the witch's servant but her boss. The familiar gave the witch her orders, which she must then obey for fear of the devil. (See below, Imp.)

According to the witch-hunters' definition, there was no need for a familiar to be visible or physically present to exist: familiar imps and demons could transform into various shapes or make themselves invisible if they desired. This had tremendous implications. Because some witch-hunters decided that, by definition, witches possessed familiars, a demonic familiar, invisible to everyone but the witch (or the witnesses who testified against her) made it possible for someone with no contact with animals to be convicted of having a familiar. The very fact that no one but the witch's accusers could see the familiar was offered as the very proof of witchcraft. Of course the witch denied having a demon imp, but what would you expect her to say? She's a witch.

These various conflicting perceptions are best exemplified by the story of Dr William Harvey and the witch, as told in an anonymous seventeenth-century manuscript. Dr Harvey (1578–1657), the discoverer of the circulation of blood, visited Newmarket with his patron King Charles I. Hearing stories about a local witch, Dr Harvey decided to investigate. He paid a call on the anonymous witch at her home at the edge of

Newmarket Heath. Her first instincts were to be wary and secretive but Dr Harvey worked to put her at ease. Engaging her in conversation, he managed to pass himself off as a fellow magical practitioner. Enjoying the company, the witch relaxed. When Dr Harvey asked to see her familiar, she obliged. Putting out a saucer of milk, the witch made some toad-like noises and a toad hopped out from under a chest to lap up the milk.

Dr Harvey gave the woman a shilling and sent her out to buy them some ale. In her absence, he caught and dissected her toad. Imagine someone coming into your home and secretly dissecting your pet. Having dissected the creature, Dr Harvey formed the scientific conclusion that the familiar was not an imp or a demon but was, in fact, really a toad and thus, in his understanding, not truly a familiar.

When the woman returned with the ale and learned what had happened, she was absolutely devastated, screaming and lunging at the doctor. He tried to calm her with gifts and explanations, all to no avail. Eventually he lost patience and identified himself as the king's physician, telling her that instead of crying for her toad, she should be rejoicing that he wasn't having her tried for witchcraft. Dr Harvey was an early scientific hero and this story is often understood as a parable recounting an early triumph of science over superstition.

Ferrets (Polecats) and Weasels

Perhaps only hyenas attract the same level of fear and revulsion as weasels. True, many people dislike cats, spiders, wolves, and snakes but that loathing tends to be mingled with grudging admiration. Even people who claim to be all-around animal lovers frequently make an exception for weasels, perceived as disgusting, bloodthirsty, evil creatures with no redeeming features. They might be surprised to know that once upon a time, in some places, weasels were admired, useful, and sacred.

The order *Mustelidae* encompasses weasels, ferrets, badgers, stoats, polecats, fishers, martens, minks, wolverines, otters, and the most famous member of the family, the skunk. It's a smelly family; the order's name derives from its members' ability to produce *must* (musk) from their well-developed anal glands.

Mustelidae are a well-distributed family and the identification of weasels with witchcraft occurs throughout Europe, Asia, Africa, and North America. Weasels and ferrets traditionally serve as witches' familiars and as a form into which witches commonly change. Weasels are understood as "witch-creatures." As with hyenas, the comparison isn't intended to be complimentary toward witches; however, negative feelings towards weasels tend to be based on misinformation, misinterpretation, and untruths.

The *Mustelidae* family has a lot of members; the names used to refer to various species are frequently used carelessly and interchangeably. Popular understanding of what is a weasel or ferret may not match scientific classification.

Weasels and ferrets are closely related species but they are not identical. Ferrets are exclusively domestic animals; they were domesticated about the same time as cats and were once far more widely distributed as pets. Few people have actually seen a weasel; wild, forest animals, they're significantly smaller than ferrets. Despite their big reputations, weasels are *tiny*. Fierce, energetic and truly fearless, they can and will successfully attack creatures many times their size, chickens only one example.

Weasels appear to be magical creatures for a variety of reasons:

* *Because they are so tiny, like a fairy creature, their ability to bring down a much larger animal appears to be magical—witchcraft. (Fairies were once understood as potentially very dangerous.)*

* *A legend exists (it happens to be untrue) that weasels hypnotize their prey with their "evil gaze" like a snake-charmer. This only adds to their sinister reputation.*

* *Sleek, slim, with tails as long as the rest of their bodies, weasels resemble furry snakes with legs. Like snakes, they burrow in Earth, disappearing within and then suddenly popping out. Their size makes them look like creatures that should be prey, not predator. Brave, fearless killers despite their size, weasels look like a magical blend of cat and snake.*

* *Weasels in Northern climates change colors magically to blend with the seasons. Usually light brown with a white belly in warm weather, many species turn snow white in winter.*

* *Weasels cannot be contained. Houdinis of the animal world, they wriggle snake-like out of cages and confinement, disappear into holes in Earth, leap and climb to precarious heights, and twist their limber bodies into all kind of gymnastic feats. Quiet, stealthy, and fast, weasels suddenly jump out like jack-in-the-boxes: pop goes the weasel!*

What seems to disturb people most, and the reason why ferrets are banned as pets in places like California, is their manner of killing and eating. People perceive that weasels enjoy killing, have fun with it and are needlessly bloodthirsty, leaving devastation in their wake. There's a vestige of truth in this observation but it's also misunderstood and misinterpreted.

As tiny creatures that kill larger animals, of course what they've killed is too much for them to eat (and weasels, unlike wolves, are solitary hunters; there's no group feast) so, typically, a weasel takes a few bites (more likely a few sips of blood) and then moves on. People see weasels as blood-thirsty, vampiric, murderous creatures and dub them "wasteful killers." (Of course, this is all relative. From a hyena's perspective, humans must be incredibly wasteful: we don't grind up bones and eat them, the way they do.)

It's difficult to understand weasels' habits unless you understand weasels. They may as well be poster animals for what was once labeled hyperactivity. Weasels and ferrets in action resemble the cartoon character, "the Tasmanian devil." Smart, fun, dizzyingly fast, they *never* stop moving, bouncing, playing—or at least not until they pass out from exhaustion, only to jump back into action as soon as they are refreshed. Not only their bodies but their minds are constantly working. Lively, joyous, curious, not shy: they are extremely fun animals to watch and play with, but they can be dangerous pets. With *very* low thresholds of boredom, their minds must be constantly engaged. Unlike many cats, dogs, or even snakes and rabbits, ferrets cannot be left alone to sleep or wait for the fun to begin. Left to their own devices, they will escape from any cage and cause havoc in their wake in their desire for fun, adventure, and stimulation.

Weasels possess an *extremely* high metabolic rate; they need small amounts of food protein more frequently than slower, more sedate, less active creatures. For these tiny creatures, even a few bites are sufficient. Squirrels cache their nuts, leopards store their meat, but this isn't the nature of the speedy little weasel. It doesn't think about what's been left behind but searches for something new. When it's hungry, it kills again. It may lap blood from its victim's throat for a quick burst of energy, lending it its reputation as a vampire. (This nature is common to weasels, polecats, and ferrets.)

Despite its name, the European ferret is originally native to the Middle East and North Africa and was domesticated there several thousand years ago. Ferrets are also commonly called polecats, indicating the confusion between cats and weasels. Once upon a time, the classification of species was based on observation, not genetics. Cats and ferrets were perceived as being closely related, although that's not scientifically true. The same name, "catta," was used to indicate both ferrets and cats. In old writings, it's difficult to determine to which the word refers. To add to the confusion, there are wild species known as polecats that are also identified as popular witches' familiars. These polecats dwell in woods, swamps and marshes, making dens in stream banks or under tree roots.

Ferrets originally played roles not dissimilar from pet cats. Long before cats became common in Europe, ferrets were used to keep homes and storehouses safe from mice, rats, and other vermin. Weasels were famously used as rat-catchers in ancient Rome.

In some places, ferrets are third in popularity as pets, following only dogs and cats. However, there is a reason cats, once they were well distributed geographically, drastically overtook the role once played by ferrets. Adult ferrets behave like crazed kittens. The phrase "curiosity killed the cat" probably applies to ferrets more than it does to felines. With more curiosity than common sense, ferrets get into a lot of trouble. They must be supervised: they get into holes in the walls, behind household appliances; every year ferrets are killed when they sneakily climb inside pull-out sofas and are then accidentally crushed.

Weasels are associated with knowledge: they can't get enough, even when it isn't beneficial to them. They possess an unstoppable urge to *know*. This concept survives in the English language when we say someone *"weaseled"* or *"ferreted out"* information.

Mythologically speaking, weasels are associated with magic, witchcraft, prophesy, sex, reproduction, death, battle, and healing:

* *Because of their shape, weasels are associated with human genitalia.*

* *Because they slip easily in and out of Earth, weasels were understood as messengers between the realms of daily reality, the after-life and the spirit world. Fearless, smart, and persistent, nothing will stop them from accomplishing a mission.*

* *Because they can dig their way out of anything, and escape from any confinement, they are associated with successful childbirth, their powers beseeched to quicken a child stalled in the womb or birth canal.*

In the North American Pacific Northwest, the mink (a form of weasel) is the embodiment of the cultural trickster hero. He prepares Earth for human habitation. Mink differs from other trickster heroes like Coyote, Raven or Rabbit because of his suave, amorous, untiring nature; he is the lover-boy supreme!

In Apuleius' tale *The Golden Ass*, a man is paid to guard a corpse from Thessalian witches. The witch ultimately approaches, stealthily and successfully, in the form of a weasel. She gets what she wants and simultaneously manages to play an enormous trick on the hero of the story, too. (See **CREATIVE ARTS:** Literature: *The Golden Ass*.)

According to Greek myth, Hera sought to prevent or at least painfully delay Hercules' mother, Alcmene, from giving birth to him. Depending on the version told, she posted either a childbirth deity or a pack of witches before Alcmene's birth chamber with instructions to delay her at all cost. Seven days of hard labor later, Alcmene was in agony and near death. The plot was finally foiled by Alcmene's devoted servant, Galanthis, who stopped the jinx with a trick. In the midst of all the angst and misery, in the presence of the goddess or witches, Galanthis laughed with gusto. Her laughter broke the spell; they assumed Alcmene had given birth and ceased their spell-work. Hera punished Galanthis by transforming her into a weasel, as a rebuke for trickery and too much cleverness. Weasel-shaped Galanthis ran off to the midwife-witch goddess Hecate, who offered admiration and respect for Galanthis' ability to provide successful, safe delivery despite formidable odds. Hecate adopted the weasel as her sacred servant.

Flies

Flies play various roles in witchcraft: as witches' familiars; as witches' weapons; as the vehicle for the shaman's wandering soul. Flies were anciently associated with the mysteries of birth and death. Once upon a time, especially in the Middle East, flies were understood as souls of the dead searching for new incarnations. Souls were believed able to travel between lives in insect form. The Philistine deity Baal-Zebub, an aspect of the masculine fertility spirit Baal, is Lord of the Flies, the Shepherd of Souls. He would eventually become demonized and transformed into Beelzebub, a synonym for Satan.

Flies also represent the shaman's journeying soul, whether literally or figuratively. Flies were envisioned as flying in and out of the entranced shaman's open mouth. Should the fly be unable to return, the soul might be stuck in limbo, the shaman forever unable to awaken from the trance.

Flies may also be spirits in disguise and not particularly nice ones either. According to Arabic legend, King Solomon once transformed a mass of malevolent *djinn* into flies, imprisoning three million of them within a black glass bottle, which was then hidden inside a well near Babylon. Centuries later, local people searching for treasure came upon the bottle and broke it, releasing the flies/*dinn*, who were free but, unable to break Solomon's transformation spell, were more spiteful and malevolent than ever.

Flies serve as witches' familiars, especially in Scandinavia. Flies journey out to do the witch's bidding (not always malevolent) and scout out information. Those imprisoned on accusations of witchcraft were often inadvertently betrayed by flies or other insects. Although they might emphatically deny the charges, even under torture, witch-hunters would claim that the presence of persistent, hovering flies was proof that the person had a familiar and was thus a witch. Of course, considering the standards of sanitation and cleanliness in a medieval prison, plus the presence of blood and pus from untreated, infected wounds incurred during torture, how could there *not* be flies?

Sometimes accused witches died before they could be executed, acquitted or otherwise released, whether because of suicide, miscalculated torture or deliberate murder. Because witch trials were legal proceedings, none of those scenarios was officially acceptable. The truth of the situation was often hushed up by blaming it on the flies; allegedly Beelzebub had sent emissaries in the form of flies to help the witches "escape" judgment.

Flies are often perceived negatively within traditional witchcraft.

❋ *Saami shamans allegedly kept flies in magic boxes to be sent out as desired to cause injury, or at least so claimed their non-Saami neighbors.*

✴ *Not all flies are bewitched flies but the ones that are may be fatal: throughout Tanzania, special flies allegedly attack and kill victims at night as directed by the sorcerers who control them.*

✴ *According to Pueblo Indian folklore, witches control flies and other insects, directing them to nefarious, destructive purposes.*

Foxes

Foxes are intensely identified with witchcraft in East Asia, and most profoundly in Japan where they are the witchcraft animal supreme. *Fox-owning* is a specific form of witchcraft, unique to Japan.

The fox's role in witchcraft may derive from its ancient importance in Japanese spirituality. Inari is the ancient but still immensely popular Shinto spirit of rice, food, and nourishment. Inari brings prosperity, fertility, and abundance and has shrines in every Japanese farming village. The fox is Inari's sacred animal, messenger and, sometimes, alter ego. Stone or wooden foxes are always found in front of Inari's shrines. The fox and Inari merge to form one being: the question of which came first, the fox or the human shape, is irrelevant. They are parallel forms of the sacred being.

You'll notice I haven't used either *"he"* or *"she"* to refer to Inari; that's because Inari's gender(s) remains subject of debate. Today Inari is most commonly depicted as a bearded man carrying bundles of rice, however Inari also manifests as a beautiful woman or as a female fox. Inari's female manifestation is believed to be older, predating the introduction of Buddhism into Japan. There is much debate in spiritual and academic communities as to whether Inari has *always* possessed both male and female manifestations or whether the original, primal spirit was female but over time, for socio-political and religious reasons, the male form became preferable and more common.

Inari in her feminine aspect is also intensely involved with sex, fertility, reproduction, and the magical arts, not only agricultural abundance. Similar but exclusively female fox spirits possessing strong ties to magic and witchcraft exist in China, India and Korea.

Once upon a time, Japanese fox spirits were protectors, teachers, and sponsors of witchcraft. Even now some fox spirits are saintly and helpful. (And the foxes that serve as Inari's messengers are miracle workers, understood as sacred and godly.) However, as centuries passed, attitudes towards witchcraft became more ambivalent, and fox spirits became feared. Why?

Fox spirits are held responsible for illness and misfortune. They possess victims, similar to possession by demons, dybbuks or zar spirits. (This isn't ritual possession or channeling; it's involuntary and unpleasant—see **MAGICAL ARTS**: Ritual Possession.) Sometimes full possession (spiritual takeover) results; sometimes only individual symptoms of possession. Symptoms of fox possession include hearing voices, insatiable and indiscriminate appetite, nocturnal feelings of suffocation plus increasing facial resemblance to a fox: The person begins to develop a visible *"snout."*

Eventually the fox may push the true individual out, taking over body, soul, and personality, either full-time or just intermittently. The fox spirit speaks through the person's mouth, often indulging in obscenities, frequently sexual, which the person would normally *never* use. (See **CREATIVE ARTS**: Dance: Tarantella.)

Specific individuals and families are believed to control fox spirits. The solitary fox-owner is most frequently believed to be a corrupt and degenerate sorcerer or exorcist, the proverbial shaman-gone-bad. Although fox familiars are disproportionately female, those humans who put them to evil use are usually male.

> Although most fox spirits are perceived as greedy or power-hungry, spiritual motivation may exist as well; what the fox spirit may really desire is a shrine and daily offerings. The only way for them to make their desire known is through a human mouth, similar to African zar spirits.

Solitary sorcerers dispatch foxes to carry out nefarious deeds. The old extortion racket may be at play: what seems like a perfectly respectable exorcist who specializes in ridding people of fox-spirit possession may actually be the source of that possession, the one who sent the fox. No wonder he can exorcise the spirit: the fox is his familiar who always does his bidding. Fox spirits may also be rented out to others for a fee, to perform their secret, dirty work as well. (Fox spirits tend to run in packs. As opposed to the concept of one familiar per person, the fox-owner may have a large number of fox spirits to work with. Seventy-five is a typical number, although there may be less. Foxes in the wild do *not* run in packs incidentally, being relatively solitary creatures.)

Fox spirits are fed daily; in return the familiar performs various magical services on the person's behalf. It is a mutually beneficial relationship although neighbors may see the fox-owner as threatening and possessing unfair advantages.

Fox spirits run in families. Families who are hereditary owners of foxes typically transmit this hereditary power through the female line. For centuries tremendous fear and social stigma have been attached to families rumored to be fox-owners. Not only is it hereditary, fox-owning may be contagious too. One becomes contaminated (at least by the social stigma) by living in a house formerly occupied by a fox-owner or by possessing his or her property. Contamination may be avoided by avoiding the fox family: don't visit them, don't socialize with them, don't engage in any financial transactions with them, don't be friends with them (but don't offend them either; you don't want them coming after you), and don't marry into their family—most especially don't marry their women.

Japan has never had European-style witch-hunts; few witches have been killed. Instead their punishment is intense social ostracism. Occasionally ostracism has evolved into violence: houses burned down as retribution and/or entire families banished.

This isn't ancient history: in 1952 a young couple committed suicide together because the woman came from a family with a reputation for fox-owning and the man's family forbade their marriage. Because fox power is transmitted through the female line, they feared its impact (perhaps magically but certainly socially) on their family.

Just like real foxes are believed to surreptitiously raid chicken coops, fox spirits are believed to rob the neighbors. (Fox-owners are believed to gain wealth at the expense of others. To become suddenly, mysteriously wealthy is to leave oneself open to accusations of malevolent witchcraft—particularly if anyone else in the area is simultaneously suffering misfortune.)

In China, fox spirits retain their positive identity. Among their primary roles is the protection of archivists and librarians. Should a document be lost, missing or otherwise unable to be located, offerings are made to the fox spirit.

After the offering is made, the archivist leaves the room for a little while to give the spirit space and opportunity to work its magic. Upon his return, the document, book or scroll should stick out or somehow draw attention to itself.

Despite the ostracism, you'd like a fox familiar. If you're not from a family associated with them, where do you begin? How does one obtain a fox familiar? A late seventeenth-century work contains an account of the *Izuna Rite*, the magical ritual by which people gain power over fox familiars:

1. Find a pregnant fox.
2. Feed her, care for her, form an alliance with her during her pregnancy but especially afterwards when she's needy and vulnerable.
3. **YOU CANNOT TAKE A CUB, NO MATTER WHAT.** This isn't "fluffy-bunny" magic; I'm not making this up. This is what the seventeenth-century text instructs. If you are meant to have a fox familiar, when the cubs are sufficiently grown, the mother will bring you one and tell you to name it.
4. Name the fox but keep the name secret. Henceforth, if you call the name, the fox will come to you in invisible form. No one else will be able to see the fox spirit, only you. Nothing is ever entirely hidden, however, so be prepared for others to attribute supernatural powers to you.

Frogs and Toads

Frogs and their land counterparts, toads, are probably the most ancient and universal fertility symbols. The toad represented the uterus for the ancient Greeks, Romans, and Scandinavians. It is a fertility symbol throughout the Semitic world. Some theorize that this association was made because of the appearance of frogs prior to the flooding of rivers, an important herald of fruitfulness in desert lands.

Frogs seemed to call the rain or maybe to announce it. Frogs herald the start of the rainy season in Puerto Rico, too. Here on the other side of the world, years before Columbus, they became the ancient Taino emblem of fertility. Frogs represented fertility to the Aztecs and Mayans and to various indigenous cultures of North and South America. The Aymara of Bolivia and Peru traditionally placed small frog images on hill tops to magically call down rain when it was needed.

Frogs are related to human reproductive issues throughout East Asia. In China, frogs exemplify maximum yin, the ultimate feminine force. There's no man in the moon, according to Chinese folklore; only a woman, a rabbit, and a frog—each one symbolic of intense yin forces as is the moon herself.

Frogs and toads are amphibians: they begin their lives as water creatures (tadpoles) but eventually shape-shift into land dwellers. According to estimates there are at least 4,360 species of frogs (including toads) worldwide. Frogs are found on every continent except Antarctica.

Maybe people perceived the link between frogs and fertility because, although they need to await proper conditions, when the frog finally does give birth, the tadpoles are so numerous. The tadpole is the Egyptian hieroglyphic for the number 100,000. Frogs appeared in great numbers during the annual Nile floods; they were harbingers of abundance and prosperity.

Maybe the shape of the tadpole and its watery environment were reminiscent of the human embryo. Modern people see a resemblance between the form of a tadpole and the shape of a sperm. Rationales are fascinating but ultimately tell us more about people than about frogs. What is significant is that very early in the development of human cultures and thought, the frog and the toad became symbols of birth and the entire regenerative process.

Eventually, the frog became a Halloween animal—a representation of the witch. This is for a reason: in Europe, frogs represented midwives. In the way that a barber's pole advises you that haircuts are available, the frog was the midwife's advertisement: "I can help you have a safe and easy birth." When midwives became denigrated as witches, the frog was condemned as her familiar, her telltale sign.

Frogs represented the force that initiates life to the Egyptians, symbolic of the sacred powers of fertility, regeneration, and rebirth. In one Egyptian creation story, the world is formed from primordial chaos by the collective efforts of four frogs and four snakes. Heket may be the most ancient of Egypt's many deities. Controller of human fecundity, the consort of the spirit of the Nile, she was revered as the *Giver of Life, Goddess of Primordial Waters*" and as "*the great magician.*" Her hieroglyphic symbol was the frog. Heket could manifest purely in frog shape as well as a woman with a frog's head. (Whether Egyptian Heket is or isn't identical to Anatolian Hecate remains subject to fierce debate.)

Not all frogs are female: ancient Celts called frogs "Lords of the Earth," identifying them with healing waters and sacred wells. Vestiges of these royal frogs linger in European fairy tales, like "The Frog Prince," where enchanted frogs lurk in magical wells awaiting transformation into fabulous princes by true love's kiss. Because toad venom may be hallucinogenic, frogs and toads are also associated with shamanism and divination.

Although most ancient associations with frogs and toads were positive, it wasn't always the case: Zoroaster declared that all toads should be exterminated because of their venomous, malevolent nature. This exception to the rule eventually became the general perception in post-Christian Europe. Toads and frogs were perceived variously as slimy or warty, disguised demons or witches' familiars.

Toads' associations with magic, fertility, and women's wisdom never disappeared but they were certainly reinterpreted. From Northern Italy upwards through Germany, Poland, and the Ukraine, toads are named by words that also indicate "*fairies,*" "*witches,*" and "*sorcerers.*" In parts of Italy, for instance, frogs are called "*fada*" or *fairy.* "*Rospo,*" the Italian word for toad, may derive from the Latin "*haruspex,*" the word used for Etruscan diviners.

By the Middle Ages frogs and toads were considered among witches' most prevalent familiars. According to Reginald Scot, author of *The Discoverie of Witchcraft* published in 1584, toads were considered second in popularity only to the cat as a witch's familiar.

In Shakespeare's *Macbeth*, when the witches say "*Paddock calls*" they refer to a familiar toad, "*paddock*" being a diminutive of the Anglo-Saxon word for toad "*pad.*"

According to testimony given during Basque witch trials (on the French side of the Pyrenees) toads were favored familiars. Great companies of witches allegedly traveled to cemeteries for the purpose of "baptizing" their toads, which were dressed to celebrate in black and red velvet with bells at their neck and feet. One young woman claimed to have seen a noble lady dancing at the Sabbat with four toads: one belled and costumed in velvet riding on her right shoulder, three more naked toads riding on her left shoulder and wrists.

Frogs and toads were perceived as diabolical, disgusting and grotesque. A Swiss woodcut from approximately 1500 depicts a dead witch lying on a table following her dissection. A large toad is shown where her heart should be: this was intended to demonstrate her depraved, inhuman, demonic nature.

Old memories die hard, however; even in post-Christian, post-witchcraze Europe, there was resistance towards abandoning this most potent and ancient of fertility symbols. According to Central European tradition frogs carried dead children's souls, thus it was unlucky to kill them. A once popular Central European tradition involves offering frog-shaped ex-votos at the Virgin Mary's shrines as part of a petition for fertility and women's gynecological health.

Ancient people considered fierce, dangerous mothers desirable. A passive mother who couldn't or wouldn't defend her children only left them vulnerable. Thus it's no surprise that many beautiful goddesses of fecundity also double as war goddesses (Aphrodite, Ishtar, Oshun). Frogs (and especially toads) may be harbingers of abundance, but they're also potentially dangerous, venomous creatures.

When attacked or injured a toad secretes a thick white poison through its skin. This sometimes hallucinogenic, often lethal substance is now called *bufotenine*. Once upon a time, it was known as *"toad's milk"* and was incredibly feared. Allegedly an ingredient in many witches' flying ointments, it is typically the key ingredient in Amazonian arrow poison. It was believed that witches dispatched toads to poison their enemies. During Scotland's North Berwick witch trials, Agnes Sampson confessed (under duress) to attempting to assassinate King James VI with poisonous toad juice. Toad venom may be among the ingredients of the formula that transforms people into *zombis*.

Goats

General wisdom states that goats were the first animals to be successfully domesticated. Goats are involved in a lot of firsts:

✳ *Goats are credited with leading people to coffee, once a sacred beverage. (For many, it still is.) An Ethiopian shepherd noticed that his goats were particularly perky; he watched as they chewed coffee berries and tried some himself, thus initiating the cult of caffeine.*

✳ *Goats brought various fragrant resins to people, most especially rock roses, among Aphrodite's holy flowers. The aromatic essence was discovered clinging to goats' beards.*

✳ *Some of the most ancient existing evidence of magical/spiritual ritual involves the unearthed funeral rites of a Neanderthal child discovered in Teshik-Tash, modern Uzbekistan. The child's partial skeleton was encircled by ibex horns, a type of wild goat, arranged vertically in pairs, the pointed ends stuck into the ground, reminiscent of later European funerary spells that involve driving spindles into the ground, usually intended to quiet the restless dead.*

Goats are responsible for the discovery of the Oracle of Delphi. Before there was ever a shrine, Delphi was a playground for goats, which thrived on the rocky terrain. Humans followed them up the slopes and domesticated them c. 1400 BCE. As legend tells it, a massive earthquake created a chasm or fissure at Delphi through which some sort of vapor emanated. (Modern science has been unable to detect or explain these vapors.) Goats exposed to the vapors were observed to act strangely, suffering spasms and bleating in odd voices. Their keepers began to have similar experiences except that their odd voices were discovered to be prophetic. Delphi eventually became an organized oracular shrine, originally dedicated to Gaia, the Earth and then to Apollo. Goats remained the ritual sacrifice at Delphi.

Goats are associated with love, knowledge, fertility, prophesy, expiation, regeneration, and rebirth. They are *intensely* associated with sex, sexual energy, and the procreative urge and power. Goats serve as Aphrodite's mount and as companions of various Middle Eastern fertility spirits, including Inanna-Ishtar and Lady Asherah. Perceptions change: once upon a time, comparing a man to a goat implied admiration. Today's "old goat" is a pathetic, foolish lecher, kind of like those dumb-ass donkeys.

According to a Germanic magic spell, goat tallow rubbed onto the penis serves as a babe magnet, irresistibly attracting women.

Goats were profoundly involved with a multitude of ancient spiritual traditions including Celtic, Greek, Jewish, Norse, Roman, and Sumerian. Goats are sacred to Aphrodite, Azazel, Dionysus, Freya, Hera, Hermes, Pan, Thor, Zeus: sexy deities, one and all.

Goats were respected, sacred, and beloved in ancient religion. Goats were people's teachers, companions and in many places, primary food animal, supplying meat, milk, dairy products, and material for clothing and tents.

Goats were not generally considered to be witches' familiars, nor do witches transform into goats. Goats do frequently serve as witches' mounts however, and many medieval woodblock prints depicting witchcraft show witches riding on goats' backs, just like Aphrodite, although this may have been intended to euphemistically suggest that witches copulate with the devil. No animal is more associated with the Christian devil than the goat. Artistic renditions of the sabbat from the Middle Ages to Goya's masterpieces depict Satan presiding over the witches' sabbat in the form of a tall man-sized upright goat. Satan is also depicted as a composite creature, frequently with bat's wings and a snake's forked tongue, but with goat's eyes, horns and hooves.

More in-depth discussion of goats' ancient spiritual roles and the part they were given to play during the Witchcraze are found in **HORNED ONE.**

Hyenas

The stereotypical African witch doesn't have a pointy hat or broomstick but she's still a night rider journeying to secret assignations with other witches. These female witches ride naked atop galloping hyenas, with one foot dragging on the ground, the other on the hyena. (Allegedly this enables the hyena to attain extraordinary speed.) The witch carries a flaming torch, fueled with hyena butter, keeping an extra supply in a gourd slung over her shoulder so there's no danger of running out.

It's the hyenas that reveal her identity. Hyenas are believed to be the telltale sign that causes someone, usually but not exclusively women, to be branded a witch in Africa. Any evidence, regardless how flimsy or tangential, linking someone with hyenas may be considered proof of sorcery in African witchcraft trials.

Witches ride hyenas. Witches keep hyena familiars. Witches *are* hyenas. Witches shape-shift into hyenas. Zambian sorcerers enter trances and send their souls into the bodies of real hyenas. In other areas, there's no such thing as *"real"* hyenas: all are magical creatures, witches in disguise or witches' familiars. There's no such thing as a hyena that is not somehow affiliated with witchcraft.

Hyenas who are witches take spiritual possession of people, creating a kind of soul-hyena: the victimized person doesn't physically transform, but inside, where a human soul should be, lurks this hyena. If your best friend doesn't act like herself, maybe it's because she isn't herself: a hyena has supplanted her soul and taken over her body.

People who are witches transform hyenas into human likenesses. They can selectively choose the likeness, too. If your best friend begins to act strangely, maybe it really wasn't him at all but a hyena in disguise. In other words, there are two of them walking around: the real one and the disguised hyena—something like a *Swan Lake* scenario but with hyenas instead of swans. Witches are also believed able to create hyenas: their bodies are molded from porridge and brought to life via rituals and herbs.

Witches are believed able to cast sleeping spells on hyenas, transforming them into their own likeness, putting them to bed beside their own husbands so that the witches can secretly slip out with no fear that the husband will ever wake up and discover their disappearance. (During European witch trials, witches allegedly used brooms, branches, and sticks in identical manner for the same purpose. Because this was generally believed, husbands testifying that their wives couldn't possibly have attended sabbats as they had been home in bed together were thus unable to provide alibis for their wives.)

According to Bantu tradition, real hyenas are perfectly capable of transforming into human form without any help from a witch. The transformation may, however, only be accomplished during the day. Some hyenas shape-shift in order to visit, harass or terrorize humans, but some do it just for the joy of shape-shifting. Whole communities of shape-shifting hyenas are said to exist; although to an outsider they may look exactly like ordinary people. Don't try to stay in their village, though, no matter how friendly the locals seem; they may look like people but they still eat like hyenas. In order to shape-shift like this, hyenas must obtain a human soul. How this is done varies but hyenas that eat human corpses, as hyenas are known to do, may have the inside track.

Throughout Africa, hyenas allegedly live and bear their young in the houses of witches who milk them daily.

In some areas, although not many, hyenas gain some level of protection from their associations with witchcraft: it's believed dangerous to kill a hyena because her witch will magically retaliate.

In parts of East Africa, every witch is believed to own at least one hyena, which is branded with her special witch-mark, something like a bewitched cattle brand, invisible to regular eyes although clearly visible to other witches. Witches allegedly refer to their hyenas as "night cattle." People swear they've seen hyenas sporting earrings, either indicating that they're transformed people or that a person pierced that ear, as even the most magical hyena still lacks the skills for employment in a piercing parlor. (None of these tales actually derive from witches themselves; all are second-hand at best.)

The art of hyena riding is apparently very challenging. Novice witches must be trained at regular bush meetings where mounted witches gather. These rendezvous are reminiscent of European sabbats with one crucial exception. Yes, witches gather for orgies, cannibalism and all sorts of evil works, but there's no devil in attendance. Like female hyenas, which are the dominant gender of their species, no need for a male director of ceremonies exists.

Observing the powerful identification of hyenas with witches in Africa that exists even today makes one think that this is how it must have been with black cats and witches during the European Burning Times. Any association between a cat and a woman was believed to betray witchcraft: witches rode cats, kept cats, transformed into cats. Even lone cats, *sans* women, were believed to be witches in disguise. There is one crucial difference though: even at the height of the Witchcraze, cats were understood to be beautiful, sensuous, sometimes useful creatures. They might be evil but seductively so. An element of longing exists: a desire to destroy what one can't possess or control.

In Africa, hyenas are associated with garbage, feces, corpses, death, cemeteries, decay, and rotten odors. (And there are places where hyenas do live on human garbage and refuse or lurk in cemeteries, although this tends to be in urbanized areas where few other alternatives remain for them.) They are the largest creatures to exist mainly from scavenging. They are ungainly, awkward creatures, shaggy, smelly, and ragged-looking. They get into garbage; they unearth graves. They are not afraid of people, stealthily entering settlements at night in search of food, their identities exposed by glowing eyes and their characteristic, eerie laughter.

Hyenas are actually extremely interesting creatures, with unusual social structures and unusual genital structures, too. Females are the dominant gender within hyena society; unlike many species, females are 10 percent larger than males. Hyena females eat first; males wait to eat whatever's left over. Of course, this was difficult to determine for a long time. Male and female hyena genitals are virtually indistinguishable from each other, at least for human observers. Female spotted hyenas have highly developed, extremely large clitorises with erectile potential. (Subservient female hyenas—not the alphas—are the only creatures who display genital erections as a sign of submission; hyenas greet each other via genital inspection.) They urinate, copulate, and give birth through these clitorises. Scientists who study sex hormones adore hyenas: females have extremely high levels of androgens, traditionally considered the male sex hormone. These androgens are converted to testosterone, of which female hyenas possess a high level, especially when pregnant. A pregnant hyena's testosterone level may exceed that of the males. (Hyenas are used in animal research to study hormones.)

Hyenas have their own family group, the *Hyaenid.* Based on fossil evidence there may have once been more than 69 species. Hyenas were once found in Europe as well as Africa and Asia, where they exist today. However, only four species survive.

Witch hyenas tend to be striped and spotted hyenas, and most especially spotted ones, which are the species commonly known as "laughing hyenas."

Animals strongly identified with witchcraft tend to be formerly sacred animals who've since lost their reputations and are now feared and despised, like witches and the magical arts. Most of these animals have former spiritual affiliations with profound life-and-death topics: sex, birth, and the after-life. Do hyenas have a similar history? It's hard to tell; very little information is available. All these tales of night-riding come from outsiders; anthropologists, witch-hunters, missionaries, and story-tellers. There are some clues however:

❀ *This association of malevolent witchcraft with an animal species characterized by dominant females with visibly large penis-sized clitorises occurs in areas where female genital mutilation (excision of the clitoris) is a traditional practice. The very lack of discussion of hyenas when discussing mythic explanations for female genital excision is revealing. (The most commonly told myth involves removal of termite hills.)*

❀ *Some African tribes traditionally dispose of their dead by putting the bodies out in the bush for hyenas to eat, something that smacks of sacrifice.*

❀ *In Harar, Ethiopia, people feed hyenas and encourage scavenging. It's become an oddity, something for tourists to see, so there's little serious spiritual discussion of the bonds between Ethiopia's "hyena men" and the animals they feed, at personal financial sacrifice and in the face of social ostracism.*

❀ *Hyenas are traditionally believed allied to vultures, scavengers who are also now feared and disliked but who were sacred birds in Egypt and elsewhere. The word for "vulture" in ancient Egyptian was synonymous with "mother."*

❀ *Medieval Europeans believed that there was a stone within the hyena's eye (there isn't), which, when placed under a person's tongue, enabled one to foretell the future.*

❀ *Hyenas are associated with smiths and other artisans, respected, required members of society who are also feared and associated with sorcery, the original professional magicians. These artisans transform raw materials (ore, clay) into practical, beautiful, sometimes spiritual goods. Hyenas are believed able to transform themselves.*

Legendary associations of hyenas and witches make for good stories but like the identification of cats with witches during the Burning Times, this is really no laughing matter.

Associations of hyenas with smithcraft and witchcraft are not only folkloric fantasy tales but have had a massive impact on people's lives, contributing to tragic prejudice. Hyenas are associated with individuals but also with ethnic groups who are thus tarred by associations with malevolent witchcraft. The word *"buda"* (also spelled *"bouda"*) indicates "hyena-person." During the day budas appear to be ordinary people but at night budas either transform into hyenas or they ride on the backs of hyenas in great packs.

Budas and hyenas are believed to possess the Evil Eye, which leaves their victims drained and debilitated. Specific ailments are also associated with the Evil Eye. There's no obvious physical attack; there may be no contact, however fleeting, with a hyena. This is a spiritual, magical attack.

Traditionally budas are ironworkers and potters. Wherever people fear the buda, there are professional buda experts, similar to European witch-finders. They are engaged to determine the identity of the buda who cast the Evil Eye.

There are various methods of lifting the Evil Eye: a simple case may be cured via incantation, but in persistent cases an expert may be consulted to determine the identity of the buda, which is believed necessary to break the spell. Sometimes the victim is made to identify the buda, even if they claim complete ignorance. The victim, who by definition is already not feeling too well whatever the cause, is interrogated (sometimes harshly, sometimes for hours) until identification of the perpetrator is made.

✴ *The victim may be brought before the alleged buda who is forced to spit upon the victim, his saliva believed to vanquish the Evil Eye.*

✴ *If the expert buda-finder is unable to determine the identity of the buda, the victim's forehead may be stamped with a hot iron brand. This signature mark will allegedly show up on the face of the guilty buda, too, providing identification. As you can imagine, buda-finders who resort to this tactic frequently are not in high demand.*

✴ *Goma smoke is another method of stopping and reversing the effects of the Evil Eye. The ability to use fire characterizes the buda (whether smith or potter). So fighting fire with fire, smoke is generated to counteract and eliminate the effects. This is not just any old smoke: goma smoke is produced by burning tires or chicken feces alongside an assortment of woods. It is not fragrant, quite the opposite. On market days when artisans pass through villages, goma is lit as protective fires before residences.*

✴ *Goma is also used to identify the buda. Perceived victims of the Evil Eye are tortured by being smoked with goma, which has an oppressively foul smell, until they name the perpetrator. Once the perpetrator is named, the guilty party is summoned to face the victim, apologize and remove the Eye. There's no such thing as inability; if they can't, it's perceived that they won't. An article of the buda's clothing may be taken (sometimes right off their body) and thrown into the goma fire. The victim inhales smoke rising from the cloth.*

The victim has no choice but to identify *someone*; he or she is not left alone until this is accomplished (and the victim is typically a child). The accused must also participate in the ritual, no matter how absurd or insulting, or risk being killed by a mob.

Although any individuals may be buda, the term buda is most frequently used in Ethiopia to refer to its Jewish community, the Beta Israel, who are simultaneously ethnic, religious, and professional minorities.

Beta Israel men are traditionally smiths, the women potters—transformative professions viewed by the majority Christian society with ambivalence. Tools and handicrafts are vital, needed, and highly valued yet the practice is despised (working the land being perceived as the only respectable, sanctified occupation) and associated with witchcraft—as are the practitioners, to whom supernatural powers are attributed. To be an artisan is demeaning, yet magically powerful. Forbidden to own land, historically the Beta Israel have worked as tenant farmers for Christians, often in share-cropper-like circumstances.

Available information regarding traditional African witchcraft is virtually always filtered through the eyes of anthropologists or missionaries but there are a few important exceptions: Hagar Salamon's *The Hyena People* (University of California Press, 1999) contains interviews with people who survived accusations of being budas. And Nega Mezlekia's *Notes from the Hyena's Belly* (St Martin's Press, 2000), a memoir of the author's Ethiopian youth, gives a brief but significant explanation from the victim's perspective.

Imps

Today, should someone suggest that you have an *impish* smile or *impish* charm, it's probably a compliment. Most likely you're being compared to a charmingly naughty child. Of course, today, should someone call you *"little devil"* or *"little demon"* that's probably a compliment too, not intended to be taken literally or as a threatening, hostile statement.

Perhaps because some people needed to believe that they were inherently superior to animals, many witch-hunters had a hard time fathoming that witches' familiars, their trusted allies and companions, were really animals. If they had superior powers, they couldn't be mere animals; they must be little demons or devils in disguise.

Imps were small demons who, commonly disguised as animals, served as witches' familiars. Because they were supernatural creatures they could be expected to perform services that no true animal ever could, like fly through the air, invisibly cause death and destruction, or mysteriously torment victims of witchcraft. In areas where witchcraft was intensely demonized, it was believed that when a new witch was initiated at her first sabbat, Satan personally gave her an imp, not so much to serve her but to act as her control, ensuring that the witch carried out her assigned quota of nefarious deeds.

Unlike traditional familiars, which behaved like the regular animals that they were, eating and sleeping in the manner appropriate to their species, imps had special needs. Because imps were vampiric, witches were obliged to feed them using their own body fluids, milk if they were mothers, blood if not. (What type of blood imps fed upon is not entirely clear.) Witches were believed to grow an extra nipple just to feed their little imp. The search for supernumerary nipples became a common feature of later witch-trials, although it might be "found" in odd parts of the body and in odd forms.

Should the witch's own fluids be insufficient, the imp might go and milk neighboring livestock completely dry. These imps would travel in the form of familiar animals like bats, hedgehogs, ferrets or cats leading to strange, implausible fears about certain animals being harmful to cattle. Hedgehogs are still commonly believed to steal cow's milk, as are bats; of course the old stories never referred to *real* animals—thefts were caused by supernatural imps in masquerade.

The root concept of the imp may derive from small shape-shifting spirits previously understood as friendly and helpful. Pagan European households, from Italy to Lithuania, once cherished snake-spirit household helpers. Some spirits weren't exclusively tied to one animal form: Finland's *para*, for instance, are domestic spirits known to assume the forms of cats, frogs or snakes. Attached to a person or family, they magically increase supplies of butter, milk, grain, and cash. (In later folklore, *para* are classified as goblins.)

As the witch-trials faded from memory, the older Pagan conception of animal-shaped, mischievous domestic spirits re-emerged. Imps, those little devils, became figures of fun, mischief, and humor, albeit sometimes with a nasty edge. Imps entered the lexicon of Halloween via Victorian postcards, where they are not depicted as animals but as bright red devils, an image borrowed from the Central European *"devil,"* Krampus, who starred in his own postcard series. This type of imp, fun, lascivious, and joyful, is drawn to perfection in Kipling West's *The Halloween Tarot*.

Iynx (Wryneck)

Iynx is the name of a nymph, a bird, and an ancient Greek love charm. The famous charm consists of a miniature spinning wheel to which a wryneck bird is attached. It's a very primitive device; it could be a child's handmade toy, except for that poor suffering bird. The wheel is ritually spun, accompanied by incantations to draw and bind a lover. As the spell-caster murmurs and chants, she spins the toy, which makes a humming noise, similar to heavy breathing.

Iynx the nymph was a daughter of Pan and Echo. She invented the device that bears her name as an attempt to get back at Hera who had stolen Echo's voice. Iynx used the device to force Zeus to fall for Io. Not to be outdone in this witch-war, the furious Hera promptly transformed Iynx into a wryneck.

What does the bird have to do with the charm? Why specifically a wryneck? The Greek word for the wryneck, a species of woodpecker, is *iynx*, named for its cry. (Allegedly the nymph announces her name so that family and friends will recognize her in her altered state.) The bird gets its English name, "wryneck," from the characteristic movement of its head. When the wryneck is endangered or otherwise stressed, its defense mechanism is to extend its neck further than one would believe it could, twist it around and simultaneously fluff up its head feathers. With that long neck and puffed-up head, the wryneck resembles a snake—.causing its predators to think twice before attacking, and causing people to draw some other sexually-oriented comparisons.

Not surprisingly, the charm was a woman's tool; its goal to make the man she desired behave like that wryneck—or at least the appropriate parts of him. (And if he wasn't easily charmed, he'd be caught like that helpless bird. This isn't a particularly nice spell—its intent is to assertively bind, rather than sweetly seduce.)

Perhaps wrynecks became scarce, perhaps the inherent cruelty became distasteful, or perhaps it was discovered that the spell worked better without the bird. Eventually the wryneck component was abandoned and the spell cast with only the wheel. Even so, it retained its name. Eventually the name came to refer to any sort of aggressive love spell, and then finally to any sort of malevolent spell, romantic or otherwise. That usage survives in English, albeit with the Latin spelling, "*jinx.*"

Jaguars

Jaguars are ubiquitously identified with witchcraft, sorcery, magic, and shamanism throughout Central and South America. This reflects indigenous belief, existing long before European contact. (European-styled Latin American witchcraft exists too; the most typical familiars are cats, bats, and black dogs. Of course, black panthers/jaguars may be understood as supernaturally giant black cats.)

In this region, jaguars are simultaneously the most feared and revered of animals, playing a very prominent spiritual and magical role. The jaguar is the largest feline in the Western Hemisphere and is considered the most successful predator. Jaguar imagery pervades Central and South America from the Andes Mountains to the swamps of Eastern Mexico. The animal's range once extended from Argentina north through the southern United States. The jaguar remains the most powerful jungle predator of Central and Upper South America, although its range has been drastically curtailed because of habitat loss, and also because it has been relentlessly hunted as a competitive species, for sport and for its beautiful fur.

The jaguar embodies Earth's untamed, primal powers. Solitary, secretive creatures, jaguars are comfortable in all possible realms: they kill monkeys in trees, tap their tails into water to attract fish, jump into water to catch caimans, and hunt all sorts of other creatures on land. Jaguars cross boundaries: they are the biggest, fiercest, smartest, most mysterious animals in the jungle. They are believed to cross boundaries of species as well: many legends tell of liaisons between male jaguars and human women.

> In Amazonian mythology, the jaguar is considered the Master of All Animals. Jaguars are often portrayed as the central image in depictions, adored by other animals.

The animal manifests in two varieties. The more common, a golden cat with black spots (really rosettes) bears a very strong resemblance to the leopards of the Eastern Hemisphere. Jaguars may also have black fur. (If one looks closely in the light, the rosettes may still be observed.) Completely black jaguars and leopards are both known as black panthers.

The Mayans associated jaguars with the night sky, especially the black panther. Spotted jaguars symbolize the stars in the night sky. Their golden color represents the sun, while their glowing eyes mirror the moon.

Tezcatlipoca, "Lord of the Smoking Mirror," Aztec Patron of Sorcerers has a jaguar as his nagual or shadow soul. Jaguars' shining eyes are identified with mirrors and Tezcatlipoca sometimes travels in the guise of his sacred creature. Among Tezcatlipoca's many manifestations is one as Tepeyollotli—"*the Jaguar Who Lives in the Heart of the Mountain*," Earth's core. According to Aztec belief, supernal jaguars live in caverns beneath the Earth, occasionally emerging as the need arises. A modern Lacandon Mayan prophecy warns that life as we know it will end when these jaguars emerge from their underground cavern home to devour the sun and moon.

Aztec and Mayan shamans specifically identify themselves with jaguars but the association permeates virtually all shamanic cultures throughout the continent. Shamans dress as jaguars. The Mayan word "*balam*" signifies both "*magician-priest*" and "*jaguar.*" The word for "*jaguar*" also indicates "*shaman*" in various unrelated indigenous languages. The jaguar protects and teaches the shaman. Many believe that the shaman actually transforms into a jaguar. Real jaguars are also believed to act as jungle shamans. In some tropical rainforest communities, snakes are believed to serve as these jaguar's familiars.

Jaguars are also profoundly associated with various Amazonian psychoactive plants. Jaguar motifs decorate paraphernalia needed for preparing brews and powders from these plants. It's been suggested that real jaguars may chew hallucinogenic vines twined around jungle trees in the manner that domestic cats sometimes chew grass. Perhaps the jaguar literally taught shamans about these plants. (This may or may not be true but the concept isn't absurd: reindeer have been known to eat the fungus fly agaric: see **BOTANICALS:** Amanita Muscaria.)

Amazonian shamans still identify with jaguars. Jaguars remain among the most popular subjects of Mexican mask makers, frequently formed with mirrored eyes.

Leopards

Leopards still roam through parts of Africa and Asia, although their range is seriously curtailed because of habitat loss and hunting. Leopards once lived in Europe as well although they are extinct there now. Large, beautiful, solitary wild cats, leopards are fierce, stealthy, nocturnal hunters who are, in theory at least, not averse to hunting a lone human.

Leopards physically resemble jaguars although they are smaller and their spots are really spots, not rosettes. Like jaguars, there are two varieties: golden with black spots and pure black. A pure black leopard would be almost impossible to see at night without illumination, except for its burning, glowing eyes. Author Bruce Chatwin posits that it's the leopard who lurks as the primordial human fear, the animal power who once scared us most.

Images dating from *c.* 5700 BCE from Anatolia show goddesses riding leopards. Leopards are integral to the myth of the Anatolian deity, Kybele, the Mountain Mother. Leopards raised her when she was an infant left exposed to die in the forest. Suckled on leopard's milk, she grew up to be the first root-worker and witch, a queen and great goddess. Leopards flank her throne. (See **DIVINE WITCH:** Kybele.)

The leopard was sacred to Dionysus, Kybele's sometime compatriot. Dionysus appears in the form of a leopard; panthers draw his chariot and appear in his entourage. As the word "panther" was also used as a synonym for Dionysus' female followers, the Maenads—it's tempting to wonder whether those panthers in his midst were intended to imply women transformed into huge black cats.

Leopards are associated with royalty throughout Africa. Many royal clans count leopards as their primeval ancestors. In some regions, wearing a leopard skin was reserved exclusively for royalty or for the most elite spiritual societies. Artifacts recovered from Tutankhamun's grave show King Tut riding on the back of a panther. Leopards are also considered ancestors and spiritual sponsors of various African shamanic societies. Leopards were identified with Kenya's Mau-Mau. Belief that the Mau-Mau could transform into leopard-men contributed to their fearsome reputation.

In Mali, the Bamana/Bambara witch-goddess Muso Koroni manifests as a black panther or as a many-breasted woman. (Some believe that the many-breasted deity from Anatolian Ephesus, commonly identified as either Artemis or Diana, is really that other leopard woman, Kybele.) Muso Koroni oversees initiations: it was believed that she stimulates menstruation by scratching girls with her leopard's claws. A nocturnal spirit, like a leopard, she rules the boundaries between civilization and wilderness, straddling the balance between chaos and order.

See **CREATIVE ARTS:** Films: Cat People; **DICTIONARY:** Maenad; **DIVINE WITCH:** Dionysus; Muso Koroni.

Magpies

The magpie is a large, curious, active bird with a harsh call and a swaggering walk. It originally inhabited scrublands, forests, and other areas with dense foliage but it is now adapted to other areas, including urban habitats. Omnivorous, it eats pretty much whatever it can find: insects, seeds, fruit, small mammals, or carrion. It is a very clever bird and has a reputation for stealing and hoarding shiny objects.

Magpies inhabit North America, Europe, Northwestern Africa, the Middle East, Central and East Asia. Virtually wherever they are found, they are associated with witchcraft either as familiars or, more frequently, as the form into which witches transform. One Russian nickname for witch is *"soroka-veschchitsa," "magpie-witch."*

> Magpies are members of the corvid family like jackdaws, crows, and ravens, but they have their own section here for two reasons:
>
> ❋ *Magpies were understood as a different type of bird. The other three very closely resemble each other in color (solid black) and nature. Magpies are dramatically* black *and* white, *although depending upon the light their black feathers may appear blue, green or purple.*
>
> ❋ *Magpies possess very different magical and mythical associations, often specifically identified with romantic and women's magic.*

Magpies are associated with female power, romantic magic, and prophesy. In *Macbeth*, Shakespeare notes that magpies were used as augurs. Russian folk belief suggests that magpies announce storms. People who live near magpies will notice that the birds often announce the arrival of visitors or other changes.

Scottish, Swedish, and Russian witches commonly take the form of magpies. Latvian witches allegedly adopt the form especially for Midsummer's Eve. Siberian witches can allegedly transform into any type of bird or animal they wish to: magpies are their most common choice.

Various legends describe Russian magpie-witches. According to one, Ivan the Terrible gathered together all the witches he could find in order to burn them, but before he could, they transformed into magpies and flew away. According to another legend, there are no magpies in Moscow because church leader Metropolitan Alexei, recognizing them for what they truly were, forbade them to fly over the city. The seventeenth-century usurper of the Russian throne, known as the False Dmitrii, had an unpopular Polish wife widely believed to be a sorceress. She allegedly escaped from Moscow by flying away as a magpie. Magpies were also occasionally burned as witches in Russia, or hung onto peasant barns as a warning to witches.

Not all magpie-witches are living transformed witches. One story suggests that murdered witches reincarnate as magpies. They are true birds but their souls remain those of witches. It's necessary to be kind and respectful to them, some even suggest saluting them, because otherwise they'll cast a spell on you.

In Russia and elsewhere in Europe, magpies became identified with Satan. In England, they're known as the devil's own bird. In Russia, flocks of magpies are associated with Satan, betraying subtle identification of witches with diabolical forces.

Chinese mythology has happier associations. Magpies form the bridge that, one day a year, permits the sacred Weaving Maiden to be reunited with her beloved husband, the Cowherd. In Chinese the epithet *"Heavenly Woman"* is shared by celestial goddesses and magpies, which may be goddesses in disguise.

Nahual, Nahualli, Naualli, Nagual

Deriving from the Nahuatl (Aztec) language, the word *"nahual"* indicates different concepts in different regions of Mexico, all having to do with animal alliances. Because the same word is used to describe these linked but different concepts confusion exists. The word is also pronounced slightly differently depending upon region; attempts to transliterate the word into English have resulted in a variety of spellings. None of them are wrong.

Nahual has been translated as "shadow soul," a human soul's animal twin. It's also translated as "mask" or "disguise." The nahual is an animal ally, although the meaning is more profound than standard modern usage where animal ally may refer to a friend, companion or animal. The relationship is deeper: the nahual may be understood as one's animal soul. It may or may not refer to a specific individual animal.

Souls and identities of humans and nahuals are bound together; they share each other's destinies. This is a very shamanic concept, and it exists in Eastern Hemisphere magic, too, or at least once did. In Hungarian witchcraft-trials, cats, dogs, hens, and frogs are perceived as doubles or second bodies of witches.

There are various definitions of nahual.

The nahual is a person who can transform, a shape-shifting witch or sorcerer. These practices were a major concern for Colonial priests in Mexico. In 1600, Fray Juan Bautista warned of native sorcerers who transformed into chickens, dogs, jaguars, owls, and weasels. The seventeenth-century priest Ruiz de Alarcón mentions specific cases and explains the power as deriving from Satanic compact. (The Spanish Inquisition was in full swing in the Western Hemisphere.) However, the concept is of indigenous origin. Satan didn't exist in the Western Hemisphere before priests brought him.

The Aztec deity Tezcatlipoca, the divine sorcerer, was believed able to transform into a jaguar. Nahuals tend to possess specific forms; in other words not every nahual transforms into the same shapes. Not limited to animals, some nahuals may also be able to transform into natural forces, like lightning or (especially) whirlwinds. Some nahuals (this human kind) can also allegedly become invisible and thus transport themselves secretly from place to place.

Nahuals were feared and respected for their power. Although the stereotype, as filtered through the Inquisition, identifies them as malevolent independent practitioner sorcerers, they also served as protectors of their communities. During the Colonial Era, nahuals lead native resistance, which may explain some of the colonizers' hostility toward them.

Secondly, the nahual may be the animal part of this dyad. Every human being has a nahual. You have a nahual but if you don't know its form, then you're only half a person, not operating at your full capacity. Under the Aztec Empire, a priest presided over a ritual on the fourth day following birth to determine a baby's nahual and bind the relationship. This nahual serves as the person's guide and protector, offering various psychic gifts and magical or physical powers. Each type of animal is capable of offering different gifts. Every Aztec deity had a nahual. If you share a nahual form with a deity, you share a bond with that deity, too.

If you didn't receive your nahual as a child, it's never too late. Another Aztec method is a do-it-yourself ritual:

1. Go into the woods alone and go to sleep.
2. Your nahual will either appear in your dreams or you will be confronted by your nahual when you awake.
3. Once the nahual is identified, you are obliged to enter into a life-long contract with it.

Furthermore, in Toltec and Mixtec traditions, the nahual is an individual's totem or fate-guardian, or perhaps the personification of one's deepest psyche. Nahual also names the reciprocal relationship between a person and their animal double.

In Oaxaca, the traditional concept is related but subtly different. Naguals, as the word is most frequently spelled there, are a form of animal ally. Every one has one; their identity is disclosed via ritual. At its most superficial level, the nagual serves as a magical assistant, it can help you accomplish your life's goals if you know how to work with it. However, the nagual may also be understood as a person's other half; they mirror each other or share a soul, or perhaps the animal is the person's second soul. Lives of human and animal are bound up together. They're not identical, not interchangeable, one is not merely the transformed shape of the other but should one die, the other one will too.

No need for a priest here: parents usually determine a nagual's identity shortly after a child's birth. Identification of the nagual reveals crucial information about the child's nature and required upbringing, not to mention taboos, which are very easy to break if you don't know about them. There are various slightly different methods of determining a nagual. Here's one:

1. Sprinkle ashes outside the place where a baby was born.
2. The first animal footprint captured by the ashes identifies the nagual and sometimes the baby's name.

Owls

"Strega," "strix," "estriё": these terms are synonyms for "witch," although literally what they mean is "owl." Owls were witches' familiars from ancient Egypt, Rome, and Asia to modern Africa and Native America, with *many* stops in between. They represent divine yin: night, darkness, magic, and sacred lunar and feminine mysteries.

Owls are associated with wisdom, both conventional and secret, witchcraft, magic, sex, death, and birth. In the Eastern Hemisphere, owls were understood as emblematic of the uterus and as embodying the Great Mother's power over life and death. Owls are sponsors of shamanism. They bestow gifts of clairvoyance and teach the arts of astral projection. They serve as guides to the realms of the spirits and the dead because, of course, owls can navigate the darkness.

There are approximately 135 living species in the order *Strigiformes*, varying in size from the six-inch elf owl to the three-foot long Great Gray Owl. Owls have a very distinctive shape. Only their silhouette may be required for identification. Compared to other birds, owls are fairly odd looking, resembling cats with wings. (If seated silently on a tree branch, it may be hard to immediately distinguish an owl from a cat, especially from a distance and in the dark.)

Their eyes are circular, evoking the full moon's shape and glow. Some owls are even horned, or at least they appear to be.

Owls announce the night like crows herald the day. *No* bird or animal is more associated with night than owls.

Owls made a very early impression on people: in *Les Trois Frères* cave in France, home of the *"Dancing Sorcerer,"* an unmistakable outline of a pair of snowy owls together with their chicks is chipped from the rock face. Paleolithic "Eye-Goddesses" may represent stylized owls.

"Striges" was the Roman name for witch, typically understood malevolently. Owls were perceived as harbingers of doom, trouble, and death—in short bad news; however the Romans also had tremendous issues with women's power. By the classical period, women were essentially

property belonging to men: their husbands, fathers or brothers. Those women who rebelled, for instance those who joined the Bacchanalia, were punished. It was not a culture innately sympathetic to women's sexual autonomy or to their sacred arts.

Strix came to be understood as a specific kind of witch: grotesque, sexually voracious, baby killing, female cannibals—all the negative stereotypes that still exist. This isn't an integral part of the word's meaning, however. *Strix* and its linguistic derivatives may also be understood to denote witchcraft's positive attributes: knowledge of Earth's powers, the ability to journey between realms, and acquisition of great wisdom, especially of crucial, secret topics.

Various sacred female spirits are profoundly identified with owls:

❊ *Owls are sacred to Athena. The small screech owl is her emblem and Homer describes Athena as "owl-faced." It was popularly believed that Athena appeared on the battlefield as an owl during a Greek battle with the Persians.*

❊ *Owls are identified with the Semitic wind spirit Lilith, whose name is cognate with "screech owl." (There are those who deny that she appears in the Old Testament because the only clear reference to her may also be understood to literally mean "screech owl.") Unlike most other formerly prominent Middle Eastern deities, Lilith, identified as Earth's real first woman, survived to star in worldwide Jewish folklore, where she serves as the prototype of the witch.*

❊ *Blodeuwedd, the Welsh magical woman, is formed from flowers. Since she is a magical being, she is immortal and cannot be punished by death for betraying and killing her husband Lleu; instead she is transformed into an owl, condemned to hunt alone at night for ever. The implication is that*

Blodeuwedd, as the embodiment of the lustful, fickle, secretive, plotting, murderous woman now displays her true form—that of a witch.

❊ *Owls fly with Tlazolteotl, Aztec witch-goddess with dominion over life, death, magic, and spiritual purification. Tlazolteotl cleans up sin like owls gobble up rats.*

❊ *Marinette, Vodou sorceress lwa, manifests as a screech owl. Those whom she temporarily possesses demonstrate her presence by behaving like owls too.*

Owls signify witchcraft. Whether this is understood positively, negatively or neutrally reflects cultural and individual perceptions of witchcraft. Owls famously serve as witches' familiars and messengers and most frequently as the guise into which witches transform.

❊ *Some Siberian shamans' coats are cut to resemble owl wings and tail.*

❊ *Apuleius witnessed the successful transformation of the witch Pamphile into an owl in his novel,* The Golden Ass.

❊ *In central and southern Africa, sorcerers are believed to fly at night like owls to steal food and valuables from their neighbors.*

❊ *African witches who prefer not to shape-shift into hyenas are believed most likely to choose the shape of an owl instead.*

❊ *Aztec nocturnal shape-shifting sorcerers were known as "tlacatecolotl," "owl-men."*

❊ *The Aztecs associated owls with caves and mirrors—the same magical world of sorcery inhabited by sacred jaguars and presided over by the divine sorcerer, Tezcatlipoca.*

Owls signify birth and women's power, especially their reproductive and sexual powers:

❋ *In Ecuador and Peru, dating back at least as far as 300 BCE, owls representing the divine mother are favored decorative motifs on spindle whorls. The deity is usually depicted in a birthing position. (These spindles strung together are found in abundance at gravesites as well as other sites associated with death, perhaps as charms of rebirth.)*

❋ *In parts of France and Wales, the hooting of owls doesn't signify death but its opposite. It's believed to foretell the birth of daughters.*

❋ *In the nineteenth century, "owl" became slang for whore or harlot.*

Pigs

Circe, the sacred sorceress, notoriously transformed men into swine; historically however, pigs are more usually identified with powerful goddesses and witches than with their transformed victims.

Perhaps no animal evokes as passionate a reaction as does the seemingly humble pig. Few cultures are traditionally neutral towards pigs; instead pigs tend to inspire either intense reverence or loathing. Some ancient cultures, the Celts for instance, perceived pigs as sacred, holy animals; other cultures understand pigs to be just the opposite. Most famously, pork is a tabooed food for Muslims and Jews. Perhaps in reaction, in certain parts of medieval Christendom, to eat pork developed almost a sacramental quality: one could prove one was a good Christian by eating pork with gusto.

So some cultures perceive pigs as *bad*, while others see them as *good*. It seems so clear, doesn't it—almost dualist? Well, when one approaches the sacred, *nothing* is ever that simple, and perceptions of pigs are no exception.

Prohibitions against consuming pork in what is now considered the Middle Eastern region pre-date both Islam and Judaism. The ancient Egyptians also refrained from eating pork under religious taboo, perhaps because of its associations with the dangerous sorcerer deity Set. Swineherds occupied the absolute lowest niche in ancient Egyptian society—the equivalent of India's Untouchable caste. (Although one wonders, if no one was eating pork, why there were any swineherds at all?)

There is a belief common to many anthropologists and scholars of religion that intense food taboos virtually always arise only when something is too holy to be eaten. In general, tabooed meat derives from an animal that is (or once was) a culturally sacred totem. In plain English, the forbidden animal was once a holy beast; too sacred to eat, often too sacred to even discuss freely, so that later generations may no longer recall or understand the true original impetus for the prohibition.

Conversely, in Christian areas, pigs were simultaneously perceived as lucky *and* treated with contempt. Today, if someone is described as a "*pig*" virtually anywhere on Earth, not only in Jewish or Muslim areas, it's almost inevitably meant as an insult.

❋ *Pigs are frequently used to represent the epitome of sloth, greed, carnal pleasures, and slovenliness.*

In medieval Christian art, the pig symbolized gross materiality and the inherent bestial nature that humans should strive to rise above.

In Buddhist iconography, the pig epitomizes desire in all its forms.

People first domesticated pigs some five to seven thousand years ago, however, like cats, there are only slight distinctions between wild and domestic pigs. Abandoned domestic pigs return to a feral state easily and are notoriously self-sufficient. The term *"boar"* is used to refer to the wild European pig once widespread throughout the forests of Europe and the British Isles and believed to be the ancestor of modern domestic pigs. *"Boar"* also names the adult male domestic pig. (The female pig is a *sow.*) To avoid confusion, the term *"pig"* is used in this section to refer to the entire porcine family, wild, feral, and domestic, unless specified otherwise.

> Pigs, in some ways, occupy a sacred niche similar to that of the bear, an animal whose sacredness is also considered too potent to even discuss. Like bears, pigs are associated with dangerous but fiercely devoted mothers, lunar deities, herbalism and root magic, and Earth's gestation during winter. Bears and pigs also featured in similar sacrificial rituals and practices. Male and female bears are also called boars and sows respectively.

Pigs are highly intelligent. Today they are frequently kept as pets and many people claim that pigs are more easily trained than dogs. However, pigs are also notoriously stubborn and strong-minded. (As they can grow to be quite formidable in size, it may also be more physically challenging to *persuade* a recalcitrant pig to change its mind.) They are potentially destructive creatures. They do not graze like sheep; instead, they famously *root*, overturning the Earth in search of the delicacies they enjoy. (It is believed that pigs introduced humans to the pleasures of truffles; from a folkloric or mythic perspective, pigs are associated with mushrooms in general, and with *Amanita muscaria* in particular.)

Pigs are large, fierce, and stubborn. Although pigs are not predatory—they do not seek to harm humans—neither will they back down from a fight. Once they are in an aggressive mode, they may even pursue a fleeing person. A fast, angry, stubborn pig is a dangerous one. The most formidable pig ancient people would have met would have been a mother pig.

Wild boars form groups called "sounders." Each sounder has approximately 20 members, although some have considerably more. Each sounder consists of several sows with their offspring; adult males only join during the breeding season but otherwise live alone. Sows are quite capable of providing for their piglets as well as protecting them independently or in conjunction with other sows.

Ancient people thus identified sows with the ideal of the fierce mother who protects her young no matter what, similar to the bear or crocodile mother. Pigs became identified with the goddesses who also epitomized the ideal of the aggressive, fervently devoted mother.

Pigs do not deserve their reputation as filthy, slovenly creatures. They lack sweat glands and thus find relief by lingering in water or wallowing in mud when they are hot. (According to one legend, the healing properties of the thermal waters of the city of Bath were discovered after pigs were observed wallowing in its mud.)

For a variety of reasons including this affinity for water, their propensity for "rooting" in Earth in the manner of a root-worker or herbalist, their identification with fecund but fierce mothers, and, not least, because of their lunar crescent-shaped tusks, ancient people identified pigs (even male ones, because of those tusks) with the female principle, with the moon, witchcraft, and with powerful magically potent female deities.

✴ *No creature is as identified with Earth's pleasures, gifts, and comforts as is the pig.*

✴ *No creature is as identified with the Corn Mother as is the pig.*

However, as Earth's pleasures became increasingly suspect, the pig's reputation sank. Part of this ambivalence toward pigs may stem from the profound role pigs once played in Pagan ritual; part may derive from the roots of *why* pigs played that role: the powerful identification of pigs with Earth's bounties as well as with fierce, fertile female power.

Pigs were associated with sex, birth, new life, regeneration, fruitfulness, abundance, prosperity, divination, and love. Pigs also epitomize male and female reproductive sexuality. Sows are emblematic of fecundity. In Italy, as well as those areas once dominated by Rome, the word "*pig*" was used as a nickname for the vulva, similar to the modern usage of "*pussy.*" Small gold and silver pig-shaped charms were worn as amulets by Roman women to ensure fertility, and cowrie shells were frequently called "pig shells" in Europe, not because of their resemblance to swine but because of their resemblance to the vulva.

Pigs are associated with almost as many deities as are snakes. In fact, the deity whom pigs are most closely identified with today, Demeter, has two sacred creatures: pigs and snakes.

✴ *The Eleusinian Mysteries, dedicated to Demeter and her daughter Persephone, was the most significant spiritual ritual in ancient Greece. Its ceremonies were initiated by the sacrifice of a pig.*

✴ *When Persephone is kidnapped, only two voluntarily assist Demeter: the young swineherd who is the only eye-witness to the abduction (some of his pigs fall into the chasm that opens up to swallow Persephone) and the witch-deity Hecate, whose sacred animals also include snakes and pigs.*

✴ *The Eleusinian Mysteries were not Demeter's only sacred rites. She also presided over the* Thesmophoria, *a women's annual autumnal mystery whose rituals involved both her sacred creatures, pigs and snakes. Because it was a "mystery" cult festival few details survive, however this much is known: during the ritual, pigs, cakes, and pine branches were thrown into underground chasms (or vaults), which were then covered so that they were contained within Earth. Snakes lived in these grottoes as guardians: they may have consumed much of the offerings. During the next year's festival, the decayed remains were removed and incorporated into ritual. This ritual may have reproduced Persephone's descent into the Underworld and her ultimate emergence.*

✴ *Ceres, the Italian Corn Mother, eventually became profoundly identified with Demeter. Pigs were kept in underground enclosures of her shrines. Those seeking healing dreams were invited to sleep among the pigs. (See below for more information regarding pigs and dreams.) Silver and gold pigs were among Ceres' votive offerings.*

✴ *Artemis' shrines were often decorated with boars' heads or with their tusks. She famously sent the Calydonian boar to ravage the land as punishment when a king neglected to offer her what she perceived as her share of first fruits of his hunt.*

Animals

* Among the deities depicted as riding pigs are Arduinna, Baba Yaga, Demeter, Freya, and Isis. Freya and Baba Yaga will eventually come to be explicitly identified as witches.

* Cerridwen, the Welsh witch-goddess, is sometimes called "The White Sow." Pigs are her sacred creatures.

* Among Brigid's many animal familiars is one known as the King of the Swine.

* The ancient Celtic deities known as hags are frequently described as having boar's tusks.

* Sometimes Hecate is depicted as having three heads facing in three different directions: although there are variations, a pig is almost inevitably among one of the three creatures. Hecate also occasionally manifests in the form of a black sow, particularly when she is in an aggressive mood.

* Ezili Dantor is the Haitian lwa who epitomizes the aggressively independent, self-sufficient mother. Her sacred animal is the black pig, and she is powerfully identified with the small black self-sufficient pigs that once ran wild through Haiti and upon which rural Haitians depended for food and income. Those pigs, like Ezili Dantor, represented economic independence: as demonstration of their economic importance, the same word was used to name these pigs and banks. (In the 1980s, these pigs were eradicated and replaced by higher maintenance white pigs during a United States-sponsored program that remains controversial.)

Pigs, and specifically pig-sties, are also identified with oracular powers. An ancient method of incubating a prophetic dream was to sleep in a pig-sty. Although it seems humorous today because pigs are now commonly perceived as silly, lazy, useless, slovenly creatures, this method was once taken *very* seriously and is common to German, Italian, Romanian, Romany, Scandinavian, and Slavic traditions.

* The one requirement is that the pen must *contain at least one sow with her young.*

* It was once a German custom to nap in the sty on either Christmas Day or the day of the solstice to obtain lucky dreams and good fortune.

* In Italian tradition, the ritual may be accompanied by invocations to St Anthony of Egypt for maximum effectiveness.

White sows have particularly powerful lunar associations. The porcine profile can change dramatically—expanding and slimming down—in response to diet, pregnancy, and birth. This rhythmic shape-shifting was perceived as similar to that of the moon. Black sows are particularly identified with witchcraft. Black pigs, particularly small, fast ones, were often understood to be transformed witches engaged in spell-casting missions. Witch-hunters accused witches of offering black pigs to Satan.

See also Bears, Snakes, Transformation; **BOTANICALS:** Amanita Muscaria or Fly Agaric; **CALENDAR:** Yule; **ERGOT; DIVINE WITCH:** Artemis; Baba Yaga; Cerridwen; Circe; Freya; Hecate; Isis; Set; **HAG; HORNED ONE:** Chimneysweep.

Rabbits and Hares

The animal once most associated with European witchcraft wasn't the cat, which for a long time was rare, but rabbits. Rabbits serve as witches' familiars and messengers and are the form into which European witches once most frequently transformed.

Most rabbit and hare species graze at twilight. Little brown rabbits camouflage well; they suddenly appear and disappear, as if by magic. Rabbits' defenses are limited to speed, brains, and fecundity. Rabbits survive and thrive because they can reproduce faster than they can be killed. No surprise, then, that the rabbit is the fertility animal extraordinaire. They are associated with sex, reproduction, and the moon. Classic tricksters, they represent success, survival and joy despite all odds, which, after all, is the primal stimulus for magic and witchcraft.

The gestation period of a rabbit is 28 days, one lunar month, akin to a woman's menstrual cycle. The Egyptian word for "rabbit" translates as *the opener*" and also indicated *"period*' in both the calendar and menstrual sense. Sacred rabbits, female and male, had dominion over women's reproductive abilities. Vestiges of that Pagan belief survive in the bunny that delivers eggs, emblematic of birth, at Easter, the Christian holiday that closely corresponds to the Vernal Equinox, the time of Earth's rebirth. Easter bunnies are most frequently depicted as sweet, juvenile purveyors of candy eggs; the hares they're based upon were understood as wild, raucous, very phallically empowered magical creatures. The consort of the Pagan goddess Ostara, whose name is recalled in "Easter," was a man-sized hare. (See **CALENDAR:** Easter; Ostara.)

Around the world, rabbits are associated with the moon, the celestial body ruling magic, romance, and reproduction. In many areas there's a rabbit in the moon, not a man.

Throughout Central America, the moon was uniformly associated with rabbits. Classical Mayan imagery depicts a beautiful, youthful woman sitting on a crescent moon, cuddling a rabbit in her arms. The Yucatan goddess Ix Chel, lunar deity of women, magic, storms, and spinning has a consort who manifests in the form of a man-sized rabbit.

In China, rabbits are associated with witchcraft, sorcery, and alchemy. According to Chinese myth, a rabbit keeps the Moon Lady company in her lonely palace—not just any old rabbit though: the rabbit on the moon is an alchemist rabbit, seen pounding out the secret elixir of immortality with his mortar and pestle.

In the US, the words "rabbit" and "hare" are interchangeable and commonly perceived as synonyms. In the UK, however, this is not the case: rabbits and hares are perceived as distinct. It is the hare that is identified with witchcraft, magic, pre-Christian traditions, and especially the moon.

Rabbits are trickster spirits in Africa and now, via transplantation, in the United States as well, the classic examples being Brer Rabbit and Bugs Bunny. They represent rabbits' powers of rebirth and regeneration: no matter how much trouble Brer and Bugs get into, even when doom seems certain, they always miraculously slip out of trouble (or resurrect) to survive and thrive. They are magical creatures, too smart for their own good; their curiosity, quest for knowledge, and inability to mind their own business inevitably leads them into trouble, which they always then manage to remedy and survive. They are somewhat dangerous creatures, too, reminding us that tricksters aren't just cuddly bunnies but typically also possess a sharper edge that can lead others into trouble, as well as extricating them again.

Historically, when English witches transformed into animals, it was most frequently a hare. Unlike on the European mainland where wolves were the most common form, there's little British tradition of werewolves. Christina Hole, author of *Witchcraft in England*, suggests that this powerful identification with hares occurred when wolves were eradicated in the British Isles.

The British Isles are filled with tales of hares serving as witches' alter egos:

✳ *According to legend, Anne Boleyn haunts her parish church in the form of a hare.*

✳ *Isobel Gowdie, perhaps Scotland's most famous witch (for reasons unknown, she volunteered her witchcraft confession), claimed that she traveled in the form of a hare.*

✳ *On the Isle of Man, gorse was set on fire on May Day to flush out the witches, believed to take the form of hares on that day.*

✳ *In Ireland, rabbits found amid cows on May Day were once summarily killed because they were believed to be shape-shifting witches with wicked designs on cattle, milk, and butter.*

Even people with little knowledge or interest in magic spells are familiar with the concept of the lucky rabbit's foot, typically carried as a gambling charm. "*Lucky for whom?*" asks the old joke. "*It wasn't lucky for the rabbit!*" Indeed. This "charm's" origins derive from magical witch-hunting techniques similar to those advocating slaughtering rabbits on May Day.

The custom of carrying a rabbit's foot charm

is now associated with gambling luck but that wasn't the original intent. The magical rabbit's foot isn't some ancient spell but is of relatively recent origin. Although popularly associated with African-American conjure traditions, the charm has British roots. Similar charms were used in nineteenth-century England to protect against witchcraft.

Not just any old rabbit's foot would do. Slightly different versions of this spell exist, some more difficult than others, but to turn the trick, it originally had to be the left foot of a rabbit killed in a cemetery at midnight, sometimes on a Friday or a Friday the 13th; on a dark moon Friday or any dark moon. Some American versions specify that it must be an African-American cemetery, which may indicate something about the spell-casters beliefs about witchcraft. Other versions stipulate that the rabbit must be killed with a silver bullet. (Silver is the moon's metal.)

There are various ways of understanding this spell:

✳ *The rabbit may be understood as a transformed witch, who is now destroyed and her power stolen for the killer's personal use.*

✳ *It may be understood as similar to traditions like nailing bats or owls to barn doors to scare away witches; an announcement that what can be done to the crucified witch can be done to others.*

✳ *It's possible that the spell-caster's goal was to obtain a rabbit familiar or even spiritual possession of the witch in rabbit form.*

✳ *The rabbit may also be understood as a revenant or powerful ghost; caught outside its grave, it's now finally* really *dead and unable to rise and walk again.*

Scorpions

Scorpions' profound association with witchcraft and magic is reflected in the astrological sign of Scorpio, the sign with dominion over magic, death, and sex. Scorpio rules the reproductive organs.

Astrological associations of scorpions with sex, death, birth, and rebirth derive from ancient Egyptian mythology. The Egyptians both feared and venerated scorpions. The power to harm is the power to heal and vice versa. Scorpions were potentially deadly, as were scorpion deities, who were worthy of fear and respect but also invoked for protection against scorpions and other deadly dangers. Scorpion-power may be understood as witchcraft; the ability to channel potentially dangerous energy positively or negatively as desired, and especially the ability to heal and over-ride damage caused by others—spiritual and magical poisons as well as physical ones.

Scorpion goddess Serket (also spelled Selket or Serqet) is among the Egyptian deities most associated with magic and witchcraft. Serket is usually depicted as a beautiful woman wearing a scorpion on her head (she also manifests in crocodile, cobra, and lion form). Serket travels in Isis' entourage. She is a protective spirit who is among the four primary deities (alongside Neith, Isis and her sister Nephthys) guarding entombed coffins. Serket's title *"Mistress of the Beautiful House"* is a euphemistic expression for that ancient funeral parlor, the embalming pavilion. Serket is invoked in many spells to protect and heal poisonous bites. She served as matron of those practitioners of magical medicine who specialized in such cases.

The scorpion-girls who serve as Isis' escorts when she is in hiding with baby Horus may be understood as witches. When the Egyptian culture-hero Horus grows up, he marries one of them.

Scorpions in Chinese magic are symbolic of great harm and danger, as well as of the power and ability to counteract them.

The mating habits of scorpions are similar to those of spiders, their relatives. The male scorpion is smaller than the female. Sex begins with a copulation dance, tails entwined. At the conclusion of the act, the male, who apparently knows what's coming, usually tries to escape; the female, for her part, tries to devour him as her post-coital snack. (She's allegedly successful only 10 percent of the time.)

Scorpions have a long pregnancy even by human standards: a year and a half before delivery. A long-lived species (15–25 years) scorpions don't reach sexual maturity until they hit the magic number seven. Scorpions are fierce, devoted mothers; after the birth, baby scorpions stay safe by riding on their mother's back for two to six weeks.

Skin-walkers

The term "skin-walker" refers to the same concept as those nahuals (sorcerers) who are able to change forms. It is the English translation of a Navajo term. Although traditional Navajo culture is shamanic, with a long tradition of magical healing and positive magical practices, the word "witchcraft" in Navajo is virtually always understood as malevolent. Use of the word "witch" almost always refers to a shaman gone bad or to a corrupt sorcerer or some sort of malevolent practitioner of magic. Traditional Navajo philosophy prizes harmony and places emphasis on the welfare of the community. Witches are understood to place individual desires above those of the group.

Navajo witches most frequently transform into wolves or coyotes. They may be distinguished from a regular wolf or coyote, at least by someone who is familiar with the genuine article:

❋ *Transformed wolves and coyotes may be unusually large.*

❋ *They carry their tails in a different manner than real animals do.*

❋ *They may betray themselves by wearing or carrying something associated with humans, like jewelry.*

Snakes

Snakes are so central to witchcraft, spirituality and magic that a thousand-page book could be devoted to that topic alone. Of necessity, this has been compressed. What follows is only a brief synopsis, the proverbial tip of the iceberg.

Snakes play a profound role in witchcraft as familiars, companions, teachers and transmitters of magic, guardians of knowledge, and as witches themselves, transformed or otherwise. A Ukrainian word for "witch" is synonymous with "snake." This may be understood as the stealthy dangerous snake in the grass or as a mysterious, powerful, holy being, however you choose.

Snakes are symbolic of birth, life, immortality, rebirth, fertility, sexuality, health, and wisdom—especially women's wisdom. Snake venom potentially kills or cures, as do shamans, healers, and witches.

Hibernating snakes burrow within Earth; emerging in the spring, they're believed to carry Earth's secrets as well as her sacred generative powers with them. No animal is as identified with the powers of Earth or Great Mother Goddesses as the snake.

Snakes are emblematic of sex, generative power, and childbirth. Snakes unite the male and female generative principles as surely as does the pestle in the mortar. Snakes are understood as animals that resemble both female and male genitalia. Male resemblance is obvious—how many blues singers boast of being "*crawling king snakes*" or similar serpentine forces? No need to make the comparison any clearer; that's a metaphor anyone can figure out. The resemblance to female genitalia is more subtle. The snake possesses an unhinged jaw that enables it to open up so wide that it can swallow prey bigger than its head. This was understood to symbolize the vagina, which magically opens to disgorge a baby.

Although snakes are associated with healing in general, they are particularly associated with women's reproductive health. In Rome, it was believed that contact with snakes improved a woman's health. It's believed in many places that snakes actually taught women the techniques of childbirth, undulating their bodies in demonstration. Snakes are literally brought into the birthing chamber in areas as far apart as China and Arabia, sometimes for the express purpose of entrancing the laboring woman for an easier, speedier, safer birth. If snakes aren't available or convenient, belly dancers substitute, especially snake or sword dancers, shimmying with sinuous movements to help lead the birthing mother in the childbirth dance.

Neolithic pottery from near Kiev shows snakes surrounding a pregnant womb, protecting the treasure within. Horned snakes were emblems of fertility, regeneration, and healing in Celtic Europe.

It has been suggested that the identification of women with snakes reveals women's attachment to Earth, to Earthly (material) things and powers—an attachment that prevents them from attaining salvation and spiritual freedom. And of course, the snake most people are familiar with is the one that tempted Eve. Based on this story, snakes eventually became identified with Satan, known as that old serpent. (Other versions prefer a female snake; identifying it with a diabolized Lilith, the former childbirth spirit who shed her skin to become the Queen of Demons.)

Because the Bible is often used to rationalize violence toward witches and witchcraft as well as hostility toward snakes, it's worth taking a brief second look. The Bible has famously been interpreted and reinterpreted to suit many purposes. The word that characterizes attitudes towards snakes in the Old Testament isn't horror or disgust but ambivalence. The snake's appearance in the Garden of Eden isn't its only appearance: snakes are a common motif in the Jewish Bible.

Various versions of the Adam and Eve tale posit a different understanding. Ancient Gnostics, who understood material Earth to be created by a deceptive usurping demi-god, not the true Creator, perceived that the snake was trying to warn and save Eve. In some versions, the snake may even be the Creator deity. A modern Hasidic take on the story suggests the snake ultimately did us a favor; no potential for human growth exists in Paradise. It's like the womb; no matter how comfortable you are, ultimately you have to get out and start living if you want to survive.

The most famous serpentine appearances include the following:

The Garden of Eden (Genesis 3: 1-24): However else you may interpret the story, one thing is true: the snake never lies to Eve. The snake speaks directly to Eve; this was once understood to mean she was more vulnerable to sin and temptation. It may also reflect women's ancient spiritual association with snakes. Eve is punished with painful childbirth—the once cordial relationship between people and snakes is broken. This may be understood as observation of the results of snake-spirituality suppression, rather than as something inevitable or even desirable. If the relationship is sundered and if snakes symbolize women's primal wisdom, the end result will be that women lack the information required for easier, less painful labor.

Rods before Pharaoh (Exodus 7: 8-13): Rods are magically turned into snakes, a trick quickly reproduced by the Egyptian magicians, because, as every anthropology book points out, this common trick is still played by Indian snake charmers. Of course, the real magic comes when Aaron's rod-turned snake eats the others. This snake is a dangerous, mysterious but sacred sign from God, who may be understood in this context to be affiliated with snakes not opposed to them.

Fiery serpent of the desert (Numbers 21: 5-9): In a bit of prophylactic magic, when the children of Israel are plagued by snakes in the desert, the Lord instructs Moses to create a brazen serpent, indicating the presence of magical metal workers. Again, the snake is not identified with any evil being or impulse but with safety, protection and with God himself.

Any identification of the snake in the Garden of Eden with Satan was not explicit until the first century after Christ. That connection was initially established in a number of first-century texts, either entirely Christian in origin or influenced by Christianity.

Hezekiah breaks fiery serpent Nehushtan (2 Kings 18: 1-4): The brazen serpent was preserved and named (Nehushtan, a name with linguistic roots similar to words for "magic") and eventually moved into the Jerusalem Temple, where it remained for 500 years as an official cult object before it was pulverized in a fit of religious reformation.

That snakes would be associated with the biblical Creator shouldn't be surprising; snakes play the role of Creators themselves in sacred stories from around the world.

✻ *In China, the goddess Nu Kua, half-snake, half-woman molds humans from clay and puts the universe into order.*

✻ *The Pelasgians were early inhabitants of Greece. According to their creation myth, in the beginning Eurynome, the All-Goddess, rose from Chaos. Dividing the sky from the waters, she began to dance on the waves. Out of the wind, Eurynome created a huge serpent and named him Ophion. They danced together, then Ophion coiled about her and she conceived. Eurynome transformed into a dove and brooded over the waters. She laid the universal egg and bade Ophion coil around it until it was time to hatch. Out of that egg emerged all of Creation, Earth's planets and all living creatures, all children of a goddess and a primordial snake.*

✻ *Wunekau, solar deity from New Guinea, is the Creator of the universe. Still actively involved with creation, Wunekau directs winds to make women conceive. Among manifestations of his divine presence is a giant snake.*

Snakes are guardians of Earth's hidden treasures and secret knowledge. Snakes protect all that is most valuable and control its distribution—wisdom, material wealth and treasure, health, and children.

Snakes are associated with the water element throughout much of the world. They are perceived as rain bringers and famously appear to people all over Earth in the form of the rainbow. There are some 50 species of sea snakes, almost all of which are venomous. Sea snakes aren't restricted to the ocean. Some live in rivers, others in swamps or lakes.

According to Carl Jung, snakes represent the underworld, primordial matter, the dark, the unknown, the primal, the Earthy, the watery, the elemental.

Snakes have a long association with worship of the Great Mother, especially in Mediterranean regions. The Egyptian hieroglyph for what would be understood today as "goddess" is expressed by the image of a cobra. Unke, the German snake guardian, is depicted as either a crowned half-fairy/half-snake or as an entire snake wearing a crown and carrying keys. She presides over a family of snake spirits, the Unken (plural), who watch over babies in their cradle. It was considered unlucky to kill or injure a snake as this might result in loss of prosperity or the death of a child.

Once holy, snake spirits would eventually become demonized just like real snakes: the Libyan snake goddess Lamia was transformed into a *strix*, a witch-like fiend thirsting for children's blood in classical Greek mythology. Semitic snake spirit Lilith later emerges as a baby-killing vampire spirit, the Queen of Demons.

These are just a few deities associated with snakes. There are many more:

✻ *Asklepios and his daughter Hygeia (Greek)*

✻ *Athena (Libyan, Greek)*

✻ *Damballah and Ayida Wedo (Damballah, the white snake, is the most ancient member of the Vodou pantheon; his wife Ayida Wedo is the rainbow serpent)*

✻ *Demeter (Greek)*

✻ *Ezili Freda Dahomey (Vodou)*

✻ *Fauna (Roman)*

✻ *Hecate (Anatolian)*

✻ *Hera (Greek)*

✻ *Hermes (Greek)*

✻ *Isis (Egyptian)*

✻ *Ix Tub Tun (Mayan snake goddess; spits rain and precious stones)*

✻ *Juno (Roman)*

✻ *Kadesh (Semitic spirit of sexuality, beloved in ancient Egypt)*

✻ *Kebechet (Egyptian: Anubis' daughter manifest in snake form; she is the purifying libation of water that revitalizes the dead)*

✻ *Lilith (Semitic)*

✻ *Mami Waters (West and Central African)*

✻ *Medusa (Libyan, Greek)*

✻ *The Nagas (Indian)*

✻ *Ogun (West African)*

✻ *Persephone (Greek)*

✻ *Quetzalcoatl (Aztec "plumed serpent")*

✻ *Rosmerta (Gaul)*

✻ *Serapis (Hellenic Egypt)*

✻ *Simbi (Congolese guardian of fountains, marshes, and fresh water)*

✻ *Susanowo (Japanese)*

✻ *Wadjet (Egyptian)*

Snakes are emblems of death. Etruscan Hades grasps a snake while his wife, Persephone, has serpents entwined in her hair—as does that other death deity, Hecate. Shiva and Kali, India's deities of sex, birth, magic, and death are also both ornamented with snakes.

Snakes are emblems of immortality too. Snakes' characteristic shedding of skin is emblematic of regeneration, rebirth, immortality, and restoration to health. They ensure that cycles of life continue, that generative powers can be renewed, revived and remain undiminished. Snakes are regarded as stimulators and guardians of life energy.

Snakes are emblems of prophecy: from the earliest times snakes have been connected to oracular power and divination. The women who served as the mouthpiece for the Oracle of Delphi (in truth, they *were* the oracle) are typically called "priestesses" in English. The actual term for them, however, was *"pythia"* or *"pythoness"*; they were understood as snake women. Originally Delphi was a snake shrine dedicated to the Earth Mother. When Apollo violently installed himself as the oracular spirit in charge, the snakes were killed. However, even afterwards, it was reputed that the vapors that stimulated prophesy emanated from the snake corpses left to rot under Apollo's shrine so, dead or alive, the snakes remained responsible for the oracle.

According to ancient European tradition, if a snake bit someone, they would inherit the ability to prophesize. Vestiges of this belief survive in the snake-handlers of the Holiness tradition of the Appalachian Mountains.

Snakes are also emblems of healing, an identification that remains today. The symbol of the medical profession is the caduceus, Hermes' double-snake entwined staff. (The emblem is often identified with Asklepios, the Sacred Physician, however his staff only has one snake.) Snakes are the original healing animals. They lived in the very first official hospitals, the temples of Asklepios, and were believed integral to the healing process. The appearance of a snake to an ill person, whether in person or in dreams or visions, was understood as an omen of healing and renewal, not death.

The *sangoma* are traditional Southern African healers, frequently female. Their medical career is often initiated when they are called by an ancestral spirit, usually during puberty. This calling manifests in various ways; frequently the ancestor visits in a dream during an illness. The person must then seek out an experienced *sangoma* for training. Resisting the call leads to illness and breakdown. Dreams vary in content; however, according to those individuals who've chosen to share their experiences, they virtually always somehow involve a snake.

The practice of handling poisonous snakes in spiritual ritual is found independently throughout Asia, Africa, Europe, and North America. Snake-charming, which now most frequently relies on illusion, is a derivative of this magical-spiritual art. Genuine snake handling survives

in pockets around the world, most famously among the Hopi Snake Dancers of Arizona, and perhaps most surprisingly in the Christian Holiness tradition of the Appalachian Mountains.

Snakes serve as personal guardian spirits and the equivalent of household familiars. Zaltys, the Baltic grass snake, was revered and kept as a living guardian in shrines. Maintaining Zaltys in one's home, in the form of a grass snake, was believed to bring blessings and good fortune. The snake was kept under the marital bed or near the home stove. In Baltic regions snakes were understood to radiate life energy and so were never killed.

Polish bishop Jan Lasicki, writing in the late sixteenth and early seventeenth centuries, reported that once a year, domestic snakes were charmed out of their hiding places by Pagan priests and offered the finest food to eat, in an attempt to guarantee a prosperous new year.

Dragons, also identified with witchcraft, are a subcategory of snakes.

* Hecate drives a chariot drawn by dragons.
* When the Norse hero Sigurd tastes dragon's blood in *The Volsung Saga*, he *immediately* understands the speech of birds—luckily for him, as this ability will save his life.
* Dragons symbolize Paganism. When Saint George and other knights slay dragons, they are emphasizing Christian victory over other traditions.
* Dragons symbolize menstruation. When Saint George and other knights slay dragons, well …

Encyclopedia of Witchcraft

In Japan snake familiars are considered similar to fox spirits. However, while fox spirits run in packs, typically there's only one snake spirit per household. The snake lives in a pot in the kitchen and is fed on the family's food plus offerings of saké. The snake is believed sent out to cause harm to others. The chief symptom of snake-spirit attack is sudden, severe pain in the joints.

Spiders

Arachne was a master weaver of fabrics and tapestries at Colophon in Lydia, the daughter of a man involved with the trade in the rare purple dye then reserved for royalty and the spiritual elite. There are various versions of Arachne's story but somehow she ended up in a tapestry-making contest with the goddess Athena, credited by the Greeks as the inventor of weaving. Both wove tapestries; the general population was permitted to choose the winner. Arachne won, with a cynical tapestry mocking the lifestyles of the gods, especially Athena's father Zeus' prodigious love life. Daddy's girl was enraged. Exactly what happened next depends on the version of the story:

❊ *Athena transformed Arachne into a spider*

❊ *Athena hanged Arachne and then changed her into a spider*

❊ *Arachne hung herself but Athena, out of pity, changed the rope into a web and Arachne into a spider, the ultimate weaver.*

Spiders are now classified as belonging to the Arachnid family, as are scorpions, emblems of Egyptian goddesses. The word *"spider"* derives from the Old English *spinan,* "to spin." It is thus closely related to *"spinster,"* which although given the colloquial meaning "old maid" with the added implication of being dowdy and undesirable, technically refers to an unwed, independent woman. Spinning was once not only an occupation and art associated with women but a spiritual and magical tradition. Spiders are sponsors of spinning and emblems of witchcraft.

There are perhaps 100,000 species of spiders on Earth. They are a *unique* species; only spiders create webs from within their bodies. The web is the spider's home and the manner in which she captures her prey. On the outside of her body, spiders possess four or six (depending upon species) spinnerets. Liquid spurts from these teat-like organs, which solidifies almost immediately on contact with air, forming spider silk. Spiders can employ one or more spinnerets as desired. Seven different types of spider silk exist; all spiders can produce three while some can produce more. The tensile strength of spider thread is second only to fused quartz.

Spider webs can be beautiful. Dew shining on spider webs in the sun resembles sparkling diamonds. Complex, artistic webs are spun by female spiders. Designs are mazelike and may have inspired labyrinths and mandalas. Spiders inspired the art of spinning; magical theory says spiders themselves taught women how to spin.

True artists, spiders spin webs out of their own bodies, in similar fashion to the way women birth babies and produce milk.

"'Come into my parlor,' said the spider to the fly …" All spiders are predatory. They suck their victims empty of fluids, leaving nothing but dead husks behind, in the manner of vampires or succubi. Various species, not only the black widow, cannibalize their mates and children.

Spiders terrify many people, disproportionately to their ability to harm. Arachnophobia is the scientific name for fear of spiders (and scorpions, too, which are also arachnids).

> This primal, irrational fear is evoked in the gigantic threatening spiders in J. R. R. Tolkien's *Return of the King* and J. K. Rowling's *Harry Potter and the Chamber of Secrets*. Shelob, the female spider in the Tolkien book, particularly evokes some kind of terrible, primal, chthonic goddess. Her hunger and ferocity transform her into a veritable guardian spirit, albeit not for Frodo.

Black Widows truly are dangerous. Once you know what they look like, they're hard to mistake: shiny, glossy black spiders, the females wear a red hour-glass shape on their underside. Their color scheme and venomous potential, combined with their conjugal habits, make Black Widows the spiders most identified with witchcraft, their name synonymous with *femmes fatales.*

Mating habits of spiders are pretty unique, too. Their mating terrifies and fascinates people, often especially men. Having consummated the relationship, the female spider, usually the larger of the two, often attempts to consume the male, quite frequently succeeding. (There's one male who won't kiss and tell!)

Spiders have been used as metaphors for the dangers of sex, both literally and also in terms of sex being the trap that leads to the death of men's immortal souls.

Because spiders give birth to huge quantities of young at one time they are also ancient emblems of fertility and female generative power. Spiders are associated with birth, death, sex, immortality, destiny, and the acquisition of

wealth, power, and magical knowledge. Because spiders (and spinners) are understood to spin and cut the threads of life, many deities take the form of spiders or are allied with them.

Spider goddesses include:

❋ *Askhe-tanne-mat, the Ainu spider goddess, manifests as a long-fingered woman who guides babies through the birth canal.*

❋ *Female spider deities are heroines of Native North American spirituality; variously known by names like Spider Woman or Old Spider Grandmother they rescue people from disaster, sponsor culture heroes and perform miraculous actions like providing people with fire.*

❋ *Morticia of the Addams Family, whose tight black spider gown is intended to evoke the magical Black Widow (although Morticia verges on the saintly!)*

In Hungarian tradition, spider webs are the gossamer thread spun by fairies. In Germanic areas, spider webs are considered threads from Mother Holle's spindle. (See **DIVINE WITCH:** Hulda.)

Chinese mythology looks at both sides of the spider controversy. Spiders are sacred to the saintly Weaving Maiden, the romantic guardian spirit of young women. On the other hand, female spiders, bored with male spiders and seeking to up the ante, transform into the shape of beautiful women. Men, Chinese folklore warns, should you meet a mysterious, seductive maiden, be on your guard! She may be a spider transformed into a girl, out to ensnare you.

Spiders show up in classic Halloween iconography; fake spider webs decorate haunted Halloween houses. Halloween witch costumes frequently may as well be spider costumes. (Several years ago a witch dress named Spiderella was popular.) A spider-witch plays the role of the Weird Sisters in Akira Kurosawa's film interpretation of *Macbeth*, *Throne of Blood*.

Perhaps in remembrance of their former sacred status, it's believed unlucky to kill spiders. To do so is to risk losing wealth and spiritual protection.

See also **WOMEN'S MYSTERIES:** Spinning.

Transformation

There are various forms of transformation:

✹ *Witches and sorcerers willingly transform into animals and back to their original form.*

✹ *Animals willingly transform into people and back to their original form.*

✹ *People are victimized, most frequently by witches, and forcibly transformed into animals. Under a spell, they lack the power to transform back at will but need magical assistance.*

Werewolf literally means "man-wolf," however there is some evidence that the word was originally used to indicate *"one who knows how to change form."* That said, that word's historical nuances and implication have cause werewolves to be unique phenomena, somewhat different from standard shape-shifting. Werewolves are discussed in depth together with wolves. See Wolves and Werewolves.

People Who Transform Willingly into Animals

Witches are famed worldwide for the ability to transform into different shapes at will, in popular terminology: shape-shifting. According to story, legend, and myth, this ability is accomplished literally. Whether witches would agree with that assessment is subject to lots of debate. In general, stories about shape-shifting are told by observers, not the witches. Of course, those very same stories frequently describe witches as secretive and evasive, so what can you expect?

According to many witches, channeling the spirit of an animal is what is significant rather than literal transformation. Others would suggest that transformation is real but occurs on a shamanic or dream level.

Whether transformation is literal, soul-journey or something else, real witches consider their magical abilities to be sacred and private and will, thus, rarely brag. How, then, do other people know of these transformations? Easy, legend says: they've been witnessed or even experienced. Although countless stories recount tales of transformation, there are basically only a few themes:

✹ *The story-teller actually witnessed the process of transformation. Thus Lucius Apuleius saw the witch Pamphile change into an owl (a strix or strega).*

✹ *Having witnessed the transformation or otherwise picked up some fragments of magical knowledge, the story-teller attempts to copy the witch and transform, too. Sometimes it works, although usually not too well—as with Lucius Apuleius, who only manages to turn himself into an ass.*

❋ *In the most common theme, an animal, initially understood as a real animal, is somehow injured. Sometimes a human is then found to have an identical injury, betraying her as a witch.*

❋ *Sometimes an injured or killed animal is discovered with something, usually an item of jewelry, that betrays their human identity.*

The classic tale of the transforming witch involves Lady Sybil of Bernshaw Tower in Lancashire, a beautiful heiress who loved to walk to Eagle Crag where she would gaze into the wooded gorge below. The power of the woods lured her; she became a witch. Beautiful, brilliant, and independently wealthy, Lady Sybil took to rambling through the ravines of Cliviger Gorge in the form of a white doe. She attracted the attention of a man named Lord William, variously identified as either being of Hapton Tower or Townley Castle. He became obsessed with her and requested her hand in marriage but she refused.

Not taking "no" for an answer, Lord William hired Mother Hellston, local witch, to prepare a spell for him. She advised him to capture the white doe and hold it captive within Hapton Tower. She gave William an enchanted silk cord and loaned him her familiar, a black dog. On May Eve, he captured the doe. At dawn, the doe turned back into Lady Sybil in her human form, under his spell.

The story now takes one of two twists:

Either, Lady Sybil renounces witchcraft and marries Will. Whether this renunciation was sincere or not initially, Lady Sybil eventually returned to her craft. One day, while she's playing in the form of a white cat at Cliver Mill, the miller *accidentally* cuts off her paw. (Italics mine; this story is usually told with a very straight face.) However, Lady Sybil's magical skills are such that she can restore her hand. (See **MAGI-CAL PROFESSIONS:** Millers.) Or, in the second version, Lord William forgets to pay Mother Hellston; the spell lasts one month and then it's broken. Sybil, now married to Will, comes to her senses, discovers herself a married captive, and wants to escape. William holds her prisoner. A servant named Robin is set to watch her. One day Robin sees a white cat slipping from the room. He cuts off its paw, which instantly transforms into Sibyl's hand, identifiable by its ring. After her hand has been chopped off, Sybil languishes and quickly dies. She's buried, as per her request, in Cliviger Gorge.

Either way, local legend says that to this day on May Eve, a white doe, a black hound, and a ghostly hunter haunt the gorge.

❋ *Throughout Africa, witches transform into hyenas, bats, nightjars, and owls.*

❋ *Throughout the British Isles, witches transform into cats and hares.*

❋ *In India and Java witches transform into leopards and tigers.*

❋ *Jewish and Mexican witches transform into bats, black cats, and black dogs.*

❋ *In Scandinavia and Finland, witches transform into flies.*

❋ *Baltic, Russian, Siberian, and Swedish witches transform into magpies.*

❋ *Siberian shamans, understood as distinct from witches, transform into bears, eagles, boar, elk, and wolves.*

Transformation stories and techniques exist worldwide. In Central America and the Andes, there's a whole hierarchy to shape-shifting. The animal into which you transform reveals your power and status. The most important and powerful sorcerers transform into eagles, jaguars, quetzal birds or natural forms that are associated with status and royalty such as lightning bolts, whirlwinds or pools of blood. The less powerful are only able to transform into lower-status creatures like mice, turkeys, and vultures—although with practice and the acquisition of powers they can move up the transformation ladder.

According to witch-hunt era Christian theology, witches could potentially transform into any form, except that of a lamb or a dove, which were perceived as utterly pure, sacred creatures.

The powerful lwa Ezili Zandor is the matron of the Haitian sorcerers' secret societies known as *The Red Sects*. Members travel at night in the form of black cats, black pigs, crocodiles, horses, leopards, owls, and wolves. Witches of the Pueblo Indian nations transform into animals for purposes of travel. It's the most convenient way to get around: easy, quick and discreet. The most popular forms into which to transform include cats, crows, canines, owls, dogs, wolves, and coyotes. Different animal forms are more prevalent in some pueblos than others.

The methods of transformation vary. According to BaKongo belief, every individual possesses multiple souls. A certain type of soul, sort of an "image soul," can adopt different appearances. These appearances are known as *yunga* or shells. The shell is an outward covering and it can be changed as desired. The most powerful

witches, sorcerers, seers, and prophets can possess and/or develop multiple yungas.

A Portuguese technique leaves the form you attain somewhat to chance:

1. Go to a crossroads during a Full Moon.
2. Spin repeatedly while howling until you get so dizzy or exhausted you collapse on the ground.
3. You will transform into the shape of the last animal to lie there.

(To avoid transformation into a vole or worm, you may wish to observe the area for several hours—or even days—prior to spell-casting.)

According to the tenets of Taoist magic, all living beings can learn the art of changing forms. It's easiest for humans, easier for animals and harder still for plants. What's stopping you from shape-shifting? It's not lack of magical ability, but laziness and lack of discipline.

Two methods of transformation exist.

1. The ethical method: study various Taoist classics and eventually the ability is gained.
2. Sex magic: the partner who first achieves orgasm gives off energy, which may be acquired by the other partner and used for purposes of transformation. One partner essentially vampirizes the other's vitality and magical powers. Yes, it's potentially harmful for the other partner.

According to another Taoist magical belief, extended longevity may earn you the ability to shape-shift. If you can live long enough, the ability may just develop naturally. Of course, there's a hidden implication in this method: how does one achieve really extended longevity? Answer: alchemy; the acquisition of the philosopher's stone. If you study alchemy intensely, one of the side-effects may be transformative power.

Other traditions use other methods of transformation:

* *Witches from the Pueblos of the American Southwest jump through twisted yucca fiber hoops. (In various legends, Coyote teaches these transformation skills.)*

* *Russian witches transform via similar athletic means. One method is to somersault backwards over copper knives thrust into the ground or into a tree-stump; to return to human form, somersault back over the knives in the opposite direction, retracing your steps, so to speak. If someone removes the knives, while you're out roaming, you're stuck.*

* *European witch-hunters believed that transformation was only possible because of a diabolical pact. The witch didn't really have the power to transform; Satan did it for her, or at least supplied the illusion. Other schools of philosophy understand the ability to shape-shift as a gift from a deity. Frequently the form into which one transforms is one that is sacred to that deity. In essence, by transforming, you become the deity's sacred animal or messenger. This may or may not be understood literally. Thus Diana's "dogs" and "wolves," sons of the bitch goddess, may not have expected to literally transform into canines.*

* *That literal transformation wasn't necessarily expected is indicated by the use of masks and costumes to transform. If you really literally expect to change forms, who needs a mask? Why go to the time, trouble, and expense? Masks, costumes, and rituals assist ritual channeling of the animal; once the spirit of the animal is received, the costume completes the picture.*

* *According to the powerful and sophisticated traditional schools of magic in Java, you can transform yourself. Javanese sorcerers most frequently transform into tigers by memorizing entire books of*

magical chants, which must then be repeated perfectly from memory during ritual. Transformation may also be effected via magical fabrics, in the case of the tiger, a special striped cloth.

* *Transformative energy may be the gift of a spirit. The Vodou lwa Ogou ge Rouge is renowned for bestowing this power, as is the Norse spirit Freya.*

* *According to some schools of magical philosophy, no method is necessary. The ability to transform, to change shapes, is hereditary. Certain animal forms run in families, kind of like the old horror film, Cat People.*

Animals Who Transform Willingly Into People

Which came first, the chicken or the egg? Shape-shifting is a hall of mirrors; one mustn't always assume that the human form is the original form. Some cultures believe that some animals have the intelligence, desire, and magical skill to assume *our* form to accomplish various purposes.

In Russian magic, it's believed that animals may be transformed witches, wizards or spirits. Spirits usually take the form of black dogs or cats while magical practitioners are white or gray.

Shape-shifting is a common theme in Japanese folklore but the typical scenario of witch transforming into animal is reversed. In Japan, animals, most typically cats, foxes, snakes, and tanuki (known as Japanese badgers), transform into human form. Transformation by snakes usually involves some sort of romantic motivation. Tanuki are mischievous and greedy but rarely malevolent. Sacred clowns, their shape-shifting may even stem from spiritual intent:

their favored form is as a Buddhist priest. The tanuki stands up on his hind legs and distends his scrotum so as to become a drum, in order to make people laugh.

Cat spirits frequently possess malevolent intent; in their transformed state as humans they may be understood as witches in the worst sense of the word. In the standard form of the Japanese legend, a malevolent cat spirit eats an old woman, usually the village blacksmith's mother, and then assumes her shape in order to harm travelers. These cats disguised as women typically lead packs (covens) of wolves. Because she looks *exactly* like Grandma, the cat gets away with evil deeds for a while but is eventually exposed by the telltale clue that she is a disguised animal: she always eats alone. (This is because she must eat like an animal with her face directly in the bowl and not as a human, sitting up with utensils.)

Foxes are far more complex: their motivation might be mischief, magic or malevolent soul-stealing. To complicate matters, transformative foxes may or may not be real foxes. Spirit foxes may be able to clothe themselves in various bodies, vulpine and/or human. Foxes may also engage in amorous adventures but it tends to be for vampiric purposes, as a method of alchemical sex magic.

Malice or revenge are typical motivations for fox spirits; and it can be for something as simple as startling it when it's asleep or stepping on its tail, escalating to killing a cub or a mate. (In this, fox spirits are very similar to *djinn*, which also take the form of animals, typically dogs or cats, which must not be harmed, frightened or molested lest the hidden *djinn* retaliate.) Other motivating factors may be greed, lust or desire. They may want sex or food, especially treats they're not likely to get in fox form.

According to Taoist belief, any fox that attains fifty years of age can shape-shift into a standard human. If the fox can make it to a hundred, he'll be a skilled sorcerer, too. There are various beliefs regarding abilities earned through longevity. An alternative view is that foxes and wolves that survive eighty years can transform into humans. If these animals can achieve one thousand years, they'll be divine. (And how does a fox or anyone live to be a thousand years old? Through alchemy.) Older people are likewise able to develop the ability to shape-shift.

A classic example from Japan: a samurai walking home one night spots a fox and shoots an arrow at it. The fox is wounded but doesn't fall. It keeps going. The samurai follows it but is unable to catch up. Even wounded, this fox is too fast. He keeps following and eventually the samurai discovers that the fox has led him home. Suddenly, the fox transforms into a man and sets the samurai's house on fire. Before the dazed and confused samurai can react, the fox transforms back into its original shape and escapes into the forest.

Victims of Transformation

Among witches' notorious "crimes" is the transformation of human victims into animal form. The most famous example is Circe, the witch goddess of Homer's *Odyssey* who transforms men into apes, pigs, and lions. Of course, one could say, as Circe does, that she isn't *transforming* them, she's revealing their true essence. (She regrets the prevalence of pigs and the paucity of lions, suggesting that Odysseus would have been a lion.) And of course, Circe doesn't come looking for these men; she lives on a rock in the middle of the sea—they come to her. The motivation of fairy-tale witches who transform victims into animals isn't always clear, but the witch is almost always depicted as the aggressor.

Victims are transformed into animals, most frequently horses. The victim isn't treated gently but ridden hard, saddled, bridled or struck with the bridle.

What's the evidence of transformation? There'll be wounds on or in the mouth, traces of the bit. Another indication is when tack or riding equipment is missing. The victim may wake up suffering from dizziness, fatigue, covered in cold sweat or black and blue marks—"blue in the face": all evidence of having been "ridden."

Another fear is that animals may be indistinguishable from all the others. This may date from guilt about the treatment of formerly sacred animals. Once transformed, the victim who, unlike self-transformed witches who always seem to retain their human capacity for speech, loses the power to speak, and so is treated just like any other animal.

* *Circe's spell is first discovered when Odysseus' hungry sailors almost eat their comrade, transformed into a pig.*

* *Artemis punishes the hunter Actaeon for a transgression by transforming him into a stag. His own dogs are unable to recognize him, he's unable to call them off, and they rip him apart.*

* *In the Japanese animated film* Spirited Away, *the heroine Chihiro yearns to rescue her bewitched parents, transformed into pigs, but they're in a pen with hundreds of other pigs, destined for the dinner table. They can't identify themselves to her and so it's an impossible task.*

Wolves and Werewolves

Depending upon what one understands a werewolf to be, the line between wolves and wolfmen may be very fine indeed. Mirror-images of each other, they can't really be separated and so are considered together.

The emotions evoked by wolves and the treatment accorded to them parallel those toward witches. Some find profound beauty, spirituality, something indescribably unique and *special* about wolves; words aren't sufficient to evoke the holiness many perceive. On the other hand, the passion, hostility, determination to exterminate wolves—out of all proportion to any damage they might possibly do—parallels emotions toward witches: the urge to kill off something wild, free, and independent.

Like witches, wolves are demonized. Wolves have historically been hunted and exterminated just like witches, shamans, and diviners.

* *By 300* BCE *Pagan Celts were breeding wolfhounds especially for killing wolves.*

* Vargr, *"wolf," was the term used in Icelandic law codes to refer to outlaws who could be hunted down like wolves. The word also implies that wolves could be hunted down like outlaws, the worst offenders.*

* *In Anglo-Saxon England wolves were sometimes hanged near criminals. The Saxon word for gallows is* "varagtreo," *"wolf tree."*

* *In France, in approximately 800* CE, *Charlemagne founded an order for the purpose of exterminating wolves, the* Louveterie.

* *In 1281, King Edward I hired a man, Peter Corbet, to destroy all the wolves he could find in Gloucestershire, Herefordshire, Shropshire, Staffordshire, and Worcestershire.*

The desire to eliminate wolves was frequently translated into what may be considered a "wolfcraze" similar to the European Witchcraze. In various parts of Europe and North America, it wasn't sufficient to merely kill wolves; instead they were brutally tortured to death. There is a sadistic quality to the history of the extermination of wolves that more closely resembles the witch-hunts than extermination of other animal species. In the United States, for instance, wolves were captured alive and dragged behind horses until they were torn to pieces. Other wolves captured alive had their jaws (and sometimes penises) wired up and then were released.

Wolves, shy and wary, very rarely attack humans. (Not a single case of a wolf killing a human has been recorded in North America.) Dogs and automobiles are responsible for a vastly greater number of human death and injury, yet both are beloved. Wolves have been known to prey on livestock, but only when humans have encroached on their territory. It's not wolves who've spread out—their territory has consistently diminished over the last two thousand years; humans have spread out, cleared and destroyed wilderness, removing wolves dining alternatives.

However, for some, wolves are the essential spirit of the wild. Without wolves, some magical earth power is also extinguished. In Lakota, the word for "*wolf*" translates as the "*animal that looks like a dog but is a powerful spirit.*"

Wolves are identified with witchcraft:

❋ *In Germanic tradition, wolves are witches' mounts and were believed to carry them to sabbats.*

❋ *In the Navajo language, the same word is used for "wolf" and "witch."*

❋ *Vargamors were forest-dwelling Swedish wild women who communed with wolves.*

❋ *The connection between wolves and witches is so powerful that when some European Romany hear a wolf howl, the automatic reaction is to advise caution as the sound may signal the approach of a witch.*

In myth and legend, wolves nurture humans: Zoroaster was allegedly suckled by a mother wolf; Siegfried, Teutonic hero, allegedly had a wolf for a foster-mother, and the founders of Rome, the abandoned babies Remus and Romulus, were found and nursed by a she-wolf.

The wolf was once Rome's totem animal. The primordial horned spirit Faunus negotiates the balance between deer and wolves, the way the Greek deity Artemis sets the balance between wolves, deer, and hunters. The Lupercalia, Rome's festival of fertility and purification, was held in honor of Faunus, also known as Lupercus, the wolf spirit. Remnants of the holiday linger in Valentine's Day traditions. And Feronia was the Italian sacred spirit of magic, prosperity, and freedom. Her sacred animal is the wolf. Once upon a time, if slaves sat on a stone in her shrine, they gained their freedom. Feronia survives but not as a goddess; her most common manifestation is as a witch who roams the marketplace, once women's place of power.

Wolves are identified with ravenous appetites, whether for food, sex or pleasure. They are identified with strong male sexuality, as in wolf whistles. A wolf is a euphemism for a sexually predatory man. One observes the evolution of demonization of wolves in the tale *Little Red Riding Hood*. The wolf Little Red Riding Hood meets in the earliest forms of the story is clearly a man. He forcibly gets her into bed; she only escapes by insisting that she needs to use the bathroom—this of course in the days prior to indoor plumbing. Later versions, cleaned up for children, suggest that the villain Little Red Riding Hood encounters is a real wolf, albeit a talking, cross-dressing one.

Werewolves

What exactly are werewolves? Monster-movie material or something real? During Europe's Witchcraze, a concurrent werewolf panic (centered mainly in France but also present through other regions of Europe) resulted in the deaths of many men. Just as witchcraft was identified with women, werewolves were identified with men.

Johannes Nider, author of an early fifteenth-century witch-hunter's manual *The Formicarius*, discusses male witches who transform into wolves. Werewolves may be nothing more than male witches. During the witch-hunts, as witchcraft became increasingly identified with women, public perception and theology may have required that men be classified differently—if men and women can both be witches, then all this theology about women being the gender more susceptible to Satanic wiles goes out the window. To wear a wolf's skin may be a euphemism for walking the shaman's or male witch's path.

European werewolves, similar to Navajo skin-walkers, may not look exactly like real wolves. They may walk upright and have no tail, which sounds suspiciously like a person. Other descriptions suggest that werewolves have a human body but a wolf's head, like an Egyptian deity or like a masked human.

Although they might or might not literally transform, once upon a time, many people strove to be identified with wolves.

* *According to Book 10 of Homer's* Odyssey, *Odysseus' grandfather was named Autolykos—"He who is a Wolf."*

* *The desire to identify with wolves is demonstrated by once popular boy's names: Adolf, Rudolph, Wolfgang, Wolfram, and plain old Wolf.*

* *The blues singer called Howlin' Wolf was born Chester Burnett. His adopted name may be understood as a magical name, a veritable boast of primal male and magical power. In many of his songs he explicitly identifies himself with the creature, as a source of pride and power.*

* *The Pawnee nation, Plains Indians from present-day Kansas and Nebraska, identified so profoundly with wolves that the Plains hand-signal for wolf is the same as the one for Pawnee. Others referred to them as the* Wolf People.

* *Odin's warriors behaved like wolves, hence the name "wolf-warriors." Sixth- to eighth-century CE helmets and scabbards found widely through Western and Central Europe were decorated with figures that may be werewolves or berserkers.*

The earliest written report of werewolves derives from Herodotus, the fifth-century BCE Greek writer. According to him, a tribe known as the Neuri, living north of the Black Sea, had members who turned into wolves for several days each year. Today, this is thought to refer to Scythian shamans.

Werewolf transformation manifests in two distinct ways:

* *those who shift back and forth between human and werewolf manifestations*

* *those who assume the form of a wolf full-time*

People become werewolves voluntarily and involuntarily. People become werewolves accidentally or intentionally. People transform themselves into werewolves or others do it for them. The second manifestation, the full-time wolf, is virtually always an involuntary transformation and is frequently the result of a curse.

How else do you become a werewolf?

* Ancestry may be blamed. Someone from a family full of werewolves may be more likely to be one.

* Simply sleeping in the moonlight may do the trick.

* Taking off one's clothes and howling in the moonlight is considered effective, too.

* The notion that being a werewolf is contagious is popular nowadays but derives more from movie traditions than from any folk wisdom. It may derive from confusion between vampires and werewolves.

* In Ojibwa tradition, eating meat that was previously tasted by a real wolf leaves you prone to transformation.

* In the Harz Mountains, the witches' playground, there is a "werewolf stream." All one must do is find it and drink the water.

* In the Balkans, there's a special werewolf flower. Pick it and transform.

* Various spells refer to magical belts which when worn help one transform.

* European werewolves allegedly concoct salves similar to witches' flying ointments to effect transformation.

* Order of birth: being born the seventh son of a seventh son or the seventh daughter of the seventh daughter is good.

* Someone born with teeth and/or a caul may indicate a potential werewolf (see **DICTIONARY**: Taltos).

* Curses cause transformation, as do evil spells: Polish witches can transform you into a werewolf via methods of "spoiling." The witches form a belt from human flesh. This is secretly placed over the threshold of a room where a wedding reception is expected. Should someone step over the girdle, they're doomed to roam as werewolves. (Doom isn't expected to be permanent; the witches' goal isn't malice, it's extortion: you can pay them to remove the spell.)

* A fairly international tradition recommends that you drink rainwater collected from a wolf's footprint.

* In Brazil, the notion of becoming a werewolf involves the acquisition of an animal alter-ego. Accomplishment takes some long-term planning: for three years in a row, intensely petition San Cipriano and roll in the ashes of St John's Eve bonfires.

According to the witch-hunt era Roman Catholic Church, one can only become a werewolf by making a pact with the devil or by being a child born outside church-sanctioned marriage. No other methods exist. (So much for being the innocent victim of a werewolf attack!) However, according to various unofficial traditions Christian transgressions may be punished by involuntary transformation into a werewolf, including:

* being born on Christmas Day, a day also associated with the winter solstice and the power of the sun. Prior to Christianity, this day was understood as falling within a time period when Earth's innate anarchistic forces were at their most powerful. Another, possibly related superstition, suggests that those born on Christmas Day possess the ability to talk with animals.

* illegitimacy

* being born a Roman Catholic priest's son

❋ *Breton folklore suggests that anyone who doesn't go to confession for ten years is vulnerable to transformation to a "bisclavret," the Breton werewolf.*

Lest one think that only male werewolves exist, there are tales of fierce, female werewolves too:

❋ *A Welsh prince allegedly had his werewolf daughter eliminate his enemies.*

❋ *In the Russian tale* Ivan of Shiganska, *a female werewolf kills the abusive husband her parents forced her to marry.*

❋ *The* loups-garoux *of Haiti and the French Caribbean are a fusion of Breton werewolf traditions and African secret sorcerers' societies. These island* loups-garoux *tend to be female. Typically the ability to transform is passed from mother to daughter.* Loups-garoux *can be violent; attacks tend to be random although children of enemies are particularly vulnerable.*

This may be lore or legend but werewolves are no laughing matter. Many people died because of werewolves: not because werewolves killed them but because they were suspected or accused of being werewolves. As with witches, despite all the talk of harm, malevolence and bestiality, it's the werewolves who have historically been victims, not victimizers.

Concurrent to the European Witchcraze, there was a werewolf-panic, most famously in France but also elsewhere. (Werewolf-panic did not strike the British Isles, perhaps because wolves were already extinct.)

Like witchcraft, it's extremely hard to prove you're not a werewolf, especially a diabolical one. The human being is allegedly taken over by the spirit of a wolf, thus transforming into a werewolf. The alleged werewolf may be sleep-

ing in bed or locked up in jail while his soul roams free. Using this kind of definition of werewolf, anyone might be convicted as a werewolf even if far from the place where the "crimes" were committed. (And they're may have been crimes; just because the werewolf didn't commit the murder doesn't mean that the murder didn't exist. One wonders how many accusations of witchcraft were used to deflect attention from true perpetrators.)

As with witch-trial transcripts it's very difficult to know which part, if *any* of the testimony is genuine. Confessions were obtained via torture, terror, and duress and aren't reliable. At the same time, hidden within some of the transcripts are interesting tales that suggest real, true witchcraft may not have been eradicated in Europe.

Among the most famous historical werewolves are the following:

Gilles Garnier: A number of children disappeared in the vicinity of the French city of Dole, beginning (as best as can be told from surviving records) in 1572. The rumor spread that a local werewolf was responsible. In response, the local government passed a law permitting the people of their district to hunt werewolves although it was *"out of season."*

At twilight on November 8, 1573, hunters, hearing screams in the woods, discovered a severely wounded little girl fighting off something lupine. The creature fled into the woods. Some of the hunters insisted that it was a wolf. Others said they recognized it as a man, Gilles Garnier, known as the Hermit of St Bonnot.

Garnier lived with his wife in a hut near where the attack occurred. He was a red-faced, long-bearded unattractive man with bad posture and a unibrow. On November 14, a ten-year-old boy disappeared in the area. Garnier was arrested and interrogated. He said that years earlier he had met a man in the woods who taught him to shape-shift into various forms, including those of a lion or leopard but, as Garnier pointed out very reasonably, wolves were most convenient because they were least noticeable. He claimed he spent most of his time in wolf-form and used his powers to obtain food for his impoverished family. Tortured, he confessed to the murders. On January 18, 1574 Garnier was burned alive and his ashes scattered to the winds.

Peter Stump: In 1590, Peter Stump was arrested in Cologne and charged as a werewolf for a series of murders, including that of his own son, which had occurred over a 20-year period. On March 31, 1590, Stump was executed as a werewolf. An illustrated pamphlet was published detailing Stump's career as a werewolf. The pamphlet was translated into different languages and was a bestseller of its time.

Jean Grenier: In the spring of 1613, children began mysteriously disappearing in the St Sever district of Gascony, France, including a baby from its cradle. An aura of fear pervaded the area. Other children began to report unusual occurrences. Finally 13-year-old Marguerite Poirier reported that while tending cattle, a huge, ferocious canine with reddish fur and a short, stumpy tail jumped from the bushes and attacked her. Marguerite fought it off with an iron-tipped staff. (This may be understood as a clue to the beast's supernatural identity. If this were really a wolf, a child with a club wouldn't stand much of a chance; iron is feared by virtually all supernatural beings. It breaks virtually every spell and offers spiritual-magical protection.)

Rumors soon spread that Jean Grenier, aged approximately 13 or 14, was boasting of attacking Marguerite. He claimed that if it hadn't been for that iron-tipped staff, he would have killed and eaten her as he did others. Grenier, the son of an impoverished laborer, traveled about seeking work with local farmers. He never lasted long at any job, usually being fired for neglect-

ing his duties. Whether he was uneducated or mentally disabled is unknown, but it was noted during his trial that he had the intellectual capacity of a much younger child. When unable to find work, he begged.

Soon 18-year-old Jeanne Gaboriaut came forward and testified under oath that while she and some other girls had been tending cows, their sheep dogs began to growl and whine at something. The girls investigated and discovered a filthy, red-haired, feral boy with a unibrow. Jeanne asked him why he looked so strange. According to her, he responded, "Because sometimes I wear a wolf's skin." The puzzled and intrigued girls asked him to explain. He claimed that a man named Pierre Labourat gave him a wolf skin that, when donned, enabled him to transform into a wolf and hunt. He boasted that he killed and ate many dogs but that these weren't as tasty as children. The girls fled to the authorities.

A search was made for the boy who was soon found and arrested. Jean Grenier claimed to come from the village of Saint'Antoine de Pizon. His father beat him so he ran away, earning a living as a cowherd and beggar. About three years earlier (this would have been when he was about 10) another boy took him into the woods to meet the Lord of the Forest, who turned out to be a tall man, dressed in black, riding a black horse. Jean met him several times and agreed to serve him. Jean described the children he'd killed and eaten. Witnesses came forward to corroborate his story. The court pronounced him a werewolf and sentenced him to life imprisonment in a monastery.

Grenier is unusual in werewolf-lore because virtually all other convicted European werewolves were burned to death, in the manner of witches. In Grenier's case however, the Chief of the Court made a speech suggesting that questions of witchcraft and diabolism should be disregarded. Instead the court should consider the boy's age and mental capacity.

Thiess, the Livonian Werewolf: In 1692, in Jurgensburg, Livonia, an 80-year-old man named Thiess was interrogated. Thiess had long been under suspicion; local Christians considered him an idolater. He allegedly killed small livestock in wolf form although he cooked the meat, not eating it raw.

Thiess perplexed and frustrated his inquisitors. Yes, he confessed to being a werewolf but insisted that he was a holy werewolf, a benevolent one, a werewolf of God. Furthermore, he wasn't alone: he belonged to a werewolf society. According to Thiess, members of this society went to Hell and back three times a year to fight the devil and his sorcerer minions. (The three nights were St John's Eve, St Lucy's Night, and Pentecost.) Thiess initially told his interrogators that Hell was at the "end of the sea." After further questioning, Thiess amended this to the more conventional "underground." He claimed there were male and female werewolves but specified women, not young girls. Thiess called werewolves "the dogs of God." He claimed there were also German werewolves but that they fight in a different hell. The werewolves fought with iron whips. The sorcerers were armed with broomsticks wrapped in horsetails. They fought for the fertility of barley and rye fields as well as the sea's bounty of fish. Sorcerers stole shoots of grain; if the werewolves couldn't get them back, there would be famine.

The inquisitors had wanted a standardized werewolf/witchcraft/heresy trial; instead they had stumbled upon a magical shamanic scenario. Exactly what fate befell the aged Thiess is unknown.

Some context may be needed to truly appreciate the Livonian werewolf: Today Livonia is in southern Latvia but in 1692, Livonia was a Baltic province of Russia, bordered on the north by Estonia and on the east by Lake Peipus. It was a true crossroads area, with various ethnic groups present including a high proportion of Swedes.

Pockets of old religion are believed to have survived as well as a shamanic tradition that may have merged with Christianity, thus creating a kind of "double-faith." Latvian werewolves belonged to the society of the Hairy Martinians, which may be understood as a male witch society. They roamed on certain nights, especially Midsummer's Eve, to drive away the demons of infertility. They gathered at full moons and at New Year in the forest. Islands in the Latvian River Brasla were among their favorite meeting places.

Count Jean Potocki: The Polish count Jean Potocki was born in 1761. A writer, traveler, and diplomat serving Tsar Alexander I, Potocki traveled widely in Europe, Asia, and North Africa, where he claimed to have flirted with various secret societies. Considered among the founding fathers of ethnology, Potocki was also an early Egyptologist. His claims to fame include his death and his mysterious novel, which was published posthumously. Chapters of *The Manuscript Found in Saragossa* were published beginning in 1797, however the novel was still incomplete at the time of Potocki's death almost 20 years later. Sections of the original text were lost; however, a version remains in print, including an English translation. The book is a complex series of intertwining stories featuring a cast of characters including Gypsies, a Kabala master, Moorish princesses, and assorted members of secret societies. It has been compared to *The Arabian Nights*.

In 1815, Potocki committed suicide using a silver bullet from a melted-down samovar, allegedly convinced that he was a werewolf.

✪ Books of Magic and Witchcraft

*S*cholars and anthropologists suggest that the need to record rituals, formulas, prophecies, spells and their results may have stimulated the creation of writing. Among the earliest surviving writings from many lands, languages, and scripts are divination results and recommended magic rituals.

(Documents pertaining to taxation are also heavily, if less romantically, represented in these early texts.)

Some acknowledgement of this history may be found in myths revealing the identity of the first book. Inevitably it's a book of magic spells. In ancient Egypt, Thoth was believed to have authored the first book, the eponymous "Book of Thoth." It allegedly contained various spells, rituals, and names of power. Names of power were words so powerful that if uttered correctly (and you had to pronounce them *just* right!) virtually anything was in your grasp: spirits would be summoned to accomplish your every desire.

The ancient Jews knew similar legends although they had a different first book: the angel Raziel, witnessing the expulsion from Paradise, felt sorry for Adam and secretly slipped him this book engraved on a sapphire tablet. Raziel knew that without a guide to spells, rituals, amulets, and talismans life would be much more difficult, painful, and joyless. Jewish mystical tradition names this book after the angel, *The Book of Raziel*.

The neighboring Samaritans had an almost identical legend, although they called their first book, "The Book of Signs." And according to Etruscan traditions in ancient Italy, their ancestors were plowing a brand-new field when a strange figure emerged from out of the Earth, with the head and body of a handsome young man but possessing snakes for legs. This sacred being identified himself as Tages and he, too, bore a book of spells, rituals, and mysticism that he gave to the Etruscans along with verbal instructions. It was upon these materials that the Etruscans claimed to have founded their great magical, oracular, and spiritual traditions.

It isn't all legend. We know that the classical Greek magicians wrote handbooks that integrated spells, rituals, and instructions for creating amulets, magical tools, and curse tablets.

Books have been used to teach witchcraft, encompassing spiritual traditions and magical arts. They've been used to store and preserve information; they've also been used as magical tools, as sacred objects of power.

Historically magical books have not represented the diverse realities of witchcraft. Women's magic, folk magic, Earth magic has traditionally been transmitted orally. Until *very* recently, what was found in books, with very few exceptions, consisted largely of ceremonial or high ritual magic. Perhaps because of the literacy factor, ceremonial magic was considered the province of adepts, while folk magic ("kitchen magic") was considered foolishness and superstition, even among occultists. This situation has changed drastically today—the pendulum may even have swung in the opposite direction—but only since the 1970s.

Because so few magical books survive and so many unknown manuscripts were destroyed it's impossible to know whether this split between male and female magic was always the case. The stereotype suggests that only men were literate but that's also misleading: once upon a time, few men could read either.

What you *won't* find in this section:

❋ Works of fiction featuring witches as characters or otherwise inspired by witchcraft. Please see **CREATIVE ARTS**.
❋ The literally thousands of "magical texts" including Books of Shadows, spell-manuals and modern grimoires published since the 1970s.

This stereotype of literate male magicians conducting high ritual in some tower while female witches played in the dirt below may be nothing more than stereotype, however: approximately thirty years before the Common Era, the Roman poet Horace wrote about exclusively female witches and their power to draw down the moon. He described them as devotees of Diana and Proserpina who celebrated in secret nocturnal ceremonies. According to Horace, these witches, too, had a book, the *Libros Carminum*, the "Book of Charms" or Incantations.

Before the invention of the printing press, making a book was an extremely laborious, time-consuming process. Everything was done by hand, one copy at a time. Very frequently only one copy of a book ever existed so when a book was lost, it was gone for ever. Each book was unique, just as each person is unique—parallels that were not forgotten when books were burned, neither by those who destroyed them nor by those who loved or valued them.

Printing was revolutionary; it changed everything. Printing is the process of making multiple copies of a document by the use of moveable characters or letters. The process was developed independently in both China and Europe. Printing made it possible to make more copies in a few weeks than would have been possible in a lifetime by hand. Johann Gutenberg began building a printing press in 1436 although it took him until approximately 1450 to perfect the process. Although the number of books expanded exponentially there were not nearly as many publications as there are today: your choices were very limited, so what existed was very influential.

Quite a few of those early books, a fairly substantial percentage, had to do with magic and witchcraft, one way or another. Among the earliest and most widely distributed publications were witch-hunters' manuals, guides for trial judges, Inquisitors and witch-finders. For years, the world's second most popular bestseller, second only to the Bible, was the *Malleus Maleficarum,* "The Hammer of the Witches." Although witches have always been eyed with suspicion by authority and various levels of persecution certainly pre-dated the printing press, perhaps without its invention such massive witch-hunts would not have happened.

On the other hand, simultaneously printing presses were used to bring magic traditions, albeit sometimes incredibly convoluted traditions, to more people than ever before. At great tremendous personal risk, printed grimoires, books of ritual magic, began to appear in Europe. They may be understood as an act of brave defiance against censorship and against the witch-hunts.

In 1951, the last law against witchcraft in the United Kingdom was repealed; this opened the floodgates of a new phenomenon: the witch as author. Gerald Gardner is credited with authoring the first factual book about witchcraft written by a self-identified practitioner. *Witchcraft Today* was published in 1954. (See **HALL OF FAME:** Gerald Gardner.)

Many people now learn magic, witchcraft, and Wicca from literary sources rather than from other people. (In many cases this is the only option.) Once upon a time, every town and village had at least one wise woman or cunning man with whom you could consult. That opportunity doesn't exist anymore and so books and authors have stepped in to fill the void.

Almanacs

Almanacs, defined as books, typically published annually, containing useful, practical advice and information, are most familiar today as standard reference books, similar to encyclopedias or dictionaries. Although some are little more than a compilation of tables of information, many are extremely entertaining. In addition to the "*useful, practical information*" many almanacs also include proverbs and sayings, little stories, humor, recipes, and assorted odd factoids and miscellany.

However, these extras are the icing on the cake: almanacs are filled with information intended to help one plan one's daily schedule and one's work schedule, especially if you still subscribe to a "traditional" occupation like farming, hunting, fishing or seafaring. The typical contents of an almanac include farming and planting information, tide tables, tables of sunrises and sunsets, weather forecasts and *ephemerides* (the fancy, technical word for astrological tables). Astrology? In a standard reference book? Yes, because the earliest almanacs were books of magic.

The modern English word *almanac* is believed to derive from the medieval Latin *almanach,* which most likely derives from the Arabic *al-manakh,* meaning "an almanac." Another theory suggests that *almanac* actually derives from the Saxon *al-mon-aght,* the name given to Norse runic clogs, carved wooden sticks detailing a year's progression.

Almanacs have extremely ancient roots; they derive from what is known as a *hemerology.* Hemerologies are magical calendars listing predictions for each day. What does each day *mean?* What blessings does each day promise or, conversely, for what inherent dangers must one prepare? Which deities or forces possess their utmost power on this day? Intrinsic to the hemerology is the notion that there is such a thing as lucky or unlucky days. Hemerologies thus serve as a guideline for avoiding disaster and maximizing good fortune.

Hemerologies list favorable and unfavorable days within each month; positive and negative actions for each day are also listed. Hemerologies existed in places as far apart as China, Egypt, India, Mesopotamia, Mexico, and Rome.

The earliest known hemerology dates back to at least the second millennium BCE in Mesopotamia. Hemerologies typically include predictions like this:

❋ *On the seventh day of the month he should not take a wife; distress will befall him*

❋ *On the eighth day of the month he may take a wife, his heart will be happy*

Daily horoscopes published in newspapers derive from this concept. Among the Aztecs and Mayans, when a baby was born, the hemerological table was consulted in order to reveal the new child's nahual, patron deity and perhaps name (see **ANIMALS:** Nahual).

With the invention of the printing press in the fifteenth century, almanacs, which were cheap to produce, became widely circulated and influential. Many people had only two books in their home, the Bible and an almanac. Scholars began producing their own almanacs, among the most renowned being Michel de Nostre Dame, better known now as Nostradamus. His predictions were first published as a feature within the almanacs he wrote, compiled, and published annually beginning in 1550. English astrologer William Lilly published his own almanacs in the seventeenth century.

By the eighteenth century, almanacs had become an extremely popular literary genre; many were bestsellers. Benjamin Franklin published his *Poor Richard's Almanac* from 1732 to 1758. Benjamin Banneker, the African-American astronomer and mathematician also published a series of best-selling almanacs. *The Old Farmer's*

Almanac, first published in 1792, is North America's oldest continually published periodical. *The Old Farmer's Almanac* was originally a guide for farmers and remains so, although many readers who have nothing to do with agriculture, simply enjoy reading it or depend upon its renowned weather predictions. *The Old Farmer's Almanac's* weather and farming advice are based on astrological wisdom, particularly moon phases. For many, these books are their only exposure to true astrology.

The Witches' Almanac

Another popular publication, *The Witches' Almanac*, falls squarely within the tradition of almanacs as books of magic. In addition to the standard practical information one expects to find within an almanac (moon phases, planting tables, and so forth) *The Witches' Almanac* is filled with information regarding spells, spirits, and practical magic. *The Witches' Almanac* was created by Elizabeth Pepper and John Wilcock and was first published as a labor of love in 1971. It is published annually coinciding with the vernal equinox. In 1980, when their publisher went out of business, *The Witches Almanac* went on hiatus until 1991 when Pepper and Wilcock revived it as an independent publication. It continues to serve all facets of the witchcraft community.

Books of Shadows

According to its most basic definition, a Book of Shadows is a book of spells or rituals copied by hand. That's crucial; by definition, a Book of Shadows is a personalized, hand-written book. No two are identical, if only because the handwriting is different. Although various authors have published their personal Books of Shadows, these are usually intended as guidelines or methods of preserving traditions. If you use a printed, published Book of Shadows for spell-casting, which many do, then by definition it is being used in the manner of a grimoire. In order to possess an authentic Book of Shadows it must be hand-written, even if all you do is copy it word for word. A not insubstantial portion of the tradition's power and beauty derives from the magical art of putting pen to paper.

Books of Shadows derive from the notion that because magical practices and/or Pagan religion were persecuted with total eradication as the goal, witches (variously defined) kept secret books. Secrecy was crucial because possession of a magical or Pagan text (and that's a distinction the Inquisition would not have made) was grounds for arrest and conviction for witchcraft. The title of the genre, which may or may not have been coined by Gerald Gardner, father of modern Wicca, refers to the necessity of keeping these books hidden or *"in the shadows."*

If one uses the purest, narrowest definition of a Book of Shadows as a hand-written, personalized book of rituals and magic, then in essence, all magical manuscripts created prior to the invention of the printing press, not least the medieval grimoires, are Books of Shadows. They were, by necessity, hand-copied. There was no other way to make a book.

However, that pure, narrow definition of Books of Shadows is rarely used, and the equation of them with medieval grimoires would horrify, appall and anger many Wiccans, because a Book of Shadows is more than just a handwritten ritual guide.

Many would object to considering medieval grimoires as Books of Shadows because these grimoires are virtually all associated with a type of selfish, frequently malevolent, male-oriented sorcery, heavily steeped in Christianity (many who used and perhaps wrote them were theologians) and with a type of magic that is diametrically opposed to traditional Earth-centered witchcraft.

Historic Books of Shadows, as opposed to those created in the wake of Gerald Gardner, are understood to have been books written by individual female witches or by covens in a desperate attempt to keep traditions alive. They are shadowy because normally this material would never have been written down but transmitted orally—but desperate times require desperate action.

This is the definition of Books of Shadows as taught by Gerald Gardner, who claimed to have learned of the tradition when he was initiated into a long-secret coven. Gardner wrote his own *Book of Shadows* together with Doreen Valiente and Aleister Crowley, and this book is among the bedrock on which Gardnerian Wicca is formed.

Since Gardner, Books of Shadows are an integral part of Wiccan religion, manifesting in various ways.

✺ *Solitary witches may create their own book to suit personal needs.*

✺ *Some traditions maintain one copy, entrusted to the High Priest or High Priestess; initiated individuals may copy from the book as needed.*

✺ *In some traditions, initiation involves copying and understanding the* Book of Shadows *over an extended period of time.*

✺ *Not all traditions create Books of Shadows; some prefer not to put everything in writing.*

In this sense Books of Shadows transcend spells. They are books of ritual. If one belongs to a specific spiritual or witchcraft tradition, this sacred book is where the laws, rituals, spells, and crucial information of that tradition are written.

This notion of the historical Book of Shadows grounded in the witch-hunts is controversial. Academics specializing in witchcraft often object to it, convinced it didn't exist. Many believe Gerald Gardner created the concept himself and only claimed that the tradition was old, similar in fashion to the way grimoires authored in the eighteenth century claim to be based on ancient manuscripts. Because so few ancient magical or Pagan texts survived, it's impossible to verify—or disprove—these claims.

Scholarly objection stems mainly from the fact that the type of witch Gardner describes tends to be female and is generally believed to be at best functionally illiterate. However, this is assumption and incredibly difficult to prove, one way or another.

Witch-trial records do show that when witches were burned, books were burned with them. However because the books were burned there is little if any evidence of what was burned. It's an old political trick: first burn the evidence, then say the evidence didn't exist. And maybe it didn't. Maybe the scholars are right. But maybe they're wrong—at least some of the time. Secrets have a way of emerging from the shadows: *one* historical reference survives. According to seventeenth-century Venetian Inquisition records, charges of witchcraft were levied against a woman named Laura Malipero. When the agents of the Inquisition searched her home they discovered a copy of the banned grimoire *The Key of Solomon*, together with a private, hand-written book of spells and rituals into which Laura had copied portions of that classical grimoire. Laura Malipero was obviously not illiterate. Her handwritten book fulfills Gerald Gardner's concept of the individual witch's

Book of Shadows and straddles the fine line between them and medieval grimoires.

And whether Gerald Gardner or someone else made up the notion of Books of Shadows may be irrelevant; it is a beautiful tradition. The completed books (and some are never complete, perpetual works in progress) are beautifully embellished works of art, power, magic, and spirituality. Some are written in magical scripts; some are illustrated. No two are exactly alike.

Wiccan Books of Shadows are traditionally kept secret. Many covens administer an oath of secrecy to initiates. You have to enter and commit yourself to that twilight world of shadows to gain access.

In 1971, the American Wiccan Lady Sheba (Jessie Wicker Bell, died March 25, 2002) was the first to publish an entire Book of Shadows, under the title *Lady Sheba's Book of Shadows*. Lady Sheba was a pioneer of Wicca as a public religion. She was among the first to officially register her religion as Wicca at a time when many people were ignorant of Wicca and associated it with Satanism. (The United States armed forces now acknowledges Wicca as a religious option, something not afforded to various Native American or African-derived spiritual traditions.)

Lady Sheba's Book of Shadows was published to tremendous interest but also tremendous animosity. By publishing her personal Book of Shadows Lady Sheba ignited a firestorm, not from outsiders but from within the Wicca community. Many felt betrayed and believed that she had violated her oath of secrecy. She was accused of making precious spiritual secrets public. (This was a time when comparatively few metaphysical works of any sort were published.)

In addition, many misunderstood the concept of a Book of Shadows being a compilation of earlier material and traditions. Because her *Book of*

Shadows was published under her name, many accused her of claiming to be the author of the material in her book, some of which was traditional. However, other material in her book had been composed by Doreen Valiente, Gerald Gardner's High Priestess and co-author of Gardner's *Book of Shadows*. Because it was never entirely clear exactly how much of Gardner's material was old and traditional, and hence in the public domain, and how much was created to fulfill the needs of a new spiritual tradition, various issues of copyright infraction, on the ethical level if not also on the legal, were raised.

Lady Sheba's response to this controversy and the hostility engendered was that the time of secrecy was over and that she had never claimed that the material was original. She was merely passing on the Gardnerian tradition as she had received it. The book remains in print. It is not a book of magic spells but of Wiccan ritual and theology.

Dream-books

Dreams are often understood to contain encoded symbolic meaning. The problem inevitably is cracking the code. Dream-books are guides that allegedly help you do just that. It is an ancient genre that retains its popularity today. The concept is found around the world.

✵ The Artemidoros, *a classical dream-book, was written in Greek in the second century* CE *and named for its author.*

✵ *Artemidoros' work was translated into Arabic in the ninth century and stimulated a rash of medieval Arabic dream-books, which in general are accessible only to those fluent in classical Arabic and its nuances.*

✵ *The Arabic dream-books' influence may be seen, however, in* The Oneirocriticon of Achmet, *a Byzantine work on dream interpretation, which was written in Greek in the tenth century and has greatly influenced subsequent dream-books, not only in Byzantine Greek and medieval Latin but also in modern vernacular European languages.*

Dream-books aren't psychological studies of dreams; instead they're mainly tables of interpretations. If you dream of something, what does it really mean? They're books of codes. For instance, if your head turns in a dream, this might indicate a change of location in your future. Eventually dream-books began to fulfill another important purpose: treasure hunting. It was believed (and still frequently is) that your dreams hold the clue to your fortune. Any dream symbol can be assigned a number; if you've got the right numbers, you might just win the lottery. The implication is that everyone has the right numbers although only a few can decipher them and put them to good use.

Although dream-books do not evoke the hostility of spell-books or grimoires, they were greatly discouraged by the Christian authorities during the Middle Ages. (Later on, they'd just be disparaged as foolishness and superstition.) Games of chance derive originally from sacred arts and it is a very small step from believing numbers are imbedded in your dreams to appreciating that benevolent guardian spirits placed them there. In fact, various Italian and Chinese spells invoke spirits to help provide winning numbers.

In a dream-book all components of a dream, anything envisioned or experienced, is assigned a number. For example, according to *Aunt Sally's Policy Players Dream Book and Wheel of Fortune* should you encounter a woman named Clara in your dreams (or even just see or hear the name) you might want to play 13, 36 or 42. *Everything* may be assigned a number and the better books are quite comprehensive, inventive, and fun.

In the late nineteenth and early twentieth centuries, inexpensive Hoodoo-oriented publications were marketed with romantic titles like *The Mystic Oracle* or *The Gypsy Dream Book and Fortune-teller*. Many were sold in conjunction with dream incense. The incense was burned before bedtime to stimulate clairvoyant dreams and then the book would help you figure them out. *Aunt Sally's Policy Players Dream Book*, published in the 1890s and still in print, features a cover illustration of a thin gap-toothed black woman with gypsy-style earrings pointing to some lucky numbers with a knowing look. The implication is that she is a conjure woman; she wears a head wrap tied to display horns of power. *Aunt Sally's* and many other modern dream-books oriented toward the hoodoo trade are believed to incorporate material from much older sources.

Grimoires

In 1277, the Archbishop of Paris issued a condemnation of *"books, rolls or booklets containing necromancy or experiments of sorcery, invocation of demons or conjuration of demons, or conjurations hazardous for souls."* In other words, grimoires.

The term "grimoire" is the name given to the genre of books of magic spells and rituals. Grimoire is a French word and is most usually pronounced *"grim-wahr."*

Variants exist in other languages like Latin (*grimorium*) or Spanish (*grimorio*) although an English variant does not exist, the French version being used instead. In general, the grimoires were a European phenomenon. Many of the classical grimoires weren't translated into English until well into the nineteenth century (S. L. MacGregor Mathers, founding member of the Golden Dawn, is responsible for some of the earliest translations).

> The closest English word to grimoire is "grammar," meaning a textbook or, more specifically, an instructive manual teaching correct construction of language. At their simplest, grammars are spelling books and so are grimoires. They just teach different spelling skills.

The first thing one must understand about grimoires, if one wants to understand the genre at all, is that they were illegal. These aren't merely textbooks of magic and magical ritual; they're *forbidden* textbooks; to be precise, *forbidden* texts of *forbidden* practices. Back in the Middle Ages, if you were caught with a magical book, punishment was dire. You'd be arrested and arrest almost inevitably led to torture. Oh, you could confess voluntarily to every charge but it gained you little. It wouldn't earn you a faster, more painless death because voluntary confession was rarely enough. Inquisitors were convinced that arrested witches and sorcerers were *always* hiding something; it was in the nature of witches to be cleverly evasive and secretive. So they'd torture you until they deemed that what you confessed under pain, terror, and duress was sufficient. Only then would you be burned alive with your magical book at your feet, lest you forgot what got you into this mess in the first place. The book prominently displayed and burned was also a warning to others to stay away at all costs from forbidden texts. There are very excellent reasons why until recently you couldn't openly buy any sort of magical work in a regular bookstore.

Historically, however, no matter how many have been willing to kill for a forbidden book of magic or spirituality, many more have been willing to risk their lives and die for these books and the knowledge they contain.

Grimoires are based on awareness of how precious and endangered magical and spiritual traditions were and how difficult they were to access. Persecution of witches and the destruction of their books pre-date Christianity. Roman authority, although Pagan, feared and wished to suppress magical information; they destroyed works by the thousands too.

There were always people, however, who regretted this loss and attempted to forestall and prevent it, albeit usually secretly. Fragments, pieces and individual pages of these magical texts were saved and preserved. Those who had read them sometimes attempted to recreate them. A black market for these invaluable suppressed magical texts soon sprang up, as did forgeries.

Magical texts, even in fragments were treasured. People copied them by hand from other people's copies. These copies, each perhaps slightly different, were circulated and copied again and again.

Few knew what to expect from these books because by definition they were scarce and mysterious. Few could understand or even read them: many texts were in archaic or unrecognizable scripts. Some are written in obscure foreign languages. And for a population that was largely illiterate, perhaps *any* writing is obscure and mysterious. Those little details didn't stop people from copying them and making attempts at translation. Some early manuscripts are written in several languages at once; your speculation as to why is as good as anyone else's. As to whether these manuscripts were authentic or whether translations were anywhere near accurate, there was rarely anyone to ask. Even if there was someone, who could trust that that person wouldn't inform the Inquisition of your curiosity, especially if they're arrested and tortured themselves?

The results of these hand-written magical manuscripts are the medieval grimoires. Pretty much across the board, they're a garbled mess. Some are believed based upon genuinely ancient magical texts. Others may contain fragments of these texts, while still others may be forgeries, written to discredit sorcerers or despised ethnic groups or just to earn small fortunes on the black market. Some are a combination of all of the above.

Grimoires as we know them began to appear in the twelfth century. Authorship is generally unknown. New editions were made by hand-copying old ones at great personal risk. It is a dream-like genre. Books were written in code, so that only adepts could understand what they were *really* saying. Some grimoires are attributed to famous names from the past like King Solomon, Albertus Magnus, and various occult masters. (Many are largely cribbed from the works of Cornelius Agrippa although this is rarely acknowledged.) Inevitably attributed authors are long dead and gone for obvious reasons: dead men tell no tales; dead men can't be prosecuted for witchcraft. Did these famous authors write the entire grimoire? Definitely not. Did they write some or any of the book? Maybe. It can't be conclusively determined.

In general, with few exceptions, these books are compilations of materials from varied sources, often reflecting very different and even contradictory traditions. Some may be "made up"—an attempt to gouge money from book collectors. Sometimes however even in a book that seems 99 percent invented, a glimmer of genuine occult wisdom suggests that at some point *something* was real.

For a living person to actually take credit for authoring a grimoire would have been tantamount to suicide, so inevitably they are always "found" manuscripts. An old trunk was opened and an old book discovered within. Or more frequently the story is that someone was minding their own business when a mysterious stranger handed them the text and disappeared. Are these stories true? Maybe. Books *were* hidden away in chests; someone transporting an illegal magical text probably wouldn't stop for a chat, tell you where they came from or give you enough information to find them later. On the other hand, maybe these mysterious stories are the required excuses needed for possession of a magical book, or maybe the person telling the story was really the one who first produced the book.

> The exclusively male orientation of this genre may be appreciated when one considers that magical books are attributed to Enoch, the Angel Raziel, the Egyptian deity Thoth, and the master magician King Solomon as well as his arch-rival, the master demon Asmodeus. Even a pope is credited with a grimoire. Why then are there no grimoires attributed to such legendary sorceresses as Isis, Circe, Medea or Morgan le Fay?

Grimoires frequently begin with an explanation of who wrote them, where, and why. Conjurers inevitably conjure up glamorous pasts and reputations for themselves. They were trave-ling in Egypt; they met a holy man in India. Are these stories true? Maybe.

The printing press was invented and popularized in Europe during the era of witch-hunting. Magical texts remained forbidden and illegal,

however the new technology offered the possibility of making these texts more accessible. After the invention of the printing press, grimoires were published and circulated in secret. Surviving classical grimoires seem to have been printed and standardized between the sixteenth and eighteenth centuries although they preserve older material within their pages, although by the time a work was published in a standard edition, it often bore little relation to the original manuscript upon which it was based.

Several versions of the same book may exist, frequently in different languages. It may be impossible to determine which was published first or whether all derive from a now missing source.

Medieval grimoires are in general not books of practical magic. They reflect the predilections, needs, and desires of their intended readers: educated male sorcerers, many with a background in Christian theology.

The grimoires were inspired by various sources. Any one grimoire may include spells and rituals based on one or more of the following:

✳ *Egyptian magical papyri*

✳ *Jewish angelology and magical handbooks including Kabalistic texts*

✳ *Pagan magical texts, especially surviving remnants from classical Greece, Rome, and pre-Christian Byzantium*

✳ *Roman Catholic ritual*, especially *rites of exorcism*

✳ *Alchemical traditions and mysteries*

In general the grimoires emphasize a school of magic known as Ceremonial Magic or High Ritual magic. Further details explaining this school of sorcery may be found in **MAGICAL**

ARTS: Commanding and Compelling. However, the basic premise is that the magician attempts, via a series of often lengthy rituals, to summon spiritual beings and command them to perform various actions on their behalf.

There are three components to this style of magic:

1. Spirits, frequently identified as demons, must be summoned or compelled to come to you.
2. Once you have them, you have to tell them what to do and enforce their compliance.
3. Finally, at the appropriate moment the spirits must be banished or compelled to leave.

The orientation is almost exclusively male. Angels and demons are summoned but not to reveal spiritual secrets, or at least not for the sake of mere knowledge. They're called upon to locate treasure or forcibly deliver the woman (frequently someone else's wife) who's already rejected you. There is relatively little herbal magic (some grimoires contain remedies, although these tend not to be practical or based on established herbal medicine), which was considered the province of women. Sorcerers weren't interested in this type of magic. Instead, grimoires are handbooks of magic for personal satisfaction, often rooted in selfish desire, rather than for the magical worker who serves her community.

As a whole, the medieval grimoires are not representative of modern witchcraft practices, Wiccan or otherwise. Those who are unfamiliar with them will likely be shocked. To describe them as mean spirited is an understatement (however this is true of many old magical documents, especially surviving texts from Alexandria). Although few if any are literally diabolical, many advocate brutal animal cruelty, magical rape, theft, and murder.

The most important surviving manuscripts from the Middle Ages and Renaissance are preserved in the British Museum in London and the Arsenal Library in Paris.

A sampling of the most famous grimoires follows. Also included in this list are a few books that are not medieval grimoires but were consciously written to follow in the tradition.

Aradia or The Gospel of the Witches

Although *Aradia or The Gospel of the Witches* is a relatively modern book devoted to magic and witchcraft, it is surrounded by an aura of mystery and controversy as powerful as that of any medieval grimoire.

Charles Godfrey Leland (August 15, 1824–March 20, 1903), who is credited as *Aradia*'s author, was an American folklorist, author, and journalist, and a respected authority on magic and witchcraft. A wealthy, cultured, well-traveled man, he went to Italy where he employed fortune-tellers and witches to serve as sources and teach him about their traditions. Leland came to believe that Italian witchcraft was deeply rooted in ancient Etruscan and Roman traditions. When he heard rumours about a mysterious manuscript setting forth the ancient doctrines of Italian witchcraft, Leland was determined to obtain it.

Among his sources was a fortune-teller named Maddelena whom he allegedly met in 1886 when he began employing her as a source. He nagged her to help him find this manuscript and, eventually, apparently she did. (How much he pressured her is subject to debate. Leland paid his sources; whether what they told him and brought him was true or was intended to please a wealthy patron is also subject to debate.)

Maddelena brought Leland the manuscript that would serve as the basis for *Aradia or The Gospel of the Witches* on New Year's Day, 1897. It was not an ancient manuscript. An older version (or any other version) of *Aradia* has never been found. Nor did Maddelena bring him the original but had copied it in her own hand, similar to the tradition of Books of Shadows and of medieval grimoires. Leland himself confessed that he did not know how much of Maddelena's handwritten manuscript was copied from another book and how much was based on oral traditions.

Having delivered the manuscript, Maddelena disappeared. Leland never saw her again, nor was he ever able to produce her in order to verify his story. He translated the Italian manuscript. *Aradia* is mainly devoted to the deity Diana, Queen of the Witches. It describes a version of her mythology and also includes a compendium of charms, spells, incantations, rituals, and folk magic. Leland added a commentary and published the work in London in 1899. (The part that he claims is derived from Maddelena's manuscript is in Italian with an English translation; Leland's own additions are solely in English.)

The tale Leland recounts of how *Aradia* came to be published is not dissimilar from the backstory explaining the existence of many medieval grimoires: the gist of the story is inevitably that a magical adept delivers a manuscript to someone and then disappears, leaving that person to present the manuscript to the world. However, Leland was no medieval sorcerer but a preeminent folklorist operating, theoretically at least, under the guise of science and anthropology, and so his book was held to a higher standard than that of the grimoires. Bitter arguments immediately sprang up regarding

whether the manuscript is really a copy of an ancient book or whether it simply purports to be. Although there is no proof that *Aradia* is based on an ancient manuscript, neither is there any proof that it isn't.

How much of it is historically verifiable and how much is "*made up*"? Since its publication, *Aradia or The Gospel of the Witches* has stimulated tremendous debate as to its *true* origins.

There are four possibilities:

1. Maddelena genuinely copied an ancient manuscript.
2. Maddelena wrote the book herself, perhaps based on her own family and personal traditions.
3. Leland made up the story about Maddelena and actually wrote the book himself.
4. Some or all of the above are true.

Because *Aradia or The Gospel of the Witches* would eventually exert tremendous influence on Gerald Gardner and Doreen Valiente and become incorporated into their vision of modern Wicca (most significantly the foundation of *The Charge of the Goddess*, among the most beloved Wiccan rituals, lies within *Aradia*), this debate regarding the book's origins has never gone away but remains fervent and perhaps even more passionate now then when it was first published over 100 years ago.

Aradia is a complicated, complex book even as to how it should be categorized. It is somewhat unique, falling midway between a witch's *Book of Shadows* and a medieval grimoire. Whoever did compose the book was familiar with both those magical literary genres. However, the book identifies itself as a *vangelo* or a gospel; *Aradia or The Gospel of the Witches* consciously intends to serve as a testament to Diana in the manner that the New Testament gospels serve as a testament to Christ.

> *Aradia or The Gospel of the Witches* explicitly states that devotion to the Madonna, particularly when she is visualized with the crescent moon, masks forbidden devotions to Diana.

In the context of medieval grimoires, *Aradia or The Gospel of the Witches* is radical because the focus is on powerful female deities (and Diana is clearly a goddess, not a demon) and because most of it is clearly intended for use primarily by women. There is no pretense toward containing hidden teachings from ancient Egypt or secret writings authored by prophets, kings or popes. Instead this is a text of witchcraft ostensibly created by witches for other witches, and humble ones at that. Simple if potentially powerful folk magic spells, the *"Conjuration of the Lemon and Pins"* for instance, are included that, one imagines, would have bored Dr Faust-style magicians with loftier pretensions.

However, *Aradia* is more than just a collection of folk magic and ritual. The book includes Leland's personal definitions of witches and witchcraft:

> … *in Italy great numbers of strege, fortune-tellers or witches, who divine by cards, perform strange ceremonies in which spirits are supposed to be invoked, make and sell amulets, and, in fact, comport themselves generally as their reputed kind are wont to do, be they Black Voodoos in America or sorceresses anywhere.*

Leland understands Italian witchcraft (*stregheria*) to be the joint product of hereditary witches and those who over the centuries, for one reason or another, joined forces with those witches: *"the witches of old were people oppressed by feudal lands*

[sic] … *holding orgies to Diana which the Church represented as being the worship of Satan,"* as well as a *"vast development of rebels, outcasts, and all the discontented, who adopted witchcraft or sorcery for a religion"* who held *"secret meetings in desert places, among old ruins accursed by priests as the haunt of evil spirits or ancient heathen gods, or in the mountains."*

In *Aradia or The Gospel of the Witches*, Diana is described as the first of all spiritual entities. Reminiscent of the Pelasgian creation tale retold in **ANIMALS:** Snakes, Diana first begets Lucifer (who may or may not be *that* Lucifer). Vain, proud, and arrogant, Lucifer rejects Diana's advances but she outsmarts him by resorting to witchcraft, shape-shifting into the form of a black cat, and so is able to conceive their daughter Aradia (Herodias), identified as the female Messiah, the first true witch.

Aradia contains no demonology comparable to medieval grimoires; the deities are treated respectfully. *Aradia* contains no commanding and compelling rituals equivalent to medieval grimoires but does share some themes in common with standard sorcerers' grimoires—most jarringly (to modern ears and in a book largely devoted to women's magic) a spell intended for use by a wizard desiring the love of woman.

He is encouraged to transform her into a dog, Diana's sacred creature, in which form she will be compelled to come to him whenever he wishes. He can then transform her back into female shape and have his way with her. She will remember nothing of the experience, it will seem like a dream. This is essentially the wizard's equivalent of a magical date-rape drug.

The image of women transformed into dogs is very powerful, however. Diana's votive imagery almost always depicts her accompanied by hounds; the implication contained in *Aradia* is that these hounds are transformed devotees, witches accompanying their goddess in disguise, and recalls that the slur *"son of a bitch"* was once intended to insinuate that a man's mother was a witch and hence sexually autonomous (or promiscuous depending upon perception), and that his father's true identity might thus be suspect.

See also Books of Shadows; **ANIMALS:** Dogs; Snakes; **DIVINE WITCH:** Aradia; Diana; Herodias; **HALL OF FAME:** Gerald Gardner; Charles Godfrey Leland; Doreen Valiente.

The Black Pullet or The Hen with the Golden Eggs

Do you remember the story of the goose that laid the golden eggs? Wouldn't you like to own a bird like that? Impossible, you say? Well, how about a chicken that can lead you to treasure? Would you settle for that? Sure you would. Now all you need is this book *and* the magical skill to put its secrets into practice.

Subtitled *The Science of Magical Talismans*, *The Black Pullet* is believed to have been first published in the late eighteenth century. Who wrote it? Who knows? The oldest extent version was written in French although it seems to have been published in Rome. According to what's written in the text, the anonymous author was traveling in Egypt when a mysterious man took him inside a pyramid and taught him occult secrets, which the author now wishes to share. *The Black Pullet* is the result.

This grimoire is devoted to talismanic magic and treasure hunting. It is divided into two sections, which may or may not have once been separate books. The first contains instructions for making magical rings that will enable you to command and control the elemental fire spirits known as salamanders. Why ever would you want to do that? Because salamanders can,

allegedly, be compelled to bestow gifts like invisibility and winning lottery numbers. The book's second section, fairly unique among grimoires, is devoted to instructions on how to create a magical chicken that can lead you to buried treasure. Don't laugh; this wasn't intended as a joke—or at least maybe it wasn't. A fairly late grimoire, with no pretense of presenting age-old information, *The Black Pullet* was produced in an era where the lines between obsessed sorcerer and mad scientist were very fine.

The Black Pullet takes a novel approach toward the prevention of piracy and copyright fraud, one that other publishers would perhaps like to consider. Similar to those curses found within Egyptian tombs or inside buried hordes of treasure, the text warns that anyone producing a pirated version will be severely punished via magic.

The Black Pullet displays more humor (or what can be interpreted as humor; maybe there was never any intention of being funny) than is customary in this genre. However, one mustn't underestimate *The Black Pullet*. It's an influential grimoire, which has been incorporated into various traditions, especially those of the Western Hemisphere including Hoodoo. The book is available in English. A Spanish translation—*Gallina Negra*—has been influential in both Afro-Caribbean and Mexican Santeria.

The Black Pullet created a new style in grimoires, resulting in a series of book with equally evocative titles. Extremely similar grimoires were published under titles like *Black Screech Owl*, *Queen of the Hairy Flies*, and *Treasure of the Old Man of the Pyramids*. A new "version" of the *Grand Grimoire* was also published around this time entitled *The Red Dragon* (see page 127).

See **ANIMALS:** Chickens; **DICTIONARY:** Santeria.

The Book of Pow-Wows or The Long Lost Friend

The Book of Pow-Wows has over the years become the work most often used to define the Pow-Wow tradition. This selection of charms and folk medicine was compiled in 1819 by Johann (John) George Hohmann.

Pow-Wow uses an Iroquois word to name the magical traditions of German immigrants to the United States. More information may be found within the **DICTIONARY**.

Unlike virtually all other books in this section, medieval and otherwise, *The Book of Pow-Wows* and its author are well-documented. Pow-Wow artist John George Hohmann (his name is variously spelled Hohmann, Homan, and Hohman) was born in Germany in approximately 1775. He emigrated to the United States as an indentured servant, arriving in Philadelphia on October 2, 1802 with his wife Anna Catherine and at least one child. Mr and Mrs Hohmann worked as indentured servants in different households in exchange for payment of their sea passage.

Hohmann served in Bucks County, Pennsylvania for 3½ years. Upon release from indenture, The Hohmanns reunited and set up a household together. Hohmann was a devout Roman Catholic and a fervent believer in faith healing. He put together a German-American spellbook, reflecting Pow-Wow tradition. The book was initially published in German as *Lange Verborgene Freund* (*The Long Lost Friend*) in Reading, Pennsylvania in 1820. It was eventually translated into English and retitled *The Book of Pow Wows or The Long Lost Friend* in 1855.

Hohmann did not want his compilation to be considered a grimoire, or at least he didn't want the local negative attention that authoring a grimoire would attract. This reflects the controversy in the Pow-Wow community between those who perceive themselves as devout Christians, with Pow-Wow as a form of Christian faith healing, and those who acknowledge and perhaps identify with other roots and influences. Hohmann certainly would have resented having his book appear on the same list as *The Sixth and Seventh Books of Moses*, a book reputed to be dangerous and diabolical although (perhaps for that reason) it was extremely popular among German magicians as well as dabblers in the occult. Many understand *The Book of Pow Wows* to be a safe alternative to that book.

Needless to say, *The Book of Pow-Wows* is intensely Christian in tone, if not ritual. Pagan Pow-Wow practitioners avail themselves of the same charms by merely deleting Christian references, many of which are easily omitted.

The Book of Pow-Wows was extremely influential outside the Pow-Wow community as well. Traveling salesmen specializing in "religious goods" carried *The Book of Pow-Wows* to the south, where it was purchased by Hoodoo and Voodoo practitioners who began to incorporate its practices and from whence it entered what would eventually become mainstream American magic transmitted to the world.

The book contains magic from various traditions including German folk magic, Romany magic, and Kabalah. As is so often the case, *The Book of Pow-Wows* seems to have offered readers more benefits than it did its author. Hohmann did not enjoy economic success; five acres belonging to him were sold in a sheriff's sale in 1825.

The Book of San Cipriano and Santa Justina

There are two St Cyprians. Both were third-century archbishops who died as Christian martyrs. One or both of them was a converted Pagan magician who renounced sorcery to allegedly become a devout Christian. As part of that renunciation process, the magician burned his substantial library of magical texts. Apparently several centuries after his death, St Cyprian began to regret his actions or at least the book-burning ones. He decided that he'd better make amends and provide people with a book containing the essence of his old collection. Now a dead man can't write, even if he is a sainted archbishop, but he can do the next best thing—he can channel.

According to the preface of *The Book of San Cipriano* the German monk Jonas Sulfurino wrote down the words dictated to him by St Cyprian in 1000 CE. Exactly who was Jonas Sulfurino? Who knows? But of course in order to be considered an official saint, by definition one must produce miracles. If a saint can produce miracles, who says he can't dictate a book?

Various slightly different versions of this grimoire have been published under the same title or very close variations on the title. The manual became *extremely* popular in Iberia, where St Cyprian (San Cipriano) is considered the major patron of magic. He is also considered patron saint of the Romany, who have exerted tremendous influence over Iberian magical traditions. Much of *The Book of San Cipriano* is devoted to finding long-lost buried treasure in Iberia. The best-known edition was printed in Spain in the sixteenth century. Still very influential in Spain and Portugal, Europeans brought the grimoire to the Western Hemisphere where it has been incorporated into various Afro-Brazilian traditions, including Candomble, Macumba, and Umbanda. As far as I know, there is as yet no English translation.

The book is intensely Christian in tone with prayers addressed to San Cipriano and Santa Elena (St Helen, mother of the Emperor Constantine, credited with discovering the True Cross in Jerusalem.) Despite this, it still bears a reputation in some quarters as a "wicked book." Some believe that owning a copy leads to evil deeds including murder and suicide.

The Grand Grimoire or The Red Dragon

Believed to have been written in the mid-seventeenth century, the earliest extent version of *The Grand Grimoire* is in French. The book includes methods of demonic conjuration and necromancy. It is not a nice book and perhaps best fulfills the stereotype of a diabolical grimoire. Arthur Waite, scholar of magic and founding member of The Golden Dawn described *The Grand Grimoire* as *"one of the most atrocious of its class"* because it directs the magician to perform acts possible *"only to a dangerous maniac or an irreclaimable criminal."*

The Grand Grimoire contains a unique ceremony of demonic conjuration to summon a spirit called *Lucifuge Rofocale*. Instructions for making a pact with Lucifuge are included, although the text suggests that this should only be used by those magicians who are unable to force the demon without resorting to a pact. Demonstrating the arrogance of this tradition, the pact contained in *The Grand Grimoire* is intended as a trick; the demon allegedly believes he will obtain the conjurer's soul after 20 years of service, however only vague promises of some type of reward are really made. Essentially these are instructions for beating the devil at his own game. Lucifuge can allegedly be compelled to locate hidden treasure and deliver it to the sorcerer.

The Great Albert

The full title of this influential grimoire is *Albertus Magnus, Being the Approved, Verified, Sympathetic and Natural Egyptian Secrets or White and Black Art for Man and Beast Revealing the Forbidden Knowledge and Mysteries of Ancient Philosophers.* Perhaps that's why they call it *The Great Albert.* (There's also a *Little Albert.*)

The book is attributed to the theologian, Christian saint and alleged magician Albertus Magnus. It is basically a collection of German folk magic and medicine with a strong Christian component. The earliest *Great Albert* currently known is a German manuscript dating to 1478. The first English edition was published in London in 1725.

The Grimoire of Honorius the Great

The Grimoire of Honorius the Great was allegedly written by Pope Honorius III, who passed away in 1227. The grimoire is occasionally attributed to one of the other popes known as Honorius, however the general consensus seems to be that *if* the grimoire was indeed written by a pope, then Honorius III is the one. Why would a pope author a grimoire? For priests to use—or at least that's the rationale given in this book.

The book's origins are unclear. *The Grimoire of Honorius* has existed in its present form since at least 1629 and was published in Rome in 1670. According to information contained in its text, a convention of sorcerers elected Honorius to write a work capturing the essence of the magical arts. The text was to be closely guarded and secretly passed from one generation to another. The anonymous author of *The Grimoire of Honorius*, whoever he was, included an introduction in the form of a papal bull from Pope Honorius proclaiming that Roman Catholic priests are now permitted to invoke demons.

The Grimoire of Honorius suggests various methods of summoning, commanding, and dismissing demons. Included in the work are prayers, assorted animal sacrifices, and instructions on how to create a magical book. Whether or not the grimoire was actually authored by a pope, its orientation is clearly Christian.

Is the concept of a pope authoring a grimoire completely laughable? Again, who knows? Since the Middle Ages, rumors have consistently circulated that before confiscated magical texts were burned, copies were secretly made and sent to the Vatican Library. Many sorcerers came from a clerical background and in many areas, such as France or Russia, priests were frequently reputed to double as sorcerers and were feared as such. Historically, priests were convicted and burned as witches. Based on their texts, some grimoires were intended for use by rogue priests.

Because the Pope had access to these stores of knowledge, many popes have had reputations, whether deserved or not, as sorcerers. One persistent conspiracy theory alleges that the European Witchcraze was at its roots really a secret attempt to eliminate everyone else possessing any kind of magical wisdom so that only a very small elite, safely hidden in the heart of the Church, would have control over this knowledge.

The Key of Solomon or Clavicula Salomonis

This may be the work that inspired all medieval grimoires. Much of the whole commanding and compelling magical genre derives from tales of King Solomon as the world's most powerful magician. King Solomon was allegedly able to command a host of spirits. Of course, back in Solomon's day there was no notion of demons as Satan's spawn, which emerged only post-Christianity. Arabic tradition, which retains many wonder stories featuring the Jewish king, identifies the spirits Solomon commanded as *djinn.* Jewish tradition suggests that Solomon obtained and maintained his power over the spirits, many of which were dangerous, through the use of a magical ring.

However, be that as it may, by the first century CE, the Roman collaborator Flavius Josephus, author of *The Jewish Wars*, noted the existence of a book written by King Solomon. Did Solomon really write this book or did the tradition of attributing manuscripts to the world-renowned already exist? Who knows? No definitive consensus can be reached. Cleopatra of Egypt is known to have authored books so it's not a far-fetched notion to imagine that Solomon could have written a manual of magic, whether he actually did or not.

People have been searching for King Solomon's magical manuscript ever since. We know that a book entitled *The Testament of Solomon* existed by the fourth century. Several handwritten manuscripts recognizable as *The Key of Solomon* have survived. The oldest surviving copy is in the British Museum. It was written in Greek and is believed to date from the twelfth century.

The Key of Solomon and its companion work, *The Lesser Key of Solomon* (*The Lemegeton*), are considered the most influential medieval grimoires. Many other grimoires including *The Grand Grimoire* incorporate information taken from *The Key of Solomon*, sometimes openly, sometimes not.

Different portions of *The Key of Solomon* as it exists today were composed at different times and by different authors. It's believed that vestiges of ancient Jewish magic survive within the text. *The Key of Solomon* is a book of ceremonial magic based on Jewish mysticism and Kabalah. The emphasis is on spirit summoning and control. The text outlines magical rituals for evoking spirits, including animal sacrifice.

Perhaps the oldest of the grimoires, *The Key of Solomon* gained a notorious reputation during the witch-hunts:

* *In 1350, Pope Innocent VI orders something called* The Book of Solomon *burned.*

* *At around the same time Nicholas Eymericus burned a book confiscated from a sorcerer entitled* The Table of Solomon. *This may or may not be a version of the* Key.

* *In 1456, a pamphlet against magic mentions the* Key *by name.*

* *In 1559, the Inquisition specifically condemns* The Key of Solomon *and bans it as a heretical work.*

* *During her seventeenth-century trial for witchcraft in Venice, Laura Malipero's home was searched and a copy of the* Key *found. A hand-written book was also found into which she was transcribing excerpts from the* Key.

The Lemegeton or The Lesser Key of Solomon

The Lemegeton is a collection of five books devoted to spirit summoning. Once again, the text is attributed to King Solomon. The earliest complete surviving manuscript in its present form was written in French and dates to the seventeenth century, although it contains references that date back to approximately 1500. Johann Weyer (1515–1588) included material that seems to derive from *The Lemegeton* in his catalog of demons, indicating its earlier existence.

What does *Lemegeton* mean? It resembles an acronym but no one is sure. The text is divided into four parts, which may or may not have originally been separate works. At least one, the *Almadel* is believed to have once been an original work. The sections are published together and individually today. Purchasing *The Lemegeton* can be tricky as sometimes the books are sold in one volume but sometimes not. Any volume sold under that name will contain the first book, the *Goetia* and possibly some or all of the others. Each book or section possesses an individual title, however.

The books are divided as follows:

1. *Goetia*: this means "sorcery" in Greek. When people refer to *The Lemegeton*, this is often what is meant. It includes a list and analysis of the 72 most influential demons, many of whom were deities, not demons, at the time of King Solomon. According to legend, King Solomon imprisoned these particular 72 inside a sealed brass cauldron and threw them into the ocean's depths. Eventually the cauldron washed ashore. It was discovered and opened in the expectation that it would contain treasure, or at least the equivalent of obliging genies in the bottle. Instead, the spirits escaped and are now loose in the world, more troublesome than ever. They can only be controlled by the methods described in this book. The *Goetia* was translated into English in a collaboration between Aleister Crowley and S. L. MacGregor Mathers, before their eventual falling out.

2. *Theurgia Goetia*: describes directional spirits and what to do with them.

3. *Art Pauline*: includes information on planetary hours and governing and guardian angels, as well as instructions on determining your own angels.

4. *Art Almadel*, also sometimes spelled *Almandel*: who needs dangerous, troublesome demons? This book includes instructions for summoning angels and convincing them to provide your heart's desire. The age and origin of this book is unknown. The earliest known reference to *The Almadel* occurs approximately 1500. Its title isn't as mysterious as those of some other grimoires: an *almadel* is a wax square upon which one may inscribe sigils. The handbook reveals how to create almadels.

There is also a fifth book, well, two of them, that are sometimes considered part and parcel of *The Lemegeton* package. The two fifth books are not identical and have different names. If you purchase a "complete" *Lemegeton*, it may contain only the four books listed above; it may contain the four books plus one of the following titles or it may substitute one of the following for one of the above:

✳ Artem Novem: *this includes rituals and prayers that it claims are necessary to consecrate the tools used in the other books*

✳ Ars Notoria *or* The Magical Art of Solomon: *also attributed to Solomon*

The Little Albert or Les Secrets Merveilleux de la Magie Naturelle et Cabalistique du Petit Albert

This is also known as *The Book of Secrets*, the same nickname given to *The Great Albert* (as opposed to the grimoire *True Black Magic*, which is also known as *The Secret of Secrets*.) Like *The Great Albert*, this one is attributed to theologian, saint, and magician Albertus Magnus, although whether some or any of it was actually authored by him is subject to debate. The manuscript originally circulated in various handwritten versions. It was later printed and standardized, reputedly first published in 1651 in Lyon. *The Little Albert* was banned by the Inquisition.

The Magus by Francis Barrett

Written in 1801 in England, this is considered a primary source for modern ceremonial or high ritual magic. For a long time it was very rare and sought after, although always very controversial. *The Magus* evokes strong reactions. Many consider it a masterwork; others consider it an act of theft. Is it a compilation or did Barrett claim to be author?

Francis Barrett was a British chemistry professor. He also taught private classes in the magical arts. He translated many occult texts previously unavailable in English.

The Magus is unusual as a grimoire written in English, which may or may not have contributed to the hostility toward it. Those who favor the book believe that Barrett compiled it in an attempt to stimulate the survival and growth of ceremonial magic, which he perceived as endangered.

The Magus is divided into sections, the last being a series of biographical sketches of various magical masters. It is somewhat out of character with the rest of book and there have been allegations that this section was added by the printer as "padding." (Adding insult to injury, some consider this the best part of the book.)

The Munich Manual of Demonic Magic

This book, written in Latin and dating from the fifteenth century, offers instructions for conjuring and dismissing demons using magic circles and words of power. Roman Catholic ritual is heavily incorporated although hardly in an approved, orthodox manner. Spells are included to obtain a woman's love when other methods aren't working, to attain invisibility, and to cause enmity between people who currently like each other.

Mystery of the Long Lost 8th, 9th and 10th Books of Moses

The Mystery of the Long Lost 8th, 9th and 10th Books of Moses is *not* a medieval grimoire but is based upon the traditions of the genre. It was first published in 1945. Its author and compiler, Henri Gamache, was a mysterious, albeit highly influential folkloric-scholar He collected the material for *The 8th, 9th and 10th Books* from medieval Arabic, Aramaic, and Coptic grimoires. Gamache's work doesn't evoke the same passions as does *The Sixth and Seventh Books of Moses* (see page 129)—it is considered neither diabolical nor inauthentic. The general consensus is that Gamache's work is based on genuine sources.

Henri Gamache's book consists of three parts. The first two include his analyses of Moses, whom Gamache describes as "the great voodoo man of the bible" and of how and why these magical texts were lost. (Basically these two parts are Gamache's explanations of why conventional wisdom regarding the Bible is wrong.) Gamache links ancient Egyptian and Jewish magic and spiritual traditions to those of sub-Saharan tribal Africa.

The third part is called *Curiosa or 44 Secrets to Universal Power* and contains various seals, nostrums, and sigils.

Rather than commanding and compelling demons, the focus is upon "practical magic" such as *"seals for love between a man and his wife"* or *"seal for whoever wisheth for a woman and her father will not give her."*

The Picatrix or the Ghayat al-Hakim ("The Aim of the Wise" or "The Goal of the Wise")

The Picatrix is highly unusual because it is a survival of an Arabic book of magic in Europe. Because it was translated into Latin at an early stage, *The Picatrix* remained accessible to Europeans when almost all other Arabic metaphysical knowledge was not.

The Picatrix was apparently composed in Andalusia in approximately 1000 CE at a time when most of what is now Spain was under Muslim rule. Although the book is attributed to the Andalusian mathematician al-Majriti who died *c.* 1005, there is little indication that this attribution is any more reliable than those of other grimoires. Some believe that the book was actually composed and/or compiled in the twelfth century. The book now popularly known as *The Picatrix* was translated into Latin in 1256 for the Castilian king Alfonso the Wise.

The Picatrix is substantially larger than other grimoires. It is a compendium of four books and may offer the most complete magical system of any grimoire. It is mainly a compilation of astral, sympathetic, and talismanic magic, grounded in Arabic and classical magic, with reference made to Hermes Trismegistus. Among the stated aims of the book's spells are the acquisition of love and longevity, healing, escape from captivity, and gaining control over one's enemies.

Although it was always rare, it was also highly influential. Latin, French, Spanish, and German translations are available. An English translation of *The Picatrix* has been published by Ouroborus Press.

See **HALL OF FAME:** Ficino; Trithemius.

The Red Dragon

If you've read *The Grand Grimoire*, you've read *The Red Dragon*. Some versions of *The Grand Grimoire* (or *The Red Dragon*) are in fact published as *The Grand Grimoire or The Red Dragon*, although each may also be published independently. Confused? Apparently that's what a publisher wanted. *The Red Dragon* is believed by many to be nothing more than a retitled, slightly different version of the earlier *Grand Grimoire*. Allegedly when a publisher wished to sell a new grimoire but lacked a new manuscript, the new title was simply tacked onto a version of the old book. An alternative explanation suggests that The *Grand Grimoire* was retitled to sound similar to *The Black Pullet*, which was then considered more stylish and nouveau than diabolical older texts like *The Grand Grimoire*, which had earned an evil reputation. (A certain cynicism may be at play here. It's been long rumored that a good percentage of those who purchase grimoires do so because they want to own something notorious and diabolical, not because they ever plan to put the book into practice or even have the capacity to read it.) *The Red Dragon* was published in 1822, although information contained in the text claims that it was really written in 1522. Again, who knows?

The Sacred Book of Abramelin the Mage

Aleister Crowley described this book as both the best and most dangerous book ever written. Dion Fortune claimed Abramelin's magical system was the most potent and complete.

The Sacred Book of Abramelin the Mage may best exemplify the mysteries, frustration, and beauty of the medieval grimoire genre. The grimoire was allegedly written by the magician Abraham ben Simeon in 1458 for his son, although whether the book itself was actually authored in 1458 or whether the date indicates when a copy was made of an earlier work is unclear. According to the story given in the grimoire, Abraham, a magician and Kabalah master from Wurzberg, spent years traveling through Europe, the Middle East, and Egypt in search of mystic wisdom before meeting his teacher, a Jewish magician in Egypt called Abrahamelim or Abra-Melin. Abra-Melin taught Abraham a magical system which he now allegedly sets down on paper for his son.

Three surviving manuscripts of this work exist, each one written in a different language: French, German, and Hebrew. They are all slightly different; it's unclear which is oldest. S. L. MacGregor Mathers first translated *The Sacred Magic* into English in 1900, using the fifteenth-century French manuscript.

Whether the story that explains the grimoire is true has been subject of deep, heated debate. There is no documentation that either Abraham, his son or the mysterious Abra-Melin ever existed, although there is also no proof that they didn't. A number of Christian references and themes in the work have lead some to believe that the author was a Christian and that the work is a forgery attributed to a Jewish magician either as defamation of character (the stereotype of the Jewish magician encouraged diabolical associations) or because in certain circles, Jewish magic was perceived as glamorous and mysterious, similar to the manner in which Egyptian magical traditions are still perceived. Others believe that later Christian interpolations were added to a book that is at heart exactly what it claims to be. Traditional Kabalah scholars have also studied this work to debate its authenticity. No consensus has been reached. No less an authority than the Kabalah master Gershom Scholem changed his mind about *The Sacred Book of Abramelin* several times. (By contrast, there is general consensus among Kabalah scholars that the grimoire known as *The Sixth and Seventh Books of Moses* has no basis in true Kabalah or ancient Jewish magic.)

The Sacred Book of Abramelin the Mage is not just a collection of seals, spells or rituals but an entire magical system. Think you'll bring the book home and knock off some spells this weekend? Think again. Abramelin's system involves *months* of purification. The book had tremendous influence over ceremonial magic. Once the system has been learned and the practitioner initiated, it promises mastery of the invocation of benevolent and malevolent spirits for material purposes, including acquiring romance and treasure, raising armies from thin air, and magically traveling through air or underwater. (Regardless of *who* actually wrote this text, this was *centuries* before submarines or airplanes.) The system is based on a series of magic squares, however the book makes it clear that the system won't work for anyone who is not an initiate.

> Raphael Patai, scholar of esoterica, was fluent in Hebrew, German, and French and so was able to read all three surviving manuscripts and compare them. Based upon these comparisons, he felt that at heart, the story presented in the manuscript was plausible and the magical system authentic, although later interpolations had obviously been made. His fascinating analysis of the three manuscripts is found in his book *The Jewish Alchemists* (Princeton University Press, 1994).

See **HALL OF FAME:** Aleister Crowley; Dion Fortune; S. L. MacGregor Mathers.

The Secret of Secrets or True Black Magic

According to this manuscript's claims, it was allegedly discovered in Jerusalem at the Sepulcher of Solomon (yes, this one is attributed to him too.) Allegedly translated from Hebrew, it seems to have first been published in Rome in 1750. The book contains 45 talismans and some instructions on how to use them. Arthur Waite identified *The Secret of Secrets* as an adaptation of *The Key of Solomon*. It is truly very similar although more malicious in tone. It was considered a diabolical, dangerous text, although this may have been a deliberately cultivated image—as demonstrated by its alternative title.

The Sixth and Seventh Books of Moses

Like the *Mystery of the Long Lost 8th, 9th and 10th Books of Moses*, the grimoire known as *The Sixth and Seventh Books of Moses* is based on the premise that the Ten Commandments were only part of the message transmitted on Mount Sinai. The Ten Commandments and the first five books of Moses (the first five books of the Old Testament) were the public information transmitted to Moses. God also gave Moses secret information.

This concept is based on some ancient Jewish mystical traditions that suggest that esoteric knowledge *was* also simultaneously transmitted. This knowledge is dangerous and so is not readily circulated. (Until recently, study of Kabalah was restricted to men who were over 40 years of age and married. It was considered too dangerous for anyone else.) However, the specific back-story of *The Sixth and Seventh Books* as revealed in its own introduction does not come from Jewish tradition.

According to the introduction, the material in the grimoire was allegedly first divinely revealed to Moses on Mount Sinai. It was then transmitted secretly, generation to generation, until it reached King Solomon, who used the material to command spirits. (In essence, through this story, *The Sixth and Seventh Books* is making a competitive claim for *The Key of Solomon*'s glory.) Following King Solomon's death, the material allegedly went underground for centuries but was then "discovered" in 330 by the Roman Emperor Constantine. Constantine retained the tradition of secrecy; however the secrets had now passed out of Jewish hands, coinciding with Rome's acceptance of Christianity as the state religion, and would eventually become the personal property of the popes. Eventually Pope Sylvester, another pope reputed to be a magician, had the material translated but commanded that it be kept secret and *never* made public under threat of excommunication. No secret stays hidden for ever; people had long whispered of these secrets, stolen glances at these manuscripts. Or so they said. In 1520, a copy of the translated book allegedly reached the Holy Roman Emperor, who finally broke with tradition and permitted publication.

To some extent, this is the conspiracy theory grimoire. Beyond whatever else, the story reveals fears of hidden knowledge, Jewish, and/or Vatican conspiracies.

So what's in these sixth and seventh books? The *Sixth Book* contains magic seals; the *Seventh* contains magic tables. The core of the book is an anthology of woodcuts allegedly copied from old manuscripts as well as incantations for summoning, commanding, and dismissing spirits. The book seems originally to have been written in some combination of German, Hebrew, and Latin, although this may be because different versions have been cobbled together. Christian and Jewish spiritual traditions are intermingled, not necessarily comfortably. A German edition was first published in Stuttgart in 1849 and attributed to Johann Scheibel (1736–1809) although scholars believe the material dates back to the fourteenth century. The first English translation was published in 1880 in New York by Wehman Brothers.

The Sixth and Seventh Books of Moses evokes passionate responses. There are scholars of ancient Jewish magic who absolutely detest this book. Various amulets and talismans are purported in the text to derive from ancient Egypt-

ian and Jewish sources; some Kabalah scholars believe that some of the seals *are* authentic, or at least based on authentic tradition. However, the text seems to have been written (or incredibly strongly amended) by a Christian author(s) with little direct knowledge of ancient Semitic magic or the nuances of Hebrew or Aramaic. Although the book claims to derive from sacred texts like the Talmud and assorted Kabalistic works, it bears little or no resemblance to them. (Because the average reader has *no* knowledge of these topics, they are not in the position to judge authenticity but are likely to take it at face value.) Some believe that *The Sixth and Seventh Books of Moses* is a medieval forgery used to implicate Jews as sorcerers, leaving them vulnerable en masse to legal persecution as witches.

The Sixth and Seventh Books of Moses contains some interesting magical seals that contain recognizable Hebrew letters as well as those of an unknown script. Portions of the manuscript were allegedly translated from Cuthan-Samaritan, a mysterious language about which little is known other than it has allegedly been extinct since the twelfth century.

The Sixth and Seventh Books of Moses became particularly popular in German magical traditions. It was transported to the Western Hemisphere by German immigrants where it remains a (controversial) part of the Pow-Wow canon. It is also favored by various African Diaspora traditions including Obeah and Vodou.

However, *The Sixth and Seventh Books of Moses* earned its fame and notoriety as perhaps the most diabolized of all the grimoires, evoking particularly strong reactions from those opposed to the practice of magic. It developed an extremely malevolent European reputation, although this may be partly responsible for the book's popularity.

The book retained great popularity in Germany up until the 1930s. When Pow-Wow artists refer to the "black book" this tends to be the one they mean (unless they're discussing Satan's personal book of records).

In the 1950s the German metaphysical publisher Planet Verlag printed and sold 9,000 copies of *The Sixth and Seventh Books of Moses*. In 1956, a coalition of German anti-occult religious and secular authorities sued the publishers, claiming that some of the spells might be construed as encouraging occult murder. A lower court found Planet Verlag guilty of "harmful publication" and imposed heavy financial penalties.

The True Grimoire or Grimorium Verum

This is a strange grimoire full of interesting details, inaccuracies, and controversy. S. L. MacGregor Mathers described it as *"full of evil magic, and I cannot caution the practical student too strongly against [it]."* Another work attributed to King Solomon, it is sometimes sold as *The True Clavicles of Solomon*. As clavicles means "keys" the implication is that this work is superior and more authentic than the renowned, popular *Key of Solomon*. This may be opinion or it may be audacity; there are those who believe that the bulk of *The True Grimoire* is cribbed from the *Key* and the *Lemegeton*.

Be that as it may, *The True Grimoire* was allegedly translated from the Hebrew by a "Dominican Jesuit" (which doesn't exist—there is no such religious order) and allegedly published by Alibeck the Egyptian in Memphis, Egypt in 1517. (Arthur Waite says Memphis is really Rome.) Its author and origins are unknown. Some experts date it no earlier than 1750 although others disagree and accept the alleged publication date. Some claim that this text was among those used by the diabolical Abbé Guibourg in the seventeenth century.

The True Grimoire offers a complete course in summoning and compelling demons and was at one time extremely popular—it was the most popular grimoire in Europe by the nineteenth century, particularly in France. Similar in style and nature to *The Grand Grimoire*, it contains instructions for conjuring and compelling demons, including sigils and descriptions of demons' powers. Like *The Grand Grimoire*, *The True Grimoire* was considered a diabolical book

Although it is now a notorious book and many avoid it for fear of being tainted by association, *The True Grimoire* is a particularly fascinating example of the grimoire genre. It is unusual in that grimoires virtually always assume that practitioners and readers are exclusively male: *The True Grimoire* uniquely contains some instructions offering variations depending upon whether the magician is male or female. It is also comparatively respectful towards demons. Instead of merely commanding and compelling, the reader is informed that such powerful spirits won't do anything without payment. This may be construed as referring to offerings or sacrifice and indeed, pretty disgusting instructions are included for preparing a sacrificial goat, although these instructions correspond to *no* spiritual traditions' notions of sacrifice.

Diabolical or not, whoever wrote *The True Grimoire* must have been a book-lover. Among the various demons and their powers that *The True Grimoire* identifies is Humot who, the text assures, will instantly provide the conjuring sorcerer with any book he or she might demand.

The World's Greatest Magician Black Herman's Secrets of Magic, Mystery, and Legerdemain

The author, who called himself "Black" Herman Rucker, was an African-American stage magician, herbalist, and hoodoo doctor. He remains highly unusual because he is among the very few to have successfully integrated simultaneous careers in legerdemain and true magic. Since the European witch-hunts, both these traditions have eyed each other with suspicion and hostility. Although each derives from shamanic arts, many practitioners of either art perceive *their* craft as diametrically opposed to the other.

Rucker published a monthly magazine from his Harlem headquarters and was famed for providing winning lottery numbers. Like many magicians, Rucker cultivated a glamorous image and origins. He claimed to have been born in Africa and to have learned mystic traditions in his travels around the world, including stops in Paris, London, China, India, and Egypt.

This is not a handbook of instructions for commanding and compelling; however it was written by someone who was familiar with the genre, particularly with those grimoires that combine folk healing with practical charms and spells.

Just because Black Herman's grimoire is modern doesn't mean it isn't steeped in mystery and confusion. The book consists of two parts: a preface and a body of main text. The preface is dated 1925, however no book in the form in which it presently exists has ever been found with a publication date earlier than 1938.

To further add to the confusion, there is also a nineteenth-century grimoire known as *Herman's Book on Black Art*. It has no relationship to *Black Herman's Secrets of Magic* other than a confusing similarity in titles. The identity of the older Herman remains unknown; that book hews to more traditional grimoire material and has been classified as a necromancer's manual. The World's Greatest Magician *Black Herman's Secrets of Magic* combines parlor tricks and legerdemain with spells, charms, horoscopes, lucky numbers, and Christian ritual.

See **DICTIONARY:** Conjure; **HALL OF FAME:** Black Herman Rucker.

Library of the Lost

These are the books you can't read. You certainly might want to; they were packed with metaphysical, magical, and spiritual wisdom, but you can't because they don't exist anymore. Now, books, even in the best of times, are fragile and perishable things. Paper burns, gets ripped or wet. Bindings break. Sometimes books that are too loved just fall apart eventually. However, that was not the fate that befell these books. These books were deliberately and systematically destroyed because someone with the authority to do so didn't want you or anyone else to read them.

The New Testament indicates the existence and suppression of magical texts. According to Acts 19:18-20 Paul encouraged his Ephesian converts to burn their vast collections of magical books. How vast were these collections? Their worth was estimated at fifty thousand pieces of silver at that time.

It's impossible to describe most of what was destroyed because nothing remains to tell, not even knowledge of existence. The following works and collections, however, are among the most prominent members of this library of the lost.

Alexandria's Library

The Royal Library of Alexandria, Egypt is believed to have been the largest depository of written work in the ancient world. It's estimated that at its peak it held between 400,000 and 700,000 scrolls, including Aristotle's own personal collection donated by one of his students. Allegedly, the Library possessed a copy of every book then in existence. How was this accomplished? Theft.

The Library belonged to the Pharaoh, whose word was law. All visitors to Alexandria were required to surrender any books in their possession. Copies would be made and the copy returned to the rightful owner, while the original was retained by the Library. Visitors didn't even have to enter the city. The Library was authorized to remove any books (scrolls) found aboard ships docking at this major port city on the Mediterranean; once again, copies were made and given to the owner.

All that remains of the Alexandria Library is information regarding its policies and the names of some of its titles, a little taste of what was lost. In addition to books of general interest, the Library possessed vast stores of metaphysical works from ancient temple collections throughout Egypt, Greece, Judea, Libya, Mesopotamia, and Nubia.

The Library is believed to have been founded during the third century BCE by Pharaoh Ptolemy II. There are various versions of how the library was lost. The version most commonly circulated until recently suggested that during Julius Caesar's invasion of Alexandria, the Egyptian fleet was burned with the fire spreading to city and library. Much of the old royal city of Alexandria ended up underwater following a series of earthquakes. Only recently has technology been developed to enable archeologists to study these ancient submerged ruins.

The old city has been recreated and mapped more accurately than ever before. It's now believed that Caesar's military actions did not destroy the library itself; instead it's believed that warehouses filled with books, perhaps intended for export, near the Alexandria docks were burned instead.

Before modern archeology, much of what was known about ancient history was filtered through the eyes of Christian monks who translated, wrote, and edited history texts. Booklovers themselves, they may have preferred the notion that Caesar was responsible for this waste and destruction. (Even reports that still hold Caesar responsible acknowledge that attempts were made to rebuild or further enhance the Library. Marc Antony allegedly gave his lady-love, the scholar pharaoh Cleopatra, a gift of 200,000 books for what was essentially *her* library.)

The Royal Library was finally shut and destroyed during the late fourth century when all other Pagan temples were destroyed. Theophilus, the second Bishop of Alexandria, requested authorization from the Emperor in 391 to destroy all aspects of Paganism and that was the end of the Library. Exactly what happened to the Library is unclear, however the Temple of Serapis was destroyed by a Christian mob that burned all texts found within the shrine.

Druid Books

Very little is known today about the Druids and even less is completely understood; we're not even 100 percent sure of exactly who they were or what their function was in Celtic society. (Yes, yes, I know. You can read a book that will definitively, *absolutely* identify the Druids, their beliefs, rituals, and actions; afterwards, you can pick up *another* book that will give you some other definitions and explanations. *Many* definitive versions exist.) Most of what we do know is filtered through the writings of Romans like Julius Caesar, who encountered them under less than friendly circumstances.

The standard explanation for our lack of knowledge regarding Druids is that they didn't write, therefore left no information behind. Celtic society was either non-literate or it was felt that it was too dangerous to commit information, particularly esoteric, valuable information, to paper, where anyone could theoretically read it, including the uninitiated or enemies. This standard explanation may very well be correct; certainly no proof currently exists to indicate that it isn't. The only clue that this might not entirely be the case comes in reports that St Patrick claimed to have burned 180 books belonging to Irish Druids.

The Etruscan Library

According to legend, Tages, Lord of Wisdom, emerged one day from out of a newly plowed field in the form of a young man with snakes for legs, bearing a book, which he gave to the Etruscan people. This book became the basis for their spiritual and mystical traditions, including their extremely sophisticated systems of divination and augury.

The Etruscans were a non-Indo-European people who inhabited northern and central Italy from approximately 800 BCE. Their memory survives in the name "*Tuscany*." Scholarly debate rages as to whether the Etruscans were indigenous to the region or immigrants from Asia Minor or the Eurasian steppes. Very, very little, in fact, is known about the Etruscans although, unlike the Druids, it cannot be said that they didn't have books. They were an extremely literate, educated, structured society, the dominant power in that area for centuries. The little that is known about them today is filtered through the eyes of their neighbors, the Romans and Greeks, who were uneasy with the Etruscans, not least because of the prominent presence and political and economic equality afforded to Etruscan women.

The Etruscans were what is known as a magical society and were viewed as great magicians. The English words "*augury*" and "*auspicious*" derive from Etruscan. *Augury*—a method of divination through the observation of birds—was pioneered by the Etruscans, while *auspice* or *auspicious* derives from "*haruspex*" (plural *haruspices*)—the title given the Etruscan priest/magician/seers.

The early kings of Rome were ethnic Etruscans. The very name "*Rome*" may derive originally from an Etruscan word. Unfortunately for them, the Etruscans found themselves sandwiched between warring, hostile Celts and Romans and bore the brunt. Although the Etruscans first dominated the Romans, they were eventually subjugated by them and not particularly nicely. Etruscans were granted Roman citizenship in 90 BCE but their leadership picked the wrong pony in a political dispute and so they ended up complete losers, their language suppressed and their culture outlawed.

Before he was emperor, Claudius (August 1, 10 BCE-October 13, 54 CE, emperor from 41–54) was a scholar. (This is the emperor who inspired the book and television series, *I Claudius*.) Claudius sought to preserve Etruscan traditions of magic, divination, and spirituality. The countryside was scoured for elderly Etruscans who were brought before him to be quizzed. The end result of Claudius' efforts was a 20-volume compilation of Etruscan history, spirituality, and knowledge. Claudius established laws protecting the haruspices and convinced the Roman

Senate to establish a library housing his 20 volumes as well as various other writings pertaining to Etruria. *The Sibylline Books* (see page 136), by then somewhat out of fashion, were moved into this storehouse of spiritual wisdom.

Christianity's rise to power sounded the death knell for what remained of Etruscan culture. Arnobius, author of *The Seven Books of Arnobius against the Heathen*, exemplified the official attitude when he wrote in approximately 300 CE that *"Etruria is the originator and mother of all superstitions."* Etruscan magical practices were still held in high regard by the general Roman population, if not the government, and thus were targeted for elimination.

The Christian general Flavius Stilicho, regent for the Emperor Honorius between 394 and 408 CE destroyed Claudius' 20-volume Etruscan compilation as well as *The Sibylline Books* and the Tagetic Books, which had been stored in Rome's Temple of Apollo. Today, we are still unable to decipher Etruscan writing; less than 100 words of the Etruscan language can be definitively translated.

Mayan, Aztec, and Mixtec Codices

Most of the cultures encountered by the first European explorers of the Western Hemisphere were non-literate, but there were exceptions. The organized, highly structured and urban civilizations of what is now Mexico were highly literate. The Aztecs (centered in what is now Mexico City) and Mixtecs (centered near Oaxaca) recorded their spiritual, magical, historical, and astrological knowledge as well as prophecies in a type of hand-written book now known as a *"codex"* (plural *codices*). These would eventually be systematically destroyed by the Conquistadors and the Inquisition. Less than 20 Mixtec codices survive and precious few Aztec

ones as well, notably the *Borgia Codex* currently housed in the Vatican.

The Mayans were beheld with awe both by their contemporary neighbors and by later observers for their mystical and astrological systems. They had an incredibly complex calendar. Most cultures base their calendars on either the lunar or solar cycles. The Mayans studied cycles of the sun, moon, *and* Venus and computed a calendar that coordinated all three.

Mayan codices were made from flattened fig tree bark, covered with lime paste (calcium carbonate, not the citrus fruit) and then folded like an accordion. They were written using an exceptionally sophisticated hieroglyphic system, which has yet to be completely deciphered and understood, and vividly illustrated on both sides. This type of paper survives and is known as *amaté* paper and is a staple of Mayan crafts designed for tourist consumption.

As far as the vast storehouse of Mayan codices goes, only three pre-Columbian Mayan texts and a fragment of a fourth remain. The sixteenth-century Spanish conquerors appreciated immediately that the Mayans had a great, literate, developed civilization. The Mayan hieroglyphic system frustrated and puzzled them. Initially, all texts were gathered together in an attempt to make sense of them but it was quickly decided that the codices were Pagan and diabolical and so they were burned.

Father Diego de Landa, second Bishop of Yucatan (November 12, 1524–April 29, 1579) is responsible for the destruction of Mayan texts. Although some books had already been destroyed, when it was brought to his attention that some Mayans, believed to have converted to Christianity, were still practicing their indigenous traditions, Father de Landa ordered an Inquisition followed by an auto-da-fé in which all the Mayan texts (and also some five thousand

Mayans) were burned on July 12, 1562. Father de Landa writes:

> We found a large number of books in these characters [the hieroglyphics] and, as they contained nothing in which were not to be seen as superstition and lies of the devil, we burned them all, which they [the Mayans] regretted to an amazing degree, and which caused them much affliction.

Not *all* books were destroyed. The Mayans rescued some, burying them or hiding them in caves. Unlike hidden manuscripts buried in the arid deserts of Western Asia and Egypt, however, the Yucatan climate isn't conducive to hiding forbidden books. Most were destroyed by humidity, the surviving pieces now impossible to read. Three codices survived in Europe, although how they got there remains mysterious as is much of their history (one codex was ultimately recovered from a garbage can). They are named after the cities in which they were found: the *Dresden Codex*, *Paris Codex*, and *Madrid Codex*. A fourth, fragmentary one is known as the *Grolier Codex*.

Missing Grimoires

How many books, whether defined as Books of Shadows or grimoires, were burned during the witch-hunts? If it's impossible to determine the number of human victims, it's even more impossible to determine the quantity of books. Magical possessions, or anything perceived as such belonging to those convicted of witchcraft, were burned, especially books. What was destroyed in these fires? Who knows? The books are gone and in general it is as if they never existed.

There is an important exception however. The Dominican inquisitor Nicholas Eymericus confiscated and burned many magical books (including such titles as *The Table of Solomon* and *The Treasury of Necromancy*) but not before he read them first. Although these books no longer exist, his descriptions do. He wrote a *Directory for Inquisitors*. According to Eymericus, confiscated books described elaborate magical systems, demons and the means necessary to command them, words of power and what Eymericus described as the diabolical pact.

The Sibylline Books

The ancient prophetesses known as the Sibyls were once rivaled only by those from Delphi. Solitary prophetesses, the various Sibyls existed in various locations; the most famous, and the only one for whom archeological evidence currently exists, is known as the Cumaean Sibyl because she prophesied from a cave near the town of Cumae (now Cuma) overlooking the Bay of Naples. At some point, for whatever reason, the Cumaean Sibyl decided to close up shop, but apparently thought the king of Rome might wish to preserve her prophecies. In 525 BCE, the Cumaean Sibyl presented herself to Tarquin the Proud, last king of Rome, ruler from 534–510. Despite her modern acclaim, he was unfamiliar with her, or perhaps he was expecting someone more impressive. She offered to sell him nine books revealing the future destiny of the world for 300 pieces of gold. She was small, bent over, shabby, and extremely aged, a veritable hag and the king perceived her as senile. He laughed at her and dismissed her.

Sometime later, the Sibyl returned to the king, offering to sell him six books revealing the future of the world for the same price as the nine. Now Tarquin was convinced she was deranged; he mocked her and sent her away. Sometime later, the Sibyl returned for the third time, carrying only three books now, for which she demanded the same 300 gold pieces. Something about her finally impressed the king and he asked to see the books. When he looked them over, he immediately recognized their value, paid the asking price and demanded to buy the other six. The Sibyl had the last laugh; she told Tarquin that she had burned them and promptly disappeared and was never seen again.

Whether one believes that story or not, *The Sibylline Books* existed. We know this because documentation survives regarding how they were stored, edited and finally destroyed.

Three books came directly from the Sibyl. Tarquin tremendously regretted not purchasing all nine. He ordered the entire College of Priests to recreate the other six as closely as possible. Envoys were sent to other Sibyls in other areas to obtain information. They did the best they could; however an aura of doubt remained as to whether *all* the crucial information had been retrieved. According to legend, because of Tarquin's failure Rome was fated to never know its future.

These books were once Rome's most heavily guarded treasure. *The Sibylline Books* were kept in a closely guarded vault beneath the Capitoline Temple of Jupiter where they were consulted by the College of Priests. The senate decreed that *The Sibylline Books* could only be consulted in cases of dire national emergency or before any momentous decision. Even the high priests were not permitted to examine them without receiving special authorization from the Senate. Anyone who attempted to defy this decree was to be sewn into a sack and tossed into the Tiber River.

In 204 BCE, when the Romans found themselves unable to defeat Hannibal of Carthage, *The Sibylline Books* were consulted. The books foretold victory if the sacred meteor representing the goddess Kybele, then housed in what is now Turkey, be brought to Rome and installed in a temple built for Kybele. History proved this prophecy correct.

Some information as to what was contained in *The Sibylline Books* survives. Some of it was agricultural information, similar to a modern almanac. There were also instructions for ending plagues and a description of the apocalyptic end of the world, which sounds remarkably like a description of nuclear disaster.

In 83 BCE, a tremendous fire destroyed the Temple of Jupiter and *The Sibylline Books* burned with it. Once again envoys were sent to various oracles in order to reproduce the texts as closely as possible. The Roman hysteria that greeted Egyptian Queen Cleopatra's love affairs with Roman leaders derived partly from rumors that *The Sibylline Books* had prophesied her eventual takeover of Rome. In 18 BCE, Cleopatra's nemesis Augustus Caesar had a second copy of the books made to protect against loss. During the process, he had one or both copies of *The Sibylline Books* carefully edited to erase all passages he deemed unacceptable.

Magic, prophecy, and mystery religions were increasingly unpopular in Rome. In 13 BCE, Augustus Caesar burned two thousand magical scrolls. Owning a magical book became a capital offense. Those who wished to preserve their books as well as their lives hid their libraries. *The Sibylline Books* were preserved but they fell out of fashion and were rarely consulted. Eventually the Roman Emperor Claudius established laws protecting diviners and prophets, including the Etruscan priests known as haruspices. He persuaded the Roman Senate to establish a library housing various writings on Etruscan religion and spirituality. Among the texts preserved in this library were *The Sibylline Books*.

Magic, prophecy, and mystery religions became even less popular once Christianity became Rome's official religion. However, for a while *The Sibylline Books* were tolerated, and even respected, because it was believed that the Cumaean Sibyl had foretold the birth of Christ. Attempts were also made to utilize the Sibylline prophecies to their best advantage. Thus we know of the apocalyptic prediction because Christians later wrote of it, explaining that although others would perish, they would survive to live forever in the Kingdom of God. However, *The Sibylline Books* were ultimately Pagan works and exceptions would not long be made for them.

In 405 CE, the Christian general and acting regent, Flavius Stilicho, burned *The Sibylline Books* as heretical texts offensive to Christianity, along with Claudius' entire library of Etruscan books devoted to divination, magic, religion, and spirituality, only stopping to scrape the gold from the doors of the Temple of Jupiter.

Because there were at least two copies of *The Sibylline Books* and because near the end they weren't as closely guarded as they had been in their heyday, rumors persist that a copy of *The Sibylline Books* is secretly kept in the Vatican Library of Forbidden Books.

Witch-Hunt Books

Like the chicken and the egg, it's impossible to determine how much the witch-hunts inspired the genre of witch-hunters' manuals and how much the manuals influenced the witch-hunts. Certainly, stereotypes of witches and the demonization of witchcraft resulted from these books. Witch-hunting was given a religious, even papal, seal of approval in mass-market print form. Regular people, even the illiterate, were able to buy picture books that enabled them to recognize a "witch" and her familiars. (Let's just say that whoever created these illustrations must have enjoyed drawing cats and bats.)

These manuals taught witch-finders how to find "witches" and instructed judges to have no mercy. Methods of torture were discussed dispassionately. This is a virulent genre; the books are worth reading if only because they still possess the ability to shock. The hatred of witches, women, nature, and foreign people and cultures is palpable.

Interspersed among witch-hunters' manuals are a few other works published simultaneously, protesting against the witch-trials or the demonization of witches. It is worthwhile to read these as well because they put the lie to the notion that the European witch-hunts occurred because of ignorance, because people didn't know any better. Balthasar Bekker and Friedrich Spee knew better, and felt strongly enough to record their beliefs in print for everyone to read, at tremendous personal sacrifice and great personal risk.

Some of the most prominent witch-hunters' manuals are discussed below although there are others in the genre. The few works that dispute witch-hunt methods stand pretty much alone, although history shows that there was a tremendous response to these works. Bekker's work in particular is believed to have drastically minimized witch-hunting in the Netherlands. Because many of the authors of the most prominent witch-hunt manuals also presided over trials, much of their historical background will be found in **WITCHCRAZE!**

Unlike grimoires, authors of witch-hunters' manuals were pleased and proud to sign their work. Publication dates and locations are reliable. There was no reason, when publishing these books, to fear the law; these authors *were* the law.

Books are listed in alphabetical order by author's name. (As you will see, in general, grimoires had snappier, more evocative titles.) None of the following titles have been lost. All remain in print.

Ady, Thomas

A Candle in the Dark, or a Treatise Concerning the Nature of Witches and Witchcraft: Being Advice to the Judges, Sheriffs, Justices of the Peace and Grandjurymen What to Do Before They Pass Sentence on Such as are Arraigned for their Lives as Witches (1656)

Ady's book argues that the Bible does *not* support the validity of witchcraft, at least in the demonic sense. Ady criticized tests used by contemporaries to determine whether someone was a witch. This book was particularly popular among Protestant critics of the witch-trials for whom the Bible was the ultimate arbiter. The book contains the first written reference to "hocus pocus," used to describe fairground conjurers who practice deceit and illusion rather than witchcraft.

Bekker, Balthasar

The World Bewitched or The Enchanted World (1690)

Balthasar Bekker, a Dutch scholar and Reformed Dutch Church clergyman (March 20, 1634–June 11, 1698) was a major force in preventing the escalation of witch-hunts in Holland. In 1690, he published *The World Bewitched*, a revolutionary work in which he argued that spirits cannot control the actions of humans and that witches do not consort with the devil, and therefore people are deluded if they fear the power of witches. Bekker suggested that Church leaders encouraged these beliefs so as to justify their practice of confiscating the estates of wealthy people convicted of witchcraft. This book is now considered the seventeenth century's most influential critique of demonology and witch-hunting.

The World Bewitched was published in Dutch and was soon translated into English, French, and German. Within two months of publication, 4000 copies had been sold in the Netherlands alone. Bekker's church did not support him. In 1692 he was expelled from the ministry because of his book. *The World Bewitched* was very influential among the Dutch populace, despite protests from local church officials, and witch-hunting in Holland was subsequently mild, never reaching the panic levels experienced in France, Germany, and Switzerland.

Bodin, Jean

Demonomania of Witches (1580)

Jean Bodin (1529–1596) was a French Carmelite monk who left the order to study law, eventually becoming a law professor and attorney. Beginning in 1561, Bodin spent 15 years serving King Charles IX of France, at which point he authored and published *Six Books of Republic*, which analyzed the concept of sovereignty, the king's right to rule. The book became extremely influential and established Bodin as a leading European political theorist. Many of his books fell somewhat foul of the Inquisition because they were understood to reveal Calvinist sympathies. Bodin has been described as "a learned and humane scholar" and praised for his early defense of religious tolerance.

Of course, that tolerance didn't extend to witches, nor was *Six Books of Republic* Bodin's only work. Bodin left the Court shortly after its publication and became a small-town attorney, public prosecutor and trial judge. Bodin was already prominent and esteemed when he wrote *Demonomania* and it quickly became among the most widely read demonological treatises of its day, going through ten editions before 1604. It was published in French, German, and Latin.

The book is essentially a professional handbook for prosecutors and judges. In it Bodin argues that it is the responsibility of all judges to treat witches harshly and then execute them by the most painful methods possible. He regretted that burning someone alive wasn't painful enough and suggested the use of green wood so as to prolong the experience. Anyone showing mercy to witches was suspect and should be tried and executed, too. Bodin suggested that Johann Weyer (see page 146), who had previously disputed the existence of witches, be among those tried. No exceptions were to be made for little witches; Bodin encouraged children to be tortured as brutally as adults so that they'd testify against their parents (and presumably against whomever else their torturers suggested).

Demonomania was used by many judges to justify cruelty and torture. Bodin himself boasted that he'd had both children and adults burned with hot irons until they confessed to any and every accusation. He died from bubonic plague in 1596.

> "Whatever punishment one can order against witches by roasting and cooking them over a slow fire is not really very much; and not as bad as the torment which Satan has made for them in this world, to say nothing of the eternal agonies which are prepared for them in hell, for the fire here cannot last more than an hour or so until the witches have died." (Jean Bodin, Demonomania)

Boguet, Henri

Discourse on Sorcery (1602)

Henri Boguet (*c.* 1550–1619) was a French attorney and author of legal textbooks for witch-trial judges. Boguet himself had presided over witch-trials as a chief judge in Burgundy and he included details of personal experience in his *Discourse on Sorcery*. As judge, Boguet condemned at least 600 people to death, including children, for whom he showed no mercy. Boguet describes how he oversaw in person the torture of an eight-year-old girl allegedly possessed by demons. Despite the common practice of strangling the condemned prior to burning their bodies, Boguet personally made sure that many of the condemned were burned alive. His textbook was highly popular, with over a dozen reprints by 1614. He held witches responsible for outbreaks of syphilis. Boguet writes as an eye-witness that Germany in 1590 was

> *almost entirely occupied with building fires [for witches]; and Switzerland has been compelled to wipe out many of her villages on their account. Travelers in Lorraine may see thousands and thousands of the stakes to which witches are bound.*

del Rio, Martin

Disquisitiones Magicarum or Investigations into Magic (1603)

Martin del Rio (1551–1608), who became a Jesuit at the age of 30, was considered a great scholar. His work was written in Latin and became immensely popular, even displacing the *Malleus Maleficarum* in certain circles. It argues that European witchcraft beliefs and practices were stimulated by attraction to Moorish culture in Spain and also implicates various heresies and the emergence of Protestantism as having influence over witches. He perceived Christianity as besieged by alchemists, sorcerers, and witches whom he classified as heretics as well as evil-doers. Del Rio's teacher at the Sorbonne, Professor Juan de Maldonado, also taught Pierre de Lancre (see page 144). A popular lecturer, he emphasized that faith was more vital than reason, and is believed to have had an impact on the witch-hunts, if only indirectly, through his famous, powerful students.

Gifford, George

A Discourse of the Subtle Practices of Devils by Witches and Sorcerers (1587) and *A Dialogue Concerning Witches and Witchcraft* (1593)

The English clergyman George Gifford (*c.* 1548–?) wrote two books arguing that witches did not possess supernatural power to harm. Only the devil himself possessed the power to work supernatural evil. Gifford believed that most self-professed witches were delusional and that witch-hunters and persecutors were stimulated by fear and hysteria, not reason. Gifford was an independent thinker; in 1584 he had been suspended from his ministry for refusing to subscribe to the articles of the established church. He lost his position despite petitions otherwise from his parishioners. Gifford did not deny the existence of witchcraft; however he amended its definition. Magical work and mystic power sought through Christian channels were not to be considered witchcraft. Gifford's works contain rare descriptions of the Essex witch-trials.

Guazzo, Francesco Maria

Compendium Maleficarum or Collection on Witches (1608)

Francesco Guazzo was an Ambrosian monk considered an expert on witchcraft and demonology. Federico Borromeo, Archbishop of Milan between 1595 and 1631 and later a cardinal, requested that Guazzo write *Compendium Maleficarum*. In 1605, Guazzo had been called to Germany because of his reputation as an expert demonologist. In Germany he was personally involved with various witchcraft trials, serving as a judge. He returned to Milan in 1608 and presented *Compendium Maleficarum* to the archbishop. It immediately became a standard text for witch-hunters and judges, used by lawyers and church official for making arguments and rendering decisions during trials.

Guazzo acknowledges in the text that some women accused of attending sabbats had witnesses who saw them simultaneously home in bed. However, Guazzo points out that these alibis aren't proof that the witches weren't at the sabbat, for two reasons:

✳ *Witches can magically journey in their dreams.*

✳ *Satan is perfectly capable of creating a "false body" that impersonates the witch well enough to fool her husband and children, making it look like she's home while really she's reveling.*

Using Guazzo's arguments, it's virtually impossible to provide an alibi or prove innocence. It wasn't necessary, incidentally, to read the *Compendium Maleficarum* either closely or in full to be influenced by it. Its very title subliminally sent a powerful message. *Maleficarum* is the feminine form of the Latin term for witches, which subtly reinforced the notion that witches were largely, if not exclusively, female. In fact, it wasn't necessary to read *Compendium Maleficarum* at all in order to understand its underlying message. *Compendium Maleficarum* is essentially an extension and update of Heinrich Kramer and James Sprenger's *Malleus Maleficarum* (1486). Guazzo's work also shows the influence of other witch-hunting authors like Martin del Rio and Nicholas Remy. However, unlike these other books the *Compendium* is a picture book. The other manuals presuppose a fairly high level of literacy. None of these books are easy to read. The language is specialized; they're full of convoluted legal arguments and theology. Unlike English witch-trial pamphlets, these handbooks were intended as texts for attorneys, clergymen, and judges, not for the average reader. The *Compendium Maleficarum* however doesn't demand literacy at all; the book is illustrated with a series of provocative, stereotypical and frequently sordid woodcuts depicting witchcraft, demons, and maleficia. The images remain familiar today; they're used to illustrate countless books on witchcraft. The illustrations, perhaps even more than the text, made the *Compendium Maleficarum* an extremely influential book.

See **CREATIVE ARTS:** Visual Arts: Medieval Woodcuts.

Gui, Bernardo

The Inquisitor's Manual (c. 1324)

Bernardo Gui (1261–1339) was Inquisitor in Toulouse between 1307 and 1323 and took personal credit for at least 930 convictions of heresy, although not necessarily of witchcraft. His book's main targets were Jews who had converted to Christianity but then "relapsed." It describes methods to be used by the Inquisition and set a precedent for witchcraft trials as well as trials for heresy. Gui makes an appearance, allegedly very much in character, as the witch-hunting Inquisitor of Umberto Eco's novel *The Name of the Rose.* Among his suggestions, Gui proposes that the Inquisition investigate "women who ride out at night."

James I, King of England

The Daemonologie (1603)

The Daemonologie attracted great attention, not least because its author was the king. It contains little fresh material and is mainly a reworking of various continental witch-hunters' manuals. James I had long held a passionate fear of and fascination for witchcraft. His ascent to the throne united the crowns of England and Scotland. In his other incarnation as King James VI of Scotland, James had participated in various witchcraft trials, most notoriously those of the North Berwick witches, accused and convicted of plotting against the throne. Scotland had a history of brutal witch panics, second in intensity perhaps only to Germany; England, on the other hand, had a relatively mild attitude towards witchcraft with little focus, until James' arrival, on demonology.

James was so enraged by Reginald Scot's *The Discoverie of Witchcraft* (see page 145) that he ordered every single copy of the book burned by the public hangman. *Daemonologie* was intended as a refutation of Scot's work, written in the year of James' ascension to the throne of England. It was popular enough to justify publication of a second edition in 1651.

Kramer, Heinrich and James Sprenger

Malleus Maleficarum or *Hexenhammer* or *The Hammer of the Witches* (1486)

The most influential witch-hunters' manual of all is often popularly described as the "witch-hunter's Bible," however it might better be considered the witch-hunters' *Mein Kampf.* For years, it outsold every other book except for the Bible.

The Hammer of the Witches, to use the English translation of the title, is a long tract written in Latin by two Dominican scholars, published in Cologne in 1486. The *Malleus Maleficarum* is a practical textbook, whose primary focus is legal advice on how to bring witches to trial and convict them.

Although it was *not* the first manual offering advice to those judging witch trials, it quickly became the most influential of such works and might be considered the first comprehensive guide to identifying, interrogating, torturing, convicting, and burning witches. It served as source material, inspiration, and justification for countless other treatises. In essence, without *The Hammer of the Witches* this section of the *Encyclopedia of Witchcraft* might not exist and most probably the section devoted to witch-hunting would be substantially briefer. *The Hammer of the Witches* provided primary source material for the Inquisition.

The authors were not unfamiliar with the Inquisition, although certainly not from the perspective of the persecuted. Heinrich Kramer, once spiritual director of the Cathedral at Salzburg, was appointed Inquisitor for southern Germany in 1474. (Heinrich Kramer is sometimes known as *Institoris*, the Latin version of Kramer.) His partner, Jacob (or James)

Sprenger, Dean of Theology at the University of Cologne, became Inquisitor for the Rhineland in 1470. Eventually he would be General Inquisitor for the German lands. The first major witch-hunt in Germany, the Ravensburger persecution of 1484, inspired Kramer to write *The Hammer of the Witches.* It was first printed in 1486. There were 13 editions by 1520 and 16 more by 1669.

The *Malleus Maleficarum* has a preface in the form of a papal bull (a bull is an official decree) from Pope Innocent VIII, essentially a Vatican seal of approval. This proclaimed to readers, most of whom were theologians and professional witch-hunters and judges, that this was more than just another book. It appeared to be an official Vatican publication.

The *Malleus Maleficarum* was revolutionary in how directly and exclusively it identified witchcraft with the female sex. Although the stereotype certainly existed prior to publication, it essentially hammered the point home so that it could not be avoided. It casts women in an extremely negative light and maliciously so. The *Malleus Maleficarum* falsely derives the word "feminine" from "fe" (faith) and "minus" (minus, less, lack). Women, according to the *Malleus Maleficarum*, are inherently lacking in faith but insatiable with carnal desire and hence vulnerable to the devil's administrations in a way that men cannot be.

The book states that disbelief in the existence of witches and witchcraft is heresy. Also, according to the book, witchcraft is the most evil of all crimes and the most abominable of all heresies.

When investigating witchcraft, not all forms of torture are acceptable, although perhaps not for reasons you might think. *Malleus Maleficarum* bans hot iron and boiling water ordeals, which had previously been used, because the devil might use these methods to help a witch escape unscathed. (Various cold water ordeals might be substituted.) Although the book doesn't go into further detail, various shamanic traditions, to this day, use hot iron and boiling water as demonstrations of power and ritual possession. Whether Kramer and Sprenger were aware of these traditions or had seen demonstrations is unknown.

The *Malleus Maleficarum* remains in print. It has been translated into English, French, German, and Italian. Although written by Dominicans, the tract was accepted by Lutheran and Calvinist authorities as well as Catholic, perhaps one of the only things, along with witchcraft, with which they were all in agreement. Interestingly, the Spanish Inquisition, which was under distinct management from Europe's other Inquisitions, was not overly impressed with the *Malleus Maleficarum* and skeptical of its value.

Lancre, Pierre de

A View of the Duplicity of the Messengers of Evil (1613)

This work was published in Paris as a justification of witch-hunter Pierre de Lancre's (*c.*1553–1630) merciless persecution of the French Basques in 1608. De Lancre's book gives extensive details of the diabolical sabbat, and drags out every stereotype of cannibal, devil's ass-kissing witches. De Lancre's book, like the *Malleus Maleficarum* is virulently hostile to women and particularly prurient. Far more is revealed about de Lancre's sexual fantasies than about any aspect of witchcraft. It also includes attacks on Jews, whom he describes as Christianity's oldest enemy.

The book does contain what may be the only known pre-twentieth-century reference to an "esbat." De Lancre claims a French witch used the word to describe a gathering of witches. It's not necessary to actually read the book incidentally; an engraving by the artist I. Ziarko graphically depicting the diabolical sabbat complete with witches in attendance, appeared as a double-page spread in the second edition of the book so that the illiterate could still appreciate the message.

Mather, Cotton

Late Memorable Providences Relating to Witchcraft and Possessions (1689)

The Reverend Cotton Mather (February 12, 1663–February 13, 1728) was a profound believer in diabolical witchcraft and involved in many of the New England witch trials, including those in Salem Village. He preached a sermon in Boston in 1689 entitled "A Discourse on Witchcraft." The sermon was included in a larger collection of writings entitled *Late Memorable Providences Relating to Witchcraft and Possessions*.

Reverend Mather was highly influential in the Massachusetts Bay Colony; at a time and place where the variety of reading material was limited, Reverend Mather's work was highly circulated, discussed, and respected. Three years after publication, Salem Village erupted in its notorious witch panic. Mather's work breaks no new ground but is consistent with those of his contemporaries in Britain.

Perkins, William

Discourse on the Damned Art of Witchcraft (1608)

Reverend William Perkins (1555–1602) was an English Puritan preacher and author of this

1608 guidebook for witch-hunters, published posthumously. The book established criteria for what constituted "legitimate" suspicion of witchcraft:

🕷 *Those who consort, are affiliated with or closely associate with witches are most likely witches too, thus encouraging arrests of husbands, children, siblings, parents, and other relatives of suspected witches.*

🕷 *If someone is cursed and then dies, the curser should immediately be arrested and charged with witchcraft.*

🕷 *Deathbed accusations of witchcraft must be heeded.*

Perkins writes that because all evil things written about witches are true, severe torture is justified to extract confessions. Essentially there is to be zero tolerance of snippy, evasive witches. All witches, regardless of crime or circumstances, warrant equal punishment: the worst. Perkins writes

> *by witches we understand not those onely which kill and torment: but all Diviners, Charmers, Juglers, all Wizzards, commonly called wise men and wise women ... in the same number we reckon all good Witches which doe no hurt, but good, which doe not spoile and destroy, but save and deliver.*

Remy, Nicholas

Demonolatry (1595)

Nicholas Remy (1534–1612) was a French priest and attorney. In 1570, he served in the Inquisitorial tribunals in Alsace. He became privy councilor to the Duke of Lorraine in France. In 1591, he became Lorraine's attorney general and presided as judge over witchcraft trials for the next 15 years. Remy was also involved with werewolf trials. He was proud to boast that he was personally responsible for the deaths of 900 witches between 1581 and 1591. According to him, this was his life's greatest accomplishment. Perhaps he could have made it an even thousand but an epidemic in 1592 caused him to flee to his country estate where, at his leisure, Remy compiled a treatise on demonology based largely on his own personal experiences. The book was published to great popular acclaim, enough to warrant eight reprintings, and was translated into German. Among Remy's arguments is that trial judges and magistrates are immune to witchcraft by virtue of their office and the divine sanction obtained by royal appointment.

Demonolatry's title comes from its focus on the diabolical relationship between witches, demons, and Satan. According to Remy, Satan craved Black Masses and manifested to people in the form of a black man or animal. Demons could enter into sexual relationships with women. If the women would not be seduced, then the demons would rape them.

Scot, Reginald

The Discoverie of Witchcraft (1584)

Reginald Scot (1538–1599) lead the skeptical opposition to the witch-hunts. Scot does a case-by-case analysis of the realities and illusions of witchcraft *and* witch-hunting. It is perhaps the earliest "rational" approach to the witch-hunts. He reveals tricks of conjuring (illusion) and so refutes notions of diabolism. It encourages the notion that if witchcraft is only conjuring and thus not "real," it's not really witchcraft and so should be safe from persecution. Scot's book is credited with saving lives. A chapter of the book is devoted to criticism of alchemy. Scot's book so aggravated King James VI of Scotland that he ordered all copies burned and was inspired to write his own treatise on the subject after he became King James I of England.

Spee, Friedrich

Cautio Criminalis or Circumspection in Criminal Cases, **also published as** *A Book on Witch Trials* (1631)

Friedrich Spee (February 25, 1591–August 7, 1635) was a Jesuit assigned to be the confessor for those condemned to die as witches in Wurzberg in the 1620s. What he heard convinced him that the unfortunate souls were innocent of the crimes of which they were accused. *Cautio Criminalis* was first published as an anonymous attack of the witch-hunts. He described torture in (non-prurient) detail, particularly the use of the rack. Spee did not deny the existence of witchcraft or even demand the abolition of the trials. Instead he demanded legal reform and an end to hysteria, panic, torture, and lies. Spee is among the heroes of the German witch-hunts. Many experts believe that his book was instrumental in abolishing the witch trials in various places, such as Mainz, and helped stop or at least reduce the terrible slaughter in Germany.

Weyer, Johann

De Praestigiis Daemonum (1563)

Weyer (1515–1588), also known as Wierus, was a student of the theologian and magical scholar Cornelius Agrippa. He was personal physician to the Duke of Düsseldorf. Although other books had debated the reality of various aspects of witchcraft and demonology, Weyer's was the first to deny the reality of witches altogether. According to Weyer, witches were not recruited and made no pact with the devil; however the whole notion of supernatural witches was a diabolical illusion. In other words, the devil, whose existence he does not deny, is responsible for the witch panic and witch-hunters are playing into his hands. The witch-hunters might be said to be operating under a diabolical illusion or they might be construed as collaborating with Satan themselves. In response, French witch-hunter Jean Bodin suggested that Weyer be burned for witchcraft. Virtually every contemporary demonologist, Catholic or Protestant (Weyer was Lutheran) attacked his suggestions and his reputation.

Weyer did not dispute the existence of malevolent sorcery, nor did he suggest that those guilty of that crime go unpunished. However, he claimed that witchcraft as presented by the witch-hunters, complete with supernatural powers and demonic pact, was an impossibility. Instead he believed the witch-hunts to be misguided attacks on harmless, if perhaps crazy, old women. (Weyer is believed among the first to use the term "mentally ill.")

Weyer published his work in 1563 in Latin and continued to publish expanded editions in 1564, 1566, 1577, and 1583. He also translated an abridged version into German in 1566, which was reprinted in 1567 and 1578.

✪ Botanicals

Although *every plant on Earth possesses* its own magic powers, some are specifically identified with witchcraft. These make up the majority of the plants featured within this section. (A few exceptions are those significant to the history of witchcraft.)

Imagine the first people on Earth, wandering through primordial forests, overwhelmed by this green world. In the beginning, there must have been too many plants of which to keep track but after a while, as with anything, individual natures would emerge. Some plants were discovered to be wonderfully nutritious or seductively delicious. Others were sources of water when none else could be found. Some plants were fonts of healing. Some eased labor pains, stimulated milk supply, or discouraged pregnancy when it was unwanted. Some plants just made you feel good. Inhaling their fragrance relieved your mind of worries. Inhaling other fragrances made you drop whatever else you might be doing and focus single-mindedly on romance instead. Other plants turned out to be the equivalent of keys: they opened the doors to other realms. Some provided portals to the spirits. And then there were those dangerous plants: should you taste even as little as a berry

or perhaps just touch the wrong leaf before putting your fingers in your mouth, the results could be fatal. One definition of modern witchcraft is that it is the surviving remnants of Paleolithic spiritual traditions focused on sacred plants and the beverages brewed from them. Witches, then, are devotees but also ritual leaders—those experts who understand the nuances, gifts, and dangers of the most volatile plants.

Formerly sacred plants evolved into witchcraft plants. The plants didn't change but attitudes towards them did. These plants, for one reason or another, tend to be ones that must be handled with care and expertise so as to avoid danger, damage, death, and disaster. Once upon a time, the skill and knowledge required to safely handle and manipulate these plants was admired.

In general, "witchcraft plants" fall into several categories. The following are not mutually exclusive. Many witchcraft plants fall into several categories at once.

* *Witchcraft plants offer power over life and death. Some exert powerful influences over the human reproductive system. These include fertility enhancers, menstrual regulators, herbal contraceptives, and abortifacients. Aphrodisiacs, those plants that promote sexual interest and ability, may be included in this category too.*

* *Just as some plants are identified with birth and life, others have associations with death, whether for spiritual reasons or because the particular plant is deadly poisonous, or both.*

* *Some plants possess the power to intoxicate; they stimulate the euphoria sometimes crucial to shamanism, witchcraft, and some spiritual rituals. They stimulate joy, exultation, and feelings of well-being, at least temporarily.*

* *The modern term "entheogen" describes substances that are gateways to visionary experiences. Used with knowledge, skill, and experience, these substances may unlock portals so that the shaman and witch can journey and fly.*

Witchcraft plants include wild, uncultivated plants that resist domestication, prickly, stinging plants that assert powerful boundaries, and poisonous and psychoactive plants. Many witchcraft plants are associated with the moon and with female reproduction and sexuality.

Warning

With the exception of linguists, most people's current knowledge of Anglo-Saxon extends no further than a few select four-letter words. However, it's vital to be familiar with at least one other four-letter word, at least before you play with *any* plants: **BANE**. Pay attention when you see or hear that word: it is a warning of danger. Bane derives from the Old German *bano* meaning death. Bane implies that a plant is poisonous enough to cause death.

Folk names tend to describe something about a plants' use; plants with "bane" in their name frequently recall the identity of those plants' primary victim, hence *henbane* or *wolfsbane*. However, beware: any plant with "bane" anywhere in its name is poisonous to some degree. That's how it earned that name.

Important: the plants in this section are included for historical purposes. Experimentation with plants, particularly with those known to be dangerous, is not encouraged. Those who are fascinated with plants might consider enrolling in the various academies of botanical knowledge or an apprenticeship with an acknowledged master.

Poisonous plants may be even more lethal today for two reasons. Firstly, *lack of knowledge*. We don't really know how or even if our ancestors administered the following plants. Practitioners were killed and chains of transmission destroyed. Their methods may have been very different from our own. Although they lacked our technical capacity, their knowledge of fine botanical nuances was almost certainly greater.

As an example, to this day traditional Chinese medicine, a still-thriving millennia-old discipline, discourages treatment by one single herb. Botanicals are almost always combined to create a buffering, synergistic effect. (Synergism means that the whole, the end result, is greater than the sum of its parts.) It is very possible that once upon a time ancient practitioners, skilled herb-witches, knew how to combine dangerous plants in such a way that they buffered each other, antidoted each other and made administration of individually poisonous substances possible. We no longer have this knowledge; it may be lost for ever.

Secondly, *concentration and isolation*. Modern understanding of plants and nature is very different from what it once was. Today we know that every botanical contains various phyto-hormones and chemical constituents including alkaloids that provide its various physical effects. In other words, once upon a time we knew that belladonna was toxic; now we know *why* it's toxic, which chemical constituents are responsible for its poisonous effect. These chemical constituents can now be isolated and concentrated. The effect of the chemical constituent on its own is almost certainly more potent and concentrated than when left as part of a complex system of interlocking components. There are herbalists who will only work with whole plants believing that any form of concentration of plant powers, including essential oils, is dangerous.

Modern scientific inclination is to isolate individual chemical constituents, refine and concentrate them, so that medicine can be standardized. Standardized synthetics may also be created that are even more potent than the whole plant. The disadvantage is that by isolating a single chemical constituent, we may remove buffering that provided a measure of safety. These standardized, concentrated forms

do not occur in nature and may, in fact, not be safer. The classic example is ephedrine, the now-banned dietary supplement derived from ephedra, a plant used medicinally since at least Neolithic times.

Safety Tips

✳ *Never use any botanicals without expert professional supervision. This extends to more than just standard internal administration. Even handling certain plants can be dangerous.*

✳ *Do not wildcraft (i.e., don't harvest from wild places), for two reasons:*

1. *This is the botanical equivalent of poaching animals; many botanicals are severely endangered in the wild.*
2. *Plants can be deceptive. It's very, very easy to assume that one is picking one plant when one is, in fact, picking another. This is particularly true with mushrooms, who bear reputations as tricksters, sometimes deadly ones. The classic example occurred in Northern California. Japanese mushroom experts, visiting the area, brought their harvest home and prepared them for dinner and were promptly poisoned, some fatally. They were genuinely experts: what they picked was* absolutely *identical to mushrooms that were safe in Japan, except that the Californian variant was lethal.*

Botanicals have local and folk names; these are the names they've been called in a specific language or region. Many of these folk names are very revealing; they tell you something about the plant's nature and uses. However, many folk names are shared. Half a dozen plants are known as *motherwort*; the only thing they may have in common is that they're beneficial in some aspect of maternity, whether conception, birth, or nursing. If you ask for motherwort, you may receive any one of these half dozen plants, at least one of which is also a powerful cardiac stimulant. However, each and every plant has only one Latin designation. That Latin designation is used internationally to describe only one single plant. Latin designations are the *lingua franca*, the common language of the worldwide botanical community. For safety's sake, because otherwise you may have no idea what plant you're working with and many plants have *profound* and sometimes dangerous physical effects, *always* use the plants' Latin classification.

Corn, rye, and other grains, as well as ergot fungus, are discussed in **ERGOT**. Fly agaric mushrooms *(Amanita muscaria)* are discussed below.

Alder

(Alnus spp.)

Other English names include: black alder, red alder, and owler. In Danish, its name is synonymous with "elf king" while in German it's called the Walpurgis tree or Walpurga.

Despite the confusing similarity in names, alders are not the same as elders, although both species of trees have powerful associations with witches and elves.

Alder is a moderately sized tree indigenous to the British Isles and most of Europe, all the way across Russia to Siberia. Alder is also native to the Caucasus, Turkey, and North Africa, from

Morocco to Tunisia. It was introduced to the Western Hemisphere during the Colonial Era and is naturalized in eastern Canada and the United States. (Some species of alder are also indigenous to the Andes region.) It is an extremely common tree and is now understood as an ecologically valuable tree because of its ability to improve the fertility of soil by fixing nitrogen from the air, although for centuries alder was a tree of ill repute.

Alder is unique for several reasons:

🌸 *Alder is renowned for its proclivity for water. Alder thrives in bogs, marshes, and swamps where other trees can't grow. Alders are allegedly attracted to water, hence the use of its wood for dowsing rods. Because its wood doesn't rot in water, it was perceived as a particularly powerful and valuable tree. Neolithic houses were built on alder stilts, as are the shacks of swamp witches. The city of Venice was built on alder. Alder loves and is beloved by water spirits and is believed to provide safety to their devotees.*

Alder is identified with water and with the color red. Water is the element most associated with magic, with the moon, witchcraft, and feminine power. Red is the color of blood and hence identified with birth (babies arrive amidst blood), death, menstrual mysteries, witchcraft, and women's power.

🌸 *Alder "bleeds." When alder is struck or cut, its pale heart wood gradually turns red. The modern scientific explanation is that this phenomenon is caused by the effects of nitrogen. The obvious non-scientific explanation is that the red color represents blood, although whose and under what circumstances has been subject to interpretation. The initial explanation, based on folklore, herbal, and magical traditions, seems to have been that alder menstruated like a woman, making it a rare, magically powerful and protective tree, and leading to its association with female deities and women's enchantments.*

Later, particularly in Northern lands alder came to be understood as inhabited by spirits. It is the spirits who bleed and mourn (and are angered) when the tree is cut. These spirits include the elven king but especially his daughter.

Alder's identification with the color red is increased by its annual production of red catkins—so-called because of their perceived resemblance to cats' tails. (In actuality, these are the tree's berries.)

Alders represent the goddess or the witch in her guise as hag or crone. The Earth Mother, the Great Mother, both gives birth and accepts the dead back into her womb, her cauldron of regeneration where souls are renewed and born again. The alder shares the essence of the Great Mother who welcomes the dead. It is a tree of death but also of resurrection.

Traditionally witches meet beneath alders. Alders, like elder, contains portals to other realms, such as those of the elves, fairies, and the dead. These thresholds are concealed within the tree but will open to those who know how to find them (and even perhaps, by accident, to innocent bystanders!).

❋ *Alder is known as the Walpurgis tree because German witches allegedly ate alder buds during their flight to the Brocken mountain on Walpurgis Night.*

❋ *Witches used alder branches to stir up and control the weather.*

❋ *Alder was particularly associated with red-haired witches. Allegedly, alder wood in the hands of a red-headed woman supernaturally boosted her own magic powers.*

❋ *Italian witches blended alder sap with madder to produce vivid red dyes that were used to color the scarlet ribbons, charm bags, and clothing so prized by Italian witchcraft.*

❋ *In Italy, alder wood is incorporated into the May Eve bonfires.*

❋ *In Ireland, the tree was used for divination, especially for diagnosis of the magical or spiritual roots of illness. In Irish tradition, it is forbidden to cut an alder. Many still hesitate today.*

❋ *Magical flutes, pipes, and whistles were carved from alder. Oracle flutes, instruments of divination, previous to being carved from alder, were formed from the bones of sacrificial victims.*

Post-Christianity alder's reputation grew ominous and negative. The bleeding tree's magic blood was explained as a reminder of the crucifixion.

Most of alder's uses were for ritual and magic (and feminine magic at that) and so it wasn't considered a "practical" botanical. Hildegard of Bingen described it as a "useless tree." There were a few exceptions: in Scotland, alder was prized for fine furniture. Scottish Bog Alder was also known as "Scottish mahogany" and was considered a luxury wood.

Alder is also a crucial component of many natural dyes. Depending upon the part of the plant, alder is used to make black, green, and red dyes as well as to tan leather.

According to the old medicinal law of similars, like is used to cure like. Just as with the similar-sounding elder, alder, the tree of witchcraft, is used to prevent and ward off witchcraft. Alder's main medieval uses were to protect against witches and vermin (fleas, lice, and mice; the sticky leaves may catch resident fleas).

A traditional remedy suggests that inner alder bark simmered in wine serves as an antidote against magic potions. On Walpurgis Night, branches of alder were crossed and placed against doors to prevent witches flying overhead from landing and entering. (Although the Walpurgis tree is so identified with witches' activities on this night, one wonders if this tradition isn't a distortion of some old witchcraft practice.)

See also Elder; **CALENDAR:** Walpurgis; **PLACES:** The Brocken.

Amanita Muscaria or Fly Agaric ☠

(*Amanita muscaria*)

Other names: Witches' Eggs

Amanita muscaria, also commonly called fly agaric, is not a botanical. It is a fungus, a type of mushroom. However, these are modern classifications. Ancient people looked for similarities of essence as well as for differences and distinctions. Mushrooms were (and are) used similarly to botanicals and so it is classified here amongst the botanicals.

Even if you know next to nothing about mushrooms or botanicals, even if you don't know what's so special about *Amanita muscaria*, it's pretty certain that you're familiar with what it looks like even if you don't recognize its name. You may never have seen a real one, but you've undoubtedly seen its picture. *Amanita muscaria* are the big red speckled mushrooms known as toadstools that are inevitable components of folkloric imagery. Look at traditional illustrations of witches, dwarfs, or fairies and you'll likely find at least one amanita tucked into a corner.

Mushrooms were understood as very special and powerful. Mushrooms pop up overnight directly from Earth or emerge from tree trunks, fully grown as if by magic. Some have psychotropic properties; many are poisonous, some to the point of fatality.

> In Germany, mushrooms in general are known as *hexensessel* or "witch's chair."

Psychotropic mushrooms, of which *Amanita muscaria* is the classic example, have historically been used in spiritual rituals worldwide. In fact there are scholars who believe that *Amanita muscaria* may have initially inspired a vast proportion of all human spiritual traditions and religions.

Among the traditions that some believe derive from mushroom cults are the Eleusinian Mystery religion, various ancient Egyptian traditions, Judaism and Christianity. Some scholars believe that *Amanita muscaria* was the mysterious biblical manna as well as Jesus Christ's *"bread of life."* There is even a Dead Sea Scrolls' scholar who has suggested that New Testament references to Jesus are actually euphemisms, eventually forgotten, misunderstood, and distorted, for *Amanita muscaria*, hence the emphasis on the host as sacrament. Others believe that soma, the mysterious brew of the Aryan people of India mentioned in the Rig Veda, is really amanita.

Amanita's associations with shamanism and ancient religion are so primordial and powerful that they transcend associations with witchcraft.

Encyclopedia of Witchcraft

Thus, images of *Amanita muscaria* show up *everywhere*, in Easter imagery as much as in Halloween's. Folkloric toys are created in the form of these mushrooms—I have a Polish carved wooden toy amanita. You remove the polka-dotted red roof to reveal carved wooden soldiers within. Even though amanita is poisonous, its image proliferates in children's books, not as scary images like spiders but friendly ones. (Can you imagine artists blithely submitting similar images of datura or wolfsbane?) Those dancing mushrooms in Disney's *Fantasia*? *Amanita muscaria*. Some even believe that the image of Santa Claus in his red and white suit may be a coded reference to amanita. Certainly his reindeer-driven sleigh can only be a reference to the cultures of the far north, where *Amanita muscaria* is intrinsically tied to shamanism, with reindeers integral to the ritual. (You'll find out why below.) Santa's habit of going up and down chimneys is also strangely reminiscent of shamans' and witches' flight.

Fly agaric is not uncommon throughout Eurasia and North America. It prefers poor soils, growing in marshes or along roads. It grows near birch, fir or pine trees, and is a traditional component of Siberian shamanism, where it's sometimes called "lightning mushroom." Based on linguistic studies, its use in that region may go back at least as far as 4000 BCE.

Amanita muscaria provokes a state of intoxication and allegedly opens portals to other realms. It has traditionally been used for divination, to contact spirits or journey to other realms and to locate lost, stolen or missing objects, especially those believed hidden in Earth.

Although *Amanita muscaria* is highly toxic, historically certain methods of preparation make it safer for use. Ibotenic acid, one of the psychotropic chemicals in amanita, is almost wholly retained in urine and not used by the body. (This is *not* true of its other chemical constituents, including the poisonous atropine and muscarine.) The traditional method of use, among the Finno-Ugric people of Finland, Lapland, and Siberia was to drink the urine of reindeer, which ate the mushrooms. (Reindeer may even have taught people about *Amanita muscaria*.) Reindeer meat may also be eaten in order to receive the hallucinatory experience. This is traditionally believed to be the safest method of use.

Amanita muscaria is among the ingredients cited in formulas for witches' flying ointments. However, it is *not* among the magical ingredients traditionally cited in medieval grimoires. Shamans desired to meet, commune, consort, and battle with spirits; medieval sorcerers just wanted to boss them around.

Medieval sorcerers, with all their emphasis on commanding and compelling spirits, weren't interested in using substances that couldn't be commanded as well. Amanita is, to say the least, unpredictable. It is also potentially fatal. It is not safe for individual experimentation under any circumstances, nor has it ever been considered appropriate for solitary sorcery. Instead amanita's use has historically been restricted to shamanism and to those folk magic practices directly descended from shamanism.

Because it is potentially fatal, *Amanita muscaria* has historically been a component of group ritual supervised by sober observers. Because dosage is so crucial, because the amanita cannot be standardized, and because there's no room for mistakes, amanita lore has always been transmitted orally and within shamanic channels.

According to Russian folklore, the presiding spirits of these mushrooms manifest in the form of small red tubular beings who are able to communicate with those under amanita's influence. (The mushroom may be understood as providing a portal for communicating with these spirits.) These spirits can be helpful and provide information, however they are also reputed to be wild tricksters with a taste for mean practical jokes, funny to them perhaps but tragic for their target. They may try to persuade the consumer of the mushroom to do potentially dangerous things—one more reason why sober supervision is so crucial.

Vivid red *Amanita muscaria* with its white polka dots may be understood as the mushroom equivalent of Amazonian poison arrow frogs. Its bold color announces its poisonous nature.

Decoctions of *Amanita muscaria* have historically been used to kill flies, hence it is also commonly called fly agaric. *Amanita muscaria*'s many other nicknames reflect its background in shamanism and witchcraft. Words used to name fly agaric are frequently connected to words for that shamanic tool the drum, and to toads. The common rationale for toad references has to do with childlike images of toads sheltering from the rain under large umbrella-like toadstools. However, among the chemical components isolated from *Amanita muscaria* is bufotenine a secretion otherwise found in toads' skins.

Apples

(*Malus pumila or Pyrus malus*)

Apples are magical fruits. Slice them in half horizontally and the star or pentacle secretly hidden within is revealed. In ancient days, apples were associated with love, lust, and pleasure, but eventually love, lust, and pleasure fell out of grace and apples became identified with witches and the devil.

The most famous apple of all may be the one with which Eve tempted Adam; the story is often told as if the apple were a euphemism for sex. Apples were already long associated with love, sex, and forbidden pleasures when Christianity came to prominence, whereupon translations then identified the apple as the fruit of the Tree of Knowledge. However, apples are native to temperate regions and are not indigenous to the region where Bible stories were first told. Many biblical scholars are absolutely certain that apples were not the forbidden fruit (figs, quinces, and pomegranates are the front-runners, although of course the argument has been made that *all* trees existed in the Garden of Eden, therefore the forbidden fruit could be anything).

Apples became synonymous with sex, sin, and feminine wiles. Fairy-tale apples, like the one the wicked witch-queen feeds Snow White, look seductively beautiful and innocently tasty but are secretly poisonous and perversely dangerous. Apples remained prized love spell ingredients—there are literally hundreds of love spells featuring little more than apples. Perhaps for this reason, apples became classified as more than just a food; they were witches' tools, especially those bright scarlet apples.

Belladonna ☠

(*Atropa belladonna*)

Atropa belladonna has many names: banewort, deadly nightshade, devil's cherry, dwale, but most popularly belladonna which means "beautiful lady," a surprisingly innocuous, even seductive name for such a deadly plant. The standard explanation for this folk name says that it derives from an extract made from the berry's juice that was used in ladies' eyes during the Renaissance to create a dilated "doe-eyed" expression, which was, at that time, considered very beautiful and seductive.

However, centuries previously, belladonna was sacred to the Roman war deity, Bellona, daughter of Mars. The plant was considered under her dominion and to share her essence. Ancient Roman priests allegedly drank some sort of elixir containing belladonna prior to ritual appeals to Bellona. The word belladonna contains the name Bellona within it, and it may have been a euphemistic pun on her name so that one could refer to her without actually calling upon this beautiful but fearsome Lady. Belladonna, like the goddess Bellona, is a beautiful but lethal killer.

Belladonna's genus name *Atropa* honors Atropos, one of the three Fates, whose name means "the dreadful," "the merciless," or "the cutter." Atropos is the Fate who cuts or terminates the thread of life.

All parts of the belladonna plant are poisonous including flowers, leaves, and roots. However the berries are the most virulently poisonous part of all: as few as three can kill a child. Do you remember those advisory stories reminding you not to assume that because birds can eat berries, that those same berries are safe for human consumption? Belladonna berries are the perfect example; many birds munch on the berries with impunity, something that is impossible for humans and for many mammal species.

Belladonna is a member of the nightshade family and is frequently equated with Deadly Nightshade. The names may or may not be used to indicate the same species. Various types of nightshade do exist that are also deadly, including Black Nightshade (*Solanum nigrum*) and Russian Nightshade (*Scopolia carniolica*), also known as Russian belladonna.

The primary toxin is the alkaloid atropine, which first stimulates the nervous system, then paralyzes it, causing muscular convulsions. Belladonna may also cause hallucinations, cramps, severe headache, mental stupor and, of course, death. Fly agaric (*Amanita muscaria*, see page 152) is the traditional antidote, however, it, too, is potentially fatally poisonous and the antidote must be administered at an incredibly fine, delicate balance and only by a skillful, professional hand.

Belladonna is a perennial that grows rampant among ruins and in wastelands. It is still found in this manner in Great Britain. It is rarely found wild in North America but is instead a cultivated plant. As its name implies, it has lovely flowers and so is often a prized component of poison gardens, where it may be appreciated visually and from a distance.

Belladonna's alkaloids are used to make atropine, an eye medication. Until World War I belladonna was not an uncommon medicinal plant. Trained herbalists and pharmacists knew correct methods of use. The main pharmaceutical crop was derived from wild belladonna growing on stone ruins in the wilder regions of the old Austro-Hungarian Empire. It was used to treat asthma, sciatica, and various other disorders.

As a beautiful and dangerous plant, belladonna was beloved and prized by herbalist wise-women who marked their skill by their proficiency with such plants. (There is no margin for error; no room for smoke and mirrors. It is impossible to fake your ability and knowledge with plants such as these; the truth will immediately be demonstrated.)

According to ancient witchcraft traditions, belladonna is at the peak of its power on May Eve (Walpurgis Night), so European witches only picked it on that night, when it is at its most powerful and magical.

See also **CALENDAR**: Walpurgis; **PLACES**: The Brocken.

Birch

(Betula alba)

Other names: The Lady of the Woods

Birch trees are unusual: their bark is white unlike the more usual brown. Birches are the botanical equivalent of the sacred white doe or buffalo. They are symbolic of light, purity, healing, and magic.

Birch is the tree of birth and new beginnings. This isn't merely mystical palaver but is based on some historical truth: birch trees are believed to have been the first to cover the land emerging from the Ice Age. Its use is certainly ancient; Ötsi, the Neolithic "Ice Man" who was found frozen in an Alpine glacier was carrying a birch bark bag when he perished. Birch is believed to epitomize female qualities. If oaks are essentially male, then birches are female. They are associated with powerful goddesses like Brigid and Sarasvati. Baba Yaga lives in the heart of a birch forest.

The name allegedly derives from Sanskrit *bhurga*, meaning "tree whose bark is used for writing upon." Birch bark is used in that manner among various Native cultures of North America, most notably the Ojibwa, who put birch to many uses, but also in Russia, where birch bark "paper" is incorporated into spell-casting to leave messages for nature spirits.

Amanita muscaria mushrooms grow beneath birches so birches are closely identified with these hallucinogenic mushrooms. The mushrooms may be understood as gifts of the tree. Birch wine and beer are also made.

Various traditions illustrate the identification of birch trees with new beginnings:

✼ *The birch is the first tree in the Ogham alphabet* (Beth).

✼ *Cradles are traditionally carved from birch wood to provide blessings and protection and a good start for a new baby.*

As the tree of new life, the birch was frequently chosen to be the maypole. Birch is among the most traditional materials for crafting a witch's broom.

Roman officials carried bundles of birch twigs as symbols of authority. A bundle of birch twigs with an axe in the center was known as a *fascis* and was originally intended as a symbol of generation and fertility. (Axes were symbols of rebirth and fertility deities, both male and female.) The *fascis* was appropriated by Mussolini and the word has since derived new meanings.

Once upon a time, bundles of birch twigs were used to slap cattle and women (gently!) to boost fertility and offer blessings and protection. Many horned deities carried similar bunches of birch twigs. English has no specific word for this bundle of birch twigs but in Hungarian the word *virgàcs* (pronounced *veer-goch*) names this item. Krampus, Santa Claus' Central European "helper" is never without his *virgàcs*. The symbol also survives among the traditional accoutrements of the chimneysweep as well as among the birch twigs used to enhance the experience of the Finnish sauna.

See also **DIVINE WITCH**: Baba Yaga; **HORNED ONE**: Krampus; **PLACES**: Bathhouse.

Coca

(Erythroxylon coca)

The coca plant is indigenous to Bolivia and Peru and has a long history of ritual and magical use there. Cocaine, the illegal stimulant, is a derivative of the coca plant; indigenous ritual incorporated the whole plant, not refined, concentrated derivatives. There is tremendous resentment among traditional ritualists for the way their sacred plant has been manipulated, corrupted, and politicized. However, controversies centering on coca began shortly after the arrival of Spanish Conquistadors.

> Caution! Potentially poisonous and, depending upon where you are, most likely to be illegal!

Coca use was discouraged by the Spanish, not because of its addictive qualities but because chewing coca leaves was associated with heathen devotion to the "*huacas*," the indigenous sacred shrines. The danger associated with coca was perceived as spiritual, not physical. Coca was a reminder of Peru's Pagan past that the Inquisition preferred to erase. For the Spanish Inquisition, coca was the plant most identified with Peruvian witches and organized opposition to the new religion and regime. However, wealthy mine-owners wished to encourage coca's use so as to stimulate worker productivity. On October 18, 1569, a compromise was reached when King Phillip II urged priests to beware of the use of coca in witchcraft and superstition but to allow its use as medicine, especially as a stimulant to encourage the heavy forced labor imposed upon the Indians.

Coca leaves were used in Peruvian love magic, as offerings to the spirits, and as an ingredient of psychotropic brews. Coca's international associations with magic and stimulation, rather than with addiction, still existed during the late nineteenth and early twentieth centuries, when power potions first became popular in the United States, including the one that bears its name, Coca Cola®.

> In 1630, an edict against stargazers (astrologers) and witches was posted on all church doors in Peru. Among their crimes, witches were accused of using "*certain drinks, herbs, and roots*" including coca, San Pedro, and datura.

Datura ⚠

(*Datura spp.*)

Datura names a widely distributed family of herbaceous shrubs with fragrant, trumpet-shaped flowers and usually spiny seedpods. There are approximately 20 species of datura growing around the world. Common folk names include angel's trumpet, devil's trumpet, devil's herb, horn of plenty, Jimsonweed and thorn apple. Many datura species have beautiful white flowers that bloom only at night, closing during the day—thus the plant possesses a profound lunar affiliation. Datura is cultivated for these beautiful flowers and various species remain staples of California's botanical nurseries.

Most species of datura are indigenous to the Western Hemisphere, however several originated in Eurasia, most probably in the region around the Caspian Sea. It is abundant in Russia from the Black Sea regions through Siberia, but thrives everywhere with the exception of very cold regions. Datura is used ritually wherever it is found, including widespread regions of Africa,

China, India, Mexico, and the North American southwest. Remains of seeds and seedpods found within a ritual context in South Texas, together with remains of other psychotropic plants, have been dated back to 2000 BCE.

Datura is used to hex and to break hexes, to induce sleep and visionary dreams. It has historically been used to communicate with other species, especially birds, and to enter other realms, especially that of the after-life. Unfortunately, it may be a one-way trip. Datura is deadly poisonous. Its active ingredient is hyoscyamine, which is similar to atropine but has a more powerful effect on the peripheral nervous system, causing powerful hallucinations.

Thorn apple is the form of datura most familiar in Western magic. Thorn apple (*Datura stramonium*) has been known in Europe since the sixteenth century, apparently introduced by the Romany who are believed to have been instrumental in datura's spread through Europe.

The most notorious datura may be Jimsonweed, which is a corruption of Jamestown Weed. There are two versions of how this species of datura acquired that name:

✻ *In 1676, soldiers were sent to Jamestown in the Virginia colony to quell a local rebellion and somehow accidentally ate the plant. This was followed by an 11-day period of delirium. The news spread throughout the colonies and Britain and the name stuck.*

✻ *The plant was named in honor of the first place in the American colonies where datura was deliberately cultivated for medical use.*

Once upon a time datura was an important medicinal incorporated into treatment for madness, melancholia, and seizure disorders. Its no longer used as such; the toxicity rate was too high and safer replacements have been devel-oped. In 1968, the United States banned the sale of over-the-counter preparations containing datura.

Elder

(*Sambucus nigra*)

The elder, known as the "witch tree," is powerfully identified with witchcraft, the magical arts and goddess-oriented Pagan tradition.

The elder is a threshold tree: it serves as a portal that allows souls to pass between realms. Ghosts, spirits, and elves can pass into the mortal realm via elder trees and bushes but, remember, one-way signs don't exist in the magical, shamanic world. Elders are also portals where *you* can access other realms.

In order to establish contact with other realms, try burning elder bark, blossoms, roots, and wood as incense. (If gathering botanical material yourself, remember to ask for permission from the plant first and always to leave a gift in return.)

The elder is sacred to the Germanic deity, Hulda, known affectionately as Mother Holle. Hulda was once an extremely prominent, important deity, so entrenched in people's hearts that, unlike some other spirits, she was never entirely banished. Unable to completely eradicate her, local Christian authority dubbed her a Queen of Witches, with the immediate implication that all who were devoted to this queen were witches themselves. In Denmark, the elder tree itself is called *Frau Hylle* or *Hyllemoer*, Danish for Mother Holle or Frau Holle. In Anglo-Saxon it was known as *Hylder* or *Hylantree*. As part of Hulda's ritual, circle dances were performed around the tree.

For the ancient Germans and Slavs, old elder trees, especially those that nestled close to a house, were the home of family ghosts. Because they are threshold trees, elders are often incorporated into funeral rites.

✳ *Heathen Frisians buried their dead underneath elders.*

✳ *In England, grave-diggers traditionally carried elder wood so as to protect them from any malevolent ghosts lingering in the graveyard.*

✳ *In other areas, it was customary for the driver of the hearse to carry a whip made of elder wood.*

Perhaps because of associations with Hulda, elder became identified with witchcraft. Elder bushes personified witches. It was believed that witches could transform into elders as surely as they could assume the form of a cat. One single solitary elderberry bush popping up in an unexpected spot might actually be a witch in disguise—another reason to treat the elder with respect. Perhaps in the spirit of that old saying *"it takes one to know one"* elders are also powerful agents used to ward off malevolent spells.

Elders have a powerful reputation as protective trees, especially for fending off malevolent witchcraft. Traditionally fingernail parings, hair or teeth are buried beneath elders so as to prevent their use in malevolent spells. Afterbirths of calves and foals are buried beneath elders so that neither the new-born animals nor their mothers can be bewitched. (These practices may also be simultaneously understood as offerings to Mother Holle, the elves or the ancestors, depending upon whose spirit resides within the particular elder.)

Elder wood is carved into amulets to prevent unwanted enchantment. Green elder branches were also buried in a grave to protect the dead from witches and evil spirits.

Elder is incorporated into many spells, especially those for love and protection. A nickname for elder sap is "blood." Sap was understood as literally the blood of the tree, in the same way that bark is its skin and leaves the tree's hair. Because the elder was believed to house important spirits, to embody Hulda's essence or to even be a witch in disguise, elder "blood" was potentially incredibly powerful, more powerful than most sap. Northern European spells that cite "blood" as an ingredient may, in fact, be requesting elder sap instead.

Elder is a short, bent, crooked tree that never grows very tall, hence the constant confusion between whether it's a bush or a tree. It is not a tall, forbidding, imposing tree. Unlike other witchcraft plants, elderberries are not toxic but tasty and nutritious—as anyone who's had elderberry preserves or wine can attest.

Unlike so many other witchcraft plants, elders are friendly plants; they're understood as a tree that likes people and is by nature helpful and affectionate. (Spirits residing within may or may not be as friendly and benevolent: Frau Holle and the elves both possess reputations for volatility, although this may be in response to defamation and loss of respect and offerings.)

Elder's roots among spiritual traditions of Northern Europe and its associations with spiritual entities and ancestral spirits were so powerfully entrenched that it created a dilemma for ascendant Christian authority. Attempts were made to either taint the tree as evil and diabolical, thus to be shunned by all righteous people, or to incorporate elder into Christian tradition, so that its use could continue under proper auspices. Both methods were historically tried.

In the days before the easy availability of wax and hence cheap candles, elder was a source of light.

Elder Candles

1. Slice the pith of elder branches into round shapes.
2. Dip these slices into oil.
3. Set the slices alight and carefully float them in water to create floating "candles."

In areas where attachment to Hulda was particularly strong, attempts were made to brand the elder as an evil tree, something to be feared. The only people who would use elder with impunity were witches. (There may be some truth to this: because it was believed spiritually hazardous to harvest any part of the elder without requesting permission from the resident spirits, only those who knew how to do this, who remembered these practices and didn't fear them, would be willing to gather twigs or berries.)

Elder retained its associations with Paganism but now Paganism was identified with the devil rather than with helpful deities. (One tradition from this era suggests that if you wanted to invite the devil over for a visit, burning an elder log in your fireplace officially extends an invitation.)

In an attempt to break chains of transmission, to seal up the portals and make people fear venturing near thresholds, Christian missionaries painted the elder as an evil tree. Various legends emerged:

* *An elder whip was used to scourge Jesus and that's why elder's branches bear cracks on the skin.*

* *Judas committed suicide by hanging himself from an elder.*

* *It was widely believed that Christ had been crucified on an elder wood cross, which is why the tree is now so stunted and bent.*

On the other hand, in attempts to ingratiate the elder into Christianity and substitute associations for the Pagan goddess with the Virgin Mary, another legend suggests that Mary hung Jesus' swaddling clothes on elder branches under which she had sought protection from a storm. (There is a northern legend that lightning never strikes elders, although whether Mary would have known this in first-century Egypt or Judea, where the date palm or tamarisk is the primary sacred tree is impossible to verify.)

Regardless of these efforts, elder's identity as a powerful spiritually charged plant was impossible to shake. Historically, date palms weren't easy to obtain in Northern climates and so the elder, that ancient local sacred plant, was a frequent substitute. In Allgau, Germany, for instance, the cross for Palm Sunday "palms" was formed from elder branches instead.

See also **CALENDAR:** Midsummer's.

Elm

(Ulmus campestris)

Elm trees are widely distributed, from as far south as Mexico, to as far north as the

Himalayas. One species, the Scotch Elm (*Ulmus montana*) is also known as the Wych Elm. In German, however, the *entire* species of elms may be classed as "*Hexenulme*" or Witch's Elm.

The elm has a reputation as a cranky tree, allegedly dropping branches onto people's heads deliberately. Elms can be very tall and as such served as local landmarks. Meeting under an elm was an easy direction to follow because elms were frequently the tallest, most imposing trees around. Witches allegedly danced around elms, particularly on May Eve.

Romany magical tradition prizes the elm as a tree of particularly powerful enchantment. Romany magic wands are traditionally crafted from elm although the wood can never be cut but only received as a gift from the tree in the form of naturally fallen branches. (Frustrated because there is no fallen branch? If the tree wants to work with you, a branch will be available, perhaps falling directly onto your head. If not, that's your signal to look elsewhere or to be patient.)

Elms were associated with death and passage into the realms of the Dead. Spirit guardians of burial mounds were believed to make their homes in elms. The wood was once used to craft coffins.

Enchanter's Nightshade

(*Circaea lutetiana or Circaea alpine*)

This is Circe's plant; the enchanter in question is the Greek witch-goddess Circe. Other names for it include Walpurgis Herb, Great Witch Herb, Sorcerer of Paris (the Trojan prince, not the city), Paris Nightshade, Magic Herb, and Great and Common Witch's Herb. In German, it's called *Hexenkraut* (Witches' Herb); its

Anglo-Saxon name was *Aelfthone*, as it was believed to counter elf-derived illnesses.

Despite its common folk name, it is not as toxic as other plants nicknamed Nightshade, such as Black Nightshade, Deadly Nightshade or Russian Nightshade. There are two species of Enchanter's Nightshade. The most common— *Circaea lutetiana*—is from Eurasia. It grows best near streams and damp, marshy places, often associated with witchcraft and magic.

A variation of the species prefers higher altitudes. Alpine Enchanter's Nightshade (*Circaea alpine*) is also called Circe of the Alps. Both plants are associated with hexes, binding charms, and love spells. Enchanter's Nightshade was one of the plants whose possession was sufficient evidence to warrant accusation of witchcraft.

Henbane ☠

(*Hyoscyamus niger*)

Hyoscyamus niger earned its English folk name because of the danger it posed to free ranging poultry. Among its other names are devil's eye, god's bean, henbell, hogbean, Insana, Jupiter's bean, and poison tobacco.

Henbane is a biennial that was originally indigenous from Mediterranean regions through Asia Minor. It's been transplanted to the United States where it now grows wild on wasteland, old, neglected gardens, cemeteries, and ruins.

Henbane's active component is hyoscyamine. It is very dangerous when used excessively or over extended periods of time. The general consensus among the ancients was that excessive use of henbane caused madness and insanity. Henbane's effect is similar to that of datura; however it was indigenous to regions of Europe where datura was unknown until late in the

Middle Ages and so henbane was for centuries Europe's most accessible, if secret, hallucinogen. (Toadstools—*Amanita muscaria*—were typically gathered from the wild; henbane is relatively easily cultivated.) For many generations it was the most prominent, beloved "witch plant" in Europe. It is also used similarly in Africa and India, although there it has more indigenous competition.

Henbane was once among the most important ritual plants of the German lands, sacred to Lord Balder. According to Germanic tradition, for optimum power the ritual harvesting of henbane must be accomplished by naked women, under the direction of magical spirits. This may indicate that the women are ritually channeling these spirits during the harvest.

Henbane was traditionally used for conjuring up those spirits as well as for divination. Henbane seeds were burned in European bathhouses, a place traditionally associated with divination and spell-casting, well into the Middle Ages. Henbane was also used as a charm in medieval weather magic. It was also once among the ingredients of a very popular medieval beer, one that apparently intoxicated in more ways than one.

All parts of the henbane plant are deadly poisonous. Allegedly even inhaling the scent of its fresh leaves may lead to intoxication and stupor. The dead in Hades were crowned with henbane wreathes, but then they were past worrying about it. Henbane is believed to have been the poison used to kill Hamlet's father in Shakespeare's play.

Although it is poisonous, henbane has historically had various medicinal uses and was believed beneficial for hernia, lung disorders, and pain relief—provided one had a herbal physician with enough skill and knowledge to administer it. Because it has narcotic properties, it has traditionally been used medicinally as an anesthetic and a sedative. It was used for various gynecological treatments. Traditional midwifery utilized henbane as a soporific during childbirth so as to create an early form of "twilight sleep." The Irish name for *Hyoscyamus niger* is *gafann*. Meted out in very carefully measured doses, it was once valued in Irish herbalism for its anodyne and sedative properties.

During the era of the Inquisition possession and use of henbane was considered sufficient proof for conviction of witchcraft.

Juniper

(Juniperus communis)

Juniper is not poisonous. Every year, juniper trees are safely brought into the home at Christmas. Its berries are found among the spice aisles of food markets, not to mention as the primary flavoring in gin. Juniper is a component of many over-the-counter medical preparations, bath oils, herbal, and cosmetic products. However, it is **not safe** for use by pregnant women or by those actively attempting to conceive.

Juniper is an evergreen widely distributed throughout the Northern hemisphere, with a long history of use in magic, midwifery, herbal medicine, and the brewing of intoxicants. Like those other small trees, elder and rowan, juniper is simultaneously identified with witchcraft and an alleged guard against it.

Long ago, in Western Asia, juniper was associated with Lady Asherah and her daughters

Anat and Astarte. Like those renowned, powerful goddesses, juniper is associated with birth, death, and prophetic ability.

Juniper earned its fame as an herbal menstrual regulator. For women who lacked periods or whose cycles were irregular, preparations of juniper could jump-start them onto the road to regularity and fertility. However, timing and need are everything: juniper was also famous as a contraceptive and herbal abortifacient. Depending upon one's perspective, juniper was understood as a woman's stalwart botanical ally, providing whatever she needed, or as an evil tree under the dominion of Satan.

Juniper is included in many love spells and aphrodisiac formulations. When administered to men, frequently in the form of a potion, it allegedly increases sexual prowess and irresistibility. When administered to women, especially if in the form of a bath or douche, as in the Hoodoo formulation known as *Hot Mama* for instance, it may be understood as being intended to have contraceptive effects. (There is as yet no conclusive scientific information verifying or disputing this historic folkloric use of juniper, although, pregnant women are strongly cautioned against its use.)

Juniper's magical uses aren't limited to love and reproduction: it was also burned to stimulate clairvoyance and for protection from disease. (The volatile oils released by the burning wood provide an antiseptic effect.) Even after World War I, French hospitals burned juniper branches alongside lavender to minimize rates of infection and the spread of disease. Juniper wood was traditionally included in Samhain bonfires to stimulate clairvoyance among those who inhaled its fumes.

Juniper was also believed by some to ward off witchcraft. If one understands "witchcraft" to be synonymous with malevolent magic, then the belief makes sense; however it remains ironic, because by the late Middle Ages and beyond in Central Europe, juniper had become almost exclusively associated with witches and midwives.

Juniper became famous for its use as an herbal contraceptive and abortifacient at a time when such things were against the law and believed by many to set one literally onto the road to Hell. This was particularly true of the subspecies *Juniperus sabina*, popularly known as savin or sabin, which grows in Alpine regions and Central Europe and is a particularly potent menstrual regulator. The phrase "*giving birth under the savin*" was a common euphemism used during the Middle Ages for induced miscarriage.

An eighteenth-century traveler visiting Swabia (now in modern Germany) writes that savin bushes served as a code, providing clear messages that couldn't be spoken aloud. Savin bushes in a garden signaled that the garden belonged to either a midwife or a barber, who at the time also frequently offered abortion services. Desperate people stole entire bushes or raided them for materials. Local authorities, on the other hand, periodically destroyed savin bushes as preventive measures. Eventually in many Central European areas, the only savin bushes to be found were discreetly hidden among other plants on private property. Bushes on public property had all been destroyed. If the botanicals don't exist, women can't use them.

Do not be in a hurry to plant savin bushes or at least not for personal use. They are beautiful, fragrant, powerful plants. However, although juniper bushes survive, the skilled practitioners who knew their secrets did not. Like the other plants in this section, administration required an experienced practitioner with a skillful hand. The wrong dosage, by a very slight margin, could cause disaster. The Brothers Grimm story *The Juniper Tree* recounts the tale of a woman who, unable to conceive, makes a Pagan-influenced sacrifice under her juniper tree. She conceives, but late in pregnancy (too late; she dies) she develops a desperate craving for juniper berries. The story is mysterious and indecipherable unless one understands the implications of that tree and those berries, inferences the Grimms' sources would have immediately understood.

Juniper's role as a component in intoxicating beverages remains today. It was once used to flavor whiskey. *Genevrette* is a French beer-like drink brewed from equal parts barley and juniper berries. The Dutch alcoholic beverage known as jenever eventually evolved into the English potion, gin.

See also **CALENDAR:** Samhain.

Mandrake ☠

(*Mandragora officinarum*, also classified as *Atropa mandragora*)

Mandrake's claim to fame lies in the magical resemblance of its roots to the human figure. Individual specimens are identifiably female or male (and a few very special ones may be both). There is no plant more identified with magic and witchcraft.

Mandrake's main magical uses have to do with love, sex, fertility, and wish fulfillment. Because it has narcotic properties, mandrake also has a long history as an early anesthetic.

In Arabic, mandrake is known as Father of Life (referring to its fertility-inducing powers) and djinn's Egg or Devil's Apple (these aren't demonic references but are instead intended to refer to mandrake's power as an aphrodisiac to provide forbidden pleasures. Islam has no demonology comparable to that of witch-hunt era Europe.) In Hebrew, the word for mandrake is translated as "love-apples," referring to its aphrodisiac properties.

The mandrake plant is indigenous to Mediterranean regions, especially Crete, Sicily, and the Levantine coast, as well as Iraq, North Africa, and Spain. It grows wild and is not uncommon in these areas. Nineteenth-century missionaries traveling to the Middle East wrote that women used this plant in the same manner and for the same purposes as described by the Bible. Mandrake's natural range extends as far north as Mount Vicentia on the southern edge of the Venetian Alps.

Although it grows rampant in warm, dry climates, it may be cultivated with care in areas not naturally conducive to its growth. The master herbalist John Gerard (1545–1612), for instance, cultivated it in his greenhouse.

Magical references almost inevitably discuss just the roots; the whole plant is lovely and useful, although potentially poisonous if taken internally. Mandrake has apple-like fruit (all those apple names aren't mere affectation) and lovely flowers possessing a strong aroma.

Mandrake is a member of the Nightshade family, many of whose members contain deadly poisons. Mandrake, too, is poisonous—the berries are particularly toxic. However, for magical purposes, mandrake is virtually always used as an amulet. It is carried, placed under the mattress, or shaped into a doll. It is safe to handle mandrake root (unlike wolfsbane, for instance, which is so toxic, even touching the plant may cause irritation) but not to take any part of the plant internally or to otherwise apply it to the body.

Many tales and legends describe mandrake's magic powers but the most famous occurs in the Old Testament. This is significant because although biblical injunctions are frequently used as the rationale for persecuting witches, in this case, the Bible recounts a magical success story. The biblical patriarch Jacob is married to two sisters. He loves the younger one, Rachel, passionately but she's infertile and desperately wants to conceive. He doesn't love the older sister, Leah (who desperately loves him) although that hasn't stopped him from fathering her many children. One day, Leah's oldest son, Reuben, old enough to understand his mother's situation, finds a mandrake root and brings it to her so that she can use it to magically gain Jacob's love. Word gets around and Rachel shows up, demanding the mandrake so that she can use it to magically conceive. The two negotiate and, ultimately, Rachel gets the mandrake, conceiving soon afterwards.

The Bible carried mandrake's reputation around the Eastern Hemisphere; the name "mandrake" developed an aura of allure and power but there was one problem: *true* mandrake doesn't grow wild in cold climates. People in these colder areas wanted mandrake too but it wasn't available. What were they to do? They began referring to local plants with similar uses and human-shaped roots as "mandrake" too. Thus the name "mandrake" may refer to a variety of different and unrelated plants. True mandrake belongs to the *Mandragora* species.

If you purchase mandrake in Greece or the Middle East or North Africa, it's quite possible that you're receiving the real thing. If you're anywhere else, you're most likely receiving some substitute. These substitutes can be very powerful—some even prefer them; however be aware that the prices charged should reflect what you're actually getting. There is no need to spend huge sums on Devil's Apple, black bryony, May Apple, white bryony or ginseng.

These all have human-shaped roots similar to mandrake. Many possess a similar magical nature and most are, like mandrake, intended for use as amulets not for internal use, because they are poisonous if consumed.

True mandrake has been an important medicinal plant for just as long as it's been an important magical one. When discussing any sort of medicinal use, that information applies **only** to true mandrake, the *Mandragora* species.

Along with opium poppies, mandrake was among the very first anesthetics in existence. Mandrake was first administered either as a potion made by boiling the root in wine, or as an inhalant made by soaking cloth in mandrake infusions. Greek physicians offered their dental patients mandrake root to chew as a local anesthetic. Hippocrates, the author of the Hippocratic oath and considered the founder of modern medicine, wrote of mandrake in approximately 400 BCE, *"a small dose in wine, less than would occasion delirium, will relieve the deepest depression and anxiety."*

Mandrake can induce deep sleep, however the incorrect dosage can cause the big sleep from which one never awakens. Fatal doses are very possible, demonstrating that, then as now, anesthesia can be among the most dangerous parts of the surgical process. The medicinal was usually prepared from the root, as is the magical amulet.

During antiquity mandrake root was used as an anesthetic, antiseptic, narcotic, and tonic. Until the early modern era, mandrake wine was used to treat insomnia.

Diluted mandrake root juice was used as an anesthetic during surgery in first-century Greece. Mandrake was used as an anesthetic by the Romans and by the renowned Arabic physicians. Its most dramatic use, however, was in Roman-occupied Judea. Crucifixion was not a unique punishment; the Romans crucified masses of people. Jewish women brewed draughts from mandrakes and soaked sponges in the liquid to offer men nailed to the crosses, causing an anesthetic effect. Depending upon the dose, this could be fatal—a mercy killing.

Sometimes, however, the person only had the appearance of death, often fairly long-term. The body would be returned to their family. Eventually they would recover. When the Romans discovered what was going on (perhaps witnessing too many dead men walking) policies were changed: it was decreed that before any man was released from the cross, his legs would be broken and/or he was to be brutally pierced with a spear.

Magically, mandrake is *always* used as an amulet and never taken internally.

❋ *For purposes of enhancing fertility, mandrake is carried as a charm or placed under the bed.*

❋ *Men traditionally carried mandrake in mojo bags to serve as love charms.*

❋ *Breton and Norman fishermen once wore jewelry made from mandrake root pieces as protective talismans.*

Even when mandrake was an important medicinal (and perhaps *because* mandrake was such an important medicinal) it has always been associated with witchcraft and magic. The ancient Greeks associated mandrakes with Circe and called it *Circaea*, although that is now the modern botanical classification for Enchanter's Nightshade, not mandrake (see page 161). Other European folk names include Witch's Herb (*Hexenkraut*), Satan's Apple (this time meant demonically), and Monster Root. Its medicinal background is recalled in the nickname Doctor Root.

In France, it was such common practice to carry a mandrake that, in 1429, the Franciscan Friar Richard denounced the practice and destroyed great numbers of them. Her inquisitors accused Joan of Arc of carrying one for wealth, although she claimed to be unfamiliar

with them. The French fairy Magloire presides over the use of the mandrake root. Some believe that the concept of the Hand of Glory (in French *main de gloire*) derives from mandrake's classical name, Mandragora.

Nowhere was the magical use of mandrake root more popular or inventive than in Germany. Historically, virtually nowhere on Earth has there been harsher treatment of witches than in Germany or more concentrated effort to exterminate them; however, ironically or not, there are equally few other places on Earth where magical and botanical knowledge has ever been more persistent. In sixteenth-century German lands, a synonym for witches was *Alraundelberin* or "mandrake bearer." "*Alraune*" already indicated a witch; it now came to mean mandrake, as well (well, really black bryony) so that mandrake and witch became synonyms.

Although technically *alraune* just means "mandrake" more is implied. The alraune describes a magical system, whereby the mandrake root (the alraune) is cared for, fed, and bathed by a person; in return the alraune provides that person with magical wish fulfillment, protection, and good fortune. This is very similar to various African rituals and to modern African-derived root-working.

The alraune became a staple of medieval German magical practice. Every Friday the root was bathed in wine, wrapped in white silk and laid in a box that was as beautiful or magically empowered as possible. One would whisper one's desires to the mandrake and hopefully watch them come into fruition.

A slightly different variation existed too: the mandrake root might be surgically enhanced to further its resemblance to a human being (a bit of plastic surgery, in effect), dressed in little clothes, and placed on a throne to serve as oracle or household guardian. Because this practice was *extremely* illegal (this was at the height of the witch-trials), the seated doll might be kept upright in a small hidden closed cabinet or box (rather than laid flat as in the other method). A popular modern collector's doll from Germany is known as the *Hexen* or Walpurgis doll; these tend to be fairly demonic creations, packaged in coffins as if they were vampires. They offend those who resent the false demonization of witches. However, they may also be understood as a corruption and continuation of this alraune tradition, the little "witch" in a box.

The concept of a wish-fulfilling mandrake doll is very ancient; allegedly Thessalian witches were able to animate mandrake mannequins and send them out to do various magical jobs. (A similar scenario exists in Abraham Merritt's pulp novel, *Burn Witch Burn.*)

Although some loved and venerated alraunes, others perceived them as diabolical conduits to Satan. Many believed that it was impossible to get rid of an alraune. One's only option was to sell it. Otherwise, no matter what you did—burn it, toss it in the sea, stamp it to bits—it would be right back, hale and hearty and intact upon your shelf.

In rural areas, people may have obtained their own alraunes, but in urban areas professionals sold them on the magical black market. The risk was tremendously great, to both purchaser and vendor, however the price the alraune demanded was very high: fortunes were made. Real practitioners may have been wary of exposing themselves; however black marketeers, often petty swindlers, knew a hot property when they saw one. You must recall that what was being sold as "genuine mandrake" was already really black bryony, a local root. By the sixteenth century it had become common practice to doctor these roots.

Mandrake roots have always been embellished to enhance their human resemblance. However what was based on tradition soon became fraud. The most authentically human-looking mandrake roots are old ones that have years' growing but who wants to wait that long to make a profit, especially when witch-hunters are expected in town? A potential buyer would explain why they wanted a mandrake (for fertility usually or for sexual magnetism); the vendor would tell them that he had a mandrake growing in a pot and to come over tomorrow. The vendor would hurry home, doctor a bryony root to look as if it would fulfill the purchaser's desires and *then* stick the root into a pot of dirt, so that when the buyer arrived it would look as if it emerged from the Earth in exactly that form. Specimens may be found today in museums in Germany as well as in London and Vienna. They are cut to resemble women, men, couples, even a woman cradling a child.

All kinds of superstitions were associated with mandrake, particularly regarding the manner in which it must be gathered. Although it can be carefully dug out the same as any other root, it became traditional to pull the entire mandrake plant from the ground in one fell swoop.

Because it's the intact root that desired, it must be pulled from Earth without damaging it. Various legends and traditions sprang up including one that suggests that pulling mandrakes is the equivalent of a game of tug-of-war. If you fail to dislodge the mandrake, it might pull you in return, causing you to disappear into the depths of the Earth.

According to another legend, mandrake screams when it is pulled; hearing the scream is fatal. Another version suggests that the first one to pull up the root dies. All kinds of complex machinations for harvesting mandrake developed: one had to stuff up one's ears with wax, tie a dog to the plant and then somehow induce him to jump away with such force that the entire root is pulled out of Earth in one piece. This practice allegedly kills the dog. Once this sacrifice has been made, the plant is believed safe to handle and use and exists as an object of wish fulfillment. (These are all superstitions, although they are based on tradition: see below. Mandrakes are grown in nurseries today; no dogs are killed during the harvest nor are there any other mandrake-induced fatalities involved in the harvest. Let's just say that if any dog ever died during mandrake harvests—and these legends may have no basis whatsoever in fact—the mandrake's scream isn't what killed it.)

A later legend that developed in places where mandrake was considered diabolical suggests that it grew only at crossroads, the home of the devil, or underneath gallows—usually erected at crossroads—where the mandrake was nourished by emanations from the corpse. (One cheerful tradition suggests that mandrake isn't any ordinary plant root but is, in fact, a hanged man's congealed urine or semen.) Along those lines, it was believed that mandrake's form reflected that of the dead man, especially if he died a virgin or lived as a congenital thief. (These legends inspired the German novel *Alrauna* by H. H. Ewers, which in turn inspired no less than five film adaptations. See **CREATIVE ARTS:** Literature.)

These superstitions are rooted in metaphysical beliefs that had become distorted and demonized. Frequently they are cover-ups for Pagan traditions, simultaneously beloved (or at least the potential results are desired) and feared. The machinations with the dog, for instance, may be cover-up for a canine sacrifice that was once intrinsic to the harvest.

The tradition that the mandrake kills the one who initially pulls it from the ground may be based on a Jewish legend (recounted among Louis Ginzburg's multi-volume *Legends of the Jews*) that Reuben found the mandrake lying near a dead donkey. (The donkey's link to the mandrake has sexual connotations that aren't immediately grasped today.) Interestingly, according to Transylvanian Romany tradition, the root of an orchid used similarly to mandrake is gathered in the same manner by attaching a dog to it. The dog doesn't die but is encouraged to lunge away by luring it with donkey's meat.

In Poland, mandrake was gathered by laying bread and money on the ground. The root was carefully pulled up; the offerings were laid in the resulting hole as payment and the hole carefully covered with Earth. The root was bathed in milk, carefully dried, and then wrapped in silk and carried home in a box. In Abruzzi, Italy, mandrake, like other magical plants, was believed best harvested on Midsummer's Eve.

Sometimes a living plant was desired, not just the root. Having a living mandrake plant on one's property allegedly brings great fortune, health, and happiness. However, one must take care in transplanting it—any injury to the plant allegedly results in insanity for the guilty party.

See **ANIMALS:** Donkeys; **DICTIONARY:** Alraune; Mojo.

Mistletoe ☠

(Viscum album)

Other names: Witch's Branch; Witch's Broom

Mistletoe is native to a region stretching from Northern Europe to Northwest Africa and east all the way to Japan. Wherever it is found, mistletoe is considered holy, sacred, powerful, and magical.

Mistletoe is unique: it was understood as a plant that wasn't a plant—a sort of magical plant. Mistletoe doesn't grow in Earth; it's a parasite that attaches itself to trees and eventually may kill them. (Identification of mistletoe with witches wasn't always meant positively. Other inferences were also intended.)

Mistletoe's poisonous berries look like tiny golden full moons. In German, these berries are known as *"witch's berries."*

Mistletoe may be the golden bough that inspired Sir James Frazer's influential book of that name. Mistletoe was sacred to the Greeks and Romans, who believed that it originated when lightning struck trees. For them, mistletoe represented life energy and generative, magic power. If Frazer is correct, mistletoe was sacred to Diana, Queen of Witches.

The Celts nicknamed mistletoe *"thunderbroom,"* uniting male and female sexual symbolism. No other botanical is as profoundly associated with Druid magic. The Druids believed that it was inauspicious for mistletoe to ever touch the ground and so created an elaborate method of harvest, which involved plucking it from the tree, using a golden sickle, with nets to catch it before it landed.

In Germanic tradition mistletoe is under the dominion of Freya, and brings blessings of love and fertility. Of course, Freya has two sides: she's a love goddess but also a death goddess.

Mistletoe's most famous appearance in mythology occurs when it is the object responsible for the death of Lord Balder. Balder has disturbing dreams; his imminent death is indicated. To forestall this tragedy, his mother, Frigg, travels about the Earth seeking assurances from every living being that they will never harm her son. Because mistletoe is so small and puny, she doesn't think it's necessary to ask. The moral of the story is an important one in herbalism: the most innocuous plants sometimes are the most lethal.

Mistletoe is used in various medicinal preparations that can only be safely prepared or administered by a master herbalist. Because of its Pagan associations, and because of this needed skill, mistletoe became associated solely with witchcraft medicine and the magical arts, except for once a year on Christmas Eve, when this formerly sacred plant is hung from the ceiling to stimulate kissing, love, and romance.

See **DIVINE WITCH:** Freya.

Mugwort

(Artemisia vulgaris)

Other names: Motherwort; The Red Goat

Caution! Mugwort is not safe for pregnant women or for those actively attempting to conceive. Mugwort Essential Oil, also known as Armoise, its French name, is unsafe for everyone and is potentially fatal. Dried or fresh mugwort herb (the whole thing, not some concentration) is safe for occasional use by most adults.

Mugwort's Latin name refers to it as common or vulgar Artemisia, as if any member of that plant family could possibly be common or vulgar. They are named in honor of the goddess Artemis. The most famous explanation is that she gave the plant as a gift to the physician centaur Chiron, who tutored Achilles and many other renowned Greek heroes. However another version suggests that the plant is named after Artemis because most of its medicinal uses involve female reproduction over which she has dominion.

✳ *Mugwort has been used to stimulate menstruation, whether to induce fertility or to terminate pregnancy.*

✳ *Mugwort has historically been used to harmonize menstrual cycles with lunar cycles. If one understands that Artemis shares the same essence as the moon, then one is harmonizing oneself with the goddess as well.*

Once upon a time, mugwort was considered among the most important of women's herbs. It was incorporated into infusions and baths and burned as incense.

✳ *The ancient Anglo-Saxons considered mugwort first among their nine sacred plants, calling it the Mother Herb.*

✳ *In Poland, mugwort, known as* bylica *and called the Mother of All Herbs, is the most powerfully magic plant of all.*

✳ *In Russian, mugwort is called* chernobyl, *which obviously has terrible modern connotations because of the disaster at the nuclear power plant in the town bearing that name. The word has long held magical significance in Russian witchcraft traditions and also makes reference to crow's beaks and has associations with the spirit, the Queen of Snakes. It is sometimes a forbidden word, not to be uttered during certain forms of spell-craft because if uttered, the spell is immediately nullified.*

✳ *In the southern Tyrol, mugwort is called "broom herb"; because of its association with witches' brooms.*

The plant allegedly protects against witchcraft, ghosts, and thieves. It is a traveler's herb, providing safety and protection. Another nickname for mugwort is Saint John's Girdle, commemorating John the Baptist, who allegedly roamed the wilderness eating wild honey and wearing a mugwort belt.

Mugwort is among the original bitter herbs; it doesn't taste good and so has very few culinary uses. Mugwort's uses tend to be restricted to women's reproductive issues and to magic. By the Middle Ages, possession of Artemis' sacred gift was considered sufficient evidence for conviction of witchcraft. Only midwives or witches (and for many, those terms were synonymous) could possibly use mugwort, a botanical that must be handled with care.

It may be used to stimulate fertility, however if used during pregnancy, it may have disastrous effects. Its potential gifts are dependent upon administration by skilled herb-doctors who understand both the nuances of the botanical and the nuances of the female body.

It doesn't grow easily from seed but grows wildly rampant in wastelands and ruins. Those who desired mugwort were often forced to gather it in the cemeteries and ruins it favors, increasing its sinister associations. (When it's happy in its environment, mugwort grows so well that in part of the North American Midwest, where it has been naturalized, it's treated as a pest, fit for nothing but eradication.)

Although dried mugwort may be easily and inexpensively purchased from herbal suppliers, living mugwort plants can be difficult to obtain today. Mugwort, the ultimate witch plant, is most frequently found today in packaged "dream teas" and "dream pillows." It is almost always the activating constituent in dream-stimulation products although, because mugwort tastes so bitter, it may be buffered by many other ingredients. As might be gathered, mugwort's other profound gift is stimulation of dreams and clairvoyance. It usually has a fairly dramatic effect: mugwort opens the portals to other realms and shoves you through. It is worthwhile remembering that Artemis the

Huntress was not a gentle goddess by anyone's standards.

Mugwort sometimes reaches heights of five feet, blooming and achieving its peak power at Midsummer's Eve. Mugwort is among the plants most associated with Midsummer's. Mugwort ashes from the Midsummer's bonfires bring good luck all year round.

See **CALENDAR:** Midsummer's Eve; **DIVINE WITCH:** Artemis.

Mullein

(Verbascum thapsus)

Mullein is a tall, straight plant with downy leaves. When dried, the down on its leaves and stem are excellent tinder. In the days before wax was inexpensive, dried mullein stalks made excellent torches. They were used as such in the rites of the dark moon goddess, Hecate, to whom they are sacred. Hecate, Queen of Witches, is completely nocturnal. She only accepts petitions after dark and she's fairly picky about forms of illumination. Mullein stalks are her favorite choice. This history is reflected in mullein's many nicknames: The Hag's Taper, or the Witch's Taper, or Corpse Candle.

Another nickname is graveyard dust. Hecate rules the frontier between death and life, often escorting people back and forth over the border. Powdered mullein, her sacred herb, is considered an acceptable substitute for true cemetery dirt called for in magic spells.

Mullein's associations with death aren't limited to Hecate or Eurasia. Mullein is also sacred to Oya, the spirit of Africa's Niger River, who has become increasingly prominent in African-Diaspora faiths where she is Queen of the Cemetery Gates. Oya is the only one among the Yoruba spirits, the orisha, who has no fear of the realm of the dead. Like Hecate, Oya is a powerful witch and herbalist who protects women and children.

Mullein is used in various herbal preparations, particularly for ear infections. It was believed to ward off wild animals. (Animals in general will not consume mullein because the downy leaves irritate their throats.) However, because of its associations with dark goddesses and Pagan magic, mullein retained a somewhat sinister reputation and was identified as a witch-craft plant.

See **DICTIONARY:** Orisha; **DIVINE WITCH:** Hecate; **HORNED ONE:** Oya.

Nettles

(Urtica dioica)

The nettles are a family of plants widely distributed over Earth and were once considered very beneficial and widely used. Cloth was spun from nettles. The plant supplied the thread used by Germans and Scandinavians prior to the introduction of flax.

The tops of the leaves may be cooked and are very nutritious. (Stinging nettles really do sting and must be picked with gloves; however once dried or cooked, the sting is gone.) Many beneficial medicinal uses exist. By the Middle Ages, however, in the same places where it had once been prevalent and much used, stinging nettles were so associated with witchcraft that possession was grounds for accusations of being a witch. How did this once beneficial plant develop such an evil reputation?

Although nettles are used to dissolve gall-bladder stones, heal wounds, and to relieve the stiffness of arthritis, its primary medicinal associations are largely female-oriented. Stinging nettles are a woman's friend. Traditional medicinal uses included soothing and hastening labor, so the nettle became perceived as a demonic plant because Eve had been doomed to suffer in childbirth. Attempts to relieve labor pains were considered Pagan, sinful, and defiant.

Stinging nettles have other uses: they are classified as a galactogogue, meaning that they stimulate and increase a woman's milk supply. That's a fairly innocuous use. However, honey mixed with the juice of Roman nettles (*Urtica pilulifera*) and applied to a strip of linen inserted vaginally prior to intercourse was an early attempt at contraception in ancient Egypt, as well as the bordellos of ancient Rome. The honey worked as a barrier. Nettle juice may have some spermicidal properties.

Nettles represented wilderness, wild women, and the general quality of being wild. Because they sting and because the juice of nettles provides the antidote for that sting, nettles were identified as the botanical equivalent of snakes, whose venom both heals and harms. Snakes were understood as the animal companion of Satan. Nettles were perceived as diabolical plants. Consuming them allegedly stimulated lust, which perhaps doesn't seem so bad today, but was, once upon a time, among those sins for which witches, especially alluring, enchanting ones, were blamed. Nettles came to represent witches; they share the witches' essence and back then that wasn't meant as a compliment.

The botanical name for what is known in English as blind nettles—*Lamium album*—derives from Lamia, often understood as a synonym for "witch." Lamia, in mythology, was a tragic queen reduced to stealing, killing, and maybe consuming other women's babies.

Stinging nettles are traditionally used in witchcraft to remove curses and break spells. They are protective, guardian plants. Their stinging, prickly nature epitomizes their watch-dog nature. What type of dog is most frequently chosen to serve as a guard? A cute, little, fluffy one or a dog that at least looks like it could inflict some damage? The trade in Rottweillers, Dobermans, and pit bull terriers says it all. Stinging nettles are their botanical equivalent. With stinging nettles on your side, who would trespass against you? Or so many thought.

The power of stinging nettles was cruelly turned against convicted witches. Witches were frequently dressed in nettle shirts when they were lead to the funeral pyres. This was for many reasons:

* *to break their magic and nullify any potential last spells or curses that the witch might cast, because the judges were afraid of their victims*

* *to visually identify them as witches, lest bystanders forget why they were being burned*

* *to signify the Satanic pact by the use of this diabolical plant*

* *to discourage others from wanting any contact with the stinging nettle—only witches would continue to use them*

* *merely to torture them even more with this botanical equivalent of a hair shirt.*

It didn't help that stinging nettles, like mugwort, grows most prolifically among stone ruins and in the cemetery. However, the fairy tale *The Wild Swans* suggests some awareness of injustice toward the nettles, magical practice, and practitioners of witchcraft. (See **FAIRY-TALE WITCHES:** Hans Christian Andersen.)

Opium Poppy

(Papaver somniferum)

> Caution! Potentially poisonous and, depending where you're located, almost definitely illegal.

There are many species of poppies, however only two, the opium poppy and the wild setaceous poppy, which may be the root ancestor species of all poppies, contain morphine in any significant amount. Opium poppies were perceived as the most powerful and magical of the species for obvious reasons. However, opium poppies tend to be illegal, even if you're only planning to add these pretty flowers to your garden, even if you have no intention of producing opium but only wish to use these plants magically or ritually. It is highly unlikely that most of us will ever have access to opium poppies. (Attempting to order them from a seed catalog will likely get you the wrong kind of attention. You try explaining to drug officials that you're only interested in ritual use.)

As with mandrake root, when discussing historical medicinal use, only true opium poppy (*Papaver somniferum*) is indicated; however, when discussing ritual or magical use, any of the many other poppy species may substitute. Vivid red corn poppies are the most popular substitute. They were also dedicated to Demeter (as are opium poppies) and serve similar magical function. Another substitute might be the red poppies classified as *Papaver strigosum* or "witch poppy."

Opium poppies are most notorious as the source of opium. This overshadows every other use the plant has ever had—the leaves were once eaten as potherbs, and poppy seeds are nutritious and a source of cooking oil.

Poppies contain a tremendous amount of seeds; they are literally countless. Because of this, poppies are among the flowering plants most associated with human fertility. They are the floral equivalent of a pomegranate. As such, they were associated with the generative powers of the Earth and sacred to powerful goddesses.

Opium has been used as an aphrodisiac and intoxicant since the Stone Age, however ancient forms of usage were different than those of modern times. It was once less concentrated, the ancients not having access to derivatives or synthetics. The ancients didn't have the technical capacity to isolate chemical constituents as is done today. There was little concept of "recreational drugs." (There still isn't in traditional societies today.) Instead opium poppies were understood as unique, sacred, both beneficial and dangerous and as packed with magic power as with seeds.

Opium has extremely ancient associations with human beings. Although its origins remain shrouded in mystery, opium poppies have been cultivated since that old time immemorial; no wild population exists. Some poppies may escape from a field and wander; abandoned poppy fields will thrive; but basically opium poppies live where people plant them.

Poppies were cultivated by European Neolithic cave dwellers. They are believed to have eventually traveled from Northern Europe to the Mediterranean during the later Neolithic period, following the amber trade route. By the Bronze Age, opium poppies were well distributed throughout the Eastern Hemisphere and used medicinally, as a food source, and as an intoxicant. The most ancient form of use, for instance, was an infusion, either opium poppy-infused water or wine. Helen of Troy's elixir of forgetfulness, *nepenthe*, is believed to have contained opium as well as those other witches' plants, mandrake and henbane.

Medicinal use of opium disappeared in Europe in the wake of the Black Death, hence its later associations with Asia where it was still used medicinally, ritually, and magically. (It was eventually reintroduced by the physician/alchemist Paracelsus in the form of laudanum.) Although gone, opium poppies were never quite forgotten: perhaps because they retained their mystique, were mysterious and powerful, and because herbal skill and knowledge was required for safe, successful administration, opium poppies became associated with witchcraft. Opium poppies are believed to have been among the ingredients in witches' flying ointments.

Because of their notoriety, it is easy to overlook the beauty of opium poppies: although they also come in other colors including white and purple, most are a vivid blood red, the color anciently identified with luck, life, and good fortune. That red color also emphasizes opium's association with fertility power and the deities who preside over it.

✻ *The Greek Corn Mother Demeter drank opium to relieve her state of grief over the loss of her daughter Persephone. She wears a necklace formed from opium pods. Although very little is known about the religious rituals known as the Eleusinian Mysteries that were devoted to Demeter and Persephone, opium poppies seem to have played a part.*

✻ *Hathor's necklace is formed from opium pods and mandrake. Hathor is the ancient Egyptian goddess of joy and intoxication. In addition to opium poppies, Hathor presided over beer, wine, and musical intoxication, too.*

✻ *Isis sometimes holds poppies, too. Thebes, in ancient Egypt, was renowned for its poppy fields.*

✻ *Poppies are sacred to the Russian forest witch, Baba Yaga. The seeds are incorporated into her initiation rituals.*

✻ *Nyx the Greek goddess of night, carries a bouquet of poppies, while her son Thanatos, "Death," wears his poppies in a garland.*

✻ *Hermes was also associated with poppies. Originally a shamanic fertility deity, associated with horned animals like sheep and goats, Hermes retains his function as messenger between realms. His home is in Mekone, which translates as "poppy town." His magic staff can cause sleep if he wills it so. That staff with its two entwined serpents remains emblematic of the medical profession. Snakes and poppies were once representative of healing and the physician's art.*

✻ *Opium poppies are associated with the sacred physician, Asklepios, Apollo's son. Visitors seeking treatment at the Temple of Asklepios were given poppy extract to induce curative dreams. Asklepios is sometimes depicted holding the readily identifiable opium capsules in one hand and his serpent entwined staff in the other. (Asklepios' staff, unlike Hermes' caduceus, only has one snake.)*

Mythic associations are based on actual observation. Poppy seeds will remain viable within Earth for a *very* long time. Should the soil then be disturbed or churned up, long dormant seeds will suddenly germinate en masse and fields of brilliant red flowers will spectacularly bloom. The ancients identified this phenomenon with the resurrection of the dead and renewal of life, and it was vividly demonstrated during World War I when fields of battle in Flanders and Northern France blossomed with countless scarlet poppies.

Somniferum, the Latin name given to distinguish opium poppies from other poppies, derives from Somnus, the Roman Lord of Sleep, hence such related words as somnambulist and somnolent.

Today opium poppies are dreaded and banned as the source of illegal and dangerous narcotics. "*Narcotic*" in modern terminology implies "*dangerous*," "*addictive*," and frequently an "*illicit*" or "*illegal*" drug. However, in traditional medicinal usage, in the word's most technical sense, "*narcotic*" indicates a substance that induces sleep. Narcotics, in the medical sense of the word, are powerful sedatives and soporifics; they relieve pain and put you to sleep, enabling healing to occur. For millennia, opium was the only reliable anesthetic in existence.

Alkaloids were first discovered by studying opium poppies—as were the entire concept of alkaloids. In 1803, a German pharmacist isolated the very first alkaloid. Discovering that it was highly narcotic and the primary active constituent of opium, he named it morphine in honor of Morpheus, the Greek Lord of Dreams. Opium has since been discovered to contain 40 other alkaloids.

Like *Amanita muscaria* (see page 152), another ancient intoxicant, the visual imagery of poppies is often divorced from the botanical's physical effect. In other words, poppies serve as ornamentation for all kinds of illustrations dedicated to children or mainstream holidays. Poppies are so deeply imbedded within human culture that the image survives even where the actual plant and the rituals within which it featured does not.

❋ *Crimson poppies decorated a great quantity of European postal cards from the classic age of postcards, especially Christmas and New Year cards, the period corresponding to the Winter Solstice when Earth is sound asleep.*

❋ *Poppies appear in the film version of* The Wizard of Oz *as the Wicked Witch's magical tool.*

Roots

An ancient synonym for witch, cunning person or wise person is root-worker, root doctor, or the gender specific root-woman or root-man. A root doctor may work with other parts of plants as well as many other genres of magic, however roots are special.

Although all parts of a plant possess their own enchantment, in general, roots are considered a plant's most profound source of magic power. Roots are buried within Earth and so it's believed that they absorb Earth's secrets and hidden wisdom.

World famous wonder-working roots include:

❋ *Mandrake* (Mandragora officinarum)

❋ *High John the Conqueror* (Ipomoea jalapa), *a species of Morning Glory*

❋ *Ginseng* (Panax quinquefoliusm *or* Panax schinseng)

❋ *Angelica* (Angelica spp. *especially* archangelica), *knowledge of this root was the gift of an archangel*

Root-workers dig into Earth to gather supplies. Once upon a time, digging into the Earth Mother without permission was tantamount to rape. But how do you ask for permission, how do you know whether you've received it and what is the proper ritual for harvest? The root-worker knows. These eventually became professional secrets, transmitted orally.

It is not necessary to kill the plant in order to gather the root, although that is what is most frequently done today. A skilled gardener can carefully dig up a plant, remove part of the root and then replace the plant, also leaving payment for whatever was taken and for disturbing its peace. This takes care and time and precision.

Roots are used for magical, spiritual, and medicinal purposes. Roots serve as lucky charms. High John the Conqueror in your pocket allegedly serves as a draw for good fortune and bestows sexual magnetism on its bearers. Other roots promise fertility or love or protection or success.

Once upon a time, knowledge of roots, the type a root-worker possessed, also implied a certain knowledge of the female reproductive system. The Bible's first command to people is to be fruitful and multiply. Ancient Jewish sacred texts discuss the contexts where it is permissible to break that commandment. Vague references are made to a *"cup of roots"* (a potion brewed from roots) that can permissibly terminate pregnancy in certain circumstances. Although the actual formula isn't specified, it wouldn't have to be: back then, the root-workers would know. This information was transmitted orally over generations; it may never have occurred to people that this basic, standard information could ever be entirely lost. Those formulas were lost, but the references to cups of roots survived. In medieval Europe, this lead to "roots" having an ominous reputation.

Many roots are treated as living beings—unlike other parts of the plant, which are almost uniformly treated as materials for use. Roots must be cared for so that in a reciprocal relationship they will care for you, too. Roots are "fed" on schedule, daily or weekly or otherwise, with sips of alcoholic beverages, sprinklings of powder, or dabs of enchanted oils. Hopes, dreams, and fears are whispered to them. They may be wrapped in silk or carried in charm bags, kept under one's pillow or slipped into one's

bosom. Mandrake roots or those roots resembling them are carved to look like little people, making it even easier to talk to them and envision them as alive.

In the twenty-first century, this type of witchcraft is most commonly associated with African-derived magical systems, particularly hoodoo or conjure, because it was marketed and so was relatively public. However root-working is international and exists with variations virtually everywhere on Earth, although it may now be secret and almost forgotten.

Rowan

(Sorbus aucuparia or Fraxinus aucuparia)

The rowan is a small tree closely identified with magic and spirituality in Northern lands. Its English name is related to the Sanskrit *"runall'"* meaning *"magician"* and the Norse *"runall'"* meaning *"a charm."* Rowan tree may also be understood to mean *"rune tree."* Rune staves were traditionally carved from its wood.

Rowan is also etymologically connected to *"alruna,"* the name given to ancient Germanic prophetesses and magical practitioners. Another nickname for rowan is *"witch tree."*

❋ *In the Scottish Highlands, use of rowan wood for any other reason but spiritual ritual was forbidden once upon a time.*

❋ *Celts in other regions made black dye for ritual robes from rowan's bark and berries.*

❋ *Rowan trees were planted around or near stone circles.*

* In Wales, rowan trees were planted to guard and protect the deceased.

* Cattle were driven through rowan hoops to generate fertility, break any malevolent spells, and offer protection.

Rowan trees were so deeply imbedded in the spiritual fabric of Northern lands that their use couldn't be prevented; instead it was redirected. Rowan's most frequent modern magical usage is to prevent witchcraft. Many will tell you that it's called "witch tree" because it prevents witchcraft. In fact, it's more of a case of "*it takes one to know one.*" Rowan is one of those unusual plants that are simultaneously identified with witchcraft and also allegedly protect against it. Rowan may be understood as possessing the power of a witch so powerful that she can negate all other spells cast.

Like other trees (but even more so), it is important not to harvest any part of it without first asking permission (and giving the tree a chance to refuse), and then offering libations and gifts in return.

* Rowan is identified with Brigid and her festival of Imbolc.

* Rowan is identified with the Norse deity Thor. As one of his sacred plants it was believed beneficial for ensuring virility.

To this day rowan is planted near homes for spiritual protection. The finest dowsing rods for locating metal are crafted from rowan. Rowan also contributes to intoxicating beverages: the berries were made into wine in the Scottish Highlands, the Welsh brew a rowan berry flavored ale and the Irish have used it to flavor mead.

See **CALENDAR:** Imbolc.

Rue

(Ruta graveolens)

Caution! Rue is not poisonous, however it is not safe for pregnant women or for those actively attempting to conceive.

Rue grows over much of Asia and Europe. Among its folk names are "Mother of the Herbs," indicating rue's importance, and "weasel"' or "weasel snout," indicating its affiliation with that magically powerful trickster animal.

Another folk name, "Herb of Grace," is intended to indicate that rue has been incorporated into Christian tradition; it is considered among the Virgin Mary's blessed herbs. Rue is used to ward off malicious magic. It's also called "witchbane" because it allegedly keeps witches away. However rue's historical association with witchcraft, magic spells, and Pagan ritual predate its associations with Christianity.

Rue is the primary plant in Italian magical traditions. It was sacred to Diana, Aradia, and Mars. In Italy and elsewhere, rue is famed for breaking the power of the Evil Eye. (Rue and weasels are among the few able to withstand the basilisk's deadly eye.) Something as simple as a sprig of rue pinned to one's clothing prevents the Evil Eye as well as many other malevolent spells. Among the other rue-associated Evil Eye preventatives is the Italian *cimaruta* amulet. Cimaruta literally means "sprig of rue." It is an amulet formed in the shape of a sprig of rue, and usually made from silver, tin or some silver-colored metal. It is enhanced by small charms that hang from the "*fingers of rue.*" Most are associated with fertility such as keys, fish, crescent moons, and horns.

Rue is believed to promote clairvoyance. It was also a primary tool of protective magic. Rue's ability to prevent malevolent magic and return negative spells may be understood to resemble that of powerful witches able to turn back malevolent spells cast by others.

Any witch powerful enough to break a malicious spell could cast one of her own, if she so chose. Rue was thus a component of ancient curses; the plant strengthening the necessary verbal component. The verb "*rue*" as in "*you'll rue the day you were ever born*" is believed to derive from these ancient practices.

However, rue's most recognized use from antiquity through the Middle Ages was as an herbal abortifacient. Armed with this knowledge, Ophelia's mad scene in Shakespeare's *Hamlet* takes on different resonance. Shakespeare's audience most likely would have understood the reference; this was fairly common knowledge, at the time, not obscure secret wisdom. Rue, thus, had a shadow reputation as a dangerous, frequently illicit botanical. Rue was also among the primary Midsummer's Eve herbs.

See **DICTIONARY:** Evil Eye.

Saint John's Wort

(*Hypericum perforatum*)

Saint John's wort is a plant with powerful solar affiliations. If mugwort is the plant of the moon, then Saint John's wort belongs to the sun. According to the ancient Greeks, while mugwort was Artemis' sacred plant, Saint John's wort epitomized the power of her brother, the solar spirit Apollo. Saint John's wort is understood metaphysically as mugwort's brother.

Saint John's wort derived its English folk name from the feast day of John the Baptist, which coincides with Midsummer's Eve and the Summer Solstice. It is when the sun is at its maximum height and it is when *Hypericum perforatum* is at its peak, too. (So is mugwort—a folk name for that plant is Saint John's Girdle.)

Saint John's wort is a *sunny* plant; it brings light and cheer and clarity where previously there was darkness and despair. It is probably the plant in this section most familiar to the average reader because Saint John's wort's magical uses have been found by modern science to be true: Saint John's wort is a modern remedy against depression. Although the concept of standardized medication is new, Saint John's wort's reputation for providing light in the darkness is ancient.

❋ In medieval France, it was traditionally used as a remedy against interference from the fairies, especially when that interference is experienced as depression and malaise.

❋ In Greek tradition, sprigs of Saint John's wort were hung over portraits of the dead so that whatever ills the deceased had suffered, whether physical, emotional or psychic, would be relieved. Their afflictions, pain, and suffering would be terminated so as not to infect the living with these emanations.

Mugwort and Saint John's wort may be understood as complementary powers or as oppositional forces, depending upon your perspective. If mugwort epitomized witchcraft, then witchhunters' believed that Saint John's wort would oppose and eradicate it. If mugwort is maximum yin—an emphatically female plant—then Saint John's wort is maximum yang, the epitome of masculinity. If mugwort is the evil sister, then Saint John's wort is the heroic brother.

The use of Saint John's wort by witch-hunters may be understood as cultural or magical appropriation. That Saint John's wort was also popular amongst witches is indicated by its German folk-name, Walpurgis Herb. However, in French Saint John's wort is called *"chasse-diable"* or "devil-chaser."

Witch-hunters fed Saint John's wort tea to accused witches in the belief that it negated the devil's compact. Negating the compact didn't mean that now everything was all right and the ex-witch could go home free. She was doomed anyway; "negating the compact" merely ensured that it would be safe to execute her. She would lack the power to execute vengeance on her judges and executioners.

San Pedro ☠

(Trichocereus pachanoi)

San Pedro is a ribbed night-blooming cactus also known as *achuma, huachuma,* and *giganton*. It grows from sea level up to altitudes of 3000 meters in South America from Ecuador to Bolivia.

San Pedro is Spanish for St Peter, the saint who holds the keys to the kingdom. San Pedro contains the potent alkaloid mescaline. It possesses a psychotropic, consciousness-altering effect and has historically been used to enter or view the spirit world. It is used as a diagnostic tool for *curanderos* (Latin American shamanic healers) to enable the diagnosis of illness and determination of the needed cure. Under the influence of San Pedro the shaman may battle ferocious animals, communicate with spirits or travel between realms.

Based on representations on pre-Columbian pottery, San Pedro has probably been used for at least one thousand years and possibly for three thousand years or even longer. The first written descriptions appeared shortly after the arrival of the Spanish within the context of the Inquisition. Seventeenth-century priests wished to eliminate Pagan practices of which San Pedro was seen as being integral. To persist in San Pedro's use was to defy the new order and the new religion and thus to be branded as a witch. Because San Pedro is not administered without strict rituals and expert supervision, it was understood as a witch's tool. Eliminating the plant eliminates the presiding practitioner's role, stripping her of function and respect.

Its use was never eradicated however. Social scientists, ethnobotanists, and chemists now find San Pedro fascinating and it has been intensely studied for over 50 years. It is still used by Peruvian *curanderos*. It is most frequently administered as part of a psychotropic infusion, meaning that there may be a lot of other stuff in the brew, too. These are sophisticated rituals that require both spiritual knowledge and botanical expertise; San Pedro is not a toy for laypeople to play with. Both benevolent and malevolently oriented practitioners create these potions, although obviously with different motivation.

Infusions are ingested as a component of spiritual and magical ritual. In other words, consumption of the beverage isn't believed sufficient. It's only part of a process, broken down into steps that must be completed properly. Plants must be gathered and prepared ritually. The brew is ritually prepared, too, with spiritual ritual incorporated at every stage.

This is not a mechanical process. Rituals are

required to enable the spirit of San Pedro to interact with human spirits. This is reminiscent of other indigenous American rituals featuring ayahuasca and peyote, leading one to wonder whether once upon a time there weren't similar rituals, similar complex brews for *Amanita muscaria* or henbane.

San Pedro is also consumed within supervised ritual. It is traditionally believed that if the consumer is not prepared by the ritual leader (*curandera*, shaman, witch) who opens and closes portals as needed, then the person under the influence of San Pedro is left vulnerable to magical attack, because these are not one-way portals …

Trees

Among the most ancient forms of religion is devotion to sacred trees. In modern usage "tree worship" sounds flat and simplistic; language doesn't do justice to the concept. Today trees are primarily understood as sources of lumber or as something to be moved out of the way so that the Earth below can be utilized for profit or practicality. In that context "tree worship" may sound primitive and silly.

In order to even begin to understand this concept, one must look at Earth with the wonder-struck eyes of magical perspective. First of all, lose the concept of "one way" directionals. If trees can be perceived as growing out of the ground, they may also be understood to penetrate the ground, as if they were moving downward, not up.

Now imagine: if Earth is a fertile female, what could those big, strong, hard trees possibly be? Genital imagery permeates ancient religion: trees often serve as huge, symbolic male generative organs.

Ritual processionals all over the world, from Japan throughout Asia and Europe, feature trees carried to represent generative energy. Sometimes they're carved explicitly and very realistically into gigantic phalluses; sometimes tree trunks are left *au naturel*, no enhancement necessary. On-lookers may reach to touch the passing tree to gain a little of that energy for themselves: for reproductive fertility, for material prosperity, for sexual prowess, and for the magical prevention of erectile dysfunction. That tree serves a lot of people's diverse magical needs. This phallic tree trunk may be pounded on doors to announce the arrival of the creative, generative spirit.

The most famous surviving phallic tree is the Maypole. A tall, hard, straight tree (often an elm) is ritually prepared, then set up within a dance ground—a magic circle. Young girls dance around it, wrapping it in silk ribbons. (Makes you wonder about that other lavishly ornamented tree, the Christmas Tree, doesn't it?)

Not all trees were masculine. Smaller, curvaceous trees like the elder or rowan are usually perceived as feminine. Fruit-bearing trees, like figs, date palms or apples, are considered female as well, although nut trees are resolutely male. The Latin classification for walnuts describes them as "Jupiter's balls" and we're not talking about baseballs, golf balls or any other round object used in sports.

Some of the oldest religious rites took place in sacred groves. These groves were sacred ground and places of oracular wisdom. Various deities maintained sacred groves of trees that shared their essence. Zeus presided over the oak grove at Dodona. The oracle was interpreted by listening to the wind whispering through the trees. Eventually "whispering" would become the domain of witches.

There is an ancient, ancient, primordial tradition of holy trees. One especially sacred motif was the snake in a tree. The snake curling its body around a tree trunk was sometimes understood as the unification of the sexes. Some have suggested that the biblical story of the snake and the tree in the Garden of Eden may be interpreted to mean that the era of that kind of religion was ending. The story is not told without regret; it is accompanied by expulsion from Paradise and foretells enmity between the sexes and between species.

Even after expulsion from Eden, however, tree worship doesn't end in the Bible. Lady Asherah of the Sea, pre-eminent mother goddess of the Western Semitic people, presided over sacred groves where women went to dance, sing and commune with nature. Trees were carved into the sacred poles named after Asherah and set up in high places as well as within the Jerusalem Temple.

For centuries, the Kings of Judea repeatedly installed, then removed and destroyed these pillars, only to have them installed once again. Although Asherah is frequently painted as a Canaanite goddess, one of the foreign deities the prophets accused the Children of Israel of whoring after, archeological evidence suggests otherwise. Lady Asherah was also an indigenous Hebrew goddess. Her image spent more time in the Jewish temple than outside; every time she was removed, someone eventually replaced her until the destruction of the First Temple. Obviously she was a controversial figure but there's no way for us to truly understand the controversy because the only surviving writings derive from those opposed to Asherah and devotion to trees. No explanation survives from those who loved her, or at least none has yet been unearthed.

Descriptions of tree-centered spirituality around the world could fill a thousand pages. Norse cosmology describes the World Tree upon which the entire world and all its realms are centered. In Uppsala, Sweden, the city dedicated to Freyr the Elven King, Lord of Generative Fertility, there was an ancient sacred grove where every single individual tree was held sacred. The Druids held their rituals within sacred oak groves. A grove is a sacred perimeter of trees, the space within is demarcated as holy, ritual, magical space. However, much of Earth was once covered with trees.

The forest is the realm of trees and their spirits. It is a place of wild, free, bountiful energy. Cutting down forests may be understood as acts of spiritual warfare against spirits in general (a denial of their existence), against those spirits who preside over forests in particular, and against their devotees. Destruction of rain forests worldwide (as well as other forests) is now attributed to needs of business or "civilization" rather than official religion but may still be understood in the same manner.

This isn't conjecture: when the missionaries Boniface and Willibrord came to convert the Frisians and Germans in the early eighth century they deliberately destroyed sacred trees. Cutting down groves was understood as a religious act; clearing wilderness makes way for "civilization" and easier administration of authority.

In Europe, forests, the realm of the trees, became refuges for outlaws, witches, Pagan hold-outs, and all those who found themselves persecuted by the New Order. When forests became perceived as solely dark and dangerous, witches maintained the forest's beneficial wisdom and secrets.

The sacredness inherent in a single tree is sometimes sufficient, however.

* *Witches were described as dancing around a tree at their sabbats.*

* *A walnut tree in Benevento, Italy is legendary as a witches' meeting place.*

❊ *According to a Northern legend, when missionaries chopped down a huge holy oak, a small pine arose from its roots. This became the first Christmas tree.*

Judaism was never able to suppress devotion to trees: Lady Asherah's sacred tree survives in the Kabalah's Tree of Life. Likewise the Christian Church was never able to suppress devotion to trees. Tree traditions survived in the Yule log, Maypoles, Easter egg trees and, most especially, in beautifully garlanded and bedecked Christmas Trees.

Witches became guardians and preservers of tree magic. Trees supply the materials for various magical tools, not least magic wands. The magic wand places the power of the tree directly into the practitioner's hands, enabling her to focus it as desired. Different types of wood are believed most beneficial for different purposes and styles of magic.

See **PLACES:** Forest; **TOOLS:** Brooms, Wands.

Vervain

(Verbena spp.)

Vervain is associated with the positive power of magic, witchcraft, and women's wisdom. Unlike other witchcraft plants whose temperaments are volatile and dangerous, vervain is friendly. No other plant is believed to have as much affection for people as does vervain. Vervain's magical uses include providing love, luck, health, and protection, changing bad luck into the best luck and transforming enemies into friends. All one has to do is touch vervain—no elaborate brews are required—to begin to receive its gifts. Vervain, however, is not a "goody-two-shoes" plant; it is a powerful and vigilant protector that may

be used to smash hexes and reverse malevolent charms.

Vervain is sacred to Isis; it is believed to have sprung from her tears. Isis was once dependent upon human mercy and learned to love people deeply. Vervain shares her essence and so reflects her feelings.

In Northern Europe, vervain was associated with smithcraft and ironworkers. (Many of the spirits presiding over metal-working are female.) Allegedly vervain was incorporated into the ancient formula for hardening steel. Because of these associations with iron, vervain is also believed to magically encourage the male member to remain as hard and firm as that metal. The Druids harvested vervain with an iron sickle.

Some believe that vervain's name derives from two Celtic words: *fer* "to take away" and *faen* "stone" or "weight." According to Druid tradition, vervain was gathered at night, during the Dark Moon. The Druids of Cornwall and Devon incorporated vervain into divinatory rituals, inhaling its fumes.

European colonists brought vervain seeds to the Western Hemisphere, where naturalized it now grows wild. At its peak, at Midsummer's Eve, vervain can reach heights of about five feet. It is used in love potions and aphrodisiacs.

Willow

(Salix spp.)

Why does that willow weep? Why, indeed? Willows are identified with some of the most powerful goddesses of all including Artemis, Circe, Hecate, Hera, and Persephone. Although they are extremely beautiful trees, many planted purely for ornamental value, willows tend to possess somewhat of a doleful, ominous reputation. They have long been considered witch's trees and witch's tools.

Weeping willows are a specific type of willow (*Salix babylonica*). They were indigenous to China but spread westward and are now widely distributed. There are many species of willow; as a whole they are also extremely well distributed—miniature willows, only inches tall, survive in the Arctic Circle, while other species may be found in deserts and tropical areas.

Willows are graceful trees with lithe boughs and an affinity for water. Like alder, willows are often found near rivers, streams, swamps, and marshes. The willow is believed to love and crave moisture (hence the weeping willow's affinity for tears) and so is under the dominion of the moon, the planetary body that rules water, women, and fertility.

Snakes are the creatures believed to most closely share the essence of the willow tree. The willow's branches and leaves are believed to resemble the motion of a snake. In ancient Greece, willow branches placed under the beds of infertile women were believed to transmit fertility-generating snake power. (No doubt a more peaceful night's sleep was to be had with willow branches beneath the bed rather than living, slithering snakes!)

Willows are also used to magically ward off snakes and prevent snakebite. Among willow's other magical uses are for wish fulfillment and healing and love spells.

Perhaps because willows were associated with such powerful lunar goddesses, the trees came to be associated with witches in ancient Greece. "Willow" has long been a popular magical or craft name among witches—as exemplified by "Dark Witch Willow," the character on the television series, *Buffy the Vampire Slayer*.

Willows are associated with fertility and birth, but also with death. In Celtic areas, willows were planted in graveyards because it was believed that they encouraged the dead to rest peacefully and to refrain from roaming.

❋ *Thin, flexible young willow branches are a traditional binding to hold handmade witches' brooms together.*

❋ *Magic wands crafted from willow are believed especially beneficial for divination.*

Wolf's Claw or Club Moss

(*Lycopodium clavatum*)

Common club moss has an amazing number of evocative folk names. In English it's known as devil's claw, wolf's claw, snake moss, witch's dust, witch's dance, or Earth Sulfur. In German, it's called *Hexenkraut*, "witch's herb." Long considered a sacred plant according to the Roman Pliny, its harvest first required a sacrifice of bread and mead. Wolf's claw was then gathered with the left hand, while adorned in white robes standing barefoot beneath a New Moon.

Although the plant has various other magical uses, the dust from its spores made wolf's claw an important shamanic tool. This yellow spore dust is known as *witches' flour, druids' flour, elven flour* and perhaps most accurately as *lightning powder*. It's oily and if tossed onto flames explodes with a burst similar to thunder and lightning. Today it's perceived as only a special effect; magical illusionists remain enamored with it, but once upon a time it was considered magical and used to great effect by shamans. (The spore powder also has medicinal use.)

Wolfsbane ☠

(Aconite napellus, Aconite vulparia)

Also known as aconite, blue rocket, friar's cap, monkshood and Venus' chariot, wolfsbane is among the deadliest of plants and very closely identified with witchcraft. It is indigenous to Eastern Europe, but was eventually grown in ancient Greece, from whence it spread to Italy and is now found as far afield as the British Isles. There are over 250 species of *Aconite*. Variants are also found throughout Asia.

Its active alkaloid is aconitum, a very potent poison. One fifth of a grain of aconitum is sufficient to produce a fatal dose. Controversy exists about whether it produces a psychotropic effect. It's impossible to determine for sure because at present, with existing knowledge, wolfsbane is basically impossible to use. (Processed derivatives are a component of Ayurveda and Traditional Chinese Medicine.) Whether it was ever genuinely used or whether those formulas calling for it are just full of bravado is equally impossible to tell. Many spells suggest brewing it, although just because a spell is "traditional" doesn't mean anyone actually ever cast it (or at least not successfully!).

🕷 *Wolfsbane is so poisonous that even handling the plant causes skin irritation and is potentially dangerous.*

🕷 *Wolfsbane is so poisonous that having ritually bathed the plant, it's no longer safe to even put your hands in the water, let alone ingest it.*

That said, few plants are as identified with witchcraft as wolfsbane.

Its natural habitat is mountains, however it can be cultivated and it will wander. It blooms in the summer. Wolfsbane is a very beautiful plant with lush flowers and is thus a favorite of traditional poison gardens. It was used to represent the dangerously alluring witch, the *femme fatale*, whose beauty masked her innately poisonous nature. Wolfsbane is known as the Queen of Poisons.

Every part of the plant is deadly, most especially the root. The name wolfsbane derives from attempts at wolf eradication. Gaulish Celts and Chinese used it as arrow poison, and the ancients concurred that aconite was the deadliest of their known poisons.

Wolfsbane is sacred to Hecate. Its origin is sometimes attributed to Cerberus, the three-headed guard dog of Hades, who may or may not be Hecate the dog goddess in disguise. Wolfsbane allegedly sprang up where Cerberus' drool touched Earth.

✷ Calendar of Revelry and Sacred Days

Witches certainly require privacy to cast spells and for certain rituals, however witches around the world are also renowned (or notorious) for their partygoing and party-giving skills. Witches have a reputation as a restless bunch: they like to get out of the house frequently (or at least so says the stereotype), especially at night and especially when the night holds promise of high spirits and magical company.

Although perhaps any time is the right time for celebration, enchantments, and revelry certain times of the year are particularly associated with witches and witchcraft.

The witch's calendar of revelry and sacred days includes celebrations of Earth and her powers, ancient Pagan festivals, and modern derivations of these festivals from Neo-Pagan as well as Christian sources.

Upon closer examination one will notice that although there are many localized names for these holidays, reflecting different cultures, languages, and spiritual orientations, most of them correspond in time to seasonal changes such as the solstices, equinoxes or periods immediately following or preceding them.

The modern perception is that people superimpose holidays and festivals on these time periods. The magical perception would suggest that ancient people were responding to Earth's moods.

The nature of the festivals (some are solemn, others wildly ecstatic) reflects Earth's natural and consistent state at that time of year. Thus the many variations on specific themes may not all derive from one source; instead they may have emerged independently, in response to a natural phenomenon that, although obvious to our ancestors, may be imperceptible to many of us today.

These celebrations may be categorized thus:

✷ *Festivals honoring and acknowledging solstices and equinoxes: Midsummer's, Mabon, Yule, and Ostara*

✷ *Anarchist festivals when rules are defiantly broken: May Eve, Midsummer's Eve, November Eve, and Yule*

✷ *Nights that witches congregate and celebrate: Halloween, May Eve, Midsummer's Eve, and Easter. (Easter? Yes, read on.)*

185

❋ The periods when the veil between realms is thin and dead souls return to visit the living: Halloween, Yule, and Lupercalia.

❋ Times devoted to ritual purification and cleansing rites: Yule, Lupercalia, and the February Feasts.

❋ Celebrations of the Harvest and the Corn Mother: Mabon, Lughnasa, and the February Feasts.

Different names are used for identical days representing different traditions, languages, cultures, and spiritual orientations.

The Anthestheria

See also February Feasts, Candlemas, Imbolc, and Lupercalia.

The Anthestheria, "the festival of flowers," heralds the arrival of Dionysus, Lord of New Life and Wine, literally. It hails the birth of the deity plus the annual ritual opening of new casks of wine. The festival was devoted to birth, death, purification, and fertility.

Only one of several annual festivals honoring Dionysus in Greece, the Anthestheria was held for three days in the month of Anthesterion (February/March). According to some analyses of the festival (much is enshrouded in myth), the festival also corresponds with Dionysus' birth. If there is such a thing as a "triple goddess" then Dionysus is the corresponding "triple god"; during this festival he is honored as infant, husband, and dying god.

Opening the new casks of wine isn't as simple and forthright as it sounds. The wine casks were half-buried in Earth during the fermentation period, so their removal is like a birth, specifically like a Caesarian section and even more specifically like Dionysus' own birth. Dionysus'

mother died before he was born; the unborn child was surgically removed from her womb and then sewed up within his father Zeus' thigh, where he was allowed to mature in peace until the time was ripe. Ritually unearthing the casks and opening them is a metaphoric re-enactment of Dionysus' birth. His devotees share in the deity's essence by consuming him; drinking the wine accomplishes this purpose.

Initially the festival was apparently celebrated by women and children, but there are many gaps in the historical narrative. Many aspects of devotion to Dionysus fall under the category of "mystery traditions" and hence secrecy was always a component. In addition, the more female-oriented aspects of his devotion ultimately became disreputable and illegal. Information regarding them was suppressed.

The first two days of the festival were devoted to honoring the deity and the new wine. The festival's days (and nights!) were punctuated by secret celebrations for mature women, rituals of initiation for children, and general revelry and celebration for all. Everyone was invited to the party, including men, ancestral spirits, dead souls, and various spiritual entities.

There are two levels to this festival, however. It was a public festival, with some aspects celebrated by all, but it was simultaneously also a mystery celebration. Dionysus' most devoted servants, the maenads and others, celebrated secret rites in his honor, apparently including the Great Rite, the sacred marriage between deity and devotee. (See **DICTIONARY:** Great Rite.)

The festival's three nights were reserved for women's mysteries. The maenads celebrated privately in the mountains and forests. Little information survives, however mature women were understood to play the role of brides of Dionysus at this time. (In some legends, Dionysus' marriage to Ariadne coincides with this festival; other legends suggest that the wedding was held on May Eve.) Among the festival's goals was the stimulation of personal and agricultural fertility.

Rituals and celebrations evolve over time. Attitudes toward ghosts changed. What seems to have originally been a day devoted to honoring dead ancestors (see Dias de los Muertos; Festivals of the Dead) eventually became a time of fear. Household doorposts were smeared with pitch in an effort to keep ghosts out. Many shrines and temples were kept tightly sealed on this day, allegedly to prevent ghosts from entering and lingering longer than their allotted time on Earth. (Another explanation suggests that this day belongs only to Dionysus and Hermes; therefore other spirits are prevented from leaving their shrines and joining the rituals.)

The festival concludes when women carry pots of cooked grains and vegetables to the marshes to bid farewell to the dead with the ritual incantation *"Begone Ghosts! The Anthestheria is over!"*

If rituals are conducted correctly, the end result is the removal and purification of malevolent ghosts, low-level spirits, and spiritual debris. Modern versions and adaptations of the Anthestheria are celebrated by some Neo-Pagans.

Beltane

See also Floralia, May Eve, and Walpurgis.

Beltane is the conventional modern spelling. *Bealtaine* is the traditional Irish spelling.

Beltane officially begins at moonrise on the evening before the first day of May. It is the Celtic festival corresponding to May Eve, which is metaphysically understood as the moment when Earth's generative, reproductive, and sexual energies are at their peak. Beltane, thus, is among the many May festivals celebrating Earth's sexual and reproductive powers; however Beltane has added resonance in Celtic lands as it also inaugurates the second half of the year.

Rituals are held during Beltane to enhance and increase the fertility of land, people, and animals. A celebratory feast welcomes the newly awakened Earth. Witches and fairies are out and about tonight.

The modern Western year is divided into quarters (spring, summer, fall, and winter). However, as well as can be understood based on limited surviving information, the ancient Celtic year was divided into halves:

❋ *The dark half is initiated with the festival of Samhain, which corresponds to October 31st on the modern calendar or Halloween.*

❋ *The bright half is initiated by the festival of Beltane, corresponding to April 30th on the modern calendar or May Eve.*

One may visualize this calendar as akin to a yin-yang symbol, with Beltane proclaiming the start of the bright yang portion.

Much of what we know of Celtic festivals (and most of what has been incorporated into modern Wicca) derives from Ireland, although the Celts once dominated a good part of Europe. There are indications that similar festivals were held elsewhere in Celtic Europe, not least by the prevalence of May Day celebrations throughout the entire continent.

Known as *Calan Mai* in Wales, Beltane is the Celtic fire festival marking the beginning of summer. The name may derive from "bel" (light) or "bil" (luck) and the general consensus is that Beltane means "bright fire." The name may also honor the Celtic deity named Bel or Belenus. Another possibility is that Bel is either derived from or identical to the pan-Semitic fertility deity Baal.

Fire may be understood as a little bit of the sun on Earth. In the spirit of the metaphysical adage *as above, so below,"* the magical power of the sun was rekindled and enhanced by the Beltane bonfires. These bonfires were known as "bel-fires" or bale fires. They joyfully celebrate and proclaim the return of fertility (life) to Earth. Beltane bonfires were ritual fires and were traditionally kindled by friction or by sparks from a flint. (To this day, some traditionalists resist the allure of matches or lighters and insist that others do so as well.)

The bonfires convey the magical, healing, energizing force of fire. In order to benefit from this positive magic radiant energy, people dance around the fire, jump over it, crawl through it once it gets low and also drive their livestock through. Although any animal can benefit from the magic of the bale fires, cattle, the sacred cows so intrinsic to Irish myth, are especially associated with Beltane. If there are twin fires or multiple fires, people will dance between them and lead animals between. The ultimate goal of these rituals is disease prevention and the termination of bad luck, as well as the renewal of fertility and creativity.

Although a sacred day, Beltane was a happy, raucous holiday, not a serious, solemn one. It is impossible to celebrate Earth's sexuality without simultaneously reveling in human sexuality too. Beltane was one of those anarchic festivals where everyday constraints were thrown to the winds. The Christian Church would eventually condemn the carnal licentiousness of Beltane rites, accusing the populace of indiscriminate copulation. Although defamatory, these accusations weren't without a vestige of truth (although it's unlikely that sexual activity was ever as indiscriminate and random as the Church postulated), however disapproval stems from perspective and perhaps a wee bit of jealousy. After all, some people were having fun when others weren't. (See May Day, page 211, for further information.) Children whose birthdays fell near the Celtic festival Imbolc, which occurs precisely nine months later, were affectionately known as "Beltane babies," and were considered to be special children with strong psychic powers and favored by the fairies.

> **According to Sir James Frazer, author of *The Golden Bough, "every woman who fetches fire on May Day"* was considered a witch in sixteenth-century Ireland.**

Beltane was understood as a witches' festival, when witches came out to play, as well as a day that was sacred to devotees of the Fairy Faith. Perhaps their very visibility on this date made those with magical or Pagan inclinations vulnerable to those with other orientations. Notions of sacrifice, and especially of sacrificial witches permeate many historic Beltane traditions, and May became a time when witches and their animal allies were persecuted.

※ Cats and rabbits discovered in the fields in Ireland during Beltane were traditionally understood as witches in disguise and frequently killed on the spot, often by being tossed into the bonfires.

※ Litters of kittens born during the entire month of May were feared as potential witches' familiars and summarily drowned.

※ A tradition known as "burning the witches" persisted in the Scottish Highlands into the eighteenth century. Young men took bits of the burning Beltane bonfires onto pitchforks. They then ran through the fields shouting "Fire! Fire! Burn the witches!" The fire is scattered through the fields to enhance their fecundity—which, in fact, it does.

The joyful aspects of Beltane have been incorporated into contemporary Wicca. Aspects of the festival devoted to the sun, human sexuality, and the regeneration of life and magic power are emphasized.

Candlemas

See also February Feasts, Imbolc, and Lupercalia.

Candlemas is the informal English name given to the Roman Catholic feast of the Purification of the Blessed Virgin. Candlemas is the oldest of the festivals specifically honoring the Blessed Mother. It coincides in time with other purification festivals dedicated to other divine mothers such as Brigid (Imbolc) and Juno (the Lupercalia).

There is confusion as to when Candlemas is celebrated; depending on which version of the calendar is used, Candlemas falls on either February 2nd or February 15th, although always beginning the previous eve. The Lupercalia, Rome's festival of purification and fertility that officially began on February 13th, was officially banned in 494 CE, although it's believed to have survived in secret for longer. Candlemas is generally understood as an attempt to replace it.

Candlemas traditions in the form they exist today can be safely dated to the eleventh century. Candlemas also marks the official end of the Christmas season; Yule greens and decoration are now taken down.

Despite its ecclesiastical name, but perhaps because of positive association with candle magic (and maybe simply because many find it easier to pronounce), the name Candlemas is often used to refer to the modern Wiccan sabbat Imbolc. In other words, although the name Candlemas is used, rituals and practices belong specifically to Imbolc (see page 204).

Other Neo-Pagans understand Candlemas as a celebration of candles, now standard everyday witchcraft tools. Traditionally candles are set ablaze in every window and the night is considered ideal for candle magic and divination.

Candelaria is the equivalent of Candlemas in Spanish-speaking countries. Oya, the warrior orisha of storms, is syncretized to the Virgin of Candelaria and shares her feast day. Oya sweeps the atmosphere clean using the powerful hurricane winds that blow annually from Africa toward the Caribbean. Oya's traditional Candelaria offerings include nine purple candles, nine small purple eggplants, and a glass of red wine.

See also **DICTIONARY:** Orisha; Santeria.

Cross Quarter Days

The Cross Quarter Days are those that mark the half-way point between solstices and equinoxes:

* May 1st, also known as Beltane, May Day, and Walpurgis

* August 1st, also known as Lammas and Lughnasa

* November 1st, also known as All Saints' Day and Samhain

* February 1st, also known as Candlemas and Imbolc

Pagan festivals and holy days correspond to each of the Cross Quarter Days. In addition, in various parts of Europe—notably Scotland and Ireland—the Quarter Days were when rents fell due to the landlord, perhaps necessitating the need for some extra magic.

Dias de Los Muertos/Mexican Days of the Dead

See also Festivals of the Dead, Halloween, and Samhain.

The Days of the Dead refers to a three-day festival that fuses pre-Columbian indigenous celebrations with those of Roman Catholicism. Because the Roman Catholic feast day that honors the deceased also incorporates a tremendous amount of older Pagan spirituality and tradition, the modern Mexican Days of the Dead is a tremendously complex celebration.One must specify *Mexican* Days of the Dead because virtually every Latin American community throughout South and Central America also has some sort of commemorative feast, as do many communities elsewhere. Although the purpose is identical, traditions vary greatly. Aspects of the Mexican Days of the Dead have become increas-

ingly influential over Neo-Pagan spirituality.

November Eve and the days immediately before and after are internationally considered the time when the dead visit the living. Depending upon perspectives toward the nature of the dead, some cultures find this a scary time. In other words, if the revenant dead can only be up to no good, then the time when they return is a time of great danger.

In traditional Mexican culture, however, the dead are welcomed, feasted, propitiated, and then sent safely on their way. This is the natural order: it is natural for the dead to appear at this time and it is natural for them to depart afterwards. The dead who are not propitiated and treated with respect, love, and honor are those who may linger and become troublesome ghosts. It is in the community's interest for this not to occur, and the Days of the Dead are celebrated by individuals and families but also by communities at large. To witness Days of the Dead celebrations in Mexican villages is to understand how festivals like Beltane, Midsummer's or Samhain must once have been an entire community's affair.

> Extremely similar festivals honoring the dead were once held at this time of year throughout Italy, most especially in Salerno. The practice was banned by the Church in the fifteenth century.

There isn't just one fixed way to celebrate the Dias de los Muertos. Traditions vary depending on location and region, however some themes and traditions remain consistent. Each day of the three-day festival is dedicated to a different community of the deceased. The dead are envisioned as a parade of spirits, arriving in scheduled hosts arranged according to age and manner of death.

The Mexican Days of the Dead is a celebratory festival, combining humor with devotion, a lust for life with an acceptance of death. Traditional Aztec culture didn't fear death. Death was understood as a period of deep sleep or true reality, while life (or lives) was the dreams experienced during this sleep/death. Modern Mexican culture revels in humorous, grotesque, defiant artistic celebrations of death, which simultaneously celebrate life, too. Death isn't a topic to be avoided but instead it is defied and mocked while simultaneously respected and revered.

✴ *Images of skeletons and skulls are omnipresent.*

✴ *Decorated sugar skulls fill the stores in the period leading up to the holiday in the same manner that pumpkins and Halloween-oriented cookies and candies do at this time in the United States.*

✴ *Special holiday foods are prepared and served only at this time of year, including certain moles (Mexican stews featuring bitter chocolate) and the "Bread of the Dead"—a sweet loaf decorated with skulls and crossbones.*

An *ofrenda*, translated into English as an "offering table" or altar, is set up in the home. The *ofrenda* serves as the magnet that guides and welcomes the spirits of the deceased. A table is beautifully decorated and laden with the feast to be shared by the living and the dead.

Technically the festivities begin the eve of October 31st in conjunction with the Roman Catholic festival of All Hallows Eve, however, depending upon region or village, it may begin as early as October 27th. Commemorations prior to the 31st are more openly Pagan in ori-

entation than the official three-day period, which is technically a Roman Catholic feast.

What follows is a standard calendar for the Days of the Dead. However be advised that this is subject to variation.

✴ *October 27th is dedicated to those who died without families, whose families have since died out or to those who, for whatever reason, have no one to welcome them and create an* ofrenda *for them. Sad, lonely, and potentially jealous and resentful, if left hungry and unpropitiated these are the spirits who can potentially become dangerous, malevolent ghosts. Bread and water is placed outside for them.*

✴ *October 28th is dedicated to those who died violently, whether by accident or through intention. They, too, are given fresh bread and water.*

In both these cases, food and drink is placed outside, not inside the home. The intention is to prevent the phenomenon of destructive, malicious, "hungry ghosts," not to have the ghosts become so comfortable that they decide to move in.

✴ *October 29th is a day of preparation.*

✴ *October 30th is dedicated to Pagan babies and babies in limbo, those children who died without baptism or unknown wandering children's souls. Bread, water, and small things that would please a child (sweets, toys, juice) are placed outside.*

Up until this point, any food offered is not shared by the living. Once given, it is left outside.

The night of October 31st may be dedicated to dead children while November 1st is for deceased adults. In some communities, however, November 1st is the *Dia de los Angelitos* (the Day of the Little Angels). Children's graves are given special attention and *ofrendas* devoted to children are erected.

✳ *October 31st is offered to dead children whom a family knew and loved. The offering is made in the home; the dead souls from this point on are welcomed into the home.*

✳ *November 1st is dedicated to deceased adults, friends, family members, loved ones or those whom one admires and wishes to honor. Offerings may be made at home or brought to the cemetery, where living and dead may feast together.*

✳ *By the evening of November 2nd, the dead should be gone, well on their way back to where they came from. Trails of shredded yellow marigold blossoms may be laid to lead them back to the family plot. Stubborn, lingering ghosts are sent on their way by masked mummers. This once would have been the shaman's job.*

Easter

See also Ostara.

In Ireland as well as the United Kingdom and her former colonies, the witches' party night is Halloween. In Germanic and Slavic lands, witches fly on Walpurgis Night. In Sweden, the witches fly on Easter Eve. *Easter?* Yes—Pagan traditions permeate Easter and not only in Sweden.

Although Easter is frequently considered the most sacred day of the Christian calendar (in some areas it supersedes Christmas) many of its beloved folk customs have nothing to do with Christianity—most obviously egg-delivering bunnies.

Easter corresponds approximately with the vernal equinox, the beginning of spring, and as

such is a celebration of new life, including flowers, eggs, and babies. The vernal equinox corresponds with the beginning of the astrological sign of Aries, the very first sign of the zodiac and hence the beginning of a new annual cycle.

Easter's name honors the Germanic deity whose name is variously spelled *Astara, Easter, Eostre,* and *Ostara* and is believed to mean "Radiant Dawn." Ostara is the spirit of spring and the returning season of fertility. Her annual return was traditionally celebrated with flowers, bell-ringing, and singing. New fires were lit at dawn.

Ostara manifests as a beautiful young woman, with flowers in her hair. Her male consort takes the form of a rabbit. Sometimes he is the size of a full-grown human male; at other times he's a little bunny that Ostara cradles in her arms. Ostara and her frisky rabbit bring the eggs that signify Earth's resurgence of fertility.

Easter celebrates the magical energy and power that encourages and stimulates new beginnings. It is a festival of fertility and efforts to enhance fertility. These aspects of the holiday may be ignored or passed over, however they are not hidden or obscure. Until not that long ago, it was traditional in French, German, and Italian villages for special phallic-shaped cakes to be carried in procession to the local church at Easter.

Easter's Pagan components include the following.

Easter Eggs

Eggs are symbolic of new life, new beginnings and fertility. They are a component of countless magic spells. Decorating, preserving, hiding, and burying eggs are only a few of the techniques used in ancient spells from around the world. The goals of most spells incorporating eggs include protection, purification, spiritual cleansing, wish fulfillment (the goose with the golden eggs), prosperity, and abundance including personal reproductive abundance. When a major fertility symbol like a rabbit presents another fertility symbol, like an egg, a very clear message is being sent. (For those unfamiliar with the basics of the birds and the bees, in real life rabbits do not hatch eggs, *ever*. Should a rabbit ever be seen with an egg, something magical is going on.) (See **ANIMALS**: Chickens; Rabbits.)

Easter eggs are decorated with magic symbols. In Greece, they were traditionally dyed red. Easter eggs are given as gifts or hidden so that hunts may be held for them. Once upon a time, the person who found the missing egg, the most eggs or the golden or otherwise special egg could expect to have all her wishes fulfilled in the coming year. (In other communities, she'll be the first to wed or have a baby.) Hard-boiled eggs may be served in their decorated shells as part of the ritual meal, or conversely chocolate eggs, often accompanied by chocolate rabbits, are seasonal treats. Old chocolate rabbit molds are now used to craft beautiful rabbit candles.

Among the most famous of Easter eggs are *pysanky* or Ukrainian Easter eggs. Pysanky (singular: pysanka) have an ancient history and were created before Christianity arrived in the Ukraine, however they are now an important component of the Easter holiday. Pysanky are beautifully decorated with beeswax and dyes.

The creation of pysanky is considered a feminine sacred art; what may seem to be merely decorated eggshells has deep spiritual resonance for Ukrainians, many of whom believe that each time a woman makes a pysanka, the devil, representing the principle of evil and blight, is pushed further down into captivity and further from humanity. Through an act of creation utilizing symbols of life and the goddess, such as eggs

and beeswax, women become spiritual warriors against forces of depravity, evil, and death. As long as women create pysanky, the powers of life prevail but it is also believed that when the last woman to make pysanky stops doing so, then evil will reign triumphant over Earth.

Pysanky are traditionally given as gifts to those one loves or wishes to honor.

Easter Witches

The Easter season is when Swedish witches (and those in parts of Finland, too) traditionally join together in celebration. The Easter witches' holiday begins on the night before Maundy Thursday (Holy Thursday). Beginning then and continuing through Easter Eve, witches mounted on brooms fly up chimneys, together with their faithful cats. Easter witches typically don't dress up in special clothing like pointy hats and cloaks. They wear regular ordinary clothing; flying on a broom is considered sufficient evidence to recognize them. Invariably the Swedish witch carries a coffee pot; that magical elixir is necessary for the long ride with its many rest-stops, as well as for the festivities once she arrives.

Not that long ago, people were scared of the Easter witches. Doors to homes and barns were locked during this time; chimney flues were closed, perhaps to keep those with wanderlust inside. Anything that could potentially be converted into a witch's vehicle (brooms, pitchforks, rakes) was locked up, lest the neighbors accuse you of helping the witches have fun. Crosses were drawn on the door with chalk to let the witches know they were unwelcome. Fires were kept burning in the hearth to keep it from being used as a portal. Firecrackers were set off in hopes that witches would be startled and fall from their brooms. On a dare, young men would hide out overnight in church bell-towers waiting for the witches. When traveling by broomstick, frequent stops for rest and refueling are necessary. Allegedly grease from church bells is among the ingredients needed to fuel flying broomsticks and so church towers are where witches congregate on their way to festivities on remote mountain peaks.

Today, Holy Thursday or Easter Eve is when Swedish children, boys and girls both, dress up as Easter hags and witches. They parade in costume and pay social calls on neighbors begging treats. There's no pretense of being scary or grotesque witches; instead these small children are very cute and completely unthreatening, dressed up as little old babushka-ladies with headscarves and old-fashioned dresses. Some children carry an empty coffee pot, which neighbors can fill with treats. Others leave small decorated cards, known as "Easter letters," which include small poems and pictures of witches, their cats and broomsticks, similar to a Halloween card elsewhere. The identity of the sender is sometimes secret; unsigned cards are slipped into mailboxes or beneath doors. It is up to the recipient to figure out the giver's identity and reciprocate with a small treat.

Esbat

The word "esbat" is believed to derive from the Old French *s'esbattre*, which means "*to frolic and amuse oneself*" or "*to celebrate joyfully*." Esbats are among the sacred, celebratory days of Wicca.

At present, there is only one known pre-twentieth-century reference to an "esbat." It derives from the memoirs of the witch-hunter Pierre de Lancre, published in 1613. The word is used in a quotation from a witch. Margaret Murray picked up the reference and used it in her writings, which were to have tremendous influence on Gerald Gardner. Esbats are now an integral part of Gardnerian Wicca and the word has entered the general witchcraft lexicon, although it is not used in a consistent fashion.

The modern definition of "esbat" is somewhat loose and one cannot assume that everyone defines the word identically. At its least rigid definition, esbats refer to any scheduled ritual. It is most often intended to indicate the meeting of a coven, however independent practitioners also celebrate esbats, and will do so in solitary fashion if they choose.

How and when esbats are celebrated depends upon how each tradition, coven or individual defines the word:

* *Some use "esbat" as a synonym for "sabbat" or to refer to one of the four lesser Wiccan sabbats (see Sabbat, page 214).*

* *Esbats may be specifically identified with lunar devotions. In this case, esbats are celebrated in conjunction with either the new or full moon, so that there are 13 annual esbats (or if the full moon is observed, the occasional additional blue moon, too). When esbats are associated with the full moon, some prefer celebrating sky-clad (without clothes) so that moonlight is better able to charge the body with its magical energy, however this depends upon coven and individual.*

* *Some covens use the term "esbat" to refer to any regularly scheduled meeting.*

See **HALL OF FAME:** Gerald Gardner; Margaret Murray.

Feast of St Lucy or Santa Lucia

The Feast of St Lucy is celebrated on December 13th. In the Germanic world, the Eve of St Lucy's is renowned (or notorious) for an upsurge in spirit activity, most notably by the passage of the Wild Hunt. Witches and practitioners go out to join the Hunters, although others may hide behind locked doors and amulets.

Before the Gregorian calendar reform of 1582, the Feast of St Lucy fell on the shortest day of the year, the winter solstice, a day of tremendous spiritual power. Apparently the calendar change means little to the spirits because they're still out riding around.

The festival officially commemorates St Lucy, an early virgin martyr. Lucy, a beautiful young noblewoman from Sicily, had made a vow of chastity. When her father made arrangements for her marriage, Lucy bet that if she literally removed her eyes, the chosen groom would change his mind and quickly retract his proposal. She wasn't wrong but luckily for Lucy, God was so impressed by her determination that he stuck her eyes back in, healed them and miraculously gifted her with sight once more. St Lucy is now the matron saint who heals afflictions of the eye and who averts and removes the Evil Eye (see **DICTIONARY**: Evil Eye).

Today the Church acknowledges that Lucy's hagiography is built on legend and folklore. Many believe that forbidden but formidable female deities hide behind the saint's respectable mask.

In the Mediterranean St Lucy is identified with the Italian deity Juno Lucina, Juno the Lightbringer (see Lupercalia). However, nowhere is St Lucy more beloved than in Scandinavia where that shape-shifting witch-goddess Freya is believed to have assumed the saint's guise. As a goddess, Freya leads the Norse warrior spirits, the Valkyries. She welcomes fallen battle heroes; half will spend joyous eternity partying in her hall, while the other half accompanies Odin. As deities of witches (or as disciples of the devil, if you prefer that perspective) Odin and Freya are among the leaders of the Wild Hunt. Freya also has dominion over love, romance, sex, and fertility. She typically manifests as a golden woman who shines like the sun. In Norway, virginal St Lucy has something of a reputation as a loose woman, even as a goblin (defined as a malevolent fairy). She even sometimes leads the Wild Hunt.

In Sweden, the Feast of St Lucy is celebrated with a beloved ritual enactment. One of a household's young girls or women, usually either the eldest or youngest daughter, ritually embodies the saint. She rises before dawn to fix coffee and breakfast for her family. Ritual foods are served such as the pastry known as *lussekatter*, "Lucy's cats," saffron buns, cross-shaped pastries also frequently flavored with saffron (saffron, the world's most expensive spice, is a potent natural dye; it turns food and drink golden), and glogg, hot spiced wine with aquavit.

The girl dresses up as St Lucy and brings breakfast to everyone else's bed. Intrinsic to the ritual is her crown of lit candles. The crown usually incorporates either seven or nine candles, although this varies depending upon household and region. The Santa Lucia crown may be built upon a wreath created from fresh greens, often rue, and is decorated with scarlet ribbons.

In Switzerland, St Lucy is a gift-giver; she strolls around together with Father Christmas (who may be her old partner Odin in disguise). She distributes gifts to girls, while Father Christmas gives gifts to the boys. In Swiss folklore, St Lucy is often understood to be Mrs Christmas, Santa Claus' wife, which one imagines would have greatly distressed that young Sicilian martyr.

In Hungary, St Lucy's Day is associated with divination. Bands of boys known as the "cacklers" or the fortune-tellers, used to proceed from house to house, singing ancient fertility songs, similar to the tradition of Yule carolers. The cacklers requested hens, geese, eggs, and blessings. The mistress of the house was somewhat obligated to welcome the singers and give them their traditional offering of dried pears as if this was done, her home was considered blessed for the year to come. If the cacklers aren't welcomed, her clutch of chickens, however many there might be, is allegedly doomed to be reduced to one blind hen. (The curse of St Lucy's eyes!)

Once upon a time, if someone in Hungary wished to know the identity of a village's witches, St Lucy's Day was the time to begin building a magical chair from nine different types of wood, put together without nails. (This spell apparently must be constructed without iron.) Known as a "Lucy Chair" one could work on it daily until Christmas when, if you hadn't changed your mind, it would be placed at the very back of the local church. Should the maker stand upon it during Midnight Mass, the witches would be identified by the horns now revealed on top of their heads. These horns are invisible to everyone but the one with the Lucy chair, who is now in the position to expose these witches.

Of course, this was no secret ritual; on the contrary someone standing on an unusual homemade chair during Midnight Mass would be quite conspicuous. Whether he saw the witches or not, they would certainly see him and so the end of the spell instructs him to run home as quickly as possibly immediately after Mass. Hopefully he's remembered to fill his pockets with poppy seeds which may be tossed behind him to distract the witches, who by now would be in hot pursuit. (Russian fairy tales also advise tossing poppy seeds should Baba Yaga ever be in pursuit.) Allegedly the witches will be forced to stop and pick up these sacred seeds. Once he was home, the chair must immediately be burned, which is perhaps why so few survive! (At least one, however, is on display in Budapest's Ethnographic Museum.)

See **BOTANICALS:** Opium Poppy; **DIVINE WITCH:** Freya: Odin.

February Feasts of Purification and New Life

The month of February leads to the spring equinox, Earth's awakening after her long slumber. It is a monumental threshold because, of course, what if Earth doesn't awake? What if the winter is endless, food-stores run out, and so forth. (This isn't mere anxiety but may reflect vestigial memories of Ice Ages.)

The spring equinox was understood as the birth of a New Year. This was eventually literalized with formal calendars. Many traditional New Years all over Earth are initiated at the equinox, not least the zodiacal calendar, whose first sign Aries begins on that day. February then is the solar month leading up to the month containing New Year's Day. Festivals in February are frequently devoted to spiritual and magical preparations for this new cycle.

The very name "February" derives from the Latin for purging and purification. This time period is devoted to crucial magical and spiritual rituals intended to protect Earth, cleanse it of accumulated psychic debris, and encourage the regeneration of fertility.

As the element with the most profound (although dangerous) powers of purification, fire is often featured in these festivals. Candle processions, for instance, are common motifs honoring Brigid, Juno Februa, Oya, and St Agatha. However, masculine fire is balanced by feminine liquid. Many of these feasts honor life-sustaining beverages. All milk ultimately comes from mothers, whether human, bovine or ewe. The February feasts celebrate and seek to protect these mothers.

Among these February festivals are the Anthestheria, Candlemas, Little Candlemas, the Lupercalia, and Imbolc, which possess their own entries; however there are also many other festivals with similar themes at this time.

the Dionysia/the Festival of St Trifon

In many cultures, milk is a drink reserved for children. Adults must find alternatives. Dionysus, Lord of Wine, is believed to have first emerged as a prominent power in Thrace, present-day Bulgaria. Wine is his sacrament; an ancient legend proclaims that Dionysus was able to convert water into wine.

Various festivals were held in his honor, characterized by ecstasy and intoxication (and also theatrical competitions!) as befitting this shamanic deity. Dionysus is not a fire deity, quite the contrary; liquid devotions are more his style. However in some areas devotion to Dionysus included snake handling and sometimes firewalking (the shamanic feat of walking over glowing coals). This particular festival corresponds to the time when casks of new wine were annually, traditionally opened and enjoyed.

When Bulgaria became Christian, names of festivals were changed. However, the celebrations survived. St Trifon is now the patron saint of viticulture. Ritual purifications of the vineyards were once held in February. Today St Trifon's Day honors the fruit of the vine, the vintners who create it, the deities who oversee

it, and all those who enjoy it. Dates of the festival vary depending upon location; sometimes it is early in February, the third or fourth day (and because of the nature of the celebration, there is a tendency perhaps to linger). Other communities celebrate St Trifon on February 15th; Valentine's Day festivities, which were largely unknown in Bulgaria until recently, have crept in and so now the wine is frequently accompanied by chocolate hearts. (See Lupercalia, page 209.)

the Feast Day of St Agatha (February 5th)

St Agatha, another Sicilian martyr, allegedly died *c.* 250 CE. She is believed to have served as direct inspiration for St Lucy. St Agatha's fate was particularly horrific and brings to mind the brutal violence so often historically (and presently) inflicted upon women. St Agatha, who according to legend wished to be a *virgin* martyr, was sent to a brothel where she was repeatedly raped. Deprived of food and water, she was then racked, beaten, her flesh was ripped by iron hooks, her breasts were cut off and she was burned with torches. Agatha was then rolled over broken potsherds and live coals until she died.

Early Christian icons depicted Agatha carrying her breasts on a plate (as Lucy carries her eyes). They were eventually confused for bells (or were they?) and so St Agatha reigns today as the matron saint of bell makers. Her symbolic objects include a bell, a brazier filled with smoking coals, and a pair of iron tongs. St Agatha allegedly once saved her hometown Catania from Mount Etna, the volcano, where Hephaestus, the Greek sacred smith, had his forge. Sacred images of Agatha almost always depict the volcano as well; it is frequently drawn so as to resemble a huge breast, threatening to overflow with milk rather than lava.

Here's the thing: if one examines St Agatha's iconography completely out of Christian context, Agatha looks amazingly like the Pagan spirit of Mount Etna. From that perspective, Agatha is a fire spirit who presides over smithcraft: her brazier and iron tongs are the symbols of that magical craft. Bells, her emblem, are magical tools of purification crafted by metalworkers. (And, in fact, St Agatha today is an official matron of metalsmiths and bell foundries.)

Even Agatha's name resonates of Paganism, deriving from a Greek word, *agathos*, meaning "good." It was also the name of a beneficial serpent deity who was widely venerated. And what was Hephaestus the Smith's sacred creature, by the way? A serpent. (Among the many gifts St Agatha bestows upon people is protection from venomous snakes. Allegedly if you drink Holy Water on her feast day, snakes will not harm you.)

It is not uncommon for female deities from Mediterranean regions to be depicted cradling and lifting their naked breasts toward their devotees as if they were nursing mothers offering comfort and nourishment to a very young child. And, in fact, St Agatha is matron saint of wet-nurses and nursing mothers as well as those who are hungry, who cry out for the goddesses' breast when there is no other food to be had.

St Agatha heals those who suffer from afflictions of the breast—not only breast cancer but mastitis and other conditions that interfere with breast-feeding or that make it painful or difficult. Of course, all those old bare-breasted deities kept theirs on their chests whereas with St Agatha it is as if all her old icons and sacred images were turned against her. The very things that were once sacred (coals, iron implements, earthenware shards, fire, sex, the female parts of the body) became vehicles of torture, humiliation, and annihilation.

There is something uncomfortably lascivious in discussions of Agatha's torture. During a time when people didn't discuss sex—*all* discussion was considered inappropriate—still there was a willingness to dwell in detail on Agatha's rape, the brothel, the amputation of her breasts and the sadistic mortification of her flesh. The word "brothel" wouldn't have been mentioned in polite company, certainly not mixed company, and yet exceptions were made in Agatha's case. Her saga, in many ways, bears the aura of violent misogynist pornography—or of elaborately detailed witch-trial transcripts. If one understands "virgin" in its pre-Christian sense, i.e., as an independent, autonomous woman beholden to no one (as in the virgin fertility goddess Artemis or in Vodou's wanton virgin Ezili Freda-Dahomey), then it is very tempting to see hidden in the tale of Agatha's torture a warning or foreshadowing of tortures and oppression to come.

Throughout Italy special breast-shaped pastries called "St Agatha's Breasts" are eaten on her feast day. Although St Agatha's official feast day is February 5th, the festivities in Catania, Sicily, her hometown, begin on February 1st. She is feted with candle processions, fireworks, music, and poetry contests.

St Agatha protects Catania from fires, earthquakes, and volcanic eruption. Her veil, which was taken from her tomb and is preserved at Catania, is said to keep Mount Etna under control. The annual display of her veil is accompanied by tambourine performances that would have done Isis or any number of Pagan deities proud. (There are those who perceive Isis, Mistress of Magic, hidden under Agatha's veil. Isis, too, has affiliations with snakes and protection.)

The Festival of Juno Sospita

Juno's name derives from the same roots as the word "one." One is her sacred number and the first day of each month is dedicated to her. The festival of Juno Sospita, Juno the Savior or Defender, was held on February 1st. Juno the Savior was considered the Mother of Rome, Matron Deity of the Republic.

On Roman coins, dating from 105 BCE, Juno Sospita is depicted clad in goatskins complete with horns. Sacrifices were made to Juno the Savior on February 1st, and young girls offered barley cakes to the sacred snakes who lived in her grove. (See also Lupercalia, page 209.)

Festivals of the Dead

Halloween, Samhain, and the Days of the Dead are not unique. Virtually every culture had, at least at one time, some sort of ceremonial honoring ancestors, dead souls or those who have passed on to the eternal Summerlands or Elysian Fields. The following are only some of the most famous.

The Egyptian Feast of the Dead

This, one of the earliest known festivals commemorating dead souls, may be the most ancient root of Halloween. The festival was held annually corresponding to modern mid-November. It commemorates the day Osiris was killed by his brother Seth.

Osiris subsequently became the Lord of the Dead. The festival specifically honored him. During the festival, people mourned for Osiris. Oil lamps were lit outside homes and left burning through the night. The days surrounding the festival were considered times of danger and vulnerability but were simultaneously highly magically charged. Osiris' dead body was sometimes depicted with corn sprouting from it. While alive, Osiris was renowned as the one who taught people the secrets of agriculture. One may understand his myth as an early retelling of the story of the dying grain, which must be cut down so that people may eat, survive the winter and have new seeds to plant for the year to come. (See **ERGOT**.)

In Abydos, the sacred city devoted to Osiris, an eight-act drama portrayed the saga of Osiris' life, death, and resurrection. According to Plutarch, the festival lasted for four days and was also a general commemorative feast for the dead.

The Feralia

One of several Roman festivals of the dead, most of what we know regarding the Feralia, the surviving information, derives from Book 2 of Ovid's *Fasti*. The Feralia began on February 21st and was the day to appease ancestral spirits.

Romans stayed home. Sanctuaries were closed. No weddings were held; only offerings to the spirits of the dead and their presiding deities were given. Visits were made to family tombs. According to Ovid, offerings typically consisted of votive garlands, sprinklings of grain, a few grains of salt, violets and bread soaked in wine. The dead had modest desires; what they wanted most of all was recognition and remembrance.

The Lemuria

The Lemuria was the second annual (but oldest) Roman commemoration of the dead. It was held on three odd days in May—May 9th, 11th, and 13th. During these days, the dead walk the Earth and must be propitiated. *Lemures* was the term used for these walking revenants, hence the name of the festival in their honor. They were understood as the angry, volatile, dangerous dead and so appeasement and protection was particularly crucial.

According to Ovid the holiday derives from the death of Remus, whose death at the hands of his brother Romulus is reminiscent of the biblical Cain and Abel. Remus' blood-stained ghost appeared to Romulus and demanded a festival in his honor. *Remuria* eventually became *Lemuria*. (There are also suggestions that the festival predates the arrival of the Romans in the region and has its origins in an Etruscan holy day.)

There is a description of the festival in Book 5 of Ovid's *Fasti*. The paterfamilias, the male head of the household, arose at midnight. He made the life-affirming gesture of the fig-hand (thumb between first and second fingers mimicking the sexual act) and then cleansed his hands in pure water. He walked barefoot through his home, spitting beans while saying *"With these beans I redeem me and mine."*

This ritual was repeated nine times. At the conclusion, the paterfamilias ritually bathed, then banged on metal pots and pans proclaiming *"Begone, ancestral spirits!"* nine times.

The Festival of Mania

The Roman Festival of Mania was held on August 24th. The modern term for "ancestor worship" is *manism*. The name derives from the *manes*, Rome's deified ancestral spirits. The goddess Mania presides over this host of spirits. On this day, Rome's "ghost stone," the cover that shielded the entrance to Hades, was lifted so that the ghosts had easy access. In addition to the ancestral spirits, the day honors Mania and Ceres, the Corn Mother. (For further information, please see **DIVINE WITCH: Mania.**)

Obon Festival

The Buddhist festival Obon is celebrated annually from the 13th to the 15th day of the seventh month of the Japanese calendar, which corresponds to the Western July 15th if the lunar calendar is used or August 15th if the solar. Obon commemorates the ancestors who are believed to return to Earth at this time to visit surviving relatives and descendants.

Rituals vary depending upon region and family, however Obon is typically characterized by lanterns, which are hung in front of houses to guide dead souls back home. Visits to the cemetery are customary. Offerings to the ancestors traditionally include cake, fruits and flowers, rice, and vegetables. These are placed on altars at home or in shrines and temples. Traditional dances (*bon odori*) are believed to comfort and please returning ghosts.

When Obon is over, the lanterns are placed in living waters, such as streams, rivers, lakes, and seas. There they float and will guide the ghosts back to their own realm.

Parentalia

This eight-day Roman festival in February honored dead ancestors. All temples were closed, no marriages took place and government officials were forbidden to wear their robes in public. Individuals visited the graves of their parents and other relatives, bringing offerings of milk, wine, honey, oil, and spring water. Some brought sacrificial blood from bodies of black animals.

Graves were decorated with roses and violets and a ritual meal was eaten at graveside. The festival's ritual greeting and farewell were the words, *Salve, sancte parens*, "Hail, holy ancestor." The Vestal Virgins, guardians of Rome's sacred hearth and fire, had their own particular rituals during this time, where they honored the group's sacred "ancestor."

The Floralia

The Floralia was the festival in honor of the Roman deity, Flora, for whom flowers are named. (Yes, there is another goddess named Fauna.) Flora was indigenous to the Roman region although she was there before the Romans. She is believed to be of Sabine or Oscan origin.

Flora is the spirit of blossoming flowers and springtime. She embodies the flowering of all nature, including human. Flowers indicate the promise of reproduction. Flowers lead to fruit as surely as sexual intercourse leads to babies. Flora is the spirit who embodies both the pleasures of the moment and the promise of the future.

The Floralia is believed to be the ancestor of all May Day celebrations. It was celebrated annually from April 28th through the beginning of May. The Floralia honored the female body. Beautiful Flora may be understood as the original Queen of the May. The festival was celebrated in the nude until the third century CE when Roman authorities demanded that revelers be clothed. The festival survived in this fashion until the next century, when all Pagan festivals were banned. Although all flowers are sacred to Flora, her favorites are fragile, transient bean blossoms.

Halloween

See also Festivals of the Dead and Samhain.

Also known as All Hallows, All Hallowmas, All Saints' Day, Hallowtide, and November Eve.

No night is more identified with witchcraft, magic, spirits, and ghosts. This is the night when the veil between realms is so thin as to be nonexistent. It is thus the perfect night for divination, magical ritual and spells, petitions to spirits and communication with the dead. The Wild Hunt rides on Halloween and the fairy mounds open up. This is one of the few nights when the trooping of the fairy folk is visible and changelings can be rescued. (See **DICTIONARY:** Wild Hunt.)

"Hallow" derives from an Old English word for *"holy."* Until the early sixteenth century, the word was usually applied only to saints and so it is essentially an archaic word for "saint." All Hallows Eve is the vigil preceding All Saints' Day, the Roman Catholic festival corresponding to ancient feasts of the dead. "Hallow" however has since gained the meaning of "holy" or "sacred," as in "hallowed ground," so Halloween may also be understood as "Sacred" or "Holy Night"—which for witches and those who love them, it is. (Those who fear them, on the other hand, would say that this is a night for staying inside because witches, demons, ghosts, and fairies are at the height of their powers!)

The Feast of All Hallows is thus synonymous with the Feast of All Saints. *All Hallows' Even* became *Hallowe'en*, which eventually became *Halloween* when the apostrophe was lost sometime during the mid-twentieth century.

In some areas (particularly those where witches are most active on May Eve or Midsummer's) the Feast of All Saints is a serious, solemn, devout festival completely devoted to Christian prayer. In other areas, historically in Ireland and the British Isles, Halloween retained

Halloween is a time for making wishes and for rituals to obtain good fortune.

This entire ritual, from the moment you leave your home until the handkerchief filled with graveyard dust is safely hidden, must be done in complete silence. Not a peep or your wishes allegedly won't come true!

1. Purchase a new cotton handkerchief before Halloween begins. Don't use it; keep it clean and reserve it for the following ritual.

2. As early as possible on November 1st, as early as one minute past midnight, leave home, taking the handkerchief, and go to a cemetery, entering by the main gate.

3. Walk along the path to the wall opposite the main gate. At some point on this walk, pick up a little dirt, put it in a corner of the handkerchief and make a wish while knotting that corner shut.

4. Retrace your steps exactly (or even walk backwards!) out the main gate.

5. Go to a second cemetery and repeat steps 2, 3, and 4, knotting the pinch of dirt up in a different corner of the hanky.

6. Go to a third cemetery and again repeat steps 2, 3, and 4. At this point you will have gathered three pinches of dirt and formed three knots in the handkerchief.

7. Go home and hide your handkerchief on a high shelf or within the rafters or somewhere where it won't be disturbed. Your wishes will allegedly come true.

its anarchic associations with witchcraft festivities and as such is a holiday devoted to fun, pranks, magic, and divination, to varying degrees, depending upon individual orientation. Maybe some witches still fly off on their broomsticks to deserted mountain peaks. Others attend Halloween parties, witches' balls, and dumb suppers. It is a sacred night for witches, the perfect moment for spells, rituals, and devotions to the spirits. For others, it's the night to dress up as witches and go out and revel in the spirit of fun and freedom that witches allegedly always enjoy.

Halloween is a complex festival with many roots. In its present form it is an amalgamation of the Celtic festival Samhain with the Roman celebration of Pomona, the spirit of crops, fruit, nuts, and seeds, and with assorted other Pagan festivals of the dead, including those devoted to the Corn Mother, as well as of magic power and women's "witch power." It is no accident that Halloween (and many festivals of the dead) fall within the zodiac sign of Scorpio, which has dominion over reproduction, the mysteries of sex, and the portals of birth and death.

Pomona, the Apple Queen, was the Roman deity of fresh fruit and fruit trees, especially apples. Her name derives from the Latin *pomum*, similar to the French word *pomme* or "apple." Pomona was a wood-nymph whose attribute is a pruning knife. (The Romans were responsible for domesticating wild apples, transforming the sour fruit into the juicy, delicious one of today.) The beautiful Pomona was sought after by many, including the goat-god Pan, but rejected them all, preferring to remain independent. She was finally wooed and won by Vertumnus, the male deity of the shifting seasons, who became her consort. Vertumnus represents the year in its guise as shape-shifter. Pomona initially rejected him too, until he gained her trust by approaching her in the form of an old woman—

a classic bit of ancient Halloween masquerading.

Halloween also falls within the period when the dead are understood to return to their old haunts. Traditionally at Halloween, children costumed as spirits of the dead or ghosts went begging from door to door, where they were given the seeds of life in the form of nuts and fruits, especially apples and hazelnuts.

Recently Halloween has become characterized by the grotesque and gross in the same manner that once suspenseful "horror" films have been replaced by gore. In Victorian days, Halloween was a romantic holiday to rival St Valentine's Day. (Both days may derive from similar roots; see Lupercalia, page 209.) Halloween cards were given to one's beloved in the way that one may now receive a Valentine's card. (Cards were frequently decorated with images of witches, more often beautiful and seductive than grotesque.) It is also the perfect night to engage in romantic divination and love magic.

Halloween is traditionally a time for games and fortune-telling. Many techniques are reserved for this night alone:

A Simple Halloween Divination: Go to a crossroads on Halloween and make an invocation to the deity, angel or ancestor of your choice. Listen to the wind or any words you hear at midnight (e.g., passing car radio or human voices) to hear your oracle for the next year.

Dumb Suppers

"Dumb suppers" earned their name because the entire ritual is conducted in silence from start to finish. No matter what happens or who shows up for dinner, it is vital to remain silent and to reserve discussion for after it is very clear that the ritual is over. Traditionally, dumb suppers serve either of two purposes:

* *Romantic divination—dumb suppers serve as divinatory methods of discovering your true love or your destined spouse (ideally but not always one and the same!) When you prepare the dumb supper, set the table for two. Allegedly your other half will come and dine with you. (This is not necessarily meant literally; expecting immediate literal results from magic spells leads to disappointment. Spells can come "true" in various magical ways.)*

* *Necromancy—the dumb supper serves as a type of séance. It may derive from rituals similar to those of the* Dias de los Muertos *celebrations where the living dine with the souls of the deceased.*

There are all sorts of variations on the Dumb Supper. Here are two:

Dumb Supper One: Starting at the stroke of midnight, set the table while consistently walking backwards, so that there are nine things on the table to eat. (Things like salt and pepper or butter count among the nine.) Then silently honor those who have passed on.

Dumb Supper Two: Set the table for two or more as desired. Each living person gets a plate; a setting is also laid for each anticipated invisible guest. Do not expect them to serve themselves. If this is a group dinner, guests are invited to bring photos or images to represent the souls of the deceased to whom invitations have been extended.

1. Leave all the doors and windows unlocked. (If possible, leave them open, although depending on where you are, nights at this time of year can be very chilly.)
2. Reverse the supper. Set the table in reverse; serve the food in reverse order, beginning with coffee, tea and dessert and working backwards.

Halloween Trees

Ancient traditions re-emerge in surprising new ways. The vestiges of "tree-worship" that have survived for so many centuries as Christmas trees, Yule logs, Maypoles and Easter egg trees have been joined in very recent years by a brand new tradition: the Halloween tree.

Similar to those other holiday "trees" named above, Halloween trees are lovingly decorated with charms and ornaments inspired by the holiday and by witchcraft. Many ornaments for instance are crafted in the image of witches or their accoutrements.

Unique and very appropriate to this holiday, however, before being decorated, Halloween trees are completely bare. Halloween trees are either deciduous trees that have dropped *all* their leaves or are, in fact, dead trees, perhaps the equivalent of ghost trees. Sometimes miniature Halloween trees are crafted from black wrought iron or other metals.

Hecate Night

November 16th is the night dedicated in honor of the witch deity Hecate. It is not the only night of the year sacred to her. Hecate claims dominion over all dark moon nights as well as the final day of each month (October 31st, the Feast of All Hallows is particularly sacred to her). Rituals and petitions to her are considered especially potent on any of these days, however the festival on November 16th recalls that Hecate was once a great goddess complete with temples and shrines, venerated by many, not only her spiritual daughters, witches. Hecate keeps nocturnal office-hours and this festival is no exception.

It begins at nightfall. Animal sacrifices were once offered in Hecate's temples in what are now Greece, Turkey, and Georgia; however those rites have been lost and are no longer appropriate. Gifts that memorialize her ancient sacrifices as well as her sacred animals *are* appropriate, however—votive imagery of dogs, wolves, pigs, horses, and snakes.

This is the night to be initiated into Hecate's Mysteries. Hecate Suppers were once held. Celebrants share a feast in Hecate's honor; a full plate for the goddess is left at a crossroads. (Whatever is left is considered given; do not use your finest china plate unless it is intended as part of the offering. It is forbidden to take anything back that has been given to Hecate.) Appropriate foods for the ritual dinner include cheese, honey, garlic, eggs, mushrooms, fish including red mullet (a scavenger which was taboo elsewhere) and honey cake for dessert. Leave the offering for Hecate and do not look back. If someone else picks it up, whether human or animal, this is wholly appropriate and Hecate's desire. Should you hear a dog bark it is highly auspicious. Allegedly Hecate roams the Earth on this night with her pack of hounds and wolves, accompanied by a host of ghosts, blessing those who left offerings for her.

Imbolc

Imbolc is among the February feasts of purification. The festival falls on the Cross Quarter Day marking the midpoint between the Winter Solstice and the Spring Equinox. This Celtic festival begins the evening of February 1st and continues through the next day. Imbolc is understood to mean "purification," however the literal translation is "in the belly" or "in the womb." This has been euphemized to mean "in the Earth" indicating agricultural promise, however, the Celtic deity Brigid who is celebrated on this day is also a spirit of fertility and sexuality. Babies conceived at Beltane would, if brought to full term, be born at this time.

Imbolc is one of the ancient Celtic pastoral holidays. It celebrates the lambing season and the first lactation of the ewes. An alternative name for Imbolc is Oimelc, which is believed to mean "ewe's milk." Imbolc celebrates the first fluttering of life in Earth's womb, the "quickening" that in the days before pregnancy testing was the first confirmation of pregnancy.

Imbolc is a fire festival celebrating light and new life. Earth awakens. Animals like bears and hedgehogs emerge from hibernation. The first spring flowers, like crocuses, begin to peek through the Earth. This is the day when the hedgehog, among Brigid's sacred creatures, comes out of hibernation. Whether it sees its shadow and returns to hibernation or not is believed to foretell the length of winter. (Migrants to North America wishing to retain this custom but lacking hedgehogs, substituted groundhogs instead.)

The Pagan deity Brigid was assimilated to the Roman Catholic Church as St Brigid. February 1st is her official feast day and is believed to be her birthday. Coincidentally perhaps, the goddess and the saint accept identical offerings.

Brigid's Pagan epithets include "*Fiery Arrow*," "*The Bright One*," "*The Flame Without Ashes*," and "*Moon Crowned Queen of the Undying Flame*." She is a spirit of healing, poetry, music, and smithcraft. She is the matron of artists, poets, craftspeople, and livestock. She may manifest as a pillar of fire or, alternately, a flame may shoot from her head. She is also sometimes depicted with a serpent wrapped around her head like a wreath. Her sacred animals include cattle, horses, wolves, and snakes.

St Brigid also has profound associations with fire. In one story she carries a burning coal in her apron but miraculously doesn't burn. In another, flames shoot out of her head or engulf her but miraculously she is not burned.

Offerings to Brigid include poetry written in her honor, dishes of milk and blackberries as well as offerings given on behalf of her sacred creatures. On Imbolc Eve, it was traditional in Ireland to place a loaf of bread on the windowsill for Brigid, together with an ear of corn for the white cow with red ears who is her traveling companion. Sheaves of wheat are woven into x-shaped crosses known as "Brigid's crosses" and hung from the rafters to serve as protection from fire and lightning.

Ivan Kupalo

Russian Midsummer's Eve, Ivan Kupalo, is the day to regenerate human sexuality and fertility. Ivan Kupalo is a magical time for witches, sorcerers, shape-shifters, and household (and other) spirits. It's a time for gathering magical and medicinal herbs. For maximum power, the morning dew should still cling to the botanicals. On the night of Ivan Kupalo, it's believed that witches traverse the land, lighting the darkness with their magical fires. They make trees talk and put silver into water.

Who is Ivan Kupalo? Good question. "Ivan" is the Slavic version of "John" and refers to John the Baptist; tacit acknowledgement that, officially at least, this is St John's Eve. The word "kupalo" is described as deriving from *kupat* "to bathe." However, Kupala is also the ancient Slavic spirit of water, magic, and fertility. Midsummer's Eve, the summer solstice, is her sacred day. The festival of St John the Baptist was superimposed over her day, which features ritual bathing as well as magical bonfires. (His associations with baptism, the holy, magical, and cleansing powers of water, lend themselves to a

Pagan water festival.) The festival, even one that remained as stubbornly Pagan as Ivan Kupalo, was more acceptable if it bore a man's name.

Ivan Kupalo, like other Midsummer's Eve festivities, celebrates the marriage of fire with water, male with female, and the subsequent bounties of Earth. Ivan Kupalo marks the consummation of Earth's marriage with the Sun. They are never closer than today. To preserve and partake of this energy, people celebrate sexual union, too.

The oldest written report of the festival of Ivan Kupalo comes from twelfth-century Russian Church chronicles, which describe girls dressed as brides who are taken to the river to dance and jump, worship Kupala, tell fortunes and bring sacred river water back to villages to sprinkle over houses and possessions. Bonfires were lit at night and villagers jumped over them.

A Midsummer's doll is made and decorated with branches and flowers. A girl is designated to represent Kupala. Holding the doll, she leads others, both male and female, to jump over the bonfires. With variations, this tradition is common to all areas with strong Slavic influence.

Fear of witchcraft is demonstrated too—the fear that some have secret knowledge that enables them to make private use of magical energy for personal (and perhaps selfish) benefit. In Belorussia, Baba Yaga is accused of leading witches, her devotees, in rituals that siphon solar energy into private magical fires during Ivan Kupalo.

Lammas

The word "Lammas" derives from the Old English *hlaf* ("loaf") and *maesse* ("mass" or "feast"). It was a harvest holiday of the early English Church celebrated on August Eve. Loaves baked from the year's first ripe grain were blessed in Church.

There are two versions of the origins of this feast:

❊ *Lammas is an attempt to integrate the Celtic Pagan festival of Lughnasa into the Christian calendar. Although also a harvest festival, Lughnasa honored the important Celtic solar deity Lugh.*

❊ *Devotion to Lugh may have been superimposed on an earlier holy day dedicated to the Corn Mother and her dying son. The Corn Mother mourns her son, eventually transforming into the* Mater Dolorosa, *the Mother of Sorrows.*

Lammas is celebrated as one of the important Wiccan sabbats. Although either name may be used, the Anglo-Saxon Lammas tends to be favored in modern Wicca.

Lammas, August Eve, is often a night devoted to romantic enchantment.

Please see Lughnasa (page 207) for further details.

Litha

The Wiccan sabbat that corresponds to the Summer Solstice and thus to Midsummer's and St John's Eve, is Litha. However, unlike Midsummer's, there is no fixed calendar date. Rather Litha is celebrated at the exact conjunction of the solstice, on whatever day it falls—approximately June 21st—when the sun is at its height, the longest day of the year.

The name "Litha" seems to derive from the ancient Germanic calendar, which was apparently divided six-fold rather than twelve-fold as is the modern Western calendar. Each year was divided into 60-day *tides*, what might be considered a "double-month." Litha seems to have named the summer tide. (See also Midsummer's Eve and Ivan Kupalo.)

Lughnasa

Pronounced Loo-nah-sa. Also spelled *Lughnasad*. See also Lammas.

Lughnasa Day is an ancient Celtic harvest feast celebrated on August 1st and for the fortnight preceding and following that date. Four weeks are dedicated to honoring the Celtic solar deity, Lugh, Spirit of Craftsmanship, Light, Victory, and War: the last two weeks of July and the first two weeks of August, which roughly correspond to the dates when the sun is in the astrological sign of Leo, the sign that belongs to the sun and epitomizes its power. In modern Irish Gaelic, the month of August is known as *Lunasa*.

Lughnasa is an agricultural rather than a pastoral celebration. It was a late introduction , at least in its present form, to Irish festivals, brought perhaps by continental devotees of the deity Lugh, a relative late-comer to the Irish pantheon. There are various legends about how and why Lugh initiated the festival that bears his name. Those legends about Lugh may be correct; however, just as Christianity would eventually transform Lughnasa into its harvest feast Lammas, so Lughnasa is superimposed on an earlier holy day devoted to the Corn Mother and her dying son.

Although the modern Wiccan sabbat is almost always devoted solely to the eve of July 31st leading into Lughnasa Day on August 1st, ancient people may have had more leisure time and more time to devote to spirituality (and fun). August 1st was merely the culmination of a month of celebrations. The three days prior to Lughnasa Day were particularly sacred and devoted to purification. Those three days are dedicated to Ireland's ancient solar goddess Ana; an earlier, more primordial deity than Lugh, the entire festival may once have belonged to her.

Although it's still hot in August, the festival marks the waning of the sun. Days are noticeably shorter than they were at the last major festival, Midsummer's Eve, which corresponds roughly with the Summer Solstice. The beginning of the end of summer is in sight.

Lughnasa is a celebration of the harvest but also a sacrifice of the Harvest King. John Barleycorn must die if the people are to live or, as that other proverb goes, you shall reap what was sown. The festival was intended to ensure a plentiful harvest. During Lughnasa, Lugh fights the Evil Lord of Blight for possession of the harvest. (See **ANIMALS:** Wolves and Werewolves: the Livonian werewolf; **DICTIONARY:** Benandanti.)

Lughnasa was a fire festival characterized by bonfires. Fire may be understood as pieces of the sun brought down to Earth. During the three days leading up to the Celtic festival, water was taboo. There was no bathing and no fishing prior to the Sacrifice of the Grain King (or the Grain Bear, Grain Horse, or Grain Wolf).

Lugh was an extremely important Celtic deity, not least because (along with Brigid) the widespread veneration of Lugh indicates the existence of pan-Celtic spiritual traditions (at one point, the Celts ruled a huge swathe of continental Europe before being forced to the very edges of the land mass). However we don't really know all that much about Celtic cosmology and ancient religion. The Celts left very little if any writing, and what exists is filtered through the eyes of outsiders, like Romans or Celtic Christian converts.

Lugh's name is spelled variously depending on location. Lugh is the Irish spelling; in Wales he is Lleu Llaw Gyffes, the "Bright One of the Skillful Hand." He was known as Lugos, which means "raven," in Europe and was an important figure in Gaul.

At least 14 European cities are named for Lugh including Laon, Leyden, Loudon and Lyon. Lyon's old name was Lugdunum, the fortress of Lugh. The city is believed to have been his cult center. Coins associated with that ancient city bore the images of ravens, which may be a reference to Lugh (or Lugos as he was known there). Carlisle in England, the former Lugubalium, is also named in Lugh's honor. (It's been suggested that many European churches dedicated to St Michael the Archangel were built over sites once dedicated to Lugh.)

Lughnasa means "the marriage of Lugh." There is a tremendous romantic component to the celebration. Lugh the sun and the Earth Mother renew their wedding vows annually during the full moon in August and invite all to gather and revel with them. Lughnasa celebrates the consummation of their sacred relationship. It precedes the spring festival of Beltane, which symbolizes the birth of the bright half of the Celtic year, by exactly nine months. It's not an affectation to say that this is the day the solar deity weds the Earth. Once upon a time, that was meant quite literally. This was the day when a High Priestess, channeling the goddess who embodied the land of Ireland, ritually wed the High King of Ireland. The consummation of their marriage enabled him to rule for yet another year.

Although the sacred marriage and the Corn Mother's sacrifice of her son or young lover no doubt precedes Lugh's associations with this date, there are also various versions of how Lugh became involved.

✳ *Lugh ordered a commemorative feast to honor his foster-mother, Tailtiu. On August 1st, a great festival was held at Teltown on the Boyne River in Ireland. The town allegedly takes its name from Lugh's foster mother who is buried there. Lugh instituted games in her honor.*

✳ *An ancient marital fair took place in Teltown, perhaps initiated by Lugh. It was a time to begin as well as formalize relationships. Men would stay on one side of the fair, women on the other, while go-betweens served as mediums to make arrangements. (Similar marital fairs still occur in rural Berber areas of North Africa.)*

✳ *Lugh has two wives, granddaughters of the King of Britain. When they died, Lugh requests that these women's lives and memories be commemorated every August 1st. His wives' names are Nas and Búi. (Búi is another name for Cailleach Bhéara—see* **HAG**: *Cailleach Bhéara.)*

Lughnasa is an occasion for blessing and harvesting botanicals for the coming year. In Northern climates, plants and their volatile oils are at the height of their power just before decomposition begins.

In Britain, Lughnasa and similar festivals weren't banished but were integrated into Christianity. St Columba, for instance, allowed his monks to maintain their Lughnasa celebrations although he renamed it the "Feast of the Ploughman." Lughnasa evolved into the festival of Lammas.

A deity who identifies himself as a sorcerer is attractive to those who practice witchcraft. Lugh or Lugos seems to have been a very important deity in Europe; post-Christianity, devotion to him seems to have gone underground, at least for a while, based upon reports of witches' sabbats held at the *Puy de Dome*, the 5000 foot peak in the Auvergne region of France, full of caves and grottoes, where Lugh maintained a sanctuary. (See **PLACES**: Puy de Dome.)

The August Herbs

In Northern Europe, August Eve, the night preceding Lughnasa, is the opportunity to create the botanical amulet known as the August Herbs. If proper ritual is followed, it's believed that these nine sacred herbs will bestow various blessings during the upcoming year including protection from malevolent magic and volatile weather. They attract love, stimulate romance, enhance sexuality, and ease labor pains as well as the passage into death.

1. For maximum power, pick the August herbs before sunrise while maintaining complete silence.
2. The original instructions suggest that the harvest must be accomplished while naked but if this is unrealistic then at least be barefoot and bareheaded.
3. Gather a bundle of arnica, calendula, dill, lovage, mugwort, sage, tansy, valerian, and yarrow. No iron can be used in the harvest, so no modern knives. Gather the herbs with your hands or with a ritual stone or crystal knife. If they're hard to pick, you can bite through the stems. Don't petition for blessings but keep a still, serene, blank mind.
4. Ornament the bundles with blue cornflowers and red corn cockles. Add a border of low growing herbs like chamomile or mother-of-thyme.
5. Place a stalk of millet, rye or other grain in the very center of the bundle, tie with a red ribbon and hang it within your home.

Lughnasa or Lammas is one of the more obscure witches' holidays. Pagan aspects of the festival were suppressed long ago and the Christian feast of Lammas was never entirely reinstated in Britain after the Reformation. Lammas is considered amongst the eight major sabbats of the Wiccan Wheel of the Year, however the roots of this holiday are so agricultural and rural that it often stymies modern Neo-Pagans, frequently no less urban than anyone else in the twenty-first century. Modern Lammas festivals often focus on the romantic aspects of the feast. It's a wonderful night for love magic as well as for enjoying the first fruits of the harvest, including grain and wine.

Lupercalia

See February Feasts, Candlemas, and Imbolc.

The Lupercalia was a complex and ancient Roman festival of purification that also served to celebrate and generate human fertility and honor wolves. Although standard explanations suggest that this festival of fertility and purification was initiated by Romulus and Remus in honor of the she-wolf who rescued and nursed them, the festival is believed to be far more ancient.

The deities who preside over the Lupercalia are Juno and the wild horned spirit Faunus. (See **HORNED ONE:** Faunus.) Faunus is the primordial spirit of wild nature, the male generative principle. He also mediates the balance between wolves and their prey and between shepherds and wolves.

The religious ceremonials at the heart of the Lupercalia purified the land and its inhabitants for the New Year. (February was the last month of the ancient calendar; the New Year began with the vernal equinox, when the sun entered the first astrological sign, Aries.)

The name "February" derives from two meanings:

❊ *Februare: to cleanse*

❊ *Juno Februata: Juno of the Fevers of Love or Juno Who Provides Purification*

Juno, the ancient Matron of the city of Rome, is the only deity with two months named in her honor: the eponymous June and February. Juno—or *Uni*—was an Etruscan deity whose presence in the Eternal City pre-dates the Romans.

During the nine days of the Lupercalia, from February 13th through the 21st, dead souls wandered the Earth, consuming the essence of the food and drink that the living offered them.

Today February 14th is St Valentine's Day, a holiday that for many signifies nothing more than the obligation to buy flowers and chocolates. The roots of Valentine's Day go deeper. February 14th marked the first day of the Lupercalia. The day honored Juno, in her fertility aspect, and the male spirit Faunus, or Lupercus. On February 14th, Juno and Faunus respond to women's pleas for fertility.

The annual festival opened with the arrival of the Luperci, Faunus' "wolf-priests," at the Lupercal, the cave on the Palatine Hill where the wolf nursed Romulus and Remus. Dogs were sacrificed for purification, goats for fertility. These were eaten by the priests.

Following the priests' meal, the goatskins were cut up. The Luperci smeared themselves with the blood and dressed themselves in "Juno's cloak," the torn patches of goatskin. Pieces of goatskin were formed into whips, known as a *februa*. Either the priests or specially chosen young boys would then run around the Palatine Hill striking at people with these whips, particularly barren women. Women struck by the februa were believed to be rendered fertile. Conception was believed ensured as was easy childbirth and healthy babies. Women positioned themselves strategically around the hill to guarantee that they would be struck, usually upon their outstretched hands.

Mabon

Pronounced "may-bon."

Mabon coincides with the autumn equinox, approximately September 21st. Day and night are temporarily equal; it is considered a time for contemplation and reflection. According to the old Celtic calendar, Mabon was the "second harvest" following Lughnasa. It is a harvest festival in the manner of traditional Thanksgiving harvests. Mabon is the time to honor the trees. Its symbol is the cornucopia.

It is among the more difficult feasts for modern people to appreciate; it is more than just acknowledgement of the equinox and the coming of the winter season. This festival was a crucial spiritual experience for those responsible for gathering their own food, whether through the seasonal harvest or the seasonal slaughter. Food production was once a communal activity; in essence, the harvest, whether flora or fauna, sacrifices their lives so that people can live. Mabon is the festival of thanksgiving and purification that attempts to maintain vital spiritual balance.

The name "Mabon" derives from a hunting deity, the child of Modron. Modron and Mabon may be titles, rather than names. Modron is believed to mean "mother" or "divine mother." Mabon may mean "young man" or "son."

Mabon is simultaneously the youngest and oldest of souls. He is eternally young and embodies male fertility. Reminiscent of stories of changelings, Mabon was stolen from Modron three days after birth and disappeared for many years; he is believed to have been held captive in the otherworld. Mabon fades into the afterworld at Samhain to emerge in spring, a male counterpart to Persephone.

May Eve

See also Beltane, Floralia, and Walpurgis.

Earth's innate sexual energy and forces are at their height on May Eve. The intent of this festival is to celebrate these forces and partake of their power. If May Eve could be characterized in one word, it would be "joy" or perhaps "ecstasy." Traditional rituals include bonfires, dancing around a maypole, gathering May morning dew and the crowning of a May Queen and sometimes also a king.

The May festival is a time for romance. Prohibitions against getting married in May (allegedly it's unlucky) didn't exist prior to Christianity. The month of May was eventually dedicated to Mary and thus to chastity. May was traditionally understood as time of rampant sexuality. Babies conceived at May Day will, if brought to full term, be born around Candlemas/Imbolc. Children born on May Day can allegedly see and converse with fairies.

Although May Eve is a fire festival complete with bonfires, it was also a water festival. Special herbal baths were known as "May Baths." Sometimes these were solitary but other times communal or group celebratory rituals.

On May Day, the radiant sun emerges to celebrate with its beautiful bride, the flower bedecked Earth. Although sex was never as indiscriminate as the Church alleged, sexual activity was once part of May Eve traditions. It is a festival that celebrates sexual energy as well as the potential for fertility (see Floralia, page 201). Sex was understood as a sacrament. By coordinating sexual activity with that of the world's male and female principles (the Sun and the Earth or fire and water) magical energy was generated, which was believed beneficial to individual participants and also to all of creation, to the whole Earth and thus to the entire community. Sex was not perceived as potentially sinful but as potentially holy.

Once upon a time, *really* way back when, major festivals were the only times when different tribes would rendezvous and intermingle. Perhaps the seeds that would eventually become distorted in witch-hunters' fantasies of orgiastic sabbats were first laid here. Throngs of people would converge at crossroads (there weren't many other roads!) or places of power; no need for a written calendar, if one follows the sun, the equinoxes, solstices and the days related to them are simple ones of which to keep track. It was the time to meet and greet and for what still exist as "marriage fairs." These were crucial because everyone within a small, closely knit tribe might be closely related; in terms of the need for genetic variety, these festivals were the time to find a mate, whether permanently or temporarily. Traditions lingered long after the technical need existed.

Communities would elect a King and Queen of the May who embodied the best of the male and female principles. The Maypole represents the unification of female and male energies; it marks Earth's pregnancy. May Day also contains vestiges of old tree worship—as demonstrated most obviously by the Maypole, a survival of tree worship and old phallic cults. The Maypole was once burned after the completion of festivities, similar to the Yule log. Ashes were kept as amulets for fertility.

Dancing around the Maypole, together with singing and feasting, are all traditional components of May Day. Special aromatic beer and May Wine are often part of the festivities.

May Eve is the night when witches traditionally gather to dance and celebrate. Conversely their enemies know where to find them. Perhaps the custom of marking the holiday by dressing children as witches began as a cover; if everyone is dressed as a witch, then it can be difficult to determine which are the real ones.

In some cases tables were turned and May Eve festivities were intended to ward off, rout out, harm or even permanently eliminate witches.

Midsummer's Eve or St John's Eve

Midsummer's Eve was originally intended to coincide with the summer solstice, the day when the Sun enters the sign of Cancer, the astrological sign that belongs to the moon, and Earth's magical forces are at their height. Midsummer's Eve is a major holiday for witches and those who love them. Because fixed calendars came into existence, Midsummer's, especially in its guise as the Feast of John the Baptist, does not necessarily correspond exactly with the solstice. (The solstice moves; the Feast doesn't.) Modern Neo-Pagans, however, frequently coordinate Midsummer's with the solstice and so this festival may be celebrated anytime, depending upon place, traditions, and participants, from approximately June 20th through the 24th. A wild anarchic joyous festival, the ancients would have had no objection to it lingering for three or four days.

Midsummer's Eve is a fire *and* a water festival characterized by ritual baths and bonfires. Bonfires are built upon carefully selected magical wood with special aromatic herbs thrown into the fires. The ashes are later preserved as amulets. Bonfires are built on the shores of lakes, rivers, streams, and oceans. Just as livestock is driven between or around bonfires, so they were once driven into the sea to be buffeted by spiritually cleansing and magically empowering waves.

Midsummer's marks the convergence of Sun and Moon. The sun is at its zenith but the zodiac has entered the watery sign of Cancer, the only sign ruled by the Moon. Children born during this 30-day period are known as Moon Children. Lunar deities like Artemis, Diana, and Hecate have powerful associations with fire and water as well as botanical magic.

Midsummer's is considered the absolute optimal moment for harvesting magical and medicinal plants. Plants are ideally picked at midnight or when the first dew forms. (Rolling in the dew is believed beneficial for people, too.) Special, unique plants such as the fern seed that provides invisibility are available only on this night. Witch-hunters claimed that this was the night witches rode off to join Satan; witches, on the other hand, claimed that this was the night they congregated to celebrate the Earth and to harvest botanicals for the coming year's spells. According to the tenets of Russian witchcraft, the most powerful botanicals in the world are ritually harvested on Midsummer's Eve atop Bald Mountain.

This is the time to stay out all night reveling and then gather plants before calling it a night. It is a magical time for divination, communing with the spirits, and finding true love—or at the very least romance, flirtation, and fun.

Although Midsummer's Eve was Christianized as St John's Eve, this is perhaps the church holiday with the thinnest veneer. In Siberia a popular name for St John's Day is *Ivan Travnik* (John the Herbalist) or *Ivan Koldovnik* (John the Magician).

In Denmark, Midsummer's Eve has been celebrated since at least the time of the Vikings and is associated with Odin. Healers gathered their botanical supplies for the year on this night. Bonfires were lit, a tradition that survives today, however, visits to healing springs were once incorporated into the festival as well. Bonfires are still sometimes built on beaches. In Scandinavia, "maypoles" are sometimes erected at Midsummer's instead.

Midsummer's Eve bonfires and water celebrations were particularly beloved in Mediterranean regions. Midsummer's pre-dates Christianity and Islam, and although the later associations have diverged from each other (on the Mediterranean's southern shore, in Muslim Algeria, Morocco, and Tunisia, the festival is identified with Fatima, the Prophet's daughter rather than with John the Baptist), the rituals and associated botanicals are virtually identical on either side of the sea.

John the Baptist is much venerated by Freemasons. There is a tremendous Masonic component in Vodoun. In Haiti, John the Baptist is considered among the lwa; his feast day is celebrated with bonfires, ritual bathing and ceremonial. Whether these celebrations arrived in Louisiana from Haiti, directly from France or even perhaps directly from Africa are unknown.

The most important annual New Orleans ceremonial during Marie Laveau's time was held on St John's Eve at the Bayou St John, the natural waterway which once connected Lake Pontchartrain, popularly known as St John's Lake, with the Mississippi River and the heart of the Vieux Carré. When these ceremonials began is unknown. Marie Laveau presided over St John's Eve ceremonials at the Bayou St John for years. (See **HALL OF FAME:** Marie Laveau.) Celebrations included bonfires, ritual bathing, ancient snake rites, drumming, dancing, singing, and a communal meal. Once secret and forbidden, the festival's reputation (and remember, ostensibly at least this is an official Church-sanctioned feast, although certain practices—those snakes!—were consistently condemned) spread and by 1831, the Pontchartrain Railroad began running special cars to the lake for the festivities for tourists and spectators, not for the participants.

Eventually St John's Eve Voodoo celebrations became a tourist attraction. Tourists, non-practitioners, and observers came to watch, not to participate. Eventually tourist shows began to be staged for which fees were charged. Once again, it became necessary to hold true ceremonials in private. Post Civil War, the tourist fascination with Voodoo culture waned, resulting in periods of great oppression. By the late 1890s, private ceremonies as well as St John's Eve celebrations at Lake Pontchartrain were routinely broken up by police.

Ostara

See also Easter.

Ostara is the Anglo-Saxon spelling of the name of the Germanic deity of spring, whose celebration closely coincides with the vernal equinox. Among her sacred attributes are rabbits, painted eggs, babies, and children. Although "Ostara" and "Easter" are merely slight variations on the same name, Ostara still holds Pagan resonance and lacks the profound identification with Christianity that Easter has; Ostara is the name most frequently used by Neo-Pagans. It names one of the Wiccan sabbats.

Celebrations and rituals of Ostara correspond with Pagan Easter practices. Further details will be found in the entry for Easter.

Sabbat

The word "sabbat" has two completely different definitions that are only tangentially related. When one hears or reads the word it is important to distinguish which meaning is intended.

* ✳ *Witch-hunters used the term to refer to mass gatherings of witches. Witch-hunters spun fantastic tales about what occurred at these sabbats that distort or have little, if any, relationship to true witchcraft practices.*

* ✳ *Modern Wicca has reclaimed the word and uses it to refer to eight holy days marking the Wheel of the Year. The four major sabbats are Beltane, Lughnasa, Samhain, and Imbolc. The four minor sabbats are Mabon, Yule, Litha, and Ostara.*

> It is crucial to emphasize that witch-hunters' fantasies may have had little to do with witchcraft practices of their own time. Their fantasies have *nothing* to do with modern witchcraft or with Wicca.

Because the two definitions are so different, they are addressed separately, in historical order.

Witch-hunters' Sabbats

At its most bare-bones definition, the pre-Gardnerian definition of a witches' sabbat indicated a mass convergence of witches. When considering the "witches' sabbat" it is almost impossible to determine what's real and what stems from the witch-hunters' fears, prejudices, and fantasies. Virtually the only surviving descriptions and information regarding European witchcraft and post-Christian Pagan practices derives from witch-hunters' records. To put this in modern context, it is as if knowledge of achievements by those of African-derived ancestry was dependent on records written by the Aryan Nations, Ku Klux Klan or similar white supremacist organizations. It is as if the only information regarding thousands of years of Jewish history were written by Nazis. And yet, regarding European witchcraft that is what there is. Nothing can be taken entirely at face value. One must constantly analyze, weigh the motivation and read between the lines.

Did magicians and devotees of ancient spiritual traditions gather secretly in remote areas such as caves, forests, mountain tops or swamps? If they did, wouldn't they do so on magically charged nights like the equinoxes or solstices or those periods when the veil dividing the realms is at its most permeable?

The very name "sabbat" is an invention of the Inquisition. Nothing indicates that witches ever used that word until it was introduced by the Inquisition. It is not a coincidence that "sabbat" sounds amazingly similar to the Jewish "sabbath." They are frequently spelled identically, with the final "h" or without. (English spelling wasn't formalized until quite late.) The spelling "sabbat" is used exclusively here, as it is in modern Wicca, to avoid confusion and demonstrate that only witchcraft is being discussed.

Attempts were made by the Church to associate witchcraft and sorcery with Jews or vice-versa; defiant, disobedient people who refused to accept Christianity were initially all lumped together. Before witches had "sabbats" the Church claimed they had "synagogues." This was not intended as a compliment or as acknowledgement of witchcraft as religion. During the Middle Ages, official Christianity considered the beliefs and rites of Jews to be the absolute height of perversion. (After Jews were banished from many regions, the spotlight would be turned on witches.) To call something a "synagogue" or "sabbat" was intended as a vile insult.

In the Middle Ages, Church authorities used the term "synagogue" to describe any gathering of heretics; it was widely used by judges and inquisitors until the late sixteenth century. Sabbat, used as a synonym, became exclusively identified with conventions of witchcraft.

Sabbat was but the most popular of the many names for conventions of witches. Scholarly synonyms included *sagarum synagoga* and *strigiarum conventus*. Popular synonyms included

✳ *Akelarre:* a Basque term deriving from *akerra* or "billy goat"
✳ *Hexentanz:* German for "witches' ball"
✳ *Striaz, striazzo* and *stregozzo:* Italian terms for meetings of witches

---

According to witch-hunt trial records, the general format of witches' sabbats is as follows:

✳ *Male and female witches gather en masse at night, usually in remote or solitary places.*

✳ *Although sometimes the staging arena is a local cave or forest, in many cases, particularly for major, very well-attended sabbats, the location was distant and remote. Participants couldn't realistically get there and back in the time allotted, usually overnight. Thus witches were said to "fly" to sabbats using different methods including ointments, transformation, vehicles like broomsticks, on animals or on hag-ridden victims.*

✳ *The witch-hunters' sabbat is presided over by a male devil or demon. First-timers must renounce the Christian faith and offer homage to the devil, who appears in various forms, human or animal.*

✳ *Then there's a big party: dancing, feasting, orgies. Before leaving, the witches receive a gift (sort of like a goody-bag) of evil ointments, especially ointments enabling them to return or to commit maleficarum (evil witchcraft).*

Negative stereotypes feature prominently in descriptions of sabbats including indiscriminate, incestuous orgies, killing babies, and ritual cannibalism, especially of babies. (Abortion wars may be at play here; images that depict women bringing baskets of dead babies to lay at the devil's feet could serve as modern anti-choice propaganda.)

Divinity is worshipped in the form of an animal; devotees copulate with the devil, often in the form of an animal, most frequently a goat, donkey, black cat or dog. They pay him homage in grotesque, obscene, sexually charged fashion.

When did sabbats allegedly take place?

The answer depends upon which trial transcript one depends upon. There are many variations.

Sabbats were held weekly for the local coven or community. Fourteenth-century depositions from Toulouse emphasize that sabbats were held on Friday evenings, similar to Jewish devotionals. The Basque *akelarre* was usually held on Friday evenings, as allegedly were Italian witches' sabbats. Why? All kinds of possibilities exist:

✳ *because of attempts to defame witches by associating them with Jews?*

✳ *because of attempts to defame Jews by associating them with witches?*

❋ because Friday belongs to the Goddess of Love?

❋ because Christ was crucified on a Friday and so this was the utmost disrespect?

There were also seasonal, ceremonial sabbats, three or four times a year, the equivalent of High Holy Days, when witches journeyed from far and wide. Meetings at the Brocken on Walpurgis or Midsummer's may be understood in this context. (See **PLACES:** The Brocken.)

> Witches' sabbats were *always* nocturnal and *always* ended at daybreak. The rooster crows and witches disperse. Before there were notions of Dracula and blood-sucking bats, the word "vampire" was used in the Balkans to refer to witches. The legend that vampires must hide from sunlight and that their power is broken at dawn may derive from this concept.

Where do witch-hunters say witches convene? At crossroads, cemeteries, and ruins (and what ruins were these? Frequently old Pagan sites; ruins were often all that was left of previously sacred places); in the woods, in a cave, sometimes at the foot of the gallows, in the churchyard (which typically serves as graveyard, hallowed ground for the faithful), sometimes even inside the Church. Huge, major sabbats were held in far-away remote areas, typically high mountain peaks like Bald Mountain, the Blokula or The Brocken. Many of these places are genuine Pagan sites or areas that witches would value as magically charged. (And not everyone understands the cemetery to be a threatening place. Those who venerate their ancestors will find comfort there.) Nothing indicates that witches didn't meet at night.

Upon what, if anything, did the witch-hunters base their distorted notions of the sabbat? Survival of the Bacchanalia? Survival of other Pagan rites? Resentment that other people were indulging in parties? Quite possibly.

How did the witches know when to attend the sabbats? According to witch-hunt era legend, witches and sorcerers have a small mark (sometimes described as "blue") somewhere on their body, which tingles or throbs at Satan's summons. (This image was evoked in *Harry Potter and the Goblet of Fire* in the death-eater's mark.)

If all the superimposed demonology is stripped away, what did witches actually do at sabbats?

They feasted. What did they eat at those sabbat feasts? According to trial transcripts, menus varied depending upon location; however, allegedly the following was served:

❋ in Alsace: fricassee of bats

❋ in England: roast beef and beer

❋ in Germany: sliced turnips, allegedly as a parody of the host

❋ in Lancashire: mutton, best if stolen

❋ in Savoy: roasted children

❋ in Spain: exhumed corpses, preferably close relatives

Regardless of what they ate, prisoners generally told their inquisitors that the food was cold and tasteless, presumably so that they wouldn't feel bad about not being invited to the party. A point is typically made that salt was omitted, as it is when offerings are made to *djinn* or fairies.

Attendees sang special songs, known as *"Litanies of the Sabbat."* During the late Middle

Ages, witches allegedly sang lists of angels, cherubim, seraphim, spirits, demons, and so forth requesting compassion, generosity, and mercy. It is fascinating to compare these songs to the contemporaneous sorcerer's practice of commanding and compelling spirits. A similar type of litany may be heard in the New Orleans musician Dr John's recording "*Litanie des Saints*," which he describes in the CD liner notes as a mixture of Gris-Gris, Voodoo, Catholic, and African religions. These medieval witches' litanies may also be understood as the practice of simply listing names of spirits, a practice which survives among modern goddess-devotees as a way of honoring spirits and keeping them alive. Sometimes the only surviving aspect of a spirit or deity is an unforgotten name.

According to witch-hunters' fantasies, it's not enough for the witches to eat, drink, and be merry at sabbats. That's not bad enough. They must also mock and desecrate Christian rites.

One can actually observe this process during witch-trial transcripts. The witches initially discuss fairies or their equivalent. The witch-hunters aren't interested. They're theologians, sometimes men of science. Old wives' tales don't hold their attention, any more than they would a modern scientist. They have bigger theological fish to fry: they desire heresy. Under pressure and torture, the fairies eventually evolve into demons.

This is clearly seen in Isobel Gowdie's testimony. Isobel Gowdie is famed as the Scottish woman who, for whatever reason, voluntarily confessed to witchcraft. She initially describes fairies. Her inquisitors were bored and dissatisfied with this. Her Fairy Queen soon emerges as a male devil.

According to early modern Hungarian witch-craft-trial transcripts, somewhat less influenced by demonology than many other regions, the sabbat might better be described as a witches' party or ball, a gathering characterized by fun and merriment, attended by witches, their spirit doubles and/or spellbound victims. (Hungarian witch trials liberally feature accusations of kidnapping by witches. Witches transport the victims to sabbats and other locations.)

Hungarian and Italian women who were accused of journeying to sabbats described beautiful fairy-like sabbats, full of music, dance, and sensuality. Wonderful food and drink is served, better than daily reality. Their sabbats are pleasure dreams, not nightmares. Going to the sabbat was akin to a trip to fairyland, reminiscent of the fairy tale "The Twelve Dancing Princesses," where the girls slip out at night to revel so hard in magical underground grottoes that their shoes wear out.

Sabbats of Modern Wicca

Witch-hunters' descriptions of sabbats have no relevance to modern practice. In Wiccan parlance, Sabbat is the term for eight seasonal festivals, marking the Wheel of the Year based on the ancient Celtic calendar.

The four great fire festivals include Imbolc, Beltane, Lughnasa, and Samhain. Samhain marks the beginning of the dark half of the year, the descent into winter. Beltane marks the beginning of the light half. These are the two portals of the year, birth and death. (Interestingly ancient Babylonian astrology also contains portals of birth and death, corresponding respectively to the Summer Solstice and the Winter Solstice, which correspond to the witchcraft celebrations of Midsummer's and Yule.) Imbolc marks the quickening, the first approach of spring. Lughnasa marks the sacrifice of the harvest, the preparations for winter.

Mabon, Yule, Ostara, and Litha are frequently described as the lesser sabbats, although some traditions do consider all of equal importance. Each of the eight sabbats is discussed within its own entry.

Samhain

Pronounced "Sow'en." Corresponds in time to Halloween.

Samhain translates prosaically as "summer's end." It marks the end of the light half of the Celtic year and the beginning of the dark half. The border between years is distinguished by the lack of the border between worlds.

> The notion of the year being split into dark and bright halves isn't limited to Celtic areas. In Russia, for instance, the dark half of the year belongs to the spirits. It's the perfect time for story-telling, magic, and divination, culminating with May Day.

The Celtic New Year begins at nightfall on October 31st—the beginning of the Gaulish month Samonios, the first month of the year. The veil between realms may be penetrated. Barrow wights, ghosts, fairies, and other spirits roam through the night. According to Irish tradition, the barrows and mounds where the fairies dwell open up on Samhain so that the fairies can come out to revel. And so, what kind of spirit-working witch would wish to stay home, at least unless she was occupied by rituals there?

Although modern Halloween celebrations and Neo-Pagan Samhain are based largely upon traditions of Ireland and Britain, there is no reason not to think that similar commemorations didn't exist throughout Celtic-influenced Europe, if only because the Church felt it important enough to create the Feast of All Saints to substitute for these concurrent festivals of the dead. It is a Breton custom to pour libations over gravestones and tombs at this time.

Metaphysics aside, Samhain was also an ancient Celtic pastoral festivity. It signaled the end of the grazing season, when only breeding stock was set aside from the end-of-the-year slaughter. The harvest was brought in at this time. There is an Irish superstition that crops left out after November 1st would be spoiled by the fairies. (Although perhaps this camouflages an older belief that crops left out after November 1st *belonged* to the fairies and hence were no longer safe to be touched.)

This may have been a time of sacrifice for the Irish Druids. Some suggest that human sacrifice may once have occurred at this time but there's no way of currently knowing whether that was ever true or whether that information is based on attempts to defame and discredit the Druids. Horses were also once allegedly sacrificed.

According to legend, the Irish deities the Dagda and the Morrigan consummate their relationship today to ensure the fertility of land, people, and animals for the year to come. The Dagda, "the good god," is the tribal father god; the Morrigan, "the phantom queen," is often described as a "battle goddess" although that only hints at her powers. She begins the Great Rite in the form of an old hag but is rejuvenated by the union, regaining her youth and beauty.

A false suggestion is frequently made that the holiday is named in honor of a deity named Samhain. There is no such deity, however a French statuette identifies Cernunos, the horned Celtic deity with the Roman deity Dis,

Lord of the Underworld. It's possible that he was worshipped at Samhain.

the three Spirit Nights

In Welsh tradition, these are the nights when all kinds of spirits and denizens of various other realms are free to ramble and roam around Earth. If you wish to rendezvous with them or you have some practical business involving these spirits, the three spirit nights provide your maximum opportunity: May Eve; Midsummer's Eve and Halloween.

time of Day

Some points of the day are more powerful than others.

At certain moments or times the thresholds between realms are more tenuous and more easily penetrated:

✳ *Noon: the precise moment at midday when the sun passes from East to West.*

✳ *Geisterstunde, "The Hour of Spirits": in certain areas of Germany, this is the hour between 11 p.m. and midnight, excellent for magic and divination.*

✳ *Midnight, the Witching Hour.*

✳ *The Hour of the Wolf: despite the name, this isn't one precise moment but the wee still hours after midnight but before dawn when sounds, emotions, and dreams are magnified in power.*

There are those who believe that the hour immediately proceeding midnight, culminating at the stroke of 12, is ideal for benevolent magic, while the hour immediately following is the most powerful for magical spells stemming from anger and a fierce desire for justice.

twelve Nights of Christmas

See also Yule.

The famous Christmas carol celebrates the gifts given on each of the twelve days of Christmas. Witches celebrate during the twelve nights. Ever wonder *why* the Wild Hunt rides at Christmas time?

According to ancient Celtic, German, Greek, Roman, and Slavic calendars, a gap in time occurs in midwinter for twelve nights, which now correspond to the Twelve Nights of Christmas. This period begins with what is now Christmas Eve and continues until what is now the Feast of the Epiphany.

During this period, there's a gap, a void where the veil between realms is particularly thin or even non-existent. During these twelve days and nights, the dead roam the Earth and the Spirits join together with their devotees.

Known in Germanic lands as the "*Zwölften*" or "*Twolven*," this was the time when Woden and Frigg held forth.

The Twelve Nights are a wild, raucous time devoted to merry-making, gift-giving, masquerading, divination, spell-casting, and magic ritual. Festivities during this period once had more in common with Valentine's Day or romantic Halloween celebrations than with modern conventional, staid Christmas devotions.

See **DIVINE WITCH**: Odin.

Walpurgis

See also Floralia, May Day, and Beltane.

Walpurgisnacht, Walpurgis Night, is the Germanic celebration of May Eve. Walpurga is a Germanic woman's name, sometimes given as Walburga or Waldborg. The earliest Walpurga was a spirit or goddess. Walpurga manifests as a beautiful white lady with long flowing hair wearing a crown and fiery shoes. She carries a spindle and a three-cornered mirror that reveals the future. Her memory survives in the popularity of spindles and thread used in divination and love spells on the night named in her honor.

Once upon a time, Walpurga was involved in rituals intended to evade the forces of winter and allow the emergence of summer. For nine days before May Day, the Wild Hunt pursues Walpurga. She is their quarry. Walpurga, in turn, seeks refuge among local villagers who leave their doors and windows open so that the Lady of Summer can find safety from frost. According to one legend, Walpurga begged a farmer to hide her from the Wild Hunt in his stack of grain, which he does, not realizing she's the goddess. By the next morning, she's gone but he finds grains of gold sprinkled amongst his rye crop.

Under Christian influence, Walpurga's Night eventually transformed into a time to drive out the forces of Paganism rather than the forces of winter. In the eighth century, Walpurgis Night was remade into a holiday honoring a saint, not a goddess or summer.

St Walpurga or Walburga, the niece of St Boniface, was an English abbess who founded religious houses in Germany during the eighth century, and is believed to have been born in approximately 710 in Wessex. She became a missionary-abbess in St Boniface's church and presided over a community of nuns in the German town of Heidenham. This Walpurga was canonized as an official saint of the Church following her death in 779.

After St Walpurga's body was interred at Eichstadt, miracle-working oil is said to have begun to trickle from her tomb. Her relics were eventually distributed amongst various churches across Europe. St Walpurga assumed many of the functions of Pagan Walpurga. She offers protection against plague, famine, crop failures, and the bites of rabid dogs. The matron saint of the city of Antwerp, St Walpurga is often depicted carrying a sheaf of grain. Above all, St Walpurga protects and defends against witchcraft.

German witches defied her by riding to their sabbats on the night before her feast day on May 1st. Villagers lit bonfires that night, allegedly to prevent the witches from landing. Others shot guns into the air so as to blast witches. According to Pagan tradition, residences and barns were ornamented with certain special May Eve botanicals. Once upon a time, these plants carried the powerful blessings of witch-deities. Ornamentation with these same botanicals continued post-Christianity, only now, allegedly, these identical plants warded off witchcraft and prevented witches from visiting.

❋ *Elder wood was hidden in barns or homes ostensibly to protect against witchcraft, although the original reasons for these practices may be forgotten.*

❋ *Others placed alder branches against their home to keep witches away on Walpurgis Night. (Alder is known as the Walpurgis tree.)*

* *Ground ivy* (Glechoma hederacea *or* Nepeta hederacea) *allegedly breaks magic spells. It's woven into garlands and worn on Walpurgis to protect from witches with evil intent.*

Walpurgis Night was the witches' major sabbat. Mass convergences of witches allegedly took place on high mountain peaks identified with the witch goddess Freya.

Yule

The ancient Germanic calendar was divided into six periods of 60 days each, known as *tides*. Each tide was the equivalent of two modern months. Yuletide refers to the two-month tide corresponding to modern December and January. The winter solstice falls within this period, as does the 12-day period commemorated as the Twelve Days of Christmas. Similar to Halloween or the February Feasts of Purification, the veil between realms is thin during this time and ghosts and spirits walk the land.

Yule may be defined either of several ways:

* *as the Nordic Pagan festival that once began at the Winter Solstice*

* *as an alternative name for Christmas; those who use that name tend to emphasize Pagan survivals within Christmas, however not necessarily to the exclusion of Christian elements. This Yule begins on the evening of December 24th, regardless of the specific timing of the Solstice.*

* *as the modern Wiccan sabbat that corresponds to the Winter Solstice*

The word "Yule" may derive from the name of a Nordic festival. Juleiss was the name of the Gothic month of celebrations and fun. In Dutch, "*joelen*" means loud, fun, raucous partying. (My Dutch source suggests that *joelen* is what the crowd does during a football match!) Yule may also derive from the Anglo-Saxon word for "wheel," commemorating the cutting and rolling of the Yule log.

Christmas is permeated with Pagan traditions. The period of time beginning with the Winter Solstice and continuing for at least the next twelve days was a popular time for festivals in the pre-Christian world. Many traditions and rituals have since been absorbed into the Christian celebrations.

These December festivals included:

* *The Nordic festival of Yule. Its elements included the yule log, the yule boar, and devotion to evergreen trees. Odin, the shaman god, sometimes resembles the jolly gift-giver alternately known as Santa Claus, Father Christmas or Old Saint Nick. Odin studied shamanism with the neighboring Saami and perhaps learned something about herding reindeer, too. Although Odin isn't the elven king—that's Freyr's job—the elves and Odin do come from the same territory.*

* *The Saturnalia and the Feast of Ops: the Roman festival in honor of Father Time, also known as Saturn, and his consort Ops. For the Romans, Saturn was king of an ancient "golden age" of perfect happiness, before people had to farm for a living. His festival looks back to that early age with nostalgia. The Saturnalia celebrated the solstice and sought to protect winter-sown crops, but above all the Saturnalia was a joyous, merry festival characterized by gift-giving, especially to children. The Saturnalia counts among the wild, anarchic festivals. There are rituals to encourage fertility. Gambling and gaming was encouraged; cross-dressing was popular. Social distinctions were reversed, so for a few days a slave could be master.*

The ancient deity Saturn also bears something of a resemblance to that white-bearded old gentleman, Good Saint Nick.

✳ *The Rural or Lesser Dionysia: allegedly the most ancient of the Greek festivals honoring Dionysus. Held at the very beginning of January, on this day even slaves enjoyed freedom. A procession was held which included a goat bearing a basket filled with raisins. An erect wooden pole carved to resemble a phallus and decorated with ivy was carried in the procession too.*

✳ *The Mothers' Night: a Germanic midwinter festival associated with the Norse deity Odin. According to the monk, historian, and scholar the Venerable Bede (c. 672–May 25, 735 CE) the Mothers' Night corresponded in time with Christmas Eve and was the most important Pagan festival in eighth-century Britain. Little information about the holiday survives. Mothers were apparently honored as were perhaps the ancient European deities known as the* Matronae *or "The Mothers." Divination was practiced at this time. Dreams on this night were believed to reveal the future.*

In Russia, the season coinciding with Christmas was a time traditionally celebrated with cross-dressing, dressing as animals, masking and mumming.

December is a time for dancing, singing, and feasting, a time when men masquerade as animals and especially as the Horned God. The Horned One carries a small broom of birch twigs with which to generate and enhance fertility power. His face is blackened with soot or charcoal dust so that he looks as if he's come down the chimney. (It's meant to emphasize his fertility and immortality, similar to the way ancient Egyptians painted Osiris black when they wished to emphasize his resurrection from the dead and the immortal life he had achieved.)

These wild defiant celebrations found their place within Christmas. To this day conservative evangelical Christians discourage Pagan elements within the holiday, suggesting that followers "put the Christ back into Christmas." Until fairly recently, Christmas, and particularly these Pagan elements, was considered somewhat disreputable. It was once considered a wild and raucous holiday, which the defiant, anarchist forces of Earth attempted to dominate.

The New England Puritans refused to celebrate Christmas, for instance, while, in 1801, the Pennsylvania House of Representatives forbade masquerading at Yule. The punishment was to be no more than three months imprisonment *and* a fine between $50 and $1000, which was an incredibly large sum of money in those days. And in 1881, Philadelphia law banned Christmas Eve masquerading. (Not a problem; revelers simply moved their festivities to New Year's Eve. Many customs now associated with New Year's Eve were once identified with Christmas.)

Why? What were people doing?

Celebrations of the Horned One, excised from May Day, Midsummer's and especially Halloween, survive at Christmas time. This is particularly apparent in the parts of Europe where Father Christmas has an official helper, like Black Pete or Krampus. Santa Claus himself may be the Horned One, albeit now in a padded suit. (See **HORNED ONE:** Krampus.) German immigrants to the United States formed a sizable community in the state of Pennsylvania. They brought their raucous Yule traditions with them.

In addition to Santa and his helpers, Pagan elements of Yule include:

✳ *The Christmas Tree: this is a survival of ancient devotion to trees. An evergreen, symbol of eternal life, is decorated, honored, and feted. Whether the* ancients would have approved of chopping down so many trees during this season is subject to debate.

❋ The Yule Log: a log (or at least a large chunk of one) is decorated and burned on the Eve of the Solstice. To put this in context, one must recall that Pagan goddesses, including Diana and Hera, were once worshipped in the form of a piece of log. The modern Yule log has powerful associations with Frigg, who is married to Odin. The Yule log is incorporated into fertility spells as well as in spells for protection. The ashes or charred bits of wood are preserved until the following Yule. The "buche-noelle" is a cake shaped to resemble a Yule log. The Yule log is often cut from a yew tree and some believe that the name "yule" derives from "yew."

❋ The Yule animal, the boar or male pig, commemorates the sacrificial boar offered to Freyr in winter. Whole roast pig is the traditional Yule feast in some regions. In Sweden, yuletide cakes are still baked in the shape of a boar. In Britain, pink hard candy pigs were once customarily presented following the Yule feast. Smashed with a hammer, the pig broke into bits so that there was a piece of the "sacrifice" for everyone at table.

❋ Have we mentioned mistletoe? The golden bough is hung over thresholds with scarlet ribbons. According to tradition, should a couple of people find themselves simultaneously under the mistletoe, they must kiss. (Much maneuvering may be spent getting people underneath the mistletoe …)

Witches play their part during Yule time too.

❋ The witch Befana gives children in Italy gifts on Christmas Day, much as Santa Claus or Father Christmas is the primary gift-giver elsewhere in the world. Befana flies on a broom or arrives riding a donkey.

❋ The German witch Lutzelfrau prefers to receive gifts. In a Yuletide version of "trick or treat" Lutzelfrau flies through the air on her broom creating havoc in the homes that have neglected to honor her with small offerings.

❋ In parts of Austria and Germany, children celebrate Christmas by going door-to-door wearing masks and costumes (frequently but not always conforming to the stereotype of ugly witches) and carrying brooms. They beg small treats in the name of the witch-goddess Perchta.

❋ Various witch-goddesses including Perchta, Hulda, Herta, and Freya lead the Wild Hunt at this time of year, sometimes in conjunction with Odin (who may or may not be the male Pagan deity who hides under the mask of Father Christmas).

See also **ANIMALS:** Pig; **BOTANICALS:** Mistletoe; **DICTIONARY:** Wild Hunt; **DIVINE WITCH:** Befana; Freya; Herta; Hulda; Odin; Perchta.

✪ Creative Arts

For as long as there have been creative arts, witches and witchcraft have served as inspiration for those various arts and continue to do so at an ever-increasing rate. Witches have *always* served as creative muse, one way or another, although how witches and their craft have been interpreted and depicted depends upon era, culture, and often the individual artist's inclinations.

Should one attempt to delete the presence of witches and witchcraft from the various creative arts, as some have periodically wished to do, there would be tremendous gaps: no *Macbeth*, no *Harry Potter*, *Lord of the Rings* or *Chronicles of Narnia*. The number of films that would disappear from history is almost unimaginable, as would be the number of popular songs in virtually every genre—from Frank Sinatra singing "Witchcraft" to Screamin' Jay Hawkins' "I Put A Spell On You" to that country music classic, "Under Your Spell Again."

The powerful presence of witches in the creative arts is highly appropriate as most of what are now considered "creative" arts were once also considered magical, shamanic, and spiritual arts:

✳ *Dance and music are historically powerfully rooted in shamanism and are traditionally used to cast spells, summon and banish spirits and generate magic energy, as well as to generate entertainment and fun.*

✳ *Although we don't necessarily understand them, based upon surviving imagery and location (deep within often difficult-to-access caves), the earliest known visual arts—cave paintings—were created for ritual and/or magical purposes.*

✳ *Western theatrical performance derives from the sacred rites of Dionysus; theatrical traditions from other parts of Earth derive from similar spiritual and magical roots.*

Witchcraft has inspired modern artists just as powerfully as ancient ones. Many of the earliest films were devoted to occult themes, especially witchcraft and witches. Most of the first comic-book heroes and heroines were inspired by tales of magic and sorcery. Various depictions of witchcraft flew off the presses virtually as soon as the printing press was invented—not only witch-hunters' manuals and handbooks of magic but also fictional depictions of witches. The book that is considered the first true Western novel (*La Celestina*) is named for the witch who is its central character.

Witches have inspired art but those works of art, many of which are powerful, profound, and influential, have also intensely shaped and influenced how people have perceived and understood witches, whether favorably or not. The following section of the *Encyclopedia of Witchcraft* explores some of these witches and the manner in which they have been depicted.

Witches have inspired literally countless works of art. Thousands of pages could be devoted to these witches alone; what follows is by necessity only a random sampling of some of the more significant witches who have entertained, informed, amused, thrilled, chilled, and served as role models, inspiration, and objects of fear over the ages. My apologies if I have omitted any of your favorites. Because these are creative arts, often meant to do nothing more than entertain, many of these witches by definition are not realistic but are figures of fantasy, or at least partially so. Characters identified as witches or similar magical practitioners are included, regardless of which definition of witchcraft they may fall under; in addition, creative works that feature witchcraft and what are often understood by at least some as its practices are also included.

Comics

What do most standard comic-book heroes have in common? Whatever their differences, most crusaders for justice share two aspects: super-natural powers; costumes, or at least distinctive clothing. Now who on Earth has supernatural powers? No need to invent back-stories or rationales about abandoned babies from outer space, or magic powers derived from scientific experiments gone awry: witches, sorcerers, and magicians come by their supernatural powers naturally or through education—or at least they do according to *some* definitions of witchcraft.

The first superheroes were occult practitioners. After all, who else has supernatural powers if not a witch? As for that distinctive clothing, in a sense, one can trace the roots of comic-book villains back to witch-hunt era woodcuts and illustrations created for penny-dreadfuls, intended to entertain, titillate, shock, and enthrall their audiences as much as to offer "moral instruction." (See page 314, Visual Arts: Woodcuts.) How would you identify the witch in those popular illustrations? Easy. By her distinctive clothing or, conversely, her total lack thereof. Those imaginary witches may be considered among the first cartoon villains or anti-heroes.

Exactly what are comics? At their most basic, comics are defined as an art form consisting of multiple sequential images that usually form a narrative or tell a story and that usually, but not always, incorporate written text. A single image or "panel" is defined as a cartoon, not as a comic. Those medieval woodcuts featuring images of witches cavorting with Satan may be understood as "cartoons."

Comics in the form they exist today blossomed as a phenomenon in the twentieth century. What is now nostalgically remembered as the Golden Age of Comics is usually dated as occurring between 1930 and 1951. Superman first appeared in 1938. His creators were influenced by magical stories of the Golem of Prague. Mandrake the Magician had already appeared four years earlier.

In the United States, comic books were eventually marketed exclusively to children and adolescents (this was not originally the case, nor was it the case elsewhere in the world, most notably in Japan; see Manga, page 297). On the one hand this added to the aura of worthlessness surrounding comics; on the other it also stimulated a powerful desire in some people to sanitize the genre so that it would be truly suitable for children, similar to the desire some have to clean up and child-proof fairy tales.

This was taken *very* seriously: in the United States in the 1940s and 1950s comics were popularly blamed for juvenile delinquency and "moral degradation." They were accused of glorifying crime and making heroes of seedy, shadowy, disreputable, morally ambiguous characters, occult practitioners not least among these (see The Black Widow). The United States Senate Subcommittee on Juvenile Delinquency investigated the influence of comic books. Schools and parental organizations held public comic-book burnings. Comic books were banned in some cities. Circulation of comic books declined sharply; only the tamest of comic books thrived in what may be considered the comic books' Dark Ages. They have only recently regained their mass popularity. Comics once again address metaphysical issues, feature occult practitioners, and are frequently targeted to a mature audience.

By definition, "comic-book witches," past or present, are not realistic. The entire genre of comic books is typically not a realistic medium but one devoted to fantasy and fun.

Changes in the last 50 years of metaphysical history may be tracked through comic-book heroes:

☀ *During the Golden Age of Comics, magicians invariably studied with ascended masters in Tibet. Frequently they had magical partners, disguised as valets or servants, who were really adepts from Africa or China.*

☀ *Modern comics, on the other hand, frequently feature what at least appear to be youthful female witches, flexing their magical muscles (some are secretly thousands of years old). These witches are often drawn to resemble a fantasy of what a modern practitioner of Wicca might look like, even though, again, be cautioned, this is not a reality-based genre.*

The following are but a sampling of the most popular and most significant comics incorporating witchcraft and the magical arts as major themes. There are many more. (If characters are identified as witches or as practitioners of the magical arts, I've included them, regardless which definition of "*witch*" the character fulfills.) I have also attempted to impose a semblance of consistency over the genre and to note the first appearance of the magical *character*, not necessarily of the comic book with which they are now most popularly associated. (Records are not always clear.)

The Black Widow

Marvel Comics, first appeared in 1940.

Is the Black Widow a heroine or a villain? That's a tough call. On the one hand, she dispatches villains like the finest superhero. On the other, she works directly for Satan; her mission is to kill evil-doers so that her boss can collect their souls. That scenario leads to all sorts of interesting spiritual, religious, and metaphysical speculation. The Black Widow is based on the stereotype of the witch as the tool of Satan; however, she is as much a crime-fighter and wrong-righter as Superman or any other hero.

Once upon a time, in her debut issue, Claire Voyant was an attractive psychic presiding over séances. Hired by a family wishing to contact a lost loved one, Satan insinuates himself into this séance and manipulates activities so that all but one member of the family ends up dead. During the séance, under Satan's influence, Claire issues a witch's curse. The client, who fails to understand the gravity of the situation, complains, *"I came for a séance, not a lesson in witchcraft."* When the family perishes, the sole survivor blames Claire and murders her.

Satan claims her soul and transforms her into "The Black Widow." (And is the inference that psychics and fortune-tellers, whether fraudulent or real, have sold their souls?) Like any superheroine she now sports distinctive clothing—a sexy, black spider-themed costume. The devil gives her supernatural powers, too.

Her first victim is her murderer: she materializes before him in a ball of flame. All she has to do is lay her hand on his forehead and he's dead, leaving a spider-shaped burn as the sole clue to her identity. After this act of vengeance, the Black Widow focuses on purging Earth of villains.

Perhaps not surprisingly, the Black Widow had a limited run, only appearing in a few comics. It was a pretty racy story for its time: its "heroine" reports to Hell and there is at least a visual implication of a sexual relationship between the Black Widow and the devil. Not only was Claire's costume sexy and seductive, but Satan himself, drawn as a horned red devil, was *very* obviously naked—with the exception of his scarlet cape, always strategically, arranged to hide his private parts.

Claire's final Golden Age appearance was in 1943. Although her character became dormant, the moniker "Black Widow" was too good to lie fallow. A new Black Widow, Natasha Romanoff, first appeared in 1964 and is now among Marvel Comics' most popular characters. Her story line has nothing to do with that of her predecessor.

Claire Voyant reemerged in 2008 in the limited series The Twelve, although her back-story was changed. Her occult background has been eliminated: she is no longer a medium. Instead, her desire to avenge her sister's murder caused Claire to fall permanently into Satan's clutches. Caped, naked Satan has been reduced to a pair of giant scarlet eyes.

See also **WORMWOOD**: Dangers of Witchcraft: Curses; **MAGICAL ARTS**: Divination; Necromancy.

Doctor Strange, Master of the Mystic Arts

Marvel Comics, first appeared in 1963.

Dr Stephen Strange was once a *brilliant* surgeon; however he was also cold, narcissistic, pompous, and selfish—in short, a jerk. He also had a dangerous tendency to hit the bottle a little too hard; one dark stormy night, driving while drunk out of his mind, Strange crashed his car, in the process killing his pregnant wife and unborn child and forever damaging his hands so that he's no longer able to practice his craft. His entire previously well-organized life is gone. Strange sinks deep into depression, hits the bottle even harder and ends up on the street, all the while, however, seeking for spiritual solace, direction, and resolution for his grief.

At the very end of his tether, he hears of a miracle-working cave-dwelling Tibetan lama, "The Ancient One," and goes to seek assistance. First deemed unworthy of assistance, although perhaps this was a metaphysical test, Strange gets stuck in the snows of Tibet over the winter. Through a series of circumstances, he proves himself changed for the better and the Ancient One accepts him as a student of magic, explaining to Strange that it's not his hands that are broken; it's his soul. Strange moves into the cave and begins to study the secrets of sorcery and the magic of the mystic arts, transforming into a superhero and a very popular one at that.

Strange remains a viable, vital character. In addition to sometimes starring in his own comic books, over the years he's made frequent appearances in various other series. He's evolved over the years: in 1988 he was promoted to Doctor Strange, Sorcerer Supreme. (See page 233, Witches.)

Hellblazer

Vertigo Comics, comic series first published in 1988.

The star of this comic book series, the master sorcerer John Constantine, first appeared as a character in the horror comic-book series *Swamp Thing*. He is a featured character in many graphic novels and is also featured in other Vertigo comics including *Books of Magic* and *The Sandman*. Constantine reportedly dated Zatanna while they were in college. (See Zatanna, page 233.)

Constantine has no standard super-powers similar to a conventional comic-book hero; his magical powers consist of magical skill and knowledge. This trench-coated, chain-smoking sorcerer anti-hero initially used these magical powers for unethical goals. (Chain-smoking eventually led to lung cancer; however Constantine was magically able to force the Lords of Hell to heal him.) He is still a brutal practitioner when needs-be in order to save his skin from his many enemies, however Constantine has now dedicated himself to realigning the world's balance towards good and righteousness. (Or at least away from evil.)

Constantine derives from the mold of the classic medieval sorcerer whose interests lie in demons and hell. Like Mandrake (see page 229), he is a master hypnotist; Constantine is also shown conducting séances and exorcisms and creating sigils. Constantine is a hereditary witch; his family includes a tremendously long line of occult practitioners. He began his own occult education during adolescence and is truly a master, however he is also an egotist who frequently overestimates his talents, landing him in scrapes from which he must magically extricate himself.

—

Ibis the Invincible

Fawcett Publications.

This turbaned crime-fighting master magician first appeared in 1940. With the exception of Mandrake the Magician, he was the most successful of the magician superheroes.

Once upon a time, some four thousand years ago, Ibis was the Egyptian prince Amentep, magical adept, student of the Egyptian mysteries, and next in line for the throne. He was also deeply in love with a beautiful Theban princess. All was going so well for Amentep—that is, until an evil magician known as "the Black Pharaoh" seized the throne, and Amentep's ladylove as well.

Through the use of a magic wand known as the "ibistick" Amentep transformed into the superhero Ibis the Invincible. He was able to rescue his beloved, Princess Taia, however unfortunately, in shades reminiscent of "Sleeping Beauty," the Black Pharaoh had placed her in a coma destined to last for four thousand years; a spell Ibis was unable to break. Not a problem: Ibis magically placed himself in an equivalent suspended animation. When the series begins, it's 1940 and the sleeping spell has finally worn off. The two ancient Egyptians, now mummified, discover themselves housed in separate European museums. Through his magic powers, Ibis is able to create a reunion. Once this is accomplished he dedicates himself to fighting evil with the magical ibistick. Targets include werewolves and vampires. (Later versions of the comic suggest that the ibistick is a gift from Thoth; the earliest versions suggest that it was a miscalculated gift from the Black Pharaoh.) (See **DIVINE WITCH:** Thoth.)

Mandrake the Magician

King Features.

This is where the tradition starts. In 1924, when he was 19 years old, Lee Falk first created the character Mandrake the Magician, initially drawing two weeks' worth of strips. Ten years later he sold the character to King Features, the company that is often credited with creating the modern comic.

Mandrake the Magician first appeared as a newspaper comic-strip character in 1934. The comic strip and the character were extremely successful. Mandrake was a popular phenomenon although attempts at converting the strip into comic books never matched that success. In 1939, Columbia Pictures released a 12-part serial inspired by Mandrake the Magician, starring Warren Hull (January 17, 1903–September 14, 1974) as the crime-fighting superhero. The Mandrake radio serial aired from November 11, 1940 until February 6, 1942. Originally slated as a three-day-a-week program, by 1941 it ran five days a week.

Mandrake the Magician was the first superpowered costumed crime fighter. His costume was that of a stage magician. Although he appeared to be a mere illusionist, nothing more than an entertainer, that was actually a cover for his deeper supernatural powers, in the same way that Clark Kent's career as a news hound was the front for his existence as Superman.

Mandrake set the standard for the superheroes of the future, magical or otherwise. According to the plot-line, Mandrake acquired his powers in Tibet where he had studied the magical arts since childhood. Among his teachers was one known as Luciphor, who eventually decided to use his power and knowledge for selfish purposes and was transformed into the evil "Cobra." Mandrake's faithful valet, Lothar, is really an African prince in disguise and another magical adept. (In response to changing times, over the years Lothar has transformed from employee to friend.)

Mandrake's success inspired a multitude of other similar characters including Marvelo the Monarch of Magicians, Tor the Magic Master, and perhaps most notably, Zatara the Magician. He still makes periodic appearances; in 1986 he was among the superheroes on an animated television series, *Defenders of the Earth*, alongside such stalwarts as Flash Gordon.

Sabrina the Teenage Witch

Archie Comics.

The character Sabrina the Teenage Witch first appeared in the back pages of an Archie Comics magazine in October 1962. Many characters make brief appearances and then disappear forever, however Sabrina from the start had that certain something, that *je ne sais quoi* that kept her from comic-book oblivion. A fun, youthful, lively witch with ordinary teenage problems (and some others as well) she would eventually become the most successful Archie Comics adaptation. Sabrina became a main character in 1969 but wasn't featured in her own comic book until April 1971. Since then she has been featured in various television animated cartoons before the hit live-action television series began in 1996. Since the success of the television show, the comic book has been revived frequently, with the actress Melissa Joan Hart (television's Sabrina) on the cover.

(See page 313, Television: *Sabrina the Teenage Witch*.)

The Sandman

DC Comics/Vertigo, first appeared in 1988.

There have been several comic series featuring a character named the Sandman, dating as far back as 1939. These characters and series are, at best, tangentially related. Our "The Sandman" refers to the series that began in January 1988.

The "Sandman" makes reference to the nursery rhyme character who enters bedrooms bearing "sleepy dust" and enables people, especially children, to sleep and dream. "Sandman" is the nickname for the protagonist of this comic series who is also called Dream, the Lord of Dreams, perhaps more familiar to lovers of Greek mythology as Morpheus, Lord of Dreams and grandson of Nyx. (See **DIVINE WITCH:** Nyx.) When the British writer Neil Gaiman was requested to revive the comic-book hero the Sandman (and it is important to note that comics aren't necessarily comedic), he was allowed to take the character in directions that interested him. His interests were obviously shared by many readers. What was initially intended to be limited to perhaps seven issues became immensely popular and led DC Comics to create their imprint Vertigo, which publishes

comics directed toward a mature audience, frequently featuring occult-oriented themes and more sexually and violently graphic than its child-friendly parent DC Comics.

According to the basic plot line, in 1916, the magician Roderick Burgess attempted to trap Death but catches Dream (our "Sandman") instead. Burgess resembles an Aleister Crowley-style magician. His devotees address him as "Magus." Having caught Dream, Burgess attempts to pry his secrets from him but can't. Rather than freeing him, he keeps Dream imprisoned under glass while attempting to negotiate with him. (Dream finally escapes in 1988 as the series begins.) In the meantime, Dream's absence has stimulated worldwide sleep disorders and spiritual havoc.

The series is heavily influenced by Greek mythology and has been collected into graphic novels.

The character Thessaly first appeared in Neil Gaiman's Sandman story "A Game of You." Described as the last and most powerful of the legendary Thessalian witches, Thess intrigued many readers. In 2004 she starred in her own four-part mini-series, published by Vertigo Comics, entitled *Thessaly Witch for Hire*.

The Scarlet Witch

Marvel Comics, first appeared in 1964.

The Scarlet Witch is the *nom de guerre* of Wanda Maximoff. She is a recurring character who has periodically starred in her own comic series as well as making guest appearances with other characters, including the Avengers, the X-Men, her father Magneto, and her twin brother, Quicksilver (Pietro Maximoff). Because she has been around for a long time, her back-story has evolved and changed, becoming more complex over the years. Wanda has been a heroine and a villain. Many comic-book characters and readers alike consider her the most powerful of Marvel's mutants, and she is both loved and feared.

As children, Wanda and Pietro were raised in Europe by their adoptive parents, a Romany couple, Django and Marya Maximoff, whose own two children were murdered in the Romany Holocaust of World War II. They live a nomadic life with the Gypsies, poor but content. Happiness is short-lived: when Django is caught stealing food for his starving family, villagers attack them. The parents are killed but Wanda and Pietro escape. They wander Central Europe for several years until eventually Wanda's emergent magic powers draw negative attention. In a burst of anti-witch mob violence, villagers attack Wanda and Pietro but they are saved by Magneto who brings them to America, where the twins begin their career, first with the Brotherhood of Mutants and then with the Avengers.

The Scarlet Witch is identified as a witch by her title; her early childhood was steeped in rural, traditional Romany culture and one might assume that she had picked up some magical knowledge and training. Perhaps this was the original intent of the storyline. Certainly *someone* involved in creating Wanda's back-story was a fan of Romany culture. Her adoptive father's name is a tribute to two real Gypsy heroes, the jazz guitarist Django Reinhardt and the author Mateo Maximoff. Although her powers are innate, Wanda is shown learning how to control, focus, and expand them. She studies with Agatha Harkness, another Marvel comic witch.

Wanda is both a trained witch and a mutant whose powers are genetically derived.

Wanda's powers are described as "hex-powers." (See **DICTIONARY:** Hex.) Wanda is able to accomplish the impossible 80 percent of the time using what she calls "hex-bolts" and "hex-spheres." (Her powers are found to be unreliable 20 percent of the time, which many witches would suggest is not a bad track record.) Wanda also conceives via hex-power. She believes her robot husband Vision is the father but really her desire has activated a magical pregnancy. She has twin sons, one of whom, Wiccan (Billy Kaplan) is a powerful witch in his own right.

Tarot: Witch of the Black Rose

Broadsword Comics, first appeared 2000.

The first issue of *Tarot: Witch of the Black Rose* was dedicated to the witches of the world. (Cemetery workers of the world, too!) Its eponymous heroine is named Tarot. A card-reading witch and member of the Black Rose coven, Tarot is the daughter of a long-line of hereditary witches, some of whom were burned at the stake because, in Tarot's words, *"they were proud enough to call themselves witches."*

The anti-heroine, if you will, is Tarot's sister Raven Hex, although she is no simple, ordinary villain. Raven Hex is obsessed with avenging crimes against *witchkind* and ushering in a new age, to be ruled by witches. Her goal is to vanquish those who are intolerant towards the Craft and bring prosperity to every sorceress. Sounds pretty good, huh? Unfortunately, as Tarot foresees, this plot is actually doomed to ignite new Burning Times. Tarot must secure the future for witches and the world in general.

Tarot is a beautiful, red-haired, scantily clad (when she's clad!), sexy fantasy witch with hereditary super-powers who resides in a mansion in Witch Hollow, Salem, Massachusetts. When girded for battle Tarot sports pentacles on her clothing, a majestic horned headdress, and a magic sword. Her faithful familiar Pooka is an adorable but fierce bat-winged black goblin cat.

Tarot: Witch of the Black Rose is unique and revolutionary because, while grounded in the tradition of comics as fun, entertaining, fantasy adventure it also displays genuine, authentic knowledge of witchcraft. Unlike other series, there is *no* ambivalence toward witchcraft: Tarot, Raven Hex, their mother, and other witches are proud, strong, autonomous, and independently powerful. The series expli-citly rejects the notion of witches as devil-worshippers. (Raven Hex informs a young would-be apprentice that witches don't believe in the existence of Satan but that if he did exist, *he* would worship *her*!)

Tarot is as sexy as any other pin-up witch but witchcraft as an art, skill, and culture is presented responsibly.

Jim Balent, creator, writer, and artist of *Tarot: Witch of the Black Rose*, worked on the DC Comics series *Catwoman* from 1993 until 1999 when he began his own independent company Broadsword. *Tarot: Witch of the Black Rose* was Broadsword's first production; subsequent works are also inspired by metaphysical themes including witchcraft and vampires.

Comic-book back pages are traditionally filled with all sorts of extras and bonuses like briefer strips featuring special characters, interviews, jokes or short stories. *Tarot: Witch of the Black Rose* features interviews with "real" witches and occult practitioners (interviewees have included Laurie Cabot, Fiona Horne, and Raven Grimassi) as well as spells or magical information. Different Tarot decks are featured monthly.

Wendy the Good Little Witch

Harvey Comics.

Wendy the Good Little Witch first appeared in 1954 in the back pages of *Casper the Friendly Ghost* comics. She was eventually popular enough to merit her own comic series and was also featured in a cartoon television show. (Harvey Comics has been "on hiatus" since the 1990s. Wendy's future, along with the other Harvey characters, remains uncertain.)

Wendy is Casper the Ghost's friend. She often shares pages with Casper, and they make appearances in each other's series. She serves a very similar function to Casper, although in witch-world, rather than the realm of ghosts. Just as Casper is the sole "friendly" ghost amidst a bunch of dour chain-clankers, Wendy is the only nice witch amongst a sour bunch.

Wendy dresses entirely in red and wears a baby's one-piece outfit complete with peaked hat/hood, although she's not an infant. Her age is indeterminate; she appears to be a small child although she comes and goes independently and quite competently. She has a magic wand with a glowing red tip and flies a broom. Her lack of green skin and warts annoys the other witches.

Wendy is seemingly the *only* good witch, an anomaly. Wendy lives with her aunts, "The Witch Sisters," typical, stereotyped green-faced crones with hooked noses. They specialize in stinky brews and trouble. Wendy serves as sort of a subtle peace enforcer, protecting people from her relatives and also protecting her aunts from malicious humans. There are various other witch characters; other little girl witches wear identical costumes but theirs are usually blue.

None are nice or intelligent like Wendy. One sorry little witch is named Dumbella while another is Bratty Lou. Although the series was meant to be "cute" it reinforces negative stereotypes. A comic book produced in 1970 shows the frustrated Witch Sisters hiring a tutor, Miss Moldee, to teach Wendy *the witch way*, defined as being "mean" and "unpleasant." The series was geared for younger children and thus nothing really *bad* can happen, there's no violence or real drama; the witches' mean spirit usually translates into their playing tricks on animals, usually transforming cute ones into less attractive species.

Witches

Marvel Comics.

Witches debuted in June 2004. A new breed of witch-oriented comic books has emerged that seems to be structured along the lines of *Charlie's Angels*. A prominent male character recruits what at least look like young witches to work their magic powers.

In the case of *Witches*, a dangerous magical book, *The Tome of Zhered-Na*, has been accidentally opened, releasing its malevolent powers. Acknowledging a new era in magic, our old friend Dr Strange (see page 227) can't do the job by himself but recruits three young female witches (Jennifer Kale, Satana, and Topaz) to help him save the world. These three represent the threefold power of women—maiden, mother, and crone—although as befitting comic-book heroines, even the one representing the crone sure looks like a sexy young witch. Dr Strange is still treated with respect; at least one young witch refers to him as "Master Strange." Various metaphysical themes emerge and eventually Lilith, who may be the comics' favorite

goddess, makes an appearance. (See **DIVINE WITCH:** Lilith.)

The Witching

Vertigo Comics, launched June 2004.

Like *Witches* (above) this similarly named series also features a trio of witches, Elsa, Kara, and Sook, however these girls don't need Dr Strange. They have the Vertigo character Lucifer Morningstar instead. (Yes, *that* Lucifer.)

"*Elsa Grimston, Witch*," as she identifies herself, represents the crone of this triad. She was conceived on what she calls a "black magick altar" during a sex magic ritual attempting to implant a lunar spirit into a human child. Her father, Henry Grimston, is a Crowley-style magician who, Elsa says, initially believed himself to be more powerful than the devil. His error was subsequently proven to him and so he turned into a devotee of the devil.

Elsa learned magic directly from the finest teachers, the fate goddesses. (See **WOMEN'S MYSTERIES:** Spinning.) When the series starts, all she really wants to do is go home to the moon for some peace and quiet, but she's ordered back to Earth to magically preserve Earth's power balance. Elsa must recruit a maiden and mother for her trinity. She discovers Sook, a fun-loving Korean girl from Texas, and Kara, a young singer whose mother is a not particularly competent spell-casting witch.

Zatanna, The Magician

DC Comics, first appeared in 1964.

In 1964, DC Comics considered reviving their old magician hero Zatara (see next entry).

Instead they created a new character, his daughter Zatanna.

According to the plot-line, 14 years after Zatara's mysterious disappearance, his daughter comes looking for him. She knows little about him or his disappearance but during the search, in which she is aided by various superheroes including no less than Batman, Zatanna discovers her own magic powers. Just like her father, by speaking backwards she can create wonderful, powerful magical transformations.

Zatanna was revolutionary because she is a female character who conforms to the theme of the illusionist who is really a magical practitioner in disguise. Like the medieval sorcerers, that type of conjurer is virtually always identified as male. (And for good reason: men do dominate the field of illusionists, most of whom today are genuinely only illusionists.) (See **HALL OF FAME:** Black Herman Rucker; Jan Eric Hanussen.)

Zatanna adapts the costume of the traditional male stage magician to suit herself, including top hat, tuxedo jacket with tails, high heels, and fishnet stockings. Zatanna made periodic appearances during the years as a guest star in various series including *Batman*, *Hawkman* and *The Green Lantern*. (She is a member of DC's Justice League.) The circumstances of her birth remained unrevealed until 1980. Without revealing any secrets, let's just say she inherited many magic powers from her mother's side too.

Eventually Zatanna succeeds in rescuing her father from his magical imprisonment and comes into her own powers as a superhero. (In one story she journeys to the magical Breton kingdom of Ys. See **DIVINE WITCH:** Dahut.)

Zatara, The Magician

DC Comics, first appeared in 1938.

Zatara made his debut in DC's Action Comics #1, the very same issue that launched the man of steel, Superman. He existed as a comic hero until 1950 when he was retired. (Considering whether to revive him inspired DC Comics to create his daughter Zatanna instead. See previous entry.) Giovanni Zatara, of Italian origin, only appears to be a simple stage magician. True, it was all he originally expected to be. He practiced the craft of illusions until he was a master. At some point, however, he discovered that he possessed genuine magic powers, which he now uses to protect the world from wrongdoers. (He attributes his powers to the possibility of unknown magical ancestors including Leonardo da Vinci.)

Zatara has a special magical trick: speaking backwards. By doing this he can cause anyone or anything to bend to his will: true commanding and compelling powers that would make any medieval sorcerer proud. Zatara eventually reappeared in the series devoted to his daughter Zatanna but was finally killed off (or so it presently seems) in 1986.

Among the many other comic-book enchantresses, sorcerers, and witches are

- ❋ *Doctor Fate*
- ❋ *Doctor Occult*
- ❋ *Encantadora*
- ❋ *Enchantress*
- ❋ *Felix Faust*
- ❋ *Jennifer Morgan*
- ❋ *Madame Xanadu*
- ❋ *Morgaine Le Fey*
- ❋ *Nico Minoru*
- ❋ *Sargon the Sorcerer*

Dance

Beyond casting spells and stirring the cauldron, when one envisions traditional witches, what are they usually *doing*? Popular depictions of witches flying through the air may be a distorted misunderstanding of shamanic soul-journeying. Witch-hunters' allegations of baby stealing, cannibalism, and incest are defamation. The single realistic and consistent description of witches shared by both those who love them and those who despise them is that witches *dance*.

This is a fairly international image: witches all over the world are described as dancers. Wherever traditional witches congregate and rendezvous, observers claim that they dance. (Witches themselves most often maintain professional secrecy.) In fact, Reginald Scot, the Elizabethan authority on witchcraft, quoted witch-hunter Jean Bodin's suggestion that witches shouldn't be defined as *night-walkers*, but instead as *night-dancers*. (See **BOOKS:** Witch-Hunt Books: Bodin; Scot.)

In fact dancing is so integral a part of historical witchcraft that among the *countless* definitions of witchcraft is one that defines it as the persistently surviving vestiges of "*Neolithic dance cults.*"

Now "dance cult," like "fertility cult," is a vague, nebulous term. What is that definition trying to express? Dancing is among the most ancient magical arts of all. It is to some extent a forgotten magical art because information regarding it is fragmentary at best. Dancing was taught by doing; although ancient images depict magical and ritual dance they are by necessity static. We see the dancer frozen at one step; we can't see the dance as a whole.

Even today among traditional spiritual traditions, an incredibly high percentage of rituals involve dance. Dance for spiritual purposes was suppressed in Christianity and Judaism. In 1231, as only one example, the Council of Rouen for-bade dancing in church. (Dance-centered spirituality survives in pockets of Islam, most notably the Sufi dervishes; however this too remains controversial and somewhat counter-cultural.) Church disapproval was based on a variety of reasons:

* *Dances retained Pagan elements—in Judaism, for instance, dancing in groves was associated with devotion to the suppressed goddess Lady Asherah.*

* *Dances incorporated cross-dressing, masking, and the impersonation of animals and deities.*

* *Dances were intrinsic components of female-centered or even female-dominant spiritual traditions.*

In modern mainstream Western society, among the majority of those who adhere to the monotheistic faiths, people dance for pleasure, entertainment, enjoyment, and exercise, and also as part of theatrical performance. Witches, however, are persistent preservers of ancient traditions. Some witches still dance with other motivation in mind. Because of course there's the crucial matter of *why* people dance.

Why *do* people dance?

Traditionally and historically there have been rain dances, initiation dances, puberty, fertility, and healing dances. There are harvest dances in particular—grain and wine dances. There are war, victory, and peace dances.

* *People dance for purposes of entrancement, to induce trances.*

* *People dance for purposes of spell-casting.*

* *Dances honor and appease all kinds of spirits.*

* *Dance is a powerful method of inviting the spirits to appear, as opposed to the commanding and compelling techniques that sorcerers depend upon (see* **MAGICAL ARTS:** *Commanding and Compelling).*

* *Dance is frequently the method by which spirits are invited to enter the dancer's body—usually a trained devotee who then temporarily serves as a vehicle for prophecy and healing (see* **MAGICAL ARTS:** *Ritual Possession).*

* *Dance, conversely, is among the methods for exorcising malevolent spirits or those who've overstayed their welcome.*

* *Dance is a method for aligning one's personal energy and rhythm with that belonging to Earth.*

* *Many people dance just for joy. Dance is one of the paths to ecstasy, the magical shamanic state. To this day some types of dance—that of the so-called whirling dervishes, for instance—are defined as "ecstatic dance."*

* *Dance is among the most accessible and powerful methods of generating fresh magical energy.*

Fire-walking, an ancient shamanic art still occasionally practiced, may also be understood as an aspect of dance. Dance is a component of the rituals leading up to the actual fire-walking; participants are as likely to dance over the glowing coals as to *walk* over them.

Although dance is fun, traditional dance can also be serious business. Many traditional societies have specific social organizations devoted to dances: these include women's societies, men's societies, cross-dressers' societies, sometimes, depending upon the dance, societies that integrate the genders so that women and men dance together, and sometimes even dance/spiritual societies for which being trans-gendered is a requirement of entry. Because harvests, health, fertility, weather, and other crucial issues are understood as dependent upon and controlled by the dance, it's crucial that the dances are performed correctly and that the dancers adhere to all the ritual and magical requirements so that disaster may be averted.

Those scholars who define witchcraft as a vestige of "Neolithic dance cults" understand witches' covens to be surviving tokens of these frequently secret dance societies, each of which had stringent initiation requirements.

This type of dance-centered spirituality still exists among Earth's traditional peoples. Witches' balls may certainly be understood as the remnants of similar traditions. (See **HORNED ONE.**)

By necessity, the information that follows is fragmentary. If only there had been video cameras to capture ancient dancers' moves.

Circle, Ring or Round Dance

Perhaps the most ancient dances of all, round dances are reminiscent of fairy rings and magic circles. Although some ring dances are complex with specific turns, steps, and sequences, at their most primal these are exceedingly simple dances: people join hands and dance around in a circle. No artistic skill is needed, nor is there need for special preparation: the simplest round dances are egalitarian. With the exception of the exceedingly frail or those whose mobility is challenged, virtually anyone can join in.

A Paleolithic drawing depicts women wearing peaked hoods dancing around a central phallic symbol: it's very tempting to see in this the ancestral roots of witches dancing around a Maypole, or perhaps around a costumed, horned figure.

Ring dances are frequently danced around something that serves as a central focus: that something might be a stone, an altar, a statue or an animal.

❋ *Some shamanic bear dances actually circled around a real living bear, although other dances circle around bear skulls or other ritual paraphernalia.*

❋ *Ring dances may circle around a person, who may be costumed and/or masked, or sometimes enthroned.*

❋ *Modern witches do the circle dance to raise the cone of power. (See* **DICTIONARY:** *Cone of Power.)*

❋ *Witches dance to demarcate the sacred circle.*

❋ *Dancers may encircle a high priestess, initiate or priest.*

❋ *Dancers may encircle living trees, as did the Italian witches of Benevento. They may also dance around cut trees, carved phallic poles, pillars or Maypoles.*

Some ritual groups include a single man together with many women; the women may dance around the man, who may or may not be costumed. This may be what witch-hunters understood as a diabolical sabbat: witches circling a man costumed to resemble a goat or a horned, hoofed deity.

Ring dances, perhaps because they are so basic and primal, have the highest survival rate of what may have once been a huge magical repertoire of dances.

Dance of the Seven Veils

Salome performed the Dance of the Seven Veils for her stepfather King Herod Antipas, the husband of her mother Herodias. King Herod was so moved by her performance that he offered to give her whatever she desired. At the behest of her mother, Salome requested that the head of the prophet John the Baptist be served to her atop a silver platter as her reward.

As with so many other legends, it is unknown whether this story is true or how much of it is true; however it is a deeply entrenched legend and many consider it to be gospel. Indeed aspects of the tale are included in the Gospel of Mark (6:21-28) and the Gospel of Matthew (14:6-11). The Gospels do not name the dance, although neither do they name the dancer. The legend as it is known today derives from an amalgamation of sources. Disagreements regarding details of this story still arouse tremendous passions, not least as to whether the Bible can be considered a historical source.

Herodias, the actual manipulator of events, the brains behind Salome's beauty, emerged as a prototype for the evil anti-Christian witch. Centuries later, Herodias would emerge as a European Queen of Witches, in the company of Diana and Lilith. (See **DIVINE WITCH:** Aradia; Diana; Herodias; Lilith.)

There are two versions of the motivation behind John the Baptist's murder. The original historical motive explains that John the Baptist, then an important prophet whom some considered to be the Messiah, publicly denounced the marriage of Herodias and Herod Antipas. Both had been previously married, she to his brother. They engaged in an extra-marital affair, eventually divorcing their respective spouses so that they could marry. Due to technicalities of Jewish law, their marriage could be construed as incest.

The House of Herod had been imposed upon the Jewish nation by their Roman occupiers and was exceedingly unpopular. John the Baptist's criticism could be understood as rabble-rousing. Herodias took this personally; taking matters into her own hands, according to the legend, she decided to eliminate John, reminiscent of the actions of that other hated biblical queen, Jezebel. The authors of the Old Testament despised Jezebel, not only because of her murderous behavior but also because she was the high priestess of Lady Asherah, Judaism's forbidden goddess.

That's the version that draws on proven historical events, as well as the basic gist of what's contained in the two Gospels. However that version didn't bewitch nineteenth-century storytellers nearly as much as the idea of beautiful, lascivious Salome dancing with a severed head. A new plot-line eventually emerged suggesting that Salome was sexually obsessed with the handsome ascetic prophet. When he rejected her advances, she decided she'd have him one way or another, dead or alive.

As traditionally told this story focuses on perverse, ruthless women. If one focuses on the dance itself, rather than on female depravity, an entirely different perspective emerges. Neither of the versions explains two aspects of the tale:

❊ *What was the dance of the seven veils?*

❊ *Why was Herod so moved?*

The Dance of the Seven Veils reproduces the goddess Inanna-Ishtar's mythological descent to the underworld, the realm of death ruled by her twin sister. Readying herself for the visit, Inanna-Ishtar dons all her finery so that she will appear as powerful and divine as possible. She begins the journey secure and arrogant in her identity as the beautiful Queen of Heaven. At each of the seven gates leading to her sister's kingdom, however, Inanna-Ishtar is forced to relinquish one item of clothing (her crown of stars, her famous lapis lazuli necklace, and so on) until finally she approaches Death completely naked, vulnerable, and powerless.

Once upon a time back in Mesopotamia, Inanna-Ishtar's priestesses channeled the deity during the annual sacred marriage and during other crucial rituals. (See **DICTIONARY:** Great Rite; **MAGICAL ARTS:** Ritual Possession.) The Dance of the Seven Veils reproduces Inanna-Ishtar's solitary journey to Hell. At the very least, the dancer impersonated Inanna-Ishtar; perhaps she also ritually channeled her. This would not have been mere entertainment but a tremendously potent act of spirituality. In first-century Judea, it would also have been a highly controversial, forbidden spiritual act, which would perhaps explain Herod's excessive reaction to what many consider nothing more than a striptease.

If Herodias did initiate the performance, than her resemblance to Jezebel might be intended to imply something about her spiritual inclinations. Devotion to the goddess may have been what earned Herodias' reputation as a witch.

The dancer sheds one veil as she passes through each gate; her final nudity may have shared as much with the *danse macabre* as it does with erotic entertainment. (See page 241, *Danse Macabre.*) Inanna-Ishtar's ancient myth may be understood literally, allegorically or as a shamanic soul-journey. Although the war goddess Inanna-Ishtar also has dominion over sex and fertility, and many of her hymns are very erotic, this particular myth is *not* a particularly titillating story—or not unless one finds *any* reference to female nakedness to be sexually stimulating, which may have been the case in medieval Europe but was not necessarily so for a king like

Herod who presumably had access to naked female flesh whenever he wanted.

The Dance of the Seven Veils developed a reputation as a bewitching erotic performance that held men irresistibly spellbound and persuaded them to commit all sorts of foolish, perverse, and evil acts. The name "Dance of the Seven Veils" retained an aura of powerful bewitchment and so was incorporated into many forbidden sex shows and theatrical performances. By the early twentieth century, the Dance of the Seven Veils had become just another version of the burlesque hoochy-coochy, only with some implied extra erotic magic powers.

The legend continues to evolve: the spiritual components of the dance have once again risen to the forefront. Ruth St Denis (1880–1968), the *grande dame* of early modern dance, described herself as a prophetess and devoted much of her life to sacred dance. Among her sacred dances was one entitled *"Ishtar of the Seven Gates."* Many modern belly dancers have choreographed their own personal interpretations of the Dance of the Seven Veils, frequently in tribute to Inanna-Ishtar.

Dances of Death

These particular "dances of death" do not refer to a specific dance but to the motivation behind a genre of witches' dances. The *danse macabre*, which is sometimes also called *the* dance of death, and is a specific type of dance, is discussed in its own entry on page 240.

Witches famously dance in the graveyard. This is true not just in witch-hunt era Europe but wherever one finds cemeteries. They don't even have to be cemeteries in terms of literal burial grounds: in India, magical practitioners devoted to Kali and Shiva dance in cremation grounds.

This is an old stereotype involving ancient legends, traditions, and practices. Witches still gather in cemeteries to dance as well as to conduct rituals, cast spells and commune with ghosts, ancestors, and spirits. Why do they do so?

Dances were once traditional components of funerals. These dances stem from many motivations and serve different purposes:

* *Dances help see the dead soul off on his journey to the next realm*

* *Dances invite (and then dispel) necessary funerary spirits—the ones who'll make sure the dead soul departs in a timely fashion and reaches his destination safely.*

* *Merry-making propitiates the spirits, honors ancestral spirits and pleases ghosts, some or all of whom may join the living dancers in their revelry.*

* *Dancing dispels fear and gloom, the existence of which increases malevolent magical powers.*

* *Dancing cheers the living.*

Because these are pre-Christian traditions, it stands to reason that they would meet with disapproval from the Church. Witches may be understood as maintaining (or at least attempting to maintain) their ancient practices. Fairy tales where the heroine is forced to gather magical materials in the cemetery inevitably find her doing so in the midst of dancing witches.

Cemeteries are also threshold areas packed with highly charged magic power (see **DICTIONARY:**

Threshold). There are few, if any, places on Earth with more power and so magical practitioners go to cemeteries to gather materials, cast spells, hold rituals, commune with spirits, ancestors and ghosts and, yes, not least, to dance. (See **MAGICAL ARTS:** Necromancy; **PLACES:** Burial Grounds.)

Exactly what kind of dances are these dances of death? Although they vary depending upon culture, region, tradition, and individual, two types of dances are consistently popular: circle dances, especially around grave markers, the cemetery's central cross or other monuments, and serpentine line dances that spiral around graves and throughout the entire cemetery.

Danse Macabre or The Dance of Death

Many of the names for medieval dances are used somewhat interchangeably and carelessly today. The French term *danse macabre* is sometimes used to refer to *any* type of dance having *anything* to do with death, cemeteries or skeletons. It is also sometimes classified among the various dance manias that swept Europe during and after the Black Death, characterized by masses of frenzied dancers unable to stop dancing. (See Tarantella, page 247.)

However, in the context of this book, "danse macabre" refers very specifically to a medieval dance in which a figure representing death leads a procession to the graveyard. It is sometimes also called the Dance of Death. Death may be personified as a black-cloaked figure or as a naked skeleton. Death is not to be confused with the devil but is an independent entity.

The danse macabre is most familiar today as a visual image. The theme first achieved popularity in the fifteenth century and was incorporated into various styles of art, including woodcuts, carvings, frescoes, and paintings on canvas. The danse macabre was painted by innumerable unknown artists as well as by masters like Hans Holbein the Younger. Images corresponding to this theme were painted or carved onto church walls, chapels, ossuaries, and family vaults. Artistic depictions still resonate even to this day: the danse macabre may be witnessed among modern Halloween imagery, although it is now favored because it is "spooky." Images of dancing skeletons hark back to the danse macabre.

The danse macabre is more than just a visual device, however; it was once an actual and very popular dance. A masked, costumed figure sometimes carrying a scythe represented Death. This person led a serpentine chain dance of the living, each person holding the hands of those on either side. Perhaps originally this procession did sometimes ultimately terminate in the cemetery but eventually it became popular enough to be integrated into public processional performances (see page 244, Processions), including those sponsored by local churches.

Although there are sufficient artistic depictions so that the dance is easily recognized, only a little information exists regarding actual dance practices. It is believed to have first originated in France as a reaction to the devastation of the Black Death. The earliest documented depiction of the danse macabre comes from Paris and is dated 1424.

The danse macabre grabbed hold of the public imagination. It spread throughout Europe. As it entered new regions, it evolved, eventually traveling far from its roots as a simple serpentine dance and transforming into elaborate theatrical productions, particularly in Denmark and the German lands.

There are two ways of understanding this image and perhaps also the motivation behind the dance. These perspectives are not mutually exclusive:

✳ *The conventional interpretation of the danse macabre suggests that Death is the great equalizer. Everyone dies, rich and poor, noble or peasant, no one can purchase or ordain immunity. In images devoted to the danse macabre, Death often leads emperors, princes, noble churchmen, leaders, and the obviously wealthy by the hand. (The theme behind this image survives in the Tarot card entitled* Death.)

✳ *It is common metaphysical practice to analyze images by looking at them out of context: in other words, what do you actually see, when you don't think about what you're supposed to see? In the case of the danse macabre, one sees the living dancing happily and peacefully with the dead, the spiritual motivation for many traditional witches' serpentine dances of death.*

A recreation of the danse macabre may be witnessed at the conclusion of Ingmar Bergman's 1957 film, *The Seventh Seal.*

The Goat Dance

Once upon a time (and still in some places) men impersonated the horned one and danced masked and costumed as an animal, frequently a goat. (See **HORNED ONE**.) Witch-hunters, perhaps initially misunderstanding reports, envisioned Satan as an upright male goat dancing amid witches during sabbats.

In either situation, "goats" are seen to dance; however *the* goat dance refers to a genre of folk dance, still existing in Greece, Romania, the Balkan region, and elsewhere, mainly centered in the god Dionysus' old stomping grounds. Although there are regional differences, there are recognizably related goat dances everywhere Dionysus once held influence.

The goat dance is danced by men traditionally dressed in goatskins, crowned with horns and/or wearing goat leather masks. There are two variations of the dance:

✳ *The goat dance is fast, frenetic, and vigorous and exemplifies the goat as a rambunctious male fertility figure.*

✳ *The goat dance is a solemn dance that re-enacts the sacrifice and sometimes eventual resurrection of the goat.*

Because the two themes are sometimes combined into one lengthy narrative, dances that incorporate only the frenetic or only the mournful aspect may be understood as edited or taken out of what once may have been a larger context. In either or both cases, the dancer who impersonates the goat may be understood to represent either a real goat or any one of the innumerable spirits who manifest in goat shape. These spirits in general are tricksters, personifying male procreative energy. In general, however, the goat dance is believed to honor, remember and, quite literally, memorialize Dionysus.

La Volta

Generally believed to have originated in Italy, this folk dance eventually became extremely popular and spread throughout Europe. Its name is translated as *"the turning."* Although no longer the rage, dance historians still consider *la volta* significant if only because it's believed to be the progenitor of the world-famous waltz.

And how did this Italian folk dance travel across Europe? Allegedly, through the powers of witchcraft. Not just any folk dance, la volta is believed to have initially been a witches' dance; it was first danced at sabbats and witches' balls. Reginald Scot, the English authority on witchcraft, suggested that witches brought this dance from Italy to France. (See **BOOKS:** Witch-Hunt Books: Scot.) Elegant, masked observers of witches' balls learned the dance and began enjoying it elsewhere.

As befitting its origins, la volta was scandalous. It is not a processional, a line or a circle dance. Instead, like the waltz, it's a partner dance for two, traditionally a man and a woman. Unlike other dances of that era, partners faced each other and held each other close—not customary during the sixteenth century. The turn for which the dance is named was executed by the man who simultaneously held the woman up in the air, holding her tightly by the waist. (La volta was a folk dance, not a ballroom dance and was considerably more athletic and vigorous than the modern waltz.)

Conservative society was quick to condemn la volta. The dance was called shameful and indecent. Dancers were warned that it would stimulate miscarriage and murder.

Nevertheless la volta continued to cast its spell: Catherine de Medici (April 13, 1519-January 5, 1589), the Italian-born queen of France famed for her love of the occult and patronage of its practitioners including Nostradamus (there were whispered suggestions that she, too, was a witch), is believed to have introduced the dance to the French court, from whence it spread to the world. Elizabeth I of England (September 7, 1533-March 24, 1603) was also reputed to be very fond of it.

Maenad Dances

When anthropologists mutter about witchcraft as surviving vestiges of dance cults, frequently what's really being implied, without being explicitly spoken because, of course, this can never be scientifically proven, is that in one form or another the Maenads survive.

The Maenads were the female devotees of Dionysus. Among Dionysus' titles is Lord of the Dance. The word "Maenad" would also eventually come to be used as a synonym for female "witch."

The Maenads were not sedate women, at least not during rituals: they danced, sang, reveled, and drank. Magical practices were incorporated, as was ritual possession. When possessed by the deity, the Maenads were wild and fierce. Whether they really tore animals to bits by hand and consumed them raw is unknown, however that was their reputation in Greece. Conventional society considered the Maenads dangerous, disreputable, and out of control. Women had few rights in classical Greece and were expected to remain quiet, discreet, and well behaved. The Maenads defied convention.

Very little information survives regarding the Maenads. What exists tends towards the sensational, written by observers and, in general, by those who beheld these independent women with vehement disapproval. Virtually the one neutral thing that can be established about the Maenads is that they danced.

The Maenads danced bull dances, erotic dances, and labyrinth dances. They danced in public ritual as part of Dionysus' processionals, and they danced in secret in moonlit forests, where they ritually channeled Dionysus and perhaps other spirits, too. (Many spirits joined in Dionysus' retinue, including Pan the goatfoot god, Hecate, and Kybele.)

The Maenads were frequently depicted in Greek sculpture and vase paintings, often in the company of satyrs and very often dancing. Much of what we know of their dances is derived from this imagery, which of course is static. However, this much is generally believed:

❋ Their dances were characterized by an absence of symmetry, thus they did not have the appearance of "orderliness" typically valued by classical Greek civilization. The women dance together in a group but each dances as an individual with slight variations.

❋ Their movements were loose and flexible, characterized by stiff or waving arms and deep back bends, followed by immediate deep forward bends. Sometimes the movements seem unconsciously erotic: in other words, there is no self-conscious attempt to titillate the viewer.

❋ They whirled, presumably whirling themselves into an ecstatic state, similar to the so-called whirling dervishes.

❋ They danced holding lit torches as well as the thyrsus, the magic wand associated with Dionysus, which consists of a stiff fennel stalk topped with a pine-cone. They struck the ground with the thyrsus.

❋ The Maenads accompanied their dance with castanets, cymbals, and frame drums. They attached small bells to their clothing.

❋ They wore swirling scarves and capes while they danced. There is no indication of veils. Instead, in some depictions, the Maenads dance so hard, their breasts fall out of their clothes, seemingly causing no distress or embarrassment.

❋ Dances involved walking, running, and leaping, often executed on their toes or on the balls of their bare feet. (This may or may not reproduce the "shaman's limp"—see The Step of Yu page 246.)

Perchtentanz or Perchta's Dance

The Perchta in question is the Germanic witch-goddess who is now among the leaders of the Wild Hunt. Perchta leads a horde known as the Perchten.

In Austria and southern Germany, Twelfth Night is Perchtennacht, when Perchta leads that horde across the night sky. At some point during the twelve days of Christmas, the dance known as the Perchtentanz is traditionally performed on solid ground. The Perchtentanz is a masked, costumed, choreographed performance, now much beloved by tourists. Scholars and historians love it too: the Perchtentanz is classified among sword dances and is related to the so-called Moorish dances, which typically re-enact battles between the forces of good and evil, light and darkness, as personified by Christians and Moors. Out of all of these dances, the Perchtentanz is believed to have retained the most Pagan elements. The performance is believed to contain vestiges of pre-Christian German devotion to Perchta. The original intent may have been to drive out the forces of winter, dispel malicious spirits, and stimulate the coming harvest.

There are regional variations in the way the Perchtentanz is performed; as an example, the Perchtentanz of Salzburg, Austria traditionally features two factions: the "beautiful Perchten" have elaborate headdresses and are bedecked with bows, bells, ribbons, and flowers, while the "evil Perchten" wear grotesque masks and tattered rags. They engage in hand-to-hand combat, reminiscent perhaps of the Italian Benandanti, the "good walkers" who magically battle the forces of evil. (See **CALENDAR:** Walpurgis; **DICTIONARY:** Benandanti; Wild Hunt; **DIVINE WITCH:** Perchta.)

Processions

The Roman victory "triumph," all sorts of parades, and modern Carnival and Mardi Gras processions complete with floats are rooted in the sacred tradition of the ancient processional. These may be further rooted in primal "follow the leader" type dances, line dances or serpentine snake dances (see Snake Dance, page 245).

Processions were frequent components of ancient spiritual festivals. An image, person or sacred object representing the deity being honored was transported in a wagon. The deity was accompanied by an honor guard of priestesses, priests, devotees, pilgrims, sacred animals, musicians, and, especially, dancers. Sideshow magicians who give crowd-pleasing "magical" performances may be understood to derive from these theatrical traditions, as do sacred clowns.

Processions would proceed in a line from one point—frequently the deity's official shrine—to a chosen destination: typically another shrine, the ocean or another sacred place. (The procession may or may not eventually circle back to the starting point.) Frequent scheduled stops might be made, as with some modern parades. There might be theatrical performances at these stops or rituals, often incorporating music and dance, masking, and guising.

Many African Diaspora spiritual ceremonials including those of Vodou and Candomble invite the spirits to join the living; the spirits are expected to arrive in a somewhat orderly fashion. This parade of spirits may be understood as similar to the ancient processionals.

Although processions were crucial to the devotional rituals of *many* spirits including Bastet, Durga, Hathor, Hera, Herta, Isis, Kybele, and Perchta, they are most famously identified with Dionysus, and his processions are believed to have served as the prototype for the medieval processions that eventually evolved into modern parades. A sacred object representing the deity, often a pine tree, phallic pole or other phallic symbol, was transported from one point to another. It was accompanied by an entourage of spirits, including Pan and often Hecate, Kybele, and others.

The Maenads danced in Dionysus' processions while accompanying themselves with percussion instruments including frame drums, cymbals, and castanets, instruments still associated with women's tribal dances. Dionysus' sacred animals were in attendance including donkeys, mules, and leopards. Participants and observers were often masked and costumed. Dionysus was Lord of the Dance and of Theater: the parade would periodically be punctuated with theatrical performances. Dionysus was also Lord of Wine and Intoxication: the sacred blends with the profane. Participants and observers often indulged in Dionysus' sacraments. Raucous, drunken, masked Carnival celebrations are in direct line of descent from the celebratory parades of Dionysus. (The famous Carnival of Rio de Janeiro remains dominated by traditional dance clubs; each club spends a year preparing choreography and costumes for their Carnival performance.)

Similar processionals—although rarely if ever incorporating the aspect of intoxication specific to Dionysus as Lord of Wine—are common to many indigenous traditions of Africa, Asia, North America, and elsewhere. The concept of a procession incorporating masked and/or costumed dancers, musicians, singers, and theatrical performances for magical and/or ritual purposes is among the oldest spiritual traditions of all.

Even after other Pagan customs were forbidden, the much beloved procession went undercover and survived until the Middle Ages in traditions associated with the Feast of Fools, the Feast of the Ass, and similar festivals. Modern Roman Catholic feast days that incorporate a parade featuring the honored saint's statue pulled on a wagon may be understood as continuing this tradition, particularly when the parade is held in conjunction with a fair. Many traditional Church processions still incorporate special dances performed only at these festivals. (See **CALENDAR:** February Feasts: Saint Agatha.) Many parades that today honor specific sacred Madonnas are indistinguishable from parades that once honored Pagan goddesses.

> The Wild Hunt reproduces the concept of the sacred processional. A sacred rider leads a procession of fairies, ghosts, and spirits. They are accompanied by animals, most notably hounds, and by music in the form of horns. The witches who allegedly join the Hunt as dancers may be understood as stepping in the shoes of the Maenads in Dionysus' old processions.

Snake, Serpentine or Spiral Dances

There are two types of snake dances:

❋ *Dancing with snakes*

❋ *Dancing the spiral or serpentine dance*

There is no animal more associated with magic, witchcraft, and women's power than snakes. Although men dance with snakes, too, snake dances are largely women's dances.

> Because he invented and forged tools devoted to agriculture, circumcision, and warfare, traditionally considered "men's business," Ogun, the West African deity of iron, is often considered a "man's deity." However, once upon a time, another aspect of Ogun's devotions, now largely abandoned, involved snake charming and dancing. Women were his chief devotees in this aspect of his cult.

Snakes are beautiful, flexible, and often good-natured: they're willing to be handled and may participate in the dance. Women from all over Earth have danced with snakes as part of magical and spiritual rites. Some belly dancers and other traditional dancers still dance with snakes; this is not an abandoned, forgotten tradition.

Historically significant snake dancers include:

❋ *The Maenads, who allegedly danced with snakes, engaged in snake charming and wore snakes in their hair as crowns. (Deities like Brigid, Hecate, Lilith, and Persephone are depicted with similar hair-dos.*

Snake-haired Medusa may also be understood to embody this concept.)

✸ *The Italian deity Angitia was the niece of the sorceress-spirit Circe. She learned her aunt's magical secrets including fire-walking and snake charming and brought them to the Roman region. (See* **DIVINE WITCH:** *Angitia.)*

✸ *Marie Laveau, the self-proclaimed Pope of Voodoo, famously danced with her snake, the Grand Zombi, during Midsummer's Eve rituals on the Bayou St John. Her snake's name often confuses because it sounds identical to the* zombis, *the living dead, of Haitian lore. However, in this case,* Zombi *is a variant of what is now most commonly spelled* Simbi *in English. Simbi is a powerful water-snake deity of Congolese origin.*

✸ *Mami Waters, currently an extremely popular West and Central African deity, is most often depicted in the guise of a snake charmer. Mami Waters was originally a water-snake spirit, similar to a mermaid. Once a minor, regional spirit, during the later twentieth century she emerged as among the most popular deities of a newly urbanized sub-Saharan Africa. An old German theatrical poster promoting a snake charmer somehow became identified with Mami Waters; it is now her most popular devotional icon.*

There is also a different type of snake dance, which may or may not incorporate living snakes. This dance is also known as a serpentine—or line—dance. A company of dancers—the more numerous the more effective—forms a sinuous, twisting line that mimics the motion of a snake. This type of dance is also commonly called a spiral dance.

> The serpentine dance is an affirmation of life and the potential for resurrection. The original *danse macabre* in its primitive form reproduced the movements of the serpentine line dance although no apparent conscious associations with snakes exist. In this context the *danse macabre* may be understood as either affirming life in the face of death or of succumbing to the despair of the Black Death.

Neolithic statuettes and other surviving stone and pottery crafts are often embellished with spirals; these spirals curve around bodies, most typically around those anatomical parts most associated with sex and procreation. These spirals are understood as representing serpentine power: they protect, preserve, enhance, and increase generative, creative power.

The twisting line of serpentine dancers essentially recreates a giant, magical snake that spirals around sacred sites, trees, mountains, and homes (or anything else); the dancers reproduce the motif of the spiraling snake; they, too, generate magical energy and blessings.

The Step of Yu

This dance step associated with Taoist shamans (and often particularly with female shamans) commemorates Da-yu (also spelled Ta-yu) or Yu the Great, the mythical founder of China's Xia Dynasty. Yu was also a great shaman, allegedly able to control storms and floods. He was partially paralyzed and walked with a limp; an imitation of his step was transformed into a shamanic dance—or so the legend says.

The earliest written reference to "the Step of Yu" (or in Chinese, *Yu-bu*) derives from the fourth century BCE with a description from the Taoist philosopher Ko Hong. The Step of Yu was a hopping dance: the dancer first leads with the left foot, then shifts to the right, in the meantime, simultaneously, dragging the other leg.

The limping step may be understood as more than mere imitation. Although the dance is named for Yu, the limping step associated with shamans may be far older.

For reasons that remain mysterious, a tremendous number of shamanic heroes from all over Earth possess myths that involve wearing only one shoe or detail an injured or somehow vulnerable (special) foot. These include Achilles, Jason of the Argonauts, Oedipus, Hephaestus, Wayland the Smith, and the biblical Jacob. The motif isn't exclusive to men: in one story Medea removes one single sandal. One way of interpreting the secret meaning of the loss of Cinderella's shoe is as a tale of successful shamanic initiation. (Shoes also represent female genitalia and so there are also other ways of interpreting the glass slipper that serves as the prince's tool for identifying his perfect match.) Cinderella is able to escape from the degradation imposed on her when she learns to access her magic and shamanic powers. Walking with one shoe on and one shoe off demonstrates her successful initiation as a shaman.

Many of the trickster spirits who are so often sponsors of shamanism are also depicted limping, most notably perhaps Africa's Papa Legba. Medieval depictions of the devil incorporated this image of the limping trickster. Satan was often portrayed during the witch-hunt era as having one shod human foot and one bare cloven goat's hoof, causing him to limp. (See **HORNED ONE**.)

In some Northern regions, dances associated elsewhere with goats are performed in honor of bears. The shaman Yu was allegedly able to transform into a bear.

Tarantella

You've heard of the dance called *"the monkey"*? How about *"the pony"*? Well, the tarantella means *"the spider."*

The tarantella was born in Italy. It was more than a mere dance; the tarantella might more accurately be described as a phenomenon that lasted some 300 years, although depending upon how you interpret its history, the tarantella's roots may stretch back much further.

Some considered the tarantella an act of magical healing; others described it as mass hysteria, and still others muttered about a resurgence of witchcraft and Pagan practices.

The tarantella arose in response to a condition known as "tarantism," allegedly caused by a spider's bite. The first victims were workers, predominately but not exclusively female, who manually harvested grain. The initial symptom of tarantism was intense melancholia followed by pain, swelling, vomiting, priapism (involuntary, often painful erections that refuse to abate), and what was described as "shameless exhibitionism." The end result was delirium and then eventually death. Victims were said to die either laughing or crying wildly.

What is believed to be the first case of tarantism was recorded in 1370 near what was once ancient Tarentum, a formerly Greek settlement on Italy's southern coast, known in modern times as Taranto. The dance, the condition, and eventually the name of a class of arachnids were named after the town. Tarantulas were named after Taranto, not the other way around.

There was only one known cure for tarantism: a magical dance known as the tarantella.

The spider's victims, known as the *tarantati*, sought relief via the tarantella—a dance that allegedly flushed the venom from the victim's body. No drugs or medicinals were used; only music and prolonged, intense, sweat-inducing dance.

Victims were made to dance for three or four hours at a time, then allowed to rest a little before once again resuming. The dance was performed continually for three to four days at a time—a veritable dance marathon!—after which the victims were consistently free from the symptoms with its fatal climax, although some victims would have repeat attacks annually, necessitating repeat performances. Tarantism was seasonal; it wasn't common during the winter but coincided with the Dog Days of summer and the local grain harvest.

The tarantella is but one of many dances included in what is now described as the *dance mania* that emerged in Europe and Northern Africa following the Black Death, most notably St Vitus' Dance. Whether or not the tarantella is related to these other dances is subject to debate. St Vitus' Dance, and other such dances, was an affliction. Dancers could not stop dancing: similar to the fairy story of the fatal red shoes, the dancer dances to death. The tarantella, on the other hand, allegedly *prevented* death. The dancer died if she didn't dance.

While dancing, the tarantati spoke and acted obscenely in a manner considered shockingly out of character for the victims. They are also described as "playing" with branches and swords. It's unclear who discovered the dancing cure; some suggested that the bites themselves incited them to dance. In other words, the spider made them do it! The tarantella, according to this description, initially emerged as an involuntary reaction to the spider's bite: the dancer might be understood to be possessed by the spider in the manner that those who engage in ritual possession dance in the manner of the specific spirit that they channel.

Although tarantism was initially blamed on the spider's bite, the condition was also contagious. It could be spread from one person to another. Although much of the criticism of the tarantati was directed toward women, men as well as women, both young and old, are described as infected with the tarantella bug. Children as young as five years old are reported as dancing. It was not restricted to Italians: Albanians, black Africans and Romanies are also described as afflicted with the illness and participating in the cure. From Italy, the tarantella mania traveled to southern France, Spain, and the Croatian coast.

Originally dancers may have whirled alone, however eventually it became considered unlucky to dance a solo tarantella. The dance evolved into either a couple's dance or a dance performed by several women. (The dance also differed depending upon region.) Sometimes a man and a woman danced surrounded by a circle of other dancers. Should one of the dancers in the center of the circle tire, someone else would immediately serve as a replacement.

This tarantella was a circle dance and was traditionally accompanied by castanets, mandolins, violins, and tambourines. The music changes tempo, speeding up as the dancers change direction. As the tarantella evolved into a group or couple's dance, the fun, pleasurable aspects of it began to transcend its origins as a shamanic dancing cure.

The tarantella as a magical healing dance reached its height in the seventeenth century. By the late eighteenth century the hysteria had declined, although the dance remained popular—as it does still. Today the tarantella is considered a romantic, sensuous dance and is often prominently featured during traditional Italian wedding celebrations, although not many recall its origins as a reaction to a spider bite.

Perhaps this is because the aspect regarding the spider bite and the tarantella's origins remains mysterious and controversial. Despite the dance's name, the culprit is not a tarantula as understood in the modern sense but is most frequently identified as *Lycosa tarantula*, the European wolf spider. This ground-dwelling spider doesn't spin a web to catch its prey but is fleet of foot and so actually chases and captures it instead. It lives in burrows in the ground and spins silk in order to cover the openings of these burrows. It is very plausible that harvesters could have encountered it in the fields and very possible that they could have been bitten. *However*, modern scientific testing suggests that no serious injury results from the bite of this spider but merely some pain, itching, and swelling. In other words, whatever was happening to the tarantati doesn't seem to have been caused by this spider.

There are many unresolved questions regarding the tarantella: did anybody actually die if they didn't dance the tarantella? (If so, it wasn't simply because of the spider's bite.) And who invented this cure anyway? In other words, exactly what was going on?

These are not new questions, nor are there definitive answers. Back in 1672, the Neapolitan physician Dr Thomas Cornelius accused the tarantati of being malingerers, half-wits, and *wanton young women*. He claimed that many, especially the women, simulated being bitten in order that they would be able to dance and rave.

Some historians have suggested that the tarantella actually masked forbidden Pagan harvest dances, or secretly surviving Maenad traditions, or even perhaps vestiges of devotions to an ancient spider spirit. (The area where the tarantella first emerged is one strongly associated with *stregheria*, the Italian tradition of folk magic.

It was an area where the Maenads once exerted their presence and where there was a history of devotion to the corn mother Demeter.)

According to Charles Godfrey Leland, an authority on Italian witchcraft, the tarantella was the "awakening dance" of the Italian witch-meetings known as the *treguenda* (see next entry).

Some historians claim to recognize the tarantella from images on ancient Greek vases and on the wall paintings of Pompeii. This dance wasn't known as the tarantella yet but was called the Lucia and the Villanella among other names.

Although the hysterical condition became very widespread, the tarantella seems to have been concentrated in a largely female core group. Certain families were strongly identified with the magical dance. Some dancers had annual attacks, typically around the Feast of St Paul.

Although there's no way to "prove" what happened, the description of normally modest, reticent people suddenly spouting obscenities and engaging in sexually explicit, usually embarrassing behavior corresponds with standard descriptions of spiritual possession, voluntary and involuntary, common to all areas of Earth and innumerable spiritual traditions. (The standard explanation given by anthropologists, for instance those who have studied Africa's zar, is that these characteristics of possession are the rationale given for women's occasional breakdowns under excessively repressive societies.)

See also **ANIMALS:** Spiders; **DICTIONARY:** Zar; **ERGOT**; **WOMEN'S MYSTERIES:** Spinning.

Treguenda or Danza Alla Strega

This Italian dance is based on a witches' ritual in which an invisible web is woven to entrap unwary travelers. Because of the connection with spiders, some historians associate the *treguenda* with the tarantella.

According to Charles Godfrey Leland's book *Aradia or The Gospel of the Witches* (see **BOOKS**: Grimoires: *Aradia*), *treguenda* is also the term used to denote a sabbat or witch-meeting. Italian witch-trial transcripts put great emphasis on dancing as an element of the witches' sabbat.

Film

Witches of all kinds cast their web of enchantment over the movies. From the very earliest days of film, witches, witchcraft, and occult themes have been popular movie subjects.

Because there are *so many* cinematic witches, some main characters, others limited to brief cameos, this list is only a sampling of some of the more significant movies featuring occult practitioners or those characters specifically identified within their respective films as witches (regardless what type of "witch" she may be). Characters identified solely as fortune-tellers have, regretfully, been omitted, most notably perhaps Marlene Dietrich in Orson Welles' *A Touch of Evil*. It is by no means a definitive list—that would entail a book of its own.

Films are filled with "witches" but what kind of witches are these? The following section examines how witches have been depicted in various films, from art-house movies to crowd-pleasing blockbusters to B-movie horror flicks. The *only* thing that unites many of them is witchcraft.

The question of whether movies depict reality or create fantasy (or some combination of the two) has been debated since cinema's invention. This is particularly significant when witches are shown on screen as the various definitions of "witch," depending upon whose opinion is counted, include both figures of reality *and* fantasy. "Reality" isn't necessarily expected when films evoke a fairy-tale quality (e.g., *The Wizard of Oz* or *The Mask of Satan*), however it's crucial to realize that many movies that appear to be *real* aren't necessarily any more realistic in regards to witchcraft than any of the more obvious fantasies.

How witches are cinematically portrayed is significant because false images and stereotypes regarding witchcraft contributed to the persecution of millions. (And whether or not millions were executed during the Burning Times, it's safe to say that millions suffered, in one way or another, from its effects.) On one hand, there's the tendency to dismiss movies as mere entertainment, not to be taken seriously; on the other, these often powerful images contribute to how modern people understand—or think they understand—witches.

Movies also too often feature historical inaccuracies: no matter how many movies you've seen that indicate otherwise, no witches were burned in Salem, Massachusetts: that's not how they were killed there. But of course, based on the movie version of witchcraft, one would think that *all* witches' ancestors once lived in Salem, and that what got those poor Puritan girls so fired up in the first place was some kind of "voodoo ritual," none of which is true. Although much of witchcraft's history is shadowy, quite a lot is well-documented, and to depict, as many films do, witches being burned in Salem is a little like filming a version of *A Tale of Two Cities* with gibbets or pyres instead of the guillotine.

Alraune

H. H. Ewers' 1911 novel *Alraune* has inspired several film adaptations. The title *Alraune* names the film's heroine (or anti-heroine, as she was actually intended); alraune, the German name for the magical botanical mandrake root, derives originally from the name for Germanic shamans, the *alraunas*. Alraune is sometimes used as a synonym for "witch." So the title may be understood to indicate a woman's name, an amuletic root or to simply mean "witch." (See **DICTIONARY:** Alrauna.) English-language versions of the film sometimes call the main character Mandrake.

The plot is based on one of the many legends regarding the magical mandrake (see **BOTANICALS:** Mandrake). According to this one, mandrakes take root when sperm, involuntarily ejaculated by a criminal as he dies by hanging, hits the bare Earth under the gallows at a crossroads. In the novel and films, this (false) legend inspires a genetic scientist to experiment by obtaining sperm from a hanged criminal and using it to artificially inseminate a street-walker, who serves as the human stand-in for Earth.

The scientist's ostensible goal is to determine whether it is environment or genetics that influences character. He raises the result of his experiment, a baby girl he names Alraune, as his own daughter, sending her to convent school so that she may have only the "purest" environmental influences. (Please see Literature: *Alraune*, page 276 for further details on the novel and its author.)

Is Alraune a witch? Her name suggests that she is intended to be perceived as one. Furthermore, the film suggests that her power to hold men spellbound is a supernatural one; she epitomizes the alluring witch, the femme fatale. Her beauty and charisma and the power she derives from them are presented as being something more than human.

Versions of *Alraune* include:.

❋ *Alraune (Mandragore)*
Director: Henrik Galeen, 1928, Germany

Also released with the English titles *A Daughter of Destiny*, *Mandrake*, and *Unholy Love*.

Starring Brigitte Helm as Alraune and Paul Wegener as the mad scientist Jakob ten Brinken, *Alraune* is considered a classic of German silent cinema. *Alraune* was intended to shock its audience: it was considered scandalous and controversial at the time of its release because of implied promiscuity, pre-marital sex, and incest.

However, much of what was considered scandalous behavior for a woman in 1928 isn't out of the ordinary today. Alraune just seems more "modern" than her fellow movie characters. Alraune smokes, has sex when and with whomever she wants, isn't intimidated by the nuns who are her teachers, and runs away with the circus. (Yes, she also encourages young men to steal and disobey their parents; however this can be understood in the context of how very few options for empowerment women then possessed, although that is not how it was intended to be understood: Alraune was meant to represent the worst dangers of womanhood—a rotten corrupting influence on everyone she meets.)

❋ *Alraune*

Director: Richard Oswald, 1930, Germany. Also known as *Daughter of Evil*.

Brigitte Helm was an important German movie star: Marlene Dietrich was only cast in the *Blue Angel* after Helm turned down the part. Helm's most famous film was Fritz Lang's *Metropolis*, however Alraune was something of a signature part for her as she played this role twice, this time in a film with sound.

❋ *Alraune*

Director: Arthur Maria Rabenalt, 1952, Germany. Also released as *Mandragore, The Fruit of Evil* and *Unnatural*.

Starring Erich von Stroheim as the scientist and Hildegarde Neff (Knef) as the title character, this version explicitly describes Alraune as a "bewitching woman." She is first witnessed in a lush garden setting so that she herself appears to be an exotic blossom. Neff's Alraune is shown nibbling an apple like Eve and complaining of being confined like Lilith. She is a free spirit with mystical powers who does as she desires. The film suggests that possession of a mandrake root enables one "to possess the powers of the gods."

Bell, Book and Candle

Director: Richard Quine, 1958, United States

John Van Druten's play *Bell, Book and Candle* was initially intended as a serious look at modern witchcraft, although its first audiences didn't appreciate this—instead they laughed in unexpected places. Rather than shelving the play, it was adapted so as to become a light comedy. In this new incarnation, *Bell, Book and Candle* opened on Broadway on Valentine's Day,

1950 with Rex Harrison and Lilli Palmer in the starring roles. It was a major success and a film version was scheduled. Jennifer Jones was initially set to star as Gillian but she became pregnant and withdrew from production.

Kim Novak, reportedly America's number-one box-office attraction in 1956, was subsequently cast in the starring role as the glamorous Greenwich Village witch Gillian Holroyd, back in the day when the Village was New York City's bohemian enclave. *Bell, Book and Candle* features very stylish, fun-loving, arty, *interesting* witches.

Gillian is but the most powerful of a pack of these witches including her aunt Queenie (Elsa Lanchester) and the regal Bianca De Passe (Hermione Gingold.) A young Jack Lemmon plays Gillian's bongo-playing brother Nicky, identified as a warlock. (The film repeatedly and emphatically makes the point that male witches are known as warlocks, although as one of the characters is a purported authority on witchcraft who is consistently shown to be something less than expert, perhaps that's meant as a sly joke.) (See **DICTIONARY:** Warlock.) The movie's true star may be Gillian's familiar, the Siamese cat Pyewacket.

Pyewacket's name derives from a famous woodcut made in 1647, which portrays Witchfinder General Matthew Hopkins alongside two accused witches seen naming their familiars. (Although the woodcut names the cat *Pyewacket*, the actual trial transcripts suggest that its name may have really been *Pynewacket*.)

Bell, Book and Candle was advertised as a bewitching comedy about an enchanted subject. The title refers to rites of exorcism that a character in the film describes incorrectly as being used to exorcise witches. (These rites are really intended to exorcise demons, however, once again, as the character, ostensibly an expert on witchcraft is consistently shown to be sorely lacking in knowledge, it's unknown whether that error was intentional—an insider's joke—or not.) There is no exorcism ritual in the movie, and the most prominent bell is the one around Pyewacket's neck.

Although the witches are smart, attractive, and fun, the movie's depiction of witchcraft is not entirely positive: Gillian is an ambivalent witch. She longs to spend Christmas Eve in a little church listening to carols rather than at the jazz club where the witches hold court. (Jimmy Stewart's character, unknowingly finding himself in this company of witches, complains that atmosphere at the Zodiac Club seems more like Halloween than Christmas.)

According to Bell, Book and Candle, witches can't fall in love, can't blush, can't sink in water, and are unable to cry. The film itself defines witches as people who live by magic and as people who possess powers that others lack.

> Bell, Book and Candle is unusual in that it prominently features a male witch, Nicky Holroyd, played by Jack Lemmon. Nicky's favorite trick—magically dimming street lights—may have inspired Harry Potter's wizard Albus Dumbledore.

The Blair Witch Project

Directors: Daniel Myrick, Eduardo Sanchez, 1999, United States

Baba Yaga lives! That's the subliminal message of The Blair Witch Project, however be forewarned; this movie has nothing to do with witchcraft but everything to do with local legends and perceptions of witchcraft. There is no witch in The Blair Witch Project; there is only fear, panic, and superstition.

Three student film-makers disappeared in October 1994 while filming a documentary in the woods near Burkittsville, Maryland. They were never found but one year later their film footage was recovered. The Blair Witch Project is that footage, the only evidence of what happened to these students. Many who watched the whole movie failed to realize that it was not a documentary but was instead really a work of creative fiction. Word of mouth parlayed this extremely low-budget "mockumentary" into sales of over $140 million in the United States alone, making it one of the most profitable independent films ever.

This is not a witch-friendly movie. Instead it feeds off fairy-tale fears of vengeful, cannibal killer witches. According to the basic plot a fervently held local legend insists that a witch (or her ghost) haunts the woods near Blair, Maryland. A woman, accused of witchcraft in the eighteenth century, was banished to the forest. Since then responsibility for two centuries' worth of strange disappearances, particularly of children, and mysterious murders, has been laid at her forest-hut's door.

What happens when you underestimate the power of the forest? If one seeks to find any true metaphysical theme in The Blair Witch Project then that question sums it up. Young people venture into allegedly haunted woods with all sorts of technical tools: maps, compasses, flash-lights, cameras plus the arrogance of youth but with absolutely no magical preparation, know-ledge or skill. The students seek to research "witchcraft" as a spooky phenomenon yet they have no preparatory knowledge of witchcraft itself.

What happens when you dabble in something or research something without actually respect-ing it enough to truly obtain an education on the subject? Once the film-makers enter the forest, leaving the realm of civilization behind, strange things begin to happen; they are completely out of their depth. They are unable to distinguish whether the mysterious craft markings, cairns, and wicker work that begin to appear are malevo-lent or otherwise. The students know how to work a camera and conduct an interview but they are clueless about magical practices, pre-sumably local ones. Once panic sets in, which doesn't take long, and the tools of civilization brought with them into the woods are lost, it becomes clear that these students don't know how to navigate and survive the forest either. *The Blair Witch Project* may be understood as warning against dabbling in dangerous areas outside one's expertise, with witchcraft and wild nature falling into that danger-zone category.

Burn, Witch, Burn!

Director: Sidney Hayers, 1962, United States

Also known as *Night of the Eagle.*

How's this for confusing: although this movie borrows its title from Abraham Merritt's novel *Burn, Witch, Burn!* it is actually the most faithful of the three cinematic renderings of Fritz Leiber's novel *Conjure Wife.* (See also *Weird Woman* and *Witches' Brew*, pages 270 and 271.)

Peter Wyngarde plays Norman, a narcissistic and somewhat pompous British anthropology professor. Janet Blair plays his American wife, Tansy. He thinks he knows everything there is to know about witchcraft and the occult, which he considers superstition rather than reality, valuable only as an academic topic. Little does he know … When Norman discovers magical charms actively in use by Tansy, he burns them and insists that she cease and desist from all magical activity. Of course, this being intended as a horror-suspense movie, all hell immediately breaks out and the professor and his wife are left vulnerable to the wiles of fellow-professor *and* witch, Margaret Johnston.

The witches are depicted as extremely con-ventional, even conservative, women. There is nothing stereotypically witch-like about them, appearance or behavior-wise. There's nary a black dress on the screen, let alone a pointy hat. There is *nothing* that distinguishes these witches from any other women and the film in fact sug-gests that *all* women are witches; men, the rational species, just aren't aware of the fact.

The spells and charms described in Fritz Leiber's novel are reasonably realistic folk magic, with a hoodoo flavor. Tansy learned them while on a research trip to the southern United States. Although *Burn, Witch, Burn!* follows the plot of the novel fairly faithfully, like the other movie versions of the book, this type of magic was apparently deemed not "dramatic" enough. In *Burn, Witch, Burn!* Tansy learns her tricks in "*the Islands,*" and the style has shifted to sensa-tional movie-voodoo with no relationship to the real thing.

As times change, different things develop and lose the power to shock. Although intended as a horror film and "midnight movie" there is little in *Burn, Witch, Burn!* to scare a twenty-first-cen-tury audience. However, what might be most shocking to modern eyes is the film's premise that it is normal and acceptable for a husband to determine what his wife may believe and practice. The film expresses no outrage that Norman should bully Tansy or destroy her personal property and handiwork. There is no suggestion that a man might consider respecting his wife's spiritual beliefs.

Although women are presented as the power behind men, men, in their turn, are presented as women's masters and the arbiters of what is spiritually acceptable. (See Literature: *Burn, Witch, Burn!*; *Conjure Wife*.)

the Burning Times

Director: Donna Read, 1990, Canada

Produced by the National Film Board of Canada, this film is the second part of the *Women and Spirituality* trilogy, which also includes *Goddess Remembered* and *Full Circle*. *The Burning Times* is a documentary tracing the history and roots of the European Witchcraze. "Witches" are defined as devotees of women-centered spiritual traditions who were eventually condemned by the Church as worshippers of the devil.

The film features original music by Lorena McKennitt and on-screen interviews with prominent modern witches and priestesses Margot Adler and Starhawk. It incorporates African-derived and Latin American traditions as well as European into its vision of what has been labeled as "witchcraft." Witchcraft is presented as genuine practice and, despite the Witchcraze, as one that is vital and continues to flourish today.

Cat People

Director: Jacques Tourneur, 1942, United States

The cat in *Cat People* isn't just some kitty-cat; it's a magnificent black panther fit for a Maenad. And the "heroine" of this film, Irena Dubrovna, comes from Dionysus' old territory: the Balkans.

What happens if a small group of persistent, defiant "witches" flee into the mountains and cling to their ancestral Pagan traditions? What happens if these witches eventually develop (or perhaps always possessed) hereditary transformative magic powers? These witches can't help it; they're born with their powers and can't shed them. And what happens if, over the centuries, these witches (or at least some of their descendants) become so indoctrinated and influenced by the dominant Christian culture that even *they* believe that witches are evil, sinful, destructive, and dangerous. This is the premise of *Cat People*.

Val Lewton produced a series of what might be termed horror-noir psychological thrillers containing vaguely metaphysical elements for RKO Pictures. *Cat People*, shot in one month on an exceedingly low budget, is considered among his finest. Its "witch" is the kittenish French film star Simone Simon as Irena Dubrovna, a Serbian fashion artist living in the United States.

Cat People's persistent motif is a Christian knight (Serbian King John) spearing a black panther, very similar to the image of St George slaying the dragon. Irena explains that the symbol isn't intended to be understood literally: the panther represents witches and ancient Pagan traditions that Irena fervently considers "evil ways." Reference is also made to the leopard as the evil beast of the Book of Revelation. The panther is Irena's alter-ego and double.

Sex and strong negative emotions (jealousy, rage) cause Irena's inner panther to take control.

Irena isn't an ambivalent witch like Gillian of *Bell, Book and Candle*; she's a tortured, anguished witch, caught between worlds and torn between desires. (Elizabeth Russell's brief but powerful cameo as another cat woman indicates that not all of Irena's compatriots suffer as she does. Her feline features accentuated, dressed in a tight black sequined dress with a hair bow tied to resemble horns, the Russell cat woman recognizes Irena as her "sister," although Irena fears and rejects her.)

Cat People is something of a Rorschach test: those who watch it may view Irena with sympathy or horror. It may also be understood on many levels: one character points out that Irena never lied, however the other characters are unable to believe her until after it's too late. Irena *knows* things that the other characters refuse to believe. On one level, the Balkan witch is surrounded by arrogant American innocents, convinced of their own superior knowledge, but the film, produced by Europeans in Hollywood during World War II, may also be understood on a political level as well as on a psychological one: Irena is terrified of her own sexuality, passion, and power—her animal nature.

Be warned: *Cat People* does not end happily for either witch or panther.

The film was remade in 1982 under the same title but it is not the same story, and the metaphysical concerns have shifted to erotica.

The Conqueror Worm

Director: Michael Reeves, 1968, United Kingdom

Also known as *The Witchfinder General*

This move derives its title from Edgar Allan Poe's poem "The Conqueror Worm" but the poem has nothing to do with the plot on any lit-

eral level. Instead, it affirms that the Conqueror Worm (i.e. death) is the hero of "… *the tragedy, 'Man.'"* Because Edgar Allan Poe was considered a sure draw for horror movie audiences, this film is sometimes titled *Edgar Allan Poe's Conqueror Worm* but this was only a marketing ploy. The movie's alternate title is more accurate: Vincent Price stars in this costume drama as the East Anglian witch-hunter Matthew Hopkins, who adopted the title Witchfinder General.

Although the film is not *exactly* accurate, it is based on historical events; its premise is that tension between Royalists and Cromwell's forces during England's Civil War resulted in women's increased vulnerability to charges of witchcraft.

Conqueror Worm was considered a very violent film when it was released. It also incorporates scenes of sexuality and doesn't shy away from the sexual satisfaction witch-finders and torturers sought from their endeavors. Because torture scenes are integral to the plot, rather than just gratuitous, witch trials lend themselves to exploitation by horror movies. *Conqueror Worm* was revolutionary because it unequivocally portrayed the witch-hunters, rather than witches, as the true source of evil. Matthew Hopkins and his henchmen are portrayed as the monsters, rather than the people he persecutes. True horror is shown to exist, not in witchcraft, but in the pleasure some take in tormenting others. See **WITCHCRAZE!:** England.

The Craft

Director: Andrew Fleming, 1996, United States

Troubled teens dabble in witchcraft, discover their power and find more trouble. That about sums up the plot of this movie. Superficially this is a witch-friendly movie but at its core it's about the dangers of playing with witchcraft.

The heroine, Sarah, has shown manifestations of psychic power since childhood. The movie begins as she moves to Los Angeles. Sarah is enrolled in a Catholic school where she meets a party of three would-be witches searching for a fourth so that each of the cardinal directions may be represented by an individual witch during rituals.

The girls are self-taught. Sarah is seen reading the *Witches' Almanac*. (See **BOOKS:** Almanacs.) They haunt an occult bookshop where the other girls encourage Sarah to shoplift. The store's proprietor, an experienced, educated witch, is the closest *The Craft* gets to a true heroine.

The film defines witches as people who "make things happen." Witchcraft is used for healing scars and protection but is most often used in *The Craft* for "getting back" at enemies. *The Craft* features the girls engaging in assorted "witchcraft rituals" that are strongly influenced by high ritual magic and Gardnerian Wicca.

On the one hand, witchcraft isn't mocked and the girls aren't shown as ridiculous for engaging in magical practices. Magic is demonstrated as genuine and valid, albeit unpredictable and dangerous. However, it's crucial to realize that *The Craft* was intended as a horror fantasy in the same manner as *Cat People* or *Burn, Witch, Burn!* One doesn't expect reality from horror fantasy and although the four young "witches" wear modern clothing and engage in rituals that resemble witchcraft, *The Craft* is not a depiction of modern Wicca or Neo-Paganism, nor is it any more real than any other cinematic version of witchcraft. If one wished to view this movie in a positive fashion, one could say that it shows that those who play with magic without knowledge or respect destroy themselves and others in the process. However scenes that allegedly depict spiritual invocation are just as false and disrespectful as the way old Hollywood movies depicted Voodoo and Pagan spirituality in general.

See **DICTIONARY:** Wicca; **HORNED ONE:** Krampus; **MAGICAL ARTS:** Ritual Possession.

Disney's Animated Witches

Walt Disney Studios has become synonymous with animated family features; wicked witches are among Disney's most popular villains. "Popular" is the proper term; although Disney's animated witches almost inevitably conform to stereotyped visions of evil witches, many adore them and consider them the true stars of the movies in which they star—their power and energy redeeming what many otherwise might consider insipid features.

❋ *Snow White and the Seven Dwarfs*
Premiering on December 21, 1937, this was the very first full-length animated film. Before its premiere, *Snow White and the Seven Dwarfs* was considered to be Walt Disney's folly, his crazy experiment; conventional wisdom suggested that no one would sit through a 90-minute cartoon. Walt Disney literally bet the house on his experiment; he mortgaged his home to pay for the film's production. Conventional wisdom was proved wrong: *Snow White and the Seven Dwarfs* became one of the biggest hits of motion picture history and set the stage for the plethora of animated films that followed.

> Another animated wicked stepmother witch-queen complete with magic hand mirror exists in the 1933 Fleischer Studio's Betty Boop cartoon *Snow White*. This witch sings *"Magic mirror in my hand, who's the fairest in the land?"* and flies on her broomstick as Cab Calloway sings *St James Infirmary Blues* over the seemingly dead Snow White.

The movie's plot is loosely based on the Grimm's fairy tale of the same name. A cartoon witch also appeared in the 1932 short, "Babes in the Woods," one of Disney's *Silly Symphonies*. She may have served as the model for Snow White's crone-witch. The actress Gale Sondergaard was among the inspirations for the coldly beautiful witch-queen. Ironically, Sondergaard would eventually be considered "too attractive" to portray *The Wizard of Oz*'s Wicked Witch of the West.

The witch in *Snow White and the Seven Dwarfs* literally has two faces: she is a coldly beautiful, villainous queen but when she wishes to appear otherwise, she is able to transform herself into the very stereotype of the fairy-tale witch: the old, bent-over, warty crone. The witch is shown as a true occult practitioner; her prize possession is an interactive magic mirror complete with accurate astrological sigils. Her pet raven serves as her familiar and she possesses an underground laboratory fit for an alchemist.

Although now considered a children's classic, Disney's *Snow White and the Seven Dwarfs* was initially considered too frightening for children. The film was considered terrifying—particularly the scene with the witch's dungeon-laboratory with its spider and skeleton. In England, censors ruled that children under the age of 16 couldn't see the film without adult accompaniment for fear that it would cause nightmares.

❋ Cinderella

There's no witch in Disney's *Cinderella*! Or is there? Hmm, who might the witch be? Could it be the evil stepmother? Well, if one subscribes to the definition of "witch" as an evil, abusive woman, then I suppose she could be made to fit the mold. However, what about that other character, the older woman with her peaked cape, magic wand, magic spells, proclivity for pumpkins, and magic chant of *"Bibbidi, Bobbidi, Boo!"* Could she be the witch? Oh, no, that's right she's the *"fairy godmother!"*

What makes her a fairy rather than a witch? Well, she calls herself a fairy godmother. Maybe more importantly, she's *good* rather than *wicked*. In truth, there's often very little difference between supernatural witches and supernatural fairies, however Cinderella's fairy godmother demonstrates the inability of Disney animated features (and many others as well) to allow for any witch other than an evil one.

That Cinderella herself, who is portrayed as conversing with animals, communing with fairies, and covered in soot like some Pagan devotee, might also be construed as a witch—or at least a witch in training—is another story …

See **FAIRIES**; **HORNED ONE:** Chimney Sweep.

❋ Sleeping Beauty

World premier: January 29, 1959.

Disney's *Sleeping Beauty*'s "witch" is the flipside of Disney's *Cinderella*'s "fairy godmother." What is initially introduced as a *"bad fairy"* quickly transforms into an "evil witch." The evil fairy-witch's very name, Maleficent, derives from *Maleficia*: the practice of negative—and often fatal—witchcraft. The word, although obscure, is most famous from its use in the titles of witch-hunters' manuals such as the *Malleus Maleficarum*. The movie's "three good fairies" take the royal baby so as to keep her safe from the "evil witch Maleficent."

The film is extremely dualist: the "good fairies" are completely good; the evil witch has no saving grace although, like Disney's other witches in such films as *The Little Mermaid* and *Snow White and the Seven Dwarfs*, Maleficent lights up the screen with her vitality and is often considered to steal the show from the "good" characters.

Maleficent is a goddess-like witch whose elements derive from traditional visions of witchcraft. She wears a black and red cape, the witches' colors. Ravens serve as her familiars; her tool is the spindle and she has a magic staff. Maleficent shape-shifts into Hecate's creature, the dragon, complete with bat's wings. (The three good fairies may also be understood as stand-ins for the Fates or the Weird Sisters.)

See **DIVINE WITCH:** Hecate; **WOMEN'S MYSTERIES:** Spinning; Spinning Goddesses.

❋ *The Little Mermaid*

This 1989 animated feature film was *very* loosely adapted from Hans Christian Andersen's fairy tale *The Little Mermaid*. (The fairy tale lacks singing crabs or a happy ending.)

Ariel, the title character, is a sea princess who'd rather be human. In this context she may be understood as descended from *Bell, Book and Candle*'s Gillian or *Bewitched*'s Samantha, except that Ariel is a mermaid, not a witch. In order to fulfill her dream, Ariel must negotiate with Ursula, the sea witch. Ursula, another of Disney's goddess-like witches, is an octopus-woman who dwells in a grotto to which she has been banished. The plot hinges on Ursula's past history as a ruler and her desire to return to power and wreak revenge on those who have supplanted her, namely Ariel's father, King Triton. Ursula's personal myth is strongly reminiscent of Lilith and of Medusa. She possesses the accoutrements of the traditional witch: she has a magic mirror, crystal ball, potions, and two eel familiars, Flotsam and Jetsam, who resemble sea snakes and venture out to do her bidding. Pat Carroll voiced Ursula's character, which (according to rumor anyway), was inspired by the actor Divine.

The Golem

Director: Paul Wegener, 1920, Germany

According to legend, the golem was a huge, powerful artificial man crafted by Rabbi Judah Loewe to serve as a magical bodyguard for the oppressed Jewish community who lived locked in Prague's Ghetto. (See **HALL OF FAME:** Rabbi Judah Loewe for further details.) The story was wildly popular and inspired many others, including Mary Shelley's *Frankenstein*. The tale also inspired no less than three Paul Wegener movies, all loosely based on the original legend. This one, the last, still exists, as does a 1914 version, although a third is believed lost. Wegener was a pioneering star of early German cinema; in addition to directing this film, he also played the part of the Golem.

The Golem presents a vision of Rabbi Loewe casting a magic circle and engaging in high ritual magic as part of the creation of the Golem. He conjures up a spirit who breathes out smoky letters spelling the magic word that will animate the clay man. It is one of the most complete and complex scenes of magical work and is also considered a masterpiece of early cinema because of the effects used and created. Occult themes inspired much of Wegener's work (see also *Alraune* and *The Magician*).

Harry Potter Film Series

Author J.K. Rowling's series of seven books about the boy wizard Harry Potter have been transformed into a series of eight films:

✻ *Harry Potter and the Sorcerer's Stone*: Director: Chris Columbus, released 2001

✻ *Harry Potter and the Chamber of Secrets*: Director: Chris Columbus, released 2002

✻ *Harry Potter and the Prisoner of Azkaban*: Director: Alfonso Cuaron, released 2004

✻ *Harry Potter and the Goblet of Fire*: Director: Mike Newell, released 2005

✻ *Harry Potter and the Order of the Phoenix*: Director: David Yates, released 2007

✻ *Harry Potter and the Half-Blood Prince*: Director: David Yates, released 2009

✻ *Harry Potter and the Deathly Hallows Part 1*: Director: David Yates, released 2010

✻ *Harry Potter and the Deathly Hallows Part 2*: Director: David Yates released 2011

The movies are fairly faithful, although edited, versions of the books and are thus discussed in depth later, in Literature: *Harry Potter*.

Häxan (The Witch)

Director Benjamin Christensen, 1922, Sweden

Born in Denmark in 1879, Christensen is considered a cinematic innovator and film-pioneer in the same league as directors like D.W. Griffith and Louis Feuillade. The surrealists found him inspirational and he is considered a major influence on the Spanish master director, Luis Buñuel. His epic silent film *Häxan* (pronounced hek-sen) was made in Sweden at the invitation of *Svensk Filmindustri*.

Häxan presents itself as an examination of witchcraft from a "cultural and historical perspective." Initially it looks just like a straightforward documentary, but Christensen constantly plays with notions of reality. *Häxan* switches back and forth from documentary mode to re-enactments of different eras told from different perspectives. The film is dizzying—like trying to define witchcraft. *Häxan* begins with ancient spirits (Pazuzu, Taweret, and Set, although *Häxan* identifies none by name) and progresses to medieval woodcuts that depict witches as grotesque. Eventually these woodcuts are brought to life. Christensen's first witches are no less grotesque than the woodcuts they inspired, nor is their magic. A love potion, for instance, is crafted of cat feces and doves' hearts.

Christensen casts himself as the devil, complete with horns and protruding tongue, and seems to have a lot of fun playing the part. Witches are portrayed making compacts with Satan and kissing his hind-quarters. (This may also be Christensen's sardonic comment regarding what actors will do to gain a director's favor.)

Häxan eventually shifts to tell the tale of witch persecutions from different perspectives and with very different witches. These witches include an old beggar woman as well as a very pretty young woman whose only crime may be stimulating lust in the heart of a repressed young priest. In general, women are depicted as susceptible to the wiles of Satan, including nuns. The witches' sabbat includes heresy and desecration of church rites.

Häxan contains some nudity and was risqué for its time. Just when you think *Häxan* is an extremely unsympathetic, negative view of witches and their persecution, the film's perspective and sympathies shift. It proceeds to demonstrate fairly historically accurate renderings of the physical and emotional torture suffered by those accused of witchcraft. (Christensen really did make an intensive study of witchcraft and the Witchcraze.) The film graphically demonstrates instruments of torture and how they were used. *Häxan* doesn't shy away from the sexual aspect of torture and the perversities of the torturers. It demonstrates how a mother's desire to do anything to protect her child is fatally turned against her. *Häxan* eventually shifts again, bringing the history of witchcraft up to its own day. "Witchcraft" is now defined as an emotional disorder linked to depression, hysteria, and kleptomania. The film quotes eight million as the number of witches burned during Europe's Witchcraze, although it does not cite its sources.

I Married A Witch

Director: René Clair, 1942, United States

Europe's political turbulence stimulated the acclaimed French film director René Clair to labor in the United States. He brought his surrealist influences with him and thus created *I Married A Witch*, a magical film about a revived Salem witch and her old sorcerer dad. *I Married A Witch* is a smart, charming, funny fantasy and thus questions of historical accuracy are irrelevant, although obviously witches were not burned in New England.

I Married A Witch was *very* loosely based on Thorne Smith's unfinished novel "The Passionate Witch." (Smith, the author of the work on which the movie *Topper* is based, died before this, his final novel, was complete.) Veronica Lake stars as the witch Jennifer, although according to Lake's autobiography, Clair initially did not want her, considering her to be little more than a starlet and fearing that she lacked the necessary comedic skills. (According to Lake, he apologized for his error within one week of start of filming.) Cecil Kellaway plays her incorrigible old sorcerer dad. (And just how old is father Daniel? He claims to be 80,000 years old. There's some discrepancy in the movie as to whether Jennifer has existed since at least the time of Pompeii or whether she is *only* 290 years old.)

Various special effects include the witches traveling as smoke, Jennifer flying on a broomstick, and disapparating, as well as a flying automobile decades before Harry Potter. Jennifer is a charming, beautiful, child-like witch with a hearty appetite for food, fun, and romance. And although she does fall in love with a mortal (unwillingly; a spell goes wrong) she doesn't suffer the angst of *Bell, Book and Candle*'s Gillian or the self-doubt of *Cat People*'s Irena. Jennifer is self-confident, determined, and happy with herself. The movie ends with the strong suggestion that this lineage of hereditary witches hasn't ended just because Jennifer married a mortal.

Kiki's Delivery Service

Director: Hayao Miyazaki, 1989, Japan

The premise of this animated children's feature film is that when witches turn 13 years old they must leave home for a year of independent study before they can become full-fledged witches. Kiki is one such student witch and the movie chronicles her adventures during this year.

Kiki's Delivery Service ostensibly takes place in France but it's really an alternative universe where towns have resident witches who provide services to the community including healing, spell-casting, and fortune-telling. (Kiki's mother, for instance, is a potions master.) There is no suggestion that witches must hide their identity or skills. Kiki gets in trouble when her shaky broom-flight almost causes a traffic accident; however had she flown well, her appearance on a broom would not have raised eyebrows.

That flying broom is among the traditional witchcraft motifs in *Kiki's Delivery Service*. (A crafty witch, Kiki makes her own brooms.) Witches look like regular people and are shown to come in various shapes and sizes; Kiki's costume includes a big red hair bow and red shoes. She has a talking black cat, Jiji, as her familiar. (Black cats are the prevalent familiars in *Kiki's Delivery Service*.) According to this movie, having a good heart is what makes a fine witch.

Macbeth

Macbeth remains among William Shakespeare's most beloved works. The play and its witches are discussed in further detail in Literature: *Macbeth*, including why certain of the play's witch scenes, including those incorporating the goddess Hecate, are most frequently omitted from modern productions.

There are many filmed versions of the Scottish play including animated feature films intended for children. The following are some of the most significant recent versions.

✳ Trevor Nunn's Macbeth
Director: Trevor Nunn, 1978, United Kingdom

Although the film was released in 1978, it features the Royal Shakespeare Company in director Trevor Nunn's 1976 production of *Macbeth* featuring Sir Ian McKellen and Dame Judi Dench as Lord and Lady Macbeth. This *Macbeth* is played in modern dress. The witches aren't portrayed in stereotypical fashion in terms of resembling Halloween witches with pointy hats but are portrayed as ragged and disheveled. They could be any homeless women; nothing about their appearance particularly identifies them as witches. (Likewise the king, with whom the film visually contrasts them, wears no crown and appears clerical, rather than royal.)

Although two of the women are fair, their clothes are dark, as opposed to the king who is dressed in glowing white and wears a prominent cross. There is a strong visual contrast between the immaculate king in shining white and the dark ragged witches during the film's opening scene. There is a primal, almost animal-like quality to these witches. The shining eyes of one of the witches suggests the ecstasies of shamanism. These dark storm-raising witches are contrasted with images of devout Christianity and are potent enough to scare and unnerve the warrior Macbeth.

Trevor Nunn's Macbeth includes depiction of image magic, the piercing of a poppet (see **MAGICAL ARTS:** Image Magic). The movie omits Act 3, Scene 5 (the scene with Hecate on the heath).

✳ Roman Polanski's Macbeth
Director: Roman Polanski, 1971, United States

Roman Polanski's Macbeth was produced by Playboy Productions. The screenplay was written by Polanski and Kenneth Tynan. The film opens with the Weird Sisters on the beach. There are no Halloween-style witch costumes but these are witches that witch-hunters would recognize. Their spell ingredients are grotesque. A gallows scene evokes witchcraze-era woodcuts. A young witch performs *ana suromai*, the ritual act of exposing the female genitals.

The story of Macbeth obviously held personal resonance for Polanski who lost his own wife and child through murder, as does McDuff. His is a very passionate version of the play. Polanski doesn't soften *Macbeth* nor does he flinch from the cruelty of its times (scenes of bear-baiting are included, for instance), or the darkness and desolation of the play. *Roman Polanski's Macbeth* powerfully depicts the true violence of what was done to McDuff's family: arson and the rape and murder of women and children. The killers enjoy themselves in the process.

An entire crowd of naked witches is shown at a sabbat, not merely the three Weird Sisters, although there is no devil present. Until Macbeth's arrival, only women are present. In Polanski's version of Macbeth, the *"something wicked"* of the infamous witches' line, *"by the pricking of my thumbs, something wicked this way comes"* clearly indicates Macbeth. The extra witches' scene with Hecate is omitted but there is a surprise ending with Donalbain, who is jealous of his brother Malcolm, seeking out the Weird Sisters.

✳ Orson Welles' Macbeth
Director: Orson Welles, 1948, United States

Orson Welles' Macbeth is not the version of *Macbeth* the director is most famous for. His *Black Macbeth*, also known as *The Voodoo Macbeth*, set in nineteenth-century Haiti was not filmed. This 1936 theatrical production was created for the Negro Theater Unit, an off-shoot of the Federal Theater Project, part of President Franklin Roosevelt's depression-era New Deal program. It featured an all black cast set in Haiti with voodooist witches. Allegedly a "genuine witchdoctor" was hired to serve as consultant. The Hecate scene was left in although the goddess was played by a man. Like his later film version, *Black Macbeth* met with snide reviews but was enormously successful, and had a sold-out ten-week run as well as a national tour.

This dark (literally!) low-budget production and expressionistic vision of *Macbeth* was completed in 23 days. Welles created a new character, a monk, to serve in opposition to the witches. His version explores the question, do the witches reveal his destiny or do they tempt Macbeth to do evil? The first image in the movie is of the three Weird Sisters, the witches as Fates. The witches brandish the Y-shaped sign of ancient womanhood (the downward facing triangle atop a staff) but are chased away by the sign of the cross. This version's Lady Macbeth, played by Jeanette Nolan in her film debut, is particularly assertive. Depending on one's definition, this Lady Macbeth may also be considered to be the play's fourth witch. She may be understood as summoning spirits but also fulfills the classical Greek definition of witch as poisoner. (She drugs the king's guards' drinks.)

The "extra" witchcraft scenes are omitted.

Orson Welles' Macbeth was the last film the director made in the United States before beginning a long European exile. His intent was to prove he could make a low-budget film. The film was not initially a success; the studio for which he made it hated it, although the film has since achieved much praise. The studio objected to the Scottish accents that Welles used to provide authenticity, redubbed the voices and insisted on sizable edits.

The Magician

Director: Ingmar Bergman, 1958, Sweden

Also known as *The Face*

Dr Vogler's Magnetic Health Theatre arrives in Stockholm in 1846. The troupe features Vogler (Max von Sydow), a traveling conjurer, his young male assistant, who turns out to be Vogler's beautiful wife disguised in drag, and his 200-year-old grandmother, a traditional witch. Naima Wifstrand plays Granny Vogler. The troupe, an old-fashioned medicine show, incorporating sleight-of-hand with healing, fortune-telling, and magical practice, is on the run from the law. They must obtain legal permission to perform in Stockholm and so attract further attention from the authorities, who seek to humiliate Vogler.

A wealthy merchant and a menacing physician conspire to experiment on Vogler to determine scientifically whether or not magic powers really do exist. Vogler's tormentors hold him captive and insist that he demonstrate his alleged powers or expose himself as a fraud. In the meantime Granny Vogler is selling her sure-fire home-made love potion underneath the nose of the authorities and a grieving mother fervently hopes that Vogler's powers are real.

Granny Vogler is a wonderful witch: smart, sharp, and confident of her power; simultaneously the genuine article *and* a con artist.

The Magician illustrates the split caused or aggravated during the witch-hunt era between various branches descended from shamanism. If sleight-of-hand artists publicly acknowledged that their act was mere tricks and illusion, than theoretically they were free from accusations of sorcery or witchcraft. Safety arises from denying magic and denouncing witches.

The Magician

Director: Rex Ingram, 1926, United States

This black-and-white silent film starring Paul Wegener as the title character is considered an early horror classic and served as inspiration for many others movies. The film is loosely based on W. Somerset Maugham's novel *The Magician*, which was inspired by Aleister Crowley. (See Literature: *The Magician*.)

Ingram read Maugham's novel shortly after it was published in 1908. Crowley was then still alive and at the height of his notoriety. The film is rumored to have contained fairly "realistic" scenes of necromancy and diabolism, although exactly what is meant by this is unknown. Critics *hated* the movie, describing it as sordid and vulgar. Maugham allegedly wasn't pleased with it either. Within a few years, the three existing prints had disappeared and have never been found. *The Magician* is believed lost forever. Only a few still photographs survive. Ingram's career, previously very distinguished, went into decline and never recovered amid some muttering about "the curse of Crowley."

The Mask of Satan (La Maschera del Demonio)

Director: Mario Bava, 1960, Italy

Also called *Black Sunday* (US) and *The Revenge of the Vampire* (UK)

Mario Bava (1914–1980) was the master and originator of *gialla*, the Italian genre of horror-thriller films. *The Mask of Satan* was Bava's directorial debut. (The cameraman/director of photography had "rescued" other projects behind the scenes, however.) The plot was very loosely based on Nikolai Gogol's story *The Vij* first published in 1835. Bava allegedly wanted to film it ever since he read it aloud to his children and terrified them.

Barbara Steele plays the dual roles of Princess Asa and Princess Katia. *The Mask of Satan* is a very dark fairy tale. Many were confused as to whom the movie was targeted and so it was a controversial film upon its release. It was clearly oriented for adults yet the story is a fairy tale complete with witches and vampires, popularly perceived as fare for juveniles, during those pre-Anne Rice, pre-occult renaissance days.

As a result, American International Pictures barred its theatrical exhibition to children under the age of 12. When the film was released in the US in 1961, it had been re-dubbed and re-scored, with over three minutes of erotic and violent content deleted. (The original director's cut is now available on a DVD from Image Entertainment.) The film remained banned in the UK until 1968. It was reassessed following the success of *Conqueror Worm* (see page 256).

Mask of Satan begins with a witch burning that takes place circa 1630 in Moldavia. Princess Asa is a vampire-witch although in this part of the world there is traditionally a close connec-tion between the two. (The belief is that witches transform into vampires when they die.) Princess Asa remains in her crypt for 200 years until a scientist inadvertently releases her and she sallies forth to wreak revenge on the descendants of those who tortured her and her beloved partner, who was also burned at the stake as a witch.

Exactly what is Princess Asa—a Satanist, witch, vampire, some or all of the above? It's never definitively clear. Although she is accused of devotion to Satan, there is nothing to indicate exactly what form that devotion takes. One could substitute the name for any Pagan deity and the film would still work. There is no traditional diabolism as in *Rosemary's Baby*, although these are traditional vampires who cringe and flee when faced with the cross.

The Grand Inquisitor is the witch Princess Asa's own brother. (There is also some question as to the relationship between the Princess and her faithful companion Juvutich. Although this is glossed over in the English dub, the original version suggests that he is another brother and that incest is their true crime.)

Although conceived as a "horror" film, the horrors are real: the witch is branded and a "mask of Satan" is hammered onto her face, practices that existed. (The film's mask is described as bronze; real-life ones would likely have been iron.) Satan's mask is tusked like a boar. Of course *Mask of Satan* is not realistic: even when lashed to the stake, Barbara Steele is very beautiful. If the film were to be true to life, all her hair, including her eyebrows, would have been shorn and she would have been naked rather than clothed, as she is here, although she is disheveled and her clothes are erotically torn.

> As the mask is hammered onto Princess Asa's face, it is filmed so that it appears to momentarily be placed over the viewer's own face. For that moment, we too are lashed to the stake and gaze through the eyes of the Mask of Satan.

This cinematic fairy tale features many elements of traditional witchcraft: the magic powers of the forest, swamp, and cemetery are illustrated. Toads, bats, and dragons appear and a portrait of Princess Asa depicts her naked with a snake. The film also includes the popular theme of the skeptical, arrogant scientist who is confronted with mysterious, unbelievable (to him) occult truths, as in *Burn, Witch, Burn!* or *Weird Woman.*

Note: this *remains* a horror film even if by the standards of the twenty-first century it is no longer quite as scary as when it was first produced. Certain touches remain grotesque: for instance, the vampires must be staked through the left eye, rather than the more customary (and discreet) heart.

Midnight in the Garden of Good and Evil

Director: Clint Eastwood, 1997, United States

This film adaptation of John Berendt's book of the same name, itself based on true events, opens with a shot of the root-worker Minerva, played by Irma P. Hall. Although she is not as significant a character as she is in the book— based on the movie alone, it's unclear how important a part Minerva plays—she still exerts her power over the film. She is shown in the courthouse, the graveyard, and in a park and is responsible for articulating one of the movie's major themes when she says that in order to understand the living, one must commune with the dead.

Minerva is a conjure woman in her own right but is also introduced as the widow of the famous hoodoo doctor, Dr Buzzard. Minerva is much more fully fleshed-out in the novel. Whether you understand *why* Minerva is introduced as the "most important person of the defense team" depends largely upon how many stories about Dr Buzzard you've heard; the movie doesn't spell it out. Dr Buzzard acquired much of his renown because of his alleged ability to magically "fix" court cases for his clientele. A flamboyant, easily recognized man, Dr Buzzard attended daily sessions of court on behalf of his clients; his was a very public presence. Minerva, as Dr Buzzard's spouse, presumably learned his tricks or maybe even taught him a trick or two. She is seen faithfully attending court, the way Dr Buzzard did; the implication is that her client's final victory may be credited to her magical skill.

Rosemary's Baby

Director: Roman Polanski, 1968, United States

Rosemary's Baby was adapted from the Ira Levin novel of the same name. Both the novel and film were extremely popular. Mia Farrow stars as Rosemary, a young, devout woman originally from the Midwestern United States, the "heartland," now living in New York City with her husband Guy, an actor. The film begins as they move into a spacious Gothic-styled apartment building, the Branford, although a trusted friend with metaphysical interests has warned them of the *interesting* people who were once tenants. Apparently some cannibal witches known as the Trench Sisters lived there at one time; another witch, Adrian Marcato, was allegedly murdered in the building's courtyard. Guy and Rosemary laugh but Rosemary, at least, won't be laughing for long. (In actual fact, the building *Rosemary's Baby* calls the Branford is really the Dakota, genuinely renowned for its interesting artistic residents, most notably John Lennon and Yoko Ono.)

Initially everything seems to be going so well for Rosemary and Guy Woodhouse: their apartment is beautiful, the neighbors are friendly, if perhaps overly solicitous, Guy's career soars, and Rosemary becomes pregnant, but odd occurrences with the neighbors and what seem to be disturbing dreams make Rosemary fear that something is very wrong. Indeed she is correct. Those lovely neighbors, an eccentric elderly couple named Minnie and Roman Castevet, played by Ruth Gordon and Sidney Blackmer, are witches, and they have big plans for Rosemary's baby.

When first released, *Rosemary's Baby* was considered shocking and surprising: the film begins so innocuously that its diabolical plot, complete with scheming, secretive devil-worshipping witches, was perceived as a surprise twist. The face of evil, in *Rosemary's Baby*, wears a kindly smile and is, at least superficially, warm and nurturing. The closest thing to a "telltale sign of witchcraft" is the witch Minnie Castevet's knowledge of herbs and her production of home-made healing potions. Spells are cast through food, most notably the delicious chocolate mousse that, as Rosemary comments, possesses an "undertaste."

Ruth Gordon won the Oscar and Golden Globe awards for best supporting actress for her role as the chatty Upper West Side witch, Minnie Castevet—the only person ever to win an Oscar for playing a witch.

Rosemary's Baby's witches correspond to the deepest fears of the medieval witch-hunters. These witches aren't just casting little money spells or playing in the herb garden; they're part of a murderous conspiracy whose *raison d'etre* is to fatally undermine the Roman Catholic Church. And how one perceives the Vatican, frankly, will color just how frightening and evil *Rosemary's Baby*'s witches will be perceived.

The true underlying theme of *Rosemary's Baby* is betrayal and whether one ever *really* knows those whom we think we know most intimately. This reflects medieval witch-hunters' warnings that one never knows where Satan and his attendant witches lie in wait.

The Seventh Seal

Director: Ingmar Bergman, 1957, Sweden

The movie's plot revolves around a fourteenth-century crusader knight and his burly squire, who have returned home to a Sweden ravaged by the Black Death. Among those they encounter is a young "witch" convicted of having carnal knowledge of the devil.

The Seventh Seal is not necessarily historically accurate for its specific time and place; however it is a reasonably accurate depiction of what was done to those accused of witchcraft at the height of the witchcraze. In other words, what is shown may be not accurate for fourteenth-century Sweden but is reasonably accurate for sixteenth-century German or French territories.

The witch is first seen in stocks. She has been accused of causing the plague. Her hair is shorn. She has clearly been tortured and is emotionally as well as physically broken. She is then transported to her execution, carried backwards in a wagon. Her hands are broken; she is tied to a ladder. Through the eyes of the various witnesses (the knight, his squire, and the motley entourage they have acquired) the witch's burning is perceived as terribly brutal, even evil (the burning, not the witch). It is vividly clear that this burning is a horrible miscarriage of justice—cruel, callous, corrupt, and pointless.

Siberian Lady Macbeth (Sibirska Ledi Magbet)

Director: Andrzej Wajda, 1962, Yugoslavia

Also known as *Fury is a Woman*

The great Polish film director Andrzej Wajda filmed this Yugoslavian production adapted from a story by N. S. Ljeskov *Lady Macbeth of the Mtsensk District*. It also obliquely draws on William Shakespeare's *Macbeth*.

Macbeth's trio of witches does not appear in *Siberian Lady Macbeth*. So then, who is the witch? There are scholars who consider that Lady Macbeth may represent a fourth witch or that if the Weird Sisters are understood to really be Fate goddesses, then perhaps Lady Macbeth is the true witch. This is particularly so if her speech in Shakespeare's Act 1, Scene 5, regarding the spirits, is understood literally. In that case, Lady Macbeth conjures her own spirits independently.

The "heroine" of *Siberian Lady Macbeth*, Katarina Lvovna (played by Olivera Markovic) doesn't know her "place." Her father-in-law suggests that she's ungodly, doesn't read her scriptures and, in short, is not a good Christian woman. She's too bold, too sexually assertive, doesn't do housework, although she brews a killer cup of tea, and is accused of infertility, which is understood as her "fault," a punishment on her ungodly ways.

The witchcraft in *Siberian Lady Macbeth* is subtle. Katarina casts a fertility spell involving a mare, which sets the rest of the plot in motion. The spell comes true but in an unexpected manner, as spells are often wont to do. *Siberian Lady Macbeth* obliquely cautions that the danger of spell-casting is that a chain of reactions is initiated that can't necessarily be predicted or stopped.

Sleepy Hollow

Director: Tim Burton, 1999, United States

Washington Irving's *The Legend of Sleepy Hollow* is most famous for its primary terror: the Headless Horseman, who has since evolved into a staple of modern American mythology. Tim Burton's film, loosely based on Irving's 1820 story, expands its inherent witchcraft themes.

There is no specific witch in the original story, but the town of Sleepy Hollow is permeated by an aura of witchcraft. Irving describes it as "under the sway of some witching power." He further explains: "Some say that the place was bewitched by a High German doctor, during the early days of the settlement; others, that an old Indian chief, the prophet or wizard of his tribe, held his powwows there …". Irving's story calls the

Horseman "the dominant spirit ... that haunts this enchanted region."

In the original, Ichabod Crane is a superstitious schoolteacher and devoted reader of Cotton Mather's *History of Witchcraft*. This is where the film begins to diverge from its source material: in Burton's movie, Crane (Johnny Depp) is a forensic pioneer and New York City detective constable with modern ideas, who is dispatched to Sleepy Hollow, then a two-day ride from New York City and a bastion of Dutch culture, to investigate a series of murders.

Who is the killer? The town elders insist that it is the ghostly Horseman. Others suggest that it may be "the Witch of the Western Wood who has made a pact with Lucifer." This is problematic for Crane, who describes himself as committed to "sense and reason, cause and consequence." (Conversely, a Sleepy Hollow local describes Crane as "bewitched by reason.")

Every significant female character in *Sleepy Hollow* is some kind of witch, including Katrina Van Tassel (Christina Ricci), described as "a strange sort of a witch with a kind and loving heart"; her step-mother (Miranda Richardson); and Ichabod's own late mother (Lisa Marie). Witchcraft is shown as something that women do to protect themselves and their families. However, men are not immune to magical practice: the local magistrate carries an ankh as a protective talisman.

The film displays a spectrum of witches and witchcraft. Witches heal, curse, and cast spells—even in church. The power of witchcraft is not denied. An oracular witch is shown to be accurate. Witchcraft is not inherently evil. Even the wicked witch has her reasons.

Katrina gives Ichabod her mother's book, *A Compendium of Spells, Charms, and Devices of the Spirit World*, advising him to keep it close to his heart, as it is "sure protection against harm." Ichabod is haunted by dreams of his mother, who was murdered during his childhood for practicing witchcraft. Ichabod describes her killer as a "Bible-black tyrant behind a mask of righteousness."

Although *Sleepy Hollow* is a lot of fun, it is not for the squeamish: bats and birds—or parts of them—are components of witches' potions. We witness an Iron Maiden in a torturer's chamber and its effects.

Spirited Away (Sen To Chihiro No Kamikakushi)

Director: Hayao Miyazaki, 2001, Japan

This animated feature film is considered to be among director Hayao Miyazaki's masterpieces. *Spirited Away* won Miyazaki an Oscar for animation and shared the prize for best film at the Berlin Film Festival.

Spirited Away plots the adventures of ten-year-old Chihiro, first observed moving to a new home with her parents. On the way, they wander into a mysterious abandoned ghost town. In a scene worthy of Circe, the parents wolf down the delicious food discovered in a deserted restaurant. As night falls and the spirits who reside in this town wake, Chihiro's parents transform into pigs.

It turns out that what appeared to be an empty landscape is actually a resort-town centering on *Abura-ya*, the Bathhouse of the Spirits. Spirits journey from all over Japan to visit the bathhouse, take the herbal baths, rest, and recuperate.

Chihiro is rescued by a mysterious boy, who tells her that the only way to save herself and her parents is to labor in the Bathhouse of the

Spirits. The manager of the bathhouse is the witch Yubaba. (Suzanne Pleshette does Yubaba's voice for the English language version of *Spirited Away*.)

Yubaba resembles an elderly, elegant Central or Eastern European lady, although she does possess the stereotypical witch's large wart. Yubaba is greedy, sharp-tongued, and hardhearted. In nature, if not in appearance, she resembles the great Russian witch, Baba Yaga. Yubaba is able to transform into a bird and fly. The plot will eventually hinge on her rivalry with her sister-witch.

See **DIVINE WITCH**: Baba Yaga; **PLACES**: Bathhouse.

Throne of Blood (Kumonosu Jo)

Director: Akira Kurosawa, 1957, Japan

Also known as *Castle of the Spider's Web*

Throne of Blood transplants William Shakespeare's *Macbeth* to sixteenth-century Japan, a period of tremendous feudal conflict. It stars Toshiro Mifune as Captain Washizu, the Macbeth role. The film is strongly influenced by Japanese Noh theatre, and perhaps because it is a Japanese film it doesn't play into Western stereotypes of witches.

The characters corresponding to Macbeth and Banquo, Washizu and Miki, are lost in the woods, in this particular case the labyrinthine "*Cobweb Forest*." There they discover a mysterious, solitary apparition, an elderly spinner who may be a witch, an old lady or a spider spirit. The witch resembles a white spider (and in East Asia, the color white is often associated with death and decay). She proceeds to sing their fate.

The "witch" or "old ghost woman" is played by Chieko Naniwa. She's identified as a "witch" or as the "woman in the forest" in the English

subtitles. The "witch" spins and sings in a little hut in the forest. Although the witch is not stereotyped, the reactions to her are. One character suggests that Washizu and Miki are "bewitched" and acting under her spell rather than responsible for their own actions, which refers to the paradox central to *Macbeth*: does a prophecy reveal reality or create it?

Eventually, Washizu goes back to the forest seeking what he calls the "Evil Spirit." The very forest mocks him. The old forest woman now manifests to him as a shape-shifting androgynous witch who prophesies near a human skull and bones, similar to a Baba Yaga-like death goddess. (See **DIVINE WITCH**: Baba Yaga.)

Weird Woman

Director: Reginald LeBorg, 1944, United States

The earliest of the three movies based on Fritz Leiber's novel *Conjure Wife*, *Weird Woman* was the second of six low-budget horror movies produced by Universal Pictures as part of its *Inner Sanctum Mystery* series. (At the time, Inner Sanctum was an immensely popular radio program in the United States; the movie series was an attempt to translate this popularity to the big screen.)

Lon Chaney Jr stars as an anthropology professor whose specialty is the occult and ancient spirituality. For him this is purely an academic subject; he has no belief in his chosen topic and even less respect for it. Anne Gwynne plays his young island bride, a white woman, a professor's orphaned daughter, brought up by Natives and thus, according to the movie, infected by their primitive superstition. Her new husband wants to return her to civilization and rid her of her superstitious beliefs, although he is not averse to using her as his primary source for authoring a bestseller.

Anne Gwynne, as the witch, is the most sympathetic character in the movie. She is sweet, sincere, spiritual, loving, and *good*. Her magic spells are cast solely to protect her loved ones. She is shown casting spells in the cemetery, however the worst that can be said of her is that she is weird and misguided. There is never a suggestion that she is evil, unlike her rival, a conniving, jealous ex-lover of the professor, who is clearly *not* a witch.

A prominent theme of *Conjure Wife* is that all women are witches. *Weird Woman* shies away from this; only Anne Gwynne and the Polynesian priestess are depicted as "genuine" witches. However, at the film's conclusion, one of the rational characters, not a witch, played by Elizabeth Russell (*Cat People's* unabashed cat-woman and *The Seventh Victim's* Mimi) casts an amazingly effective and deadly spell without realizing what she's done. Although at the last minute it's rationalized as a spooky coincidence, *Weird Woman* clearly shows that anyone—or at least any women—possessing passion and motivation can cast a spell.

Vavra, the renowned Czech director, became fascinated with the topic of the witch trials. He sought out an archivist who translated the original accounts of approximately two hundred seventeenth-century witch trials. Authentic quotes were incorporated into the screenplay, which was written by Vavra himself together with screenwriter Ester Krumbachova.

Kaplicky's novel is a straightforward tale of the effects of witch-hunting on a Moravian town and its inhabitants. However, in the film version, similar to Arthur Miller's play, *The Crucible*, the witch trials were intended to serve as a political metaphor. In his autobiography Vavra said that the witch trials reminded him of the political trials staged by the Communist government in the 1950s.

In post-1968 Czechoslovakia, witch trial as metaphor was only too clear: fearing that it would stimulate discussion and rebellion, government authorities refused to allow screenings of *Witch Hammer* in Prague. *Witch Hammer* was only shown well outside the city but was still a very successful film in Czechoslovakia. It was also shown throughout Western Europe and in Canada. *Witch Hammer* won a special award for artistic achievement at the Mar del Plata International Film Festival in 1971.

Witch Hammer (Kladivona Carodejnice)

Director: Otakar Vavra, 1969, Czechoslovakia

Witch Hammer is adapted from Vaclav Kaplicky's novel of the same name, which recounts the disasters that befall when witch-hunters are invited to investigate witchcraft in a Moravian town during the seventeenth century. (See Literature: *Witch Hammer*, page 295.)

Witches' Brew

Director: Richard Shorr, 1979, United States

The third and most recent version of Fritz Leiber's *Conjure Wife* featured Richard Benjamin as the professor, Terri Garr as his witchy wife, and Lana Turner in her final role as Vivian, the powerful older witch. (See *Burn, Witch, Burn!*, page 254 and *Weird Woman*, page 270.)

The basic framework of the story is retained: a professor of ethnology is successful because his wife has cast various spells. He refuses (or is unable) to believe in magic; when the spells are removed, however, all hell breaks loose, disaster strikes. The wife becomes vulnerable and he himself is forced to resort to witchcraft to save her.

Witches' Brew takes place on a modern suburban campus. The witches are depicted as suburban matrons. Their spells are disgusting, rather than seductive (ingredients include lamb's blood, cat urine, and bat guano) and lack any basis in *any* magical tradition whatsoever.

Unlike the book or the two earlier filmed versions, the witches now openly practice on their husbands. The husband doesn't believe in magic any more than in other versions, however in *Witches' Brew* he humors his wife and cooperates with her spells: he describes witchcraft as his wife's "hobby." The notion that a husband can destroy his wife's personal property and order her about was deemed too old-fashioned for this version of *Conjure Wife*. Instead, the aggravated wife takes a "vacation from witchcraft" to teach her disbelieving husband a lesson. She voluntarily removes all spells herself, leaving herself as well as her husband vulnerable to magical attack.

Also for the first time, the witches are implied to be diabolical; some of them hatch Lucifer from a stone egg. *Witches' Brew*'s witches and their spells and rituals lack any basis in any historical, folkloric or spiritual magical tradition: according to the film the rule of witchcraft is *"use only as much force as needed to get the work done."*

The Wizard of Oz

Director: Victor Fleming, 1939, United States

The 1939 MGM film based loosely on L. Frank Baum's novel of the same name is considered a film classic, an exciting modern fairy tale for children. The story recounts the adventures of young Dorothy Gale of Kansas who gets caught up in a whirlwind with her loyal dog Toto and lands in the magical land of Oz, from where she desperately strives to return to Kansas. Along the way she meets all kinds of interesting creatures, not least being two powerful witches: a good one dressed in pink, and a green-skinned wicked witch whose image draws deeply upon traditional witch-lore.

L. Frank Baum intended his book to serve as a modern fairy tale for modern children. (See Literature: *Wicked*; *The Wizard of Oz*.) MGM Studios was inspired by the success of Disney's *Snow White and the Seven Dwarfs* to create a family-friendly fantasy film. The movie was not easy to make: there were dilemmas regarding casting (it was originally envisioned as a vehicle for Shirley Temple, not Judy Garland) and direction. Several versions of the script were written and doctored by several different people before *The Wizard of Oz* was completed.

Baum's book *The Wizard of Oz* has Dorothy encountering many threats and obstacles in an Odyssey-like journey to get home. In the movie, only the Wicked Witch remains. The book is about Dorothy's Odyssey; the movie is almost as much about killing the witch as it is about getting home. Margaret Hamilton's witch only appears for a total of 12 minutes on screen and yet her presence is absolutely pervasive.

The word "witch" pops up early in the movie, well before Dorothy's arrival in Oz: Dorothy calls Miss Gulch *"a wicked old witch"* with "witch" intended in its pejorative sense. When Dorothy runs away, she meets Professor Marvel, a medicine show conjuror. He is an occultist or at least pretends to be one, illusionist, *and* bona fide scam artist. His Gypsy caravan, crystal ball, occultist's turban, and the mask over his door all evoke actual witchcraft traditions. And the cyclone itself may be interpreted as a sign of witchcraft, as it would be in many places from rural Mexico to Russia. Witches traditionally travel in the form of destructive whirlwinds. (Dorothy's first glimpse of the Wicked Witch on her broom comes in the midst of this storm.)

L. Frank Baum's book initially had four witches: the movie reduces them to three but only two are actually shown on-screen. No Miss Gulch exists in Baum's book. The screenwriter Noel Langley, assigned by MGM to write a treatment for the *Wizard of Oz*, invented Miss Gulch, who then reappears as the Wicked Witch of the West.

Glinda the Good Witch announces "Let the joyous news be spread, the wicked old witch is dead!" An incredibly joyful, catchy song follows as everyone celebrates "*Ding dong! The witch is dead!*" Can you imagine if *any* other profession, ethnic, religious or spiritual group were substituted for the "witch" in that song? It is hard to envision that so many would sing it so blithely, carelessly, and happily although it is truly an extremely infectious tune.

The Wizard of Oz turns the notion of witch-burning on its head: instead of *burn, witch, burn,* it gives us *melt, witch, melt.*

The Wizard of Oz displays some double-standards when it comes to the Wicked Witch and her alter ego, Miss Gulch:

❋ *Why exactly is the Wicked Witch wicked? Dorothy manages to kill two witches and is not described as "wicked." Although she never intentionally meant to kill them, neither does she show even a moment's remorse. Dorothy returns to the Wizard quite happily bragging about melting the witch.*

❋ *What was Toto's crime? In the words of Dorothy, he chased Miss Gulch's "nasty old cat." (The cat is the stereotyped witch-animal.) Why is Miss Gulch not expected to defend her pet in the manner that Dorothy defends Toto? Like Rapunzel's father, Toto and Dorothy have been repeatedly trespassing in the witch's garden and although this is glossed over, apparently Toto bit Miss Gulch. Would the movie be this light-hearted if an animal had bitten Dorothy?*

When Dorothy says witches are old and ugly, Glinda's response is that "only bad witches are ugly." Compare this to the response of the old grandmother witch in Ingmar Bergman's *The Magician*. When a pretty young girl comments on how old and ugly the witch is, she calmly responds that the girl will look no better herself when she reaches the witch's advanced age.

Like the *Blair Witch Project* (see page 253) and so many fairy tales, Dorothy's journey through the woods is characterized by fear; fear of darkness, wild animals, lions, tigers, and bears. The Wicked Witch, however, is at home in the "Haunted Forest" just like fairy-tale witches and assorted witch-goddesses from Artemis and Kybele to Baba Yaga.

Dorothy is unhappy in the woods but comfortable and secure in the Emerald City, where everything is artificial and completely controlled. Even if everything is green in the Emerald City, there's no natural foliage. It is a world of illusion (good, acceptable magic because it isn't really magic) versus the primal symbolism of the Wicked Witch.

What kind of a witch is the Wicked Witch? In some ways she's a supernatural witch: she throws fireballs by hand and literally rides through the sky on her broomstick. On the other hand, she's also associated with traditional and very realistic elements of witchcraft and magical practice: the Wicked Witch is a crystal gazer. She's also seen with a mortar and pestle, the pestle stained red. She casts a sleeping spell on Dorothy with red poppies, flowers that are not only traditionally identified with anesthesia but also with women's primal menstrual power and that are sacred to many powerful goddesses. (See **BOTANICALS:** Opium Poppy.)

The witches were initially *not* considered central to the movie. Look at early posters and advertisements for *The Wizard of Oz*: Judy Garland, her three pals, and even the Wizard are featured prominently, but rarely is either the good or wicked witch. The witches were initially understood as so unimportant that an earlier *Wizard of Oz* movie, director Larry Semon's 1925 silent version featuring Oliver Hardy (of Laurel and Hardy fame) as the Tin Woodsman, doesn't even include witches at all. (The wizard does appear as a shyster illusionist identified by the title cards as a "Wizard of the Black Art.")

Nor was the Wicked Witch of the West originally envisioned as a grotesque green crone. She was initially envisioned being as beautiful as Glinda the Good Witch. The producer's original plan was to cast Gale Sondergaard, who specialized in playing cold, villainous but gorgeous anti-heroines, as a glamorous, wicked witch. However there were objections from too many people who insisted that a witch must be ugly and hateful. (This early concept of the Wicked Witch as evil and sinister but also seductively beautiful was influenced by Disney's *Snow White*'s witch-queen: a glamorous, fascinating, alluring woman.) Screen tests of Sondergaard as a "glamorous evil witch" left viewers dissatisfied: they didn't fulfill audience fantasies of what a "witch" should be. (Columnist Louella Parsons noted at the time that Sondergaard was "too pretty" for the part of the wicked witch.)

Exit Sondergaard and enter Margaret Hamilton. Initially she was merely intended to look disheveled, but her appearance was gradually adjusted: her nose and chin were restructured to appear scary and grotesque, and her hair was restyled, pulled back tight so as to emphasize her new jagged profile.

Attempts to create a scary witch were almost too successful: in addition to trimming the movie for reasons of length, the director Victor Fleming decided, based on the reactions of preview audiences, to tone down some of the more threatening aspects of the Wicked Witch. Children were apparently terrified; some scared enough to run from the theater. At least a dozen of Margaret Hamilton's lines were cut from various scenes, including some verbal threats to Dorothy and her friends. Her skywriting threat was edited from "*Surrender Dorothy or die WWW*" to just the first two words.

Of course, the Wicked Witch of the West is not the only witch in the movie. Billie Burke, the widow of the impresario Florenz Ziegfield, played Glinda, the Good Witch. (Billie Burke was also not originally envisioned in that role; among the first casting suggestions for Glinda were Fanny Brice and Beatrice Lillie.)

Glinda emerges from a bubble, and wears a high crown and wings. While described as a witch, she corresponds to the stereotype of the fairy queen. Although Glinda *looks* beautiful and is self-identified as a "good witch" she's not always very nice: Glinda teases the Wicked Witch with the ruby slippers, then slips the shoes onto Dorothy's feet. After the Wicked Witch goes up in red smoke and flames, Glinda advises Dorothy that the young girl has made a "bad enemy" of the Wicked Witch, but it is Glinda who has orchestrated it.

Literature: Novels and Plays

Witches feature in literature of all kinds, from classical to Gothic to pulp fiction to fantasy to reality-based historic novels. There are so many witches featured in literary works that what is discussed here may be considered only the tip of the iceberg. Included below are *some* of the most historically significant, popular or influential literary works including witches. The *only* thing many of these works have in common is their inclusion of witches or witch-craft themes.

Obviously it is unfair to limit great works of art such as *Faust*, *Macbeth* or *The Master and Margarita* to discussions of witchcraft, however the interested reader will find a tremendous quantity of literary analysis devoted to these works. In general, the magical aspect in these analyses is ignored in favor of "greater" themes. However, as this is an Encyclopedia of Witchcraft the opposite tack has been taken. Discussion and analysis is devoted to each work's witch or magical practitioner including how witches and witchcraft are portrayed. Significant meta-physical elements that may be overlooked or misunderstood by the general reader are also pointed out.

Warning! Spoilers! Unfortunately it is sometimes impossible to discuss aspects of literature and witchcraft without revealing important plot details, mysteries, and secrets.

It cannot be overemphasized that this is only the tip of the iceberg: given space, one could include literally thousands more books. An interesting phenomenon has been the rise at the very end of the twentieth century of the witch as a character in literature targeted to children and young adults. Several hundred years before, witches were banned and burned. Even up until the later part of the twentieth century, witches, Pagans, and magical practitioners were perceived as disreputable, and hardly good role models for children. And yet, in the post-*Harry Potter* world, children's books are filled with witches who are as likely to be positive or humorous as they are to be scary and malevolent.

Alraune

Hanns Heinz Ewers (1871–1943) was a notorious, scandalous, commercially successful and very prolific German author, the bad boy of German popular literature. At the height of his popularity he was lauded as the "new Edgar Allan Poe." Ewers specialized in supernatural tales of the occult, laced with lots of decadence, sex, blood, and violence. He wrote novels, stories, radio plays, and opera librettos. Ewers wrote the screenplay for the 1913 German silent movie *The Student of Prague*, whose story involves a student's compact with Satan and which featured Paul Wegener, who would eventually star in a movie version of *Alraune* (see Films: *Alraune*, page 251).

Ewers was a fervent nationalist in the 1920s, although he apparently never actually joined the Nazi party. He mingled with Nazi bigwigs, among them Adolf Hitler, a social acquaintance who, according to Ewers, personally requested that he write an "official" biography of Horst Wessel, the Nazi "martyr."

Although the Nazis initially found Ewers attractive, he soon fell from their favor. By 1935 his works were banned, existing copies were destroyed and Ewers was branded a non-person and reduced to abject poverty. (He died of tuberculosis sometime in 1943.)

Conventional wisdom suggests that various Nazi officials, initially impressed by Ewers' celebrity, eventually actually *read* his books and found their decadent contents offensive and inappropriate. In addition, based on the content of his books, especially *Vampire*, some believe Ewers may have been a *philo*-Semite, rather than its opposite, which could also have been problematic. He traveled in the same circles as Erik Jan Hanussen the clairvoyant, who also fell from Nazi graces, albeit, in his case, fatally. Ewers also corresponded with Aleister Crowley who published his fiction. (See **HALL OF FAME:** Aleister Crowley; Erik Jan Hanussen.)

Alraune, first published in 1911, was the second part of a trilogy of novels devoted to the *ubermensch* Frank Braun, all of which have metaphysical themes. (Some elements are believed autobiographical.) The other two books in the series are *The Sorcerer's Apprentice* (1907) and *Vampire* (1921).

Alraune was a major commercial success and established Ewers as among the most popular supernaturalist fiction writers. "Alraune" is a German name for mandrake; it derives from "*alrauna*," the title of ancient Germanic prophetesses. *Alraune* also eventually became a synonym for "witch" and so the title of the novel may be understood to imply "*Witch*."(See **BOTANICALS:** Mandrake; **DICTIONARY:** Alrauna.)

Many legends explain the supposed origins of the mandrake root and *Alraune* is based on one of these. Men frequently ejaculate as they are hanged to death; allegedly mandrakes spring up where this sperm hits Earth beneath the gallows at a crossroads. Ewers' novel is also believed influenced by the Christian writer Tertullian (*c.* 160-*c.* 225), who described the female genitalia as the gateway to Hell.

Burn, Witch, Burn!

The American author Abraham Merritt (January 20, 1884-August 21, 1943) was one of the most popular and prolific producers of a literary genre that goes by many names: "*fantastic fiction*," "*post-Gothic*," or perhaps most accurately "*supernaturalist literature*." Many of his stories and novels were inspired by metaphysical themes, including witchcraft. His witches are powerful and magically charismatic figures of horror.

Burn, Witch, Burn! was published in 1933 and recounts the adventures of a mafia don and a prominent physician, strange bedfellows who team up to solve a series of perplexing murders. All clues lead to a mysterious shop selling extremely beautiful hand-made dolls. Its proprietor, Madame Mandilip, is eventually identified as a witch who kills via magical means. Her weapons are her magic powers and those cunning dolls.

Burn, Witch, Burn! was intended as a horror novel and Madame Mandilip is a terrifying character: brilliant and powerful but irredeemably evil. For most of the novel, she is also presented as physically grotesque and the opposite of the current feminine ideal: huge, ugly, imposing, sharp-tongued and -featured.

The movie known as *Burn, Witch, Burn!* uses Merritt's title but has nothing to do with his book; instead it is a version of Fritz Leiber's *Conjure Wife* (see page 280). The novel *Burn, Witch, Burn! was* made into a movie, directed by the legendary Tod Browning (*Dracula, Freaks*), and named *The Devil Doll* (1936). Erich von Stroheim co-authored its screenplay.

The Devil Doll is not included among the films in this Encyclopedia for the same reason its evocative old title could no longer be used: there's no witch left to burn. She's been transformed into a mad scientist. The witch isn't a woman anymore either: Lionel Barrymore played Madame Mandilip in drag. The entire plot was softened; Mandilip is no longer an evil witch plotting world domination but an innocent wronged man seeking justice and revenge, forced to hide disguised as a woman.

La Celestina

La Celestina, a Spanish novel written in dialogue, is considered the first true novel to appear in the West and a classic of Spanish literature. (English, French, German, and Italian translations exist.) Its title character, Celestina, a witch, dominates its pages. *La Celestina* was immensely popular: there were 80 Spanish editions by the end of the sixteenth century and 18 editions of the Italian translation appeared by 1551, although it is less well known in English.

Initially published anonymously in 1491, the origins of *La Celestina* are shrouded in mystery; the name Fernando de Rojas appeared in acrostics on the second edition (1501) and he is generally acknowledged as the author. De Rojas was a Jewish *converso* from near Toledo, Spain, a city renowned (or notorious) for its magicians, alchemists, and occultists.

The book was first published anonymously for good reason: *La Celestina*, published at the height of the Spanish Inquisition, mocks the gentry, while simultaneously expressing empathy for witches, prostitutes, and poor struggling women in general. In the novel, spells are cast; the witch mutters and uses herbs. Although Celestina the witch is responsible for these actions, characters don't create themselves: obviously the author had some knowledge of the topic—or so the Inquisition might have said. Writing a novel like *La Celestina* was a risky proposition as the author was aware: witch persecutions are mentioned in the book; Celestina was once publicly punished in stocks.

Celestina is not only a spell-casting witch: she's a perfumer, midwife, herbalist, healer, a procuress, madam, and professional go-between. Her specialty is renewing female virginity via her sophisticated sewing skills. The novel's plot involves a nobleman who hires Celestina to help him seduce a young noblewoman. The lovers are narcissistic, selfish, and empty headed, their lives manipulated by their servants. Celestina and her prostitutes are sharp, smart, and lively. Celestina is described as the center of merriment wherever she goes, although genteel, respectable characters are shown recoiling from the "Old Whore" or at least in public.

La Celestina examines the professional urban witch. Witchcraft, magical healing, and prostitution: all were illegal and disreputable but all ranked among the very few options then available to women who lacked male economic support. This is articulated in the novel; when objection is made to her professions, Celestina asks whether she's expected to live on air.

Chocolat

This best-selling novel by Joanne Harris, published in 2000, begins with the arrival of Vianne Rocher in a French village during Carnival. Vianne decides to stay and opens up a chocolate store where she weaves enchantment.

Vianne's mother was a witch, or at least she called herself one, as Vianne points out. She taught Vianne various magical skills, most notably the transformation of bad luck into good. Although Vianne avoids the label "witch" the neighbors assume that she is one and she is shown privately engaging in practices such as Tarot card reading that would confirm their suspicions.

There is also another witch in the novel: an elderly neighbor Armande Voizin asks Vianne whether she is a witch. When Vianne asks why she asks, Armande says it takes one to know one. Armande has a reputation in the village as an old witch; she wears scarlet, the witch's color. Reference is made to her red scarf and red petticoats.

Vianne opens her store during Lent; it is located directly opposite the village church and is kept open on Sundays, tempting church-goers with her chocolates. Its presence encourages parishioners to break their Lenten vows. And Vianne's chocolate is not just any chocolate. The psychically attuned Vianne magically knows each customer's desires and needs. People are transformed after contact with Vianne and consumption of her chocolate.

Among the themes expressed in *Chocolat* is witchcraft as resistance to the Church, a theme quite familiar to the witch-hunters who exerted their presence in rural France for centuries. However in *Chocolat*, this theme is expressed through the perspective of the witch. (In the very popular film adaptation, *Chocolat*'s spiritual, magical, and religious aspects were muted. Significantly, the character of the parish priest, Vianne's primary opponent, was transformed into a mayor, a secular authority.)

Inspiration for the novel came from the author's own family background. According to the biographical information on the novel's jacket, Harris was born in her grandparents' candy shop in France and is the great-granddaughter of a woman known locally as a healer and witch.

The Chronicles of Narnia

C. S. Lewis (November 29, 1898-November 22, 1963) was a scholar, professor, and author of many popular works. Fascinated by fairy tales since childhood, Lewis was a tremendous spiritual seeker. As a teenager, he was fascinated by Norse mythology and Wagner's Ring Cycle, temporarily abandoning his Christian faith. He eventually became a theist and then on September 28, 1931, following a conversation with his close friend, author J. R. R. Tolkien, himself a devout Roman Catholic, Lewis again deeply embraced the Christian faith. Christian themes are highly significant in his work.

The Chronicles of Narnia, his beloved adventure series, consists of seven novels written between 1950 and 1956. They may be enjoyed purely as children's fantasy or as subtle Christian metaphor. A witch is a prominent character in three of the books.

The Lion, The Witch and the Wardrobe (1950) was the first book of the series to be published. The witch of the title is Jadis, the White Witch. Four children are evacuated from London during the air raids of World War II and sent to live in an old house in the countryside belonging to one Professor Kirke. While exploring the house, the children discover a portal to another realm, Narnia. Narnia suffers under a spell cast by the White Witch: it is perpetually winter. (This draws from the old theme of the witch as Snow Queen; the witch, a spirit of desolation, is represented as a force *against* fertility.)

Jadis makes a second appearance in *The Magician's Nephew* (1955), something of a prequel explaining how Narnia fell under Jadis' spell. Two children, Polly Plummer and Digory Kirke, live next door to each other in London. Digory is the title character: he lives with his uncle, an evil magician. The uncle straddles that razor-thin margin dividing sorcerer from mad scientist; as a result of his magical experiments, Polly and Digory are transported into another realm—not Narnia but the desolate land of Charn, ruled over by Queen Jadis, already powerful but not yet the White Witch.

Although the *Chronicles of Narnia* may be read purely as an exciting story, it *is* Christian allegory: witches and magicians do not fare well. However Jadis has tremendous energy and vitality; although intended as evil, she is a lot of fun, particularly her detour into the real world (portals in the *Chronicles of Narnia* are presented according to conventional magical wisdom: they are accessible from either direction), where she creates havoc in London. Many consider Jadis their favorite character.

The Lady in the Green Kirtle is more subtle and insidious than Jadis. This mysterious unnamed witch is the villain of *The Silver Chair* (1953), the fourth of the seven novels to be published. A beautiful serpentine witch bent on world domination, her weapons include glamour, enchantments, murder, and lies.

The Conjure-Man Dies: A Mystery Tale of Dark Harlem

The conjure man is dead. Or is he? And if he is, who killed him? That's the mystery at the heart of *The Conjure-Man Dies*, published in 1932 and thought to be the first published mystery novel written by an African-American. Its author, physician Rudolph Fisher (May 9, 1897–December 26, 1934) is considered among the principal writers of the Harlem Renaissance.

N'Gana Frimbo, the conjure man of the novel's title, is a Harvard-educated African king living in 1930s Harlem who mysteriously chooses to work as a conjure-man, a fortune-teller and spell-caster for hire. (The sign on his door advertising his services reads "N. Frimbo, Psychist.") Frimbo is not just any card or palm reader. He doesn't pander to his clientele nor is he shown engaging in stereotyped behavior. Frimbo possesses unique, elaborate, and intimidating methods of consultation whereby he sits in complete darkness while his client is bathed in intense light, similar but even more extreme than old-fashioned police interviews.

When Frimbo is found dead, his clients come under suspicion. In addition to its historic value, *The Conjure-Man Dies* is a good mystery and offers a vivid portrait of pre-World War II Harlem, although Frimbo is clearly not your standard conjure-man. All characters, including the conjure-man and his clients, are treated respectfully. Frimbo is a man of superior intellect and insight. Consulting a fortune-teller is portrayed as being no different than consulting any other professional.

Conjure Wife

Fritz Leiber (December 24, 1910-September 5, 1992) is considered a pioneer of supernaturalist fiction and one of its greatest exponents. (He himself coined the term "swords and sorcery" to describe the genre.) *Conjure Wife* was his first novel. First serialized in the magazine *Unknown Worlds* in 1943, *Conjure Wife* was repackaged as a novel in 1953.

Conjure Wife envisions witchcraft in a university setting. It was conceived as a modern horror story: witchcraft is modern and contemporary, not antique, ancient or a relic from lost worlds. *Conjure Wife's* witches are thoroughly modern and very well-educated women.

Its protagonist, Norman Saylor, is a rationalist professor of ethnology. (His papers include "The Social Background of the Modern Voodoo Cult" and "Feminine Element in Superstition.") When he discovers Tansy, his wife, putting his fieldwork in "Negro Conjure Magic" into practice, he forces her to stop and burns all her protective charms and amulets. Hell immediately breaks loose: a student threatens him with a gun, another falsely accuses him of sexual abuse, and he is passed over for a promotion that appeared guaranteed.

Tansy reveals that she's not the only witch on campus; her actions have protected Norman from other spell-casting faculty wives who are now exploiting the Saylors' lack of magical protection. A bad situation gets worse and Norman is forced to resort to magic himself in order to save Tansy's life. Witchcraft is the only solution.

Conjure Wife is considered the most influential of the supernaturalist novels having to do with witchcraft and was extremely popular. Three Hollywood film adaptations were made. (See Films: *Burn, Witch, Burn!*; *Weird Woman*; *Witches' Brew*.) *Conjure Wife* was also adapted as an episode of the American television program, *Moment of Fear*, in 1960.

Although this is ostensibly a horror novel, witchcraft is treated seriously: its existence isn't questioned and it may be understood as a necessity: since everyone else is casting spells, one must do so also just to survive. The witches are not treated as supernatural monsters as in other examples of this genre such as *Alraune* or *Burn, Witch, Burn!* (see pages 275 and 276) but are "normal" women with comprehensible motivations. The novel may be interpreted as mocking ethnologists, rather than magical practitioners.

The magical practices depicted in *Conjure Wife* are drawn from southern-style Hoodoo and Conjure. Norman discovers Tansy's boxes of graveyard dirt, herbs, horseshoe nails, lodestones covered with iron filings, and old silver coins as well as squares cut from flannel with which to create mojo hands. These magical practices are real and authentic, but they are often a disappointment to those familiar with witchcraft only as fantasy who expect greater drama and more spectacular "special effects." Although each of the three movie versions of *Conjure Wife* has retained the novel's basic plot, each has also changed what it is that the witches *do* so as to appear more dramatic and sensational. None of the magical practices depicted in any of the films demonstrates magical reality as do some, although not all of the practices in Fritz Leiber's novel.

Creep, Shadow, Creep!

Author Abraham Merritt returns to the scene of the crime last witnessed in his earlier novel, *Burn, Witch, Burn!* (see page 276). This follow-up was published in 1934.

Madame Mandilip, villain-witch of the earlier book, has been dispatched but her old sorcerer companion still lives, as does his beautiful daughter Dahut, and they have some nefarious plans of their own. The plot of *Creep, Shadow, Creep!* is based on the saga of the Breton witch-goddess Dahut (see **DIVINE WITCH:** Dahut) and the lost city of Ys, although *Creep, Shadow, Creep!* takes place in the modern era and Dahut has been reduced to an evil goddess-like witch. Other magical motifs include the goddess' hell-hounds and the standing stones of Carnac.

The Crucible

Arthur Miller (October 17, 1915–February 10, 2005) was already a successful playwright (*Death of a Salesman*) in 1953 when his play *The Crucible* was first produced and published. The play is inspired by the infamous witch trials that occurred in Salem, Massachusetts in 1692. The initial Broadway production was very popular, winning a Tony award. There have since been two television productions, one made in the United States and the other in Great Britain, as well as two film versions, one French and one American.

Two questions invariably arise when discussing *The Crucible*:

* *Does* The Crucible *accurately depict what* really *happened in Salem?*

* *Is* The Crucible *really about the Salem witch trials or is it actually about something else entirely?*

Second question first: *The Crucible* is frequently understood to use the witch trials as a metaphor, although specifically as to what remains subject to debate. The most popular theory is that *The Crucible* is *really* about the United States' Congressional investigation of political subversion during the late 1940s and early 1950s when Sen-

ator Joseph McCarthy was at the height of his influence. Another theory suggests that the play is really about the case of accused Communist spies, Ethel and Julius Rosenberg, who might have saved themselves from execution had they confessed.

The Crucible may also be understood as a more general political analogy, transcending specific eras and situations. Regardless how *The Crucible* is interpreted however, what is literally shown on-stage *is* the Salem witch trials. Names of characters and the events portrayed in *The Crucible* are all borrowed from historical events. However it is *not* a literal depiction of what actually occurred in Salem. Miller himself has said that he was writing a fictional story about a historical event and that what fascinated him about Salem was the personal integrity and heroism of the victims of the witch hunts.

Much of the play is fictionalized:

* *There are fewer girls in* The Crucible *than actually existed.*

* The Crucible *suggests that the witchcraft accusations stem at least partially, if not entirely, from a love triangle between Abigail Williams and Elizabeth and John Proctor. This is not based on historical fact or even innuendo, nor is it very likely to be true as at the time of the witch trials Abigail was really only 11 years old and Proctor was over sixty. (In the play, Abigail is older.)*

* *The magical practices that initially stimulated accusations of witchcraft have been altered, whether for the sake of theatricality or because it is inconceivable to modern audiences that simple folk magic could stimulate such hysteria. In* The Crucible, *young girls are accused of conjuring spirits in the forest. It is suggested that at least some of the girls danced naked. As far as is known and documented, the only magical activity in*

which the girls engaged was simple household divination.

❋ *Tituba, an enslaved woman from Barbados, a stranger from another culture, immediately fell under suspicion of witchcraft.* The Crucible *suggests that she led the girls in "voodoo-style" rituals but this too is more sensational than what actually occurred: Tituba entertained the girls with thrilling stories and also later baked a witch-cake, a magical method of determining whether the child Betty Parris had been bewitched and, if so, by whom.*

The Crucible however does depict some of the Puritan anxieties that may have stimulated Salem's witch hysteria: not only sexual repression but also their terrible fear of the forest, the wild nature that encircled them. Miller is able to make this point by moving the magical activity into the forest. The Puritans considered themselves God's tiny outpost on the edge of the wilderness, which they perceived as the devil's citadel, filled with heathens, the dispossessed Native Americans whom the Puritans feared were in league with the witches.

See **WITCHCRAZE!:** British Colonies.

Faust

The legend of the sorcerer and/or alchemist Dr Faust has served as the basis for *many* works of fiction. Further information about the historical Dr Faust and the legends surrounding him may be found in **HALL OF FAME:** Faust. Two basic themes, however, are central to the works that these legends have inspired:

❋ *The immortal human soul may be sold to the devil in exchange for something (and that* something *is negotiable).*

❋ *Great occult power can be gained in exchange for the immortal human soul.*

The first point was revolutionary: the legend of Dr Faust emerged in the midst of the European witchcraze. Witch-hunters accused witches of *giving* their souls to Satan, of dedicating their lives to him, but this was frequently understood as a one-way bargain: the witches gained little if anything from the compact. The witches were servants of Satan forced to do his bidding. Yes, they received familiars, but these familiars often bossed them around and sucked their blood. Yes, they could fly, but that's because they were required to show up wherever and whenever Satan commanded. Satan's final joke on witches, many believed, was his failure to rescue them during witch trials. Women were believed most susceptible to the wiles of Satan because women were believed to be utterly carnal, uncontrollably lascivious creatures. There was no *logical* reason to make a deal with the devil. Only women were believed stupid enough to offer themselves to Satan for nothing; most men were too smart to fall for the devil's tricks, or so the witch-hunters claimed.

And yet, men *were* sorcerers—and not just any men either. Among the men suspected, accused and/or convicted of witchcraft were theologians, physicians and other exceptionally well-educated men. *Men* wrote, compiled, published, and studied grimoires. These men could not be dismissed as stupid or ignorant and yet they too were fascinated with occult, forbidden knowledge. The legend of Faust attempts to reconcile these contradictions. The immortal soul is not given away for nothing: instead it is the prize with which one can negotiate with Satan to obtain one's heart's desires or the solution to dire emergencies.

The second theme regarding the acquisition of occult knowledge is more subtle. At issue is the cost of knowledge and whether the thirst for knowledge is innately diabolical or whether it is a commendable, valuable, honorable pursuit.

The legend of Dr Faust as well as exploration of one or both of these themes has served to inspire various works of fiction and drama. The original Dr Faust was a magician and alchemist; stories that hew closely to the original legend possess an inherent metaphysical theme. Some works, most notably Goethe's *Faust* and those that take their inspiration from it incorporate additional scenes of traditional witchcraft and magic. However, later works from the modern era frequently present the deal with the devil metaphorically rather than literally, and completely ignore witchcraft or metaphysics.

Works devoted to the legend of Dr Faust are listed below in chronological order:

✳ *J. Spies collected various legends of Dr Faust and published them in German in 1587 as* Historia von Doctor J Faustus. *The gist is that Faust sells his soul to the devil in exchange for wealth, power, and pleasure. Translated into various languages, it became popular all over Europe.*

✳ *An English translation began to circulate in England in the form of a chapbook in approximately 1587.* The History of the damnable life, and deserved death of Doctor Iohn Faustus *was translated by P. F. Gent and recounts the sins of the historical Dr Faust. It was published at a time when chapbooks (inexpensively printed pamphlets, the tabloids or pulp magazines of their time) featuring tales of witches and sorcerers were all the rage. This particular chapbook has two claims to fame:*

1. It inspired Christopher Marlowe to write his own rendition of the Faust legend (see below).

2. In virtually all subsequent workings of the Faust legend, Satan is called Mephistopheles, a mysterious name of unknown origin. This chapbook is believed to contain the earliest reference to that name.

✳ The Tragical History of the Life and Death of Dr Faustus. *This was the first dramatized version of the Faust legend; it served as inspiration for Goethe's now more famous drama.* The Tragical History of Dr Faustus *was Christopher Marlowe's most often read and performed play. It is believed to have first been performed in 1589, although it is unknown exactly when it was written. The text was first printed in 1604, 11 years after Marlowe died. A second version is dated 1616; considerably longer, the tone has changed somewhat (many perceive Mephistopheles to be more seductive in the earlier version), and it is generally believed to have been extended by unknown hands following Marlowe's death.*

Christopher Marlowe (baptized February 26, 1654–May 30, 1593), the Elizabethan dramatist and poet, was vilified as an atheist, a Roman Catholic, a sodomite and a tavern-brawler with an unhealthy interest in unsavory subjects like the occult. He was also rumored to be a spy for the Queen's Spymaster. At the time of his death Marlowe faced charges of blasphemy and heresy. (The man who accused him did so under torture.) Marlowe allegedly died, at age 29, following a fight in a London tavern, which may or may not have been related to espionage. Charges against those who killed him were dismissed. Some believe that Marlowe did not die but was forced into hiding, where he wrote plays under William Shakespeare's name.

Faustus is described as a necromancer; he conjures and raises spirits. A large portion of the play is spent watching Faust enjoy his devil-begotten powers. "Sweet Mephistopheles" is Faustus' constant companion. Although in other versions of Faust, *the devil is ultimately cheated of his prize, Marlowe's Faustus must pay the price and is quite definitely damned.*

✳ *Goethe's* Faust: A Tragedy. *When the average person thinks of Faust, this is the version most commonly considered.* Faust: A Tragedy, *by Johann Wolfgang von Goethe (August 28, 1749-March 22, 1832) was written in stages, occupying Goethe for the best part of sixty years. The drama consists of two parts; the first part was published in 1808 but it was only published in its entirety after Goethe's death.*

Goethe was a poet, dramatist, politician, philosopher, humanist, and scientist. (He was among Charles Darwin's inspirations.) It is impossible to overstate his influence over the nineteenth century, particularly in German-speaking lands. Faust, *his masterpiece, is more than just a play or a piece of literature; it is considered* the *masterpiece of the romantic era. It is often interpreted metaphorically:* selling one's soul to the devil *for immediate physical gain has been interpreted as referring to the terrible human price paid for technological and industrial advances. Goethe's* Faust *also inspired many later works that equate deals with the devil with various twentieth-century social and political situations.*

That said, if you want witches and sorcery, this is the version of Faust *that has them. Faust has an alchemist's laboratory; he visits a witch's kitchen. Faust creates a homunculus with Mephistopheles' help. Moreover, Faust attends not one but two witches' sabbats: a traditional Walpurgis Night sabbat at the Brocken Mountain (see* **PLACES***: The Brocken) and a "classical" sabbat attended by figures from Greek mythology. Among the "witches" attending the classical sabbat are Baubo, Lilith, and Medusa. With Mephistopheles help, Faust enters into a love affair with Helen of Troy.*

Marlowe's Tragical History of Dr Faustus *was popularly performed as puppet shows in*

Germany. *This is how Goethe first encountered Marlowe's work. Goethe was also inspired by the life of the magician Cornelius Agrippa. The drama may be understood to be about Agrippa as much, if not more, than about the historical Dr Faust. Many of the details seem taken from Agrippa's life: Mephistopheles first appears to Faust in the form of a black poodle; Agrippa owned a very beloved black poodle, popularly rumored to be a demon in disguise.*

Faust is not damned at the play's conclusion but is saved and redeemed at the last minute. Mephistopheles is cheated of his prize.

Goethe's Faust *inspired many other works of creative fiction. Some of the most significant include:*

Klaus Mann's *Mephisto* (1936)
Thomas Mann's *Doctor Faustus* (1947)
Michael Swanwick's *Jack Faust* (1997)

The Golden Ass, also known as the Transformations of Lucius

The Golden Ass, written in the second century CE, is the only Latin novel to survive in its entirety and as such is very famous. Even though it is ancient, it is still accessible and highly readable. Much of *The Golden Ass* is devoted to tales of witchcraft.

Lucius, the hero of *The Golden Ass* (and the name of its author), is a young man completely enthralled by magic, witchcraft, and the occult. He travels to Thessaly where he hears horrible, shivery stories about the legendary Thessalian witches. Lucius gets his chance to see these witches, up close and personal. His host's wife turns out to be the renowned witch Pamphile.

Lucius is warned not to pry and meddle but he's determined to learn some magical secrets.

He courts Pamphile's maid, persuading her to let him spy on her mistress in action. He peeps through a crack in the door and watches Pamphile strip naked, apply unguents to her body, transform into an owl, and fly away. (She is literally a *striga.*)

Lucius begs the maid to steal the unguent for him; unfortunately she lifts the wrong box and instead of an owl, Lucius is transformed into an ass. The novel follows his adventures until the goddess Isis lifts the spell and he becomes her devotee.

The novel is believed to be somewhat autobiographical. Its author, Lucius Apuleius, was a Romanized Berber born in a Roman colony in what is now Algeria. Lucius studied in Carthage, Athens, Asia Minor, and Egypt. He was genuinely initiated into the Mysteries of Isis, was a metaphysical adept, and was brought to trial on charges of using witchcraft to gain the fortune and favors of a widow (her stepchildren brought the charges).

The witches in *The Golden Ass* are powerful, but although some are physically beautiful, they are not attractive. The book (or at least the first part; the latter half is more spiritually inclined) was intended as an entertaining tale of horror. Women's magic and the magic of the poor was held in ill repute; many of the stereotypes popular in the witch-hunt era and that still exist today may be traced to the classical age. Of course, Isis, too, the compassionate savior of *The Golden Ass,* has her associations with magic and witchcraft: how much of *The Golden Ass* was meant literally and how much was meant as fun is subject to interpretation.

See **ANIMALS:** Donkeys; Ferrets and Weasels; Owls; **DIVINE WITCH:** Isis; **PLACES:** Thessaly.

Harry Potter Series

Harry Potter names a series of books devoted to the adventures of a boy-wizard, but it also names a literary phenomenon that has impacted the history of witchcraft.

Harry Potter is an orphan living with his abusive only relatives, the Dursleys. On his 11th birthday, everything changes. Harry receives information that transforms his life: he learns that he is not an ordinary person, but that he is really a wizard with innate magical powers that he can learn to enhance, control, and manipulate: Harry has been accepted as a student at Hogwarts School of Wizardry and Witchcraft.

Harry learns that there is an entire alternative witch universe with various portals linking the worlds of witches and wizards with those of the muggles, the name given to non-magical folks. In the muggle-world, Harry is pathetic and deprived but he quickly discovers that in the magical world, he is a wealthy celebrity. Harry's parents did not die in a car accident as the Dursleys have always maintained; instead they died protecting Harry from He-Who-Must-Not-Be-Named, Lord Voldemort, the Dark Lord of the Witchcraft World, ending Voldemort's fascist regime of terror in the process.

Harry's arrival in this magical world coincides with the gradual emergence of Voldemort, who had been forced into hiding following the deaths of Harry's parents—as had Harry in only one of many parallels between them. Voldemort wants his power back and Harry discovers that he is Voldemort's primary opponent and target.

The first novel in the *Harry Potter* series was published in 1997. According to author J.K. Rowling (born July 31, 1965) the Harry Potter story appeared in her head fully formed while traveling on a train between Manchester and London. A single mother of an infant, she famously wrote the first manuscript by hand in a café, one hand rocking the baby, the other scribbling.

There are seven books in the series:

✳ *Harry Potter and the Sorcerer's Stone* (US title)/*Harry Potter and the Philosopher's Stone* (UK title) (1997)

✳ *Harry Potter and the Chamber of Secrets* (1998)

✳ *Harry Potter and the Prisoner of Azkaban* (1999)

✳ *Harry Potter and the Goblet of Fire* (2000)

✳ *Harry Potter and the Order of the Phoenix* (2003)

✳ *Harry Potter and the Half-Blood Prince* (2005)

✳ *Harry Potter and the Deathly Hallows* (2007)

The Harry Potter phenomenon cannot be overstated. Books flew off the shelves at publication. Children who previously resisted reading embraced the novels. The books hit the tops of best-seller lists and remained there. The series has been translated into over sixty languages. Moreover, the books are just as popular with adults as they are with children. There is also a parallel movies series, complete with tie-in merchandising.

Not all the attention garnered by *Harry Potter* has been favorable. Fundamentalist Christian groups have objected to the series claiming that it glorifies the occult, and the books have been frequent targets of book burnings. This is somewhat ironic, as the books are clearly fantasy, written by someone outside the modern witchcraft community. Although witchcraft is portrayed as powerful and glamorous, in Harry Potter's world, not just anyone can become a witch, no matter how badly you desire to be one.

Defining exactly who is a witch/wizard is part of the book's plot; although witchcraft is hereditary, magical power is not guaranteed. Sometimes muggles are born with magic powers; with education and training, they can then become part of the magical world although many of those who perceive themselves as "pure-blood" retain prejudices against them. Witchcraft is a combination of training and innate ability; without that ability, one is doomed to remain a muggle forever.

Harry Potter is not *about* magic; witchcraft and wizardry are an entertaining motif. Thematically, *Harry Potter* may be understood as descended from Charles Dickens' novels, just with added magic. (Poor, deprived, orphaned, noble youth, forced to live with terrible people who don't appreciate him and oppressively make him labor until his true inheritance is miraculously discovered: this could as easily be Oliver Twist as Harry Potter. And to Oliver, the London underworld is, at least initially, a magical new world filled with danger.)

Harry Potter no more offers a realistic perspective of witchcraft than it does of boarding school. Superficial elements are borrowed from traditional witchcraft and sorcery (wardrobe, broomsticks, the concept of familiars and the animals depicted as such: owls, cats, snakes). However the series does offer an original vision of witches and wizards that is neither rooted in the traditional folkloric witch, nor in modern Wicca or Neo-Paganism.

Although the Harry Potter books do not contain a realistic depiction of either witches or magic, because the magical world it does depict is so interesting, fun, and attractive, because the witches and wizards are such magnificent characters and because many of the muggles in the book are either unpleasant or played as fools, the series of books offered a sense of pride to those who consider themselves magical rather than muggle, and is as popular within the magical community as without.

The *Harry Potter* series opened a doorway to discussions of witchcraft and magic that previously did not exist. For many it was a fascinating introduction to a topic that was previously considered somewhat unsavory. It also changed the perception of books about magic from marginal, often disreputable publications to best-selling blockbusters. *Harry Potter* opened the floodgates for countless other publications involving witches and magic targeted to both adult and juvenile audiences.

However, *Harry Potter* also introduced the notion that witchcraft and magic were topics intended for children. Because the series now serves as an introduction to magic for many, those who assume this notion to be true are often surprised and disconcerted at the adult nature of much traditional witchcraft and magical practice.

His Dark Materials

Witches are heroic, brave, fierce, and female in the trilogy of novels entitled *His Dark Materials* written by Philip Pullman (born October 19, 1946). The title of the series derives from John Milton's *Paradise Lost*. The trilogy comprises:

❋ The Golden Compass *(US title)*/Northern Lights *(UK title) (1995)*

❋ The Subtle Knife *(1997)*

❋ The Amber Spyglass *(2000)*

The novels feature the adventures of the young heroine Lyra Bellacqua and her compatriots in an alternative universe populated by witches, angels, fearsome cliff ghosts, talking armored bears, and a mysterious tribal shaman.

This alternative universe (*everyone* lives in this universe, not just the witches) is somewhat recognizable as our own but also very different. Lyra's hometown is a university town called Oxford but it's not *exactly* that Oxford. The human characters are also very similar to regular humans but also very different, particularly as regards to their *daemons*. These are an intensive form of soul-sharing animal ally; everyone possesses a personal daemon, a life-long animal companion that is born with you and vanishes when you die.

The books' heroes include witches, the "Gyptians" (a distinct ethnic group, whose name and various characteristic elements clearly derive from British Gypsy culture) and the armored bear (a shamanic animal).

The witches are a distinct species:

❋ *Witches fly on cloud-pine branches and wear strips of black silk.*

❋ *Witches are not immortal but live extremely extended lives; the eldest is nearly one thousand.*

❋ *Witches are exclusively women, like Amazons; men serve them or are their lovers or husbands.*

❋ *Witches have their own goddess, Yambe-Akka, the joyful deity who comes to witches as they are about to die.*

Yambe-Akka's name resembles those of Saami goddesses, and Lyra's adventures begin when she travels to the polar regions in a desperate attempt to rescue kidnapped children from the nefarious clutches of evil scientists and religious authorities acting in collusion.

The witches are fierce, beautiful, and righteous. They provide safety for children rather than attempting to harm them. Clearly in these novels, the witches fight on the side of justice and freedom.

His Dark Materials is notable for providing some of the most profound, realistic depictions of the divination experience from the perspective of the seer. Although the divination device (the "*alethiometer*") is unique to the novels, the descriptions of the divination process will fascinate those familiar with those arts. One character also utilizes the I-Ching, the traditional Chinese method of divination.

Like the *Harry Potter* series, the books have been accused of being anti-Christian. Some have also suggested that *His Dark Materials* is a direct rebuttal of C. S. Lewis' *Chronicles of Narnia* series. Both series begin with a young girl hidden in a wardrobe or cabinet, and there are other parallels. However, the witches of *His Dark Materials* help rescue civilization, rather than freeze or destroy it, as does *Narnia*'s White Witch.

Because it is a fantasy-adventure tale featuring youthful heroes, *His Dark Materials* is targeted toward a juvenile market. However, even more than the *Harry Potter* or *Narnia* series, these are not merely "children's books." Although *His Dark Materials* may be read as nothing more than a thrilling adventure series, it does contain deep spiritual, magical, and theological content. *His Dark Materials* subject matter is deeper, darker, and more *adult* than that of the other two series.

The Jungle Book

What do you call a boy raised by wolves? How about a witch? Most modern audiences are familiar with Mowgli, the feral hero of *The Jungle Book* from movies and animated versions, however the aspects of the story relating to witchcraft are almost invariably deleted from these adaptations.

The Jungle Book (1894) is a collection of stories written by Rudyard Kipling (December 30,

1865–January 18, 1936), the British author and poet born in India (*The Jungle Book*, however, was written in Vermont). Kipling was immensely popular and influential at one time, not only on a literary level but also socially; he is credited with coining the phrase "*the white man's burden.*" Among those inspired by his work was Gerald Gardner, father of modern Wicca.

The Jungle Book was followed by *The Second Jungle Book* (1895), where the witchcraft theme is further expanded. In the story "Letting in the Jungle" Mowgli is accused of sorcery and driven out of the village. He eventually returns to discover his adoptive mother Messua and her husband have been charged with witchcraft because of their relationship with Mowgli. They are about to be executed but Mowgli rescues them.

Lives of the Mayfair Witches

A witch is a person who can attract and manipulate unseen forces, or so witches are defined in the pages of the trilogy of novels known as *Lives of the Mayfair Witches*.

Their author Anne Rice (born October 4, 1941) is most famous for her very popular series of vampire novels, most notably *Interview With The Vampire*, *The Vampire Lestat*, and *Queen of the Damned*.

The individual novels of *Lives of the Mayfair Witches* include:

✳ The Witching Hour *(1993)*

✳ Lasher *(1995)*

✳ Taltos *(1996)*

The Witching Hour introduces a dynasty of powerful witches beginning with Suzanne of the Mayfair and culminating with her descendant, Rowan Mayfair, a witch of the thirteenth generation.

Suzanne conjured up a spirit that she named Lasher; Lasher becomes passionately attached to the family, choosing an individual witch in each generation as his consort, although some maintain marriages or relationships as well. Whether Lasher protects the Mayfairs or drives them to their doom is subject to interpretation and debate. (The Taltos of the third novel belongs to a race of supernatural beings; other than the name the concept has nothing thing to do with the historical taltos, the traditional Hungarian shaman. See **DICTIONARY:** Taltos.)

Lives of the Mayfair Witches offers readers a tour of Western witchcraft history, beginning in Scotland, traveling through Europe (Holland and France), and then on to the Caribbean, Louisiana, and California. Two witches are burned, one in Scotland, the other in France. The descriptions are explicit: Rice accurately depicts how witch-burnings served as popular Church-sanctioned mass entertainment.

Some of the witches' powers are innate; witches heal and kill via magical means. Doll magic is prominently featured (see **MAGICAL ARTS:** Image Magic), as is telekinesis. Methods depicted of raising and conjuring spirits are *not* traditional and some of the witches' magical experiments verge on mad science that would not be out of place in *Alraune* or *Burn, Witch, Burn!* (see pages 275 and 276).

Merrick, a later novel by Anne Rice (2001), may be read as a continuation of *Lives of the Mayfair Witches*. Merrick, described as a "voodoo-witch," is a distant relative, descended from the wealthy Mayfairs and their Haitian slaves. Merrick is extremely beautiful, tough, hard-drinking, and maybe the most powerful witch of all. Rice merges two of her genres: *Merrick* is a witch/vampire novel. Some of Rice's most beloved vampire characters (Louis, Lestat, Claudia) make guest appearances.

Different witches possess different skills. Suzanne, the first Mayfair witch, is a Scottish healer; Stella, a New Orleans witch, is described as a "real voodoo queen" familiar with powders, potions, and ceremonials. She also tells fortunes with cards. (Magical arts, in general, are described rather than witnessed; there are no depictions of true Vodoun or traditional witchcraft.) The witches are powerful, brave, beautiful, glamorous, alluring, and tragic. Their characters are complex: whether they are evil, heroines or victimized is subject to interpretation. There is also a male Mayfair, Julien, who may or may not be among the 13 Mayfair Witches.

Lord of the Rings

The wizard Gandalf may be considered a peer of such magical masters as Merlin or Dr Faust and yet unlike those legendary characters, Gandalf is not based on a historical personality but is the literary creation of J.R.R. Tolkien (January 3, 1892- September 2, 1973). Tolkien was a university professor, scholar, etymologist, and prolific author. Although his works do not contain witches, several prominently feature powerful, archetypal wizards, especially Gandalf the Grey.

Gandalf makes his first appearance in *The Hobbit* (1937) initially targeted toward youthful readers. He then reappears, alongside his sometime ally and sometime rival Saruman, in *The Lord of the Rings*, a trilogy of novels comprising:

✾ The Fellowship of the Ring *(1954)*

✾ The Two Towers *(1954)*

✾ The Return of the King *(1955)*

Tolkien was a master of etymology, the study of words and language, so it's unlikely to be a coincidence that although explicitly identified as wizards, Gandalf and Saruman are also linked to witches:

✾ *Wizards are known as* Istari *"the wise ones" in the Elven tongue.*

✾ *Saruman's Elvish name translates as* "man of skill" *or cunning-man.*

Gandalf may be crotchety and secretive at times but he is *good* and righteous and fights exclusively on the side of justice. He does not allow himself to be tempted by the forces of Sauron, the Dark Lord, as does his compatriot wizard Saruman. The wizards resemble Merlin-type magicians; they possess magic swords and staffs. Great books of power and crystal ball-like "seeing stones" also appear in the trilogy.

Gandalf appears most frequently as a dusty, elderly traveler, an old grey-bearded man wearing a grey cloak. In this guise, he is reminiscent of the Norse warrior-shaman deity Odin, himself a master magician. (Odin, too, has alliances with dwarves and elves.) Gandalf, like Odin, is also occasionally mistaken for a simple conjurer.

The Lord of the Rings inspired a highly successful trilogy of movies directed by Peter Jackson, beginning with *The Fellowship of the Ring* (2001). Each of the two subsequent films was released one year later. Sir Ian McKellen and Christopher Lee respectively starred as the dueling wizards, Gandalf and Saruman.

Love Medicine

The Ojibwa (also known as the Anishinabe or Chippewa) are the third largest Native American community in the United States. They live in the Northern United States as well as in Canada. *Love Medicine*, published in 1984, is the first of several novels by Louise Erdrich (born June 7, 1954) that take place in the Ojibwa community over an extended period of time. Although the novels are not officially a "series" they feature many of the same characters and may be read in the manner of a series. These other novels include:

✾ The Beet Queen *(1986)*

✾ Tracks *(1988)*

✾ The Bingo Palace *(1994)*

✾ Tales of Burning Love *(1996)*

✾ The Last Report on the Miracles at Little No Horse *(2002)*

Louise Erdrich's novels are often categorized as "magical realism," however they are deeply influenced by the extensive and sophisticated system of traditional Ojibwa folklore and spiritual and magical practices. Many of these practices are respectfully incorporated into her novels.

Erdrich herself is of French, German, and Ojibwa ancestry. The novels' characters are equally complex: some embrace their ancient traditions, while others, now devout Christians, fervently reject them.

The books are not written in chronological order, which lends a magical dizzying effect. In other words, *Love Medicine* was the first book written and published but in terms of chronological events it could be the third book: the witch character Fleur Pillager is an elderly woman, whereas she is young in *Tracks*, which recounts earlier events.

Fleur terrifies people; she has a reputation of placing powerful spells on those who've crossed or wronged her. She is not above playing tricks of all kinds; magic is shown as both real and illusion. Fleur is wild, defiant, and autonomous. She appreciates the power of her reputation as a witch and cultivates it.

Macbeth

"By the pricking of my thumbs, something wicked this way comes …"

Macbeth's Weird Sisters are among the most famous, influential literary witches of all time. William Shakespeare (baptized April 26, 1564–May 3, 1616) composed his play *Macbeth* in approximately 1605; it had its stage premier in 1606. *Macbeth* did not appear in print until the First Folio version in 1623.

Macbeth was inspired by the need to court royal favor; Shakespeare had been successful under Elizabeth I and wished to maintain this success under the reign of her successor, James I. James came from Scotland and was passionately interested in witches and witchcraft. He himself composed a book of demonology, a rebuttal to Reginald Scot's rationalist view of witchcraft, and also personally presided over several witchcraft trials, especially those of North Berwick. (See **BOOKS:** Witch-Hunt Books: James I.) James believed that the North Berwick witches had attempted to kill him via magic. A Scottish play that made favorable reference to his ancestry and that featured scenes of witchcraft was believed able to please the king. *Macbeth* remains among Shakespeare's most beloved and most frequently staged plays.

The story of *Macbeth* derives from various sources, but mainly from Raphael Holinshed's *Chronicles of England, Scotland and Ireland*, a popular history book of his day. Shakespeare, however, combined, altered and embellished several of the stories recounted by Holinshed.

The question posed of the Weird Sisters since *Macbeth* was first produced is do the witches foretell the future or do they actually set the future in motion?

The witches open the play with their words, *"When shall we three meet again …"* *Macbeth*'s witches are active at night. They have a cauldron full of eerie ingredients. They invoke Hecate as their goddess and conjure up apparitions for Macbeth as requested. The three witches resemble Fate goddesses or Norns; "Weird Sisters" names the Anglo-Saxon variation on that theme. (See **WOMEN'S MYSTERIES:** Spinning.) Some understand Lady Macbeth to be a fourth, solitary witch. Her speech requesting spiritual assistance (*"Come you spirits that tend on mortal thoughts!"*) might be understood literally, although contemporary audiences rarely interpret it this way.

Macbeth features several scenes of witchcraft; however, how many of these you are able to enjoy depends upon the theatrical production. Back in the seventeenth century, witches were a huge draw: there is some scholarly belief that *someone*, not Shakespeare, added extra scenes of witchcraft. Although some may find this unbelievable, others feel that these extra witchcraft scenes detract from the plot and pacing and so they are most often deleted. Two songs, in Act 3, Scene 5 and Act 4, Scene 1, are believed to have originated in Thomas Middleton's play *The Witch* and to be later interpolations. The scenes in which Hecate appears are also believed to be interpolations.

See Films: *Macbeth*, page 262, and **WITCH-CRAZE!:** England; Scotland.

The Magician

W. Somerset Maugham (January 25, 1874-December 16, 1965) met the magus Aleister Crowley in Paris. They traveled in the same circles and dined at the same restaurant *Le Chat Blanc* (the restaurant appears in the novel). Maugham disliked Crowley but was fascinated by him and he was thus inspired to write his novel, *The Magician.*

Maugham wrote the novel in the first half of 1907 but his publisher then declined to release the book as its subject matter was deemed excessively shocking. A new publisher was found and the book was eventually published in 1908.

Crowley served as the model for the magician of the title, Oliver Haddo, although he merely inspired the character. When another character humiliates Oliver Haddo, who claims to be a powerful magician, Haddo wreaks revenge by magically stealing and destroying his enemy's fiancée. The book has nothing really to do with Crowley, with whom Maugham was only slightly acquainted, and the story itself is fic-tionalized—although the character of Margaret Dauncey, the erstwhile fiancée, is allegedly based on that of Crowley's wife, Rose Kelly.

See Films: *The Magician*, page 264; **HALL OF FAME:** Aleister Crowley.

The Master and Margarita

The devil visits Moscow in the 1930s and masquerades as Woland, the Master Magician, a theatrical conjurer who carries a poodle-headed cane, reminiscent of the black poodle that transforms into Mephistopheles in *Faust.* He is accompanied by an entourage including Hella, a naked red-headed witch, Behemoth, his huge, talking, vodka-quaffing, chess-playing black cat, and the evil but sometimes helpful angels, Azazelo and Asmodeus. As they say, all hell breaks loose.

The Master and Margarita, written by Mikhail Bulgakov (May 15, 1891-March 10, 1940), draws much of its inspiration from Goethe's *Faust* (and from Gounod's opera, which derives from Goethe). It is Margarita who makes the deal with the devil in order to rescue her beloved Master, an author who has been pilloried for daring to write a novel about Jesus Christ in the officially atheist Soviet Union. (*The Master and Margarita* contains two parallel novels: one recounting a dialogue between Christ and Pontius Pilate, the other the Faustian bargain.) By making this deal, Margarita is transformed into a witch.

Margarita is the heroine of the novel; she is not damned or evil. She is instead perhaps the kindest, most sensible character in the novel. Whether Woland and his entourage are evil is subject for debate: certainly they are not gentle but dispense punishment to the rude, greedy, stupid and/or bad-mannered Muscovites they meet. They are dangerous figures and not to be trifled with, but when compared with some of the human inhabitants of the book, it's debatable exactly where evil lies.

> The Rolling Stones' song "Sympathy for the Devil" with its devil who demands sympathy and taste was allegedly inspired by *The Master and Margarita*.

The Soviet novelist and physician Bulgakov was from Kiev, near Bald Mountain, famed home of Slavic witches' sabbats. He was briefly Josef Stalin's favorite playwright, which may have saved him from the dire fate that awaited many of his contemporaries. Several of Bulgakov's works mocked the Soviet regime and he eventually fell out of favor. In 1929, all his works were banned. He couldn't publish anything and was refused permission to emigrate.

Bulgakov started writing *The Master and Margarita* in 1928. He completed the manuscript but continued to revise it until his death. A censored version was published in 1966–67. It was finally published in its entirety in Moscow in 1973 and it is considered a classic among modern Russian novels. Four English translations are available.

The Monk

First published in 1796, *The Monk* was a scandalous novel full of sex, sacrilege, and violence. It is considered among the first and finest of the genre of Gothic novels and was so popular that its author, Matthew Lewis, is still sometimes called *Monk* Lewis.

Lewis (July 9, 1775-May 14, 1818) was the son of a wealthy landowner in Jamaica who eventually became the British Deputy-Secretary of War. Matthew's mother, Frances, left her husband and children to run away with a music master, causing a major public scandal. Matthew grew up to be the intermediary between his parents. *The Monk* is characterized by his sense of compassion for women in tight situations. The vulnerability of women and their reputations as well as women's economic dependence on men are major themes of *The Monk*.

Lewis graduated from Christ Church, Oxford in 1794, determined to pursue a theatrical career. He traveled extensively in France and Germany, where he met Goethe. (The primary character in *The Monk*, the monk Ambrosio, sells his soul to the devil, as did Faust.) He eventually became a Member of Parliament.

The Monk was extremely popular but also extremely controversial and scandalous. Many perceived it as a work of blasphemy. It is as much or more about the dangers of celibacy and sanctimony as it is about witchcraft. The British author held negative opinions regarding Roman Catholicism and the Spanish Inquisition and these were expressed in the novel.

The Monk features magical books of power, necromancy, magic circles, and mirrors plus a poisoner-witch. Sorcerers conjure up spirits in the crypt. They summon, command and compel no less than a reluctant Lucifer to do their bidding (and *The Monk* features a beautiful Lucifer; there's no hairy horned goat.) The witch compels Satan to commit the crime. Ambrosio the monk is primarily guilty of pride, hypocrisy, and lust. Tellingly, having already confessed to rape and murder, the monk can't bring himself to admit sorcery, despite torture.

The Secrets of Dr Taverner

Dion Fortune (December 6, 1890–January 8, 1946) wrote six books of metaphysical, esoteric fiction but *The Secrets of Dr Taverner* was the first, published in 1926. Many consider it to be her finest work of fiction although all her novels have their adherents. Fortune was among the most influential and significant occultists during the first half of the twentieth century. She was a prolific writer and published books and pamphlets on many subjects including magic, psychic self-defense, vegetarianism, and contraception.

The Secrets of Dr Taverner consists of one dozen short stories recounting the psychic adventures of a detective similar to Sherlock Holmes. Taverner is a healer who nurtures ailing souls using esoteric techniques. Many of Fortune's characters were based on real people; Dr Taverner was allegedly based on Dion Fortune's teacher, Dr Theodore Moriarty, who specialized in what she described as astro-etheric psychological conditions. The short stories are dictated by Taverner's assistant Dr Rhodes, who plays the part of Dr Watson.

Dion Fortune remains beloved in metaphysical circles but she can be difficult to read as her work frequently expresses the ethnic and racial bigotry common to her time. Her other novels may be described as metaphysical romances, for example, in one book the heroine is rescued from being sacrificed at a Black Mass. Fortune's heroines would be understood today as witches; however her novels were written before the repeal of the witchcraft laws and the emergence of modern witchcraft, and so these heroines are identified as priestesses. Roots of Neo-Paganism may be observed in Fortune's books and much magical information is incorporated into the texts.

Her other esoteric fiction includes: *The Demon Lover* (1927); *The Winged Bull* (1935); *The Goat Foot God* (1936); *The Sea Priestess* (1938) and *Moon Magic* (published posthumously in 1956; incomplete at the time of her death, the last section of the novel was channeled by a medium).

The Tempest

One of William Shakespeare's last plays *The Tempest* was performed for the first time on November 11, 1611 in London. It recounts the tale of the sorcerer Prospero, formerly the Duke of Milan, and his daughter Miranda who have been banished to an enchanted desert island, where they are served by the spirit Ariel, summoned at will by Prospero.

The witch Sycorax, who had also been exiled to the island but who had died before Prospero's arrival, was responsible for enchanting the island (and Ariel). Her son Caliban is compelled to labor as Prospero's servant. Prospero treats him harshly because Caliban lusts after Miranda.

The character of Prospero is believed to have been inspired by Dr John Dee, who served as Queen Elizabeth's astrologer and advisor. Her successor King James was rather less tolerant of the occult and although not officially banished, Dr Dee's retreat from court to the safety of his home at Mortlake may have resembled exile.

Wicked: The Life and Times of the Wicked Witch of the West

Although the movie and book versions of *The Wizard of Oz* remain extremely popular, many find them puzzling and frustrating. Why, for instance, is the Wicked Witch of the West called wicked? What exactly is it that she does to be characterized that way? The Wicked Witch never lies, unlike say "the Wonderful Wizard of Oz" or Glinda, the *Good* Witch, who at best plays fast and loose with the truth. These musings inspired Gregory Maguire's bestselling novel, *Wicked: The Life and Times of the Wicked Witch of the West* (1995)—an exploration of the nature of evil and how "wickedness" is defined.

Maguire draws his inspiration from both the literary and cinematic versions of L. Frank Baum's *Wizard of Oz*, however he uses them as a jumping-off point for his own original vision. The Wicked Witch has previously been nameless. Maguire bestows upon her the name Elphaba, derived from her creator Baum's initials.

The characters and events of Baum's books provide the framework for *Wicked*. The anti-witchcraft bias of the older book and movie is made clear: Dorothy and her companions make brief appearances, wreaking havoc wherever they go: they kill Elphaba's beloved dogs, crows, and bees. Elphaba's sister, Nessarose (another witch) is also killed, as is eventually Elphaba.

Elphaba's green skin and various other unusual characteristics were perceived by her fundamentalist religious father as being punishment for her mother's sins. Elphaba eventually goes to college in the Emerald City where she rooms with the shallow but beautiful Galinda, not yet Glinda the Good Witch. The Wizard has taken over the government of Oz in a political coup; indigenous people are exploited and oppressed. Their land is raped for its resources; an ancient goddess-oriented religion has been suppressed. Elphaba becomes involved in animal rights and eventually in the underground political resistance to the Wizard of Oz. From the perspective of the oppressor Wizard and his collaborators, Elphaba is wicked and, because she is powerful, she must be eliminated.

Wicked also includes brief, mysterious but evocative appearances by Yackle, a character who more closely corresponds to the traditional image of a witch than does Elphaba.

Witch Hammer

In 1680, the midwife in a Moravian hamlet discovers that her cow is dry. She fears it's been bewitched and pays a local beggar-woman to steal a Communion wafer for her so that she can use it in a spell to counteract the malevolent spell. The beggar-woman is caught and this small incident touches off a murderous witch-hunting frenzy that lasts two decades.

These incidents form the basis of the Czech novel *Witch Hammer* by Vaclav Kaplicky (1895–1982), first published in 1963 to popular acclaim and commercial success in Czechoslovakia. An English translation was published in 1990. *Witch Hammer* derives its name from the infamous witch-hunters' manual *The Malleus Maleficarum* or *The Hammer of the Witches* (see **BOOKS:** Witch-Hunt Books: *Malleus Maleficarum*). The novel is based on real events that occurred in seventeenth-century North Moravia, now part of the Czech Republic but then an ethnically mixed, heavily German-influenced area. Kaplicky derived his source material from actual witch-trial transcripts.

The protagonist is a kind, tolerant priest who watches in horror as witch-hunters are invited to the small town to examine the witch. The witch-hunters' motivations are selfish: they are well aware of the power they exert over all inhabitants, including the wealthy and noble who initially see no danger for themselves.

As the witch-hunters' web tightens around the inhabitants, the book is almost painful to read. Although people engage in folk magic, no one corresponds to the witch-hunters' vision of diabolical witchcraft, although the witch-hunters have methods of making anyone confess to whatever charges are brought.

The Wonderful Wizard of Oz

The Wonderful Wizard of Oz was written by L. Frank Baum (May 15, 1856-May 6, 1919) in 1899 but published in 1900 to coincide with the new century, perceived as a new age. It was intended as a new kind of fairy tale for a new nation on the brink of a new century, completely independent of the standards of older European fairy tales, their enchantments and cruelty. The book's first illustrations were drawn by W.W. Denslow.

In his introduction, Baum wrote that *"… the time has come for a series of newer 'wonder tales' in which the stereotyped genie, dwarf or fairy are eliminated …"* But not, apparently, time for the stereotyped witch to disappear.

Those only familiar with the MGM musical *The Wizard of Oz* may find the book upon which it is based very surprising. The book features two good witches and two wicked witches, four witches all together, but there is no Miss Gulch, who was an invention of the 1939 movie's screenwriters.

❋ *The film's famous ruby slippers were originally silver.*

❋ *Dorothy is identified as a sorceress because she wears white and, according to the book, "only witches and sorceresses wear white."*

❋ *The Wicked Witch of the West has but one eye, "as powerful as a telescope and could see everywhere."*

The premise of the story is that the Wizard of Oz will not send Dorothy home to Kansas unless she performs the service of killing the Wicked Witch of the West. No one questions why and no explanation is given. It seems natural that the wise and powerful should wish to exterminate a wicked witch. The Wizard asks for a wicked thing but since the Witch is a "wicked witch" no one questions his actions.

The Wicked Witch of the West is served by talking wolves, crows, and bees. They do not survive Dorothy and her friends: the Tin Man kills forty wolves. The scarecrow kills forty crows (he wrings their necks). The bees are killed by trickery.

A nameless witch of the north kisses Dorothy at the beginning of her journey leaving a protective mark, something like the Mark of Cain. No one will touch her including the Wicked Witch, although Dorothy is not made aware of this.

Dorothy is forced to labor for the Wicked Witch, in the same manner that Vasilisa must labor for Baba Yaga. (See **FAIRY-TALE WITCHES:** Vasilisa the Wise; **DIVINE WITCH:** Baba Yaga.) Dorothy must keep the witch's fire fed with wood, except that, unlike Vasilisa, Dorothy is really a saboteur. Dorothy throws water on the witch because through trickery the witch has stolen one of Dorothy's silver slippers. She puts an iron bar in the middle of the kitchen floor, casting a spell over it so that it is invisible. Dorothy trips over it and one shoe flies off which the witch immediately puts on her foot. The motif of having one shoe on and one shoe off links both female characters to the archetype of the limping shaman. (See Dance: The Step of Yu, page 246.)

The Wizard is a charlatan with no magical powers but witches are described as able to do *"wonderful things."* *"Good"* witches, however, won't harm the wizard.

Baum intended for readers to see Oz as a real

place, an alternate realm where a real child one day discovered herself. (The movie transforms Oz and Dorothy's adventures into a dream.)

Manga and Anime

Manga are Japanese graphic novels; anime are Japanese animated films. They differ from American-style comics and animation in terms of style and artistry; aficionados of either genre may find that appreciating the other requires some adjustment.

American-style comics and Japanese manga both fall under the category of sequential art. The traditions arose independently: the roots of manga stretch back to medieval Japanese woodblock prints. The term *manga* (usually translated as *"whimsical sketches"*) was first coined by the renowned artist Hokusai in 1814 to describe his sketchbooks filled with drawings.

Fans of the Japanese genre bitterly resent having manga defined as *"Japanese comics."* The schism between fans of manga and comics can sometimes be almost as profound as that between magical illusionists and magical practitioners. Because many, on both sides of the divide, passionately feel that the differences between these closely related genres are extremely significant, comics and manga have been categorized separately in this book.

Although manga can be devoted to anything, as with comics, a good percentage features occult, mythological or folkloric themes including witches and other magical practitioners. What is listed below is, once again, only a snapshot.

Manga is a vibrant, vital genre; once exclusive to Japan, it now has global popularity particularly among young readers. As fans outside Japan began to create their own manga, the genre continues to evolve: Korean-style manga is technically known as *manwha*. *Under the Glass Moon*, for example, listed on page 299, is technically a manwha, as is *Demon Diary*.

This is an extremely fluid genre; it can be very difficult to separate manga and anime. The same story or its characters may appear in manga form, as a televised anime series, and also sometimes as feature films. Characters from one series also sometimes pay visits to other series, as do American-style comic-book characters.

The following are some of the more significant manga and anime featuring witches or witchcraft. All are available in English translation. Like comics, this is a genre devoted to fantasy and entertainment; while some elements may derive from authentic tradition and reality, don't expect realistic depictions of witches, witchcraft or many other things for that matter.

Manga are created by artists and then published. Each publishing house has its personal specialties, artistic vision, and flavor, in the same way that DC Comics, Harvey, Vertigo, and Marvel comics each possess distinct flavors and visions.

Card Captor Sakura

Creator: CLAMP; Publisher: TOKYOPOP

CLAMP is a popular all-female manga-creating team comprising Nanase Ohkawa, Mokona Apapa, Mick Nekoi, and Satsuki Igarashi.

Once upon a time an English sorcerer, Clow Reed, combined Western and East Asian magic to create a magical deck of cards, the Clow Cards. For decades these cards lay hidden inside a big, dusty book until one day a young Japanese girl named Sakura was poking around in her father's library. She picked up this curious book, opened it … and all the cards flew out! Sakura managed to catch only one.

A strange-looking creature also emerged from the book (he's supposed to be a winged lion), identifying himself as the book's gatekeeper and guardian. Cerberus, or *Kero-chan* as he is affectionately known, informs Sakura that, having opened the book, she is now the *Cardcaptor* and it is her responsibility to retrieve the missing cards. The cards, which somewhat resemble Tarot cards, bestow magical power. Eventually, after many adventures, Sakura collects them all, becoming the powerful Master of the Clow. (Kero-chan serves as her familiar, as well as Guardian of the Clow. Another familiar in the series sometimes takes the form of a winged black cat and sometimes of a panther.)

Card Captor Sakura was extremely successful: there is a series of manga as well as an animated television series and two feature films. There is even a *Card Captor Sakura* board game. *Card Captor Sakura* was also briefly featured on American television, debuting on July 20th, 2001, where it became embroiled in controversy. In January 2002, Taco Bell proposed giving out replicas of the magic Clow Cards as a prize-promotional included in a children's meal. This promotion was terminated when the Christian organization American Family Association protested, complaining that it encouraged children to dabble in Tarot and the occult.

Tokyo Babylon

Creator: CLAMP; Publisher: TOKYOPOP

Subaru Sumeragi is the 13th Head of the Sumeragi Clan, although he's a mere youth. Subaru describes himself as just an "ordinary Onmyoji" but there's no such thing. The Onmyoji are Japanese magical practitioners; the term is sometimes translated as "yin-yang magician." Part shamans, part exorcists, part wizards, the Onmyoji magical tradition is extremely powerful and Subaru is the current master. Subaru is a hereditary magician; his grandmother was the last Head of the Clan and helped train him in the art. Subaru keeps Tokyo safe from magical harm.

Assisted by a revolving cast of fellow practitioners from various magical traditions, including his twin sister, Subaru solves supernatural mysteries. Although *Tokyo Babylon* is frequently classified as an "*action-fantasy*" series, it is perhaps the series most strongly rooted in traditional, realistic occult practice. Constant reference is made to magical traditions; Subaru's wardrobe and as his magical methods resemble those of the historic Onmyoji practitioner.

Tokyo Babylon appears as a manga series; two anime episodes were also created.

See **DICTIONARY:** Onmyoji.

Under the Glass Moon

Creator: Ko Ya-Seong; Publisher: TOKYOPOP

Luka Guillaume Reinhardt is currently the world's greatest Dark Wizard; he and his sorcerer brother live next door to a witch, Madame Batolli and her young witch-apprentice daughter Nell. Luka has his own apprentice; having all these powerful magical practitioners in such close quarters encourages not only magical battles but also some love triangles. Because the male characters are so androgynous (as they tend to be in many manga), trying to determine exactly who is interested in whom and the nature of the relationships can be dizzying. Madame Batolli periodically saves the day; she dresses for action in traditional, albeit sexy witch garb including pointy hat and a *very* short black dress. She flies an industrial strength broom-thruster capable of speeds that break the sound barrier.

Under the Glass Moon appears as a manwha.

Witch Hunter Robin

Creators: Sunrise and Bandai Entertainment

STNJ is a covert government operation that captures witches. They used to kill them but new methods have been developed to deactivate their power, rendering the witches harmless, and so capture is now preferred as the more *humane* method. Anyone familiar with historical witch-hunting may find the title and premise of this anime chilling, although the plot is somewhat more complicated.

The witches aren't exactly witches; the finest witch-hunter is a witch. Witches, as defined in *Witch Hunter Robin*, seem like normal people but possess special supernatural powers. These powers are usually hereditary, which helps the organization keep track of witches: they know who to watch based on ancestry. Not every member of these lineages develops into a witch; often individuals aren't aware that they are *"witches"* until their powers suddenly awaken. There's nothing particularly magical, witchy or shamanic about these witches: they're more like rogue humans with supernatural powers. There's nothing metaphysical or spiritual about them.

The mysterious STNJ captures these witches, deactivates their powers, and sends them to the mysterious Factory—although for what purpose or fate is unknown.

The witch-hunter of the title is Robin Sena, born in Japan but raised in an Italian convent. At age 16 she returns to Japan where she joins the STNJ as their newest witch-hunter. Robin is a genuine witch although she initially keeps this fact secret; to distinguish her from her quarry, she is described as a "craft user." Her character is intended to at least superficially resemble a young practitioner of Wicca, although nothing really resembles Wiccan tradition. Robin's methods are vaguely like those of an Onmyoji. She is considered the most powerful witch in the series, able to exert considerable powers over fire.

XXXHolic

Creator: CLAMP; Publisher: Delrey/Kodansha

Watanuki Kimihiro is haunted by visions of ghosts and spirits. He can see them but is unable to control these visions, turn them off when they threaten to overwhelm him, or put his innate powers to practical, positive use. His most fervent wish is for these visions to cease. One day, pursued by nightmare visions, he feels compelled to enter a mysterious building, where he discovers Yuko the Witch awaiting him.

Yuko, the "Time-Space Witch," is the proprietress of a wish-granting store. She is poised, beautiful, serene, and mysteriously omniscient. She asks the boy his name and birthday, only later cautioning him that if someone knows your name, they can control your soul and that astrological information allows someone to plot another's life path. Without being told, Yuko knows of Watanuki's powers, his predicament, and his secret wish. She promises to help him. Of course, Watanuki must first pay for her services that he hasn't exactly asked for by laboring in her store. *XXXHolic* is related to those fairy tales where the protagonist must labor in the witch's kitchen as a form of initiation, like *Vasilisa the Wise*, *Mother Holle* or *Hansel and Gretel*. (See **FAIRY-TALE WITCHES**.)

XXXHolic appears as a manga and anime.

Yu Yu Hakusho

Creator: Yoshihiro Togashi; Publisher: Shonen Jump

Yusuke Urameshi, a 14-year-old juvenile delinquent, spontaneously saves another child from being hit by a car but in the process is fatally run over himself. No one in the Spirit World ever expected Yusuke to behave so nobly and so his demise wasn't anticipated: there's no allotted space for him in the Afterlife. Yusuke's ghost is sent back to Earth where after a complicated, convoluted plot he emerges as a supernatural detective solving mysteries involving demons, ghosts, and spirits.

He's not the witch although there is one in the series: Botan, Yusuke's compatriot and assistant as well as the ferry-girl responsible for ferrying souls over the River Styx. (Old Charon from Greek mythology must finally have retired, or maybe Botan is in charge of the Japanese division.) Botan rides an oar rather than a broomstick and possesses some magical healing powers.

Virtually all the female characters in *Yu Yu Hakusho* display magical inclinations, and *Yu Yu Hakusho* exists as manga, anime, and as a feature-length animated film.

Music

Other than spell-casting, dancing is the activity most often traditionally associated with witches. Dancing is inspired by music. Music is among the primordial shamanic arts.

Greek mythology considered Earth's greatest musician to be the shaman Orpheus, and music has been an integral part of global magical and spiritual rites since that proverbial time immemorial. According to traditional wisdom, music possesses extremely potent magic powers, which have historically been used for the following purposes:

❋ *To inspire ecstasy*

❋ *To generate additional magic power*

❋ *To foretell the future*

❋ *To beckon and exorcise spirits as needed*

❋ *To communicate with spirits*

❋ *To appease ghosts*

❋ *In healing, and in particular the treatment of mental and emotional illness and imbalance.*

Many anthropologists believe that shamans were among the first to invent and play musical instruments. Instruments were incorporated into magical, spiritual, and religious rites not only in the Pagan world but also in Jewish and Christian traditions, and although dancing in Church would eventually be forbidden, music remained. By the early Middle Ages, the Church taught that individual musical notes and the melodies formed from them potentially held certain spiritual powers. Music here is considered from two perspectives: The musical instruments most powerfully identified with witchcraft—flutes, drums and percussion instruments, and the violin—and, how witchcraft and witches have served as inspiration for composers, musicians, and songwriters. Some of the most significant instances are listed below.

Drums and Percussion Instruments

Drums and other percussion instruments are *the* most ancient, most widely distributed and most ritually significant musical instruments of all. There are drums or percussion instruments for every conceivable magical or ritual use. Drums are so primordial that their origins are unknown. (Although the most ancient surviving instrument is a flute (see page 303), this is believed to be because ancient drums were made from perishable materials.)

Drums evoke the heartbeat: the first sound a human being hears is that of his or her mother's heart while still in the womb, as well as the percussive pulsing of her blood. It is no accident that according to myth, drums were invented by the primal mother deity, Kybele: despite modern associations of drums as a masculine instrument, they were once almost exclusively associated with women and goddess-oriented spirituality, particularly the frame drum.

Drums and percussion instruments were women's instruments:

✸ *The Maenads are commonly depicted with castanets and tambourines; both would also be integral to the tarantella (see Dance, page 248) as well as to modern belly dance.*

✸ *The Hebrew prophetess Miriam led the women in dance to the accompaniment of tambourines.*

✸ *Deities like Hathor, Isis, and Kybele are commonly depicted with drums.*

✸ *Male deities closely identified with drums, such as Bes, Shiva, and Shango, tend to possess powerful associations with women as well.*

As modern drums have become larger and more physically imposing, they have become stereotyped as "male" instruments; the tambourine, however, still retains its feminine associations—as legions of tambourine-shaking female backing singers can attest.

Drums are commonly viewed, in traditional magical perspective, as possessing and radiating primal female power: they represent the womb or the vulva and are the counterpart to the male flute. Both flutes and drums are shamanic instruments and are frequently played in conjunction—as they were during witches' sabbats, allegedly. (They are also frequently paired outside the magical context, as with fifes and drums.)

Drums traditionally associated most exclusively with women are usually played with bare hands, as with the frame drum or *dumbek*. Drums most closely associated with shamanism, however, whether played by women or men, are often struck with a bone, horn or stick. (The nickname given a cooked leg of poultry, the "*drumstick*," recalls what would once have been the bone's eventual fate.)

Flutes aren't the only phallic symbol used to balance the feminine drum; the drumstick serves the same purpose. Playing the drum with the stick is magically akin to grinding the pestle within the mortar or hammering nails in a horseshoe: all echo sexual intercourse and magically affirm the creative power of generation.

Drums are used for various magical purposes, most especially:

✸ Spirit summoning: drums are used to invoke spirits. In African Diaspora traditions, every spirit possesses its own specific rhythm with which it may be summoned, with which it announces its arrival (drummers are psychically inspired to play the rhythm) or which can be used as a mode of communication.

✸ Childbirth: drumming was once an integral part of childbirth rituals, intended to entice and direct the baby's path from the womb as well as to entrance, relax, and direct the laboring woman.

✸ Spiritual cleansing: the sound of percussion, especially when the instruments incorporate metal, allegedly drives off low-level spiritual entities and removes spiritual debris, thus creating a magical cleansing and purification effect. This may be understood as bonus effect that occurs even when drums are intended for other purposes.

✸ Shamanic journeys: what in English is described as a "soul-journey" was, for the Saami people in what is now northern Norway, Sweden, Finland, and north-west Russia, known as "the way of the drum." Drums were used to guide and stimulate global shamanic forays into other realms and to assist the return journey.

✸ Achievement of ecstasy: this was considered crucial in witchcraft and shamanic ritual. Ecstasy generates fresh magical energy.

✸ Trance: drums are used to mesmerize and entrance. In this manner, they are also used for divination and prophecy, as well as to help ease ritual possession.

✸ Divination: the most famous drums used as divination tools belonged to the traditional nomadic Saami people of the European Arctic. Magical designs were painted on the drumheads. Each drum was unique; inspiration for the design came to the shaman in dreams. Bones were placed on the drumhead: when the drum is beaten, the items jump and dance. Interpretations are made based on their movement, sound, and also the manner in which the items interact with the painted designs. Similar drums were popular as fortune-telling devices until recently among traditional Hungarian and Romany shamans and witches, although designs tend to be less complex and beans, rings or other small objects usually substituted for bones.

Various types of percussion have traditionally been identified with witchcraft and women's spiritual traditions.

✸ Castanets (finger cymbals) are so ancient their origins are lost in the mist. Castanets were widely distributed at a very early date in ancient Egypt, Phoenicia, and throughout the Mediterranean. Castanets were identified with Kybele and with the Maenads.

✸ The damaru is an hour-glass shaped drum traditionally formed from two human skulls. It is not intended to be grotesque or "spooky" but to serve as a reminder of the transience of life and also that new life emerges from death. This Himalayan instrument is considered a shamanic tool and is most often identified with Shiva, although Durga, India's warrior-goddess, also plays the damaru. Damaru are also made from ivory or wood carved to resemble skulls.

✸ Frame drums and tambourines. No instrument is more associated with female spirituality and power than the frame drum (tambourines are frame drums with jingles attached). Female deities are often depicted holding frame drums; although some are anonymous, others can be identified—most notably Kybele. The frame drum is used to empower and spiritually and magically reinvigorate women.

* *The sistrum is an ancient rattle consisting of a metal or wooden frame with perforations through which rods and discs are strung. The instrument is most associated with the Egyptian deity Hathor.*

* Slit-drums *of Central and South America are believed to potentially possess human or animal powers, particularly those of the jaguar. One style of drum made by indigenous people from Columbia has a woman's head at one end and an alligator at the other.*

The primal association of drums and percussion with witchcraft and women's power survives in the tradition of *Halloween noise makers*. Although no longer so popular, until approximately the end of the first half of the twentieth century, in some communities, Halloween noise makers were as integral a part of Halloween festivities as costumes or trick-or-treating. Halloween revelers, children and adults, took to the streets with inexpensive rattles, tambourines, and similar noise makers. These noise makers, in addition to providing the joy of annoying the neighbors, were believed able to magically provide safety for their bearer while amidst the ghosts and spirits of All Hallows' Eve. These instruments were customized for Halloween and so, like ancient magical drums, they were decorated with witchcraft motifs, most especially witches, black cats, owls, bats, spiders, and ghosts.

Further reading: Layne Redmond's *When the Drummers Were Women* (Three Rivers Press, 1997).

See Dance: Tarantella, page 247; **DICTIONARY:** Maenad; **DIVINE WITCH:** Kybele; Shiva; **MAGICAL ARTS:** Divination; Spirit Working.

The Flute

The oldest surviving musical instrument on Earth is a Neanderthal flute crafted from a cave bear's femur with four holes discovered in what is today Slovenia. Its age has been estimated as between 43,000 and 82,000 years old. Not only are flutes among the most ancient musical instruments, they are also among the most widely distributed.

Flutes may have initially been discovered accidentally by blowing into hollow bones, stems (bamboo or reed) or pipes. Eventually instruments were created which could produce tones. (Experts believe that the Neanderthal bone flute replicates the modern do-re-mi scale.) They come in two varieties:

* *Vertical flutes*

* *Transverse flutes, which have a side hole like the modern flute*

Although the transverse is now the standard modern flute, it is a far more recent invention than the vertical flute: the earliest depictions of transverse flutes come from tenth-century Byzantium. Vertical flutes, of which there are many variations including Pan pipes, are the ones most identified with magic and witchcraft.

Flutes are understood to magically posses and transmit primal phallic power:

* *Women were forbidden to play flutes in many traditional societies.*

⁕ "Playing the flute" is a metaphor popularly used in Chinese erotic texts to discuss certain sexual acts; the image of a female flute player may be understood as a visual euphemism.

⁕ Flutes, according to traditional magical wisdom from New Guinea, may be used by men to curtail women's power.

Among the magical purposes ascribed to the flute are romance, fertility, and renewal of life.

⁕ Flutes were used in magical healing rituals and were a popular component of funerary rites.

⁕ Flutes were buried with the dead and carried as amulets by the living.

⁕ Flutes are used to disperse ghosts or to shamanically guide them to their next destination.

⁕ Flutes are also used for spirit summoning and for magical communication with animals.

As the earliest flutes were crafted from bone, flutes were considered powerful tools for necromancy (communication with the deceased) as well as exorcisms. The type of bone used to craft the flute would influence its powers. According to legend, Eastern Slav magicians once crafted flutes from human leg bones, which when played, forced all within earshot, except presumably the flautist, to fall sound asleep.

Deities associated with flutes include Athena, Dionysus, Hathor, Kokopelli, Krishna, Mami Waters, Pan, Tammuz, and Tezcatlipoca. Greek mythology credits Athena with inventing the flute. The sound of wind blowing through hollow bones reminded her of the hooting of an owl, her familiar. (And if one understands the owl to be Athena's alter ego, then the sound of the flute is the sound of Athena herself.) Athena

created a bone flute, which intensely delighted her—as it did her fellow deities, animals, and humans. She played it constantly until one day she realized some of those fellow deities were snickering at her. Puzzled, she caught sight of her reflection while blowing and became aware that she looked silly and undignified with her cheeks puffed out. She immediately threw the flute away and never touched it again, although the flute remained among her attributes.

Athena is a deity with an extremely complex history; she transformed herself from an ancient Libyan snake spirit with dominion over women's mysteries into the staunchest upholder of Greek patriarchy, and thus her act of throwing away the flute, the instrument most associated with snake charming, may be understood metaphorically.

Yet another legend suggests that Athena was inspired to invent the flute by the sounds made by the hissing snakes on Medusa's head as she was decapitated. Athena's later impulse to distance herself from the flute came when she realized that, while playing, her face resembled the Gorgon's mask.

Pan is credited with creating the variation of the vertical flute named in his honor, the Pan pipes. By the classical era, Pan pipes represented wild, carnal, elemental, physical nature and were looked down upon, as opposed to stringed instruments like the harp or lyre, which were under the dominion of Apollo and associated with order and "civilization." Pan pipes were associated with stubborn rural backward culture, the type that would eventually become labeled "*Pagan*," rather than with sophisticated, educated, urban musicians. Pan pipes had powerful associations with goat herds and unruly horned deities. Pan pipe-style flutes are indigenous to Africa, Asia, and South America as well as to Europe.

See **DIVINE WITCH:** Dionysus; Tezcatlipoca; **HALL OF FAME:** Cagliostro; **MAGICAL ARTS:** Necromancy.

Violin

The violin as it exists today first appeared in Italy in the latter half of the sixteenth century but did not gain widespread popularity until the early seventeenth century. The folk name for violin is "fiddle" and both names are sometimes used to refer to any sort of lute-type instrument played with a bow. The use of the bow for playing the lute arose sometime prior to the ninth century, most probably in Asia.

Despite being a relatively recent invention, it quickly developed a reputation as a potent magical tool. Because the phallic bow is used to evoke music from the instrument's curvaceous wooden body, playing the violin is magically understood as a metaphor for the act of creation; the instrument combines male *and* female primal power. In addition, the sound of the violin is identified with the human voice.

The violin evoked passionate responses. European Jews and Romany *adored* the violin. It is virtually impossible to envision Jewish klezmer music without violins, and many find it utterly impossible to envision Romany music without the instrument either.

Violins were not merely musical instruments however: European Jews and Romany perceived that the violin shared and expressed the soul-essence of their cultures. They had tremendous

symbolic value. Violins were considered powerfully magical, bordering on the sacred:

* *Images of violins were carved on Jewish tombstones.*

* *Violins were painted on a synagogue ceiling possessing an astrological motif in Vaslui, Romania.*

* *Violin strings were used as Romany amulets, wrapped around a child's wrist for protection in the manner that other cultures use red string or ribbon.*

In both cultures violins are used for summoning spells and, especially, for romantic magic. As a Jewish proverb states, "A wedding without a violin is like a funeral without tears."

This favorable perception was not universal; the opposing reaction was equally passionate and intense. Up until the last century Christian folklore considered the violin the devil's own instrument: violins were potentially diabolical and spiritually dangerous. This perception gave rise to a complex folklore—for instance when you play the violin, you communicate directly with Satan. Not that you'll ever play as well as he does or at least not without his help: among the professions Satan sometimes assumes is that of violin teacher. Master violinists were believed to have obtained their skills directly from the devil. To request private lessons, meet him at the crossroads.

According to European superstition, should you dance to the playing of an unknown fiddler, your soul could be in danger. A commonly told story, an antique version of what would now be called an urban myth, describes an innocent, unsuspecting maiden who meets a group of women joyously dancing to the sound of one lone man playing the violin. He's usually either described as a black man or he's dressed in black; he frequently wears a black cape. The man is either sinister and scary, or exceptionally handsome, or both. The girl joins the party but discovers by the end of the dance that she has unwittingly been irrevocably initiated as a witch.

> Another old legend says that fairies dance to violins. If a human joins them, he or she will fall under their power, becoming bewitched and enchanted. Whether this is a problem or a privilege depends upon one's perceptions of fairies.

According to Christian folklore, Satan doesn't just play the violin for his own pleasure; he plays it specifically so that witches can dance. And of course, the violin *has* been known to inspire wild, wear-your-shoes-out dancing. Those who only associate violins with staid classical music should listen to Romany and klezmer music, both of which prominently feature violins that once fueled week-long wedding festivities. The violin's powerful associations with the tarantella also did not help its reputation.

The violinist most identified with the violin's magical and diabolical associations was Niccolo Paganini (October 27, 1782-May 27, 1840). Paganini was acknowledged as the greatest violinist in his native Italy and throughout Europe; people speculated about how he became so great and soon rumors began to fly. Paganini developed a demonic reputation; his brilliant playing was attributed to a Faustian deal with the devil. He was even labeled a *"Hexensohn"* (witch's brat). Paganini seemed to enjoy these rumors; he never denied them but instead seem to encourage them. He dressed completely in black and would arrive at his concerts in a black coach drawn by black horses. Among his most famous compositions was *Streghe*, translated as *The Witches* or *Witches' Dances*.

(Rumors about Paganini's deal with the devil weren't laid to rest when he died. On his deathbed, Paganini refused the final sacraments; the Church refused to bury him. His body was kept in a basement for five years until finally his family's petition to have him buried was accepted.)

Madame Helena Blavatsky is renowned for writing serious metaphysical tomes like *Isis Unveiled* but she also wrote horror stories. In her story *The Ensouled Violin* (1891), an occultist turned passionate violinist hears Paganini and becomes incredibly depressed, fearing that he will never achieve such greatness. Instead of just telling him that practice makes perfect, his violin teacher attempts to comfort him by advising that Paganini only achieved his unworldly mastery with Satan's help and, furthermore, that Paganini's violin has unique strings, crafted from the intestines of a human victim who willingly offered his body for music's sake.

> Further information: American Violinist Rachel Barton's CD *Instrument of the Devil* explores the mythic and literary associations of the violin. Selections include Paganini's *The Witches* (Cedille Records, 2003).

The violin teacher assumes that this information will appall his student, leaving him satisfied with his normal human talent, but, of course, one must never assume. The student's reaction? *"By the witches of Thessaly and the dark arts of Circe!' he exclaimed, with foaming mouth and his eyes burning like coals; '... I now swear ... never to touch a violin again until I can string it with four human chords."*

Music of all kinds has been inspired by witches, witchcraft, and the magical arts.

❋ *Operas incorporating images of witches:*

Arabella (Richard Strauss)

Dido and Aeneas (Henry Purcell)

Hansel and Gretel (Englebert Humperdinck)

The Love for Three Oranges (Sergei Prokofiev)

Macbeth (versions by Giuseppe Verdi and Ernest Bloch)

The Magic Flute (Wolfgang Amadeus Mozart)

The Masked Ball (Giuseppe Verdi)

The Medium (Gian-Carlo Menotti)

Ruddigore or The Witch's Curse (W. S. Gilbert and Arthur Sullivan)

Rusalka (Antonín Dvořák)

Il Trovatore (Giuseppe Verdi)

❋ *Popular songs inspired by witches, witchcraft and magical practices include:*

Black Magic Woman (Fleetwood Mac, Santana)

Ju Ju Man (Brinsley Schwarz)

Rhiannon (Fleetwood Mac—Rhiannon is the name of a Welsh deity; however the song's composer Stevie Nicks has described it as being about *"a Welsh witch"*)

Season of the Witch (Donovan, Brian Auger's Trinity featuring Julie Driscoll)

That Old Black Magic (Harold Arlen classic popularized by Sammy Davis Jr, Ella Fitzgerald and countless others)

Under Your Spell Again (country music classic covered by Buck Owens, Gram Parsons, Waylon Jennings and countless others)

Witch Doctor (David Seville, Alvin and the Chipmunks)

Witch Queen of New Orleans (Redbone)

Witchcraft (popularized by Frank Sinatra, this standard by Carolyn Leigh and Cy Coleman has also been covered by Chris Connor, Julie Wilson and countless others)

Witchy Woman (The Eagles)

❋ *Blues and Rhythm and Blues*

Blues and its descendant, rhythm and blues, must be considered separately from other forms of popular music because of the unique nature of its references to witchcraft, divination, and magical practices.

With very few exceptions, references to witches, witchcraft, spells or other magical practices in other genres of popular music are intended as metaphor; in blues and rhythm and blues references to fortune-tellers, swamp witches, and mojo hands are meant literally. These references are also unique because of their matter-of-fact nature. They are totally lacking in sensationalism or diabolism: when Benny Spellman sings of going to see the fortune-teller it seems like the most natural thing in the world, just like consulting any other professional. And when Muddy Waters sings of going down to Louisiana to get a mojo hand, it is absolutely matter of fact, totally without shame or sensationalism. (Of course this matter-of-fact acceptance of magical practice, in conjunction with its celebration of carnal pleasures, may have helped earn the blues its old sobriquet, *"the devil's music"* ...)

In what other genre does a man boast of the efficacy of his amulet as does Muddy Waters in "I Got My Mojo Working," a concept so foreign for many that they presumed the song must be about something else, leading to new definitions for "mojo" as in the *Austin Powers* movies? In what other genre of popular music could a paean to divination as sweet and sincere as Bettye Lavette's *Fortune Teller* even exist?

The following songs are but the tip of the iceberg:

Fortune Teller (Benny Spellman)
Fortune Teller (Bettye Lavette)
Gypsy Woman (Muddy Waters)
Hoodoo Lady (Memphis Minnie)
Hoodoo Man Blues (Junior Wells)
Hoodoo Party (Tabby Thomas)
I Got My Mojo Working (Muddy Waters)
I'm Blue (The Ikettes)
I'm A Mojo Man (Lonesome Sundown)
I Put A Spell On You (Screamin' Jay Hawkins)
Louisiana Blues (Muddy Waters)
Mojo Hand (Lightning Hopkins)
Mojo Hannah (Betty Harris)
Seventh Son (Willie Mabon)
Somebody Done Hoodooed the Hoodoo Man (Louis Jordan)
Two Headed Woman (Junior Wells)

Television

Witches are comparatively sparsely represented on television, especially in comparison to the multitudes featured in books and movies. Why this should be so is subject for speculation. Television, at least up until the advent of cable, has been a notoriously conservative medium. American network television, in particular, is dependent on the favor of advertisers who generally prefer not to associate themselves with witchcraft or the occult. Television programming is, in essence, also brought directly into the home in a way that other media aren't. Witches are often considered controversial company, not suitable for children.

There is always an exception to the rule of course; many television programs, in particular comedies, feature annual Halloween episodes.

These frequently feature witches. However, in general, these are merely cameo appearances with little character development or nuance; what is presented are caricatures of witches.

Few television witches display depth of character; most of those that do are listed below. Perhaps because of the nature of television—shows appear weekly (or even daily as with *Bewitched* or *Dark Shadows*)—characters can become very familiar to viewers; in general, recurring characters identified as witches are treated sympathetically and with affection. Even a character intended initially as a villain, like *Dark Shadows'* Angélique or one who becomes dangerous, like *Buffy the Vampire Slayer's* Willow, are audience favorites.

The Addams Family

Among the most beloved television series, *The Addams Family* ran from September 18, 1964 until September 2, 1966. Gomez and Morticia Addams lived in a spooky, Gothic mansion along with their unusual, eccentric family in an otherwise conventional town. They were Gothic before "Gothic" existed. The deathly-white skinned Morticia sported long black Lilith tresses and always dressed in a skin-tight black gown reminiscent of a spider. (Arguments could also be made for that other witch creature, the octopus.) Always serene and soft-spoken but nonetheless a powerful, committed matriarch, everyone in her family adored her.

The series was inspired by the cartoons of American artist Charles Addams (January 7, 1912-September 28, 1988) that appeared in *The New Yorker* magazine from 1935 until 1988 and which remain available in several published collections. The original characters had no names. The television show bestowed names upon them and fleshed out their personalities and relationships.

The relevant question of course is whether the beautiful and brilliant Morticia (played by Carolyn Jones) is a witch. Many assume that she is; certainly the standard mass-marketed Halloween witch costume is now based on Morticia's tight-fitting black spider gown. However, Morticia is never actually explicitly identified as a witch. She does possess some supernatural powers (when Morticia smokes, her body literally smokes; there's no need for cigarettes) and she does know how to conduct a séance, but whether that is sufficient to consider her a witch is subject to debate. Morticia certainly fulfills many expectations of what a witch *should* look like. (There is also a school of thought that considers Morticia to really be a vampire, however this too is based purely on superficial evidence—mainly her extreme pallor and languor.)

The Addams Family does have other characters explicitly identified as witches, most notably Morticia's mother-in-law, Grandmama (Blossom Rock). The show's joke was that the witch was in many ways the most conventional member of the family. In addition, Margaret Hamilton, the Wicked Witch of the West from the MGM musical *The Wizard of Oz*, made two appearances as Morticia's mother, Grandma Hester Frump, and is identified as a witch. If witchcraft is hereditary, then Morticia is a witch.

Witchcraft occasionally emerged as a theme on the show as well. In one episode, the Addams children are terrified by the fairy tale *Hansel and Gretel*, which Morticia deems too violent for children because of the murder of the witch.

In the 1965 Halloween episode, Gomez and Morticia attempt to counter the falsehood taught to their children by outsiders that there's no such thing as witches. This would have been the moment for Morticia to emerge from the broom closet and announce her identity; notably she does not. However, she does conduct a séance in an attempt to contact her Great-

Great-Great-Aunt Singe, a witch who was burned at Salem so that she'll tell the kids the truth: witches really do exist. When others express doubt as to whether Singe will materialize, Morticia says confidently, "What right-thinking witch would turn down a child on Halloween?"

The Addams Family refuses to die. After the demise of the original show, it continued in syndication, remaining a cult favorite. The original cast reunited for a 1977 Halloween special. *The Addams Family* has since inspired a televised cartoon series and two feature films, *The Addams Family* (1991) and *Addams Family Values* (1993). Anjelica Huston played Morticia in both movies; Judith Malina portrayed Grandmama in the first while Carol Kane assumed the role for the second.

Bewitched

Bewitched aired on the ABC network from September 17, 1964 until July 1, 1972. The show was incredibly popular (in its first season, it was second in ratings only to the Western classic *Bonanza*.) *Bewitched* was not only a weekly series; in addition, beginning in January 1968, ABC replayed episodes *daily* until September 1973. *Bewitched* held the record of highest-rated half-hour weekly series ever to air from its inception until 1977.

Bewitched was revolutionary: the witch was completely and unambiguously the heroine. Samantha is a fantasy witch blessed with supernatural powers. Seemingly all she had to do was wiggle her nose and whatever she envisioned was accomplished, although every once in a while she was shown struggling to master a spell.

Samantha was beautiful, intelligent, kind, ethical, and in many ways utterly conventional.

The only ambivalence shown to witchcraft comes in Samantha's own attitude toward it: she'd prefer to be an ordinary human and periodically vows to abandon witchcraft for good. Her preference for doing household chores manually rather than magically is the only sign indicating that Samantha might be somewhat less than brilliant. Morticia surely would not make that mistake, and neither did Samantha's mother.

Bewitched had two witches appearing as series regulars: Samantha was played by Elizabeth Montgomery; Endora, her sardonic mother who was less than enchanted with Samantha's fascination with all things human, was played by Agnes Moorehead who, unbeknownst to most television viewers, had an illustrious career behind her: she was a founding member of Orson Welles' Mercury Theater, appeared in his *Citizen Kane*, and earned multiple Academy Award nominations. Endora thought Samantha a fool for missing out on all the fun, excitement, and glamour of witchcraft; she disapproved of her attempts to behave as a "mortal" and was the epitome of the evil mother-in-law, constantly casting (very funny) spells on Samantha's beloved.

The seeds of *Bewitched* derive from the films *I Married A Witch* and (especially) *Bell, Book and Candle,* whose leading lady Gillian epitomizes the ambivalent witch.

Nicole Kidman played Samantha in the 2005 film version of *Bewitched.*

Buffy the Vampire Slayer

Can a cheerleader slay vampires? That's the dilemma posed by the television series *Buffy the Vampire Slayer. Buffy* derives from a dualist premise: if forces of evil exist then the forces necessary to combat them must exist too (see the Introduction for a discussion of dualist thinking). In every generation, according to this television show, there is a "Chosen One," the "*Slayer*" who stands fast against these forces of evil. Who could possibly defend the world from evil more effectively than a 5'3" blonde high-school cheerleader from California named Buffy?

Buffy the Vampire Slayer premiered on March 10, 1997 as a mid-season replacement; it was not expected to do particularly well. Defying expectations, *Buffy* seized the public imagination, becoming a very popular program. The television series was inspired by Fran Rubel Kuzui's movie *Buffy the Vampire Slayer* (1992), which was not a financial success but lingered as a cult favorite.

The vampires of *Buffy* are not classic Count Dracula-style vampires nor do they conform to traditional Balkan vampire mythology. They are perhaps better characterized as vampiric-demonic beings. It's Buffy's destiny to preserve the world from them, even at the risk of her death. Buffy is not a witch, however characters explicitly identified as "*witches*" and themes related to witchcraft appear consistently.

Buffy's not the witch but her best friend becomes one. Willow Rosenberg is a brilliant computer geek played by Alyson Hannigan. Willow is not only Buffy's friend but her ally and assistant. She is the only character aside from Buffy to appear in every episode of the series.

Originally Willow researched computer websites devoted to magic spells, witchcraft, Wicca, and Neo-Paganism only in order to assist Buffy in her exploits; soon she gets hooked by the topic however and delves deep in the world of the magical arts and Wicca. Eventually Willow becomes an accomplished spell-caster and a dedicated practitioner. She is explicitly identified as a Wiccan, although *Buffy the Vampire Slayer* is no less devoted to fantasy than *Bewitched*: its depictions of Wiccans, witchcraft or metaphysical themes in general should not be considered realistic by any means.

Willow's interest in witchcraft eventually leads to obsession and disaster. Although Willow is treated sympathetically the underlying message is that practicing the magical arts is dangerous. Determined to save Buffy's life, which is hanging in the balance, Willow summons *"the Books of Dark Magic"* and drains them of their contents, absorbing their knowledge into her own body: her normally red hair turns black and her eyes darken. Thus transformed into *Dark Witch Willow*, Willow goes to the hospital, orders the doctors and nurses to leave, and magically heals Buffy.

Buffy the Vampire Slayer has provoked some serious philosophical discussions and has even been the subject of university seminars. Beneath the humor and fantasy, the show can be interpreted more seriously as depicting a dualist battle between forces of evil and righteousness.

Charmed

Charmed premiered in October 1998: the three Halliwell sisters, Prue, Piper, and Phoebe, are reunited at their childhood home in San Francisco following the death of their grandmother. They discover a Book of Shadows in the attic that foretells of "The Charmed Ones"—three witches who will become the most powerful of a long line of "good witches." Each of the Charmed Ones shall inherit one power:

❋ *The power to manipulate objects*

❋ *The power to freeze time*

❋ *The power to see the future*

The Halliwell sisters realize that they're the Charmed Ones! They learn that they must stay in the mansion and assume their role.

Charmed, described as a "supernatural drama," is based on an interesting concept: witches as enemies of demons rather than their allies. Reminiscent of the Italian magical practitioners, the Benandanti, *Charmed* depicts witches as protectors of the innocent and enemies of the wicked. Evil forces are relentless in their attempts to destroy the Charmed Ones and usurp their powers.

Shannen Doherty, who originally played the part of Prue Halliwell, allegedly refused to sign a two-year contract extension in June 2001 and so Prue was thrown through a wall in the last episode of the third season and is now presumed dead. The Charmed Ones were at a loss; the show's premise is rooted in the concept of the power of three—as in the Triple Goddess and the three stages of women (maiden, mother, crone). In order to achieve maximum power, the Charmed Ones needed a third witch. Luckily, Paige Matthews (played by Rose McGowan) soon appeared, a long-lost sister of the Charmed Ones.

The Charmed Ones' lineage began with their maternal ancestor, Melinda Warren, who although born in Virginia eventually moved to Salem, Massachusetts. She possessed all three of the Charmed Ones' powers. A warlock tricked her, copied her powers and turned her over to the authorities. (On *Charmed*, warlocks are not male witches but evil ones who happen to be male.) Melinda was burned at the stake during the Salem witch trials. (And no, witches were *not* burned at the stake in Salem, or elsewhere in New England. They were hung, a fate that never seems sufficiently grizzly for fantasy versions of witchcraft.)

Charmed draws deeply on Wiccan terminology and ritual, although this show is also a fantasy and should not be taken as representing the reality of Wicca, witchcraft or metaphysical practice in general. That said, *Charmed* treats Wicca with respect and it has a following in the modern witchcraft community.

See **DICTIONARY:** Benandanti; Wicca.

Dark Shadows

Dark Shadows was a Gothic soap opera that recounted the tangled history of the Collins family of Collinsport, Maine. It was the first daytime serial devoted to vampires, werewolves, and witches and featured mortals-vampire romances decades before *Buffy the Vampire Slayer*.

Dark Shadows debuted on June 27, 1966 and ran for five years until April 1971. A daily half-hour soap opera, the show was televised in the late afternoon and so became popular as an after-school program for older children as well as for adults.

It was originally merely a Gothic-flavored soap opera, which was not initially very popular until, nine months into the program, the character of the vampire Barnabas Collins was introduced. Barnabas caught the public eye as he did that of many of the program's female characters. Once the vampire theme was introduced, the show genuinely became suspenseful and even scary.

Barnabas was released from his slumber in the family mausoleum in a plot-line reminiscent of what was then a cult movie favorite, *The Mask of Satan* (see Films, page 265). His vampiric condition was caused by a witch: in 1795, he had scorned her love and she cursed him. As that old saying goes, hell hath no fury … the witch, Angélique, periodically made appearances on *Dark Shadows* just to make sure Barnabas never re-attained mortal status.

Angélique made her first appearance on the show during a séance conducted for the purpose of revealing Barnabas' history. She then made several appearances in various incarnations and under different names, most notably the modern character Cassandra. In the guise of Cassandra, she continues to study and practice witchcraft.

Lara Parker played Angélique in all her incarnations. Angélique is a beautiful, seductive blonde displaying lots of cleavage. Although she was a "villain" she was not portrayed unsympathetically. *Dark Shadows* drew much of its inspiration from Gothic novels and imagery; its vision of malevolent witchcraft does not contradict that of traditional folklore. Malevolent witchcraft is fueled by anger, jealousy, and rage; in this particular case, Angélique possessed tremendous resentment of the class barriers obstructing her relationship with Barnabas Collins whom she desired, loved, and despised simultaneously.

Dark Shadows did not lack controversy. Fundamentalist Christian groups protested its presence on television, describing *Dark Shadows* as "Satan's favorite television show." Witches and vampires may have been dangerous but they weren't the show's true villains; that role was assumed by stern, conservative patriarchs and hypocrite preachers. It was also not a light comedy like *Bewitched* or *The Addams Family* with witchcraft played for laughs; instead the primary witch and vampire were *very* seductive.

Various attempts have been made over the years to resurrect the television series with a new cast. *Dark Shadows* has also inspired several films. Eva Green plays Angélique in the 2012 movie starring Johnny Depp as Barnabas.

Sabrina the Teenage Witch

Sabrina the Teenage Witch has had many incarnations over many years:

✳ *She debuted in the comic book* Archie's Madhouse *in October 1962.*

✳ *She emerged as a lead character in* Archie's TV Laugh Out *in December 1969.*

✳ *In September 1971, Sabrina was featured in the animated television series* Sabrina the Teenage Witch. *She also made appearances on another series* The Groovy Ghoulies.

✳ *In 1994, actor Melissa Joan Hart was cast in a made-for-television movie, inspired by the comic character, as Sabrina Sawyer—a young girl who learns she's a witch after she goes to live with her two aunts.*

✳ *Finally Hart went on to star in this popular television series, which ran from September 1996 until April 2003. The character of the young witch learning to use her powers was renamed Sabrina Spellman. Her two witch aunts were Hilda (Caroline Rhea) and Zelda (Beth Broderick).*

The show is a light comedy in the vein of *Bewitched*. Sabrina, like Samantha, is ambivalent about being a witch: it deprives her of much of the fun of a regular teenager. Her aunts are stricter than *Bewitched*'s Endora, or perhaps *Sabrina* merely has a more responsible vision of witchcraft. Although she is a hereditary witch, one of those semi-immortal supernatural beings who just look human, there are still many rules and regulations for Sabrina to learn and abide by in order for her to become a full-fledged witch. Sabrina lives with her aunts in a conventional community; although they may appear a little eccentric, they must keep their identity as witches secret.

Sabrina the Teenage Witch draws its witchcraft imagery from traditional folklore: Sabrina has a huge interactive grimoire. The family includes a sardonic, talking black cat named Salem. (Salem is a transformed witch; he was punished by the Witch Council for attempting world domination.)

Visual Arts: Paintings, Postcards, and Woodcuts

Witches and witchcraft have inspired artists and served as their muse but, conversely, artists have also exerted tremendous influence over popular perceptions of witches and witchcraft. Artists have continually shaped and reshaped how the general public views and understands witches and witchcraft. This was especially true when there was little competition from any other media.

Images of powerful women have *always* held people spellbound. Among Earth's oldest surviving works of creative "art" are Paleolithic and Neolithic carvings of powerful females (see the Introduction).

One may trace changing perceptions of witches (and of women in general) through centuries of art. There are *countless* artistic depictions of witches or themes related to witchcraft, too many to ever include in one book; however certain eras, schools of art and individual artists are *especially* identified with the topic:

✳ *Medieval woodcuts*

✳ *The Northern Renaissance*

✳ *The Spanish painter Francisco Goya*

* *Victorian-era painters including the Pre-Raphaelites*

* *Halloween postcards from the turn of the twentieth century*

As with masterpieces of literature or film, some may consider it unfair to reduce some of the world's finest artistic representations to discussions of witchcraft, however that is what ties these very disparate styles, eras and perceptions together. It is also not usual for fine art and popular culture to be considered side by side; however in terms of historical impact, popular forms like woodcuts or postcards have exerted extraordinary influence over how witchcraft is portrayed and perceived. The anonymous masters of propaganda who created those medieval woodcuts also helped create the image of the witch as monstrous consort of Satan. And the early twentieth-century fine artists, often equally anonymous, who strove to earn a living by painting postcards, conversely helped redeem witches, popularizing the notion of the beautiful, playful or sweet witch.

Popular perceptions of witches were shaped by the paintings and engravings of acclaimed masters like Goya, Dürer or Hans Baldung Grien, and also by popular penny-dreadfuls, broadsides, and turn-of-the-twentieth-century postcards. Whether they are equally worthy as art is subject to debate; they are equal in terms of their impact on witchcraft.

Medieval Woodcuts, Engravings, and the Northern Renaissance

Although these genres are usually considered separately, when the main focus is on depictions of witchcraft, they are almost impossible to separate as the masters of the Northern Renaissance often used the same production techniques as those used by the anonymous illustrators of penny-dreadfuls and broadsides. The significant difference between the genres is the level of artistic skill of the renowned masters and the almost absolute anonymity of the medieval craftsmen.

The invention of the printing press not only promoted notions of general literacy; another by-product was the then-revolutionary concept of "popular art." Up until the fifteenth century European art was almost completely religious in nature. Religious topics were the only topics with very, very, very few exceptions. The concept of art as popular entertainment or mass secular information had yet to be born.

"Woodcut" and "engraving" refer to methods of creating art. These methods were incorporated by the masters of what is now considered the Northern Renaissance in addition to conventional painting, however the term "medieval woodcuts" is also often used as a blanket term to refer to illustrations made using that method in the popular media of the day.

Woodcut is a printing method in which images are carved onto the surface of a flat block of wood. The printing parts remain level with the surface; the non-printing parts are removed usually with a chisel. Ink is rolled over the surface using a roller; the ink is only applied to the flat surfaces. Paper is then placed face-down on the inked woodblock and pressure applied to its back. Ink is transferred to the paper and a mirror-image of woodblock is created. Multiple colors can be printed although the simplest woodcuts are monochromatic.

Woodcuts and the new printing process made it possible for inexpensive illustrations to be created for mass consumption. Literacy was still rare but anyone could view and comprehend pictures. And as the name of one type of publication, the penny-dreadful, indicates, soon almost anyone could afford them.

Medieval woodcuts as a genre tend toward the sensational and macabre: witches are a favorite theme. There are countless of images of witches in that genre: witches flying to sabbats or applying ointments, witches casting spells or curses, witches cavorting with Satan or witches just being generally evil and disgusting. These images were *incredibly* influential: many who previously had no idea what a witch looked like were convinced they did once they had seen these images.

If you didn't fear witches before you saw these broadsides and penny-dreadfuls, you likely would afterwards. Witches were typically given grotesque features: warts, hooked noses, many are deeply wrinkled and look ancient. During an era when life expectancy was low and when death during childbirth was common, women of advanced age were popularly considered *unnatural.* Merely to be a very old woman was sometimes considered among the sure telltale signs of witchcraft or diabolical affiliations.

Witches are not only identified by their pointy hats and broomsticks. In addition, certain motifs are fairly unique to depictions of witches:

- *Witches are commonly depicted reading. This may not seem unusual today, however up until the eighteenth century artists rarely depicted women in the act of reading with two significant exceptions: women who are clearly studying devotional material and witches who study books of magic.*

- *Witches are commonly depicted naked. During very conservative eras, the only women who frequently appeared naked were witches, which just went to prove what kind of women they were, even if they had been forcibly unclothed. (During public executions, condemned witches frequently died unclothed, as did Joan of Arc; it was considered the ultimate punishment and humiliation.)*

It is surmised that Albrecht Dürer and other witch-hunt era artists painted witches specifically because they desired to paint the female nude, and the only women whom it was considered acceptable to paint naked were witches.

There is a powerfully sadistic, pornographic quality to much popular witch-hunt era imagery; there are tremendous quantities of naked witch imagery, in many of them witches are engaged in various sexual acts with Satan, demons, familiars, each other, men, you name it. Other images depict the accused undergoing torture and physical examination. Often the unclothed woman (if she has clothes, they may be ripped to shreds) is chained to a board, chair or pole while a pack of men examine or torture her. Witch-hunt era images are direct precursors of similar imagery found centuries later in many pulp or pornographic magazines.

A tremendous quantity of medieval woodcuts survive; however, virtually all the illustrators are anonymous.

The Northern Renaissance

Renaissance means "rebirth" and usually refers to the flowering of artistry and intellect in Italy beginning in the fourteenth century and spreading throughout Northern Europe during the sixteenth. It is considered the transitional period between the end of the Middle Ages and the beginning of the Modern Age.

The Northern Renaissance occurred concurrently with some of the most virulent witch-hunts. Whatever their personal opinions (and many of these works are considered ambiguous), images of witches and their sabbats became popular in high art as well as low, with images of witches' sabbats created in woodcuts, engravings, and paintings by masters of the Northern Renaissance. Although the artistry may be finer and the techniques more sophisticated, many of the themes, images, and topics are no different than those of the anonymous medieval carvers. Witch-hunts were current events for these artists; they were aware of popular depictions of witchcraft and drew their inspiration from the same sources.

The Northern Renaissance artist most associated with themes of witchcraft is Hans Baldung Grien (c. 1484–1545), who is considered responsible for introducing erotic and supernatural themes into German art. Witches were among his favorite themes.

Grien received part of his artistic training in Albrecht Dürer's workshop as designer of graphic illustrations (1505–1507) and is considered among Dürer's most gifted students. He eventually became a member of his workshop. Grien painted religious pieces as well as practitioners of the magical arts. His best-known work is the High Altar of the Cathedral at Freiburg in Germany.

Grien was a member of the Strasbourg Town Council and official painter to the Episcopate. He lived in Strasbourg during a time when the city was preoccupied with witch-hunting. The Pope had appointed the Bishop of Strasbourg to supervise enforcement of witchcraft laws in the area and to discover hidden witches. Grien became a wealthy property owner who took an active role in Strasbourg civic life during this time.

His witchcraft-themed works include:

* The Witches' Sabbath *(1510); considered among his masterpieces, it featured a new technique known as chiaroscuro or tonal woodcut that resulted in a print resembling something between a woodcut and a painting*

* Scare of Witchcraft *(1510)*

* The Witches *(1510)*

* Witch with a Monster *(1515); the monster, a dragon, anally penetrates the young, naked blonde witch with his incredibly long tongue.*

* Two Weather Witches *(1523)*

* Departing for the Sabbath *(date unknown)*

* Three Witches *(date unknown)*

* The Bewitched Groom *also known as* Sleeping Groom and the Sorceress *(1544)*

Other artists and their works associated with witchcraft themes include:

* *Niklaus Manuel Deutsch (1484–1530):* Witch Porting the Skull of Manuel; Old Witch; Female Flautist

* *Albrecht Dürer (1471–1528):* The Four Sorcerers; The Witch; Witch Riding a Ram Backwards

* *David Teniers the Younger (1610–1690):* Witches Preparing for a Sabbat

* *Hans Weiditz II (also sometimes spelled Wyditz) (c. 1495–c. 1536). This Flemish artist is considered a master of the Northern Renaissance. He specialized in woodcuts and is an important exception to the rule regarding the anonymity of this genre. His woodcuts include:* Witch Turned Werewolf Attacking Travelers; Witches Celebrating; The Alchemist; Witch Fighting a Devil; Witch Brewing Potion; and Devil Seducing Witch

Goya

When it comes to witchcraft (and perhaps in other ways as well) the artist who was born Francisco de Goya y Lucientes (March 30, 1746–April 16, 1828) transcends genres. Goya created a prodigious output of work; a high percentage involved witchcraft themes including a series of paintings known as *The Witchcraft Paintings*.

Goya's mother came from the lowest rung of Aragonese nobility. His father, a master gilder, traced his family's roots to Basque ancestry. The Basque region was identified with witchcraft and had earlier been the site of one of the few major Spanish witch-hunts (see **WITCHCRAZE!**: Spain). The Basque word for sabbat, *Aquelarre*, is the title often given one of Goya's most famous paintings, called in English *The Witches' Sabbat*.

His depiction of witchcraft is ambiguous and there is much speculation as to his true beliefs. His witches are grotesque but powerful. They are consistently painted in conjunction with the devil in the form of a human-sized goat. However, Goya also created images of individual witches punished by the Inquisition and these may be interpreted as being quite sympathetic. Goya had his own troubles with the Inquisition himself, although they did not include charges of witchcraft.

Goya was perhaps the first master of social or political art and so often interpreters seek metaphors in his works devoted to witchcraft. However, scenes of Spanish witchcraft (*brujeria*) were very popular in late eighteenth-century Spain, if only as a joke about ancestral superstitions, and were a favored theme not only in visual art but also in literature: many plays about witchcraft and diabolism (assumed to be intrinsically related) were produced in the Spanish theater during Goya's time. Antonio de Zamora, the Spanish playwright and author of *The Stone Guest*, is believed to have helped inspire Goya's *Witchcraft Paintings*, for instance. Few of these witchcraft-related works are familiar to English speakers and thus Goya's work is often interpreted out of context.

Although Goya painted witches throughout his life, they are prominently featured in three specific series:

✳ Caprices

This series of numbered satirical prints are known as the Caprices, *Capriccios* or *Caprichos*, and consist of etchings with acquatint. They are named and numbered. The word "caprice" derives from the unpredictable jumping and hopping of a young goat. Approximately one-quarter of the 80 final plates in the Caprices represent witches or witchcraft. They were published in 1799 but attracted the attention of the Inquisition. Goya withdrew them from public sale and offered them to the Spanish King. They appear in the royal inventory of 1803.

Examples of the nature of witchcraft-related caprices:

All Will Fall: Capricho 19 possesses a hallucinatory quality. It depicts winged malevolent spirits including a traditional siren (a bird-woman, not a mermaid) high in a tree overlooking three women, presumably witches. The old grotesque woman/witch looks up while two younger, attractive, buxom women amuse themselves by anally penetrating a captured flying demon (or bird) who suffers in their hands.

There Was No Remedy: Capricho 24 depicts a female victim of the Inquisition riding on a donkey. She is often interpreted as a witch although her "crime" is unclear. She's bare-breasted, wearing the long peaked, striped hat of humiliation. (Stripes were once representative of criminality as in some modern prison garb.) The woman shines white and luminous while the crowd leers and jeers at her from the darkness.

Other caprices with witchcraft themes include Capricho 60: *Trials*; Capricho 61: *Volaverunt*; Capricho 67: *Wait Until You've Been Anointed*; Capricho 68: *Pretty Teacher* (a young naked witch clings to a wizened elderly cone on a flying broomstick).

✳ Witchcraft Paintings

Goya painted six oil paintings devoted to sorcery and witchcraft during 1797 and 1798. The series consists of six individual paintings, thematically related but not forming a coherent narrative. Two are now lost. In June 1798, the so-called Witchcraft Paintings were sold to his patron the Duke of Osuna who, together with his wife, is believed to have commissioned them. The surviving paintings comprise:

Aquelarre or *The Witches' Sabbath*
The Bewitched
The Flying Witches
The Spell or *The Incantation*

✳ The Black Paintings

In 1819, Goya bought a country home known as "The House of the Deaf Man." (*Quinta del Sordo*). Ironically, although Goya was deaf (he became permanently deaf in 1792), the house was *not* named in his honor; the previous owner had been a deaf farmer. Between 1820 and 1823, Goya created 14 paintings directly on the plaster walls of the house. (There is also a school of thought that suggests these paintings were actually made by his son.) They are now known as the "Black Paintings" both because of their literal color and the darkness of their mood. In

several of the works, Goya once again returned to the theme of witchcraft.

In 1860, long after Goya's death, the paintings were removed from the walls, restored and transferred onto canvas. In 1881, the then owner of the house gave the paintings to the Spanish State, which passed them on to Madrid's Prado Museum where they remain today. The house itself was demolished to make way for a railway siding, which now bears Goya's name. Among the Black Paintings devoted to themes related to witchcraft are *The Goat* and *Las Parcas* (*The Fates*).

Nineteenth-century Paintings Including the Pre-Raphaelites

The nineteenth century was characterized by a reassessment of art and women's societal roles in general, and of witchcraft and witches in particular. Among other artistic movements, the Pre-Raphaelite Brotherhood was founded by a group of seven English painters in 1848 as an extension of the Romantic movement dedicated to re-defining "art." They, together with other artists, were fascinated by mythology, mysticism, and women's mysteries, which became extraordinarily popular themes and remain so today.

Once again witches and sorceresses became a common artistic motif, although the witches now being produced were like nothing ever seen before. Previously, one could safely say that depictions of witches were generally grotesque, at best ambiguous. Images of witches created during this era were frequently *at worst* ambiguous; in general, they are beautiful, powerful, and mysterious even when they are threatening.

These witchcraft paintings remain extremely popular; although many are unfamiliar with the artists' names, the images themselves are often incredibly familiar, appearing all over the Internet on sources devoted to Wicca and witchcraft. They appear on the covers of multitudes of books devoted to witchcraft as well as other unrelated topics. It can be difficult at first glance to distinguish between the several books currently available all featuring John William Waterhouse's *The Magic Circle* on the cover, for example.

A popular artistic theme during this era was the mysterious power of women. (This was a period where women were first beginning to demand political rights and social and economic equality.) These artistic depictions may not have been intended favorably although modern eyes tend to view them in a positive manner. The concept many of these paintings intended to convey was that of the *femme fatale, the belle dame sans merci.* Although beautiful, seductive, and alluring, this woman is ultimately deadly: a Salome or a Jezebel, a Circe or a Medea, or even just some generic sorceress or witch.

Witches were still dangerous but they were beautifully so rather than grotesque. Whether this style of art reeks of misogyny or celebrates these magical, powerful women is subject to interpretation and strong cases have been made for both sides of that particular argument.

Among the artists most devoted to painting witches and sorceresses was John William Waterhouse (April 6, 1849-February 10,1917). Waterhouse enjoyed painting the theme of the *femme fatale.* Among his many works featuring themes relating to witchcraft are:

- The Household Gods *(1880)*
- Consulting the Oracle *(1882)*
- The Magic Circle *(1886)*
- Circe Offering the Cup to Ulysses *(1891)*
- Circe Invidiosa *(1892)*
- The Crystal Ball *(1902)*
- Jason and Medea *(1907)*
- Circe *(1911), also known as* The Sorceress
- The Charmer *(1911)*
- The Love Philtre *(1914)*
- Tristan and Isolde with the Potion *(c. 1916)*

There are too many paintings related to witchcraft in this genre to ever count. However, some other significant paintings from this era include:

- A Bacchante *Arthur Hacker (1913)*
- Circe *John Collier (date unknown)*
- Circe *Arthur Hacker (1893)*
- Circe *Lucien Levy-Dhurmer (1895 and 1897)*
- In the Venusberg (Tannhauser) *John Collier (1901)*
- The Laboratory *Dante Gabriel Rossetti (1849)*
- Lilith *John Collier (1887)*
- The Love Potion *Evelyn de Morgan (1903)*
- The Magic Crystal *Sir Frank Dicksee (1894)*
- Medea *Anthony Frederick Sandys (1878)*
- Priestess of Delphi *John Collier (1891)*

* The Prophetess Libuse *Vitezlav Karel Masek (1893)*

* The Sorceress *Lucien Levy-Dhurmer (1897)*

* The Sorceress *Henry Meynell Rheam (1898)*

* The Vision of Faust *Luis Ricardo Falero (1878)*

* Witch *Gustav Klimt (1898)*

* The Witches' Sabbath *Luis Ricardo Falero (1880)*

Halloween Postcards

The very first official government-sanctioned postal card was unveiled in Austria on October 1, 1869. Postcards were an immediate hit: it is estimated that nine million of them were sold in their first year of existence and sales continued to increase exponentially.

Originally postcards were intended as a very simple, less-expensive method of postal communication. The first postcards were uniform and had minimal imagery. In 1878, standard dimensions were assigned at the World Congress of the Universal Postal Union. In the 1890s, governments began relinquishing control of this profitable product, granting publishing licenses to private industry.

Simultaneously, refinement of a color-printing technique known as chromolithography occurred. Postcards could easily and inexpensively have individual images on one side, leaving room for written messages and address information on the other.

The first chromolithograph centers were in Germany, where most early art-postcards were produced. These cards are characterized by their long-lasting vibrant colors—colors created by toxic materials that are now no longer in use. The artwork on turn-of-the-century postcards, thus, is often more vivid and exciting than on more recent examples and as such are highly valued by modern collectors.

Postcards emerged in all different varieties. From approximately 1900 until 1930 sending Halloween postcards was as popular as sending Christmas cards remains today, and perhaps even more so. *Hundreds* of postcards were produced featuring Halloween imagery, especially witches. Many were also devoted to divination techniques. Today they are highly prized collectibles, and the finest ones in mint condition fetch extremely high prices. For many, this financial value is the most significant aspect of antique postal cards. However, from a witchcraft perspective, these postcards created a magical image of witchcraft perhaps never seen before.

"Fine artist" unfortunately too often translates to "starving artist"; however, postcard-production created job opportunities for many talented artists. Many labored anonymously but some postcards are signed and now are avidly collected. Because the goal was to sell postcards, images might be attractively spooky or even a little shivery but they were rarely truly grotesque. The artists had fun creating the images: many are very playful and thus express the side of witchcraft that is fun and joyful as well as powerful.

These postcards rely on mythic, folkloric, and modern imagery. Popular turn-of-the-century Halloween postcard imagery include vegetable people and other harvest motifs including Corn Mothers masquerading as witches, fortune-telling and other divination techniques, Halloween pranks, and (especially) witches and the fertility-based motifs most associated with them: owls, bats, cats, cauldrons, spiders, broomsticks, and so forth.

Relatively few witches are grotesque; even the old crones are powerful, evocative, and drawn as worthy of respect. Witches wear green, black, and red—especially red: red shoes, ribbons, bows, dresses, and stockings. There are child witches and beautiful witches (even very occasionally male witches). In general (and there *are* exceptions), they may be characterized as fun *and* powerful and welcoming. Often witches are shown interacting with conventional people, usually assisting young women with romantic divination or observing Halloween festivities.

Some of the most popular publishers of these postcards include American Postcard Company, Gibson, International Art Publishing Company, Lubrie & Elkins, Tuck, Valentine & Sons, Whitney, John Winsch, and Wolf Brothers.

Some of the most popular artists responsible for classic Halloween postcards include Francis Brundage, Ellen Clapsaddle, Jason Freixas, H.B. Griggs, and Samuel Schmucker.

Witches also appear on Easter postcards from Sweden and Finland. They are characteristic of Swedish Easter witch tradition and are usually depicted with their coffeepots as well as their brooms and cats.

Dictionary of Witchcraft: A Magical Vocabulary

The vocabulary of witchcraft includes words that are mysterious and obscure as well as others that seem familiar but reveal hidden depths when examined: if your blind-date is described as *"fascinating"* or *"alluring"* should you be pleased … or alarmed?

Words included in this section are associated with various facets of witchcraft and magical practice, as well as with those spiritual traditions sometimes confused or identified with witchcraft.

The English word "witch" has evolved into something of a catch-all for all kinds of practitioners of magical arts and traditional spirituality. Words in other languages naming practitioners of these arts or traditions are inevitably translated into English as *"witch."* In one sense, this does reflect the reality of an international community of magical practitioners who may share certain perceptions and worldviews; however this practice also denies the complexity of these traditions. Translation as "witch" was intended as dismissive and derisive.

Words translated into English as "witch" frequently describe negative practices and have negative implications. One must appreciate the powerful role that missionaries have historically played in the transmission and translation of languages. (Protestant missionaries, in particular, emphasize translation of the Bible into local languages and so are often responsible for creating the first—and often *only*—dictionaries of indigenous languages.) These are not unbiased sources.

When missionaries ask for the local word corresponding to "witch" they have not historically requested a word indicating *"beneficial female practitioner of positive magic"*; missionaries define "witch" in the most negative light and so their sources respond in kind: *"What's the word for an evil female practitioner of harmful malevolent magic?"* Inevitably, languages do have a word for this type of practitioner. However, it is rarely their *only* word for a magical practitioner nor is it typically inclusive of *all* magical practitioners.

🐜 🐜 🐜

Àjé: Yoruba word usually translated as *"witch-craft."* Technically it means *"Our Mothers"* and names mystical female powers that may be used either constructively or destructively. Àjé is tremendously beneficial to the entire community when balanced and directed benevolently, however, as with "witchcraft" some people only use the word àjé to express exclusively negative manifestations of this power. (The word is also cognate with another meaning "prosperity" and "wealth".)

Àjé refers to the power (magical energy) and also to those who embody and manipulate it. Elderly women are most strongly identified as àjé, although theoretically any woman could be. Although àjé are human, they are frequently envisioned as birds and are led by the orisha Oshun who has powerful associations with witchcraft, birds, *and* feminine power. Àjé are also affiliated with the male orishas Oko and Ogun. See page 347, Orisha; **DIVINE WITCH:** Oshun, Orisha Oko; **MAGICAL PROFESSIONS:** Metalworkers.

Akelarre: *Akerra* means male goat in the Basque language. The term was used by witch-hunters as a synonym for witches' sabbats, which they envisioned as presided over by a goat. The word is most famous as the title of the witchcraft painting by Goya, which depicts witches in the company of a huge male goat. The equivalent word in Castilian is *Aquelarre.* See **CREATIVE ARTS:** Visual Arts: Goya.

Alchemist: A practitioner of alchemy; the word is sometimes used as a synonym for magician or sorcerer; some but not all alchemists engaged in other magical arts. (See **MAGICAL ARTS:** Alchemy.)

Allure: Today this word usually means *"enticing"* or *"seductive"* and is most often used to describe beautiful women. So if someone calls you alluring, should you be flattered? Maybe. In its original Middle English usage, "allure" was intended to describe something threatening and negative. It derives from the same root word as lure, indicating *"bait"* or *"hunting decoy."*

Allure was initially defined as the power with which women entrapped men: women's magical erotic powers. Even now, the dictionary definition of allure suggests that it means "to entice by *charm* or attraction." Charm may now imply a pleasing personality but was once commonly understood as synonymous with "spell." See also charm, fascinatrix, glamour.

Alrauna, Alraune, Alruna, Alrune: This word has been used for centuries as a German synonym for "witch." Historically, however, it originally referred to pre-Christian Germanic women, also described as priestesses, prophetesses, shamans, and magical practitioners. *Alrauna* appears to derive from the same roots as "rune" and "rowan." Very little information regarding the alrauna survives. What remains derives almost exclusively from Roman observations: Tacitus described the *"aurinia"* as being endowed with magic power, while Aventinus described them as *"loose haired, bare legged witches."* There are also obscure references to *"crossroads goddesses"*; alrauna may have originally (or additionally) indicated the spirits these prophetesses served. Alrauna also refers to mandrake roots.

See Haljoruna, Rune; **BOTANICALS:** Mandrake, Rowan; **CREATIVE ARTS:** Films: *Alraune*, Literature: *Alraune.*

Alraundelberin: Germanic synonym for "witch" first used in the sixteenth century. It literally means "alraune bearer" and refers to the magical use of mandrake roots. See also Alraune, Haljoruna; **BOTANICALS:** Mandrake.

Asatru: A modern spiritual path based on ancient Nordic traditions; the term has been used since the late nineteenth century to describe adherence to and preservation of pre-Christian Nordic religion and means *"trust in the Aesir."* In Scandinavia this tradition is also known as *Forn Sior* (Ancient Way) or *Hedensk sed* (Heathen custom). Asatru was granted status as an official religion in Iceland in 1972.

Ashé: Also spelled *asé* and *axé* but consistently pronounced *"ah-shay."* This Yoruba term indicates metaphysical energy and is synonymous with the magical generative powers that fuel Earth. Ashé also indicates "command" or "authority." A person (or deity) possessing ashé has access to tremendous founts of magical energy and power. The word itself is believed redolent with this power. (See also Baraka, Chi, Heka, Mana, Nyama.)

Ba'al/Ba'alat (m/f): This pan-Semitic word literally means "master," "mistress," "lord," or "lady." Baalzebub (commonly spelled *Beelzebub* in English) thus literally means "Master of the Flies." Baal is the title of an important Semitic deity. The literal meaning of the word is often incorporated into titles for various shamanic masters:

❈ *Ba'al Shem—"master of the name"—refers to Jewish miracle-workers who acquired power by mastery of Names of Power. The ba'al shem traditionally creates written amulets for the purposes of physical healing, exorcism and renewal of fertility. (See Names of Power, page 346.)*

❈ *Balazar—"master of the zar"—an Ethiopian name for shamans who mediate between people and zar spirits. In some regions other names for the same function are also used, for instance* shykha *(Ethiopia) and* kodia *(Egypt). See Kodia, Zar.*

❈ *Baalat ob—"mistress of an ob"—mysterious Hebrew title for some sort of magical or shamanic practitioner, not least because no definitive translation of "ob" exists. The term might have languished in obscurity except for the dramatic appearance made by a Baalat ob in the Bible, better known as the "Witch of Endor." (See* **HALL OF FAME:** *Witch of Endor.)*

Baba: This Russian word has many nuances and may indicate any, some, or all of the following:

❈ *Grandma or other familiar term for "grandmother" or any elderly woman*

❈ *a midwife*

❈ any *woman, although usually a married one*

❈ *a magical practitioner or witch*

It may be a term of affection and respect or used derisively. See **DIVINE WITCH:** Baba Yaga, Jezibaba.

Babaylan: Priest(ess), shaman, magician, healer, or medium in the Visayan dialect of the Philippines. It derives from the root word *baylan*, "to guide."

Bacchanal: Celebrants of the Bacchanalia. The god Dionysus was popularly called Bacchus in Rome; his female devotees, known elsewhere as Maenads, were Bacchanals. See also Bacchanalia, Conjure, Maenad.

Bacchanalia: Dionysian celebrations and spiritual rituals; modern usage usually ignores the spiritual connection and uses this term exclusively for any orgiastic gathering characterized by *lots* of sex, alcohol, general intoxication, and/or a raucous atmosphere.

Bagatella: Italian word usually translated as *"magician"* deriving from a root word for *"stick"* or *"wand,"* thus Bagatella is typically interpreted as a practitioner with a magic wand. In older Italian Tarot decks, this word often labels the card more familiar as *The Magician*. In some regional dialects, *bagatella* also means a shoemaker and so some Tarot decks depict the Magician with a half-completed shoe. This reference to shoes may be an allusion to shamanism. See Mountebank; **CREATIVE ARTS:** Dance: Step of Wu.

Banshee: This anglicized spelling of the Gaelic words *bean sidhe* literally means *"Fairy Woman"* or *"Barrow Woman."* (Barrows are ancient burial mounds, sometimes filled with treasure, that dot the Asian and European landscapes.) The Hollywood version of the banshee is a horribly scary female monster with a fatal screech, a corruption of the tradition of personal psychopomps attached to certain Irish families. Discussion of fairy banshees is found under **FAIRIES:** Solitary Sidhe, however the word has historically been used to describe living women, too.

Among the earliest references to a banshee occurred in medieval Scotland and involved a mortal woman, a prophetess who foretold the death of King James I in 1437.

Similar references to human banshees are found among Scottish and Welsh Romany lore; the word seems to have been intended as synonymous with wise-women, fortune-tellers, witches, and healers.

Baraka: Depending upon region this Arabic word may be interpreted in various ways, which are not mutually exclusive:

✸ *"Blessing" or "power"*

✸ *Allah's sacred grace*

✸ *The sacred magical energy that permeates Earth and all living beings*

Acquisition and enhancement of baraka is the goal of the magical practitioner. More baraka equates to more power, more blessings, and greater possibilities of success, protection, and happiness. See also Ashé, Chi, Heka, Mana, Nyama.

Benandanti: Northern Italian shamanic society charged with witchcraft by the Inquisition. Benandanti literally means *"good walkers."* Inquisition records for the Benandanti cover the years 1575 to 1647 and most information regarding the Benandanti derive from these records.

The Benandanti caused the Inquisition no end of frustration: they did not deny practicing shamanic, obviously Pagan rites, in fact they initially elaborated on their activities but denied that they were "witches"—or at least not hateful, diabolical, evil "witches" as defined by the Inquisition. Instead, they considered themselves magical practitioners who served God and their community by battling other practitioners. These Northern Italian peasants challenged the Inquisition's definition of witchcraft. Their night battles in the District of Friuli allegedly continued until 1610.

The Benandanti claimed that they were compelled to serve their communities during the Ember Days. At midnight they were summoned by angels or drums. Should they resist the call, they explained, they would be severely beaten. Their bodies didn't travel: instead the Benandanti fell into trances so that their souls could depart to engage in ritual combat with those they described as Malandanti (*"evil walkers"*). They did not volunteer to become Benandanti but were predestined at birth, their identity revealed by a caul.

The Benandanti fell into coma-like trances. In this state their souls traveled, usually in the form of an animal that crept forth from the mouth, typically cats, rabbits, butterflies or mice. In this form they journeyed to the center of the Earth where they encountered an opposing shamanic army.

Shamanic battling was dangerous. If body and soul were not ultimately reunited, the body died while the soul was doomed to wander Earth until the person's destined lifespan was up. If the soul is in the form of an animal, then the Benandanti is doomed to remain in that shape for the rest of his life.

The Benandanti dueled with fennel stalks; their opponents used stalks of sorghum. The Benandanti were also armed with rue, the most powerful botanical in the Italian magical arsenal. They invoked Saint Lucy for assistance. Both rue and Saint Lucy provide psychic visions and guard against the Evil Eye, whose withering effect is similar to what would happen should the Benandanti fail to be victorious. If the Benandanti win, then crops and herds will be abundant during the next year but if not, local abundance is doomed to wither away.

The Benandanti fascinate modern anthropologists as much as they frustrated the Inquisition: their testimony indicates the lengthy survival of European shamanism.

> Further reading: Carlo Ginzburg's *The Night Battles* (Penguin Books, 1983) and its follow-up, *Ecstasies* (Penguin Books, 1999).

See also Caul, Ember Days, Fetch, Kresnik, Soul-journey, Táltos; **BOTANICALS:** Rue; **CALENDAR:** Feast of Saint Lucy.

Binding: There are two types of binding spells. Should someone threaten you with one, it's best to know which type they mean.

✳ *Spells to bind two people together, as in an eternal marriage of souls*

✳ *Spells to bind someone's power, usually to prevent them from causing harm*

Black Mass: The Black Mass mocks the Roman Catholic Mass, the central ritual of Catholicism. The Black Mass generally involves sexual behavior and sacrilegious language and invokes Satan, not God.

The Black Mass is only sacrilegious and powerful for those spiritually or emotionally invested in Roman Catholicism. One must possess a Christian orientation or background in order for the Black Mass to have any meaning. It is Christian heresy and has *nothing* to do with witchcraft *per se*. The Black Mass is *never* celebrated in modern Wicca.

What is perhaps very shocking to many outsiders is how irrelevant Christianity is to Wicca and witchcraft. There is no reason to hold a Black Mass, or any other kind of Mass for that matter. That said, participants in a Black Mass might describe themselves as "witches" because they subscribe to the witch-hunt era definition of witchcraft as Christian heresy. However their definition does not correspond to those of "mainstream" witchcraft, Wicca or Neo-Paganism.

The Black Mass is not an ancient rite but seems to have first been performed during the reign of French king Louis XIV (1643–1715). It may have emerged in response to the fantasies of witch-hunters who defined witches as Christian heretics and tortured people into confessions corresponding to these fantasies.

Practitioners of the Black Mass have also taken inspiration from literary sources. Whether these literary depictions are based on reality is subject to ferocious debate. Two particularly significant sources include *Justine*, the 1791 novel by the Marquis de Sade (June 2, 1740–December 2, 1814) which featured a Black Mass performed by an evil monk, and *Là Bas* by French author Joris-Karl Huysmans (February 5, 1848–March 12, 1907), which was published in 1891. The title literally means *Down There* or *Down Below* but is usually more sensationally translated as *The Damned*.

Bokor/Bòkò: A Haitian sorcerer, a bòkò is traditionally described as a practitioner who "works with both hands," meaning that he is willing to use his powers for harm as well as good. (The bòkò is usually male.) Power is used for individual benefit rather than for the greater good, either because it is channeled for personal benefit or because as a magician for hire the bòkò will do whatever the client wishes for a fee. This is a generally negative term although not exclusively so: the bòkò has the capacity to do good as well as evil.

Bomoh: A Malay witch-doctor or practitioner of folk magic, also known as a *dukun* or *pawang*. Massage and botanicals are incorporated alongside spiritual and magical healing techniques. Bomoh remain popular but as their practice derives from pre-Islamic traditions, is often considered disreputable and backward. Many bomoh now also incorporate Islamic spirituality into their practice.

Bonoeman: Surinamese "witch-doctors" and folk healers; they mediate with spirits and perform healings.

Bosorka/Bosorkania: Carpatho-Ukrainian synonym for "witch." The bosorka is always female. There are different ways one becomes a bosorka; sometimes it is destiny—the seventh daughter in a family is fated to be a bosorka, and the third generation in a family boasting three generations of women born out of wedlock also becomes one. Should these accidents of birth fail you, there's always another method: a dying bosorka may transfer her powers to a living one.

The word is also used to indicate a supernatural being who manifests as a woman in white with long thin arms and chicken's feet. See also Boszorkány.

Boszorkány: This Hungarian synonym for "witch" is obviously related to *bosorka* (see above) but is more straightforwardly defined as a practitioner of magic or witch. The words are believed to be of Turkic origin.

Brauche: German magical folk healing.

Brauchen: Literally meaning "to use," this Pennsylvania Dutch euphemism indicates "charming" or "spell-casting."

Braucher: A "charmer"—someone who casts verbal spells. A synonym for "spell-caster," "sorcerer" or "Pow-Wow artist."

Bruja, Brujo, Brujeria: In modern Spanish, brujeria indicates witchcraft; bruja is a female witch, the brujo her male counterpart. Brujo is sometimes translated as "sorcerer." The words derive from an older term that originally meant *"unwholesome night-bird,"* however it has became a simple synonym for "witch." The original implications survives in the Portuguese variant Bruxsa (see below) See also Strix.

Synonyms for "witch" deriving from the same source include:

* *Broxa (Jewish)*

* *Bruja (Modern Spanish)*

* *Bruxa (Classical Spanish)*

* *Bruesche (Provençal)*

Bruxsa: This Portuguese word refers to a female vampire-witch who transforms into a night bird to fly off to sabbats or rendezvous with lovers.

Candomblé: Afro-Brazilian spiritual tradition, once outlawed and thus only practiced surreptitiously. However it is now acknowledged as among Brazil's official religions with devotees deriving from all social classes and ethnic backgrounds and tens of thousands of temples (*terreiros.*) In recent surveys, approximately two million Brazilians have declared Candomblé as their religion, although many others also practice it in conjunction with other faiths. (See also Macumba.)

Caul: Some babies are born with a membrane enveloping their head: this membrane is the caul. Being born with a caul marks the infant as unique and powerful; different cultures interpret this power in different ways:

* *Being born with a caul may indicate that the child possesses psychic gifts like second sight or the ability to soul-journey.*

* *Being born with a caul may predispose (or doom, depending on perspective) a baby to enter into certain magical societies or to practice magical arts.*

* *In parts of Europe, the saying "to be born with a caul" has the added modern meaning of indicating a lucky person.*

Charm: This literally means a verbal spell, either spoken or (once more frequently) sung. The word derives from the name of a Greek oracular spirit Carmenta who became very popular in Italy. The Romans associated witchcraft mainly with incantations (*Carmentis*), as opposed to the Greeks who envisioned witches as mainly practitioners of botanical magic. Incantations and charms are synonymous; the rhymes accompanying many spells are "charms." Many spells consist of nothing other than a charm. This usage of the word "charm" remains popular in the magical community. To be charmed is to be "spellbound," although hopefully pleasantly so.

Charm has also developed a secondary modern definition indicating an object with magical power such as a talisman or amulet. Small charms are worn on charm bracelets for instance. When people refer to "lucky charms" this is what they mean. Outside of the magical community, this definition is much more common, and is often the only definition with which people are familiar.

Charmer: Spellcaster, witch.

Charovnik: This Russian term means "spellcaster" or "wizard" but also indicates a book of spells or grimoire. Among the legendary volumes listed in an old Russian index of prohibited books is something called *Charovnik* allegedly dedicated to teaching transformation skills. No copy of the book is currently known to exist.

Chervioburgium: This literally means "cauldron carrier for a witch" and was among several terms used by the Franks to indicate a male magical practitioner and/or devotee of a Pagan faith. Other synonyms include *Herburgius*, "one who carries the cauldron to witches' meetings" and *Strioportius*, "witch's porter."

Although they sound neutral today, these were intended as insults. It was considered more denigrating to suggest that the men served female witches than to suggest that they were magical practitioners themselves.

Chi, Qi: Literally "energy" or "life force" in Chinese; according to Taoist philosophy, chi is the energizing force that fuels the universe; the sum of yang and yin. Chi is inherited from our parents at birth but it may also be acquired, lost, channeled beneficially or misdirected. Without sufficient chi flowing through proper channels there is no luck, health or success. See also Ashé, Baraka, Heka, Mana, Nyama.

Ciaraulo/Ciaraula/Ciarauli (m/f/pl): Sicilian shamanic healer and/or snake charmer, sometimes also known as *serpari*. The age-old association of snakes and healing survives in the ciarauli who allegedly possess power over snakes and their venom and are spiritually obligated to use these powers to serve their community. Like the táltos or Benandanti, one is born a ciaraula. Circumstances of birth confer power over snakes and protection from them.

✳ *Seventh sons and daughters are destined to be ciaurauli.*

✳ *Predestined ciaurauli are born with "snake-charmer's marks": the shape of a snake and spider under the tongue and on the right arm.*

When the ciaraula is approximately seven years old, another ciaraula will approach and teach her the needed charms. This tradition is believed to be a survival of ancient healing traditions associated with deities like Asklepios, Angitia, Fauna, Hermes or Hygeia, all associated with snakes. (See also Benandanti, Táltos; **DIVINE WITCH:** Angitia.)

Chovihano/Chovihani (m/f): Romany witch, sorcerer, traditional healer, and/or shaman.

Cone of Power: Energy raised, held, and concentrated within a circle for magical purposes. It is released when it is at its peak.

Conjure: Almost as confusing a word as "witch" this one is also used by different people to indicate different concepts.

"Conjure" derives from Latin roots indicating *"conspiracy."* The original *conjurari* were devotees of Women's Mysteries and the Bacchanalia. The Republic of Rome considered them a threat and brutally outlawed them in 186 BCE, charging them with conspiracy. The word was intended as derogatory, similar to "warlock"; over the centuries the original meaning was forgotten but its connection with magical practices remained.

When used as a verb, modern dictionary definitions include *"practice of the magical arts," "the practice of tricks like juggling"* as well as *"to summon, especially by invocation or incantation,"* with the added implication that what is being summoned or conjured are spirits.

Conjure also refers to a specific African-American magical tradition. The word is sometimes used synonymously with Hoodoo, however although Hoodoo's framework derives squarely from African traditions, many of its practitioners are white and some ignore (or are ignorant of) these roots. Conjure is used virtually exclusively to describe African-American tradition. See also Hoodoo, Warlock; **WITCH-CRAZE!:** Rome.

Conjure Man, Conjure Woman: A witch or magical practitioner. The word is traditional in the British Isles, the Southern United States, and the British West Indies.

Conjurer: If someone asks if you're a conjurer, what are they really asking? This is another of those words that mean different things to different people:

✳ *Most loosely it is used to indicate any kind of magical practitioner*

✳ *Specifically it indicates a practitioner of the African-American art, Conjure*

✳ *It can refer to a magical practitioner whose specialty is conjuring spirits*

✳ *A synonym for illusionists and sleight-of-hand artists*

Coven: An organization or society of witches. The word seems to have been first used in sixteenth-century Scotland. Related words include *"convene," "convention," "convent,"* and *"conventicle." Convent* and *conventicle* specifically indicate spiritual gatherings of women.

"Coven" describes a society of witches, although that society may include men as well as women. Covens may be loosely or formally organized. Some traditions believe that each coven must have 13 members; others prefer different numbers including nine, three, and four, while others have no fixed number.

Cross: A shape that is famous as the emblem of Christianity; the actual English word "cross"

derives from the Latin *cruciare* "to torture," as does the word crucifix. The Cruciatus Curse, which first appeared in the fourth *Harry Potter* novel, derives squarely from this source. In magical parlance, "crosses" are life's challenges and trials. Someone suffering from a "crossed condition" exists under a dark cloud. Uncrossing spells remove these crosses. Cross candles are burned to eliminate life's hardships.

Cunning Folk, Cunning Man, Cunning Woman: Practitioners of traditional British folk magic, British magical practitioners or witch-doctors; the word literally means "the knowledgeable ones." Their tradition might be considered similar to British Hoodoo and, in fact, much British folk magic has been incorporated into the American art.

Little emphasis is placed on spirituality: this tradition coexists with (or without) any spiritual system. The emphasis is on functionality, service, and practical magic. Many cunning folk were hereditary practitioners, although whether they "inherited" their powers or were simply following in their parents' professional footsteps (as did so many others) is open to conjecture. To be the seventh son or daughter was a major advertisement of power. Specialties included divination, hex-breaking, and healing. Cunning folk enjoyed their greatest popularity during the eighteenth and nineteenth centuries, but they still exist.

Curandero/Curandera (m/f): Latin American traditional healer, shaman, and/or magical practitioner. The curandera typically has tremendous botanical knowledge.

Dakini: In modern Hindi, this is sometimes used as a synonym for "sorceress" or "witch." Technically dakini refers to Tantric initiates and to a host of female spirits, acolytes of the great goddess Kali.

Deasil, Deosil: Moving in a clockwise or sunwise direction; the opposite of widdershins. Rituals and spells may demand that one must move in a specific direction.

Demonologist: Biologists study biology, angelogists study angels, so demonologists study demons, right? Wrong. *Demonologist* is the name applied to those judges, lawyers, and theologians who specialized in witches and sorcery.

Divination: The art of prophecy. The practitioner of divination is a diviner; she serves as an oracle or medium. Divination is the fancy, esoteric term; a less pretentious but less impressive synonym is fortune-telling. *Endless* methods of divination exist including card-reading and scrying. (See **MAGICAL ARTS:** Divination.)

Djinn, Jinn, Jinni, Jnun: Depending upon regional dialect, djinn or jinn may be singular or both singular *and* plural. The plural is sometimes jnun. "Djinn" is frequently translated into English as "demon," however this is simplistic and inaccurate unless you subscribe to the notion that *all* spirits are demons.

Jinn are the spiritual entities native to the Middle East and North Africa. "Genie" derives from their name. An awareness of Jinn is shared by all residents of that region, including Berbers, Jews, Muslims, and Samaritans.

It is not considered safe to call Jinn by name needlessly or carelessly. Euphemisms include *"the others," "the neighbors," "the other side,"* or *"the ones outside."* Merely pointing to the ground is sufficient in some communities to identify them.

Drabarni: Literally, "herb woman." Drabarni indicates a Romany practitioner who serves as midwife, healer, shaman, herbalist, and/or general worker of enchantment.

The word is believed to derive from Vedic India: *"darbha"* indicates "sacred grass." In modern Romany, *"drab"* may indicate grass, herb, tobacco or a magical plant.

Drabengro: The male counterpart of the Drabarni (see above). The Romany word is translated variously as "healer," "doctor," "medicine man" or "man of poison."

Drago: Literally, "dragon"; in Sicily, a traditional synonym for "wizard," "sorcerer" or "male witch." See Mama-Draga.

Drude, Druden (pl): Originally indicated a species of South German spirit, however drude eventually became synonymous with *hexe* or "witch." In Moravia, drude refers to a male shamanic figure similar to a táltos (see page 355).

Druid: "Druid," like "witch," means different things to different people who may all passionately believe that their definition is the sole correct one. Coincidentally perhaps, "druid" has historically been used as a synonym for "witch," "wizard," "sorcerer" or "magician." Nineteenth-century references to Druids might indicate *any* sort of magical practitioner, even those with no relationship to historic Druidry; some still use this word in that manner.

The word "druid" is generally believed to derive from the Indo-European root *"drù"* or oak; this accords with the first century CE reports of Pliny the Elder. Modern Celtic scholars Caitlin and John Matthews, in their *Encyclopedia of Celtic Wisdom* (Element Books, 1994), suggest that druid derives from the Sanskrit root word meaning "to see" or "to know."

This much is historical fact: in the ancient Celtic world, Druid named a profession, spiritual vocation and/or societal class. There were female and male Druids who served as royal advisors, keepers of the oral tradition, and mediators between humans and spirits.

The history of Druidry is complex and mysterious. The Druids relied entirely on oral transmission of information: no records written from *their* perspective exist. (See **BOOKS:** Library of the Lost: Druid Books.) Surviving information regarding the Druids comes *entirely* from outside observers who were usually hostile to them, including such historically important Roman sources as Julius Caesar and Pliny the Elder.

"The Druids—that is what they call their magicians ..." (Pliny: *Natural History* XVI, 95). According to Julius Caesar, Druids officiated over spiritual ceremonials, supervised religious sacrifices and served as spiritual arbiters, making decisions and rulings on religious questions. He reported that Druids trained for 20 years before being considered masters of their arts.

Druids are prominently featured within Irish and Welsh mythology, however these sacred Pagan tales were first set down on paper by Christian monks, who could not be called unbiased (although these scribes may have been the Druids' descendants). These tales include:

❋ The Ulster Cycle, *compiled between the seventh and twelfth centuries but believed to reflect ancient oral traditions*

❋ The Chronicles of Saint Patrick, *where the Druids are his adversaries*

❋ The Fenian Cycle, *recorded in the twelfth century. Its hero, Finn, is raised by two holy foster-mothers, one a "wise woman"; the other a "Druidess."*

The Druids *were* magicians, however these magical practitioners were not marginal characters hidden in society's shadows but important, significant, influential, and *politically* powerful figures, considered worthy of respect from the general population. The "honor price" for a Druid (required compensation for injury or insult) was comparable to that for a king.

There are many ancient references to Druids as "magicians." However these references come from Romans with negative opinions regarding magical practice and who believed that in order to overcome the Celts, formidable opponents, they must first disable and eliminate the Druids who lead an active resistance movement against the Roman invaders of Britain.

Following the Roman invasion, Druidry was proscribed and forbidden in Britain, and the Druid stronghold at Anglesey, an island off the coast of northwestern Wales, was destroyed. Tacitus described the scene: *"black-robed women with disheveled hair like Furies, brandishing torches. Close by stood Druids, raising their hands to heaven and screaming dreadful curses."* (Tacitus: *Annals* XIV 30.)

Although Druidism was banned and Druids were persecuted by Rome during the first century CE, Druidesses did serve as fortune-tellers for the emperors Severus Alexander and Diocletian in the third century.

A legend explains Diocletian's respect for the Druids. While still in the Roman army ranks, Diocletian was criticized for leaving a stingy tip by a Druidess who observed him paying his bill in a tavern. Diocletian joked that he'd be more generous when he became emperor. The Druidess scolded him for being flippant but then predicted that he would indeed become emperor "*after he killed the boar.*" Her prediction was accurate: Diocletian became Emperor after killing the Prefect of the Praetorian Guard whose name was Aper, Latin for "boar."

Druidic practices in Ireland continued even after Christianity became a major force in the fifth century. Christian texts frequently depict Druids as opposing Christianity. The seventh-century *Life of Saint Berach* details a long conflict between that saint and local Druids determined not to be supplanted by Christianity nor deprived of their lands. Satanism was evoked: Berach condemns a Druid by saying "*Your father, Satan, having been cast out of heavenly inheritance … you therefore are not fit to possess this land dedicated to God.*" Early eighth-century Irish canons declared that kings must obey the injunction not to heed the superstitions of Druids, augurs, and sorceresses.

Various modern Neo-Pagan traditions are dedicated to reviving and preserving the spirit of Druidry.

> The Druids left no monuments: they preferred nature to buildings and taught in groves and caves where they also conducted rituals. The French cathedral of Chartres was built over a sacred Druid site.

See **DIVINE WITCH:** Dahut.

Dybbuk: Literally means "attachment"; in Jewish tradition it indicates transmigrating souls who for one reason or another "attach" themselves to a living person. Attachment typically manifests as involuntary possession: the dybbuk takes over the personality of the victim. Dybbuks are popular motifs in Yiddish folklore, literature, and theater, however these reflect historical reality: records of possession by dybbuks exist—there was an epidemic of possession in the sixteenth century. Similar to zar possession, women were common victims, but unlike zar, which are spirits, dybbuks are ghosts, the souls of once living people who must be exorcized, not accommodated. See Zar.

Ember Days: Ember Days come shortly before an equinox or solstice and are dedicated to purification and protection. These are threshold times and as such are powerful but vulnerable to malevolent forces. Traditionally, magically protective bonfires were lit.

According to official Church explanation, the term "ember days" has nothing to do with bonfires but is a corruption from the Latin *Quatuor Tempora*, meaning "*four times,*" indicating how many Ember Day periods there are in a year. Three days of abstinence, fasting, and spiritual purification were ordered by the Church at the beginning of each season.

However, the Church inherited the custom of Ember Days from Pagan Rome, where it was customary to plead for help from the presiding spirits and undergo spiritual ritual prior to initiating important agricultural activities. Virtually the entire month of February was devoted to ritual purification before the beginning of their New Year (see **CALENDAR:** February Feasts, Lupercalia) and so the Romans originally had but three periods of Ember Days:

✳ *In June, when preparing for the harvest*

✳ *In September, when preparing for the annual wine vintage*

✳ *In December, in preparation for seeding the fields*

Pagan Italian traditions associated with the Ember Days survived, as demonstrated by the Benandanti who engaged in shamanic battles during the Ember Days in order to save the community's seeds, crops and harvest. See Benandanti.

Enchant: This synonym for "bewitch" derives from the same source as "incantation." The dictionary also suggests that this indicates *"to influence (as if) by charms and incantations"* as well as *"to rouse to ecstatic admiration."*

Enchantment: The craft of enchanting, often a synonym of "witchcraft." Practitioners of enchantment are enchanters and enchantresses.

Enochian Magic: A system of angel magic conveyed to Dr. John Dee via the medium Edward Kelley. The angels with whom Kelley had contact were allegedly the same angels who communicated with the biblical Enoch, hence the name. Dee and Kelley first deciphered the Enochian language, an angelic tongue, in 1581. Aleister Crowley was among the first modern occultists to employ the Enochian language. In his book *Magick in Theory and Practice*, he advocated its use by all witches.

Further information may be found in Donald Laycock's *The Complete Enochian Dictionary: A Dictionary of the Angelic Language As Revealed to Dr. John Dee and Edward Kelley* (Weiser Books, 2001).

See **HALL OF FAME**: Aleister Crowley, John Dee, Edward Kelley.

Ensorcell: To bewitch or enchant; from same derivation as sorcery.

Ensorcellment: Enchantment, sorcery, witchcraft.

Envoûtement: This French word is often translated into English as "bewitchment" but literally indicates image magic: the magical use of dolls or photographs. Envoûtement technically derives from Middle Latin *invultuor* "a sorcerer who makes a voult." What is a voult? "Voult" derives from the Latin *voltus*, "face" and so indicates the image of a person. (See **MAGICAL ARTS:** Image Magic.)

Erberia: In medieval Venice, this word, literally indicating "herbalism," was a synonym for witchcraft, sorcery or brujeria.

Estrie: Old French word deriving from the Latin *strix* and *striga* (see page 354). By the early Middle Ages it was synonymous with *hexe* or "witch" in mainstream society.

However the word also entered the Jewish community, where it evolved new meanings—or retained old ones, who knows? The Jewish estrie is a liminal figure, associated with Lilith in her guise as Queen of Demons and Witches. The estrie straddles the boundary between malevolent magical practitioner, supernatural witch, demon-possessed woman, and malevolent spiritual entity. Depending upon region and community, estrie may indicate any, some, or all of those meanings.

The estrie takes various forms: she shapeshifts at will. She can allegedly take any form although black cats are favored. The estrie is vampiric: her diet is human blood. Children are her favorite food although adults shouldn't count themselves safe either.

The estrie operates in secret. Should someone

wound the estrie or recognize her true form, the estrie will die *unless* she eats some of that person's bread and salt. According to one legend, a man was attacked by a cat at night but fought back and escaped. The next day, a somewhat beaten-up looking woman approached him and begged for bread with salt. He was about to give it to her when another man protested, warning that if he saved the estrie, she'd only harm others.

Fascinate: Originally "fascinate" was synonymous with "bewitch" or "allure." Another meaning is *"to transfix and hold spellbound by means of irresistible power."* It was once believed that snakes and weasels *fascinated* their prey which, having made fatal eye contact with the predator, were transfixed, paralyzed, and unable to escape.

"Fascinate" derives from Fascinus, a Roman deity with the power to repel the Evil Eye and counteract its effects. Fascinus was the anti-Evil Eye. His power caused the opposing effect: he could make new shoots spring from dried-up withered plants and restore fertility to barren women.

Fascinus was symbolized by a phallus, and his power and protection was accessed through the use of phallus amulets. Phallic amulets similar to modern mobiles or wind chimes were combined with bells and slogans like *"Here lives happiness!"* and hung over doorways. Examples were recovered in the ruins of Pompeii. This practice of placing protective images of phalluses on houses continued into medieval times and was even found on church walls. See **ANIMALS:** Ferrets (Polecats) and Weasels, Snakes.

Fascinatrix: A classical synonym for "witch." This witch casts her spell through the power of fascination or allure.

Fetch: A synonym for "double," "doppelganger" or "shadow soul"; in horror fiction "fetch" sometimes indicates a wraithlike ghost. The word derives from Nordic shamanism: the fetch is technically a human soul that can be trained to leave the body, travel, and return while the shaman is entranced. This is more than just dream-journeying: the fetch actually manifests physically, usually in the form of a small insect or animal, typically flies, mice, butterflies or cats. (Sometimes the fetch looks like the shaman's twin, hence "double" or "shadow.")

The fetch may be an individual's animal soul; the acquisition of different animal forms may be demonstrations of shamanic power. Fairy tales of transformation may really be allusions to the fetch.

See also Benandanti, Garaboncias, Kresnik, Táltos; **ANIMALS:** Nahual, Transformation; **FAIRY TALES**.

Fjolkunnigir: This Norse euphemism for "magician" refers to *"great knowledge."* It is similar in linguistic derivation to *"cunning."*

Flagõ: A term from the Nordic Eddas variously translated as "witch," "troll-woman" or "she-wolf." Sometimes also used as a generic term for "monster." See also Trollkvinna; **DIVINE WITCH:** Angerboda, Hella.

Freemasonry: Worldwide fraternal order whose members, now both male and female depending upon Rite, share metaphysical ideals and a belief in a Supreme Creator. Freemasonry has historically been described as a secret society, although many Freemasons prefer to describe themselves as a society with secrets. Freemasonry is an initiatory system of degrees, based on the allegory of rebuilding the Temple of Solomon, with alleged roots in medieval guilds of stonemasons. Some believe these traditions go back further, to the Builders of the Adytum, the masons who built Solomon's Temple.

According to legend, after the suppression of the Knights Templar in 1312, surviving Templars went into hiding in Scotland where they eventually resurfaced as Freemasons. An "Unknown Master" received these Templar secrets and fashioned seven degrees linked to knightly titles.

Gradually as Masonry spread, local, regional, and national characteristics evolved. Some new rites were derived from alchemical and hermetic mysteries. Freemasonry has also exerted influence over various spiritual and magical traditions including High Ceremonial Magic, Umbanda, and Vodou.

As the European Witchcraze died down, hostility arose towards Freemasons instead. Freemasonry was banned, on pain of death, by a papal bull in 1738. The Vatican was troubled by the success of this secret organization among the wealthy and powerful. They suspected it of encouraging occultism, Protestantism, *and* atheism.

Freemasons, like witches, were accused of plotting world domination. Prominent Freemasons include Count Cagliostro and his wife Seraphina, Casanova, Mozart, Herman Rucker, and Harry Houdini. (See **HALL OF FAME**: Count Cagliostro, Black Herman Rucker.)

Garaboncias (Hungarian), Grabancijas (Southern Slav): This word has its origins in Italy: *necromancia* became *nigromanzia* further corrupted into *gramanzia* and from there to these modern terms. Both refer to the identical concept: a supernatural being born in the form of an extraordinary wonder-child who acquires and works magic through shamanic trance.

The child's destiny is indicated at birth because he is born with teeth and/or an extra finger. In his seventh or fourteenth year, the child must battle a magical opponent in the form of a bull. (No need to search for this opponent; it will find you.) Magical power is obtained while levitating in shamanic trance.

The garaboncias is traditionally envisioned as a wanderer with a magical black book. He rears snakes that transform into dragons when he wishes to ride them through the air. The garaboncias craves dairy products. He uses his powers to reward kindness and punish evil and injustice. The garaboncias can locate treasure and stolen or lost items, animals or people using his magic staff or a mirror. See also Táltos.

Glamour, Glamoury: Glamoury is the art of enchantment, the magical art of optical illusion. Those who possess this art possess glamour and are thus able to disguise their appearance and make the viewer see whatever the viewed wishes them to see. This is an extremely powerful, seductive art, powerfully associated with Fairies.

Goes/Goetes (s/pl): A common Greek word for "magician" used at least as far back as the dawn of the Common Era; "goes" literally means "howler" and may have originally indicated someone who howled incantations, or was a reference to wolf shamanism.

The original goes was a Greek ritual healer, a singer of charms, a medium and seer, similar to what is now called a shaman. Transformational skills may be possessed; Herodotus suggested that the Scythians who claimed to be able to temporarily transform themselves into wolves might be goetes.

The word eventually came to be used loosely and was applied to professional practitioners of mystery traditions (e.g., Orphic or Dionysiac rites), charlatans, fortune-tellers, and mountebanks. Nor did the goes have to be Greek: the word was eventually applied to any similar practitioner.

Flavius Josephus, the first-century chronicler of Rome's war with Judea, described the goetes as men who do or promise miracles, including *"overpower the Romans."* Some of his contemporaries classified Jesus Christ as among the goetes.

This was folk practice; it wasn't necessary to be educated to be a goes. The word developed lower-class connotations and eventually was virtually always meant contemptuously, or at least in the surviving records. And the community that the goes served *was* largely illiterate. Goetes became increasingly disreputable. By Plato's time, in some cities goetes were liable to be arrested.

See also Magician, Mountebank, Strix; **HALL OF FAME:** Jesus.

Goetia, Goeteia: Literally "sorcery" or "witchcraft" in Greek. The term technically refers to the craft practiced by a goes (see previously). In classical times, goetia's scope included charms, curses, mediumship, necromancy, and shamanic contact with the realm of the dead.

During the classical Greek era, distinctions were drawn between types of magic.

Goetia was considered 'low' magic while theourgia (theurgy) was higher. Theourgia emphasized inner knowledge and spiritual questing. Goetia involved paid professional services to the community. Theourgia was the province of the up-market educated elite while goetia was identified with unruly, defiant, lower classes and the rabble, not with cultured, civilized, educated, rational people.

By the Middle Ages, goetia was synonymous with "low magic" and specifically identified with malevolent scary magic. See also Goes, Goetic Magic, Theurgy; **BOOKS:** Diabolical Books: Grimoires: *Lemegeton.*

Goetic Magic: A method of summoning spirits, a modern system of magic named for the grimoire *The Goetia* and utilizing its techniques for spirit summoning. See **BOOKS:** Diabolical Books: Grimoires: *Lemegeton.*

Golden Dawn: Short name for *The Hermetic Order of the Golden Dawn*, an incredibly influential order of magicians founded in London in 1887. Its membership included some of the most prominent contemporary occultists including Samuel L. MacGregor Mathers, Moina Bergson Mathers, Arthur E. Waite, William Butler Yeats, Aleister Crowley, and Dion Fortune. The Golden Dawn transformed the Western practice and perception of the magical arts.

The Good People: Seventeenth-century English euphemism for witches and devotees of pre-Christian deities and traditions.

Goodfellow: This innocuous word historically hides subversive meanings. Today "goodfellow" is a euphemism for a Mafioso; in seventeenth-century England it was a euphemism for witches and devotees of pre-Christian deities and traditions.

Great Rite: The sacred union of female and male forces. In essence, *every* act of sexual intercourse could theoretically reproduce the Great Rite, however the term usually indicates ritual sex for a conscious purpose including healing, fertility, and magic. In many ancient civilizations (Sumeria, Celtic Ireland) the male ruler must annually unite with a specific Goddess, as channeled into the body of her priestess, in order to legitimize his right to rule. Sacred prostitution is based on this concept, as is sex magic. The Great Rite survives in some modern spiritual traditions, although now often reproduced symbolically rather than literally—thus the ritual blade in the chalice may represent the Rite.

Grimalkin: In Shakespeare's *Macbeth*, one witch suddenly announces "*I come, Graymalkin.*" She is responding to a summons from her familiar. Graymalkin literally means "gray cat."

"Malkin" was a nickname for Maud or Matilda, once very popular women's names. Eventually the term was adopted as a general name for a cat (sometimes rabbits, too) in the manner that "Rover" is now understood to refer to a pet dog. However, the word also had a secondary meaning indicating an "untidy woman." By the 1630s, the word was most commonly spelled "grimalkin."

Gris-gris: The word derives from the Mande language of West Africa and originally referred to ritually prepared magical objects, similar to what the Portuguese called "fetishes." Traditional gris-gris were formed in the shape of dolls or cloth packets. The word does *not* derive from the French *gris, gris*, meaning "*gray, gray*," indicating "gray magic" that blends "black" and "white."

Gris-gris is now sometimes used to indicate any magical object, charm bag or spell. Some also use it as a synonym for magic, although properly gris-gris indicates a magically charged object created for protective purposes. See also Mojo, Paket Kongo; **MAGICAL ARTS:** Charm Bag.

Haegtessa: "Hedge witch"; an Old English term for a prophetess. The Dutch variation is *hagedisse.*

Hag: Commonly used as a synonym for "witch," this is another word possessing multiple definitions. According to the dictionary, hag may mean a witch, a demon or an ugly, slatternly or "evil looking" old woman. To further complicate

matters, there are also ancient pre-Christian hag goddesses. The word derives from the same etymological roots as "hedge." Further information is found in **HAG**.

Haljoruna: Gothic synonym for "witch." According to the sixth-century Gothic historian Jordanes, King Filimer of the Goths, a Christian convert, conducted a census and discovered to his dismay many "witches" or *haliorunnae*. He exiled these exclusively female witches to barren lands, where they had carnal relations with desert spirits and conceived children who became the Huns.

The story was intended as an insult to the Pagan Huns, competitors of the Goths. The story excites historians, however, because of the resemblance of "Haljoruna" to "Alrauna." Whether they are one and the same is open to discussion: Haljoruna literally means "*Hal* (or *Hulda) the runester*" or "*rune-caster*" and so may indicate affiliations with the deity Hulda and/or runic magic. See also Alrauna.

Heathen: This Anglo-Saxon word literally means "dweller on the heath." The heath is the area outside the settlement; post-Christianity, those wishing to maintain old traditions retired to the heath, hence the name. It came to be synonymous with "Pagan," sometimes with the added implication of rude, ignorant barbarian. The word has been reclaimed by Neo-Pagans subscribing to Northern European traditions and today is used with pride. See also Asatru.

Hechiceria: Spanish synonym for "witchcraft" or "magic"; it corresponds to "the craft."

Hechicero/Hechicera (m/f): Spanish word usually translated as "sorcerer" although that isn't a literal translation. Hechicera suggests someone who "makes" or "creates" things—a crafter. The Spanish Inquisition used the word to describe any adherent or practitioner of indigenous Andean spiritual traditions. See also Malefactor.

Hedge: When humans clear a forest for settlement, the hedge serves as the division (the threshold) between wild nature and "civilization." Depending upon your perspective, the hedge is either a sacred area filled with liminal power or a place of imminent danger where harmful forces lurk. In either case, witches were understood to inhabit (or at least spend a lot of time) in the hedge. See **HAG**.

Hedge-rider: Northern European synonym for witch: *"she who rides the hedge."* See **HAG**.

Heid: Literally "gleaming"; in the Norse sagas the word implies "honor" but it was also a common name or epithet for witches and prophetesses. See **DIVINE WITCH:** Angerboda.

Heka: An ancient Egyptian term for sacred natural magical energy and power. Heka is also used as a synonym for "witchcraft." It is personified in a deity who bears that name.

Herbaria: "Little herbal mother." Medieval ecclesiastical synonym for "witch."

Hex: The English word "hex" derives from the German *hexe* and is among those wonderful words that serve as nouns, verbs, *and* adjectives.

✸ *Hex indicates a spell-caster and/or her spell. Although any spell can be considered a hex, it has taken on the additional meaning of a malevolent spell or a curse: "The hex cast a hex."*

✸ *Hex also indicates the act of spell-casting, thus one can threaten "I'll hex you!"*

✸ *To be hexed is to be spellbound, cursed or bewitched, literally under the power of the hex, thus "The house was hexed."*

Hexe: A witch or sorceress in German. (Plural *hexen*.)

Hexenmeister: Literally, "Master of the Witches." The hexenmeister is a magical practitioner in Pow-Wow tradition. He can cast spells but perhaps more importantly can undo spells cast by others, remove the Evil Eye, and break hexes, curses, and jinxes.

The hexenmeister may be a devout, conservative Christian who resents being categorized as a magical practitioner. Others use the term as self-description to indicate that they are magical practitioners: it may also be understood to mean "Master of Spells."

Hexerei: German synonym for "witchcraft" or "sorcery." The craft practiced by the hexe.

Hoodoo, Hoodoo Doctor, Hoodoo Man, Hoodoo Woman: A melting pot American magic, Hoodoo was born when enslaved African magical practitioners, deprived of their traditional materials, were forced to develop an entirely new botanical repertoire to fuel their emergency magic. These practitioners exemplify the ideal of the questing, curious occultist: they took wisdom from all available sources, applied it to a blended West and Central African framework and created a powerful new system of practical magic. In addition to African traditions, Hoodoo incorporates Native American, European and Romany traditions, Freemasonry, Kabalah, and Pow-Wow.

Hoodoo may be used as a noun or verb:

✺ *Hoodoo names the magical tradition.*

✺ *Hoodoo names the action of spell-casting: "I will hoodoo you."*

✺ *Hoodoo names a state of bewitchment: "I've been hoodooed."*

Unlike hex or jinx, Hoodoo is a neutral term: one can be Hoodooed with love and blessings as well as curses.

Further Reading: Catherine Yronwode's *Hoodoo Herb and Root Magic* (Lucky Mojo, 2002).

Hover: Hebrew euphemism for "witch"; it literally means "binder" and derives from root words meaning "tie, untie, join." Hover indicates a practitioner of knot magic.

Huna: Literally "secret," the equivalent of "occult." It refers to esoteric Hawaiian magical, healing, and spiritual traditions. See also Kahuna.

Incantation: Spells or verbal charms that are sung, spoken or chanted.

Istinzal: Moroccan ritual divination whereby a healer utilizes a child as a medium. The child is placed close to a source of light. A small quantity of either ink or oil is poured into the child's palm. Incense is burned to beckon the spirits closer. The child gazes into the liquid as the healer chants incantations and petitions the spirits. Although the adult healer supervises and directs the ritual, it is the child who actually sees and describes the spirits. Istinzal is but one of a

number of similar practices whose roots stretch back at least as far as second- or third-millennia BCE Babylonia.

Jězě: Old Czech for "witch." See **DIVINE WITCH**: Jezibaba.

Jedza: This Polish word can mean "witch," "evil woman" or "fury" and is related to the root verb "to get angry."

Jinx: "Don't jinx me!" people plead. Although the notion of the jinx as preventing success remains, the word has now entered common usage and many never connect it with occultism. "Jinx" derives from the Greek *iynx*, indicating a bird associated with spellcraft. (See **ANIMALS**: Iynx.) In the southern United States, jinx has come to be synonymous with "hex." Jinx, unlike most other forms of magic, is *always* negative. There is no such thing as a positive or even neutral jinx.

✺ *Jinx can be a noun, indicating a malicious spell that often has a binding effect, preventing success, victory, and achievement: "She put a jinx on me."*

✺ *Jinx can be a verb, indicating the action of placing a jinx: "I'll jinx you!"*

✺ *Jinx can also be an adjective: a team that never wins, a project that is never completed can be described as "jinxed."*

Juju: This African word, possibly of Hausa origin, originally indicated a priest-king. It also refers to the ancestral spirits of past priest-kings and to their power that is concentrated in amulets, fetishes, and other objects maintained by religious specialists.

So, technically, juju referred to specific human beings, both living and ancestral, and to their residual power that can be concentrated in an object via specific ritual. Europeans misunderstood the subtlety and complexity of this term and applied it to the amulets and objects themselves. (In other words, juju refers to the power that is concentrated, maintained, and cultivated *within* the sacred objects—not merely to the objects themselves.)

Juju Man, Juju Woman: Indicates a practitioner of magic and/or pre-Christian spirituality. It originally implied someone steeped specifically in African magical traditions and spirituality (see Juju, above). However in some regions it has become synonymous with any powerful practitioner of Earth, practical or folk magic.

Kahuna: In Hawaiian, the Kahuna is literally a specialist or master of an art. There are different types of Kahuna; some are masters of healing or various magical arts.

Kaula: A traditional Hawaiian diviner, prophet or seer. The female variation is the kaula wahine.

Kimbanda, Quimbanda: Afro-Brazilian magical and spiritual traditions deriving from similar Congolese sources as Palo (see Palo, page 348).

Kodia: Term used in Egypt for the female ritual leader of zar ceremonials. The position is often hereditary, passed from mother to daughter. See Zar.

Koldun/Koldun'ia/Kolduny (m/f/pl): Russian words translated as "witch." The koldun is a local practitioner or village witch or magician. Episcopal instructions from the sixteenth century direct Russian parish priests to root out *"women fortune-tellers and kolduny"* and hand them over to secular legal authorities.

The word is commonly considered pejorative and is usually intended in the negative sense. Kolduny are popularly envisioned as gloomy, dour, solitary practitioners who possess powers of spoiling.

Kraut: Literally "herb" in German, but it also has the added meaning of "magical substance."

Krauthexen: German for "herb witch."

Kresnik: The kresnik from Istria and Slavonia is similar to the Benandanti: their destined ability to combat malevolent "witches" is indicated by the caul with which they are born. At night the kresnik lies entranced; a large black fly emerges from his mouth and journeys to shamanic battles. The natural opponent of the kresnik is the vucodlak.

Using sticks, kresniks battle their opponents in the air at crossroads. Kresniks are also said to cross the sea in eggshells to do battle above St Mark's Square in Venice.

Kresniks can shape-shift into any animal form, although the most popular are bullocks, goats, and horses. See also Benandanti, Fetch, Vucodlak.

Lamia/Lamiae: During the Middle Ages witches were sometimes called lamiae. Lamiae combined the horrific features of the strix and succubus: they crept up on sleeping men, and held them spellbound with sexual fantasies while sucking their blood and consuming their flesh. In the nineteenth century lamia was used to indicate a *femme fatale* with powers of alluring enchantment. See also Strix.

Lamina: "Little wood mother"; a medieval ecclesiastical synonym for "witch."

Larva: Latin word indicating masks and the spirits of the dead (ghosts). See Larvatus below.

Larvatus: Latin term used in the Middle Ages to refer to someone wearing a mask and/or possessed by spirits.

Lookman, Lukuman: "The one who looks"—spiritual advisors, healers, seers, and diviners from the African-derived traditions of Surinam, Trinidad, and elsewhere in the Caribbean. Despite the name, Lookman are not exclusively male.

Lwa: Sacred spirits of Vodou. Devotion to the lwa is the basis of Vodou. *Lwa* is the standardized Kreyol spelling; *loa* is an older French variation. These spirits are also called *mystères*.

Macumba: Afro-Brazilian spiritual tradition; the word is sometimes used synonymously with Candomblé, however others use it as a synonym for "witchcraft." Macumba is powerfully associated with magical aspects of spiritual tradition; whether the word is used positively or pejoratively may reveal the user's attitudes towards magical practice.

Maenad: A female devotee of Dionysus. In many ways, the Maenads served as the prototype of the wild, free, ecstatic female witch. Eventually they too would come to be hysterically persecuted and outlawed. Among the theories of historical witchcraft is that it is a surviving vestige of Dionysian spirituality. See **CREATIVE ARTS:** Dance: Maenad Dances; **DIVINE WITCH:** Dionysus; **WITCH-CRAZE!:** Rome.

Maestra: Female master or teacher of magic. The male equivalent is the maestro.

Maga: This word derives from the same roots as "mage," "magus," and "magician"—although these words are almost inevitably used for male practitioners. Maga is the feminine version and remains a popular Spanish synonym for "sorceress" or "female magician."

Mage: "Magician"; the term is synonymous with "magus" (see Magus, page 343).

Magi: The plural form of "magus." Originally the Magi were a very learned class of Medes and Persians who practiced magical arts and indigenous Iranian spiritual traditions, which preceded and were supplanted by Zoroastrianism, although the Magi maintained some sort of official position. The Magi existed up to the Christian era.

Their reputation was such that the very word for "magic" derives from their name. For further information, see Magician.

Magic: A vague word that may indicate any, some, or all of the following:

❋ *The magical arts*

❋ *The arts of illusion*

❋ *The natural energy and power that magical practitioners manipulate in order to cast spells and effect change*

❋ *A supernatural, otherwise unexplainable occurrence or event*

This English word derives from the Greek *mageia* and the Latin *magia* meaning *"art of the magus or magician."* These words in turn derive from the Magi, a Persian caste of priests, spiritual practitioners, and masters of astrology and divination. (See Magi, Magician.)

Magician: Literally, a practitioner of magic. The Greek *magos* (plural: *magoi*) was Latinized and Anglicized as *magus* and *magi*. The original Magi were a priestly clan from Media who first had significant contact with the Greeks in the 540s BCE when Cyrus, King of the Medes and Persians, conquered the Greek cities of Asia Minor.

Herodotus (*c.*490–425 BCE) refers to the *Magoi*, a secret Persian group, responsible for royal sacrifices, funerary rites, and interpretation of dreams and omens. They also actively participated in Persian spiritual ritual, supervising sacrifices. Because they represented pre-Zoroastrian traditions, they were already somewhat disreputable in Persia. Following Persian military losses against the Greeks in the early fifth century BCE, many Magi preferred not to return home but remained to ply their trade in Greece as independent practitioners. These former royal employees became the prototype of the wandering magician.

By Plato's time (427–347 BCE) the term *magoi* had acquired negative connotations, denoting beggar priests and fortune-tellers who traveled door to door. During the Hellenistic period, the words *Mageia* and *Magikos* developed negative connotations, which were transmitted to the Romans. Magicians were perceived as charlatans and frauds or, on the other hand, *if* their magic worked, as evil and malevolent. (See also Mountebank.)

Magick: The English language was only relatively recently formalized and so older documents are characterized by creative spelling. "Magic" is often spelled "magick" but the words were intended synonymously.

"Magic," like "witch," is an imprecise word that means different things to different people. Some practitioners of the occult find it insulting to be lumped together with practitioners of illusion (and the feeling is often mutual). Thus a "k" is added so that it is clear to readers exactly what type of magic is being practiced. Aleister Crowley was the first to consciously and explicitly use this spelling to distinguish the occult arts from the tricks of stage magicians.

Magus: In modern usage, "magus" implies a master magician and is a title of tremendous respect. Although the word "magician" is used to refer to both occult practitioners and masters of illusion, magus refers exclusively to male masters of the occult arts, and so many practitioners prefer it because it clearly distinguishes between the arts.

Mala Mujer: An "evil," "wicked" or "bad woman"; a Latin American euphemism for "witch" and "sorceress." The term was popular during the Colonial Era Spanish Inquisition.

Malefactor: Literally, someone who works, does or creates evil; a term still popularly used although modern usage merely indicates an evil-doer or harm-causer. Once upon a time however, the word was understood to contain occult implications and thus was a euphemism for malevolent magical practitioners. (See also Hechicero, Maleficia.)

Maleficarum: The Latin ecclesiastical term for "witches," as exemplified by the most famous and influential witch-hunter's manual, *Malleus Maleficarum* or *Hammer of the Witches*. Maleficarum specifically indicates female witches and is linked by linguistic root to words indicating *"to cause harm"* or *"to do evil."*

Maleficia: Deeds of harmful magic, often implying death or injury caused by magic. Maleficia named the crime of witchcraft as defined by the Inquisition.

Mama-Draga: Literally, "Mother Dragon"; Sicilian synonym for "sorceress" or "witch."

Mana: Polynesian word for the sacred energy and magic power that fuels Earth.

Masca: A classical Latin synonym for "witch," masca literally means "mask." Attendees of medieval witches' balls were often masked in order to protect their identities; masks are also profound magical tools. The term survives as a modern Northern Italian synonym for "witch." See also Larva, Larvatus; **TOOLS:** Masks.

> Among the words used for "witch" in Low Latin were *masca*, *stria*, *striga*, and *strix*. The latter three survive in modern Italian as *strega*.

Mascot: An Old French word meaning "witch," mascot eventually evolved to indicate "a protector against witches." Continuing to evolve, it now indicates "a person or thing that brings luck." The most common modern mascots are those of sports teams.

Mau: Mau is the common prefix for the titles of practitioners of the indigenous spirit cults of Thailand. These spirit cults are less concerned with religious ideals like the achievement of salvation or Nirvana than on the everyday needs of individuals and the community, especially healing and human and agricultural fertility. Practitioners invoke pre-Buddhist guardian spirits in their work. Many, if not most, of these technicians of the sacred are female. Their professional titles are characterized by the prefix, thus:

❋ *Mau Du (astrologer)*

❋ *Mau Lek (fortune-teller)*

❋ *Mau Ram (spirit medium)*

❋ *Mau Song (diagnostician, diviner)*

❋ *Mau Tham (exorcist)*

❋ *Mau Ya (traditional herbal doctor)*

Medium: Someone who serves as a go-between, channel or bridge between the human realm and other realms, especially those of spirits and the dead. Some define any practitioner of divination as a medium.

Miko: Mikos are Japanese female shamans who traditionally engage in trance, telepathy, and divination. The word is also translated as "witch," "priestess," and "shrine-maiden." As mediums, they communicate with the spirit realm as well as with those humans who have passed over into the realm of the dead. The tradition harks back to the era when shamanism was dominated by women. (Ancient East Asian shamanism had particularly strong female associations.)

The oldest reference to Japanese female shamans occurs in a third-century CE Chinese chronicle and describes one named Himiko who ruled an early Japanese political federation. The miko is still found in small villages and isolated areas. In larger cities, her role has largely been absorbed by Shinto ritual.

M'kashephah: A commonly used word in late Hebrew literature that is typically translated as "witch." It derives from a root word indicating "cutting," especially herbs.

M'na-hesh: Hebrew synonym for "witch" that literally means "hisser" and derives from the Hebrew word for snake: *nahash*. It recalls the powerful identification between serpents, occult wisdom, and magical practitioners. In the Middle East, as elsewhere, snakes were associated with feminine spiritual traditions and so the added implication is that the m'na-hesh is a devotee. M'na-hesh may also indicate that the practitioner has a snake familiar, a snake double, that she hisses like a snake during spells or rituals or otherwise draws upon serpentine power.

Mojo: Mojo doesn't mean sex appeal, sexual prowess or that certain irresistible *something* that some men possess. Mojo is a talisman that enables someone, male or female, to achieve their goals and desires, whatever they may be. Mojo is always a positive talisman, used for success and victory.

Mojos frequently come in the form of packets or bags. Many magical practitioners are skilled creators of mojo bags. The practice is universal; however this specific term derives from African roots, first utilized in Hoodoo and Conjure.

Scholar Robert Farris Thompson traces "mojo" to the Kongo word "mooyo," meaning "the indwelling spirit of a talisman." Mojos are popular subjects of blues songs; when blues became popular in the greater community, many new fans lacked familiarity with magical terminology. In attempting to make sense of the word they confused mojo with one of its desired results. See also Gris-gris.

M'onen: Hebrew synonym for "witch" that literally means "crooner" and indicates one who croons or sings a spell, similar to "charmer" or "enchanter."

Mountebank: Originally a synonym for "magician"; the negative implications of mountebank derive from negative perceptions of magicians, not vice versa.

"Mountebank" derives from Italian sources and historically indicated *"someone who mounts a platform,"* usually to hawk potions and elixirs. Mountebanks were once traveling occult practitioners, sometimes solitary, sometimes in the company of a medicine show. Some were genuine practitioners, others were charlatans, and still others corresponded to all possible definitions of "conjurer" simultaneously. (In other words, just because someone is a charlatan and illusionist doesn't mean they can't also be a genuine practitioner, or vice-versa.)

Mountebank is now frequently considered synonymous with "scoundrel"—especially those who arrive in town, cause trouble, and then disappear. Older variations of the Tarot card "The Magician" are sometimes titled "The Mountebank." Even when named "The Magician" the mountebank's table usually remains in the picture. See also Conjurer, Goes; **MAGICAL ARTS:** Tarot.

Mudang: This refers to a female Korean shaman. Korean shamanism is related to that of Siberia but developed its own path over the past two thousand years and remains a potent, thriving tradition despite tremendous oppression and continued efforts at suppression. Mudang were persecuted both by Confucian rulers and Christian missionaries. They were driven underground during the Japanese occupation of Korea. Mudang communicate with the spirits, mediating between them and people, and serve as healers and diviners. Mudang were invited to perform at the 1988 Seoul Olympics.

Further Reading: Laurel Kendall's *Shamans, Housewives and Other Restless Spirits* (University of Hawaii Press, 1985).

Nachtfrau: German synonym for "witch"; literally "night woman."

Names of Power: If words radiate power, then sacred words transmit sacred power. Sacred names of the Creator, deities, angels, and spirits annul curses, provide success, and heal illness and injury. The tradition existed in various areas of the ancient world, notably China, Egypt, and Mesopotamia. The practice survives in Islamic, Japanese, and Jewish magic traditions as well as in Western High Ritual magic.

Necromancer: Often incorrectly used as a synonym for "sorcerer" (and a malevolent one at that), technically necromancer indicates a practitioner of necromancy, the art of divination via communication with the dead. (See **MAGICAL ARTS:** Necromancy.)

Neo-Paganism: Modern Earth-centered spiritual paths based on ancient traditions that are polytheistic to varying degrees. See Pagan.

Ngaka: A term from Zambia most often translated as "doctor" but may be understood as a specialist magical practitioner. For example, ngakas of the rain specialize in raising or terminating storms, similar to a European weather witch. Every animal—especially dangerous ones—is affiliated with ngakas who either protect people from the species or send the species after people. The ngaka shares the essence of their affiliated animal; they can communicate with their specific animal as well as transform into the creature whose nature she shares.

Nganga: Literally "force," "mystery" or "soul"; this pan-Bantu word indicates practitioners of the occult arts, including herbalists, magicians, shamans, and witch-doctors. There are nganga families whose lineages go back generations. Boys are trained by their fathers or other male relatives while girls receive training from their mothers or female relations. Individuals also receive guidance from deceased ancestors who communicate via divination, dreams, and ritual. Depending upon regional dialect, nganga may refer to magical and spiritual traditions as well as to the practitioner. See also Palo.

Nyama: This Mande word names a natural magical energy or force that permeates the world, similar to ashé, chi, heka or mana. It is the energy that fuels Earth; without nyama nothing can be accomplished. Nyama is the energy that fuels all actions and is a by-product of every act; the more strenuous and challenging the task, the more nyama demanded and simultaneously produced. However, massive, uncontrolled, undirected quantities of nyama are potentially dangerous. Sorcery is the method of controlling nyama and channeling it in positive (or desired) directions.

Obeah: African-derived magical traditions of the British West Indies. The word may indicate the system or it may indicate a practitioner, who may also be called an Obeah Man or Obeah Woman. The word is believed to derive from what is now modern Ghana; in the Twi (Akan) language *obayifo* indicates a sorcerer, witch or wizard.

Obeah was frequently outlawed because colonial authorities recognized that Obeah men and women encouraged and organized resistance to slavery. Like Hoodoo and the arts of the Cunning Folk, Obeah tends to be more concerned with practical magic and somewhat less with spirituality. This may be the result of living under Protestant authority, which offered less leeway for the surreptitious preservation of non-Christian spiritual traditions than Roman Catholicism, under whose rule Candomblé, Santeria, and Vodou survived and evolved.

Onmyo-Do: Japanese mystical tradition deriving from various roots including Taoism, astrology, divination, and assorted *ars magica*. Its underlying philosophy has to do with the interplay of the universe's male and female forces or yin and yang. Onmyo-Do may be understood as the magical mastery of yin and yang forces as well as those of Earth's five elements. (Although Western philosophy counts four elements, Chinese tradition acknowledges five: air, earth, fire, water, *and* metal.)

Onmyoji: A practitioner of the Japanese magical tradition Onmyo-Do, usually translated into English as "Yin-Yang Master." The term is also sometimes translated into English as "wizard," "magician" or "sorcerer." See **CREATIVE ARTS:** Manga: Tokyo Babylon; **HALL OF FAME:** Abei no Seimei.

Ordo Templi Orientis (OTO): Also known as *The Order of the Oriental Templars* or *Order of the Temple of the East*. A magical organization and metaphysical society founded in the early 1900s by Karl Kellner, a German Freemason and occultist. OTO was intended as a modern form of Templarism, drawing inspiration from the medieval Knights Templar. Kellner traveled to India where he studied Tantra and was influenced by followers of the American occult master Pascal Beverly Randolph. Randolph had traveled widely through the Eastern Hemisphere and claimed possession of the key to all Hermetic and Masonic secrets via sacred sexual magic, as well as through Templar occult methods.

The OTO was based on using sexual energy in ritual magic. Trained adepts channel energy generated by erotic arousal for transformational purposes. Kellner died in 1905 and Theodor Reuss assumed leadership of the Order. He invited Aleister Crowley to form an English branch of the Order in 1912. When Reuss resigned in 1922, Crowley became the Order's leader. There are currently active branches of the OTO in several countries. (See **HALL OF FAME:** Aleister Crowley, Pascal Beverly Randolph.)

Orisha: During the slave trade, these African spirits traveled to the Western Hemisphere alongside their human devotees. In areas especially devastated by slavery, some local orisha no longer exist in Africa but only in Western Hemisphere traditions. They form the basis of Candomblé and Santeria.

Orixa: Portuguese variation of orisha; this spelling is used by Afro-Brazilian traditions. The pronunciation is identical: *"o-ree-sha."*

Pagan: Signifies any non-monotheistic faith, devotee of that faith or someone who resists Christianity—with the exception of Jews and Muslims whom the Church classified as infidels instead. Pagan literally means "rural," "from the country" or "rustic," from the Latin root word, *pagus*.

Some explain the term by suggesting that only hicks stubbornly held on to superstitious beliefs, as opposed to sophisticated urbanites who embraced Christianity, but this is incorrect: Roman soldiers used *Paganus* as contemptuous slang for civilians, non-combatants or "stay-at-homes." Early Christians, who envisioned themselves as Soldiers of the Holy Cross engaged in sacred battle, picked up this slang but used it to refer to those not enlisted in the army dedicated to Christ. By the fourth century Pagan referred to anyone who offered devotion to local spirits or deities.

Ancient people didn't classify themselves as Pagan. They called themselves by whatever name was used for their specific tradition, clan or community. Christians identified other people as Pagans because of their resistance to Christianity: thus Pagan identified what you're *not*, not necessarily what you *are*.

Modern spiritual devotees now sometimes classify themselves with pride as Pagans. Pagan in this sense doesn't specify one faith but encompasses non-Christian or non-monotheistic traditions, including Wicca. See Neo-Paganism.

Paket Kongo: A type of Vodou amulet or talisman, paket kongo are cloth-bound packages containing botanicals and powders. Many are extremely beautiful, created from lush fabrics, bound with silk ribbons and ornamented with feathers, mirrors, and/or sequins. Because they are so beautiful, empty paket kongo are sometimes crafted by artisans as *objets d'art*. Genuine paket kongo are magically empowered and hand-crafted during spiritual ritual. They are created under the aegis of Simbi, patron snake lwa of magic. The size, color, and contents depend upon their purpose and the spirit to which they are dedicated or which they are believed to contain. See also Gris-gris, Lwa, Mojo, Talisman; **DIVINE WITCH:** Simbi.

Palo: Afro-Cuban spiritual and magical tradition that evolved from Nganga (see page 346). In addition to its African roots, Palo may also incorporate Freemasonry, Roman Catholicism, and Spiritism. There are various branches including Palo Mayombe and Palo Monte.

Palo is strongly rooted in necromantic traditions; central to its practice is the ritual creation and maintenance of a cauldron (*prenda*) containing various items including human bones. Creation of the prenda involves a pact between the palero and the spirit of one who has died. (See **MAGICAL ARTS:** Necromancy.)

"Palo" literally means "stick" (as in a small branch) and refers to ritual practices. Deities are sometimes known as orishas as they are in Santeria, but also as nkisi. They may be syncretized to Roman Catholic saints. Many nkisi are unique to Palo, however others are shared with Santeria and Candomblé although they may bear different names. Thus Zarabanda is recognizable as Ogun, the Spirit of Iron, while Lucifero names Elegba the trickster.

Palo has frequently been outlawed and has historically been a private society whose secrets were only known to initiates. Only recently have practitioners begun sharing their tradition with outsiders.

Further Reading: *The Book of Palo* by Baba Raul Canizares (Original Publications, 2002).

Palero: A practitioner of Palo.

Path: Human beings may have spiritual paths but deities have "paths" too. Some deities have the equivalent of multiple personalities, different guises, different simultaneous incarnations or "paths." These paths are the different ways a deity manifests.

Pharmakis: Greek for "herbalist" and/or "witch."

Pharmakon/Pharmaka: This Greek word simultaneously means magical substance, medicine, contraceptive, and/or poison. It is the root of the modern "pharmacy," "pharmacist," and "pharmaceutical" but in antiquity also referred to "witchcraft." Greek sorceresses and witches were called *pharmakides* or *pharmakeutriai*. Pharmakon could refer to the products of their craft, which might be used for healing or harm. Plato suggested that the Greek term for poisoning had a double meaning:

✳ *Damage done by physical substances*

✳ *Harm caused by "tricks, spells, and enchantments"*

Piseog, Pishogue: From the Irish Gaelic *pisreog*, pronounced "*pish-rogue*"; a diminutive for vagina but it also indicates a charm or spell intended to do harm, similar to "hex" or "spoiling." Piseogs cause illness, make cows go dry, and kill agricultural and human fertility. It is similar to the Evil Eye except that it is clearly intentional.

Typically something organic is left to rot on someone's property. For instance, a rotten egg, rotting meat or a used menstrual rag is hidden within a haystack. The item is the piseog: as it rots, so does the target's luck, health, fertility, and so on.

Allegedly shamrocks provide immunity from piseogs, as well as from glamour (see Glamour, page 336). Keep one on your person to keep yourself safe at all times. However, if one suspects that one is under the power of a piseog, the following serves as an antidote:

1. Discover the item.
2. Sprinkle it with Holy Water.
3. Remove it with some sort of disposable makeshift shovel.
4. Burn the piseog *and* this shovel in a ditch or far corner of a field.
5. Pray, petition, and keep sprinkling Holy Water. Prayers directed to St Benedict are believed particularly effective.

> The modern tradition of tossing rotten eggs at neighbors on the night preceding Halloween is believed to be rooted in the piseog.

Pishoguery: The system of Irish malevolent magic that entails the creation of the piseog or pishogue (see previously). Pishoguery is based on the notion that only a limited amount of prosperity exists on Earth, therefore if one person gains it, it is inevitably at another's expense.

Ancient rituals became confused with malicious magic. It was traditional to collect May Day's first morning dew and sprinkle it over crops and cattle for abundance and luck. This practice was eventually performed surreptitiously because of associations with forbidden Paganism. Surreptitious behavior attracted suspicion: individuals were accused of stealing good fortune. Pishoguery was the response: initially protective magic that attempted to balance and redirect prosperity energy, it degenerated into harmful, malicious magic instead.

Power Doctors: Traditional magical practitioners from the Ozark Mountains of the United States.

Pow-Wow: One of the earliest Algonquian words recorded by Europeans. According to seventeenth-century European translation, a pow-wow was a conjurer, diviner, ceremonial leader, and healer. The term also indicated places that contained healing power used for healing rituals and other ceremonials.

The term now names two completely distinct concepts.

❊ *In Native American usage, pow-wows are celebratory gatherings devoted to indigenous traditions.*

❊ *Pow-Wow is the name given Pennsylvania Dutch magical and spiritual traditions.*

The Pennsylvania Dutch were German immigrants who brought their rich magical traditions with them to the New World. These traditions evolved, incorporating new influences including those of local Native Americans. The name pays tribute to that influence.

Practitioners of Pow-Wow are known as Pow-Wow artists and sometime as Pow-Wows, corresponding to the seventeenth-century definition of the word. Two branches of Pow-Wow exist. Some Pow-Wows are devoutly Christian and consider their craft faith healing, not magic. Other Pow-Wows artists are discreetly Pagan (or at least, less devoutly Christian).

German territory suffered the most brutal witchcraze of the Burning Times; among the many migrants to the United States were occultists who hoped to find safety and perhaps a little freedom to practice their arts.

Psychopomp: The Greek word for a spirit who serves as an escort between the realms of the living and the dead. Among the psychopomps are Hermes, Hecate, Circe (when she wants to), and many fairies. (See **DIVINE WITCH:** Circe, Hecate, Hermes; **FAIRIES**.)

Qosem: A Hebrew word that is often translated as "witch" but literally meaning "divider." That may sound malevolent, as if the qosem's specialty is dividing people or causing dissension, however that is inaccurate. Qosem derives from a root word meaning *"to divide or assign, especially lots"* and so is a type of diviner. This linguistic usage of "divide" doesn't translate well into English: it sounds more threatening than it is. The qosem may be understood as dividing lots in the manner that fortune-tellers deal cards.

Rhizotomoki: An archaic Greek term for "root-gatherer" or "root-worker," as used by Homer and other ancient Greek writers.

Root Doctor, Root Woman, Root-worker: Witch, healer or magical practitioner, especially an herbal specialist. Root-workers use all parts of plants, however roots are generally acknowledged as containing the strongest magic power.

The term "root-worker" also implies power and knowledge and a special relationship with Earth and her protective spirits. The ability of root-workers to "root" around in Earth is the clue to this power: once upon a time, it was not considered safe to disturb Earth, unless one knew proper rituals and had received permission to dig.

Root-working is an especially ancient form of magical practice. It is believed that bears, pigs, and snakes first taught people the art: these are animals that "root" in Earth. Root-worker is sometimes used as a synonym for Hoodoo Doctor or Conjurer.

See **ANIMALS:** Bears, Pigs, Snakes; **BOTANICALS:** Mandrake, Roots; **DIVINE WITCH:** Kybele.

Rune: Alphabetic system powerfully identified with Nordic traditions. Runes are more than an alphabet, however: each rune radiates a specific power. They are used for divination, spell-casting, and other magical or spiritual practices. See **MAGICAL ARTS**: Runes.

Rune-caster: A practitioner of runes. This usually indicates a diviner—runes are first cast or thrown, then read—but the term may also imply "spell-caster" or "wizard."

Sabbat: There are two completely distinct meanings of the word:

❋ *The eight major festivals of Wicca celebrating the Wheel of the Year: Samhain, Yule, Imbolc, Beltane, Lughnasa, Mabon, Litha, and Ostara. Further information may be found in **CALENDAR**: Sabbat, and under entries for each sacred day.*

❋ *The term used by witch-hunters to indicate mass gatherings of witches. "Witches' ball" might be the most accurate, neutral synonym, especially because attendees are described as dancing, feasting, and generally celebrating.*

The use of the term sabbat to indicate the convening of witches was apparently first documented in fourteenth-century Inquisition records of trials in Carcassonne and Toulouse.

"Sabbat" derives from the same roots as Semitic words for "seven" and may derive from the Sumerian *shabbattu*, "a calming of the heart," observed as a holiday every seventh day beginning with the Full Moon festival for the lunar deity, from whence this concept traveled to Judaism. Roman Catholic theologians used the word for witches so as to imply that they were damned heretics similar to Jews, and/or that Jews were witches. (See also Akelarre; **CALENDAR**: Sabbat.)

Sagae: "Feminine wisdom"; this term literally translates as "wise woman" or "sage woman" but by the classical Roman era was a euphemism for "witch." Columella, the first-century CE Roman writer, advised masters to forbid their slaves to consult sagae.

Santero/Santera (m/f): Priests and priestesses of Santeria (see below); in order to achieve this status, one must acquire extensive knowledge of botanicals. Santeras lead ceremonials and perform divination, rituals, and other services to the community.

Santeria: The religion of the saints—but not just any saints. Kidnapped Yorubans enslaved in Cuba were determined to preserve their ancestral spiritual traditions and maintain devotion to the orishas. African spiritual traditions were outlawed and forbidden by the colonial authorities; those who defied the decree were subject to brutal punishment. What to do? Slaves were ordered to convert to Roman Catholicism; to facilitate the conversion of people forcibly kept illiterate, the Church offered visual images of the Holy Family and saints. Santeria was born.

Individual orisha were identified with specific Roman Catholic holy figures through the use of corresponding images. Thus Ochossi the Sacred Archer took on the guise of St Sebastian, whose votive imagery shows him pierced by arrows.

Sometimes this syncretism seems natural: a saint and an orisha might share much in common, but sometimes the connections are bizarre. Chango, Spirit of Male Sexual Prowess, Master of Thunder and Lightning, was syncretized to the young virgin martyr St Barbara because her votive image displays lightning.

Syncretism offers safety: one could appear to be devoutly petitioning St Barbara while really communing with Chango. However, syncretism also leads to complexity. Modern Santeria retains a Yoruban spiritual framework with added Roman Catholic influence, as well as influences from other African traditions, indigenous Taino Indian influences, and others.

Some devotees of Santeria are intensely Roman Catholic while others now reject syncretism, believing that the time for masks is over. Many others walk a middle path. However in all cases, devotion to the orishas/saints and communion with them is the primary focus of Santeria. See also Orisha, Vodoun.

Scobaces: Literally, "women with brooms"; a Norman euphemism for "witch."

Scry: A method of divination that involves gazing into a clear surface. Crystal ball or mirror gazing is scrying; one can also scry in a pan of water or ink or any smooth surface. See **MAGICAL ARTS**: Divination.

Second Sight: Psychic vision or ESP.

Seer: Literally "see-er" or "one who sees"; may also derive from the same roots as seiòr (see below).

Seidh, Seiòr: Specific form of Norse oracular practice involving prophesy via trances and summoning spirits. Throughout Scandinavia and Iceland, women performed what is defined as "ritual trance prophesy" or seiòr. Seiòr was under the dominion of Freya.

The seeress sits on a raised seat or platform where, with help from ritual assistants, she enters into trance, a process known as *ùtiseta* or "sitting out." In Christian texts, seiòr evolved into a very derogatory term. However, the tradition of "sitting out" survived until the mid-seventeenth century with the Dutch *Witta Wijven* (wise wives). In recent years, the practice has been revived. See also Völva; **DIVINE WITCH**: Freya, Odin.

Siedkona: A woman skilled in seidh (above). See also Haegtessa, Völva.

Shikigami, Shikijin: Japanese spirit familiars who serve as sorcerers' assistants.

Sibyl: Now used loosely as a synonym for "female seer" or "diviner," sibyl technically names a type of prophetess once found throughout the ancient Mediterranean world. The word is etymologically related to "Cybele" or "cave"; the Sibyls prophesized from their homes within caves. The most famous Sibyl was from Cumae, now in modern Italy. See **BOOKS**: Library of the Lost: Sibylline Texts; **DIVINE WITCH**: Cybele, Sibilla.

Skhur: North African term usually translated as "sorcery" or "witchcraft."

Depending upon regional dialect and local usage, skhur may refer to the art, the practitioner or both. It often, but not exclusively, implies malevolent magic—skhur is traditionally believed motivated by envy, jealousy, resentment, and/or the desire to settle old scores, which, depending on circumstances and perceptions, may be interpreted as a desire for justice.

Skhur is rarely initiated randomly or by strangers. Instead it tends to be a passive-aggressive method of settling scores within a family or community. Usually neighbors or relatives seeking magical satisfaction instigate skhur by secretly hiring a professional magical practitioner whose skills include spell-casting and spirit-working. These practitioners are also hired to remove skhur and heal its effects.

Solitary: An independent magical practitioner; one who works solo.

Sorcellerie: French synonym for "witchcraft."

Sorcerer, Sorceress: Now synonymous with "wizard," "witch," "enchanter" or "magician" but once sorcerer referred specifically to practitioners of sorcery (see below).

Sorcery: Now fairly synonymous with "witchcraft," originally this word reflected attempts to distinguish one type of magical practice from another. "Sorcery" first appeared in English in the fourteenth century in reference to astrology and other divinatory arts. By the sixteenth century, sorcery encompassed other forms of magic too.

When attention is paid to the nuances, "witchcraft" is often used to refer to folk practices, with an emphasis on botanical magic; "sorcery" implies High Magic, the type that requires education and literacy and incorporates lengthy rituals demanding privacy and leisure. Sorcerers tend to be male; the exceptions are wealthy, educated, independent women.

Sorcier/Sorcière (m/f): The French equivalent of "sorcerer" and "sorceress"; sometimes translated into English as "witch" or "wizard."

Sorguiñe: Spanish word indicating Basque witches. It derives from the Basque word that is translated as "witchcraft"—*Xorguinería*—and literally means "one who foretells" or "one who makes fortunes." The word is also related to the name of cave-dwelling spirits who travel in the witch-goddess Mari's host. See also Xorguina, Xorguinería; **DIVINE WITCH:** Mari.

Soul-journey: The English language has no word for shamanic traveling. Shamanic traditions acknowledge the existence of a "soul" that can be trained to leave the body, perform various functions such as traveling to the realms of the spirits or the dead, and then return to its body. While the soul is traveling, the shaman is typically entranced, asleep or may appear to be in a coma. This is a dangerous process; success is not always guaranteed, The soul may become lost, injured or be unable to rejoin the body leading to fatal consequences. "Soul-journey" is the closest approximation to this concept and so the term has entered metaphysical language. See also Benandanti, Fetch, Kresnik.

Spiritism: This is not a synonym or misspelling of Spiritualism (see below) but a specific philosophy based on the teachings of Allan Kardec. It is an instructional system describing the existence of spirits and their interaction with the material word. Spiritism was highly influenced by Christianity and in turn has been a tremendous influence on Afro-Brazilian spiritual traditions such as Umbanda.

Spiritualism: A religion or practice in which contact is made with the spirits of the dead via a medium. Modern spiritualism emerged in the mid-nineteenth century in the United States and attracted genuine metaphysical practitioners as well as con artists who preyed on the vulnerability of grief-stricken people wishing to contact loved ones.

Spiritualism was originally characterized by séances, table-tapping, and physical manifestations such as ectoplasm. However because these physical manifestations are easily faked they are no longer emphasized by modern practitioners. See **MAGICAL ARTS:** Necromancy.

Spoiling: Slavic malevolent magic. Spoiling may be similar to the Evil Eye: the spoiler radiates such intense rage, resentment, envy, and malevolence that no further or even conscious action is necessary—their very presence generates spoiling. It may also be consciously accomplished via object-driven hexes and spells. The effect of spoiling is similar to the Evil Eye:

plants, animals, people and their possessions wither away.

⚜ *Spells against an individual are accomplished via magical packets secreted onto their person or property.*

⚜ *Spells targeting a community may be accomplished by manipulating vegetation, such as a twist of rye.*

⚜ *Spoiling may also be accomplished by Whispering (see page 361).*

Strega: Italian magical traditions were remarkably persistent, surviving underground despite discouragement and persecution. "Strega" names the Italian witch; "stregheria" her entire art of practical magic. The word has lingered from old Roman times. It derives from *strix* (see below), although the vampire bird associations have been lost. Although strega may be used negatively, it is also a title for a lovingly respected witch, similar to *"Baba"* in Russian or *"Mother"* in English (as in Mother Shipton). The heroine of Tomie DePaola's series of children's books is an Italian witch named Strega Nona, *"witch grandma."* The male equivalent is "stregoni." In some Italian regional dialects, strega also refers to the entire system of stregheria, thus one practices strega. See also Stregheria, Strix.

Stregheria: The craft of the Strega; Italian witchcraft and magical traditions.

Strigoii: Romanian word indicating night-flying witches. Romanian is among the Romance languages deriving from Latin; the word derives from *strix* and is closer to the malevolent, bird-like implications of the old Latin term than it is to modern Italian *strega*.

Women born with a caul, especially if also blue eyed and red haired, were believed extra likely to become strigoii. In this part of the world, being born with a caul tends to indicate shamanic or magical ability; the extreme negative stereotype of the strigoii may derive from Christian perceptions of ancient traditions and female practitioners.

Strigoii rendezvous in forests and graveyards. Strigoii never completely die: they lie in the grave with only their right eye closed. The left eye, the one on the sinister side, is perpetually open and observant. Thrusting nine spindles into their grave won't kill the strigoii but does prevent them from rising again. See also Widdershins; **WOMEN'S MYSTERIES:** Spinning.

Strigula: Romanian for "witch," "vampire" or both. See Strigoii, Strix, Vampire.

Strix, Strigae: Strix literally means "screech owl" but is also translated as "witch." It derives from the Greek "to screech." The word may be related to *goes*, which indicates "howler." It may originally have indicated practitioners of Women's Mysteries: owls are associated with birth, death, and important female deities like Athena and Lilith.

However, the Romans adopted the word to indicate a specific type of shape-shifting magical practitioner. Classical Roman culture was tremendously suspicious of magical practice as well as of female power; these fears manifest in the strix.

The Latin grammarian Fastus defines the Late Latin word *strigae* as "the name given to women who practice sorcery."

The strix is *always* female. Human by day, they transform into birds at night, flying through the air ravenously hungry for human flesh and blood, especially that of babies. Like a succubus, strigae also lust after sex and human vitality or life essence.

According to legend, women removed their clothes and rubbed unguents onto their bodies, which enabled them to shape-shift into owl form and fly off into the night to do mischief. Roman literature from the first two centuries of the Common Era is packed with references to strigae: they flew around at night, emitting ear-piercing screeches. They had feathers and laid eggs but had women's heads and breasts filled with poisonous milk.

A strix appears in Lucius Apuleius' second-century Latin novel *The Golden Ass* (see **CREATIVE ARTS:** Literature). Pamphile the strix regains her own form after drinking a potion and bathing in an anise-bay laurel potion.

Whether originally the strix was intended to be taken seriously is unknown. If visitors from the future, lacking any context, watched modern monster movies would they appreciate that these were merely entertainment?

The strix resembles mythic accounts of spirits like Lilith and Lamia. Were the original strigae devotees of these spirits? This isn't just speculation; there may indeed have been some sort of spiritual connection: late Roman sources describe Diana as a leader of the strigae, although this may have been an attempt to defame Diana.

> The strix may also be associated with the sirens and harpies, spirits with women's heads and avian bodies.

The concept of the night-flying, shape-shifting, sexually voracious, baby-killing witch returned with a vengeance during the European witch-hunts.

See also Goes, Lamia; **DIVINE WITCH:** Diana, Lilith; **WOMEN'S MYSTERIES:** Midwifery, Spinning.

Talb: North African term usually translated as "magician." The talb may be able to command, control, or at least work with jinn.

Táltos: Hungarian shaman/wizard, also translated as "magus," "magician" or even "physician," similar to "witch-doctor" and now used to refer to any fairy-tale character with magic powers, whether human or animal. In fairy tales the táltos is invariably male, but Hungarian witch-trial records indicate that women were charged as táltos, too.

Hungary possessed powerful shamanic traditions that were suppressed following the country's conversion to Christianity in the tenth century. The traditional táltos was a shaman who specialized in locating lost or missing object, divination, healing, and weather magic.

One does not choose to become a táltos; one is destined to become one. A táltos is identified at birth by being born with a caul or at least one tooth. If the tooth is pulled out, this does not guarantee that the child will not become a táltos, however the shamanic path is challenged and powers may be more difficult to attain.

Future táltos tend to be silent, morose, sullen children with unusual physical strength and energy. They crave dairy products and eggs. Eventually, around the age of seven, the budding táltos receives a vision. An older táltos appears to them, usually in the shape of a bull or stallion, and engages the youngster in battle. In order to become a full-fledged táltos, the younger one must beat the older. Other traditional initiatory tests include climbing the World Tree or a ladder to the sky with rungs formed from iron hooks. Others report classic shamanic initiations—they get chopped into bits, cooked in a cauldron, and then revived.

Like the Benandanti, táltos battle other táltos at scheduled intervals, usually incorporating the magic numbers 3 and 7 (three times a year, for instance, or once every seven years). They duel in the form of bulls, flames, and stallions. The táltos differs from the Benandanti in that there is no sense of battling outsiders: each táltos is an independent practitioner; they wage psychic battles against each other.

According to legend, the first táltos was fathered by a wolf (shades of *Little Red Riding Hood*, the mother being a young woman who was lost in the forest; the Huns, accused of being the offspring of witches and desert spirits, are among the tribes that formed the Hungarian nation. See page 338, Haljoruna.) This may link the táltos tradition with those of wolf-shamans and wolf-warriors, or perhaps with traditions of ritual possession in the forest where one person is possessed by a wolf-spirit. (See **ANIMALS:** Wolves and Werewolves; **MAGICAL ARTS:** Ritual Possession.)

There are also táltos horses and bulls, who may be familiars of the human táltos or their doubles. However they may also be independent entities. The táltos animal may be responsible for teaching and initiating the human táltos.

Theurgy: The ancient Greeks believed that people could train themselves to be possessed by deities. While ritually possessed, individuals served as oracles. Theurgy, literally "god-working," was the last major manifestation of Pagan spirituality, serving as a foundation for later magical traditions.

The term "theurgy" was introduced by Julianus the Chaldean, who wrote *The Chaldean Oracles* in *c*.170 CE. Hecate was a particularly significant deity in Theurgy. Theurgy's stated purpose was the promotion of divine knowledge for the individual magician. Different methods existed:

❋ *Based on Egyptian traditions, theurgists chant incantations that encouraged spirits to inhabit statues. Questions could then be addressed to the statue.*

❋ *Trance states were induced in children who served as mediums (see also Istinzal).*

❋ *The spirit mounts, or temporarily possesses, the individual theurgist who facilitates ritual possession through the use of costumes, tools, and music similar to modern Santeria, Vodou, and Zar.*

When Christianity came to prominence, Theurgy was branded as diabolical. Emperor Julian, the last Pagan Roman Emperor, was an initiated theurgist who appointed other theurgists to high government positions. Julian's brief reign was followed by that of a Christian Emperor—the theurgists were removed from office and again subject to Christian persecution.

Proclus (February 8, 411–April 17, 485), the last of the great theurgists, lived in Athens and taught Theurgy at the Academy founded by Plato. In 529 the Emperor Justinian banned Theurgy alongside all other Pagan practice.

Transvection: Magical flight.

Trollkvinna: Say it out loud: in English, it sounds like "troll queen." Troll doesn't just refer to those big, stupid giants. In English, troll also means "to cause to move around," "to celebrate in song" or "sing loudly," "to sing or play" or, most tellingly, "to fish by trailing a lure or baited hook." (see also Allure). In Swedish, *trollkvinna* is a witch.

In Scandinavian folklore, there are witches who are not female trolls; female trolls however are indistinct from witches. Although male trolls are invariably unattractive and stupid, female trolls are often (but not always) beautiful and clever. Some scholars believe "troll" actually refers to surviving Neanderthals.

Umbanda: Afro-Brazilian spiritual tradition incorporating Kardecian Spiritism alongside Roman Catholicism and African traditions. Umbanda first emerged in the 1920s.

Unholden: German word for "witches" that derives from Hulda. See Haljoruna; **DIVINE WITCH:** Hulda.

Upir: This Russian word literally translates into English as "vampire" but encompasses vampires, werewolves, and witches—all closely linked in the cosmology of the Balkans and Eastern and Central Europe. Werewolves and witches transform into vampires when they die. "Upir" is believed to have originally referred to votaries or priests of lunar deities. See also Vampire; **ANIMALS:** Wolves and Werewolves.

Vala: See Völva.

Valkyrie: In Norse mythology, "Valkyrie" indicates female warrior spirits lead by Freya; they are also sometimes called "Odin's daughters." Valkyries rode wolves into battle and could transform into ravens and swans.

In the early eleventh century, England was chastised by a Christian preacher who complained about the proliferation of "wiccan" and "waelcryrian," which in modern English means "male witches" and "Valkyries." These Valkyries were not spirit-maidens but the female counterpart of the male witch: living women practicing magical arts and Pagan traditions. Valkyrie may also indicate a priestess of Freya. See **DIVINE WITCH:** Freya, Odin.

Vampire, Vampyr: Yes, yes, yes, *everyone* knows about Hollywood-style vampires who only come out at night, want to drink your blood, and are vanquished by Christian emblems like crosses and Holy Water. *Those* vampires have nothing to do with witches—unless they both happen to appear in the same horror movie.

That type of blood-sucking vampire is based on the writings of Bram Stoker, author of *Dracula*. Stoker was fascinated by Central and Eastern European folklore, as well as by the recent European discovery of South American blood-consuming bats. Stoker, applying literary license, combined many legends and added his own personal vision to create a concept that continues to entertain and enthrall millions.

However, his concept has little to do with the original European vampire.

The concept of the "vampire" transcends linguistic boundaries. Similar-sounding words referring to similar concepts exist in virtually all Central and Eastern European languages, whether Slavic, Finno-Ugric or Romance. Linguists believe these words derive from "uber," translated as "witch," which first appeared in the language of the Turkic tribes of Asia. Variations include *upir, wampir, vampyr, upior,* and so forth.

You thought the word *witch* was confusing? In the Balkans, one word (*vampire, vampyr, upir*) may indicate witch, vampire, and/or werewolf.

In Slavic areas, vampires were understood as revenants, living corpses of witches/sorcerers/magical practitioners who, for one reason or another, rise from the grave. At their most neutral, they are harmful merely because they are not obeying natural laws; at their worst, they rise with the deliberate intention of causing harm.

Little or no notion of blood-sucking exists in the original conception. Because the vampire is in a liminal state, between death and life, they require life-energy (mana, magic power, chi). This is best absorbed from living people. (Significantly, vampire bats almost never bother people.) However life force is more likely to be absorbed via sexual energy or fluids or siphoning off mana or chi than by sucking blood.

Another interpretation suggests that the vampire is not dead but a living practitioner who is able to send out his shadow soul (and recall it when desired), and that this soul is interpreted as a vampire.

Further Reading: Nigel Jackson's *Compleat Vampyre* (Capall Bann Publishing, 1995).

Vanir, Vana: Alongside the Aesir, one of the two pantheons of Norse spirits. The Vanir, the indigenous deities, were identified with magic power, prophecy, and witchcraft. Occult tools and skills such as runes or seiòr derive from the Vanir. See Aesir, Seidh/Seiòr; **DIVINE WITCH:** Angerboda, Freya, Hella, Odin.

Ved'ma, Ved'mak, Ved'mar: Russian synonym for "witch"; literally, "one who knows." Variations include the Ukrainian *vid'ma* and Belorussian *vedz'ma.*

Veneficia, Venefica: In Roman literature, *veneno* indicated poison and/or magical substance. A veneficia was a woman who created magical potions and/or poisons.

Vetulae: Although this term literally means "old woman" it was a medieval synonym for "witch." It was not a neutral term but one of derision. As its associations with witchcraft intensified, its literal meaning lessened: Henri de Mondeville (*c.*1260–1320) defined vetulae as a pejorative against all "bad women" including, according to him, barbers, fortune-tellers, converted Jewesses, midwives, and prostitutes.

Vjestica: "One who knows"; Slavic euphemism for "witch." Derived from the same root source as the English "witch" or "wicca" and the Russian "ved'ma," slight variations exist in many Slavic languages—for instance in Bulgaria, *vjescirica* indicates female witch while *viestae* is male.

Volkhv/Volkva (m/f): Russian term indicating a Pagan magician, priest or shaman. The term was used in the earliest Old Russian and Slavic texts for Finno-Ugric and Slavic shamans and Pagan practitioners. The word is believed to be Finno-Ugric in origin and thus may actually have once named a specific practice, practitioner or tradition. It seems to derive from a root word for "wolf" and so may once have indicated a wolf-shaman or werewolf. The word was also used to translate the Greek *pharmakos* (see above).

Völva: Also sometimes given as Vala. The sibyls of the North-land, the Norse term for female magician or magical prophetess. The term derives from *völr* or "stick." This stick (also known as a *stafr* or *gandr*) was used in magical rituals.

The völva presided over the divination rite know as seiòr. The völva traveled, offering her services and in turn being feasted and celebrated. She reproduces the traditional processional where a deity or sacred object is transported by wagon. A written document of these practices survives from a village in Greenland, suffering from famine and eagerly awaiting the arrival of the völva.

She was greeted with a lavish ritual meal that featured the hearts of every possible different animal. After the feast, the völva mounted a platform, wearing calfskin boots and cat's fur gloves (furry side on the inside). She sat on a cushion stuffed with hen's feathers and. requested that a villager sing the entrancing incantations. A young woman, identified as a Christian volunteered saying that she learned the songs in childhood.

The Voluspa (translated as *The Sibyl's Prophecy* or *The Völva's Prophecy*) is a Norse poem from Iceland written down in the late tenth century or early eleventh, but believed to reflect older traditions. It is considered among the most important poems in the *Poetic Edda,* if not *the* most important poem. The poem takes the form of a monologue delivered by a völva in response to Odin's questioning.

When the völva emerged from her trance, she praised the singing: the spirits had flocked to hear it. She was able to learn from these spirits that the famine would soon end as well as other information, including the destiny of the singer. According to one witness: *"Little she said went unfulfilled."*

See also Seidh/Seiòr; **CREATIVE ARTS:** Dance: Processional; **DIVINE WITCH:** Herta.

Vodo: Variation of Vodoun practiced in the Dominican Republic. See Vodoun.

Vodou, Vodoun: This word literally means "spirit" in the Fon language of West Africa. "Spirit" refers to the lwa; Fon spiritual traditions center on devotion to the lwa and interaction with them, and Vodou names this spiritual tradition. Vodou still exists in West Africa (in Togo, Benin, and elsewhere), but the word is now usually identified with African-derived Haitian spiritual traditions.

The framework of Vodou derives from Fon tradition but evolved in Haiti to incorporate other African influences, as well as those of Europe and Freemasonry. Indigenous Caribbean traditions were also incorporated into Vodou.

Although the colonial authorities attempted to suppress African spiritual traditions, and Vodoun was banned on pain of death, it flourished through syncretism: the lwa were identified with Roman Catholic saints. Thus Ogou, Spirit of Iron, wears the mask of St James the Greater who is always depicted brandishing a sword. That sword is the clue to the identity of the forbidden spirit.

Vodoun is practiced more openly now but is still subject to periodic discrimination and persecution. Vodoun and Vodou are the spellings preferred by most devotees, as they are considered more respectful than the variant Voodoo.

> Mambo are the initiated priestesses of Vodou, also spelled Manbo. Houngan is an initiated Vodou priest.

See also Lwa, Santeria, Voodoo.

Voodoo: Historically, Vodou, and traditional African spirituality in general, were not treated respectfully by outsiders, to put it mildly. Vodou was considered the lowest bastion of Paganism and primitive superstition and was mocked, denigrated, and outlawed.

Voodoo is the spelling popularized by American outsiders to the tradition. Vicious, racist distortions of Vodou were once popularly featured in horror movies and pulp novels (see Zombi). Many practitioners thus find this spelling inherently insulting and prefer Vodoun or Vodou, the official Kreyol spelling. The use of "Voodoo" as an insult word survives in mainstream society—hence terms like "*voodoo economics.*"

However, Voodoo is also used to distinguish the spiritual traditions that emerged in New Orleans following the mass emigration of Haitian refugees during the Haitian Revolution that began in 1791. The word is used in that context in this book.

Outsiders also frequently used "Voodoo" to refer to *any* magical practitioner or witch particularly one of African descent, as for instance Lafcadio Hearn's famous eulogy of Dr. John Montanet, *The Last of the Voodoos*. This is also considered insulting and incorrect. Many practitioners prefer *Voodooist* or *Vodouienne*. (See **HALL OF FAME:** Dr. John Montanet.)

Vucodlak: Usually translated as "werewolf," vucodlaks soul-journey in the form of a wolf. They do battle with their natural enemies, the Kresnik, also renowned shape-shifters. Significantly, although the kresnik can allegedly transform into any animal form, their favored shapes are livestock like goats or horses, natural prey for a wolf. It is possible to understand these clashes between kresniks and vucodlaks as witch wars rather than dualist battles between good and evil—clashes of occultists representing different communities or clans. See also Kresnik.

Wanga: Technically a Haitian term for a malevolent magical object or packet intended to cause harm, however it has also come to be a catch-all phrase for any sort of amulet or talisman. It is also sometimes used to indicate a charm bag or mojo hand and may be spelled "huanga." Practitioners of other traditions may perceive it as a neutral term, not intrinsically malevolent.

Ward, Warding: As in "to ward off"; protective, vigilant spells and rituals for safety and protection.

Warlock: Historically "warlock" has been used to designate a male practitioner of the magical arts. It was particularly popular in Scotland as a synonym for "male witch" and remains popular in the mass media, although certainly *not* within the modern witchcraft community.

It is a controversial word whose use enrages many magical practitioners. Its use also tends to indicate that the person using it is an outsider to the magical community, unaware of nuance and etiquette. There is debate as to its origins; the two possibilities are not mutually exclusive:

❋ *It evolved from the Old English* waeroga, *literally "oath breaker" but also historically used to indicate "devil." Waer* indicates a covenant, while loga *means "betrayer," from the root word meaning "to lie." That evolved into the Middle*

English warloghe, *also spelled* warlache, *and eventually into its modern spelling. This reference to "oath-breakers" links the warlock to Christian apostasy.*

✳ *It evolved from the Norse* vardlokkur, *which may mean a wise man who guards (locks) the gates of knowledge. He binds evil spirits to prevent them from entering through portals, thus creating* wards. *This warlock is a spiritual warrior and a practitioner of protective magic, especially defensive runes. If the word derives from* vardlokkur *then it derives from Pagan sources and refers to genuine Pagan tradition.*

> *Vardlokkur* may name the practitioner but it may also name the magical tradition of using runes to bind harm and provide protection.

"Warlock" may be derived from both roots and may reflect British Christian perceptions of Pagan Norse invaders. Regardless of its origin, however, the Anglo-Saxon term emerges squarely from Christian tradition. It is a Christian word used to describe those whom Christians held in contempt, and at some point it came to mean a "backsliding Christian." Witch-hunters applied it to their prey. The sting of this word still remains and it will raise hackles in many, if not most, witchcraft communities. (Exceptions are those practitioners drawing heavily or exclusively on Norse traditions, who may even favor the name.)

Although Neo-Pagans are offended by the notion of lying witches, the point is that the word was coined by the Christian authorities. The broken oath wasn't to other Pagan practi-tioners but to the Church. Pagan practitioners may have attempted to preserve their traditions through subterfuge, as was done successfully elsewhere (see Santeria, Vodou), playing for time and safety by swearing allegiance to the Church with their fingers crossed. When caught, they were prosecuted as "oath-breakers." The warlock may be understood as the British equivalent of Spain's Muslim Moriscos and Jewish *conversos*.

Whispering: A synonym for "spell-casting." Methods of spell-casting traditionally incorporate murmuring, muttering or whispering charms, prayers, incantations, blessings or curses. However, use of this word eventually lead to dangerous stereotyping: any woman, especially elderly, raggedy, and/or belligerent ones observed muttering or whispering to themselves were subject to accusations of witchcraft.

Wicca: This term may be used to indicate pre-Christian spiritual traditions of the British Isles, the revival of these traditions as formalized by Gerald Gardner, and/or magical practice in general. "Wicca" is also the Old English word indicating a male practitioner of these magical arts and/or spiritual traditions.

Different explanations of the word's origins exist, all of which may be related and none of which are mutually exclusive:

✳ *Old English* Wicca *(m) and* Wicce *(f) took the form* Wicche *in the Middle Ages for both genders. These words derive from the root verb "to know"*

✳ *The Indo-European root word* wic *or* weik *meaning "to bend" or "turn";* witches *bend the forces of nature to achieve their goals*

* *The Germanic* weiha, *"dedicated to the spirits"*

* Vigja, *Old Norse, meaning "sacred, numinous, worshipped"*

* *Indo-European root words* wid *"to know" and/or* wat *"to prophesy." Other words deriving from this source are the Russian* ved'ma, *Norse* vitki, *and Slavic* vjestica.

See also **HALL OF FAME:** Gerald Gardner.

Widdershins: Literally, "the left-hand path." When one circles counter-clockwise, one is circling widdershins, walking or dancing in the direction opposite to that of the sun. Traditional magical wisdom associates the left side with the moon, women, and yin forces. Non-dualist societies perceive "left" as neutral and necessary: there is no "right" without "left" and vice-versa, however dualist philosophy associated "left" with the evil side of the eternal chessboard of dueling forces. (See **ELEMENTS OF WITCH-CRAFT**.) Modern usage betrays these implications: *Mr. Right*, the *right* decisions, the *right* way versus *left-handed compliments* and *the left-hand path*. In Latin, the left side is the *sinister* side; need we say more?

Post-Christianity, circling widdershins was known as the *"witches' way"* and the *"devil's way."* Being observed circling widdershins was sufficient grounds for an accusation of witchcraft. Observing someone circling widdershins inspired fear in those convinced that witches were evil malefactors.

Many spells incorporate widdershins movement, as they do its opposite—deasil. Eliminating either one eliminates balance. However suspicion of widdershins survives, including within many, although not all, Wiccan traditions who associate widdershins with baneful magic. Those who incorporate widdershins into magical practice tend to use it for banishing purposes.

Wild Hunt: A wild processional of spirits. The Wild Hunt rides on windy, stormy nights as well as on specific dates of the year—Halloween, May Eve, Midsummer's Eve, and the period now designated as the Twelve Nights of Christmas.

Reactions to these processions vary: these spirits are powerful and unpredictable and it is usually considered advisable to stay out of their way. Magical practitioners, however, often wish to observe, join or somehow encounter this parade of spirits.

> The tradition of a parade of spirits who may or may not be accompanied by spirits of the dead and living devotees appears around the world, including areas as isolated as Hawaii.

In some European traditions, during the twelve intercalary days preceding the start of the New Year, dead souls travel in procession to visit families and loved ones. They are traditionally led by deities who bridge thresholds of death and life, goddesses of fertility and death like Freya, Herta, and Hulda, all of whom serve as leaders of the Wild Hunt.

* *In some areas those twelve intercalary days were interpreted as corresponding to the Winter Solstice or Yuletide.*

* *In others, the time period corresponds to Halloween and the beginning of the Dark Half of the Year.*

In other areas, this period precedes the Vernal Equinox and so corresponds in time to various purification festivals in February.

According to Nordic myth, Odin periodically rides his horse at night leading a tremendous procession of deities, spirits, heroes, and heroines. His passing is signaled by storms featuring lightning, thunder, and powerful winds. It was recommended that people stay safely indoors because should they encounter you, these spirits possessed the power to force you to join them. (This may refer to fears of involuntary possession or because being caught celebrating the Wild Hunt left one vulnerable to accusations of witchcraft and maintaining now-forbidden traditions.)

In ancient Germany and Scandinavia, this Wild Hunt—Odin's Host of Spirits—rendezvoused with Dame Hulda's Host of Witches, especially during the Twelve Days of Yule.

> In Iceland, the twelve days of Christmas are known as Odin's Yule Host. Santa Claus flying through the air in his reindeer-driven sleigh may be interpreted as Odin riding solo.

The Wild Hunt may enforce justice: a Danish runestone (gravestone engraved with runic inscriptions) concludes with the warning *"a rati be he who destroys this stone."* The *rati* is a person whose soul is taken and driven by the Wild Hunt.

Under the influence of Christianity, the nature of the Hunt changed; it was no longer considered sufficient to merely avoid the Hunt for fear of being swept up, it was now sinful to even watch the Hunt as it passed. The Hunt was associated with witchcraft and evil. Human participants were believed to be witches punished by God for their diabolical, Pagan practices.

The Wild Hunt became associated with the punishments of Hell; the spirit who heads the hunt was literally a head-hunter, out searching for transgressors against Christianity who would be forced to join the Host for ever.

The Host of the Hunt consisted of those who somehow fell outside Church sacraments: unbaptized babies, illegitimate children, major sinners, those who died violent deaths and/or are deprived of funeral rites. Heathens, Jews, and witches were allegedly among those riding with the Hunt. Allegedly the traveling souls of shamans (double, fetch, dream-soul), if unable to return to their bodies, are fated to join the Wild Hunt.

There are two ways of interpreting this, depending upon personal perception. Either disobedience to the Church dooms you to this parade of the damned, or that those uninterested in Church sacraments revel in this sacred carnival.

The Wild Hunt is but one of many names for this procession of spirits. Others include:

* *Asgard's Chase*

* *Spirit's Ride*

* *Holla's Troop*

* *Cain's Hunt*

Among the leaders of the Hunt are Dame Goden, Diana, Freya, Harlequin/Herlichinus, Herne the Hunter, Herodias, Herta, Hulda, King Arthur, Odin/Wotan/Woden, Perchta, and St Lucy.

See also **CALENDAR:** Day of the Dead, Festivals of the Dead.

Witch-doctor: This term originally indicated a magical practitioner skilled at counteracting malevolent magic. *Doctor* is a title of respect given to magical practitioners in the African-American community and in those white communities strongly influenced by their practices.

Doctor is not only a title of respect but it indicates a healer, as curses and hexes are believed to manifest as physical illnesses in many traditions, impossible to cure by conventional medicine. Harmful substances are actually introduced into the target's body (either by magical or actual physical methods). The witch-doctor must remove these harmful substances and effect the cure.

Witch-doctor has become a term of disrespect and denigration toward shamans and traditional healers, however some modern magical practitioners (like author Draja Mickaharic) embrace the title. (See **HALL OF FAME:** Doctor Buzzard, Doctor Yah-Yah.)

Wizard: "Wizard" derives from the Middle English *wizard,* "one who is habitually or excessively wise," and may be understood to derive from similar Indo-European root sources as "witch," "wicca," "ved'ma," and other words for occult practitioners. It was first used in fifteenth-century Britain and continental Europe to indicate village sorcerers.

Wizard has largely become a literary term now; few describe themselves as "wizards" (although this may change with the advent of *Harry Potter*). It was, however, a common term in the sixteenth and seventeenth centuries and was applied to both male and female practitioners.

Worker: A euphemism for a practitioner of Hoodoo or other magical arts.

Xorguina: This Basque (Euskadi) word indicates witches, fortune-tellers, and other magical practitioners. The word is also used to designate fairies, although whether these fairies are intended to be understood as spiritual entities or as human women is subject to interpretation. The word is also spelled Jurgina.

Xorguinería: Basque (Euskadi) word translated as "witchcraft." Traditional xorguinería derives strongly from Women's Mysteries, particularly spinning. The xorguina spins her spells at night at the crossroads bathed in the moonlight. Many xorguinería practices appear to derive from rituals associated with the Basque witch-deity Mari. See **DIVINE WITCH:** Mari.

Yama-Oba, Yama-Uba: Her name signifies "old mountain woman"; this Japanese being is sometimes identified as a benevolent spirit, a demon, a witch, a cannibal-ogre, or all or some of the above. Mountains are extremely sacred and powerful in Shinto cosmology and thus divinity may lurk in the Yama-Oba's past. The name may also be a title similar to that of the great Eurasian goddess Kybele, "The Mountain Mother." Yama-Oba (there may be one or many of them) manifests as a woman with long disheveled hair. According to folklore, her hair transforms into snakes and back as desired. See also **DIVINE WITCH:** Kybele.

Yidoni: Hebrew euphemism for "witch"; literally means "knower."

Yogini: Technically this refers to a female yogi, a practitioner of yoga, however it is also used to refer to mysterious females (spirits or humans) who are able to affect change that is ultimately beneficial, although this is not always immediately apparent. Among the powers of the yogini is the capacity to transform others into animal forms.

Yogini can also refer to female masters of Tantra. The word is sometimes used as a synonym for "dakini," itself sometimes used as a synonym for "witch."

Zar: Zar names a sub-category of djinn, the ceremonies through which they communicate, and the tradition of interacting with these spirits.

Zar often first manifest themselves through involuntary possession of an individual or by stimulating illness and misfortune for that person. Misfortune and illness cannot be alleviated without *appeasing* the zar. This is significant: it is more typical for invasive spirits to be exorcised. The zar aren't going anywhere; they refuse to be exorcized. Forced exorcism inevitably causes worse harm than the effects of possession, and so a system of appeasement has developed.

Trance is induced, so that the zar can speak through the possessed person to a skilled zar specialist, such as a kodia or balazar, who is able to interpret their desires and work out a plan of action. Usually gifts, offerings or some sort of schedule of devotions is demanded in exchange for alleviation of symptoms. Following the ceremonial, the zar spirit does not depart but is now transformed into an ally. The person is still possessed in other words, but possession is transformed into a mutually beneficial relationship.

Zar spirits may be male or female but their targets are almost exclusively women. Many believe that the zar represents surviving vestiges of Pagan traditions. The ceremonials are reminiscent of those of Vodou or Santeria. Whether these traditions arose independently or share common roots is unknown. Zar involves trance, dancing, and drumming. Sacrifice is often incorporated—either animal sacrifice or botanical offerings.

Zar activity occurs predominately in Muslim communities. In many areas, zar is a controversial practice and religious authorities continue efforts to eliminate it. See also Kodia, Santeria, Vodou.

Zauberei: German synonym for "magic."

Znakhar/Znakharka (m/f): "One who knows." This Russian term indicates a magical practitioner, similar to English cunning folk. The znakharka is a folk healer whose specialties include distance healing, dream interpretations, Evil Eye removal, the location of lost or stolen property, and the identification of thieves. The znakharka may also be a midwife. See also Cunning Folk.

Zombi: A word deriving from Vodou terminology indicating people who *appear* to have died and so are buried. However, the semblance of death was really caused by a sorcerer who concocts complex poisons from various botanical, mineral, and animal sources.

The sorcerer and whoever paid him (in Haiti this type of magic usually features male practitioners although this may not be true elsewhere) is well aware that the person is not really dead. When the coast is clear, the "corpse" is dug up and an antidote administered. However the effects of the initial poison—and perhaps the trauma of burial—usually cause brain damage. That person will never be the same again; they have been transformed into a *zombi*, which is the correct Kreyol spelling and may be plural as well as singular.

In Haiti, zombi are inevitably forced to labor as agricultural slaves. The concept of the zombi exists in Africa as well as in Haiti, although the same word may not be used to name that concept. Based on funerary practices that ensure that the deceased is *really* dead (graveside vigils, stakes through the heart ...) the concept may have existed elsewhere, too.

United States' forces occupied Haiti from 1915 until 1934. Haiti, an independent black republic, evoked strong reactions from white Americans—this period corresponded to an era of intense racial segregation and discrimination in the States. Fear and disapproval was laced with fascination, and distorted aspects of Haitian culture were incorporated into American mass entertainment, and especially into horror movies. "Zombies" and "Voodoo-doctors" became popular staples of the genre, objects of horror with rarely any relationship to the original concept. The Hollywood spelling "zombie" refers to this distortion.

Ethno-botanist Wade Davis, a Harvard scientist, traveled to Haiti to research zombies, in the hope that this information could be used to improve methods of anesthesia. His adventures and findings, including a formula to create zombis, are recorded in his book *The Serpent and the Rainbow* (Simon & Schuster, 1985). The 1988 film adaptation is a horror-movie and does not substitute for the book.

The Divine Witch: Goddesses and Gods

How's this for a notion? Although witches have been diabolized and accused of being in league with Satan, throughout history witches have also been worshipped: divinity envisioned in the form of a witch, shaman or sorceress.

If one defines witches as stubborn devotees of forbidden spiritual traditions, then any deity belonging to those traditions could be associated with witchcraft. The reality is that many magical practitioners work with a multitude of spirits, different ones for different needs. In financial distress? Consult a spirit of prosperity. Need help getting pregnant? Find a fertility spirit (or saint or angel).

The list of potential spirits is endless, therefore included here are only the following:

✳ *Spirits whose identity as magical practitioners is central to their myth*

✳ *Spirits identified in witch-trial testimony as significant to witchcraft traditions*

Witch-goddesses (and a few gods, too!) do more than cackle and play trick or treat. Among our company are several Supreme Creators, a few first women in existence, and spirits who once had national cults and were venerated by the masses. (A few, like the orishas and India's Kali and Shiva, still are.)

All too often, very little information regarding these spirits exists. Sometimes little more than a name is known, thus some entries are more complete than others. This section is based on available information: we don't know the identity of Herta's sacred number, or even if she had one.

Many spirits are hazy: it's not always even clear whether they are distinct spirits or just different names for the same one. This is particularly true in Northern Europe—it is unclear whether Hella, Hulda, Herta, and Perchta are distinct spirits or whether they are one and the same. So much information has been lost or distorted that it may now be impossible to ever conclusively determine. Similarly, there is often confusion between Frigga and Freya, although in this case enough mythological information survives to determine that two distinct spirits exist.

Surviving information regarding Pagan spirits almost invariably derives from texts written by outsiders—most typically Church chroniclers who disapproved of Paganism in general. By definition, spirits in the form of deified magical practitioners were vilified, *especially* when simultaneously manifesting as sexually assertive females.

Thus in order to receive an unbiased picture one must read between a lot of lines and connect a lot of dots. (The sole exception is those spirits deriving from African Diaspora traditions: information regarding lwa and orishas deriving directly from devotees is available.)

Ironically, the Pagan deities we know the most about are those the Church particularly despised: Freya, Hecate, Holle, and Kybele. Because they evoked such passions they were written about frequently. Although they were condemned and vilified, the ultimate effect is that these spirits survive with greater clarity than do so many others.

During the witch-trial era, certain deities were labeled Queens of Witches by the Inquisition: the implication being that if the deity was the Queen, her devotees were, by definition, "witches" and thus subject to prosecution. Among these Queens of Witches are Diana, Freya, Herodias, Herta, and Hulda.

Are there countless individual, independent, autonomous spirits or are these spirits all aspects of the greater divine? Are all goddesses manifestations of one Great Goddess? This is an ancient debate subject to personal interpretation. All spirits are discussed as if they are individuals here: further conjecture is up to you.

Magic, spirituality, and witchcraft are unruly, fluid, boundary-defying topics: spirits can be difficult to categorize neatly.

❋ *Spirits generally considered to be exclusively spiritual entities are included here.*

❋ *Spirits generally considered to have begun their incarnations as humans are found in* **HALL OF FAME**, *even though they may have since proved immortal.*

Thus Morgan le Fay is categorized here among Divine Witches, while her old compatriot Merlin is found in **HALL OF FAME**. *This is somewhat arbitrary: Circe is clearly a goddess and so is found here; her niece Medea is generally (but not always) considered human and so is in* **HALL OF FAME** *instead.*

❋ *Corn Mothers are found in* **ERGOT**.

❋ *Deities exclusively identified as hags are found in* **HAG**.

❋ *Deities exclusively identified as horned spirits are found in* **HORNED ONE**.

❋ *Deities strongly associated with spinning are found in* **WOMEN'S MYSTERIES**.

Abondia

Also known as Dame Abundance, Dame Habonde, Habondia.

Abundantia was the ancient Roman spirit of abundance. When Christianity became Rome's official religion, Abundantia was outlawed with other Pagan spirits. Some devotees were ambivalent about banishing prosperity and so Abundantia went underground, eventually re-emerging in medieval Europe as Dame Abundance.

During the Middle Ages, she was worshipped only in secret and, finally, only by witches. (By definition, if you worshipped her, you were a witch.) The Inquisition accused Dame Abundance, a night-rider, of leading the Wild Hunt and witches' nocturnal jaunts. According to the testimony of accused witches, Dame Abundance visits the homes of her devotees at night, bringing good luck and prosperity with her.

The Inquisition described Abondia as a Witch Queen. Some Italian women charged with witchcraft during the Burning Times acknowledged venerating Abondia, calling her a Fairy Queen. She entered English folklore in the same capacity. Abondia was described as a beautiful young woman with dark braided her, crowned with a golden tiara on which there was a star.

Angerboda

Also known as Gulveig and Heid.

"East of Midgard, in the Iron Forest, sat the old witch …" (*The Voluspa*: 40-41).

According to Norse mythology, Loki the Trickster fathered three dangerous children:

✷ *The Fenris Wolf, also known as Odin's Bane, destined to slay Odin*

✷ *Jormungard, the Midgard Serpent, fated to slay Thor*

✷ *Hella, Ruler of the Dead, destined to lead an uprising of rebellious spirits and ghosts*

Loki's three children will allegedly be responsible for the apocalyptic twilight of the gods. Ever wondered who their mother was?

Angerboda, Witch of the Iron Wood, Mother of Wolves.

Angerboda manifests as a witch so beautiful she shines, as an iron-gray hag, as a fertility spirit, and as the Mother of Destruction. It is not clear which, if any, of her names is her true one. Angerboda is generally believed to be but one name for the spirit also known as Gulveig. Angerboda and Gulveig feature in myths that, if strung together, form a cohesive narrative.

Among the central themes of Norse mythology is the confrontation and eventual semi-merger of two pantheons of spirits, the Aesir and Vanir. Norse mythology is generally told from the perspective of the Aesir or, perhaps more accurately, from the perspective of later Christian chroniclers who identified more closely with the Aesir. Surviving Norse myths, originally part of a vast oral tradition, were written down in the thirteenth century by Christian monks. The monks preserved these ancient sagas but also edited and transformed them in the process.

The Vanir are the indigenous pantheon of spirits. "Aesir" is believed cognate with "Asia"; many scholars believe that they may have originated in what is now Turkey. Important Aesir spirits include Odin and Thor. The Aesir were more aggressive than the Vanir, with a patriarchal orientation, and they were comparatively technologically advanced. Far less is known about the Vanir: theirs was a magical fertility orientation; they seemed to offer women more power. Important Vanir deities include Freya and Freyr.

Angerboda's name is related to "foreboding" or "premonition of harm." She may be a giantess, a troll-queen, a witch, a member of the Vanir pantheon, or some or all of the above. She is a shape-shifter, which may account for some of this confusion. Angerboda may be a spirit of fertility and/or Freya's personal messenger: when a childless king and queen petition Freya for assistance, she sends Angerboda to them in the form of a crow, bearing an apple of fertility. The queen quickly conceives and bears a healthy child.

The Vanir are not confrontational; when the Aesir arrive in their territory, they initially observe them from a distance. The Aesir construct halls, including Valhalla, from such massive quantities of gold that they shimmer and shine. The Vanir lack halls but live in a misty realm woven from magic spells. The gold awakened a longing and so they sent Angerboda, in her guise as *"the witch Gulveig,"* to see if she could get some. Gulveig means "power of gold." She is identified as a beautiful witch and also known as Heid, the "shining" or "gleaming" one. Like Freya, she glistens like gold.

Gulveig addresses the Aesir and speaks passionately of gold, gold, and more gold: red gold, white gold, yellow gold, burning gold, shining gold, gleaming gold, gold that reflects the heart's desires. She requests a gift of gold for the Vanir.

The response? The Aesir identify Gulveig as a witch and condemn her to death. Thor seizes and binds her. A pyre is raised in Valhalla; Gulveig/Angerboda is pierced with spears like a pig on a spit and held over the flames to burn as a punishment for witchcraft.

With her witch's power, Gulveig walks unscathed from the fire. (Norse deities, notably, are *not* immortal: she was expected to die.) She burns, her ashes are scattered, and yet miraculously she reappears, good as new. The Aesir recapture her and repeat their actions. Angerboda/Gulveig is burned and resurrected three times.

The obvious question is why, if her witchcraft is so powerful, doesn't it protect her from the Aesir? No explanation is offered. The story itself is somewhat hazy; it's unclear *exactly* what sparked the rage of the Aesir. The story may have been tweaked by later chroniclers to justify witch-burning. There are two ways of understanding Gulveig/Angerboda's threefold resurrection, depending on perspective: evil is eternal or magic never dies.

The final time she's burned, her heart remains unconsumed by the flames and Loki swallows it. This heart is blamed for his increasingly bitter, mean-spirited, and dangerous nature. (It's unclear exactly when Loki's liaison with Angerboda occurs or precisely when their children were born. Angerboda, like Loki, may be a *Jotun* or giant.)

Christian commentators blamed Angerboda for fostering Loki's ambition to be chief of the gods, supplanting his blood-brother Odin. Eventually Loki became identified with Satan, and Angerboda as an ugly, wicked witch.

The third time Angerboda was resurrected, she found herself back in the Iron Wood (*Iarnvid*), the deep forest at the world's end, home of witches and wolves. She never re-enters Asgard (the Aesir's realm) because the Aesir still long to destroy her. Instead, Angerboda returns to the Vanir empty-handed. Appalled at her treatment, they declare war on the Aesir and attack via magic spells, precipitating a brutal war between the pantheons.

In some versions, this war results in stalemate; in others, the Vanir conquer the Aesir and occupy Asgard for nine years, but when both are threatened by Frost Giants they must forge an alliance. Each side gives hostages to the other to ensure preservation of peace and an end to hostilities. Honir and Mimir go to live among the Vanir while Njord and his children Freyr and Freya join the Aesir.

Encyclopedia of Witchcraft

Although physically unscathed, Angerboda did *not* forgive the Aesir for her treatment. She raised her children in the Iron Wood and taught them to resent the Aesir.

An uneasy Odin consulted a völva (prophetess) who revealed that these children would be ultimately responsible for the destruction of Asgard. This foretold destiny is the rationale for the brutal entrapment of all three although perhaps some of the anxiety toward the mother was transferred to her children.

See also Freya, Hella, Herta, Odin; **ANIMALS:** Corvids, Wolves and Werewolves; **BOTANICALS:** Apples; **DICTIONARY:** Aesir, Heid, Trollkvinna, Vanir, Völva; **FAIRIES:** Nature-spirit Fairies: Trolls.

Angitia

The Marsi, an ancient Central Italian tribe, claimed descent from Circe's son. Their chief deity was his daughter, Angitia, a snake-charming sorceress who learned her craft directly from her grandmother. The Marsi themselves were renowned as magicians and healers. The Romans considered their territory "the home of witchcraft."

Very little concrete information survives regarding Angitia: a sacred grove was dedicated to her on the shores of Lake Fucinus, as was a temple where the arts of herbalism and snake charming were practiced and taught. Earliest recovered regional inscriptions include votive offerings to Angitia recovered from the lake.

The Marsi made an alliance with the Romans in 304 BCE but revolted two years later. The Romans ultimately reasserted their authority; the Marsi lost political autonomy and were absorbed into the Roman Empire. However, they retained their magical reputation. As late

as the second-century CE their presence as fortune-tellers plying their trade on the streets of Rome was noted. The Marsians were also reputedly magical healers, with power over bites of venomous snakes and rabid dogs.

Some believe that when Medea fled from Jason and Greece, she went to Italy and became Angitia. See **HALL OF FAME:** Medea.

Angitia's power was not forgotten post-Christianity but was transferred to San Domenico (951–1031). Much of what is known regarding Angitia is derived from rituals re-dedicated to San Domenico, especially the *Festa dei Serpari* (The Procession of the Snake Catchers or Snake Charmers) in Cocullo, Italy. The earliest historical evidence of this festival dates from 1392. By the sixteenth century, the festival was held on the first Thursday in May, as it is today.

Snake catchers (*serpari*) begin capturing local snakes during the Vernal Equinox. A standard Mass is held within the Church on the day of the festival but afterwards a votive image of San Domenico is brought outside so that snake charmers can cover it with live snakes.

The *serpari*, carrying the serpent-covered statue, lead a processional through Angitia's old stomping grounds. Roman Catholic priests provide an escort while costumed young women carry snake-shaped cakes. Live snakes are draped around other *serpari* as well as those wishing to demonstrate their devotion to the saint.

See also Circe; **ANIMALS:** Snakes; **CREATIVE ARTS:** Dance: Processions and Snake Dances; **DICTIONARY:** Ciaraulo.

Aradia

In the beginning was Diana, primordial Spirit of Darkness. She divided the world into complementary opposites: yin and yang, male and female, light and darkness.

The light half evolved into her brother Lucifer. Diana desired him and wished to unite and merge with him. Lucifer, on the other hand, wanted light to remain completely distinct from darkness. Proud Lucifer refused to merge. Diana pursued him but he resisted.

Eventually she learned that he had a favorite cat that slept with him. Diana persuaded the cat to switch places with her and so, in the form of a black cat, Diana seduced her brother Lucifer. From this union, the world's first witch was conceived: Aradia, Messiah of the Witches.

Diana sent her daughter to Earth with the mission of teaching humans witchcraft, the sacred arts of Diana, Queen of Witches.

That's the first coming of Aradia the Messiah and the history of the world, according to *Aradia or The Gospel of the Witches* anyway. Aradia returned for a second coming too.

This Aradia was born in Volterra, Italy on August 13, 1313 (August 13th being Diana's sacred day) and stimulated a revival of Italian witchcraft and pre-Christian traditions that had been driven into hiding by the Church. She herself had learned the Old Ways from her family and proceeded to teach them to others. Aradia was eventually caught by the Inquisition and burned as a witch, but not before she left a manuscript that allegedly serves as the framework for the testament *Aradia*.

No documentation regarding either Aradia exists prior to C.G. Leland's 1899 publication of *Aradia or The Gospel of the Witches*; however in 1508, Italian Inquisitor Bernardo Rategno noted in his *Tractatus de Strigibus* that a rapid expansion of witchcraft had occurred a hundred and fifty years earlier, which corresponds with the second coming.

The story of Diana as Creator of the World, Mother of Witchcraft corresponds with nothing from classical mythology, although that in itself does not prove anything; many myths—and deities—survive based on only a single source (much of Celtic and Norse mythology, for instance). This could be but another instance of a lone survival of an ancient myth, but it could also be a Christian tale intended to portray Diana and witches in a negative light.

Classical mythology suggests that if one identifies Diana with Artemis, then her brother is Apollo, a god of light. The name Lucifer ("light-bringer") pre-dates Christianity and was a title given to various Roman deities, female as well as male, and was intended as benevolent, not malefic. However during the medieval period when *Aradia* was allegedly written, Lucifer had become exclusively identified with Satan, the proud handsome fallen angel. Simultaneously, Inquisitors branded Diana the bride of Lucifer in order to damn and defame her and her devotees.

Thus this legend may be interpreted in various ways. However, no matter how it is interpreted, it is never *entirely* complimentary. Diana engages in deception, the inference that witches are daughters of Satan …

The name Aradia clearly resembles that of Herodias, another witch-deity of importance in Italy, and perhaps they are one and the same.

❋ *Is the fourteenth-century Italian witch a distortion of the biblical legend of Herodias?*

❋ *Was an actual woman named in Herodias' honor?*

❋ *Was the legend of the biblical Herodias superimposed on a Pagan Italian spirit?*

For his part, Leland believed that his Aradia was really based on a distortion of Lilith as the true first woman, rather than on the Herodias of the New Testament. Italian Jews do identify Lilith with black cats.

See also Artemis, Diana, Herodias, Lilith, Nox; **ANIMALS:** Cats; **BOOKS:** Grimoires: *Aradia or the Gospel of the Witches.*

Artemis

Artemis is among the most ancient indigenous spirits of Greece. Her earliest incarnation seems to have been as a bear-spirit, perhaps deriving from traditions dating back to the second millennium BCE that involved devotion to a deity in the form of a nursing mother bear.

In the *Iliad*, Artemis is called *"Mistress of the Animals"* and may be traced back to the Minoan era in this capacity. By the classical era, she was absorbed into the Olympian pantheon as the spirit most associated with witchcraft, lunar magic, and women's mysteries.

According to her Olympian myth, Artemis was born on the island of Delos, the daughter of Leto and Zeus. Her very first act upon drawing breath was to assist Leto in the long, difficult delivery of her twin brother, Apollo, spirit of the sun and masculinity to her spirit of the moon and femininity.

Zeus offers to grant Artemis her deepest wish: she requests never to be forced to marry. This may be understood as a demand to maintain female autonomy and independence.

Artemis is Mistress of the Hunt: she protects the wilderness from excessive human encroachment and regulates sacred hunting rituals. She influences and grants fertility to humans, animals, and plants. Through her association with the moon she regulates menstrual cycles.

Artemis is a magician and a shape-shifter who takes many forms. Her most common is as a youthful female athlete, usually accompanied by a stag and/or a pack of hunting hounds, but she also manifests as a doe or female bear.

> Artemis' colors are white and silver. Her metal is silver, too. Her planet is the moon; her earthly domain the forest but she is also associated with natural springs. She is the Lady of the Beasts: all wild animals are sacred to her but especially bees, bears, boars, deer, dogs, dolphins, goats, fish, wolves, and all kinds of cats. Her chariot is drawn by stags.

The moon was perceived as Artemis' spinning wheel, upon which she spun the fate of human beings; spindle whorls, shuttles, and assorted weaving tools have been found in nearly all her shrines (see **WOMEN'S MYSTERIES:** Spinning).

Although Artemis is often described as a solitary spirit, she is often found in the company of others. In addition to her animal companions, she has a band of nymphs to serve and accompany her. Among the spirits, her cousin Hecate is her favorite companion.

Artemis is closely identified with Diana and is also sometimes considered part of a trinity of goddesses:

✳ *Artemis, Hecate, and Selene represent three aspects of the moon*

✳ *Artemis, Persephone, and Hecate represent three realms: the living, the dead, and the spirits*

The most prominent manifestation of Artemis two thousand years ago was not, however, that classical woodland goddess.

The Many-Breasted Artemis of Ephesus

Or is that the Many-Breasted Diana of Ephesus? Either way, the image of Artemis (or Diana) celebrated for centuries in this ancient city, doesn't correspond to the classical image of those deities still so recognizable and familiar: youthful, "virginal" athletes and hunters.

During the Hellenistic period, when Greek was the lingua franca of the Mediterranean world, the deity worshipped in Ephesus was commonly called "Artemis"—or at least in surviving writings. As Rome became the dominant power, this deity was familiarly called "Diana." Significantly, both those deities, whether they are one and the same or not, lingered on the outskirts of official state pantheons—both stubborn reminders of an ancient matrilineal fertility orientation.

Frankly, the famous votive image venerated in Ephesus corresponds more closely to the great Near Eastern Mother Goddesses. This may indicate something about the hidden history of Artemis/Diana, or it is also possible that another deity (Kybele, Asherah or unknown) lurks beneath the Greco-Roman names.

This isn't obscure history: the Temple of Artemis/Diana in Ephesus, now in modern Turkey, was among the Seven Wonders of the Ancient World. Although the temple was destroyed (as was the original votive statue), the Shrine of Artemis was a major tourist and pilgrimage site: vendors sold reproductions of the statue in the same manner that modern visitors to any monument favored by tourists will find countless vendors selling countless souvenir replicas.

Reproductions of the statue of Many-Breasted Artemis survive so we know that it depicted a beautiful, regal, crowned woman, her torso completely covered by multiple breasts indicating her capacity to nurture and provide for all, her long tight skirt containing bands of animals and birds in relief.

The shrine was ancient and was destroyed and rebuilt several times. The deity herself chose the site by falling there in the form of a meteorite, which landed upon a date palm, and the shrine's single most sacred object was a meteor contained within her crown, believed to house the very essence of the deity.

Historical records indicate that the earliest temple was built in the eighth century BCE as a simple tree shrine, allegedly by Amazons, passionate devotees of the goddess. The deity was originally not depicted as a woman but in the form of that original date palm hit by the meteorite.

That first simple tree shrine was destroyed by Cimmerians in 650 BCE. The Amazons lost control of the shrine but it survived and the temple was continually rebuilt:

✳ *A temple shrine was built in 580 BCE but sacked, rebuilt, and then sacked again.*

✳ *A fourth temple, crafted from priceless white marble, was sponsored by King Croesus of Lydia.*

✳ *In October 356 BCE, a man wishing to immortalize his name by committing a crime so tremendous it could never be forgotten, set the temple's wooden precincts aflame, causing its destruction.*

An indignant population joined together to rebuild the shrine, and *this* temple is the one that was called the greatest of the Seven Wonders.

The lintel was so huge that the architect Dinocrates despaired of ever adjusting it correctly; he was on the verge of suicide when Artemis appeared to him in a dream and assured him that the lintel was now perfectly in place, she had taken care of it. When he awoke, it was.

Ephesus was a great city, its economy based on the Temple of Artemis/Diana. Small figurine renditions of Many-Breasted Diana of Ephesus were sold to *thousands* of annual pilgrims, as documented in the New Testament (Acts 19). Many reproductions are adorned with a necklace of a scorpion-like creature with a half moon or horns pointing down.

St Paul's criticism of Diana led to rioting and his expulsion from Ephesus. As Christianity gained influence, his expulsion would be revenged:

* ✱ *The statue was destroyed in 400 CE by a Christian zealot who boasted of having overthrown the image of* "Demon Artemis."

* ✱ *In 406 St John Chrysostom preached against the Temple of Artemis at Ephesus. It was looted and burned soon afterwards.*

* ✱ *A fifth-century inscription mentions the replacement of a statue of Artemis with a cross.*

See also Aradia, Diana, Hecate, Kybele; **BOTANICALS:** Mugwort, Saint John's wort, Trees.

Baba Yaga

Baba Yaga, the cannibal "wicked witch" of Russian fairy tales, has become a boogie-woman used to threaten children into obedience: *"be good or Baba Yaga will get you …"* She epitomizes the scary witch but is also grand, transcending the stereotype. Baba Yaga doesn't just eat children; she sometimes defends them by dispensing justice to evil stepmothers.

Baba Yaga features in many fairy tales; she has a striking personality and appearance. Once familiar, she's not easily confused with anyone else. It is generally believed that beneath the fairy-tale witch lurks an ancient Slavic deity, perhaps a Corn Mother banished to the woods post-Christianity.

She is an underworld goddess who controls forces of life and death. Baba Yaga may be petitioned for fertility for those who lack it. She performs miracle cures. On the other hand, according to fairy tales, personal encounters with Baba Yaga are often fatal; whether this was meant literally or shamanically is unknown. Either way she is potentially very dangerous.

Baba Yaga forces one to acknowledge the complexity and ambiguity of the witch. She possesses powers of healing and destruction; she may be unspeakably hostile or amazingly generous. She allegedly knows every botanical healing secret in existence; whether she can be persuaded to reveal these secrets is another story.

She is the Mistress of All Witches, the Primal Mother who rescues, nurtures, *and* destroys. She is a sacred being but she doesn't live in the Heavens, underground or in an underwater palace. Baba Yaga lives in a house like a human and demonstrates needs and desires like a human: she eats, sleeps, and drinks—and with gusto!

Baba Yaga lives in the heart of a deep, birch forest in a little hut named Izbushka that usually stands on stilt-like chicken's feet but occasionally on goat's legs or even on spindle heels. Baba Yaga's hut obeys orders. Say *"Izbushka, Izbushka! Stand with your back to the forest and your front to me"* and it does as directed.

The house is formed from bones, personally collected by Baba Yaga herself. The doorposts are leg bones; a mouth with sharp teeth serves as the lock, the bolt is a hand. The fence is formed from bones crowned with skulls whose empty eye-sockets glow in the dark.

In alternative versions, Baba Yaga is a spinner. Her house stands on a spiraling spindle spinning thread from human bones and entrails. Sometimes three Babas exist, similar to the three Fates.

The house is dominated by an oven that symbolizes birth, fertility, creation, nourishment, and death. It is akin to a cauldron of regeneration, and Baba Yaga stories may be understood as tales of initiation, sometimes (but not always) successful.

She is also called *"Baba Yaga Bony Leg"* which rhymes in Russian and has a resonance that's lacking in English translation. Her unusual leg indicates her shamanic connection. In some stories the leg is formed from clay, gold, iron or steel. Sometimes her leg is an iron pestle. (In other versions, she is a woman from the waist up, a snake from the waist down.)

Baba Yaga has iron teeth that protrude like boar's tusks. Her hands are tipped with bear claws. She wears a necklace of human skulls and likes to smoke a pipe. Euphemisms for her include *"Iron Nosed Woman"* or *"Iron Nosed Witch."* She flies through the air in a mortar, steers with a pestle, sweeping away her traces with a broom. Seated in her iron mortar, holding her iron pestle, she grinds out life and death like a Corn Mother. Stories of her cannibalism may be references to ancient blood sacrifices.

Baba Yaga is the protector of wild animals, who serve her. Her flights are accompanied by crows, ravens, and owls: these birds signal her dominion over day and night. They are not normally compatible: crows and ravens are intensely diurnal while owls are identified with night.

Baba in Old Russian may indicate "witch," "fortune-teller" or "elderly woman." It may be used affectionately or pejoratively (see **DICTIONARY**: Baba). Yaga may derive from Slavic words for "horror," "shudder," "illness," "snake," "wood nymph" or "witch." Yaga is also sometimes used as a pejorative to indicate an old, argumentative and/or ugly woman.

Baba Yaga is invoked in this Russian love spell. Murmur the following charm:

In the ancient realm, there is an open field
In the open field, there is a wizened oak
Around the wizened oak dance thrice-nine maidens
From beneath the wizened oak emerges Baba Yaga
She lights thrice-nine oak-wood fires
Burn for me [Name of spell's target] as fierce, hot and pure as Baba Yaga's thrice-nine fires!

According to one interpretation, Baba Yaga is the moon. She cannibalistically eats her own body and then regenerates, waning and waxing as she regulates the fertility of women, animals, and Earth. Her hut turns on its chicken's feet in rhythm with the moon's phases. When the Moon is full, her door is open and the hut is accessible to the living. Baba is fat, happy, and pregnant. When only the crescent moon is visible watch out! Baba's womb and belly are empty and she's hungry … Baba Yaga also has dominion over the sun.

In some legends she is completely solitary, but in others she is a midwife spirit who is the mother of three sons or three dragons. Sometimes there is one Baba, sometimes there are three: three sisters or one mother and two daughters. Sometimes she is married to an eagle who maintains flocks of goats. In other tales she is allied or even married to another beloved villain of Russian folklore—the powerful sorcerer Koschei the Deathless.

Baba Yaga was a popular character in seventeenth- and early eighteenth-century Russian woodblock prints, where she was often depicted in Finnish national costume. This is believed to be an oblique reference to her shamanic connections and at that time was intended as an insult.

See **ANIMALS:** Chickens, Corvids, Owls, Pigs, Snakes; **BOTANICALS:** Birch; **CREATIVE ARTS:** Dance: Step of Wu; **ERGOT:** Corn Mother; **TOOLS:** Brooms, Mortar and Pestle.

Befana la Strega (Befana the Witch) / Befana la Vecchia (Befana the Aged)

Also known as Befania.

Befana is a benevolent Italian witch who brings gifts to children on the night of January 6th, the Feast of the Magi: she fills children's stockings with gifts just like Santa Claus elsewhere in the world. This tradition is believed to derive from the Pagan practice of leaving woven goods, such as stockings, for the Goddess of Fate on this date.

The name *Befana* is believed to derive from Epiphany. Befana manifests as an old lady who flies through the air on a broom or goat. She carries a heavy sack on her back filled with gifts, or is a hunchback. She is believed to have originally been an ancient deity of ancestral spirits, forests, and the passage of time.

Befana is invoked in many Italian spells, especially those for good fortune.

According to Christian legend, when the Magi were searching for the Christ Child, they encountered an old lady and invited her to join them. She declined because she was too busy cleaning but later had regrets. She attempted to catch them up but became hopelessly and eternally lost. Still in the process of searching, on encountering homes with children, she leaves treats for good ones and tricks, like coal and rocks, for the disobedient.

Different regions of Italy celebrate Befana in different ways:

❋ *The most prevalent method of celebrating Befana throughout Italy involves creating a wooden effigy of the witch holding her distaff and spindle, which is then filled with sweets. The figure is broken open like a piñata to disperse the treats and is eventually burned on a pyre. This may be intended to resemble the Yule Log, although obviously any reference to bashing and burning witches is easily interpreted otherwise.*

❋ *In Tuscany, images of Befana are carried in street processionals.*

❋ *In Rome, people assemble to make a noise in her honor with drums, tin horns, and tambourines.*

❋ *In other areas, rag-doll Befanas are placed in windows.*

See also Mana; **ANIMALS:** Goats; **DICTIONARY:** Magi; **TOOLS:** Brooms.

Cerridwen

Cerridwen is a shape-shifting lunar deity, master magician, and herbalist. Described as the *"Old One,"* she can take *any* form but favors that of a woman or a great white sow. She is described as a witch and Keeper of the Cauldron of Knowledge, Inspiration, and Transformation. Cerridwen's most famous myth is preserved in the *Book of Taliesin*, a thirteenth-century manuscript named for the sixth century Welsh poet.

In this myth, Cerridwen is married to a giant, Tegidfoel, by whom she has two children—a daughter Crearwy, whose name means "Beautiful" or "Light," and a son Afagddu, whose name means "Ugly" or "Dark." Her children may represent the complementary forces that fuel Creation: yin and yang, female and male, night and day, summer and winter.

Cerridwen wishes the best for her children. She doesn't worry about her daughter but fears that her son lacks sufficient gifts for success, and she decides to brew a potion for him to compensate.

Once tasted, this potion bestows *all* knowledge, magic power, oracular and shamanic powers. Only Cerridwen knows the formula: it takes a tremendous variety of botanicals, which must be carefully gathered and then added at just the right moment. In addition, someone must continually stir the brew, which must be kept steadily boiling for a year and a day. Cerridwen finds a poor, ignorant child to watch the pot.

Gwion is an orphan, completely unloved: no one misses him. Cerridwen, a wonderful mother to her own children, abuses the boy, barely feeding him, forcing as much labor out of him as possible, sometimes beating him. Gwion doesn't understand the contents of the cauldron or its purpose.

The year and a day just about complete, Gwion gets careless (or is blessed by his constant proximity to Cerridwen's cauldron). A few drops of scalding liquid fall on his hand. In pain he sucks his finger. At that very moment, from those few drops, Gwion knows *all*: he is instantly transformed into a master shaman, shape-shifter, and seer. He understands everything and *knows* that Cerridwen is on her way to kill him.

He escapes by shape-shifting. She pursues him similarly. If he becomes a fish, she becomes a bigger one, if he becomes a bird, she becomes a raptor, and so on, until finally Gwion transforms into a grain of wheat, hiding in a bushel. Cerridwen transforms into a hen and eats him. He gestates in her belly (Cerridwen *is* the Cauldron of Generation) and is re-born as a beautiful, shining child, still in possession of the magical powers attained.

Circe

Circe's very name is synonymous with "sorceress." Daughter of the Sun and an ocean spirit, Circe's most famous appearance is in Homer's *Odyssey*.

According to Homer, Circe dwells in a marble *palazzo* on the Isle of Aiaia (also spelled Aeaea), where she was banished after poisoning her husband, the King of the Sarmatians. (She does travel, though: according to other reports, she lives in Lazio, a region of west-central Italy.)

Circe is a witch but she is also clearly divine: Homer calls her *"the fair-haired goddess."* Circe spends her days singing and weaving, habits associated with the Fates. (See **WOMEN'S MYSTERIES:** Spinning.) Her name derives from the same root words as "circle" and "falcon" (falcons notably circle in the sky). Circe's name also resembles *kerkis*, which means "weaver's shuttle."

Circe is a shape-shifter but is most famous for transforming others. When Odysseus and his crew, trying to return home from the Trojan War, land on Aiaia, they discover an island paradise ruled by the goddess and populated by her beautiful female handmaidens, as well as by strangely human-seeming wild animals.

Circe transforms her male visitors into animals—lions, baboons, and others, but mainly pigs. One might say that the pig is the sacred animal of the goddess. One might also say that Circe reveals the true animal identity hidden within each man. Odysseus alone is saved from this fate when Hermes warns him, offering him an herbal antidote to Circe's magic—a mysterious plant called moly. Hermes also advises Odysseus not to reject Circe's advances: ultimately he stays with her for years, fathering her son Telegonus.

Circe initiates Odysseus into shamanism, advising him how to journey to Hades, interview dead souls, and return. She is his primary tutor. Foretelling the future, she offers Odysseus invaluable advice, ultimately enabling him to return home. It is safe to say that without Circe, Odysseus would never have reached his home again.

Circe inspired what is historically considered the first ballet, in 1581. Catherine de Medici, mother of the French king and an alleged sorceress herself, sponsored a dance company, *La Ballet Comique de la Reine*, whose first production was an over six-hour-long extravaganza featuring dance, songs, and elaborate floats devoted to the saga of Circe.

Although there are relatively few myths involving Circe, she captured the heart of artists from the classical era until today. She is a frequent character in literature, movies, and comic books, as well as perhaps the most popular witch among fine artists. During the nineteenth century in particular, many artists painted portraits of Circe.

Plants associated with Circe include alder, enchanter's nightshade, juniper and mandrake. Entries for all these are found in **BOTANICALS**. See also Angitia, Hermes; **ANIMALS:** Pigs; **CREATIVE ARTS:** Visual Arts: Nineteenth-century Paintings; **HALL OF FAME:** Medea.

Dahut

Breton witch-princess-mermaid-goddess, only one tale about Dahut survives and it derives from Christian sources. The story is hazy and has many gaps.

Dahut was the daughter of Gradlon, King of Cornwall and a Druid. Her mother is Malgven, Queen of the North, a magical character, perhaps another witch-goddess. Her father and mother spend a year at sea, where Dahut is born, but her mother dies.

Dahut loves the sea and is inspired to build a miraculous crystal-walled city in Brittany named Ys, built below sea level so that it seems to emerge from the sea. To prevent flooding, a high dyke is built and locked with a unique brass key. Only one copy of this key exists and King Gradlon has it.

The legend implies that Dahut is a sea spirit or a priestess of the sea. It is not a particularly complimentary tale: Dahut is portrayed as a *femme fatale* who seduces a different man each night. According to the story, Dahut insists her lovers wear a black silk mask that transforms into deadly metal claws in the morning, killing him so that she can feed his body to the sea.

Ys was fabulously wealthy. Dahut had a sea dragon who did her bidding and brought the treasures of the sea to her. Dahut ruled the city, maintaining Celtic traditions and Pagan deities. Eventually, she had a confrontation with Corentin, Bishop of Quimper, and shortly afterwards disaster struck.

Dahut was always on the lookout for new lovers/sacrificial victims. One day a stranger dressed in red rode up to the palace; she fell madly in love with him and wished to keep him, rather than kill him. Unbeknownst to her, according to the standard version of the story, it was Satan on a mission of punishment from God. Because of the sins of Ys, the magical crystal city was about to be transformed into the equivalent of an underwater Sodom and Gomorrah.

In order to prove her love, the mysterious red stranger demanded the key to the dyke. Dahut stole it from her father and Satan opens the dyke and the sea floods in. St Guenolé, a resident of the area, appears, ordering King Gradlon to repent. Gradlon tries to escape from Ys on horseback, together with Dahut whom he wishes to rescue. Guenolé however strikes him, insisting that he abandons Dahut as the price of survival, which ultimately Gradlon does. Gradlon and Guenolé are the only two survivors.

Following the deluge, Gradlon renounces Druidry and Guenolé converts him to Christianity. Gradlon became ruler of the city of Quimper where a statue of him gazing in the direction of Ys still stands at Corentin Cathedral.

Dahut was allegedly transformed into a mermaid, in which guise she survives.

Although the story was told to emphasize the powers of St Guenolé, it may be based on an actual fifth-century disaster. Several Roman roads now leading into the sea, allegedly once led to Ys.

Dahut's tale is (unsympathetically) retold in Abraham Merritt's 1934 pulp novel *Creep, Shadow, Creep*.

See **CREATIVE ARTS:** Literature: *Creep, Shadow, Creep*; **DICTIONARY:** Druid; **FAIRIES:** Nature-spirit Fairies: Korrigans.

Diana

No spirit is more associated with witchcraft than Diana, Mother of the Forest. Indigenous to Italy, preceding the Romans in the region, perhaps an Etruscan spirit, she traveled with the Romans throughout Europe and became well known all over that once heavily wooded continent.

Over the centuries Diana became intensely identified with the Greek goddess Artemis; their names are often used interchangeably and it can be difficult to distinguish between the two, although they apparently began their incarnations as distinct spirits.

Diana was adored throughout Europe. Other versions of her name include:

✴ *Jana, Tana (Italian)*

✴ *Debena, Devana (Czech)*

✴ *Diiwica (Serbian)*

✴ *Dziewona (Polish)*

Diana has the same attributes and interests as Artemis although Diana's associations with night, darkness, and magic are stronger. She is less ambivalent toward men and sex than Artemis too—her myth makes no pretense of virginity. Diana lives in the Forest of Nemi together with her consort Virbius, a male horned spirit.

Sir James Frazer's epic *The Golden Bough* took its title and initial inspiration from rituals conducted in Diana's sacred Forest of Nemi.

Diana also had a Roman temple on the Aventine Hill. In Celtic Europe she was worshipped in the form of a log. Men worshipped Diana as passionately as women: what are described as werewolves may really be male wolf-shamans or lunar priests dedicated to Diana.

Most surviving information regarding her worship and influence comes from her enemies—Paul of Tarsus and other early Christian writers. Although originally a local deity, Diana's cult became so popular throughout Europe and Asia Minor that the early Christians perceived it as among their major rivals.

Was the subsequent destruction of Europe's forests and wildlife, especially wolves, a method of eradicating Diana's power and spiritual traditions?

When Christianity achieved political power, Diana was completely vilified. Associated solely with witchcraft—her name evoked during Europe's witch-hunts as Queen of the Witches—the Inquisition described her as Satan's bride. In 1487, Spanish Inquisitor Tomás de Torquemada stated: "*Diana is the devil.*"

Diana's devotees were particularly persistent:

✴ *Gregory of Tours describes a sixth-century Christian hermit destroying a statue of Diana that had been worshipped by peasants near Trier.*

✴ *Diana's cult was vigorous until at least as late as the late seventh century in what is now Franconia (northern Bavaria).*

✴ *British missionary St Kilian (c.640–c.689) was martyred when he tried to convert the Eastern Franks from their devotion to Diana.*

✴ *In 906, Regino of Prüm noted the worship of Diana in what he called "The Society of Diana."*

"*The Society of Diana*" was among the Inquisition's terms for witchcraft. No deity was more associated with witchcraft during the Burning Times than Diana. Each of the four instances above occurred in areas that would suffer particular virulent witchcrazes, however Diana was associated with witchcraft throughout Europe.

Devotion to Diana survived the Burning Times and remains persistent. She is among the most beloved of contemporary deities and is central to the Italian witchcraft tradition, Stregheria.

See also Aradia, Artemis, Hecate, Herodias; **ANIMALS:** Dogs.

Dionysus

Also called Bacchus.

Popularly called the God of Wine, Dionysus is much more than that: the spirit of vegetation, fertility, and generation, Dionysus presides over the mysteries of life and death. He is the spirit of untamed wilderness and irrepressible male procreative energy, intoxication, shamanism, magic, joy, madness, and sexual healing.

Dionysus is the Green Man. His images are adorned with grapevines and ivy.

Among his epithets is "the night prowler."

He was the last of the twelve deities incorporated into the Olympian pantheon and is thus usually classified as a "Greek god." However his original homeland is believed to be Thrace: modern Bulgaria and Romania both claim to be the location of his birthplace.

According to archeologist Marija Gimbutas, Dionysus was the most ancient non-Indo-European god of Old Europe and was initially a botanical spirit.

Dionysus was originally served only by women. His female devotees were known as Maenads (in Greece) or Bacchanals (in Rome). Although men served him too, women were the leaders and initiators in the Dionysian rites, and certain rites were celebrated solely by women. Witch-hunters' later descriptions of naked, wild-haired women dancing in the forest around the figure of a lone virile, horned man could theoretically describe Dionysian rites.

Dionysus was twice born, first as the child of Zeus and his daughter Persephone (in one version, Zeus in the form of a snake either rapes or seduces Persephone). Zeus named him Zagreus and designated him his heir over all his other children. Jealous Titans kidnapped Zagreus, ripped him to pieces and ate him, except for his heart which Athena rescued.

Livid, Zeus reduced the Titans to ashes and formed humans from these ashes, thus all people share in Dionysus' (Zagreus') essence. Zeus then brewed a love potion from Zagreus' heart and fed it to Princess Semele. She conceived Dionysus once again but died before giving birth.

Zeus rescued the unborn child, removing him from his mother's body and sewing him up in his own thigh to incubate until ripe and ready to be born. Dionysus was then hidden away for his own safety; he grew up in the wilderness of Thrace where he was nursed by goats.

Always loving toward women, Dionysus' first act as a full-fledged god was to travel to Hades and bring his mother Semele up to Olympus to share in his glory. Dionysus is also the only Olympian god to be happily married. There are conflicting reports as to whether May Eve or Midsummer's Eve marks Dionysus and Ariadne's wedding anniversary.

Reaching maturity, Dionysus led a caravan through the Middle East, North Africa, and India, accompanied by a parade of Maenads, satyrs, and panthers. Wherever Dionysus traveled he taught people assorted agricultural and artisanal arts, especially viniculture—the creation of wine. In addition to wine, Dionysus was also associated with opium and mushrooms. (See **BOTANICALS:** *Amanita muscaria*, Opium Poppy.)

Dionysus' festivals featured nocturnal processions with music and masked, costumed revelers. The floats, masks, clowns, dancing, public drunkenness, and erotic theater that characterize modern Carnivals and parades are descendants of Dionysian festivities.

> Dionysus manifests in the form of a man, a bull or a goat. In Dionysiac processions, the deity was represented by a huge phallus. Dionysus *is* wine; by drinking wine one shares the sacrament of Dionysus' body.

His was a widespread cult: a fourth-century CE report states that women crowned with leaves danced and performed rites of Bacchus in Britain's Channel Islands. According to the report, they *"shouted even louder than the Thracians."*

Dionysus' symbols include cymbals, frame drums and other percussion instruments, leopards and panthers, garlands, vines and snakes, mules, donkeys, and lions. His primary attribute was the *thyrsus*—a wand (often a stalk of fennel) topped with a pinecone. (See **DICTIONARY:** Benandanti.)

Dionysus is a friendly god who is most frequently surrounded by a retinue including devotees, sacred animals, and other deities. Among the deities closely allied with Dionysus are Pan, Hecate, Kybele, Demeter and Persephone, and Apollo. Dionysus eventually became Apollo's altar-equal at Delphi, taking over the shrine in winter. He was considered Apollo's opposite, representing hot ecstatic energy rather than Apollo's cold rationalism.

Dionysus' cult survived until well into the Christian era. Outlawed and driven underground, surviving pockets of Dionysian tradition were demonized by the Church. Maenads fled to the forest.

See **CALENDAR:** February Feasts: Dionysia; **CREATIVE ARTS:** Dance: Maenad Dances, Processionals.

Feronia

The spirit of Feronia allegedly still haunts the traditional marketplaces of Italy, territory she once ruled. Having been banished, post-Christianity, alongside the rest of the Pagan spirits, Feronia apparently refused to abandon her old stomping grounds but transformed from a benevolent spirit of freedom and prosperity into a bad-tempered witch in the guise of a shabby, elderly, muttering beggar-woman.

Don't let her disguise fool you: she's still working magic. Those she approaches who behave politely and generously find themselves blessed with good fortune. Those behaving otherwise are treated to *very* effective (and feared) curses.

Folklorist C. G. Leland reported in his 1892 book *Etruscan Roman Remains* that nineteenth-century Tuscan peasants classified Feronia as a *strega-folletta* or "witch-spirit." He described her as a *"wandering witch who exacts offerings."*

Little is now known about this ancient, mysterious deity. Feronia may have originated as an Etruscan or Sabine spirit. Her rites included fire-walking. Devotees walked or danced over glowing coals and burning ploughshares.

Feronia's sacred animal was the wolf. She is friendly with those other Italian spirits associated with witchcraft, Mania and Proserpina (see pages 401 and 409). Feronia was the protectress of paupers, slaves, and refugees. She had various temples including one in the heart of Rome that contained a sacred stone. If a slave sat on the stone, freedom was instantly granted. (It's not clear what kind of machinations were necessary in order to reach this stone.)

Freya

Freya is the most beautiful of the Norse spirits with dominion over love, sex, fertility, magic, witchcraft, death, pleasure, and glory. "Freya" literally means "Lady" and may be a title, not a name. (Her twin brother is Freyr or "Lord.") She is simultaneously a spirit of fertility and death, beauty and war.

Freya is the daughter of Njord and Herta (Nerthus), Sea and Earth. She is among the Vanir hostages who joined the Aesir to maintain spiritual peace. Freya, however, is so powerful that she quickly became a dominant force in her new realm.

Freya is clearly identified as a witch. When she first arrives in Asgard (the Aesir's realm), she teaches the Aesir how to craft charms and potions. It is Freya who introduced Odin to the concept of runes. Völvas and Valkyries serve as her priestesses.

Golden Freya most often manifests as a woman, although she owns a falcon feather cloak that enables her to fly like a falcon and shape-shift as she pleases (see also Circe, page 378).

Most other surviving Norse goddesses are identified as "wives"; Freya is an independent single woman who answers to no one. She *was*

married, but her husband Od mysteriously disappeared. She weeps golden tears for him that transform into amber, but takes her pleasure as she pleases.

Sacred Creatures: Cats, rabbits, boars
Attributes: Gold, amber, honey
Plants: Cowslips, flax, hemp

Two large gray cats, possibly lynxes, named *Bee-gold* (Honey) and *Tree-gold* (Amber) pull her chariot. They embody Freya's twin qualities of ferocity and fecundity. She rides a boar into battle (as does her brother Freyr). Her sacred day was Friday; her sacred number 13, the number of months in the lunar calendar. Friday the 13th is thus especially sacred to her, leading to its later malevolent associations under Christianity.

No spirit annoyed Christian authorities more than Freya. Ironically, the result was that Freya survives more vividly than any other female European spirit. Constant condemnation kept Freya from fading into obscurity.

An insult levied at Freya at the Althing (Parliament) of Iceland initiated the final round of a debate over that country's Christianization: a Christian described Freya as a *"bitch goddess."*

Freya was denounced as a Queen of Witches. Women who venerated her were therefore automatically branded "witches." And of course,

Freya's rites and traditions *did* encourage magical practice, mediumship, shamanism, and female autonomy, with Freya herself as the role model—behavior the new regime considered abhorrent and sinful.

Freya was not an obscure spirit but was beloved and worshipped over a vast European territory including Scandinavia, Iceland, Greenland, the Germanic lands, Holland, and Anglo-Saxon Britain.

Thirteenth-century Icelandic chronicler Snorri Sturluson recorded and preserved many old sagas and poems. He says Freya was the most renowned of all the goddesses, and was still worshipped in his day.

Freya's last surviving temple, in Magdeburg, Germany, was destroyed by edict of the Emperor Charlemagne. Devotees refused to surrender their faith, however: in 1668, *"the worship of Frau Venus"* was allegedly still prevalent among the Saxons of Magdeburg.

Freya was banished to the mountain peaks of Norway, Sweden, and Germany to dance with her devotees, especially in The Brocken, the highest peak in the Harz Mountains of central Germany, where she presides over annual Midsummer's and Walpurgis festivities. Freya remains among the most beloved deities among modern Neo-Pagans.

See also Angerboda, Frigga, Herta, Odin; **ANIMALS:** Cats, Pigs; **DICTIONARY:** Aesir, Valkyrie, Vanir, Völva; **PLACES:** Blokula, The Brocken.

Frigga

Also called Frigg, Fricka.

Frigga is a spirit of divination, fertility, matrimony, and childbirth. Her husband is Odin the Allfather, Leader of the Aesir. Her father is Fjorgin. The identity of her mother is unclear. It is also not entirely clear to which Norse pantheon Frigga herself belongs: Aesir, Vanir or other.

It can be difficult to distinguish Frigga from Freya. Clearly distinct spirits in Scandinavia, the two may have merged into one spirit in ancient Germany, although as so much information has been lost, suppressed and garbled it's now impossible to definitively determine.

Frigga is a shadowier spirit than Freya. Ironically, because Christians despised Freya so intensely, more lucid, substantial information regarding her and her traditions survive.

Frigga seems to have been a less overtly sexual spirit, although her name survives as an English obscenity indicating sexual intercourse. Frigga's sacred bird is the stork, leading to jokes regarding the true origin of infants. Her primary surviving myths involve her identity as wife and mother. She battles Odin's infidelities and actively attempts to save their doomed son, Baldur.

Frigga knows every person's destiny but will not reveal it. She is a spinning goddess associated with the Norns (Fates)—she spins the thread they weave and cut. Her sacred emblem is the distaff: *"the distaff side"* still indicates a wife or maternal descent.

She wears a girdle hung with keys, indicating her ability to unlock all doors and her oracular ability. Frigga has powerful associations with mediumship. A quiet, less flamboyant witch than Freya, Frigga lives in the company of masters (Odin, Freyr) and manages to hold her own.

A thirteenth-century mural in Schleswig Cathedral in Northern Germany depicts Freya and Frigga in the guise of naked witches: Freya rides through the air on a giant cat alongside Frigga astride a distaff.

Hecate, Hekate

"… *witchcraft celebrates/Pale Hecate's offerings*" (Shakespeare, *Macbeth* Act II, Scene 1, lines 51–2).

"*Hekate, whose name is shrieked at night at the crossroads of cities*" (Virgil, *The Aeneid* 4:609).

Hecate is Queen of the Night, the Spirit World, and Witchcraft. Her epithets include "*She Who Works Her Will.*" Although today most associated with Greek mythology, her name, meaning "influence from afar," acknowledges her foreign origins.

Lauded by poets long before Shakespeare, the sixth-century BCE Greek poet Sappho called Hecate *"Queen of the Night."*

Generally believed to have first emerged in what is now Turkey, she was not an obscure goddess. Hecate was at one time chief deity of Caria, now western Turkey, and was eventually widely worshipped throughout Europe, Western Asia, and Egypt. Records of formal worship date from the eighth century BCE to the fourth century CE, although as magic fell from grace she became an increasingly disreputable spirit. All Hecate's myths clearly identify her as a witch and matron of magical arts.

Hecate holds dominion over life, death, regeneration, and magic. She rules wisdom, choices, expiation, victory, vengeance, and travel. Hecate guards the frontier between life and death. She is an intermediary between the spirit world and that of humans. She is the witness to all crimes, especially those against women and children.

Hecate has been known to assume the shape of a black cat, a bear, a pig or a hen but most typically manifests as a mature woman or black dog. She has a particularly strong bond with dogs. Even when manifesting in human form, Hecate is usually accompanied by hounds. Somehow there will be a canine reference. When manifesting as a woman alone, Hecate often circles in the manner of a dog.

Artistic renderings of Hecate usually attempt to capture her spiritual essence. She may be depicted with three bodies, each facing a different direction. One hand holds the knife that is the midwife's tool, another holds a torch to illuminate the darkness, the last bears a serpent representing medical and magical wisdom. Sometimes Hecate is depicted with a woman's body but three animal heads—those of a dog, a horse, and a lion.

Hecate's sacred time is black night. All her festivities and ceremonies are held after dark; the only acceptable illumination is candles or torches. She only accepts offerings and petitions at night. Hecate is identified with the Dark Moon, the time of her optimum power.

The last day of each month is dedicated to Hecate. She also shared a festival with Diana on August 13th in Italy. Modern Wiccans, for whom Hecate is an important deity, celebrate November 16th as Hecate Night.

Her sacred place is the crossroads, specifically three-way crossroads. Among her names is

Hecate Trivia. That doesn't indicate that Hecate is trivial or that worshipping her was a trivial pursuit: *Trivia* literally means *"three roads."* Hecate is Spirit of the Crossroads: her power emanates from their point of intersection. Hecate's image was once placed in Greek towns wherever three roads met.

Sacred Creatures: Dogs, toads, snakes, dragons
Color: Black
Number: Three
Attributes: Key, Cauldron, Broom, Torch
Plants: Garlic, lavender, mandrake.
Fruit: Pomegranate
Trees: Black poplar, yew, date palm, willow
Planets: Moon and Sirius, the Dog Star

Hecate is most prominent in Greek myth-ology for being the sole deity to voluntarily assist Demeter in her search for her abducted daughter, Persephone. Later, after Persephone eats Death's six pomegranate seeds and is condemned to spend half the year in Hades, it is Hecate who accompanies her as Lady-in-Waiting. In some legends, she even becomes Hades' co-wife. Cerberus, three-headed hound of Hades, may be Hecate in disguise.

Hecate becomes Persephone's link to her mother and the land of the living. She guarantees that Death cannot break the bond between mother and daughter. Hecate is the Matron of Necromancy.

Hecate, daughter of the Titans Perses and Asteria, is older than the Olympian spirits. The eighth-century BCE Greek poet Hesiod writes that Hecate's power dates *"from the beginning."* Zeus was crazy about her: he eliminated all other pre-Hellenic deities (the Titans) but, having fallen madly in love with Hecate, he let her be.

Hecate is understood to be a triple goddess by herself, appearing as maiden, mother, and crone. She is also part of a lunar triplicity with Artemis and Selene, and also with Demeter and Persephone. Hecate dances in Dionysus' retinue and is a close ally of Kybele.

Alongside her intense lunar identification, Hecate is also associated with the element of water: her first love affairs were with sea gods including Triton. Her great-grandfather was Pontus the Sea. Her maternal great-aunt was the sea monster Keto. Hecate is also related to the Gorgons and Sirens and may be the mother of Scylla, who was transformed into a sea monster by another relative, Circe. Prior to her transformation Scylla was a beautiful woman from head to waist, with canine hips terminating in a fish tail.

In *Philopseudes ("Lovers of Lies")* by the Greco-Syrian author Lucian of Samosata (*c.*120–*c.*180), a sorcerer invokes Hecate. She manifests in female form, albeit snake-footed with snakes in her hair, carrying a torch in her left hand and a sword in her right.

Hecate led a host of shape-shifting female spirits known as *Empusas*, whose usual manifestation was as a beautiful woman with one brass leg and one donkey's leg; Hecate herself sometimes takes this form. The Empusas patrolled roads and apparently sometimes had fun terrorizing travelers. If one invoked Hecate, however, they left you alone.

Devotees feted the goddess by holding rituals known as Hecate's Suppers at the end of each month at a crossroads. (The end of the month in lunar calendars corresponds to the Dark Moon; the new month begins with the first sighting of the new moon.) A typical menu is found in **FOOD AND DRINK**. The Church was still trying to eradicate Hecate's Suppers in the eleventh century.

Post-Christianity, Hecate became among the most intensely demonized spirits, her very name synonymous with "witch." Her symbols (toad, cauldron, broom) are inextricably linked with stereotypes of witchcraft. What were symbols of fertility became symbols of evil. Her sacred dogs were converted into the Hounds of Hell. This denigration served to camouflage Hecate's origins as a deity of healing and protection.

Further Reading: Jacob Rabinowitz's *The Rotting Goddess* (Autonomedia, 1998).

See also Artemis, Baba Yaga, Circe, Dionysus, Kybele, Proserpina; **ANIMALS:** Cats, Chickens, Dogs, Pigs; **CALENDAR:** Hecate Night; **MAGICAL ARTS:** Necromancy; **HALL OF FAME:** Medea.

Hella or Hel

Once upon a time, being sent to Hel (or Hella as she is also known) may have been inevitable but it wasn't perceived as punishment: Hella, daughter of Angerboda and Loki, rules the Norse realm of the dead. She is the keeper of the souls of the departed and determines the fate of the deceased. Those who died at sea or in battle had other destinations; everyone else went to Hella who welcomed them into her home, *Helhaim*, regardless of whether they were good, bad, sinful or saintly. It's just the realm of the dead.

Hella's realm was not envisioned as a sulfurous fiery torture chamber but as a kind of inn or waystation for the dead, although once checked in, one could *never* check out. It was a bleak, gray, damp, foggy, misty realm: the concept of heat as punishment was imported from hotter, southern climes alongside Christianity. *"Lack of warmth with no hope of Spring"* was the Norse equivalent of desolation.

Hella rides a black mare and has a pack of dogs, the original Hell Hounds. She is attended by two servants, named Delay (male) and Slowness (female). Her name derives from the Old German *halja*, "covering." Her sacred creatures are horses, dogs, and wolves.

Hella and her brothers, a wolf and a snake, were raised by their mother, the witch Angerboda, in the Iron Wood. Prophecy suggested that the siblings would someday lead a Host of Destruction against the ruling Aesir pantheon of gods, and so Odin had them "brought" to the Aesir's territory of Asgard, where each would ultimately be entrapped. Odin personally seized Hella and flung her as far as he could: she landed in the Realm of Death and became its Queen.

Unlike Persephone who *lives* in the Realm of Death, Hella is simultaneously half-dead and half-alive. Half of her body is that of a fair, beautiful woman; the other half is necrotized flesh—hence her sacred colors are black and white.

Christianity would borrow Hella's name for its realm of eternal punishment, although she would be demoted and the male Satan placed in charge. Her associations with death remained: she was re-envisioned as a feared witch/angel of death:

✴ *The Black Death was particularly devastating in Norway and throughout Scandinavia. Allegedly Hella traveled the land armed with a rake and a broom. Villages totally wiped out by the plague had been swept with her broom; where some survived, Hella had raked instead.*

✴ *Hella or a pale, red-headed vampire-witch named in her honor, appears in Mikhail Bulgakov's novel* The Master and Margarita. *(See* **CREATIVE ARTS:** *Literature.)*

See Angerboda, Freya, Hulda, Mania, Odin; **ANIMALS:** Dogs, Wolves and Werewolves; **DICTIONARY:** Aesir.

Hermes

Hermes began his incarnation as a fertility spirit in Arcadia. The son of Zeus and Maia (whose name is recalled by the month of May and therefore May Eve), Hermes was born in *"Poppytown"* and has powerful associations with opium, shamanism, and botanical magic.

His sacred animals include horned livestock: cows, goats, and sheep. Hermes occasionally takes the form of a horned deity but by the classical Greek era he was most commonly depicted in the guise in which he is most familiar today—as messenger of the gods in winged cap and sandals, bearing the *caduceus*, a magic wand

entwined by two snakes, his other sacred animal. Snakes symbolize Hermes' mastery of the healing and magical arts. The caduceus remains the emblem of the modern medical profession.

Hermes is able to travel between the realms of the living, the dead, and spirits because he is a master shaman. He is also a psychopomp: a spirit who escorts the newly dead to their next realm:

✴ *Hermes served as guide when Orpheus traveled to Hades to rescue Eurydice*

✴ *He is Persephone's escort as she travels between Life and Death*

✴ *He is a spell master, providing Odysseus with the antidote against Circe's magic*

Hermes is Patron of Thieves and Tricksters but he also protects devotees against tricks and theft. He famously enjoys cleverness and despises violence, only protecting non-violent criminals—those using wit, not brawn.

In addition to shamanism and botanical spells, Hermes sponsors other aspects of magic:

✴ *As Hermes Trismegistus he was identified with alchemy and ceremonial magic*

✴ *He is the model for the mountebank, the traveling conjurer who may be a true magus, a master illusionist, a charlatan, or all or any of the above*

> Hermes, dressed in his traveler's cap, formed the prototype for the Tarot card, The Magician.

See also Circe, Dionysus, Hecate, Proserpina, Thoth; **ANIMALS:** Goats, Snakes; **BOTANI-CALS:** Opium Poppy; **CALENDAR:** May Eve; **DICTIONARY:** Mountebank; **MAGICAL ARTS:** Alchemy, Cards; **HALL OF FAME:** Hermes Trismegistus.

Herodias

The historical Herodias, granddaughter of Herod the Great, was the wife of King Herod Antipas of Judea. He was her second husband; her first was Philip, the brother of Herod Antipas. (This is according to the Gospels of Mark and Matthew; some historians suggest that her first husband was yet another Herod, her paternal half-uncle.) Philip and Herodias had a daughter named Salome. During a trip to Rome, Herod Antipas and Herodias fell in love; she abandoned his brother, he divorced his royal Nabatean wife and they married. Due to the technicalities of Jewish law, this might be construed as incest. Herod, Rome's puppet ruler in Judea, was already widely unpopular among the masses: the marriage was a major public scandal, earning the condemnation of John the Baptist (see **CREATIVE ARTS:** Dance: Dance of the Seven Veils).

Herodias didn't take this criticism lightly: according to the New Testament, she was the actual instigator of the murder of John the Baptist. She instructed her dancing daughter Salome to request the prophet's head served to her on a plate as a reward.

In real life, the Roman emperor Caligula banished Herod to Gaul in 39 CE. Herodias accompanied him, dying there in c.47. To early Christians, Herodias epitomized the Wicked Woman; she emerged as the New Testament's primary female villain and was even reputed to be a demon.

Her name was used by Christians to rail against Pagan goddesses. At some point she evolved into one herself, although it is unclear whether Herodias herself emerged as a witch-goddess or whether her name was used to mask or camouflage another.

The spirit called Herodias bears little or no relationship to the historical Herodias but was worshipped alongside Diana in Italy. Herodias and Diana are the deities most mentioned in Italian witch-trial transcripts. This pairing clearly corresponds to Diana and Aradia in the grimoire, *Aradia or The Gospel of the Witches.* Together they lead the Wild Hunt and night parades of witches.

Herodias may be any of the following:

❋ *The biblical Herodias, re-emerged as a spirit*

❋ *A Pagan spirit also named Herodias, or perhaps renamed after the biblical queen*

❋ *Lilith, in disguise*

She was perceived as a figure of power: Ratherius, Bishop of Verona (c.887–April 25, 974), complained that many saw Herodias as a queen, even a goddess (as though, he remarked, this was her reward for killing John the Baptist.) In 936 a movement, outlawed by Ratherius, arose in Italy claiming that Herodias ruled one third of the world and was thus worthy of petition and devotion. By this time she was also identified with Hecate.

During the Medieval Era, Herodias and Salome were conflated and confused. (And of course, Salome plays the more dramatic role in the legend, even if Herodias was the brains behind the operation.) In some versions both mother and daughter are called Herodias; in others, the emphasis is on a daughter called Herodias. In one legend, Herodias is doomed to ride with the Wild Hunt until Judgment Day, carrying the head of the Baptist.

In Romania, Herodias manifests as the spirit Irodeasa. Her sacred number is nine. Masked dancers riding hobby-horses and carrying clubs and swords undertook nine-day rituals in her honor. They visited nine boundary points and filled ritual vessels with water from nine springs. At the end of the ninth day, a sacred pole was cast into the river.

> In Russia, there isn't one solitary Herodias; instead the troop of female fever demons called Herod's Daughters number either nine, twelve, forty or seventy-seven spirits, the youngest named Salome. (Sometimes these spirits are Herod's Sisters instead.) They are either conflated with Lilith's Daughters or are amazingly similar: several myths are virtually identical.

See also Aradia, Diana, Hecate, Lilith, Odin; **BOOKS:** Grimoires: *Aradia or The Gospel of the Witches*; **DICTIONARY:** Wild Hunt; **FAIRIES:** Nature-spirit Fairies: Keshalyi.

Herta

Also known as Hertha, Eartha, Erda, Nerthus.

Herta is a mysterious Germanic goddess, eventually demonized as a Queen of Witches. In that guise, she leads the Wild Hunt. Although little information regarding Herta survives, her name remains sacred and familiar as it is the one given our planet, Earth.

Tacitus called her *Mater Terra*, "Mother Earth." Archeological evidence suggests that Denmark was the epicenter of her cult. She had a sanctuary amidst the groves on the Baltic Isle of Rügen, now German territory but once part of Pomerania and once ruled by Danes. The highest point on Rügen is still known as the Hertaburg. Ruins of Hertha Castle near deep Hertha Lake on Rügen are believed to be the remnants of her shrine.

She appears in Norse mythology as Nerthus (Earth), sister-wife of Njord (Sea) the father of Freya and Freyr, primary deities of the Vanir. Njord and his children went to live in Asgard, Aesir territory, as Vanir representatives/hostages. In some versions, Nerthus is Njord's first wife and Freya and Freyr's mother, but because the Aesir disapprove of marriage between siblings, she remains behind on her island sanctuary. Eventually, however, Odin comes calling; the Valkyries, lead by their half-sister, are the daughters of Nerthus and Odin, representing the true union of Aesir and Vanir.

Herta, alongside Hulda and Freya, was among those witch-goddesses Germanic women charged with witchcraft were accused of worshipping. She appears under the name Erda in *Das Rheingold*, the first part of Richard Wagner's cycle of operas *The Ring of the Nibelungs*, loosely based on the *Volsung Saga* and the *Nibelungenlied*. In Wagner's cycle, Erda is identified as the mother of the Norns (the Fates) as well as the Valkyries.

She is sometimes identified as swan or goose-footed, which may link her to shamanism or to Mother Goose. In 1867, the poet Algernon Charles Swinburne (1837–1909) included "Hertha" in his collection *Songs Before Sunrise*. In this poem she is identified as the origin of all Creation: Hertha the eternal Gaia.

See also Freya, Hulda, Odin; **DICTIONARY:** Aesir, Valkyries, Vanir; **FAIRY-TALE WITCHES**.

Hulda

Also known as Holda, Holle, Frau Holle, Hulle, Mother Holle, Frau Wode.

Hulda, Queen of Witches, the Elven-Queen, was once a hearth deity who, through demonization, became associated with the fires of Hell. She eventually diminished into a figure used to scare children into good behavior although devotion to her never entirely disappeared. A revival of her worship is currently underway.

Familiarly known as Mother Holle, she is the leader of a band of spirits, the *Hulden* (Hill Fairies), who may be friendly or punitive. Mother Holle receives the souls of the dead and releases newborns from the underworld.

She is a weather spirit. When she shakes her featherbed, it snows on earth. Rain falls from her laundry rinse water. She may be a solstice goddess who births the New Year.

Hulda may or may not be identical with Hella, Perchta, Herta or Frigga. Her associations with rabbits also link her with Ostara. There are tremendous gaps in the surviving information and so this is subject to interpretation.

Hulda may appear in any of the three manifestations of women's power: maiden, mother or crone. Sometimes she appears as a woman when seen from the front and a tree from the back. She guards and nurtures all the growing things of the forest. Mother Holle is followed by a retinue of torch-bearing rabbits.

In Lower Saxony, Mother Holle is known as the *Waldmichen*, the wood nymph. She lives in a grotto where the souls of unborn babies frolic, and she owns a mill where she grinds old men and women into new souls again. She has a retinue of rabbits: two hold up her train while two hold candles to light her way.

Hulda was known throughout Northern Europe. Holland is her namesake. She lives in mountain caves and inside wells, believed to be a source of children. She bathes at midday in a fountain from which babies emerge—a well of life.

Sacred Creatures: Wolves, rabbits
Color: White
Plants: Holly, elder, juniper, flax. According to legend, Frau Hulda first introduced flax and taught women how to create linen.
Sacred Time: The winter solstice is Mother Holle's feast day. The twelve days between December 25th and January 6th are also sacred to her.

Hulda is involved with spinning, weaving, ploughing, childbirth, and the planting and gathering of botanicals. She guards and releases unborn souls. One of her feet is reportedly deformed because of excessive treading of her spinning wheel. The deformed foot may also be an allusion to shamanism. She is "the white lady," a snow queen who wears a mantle of frost while she spins destiny.

The mysterious Norse deity Holler (Uller, Wulder) seems to derive from the Vanir pantheon of spirits. He is the Frost King: when Odin leads his Host during Yuletide, Holler rules Asgard in his place. Holler may or may not be Hulda's twin brother; in one myth he becomes her husband but before he'll marry

Hulda, he tests her with a riddle: she must come to him not dressed and not naked, not riding or walking, not alone or with company, not in light or in darkness. Hulda arrives at twilight, wrapped in a fishing net, perched on a donkey with one foot dragging on the ground, and accompanied by 24 wolves.

Mother Holle, once the provider of children, was transformed, post-Christianity, into a Teutonic demon-witch with disheveled hair and a propensity for attacking infants. The *Hulden*, once dancing hill-fairies, turned into a band of malevolent female spirits. Women suspected of witchcraft were said to ride with Hulde. Souls of unbaptized babies were condemned to her realm in the sky.

Mother Holle, a supreme and benevolent spirit, was transformed into the female equivalent of the boogieman. Country people warned their children that if they weren't obedient, Hulde would "get" them.

Frau Holle was identified as *the devil's grandmother*—the one who taught him everything he knows.

In Wurzburg, Frau Holle travels the streets on Christmas Eve in a hooded white cloak carrying a rod and sack with which to beat and carry off "bad" children, similar to Santa's European helpers, Krampus and Black Peter.

Some see Santa as Odin in disguise; by the Middle Ages, Hulda was frequently identified as Odin's consort and female ally. Sometimes she leads the Wild Hunt as his partner; other times she leads her own nocturnal host, accompanied by a host of dead souls including those who have died without being baptized. Her associations with Odin may go back further; in one legend, she was the one who first gave him his ravens.

While some feared Hulda, others, identified as "witches," still adored her: she travels during the twelve days between Christmas and Epiphany bringing gifts of fruitfulness, fertility, and abundance to people. Some fled from her but devotees of her cult wished to join her night train: the terms *"Holle-riding"* or *"Holda-riding"* were synonymous with witches' flight in Germany as late as the nineteenth century.

Jakob Grimm reported that Hulda and her train of "elves" openly wended their way through Germany in processionals as late as the fourteenth century. She led a ring of dancers in what Grimm called "witch dances."

See also Freya, Frigga, Hella, Herta, Lilith, Odin, Perchta; **CALENDAR:** Saint Lucy's Day, Ostara, Yule; **DICTIONARY:** Elf; **FAIRIES:** Nature-spirit Fairies: Elf.

Isis (Au Set)

The Egyptian deity Isis has countless epithets: *"Mistress of Magic," "She Who is Rich in Spells," "Great of Sorcery," "Speaker of Spells," "The Great Witch,"* and *"The Many Named"* are just a few.

Magic and witchcraft are central to her myth and identity: Isis casts spells and utters incantations. According to the Egyptologist E.A. Wallis Budge, in his book *Legends of the Egyptian Gods*, her *"mouth was trained to perfection and she made no mistake in pronouncing her spells."*

Isis was not an obscure goddess but was worshipped as a primary deity for thousands of years. Originating in Egypt, her worship eventually stretched from East Africa throughout Western Asia and Europe as far as England's Thames River.

Magic enters Isis' life even before her first breath. Because her mother's pregnancy breaks a spiritual injunction, she is cursed and unable to give birth. Lord Thoth, Egypt's baboon-headed inventor of magic, secretly loves Isis' mother. He creates the magical device of dice and gambles with the moon god, who controls the calendar. Thoth wins and is able to magically reconfigure the calendar, enabling his beloved to deliver quadruplets: Isis, her sister Nephthys, and brothers Set and Osiris.

Osiris and Isis fell in love in the womb; their love will transcend death. The two epitomize soulmates, albeit star-crossed ones. Thoth adores Isis and serves as her godfather, instructing her in the magical arts until her powers outshine his. Isis repeatedly proves herself to be the Mistress of Magic:

❋ *She learns Ra's true name, the ineffable name of power, with which she can stop the sun in the sky.*

❋ *She resurrects her brother-lover Osiris from the dead to magically conceive their son, Horus.*

❋ *She performs miraculous acts of healing magic.*

Isis is associated with snakes, crocodiles, cows, scorpions, and kites (a type of raptor). Her sacred mineral is bloodstone; her botanicals include vervain and myrrh.

Isis is also associated with water and the moon. She protects travelers at sea and is identified with the constellation Virgo. She is a grain spirit, too—a Corn Mother. No blood sacrifice existed among Isis' rites. She accepts offerings of milk, honey, flowers, herbs, and incense.

The cult of Isis was officially introduced to Rome in 86 BCE and became very popular because, unlike other cults, hers was open to all: not only free men but women and slaves. The tradition developed a bad reputation in conservative Rome because of the alleged licentiousness of its rites and it was suppressed at least five times between 59 and 48 BCE.

The last official temple of Isis stood on the southern Egyptian island of Philae. In 537 CE Narses, Commander of Emperor Justinian's Egyptian troops, ordered the temple closed.

Isis went underground. Devotees refused to abandon her but found masks with which to camouflage their rituals, including those of Kwan Yin and the Virgin Mary. Statues of the Madonna and Child are identical in form to those of Isis and baby Horus. One interpretation of Europe's Black Madonnas is that they represent Isis. Images of Isis, Horus, and his elder half-brother Anubis (the "fore-runner") may be understood to survive in images of the Madonna, Baby Jesus, and his elder cousin, John the Baptist (the "fore-runner").

See also Thoth; **ERGOT:** Corn Mother: Isis.

Jezibaba

Jezibaba seems to be Baba Yaga's Czech sister. A forest goddess, the name "Jezibaba" literally means "Granny Witch." Like Baba Yaga, Jezibaba lives in the forest in a little hut, although hers is on the shores of a lake. Her personality is somewhat milder than Baba's: she's not quite as scary. Less emphasis is placed on cannibalism or initiation; devotees request her assistance with love and fertility.

Jezibaba may be an incarnation of the ancient Semitic deity Yahu or Yahi, female ruler of menstrual power. Jezibaba's children are the Jezinky—sometimes hostile cave-dwelling spirits. Some scholars think the Jezinky are really djinn.

See also Baba Yaga; **DICTIONARY:** djinn.

Kali

Kali is such a crucially significant, transcendent goddess that, as with Isis, reducing her to just one aspect, witchcraft, is unfair. Kali Ma, *"Mother Kali,"* is India's Great Mother; a pre-Aryan deity, she remains venerated by millions.

Her name means "black" and also derives from the root word for "time." She is reputedly the most difficult of all spirits to understand. Her devotees claim that the attempt to comprehend her ultimately frees them from all fear. She is the Mother in her destructive aspect—the Corn Mother who simultaneously grinds out life and death. Her stereotype depicts her as a scary, bloodthirsty, out-of-control demon but this ignores her tremendous gift-giving and fear-allaying aspects.

Fiercest of the fierce, Kali backs away from nothing. To fully appreciate joy and life, suffering and death must be faced. Kali is responsible for life from conception to the grave. She maintains the world order. Kali protects the helpless, particularly women and children. She is also the Matron of Witches. Her attending spirits are the Dakini, whose name is synonymous with "witch" in modern India. Kali is the chief Dakini and sometimes is called by the name Dakini.

Her appearance is meant to terrify. Kali is garlanded with severed heads and wears a girdle of severed hands. Her earrings are children's corpses. She wears cobras as garlands and bracelets. Her mouth is smeared with blood. Her tongue sticks out. Her hair is disheveled. She is adorned with gems possessing the brilliance of the sun and the moon and is usually depicted with four hands, demonstrating her contradictions: two are actively involved in destruction while the other two confer benefits:

❋ *Her upper left hand wields a bloody sword*

❋ *Her lower left hand holds a demon's severed head*

❋ *Her upper right hand forms the gesture of fearlessness*

❋ *Her lower right hand bestows blessings and protections*

When depicted by herself Kali is usually shown dancing, but she is often shown together with her beloved Lord Shiva. Typically she stands upon his prone body or they are shown in sexual union with each other. One famous image shows Kali squatting over Shiva's prone body devouring his entrails while simultaneously offering him her breast. She also manifests as a jackal-headed woman.

Sacred Creatures: Crow, Snake
Colors: Black, red
Attributes: A black cauldron, a mirror, a cup containing blood of a head she has severed (sometimes this cup is a skull)
Planet: The moon, especially in the dark and waning phases

The deities closest in nature to Kali are Baba Yaga, La Santisima Muerte, and the Corn Mothers, especially Anat. Lilith claims that one of her alternative names is Kali.

See also Baba Yaga, Lilith, Santisima Muerte, Shiva; **ANIMALS:** Corvids, Dogs, Snakes; **DICTIONARY:** Dakini; **ERGOT:** Corn Mothers: Anat; **FAIRIES:** Nature-spirit Fairies: Dakini.

Kamrusepas

Kamrusepas, Hittite Spirit of Healing and Magic, represents the goddess as a powerful and talented practitioner of witchcraft. The Hittites were an ancient people who at the peak of their power in the second millennium BCE controlled much of Anatolia and the Middle East. Comparatively little is known about Hittite mythology: only fragments survive and have been translated. Kamrusepas plays a pivotal role in one though: in a flood myth, reminiscent of Noah's Ark, Earth is saved by a witch.

Telepinu, the Divine Farmer, grew so disgusted with Earth and her inhabitants that he decided to leave, which leads to spiraling disaster. As a result of his departure:

❀ *logs won't burn*

❀ *burnt offerings can't be made*

❀ *prayers fail to reach the deities*

❀ *deities and people alike begin to starve.*

Hannahanna, Supreme Mother Goddess, goes to Telepinu's father, Spirit of Weather, and demands that he bring his son back. He searches for him in the guise of an eagle but can't find Telepinu.

Exasperated, Hannahanna decides to send her own sacred creature, the bee, after him, although the Weather Spirit scoffs: if an eagle can't find Telepinu, how can a humble bee? The bee, in fact, locates Telepinu asleep in the wilderness. She stings Telepinu's hands and feet and smears beeswax over his eyes.

Hannahanna thinks this will do the trick and bring him back, but it only further enrages Telepinu, causing a flood: houses, people, and animals are swept away. *Finally* Kamrusepas, Spirit of Witchcraft is called. She arranges a ritual and stands atop a mountain with twelve rams as a sacrifice. She hangs a ram's fleece on a wooden cross and surrounds it with grain, wine, and cattle, and then cries out to the Gatekeeper of the Spirit Realm:

*Draw back the seven bolts! Open the seven doors!
Into your seven bronze cauldrons receive all
Telepinu's fury and anger and keep them!
Never let them out!*

Telepinu emerges riding on an eagle, sees the offerings, and is appeased.

Kapo

Hawaiian spirit Kapo's fame derives mainly from her reputation as a witch and sorceress possessing oracular powers. Traditionally Kapo was considered the deity of choice for occult practitioners wishing to use their knowledge to further their personal aims. She is the matron of the legendary powerful sorcerers of Molokai. Kapo is also famed for being able to reverse any curse or malevolent spell. She is feared, respected, and admired.

Kapo is powerful and unpredictable. She is a spirit of fertility and childbirth; also under her domain are miscarriage, abortion, and death. She is among the pre-eminent spirits of hula dancing, which originally derived from sacred ritual. Some legends credit her with the invention of hula although others suggest that the primary sacred matron of hula is Laka, the Hawaiian Spirit of Beauty.

The exact relationship between Kapo and Laka is unclear. Some legends describe them as sisters. Another tradition considers Kapo to be Laka's mother. The most generally accepted theory is that they are aspects of one another—two sides of one coin—with Laka being the consistent, life-affirming aspect and Kapo the unpredictable, shadow side.

Kapo's mother is the lunar spirit Haumea; her more famous younger sister and sometime traveling companion is the volcano spirit, Pele. Kapo was born in Tahiti but was already in Hawaii when Pele arrived. Upon her own arrival, Kapo is rumored to have established a hula school on each Hawaiian island.

Like the other Hawaiian deities, Kapo manifests in any form she chooses—human, animal, botanical or mineral. She can be stormy and fearsome or alluringly beautiful. In addition to beauty, Kapo possesses a magical detachable flying vagina that she flings and retrieves at will. Her sacred plant is the pandanus.

Kapo was once widely adored throughout Hawaii. The imprint of her detachable vagina can still be seen on the eastern side of the hill Kohelepelepe (literally "detached vagina") at Koko Head in Oahu.

Kybele

Also known as Kubaba, Kuba, Cybele.

Ancient Anatolians called Kybele the Mountain Mother; the Romans called her *Magna Mater* or Great Mother. She seems to have originated in what is now Turkey and then traveled to the Middle East. The Hittites called her Kubaba, which evolved into the Phrygian Kybele and eventually the Roman Cybele. Some associate Siduri, the sacred harlot-barmaid at the world's end in the story of Gilgamesh, with Kybele. "*Baba,*" as in Baba Yaga or *babushka,* may also derive from Kubaba.

Kybele is usually translated as "Place of Caves" or "Cave Dweller." Kybele and the Sibyls are both associated with caves and prophesy, and it's believed that the original Sibyls were Kybele's priestesses although eventually at least some became independent practitioners.

Legend has it that Kybele was an unwanted child, left exposed to die in the wilderness. Instead of consuming her, the leopards and lions who dis-covered her raised and nurtured her, a leopard serving as her wet-nurse. Living alone with animals in the woods, Kybele became a witch so powerful she evolved into an immortal goddess.

In her oldest manifestations, Kybele is a deity of healing, witchcraft, fertility, women, and children. Rites were held in forests and caves and included ritual possession, ecstatic dancing, intoxication, music, and sacred sex. She is closely identified with Dionysus and Hecate.

Before her arrival in Rome, Kybele was associated with women, slaves, and the poor, not with the elite, and already bore a somewhat dangerous reputation.

In Christa Wolf's novel *Cassandra* (Farrar, Straus & Giroux, 1984), when the Olympian gods fail them, royal Trojan women turn to the forbidden goddess, Kybele.

Kybele manifests in various ways: her typical human manifestation is as a mature, beautiful woman wearing a crown and carrying keys. She also frequently manifests in the form of rocks and as Earth herself. To enter a cave is to enter Kybele. Her most sacred manifestation, however, was as a meteorite.

In 204 BCE, on the advice of the Oracle of Delphi, the Romans fetched Kybele in the form of a meteor from her shrine at Pessinus, near modern Sivrihisar in central Turkey. Delphi had predicted that Rome would never defeat Hannibal of Carthage unless Kybele was brought to Rome. The Romans traced their descent from Trojan refugees and so basically the Oracle was instructing them to go fetch Mom to get them out of trouble. The prophecy proved correct: Kybele was brought to Rome in a triumphant procession and, in 202 BCE, Rome defeated Hannibal's forces.

The black, fist-sized meteorite had been set on the face of a silver statue. The Romans built her a temple where St Peter's Basilica now stands. It was the center of her veneration until the fourth century CE when the site was taken over by Christians.

In Rome, Kybele's rites evolved: she became a feared, scandalous, notorious goddess. Secret rituals that had once occurred in hidden caves and forests now occurred in public streets during processionals attended by thousands.

Under Roman law, women could not be chief officiators of official state cults and so men assumed positions of authority in Kybele's Roman cult. Kybele's response to this led to further notoriety, scandal, and controversy.

Still strongly associated with illiterate women, in Rome Kybele was served by priestesses and transgendered clergy known as *galli* (literally "hens" or "roosters"). In order to become galli, self-castration was required; the galli dressed and lived as women. Many were not mere eunuchs. Kybele's clergy were also skilled medical practitioners: through surgery, replica vaginas (caves) were crafted through which the galli could engage in sacred sex rituals.

Sacred Creatures: Bees, bulls, big cats especially leopards and lions, vultures
Attributes: Cymbals, a frame drum painted red or decorated with a rosette
Trees: Pine, Pomegranate
Flower: Rose
Element: Earth
Day: The Vernal Equinox

Kybele's festivals became notorious: men suddenly seized by the spirit of the goddess would feel compelled to castrate themselves on the spot using potsherds (terracotta, Earth, so Kybele is the knife herself, metaphorically or literally depending how you understand the goddess). The detached organ was flung aside; the house that it hit was considered blessed—its owner was expected to purchase the ritual wardrobe for the new galla.

Kybele's primary myths (or at least those that survive) also involve castration, death, and resurrection. It became a scandalous faith and was periodically suppressed for fear that it was damaging Rome's "moral fiber."

Kybele's shrines were temples of healing; her priestesses were skilled healers and midwives. In her role as Rome's Great Mother, Kybele is depicted seated upon her throne surrounded by lions. She sometimes holds a lion cub in her lap. She wears a crown in the form of crenellated towers or a city gate.

Her chariot is pulled by lions. She holds a pan of water in which to scry, representing her prophetic ability and her willingness to bestow this skill upon others. Kybele is credited with inventing drums, pipes, and percussion instruments. Her sacred animal, the leopard or panther, was closely identified with the Maenads, as were cymbals and tambourines.

Among other reasons, the early Church despised Kybele for the prominence of women and the presence of homosexuals, lesbians, and the transgendered in prominent cult positions. In Rome her cult had a higher percentage of men, intellectuals, and the elite as followers, but still remained extremely popular among the poorer classes and so was perceived as strong competition for Christianity and was thus particularly brutally suppressed.

St John Chrysostom (*c.*347–September 14, 407) led what would today be described as a "death squad" through Phrygia (located in the mountains of what is now Western Turkey) in 397 CE, targeting devotees of Kybele.

In 405, Serena, wife of the Christian general and acting regent Flavius Stilicho, personally entered the Roman shrine of Kybele, removed the precious necklace that hung around the neck of the votive image, and left wearing it around her own. The Emperor Justinian (c.483–565) particularly despised Kybele. He ordered her remaining temples torn down and the murder of her priestesses and *galli*. Her sacred texts were burned.

Although her veneration was widespread, *none* of Kybele's temples remain. Various ruins may be visited in Turkey, in Sardis and Prienne. St Peter's Basilica in Rome was built directly over her temple—parts are believed to survive under the foundations. Some believe that her meteorite is buried there as well.

Kybele retreated to her strongholds: devotion survived in mountain caves. Surviving galli are believed to have taken refuge in the Anatolian mountains. Kybele allegedly still haunts the mountains and forests of Anatolia accompanied by trains of wild torch-bearing attendants banging percussion instruments, blowing on flutes, and dancing.

See also Artemis, Dionysus, Hecate, Kamrusepas; **BOOKS:** Library of the Lost: Sibylline Books; **DICTIONARY:** Sibyl; **HORNED ONE:** Attis; **PLACES:** Forest.

Lilith

Earth's first woman was a witch. And no, we're not talking about Eve, although the Inquisition laid some aspersions at her door, too. According to Jewish mystical traditions, another woman existed prior to Eve; her name is Lilith and she initiated Earth's first divorce, preferring to run away and dance all night with demons in the most desolate regions of Earth to living in Paradise with someone who wished to dominate her.

No spirit possesses a more fabulous history than Lilith. She remains very vital and alive, feared and adored. Spirit of darkness, night, and feminine independence, Lilith is associated with witches, angels, djinn, demons, and vampires.

Lilith is a bird woman with powerful associations with cats. Her Hebrew name means "screech owl," which is cognate with *strix* or *strega*. "Lilith" is also related to the Semitic root word for "night."

Lilith's earliest incarnation seems to have been as a wind spirit from Mesopotamia associated with childbirth. The Burney Plaque, dating from a late period of Sumerian art (c.2300 BCE) is believed to portray Lilith: it depicts a beautiful winged woman, flanked by large owls, naked but for her horned cap. She stands atop two lions on her bird's feet. She holds the ring and rod of power in her hands. The plaque was discovered in what appeared to be a personal shrine.

According to her numerous legends, Lilith possesses many forms, appearing as an old hag or a beautiful young woman. Sometimes she is a beautiful woman from head to waist, pure flame underneath. Sometimes she is a snake from the waist down. Often dressed in red, Lilith's long hair is alternately described as black or red. It tends to be distinctive, either because it is beautiful, or because it is wildly disheveled, or both. In cultures where women bind or hide their hair, Lilith's is defiantly loose.

She manifests in animal form too, usually as a large black cat, an owl or snake. Even when in apparently human form, Lilith often displays aspects of a bird: feet, claws or wings. Helen of Troy and the Queen of Sheba are reputedly among her avatars.

Lilith may also have early roots as a tree spirit. In any form, she cannot be tamed. In the Sumerian myth *The Huluppu Tree*, "Dark Maid Lilith" lives in the sacred tree together with a snake and a sacred bird. When the formerly wild goddess Inanna makes the transition to an urban, settled, agricultural environment, she chops down the sacred tree Lilith calls home. Lilith flees, remaining a spirit of the wilderness.

Traveling westward, Jewish legend identifies Lilith as Adam's first wife, the true first female, created not later from Adam's rib but from Earth simultaneously with him. (And Genesis does contain two versions of human creation.)

Adam and Lilith's relationship quickly became contentious. She refused to be subordinate—specifically refusing to always lie beneath him during sex. Lilith demanded to be treated as an equal, basing her claim on their common origin.

When Adam attempted to force her, Lilith uttered the secret, ineffable name of the Creator, giving her the ability to fly away. (In myth, only Isis also knows this Name of Power.) Adam appealed to YHWH to send his woman back. Three angels were dispatched to fetch her but through the power acquired from knowledge of the Creator's name, Lilith was able to defy them.

The angels threatened her but Lilith threatened them right back, warning that she intended to spend eternity killing human babies and striking adults infertile. Instead of dragging her back to Eden, the angels end up negotiating with Lilith: she agrees not to harm babies in homes where her name is posted. Significantly her name does not appear in the Bible (the one possible reference to her in the Book of Isaiah is encoded; it may refer literally to screech owls); however, its presence is ubiquitous in Jewish amulets.

According to some legends, Lilith is infertile herself and burns with rage, hence her resentment of human mothers. In other legends, Lilith is the mother of a host of demons, the *Lilin* or Daughters of Lilith. Their father may be the fallen angel Samael or the dangerous spirit Asmodeus, both eventually identified with the devil. On the other hand, their father may be Adam, who allegedly reunited with Lilith after his expulsion from Eden. Another legend suggests that Lilith is the original succubus: she secretly seduces men while they sleep, their nocturnal secretions become her children.

Christian legend would ultimately claim that the snake in the Garden of Eden was Lilith in disguise, spitefully returning to take revenge upon Adam and her replacement. Some now feel that perhaps she was attempting to share her knowledge with her sister.

Sacred Creatures: All wild animals but especially jackals, hyenas, wild cats, ostriches, snakes, and unicorns. The owl is her sacred bird and messenger
Element: Lilith has all the bases covered, having associations with air, water, earth, and fire
Planet: The Moon. Her strength increases with the waning of the moon
Time: Solstices, equinoxes, and during the astrological sign of Scorpio

Although she is known throughout Semitic areas, it is in Jewish folklore that Lilith survives strongest. Lilith is a major player in Jewish fairy tales where, just as in Sumeria, she is still found living within trees. She retains her goddess-like features although whether she is a dangerous benefactor or a sometimes-benevolent demon is subject to interpretation.

Among Sephardic Jews, La Broosha ("the witch") is a euphemism for Lilith. Here she usually manifests as a large, black cat, which may account for the irrational fear that cats will suck a baby's breath out of its body.

Lilith continues to weave her spell: she is invoked in modern works of fiction more than any other witch-spirit, from the Victorian novels of Marie Corelli to comic books like *Vampirella*. Feminists have adopted her as a role model, as have witches, Neo-Pagans and Jewish-Pagans.

See also Aradia, Herodias; **ANIMALS:** Cats, Owls, Snakes; **CREATIVE ARTS:** Comics: *Vampirella*; **DICTIONARY:** Bruja; **FAIRIES:** Nature-spirit Fairies: Keshalyi.

Louhi

Louhi, Mistress of the North Country, appears in the Finnish national epic, the *Kalevala*. She is a Finnmark (Finno-Ugric) witch who protects the *Pohjola*, the back country. Louhi controls winds, fog, illness, and wild creatures. She is a master spell-caster and the mother of the beautiful and charming Maid of the North.

Female characters are given little emphasis in the heroic epic, the *Kalevala*; most interpretations of Louhi are somewhat negative. An exception is a retelling of the portion of the saga devoted to Louhi and her daughter in Ethel Johnston Phelps' *The Maid of the North* (Henry Holt & Company, 1982).

Louhi features prominently in the myth of the Magic Sampo, an enchanted device that grinds out salt, flour, and gold from thin air.

See also **MAGICAL PROFESSIONS:** Millers.

Mana

Also known as Mania, Manuana.

This is where the term "mania" comes from. Mana or Mania began her incarnation as the Italian deity who supervised the Manes, Spirits of the Dead. Mania is the Mother Superior of the Manes, their leader and overseer, Goddess of the Dead. Her "mania" (lunacy, moon-illness, lunar-inspired madness) was perceived as a conduit to the divine.

The Manes were originally envisioned as the "benevolent dead" who must, however, be consistently propitiated to stop them from becoming the threatening dead, like the Lemures. Manes eventually became a looser term and incorporated assorted spirits of the dead in addition to dead souls, such as guardians of tombs and burial grounds. Mana supervises them all.

Mania governs the subterranean Land of the Dead. This wasn't just some abstract realm someplace underground. An entrance to the realm could be located in the pit beneath the *lapis manalis* in the Roman Forum. This stone was lifted three times a year in order to release the Manes who emerged to accept offerings from the living. Mania leads them wearing a mask; her face is never revealed.

Although the Manes were sometimes described as the "benevolent dead" they weren't always *that* benevolent, and neither was Mania. At the New Moon near November 1st, windows were shuttered, houses sealed up, and mirrors turned to face the wall: the Manes were loose. It was feared that these wandering spirits of the dead would steal children.

Speculation exists that in ancient days, young boys were sacrificed to Mania at the Festival of the Crossroads (*Compitalia*) in exchange for her protection of the remaining family. The custom was allegedly abolished by Lucius Junius Brutus following the expulsion of the Etruscan kings in 510 BCE and the establishment of the Roman Republic. Garlic and poppies were then substituted for human sacrifice. At the Feralia festival, corresponding to February 13th, the Manes were offered beans, bread, eggs, honey, milk, oil, wine, and roses.

One version of her myth suggests that Mana began her incarnation as a naiad (water spirit) using the name Lara or Larunda. She had a liaison with Mercury (Teramo, Hermes), which produced the guardian spirits, the Lares. Lara/Mana was perhaps not as discreet as she could have been: overheard criticizing Jupiter's infidelities, the chief deity punished her by cutting her tongue out. She evolved into Muta, a fierce, frightening spirit, used to frighten Italian children ever since.

Post-Christianity, Mana would lose her goddess status but would survive in Italy as a feared night-witch who haunts people's dreams.

Mari

Mari, eldest of the Basque deities, is a Basque mountain goddess, the very beautiful Queen of Witches. She rides through the air encompassed by flames. No need for a broom, Mari rides a bolt of lightning.

Mari's veneration survived Christianity; she was (and remains) a very popular goddess. The Inquisition would brand her devotees as witches.

Mari rules Earth and her elements. Her husband Maju, also known as Sugaar, is the Dragon Lord of Thunder. Mari brings and ends storms.

She is depicted as a woman with the Full Moon behind her head. She lives in deep caverns within the Earth filled with gold and precious stones. (Should these gems be stolen from her, they transform into coal.)

Mari is also venerated in stone circles and atop mountain peaks. She is believed to inhabit the highest peaks of mountains like Aizkorri, Amboto, and Muru.

Morgan le Fay

Also known as Morgana le Fay, Fata Morgana.

Morgan le Fay literally means Morgan the Fairy. *Morgan* probably derives from the Welsh word for sea *"mor"*; Celtic mermaids are known as *morgans* or *merrow* in Ireland, from the Gaelic *"muir."* Most famous today as King Arthur's half-sister, she is probably more ancient than the Arthurian Saga. One theory suggests that Morgan was originally a Celtic death goddess, similar to an angel of death or psychopomp.

Morgan is no simple woodland spirit but has substantial real estate holdings:

* *She rules an underwater kingdom possibly near Brittany*

* *She rules a fairy paradise near Mount Aetna called Mongibello (or Mongibel)*

* *She has a castle near Edinburgh staffed with beautiful fairies*

* *She lives on the magical Isle of Avalon, which she may or may not rule*

In Arthur's saga, the fairy-princess became a witch-princess, a wealthy, skilled sorceress and the primary villain of most versions. From a dualist perspective, this may be necessary: once Merlin was permitted to be a "good" wizard, someone had to be the evil witch. Depending on the version, Morgan is Merlin's teacher, student, lover, and/or rival.

Even in the King Arthur stories however, Morgan was not always wicked. She first appears in Geoffrey of Monmouth's twelfth-century *Life of Merlin* as a healer and leader of the Nine Holy Women from Avalon who tend Arthur's wounds following the final Battle of Camlan.

In this version, she's not identified as Arthur's sister: she falls in love with him and he promises to stay with her in Avalon. By the end of the twelfth century she was portrayed as Arthur's sister but was still benevolent. By the thirteenth century, however, a different story emerged.

Cistercian monks composed the *Prose Lancelot* (also known as the *Vulgate Cycle*) between 1230 and 1250, which describes the adventures of Lancelot of the Lake and the Quest for the Holy Grail.

Frustrated by the popularity of romances with not-so-hidden Pagan sympathies, the Cistercian scribes determined to remake these romances into religious allegories and, in so doing, demonstrate the superiority of spirit over flesh, male over female, Christian over Pagan. They believed it was blasphemous to attribute powers of healing and prophecy to women who were unaffiliated with religious orders. (Some Cistercians also openly debated the existence of the female soul.) New elements were added to the story: incest and demonic possession, with Morgan as the villain witch.

Morgan is the sorceress supreme, an expert in botanical magic, especially poisons, a skilled shape-shifter; she was consistently portrayed as a heartless, plotting but beautiful monster. This has only changed recently, most notably in Marion Zimmer Bradley's 1982 novel *The Mists of Avalon*, which re-envisioned Morgan as a Pagan priestess and heroine. Morgan's status as goddess has been reaffirmed by modern Pagans, amongst whom she is very beloved.

Morgan also has strong, ancient roots in Italy where she is known as Fata Morgana. *Fata* is Italian for "fairy." She has a home in Calabria as well as a palace near or on Mount Aetna. Fata Morgana is also the name of a fatal mirage, an optical illusion that lured sailors to their deaths in the Straits of Messina. Morgan was held responsible.

See also **ANIMALS:** Corvids; **FAIRIES**; **HALL OF FAME:** Merlin.

Muso Koroni

Muso Koroni, leopard-goddess of Mali, is a deity shared between Bamana (Bambara) and Mande traditions. According to legend, she is the world's first female—Mother of Chaos, Creation, and Witchcraft. The first male was a blacksmith: Muso Koroni is among those spirits involved with the magical traditions of smithcraft.

Muso Koroni's name is usually translated as *"the pure woman with the primeval soul."* She is also known as *"the knowledgeable one."*

She manifests as a black leopard or panther; her black color is associated with fertility and black fertile soil. Smiths create metal images of her in the form of candelabra: her spirit is invoked when the lamp's cups, filled with shea butter, are lit.

Muso Koroni is also invoked in love spells, however she is now considered a dangerous spirit who must be carefully controlled. She is the epitome of primal womanhood, which is perceived as chaotic and unruly: every human being is believed to possess a fragment of her wild primeval nature. This wild part is called *wanzo* and, in Mande tradition, is the feminine force of chaos and disorder which is excised from men through circumcision, in order for them to be entirely, wholly masculine.

See above Lilith; **ANIMALS:** Leopards.

Nicnevin

Nicnevin, the "Bone Mother," is a Scottish witchcraft goddess. Her name is believed to be an Anglicized version of *Nic an Neamhain,* or "Daughter of Frenzy." Like the Nixies, Nicnevin is a water spirit. She can transform water into rocks, and sea into dry land. She wears a long gray mantle and carries a magic wand.

Nicnevin flies through the night; although she is usually invisible, her presence is announced by a cacophony of geese, her sacred birds. Nicnevin is among the spirits associated with the Wild Hunt and was reclassified, post-Christianity, as both a demon and a fairy.

Samhain is Nicnevin's sacred night. She is traditionally honored with celebratory feasts and toasting; some Neo-Pagans hold rituals in Nicnevin's honor on November 1st.

Nicnevin traditionally answers petitions and grants wishes on Samhain. At that time she makes herself visible as she flies through the air, accompanied by a retinue of witches and honking geese. Once upon a time, women of Fife took care to spin off all the flax on their distaffs before Samhain commenced otherwise, allegedly, Nicnevin would claim it.

Nicnevin manifests as both a beautiful woman and an old hag. In her Hag aspect, Nicnevin is known as Gyre Carlin. She may be the Cailleach of Lothian and the Border counties; some believe that Nicnevin is but another name for Cailleach Bheara. The Romans identified Nicnevin with Diana. Nicnevin is also considered the Queen of Fairies of Fife, Scotland.

See also Diana; **CALENDAR:** Samhain; **FAIRIES:** Nature-spirit Fairies: Nixies; **FAIRY-TALE WITCHES:** Mother Goose; **HAG:** Cailleach, Cailleach Bheara; **WOMEN'S MYSTERIES:** Spinning.

Nox, Nyx

A primeval Greek goddess, during the medieval age Nyx evolved into a witch who haunted the night. Goddess of Night, Nyx is the second being in one all-female Greek creation saga: first there was Chaos or the Void. Nyx was her daughter, her eldest child. Chaos had more children including a son, Erebus, with whom Nyx united and conceived a daughter Hemera (Day). Nyx shares a house with daughter Hemera although they never see each other: when one comes home through the back door, the other leaves through the front.

Nyx is also the mother of the Fates, the Hesperides, Hypnos (Sleep), Morpheus (Dream), Eris (Discord), Thanatos (Death), and Momus (Ridicule). She is the mother of all things mortal and immortal. Even Zeus feared her.

In an Orphic myth, Nyx existed from the beginning; no creation was necessary. She was a great black-winged bird hovering in endless darkness. This solitary bird laid an egg, which cracked in half: Eros, the beautiful gold-winged Spirit of Love emerged. One half of the eggshell became Gaia, the Earth, while the other half became Uranus, the Sky and Celestial Realm.

Nyx is attended by an owl and wears a black veil studded with stars.

See also **ANIMALS:** Owls; **CREATIVE ARTS:** Comics: *The Sandman.*

Ochossi, Oxossi

An increasingly prominent orisha, Ochossi is most famous as the Orisha of the Hunt, although like Artemis, he is so much more. His ability to "hunt" may be interpreted metaphorically.

Ochossi's name derives from a root word for "secret." Some translate his name as *"Left Handed Sorcerer."* Ochossi is a great magician. He knows *everything* about the powers of the forest, and about botanical power in general. Ochossi makes deadly arrow poison but also knows the rare antidotes. He is a master healer when he chooses. However, Ochossi's arrows *never* miss their mark.

Ochossi lives in the forest with his brothers Elegba, the trickster spirit and Ogun, the divine ironworker who forges and blesses Ochossi's tools. Together they are the hard-working magician-spirits classified as Santeria's *Warriors.*

Ochossi is especially popular in the African-Diaspora traditions of Brazil and Cuba. Most of the orishas are envisioned as Africans; Ochossi, however, often manifests as a long-haired Native American hunter. Because anthropologists were unable to locate branches of his tradition in Nigeria, many assumed that Ochossi was an Indian addition to the African pantheon.

Further research however indicated that Ketu, the Yoruba kingdom where Ochossi was originally venerated, was utterly decimated by the slave trade from 1789 onwards. The majority of Ochossi's priests were enslaved and transported to the West. His tradition ultimately *only* survived in the West, where he became an important, significant orisha. Ochossi is Patron of the Maroons, escaped communities of slaves living in remote, heavily wooded areas who appealed to him for protection.

Ochossi's shrines are decorated with antlers, animal horns, and feathers although he has transitioned from forest-spirit to urban deity. In this guise his popularity has increased exponentially.

Ochossi has simple tastes, favoring offerings like a dish of honey, trail mix or roasted peanuts. He accepts a glass of milk with cornmeal and honey added, although he likes alcoholic beverages, too. His colors are lavender and brown; his sacred number is two. Ochossi is syncretized to Saint Sebastian, whose votive image always depicts him pierced by arrows.

See also Artemis; **DICTIONARY:** Orisha, Santeria; **PLACES:** Forest.

Odin

Also known as Odhinn, Wotan, Woden.

Odin, the All-Father, is the leader of the Aesir spirits, Lord of Asgard. Devotion to Odin once spread across the entire Germanic and Norse world. One-eyed Spirit of War, Wisdom, and Death, he is married to Frigga, a birth goddess: theirs is a marriage of complementary forces. Odin is Lord of ecstasy, shamanism, and occult wisdom. He is a patriarch, occult master, wandering wizard, trickster, and shaman.

Odin loves women, knowledge, and hospitality. He is a spiritual seeker himself. His thirst and quest for occult wisdom is endless. He willingly paid the price of an eye in order to drink from the Well of Knowledge.

Freya was his first teacher: she taught him charms and spell-casting. Ultimately his quest for occult wisdom is a solitary pursuit: Odin famously pierced himself and hung for nine days and nights in shamanic ritual from the World Tree (Yggdrasil), dying a shamanic death in order to become a rune-master. The Tarot card The Hanged One may be understood to depict this ritual rather than a literal hanging.

Odin's curiosity has no bounds; he refuses to be limited by boundaries of tradition or by restrictions of gender. Odin is curious and respectful toward what was traditionally "women's magic." His myth demonstrates that he is not ashamed to learn from women.

✳ *Freya taught seiòr to Odin, although men historically did not practice this style of prophecy; it was considered a woman's art.*

✳ *When Odin gathers herbs and roots for healing, he dresses as a woman.*

> In the Eddas, Odin is accused thus: *"They say you have practiced magic … that you have cast spells like any Vala: you have wandered through the country disguised as a witch."* (See **DICTIONARY**: Völva.)

Odin wanders Earth dressed as a shabby, dusty traveler with a black hooded cloak, learning everything he can incognito. Those who are gracious to him in this guise are rewarded. Odin traditionally appears with a wide-brimmed hat sloping over his face to hide his missing eye. Similar images frequently appear on the Tarot card, The Magician. Some historians believe that the traditional stage magician's uniform is based on that of Odin, although others feel it honors Hermes, another wandering magician.

Odin has two ravens, Hugin and Munin—Thought and Memory. Every morning they fly all over Earth, then return full of news, gossip, and secrets to whisper in his ear.

Odin's familiars are two wolves. He rides a magical eight-legged stallion, Sleipneir, whose teeth are engraved with runes. Odin rides where he will, all over the Earth but also over the Milky Way and through the sky. He is a restless spirit, traveling and riding; post-Christianity, Odin continues to ride.

Post-Christianity, Odin's martyred son Baldur remained an appealing deity who was identified with the second coming of Christ. Odin was resolutely Pagan. Odin became the Wild Hunter himself, leading the Wild Hunt, which was now understood as a parade of the damned rather than of Odin's favorites. Sometimes Odin heads the Wild Hunt alone, at other times with a female co-leader—Freya, Hella, Hulda (Frau Wode), Perchta or Herta. In the guise of Chief Hunter, Odin was sometimes identified with the devil in medieval Europe.

> Wednesday is literally "Woden's Day" and is the best day to petition his help and make offerings for him. His numbers are three and nine. His sacred animals include wolves, ravens, snakes, bears, and horses. His attributes include a magical wand and spear. The *ansuz* rune may be used to request Odin's protection.

Vestiges of Odin linger in Santa Claus (Odin as gift-giving traveler). Odin too is a bearded, white-haired man, dressed in a hat and cloak with a magic staff. Santa Claus' Dutch sidekick, Black Peter, may be Odin's old friend Loki in

Encyclopedia of Witchcraft

disguise. A kinder, gentler Odin, complete with ravens and wolves, appears in the guise of the king in the 1994 Swedish fairy-tale film *The Polar Bear King*.

See also Herta; **ANIMALS:** Bears, Wolves and Werewolves; **DICTIONARY:** Seidh; **ERGOT:** The Rye Wolf.

Ogun

Also known as Ogou, Gu.

Ogun is the West African Spirit of Iron and Patron of Metalworkers who, in many traditional communities, also serve as shamans, sorcerers, healers, and ritual leaders. Ogun has various aspects or "paths": he is a sweaty, laboring blacksmith, a sharply dressed politician, a solder, a surgeon, and also a magician.

Ogun epitomizes the solitary forest-dwelling witch-doctor. He knows all the magical secrets of metalworking but also lives in close proximity with hunters and herbalists, so he has access to all branches of occult wisdom. In modern Vodou, Ogou is among the spirits most closely identified with transformational magic and *loups-garoux*—werewolves. In his guise as magician, Ogou is often paired with the female lwa Ezili Dantor.

Ogun remains popular throughout West Africa as well as in virtually all African-Diaspora traditions. (He is called Zarabanda in Palo.) His colors are red and black; his numbers are three and seven.

See also **ANIMALS:** Snakes, Wolves and Werewolves; **DICTIONARY:** Lwa, Orisha, Palo, Vodou; **ERGOT:** Corn Mother: Ezili Dantor; **MAGICAL PROFESSIONS:** Metalworkers.

Orisha Oko

In standard descriptions of the orishas, Orisha Oko is usually described as the judge who settles disputes, especially among women. Those aren't just any disputes: they are usually accusations of witchcraft.

It takes one to know one: Orisha Oko is the wise sorcerer of Earth magic who protects against witchcraft and heals its effects. Orisha Oko's main cult center, Irawo in the far northwest of Yorubaland, was an important shrine for the settlement of witchcraft accusations.

Disputes regarding accusations or suspicions of witchcraft were traditionally resolved by ritual in his shrines. His devotees are largely female; devotion to Orisha Oko is hereditary. Accusations of witchcraft forge links to this orisha. Once accused (and presumably if one survives the accusation) then one is expected to form a relationship with Orisha Oko that will continue through generations.

Orisha Oko is variously described as female or male. He is most commonly represented in myths as a hunter who has decided to farm instead. He is closely associated with rituals of agricultural magic. His attribute is an iron stave made from a hoe blade. He works closely with Ogun who forges his tools.

Orisha Oko manifests his anger through unyielding, infertile Earth and barren, infertile women. His colors are red and white. He accepts yams as an offering.

See also Ogun, Oshun; **DICTIONARY:** Àjé, Orisha; **ERGOT:** Corn Mother; **MAGICAL PROFESSIONS:** Metalworkers.

Oshun

Also known as Ochun, Oxun.

The sweetest, youngest, most beautiful of the orishas, Oshun is the spirit of sweet water, beauty, women, and witchcraft. Her epithet "The Source" indicates that she is the source of rivers, oceans, and children.

Oshun is the embodiment of love and romance, the Yoruba spirit most associated with providing and healing fertility. She has tremendous magical knowledge. Oshun's power extends over various parts of the human anatomy, particularly the reproductive organs. Without her blessing (or at least her sanction) there is no healing, no rain, no growth, no prosperity, no babies, no joy.

She is the orisha of luxury and wealth. Countless money spells incorporate petitions to Oshun. She is particularly sympathetic as, unlike many other spirits, Oshun too has been utterly desolate and poverty-stricken and so understands hardship and crisis.

Oshun may manifest in the form of her sacred birds: peacocks, parrots or vultures.

> Oshun is the leader of the Àjé. The importance of this female power is suggested in the birds that top beautiful Yoruba crowns. (See **DICTIONARY: Àjé.**)

Her most common manifestation is as a breathtakingly beautiful woman, usually dressed in yellow or gold. She wears five brass bracelets and a mirror at her belt, the better to be able to stop and admire herself whenever she wishes. Oshun bears a pot of river water, her gift of healing magic. She removes malevolent spells from her devotees, especially those cast using the power of botanicals.

That's the standard, most typical vision of Oshun. The orishas, however, possess multiple paths (manifestations) simultaneously. Thus there is Oshun the Goddess of Love and Fertility, her most familiar manifestation, but there are also other specialized visions of Oshun. Oshun also has paths identified with witchcraft.

❊ *As Oshun Olololdi she is the Mother of Divination. She is wed to Orunmila, Spirit of the Oracle, and is intensely involved in the process of divination. Oshun Olololdi manifests as a waterfall.*

❊ *Swamps are fresh water too: as Oshun Ibu Kolé she is the Buzzard Mother, a powerful swamp witch.*

Oshun Ibu Kolé is Oshun down on her luck. She is dressed in rags and has ragged, disheveled hair. She lives in marshes, swamps or muddy waters. Her sacred creatures include vultures, alligators, and crocodiles. Buzzards share their carrion with her so that she doesn't starve.

Perchta

Also known as Berchta, Frau Berta, Eisen Berta, Berchtli.

A Pre-Christian German divinity, Perchta manifests as a beautiful woman with pearls braided into her golden hair. A white veil obscures her face. She carries the keys to happiness in one hand and a spray of mayflowers in the other. Perchta lives in a subterranean palace, which has a fabulous garden where she welcomes the souls of children who died in infancy.

She has another face, too, also manifesting as an old decrepit hag with long, unkempt, gray hair and disheveled clothes. In this guise, she carries a distaff. It's unknown now whether she always had these two aspects (and it's very possible) or whether she was transformed into a hag following the arrival of Christianity.

Perchta had many devotees and so post-Christianity was aggressively denigrated. She was demonized as a Queen of Witches and is among the leaders of the Wild Hunt, where she usually leads a parade of unbaptized babies.

Perchta travels with a retinue of spirits known as the *Perchten*. According to Christian legend, the devil rides in their midst, although this may merely indicate the existence of a male deity who once accompanied her.

Perchta is used as a threat to make children behave before Yule. She allegedly personally punishes "bad children," although she gives gifts to good ones.

With the coming of Christianity she became the personification of the night preceding Epiphany (January 6th). In German tradition, this is known as *Perchtennacht*. (Epiphany is also called *Perchtentag*—Perchta's Day.) Modern Perchten processions are characterized by grotesque masks.

Perchta possesses various paths:

✳ *As* Butzenbercht *she comes bearing gifts*

✳ *As* Spinn Stubenfrau *("Spinning Room Woman") she visits homes at night*

✳ *As* Stomach Slasher *she inflicts severe punishment on women who do not leave her traditional Yule offerings of pancakes, dumplings, and herring. She rips open their stomachs, removes what she wants, and roughly sews them up again*

Vestiges of devotion to Perchta survive. In some Alpine villages it is still customary to place offerings of food for her on rooftops.

See also Befana, Herta, Hulda; **CREATIVE ARTS:** Dance: Perchtentanz; **ERGOT:** Corn Mother: Perchta; **TOOLS:** Masks; **WOMEN'S MYSTERIES:** Spinning.

Proserpina (Persephone)

Persephone is the young Greek spirit, kidnapped and raped by Hades and forced to become Queen of the Realm of Death for half of each year. During the other half of the year, Persephone is permitted to live with her mother Demeter on Earth. Persephone and Demeter were the central figures in various spiritual rituals and traditions, most notably the Eleusinian Mysteries.

Whether Persephone was invoked by individual witches is unknown. According to Horace's *Epodes* (30 BCE), witches worshipped Proserpina. Proserpina is the Roman name given to Persephone.

Are Proserpina and Persephone one and the same? It's no longer entirely clear. In Rome, Demeter was identified with the Italian Corn Mother Ceres and their myths merged, although in this case they clearly were once distinct independent deities. Ceres is the mother of Roman Proserpina. One version of Persephone's abduction suggests that it occurred on Sicily, once a thriving Greek colony.

Whether they are identical spirits or whether two distinct spirits have merged, Proserpina manifested somewhat differently in Italy, in particular in regards to her close identification with witchcraft.

Proserpina is the spirit who goes to Hades and back, traveling back and forth like a shaman. She is a liminal figure who survives in both realms. Persephone is the Matron of Necromancers. She presides over death: she is the

Queen of the Dead but she herself is not dead.

The name Proserpina derives from the Latin *serpere*, "to creep" or "to crawl" like a serpent. *Proserpere* means to crawl forward. (*Persephone*, on the other hand, is frequently translated as "destroying face" or "light-bearing face.")

Sacred Creatures: Snakes and fish
Attributes: Keys and a torch, emblems she shares with Hecate
Plants: Rue and parsley

Proserpina is often depicted holding a fish and a key. A fish containing a key is a secret reference to Proserpina. Proserpina is the secret deity at the heart of April Fool's Day. References to "All Fools Day" first appeared in Europe during medieval times but may be traced back to Roman rituals involving the myth of Proserpina and her mother.

When Pluto, Lord of the Dead, abducted Proserpina she called out to her mother for help. Ceres, who could only hear the echo of her daughter's voice, searched in vain for Proserpina. The fruitless search of Ceres for her daughter (commemorated during the Roman festival of Cerealia) is believed to be the mythological antecedent of the fool's errands popular on April 1st.

In France and Italy, April Fool's Day is known as April Fish Day. People once played tricks by pinning paper fish to other's backs. Old French April Fool's postcards often depict a beautiful woman holding a big, floppy fish.

See also Dionysus; **ANIMALS:** Snakes; **DICTIONARY:** Necromancy; **ERGOT:** Corn Mother: Ceres, Demeter; **MAGICAL ARTS:** Necromancy.

Ragana

The name of this Baltic deity from Latvia and Lithuania derives from the root verb "to see" but is now synonymous with "witch." Ragana is a powerful prophetess who reveals the future. Post-Christianity she became demoted to a witch who allegedly brings misfortune to humans and animals.

See **FAIRIES:** Nature-spirit Fairies: Lauma.

Rübezahl

Rübezahl, a male dwarf, is the most famous of the German mountain spirits. He dwells in Riesengebirge, between Bohemia (now the Czech Republic) and Silesia and in the caves of The Brocken, where he allegedly enjoys leading travelers astray although he welcomes respectful witches.

Rübezahl wraps himself in a large cloak to mask his face, reminiscent of Odin. He has the power to manipulate weather. He is the Lord of Magical and Medicinal Plants and Patron of Root-workers.

As late as 1814, inhabitants of the Silesian mountains still made pilgrimages to a mountain summit near the source of the Elbe River, where they sacrificed black hens and roosters to Rübezahl to keep him pacified and prevent flood waters from rising, even though a chapel built at this spot in 1681 was dedicated to Mary in an attempt to divert worshippers. Rübezahl's devotees returned home with water, herbs, and roots, which were used in cleansing and protective rituals.

Rübezahl carries a trident. His bird is the raven. The Church identified him as a demon or even as Satan himself.

According to a German fairy tale, Rübezahl

kidnapped a princess and, to please her, planted a huge field of turnips (*rüben*). She asked him to count (*zahlen*) them. While he was doing so, she escaped. This tale is featured in Andrew Lang's *Brown Fairy* Book, as well as in a German silent movie *Rübezahl's Wedding* starring Paul Wegener and Lydia Salmonova.

See also **ANIMALS:** Corvids; **BOTANICALS:** Roots; **DICTIONARY:** Root Doctor; **FAIRIES:** Nature-spirit Fairies: Elf; **PLACES:** The Brocken.

La Santisima Muerte

La Santisima Muerte, Blessed Death, is an unofficial saint increasingly popular in Mexico. Santisima Muerte is the goddess in the form of a skeleton. She is robed and sometimes carries a scythe like the Grim Reaper. She is reminiscent of other goddesses identified with Death such as Kali or Baba Yaga. Like Kali and Baba Yaga, La Santisima Muerte is both fear and loved.

She traditionally helps women get errant husbands and lovers back, although you have to be reasonably desperate to petition her as by doing so you are literally conjuring death. It is dangerous to invoke her but she can do everything, has access to all knowledge, and fears nothing. (After all, she *is* Death.) Because she is hard to handle, it's traditional to invoke her simultaneously with powerful but more benevolent spirits like saints Anthony or Elena or Archangel Michael, so that they'll keep her in line if necessary.

La Santisima Muerte is believed to be a modern manifestation of the Aztec deity Mictlancihuatl, "*Lady of Death.*"

La Santisima Muerte is particularly popular amongst prostitutes and magical practitioners, who must both often tread in dangerous territory and encounter dangerous characters. Once obscure and outlawed by the Roman Catholic Church, La Santisima Muerte is growing in popularity; her images are now found frequently in *botanicas*, Latin American shops selling magical and herbal supplies.

See **DICTIONARY:** Curandera.

Set, Seth

Set is the Egyptian Lord of the Desert and Lord of Chaos and Disorder. He is among the set of quadruplets born to the Earth and Sky; his siblings are Osiris, Isis, and Nephthys.

Both Osiris and Set love their sister Isis but she chooses Osiris. Set marries Nephthys but she also loves Osiris, and so theirs is not a happy marriage.

Osiris is initially Ruler of the Black Land, the fertile belt of civilization around the Nile River. Set is the Lord of the Red Land as the Egyptians characterized the harsh, barren desert. It, too, however, is a place of power.

Set was a powerful magician, second only to Isis. Appeals are made to Set to keep bad weather far away; he has dominion over rainstorms, sandstorms and windstorms.

He is the master of love and sex magic and is petitioned for assistance with contraception and abortion. Set appears on many ancient uterine amulets. Some of these amulets were employed to "open" the womb, requesting assistance with menstruation, conception or birth. Set is also featured on amulets to "close" the womb. These amulets were used to procure contraception or abortion.

Sometimes a hero, sometimes a controversial figure, he is most famous for his rivalry with Horus, his nephew. In modern retellings of the saga, Set is usually presented as the villain, however it may be more complex than that: the myth may be a metaphor for the historic rivalry between Upper and Lower Egypt, which Lower Egypt (Horus' territory) ultimately won.

Set's main cult centers were at Tanis, Ombos, and Naqada. His color is red. His sacred creatures include crocodiles, hippopotami, and pigs, as well as something called the "Set beast" which has never been conclusively identified. The Set beast may be an extinct creature, a creature that only exists in the spirit realm, or an anteater.

See also Isis **ANIMALS:** Pigs; **ERGOT:** Corn Mother: Isis.

Shiva

Lord of the Moon, Storms, and the Himalayas, Shiva is the Lord of Death for the sake of Rebirth. He is a great healer, described as the greatest of physicians. Deity of the forest, hunting, and fishing, he is Patron and Ruler of Untouchables and Demons.

Shiva is often portrayed with blue skin, four arms, and four faces—with three eyes each. His third eye, located in the center of his forehead, possesses the powers of creation and destruction.

Shiva, also known as "the howler" is described as the "*destroyer of rites and social barriers.*" He was a knowledge sharer, accused of teaching sacred texts to the low-born who previously had been denied access to such secrets.

He haunts cemeteries in the company of ghosts and less reputable spirits.

Shiva is accompanied by a retinue of witches, ghosts, spirits, and gnomes (Earth spirits). He is naked but adorned with snakes and scorpions, and he wears a necklace of skulls. His hair is hopelessly tangled and matted. His face is covered with ashes from cremations.

Shiva is an indigenous, pre-Aryan deity of India. The Aryan invaders initially disliked Shiva but were eventually forced to integrate him into their pantheon, although he is still considered chaotic, dangerous, and unpredictable.

He is the protector of those who do not fit easily into conventional society or who do not fit at all. Shiva presides over the realm of the dead. His statues are erected near funeral pyres or in cemeteries. Shiva is often found wandering in cemeteries. He also lives within mountain caves.

Shiva's sacred creatures include bulls, snakes, and tigers. He is the protector of trees, animals, and wild nature. He has compassion for the demons he rules despite their wicked dispositions. His colors are blue, red ochre, and saffron.

Many consider Shiva to have originally been identical with Dionysus, who once traveled through India. Like Dionysus, he is identified with intoxicating substances and sex magic. He is often portrayed in the form of a phallus (the "Shiva lingam"), as is Dionysus. Both lead parades of dancing witches and spirits. Like Dionysus, Shiva is happily wed: Shiva and his consort Parvati symbolize the perfect union of complementary powers.

Sibillia, Sibilla

According to Italian legend, the Cumaean Sibyl took refuge in a cavern in the Apennines. Her underground paradise was reached through a grotto filled with snakes in the mountains of Norcia, a region renowned for its witches and mushrooms. In this cavern, Sibilla teaches the magical arts to those who wish to learn them.

Sounds like a fairy tale? A real-life shrine, the Ridge of the Sibillini, once existed below Mount Vettore. During the fifteenth century visitors from throughout Europe traveled to Norcia to see the cave, some bringing grimoires to consecrate at Sibilla's lake.

By the Middle Ages, the ancient prophetess had emerged as a goddess of witches. In Ferrara, Italy, Sibilla, in the guise of *La Signora del Corso*, presided over the witches' flight and witches' ball. At the end of the feast, she touched all bottles and platters with her golden wand; they immediately replenished. In re-enactments of ancient shamanic rituals, the witches gathered up all the bones from the meal they had completed. These were placed within animal skins. Sibilla touched the rolled-up skins with her wand and hey presto! The animals returned to life.

Sibilla is a hospitable spirit: according to legend, Diana and Fata Morgana frequently live with her. By the end of the fifteenth century, the Church had a standing order to excommunicate anyone who made the pilgrimage to the shrine at Norcia. (Of course, on the other hand, those who defied the decree and visited the shrine were allegedly blessed by Sibilla with a lifetime of joy.) Should you stay in Sibilla's cavern for over a year, you would never be able to leave but would remain ageless and alive, living amidst abundance and revelry in a witches' paradise.

Of course those are the positive legends: witch-goddesses usually weren't permitted such good press and so other stories exist too, although even these may be interpreted in various ways:

❋ *Sibilla sprouts a snake's tail every Saturday.*

❋ *The legendary Wandering Jew allegedly finally stopped wandering, transformed into a snake, and serves as Sibilla's door guardian.*

❋ *According to another legend, at night, all the inhabitants of Sibilla's paradise turn into snakes.*

❋ *In another legend, in order to gain admittance to Sibilla's Cave, one must have sex with snakes.*

See also Kybele; **ANIMALS:** Snakes; **BOOKS:** Library of the Lost: Sibylline Books; **DICTIONARY:** Sibyl.

Simbi

Who says magicians need to be human? This most powerful of magical practitioners manifests in the form of a great snake.

Simbi names a family of Congolese water spirits who have gained prominence among the lwa of Vodoun. The various Simbis may also be understood as different aspects or "paths" of one spirit.

Simbi rules all aspects of magic. In the guise of Simbi Makaya, he is a powerful botanical magician. Simbi protects magical practitioners and offers them his tutelage. Legends describe children who go missing, stolen by Simbi, only to return to their homes years later, masters of magic.

In addition to magic and witchcraft, Simbi has dominion over communications, crossroads, and currents. As the ruler of currents, Simbi has dominion over the flow of information and energy: this ancient magician has become Patron of Computers and the Internet. Placing images of a snake on your computer (or as a screen-saver) allegedly protects it and reinforces its power.

Simbi accepts offerings of milk and water (especially rainwater), as well as alcoholic beverages such as whiskey or rum.

Milo Rigaud, a scholar of Vodou, identifies Simbi with Hermes. In the Vodou tradition, Simbi is also syncretized with Moses. Simbi represents The Magician in The New Orleans Tarot Deck.

New Orleans Voodoo Priestess Marie Laveau danced with a serpent known as *"The Grand Zombi." "Zombi"* may be understood as a corruption of *"Simbi,"* not as a reference to the living dead.

See **FAIRIES:** Changelings, Fairy Doctors, Fairy Magicians.

Tante Arie ("Aunt Arie")

Also known as Tantairie.

It's unclear whether Tante Arie, from the Jura canton of Switzerland and Montbéliard in France, is a witch or a fairy or both. She manifests in the form of a snake or giant and lives in a cave filled with treasure chests brimming with gold. She wears a diamond crown, has iron teeth and goose's feet, like a combination of Baba Yaga and Mother Goose.

Tante Arie has dominion over spinning and spinners. She rides through the region on Christmas Eve on her donkey, distributing gifts to those deemed deserving but punishing disobedient children.

See also Befana, Perchta; **ANIMALS:** Snakes; **FAIRY-TALE WITCHES**.

Tezcatlipoca

The Aztec Lord of Night, Tezcatlipoca means "Smoking Mirror." He is the Patron of Sorcerers, Shamans, and Witches.

Tezcatlipoca is an omniscient, all-knowing, all-powerful, somewhat dangerous figure who sees *everything* in his obsidian mirror. He is most famous as the rival of the god Quetzalcoatl, the Plumed Serpent, whose fall from grace is maneuvered by Tezcatlipoca's smoke and mirrors.

Because post-Christianity, Quetzalcoatl became identified as a Christ-figure, Tezcatlipoca, the unrepentant sorcerer, became identified with Satan. In many of his existing myths he appears threatening and malevolent; it is unclear whether this was always the case or whether his malevolence has increased with time and distortion.

He is a shape-shifter: his traditional forms include coyote, jaguar, monkey, owl, and skunk. His sacred bird is the turkey. Tezcatlipoca's sacred animal and nahual is the jaguar. He manifests in jaguars and in obsidian. He lives in the core of the Earth in a mirrored realm filled with jaguars.

See **ANIMALS:** Jaguars, Nahual.

Thoth

Lord Thoth is such an ancient deity that, according to Egyptian myth, he existed prior to creation. In some versions, he is the supreme creator. Even when this is not so, Thoth did his share of creating. Among his inventions are writing and magic spells, inextricably linked in Egyptian witchcraft as well as in many other traditions.

In his guise as Patron of Scribes, Thoth has an ibis' head. As a master magician, he manifests as a baboon. Thoth is Ra, the Creator's, right-hand man; without Thoth, Isis and her siblings would never have been born. He taught Isis everything he knew; she is perhaps the only one who surpasses his magical knowledge although, according to myth, even Isis still needs his assistance and advice once in a while.

He is what is considered a "cool" deity; he calms and relaxes impassioned situations. In one legend, only Thoth can safely subdue a rampaging goddess threatening to destroy Earth.

As befitting a shaman, Thoth lives in many realms at once: he journeys among the land of the living, teaching his magical skills. He serves in the Hall of the Dead as the scribe who records the accomplishments and sins of the deceased. He also rides in the solar barq beside Ra and thus lives in the realm of the spirits.

Thoth was the prototype for Egyptian priests and magicians. After Egypt came under Greek rule in 332 BCE Thoth was identified with Hermes and his cult city Khmun was renamed Hermopolis. Because the legendary magician Hermes Trismegistus came from Egypt, where he composed the books known as *The Hermetica*, many believe he is either Thoth or one of his particularly accomplished priests in disguise.

See also Isis; **HALL OF FAME:** Hermes Trismegistus, Moses.

Tlazolteotl

Tlazolteotl's most famous manifestation is as a statue of a naked, grimacing, squatting, laboring woman: this statue appears as the stolen idol in *Raiders of the Lost Ark*. Tlazolteotl has other images too: she is again depicted naked but for a peaked barked hat, riding on a broomstick in the company of owls, ravens, and bats.

The Spanish Conquistadors were shocked and perplexed when they first saw these images of the Aztec goddess—they thought they left images like these back in Europe with the witch trials. Witchcraft is international.

Tlazolteotl is the spirit of magic, healing, love, sex, desire, cleansing, and garbage.

Her name means "Eater of Filth." In her capacity as the Spirit of Filth, Tlazolteotl cleanses individuals and Earth of spiritual debris, sin, and shame. Not surprisingly, Tlazolteotl is credited with invention of the Aztec sweat bathhouse, the temescal.

She is the Matron of Female Healers, Midwives, and Weavers.

The White Women

The White Women are spirits who live in German forests where they assist travelers, practice divination, and dance fertility dances. Their exact identity and nature is unclear: they have been variously identified as spirits, lingering ghosts of witches, or goddess-worshipping witches.

Various forest-dwelling female Slavic spirits including the Rusalki and Vila are described as being dressed in white.

See also Hulda; **FAIRIES:** Nature-spirit Fairies: Rusalka, Vila.

Yemaya

Yemaya is the Great Mother of Yoruba tradition, the ultimate expression of female power. The translation of her name, *"The Mother Whose Children are Fish,"* indicates that Yemaya's children are innumerable. She is the mother of most of the Yoruba spirits, the orishas. She represents the epitome of motherhood and manifests all aspects of maternity to their fullest degree. Yemaya is among the most beloved of the orishas.

Yemaya is associated with the sea and salt water. She resides in the sea, she is the spirit of the sea, and she is the sea, specifically the upper portion of the ocean, all simultaneously. (Another orisha, Olokun, rules the oceans depths and floor.)

Her name also indicates that all humans begin their life in their mother's amniotic sea. Although most typically manifesting as benevolent and nurturing, Yemaya also has a destructive aspect: oceans have riptides, tidal waves, and whirlpools.

Despite her modern associations, in Yemaya's earliest incarnation, she was the spirit of Nigeria's Ogun River. According to one legend, Yemaya was once the Queen of the Cemetery until she tricked the orisha Oya into taking her place.

Yemaya wears seven skirts. Her attributes include a silver mask and a snake. Amongst her various "paths" or manifestations is Yemaya Mayalewo (also Mayaleo). In this path she is identified as a witch who lives a solitary existence in wooded lagoons, such as mangrove swamps where salt water merges with fresh. In her witch path, Yemaya works closely with Ogun and is powerfully associated with the production and magic powers of indigo, her sacred color and substance.

See **MAGICAL PROFESSIONS:** Metalworkers; **PLACES:** Swamps.

Ergot, The Corn Mother, and The Rye Wolf

Mysteries of Corn

Classic Halloween postcards are packed with evocative images of witchcraft. They have to be: the artists were given a very small frame in which to work their magic and so these little cards are studded with images that are the visual equivalent of short-hand, intended to evoke the haunting ambience of Halloween. These images are the iconography of Halloween. Most are familiar and predictable: witches, of course, but also black cats, bats, spiders' webs, cauldrons, and corn. Witches are depicted engaged in a variety of activities including flying on broomsticks, stirring cauldrons, scaring children, performing divination, reading grimoires, and sitting in cornfields.

Bats, broomsticks, black cats, OK; but what's the witchcraft connection with cornfields?

The standard modern explanation for the corn connection is that in North America, Halloween corresponds with the corn harvest (pumpkin harvest, too) and so these vegetables have become coincidentally associated with the holiday. This is a superficial explanation however: the connection of corn and witchcraft has deep roots and is hardly limited to North America.

The first mystery of corn may be determining exactly what is under discussion. The word "corn" sometimes causes confusion. In the United States, the only *corn* is maize corn, sacred to Native Americans, the corn first encountered by Europeans in America.

That colonists were previously unaware of maize is drummed into the heads of American school children, who are then confused to learn that Demeter is the ancient Greek "Corn Goddess." With no knowledge of corn, how could it have a goddess?

In the rest of the world, "corn" indicates grain of any sort. Thus *Corn Mother* really means *Grain Mother* and frequently really *Rye Mother*, as explored in this section.

In mainstream modern Western culture, animals and humans are commonly acknowledged as living while plants, although theoretically acknowledged as "alive," are often considered little more than inanimate objects. Most people do not believe that plants have consciousness and emotions, can communicate or that they suffer when picked or harvested.

There is no way to understand the mysteries of agricultural magic and the Corn Mother without accepting that plants are living beings possessing souls and spiritual protection, similar to animals and humans, even if they're not mobile, even if they're not *alive* in the exact same manner that humans and animals live.

> The notion of the Corn Mother is predicated on the belief that plants are killed when harvested in the same manner that animals (or people) are killed when they are slaughtered, even if there is no blood, even if the plants show no fear or resistance.

Earth's earliest peoples were foragers and hunter-gatherers: they lived solely from what Earth gave them. Earth was the mother who provides—when she didn't, one performed rituals of appeasement to coax more bounty from her and/or one moved nomadically until sustenance was found.

The concept of agriculture, of setting down roots in one spot, of working the land, planting, determining crops and harvesting them— taking what you planted rather than simply accepting what the Earth Mother gave you— was a radical human development, a revolution that caused shifts in spiritual and mental perceptions and even in the human body. The first permanent blood-type mutation (Type A) occurs at this time, apparently in response to this agricultural and dietary revolution.

This agricultural revolution did more than permit people to settle in one place: it stimulated

a new way of understanding Earth, and new fears and rituals so deeply imbedded they *still* permeate our culture even if we no longer understand or completely recognize them.

Previously people avoided digging too deeply in Earth: similar to mining, rooting around in Earth's female body was uncomfortably close to rape. In the beginning, people were still asking permission. In the beginning, prior to the invention of the plough, agriculture was considered to be a part of women's mysteries.

Planting and harvesting were accompanied by elaborate rituals requesting permission and of appeasement and self-protection. Priestesses communed with Earth so as to work together with her to reap a satisfactory, blessed harvest.

> Among the forms of the early Neolithic Earth goddess is the sow. Pigs are associated with women's agriculture prior to the invention of the plough. It's believed that observing the rooting of pigs led to the first *sowing* and reaping. The pig remains the alter ego of the Corn Mother.

The Earth Mother is the metaphorical mother of people but she is the actual mother of plants. Seeds are placed within her womb to grow. They emerge alive and would theoretically remain alive for their natural lifespan if left unharvested.

In order for the Earth Mother's human children to survive, however, they must sacrifice what are effectively their own siblings, the plants. Furthermore, this must be accomplished without angering the Earth Mother so much that she withholds next year's harvest.

Grain, the crop that stimulated the agricultural revolution, is harvested in autumn, often in late October, corresponding to what is now Samhain/Halloween. Corn, sacrificed so that people can live, was traditionally cut with a scythe or sickle, harvest tools still associated with the Grim Reaper.

A complex system of agricultural magic developed, some involving the entire community, others exclusively women's mysteries. Among the most prevalent components of traditional agricultural magic are:

* *Offerings of menstrual blood*

* *Ritual sex in the fields*

* *Ritual dancing involving leaping (flying) to encourage the plants to grow*

* *Ritual dancing involving broomsticks (women) and pitchforks (men)*

* *Shamanic battles to protect the harvest*

Many of these traditions, often long divorced from their agricultural origins, remain significant components of witchcraft, its traditions, and myths.

Sacrifices were offered to the Earth Mother as reciprocal gestures: she was expected to sacrifice her botanical children. *Every* harvest thus is a sacrifice. As agriculture changed from an exclusively female art the nature of reciprocal sacrifices changed too—menstrual blood, once so holy and powerful that it was secret and not publicly discussed, transformed into something rarely discussed because it was perceived as shameful and dangerous. If menstrual blood is the preferred offering, however, agricultural power is squarely in the hands of women.

Moving away from menstrual blood offerings also changes the nature of the sacrifice: menstrual blood was once understood as potential children. (Lack of menstruation during pregnancy was interpreted as menstrual blood being used to form the child's body.)

Women's potential children were given as offerings of thanks and appeasement for the harvest. Menstrual blood is the *only* blood that can be offered without injury or death: substitutes inevitably involved animal or human sacrifice—someone's real child was offered as gratitude and appeasement.

Earth, like a woman, was understood to have her own menstrual blood: iron ore. Ironworking placed the equivalent of menstrual power in men's hands. The creation of iron agricultural tools changed the power structure of agriculture: it became heavy labor suited to men's physical strength. Iron knives also changed the nature of sacrifice—different types of blood sacrifice became available, yet still, because of iron, tangentially related to menstruation.

Tension between men and women, anxiety about exactly where power lies, would also lead to fears of malevolent witchcraft. If women have the power to stimulate growth, then presumably they have the power to stunt it as well. Among the primary accusations of malevolent witchcraft throughout history is causing blight and harming the harvest.

See **DIVINE WITCH:** Orisha Oko; **MAGICAL PROFESSIONS:** Metalworkers.

Corn Mother

The classic attribute of the Corn Mother is that she simultaneously destroys and creates. In the act of killing, she gives life and vice versa. Even the most terrifying Corn Mother—and some are truly monsters—provides nourishment; even the most benevolent is potentially a killer.

Nourishment generously given can also be inexplicably withheld and vice versa.

❋ The Corn Mother is the loving, devoted mother who provides for her children's needs.

❋ The Corn Mother is the mad, raging, out-of-control mother (see Ergot, page 426).

Her aggressive act of grinding transforms grain into meal. Destruction and sustenance emerge from the identical source.

Mother was intended literally. In Assyrian, *bar* means both "son" and "corn"—a concept also reflected in classical Greek where *stachys* refers to a spike of wheat but also implies a child. Their identification as mothers is intrinsic to the identity of many Corn Mothers including Demeter, Isis, Ezili Dantor, and the Virgin Mary.

Virgo is the constellation identified with the Corn Mother. The astrological sign's modern image remains based on its ancient Babylonian depiction: a woman carrying a sheaf of corn. Originally, this sheaf was understood to simultaneously indicate a child.

The Earth sign Virgo is thus represented by a Virgin (originally meaning an independent woman) holding her child, which is simultaneously a human infant and a stalk of wheat. This is the basis of many mystery religions: the child is the mystery; the mother is the deity.

By the Middle Ages, European Corn Mothers were scary cannibal hags who lay in wait in the cornfields to seize unwitting children, perhaps attempting to take sacrifices (payment) no longer offered. Sometimes these Corn Mothers are explicitly identified as witches: witches, too, are feared (or respected) as potentially dangerous but also are potential sources of wisdom, healing, protection, and joy.

The frequent associations of Corn Mothers with iron betray their affinity with certain spiritual traditions, witchcraft, and women's ancient blood magic.

Corn spirits aren't only fierce, raging hags; sometimes they are beautiful, benevolent grand goddesses. Sometimes they are both, as in the Greek spirit who epitomizes the Corn Mother, Demeter.

Demeter

"*De*" refers to divinity, as in *deity, dei* or *deva*; "*Meter*" is literally *mother*, and so Demeter is the *Divine Mother* or the *Deified Mother*. Another suggestion is that her name derives from *deai*, the Cretan word for barley and thus her name would mean *Barley Mother*. (Barley was among the very first grains cultivated in that region and frequently the most successful; Crete was a particularly early area of cultivation.)

Demeter's votive imagery shows her holding wheat in one hand, poppies in the other while snakes writhe around her. Sometimes she brandishes a pomegranate too. She famously has golden hair like a field of ripe wheat. Her sacred animals include pigs, horses, and snakes.

Demeter is not an Earth goddess; she is specifically the spirit of cultivation and crops. Her most famous myth is the saga of the kidnapping of her daughter Persephone.

Instead of residing in Olympus, Demeter prefers to live on Earth. Although she has liaisons (notably with her brother Zeus, Persephone's father), she is an independent, unmarried woman. She raises her daughter herself.

One day, Persephone, usually identified as the Spirit of Spring, spots an unusual and beautiful black narcissus. It's a trap. When she plucks it, Earth breaks open beneath her feet. Hades, her uncle, Lord of the Dead, rides up in his chariot, grabs Persephone and pulls her down to his realm. In a moment, Earth closes up, as if this incident never occurred.

Persephone just has time to scream; Demeter hears her and comes running but is unable to locate her. Persephone has been playing with various maidens but not one has witnessed her kidnapping.

Demeter proceeds to behave like any parent who has lost a child; she runs around hysterically searching, with absolutely no success. She continues to search; she beseeches help from her fellow gods. *Only* Hecate, lunar Spirit of Witchcraft, offers her assistance.

Demeter searches all over Earth on a fool's quest looking for Persephone, who, of course, is nowhere on Earth. She's down below, locked in gloomy Hades, Realm of the Dead.

Demeter's search for Persephone is a lengthy epic saga; she has many adventures and encounters many characters. She eventually receives information from two sources: a young swineherd, the sole witness to the crime; several of his pigs fell into the chasm together with Persephone. Hecate also brings Demeter to Helios the Sun, witness of everything that occurs during the day, who confirms that Hades has kidnapped Persephone.

Demeter demands that Zeus, King of the Gods, force Hades to return Persephone. This is when she discovers that technically Hades *didn't* kidnap Persephone—or at least not from his perspective, as Persephone's father Zeus *gave* her to him. Neither bothered to consult with mother or daughter/bride. Hades refuses to send her back; Zeus isn't interested in attempting to force him.

In response, beautiful, golden Demeter transforms into the Corn Mother's shadow side. She abruptly withdraws her gift of fertility from Earth: nothing grows. She begins to wander in the guise of an old, gray, bitter, gloomy, humorless, and *dangerous* hag; she still has her goddess powers; she is still grand. It is during this period that she founds the Eleusinian Mystery religion. A reaped ear of corn (wheat) was displayed as the central mystery at Eleusis.

> Another myth involving Demeter suggests that she was the very last Greek deity to stop accepting human sacrifice.

People begin to starve. Customary offerings to the gods are no longer forthcoming and so the gods begin to starve too. Eventually the protests of the other gods, as well as the potentially disastrous weakening of their powers normally fueled by offerings, finally forces Zeus to order Hades to return Persephone to Demeter. Hermes is sent to fetch her.

Meanwhile in Hades, Persephone has been raped and set on the throne as the queen of Hades. In a parallel action to her mourning mother, she has been on a hunger strike. However, she has consumed six seeds from one of Hades' pomegranate trees and so Hades refuses to let her leave with Hermes. By eating the food of the dead, she has joined their ranks.

A compromise is reached: Persephone will spend half the year with her mother on Earth, half with her husband in Hades. The time spent with Hades corresponds to the period following the harvest when crops are dormant; she emerges on Earth with the first breath of spring. When she is in Hades, her mother mourns and nothing grows; when Persephone emerges in springtime, her mother rejoices and crops are abundant.

This story is ages old; countless interpretations exist, the most obvious that Persephone, daughter of the Corn Mother, is a metaphor for grain.

Hidden undercurrents, however, lie beneath the tale of Persephone's kidnapping and Demeter's subsequent grief, desolation, and rage. It is more than the tale of one mother's loss and more than just an allegory of the harvest.

✻ *If Persephone represents grain then the story may also be understood as a metaphor for the transfer of power over agriculture and its rituals from women to men with different spiritual orientations. Persephone is now a prize to be violently taken without consulting the Corn Mother.*

✻ *Who owns the child? Previously the child belonged to its mother; Zeus asserts father-right, a radical concept at one time. Hades does not actually kidnap Persephone—her father gave her to him. The two men (father and prospective husband) negotiated the deal without input from mother or daughter, a scenario that replays daily in much of today's world.*

✻ *Demeter the Corn Mother lives humbly on Earth, not in the palaces of Olympus. Her traditional offerings included raw grain, raw honeycombs, and unspun wool—simple offerings that indicate that Demeter was a deity of the ordinary people. If Persephone is a metaphor for grain, then who owns the grain? Among the underlying themes of the saga are class and property issues very relevant to emergent agrarian societies: rank exists in all societies but* peasants *don't exist among hunter-gatherers.*

See **ANIMALS:** Pigs, Snakes; **BOTANICALS:** Opium Poppy; **DIVINE WITCH:** Hecate, Hermes, Proserpina; **MAGICAL ARTS:** Necromancy.

✻ ✻ ✻

Among Earth's many other Corn Mothers are the following:

Anat

In a Canaanite myth, Baal, Spirit of Rain, Lord of Grain, is the brother and consort of Anat, fierce goddess of war, sex, and fertility. During a drought, Baal becomes weak and depleted. Mot, Lord of Death, takes advantage of his condition and kills Baal. He hasn't reckoned on Anat: in a fury, Anat cleaves Mot with her sickle. She scorches him, winnows him in her sieve, personally grinds him up in a mill, and scatters what's left over Earth.

Baba Yaga

In some legends, Baba Yaga lives in Russian rye fields while they ripen. Because she is fierce, unpredictable, and dangerous, her very presence protects the fields: she'll eat anyone who dares damage her grain. However, during the harvest, in order to even have a harvest, she must be driven into an unharvested area or away into the forest. Sometimes, a small patch at the very end of the field was braided, ornamented, and left uncut as an offering—or resting place—for Baba Yaga. (See **DIVINE WITCH:** Baba Yaga.)

Ceres

The word "cereal" derives from her name. This Etruscan goddess has now become almost completely identified with Demeter but was originally an independent deity closely allied with Tellus, the Earth Mother. Tellus is the Earth herself; Ceres, her closest companion, is the Spirit of Grain and Cultivation. They shared a festival, the Sementivae, from January 24th through 26th, during which they were petitioned to protect seeds and their sowers.

Ceres had a temple on Rome's Aventine Hill not far from that of Diana. She was originally associated with women's mysteries. By the third century BCE, her worship in Roman territory was heavily influenced by Demeter and the Eleusinian Rites, and she was identified as the mother of Proserpina.

Priestesses originally led her rites, but in the Roman republic few women were allowed positions of spiritual authority. Eventually the official Roman state cult of Ceres would be supervised by the male *flamen cerealis*. Perhaps in protest, the names of paternal relatives were never pronounced in the precincts of Ceres, unusual in intensely patriarchal Rome.

Ceres' attributes include a scepter and a basket overflowing with flowers and fruits. She is adorned with garlands of grain. Her sacred animal is the pig. Pigs were kept in grottoes beneath her Italian temples, and sleeping among these pigs was a sacred method of incubating dreams. (See **ANIMALS**: Pigs.)

Corn Mother

The Arikara Corn Mother, from North America's Great Plains, emerged through Earth in order to teach people how to cultivate corn/maize. In addition, she taught them astronomy, astrology, and the mysteries of sacred medicine bundles. She charged humans with the obligation of making regular offerings to the deities.

The Corn Mother

In Austria, the Corn Mother is an old witch who sits in the cornfields. She's black, naked, and has red-hot iron fingers with which she will prick, sting, and hurt children if she can. These fingers may be ergot. Given the opportunity, she'll roast and eat children, too, just like ears of corn. Parents invoke her presence to keep children from entering cornfields.

Ezili Dantor

The fiercely devoted single mother of the Vodou pantheon, Ezili Dantor has a dangerous, unpredictable temper and is skilled with knives. Like Demeter, she has one daughter. Although not an ancient grain goddess, she is often identified as a Corn Mother as she epitomizes the effects of the traditional Corn Mother who, in the act of destruction (slashing at the corn with her daggers), simultaneously transforms death into nourishment (grain is ground into meal).

Corn is also a conduit to the sacred: in Vodou tradition, vèvès, the sigils created to celebrate the lwa and communicate with them, are often drawn with corn meal.

Ezili Dantor's sacred animal is the black Haitian pig. Her traditional offerings include fried pork, corn sprinkled with gunpowder, and omelets filled with corn and peppers. Ezili Dantor is syncretized to Black Madonnas, especially Our Lady of Czestochowa, although Ezili's devotees perceive the child in the traditional image of the Madonna and child as a daughter.

See also **ANIMALS**: Pigs; **DICTIONARY**: Lwa, Vodou; **MAGICAL ARTS**: Sigils.

The Iron Woman

This old hag who lives in the grain fields of Ukraine is sometimes explicitly identified as a witch. She has pendulous iron breasts. With her iron hook, she captures children who wander into the fields and throws them into her iron mortar to grind them up and eat them. She bears a strong resemblance to Baba Yaga; if they are not one and the same, they are cut from the same cloth.

Isis

Isis has so many facets that she transcends classification, however at the very root and basis of her myth she is identified as a Corn Mother.

Isis, according to legend, was the first to discover wild barley and wheat. At her festival, stalks of these grains were carried in procession.

After Isis' discovery of grain, her brother/lover Osiris traveled around Egypt (and eventually the ancient world) introducing the concept of its cultivation. Because of these actions, Osiris is credited in Egyptian mythology as the founder of civilization.

To complicate matters, Osiris does not just teach about grain: he *is* the grain and thus is eventually cut down in his prime, his body is chopped up and scattered throughout Egypt. Although Isis mourns him, she is also actively involved in the process of the harvest: she unearths each piece of Osiris' body, collecting it in her winnowing sieve. Isis' actions may have served as role models for later harvest rituals. Harvesting was a solemn occasion; one mourned for the grain even though it was necessary to cut it down, winnow, and grind it. At harvest-time, when ancient Egyptian reapers cut their first stalks, they beat their breasts in lamentation while calling upon Isis.

The Mamayutas

These Andean Corn Mothers, Spirits of Fertility, transmit generative powers to women, their descendants. They are perceived as the ultimate female ancestors—the first, primordial female ancestor, founder of the female (or matrilineal) line.

Descriptions of rituals conducted for the Mamayutas may be found in witchcraft and idolatry trial transcripts of the Spanish Inquisition, operating in the Department of Arequipa, now Peru. Women presented the Mamayutas with offerings of their aborted fetuses and still births. Inquisitors were horrified by what they labeled witchcraft, unable or unwilling to comprehend the emotional resonance of this spiritual transaction.

Mary

The Virgin Mary is often interpreted as a Corn Mother with Jesus as her fruit, cut down in his prime, sacrificed, and then resurrected. In votive imagery, Mary is often depicted holding her infant in the same manner that ancient Corn Mothers hold stalks of wheat.

This relationship is also insinuated through the sacrament of Holy Communion, wherein Jesus' body is consumed in a wafer made from wheat. (And the Vatican is adamant that communion wafers be made from wheat; attempts by the family of an American girl with wheat allergies to obtain a wheat-free communion wafer have been consistently rejected.)

Despite the Inquisition's perception of this practice as intentionally and malevolently sacrilegious, use of communion wafers in Roman Catholic folk spells are almost always intended for purposes of agricultural benefit or healing—the equivalent of scattering a sacrificed Pagan grain god's ashes over the land. The desire was not to further injure Christ, as the Inquisition charged, but to benefit from the power of his body.

Mary, too, is associated with the astrological sign Virgo, although obviously the concept of the virgin is understood in its modern, literal, physical sense.

See also Anat, Isis; **CREATIVE ARTS:** Literature: Hammer of the Witches.

Perchta

Among her guises, Perchta also serves as the guardian of cornfields. If they are left unattended, she afflicts humans and/or their livestock with plagues.

Masked dancers known as Perchten dance in the fields of the farmers providing the harvest. Presumably once upon a time these were genuine devotees of the goddess Perchta. Some dancers impersonate beautiful Perchten; others represent hag-like, ugly ones. Their goal is to drive off any lingering malevolent spirits.

Perchta also supervises and guards barns that store grain.

See **CREATIVE ARTS:** Dance: Perchtentanz; **DIVINE WITCH:** Perchta.

Poludnica, The Noon Woman

This Russian Corn Mother (known as Psezpolnica in Serbia) resides in rye fields. She may appear as an adolescent girl, a beautiful woman or an old hag but she only makes appearances at noon. She wields a scythe, steals children, and tickles people to death. She leads children astray in the fields.

Poludnica makes appearances in the fields where she stops people to ask questions or engage them in conversation. If they are impolite or perhaps give the wrong answers, they are immediately struck with illness, cut down as if with a scythe. The Wends are familiar with her as well but say she carries shears, an emblem of death. (The Fates use shears to cut the thread of life.)

She is responsible for the heat stroke that strikes healthy people down at noon, when the sun is most powerful. Archeologist Marija Gimbutas describes her as the personification of sunstroke.

Rugiu Boba

"Grandma Rye" is the Baltic Corn Mother. She is present in the last sheaf of the harvest. Her breasts may be filled with poisoned milk, dangerous to children (see page 426, Ergot).

Saning Sari

This Rice Mother from Sumatra is so closely identified with rice that it is sometimes called by her name. Rituals dedicated to her are performed at planting and harvest.

Before sowing, in this community, rice is traditionally germinated and allowed to sprout. The finest sprouts are identified as Saning Sari and are then planted in the very center of the paddy. Rice grows around her and so when it's time for harvest, she must be located once more. (She may not have stayed in one spot; the spirit of the Rice Mother may have moved around.)

A witch is traditionally sent to find her; alternately the eldest woman of the family searches. The unharvested rice is observed: the first stalks seen to bend in the wind identify the Rice Mother. These stalks are carefully tied together and left uncut until after the first fruits of the harvest have been served as a festive meal for people and animals alike, because Saning Sari wishes animals to enjoy her bounty too. Finally that last sheaf is cut and carried carefully under an umbrella and accompanied by an honor guard to the barn where it will be kept in order to protect and enhance stored crops.

Saramama

This Andean Corn Mother (also spelled Zara-mama) is the daughter of Pachamama, "Earth." Images of Saramama in the shape of an ear of corn were carved from stone. She was also adored in the form of a doll (*huantay-sara*) made from stalks of corn following the harvest.

> Other Andean Grain Mothers include Quinoa-mama, Coca-mama, and Axomama, the Potato Mother.

Ergot

The Rye Mother who hides in the cornfields waiting to seize and eat children doesn't have to literally catch them. According to legend, the blackish ergots sometimes affixed to rye grain are the Rye Mother's iron nipples, which she gives children to suck so they'll die.

Ergot (*Claviceps purpurea*) is a parasitic fungus that grows on various plants, especially on grains, especially on rye, and especially on a specific strain of rye (*Secale cereale*). It is visible, covering the stalks with black growths called sclerotia.

❋ *Ergot is sometimes identified as the Rye Mother or, specifically, her nipples*

❋ *Ergot is a tool of healers, midwives, witches, and shamans*

❋ *Ergot causes deadly, frightening epidemics*

❋ *Some historians consider ergot the root cause of Europe's witchcraze*

Among the school of anthropologists and historians who prefer physical or scientific rationales for events (cause and effect), a popular explanation for the witchcraze is that it was stimulated by ergot. For what it's worth, however, rye grain was especially prevalent in England and Russia; compared to other parts of Europe, neither country had particularly virulent witchcrazes.

Ergot is not innocuous but, like the Rye Mother herself, dangerous yet potentially benevolent at the same time.

Ergot produces alkaloids known as ergotamines. In carefully monitored doses, ergotamine causes contraction of smooth muscle fiber and is used to control hemorrhage, promote contraction of the uterus during childbirth, and treat migraines—its primary modern use.

> Although outbreaks of ergotism are now rare, they are not entirely a thing of the past; outbreaks have occurred in recent history. There were 10,000 reported cases of ergotism in Russia in 1927/28, and in August 1951, ergot poisoning caused six fatalities and over 130 people to be hospitalized in the town of Pont St Esprit in Provençe, France. Victims had visions of being attacked by animals (snakes and tigers) and also perceived that they had transformed into animals themselves.

Removed from the food crop, ergot is part of an herbalist's pharmacopoeia. However, if ergot-contaminated grains are harvested, threshed, ground into wheat, and baked into bread, ergot poisoning can afflict an entire community.

The term is obscure today: because of various developments (including modern milling techniques) ergotism now rarely occurs. However, it was once frequent because of the widespread diffusion of rye throughout Europe: it's a hardier grain than wheat.

Two forms of ergotism exist:

❋ *Gangrenous ergotism attacks the extremities causing wasting (atrophy) of the limbs accompanied by sensations of burning. This form was prevalent in Western Europe.*

❋ *Convulsive ergotism causes hallucinations, painful muscular contractions resembling those of epilepsy, violent cramps, purging (diarrhea and vomiting), delirium, psychosis, the skin feels as if it's crawling, the body feels as if it's burning, and periodic loss of consciousness, generally for six to eight hours. This form was prevalent in Central and Northern Europe.*

Both forms of ergotism are accompanied by visions or hallucinations.

Among the effects of ergotism are reduced fertility (including infertility and miscarriage) and tremors, sometimes to a severe degree ("the shakes"), hallucinations, and death.

Ergotism is also known as St Anthony's Fire. This condition is not named for Anthony of Padua, the miracle saint invoked in so many magic spells, but the sainted third-century Egyptian hermit tempted by Satan, whose diabolical tools included visions and hallucinations. *The Temptation of St Anthony* was a favorite topic of medieval painters, especially Hieronymus Bosch, who vividly depicted Anthony's feverish hallucinatory visions. Ergotism was known as St Anthony's *Fire* because of the burning sensation felt by victims, described as feeling like being burned at the stake.

St Anthony's Fire devastated Europe. It was untreatable: The Order of the Hospitallers of St Anthony was created to offer refuges for victims. The affliction was not necessarily associated with ergot; instead victims were believed possessed by demons or afflicted by witchcraft.

Ergot contains potent chemical constituents. When heated (cooked) ergotamine transforms into lysergic acid diethylamide (LSD), as occurs when flour made from ergotized grain is baked in an oven.

LSD was first synthesized in 1938 by Swiss chemist Dr Albert Hofmann during a research project devoted to ergot alkaloids; its hallucinatory effects were unknown before 1943 when Hofmann returned to work on it and apparently accidentally absorbed a microscopic quantity through his skin. When LSD was first made, it was made directly from ergot although it is now made from synthetic ergotamine.

A common folk name for ergot spores is "Mother Rye." The power of ergot was understood as the long arm of the Rye Mother. Associations with maternity were no coincidence: midwives used ergot to hasten long labors as well as to provide abortions.

Awareness of ergot's relationship with fertility is apparently ancient. The Mesopotamians seem to have associated ergot with miscarriage. Ancient Greek references to "diseases of sterility" are now understood to refer to ergotism.

Ergot is difficult to use intentionally because it's hard to control the dosage. It seems to cause abortion only in the later stages of pregnancy when abortion by nature is most hazardous. It cannot be safely self-administered but can be a potent herbal drug in the hands of a skilled, knowledgeable practitioner familiar with its quirks and effects. Even today ergot rye is sold as a folk medicine in herb markets around the world.

Ergot was an early component of women's pharmacology.

❋ *In communities where "wise women" existed, ergot's effects were known properties.*

❋ *In the hands of trained, supervised shamans, ergot was a visionary tool.*

❋ *Set loose in a community without comprehension and an inclination to see visions as evil, ergot is scary and dangerous.*

Ergot's associations with grain goddesses established its link with Paganism. Where traditional midwives and shamans existed, ergot was a known quantity; in communities ambivalent to midwives, abortion, and/or shamanism, ergot was a forbidden and perhaps eventually forgotten topic—with potentially disastrous consequences for the community.

People were discouraged from learning about ergot because of what that knowledge could provide; however lack of knowledge (and once witches and shamans were eliminated, there might be no one to pass down this information) led to epidemics of ergotism, which, in a vicious cycle, led to witch panics.

Some historians suggest the entire witch-craze phenomenon stems from ergot; others suggest ergot is responsible for specific outbreaks, notably that of Salem Village.

Descriptions of victims allegedly attacked by witchcraft sometimes correspond to symptoms of ergot poisoning. Other historians argue that this is oversimplifying a complex historical situation: it is very likely one among many factors.

The German folk name for ergot is *Mutterkorn* or "Mother Corn," the reverse of *Kornmutter* or "Corn Mother." Other folk names include *Tollkorn* (German for "mad corn") and the French *seigle ivre*, "drunk rye." Other German nicknames include

❋ *Roggenmutter* (Rye Mother)

❋ *Roggenwolf* (Rye Wolf)

❋ *Roggenhund* (Rye Dog)

and sometimes plain old *Wolf* or *Wolfzahn* (wolf's tooth).

Some historians suggest that ergot wasn't recognized as a fungus until the scientific revolution in the mid-nineteenth century. Before that, people allegedly thought that these were "sun-baked kernels." This may indeed have been true in communities that eliminated wise women, midwives, and visionary shamans. However, awareness of ergot is ancient: ancient Greeks and Mesopotamians seem to have been familiar with it.

Passages in cuneiform texts indicate that plagues, infestations, and recovery periods were predicted by tracking weather patterns. Ergot flourishes during cold winters and follows certain seasonal patterns. In order to grow, ergot must have optimal weather conditions: it must be cold in winter *and* spring and warm in the summer. Northern Europe is thus particularly conducive to the growth of ergot.

Some scientists believe that ergot may be responsible for periods of population decline in Western Europe occurring between the 1430s and 1480s and between 1660 and 1739. Climatic conditions during this period were favorable to ergot alkaloid production. Researchers have found statistical correlations between 1660 and 1739 of optimum weather conditions for ergot combined with low birth and high mortality rates.

Although ergot may have been forgotten in certain regions or specific communities, it was clearly not forgotten elsewhere because it remained part of pharmacopoeia.

Although authorities sometimes forbid the use of ergot (e.g., Hanover, in 1778), by the beginning of the nineteenth century it was recognized by official medical authorities for its use in stimulating labor.

✳ *1582: use of ergot-infested rye for the purpose of assisting in childbirth or terminating pregnancy is first (officially) reported by Adam Lonicer in the German herbal* Krauterbuch

✳ *1807: reports in the United States of ergot used medicinally for (legal) abortion*

✳ *1824: ergot is recommended for control of postpartum hemorrhage in the United States*

✳ *1832: English sources report that ergot is used regularly by midwives in Germany*

✳ *1836: ergot is admitted to the London Pharmacopoeia for its use in stimulating labor*

Further Reading: an analysis of how and why traditional medicinals once commonly associated with reproduction were eventually suppressed or forgotten may be found in John Riddle's *Eve's Herbs* (Harvard University Press, 1997).

The Rye Wolf

"The werewolf sits amid the grain ..." or so says a German proverb. A German synonym for werewolf is *Roggenwolf,* "Rye Wolf." Rye wolf is also a folk name for ergot.

Throughout Europe, but especially in France, Germany, and various Slavic regions, a benevolent spirit in the form of a wolf guards the grain fields. This spirit is known as the Rye Wolf or Corn Wolf. He's the wild watchdog of the grain. When the wind sets the grain stalks moving in a wavelike motion that means *"the wolf is moving through the rye."*

The rye wolf is the ally or familiar of the Rye Mother. In German folklore, packs of rye wolves (*Roggenwolf*) run with the Rye Mother (*Roggenmutter*), also known as the *Tittenwif* whose long breasts tipped with ergot sclerotium are filled with poisoned (ergot-infested) milk. She offers them to children to drive them wild.

Hollywood movies approach werewolves literally: when the full moon rises, Lon Chaney Jr. or Professor Lupin transform into wild wolves with no self-control. Notably they are aggressive; real wolves are shy and prefer to hide from people rather than attacking them. But then, why would these films be any more realistic about real wolves than about werewolves?

The reality of werewolves may sound absurd and contradictory but these realities exist.

If one does not expect literal transformation, then there are other ways of considering the werewolf. One theory suggests that werewolves were members of wolf-shamanic societies in the same manner that some Native American shamanic healing societies are "Bear Societies."

Conversely, werewolves may be understood as priests or devotees of lunar and grain goddesses. Wolves are associated with many witchcraft goddesses, notably Diana, primary goddess throughout a broad swathe of Europe. Wolves are also the primary allies of the Rye Mother. These possibilities are not mutually exclusive.

Wolf-shaman societies would meet under the full moon; many were visionary societies associated with *Amanita muscaria*, but ergot may also have been among their tools. (See **BOTANICALS:** *Amanita muscaria*, San Pedro.)

Among the responsibilities of wolf-shamans was protecting the grain from other magical practitioners who might wish to drain or divert its aura of power for private use rather than for the benefit of the community. These competing magicians (or shamans) might be independent practitioners or rival shamanic societies from other communities.

Remnants of these societies and their traditions may be witnessed in the Benandanti and Kresniks (see **DICTIONARY**). Some trial testimony deriving from the European werewolf craze that ran concurrently with its witchcraze, notably that of Thiess, the Livonian werewolf, also suggests the survival of these ancient traditions.

Traditionally, people escape from werewolves by running into rye fields or into barns packed with rye straw. The standard explanation for this practice is that werewolves have an aversion to rye. Another possibility is that rye fields are the sacred precincts of the Rye Mother and her familiars and are thus zones of safety.

Many folk names for ergot identify it with werewolves, the rye wolf or with wolves in general. The implications are innumerable.

In East Prussia, peasants once watched for real wolves coming through the rye at harvest time, not to shoot them but to foretell the future:

❉ *If the tail was held high, one could expect poor weather and poor crops next year*

❉ *If the tail was down low, one could anticipate fertility and a good crop next year*

Odin, the Nordic shamanic-warrior deity, was the spiritual sponsor of the dread warriors known as Berserkers or "Bear Shirts." These men eschewed battle armor and, sometimes, even weapons—who needs anything else when you're armed with the spirit of the bear?

They were incredibly feared and allegedly pretty invincible. Ordinarily normal men went *berserk*: they made such an impression that the word still lingers and is easily understood. The berserkers fought under Odin's protection, these shaman warriors who channeled the spirits of bears, so that it was the bear who fought inside a man's body. It is now commonly believed that the berserkers fought under the influence of hallucinatory substances, notably *Amanita*.

However, not all Odin's warriors were berserkers. Another branch, now less famous, was the *Wolf Warriors*. These men channeled the spirits of wolves so that, temporarily, they were wolves within, men without: werewolves. They too were fierce, crazed, and may have used visionary substances to induce their condition; it's believed possible that among the ingredients of their wolf-potion was ergot.

See **ANIMALS:** Wolves and Werewolves; **DIVINE WITCH:** Diana, Odin.

Fairies

Just as the word witch is frequently used to encompass all sorts of occult or spiritual practitioners, the word *fairy* is often used as a catch-all for all kinds of disparate spiritual entities. Like "witch" "fairy" is used by different people to express different concepts. Fairies, thus, can be very difficult to discuss unless one determines exactly how the word is being defined.

The English word "fairy" has historically been used to encompass the following:

🌟 *Miniature winged flower fairies or devas—each individual flower has a petite presiding spirit. These tiny, charming spirits ride butterflies, birds, and dragonflies and are the prototype of what many modern people understand as "fairies." Because of their small stature, they seem sweet and harmless; however, flower fairies share the essence of their respective flowers, thus not all flower fairies are gentle: beautiful, poisonous wolfsbane possesses flower fairies, too.*

🌟 *Human-sized fairy folk are the subject of a high proportion of fairy tales and folk ballads. In stories at least, fairies are often aggressive, stealing human children and adults. Those who assume that all fairies are two inches tall sometimes find these stories confusing.*

🌟 *Different types of spirits from all over the world with distinct names in their own languages are commonly categorized as "fairies" in English translation, as if "fairy" was a generic term for "spirit." In English, all these spirits are known as fairies, sometimes spelled* faeries *or* fées. *Thus one speaks of "Hungarian fairies" or "Russian fairies," rather than* Tündér *and* Rusalka, *distinctly different types of spirits and both distinguishable from* sidhe, *the Irish fairies.*

🌟 *Fairy is used as a generic term for ancient pre-Christian spirits. In essence, it's a demotion: deities who've refused to fade away (or whose devotees stubbornly cling to them) are removed from the pantheon of gods but permitted a lesser role as "nature spirits."*

🌟 *Fairy has also been used historically to indicate devotees of pre-Christian spirits. In seventeenth-*

century England, "fairy" was a synonym for "witch" and/or "Pagan practitioner." This may be the root of the modern usage of "fairy" as a pejorative for homosexual men.

In stories, legends, and fairy tales, witches and fairies are often treated as mirror images of each other: both are powerful beings, predominately female using similar tools—charms, magic wands, and spells. Both are reputedly shape-shifters. Older stories blend the boundaries: not all witches are evil, not all fairies are sparkly and benevolent.

Modern versions of these fairy-tales often take a dualist approach: witches are exclusively malevolent while fairies are exclusively "good."

Historically this has not been the case. Witches and fairies have been linked for centuries; the dividing line between them has not always been distinct. In many parts of Europe, accusations of "witchcraft" were technically accusations of consorting with fairies: *witchcraft* was considered synonymous with *fairy-craft*. Witch-trial testimony from Hungary, Italy, and Scotland indicate that powerful, largely female-oriented fairy spiritual traditions did exist.

The English word *fairy* derives from the Old French *feie* or *fée*, which in turn derives from the Latin *fatua* (female seer) and *fatum* (fate or destiny). This concept is demonstrated with more clarity in Italian, where the word corresponding to *fairy* is *fata*. Thus Celtic fairy goddess Morgan le Fay is *Fata* Morgana in Italy. The Fates may as well be called *The Fairies* or vice-versa.

This is now largely unfamiliar partly because, in recent years, as fairy tales have become relegated to nursery tales, fairies have become sanitized. To the modern ear, "fairy" often has a whimsical aura, but this was not always the case:

❋ *Fairies were once respected to the point of fear*

❋ *Fairies were perceived as dangerous spirits and for good reason: "fairy" derives from "fate"*

Many fairies resemble the Middle Eastern/North African spirits known as djinn. Both are shy, volatile, nocturnal spirits who frequently distrust people and are reputedly temperamental, easily offended, and potentially dangerous. In both cases it's considered hazardous to call them by name and so euphemisms like "the neighbors" (djinn) or "the good people" (Fairies) are substituted. (Nicer, sweeter, more benevolent female djinn are sometimes classified as "fairies" in those English-language fairy tales where "djinn," unlike "fairy," still retains an aura of volatility.) Both dislike iron and salt, although djinn allegedly formed from fire, as people were formed from Earth, do not fear that element as some fairies, notably the sidhe, reputedly do.

"Fairy" is sometimes used to encompass any kind of spirit or fabulous being. Thus mining spirits, dwarfs, kobolds and goblins are all labeled "fairies," as are the Black Dogs of Britain and other supernal animal creatures. One thousand pages devoted to this vast array of spiritual entities alone wouldn't do them justice and so in these pages "fairy" is more narrowly defined.

Two types of fairies are discussed in these pages, together with their human devotees:

* *Spirits that determine human fate and destiny*

* *Spirits of wild nature: those spirits with dominion over animals, botanicals, fertility, birth, love, sex, and women's power*

Sometimes these two types of fairies overlap. Both types also are often involved with death and transitions between life and death. Many serve as psychopomps (see **DICTIONARY**) and thus encounters with them are often unwelcome and perceived as threatening.

Birth-spirit Fairies: the Fates

In the famous story *Sleeping Beauty*, following the birth of a long-awaited royal heir, her parents, the king and queen, hold a banquet for fairies who come to celebrate as well as bestow the baby's fate. Each fairy bears a blessing as a baby-gift.

Different versions of the fairy tale posit different reasons: sometimes it's an accidental oversight, other times an intentional omission, but one fairy inevitably is not invited. Sometimes she shows up anyway and is welcomed, but the unprepared parents are unable to provide the same beautiful golden plate engraved with her own name as is given her sister-fairies. The end result is that, angered, she retaliates with a deadly curse for the baby.

This scenario is no mere fairy tale but a description of spiritual rituals long performed throughout Europe, in French, Slavic, Celtic, and other regions as well as among the Romany.

Following a baby's birth it was customary to lay an offering table for fairies who were expected to arrive and bestow the baby's fate.

Details differ as to the specific spirits to whom the ritual is devoted. Most frequently, three spirits are anticipated but sometimes there is only one and sometimes as many as twelve, as in the original version of *Sleeping Beauty*. Usually the spirits are female but the Romany, for instance, have intermingled male and female birth spirits.

The offering table is the crucial element: this is not necessarily the equivalent of an *altar*, although it bears resemblance to the *ofrendas* of the Mexican Days of the Dead (see **CALENDAR:** Dia De los Muertos). A table is laid as if for a festive meal. Fairies as honored, desired guests are expected to come and dine: food and drink are offered. The table must be beautifully set with individual place settings, napkins, glasses, the works. (Each tradition will specify how many fairies are expected although as in *Sleeping Beauty*, it's usually best to be prepared for extra guests.)

* *Fatit are South Albanian fairies (singular: fati), also known as* miren *from the Greek* Moirae *or Fates. The fatit ride butterflies. On the third day following a baby's birth, three fatit approach the cradle and determine the baby's destiny.*

* *Oosood are Serbian spirits described as a sub-species of Vila (see page 443), which is interesting because it links Fate Fairies with Nature-spirit Fairies. Oosood arrive on the seventh day following a birth and are visible only to the mother. In addition to food, they appreciate flowers.*

* *"Our Good Mothers" is the Breton euphemism for these Fates who typically appear in groups of three. Their leader is named Béfind. They prefer lavish multi-course meals complete with champagne, whiskey, wine, and pastry, as well as the fruits and nuts more familiarly associated with fairies.*

* The Seven Hathors may be the earliest clear manifestation of this tradition. Hathor is the primordial Egyptian goddess of love, sex, birth, pleasure, intoxication, music, and death. She is a famed shape-shifter: the Seven Hathors may be aspects or avatars of Hathor although they may also be her daughters or attendant spirits. They appear at births to pronounce the baby's destiny. It is unknown whether food offerings were given to them, although this was customary in Egyptian tradition. They were, however, offered seven red ribbons, one for each Hathor.

Nature-spirit Fairies

Among the spirits categorized as fairies are a preponderance of what are commonly called "nature spirits." Folklorists divide these fairies into categories:

* Trooping fairies live in sophisticated societies similar to those of humans and often accumulate wealth. "Trooping" indicates that at least once a year, fairies leave their home and travel in processional.

* Solitary fairies are not all literally solitary, although some are. Many live in packs. These fairies do not troop: they are wild or feral spirits and are described as solitary because they live a stark, simple existence in the forest or underwater away from civilization.

Baobhan Sith

Pronounced *Buhvan shee*, Baobhan Sith, literally "Fairy Women," are spirits of the Scottish Highlands. Their name is cognate with *banshee* but they have a different nature, more closely resembling Vila. (See Sidhe, Vila, pages 440 and 443.)

Baobhan sith are shape-shifters, usually taking the form of hooded crows or ravens. They also manifest as women typically, but not always, dressed in green; the true giveaway as to their identity is in their feet. Rather than human feet, these ladies sport deer hooves.

Baobhan sith love to dance all night. According to some legends, they seduce men, dance with them and then kill them, draining them of their blood, and so are sometimes described as "Scottish vampires."

As with all these stories, it's difficult to tell whether this was always the nature of the baobhan sith, whether these are stories invented post-Christianity to discourage potential devotees from joining in the fairies' dance or whether, once sufficiently angered, previously neutral or benevolent spirits transform into malevolent ones.

As the baobhan sith's favorite victims are reputedly young hunters out on the moors, one suspects that like Vila, they may be animals' guardian spirits who guarantee that only spiritually initiated hunters who've performed the correct hunting rituals are permitted to hunt. (Without these rituals, animals are unable to resurrect and return to life.)

Bereginy

Bereginy refers to a host of Slavic water spirits in the retinue of a primal goddess named Bereginia (also Berehinia, Perehinia). *Bereginy* is Russian; the Polish variant is *Bóginki*.

Bereginia means "earth" and "shore," and so perhaps indicates the threshold where land and water meet. River, forest, and lake spirits, the Bereginy are often depicted in the guise of double-tailed mermaids. Some believe these primeval Slavic spirits are the ancient ancestors of the Rusalka and Vila (see pages 439 and 443); others suggest that they are sister spirits, with the Bereginy inhabiting banks overlooking the waters where the Rusalka dwell.

The first recorded historical reference to Bereginia is from a sixth-century Greek lexicon naming gods and goddesses who were taboo for Christians. Among the spirits listed to avoid is *"the Berehinia."*

The Bereginy, however, remained publicly honored by Slavic women as late as the Middle Ages, with secret devotions continuing long after. Christian chroniclers complained that the Bereginy were dangerous spirits because of the persistence with which women continued to serve them secretly. Rituals once held openly on the banks of rivers would eventually be held in sacred, secret, private places like the bathhouse. (See **PLACES:** Bathhouse.)

Dakini

Dakini are Himalayan attendants of the goddess Kali, also known as "Cloud Fairies," "Sky Dancers," and "Celestial Women." In English, dakini is alternatively translated as "fairies," "furies" or "yoginis." They are sometimes defined as "Spirits of Wrath."

In pre-Buddhist times, the Sanskrit word *dakini* denoted a female death spirit, perhaps similar to a Valkyrie, found at battlefields, cemeteries, and cremation grounds.

In modern Hindi, *dakin* indicates "witch."

From the ninth through at least the thirteenth centuries there was an active, vital spiritual tradition involving veneration of dakini with temples throughout India. Shrines centered on Tantric practice and adoration of 64 dakinis. Dakini rituals were practiced well into the sixteenth century when for now unknown reasons they began to fade from mainstream

Hindu religion. Temples were eventually abandoned, although many buildings still remain and may be visited. (They were architecturally unique in India as they lack roofs, perhaps to allow the dakini to fly in and out.)

French explorer and magician Alexandra David-Neel, author of *Magic and Mystery in Tibet* (1932), translated dakini as "fairy." See **HALL OF FAME:** Alexandra David-Neel.

Dakini can fly and possess magical powers. Although often described as dangerous (some allegedly have a taste for human flesh), they sometimes operate as personal guardian spirits and are invoked for initiation into the secrets of Tantra.

See **DICTIONARY:** Dakini, Yogini.

Deives

Deives are Lithuanian spirits who sport two faces: they manifest as fierce old hags and as big-breasted, blue-eyed beautiful women with long blonde hair. Deives protect women, supervising their work and spiritual traditions. Rules of the deives included no laundering after sunset (that's when the deives go swimming), and no spinning on Thursdays. They punish men who fail to respect these rules and force women to break them. Deives also allegedly dislike greed, excessive acquisitiveness, and selfishness.

Dones d'Aigua

These are Catalonian spirits whose name literally means "Ladies of the Water." They live anywhere where clean, fresh water can be found: springs, fountains, wells, and lakes including those within caves and forests. These Ladies of the Water guard hoards of treasure although, according to reports, they are usually very friendly and helpful to humans. They typically manifest as mermaids (half-woman/half-fish) or as sirens (half-woman/half-bird).

Dryads

Dryads are ancient Greek female woodland spirits. Attendants of Artemis, they are the guardians of trees, groves, and forests. The dryads live in trees but should not be confused with *hamadryads*, who are stationary spirits of individual trees that die when a tree is felled. Dryads, on the other hand, move around quite easily. To see them was considered unlucky, although this may be because as vigilant guardian spirits they most frequently made themselves visible when displeased and intent on inflicting disciplinary action. Dryads are appeased and propitiated with offerings of milk, water, wine, oil, and honey.

See **BOTANICALS:** Trees; **DIVINE WITCH:** Artemis; **HALL OF FAME:** Paracelsus.

E Bukura e Dheut

E Bukura e Dheut is an Albanian fairy whose name means "Earthly Beauty." She lives in a fairy-tale castle atop a mountain guarded by fabulous beasts and creatures. E Bukura e Dheut rules over a host of other beautiful spirits, her sister fairies. They are volatile and capricious and thus utterly unpredictable: when encountered they may be generous and kind or maliciously destructive, although E Bukura e Dheut herself is often used to represent the epitome of beauty and happiness.

Elf

Elf, an Anglo-Saxon word, refers to the indigenous spirits of the Teutonic lands. The words *fairy* and *fée* are of French derivation and began to replace "elf" in the fourteenth century. The words are now somewhat interchangeable, although "elf" is more specific and is never a generic term like "fairy."

Orisha originally came from Yorubaland, Lwa from Dahomey. Rusalka derive from Russia, Sidhe from Ireland, djinn from the Middle East, and so forth. Who are the indigenous Anglo-Saxon spirits and what are they called in plain English? Some would say there are none but this just demonstrates the intensity with which traditions were suppressed. Indigenous Anglo-Saxon spirits are Elves.

Elves feature prominently in the spells and charms of the Anglo-Saxons. Many of these charms were intended to protect from elves and so a hostile relationship is presumed; however some perceive that pre-Christianity, spiritual alliances existed between elves and people. Once this alliance ended, embittered elves, previously helpful, turned dangerous or, conversely, people were taught to fear elves specifically so that they would *not* continue Pagan devotions. Clues that this was the case arise in Teutonic mythology devoted to Freyr and Hulda, Elven King and Queen. (See **DIVINE WITCH:** Hulda.)

Like fairies, elves have now been cleaned-up and made-over to suit sanitized children's fiction, often portrayed as miniature, whimsical busy-bees: Santa's little helpers. Originally elves were human-sized, sometimes taller, and were renowned archers, healers, and artisans. Author J.R.R. Tolkien's portrayal of the sacred but dangerous elven folk in *The Lord of the Rings* trilogy of novels hews closely to mythological tradition.

Elves had their own kingdom paralleling those of humans. Like fairies, elves could be benevolent and helpful but were also feared: elves reputedly had a tendency to be hostile to humans, sometimes striking them with the poison darts known as elf-shot, which lead to illness and malaise.

Among theories surrounding elves is that they were the indigenous people of North-western Europe, eventually pushed deep into caves, forests, and mountain halls by Indo-European invaders.

Keshalyi

Keshalyi are the Romany fairies. Their name is believed to derive from a word for "spindle" and so they may be associated with those deities who spin the threads of fate.

They live in remote forests and mountain glades, especially in Transylvania.

The Keshalyi are gentle, beautiful, and benevolent, but theirs is a tragic saga:

Ana, the beautiful, kind, generous Queen of the Keshalyi lived in a fabulous castle in her mountain paradise, until the King of Demons fell in love with her. (These aren't Christian demons but malevolent spirits known in Romany as *Loçolico*.) She refused his advances

and proposal of marriage until the King with his horde of evil spirits stormed her palace and began devouring her fairy entourage. To spare the rest, she agreed to the marriage.

Ana as the spirit of fertility is marvelously fertile herself. Unwillingly, she becomes pregnant time and time again. The fruits of her union with the King of Demons are horrific disease spirits. A lengthy fairy-horror tale cycle recounts each pregnancy and names the child and the diseases it causes. Some but not all her pregnancies result from sex. For instance, Ana develops a skin infection. A cure is suggested that involves mice licking her sores; one mouse enters her body to be reborn as the disease spirit Lolmischo who, in the form of a demonic red mouse, inflicts eczema and other skin ailments.

The saga of the liaison between Ana and the King of Demons is the history of the introduction of diseases, both physical and emotional. However, the detailed saga may also be used by shamans and fairy magicians for purposes of diagnosis, and to affect magical cures via negotiation and control of the spirits.

Utterly horrified and in despair following the birth of her ten children (including one, Lilyi, who sounds remarkably like Lilith reborn as a Romany disease demon; she inflicts catarrhal infection), Ana finally convinced the King of Demons to liberate her. In exchange she agrees that whenever a Keshalyi reaches 999 years of age, she will marry one of his Loçolico. Consumed with remorse and shame, Ana now hides within her palace, only very occasionally venturing out in the form of a golden toad.

See below Fairy Magicians, Sicilian Fairy Cult; **ANIMALS:** Frogs; **DIVINE WITCH:** Herodias, Lilith.

Korrigans

The Korrigans (also spelled Corrigans) allegedly did not begin existence as spirit beings; once upon a time they were Pagan Breton princesses who opposed Christianity and were transformed into fairies, whether as punishment (the "official" story) or reward is subject to interpretation. Another explanation suggests that they were Druidesses, although theoretically there's no reason they couldn't be both.

As spirits, they now manifest either as mermaids or as land-living fairies. They are usually described as beautiful, long-haired women wearing flowing white garments, but they can also manifest as fierce hags, especially when encountered in the daylight.

The Korrigans are most frequently encountered in the forest or by streams. They travel in packs and like to have fun, dancing among stone circles and menhirs and leading travelers astray with their beautiful voices and mysterious fairy torchlight. Allegedly, they especially enjoy playing tricks on priests.

The Korrigans helped Princess Dahut build the magical crystal city, Ys. They are among those spirits accused of stealing human babies and leaving changelings behind.

See below Changeling; **DIVINE WITCH:** Dahut.

Lauma

Lauma (Lithuanian: Laumé; Latvian: Laūme) are Baltic fairies. The entourage of the witch-goddess Ragana, they are most frequently encountered bathing in springs at night and spinning and weaving in the moonlight—significant activities as they link the worlds of Fate Fairies with those of the Nature-spirit Fairies.

Originally Lauma were guardians of the poor and protectors of orphan children, however post-Christianity they have developed hag-like features and are sometimes described in terms similar to Baba Yaga. (See **DIVINE WITCH:** Baba Yaga, Ragana.)

Nixie, Nixy

These are female German water spirits and freshwater mermaids. Their male counterparts are the Nix. They live in societies that parallel those of humans, in underwater cities.

Male nixes have a bad reputation amongst people; they have green teeth and resemble drowned corpses. Nixies, on the other hand, are typically described as seductively beautiful although, as they are shape-shifters, their appearance may be a matter of choice. (In addition to appearing human, gray horses are favored forms.) Nixies reputedly entice mortal men to their doom.

Nixies typically manifest as mermaids, but have a passion for shopping and so like to attend local fairs and markets. No "Little Mermaid" angst regarding lack of legs for nixies. When they wish to walk on land, they sprout legs; when they wish to live in the water, legs are replaced with tails, just like that. Allegedly, the clue to the true identity of two-legged land-walking nixies is dripping water: they are always wet. Once upon a time, their apron strings were always soaked; now that aprons are out of style, it might be any item of clothing.

"Nixy" derives from the Old High German *nihhusa*, translated as "female water sprite." (The male is *nihhus*.) Various water spirits throughout Northern and Western Europe have similar names; most are threatening and malevolent.

Peri

Peri are Iranian fairies, tiny, sweet, gossamer beings nourished solely by the aromas of fragrant flowers and trees. Iran is the home of dualism; the philosophy permeates their fairy tales, too. Malicious spirits called *deevs* (possibly the root origin of "devil") constantly attempt to capture peris by hanging iron cage-traps from treetops. Peris who accidentally fly in are trapped. Their sister spirits, however, sustain these trapped peris by feeding them perfume, which in turn repulses the deevs so that they are unable to complete their nefarious plans.

Rusalka

These are Russian nature spirits associated with water, fields, and forests. They often appear in groups. Rusalka are exclusively female: they may be young and beautiful or old, fierce, and scary, but they are *never* feeble old ladies. When manifesting as crones, they are ancient hags of power.

There are fierce debates as to the true identity and origin of Rusalka and to some extent their appearance depends upon which version of events is believed. The Rusalka are shapeshifters and perhaps willing to conform to expectations.

"Rusalka" derives from the same roots as *Rus* and *Russia*, and so they are often classified as primal Russian ancestral or totemic spirits. Spirits of moisture, they officially bless the land once a year with fertility.

Another suggestion is that Rusalka are the transformed souls (ghosts) of young women who've drowned, either as a result of accidents (perhaps lured in by spirits including other Rusalka), suicide or murder: many legends suggest they were pushed in by their mothers, per-

haps referring to ancient traditions of human sacrifice.

Christian-oriented explanations suggest that Rusalka are the souls of girls who've died unbaptized, with the added inference of "So, young lady, if you're not baptized, you're doomed to become a damned Rusalka too!"

Sometimes the Rusalka are described as beautiful, wild-haired, big-breasted women—which is quite apparent as when encountered they're usually naked, although sometimes they wear white and twine poppies in their hair. Others describe them as resembling cadavers, pale and bloated like drowned corpses. They are also envisioned as incredibly beautiful mermaids.

Although they can be benevolent and were venerated for centuries, they can also be dangerous if they choose. Rusalka sometimes live in rye fields as attendants of the Corn Mother, Baba Yaga, and act as guardians of the rye. Like Baba Yaga, they are powerfully identified with birch trees and poppies.

In the Ukraine, Rusalka perch in birch trees like birds. In the spring, they move out to the branches where they sit, washing and combing their abundant hair and weaving linen garments, which they wash and hang from branches to dry. Another legend suggests that Rusalka live in beautiful underwater palaces during the winter but move to the trees when the weather heats up.

The Rusalka's ritual act of ornamenting trees with fine handiwork serves as a role model for women who weave and embroider special cloths, which they drape on birch trees as offerings to the Rusalka and the trees. Rusalka expect veneration and offerings from women as their due. They ask passing girls for gifts. Girls decorate birches with ribbons and embroideries.

Sometimes the Rusalka get bored living quietly in the forest, at which time they allegedly seduce, and then kill men. Whether this is Christian defamation and completely untrue, or whether this refers to now-forgotten human sacrifice is now unknown.

Rusalka come down from the trees at night to circle-dance in the moonlight. Allegedly if caught in the act, they drown observers. Water is the Rusalka's natural element and home but also their weapon. On the other hand, the Rusalka's water also cures: Rusalka own secret wells in the forest with miraculous powers of healing. They can be petitioned for assistance.

See **BOTANICALS:** Birch, Opium Poppy; **DIVINE WITCH:** Baba Yaga; **ERGOT:** Corn Mother: Baba Yaga.

Sidhe

Sidhe (pronounced *shee*) is the Gaelic word commonly translated as "fairy." "Fairy folk" is *daoine sidhe* or *deenee shee*.

Sidhe is also the Gaelic word for barrow or tumulus; ancient burial mounds, long grown over with grass and sometimes filled with treasure. Many fairy-sidhe reside within the barrow-sidhe. Whether these spirits received their name from the barrows, whether the name is a euphemism for the spirits—referring to them by their address (in the way that djinn are sometimes referred to as *"Down There"*)—or whether the double-word is meant to imply deeper spiritual traditions is now unknown.

Many consider sidhe the true and only "fairy folk." Various explanations are offered:

They are the ancient Celtic gods: sidhe exist in Ireland, the Isle of Man, and the Scottish Highlands.

They are specifically the Pagan spirits of Ireland known as the *Tuatha de Danann* who, deprived of offerings and devotion, have withered. *Tuatha de Danann* means "Children of

Danu" or "Dana" and refers to a legendary race that overthrew the indigenous inhabitants of Ireland. When the *Tuatha de Danaan* were, in turn, defeated by invading Milesians they took shelter in earth barrows (sidhe) and eventually came to be known by that name. Allegedly the *Tuatha de Danann* were once also known as *Marcra shee* ("fairy cavalcade") or *slooa-shee* ("fairy host").

An alternative Christian suggestion explains that the fairies are Fallen Angels—not quite bad enough to be damned to Hell but not good enough to be forgiven and saved.

They also may not have "come" from anywhere but may just be indigenous spirits who interact with people. Thus some consider the sidhe to be god-like, while others perceive them as demons caught on Earth, an important distinction when considering responses to the Fairy Faith. (See page 448; see also Fairy Witch.)

Another suggestion is that the sidhe were not spirits at all but aboriginal pre-Celtic people of the British Isles who possessed a powerful, mysterious, magical culture with a strong emphasis on herbalism and shamanism. They retreated to remote areas, including underground dwellings, in the face of aggressive invaders.

The sidhe are proud spirits who perceive themselves as worthy of veneration and intense respect: they accept (and perhaps expect!) small but consistent offerings, such as dishes of milk placed out overnight on the windowsill or doorstep.

There are male and female sidhe. They have an elaborately structured society that parallels that of humans and are considered to be trooping fairies, although some solitary spirits are also classified as sidhe. (See below, Solitary Sidhe.) Although some seem to bear a measure of hostility toward people, fairies often show considerable interest in human society and interaction with humans.

Sidhe stand accused of stealing humans, especially babies, children, midwives, and wet-nurses. The milk they expect as an offering may not always have been bovine; legends tell of fairies accosting women and begging for a sip of human milk.

"Leprechaun" derives from the Gaelic *leith brog* "one shoemaker." He is a cobbler, the sole professional sidhe; he is, however, always seen working on only *one* shoe rather than a pair, which may be a reference to shamanism. He works on shoes continually, with time off only for an occasional spree. The leprechaun is fabulously wealthy: he buries his treasure in pots and is reputedly a tremendous and not always nice practical joker. See **CREATIVE ARTS:** Dance: Step of Wu; **DICTIONARY:** Bagatella.

Their real passion, however, is for dancing and pleasure. Little industry exists among them: Irish fairies keep cows and sell or trade them at fairs. (Pre-Christian Irish deities were intrinsically involved with cattle.) The sole exception is the leprechaun who labors as a shoemaker. William Butler Yeats speculated that this was necessary as the rest of the sidhe constantly wore out their shoes dancing; he describes a woman who lived among the sidhe for seven years. When she returned home, her toes were gone: she had danced them right off her feet.

The sidhe have an intense relationship with people characterized by both love and hostility. Once upon a time, they were the subject of passionate human veneration: hidden within fairy tales and legends are suggestions of Pagan devotion and voluntary channeling of spirits, similar to modern spiritual traditions such as the African Diaspora faiths and the Zar cult. (See **DICTIONARY:** Candomblé, Santeria, Vodou, Zar.)

Solitary Sidhe

Solitary sidhe are *not* trooping fairies. Some perceive that they are a separate species of spirit, now lumped in with the sidhe. (And perhaps, in Gaelic, *sidhe* eventually became almost as generic as *fairy* in English.) Many are associated with death; some serve as psychopomps or death-knells.

The most famous is the *bean-sidhe* or banshee, which literally means "Fairy Woman" or "Woman of the Fairy Mound." It is worthwhile to recall that "fairy mounds" are another name for the often treasure-filled barrows, ancient burial mounds that stud Europe and Asia (where they are known as *kurgans*).

In the Hollywood version of the banshee, hearing her voice causes death and so she has become a staple of horror entertainment. This is unfair: the banshee doesn't kill or injure anyone nor does she scream for just anyone. She is a spirit who is attached to a specific family. (And it is a typically elegant family at that!)

She is the family's personal escort to the realm of the dead. She does not kill but awaits death and mourns. Should a member of her family be about to die (for *any* reason; it could be a natural death of someone aged 102) she manifests herself and audibly *keens*, the traditional Celtic mourning wail. Obviously, however, she is a dreaded guest: her presence, usually both visible and audible, indicates imminent death and advises the family to begin making appropriate preparations.

The banshee manifests in various forms, including:

❧ *An old woman dressed in green with glowing red eyes in hollow sockets and long, wild, white hair*

❧ *A deathly pale woman dressed in white with long, wild red hair*

❧ *A beautiful woman, veiled in white*

❧ *A shimmery, silvery woman with long, beautifully abundant silver-gray hair*

❧ *A headless woman, naked from the waist up, often carrying a basin of blood*

See **DICTIONARY**: Banshee.

Also among the solitary sidhe are the *Leanhaun shee* or "fairy lover." This beautiful fairy haunts wells and springs in Ireland and the Isle of Man in search of human lovers. If they accept her love, they are doomed to be hers forever. She vampirically feeds off their life essence and so her lovers aren't long-lived. However, there is some compensation: she infuses them with tremendous poetic and literary skills. The Leanhaun shee is blamed for the brief lives of many of Ireland's greatest poets but credited with bestowing their talent.

Trolls

Trolls are skilled shape-shifters. Modern children's stories suggest that trolls are generally hulking, stupid, and ugly. Folk wisdom agrees that trolls can be fierce and scary-looking but this is only half the story—the male half. Female trolls are fierce but beautiful.

Trolls live in communities paralleling those of humans, under hills and in barrows and caves filled with so much treasure that they glow in the dark. They love music and dancing and have been known to abduct musicians to play for them. They don't like noise, especially the ringing of church bells, and thus try to live far from human habitation—although humans habitually encroach on their turf.

> Trolls, like elves and sidhe, may refer to Pagan spirits, to human devotees of those forbidden spirits attempting to maintain their traditions apart from mainstream society, or to aboriginal people pushed to the margins by Indo-European invaders. In all cases, they are identified with magical arts, herbalism, and ironworking. In parts of Scandinavia, *trollkvinna*—"troll queen"—is synonymous with "witch." (See **DICTIONARY**: Trollkvinna.)

Despite their negative reputations, many tales exist of benevolent, helpful trolls. On the other hand, they are also among those spirits frequently accused of stealing women, children, and valuables. Trolls are expert spell-casters, herbalists, and master ironworkers. They are nocturnal. Stories suggest that they turn to stone when exposed to sunlight.

Tündér

Although Hungary also has malevolent fairies, the Tündér are charming, beautiful, and benevolent. Hungarian fairy tales describe Tündér protecting orphans and saving the destitute with gifts of the priceless pearls that they wear in their hair.

Tündér are virtually exclusively female. They are fabulously wealthy, living on remote mountaintops in amazing castles surrounded by beautiful gardens. They passionately love dancing and music and will dance the night away under the moonlight. They have powerful magical powers and own magical jewels and herbs with which they cast spells. Their body fluids, including tears, milk, and saliva, have magical properties as well and are tools of enchantment.

Legends regale the magic powers and charitable, righteous actions of specific Tündér, who are known by name. The most prominent is Tündér Ilona ("Fairy Helen"). Others include Tündér Maros, Dame Rampson, and Dame Vénétur.

Unlike many other spirits classified as "fairies" Tündér are addressed by name, although always preceded by an honorific. The Hungarian word translated into English as "Dame" indicates tremendous veneration, adoration, and respect, akin to the original usage of *Ma Donna* or "My Lady." Testimony from Hungarian witch trials indicates that these spirits may once have been intensely venerated.

See Fairy Magicians, Sicilian Fairy Cult, Witchcraft Trials.

Tylwyth Teg

Tylwyth Teg are Welsh spirits usually described as resembling humans although manifesting in assorted sizes: some are human-sized, some are approximately the height of a man's knee while others are tiny, although, as they are also renowned shape-shifters, perhaps this is a moot point. Their name means the "Fair Family" but this may be a euphemism for these Welsh fairies.

Tylwyth Teg live in organized societies ruled over by a king, Gwyn ap Knudd. There are both male and female Tylwyth Teg. They typically dress in green although the king's court allegedly wears blue and red silk.

Tylwyth Teg prefer to live in remote places: wooded areas in the mountains, or lonely islands within lakes or off the Welsh coast. They are nocturnal, emerging at night to make music and dance in the moonlight in fairy rings. They adore music and have been accused of kidnapping particularly skilled human musicians and forcing them to stay and play for them.

A human caught within a fairy ring is obliged to dance with the Tylwyth Teg for a year and a day, although carrying a rowan twig grants you free passage through their territory. Plough through one of their fairy rings, even by accident, and be cursed for life. Their mainstay meal is milk with saffron. They dislike salt and iron and are among the fairies accused of stealing children and leaving changelings behind.

Vila, Wila, Veles, Veela, Vily

Vila are shape-shifting, dancing, forest spirits. The many spellings of their name indicates how widespread they are throughout the Balkans, Central and Eastern Europe.

Vila frequently manifest as swans, horses, snakes or wolves. Most famously they appear as beautiful women with long hair. Sometimes they dance naked; sometimes they dress in diaphanous white. They are magical dancers, skilled healers, and witches.

Vila are guardians of the forest and its animals and will punish hunters who fail to perform sufficient spiritual rituals. They are also guardians of women and allegedly punish men who betray women or leave them waiting at the altar. This legend is the basis of the still popular nineteenth-century ballet *Giselle*.

> Some identify Vila as Valkyries let loose in the forest because of the resemblance of their names, their shared associations with death, and both are closely identified with wolves and swans.

Vila, on the other hand, don't seem to worry about marriage. An all-female society, they occasionally have children fathered by human men. They teach magical and shamanic arts to women as well as to those men whom they favor.

They seem to prefer passive-aggressive modes of punishment. First the Vila seduce men with their beauty and charm, luring them deeper into the forest and encouraging them to join their dance. When the men tire and have enough, or think they'll move on to activities beyond dancing, they realize they're unable to stop: the Vila dance them to death. Other legends suggest no seduction is needed; men wandering into the wrong neck of the wood suddenly find themselves compelled to dance, as in the Tarantella or St Vitus Dance. Again, the dance only stops with death.

> Fear of the Vila inspired the phrase *"that gives me the willies."* Such legends inspired Fleur Delacour in J.K. Rowling's *Harry Potter and the Goblet of Fire.*

Sometimes dancing has nothing to do with it: other legends describe men who chance upon Vila in the forest and, enchanted, fall hopelessly in love forever. Their love is unrequited and so the men waste away, eventually dying.

There are no legends regarding Vila punishing or killing women. Instead, women sometimes join the Vila in the forest to dance and receive instruction in herbalism and other magical arts.

In Slavonia, Vila live in mountain caves where people once left offerings of flowers for them. In Bulgaria, Vila ride deer, using snakes as bridles. Both, of course, are creatures that transform themselves, shedding antlers and skin.

See **ANIMALS:** Snakes, Wolves; **CREATIVE ARTS:** Dance: Tarantella, Literature: *Harry Potter.*

Having looked at the different types of fairies, we will now explore various topics associated with fairies and fairy-witchcraft.

Changelings

Among the accusations hurled against fairies is that they steal humans. Sometimes this is simple kidnapping—someone simply disappears—but traditionally fairies leave a substitute from among their own race. *Changeling* technically names this fairy replacement but the word has also come to include the entire phenomena as well as the abducted human.

Not everyone is equally vulnerable to being stolen. Common victims include:

✳ *Midwives and wet-nurses, ostensibly stolen to serve fairy mothers*

※ *Handsome young men stolen to become lovers and/or prisoners of fairy queens, as in the folk ballad* Tam Lin

※ *Babies and young children*

The abduction of children is the most feared changeling phenomenon. Two types of children are at risk: particularly beautiful, vigorous children and absolutely ordinary, run-of-the-mill healthy children. Frail children are not at risk; however the changeling left in exchange is often frail, sickly, and wizened.

One common explanation suggests that fairies, a dwindling, scarce race, believe that humans are sturdier, healthier, and more prolific, and thus seek to incorporate human bloodlines into their communities to strengthen them. Small children and infants are easiest to integrate into their communities. (The added implication is that fairies secretly observe human communities and individuals *very* closely.) The kidnapping of midwives and wet-nurses is also intended to serve similar purposes. (And once upon a time, midwives did more than just deliver babies; they performed blessing rituals believed necessary for the baby's good health and fortune.)

Changelings occur in many traditions as far afield as North Africa and the Middle East. Trolls, nixies, and Korrigans are accused of stealing children, as are sidhe; however Irish legend has a particularly extensive catalog of changeling lore and so changelings are often understood as a purely Celtic phenomenon. It is possible however that this intensive attention to changelings masks Pagan spiritual, magical, and healing traditions.

Because, of course, there's more to it: fairy tales inevitably end with the return of the old person or personality. The unspoken story is that "changeling" is also the name given to people who voluntarily went to live with fairies, often eventually returning to their communities in a changed state. Their personalities are described as "*changed*" or "*different,*" often distant, although, as these tales are never told by the changelings themselves but by (often hostile) observers, one may assume that the changelings may have had reasons to keep their distance. They also traditionally return as masters of herbal and magical knowledge.

Changelings serve as conduits between people and the fairy community. They also initiate and train fairy doctors, teaching them fairy-healing techniques.

Fairy tales and folklore often focus on methods of reversing the switch—of getting the old person back and returning the changeling to the fairies. Three traditional methods exist:

※ *Trooping fairies leave their fairy mounds and strongholds several times a year. A direct exchange may be made during this time, although to be successful, specific magical spells and rituals are required.*

※ *The fairy changeling, often weak and frail, must be nurtured so that he or she transforms into a happy, healthy, vigorous child. Supposedly when this occurs, the fairies will prefer having their own child back and will affect the change themselves.*

In general, one must be kind to the changeling if one ever wants to see one's own child again. The unspoken threat is that if the changeling is misused or abandoned, the fairies will inflict similar treatment (or worse) on the human child. The exception to that rule emerges in the school of fairy exorcisms.

※ *If fairies are perceived as demons then the "stolen victim" hasn't been kidnapped; instead they are possessed. Fairies are exorcized like demons. Exorcism rites from around the world often involve beating or torturing the possessed victim in the belief that when life within the host becomes sufficiently unpleasant, the resident demon will voluntarily withdraw or can be forced to leave.*

The danger, as noted by many traditions, is that these intensive exorcism rites may end up doing more damage (sometimes fatal) than the possession itself. Because sidhe, unlike zar, are allegedly afraid of fire, victims of fairy possession have been burned in efforts to make the fairies depart.

What if efforts are not made to affect a switch or if attempts are unsuccessful?

The fairy child abandoned to live with humans often grows up to be a sniveling, dull-witted person. No longer a child, he was no longer classified as a *changeling* but as an *ouphe*, the original "oaf."

And what of the stolen human? Reports vary: some are reported to yearn for their human life and lost friends and family. Others are reportedly happy among the fairies, living a life of joy, music, and dance.

The most famous changeling was Thomas the Rhymer, a thirteenth-century Scottish prophet, a historically documented individual also known as Thomas of Erceldoune, subject of a famous ballad. Depending on the version of his legend, Thomas either kissed or made love to a Fairy Queen; he was either instantly transported to Fairyland or rode together with the Queen on her white horse. After seven years, she either transported him back or he grew homesick and requested leave to go. The Fairy Queen offered him a choice of gifts: he could become a harper or a seer. Thomas chose the latter.

See also Fairy Doctors, Fairy Faith, Fairy Magician, Fairy Witch; **ANIMALS:** Foxes; **DICTIONARY:** Dybbuk, Zar; **MAGICAL ARTS:** Ritual Possession.

Fairy Cats

Cats, especially black ones, are the favored form of many species of spirits and fairies are no exception. One Celtic tradition suggests that gazing into a cat's eye is a method of viewing fairies and magically entering Fairyland. Cats are also identified as Fairies. Who says fairy tales aren't true?

The *Cait Sith* (pronounced *"cat shee"*) is the fairy cat of the Scottish Highlands, described as being as large as a dog or calf and black, with a white star on its breast. This is no little cuddly kitty but is an exceptionally fierce animal, spitting and growling when encountered. It is described as having an arched back and bristles, although that's typical of any angry cat. Apparently, many Highlanders once also believed these cats were transformed witches on the prowl.

The *cait sith* is no forgotten legend: in recent years, Scottish police have received over a thousand reports of sightings of huge black cats.

Although the *cait sith* was long considered a creature of fantasy, it is now believed to be what is called the Kellas Cat, named after the village in Morayshire where it was first identified in the mid-1980s. At least eight have since been killed and studied.

Generally believed to be a cross between feral domestic cats and indigenous Scottish wild cats (*Felis sylvestris grampia*) some believe that Kellas cats are a unique species instead. Kellas cats are usually completely black with a white blaze (star) on their chest, and they are large: the maximum recorded length for a male Kellas cat has been 43 inches from nose to tail although larger ones have been reported.

See **ANIMALS:** Cats.

Fairy Dart

In Ireland, this was the name given to a painful inflammation of the joints, usually in the hands or feet. Fairy doctors (see below) specialized in the removal of fairy dart. It was removed via an herbal ointment made with unsalted butter. An actual physical dart was often removed, which was frequently kept and displayed.

Darts are also associated with elves; some folklorists believe references to these darts and the illnesses (or death) they cause may actually describe the use of poisoned arrows by aboriginal peoples who are known as fairies.

Fairy Doctors

Various illnesses, conditions, and afflictions are allegedly caused by fairies, sometimes but not always because of direct contact. In addition to fairy dart (see previously), tumors that arise suddenly, as well as paralysis, are described as "fairy blast" or "fairy stroke" in Ireland.

Fairy-associated illnesses are not restricted to Irish tradition: in Hungary, for instance, typical fairy illnesses include muteness, paralysis, and "shrinking," which perhaps describes stroke.

Irish fairy doctors traditionally acquired the gift of healing directly from fairies or from changelings, understood to serve as representatives of the fairies. Many fairy doctors were returned changelings themselves.

> Similar tales are told of children stolen away by the Congolese magician spirit, Simbi. See **DIVINE WITCH**: Simbi.

The most distinguished and renowned fairy doctors are those whom the fairies love. Often these are the children for whom changelings were exchanged. The human child lives with the fairies, usually for seven years, then returns full of fairy lore and craft and able to retain contact with the fairies.

There is also a theory that Irish fairy doctors are the descendants of once socially prominent Druids, especially female Druids (the *drui-ban*) who post-Christianity evolved into independent practitioners. Both male and female fairy doctors exist but the Church traditionally reserved its severest condemnation for female fairy doctors, who were accused of being unfeminine and engaging in behavior unseemly for women. Indeed, many did drink, smoke, gamble, and look men straight in the eyes. They were also suspected of maintaining female-friendly Pagan traditions more than were male fairy doctors.

> Balkan fairy doctors serve four-year apprenticeships with fairies who teach them herbalism. Even after returning to their communities, doctors periodically visit the fairies, who offer further instruction in exchange for information about local people and events.

Disapproval from the Church was not the only hurdle facing Irish fairy doctors. They were perceived as competition by medical doctors. Fairy doctors didn't only treat fairy-related conditions: they also treated common physical maladies, serving as bonesetters and preparing herbal salves, tinctures, and balms. Many were skilled midwives. They traditionally did not charge for prayers, charms, and incantations but did for herbal remedies. Clients were expected to pay in silver, although obviously this was not always possible.

Fairy doctors are not restricted to Ireland or Celtic regions. The fairy magicians of Central and Eastern Europe (see page 450) incorporate many of the skills of the fairy doctor. They too learn directly from the fairies, although here there was greater (or at least more openly acknowledged) incorporation of shamanic techniques like voluntary possession.

Fairy doctors sometimes achieved great renown:

❋ *Biddy Early (1798–April 1874), née Biddy O'Connor (or Connors), known as the "Wise Woman of County Clare," was born at Faha, near Kilanea, County Clare. At the age of 16 she apparently moved by herself to either Ayle or Carheen, where she lived in an outhouse and contracted herself out as a servant. Her fortunes rose, although ultimately she died in abject poverty.*

*She had a complex romantic and marital history, being married at least four times including once to a much younger man late in her life, whom she was accused of "glamouring" (see **DICTIONARY**: Glamour).*

As a healer, she was honest enough to tell people when nothing could be done for them, although she allegedly performed miracles.

Biddy Early appeared in court at Ennis in 1865. The local clergy hated her. She ran card schools and was allegedly a great card player. There were rumors of alcohol abuse as well, although, as usual, all reports come from outsiders, not from Biddy herself. She had a powerful local reputation and many stories were collected about Biddy after her death. Famously, Biddy Early possessed a small blue bottle, which was either won in a game of cards with a fairy man or presented to her at a fairy fort (see page 450) by the ghost of her husband. She was never without this bottle, however it disappeared upon her death.

❋ *Maurice Griffin, a fairy doctor of Kerry, was by profession a cow herder, the old sacred animal of the Pagan Irish gods. According to legend, Griffin could cure animals with his gaze. He allegedly gained his powers of healing by drinking milk from a cow that had eaten grass touched by what is described as "fairy cloud" or "fairy foam" (a cloud-like white foamy substance fell from the sky; a cow licked it up or ate the grass upon which it melted, depending on version). He achieved great local renown as a prophet as well as a healer. Tales of Maurice Griffin may be found in Jeremiah Curtin's book* Tales of the Fairies and of the Ghost World, *published in 1895.*

❋ *Murough O'Lee, a renowned healer, lived in Connemara. He allegedly fell asleep one day in a fairy fort. When he awoke, he was in Fairyland where he lived for a year. The fairies taught him healing arts. Before he went home, the fairies gave him a book that they said contained cures for all diseases; however, Murough was forbidden to use the book—or even to open it—for seven years.*

He held out for three. A severe epidemic caused him to break down and open the book. Nothing bad happened. However, because the full seven years hadn't passed, he was never able to perform all the cures, only some of them.

See also Fairy Magician, Fairy Witch.

Fairy Faith

Sometimes stories are merely entertainment but story-telling is also among the sacred arts associated with religion and spiritual traditions. Thus, folktales and legends often include detailed spiritual information and instruction regarding their respective traditions. Some stories are intended literally, others are intended as metaphor, many may be appreciated on multiple levels simultaneously.

Thus the Bible may be understood as a historical source, as stories chronicling spiritual interaction with God and the spiritual experiences and journeys of various people, and as an explication of the sacred and a list of spiritual injunctions. Similar traditions exist elsewhere: in Santeria, the *pataki* are stories of the orisha. Pataki detail the lives and interaction of the orisha but also contain deep spiritual truths as well as ethical and moral information and spiritual instruction. Greek and other mythologies may be understood similarly.

"Fairy tales" are often understood as distinct from "sacred myths" because they are considered pure entertainment or whimsy, *even though* they detail the lives and actions of spiritual beings (Fairies), interaction between these beings and humans, and often detailed spiritual and ethical instructions. What if this was not really the case? What if fairy tales were intended to be as sacred as myths?

What if, in the face of oppression—and during the era of the witch-hunts!—these stories were deliberately downplayed as being solely entertainment in order to protect and preserve desperately endangered Pagan traditions?

That's the theory of the Fairy Faith. All those stories detailing changelings, encounters with fairies, offerings of milk, whiskey or trinkets, which incidentally closely resemble the sort of humble offerings given on a daily basis to African-Diaspora spirits, may actually be offering detailed spiritual instruction in code.

For instance, in the Isle of Man it was once believed that if water was not left out for fairies, they would break into houses and vampirically suck the blood of sleeping humans. Was this always believed or was this a created rationale that enabled people to continue making offerings to their ancestral spirits?

This type of instruction is by necessity hidden, secret or encoded: sincere continuance of these practices was illegal, potentially heretical, and subject to severe punishment including death.

> The Fairy Faith may represent vestigial remnants of Druidic religion.

Rumors and allegations that fairy tales were more than mere stories were rife throughout Ireland for centuries. Until the nineteenth century, Church control (and attendance) in much of rural Ireland was lax and country customs discreetly continued. This was an open secret: many fairy doctors openly communed with fairies. Ancient traditions were preserved, even if they were disreputable. Some fairy doctors, especially many female ones, may be understood as more than healers: they were also practitioners and leaders of the Fairy Faith.

In the nineteenth century, two conflicting phenomena arose that threatened this age-old practice:

❋ *Church control expanded throughout Ireland with attempts to standardize worship*

❋ *The burgeoning Age of Rationalism increased doubt in the existence of fairies, spirits or any sort of spiritual entity, including God. Traditions like the Fairy Faith were identified by many as primitive, backward beliefs associated with the foolish and ignorant*

This had particular implications in Ireland: by the late nineteenth century, fairies and the Fairy Faith had become an embarrassment and humiliation to the Irish Nationalist Party. Their fear was that no one would seriously consider granting political independence to a nation whose population still believed in fairies.

Both Nationalists and Unionists despised devotees of fairies. The Fairy Faith was dismissed as the worst superstition. In the wake of Neo-Paganism, however, the Fairy Faith has been revived and reinvigorated.

Further Reading: *The Fairy-Faith in Celtic Countries* by W.Y. Evans-Wentz, originally published in 1911 but recently republished (Citadel Press, 2003) is considered the classic text regarding the Fairy Faith. Based on Evans-Wentz's Oxford doctoral thesis, it incorporates information from anthropological, folkloric, and historical sources including field reports from Brittany, Ireland, the Isle of Man, Scotland, and Wales. Evans-Wentz was not a sensationalist but a serious scholar of spiritual traditions, eventually becoming a leading authority on Tibetan Buddhism.

Fairy Forts

Fairy forts, also known as ring forts or stone forts, are roughly circular earthen banks or stone walls. There were once as many as 60,000 of these circular earthworks in Ireland. Local names for them include *cashel*, *forth*, *rath* or *rusheen*.

The majority of them appear to have been built as enclosures for dwellings in the latter half of the first millennium of the Common Era, and they are classified as archeological remains of early medieval dwellings, now long deserted.

Ring forts became known as fairy forts because allegedly they are among the favorite haunts of fairies. According to common international metaphysical wisdom, ruins attract spirits: in North Africa and the Middle East, children are advised to avoid ruins so as to avoid encountering djinn, just as Irish children were taught to stay out of ring forts for fear of fairies.

Of course, those who wish to encounter the spirits know where to go to find them. Being observed exploring a ruin such as a ring fort was most often interpreted as attempting to contact these spirits and was actively discouraged, although those who wished to commune with fairies persisted in this practice.

Ring forts are usually overgrown with vegetation. They are wild, mysterious places, considered the homes of spirits, the haunts of fairies. Ring forts can be physically as well as spiritually perilous, as many contain underground passages.

See also Fairy Faith, Fairy Witch.

Fairy Magicians

"Fairy magicians" describes Central and southeastern European healers and practitioners. Fairy magicians incorporate the herbal and folk-healing skills of the Irish fairy doctors but also more openly acknowledge engaging in shamanic spiritual possession. In addition to healing, many also practiced other magical arts. In areas where witches were persecuted, the entire practice was conducted secretly: there was perhaps no conception that their traditions could be entirely distinguished from magical practice or witchcraft as the fairy doctors sometimes attempted to claim.

Fairy magicians were generally female spiritual mediators who maintained ritual connections and communication with fairies, including the Keshalyi, Tündér, and Vila among others. (See Nature-spirit Fairies, page 434.)

They were skilled in healing illnesses caused by fairies. In addition, these magicians were sometimes also fortune-tellers, necromancers, and magical practitioners who specialized in protecting against malefic magic and healing its effects.

Fairy magicians are initiated directly by the fairies. Initiates communicate with spirits via dreams and visions. Sometimes communication is via trance, which may be induced by music and/or dance. Dancing all night in the moonlight with fairies is thus a spiritual exercise as well as fun.

❋ *In Romania, healers gathered together at night for rituals presided over by Fairy Queen, Doamna Zónelor.*

❋ *In the Balkans, "fairy societies" heal fairy-derived illnesses. Anthropologists describe these fairy societies of Bulgaria, Romania, and Serbia as "possession cults."*

❋ *Also in the Balkans, the goddess of the fairies is known as "Saint Helen," who may be Tündér Ilona in disguise.*

Following initiation, members of these "fairy societies" are able to contact the fairies through sacrificial ritual and ecstatic music and dance. Fairies ritually possess society members in similar fashion to the way zar spirits, orisha, and lwa take temporary possession of their initiates. The spirit "mounts" the initiate and communicates through their voice and body. Fairy societies consider this a dangerous practice as it can stimulate illness (in the initiate) as well as healing.

See above Fairy Doctor, Fairy Faith; **DICTIONARY:** Lwa, Orisha, Zar; **MAGICAL ARTS:** Ritual Possession.

Fairy Roads

For centuries, legends suggested that Fairies, living in alternative, parallel societies, possessed roads on which they traveled and of which they were quite protective.

Fairy roads were invisible to most humans (although fairy doctors and specialists could distinguish them) and herein lay the danger. Accidentally stumbling onto a fairy road left one vulnerable to the fairies' volatile temper. Even worse, should one accidentally—or deliberately—build a house or structure on a fairy road, disaster could ensue as the fairies sought to remove the obstruction.

With the exception of fairy devotees, fairy roads were largely classified as fantasy, or at least existing only on some alternate plane, until the early twentieth century. In June 1921, Alfred Watkins (1855–April 15, 1935), a successful Herefordshire businessman and amateur archeologist, was examining some maps. He noticed that various ancient sites including barrows, standing stones, and stone circles seemed to occur in alignment. Straight lines could be drawn connecting them. Further study indicated that old churches built atop ancient Pagan shrines could also be similarly aligned. Watkins believed these lines indicated prehistoric trading roads and named them "leys" from the Anglo-Saxon word for "cleared strip of land" or "meadow." He published a book detailing his findings in 1925, *The Old Straight Track*.

His concepts were not accepted by conventional archeologists and historians who, in general, believed that the ancient Britons lacked the sophistication and technological prowess to create what Watkins proposed. However, similar theories (fairy roads, dragon lines) had long existed in the metaphysical world, and so the concept of ley lines made sense to many magical practitioners, notably Dion Fortune who incorporated the idea into her novel *The Goat Foot God*, from whence it entered the general metaphysical lexicon. (See **CREATIVE ARTS**: Literature: *The Secrets of Dr Taverner*; **HALL OF FAME**: Dion Fortune.)

Ley lines became associated with fairy roads and subject to controversy. Were there ever actual roads there or not? In some cases, archeology suggests there were but not consistently enough for conclusive scientific proof.

Metaphysicians often understand these "roads" or "lines" to be paths of power or paths of energy, and thus the actual physical presence of roads one can happen upon is irrelevant. (That said, others are convinced that the roads do exist; this passionate argument continues to rage.) What is important is that energy is not obstructed: in this sense, ley lines or fairy roads resemble the dragon paths of Chinese feng shui.

Author Rhiannon Ryall, in her book *West Country Wicca* (Phoenix Publishing, 1989), a description of pre-Gardnerian Wicca, describes "Fairy Paths" or "*Trods*" as a generally straight line seen in some fields that is a deeper shade of green than the rest of the grass. She, too, associates these fairy paths with ley lines.

Another theory harks back to the concept of fairy roads: these lines indicate roads used by spirits alone, often especially Spirits of the Dead.

One suggestion is that they are Stone Age roads linking ancient burial grounds and so are often also known as Corpse Roads.

These roads are not restricted to the British Isles but have been discovered elsewhere. German *Geisterwegen* (Ghost Roads) are roads linking medieval cemeteries.

Further Reading: Among the books devoted to this subject are Paul Devereux's *Fairy Paths and Spirit Roads* (Vega Books, 2003).

the Fairy Witch

Are you a witch?
Are you a fairy?
Are you the wife of Michael Cleary?

This Irish nursery rhyme memorializes Bridget Cleary (February 19, 1867–March 1895), often described as the last witch burned in Ireland, and popularly known as the Fairy Witch of Tipperary.

Although Ireland had among the mildest witchcraft persecutions in Europe, it is often credited with hosting the first and last witch burnings of Europe. Books sometimes chart the entire witchcraze from Petronilla of Meath, as the first woman officially burned as a witch, to Bridget who died at the tail end of the nineteenth century aged 28.

In neither case is the parallel exactly accurate: women were burned as witches prior to Petronilla and continue to be burned today, although now in different parts of the globe.

Furthermore, Bridget Cleary's death was not typical of a victim of the witchcraze.

Witchcraft was a crime during the Burning Times. Whether or not individuals were indeed practitioners of any sort, they were officially charged with crimes, tried according to an official process, convicted, and condemned to capital punishment. Their deaths, however horrific, were legal. No one was charged and punished for these deaths.

Those convicted as witches were considered the guilty parties.

Bridget Cleary, on the other hand, was killed by her husband in the process of what he described as an exorcism: he allegedly believed that she was a changeling and was attempting to get his wife back. Michael Cleary was subsequently arrested and charged with the murder of Bridget Cleary. He was convicted and served a prison sentence.

It is probable that what happened to Bridget Cleary was not unique: what was unique—and remains so in much of the world—is that someone was held responsible and punished for causing the death of a woman many believed to be a witch. Her story pulls the blankets off the suppressed subject of the Fairy Faith, both its genuine practitioners and those intensely opposed to it.

Bridget Cleary's story is also very revealing regarding the perceived blending or interchangeableness of witches and fairies. The ordeal that she underwent at the hands of her husband, neighbors, and family is certainly reminiscent of witch-trial ordeals.

Her maiden name was Bridget Boland. She attended school, off and on, until she was 14. At the age of 20, she married Michael Cleary, a cooper, on August 5, 1887. He moved into the house Bridget shared with her parents. The two couples lived together in that house until the death of Bridget's mother, one year before her own death. Bridget Cleary's mother, Bridget Keating Boland died on February 1, 1894, leaving Bridget Jr. alone in the house with the two men who would both be implicated in her death.

According to her father's court testimony, Michael Cleary asked him *"Don't you know it's with an old witch I am sleeping?"* Whether this meant Michael believed her to be a changeling or whether this meant he opposed her forays into the Fairy Faith is subject to interpretation.

Both Bridget's and Michael Cleary's mothers were reputedly fairy doctors. It is possible that Bridget Cleary was training to become one as well.

Bridget had a strong independent streak, noticed and resented by some. She had a reputation of being haughty, proud, and "fine" and was disliked by some of her peers, young women who mostly lived a very different existence from Bridget.

Bridget Cleary was independent and enterprising: she owned a Singer sewing machine and kept chickens; thus Bridget, unlike most other women in her community, had an independent income. Keeping poultry was among the very few ways to evade complete male control of the purse strings: she sold the eggs and also took in sewing.

Also unique among her female contemporaries, after eight years of marriage, Bridget was childless and rather than seeming to mourn this, she seemed to relish her freedom. With no children, Bridget could come and go as she pleased and she did. She sewed, sold eggs, earning her own money, giving her a measure of economic independence.

In the wake of the scandal following her death, Bridget's neighbors and family were interviewed about her. According to reports, she had a defiant streak and wasn't easily cowed by authority. Joan Hoff and Marian Yeates, authors of *The Cooper's Wife is Missing*, describe Bridget as possessing what neighbors perceived as a "disturbing habit" of looking men in the eye, a trait allegedly characteristic of Pagan women.

Bridget's mother had a reputation as a "fairy expert" and bore something of a reputation as a witch. Perhaps Bridget inherited her interest in the Fairy Faith from her mother. Certainly she displayed a fascination with fairies and, especially in the last year of her life, following the death of her mother, was often observed visiting two local fairy forts, leading to gossip by neighbors who speculated as to her motivation for the visits. Among the reasons suggested:

✳ *She was trying to make contact with the soul of her dead mother*

✳ *She was rendezvousing with a lover*

✳ *She was irresistibly lured there by the fairies*

Michael Cleary had his own personal history with the fairies: as a boy, his mother (also named Bridget) had allegedly run off with the fairies, disappearing for three days. Following her return, she allegedly began operating as a fairy doctor. Michael Cleary had strong feelings about fairies, too: he feared and hated them, and was obsessed with the notion that they would abduct Bridget—or that she would willingly join them.

The first known indication of dissension between Michael and Bridget occurred around Yuletide 1894. Michael allegedly feared she'd been abducted by fairies, and he ordered Bridget not to go to the fairy forts. She defied him and continued to go. (After her death, witnesses came forward saying that Michael Cleary had threatened to burn her if she went back.)

She was observed visiting a fairy fort on February 1, 1895, the first anniversary of her mother's death.

On March 6, 1895, Bridget Cleary returned home in the late afternoon, ostensibly from delivering eggs, complaining of feeling unwell. (Witnesses suggested that she had been observed at the fairy fort that day.) She exhibited signs of fairy-related illness: aches, pains, and chills. She was irritable, described as "distant," and demonstrated some memory loss. Changes in temperament and appearance are among symptoms of fairy abduction. (In other words, a fairy is believed to have replaced or be impersonating the person believed to have been abducted. See page 444, Changelings.)

Initially, the family requested conventional medical attention. A local physician was requested to pay a house call. It took the local doctor four days to respond following repeated requests. He examined Bridget, and determined nervous exhaustion and slight bronchitis.

Despite requests for the doctor's arrival, Michael Cleary allegedly suspected that his wife had been abducted by fairies, who had replaced her with a changeling. Michael perceived that Bridget was now two inches taller than previously and that she seemed, in his words, "more refined."

For nine days, Bridget lay ill with a mysterious ailment. During these nine days, assorted friends, neighbors, and relatives came in and out. Her husband, convinced that his wife had been abducted by fairies, searched for help from two sources—the Church and fairy experts. He was heard arguing with Bridget who was allegedly heard to cry out, "*If I had my mother, I would not be this way.*"

> Nine was a magic number; one theory, allegedly subscribed to by Michael Cleary, suggests that if the return of the abducted person is not affected within nine days, they are lost for ever, although this contradicts the many tales of changelings returning after seven years in Fairyland.

On at least three occasions, requests were made for a priest's assistance. Priests were traditionally called in to exorcize fairies, considered akin to demons. This is "folk Catholicism" and was not standard practice even then. Theoretically it was not permitted, although allegedly it was common practice.

A priest met with Bridget twice. Father Ryan spoke to Bridget for over 20 minutes, later describing her as coherent and intelligent. He said he thought her behavior might indicate the onset of "brain fever" and so decided to administer the last rites, just in case … She allegedly did not swallow the communion wafer: one witness claimed that she spat it out surreptitiously, thus further confirming suspicions that Bridget Cleary had been abducted and that what lay in her place was a changeling.

Shortly afterwards, with the participation of other neighbors and family members including her father and cousins, Bridget Cleary was killed by her husband and another relative, John Dunne, a local "fairy expert."

Dunne was not a fairy doctor in the traditional sense. Two types of "fairy experts" existed:

❋ *Fairy doctors, practitioners of the Fairy Faith, who were enthralled by fairies, trained by them, and practiced arts associated with them*

❋ *What are essentially fairy exorcists, whose techniques drew heavily on Roman Catholic rites of exorcism and witchcraft trial ordeals; fairies were believed by these practitioners to be akin to demons; those allied with them were akin to witches.*

Bridget was prescribed an herbal formula created from bitter herbs called "Seven Sisters Kill or Cure." It did neither. Michael Cleary then purchased an herbal cure called "Nine in One Cure," more potent and more exceedingly bitter than the Seven Sisters mixture.

In these nine days, Bridget had not been permitted to leave her home; she was in a weakened condition from her mysterious illness and perhaps from lack of nourishment: attempts were made to starve out the changeling. She was apparently afraid for her safety and requested that the police be called. This was not done.

Witnesses described the final ordeal of Bridget Cleary. A 16-year-old neighbor stood in the corner of the room holding a candle for illumination. John Dunne sat on the bed gripping Bridget's hair. Two other men held her body down, each pinning down one shoulder while another man pinned down her feet. Michael Cleary attempted to force Bridget to swallow the Nine in One herbal cure in new milk, yelling at her to *"Swallow it, you devil!"* and *"Take it, you old witch!"* Her mouth was pried open: Bridget fought back, only confirming the belief that she was fairy-possessed. It ultimately took six men to pour the liquid down her throat.

After Bridget was forced to swallow the Nine in One cure, the family waited three hours for a "change." When none was forthcoming, the "exorcism" escalated and the threat of fire was introduced.

At midnight on March 15th, Bridget was dressed in her finest clothes including a red petticoat in order that she could *"go amongst the people"*—however one interprets this. ("The People" is a euphemism for fairies.)

Urine was then thrown over her. She was choked, force-fed urine and herbs and pushed to the ground, her head knocking against the floor. Her clothes were stripped off. Bridget was shoved over the grate into the four-foot by four-foot fireplace, like some fairy-tale character (the witch in *Hansel and Gretel* for instance) in a fetal position with her legs sticking out.

According to a witness there was a low fire burning in the fireplace, hot enough to heat an iron grill but not hot enough to boil water. She was threatened with a hot iron poker. (Fairies allegedly fear both iron and fire so the combination was perceived as doubly powerful.)

Michael Cleary poured the contents of a can of paraffin oil over his wife and set her on fire. A witness claimed that the two women present attempted to put out the fire but Michael Cleary pushed them away, threatening to "roast" them as well. He proceeded to pour more oil over her burning body. According to a witness, Michael Cleary said he wasn't burning his wife; he was burning a witch who would go up the chimney.

Another witness (Protestant neighbor Minnie Simpson) later asserted to the police that the family members believed that the person was not Bridget but a witch, although she claimed that she herself (Minnie) did not. She did not explain, however, why in that case she didn't help Bridget, nor did she point out that she was among those who supplied the urine thrown on Bridget.

At this point, people allegedly thought Bridget was "cured" and left. Michael Cleary asserted that he wasn't sure and wished to remain with Bridget for further observation, promising to meet up with family members later at his father's house, although he apparently never arrived.

Based on the testimony of witnesses, Bridget Cleary was still alive when they left. It is unclear exactly when she died, however her dead body was discovered on March 22, 1895, 1300 yards from the Cleary home, wrapped in a sheet and buried in a shallow grave. Her entire back and lower abdomen had been burned: roasted clear to the bone, her internal organs visible. Her right hand was severely burned but her face, hair, breasts, shoulders, neck, legs, and feet remained unscathed. There were marks about her face and mouth and bruises on her neck, believed to be the result of choking. Death was caused by extensive burns, with the official cause given as "shock due to burns."

Eleven people were arrested in connection with the murder of Bridget Cleary, including the 16-year-old neighbor who stood quietly in the corner, holding the candle.

There are two ways to understand the saga of Bridget Cleary:

✳ *There is no possession, there's no such thing, therefore it's deadly superstition or an excuse for fatal spousal abuse. (And local gossip alleged that Bridget had a lover.)*

✳ *Regardless of whether Bridget was or was not possessed her husband and family feared rather than understood fairies. The Fairy Faith was not charming to them. Fairies were considered devils to be exorcized; the "changeling" was considered a witch to be burned, as were perhaps practitioners of the old Fairy Faith.*

Bridget Cleary's mother was locally rumored to be a witch. If one believes that Bridget Cleary was attempting to follow in her late mother's and mother-in-law's footsteps and become a traditional fairy doctor herself, perhaps she was burned as a witch to prevent achievement of her goals.

The methods of exorcism to which her family resorted were not typical of the Fairy Faith, whose practitioners openly derived their skills from fairies. Instead the herbal cures and rituals were heavily influenced by Roman Catholic rites of exorcism and also by published accounts of witch-trial ordeals. Trial testimony indicated that invocation of the names of the Father, Son, and Holy Ghost formed a significant part of the exorcism ritual.

Although Michael Cleary was mocked for believing in fairies, his actions were not those of a practitioner of the Fairy Faith but were grounded in folk Catholicism. Bridget's screams were ignored because they were considered the screams of the invading spirit (fairy and/or demon). Lying in bed, Bridget told a visiting cousin that her husband was *"making a fairy of me now"* and that *"He thought to burn me about three months ago."*

How to interpret these statements? Did Michael Cleary genuinely believe she was a fairy or beneath the mask was this just a case of spousal abuse or both? Was the goal to break the fairies' charm or to break the spirit of an independent woman?

The crime was a major public scandal; the "fairy murder" was popular with the media and drew international attention, much to the displeasure of the local authorities who felt it made the region appear primitive and ignorant. Although Michael Cleary and Bridget's family was arrested for her murder, there was ambivalence toward Bridget as well. She had not been generally beloved; whether "abducted" or not, she had clearly been dabbling with fairies.

Attitudes toward Bridget may be demonstrated by her funeral, or lack thereof:

In a macabre dénouement, Bridget's body could not be released to her family, all of whom had been arrested and were confined in Clonmel Gaol. Police called for the clergy but no priests in the district responded: Roman Catholic priests were strictly charged against performing sacraments where fairy-craft was suspected. Those who died under suspicion were refused Church burial.

The body of Bridget Cleary was finally buried at night by four policemen who read part of the burial service over her body. They had obtained a simple coffin for Bridget and brought her body to the Roman Catholic cemetery at Cloneen, where she was buried outside the church walls beside the unmarked grave of her mother near an oak tree. Bridget Cleary and her mother lie together in unmarked graves outside the church walls. No headstones exist but two stones mark the site.

During the trial, absolutely *no* discussion of fairies, or even any reference to them, was permitted. Michael Cleary was found guilty of manslaughter, not murder, and sentenced to 20 years' imprisonment, of which he served 15. Other defendants received lesser sentences depending upon perceived involvement.

Further Reading: Angela Bourke's *The Burning of Bridget Cleary* (Viking, 1999) and Joan Hoff and Marian Yeates' *The Cooper's Wife is Missing* (Basic Books, 2000).

The Sicilian Fairy Cult

Sicily was ruled by Spain between 1479 and 1713. Spanish Inquisition archives contain accounts of trials of Sicilian witches occurring between 1579 and 1651. These transcripts are fascinating as they reveal the possible existence of genuine metaphysical practice.

The official Church position at this stage was that witchcraft was Christian heresy and that witches worshiped the devil. Those charged in Sicily argued that this was not the case and attempted to explain their true activities, which they did not perceive as diabolical. Theirs was a fairy cult.

> Trials were characterized by actual torture as well as *constant* threat of torture; it's impossible to clearly distinguish genuine testimony from that uttered under duress.

Testimony documents beliefs about the Donna di Fuora, a fairy-like being who accompanied witches on their night flights. Witches joined fairies for pleasure-balls and invoked their presence for purposes of healing.

Members of the fairy society claimed to heal misfortunes and illness caused by fairies. "Witch's touch" was the term used in this region for illnesses whose root cause derived from offending fairies. These illnesses manifested in various forms, ranging from "indisposition" to epilepsy. Notably, in the ancient Mediterranean, epilepsy was strongly identified with Hecate who both healed and wielded it as an instrument of punishment against those who offended her. (See **DIVINE WITCH:** Hecate.)

These fairy healers conducted nocturnal meetings in which they attempted to persuade the fairies to remove the illness or affliction. As part of the ritual, the family of the afflicted was obliged to offer a ritual meal in the patient's bedroom.

According to trial testimony, an offering table was laid with bread, honey-cake, sweetmeats, water, and wine. The table was beautifully set with napkins, utensils, and so forth. The fairy healer decorated the ailing person's room, perfuming the air and covering the bed with red cloth. She alone awaits the fairies, who arrive when everyone else is asleep.

The fairy healer does not sleep: she paces through the room, actively petitioning the fairies, talking with them, offering them food and beverages, pleading with them, and playing her tambourine near the ailing person.

Humans were not the only ones vulnerable to witch's touch. If donkeys and horses were struck, fairy doctors conducted rituals in stables; if crops were afflicted, rituals were held in the field.

Based on trial transcripts, members of these secret fairy cults were poor. Those charged with membership, heresy, and witchcraft identified in trial transcripts included the following:

❋ *Farm laborers and their wives*

❋ *Fishermen and their wives*

❋ *Workmen and their wives*

There were more women than men. The majority of those accused were practicing wise-women, allegedly skilled in magical healing and witchcraft. Others identified in trial transcripts include a shoemaker and his wife, a deacon, two Franciscan begging nuns, a tailor, a charismatic healer, a laundress, two prostitutes, some widows, and two "Gypsy" women.

According to the Inquisition trial records, Sicilian fairy cults were organized into companies. Attending fairies were described as beautiful women dressed in black or white with cats' paws, horses' hooves or "round feet." Some have

Encyclopedia of Witchcraft

pigs' tails. Women, fairy and human, danced together while a male fairy minstrel played a lute or similar instrument.

In 1588, a fisherman's wife from Palermo confessed to the Inquisition that in a dream, she and her company rode on male goats through the air to a country called Benevento, which belonged to the Pope, perhaps implying that the devil did not have dominion. There the company worshipped a Queen and King who, they were told, would bestow wealth and beauty upon members of the company. The King and Queen would also give them handsome young men with whom they would have fabulous sex. After rituals of worship, the company joined in celebrations of feasting, drinking, and sex.

The fisherman's wife also told the Inquisition about another witches' assembly entitled "The Seven Fairies." During the Seven Fairies, witches transformed into animal shape before going out to kill boys and commit mischief and vandalism.

According to trial transcripts, the fisherman's wife confessed the error of her ways. She said she hadn't realized her actions were diabolical. According to her, motivation for her actions were pleasure (fun) and because the Queen and King gave her remedies for healing the sick.

Witchcraft Trials Involving Fairies

Fairies may seem whimsical, sweet, and harmless today but demonstrating an interest in them was once considered witchcraft. Early in the witch-trial era, particularly in France, devotion to fairies and membership in fairy societies was among the forms of witchcraft that the Inquisition wished to prosecute and eliminate.

Bernardo Gui's *The Inquisitor's Manual*, published *c.*1324 and among the earliest witch-hunters' manuals, instructs Inquisitors to question sorcerers, diviners, and necromancers *"on the subject of fairies who bring good fortune, or it is said, who run around at night."*

Later on, as witchcraft became associated with diabolism and Satan-worship, the Inquisition was no longer interested in fairies unless devotion to them corresponded to what the Church considered standardized Satanic practice. Some of those charged with witchcraft disagreed: some, particularly in Hungary and Italy, acknowledged membership in fairy societies. Some even acknowledged these to be witchcraft, but denied that these practices had anything to do with Satan. Instead of worshipping Satan, these practitioners claimed devotion to beautiful, benevolent fairy queens who provided them with pleasure and material gifts, including food.

Trial transcripts are fascinating (from a distance!) because one observes that this talk of fairies and feminine rites (a lot of attention is paid to the fairies' beautiful clothes, jewels, and coiffeurs) bores the male ecclesiastical Inquisitors: *they* want to talk about heresy, sacrilege, and the devil. Eventually, presumably after application of threats and torture, the witnesses' discussion of fairies inevitably transforms into standardized descriptions of sacrilege (sex with the devil, ritual mutilation of Communion wafers, etc.). Because lengthy transcripts of the trials survive, this transformation may sometimes be observed.

* On March 18, 1430, judges at Rouen asked Joan of Arc whether she knew anything about those who "went or traveled through the air with the fairies." She denied first-hand knowledge but acknowledged being aware of this practice. She describes it as "sorcerie" and reported that it took place in her region on Thursdays.

* Alison Peirsoun of Byrehill, Scotland, was visited by the ghost of a dead relative, William Sympsoune, who took her to see elves and fairies. Fairies taught Alison to prepare healing ointments so skillfully that when Patrick Adamson, Archbishop of St Andrews (c.1543–1591) was ill, he sent for her. She did, in fact, cure him. Having recovered, the Archbishop reconsidered the situation. He refused to pay Alison her fee, attributing her skills to the devil. She was charged with witchcraft. Alison was arrested and tortured. She subsequently confessed and accused many others of consorting with elves. She was burned at the stake.

* In 1662, Isobel Gowdie of Scotland volunteered a confession of witchcraft. She claimed that she went to the Queen of the Fairies who gave her meat—more meat than she could possible eat. Transcripts indicate that Inquisitors became bored with Isobel's story, her fairy-tale descriptions of the Queen of Fairy. They wanted to hear about the devil, and soon Isobel indeed changed her testimony. (Isobel Gowdie is among the mysteries of the Burning Times. It is unknown why she voluntarily confessed to witchcraft, nor what ultimately became of her.)

* During a 1745 Hungarian witchcraft trial, several women including an Erzsébet Ràcz argued they were not witches but members of the "Convent of Saint Helen," which may perhaps be understood as the "Society of Tündér Ilona." (Saint Helen is also the name given the Fairy Goddess in the Balkans.)

See also Fairy Magician, Sicilian Fairy Cult, Tündér; **WITCHCRAZE!**

Fairy-Tale Witches and Mother Goose

Witches play complex, crucial roles in fairy tales. They are the villains of countless tales: they kill, kidnap, maim, raise havoc, behave maliciously, and last but very much not least, entrap and eat children. Witches are demonized in fairy tales: "happy endings" often include torturing and killing witches.

Witches are also the heroines of countless fairy tales. They rescue, heal, revive, provide guidance, instruction, and magical tools. Witches are often the sole sources of salvation in desperate circumstances, although, quite often, when witches play a positive role, they are labeled something other than "witch."

Sometimes the very same witch plays both roles (villain and heroine) in the very same story. Sometimes, although a story might *officially* and explicitly label a witch as a villain, undercurrents within the story suggest a more complex role instead. This is particularly true among Jewish fairy tales starring Lilith and Russian fairy tales starring Baba Yaga.

Fairy tales helped perpetuate the worst stereotyping of witches, but fairy tales also helped preserve and transmit witchcraft and shamanic traditions.

When most English-speakers consider *fairy tales*, they generally think of Hans Christian Andersen and the Brothers Grimm. Ironically, both are fairly fairy-free; there are virtually no fairies in Hans Christian Andersen and even fewer in the Brothers Grimm.

In comparison, Irish fairy tales include a high proportion of stories about fairies (*sidhe*) or featuring fairies in prominent roles. Tales from the Balkans, France, Hungary, and Italy are also packed with fairies. As a classic example, Charles Perrault's French version of *Sleeping Beauty* features thirteen fairies; the Brothers

Grimm version of that tale, *Briar Rose*, features thirteen "wise women" instead.

Wise women is a euphemism for a single, less polite word rooted in identical etymology, although that certain less polite word is fraught with nuance and loaded down with baggage.

Significantly, twelve of the "wise women" in *Briar Rose* are "good" and bless the baby; the thirteenth is angry and curses her. That certain word cognate with "wise woman" is, of course, "witch": had it been used instead, the Brothers Grimm would have had to acknowledge that twelve out of the thirteen were *not* wicked.

The borderline dividing witches, wise women, and fairies can be very nebulous. When I asked my primary Hungarian source to confirm the English translation of *boszorkány* (see **DICTIONARY**), she automatically replied, "*witch.*" When I requested further details, the finer nuances of the *boszorkány*, she immediately responded, "*an ugly, mean, wicked witch.*" But, I inquired, is the *boszorkány* "wicked" by definition or could she also be a beautiful, benevolent witch? The response was a blank stare. I pressed on, "*Well, what would you call such a witch? What do you call a beautiful, powerful, essentially good, female practitioner of magic?*" The light of recognition dawned: "*That's a fairy!*" she instantly responded.

Sometimes "fairies" refers to different species of spirits but sometimes it doesn't. "Fairy" is often a euphemism or stand-in word for "witch," often with the added implied nuance of "beautiful witch" although not always. (And, of course, not all fairies are uniformly benevolent or beautiful, not even in Hungarian fairy tales.)

During Europe's Burning Times, in some regions, notably France and Italy, consorting with fairies was included among charges of witchcraft. Fairies were *not* officially considered sweet, harmless, and suitable for children's tales;

instead they were dangerous relics of Paganism. Consorting with fairies and telling tales glorifying them was a criminal act. (See **FAIRIES:** Sicilian Fairy Cult, Witchcraft Trials.)

The existence of Balkan fairy societies (see **FAIRIES:** Fairy Magicians) and assorted fragments of witch-trial testimony suggest that the Inquisition was not entirely fantasizing about devotion to fairies. When witchcraft became diabolized (i.e. witchcraft was defined as a Satanic cult) some of the accused witches protested that they did not worship Satan but were devotees of the beautiful, generous, benevolent Fairy Queen.

If "Fairy Queen" is a euphemism for the Goddess, then fairies are her devotees, those who remember old, forbidden, suppressed knowledge. They are the "*ones who know*"—the definition at the heart of the word "witch." *Fairy tales* thus might just as easily be called *witch tales*.

In the Grimms' fairy tale *The Twelve Dancing Princesses* (also called *The Dancing Shoes* and *The Shoes Worn to Pieces*), twelve beautiful sisters each mysteriously wear out a pair of shoes nightly. They refuse to reveal where they've been or what they've done. Those who investigate are foiled. In order to prevent their mysterious escapades, the princesses are locked into the bedroom they share every night but to no avail: every morning their shoes are still worn through. Eventually it is revealed that the princesses journey to a magical subterranean grotto to join other nocturnal revelers in dancing the night away.

Although not explicitly stated, these revels may be understood as witch-balls or, in the Inquisition's term, *sabbats* (see **DICTIONARY**). The description of their magical dance-realm corresponds to witch-trial testimony in which Italian and Hungarian women described visits to their Fairy Queens—visits the Inquisition labeled diabolical witchcraft, punishable by death, a crucial reason why the princesses keep their destination secret and why they maintain silence as the young men who try but fail to discover their secret are doomed to die.

The princesses are not necessarily as cold and heartless as the story implies (but this may be understood as another clue to their secret identity; their talent for concocting sleeping potions is another). The sisters' escapades are dangerous and forbidden—hence their dire need for secrecy. The youngest sister notably is terrified of being discovered.

The story contains mixed messages and is ambivalent toward the princesses: its hero is the man who discovers their secret. By the end of the story, the princesses' dancing has (presumably) been curtailed, but they are not punished, they are not presented as grotesque, and they are not called "witches" even though they have been faithfully attending those nocturnal balls.

The concept of "fairy tales" as a distinct literary genre (as opposed to a vital oral folk tradition) was born in the nineteenth century; in the context of that time, the name "fairy tale" was innocuous but implicitly dismissive and condescending. Even now, describing something as a "fairy story" often implies that it is untrue or only believed by the gullible.

By the nineteenth century, most educated people didn't believe in the existence of "fairies" and assumed others didn't either. (Many had doubts about witches, too.) By this time belief in fairies was socially acceptable only for *very* young children. Suspension of reality is often considered part and parcel of fairy tales. Many assume "fairy tale" to be synonymous with "fantasy tale," and so fairy tales are stories to be enjoyed but not believed.

And yet *other* compilations of ancient stories, also former oral traditions, are widely held sacred:

❋ *The Bible is a sacred text incorporating a series of stories including fantastic occurrences, heroic adventures, and even a witch. Although many publications of these stories are oriented toward children, they are understood as being more than "children's tales." Many, adults as well as children, understand these tales to be literally true, while others perceive them as founts of spiritual wisdom and metaphor.*

❋ *"Mythology" literally means "sacred stories"; while most modern Western people may not accept ancient Greek, Egyptian or Norse myths as literally true, most believe they contain ethical lessons and allegories as well as being entertaining at the same time.*

❋ Patakis *are the sacred stories of Yoruban spiritual traditions including Santeria. These often very entertaining legends of the orishas simultaneously transmit sacred information. (See* **DICTIONARY***: Orisha, Santeria.)*

In addition to possessing spiritual truths, all of the above are acknowledged to contain traces of history.

What if some fairy tales could be considered in the same way?

What if some fairy tales weren't entirely fantasy or nonsense tales?

What if instead, secretly imbedded in a substantial percentage, there are hidden magical, mystical, spiritual, and shamanic secrets as well as lingering vestiges of history?

The way fairy tales are most often experienced today is not the way they were originally experienced, or intended to be experienced. In the late seventeenth century, at the tail end of the witch-hunts, men began to collect and publish fairy tales, culminating in the nineteenth-century publication of massive collections by the Brothers Grimm in Germany, Aleksandr Afanas'ev in Russia, and others elsewhere.

Although virtually all national collections of fairy tales compiled in the nineteenth century were compiled by men, their sources were largely female. Despite the fact that fairy tales are now usually read from books, fairy tales were originally part of a vast, and largely female, oral tradition.

> Although both men and women are story-tellers, many scholars consider the more magical, "supernatural" fairy tales to be almost exclusively female in origin. In essence these stories could be classified as "Women's Mysteries."

The goals of the nineteenth-century story-collectors did not necessarily parallel those of their sources: Jakob Grimm, for instance, wished to create a unified Teutonic folklore that expressed the German *"folk-soul."* Many collectors had nationalist goals. Others wished to preserve what they perceived as an inevitably vanishing treasure—this world of stories, this formerly oral tradition. Women's world of magic tales was expected to disappear in the face of science, industry, and rationalism; men would save and preserve whatever was worthwhile for posterity, and fix it up a bit in the process.

Fairy tales, once the province of adults, were transformed into nursery tales for "nice" middle-class children, and so were tailored toward what was considered suitable for that market: explicit references to bodily functions and sex were deleted, including sexual double entendres. Many magical double entendres remain however—maybe because the compilers didn't fully understand or recognize them. (And in all fairness, many of their sources probably no longer recognized them either.) Thus references to *"wearing out iron shoes"* and *"spinning in the moonlight"* merely sounded magical in a nonsensical, charming kind of way.

For centuries, the intended audience for these stories had not been only or even mainly children; the stories were told by women to other women. Young children heard them because of their constant proximity to women. Tales were told wherever women congregated together, particularly without men, particularly in spinning circles.

Fairy tales are sometimes accused of encouraging female passivity. With all due respect, this opinion usually reveals someone who hasn't delved deeply into fairy lore, which is just *packed* with brave, clever, inventive, powerful women. For those only familiar with the Disneyfied versions of fairy tales, this may be news. Yes, in fairy tales brave princes do rescue catatonic beauties, but more often women must rescue men, often by developing previously untapped magical, shamanic powers.

Pagan elements survive in *many* of these stories, although in general these are oblique. The elements must be recognized by the listener; they are rarely spelled out and for a critical reason—the stories that reach us today survived the witch-hunts. Many contain material that if told explicitly would have earned the teller (and most likely the listeners, too!) devastating punishment and even death.

> In Russia, telling stories was condemned by church officials, including St Kirill of Turov (*c.*1130–April 28, 1182), who described the punishments awaiting story-tellers in the next world.

Fairy tales served different needs: they simultaneously entertain and instruct. They were told by different people with different and complex motivations. Some fairy tales may be seen to counter other fairy tales. Some caution against witches and witchcraft; others preserve and transmit witchcraft traditions.

Fairy tales often sound fantastic to those unfamiliar with magical and shamanic themes. Stories are funny, thrilling and entertaining but nothing more. For those seeking shamanic, magical, and spiritual instruction, however, information may be transmitted in relative safely in the context of public story-telling.

Hidden clues lurk encoded in stories that no one was officially expected to take seriously. They were told to people—women and young children—that no one officially took seriously either. Those fairy-tale clues include the following.

✳ **Spinning:** *more than just a household chore. See* **WOMEN'S MYSTERIES:** *Spinning.*

✳ **Old fertility symbols:** *pots, cauldrons, ovens, stoves, mortars and pestles,* particularly *if they're iron or earthen.* Any *reference to iron is worth a second look. References to chopping, grinding or winnowing, particularly if what is being processed is a human body, recall the Corn Mother. (See* **ERGOT**.)

✳ **The color red:** particularly *in reference to shoes and* particularly *when the red item is extremely significant, magically powerful, and/or controversial. Some, though not all, references to red refer to menstrual power and old spiritual traditions. Should a hero be advised to bypass shiny new swords in favor of a red rusty one, that's usually a good indication.*

✳ **Limping, hobbling, crutches:** *pay attention to people who limp, hobble, use crutches or a prosthetic leg or who are identified as having one "different" or vulnerable leg or foot. Sometimes the person*

wears their shoes on the wrong feet or is missing or loses a shoe. For reasons not now entirely clear, that limp or shuffle is often indicative of shamanic power and capacity. This ancient motif appears in myths (Achilles, Jason, Oedipus, Odysseus) and the Bible (Jacob/Israel). Shamans performed their shuffling dance (perhaps in imitation of bears?) throughout Asia and North America. Trickster spirits (such as Africa's Elegba), and crossroads spirits who "open doors" also often limp—as does the Christian devil. (See **ANIMALS:** *Bears;* **CREATIVE ARTS:** *Dance: The Step of Wu;* **DIVINE WITCH:** *Baba Yaga, Hecate;* **HORNED ONE:** *The Devil, Krampus.)*

✳ **Speaking animals:** *sometimes having humans and animals communicate is merely a story-teller's device but sometimes not. If one begins to read fairy tales, it is amazing just how many characters are able to communicate with animals, particularly female characters. This is not merely literary license: acquiring the power to communicate (to varying degrees) with animals is traditionally among the first shamanic or witchcraft skills acquired.*

✳ **Shamanic resurrections:** *here's a standard motif: someone, the hero or sometimes an animal, is killed and dismembered. Not to worry, this is a fairy tale: someone else will gather up all their bones and wrap them in a magic cloth or an animal hide. From this point, details vary. Sometimes magic words are said, sometimes the "water of life" is sprinkled, sometimes it's sufficient to point or wave a magic wand and hey presto! The person returns to life, all in one piece, better than ever. This motif is at least as old as Inanna-Ishtar's descent to the Realm of the Dead and her subsequent resurrection (see* **CREATIVE ARTS:** *Dance: Dance of the Seven Veils) and may be understood as pure fantasy, but amazingly this motif occurs all over the world.*

A Native American variation from the Pacific Northwest insists that, once salmon is consumed, all bones be carefully preserved and ritually disposed so that the salmon can resurrect and return the following year. In a Norse myth, two goats pull Thor's chariot. When there is no food, he slaughters and eats them then ritually gathers and prepares their bones, so that they repeatedly return to life.

Standard steps involved in this resurrection mimic those of shamanic initiations. Shamans from all over the world have described initiations in similar terms: they are "killed," chopped up, cooked, and consumed by spirits who, if all goes right, will then resurrect them. Once reborn, the shaman has powers previously unpossessed; once resurrection is complete, a story's hero can accomplish tasks he was unable to before.

Tales of Baba Yaga eating people may be understood in this context. (Without context or explanation, it just sounds like cannibalism.) A classic example occurs in the Russian fairytale Koschei the Deathless (see page 496). (See also **DIVINE WITCH**: Baba Yaga, Cerridwen.)

✳ **Shamanic battling:** *details of the initiation process of European shamans, from Hungary's* táltos *to Italy's* ciaurauli, *feature some consistent details. The person is destined to be a shaman; it is not a matter of choice: one way or another, they are "called." No need to seek initiation; the initiator finds them. When the shaman-to-be reaches a specific age, usually seven, an older member of the shamanic society appears and begins their training. Then at a later age, usually fourteen, in order to complete initiation, another shaman or a psychic apparition must be battled and defeated.*

This is magical battling: it's not a boxing match. In fairy tales this type of story often involves an oven: someone, either the witch or the initiate, must be cooked within it. This motif is popular in Russian Baba Yaga stories: Baba Yaga gets roasted a lot but never dies. By getting Baba Yaga into the oven, however, the initiate effectively becomes the witch.

Because burning was the Church's method of eradicating witches, and because stories were told during the Burning Times by narrators with varying orientations, these stories must be read closely: is the story an anti-witchcraft story or a tale of initiation? (See **DICTIONARY**: Benandanti, Ciaraulo, Kresnik, Táltos, Vucodlak.)

✳ **The motif of two sisters:** *frequently half- or stepsisters; one is "good" but unappreciated, abused, neglected, and exploited. Notably she does not complain about her abuse but submits and endures. She journeys to the goddess from desperation or other sincere reasons, behaves kindly, honorably, and respectfully, works hard and is rewarded.*

The other girl is selfish, lazy, and indulged. Her mother pretends she is "good" although the story inevitably makes it clear that she's really a mean brat. This girl journeys to the goddess for selfish, acquisitive reasons, but her true character is exposed by the goddess and she is punished.

Pagan symbolism lurks very close to the surface in these stories: sometimes the goddess, wearing the mask of a witch, is even named. (See page 469, Grimms' Fairy Tales: Mother Holle; *Russian Fairy Tales:* Baba Yaga.)

Fairy tales may be interpreted in various ways and understood on many levels. Beyond the Freudian, Jungian, and moralistic interpretations frequently given this motif of the sisters, two other additional levels may be considered:

✳ *The story is instructional: should you, dear listener or reader, ever be forced to journey to Baba Yaga's hut, the story demonstrates which behavior enables survival and success versus the behavior guaranteed to result in your destruction.*

✳ *Within this story motif may also be heard silent howls of protest from "wise women." The daughters of the goddess (notably the "good" sister, with whom* the narrator identifies, inevitably lacks a human mother) are persecuted, beaten, starved, dressed in rags, and made to labor for others—their once-sacred tasks turned into enslavement and drudgery. They are denied their birthright while others who pretend to be good, pious, and lady-like (and are afforded the opportunity to be so) contribute to their persecution. But ultimately the goddess knows and in the end will reveal all ...

Warning! Spoiler alert! It is not always possible to discuss stories without revealing crucial plot twists. For those who care, please read the story first. All stories mentioned here are in print.

Some of the difficulty in understanding these tales involves modern perceptions of traditional "women's work." Spinning and weaving were once sacred arts, not chores, in the manner that fertility was once a sacred power, not an obligation. In fairy tales, heroines aren't darning socks at home; instead they spin outside in the moonlight, seated at crossroads, by sacred wells or in trees and caves. See **WOMEN'S MYSTERIES**: Spinning.

❋ ❋ ❋

What follows is a *brief* overview of witches in fairy tales and folklore. This is an *endless* topic and so emphasis is placed on the Western canon (Andersen, the Brothers Grimm, Mother Goose) as well as tales from cultures with interesting perspectives on witchcraft or where witches play a particularly significant role. Hidden, oblique magical, shamanic and Pagan elements are subtle and often unfamiliar and thus are emphasized here.

Fairy tales focusing on millers, their daughters, sons, and cats are discussed in **MAGICAL PROFESSIONS**: Millers.

African-American Conjure Tales

Conjure tales first emerged among the African-American population of the pre-Civil War United States. Conjure tales, as their name suggests, focus on conjurers. (See **DICTIONARY**: Conjure, Conjurer, Hoodoo.)

What is fascinating about this genre from a witchcraft perspective is its lack of sensationalism and moralizing: conjurers are presented as a fact of life.

❋ *Both conjure women and men appear.*

❋ *Conjurers are heroes and villains of this genre. Some behave malevolently and selfishly and abuse their power; others however are heroic, righteous, and valiant and serve justice.*

❋ *Some conjurers are enslaved; others are explicitly identified as free black people.*

❋ *Conjurers serve both an African-American clientele and a white one.*

Magical practices are described matter-of-factly with little hocus-pocus. Conjurers are paid professionals: stories tell exactly what was bartered or how much the conjurer earned. (Important information for those seeking these services.) If a job is strenuous, the conjurer may reject the first offer of payment to request more. Conjurers are skilled practitioners with a sense of their own worth. Significantly, conjurers are shown serving their community, often providing the only venue for justice or safety.

Conjure tales were originally part of an oral tradition. In their written form, they are now most associated with lawyer and educator, Charles W. Chesnutt (1858–November 15, 1932), who collected and embellished them and, like Hans Christian Andersen, also created original stories within the genre. His first published story, *The Goophered Grapevine*, appeared in *Atlantic Monthly* magazine in 1887.

> Goopher, now most frequently spelled goofer, derives from a Kikongo word indicating "killing curse."

A collection of conjure stories, *The Conjure Woman*, followed in 1899. Chesnutt retells the stories via the interplay of two narrators, Uncle Julius, a former slave on the McAdoo plantation and John, the Northern man who purchases the old estate, ultimately employing Julius as his coachman. (See **MAGICAL PROFESSIONS:** Coachmen.) Julius relates his conjure tales to John and John's ailing wife; his speech is rendered in the African-American dialect of North Carolina.

Chesnutt treats conjurers and their clients with respect, not mockery or condescension. Conjurers are mentioned by name, especially Aunt Peggy, described as a "witch" as well as a conjure woman. His stories are set on the pre-Civil War plantations of North Carolina. Unlike other writers of his time or later, he does not gloss over the bitter realities of slavery.

In *The Gray Wolf's Ha'nt* (Haunt), Dan, a slave, loves his wife profoundly. Another man makes unwelcome advances toward her; she complains to her husband. Dan approaches the other man and a fight ensues. Without warning, the other man draws a knife; Dan, a large, strong man, hits him before the knife can be used but he hits him too hard, inadvertently killing him. There are no witnesses and, as the narrative points out, because the victim is a free black man, the local white authorities—the only legal authority—have no interest in prosecuting his murder or discovering his murderer. (The point of prosecution wouldn't have been justice but economic compensation for a slave-owner, the equivalent of loss of property-value. Since the victim is free, this isn't an issue. No one in a position to provide legal justice cares.)

It would seem that Dan could safely and secretly walk away from this crime, except for one thing: the dead man is the son of a local conjurer whose *only* course of justice for his son is magical. The stories make clear that when conjurers work their roots, all is revealed and so Dan, well aware of his victim's identity, has no doubt that he will be the target of vengeance.

Terrified, Dan goes to a competing conjurer, Aunt Peggy, and begs for help. Unable to directly counteract the other more experienced conjurer she offers Dan a *"life charm"* for protection, crafting it from Dan's hair, roots, herbs, and red flannel and receiving a piglet as payment for her efforts.

The victim's father does uncover Dan's identity but, realizing a counter-charm has been worked, he sends his animal allies to uncover it. In this epic tragedy, the conjure man gets his revenge by tricking Dan into killing his own beloved wife, the innocent woman whose beauty sparked the initial quarrel. Dan in turn kills the conjure man: both have avenged the respective deaths of their loved ones. Aunt Peggy alone survives to appear in other tales.

Conjuring is depicted as pre-Christian or as something forbidden by Christianity. However in Chesnutt's renditions, conjuring is not intrinsically bad or evil. In *Poor Sandy*, Tenie is a conjure woman who hasn't practiced in 15 years since she became Christian. When she reveals her identity and skills to her new husband, he is impressed, not horrified.

Charles W. Chesnutt's stories are reprinted in their original form in *The Conjure Woman and Other Conjure Tales* (Duke University Press, 1993). *Conjure Tales* (E.P. Dutton, 1973) features the stories revised as thrillers for children. Narrators and the sub-plots attached to them are deleted, as are the dialect and loop-holes allowing readers the option of not believing the tales. However, the harsh realities of slavery (forced separation of families is a major theme) are retained.

In Chesnutt's tales, conjuring is not reserved for slaves, the uneducated or African-Americans. You don't have to "believe" in it for it to work. Although white people are depicted professing not to believe in conjure, Chesnutt makes clear that many of them do and that their slaves are well aware of this. White people, including plantation owners, hire conjurers too. Sometimes conjurers cast spells for these owners that do not benefit their own community. In *The Goophered Grapevine*, Aunt Peggy is hired (and paid ten dollars cash, a significant sum) by a slave-master to goopher or fatally curse his scuppernong grapevines so that his slaves can't nibble on the harvest.

See **ANIMALS:** Allies; **BOTANICALS:** Roots; **DICTIONARY:** Root Doctor.

Grimms' Fairy Tales

The Brothers Grimm, Jakob (January 4, 1785–September 20, 1863) and Wilhelm (February 24, 1786–December 16, 1859), first began collecting these stories in 1806 largely from female sources. Two hundred and ten stories would be published although not all in the same edition. Their original intent was to preserve the folk tradition that they perceived as the expression of the German soul. (Ironically many of the stories derive from French-Huguenot sources.)

Jakob Grimm was also the author of the massive four-volume *Teutonic Mythology* (1835). He himself drew parallels between folktales and mythology, especially the *Song of the Nibelungs*.

The massive popularity of Grimms' fairy tales sparked the modern field of folkloric studies. Unlike Hans Christian Andersen or Oscar Wilde, the Brothers Grimm didn't create their own stories but relied entirely on sources. Yet, at the same time, they didn't merely transcribe the narrator's voice as today an anthropologist theoretically would, but selectively edited, polished, and revised these stories. The brothers admitted deleting phrases and topics they considered unsuitable for children but insisted that they preserved the "spirit" of the tales.

The Brothers Grimm, Jakob in particular, did not initially perceive that they were writing for a children's market but envisioned a readership of other scholars and folklorists. "Folklore" however had not yet emerged as a respected academic subject; the topic confused many people. In the rational, industrialized nineteenth century, the stories seemed like they *should* be intended for children, yet the subject matter of many of these tales (sex, pregnancy, child abuse, incest) was not exactly conventional middle-class bedtime-story material. Grimms' fairy tales were initially criticized as inappropriate for children.

Their publisher—and Wilhelm—realized the commercial potential of their work (although the Grimms themselves never made much money from their tales). Subsequent editions were revised to be more appealing to middle-class parents:

❋ *While in some cases stories became* more *violent, sexual references were deleted.*

❋ *Evil but formerly biological mothers transformed into wicked stepmothers.*

❋ *Christian references were inserted and emphasized. Greater emphasis was placed on rites of marriage and church attendance. (In early versions of* The Frog Prince, *for instance, once the frog has transformed back into a handsome prince, he and the princess hurry to bed; in later versions, they hurry off to church to be married first.)*

The first edition of *Kinder- und Hausmärchen* was published in 1819. Eventually seven editions featuring substantial revisions would be published.

While there are witches, elves, goblins, millers, and devils aplenty in Grimms' fairy tales, there are almost no "fairies." The original German title does not actually refer to fairies, or to any other type of supernatural creature for that matter. The title is more accurately translated as *Children's and Household Tales* or *Nursery and Household Tales* and frequently as *Grimms' Tales for Young and Old.*

Witches appear in many of the tales, including the following.

Briar Rose

This German version of *Sleeping Beauty* has one significant difference: lack of fairies. The king is so delighted by the birth of his long-awaited daughter that he invites not only his relatives, friends, and acquaintances to a feast but also twelve *Wise Women*. Significantly, although there are thirteen Wise Women in his kingdom he only has twelve golden plates for them, and so one must stay home.

No specific reason is given as to *why* the thirteenth Wise Woman isn't invited; it is the number thirteen itself that seems to be the problem.

❋ *Thirteen is associated with the traditional number of witches in covens*

❋ *Thirteen is traditionally identified as an anti-Christian number, hence the superstition against thirteen at table and the perception of thirteen as an unlucky number*

Coincidentally or not, when the disgruntled thirteenth Wise Woman gatecrashes the party, her curse is that at the age of fifteen, the princess will prick her finger on a spindle, ancient emblem of Women's Mysteries, and die.

In response, all spindles in the kingdom are destroyed except for one. The princess is kept ignorant of her history and is not forewarned.

She can't even recognize a spindle when she finally sees one nor does she know enough to be wary. In essence, she is not rooted in women's spirituality and thus lacks its protection. (The story could also be interpreted in the opposite way, read as a warning suggesting that these forbidden women's traditions, which persist right under authority's nose despite vigorous attempts at their extirpation, are dangerous to young women.)

The day she turns fifteen, her parents are away and the unsupervised princess spends her birthday exploring the castle. She discovers one room with a rusty key in its lock. (Red rust is a traditional substitute for menstrual blood in many spells and rituals.) Using the key to open the door, she discovers an old woman spinning. Ignorance is what really "kills" the princess. She doesn't know not to handle (or how to handle) what is dangerous or taboo for her.

Of course she doesn't die but merely falls into a faint. A hedge, symbol of shamanic witchcraft, grows protectively around the castle to serve as a test: the only one capable of breaking the Wise Woman's curse, the prince who is worthy of Briar Rose, proves himself by his ability to navigate this hedge.

See **DICTIONARY:** Hedge; **WOMEN'S MYSTERIES:** Spinning.

The Devil with the Three Golden Hairs

In this Teutonic equivalent of a *táltos* tale, a poor woman bears a son born with a caul, indicating his special destiny. A fortune-teller is called in: she prophesies that at age fourteen the boy will marry the king's daughter.

✳ *The reference to the fortune-teller is matter-of-fact and non-judgmental*

✳ *Fourteen is the age when táltos and similar shamans traditionally undergo initiations involving battling.*

The king learns of the prophecy and, appalled by the idea that his daughter could marry a peasant, arranges to kill the child. The baby is placed in a box and thrown into the river but is rescued by a miller.

When the boy turns fourteen, the king discovers that he's not dead and again attempts to kill him. The boy consistently survives and outwits all attempts on his life until finally the king announces that the boy can marry his daughter if he journeys to Hell and brings back three gold hairs from the devil's head. *This* is the shamanic journey, the journey to the other realm, and confrontation or negotiation with the spirits.

Upon reaching Hell, the boy finds the devil away but the devil's grandmother at home. (According to legend, the devil's grandmother taught the devil everything he knows.) She is sympathetic to the boy, offers her help, and protects him by allowing him to crawl into the folds of her skirt where it is safe.

Significantly she doesn't perform the boy's task for him. She instructs him to listen closely to her conversation with the devil; *if* he has the ears, skill, and talent, he will accomplish his task, survive, *and* vanquish his opponent. If not, he loses all.

See **DICTIONARY:** Caul, Táltos; **HAG:** The Devil's Grandmother; **HORNED ONE:** The Devil; **MAGICAL PROFESSIONS:** Millers.

Fitcher's Bird (sometimes called Fowler's Fowl)

A wizard misuses his powers in this Bluebeard-type tale to become a serial killer of women. Having already murdered many women, he kidnaps three sisters, one after the other. The first two fall prey to his wiles; the third has shamanic skills and is able to resurrect her sisters by reassembling their dismembered parts. The wizard is ultimately burned alive.

The wizard is clearly a villain and so there's little sympathy for him (his is a flat character, *nothing* is revealed about him other than he's an evil wizard/serial killer); however he is also the only person explicitly identified as a magical practitioner. The third sister has her skills too, although this is *not* made explicit: for those unfamiliar with shamanic ritual, it may seem completely coincidental that she just happens to know how to resurrect her sisters. What is perhaps not coincidental is that the one figure clearly identified as a magical practitioner, the wizard, is burned.

Frau Trude

No Disneyfied version of *Frau Trude* exists—the harsh, brief story of an unnamed little girl who is stubborn, insolent, and disobeys her parents. While this is explicitly stated in the story, none of her bad behavior is witnessed. What is witnessed is that she is curious and brave (or perhaps reckless).

One day the little girl announces that she intends to visit *"Frau Trude"* because she's heard so much about her and is curious about her interesting house containing unusual things. The parents forbid her to go, telling her that Frau Trude is a wicked woman who does "god-less things" and that if she disobeys, then she's not their child any more. The story contains no further identification or information regarding Frau Trude, although notably she is the only character in the story with a name. The girl disobeys and visits Frau Trude.

The story is abrupt and vague; the little girl's approach or her initial meeting with Frau Trude isn't retold. Instead it jumps to a dialogue between Frau Trude and the little girl regarding why the little girl has become so exceedingly frightened.

Frau Trude asks what scared her: the little girl says she saw *"a black man"* on Frau Trude's steps. Frau Trude identifies him as the charcoal burner. Frau Trude doesn't ask more questions but the little girl keeps talking: she saw *"a green man,"* too. Frau Trude identifies him as a hunter. The little girl then volunteers that she saw a *"blood-red man"*; Frau Trude identifies him as the butcher.

The little girl doesn't know when to stop; she tells Frau Trude that she looked through the window and didn't see Frau Trude but saw the devil with a fiery head. Unluckily, she's said the magic words: Frau Trude reveals that the girl saw *"the witch in her true headdress"* and that she's been waiting and asking for this child who will *"burn bright"* for her. She transforms the girl into a block of wood and throws her on her hearth fire.

There are different ways of interpreting this mysterious and depressing little story.

One way is as an anti-Pagan, anti-witchcraft tale:

✳ *"The black man" was a very common witch-hunt era (and later) euphemism for Satan. A high percentage of those who heard this story, especially in the nineteenth century, would assume this reference was to the devil.*

* The "Green Man" explicitly names the Pagan spirit of male procreative energy, although it sometimes specifically indicates Dionysus, too. In either case, the Green Man is a deity associated with witchcraft; devout Christians might consider the "green man" another euphemism for the devil, too.

* "The red man" is another euphemism for Satan, sometimes envisioned as a red devil with horns and forked tail. Krampus, a spirit identified with the devil and popular in southern Germany, is often depicted in this fashion.

* The implication of the little girl's fourth and final vision is that she has witnessed Frau Trude's true form; Frau Trude is a devil too and will not permit the little girl to live to tell the tale.

If you subscribe to this interpretation then the story contains the following morals:

* Children should obey their parents who know best.

* Witches are evil child-killers who should be avoided at all costs.

* Witches are in league with the devil or may even be the devil.

There is, however, another very different way of interpreting *Frau Trude*, provided various story elements are recognized:

* Blocks of wood were associated with divine female spirits in pre-Christian Europe. The fiery goddess Diana, for instance, was worshipped as a block of wood throughout Europe. The Yule log, identified with Frigga, was burned at Yuletide and its ashes preserved throughout the year for good fortune and protection. The story ends abruptly; if it continued, perhaps the girl would resurrect.

* The three different-colored men witnessed by the child don't have to be interpreted as devils: the Green Man's popularity, for instance, remains undiminished in the twenty-first century. Neo-Pagans consider him a god or positive sacred force. Although red Krampus was identified by Christians as the devil, he is, in fact, a stubbornly persistent male horned deity, a concept much older than the Christian conception of the devil. Frau Trude specifically identifies the black man as a "charcoal burner." Before Christianity associated it with Satan, black was the color of fertility and life-everlasting; Europeans masked their devotion to blackened male fertility spirits, like Krampus, by disguising them as charcoal burners and chimneysweeps.

* Most importantly perhaps, who exactly is the mysterious and deadly Frau Trude? What does it mean to be "a witch in her fiery headdress?" Is she, as the story implies, the devil or is she, like Mother Holle (see page 477) a disguised goddess and potential initiatrix?

Frau Trude and Mother Holle are the only witches with names in *Grimms' Fairy Tales* and so comparison between them is inevitable. Their eponymous stories are somewhat parallel as well; in both cases, young girls visit them.

In *Mother Holle*, two girls make the journey, the first passes Mother Holle's tests and is rewarded; the second girl doesn't. *Frau Trude* can be understood as recounting disasters that befall failed initiates or what happens to those who lack preparation.

Frau Trude has even more parallels with the Russian *Vasilisa the Wise*, which features another solitary girl's visit to a witch with an interesting house containing unusual things, albeit Vasilisa isn't there by choice.

Vasilisa never volunteers information or voluntarily seeks information. When finally pressed by Baba Yaga to ask questions, she inquires about the white, red, and black riders she witnessed riding in the forest. Baba Yaga identifies them as her servants. Vasilisa accepts her answer without requesting further explanation. When Baba Yaga invites further questions, Vasilisa politely declines. Baba Yaga compliments her on her wisdom, explaining that if she'd asked about anything inside the house, Baba Yaga would have been obligated to kill her.

The little girl in *Frau Trude* is destroyed only when she asks about what she has seen within the house. Unlike Vasilisa, the little girl in *Frau Trude* doesn't have maternal magical guidance and spiritual protection; instead her parents disown her. They offer no instruction or protective blessings and so she is doomed.

See Russian Fairy Tales: *Vasilisa the Wise*; **BOTANICALS**: Trees; **DIVINE WITCH**: Baba Yaga, Diana, Dionysus; **HORNED ONE**: Chimneysweep, The Devil, Krampus.

Hansel and Gretel

Now among the Grimms' signature fairy tales, *Hansel and Gretel* is extremely hostile towards witches and to adult women in general. In the context of fairy tales, its witch is particularly virulent: she's portrayed as physically grotesque; a cannibal who lusts for children and insidiously lures them to her. The resemblance of witches to animals is pointed out; in nineteenth-century Europe, this was no compliment.

Nothing ultimately happens to the witches in *Frau Trude*, *Rapunzel*, and *Jorinda and Joringel*: in *Hansel and Gretel* the witch is graphically killed by incineration in an oven. In the twenty-first century, this evokes thoughts of Auschwitz but ovens were first developed as execution tools in Germanic lands to kill witches during

the Burning Times. (See **WITCHCRAZE!**: Germany.) *Hansel and Gretel* thus is not entirely a fantasy tale.

Hansel and Gretel was among those stories initially thought unsuitable for children—not because of the violent killing of the witch but because the concept of parents' abandoning their children was considered too disturbing. The story was periodically revised by Wilhelm Grimm.

Hansel and Gretel's parents are identified as a woodcutter and *"his wife."* In the earliest published versions of this story, the female parent is the biological mother. Wilhelm Grimm did not revise the tale by making her kinder; rather she became increasingly villainous but, by the fourth edition, had become a *stepmother*. The father, however, was increasingly exonerated in subsequent editions: his wife *made* him do it.

The family is starving; they have no food. They live on the edge of the forest yet seem unable to reap the forest's bounties. There is no indication that attempts at hunting or foraging in the forest have been made. In *Hansel and Gretel*, the forest seems useful only for chopping wood or abandoning children.

The mother convinces the father to abandon the children in the heart of the forest. The children eavesdrop (or overhear) the parents' private conversation and so are aware of impending doom. Hansel famously scatters a path of white pebbles behind him to lead them home. This works, but the second time the kids are abandoned in the forest, Hansel tries to blaze a trail with bits of stale bread instead. These woodcutter's children, raised right on the threshold of the woods, are so unfamiliar with nature's ways that they cannot foresee that inevitably there will be no trail home: of course, birds, insects, and forest animals eat the bread. Hansel and Gretel wander lost in the forest for three days until a lovely snow-white songbird leads them to the witch's house.

Beautiful white songbirds usually lead fairy-tale heroines to safety; the bird's presence in *Hansel and Gretel* indicates that perhaps this story once followed different paths. (See page 479, *The Old Woman in the Forest*.)

The house is made from bread, the roof from cake, and the windows from sparkling sugar. Faced with this miraculous house, Hansel and Gretel just begin to eat; they eat the witch up, house and home.

A major fairy-tale theme is that witches have food when others do not. The less remarked upon flipside is that, in fairy tales, food (and other valuables) is stolen from witches although the theft aspect is consistently glossed over.

Now one could argue that Hansel and Gretel are too overwhelmed and famished to remember their manners, yet even when the witch inquires from within *"Nibble, nibble little mouse, who's that nibbling at my house"* they evade the question. (They reply: *"The wind so mild, the Heavenly Child."*)

They do not apologize, introduce themselves, ask permission or seem at all curious or nervous about whose house it is that they are eating. What is wrong with these children? Have they no manners? Have they no *sense*? They discover a *magic* house in the woods yet show no awe, respect or caution. Houses made of bread and candy in the middle of the forest cannot be any more common than houses revolving on chicken's legs but Hansel and Gretel seem to assume that it is theirs for the taking.

The narrator blames the witch: the story states that she deliberately built her edible house to entice children, even though she is in the middle of the forest where, presumably, lone children rarely wander. This is only logical if one assumes, as many do, that the wicked witch and the wicked mother are one and the same and so Hansel and Gretel's arrival was anticipated.

The witch, on making her first appearance, is identified as a hobbling old woman with a crutch. The witch feeds them a fine meal of *"milk and pancakes, sugar, apples, and nuts."* She gives them a beautiful, comfortable bed but by the next morning it's all revealed as deception: Hansel is imprisoned behind iron bars and Gretel is ordered to work for the witch, like Vasilisa the Wise in Baba Yaga's hut. (See page 494, Russian Fairy Tales: *Vasilisa the Wise*.)

Gretel contrasts with Vasilisa:

❀ *Vasilisa serves Baba Yaga. She is careful to behave like a servant: she's aware that her life is in the witch's hands. Baba Yaga is not nicer to Vasilisa than the nameless witch is to Gretel; the threat of death is just as explicit and ever-present in Baba Yaga's house. Baba Yaga explicitly does not offer Vasilisa food but Vasilisa is just grateful to survive.*

❀ *Gretel is annoyed that she only gets crayfish shells to eat (lunar food; the crayfish, as depicted in the Tarot card, The Moon, was emblematic of the moon in*

Central Europe). *For a child who just days before was starving in the woods, who has been abandoned by her own parents specifically because of lack of food, this is fairly petulant behavior. And these shells, while obviously not ideal fare, are edible if one is starving; Gretel isn't offered grass or stones. (An opposing interpretation might suggest that Gretel is righteously rejecting the witch's lunar, magical diet.)*

❋ *Vasilisa has a secret magic weapon (her doll) that allows her to pass Baba's initiation, but she also behaves with dignity, works hard, has good manners, and faces her fears.*

❋ *Gretel cheats, snivels, and doesn't pass her initiation. But of course, there's a significant reason why she doesn't: Vasilisa's doll represents her mother's undying love and devotion, and this maternal relationship is the crucial element Gretel conspicuously lacks.*

❋ *Both Vasilisa and the witch survive in* Vasilisa the Wise: *when her initiation is complete, Baba Yaga insists that Vasilisa take the gift that ultimately transforms her into a tsarina.*

❋ *In* Hansel and Gretel, *the witch is burned to death in her own oven—the symbol of what should be a cauldron of regeneration.*

According to *Hansel and Gretel*, witches have red eyes and limited vision but have a keen sense of smell, like animals.

The witch wishes to fatten Hansel, the better to eat him. She stuffs him like a goose, feeling his finger periodically to see if he's sufficiently fat.

Clever Hansel fools her by offering a chicken bone to feel instead. (And if her eyesight is so poor that she can't even see Hansel right in front of her, why can't he slip Gretel some of his larder?)

Finally, impatient, she decides to cook him anyway, and bake Gretel in the bargain. The witch asks Gretel to test the oven's heat: until now Gretel has been the passive child but she sees what's coming and determines to trick the witch.

This scenario is not uncommon in fairy tales, particularly among Baba Yaga tales. There's a game aspect to it, and it's usually accompanied by verbal banter. The witch wants to cook someone who turns the tables on her, effectively assuming the witch's role: it's an initiation story. Having gotten the witch in the oven, the person quickly escapes and the witch survives to initiate more visitors. *Hansel and Gretel* takes this format but distorts it. There's little verbal banter but graphic violence instead.

Japanese manga artist/author Junko Mizuno re-envisions *Hansel and Gretel* (Viz, 2003): Gretel Sakazaki, high-school warrior, rescues her entire community from the witch's enchantment with a little help from her twin, Hansel, and a magic doll. There is no stepmother: both mother and father are nurturing but bewitched. No one is robbed, eaten or killed; all characters including the witch are eventually reconciled. Even the witch's motivation is explained.

Gretel shoves the witch into the iron oven; the story emphasizes the flames and her shrieks as she dies. Once she's dead and the children have nothing to fear, they do not run away but rob the dead witch blind. They steal everything in the house including precious jewels. Only then do the children rush home to the parents who have twice abandoned them. Miraculously, considering how lost they were before they now have no trouble finding their way home.

Proximity to the witch has paid off: Gretel is now the leader. She has gained the capacity to speak with ducks, allowing the children to return home where their father is delighted to see his now-wealthy children. The father's wife "coincidentally" died at the same time as the witch, leading many to interpret that they are one and the same.

See page 494, Russian Fairy Tales: *Vasilisa the Wise*; **CREATIVE ARTS:** Films: *Blair Witch Project*, Manga; **PLACES:** Forest.

Jorinda and Joringel

This story could be subtitled "In Praise of Menstrual Magic." It combines a magic-friendly narrative with a wicked witch who lives in an old enchanted castle inside a great, dense forest. During the day the witch transforms into a cat or owl but at night she takes human form. Her crimes are listed as follows:

❋ *She catches birds and game, kills them, and then boils or roasts them, although why it is a crime for her to do what any hunter does is unexplained.*

❋ *She has cast a spell so that anyone coming within a hundred steps of her castle is frozen in their tracks until she chooses to release them with another spell.*

❋ *Should one of those frozen souls be an "innocent girl," rather than releasing her the witch transforms the girl into a bird and shuts her in a wicker cage.*

Why she does this or what she is planning to do with these girls is unclear but the story advises that she has seven thousand of these rare birds, all locked up.

Jorinda and Joringel, a young betrothed couple seeking some privacy, wander into the wood. Joringel warns Jorinda not to get too near the castle. However, they get lost and discover themselves near the castle walls. Joringel is frozen; Jorinda is transformed into a nightingale. The witch appears as both an owl and as a woman: as a woman she has big, red eyes and a crooked nose, so long that the end touches her chin.

Joringel eventually saves his beloved, not by force but through magical means. The solution appears in his dreams: a blood-red flower with a large pearl within. In his dream, whatever he touches with this flower is freed from enchantment. Joringel doesn't dismiss his dream but searches tirelessly through the forest for the flower, finding it only on the ninth day.

His dream come true, the flower antidotes spells and serves as his key to the enchanted castle, where he discovers the witch feeding her seven thousand birds. She is unable to get near him because of the flower. All the women are rescued and nothing violent befalls the witch: Joringel touches her with his blood-red flower and the worst that happens is that she loses her power to work magic.

See **ANIMALS:** Cats, Owls; **BOTANICALS:** Opium Poppy; **WORMWOOD:** Dangers of Witchcraft: Menstrual Power.

Mother Holle

The Goddess lives; she's underground, can be reached via a sacred well, and can still dole out punishment and reward just as she did in her heyday.

Unusually, in the story *Mother Holle* the witch is named. That name isn't random but very specific: amongst all Grimms' fairy tales, this one's Pagan references are most explicit:

❋ *Some would recognize the ancient Germanic goddess Hulda*

❋ *Some would recognize Frau Holle the Witch Queen, Storm Goddess, Elven Queen, Wild Hunter, alleged child-stealer, and bogie-woman*

A widow has two daughters, one identified in the story as beautiful and hard-working, the other ugly and lazy. In the earliest version the widow is the biological mother of both girls; later renditions make her the heroine's stepmother. She prefers and favors the ugly, lazy girl although the narrator clearly identifies with the other.

The beautiful girl plays the Cinderella role, laboring for the family as household drudge. Among her daily chores she sits beside a well near a roadside and spins until her fingers bleed. One day, when the spindle is covered with her blood, she dips it into the well to wash it off, but it slips from her hands and falls into the depths. She runs home weeping to her mother, who unsympathetically tells her that since she dropped it, she can just go retrieve it. The girl goes back but doesn't know what to do; she finally jumps into the well after the spindle.

In one version, although the girl still spins by the well, the scenario with the blood is deleted; instead she simply falls or jumps into the well, implying depression and suicide.

The girl loses consciousness and awakens in a beautiful meadow filled with flowers. She begins to walk, encountering various strange situations. In all cases, she is respectful, helpful, and kind. She finally reaches a little house where an old woman looking out the window sees her. The old woman's teeth are so huge that the girl is afraid and starts to run away.

The toothy old woman calls out to her, invites her to stay in her house, reassuring her that if she does her chores properly, she won't regret it. The woman identifies herself as Mother Holle: she is the *only* character in the story with a name.

The girl does her job well; Mother Holle is kind to her, never speaks a harsh word, and gives her meat to eat every day. Eventually, however, the girl becomes homesick, saying *"I know how well off I am down here but I must go back to my family."* Mother Holle expresses approval: she is pleased that the girl wishes to go home.

Because her service has been faithful, Mother Holle personally guides the girl back. No trip up the well this time—she takes the girl's hand and leads her through a door. As the girl passes through, she is showered with gold so that she is entirely gilded. Mother Holle also returns the spindle that began her quest.

The girl discovers herself back home. Mother and sister are impressed that she is covered with gold. She tells them her adventures; the mother determines that the same good fortune should befall her favored daughter.

The sister is sent to sit by the well. She doesn't spin but pricks her fingers and hands with brambles until they bleed and then throws the spindle down the well, jumping in after. She discovers herself in the same beautiful meadow. She too begins to walk, encountering the same odd situations: she is not helpful but mean-spirited, selfish, and rude. She has heard about Mother Holle (or so she thinks) and so is not afraid or filled with awe. Mother Holle recruits her; the sister works hard for one day but then slopes off. Mother Holle dismisses her, telling her to go home. The girl anticipates being showered with gold: instead as she passes through the gate, she is showered with irremovable pitch. (Other versions suggest excrement.)

See also *Frau Trude*; **DIVINE WITCH:** Hulda; **WOMEN'S MYSTERIES:** Spinning; **WORMWOOD:** Dangers of Witchcraft: Menstrual Power.

The Old Woman in the Forest

A party riding through the forest is set upon by robbers; everyone is murdered except for one servant girl who jumped out of the carriage and hid. She wanders alone, hopeless and hungry through the vast forest until a white dove appears with a golden key in its beak.

The dove speaks to her, advising that the key opens a lock found on a large tree. The girl opens it and finds bread and milk inside the tree. The dove gives her another key, which opens another tree: this one contains a bed. A third key opens another tree; this one is filled with beautiful clothes, gold, and gemstones. The girl lives happily in the forest with the dove's protection.

Eventually the dove, asking for a favor in turn, leads the girl to a hut (shades of *Hansel and Gretel*). Before she enters, the dove offers instructions: inside the hut will be an old woman seated by her stove. Even though the woman will greet her politely, the girl is advised not to answer or even pay attention but to quickly enter another room where she will find a table laden with rings, many with magnificent sparkling stones. The girl must bring back only the plainest ring.

The girl follows these directions although the old woman tries to prevent her. She searches through the rings but no plain one can be found, until the girl notices the old woman slinking away with a birdcage. She runs to see; the bird within the cage holds the ring in its beak. She grabs the ring, runs back to the tree and awaits her dove, who does not arrive. Instead, suddenly the tree's branches twine around her. The branches transform into the arms of a handsome young man. He had been bewitched by the old woman (now identified as "*a wicked witch*"), who transformed him into a tree but allowed him to fly around as a dove for several hours a day.

See page 474, *Hansel and Gretel*; **BOTANICALS:** Trees.

Rapunzel

The premise of the story is that Rapunzel's parents live next door to a witch; their house overlooks her garden. (Although the witch in this tale is usually explicitly identified as a witch, in some translations she is identified as a "fairy.")

The witch's garden, according to the story, is surrounded by a high wall. No one dares enter it for fear of the witch. But why should someone "enter" someone else's garden and take her vegetables? Why don't they knock on the door politely and ask for some or, better yet, offer to pay or barter for it?

> The implication in this story is that the witch with her beautiful walled garden is wealthier or of higher social status than her neighbors, traditionally a vulnerable position for a solitary woman during the Burning Times.

Rapunzel's mother is pregnant and desperately craves food from the witch's garden. For whatever reason, she will not ask for it. There is no information about the witch other than she possesses this garden and that people are afraid *because she is a witch*. The woman languishes dangerously, finally telling her husband that she will die unless she can eat some rapunzel (a type of vegetable) from the witch's garden. The husband determines to save her, announcing that "*cost what it may*" he will get her some rapunzel. Despite his announcement, he does not offer to pay any cost whatsoever; instead he steals some.

That it's plainly theft is clear from the father's actions: he doesn't openly go over the wall in daylight; he waits until dark, sneaks over the wall, grabs a handful, and flees.

He gets away with it once; the second time, the witch catches him in the act, looks him in the eye, and names his crime: "*How dare you sneak into my garden like a thief and steal my rapunzel!*" She threatens justice but the man pleads for mercy, saying that he feared his pregnant wife would die from her food cravings. The witch calms down and strikes a bargain: as much rapunzel as they'd like in exchange for the child. She vows to care for it like a mother. This is ironic because, of course, the child's biological parents trade her for salad. The husband could refuse the witch's offer. Although the story specifies that he agrees "*in fright*," nothing in the story indicates that the parents bargained, plotted or schemed to prevent giving away their child. As soon as the baby is born, the witch comes to claim her and the parents disappear from the story.

Rapunzel is well treated. She grows up to be the loveliest child in the world, her excessively long hair emblematic of psychic power obtained under the witch's tutelage.

When Rapunzel is twelve, the witch shuts her up in a tower without stairs or doors in the middle of the forest. No explanations are offered but this is clearly some sort of initiatory ritual. The witch visits her daily by climbing up Rapunzel's strong braids and climbing in through the window.

> In an Italian fairy tale that mingles elements of *Rapunzel* and *Hansel and Gretel* there is no father. The mother steals from the witch. When caught, she agrees to give up her child as a ploy but without any intention of ever doing so, and later attempts to renege on the bargain.

Eventually a young prince passing through the forest discovers Rapunzel in her lonely tower; he too begins to climb up her braids daily. This goes on for an extended period of time; they enjoy themselves. In the earliest version, Rapunzel's pregnancy eventually gives them away. The Grimms' were uncomfortable with sex, and in later versions Rapunzel accidentally reveals her trysts when she foolishly asks the witch why she's harder to pull up than the eager young prince.

The witch's response is to cut off Rapunzel's hair (her psychic power) and banish her from the tower and the forest. Contrary to popular belief, she doesn't harm or blind the prince. She confronts him in the tower (during this confrontation, she identifies herself with a cat); in despair, he jumps out the window, falling into brambles, which blind him.

See **ANIMALS:** Cats; **FOOD AND DRINK:** Rapunzel.

Snow White

The most familiar version of this story is now Disney's animated film. The "witch" is the star of both versions. (The fairy tale is devoted to her attempts to kill Snow White.) But is she, in fact, really a "witch"?

In the Disney version, she's explicitly identified as one; Grimms' version is slightly more ambiguous. Whether she's a witch or just viciously evil depends upon perceptions; she is never explicitly called a witch but is initially introduced as the woman who weds Snow White's recently widowed father. She is described as a beautiful lady, but proud and unable to tolerate the thought that anyone might be more beautiful. *Why* she feels so passionately is never made clear: is this just vanity or does perhaps her status, marriage or even life depend upon her being the fairest in the land?

The queen does have a magic mirror. Is possession of a magic mirror sufficient to be identified as a witch? Interaction with the magic mirror is the single magical action performed by the queen. It is a pivotal action: the queen's attempts to kill Snow White are all predicated on the mirror's responses to her famous question:

> *Mirror, mirror on the wall*
> *Who is the fairest of them all?*

Although she can communicate with the magic mirror, the queen is never observed casting a spell. Her attempts on Snow White's life rely entirely on violence and poison. If the queen is a witch, then she corresponds to the classical Greek definition that doesn't distinguish between witches, herbalists, and poisoners.

In Disney's version, Snow White is under a spell, finally broken by the prince's kiss. In Grimms' version, Snow White is the victim of sophisticated poison: she appears to be dead but isn't, somewhat like a *zombi*. Because she still looks so beautiful and lifelike, the seven nameless dwarfs can't bear to bury her underground but craft a glass coffin for her. Snow White lies in that coffin, the story says, *"a long, long time,"* but her body, like that of a miracle saint, does not decay.

When the handsome prince stumbles upon her gravesite, he falls in love with the beautiful corpse and begs the dwarfs for the body. They acquiesce and the prince, who has no expectations of her resurrection, has his servants carry the dead woman home. During the journey, however, the coffin is jostled. The jolt dislodges the poison apple caught in Snow White's throat and she awakens. Nuptials are planned for Snow White and the prince.

When the wicked queen hears of the wedding, she cannot stay away but feels *compelled* to witness it herself. Who's casting spells now? Coincidentally perhaps, the wedding party is anticipating her arrival: iron shoes have been heated over burning coals. The queen is forced to don what the story calls "red-hot" shoes and dance until she dies.

See **BOTANICALS:** Apples; **CREATIVE ARTS:** Film: Disney Witches; **DICTIONARY:** Pharmakon, Zombi.

Hans Christian Andersen's Fairy Tales

Hans Christian Andersen (April 2, 1805-August 4, 1875) did not collect folktales like the Brothers Grimm. He learned them at home from his mother.

Most famous for his 124 fairy tales, Andersen would have preferred renown for his novels and poetry. Many of the fairy tales are his own creations; all were embellished though some are based on ancient folktales. The shamanic quality of many of these stories emerges, perhaps despite Andersen's intentions.

Andersen grew up in Denmark amidst terrible poverty. His father died when he was eleven. His mother, Anne Marie Andersen (c.1774–December 1833), is usually described as an "*alcoholic*" and intensely "*superstitious*." She may indeed have been an alcoholic but she was also a devoted, protective mother who made it a condition at the first school Andersen attended that he was never to be beaten.

Descriptions of Anne Marie as "*superstitious*" may be understood to imply "*rooted in Pagan tradition*." She practiced divination with Saint John's wort and consulted fortune-tellers, sending her son to them in times of crisis. In April 1816, when Hans was eleven, his father was deathly ill. His mother did not send Hans for a doctor but instead sent him to a wise woman, Mette Mogensdatter, who performed what one of Andersen's biographers describes as "*magic tricks.*"

Anne Marie's own mother, Anne Sorensdatter (born c.1745), bore three daughters out of wedlock. Although at the time this was associated with ignorance and promiscuity (as indeed it was by her deeply embarrassed grandson), it was also associated with Paganism or, conversely, with lack of devotion to Christian piety and ritual. Sorensdatter spent a week in prison in 1783 because her daughters were born out of wedlock.

Andersen, a devout Christian, was embarrassed, ashamed, and disapproving of his maternal background, yet he also drew on the wealth of tales learned at his mother's knee to create his own fairy tales. Andersen's fairy tales reveal his conflicting emotions towards Pagan spiritual traditions and female sexuality and power.

His stories often shock modern readers. Female characters suffer tremendous physical pain in his tales; some suffering physical mutilation. Intensely tragic, sad stories, few possess anything remotely like happy endings. The little match girl freezes to death; the girl in *The Red Shoes* is "saved" by having her feet amputated.

Among Andersen's stories with themes related to witchcraft are the following.

the Little Mermaid

The Little Mermaid is most familiar to modern audiences via Disney's animated version. Tremendous liberties were taken with Andersen's story in order to make it a "feel-good" children's movie, not least providing a happy ending, conspicuously lacking in the original.

Andersen's *The Little Mermaid* tells the tale of the unnamed daughter of the Sea King, the youngest of six sea-princesses. The point is early made and continually emphasized that only humans have immortal souls; sea-spirits do not. Good deeds aren't sufficient: the only way for our little sea-princess to win an immortal soul is if a human man falls *completely* in love with her, marries her in a church ceremony, and is faithful throughout eternity. (Thankfully these aren't requirements for human women!) If this happens, the man's soul will flow into the sea-spirit: his soul is large enough for both of them.

In Andersen's story, this immortal soul is as attractive to the sea-princess as the handsome prince she saves from a shipwreck. She decides to try to win him *and* an immortal soul. To do so, she journeys to the sea-witch, who resembles an underwater Baba Yaga.

The nameless witch knows what the nameless sea-princess wants without being informed. She describes her desire as "*stupid*" and explicitly informs the little mermaid that it will bring misfortune. The price of the potion that creates legs is the little mermaid's beautiful voice, not because (as in Disney's version) the witch craves it for herself but because the mermaid must pay the best thing she owns in exchange for this valuable potion containing the witch's own blood. (The sea-witch is depicted drawing drops of *"black blood"* from her breast, lest anyone suspect any other kind of blood was used.)

The plan, as the witch foresaw, does not succeed. The sea-witch makes one final appearance, albeit offstage. When the little mermaid's plan fails, her five sisters trade their hair with the sea-witch in return for a magical knife. If the little mermaid will use this knife to stab her beloved prince, who's now married another, in the heart, allowing his blood to drip on her feet, her tail will reappear and she may resume existence as a mermaid. The mermaid considers this briefly, but throws herself and the knife overboard instead.

The Little Mermaid derives from Andersen's imagination, not ancient folk-tradition. Rusalka and Nixies notably sprout mermaid's tales in the water, effortlessly and painlessly developing legs whenever they wish to walk on land. Rusalka and Nixies are notoriously athletic; they enjoy dancing, and nimbly climb trees— as opposed to the Little Mermaid whose legs are described as feeling as if they're being run through with a sharp sword.

Commentators typically interpret this as the little mermaid's ultimate rejection of "black magic" and thus as the act that earns her ultimate "reward": she does not dissolve into sea foam as feared but is gathered up among the *"daughters of the air."* Like sea-spirits, they lack souls but, unlike them, they are able to earn souls by doing good deeds for three hundred years.

The Little Mermaid concludes as a morality tale: children's good behavior shortens the time required for these daughters of the air to acquire souls. Bad, disobedient children lengthen this probationary period. The moral of the story thus is that next time, dear child, you consider not obeying your parents remember that you are personally lengthening the little mermaid's purgatory.

See also Russian Fairy Tales; **ANIMALS:** Frogs, Snakes; **CREATIVE ARTS:** Films: Disney Witches; **DIVINE WITCH:** Baba Yaga; **FAIRIES:** Nature-spirit Fairies: Nixie, Rusalka; **WORMWOOD:** Dangers of Witchcraft: Menstrual Power.

The Snow Queen

The Snow Queen is not a witch but a frost goddess. The story recounts the shamanic journey of its heroine, Gerda, to redeem her beloved playmate Kay frozen in the Snow Queen's realm. Gerda and Kay are both depicted as children. When Kay mysteriously disappears, Gerda searches for him.

Her first step is to make a Pagan-style offering of her precious red shoes to the river so that, in exchange, it will return Kay. The river responds: when Gerda climbs into a boat, it simply floats away with her, taking her on a journey that ultimately leads to Kay.

How does Gerda know how to do this? Her grandmother is described as speaking the language of crows, i.e. she is a shaman.

Gerda's first stop downriver is a little house with toy soldiers standing guard. It is a witch's house: she is described as an old, old woman leaning on a crutch. Although the woman can work magic, we are advised that she is not a "*wicked witch*," only a dabbler. She adores Gerda and would like to keep her but intends to care for her, not harm or eat her, although she is obstructing Gerda's path. She enchants Gerda so that she temporarily forgets her quest. From a shamanic-journey perspective, the old woman is a test: will Gerda become so comfortable that she gives up?

✳ *Gerda is able to speak to plants, and so eventually recalls her mission.*

✳ *She is able to speak to crows, and so is given information bringing her closer to Kay.*

In the process of rescuing Kay, Gerda must visit the houses of two more wise-women: one identified as a Saami woman, the other as a Finnmark woman, both identified with Pagan traditions and Finno-Ugric shamanism.

These three women serve as Gerda's shamanic initiators. Gerda passes all tests, behaves with purity of heart and single-minded focus, and is able to rescue Kay from permanent frost (coma?). In true shamanic style, the journey is retraced step-by-step until Kay and Gerda are safely home with her proud, welcoming grandmother.

See **ANIMALS:** Corvids; **HAG:** Gerda, Skadi.

the Wild Swans

A wicked stepmother-witch queen curses her eleven stepsons, transforming them into wild swans. Her one stepdaughter, Eliza, is left untouched but is sent away to be raised outside the castle. When she returns in the prime of adolescence, beautiful and *good*, the witch stepmother desires to transform her.

She offers Eliza an enchanted bath in her own beautiful, luxurious bathtub. While the bath is

drawn, the witch kisses three toads, directing one to sit on Eliza's head in the bath so that she'll become stupid as a toad, the second to sit on her forehead so that she'll become ugly as a toad, and the last to sit on her heart so that she will become evil-tempered like a toad. When the toads are placed in the clear water, it turns green.

> Toads, ancient symbols of prosperity, immortality, and female reproductive power are transformed into emblems of stupidity, ugliness, and evil.

The witch's plot is foiled because Eliza's innate goodness and "*purity*" antidote the spell. When Eliza enters the bath, the toads are transformed into scarlet poppies—the story informs us that they would have become roses (the Virgin Mary's flowers) except for the toads' venom and the witch's kiss.

Magic won't work on Eliza and so the witch takes a different approach. She rubs Eliza with walnut juice, staining her skin brown, and disarranges her formerly neat hair so that it hangs in wild disarray. She transforms Eliza into the stereotype of a witch (although notably the witch-queen herself is elegant and conventionally beautiful); however in Andersen's Denmark this description would also have had recognizable ethnic connotations. Eliza has been made to resemble the stereotype of a Romany girl.

Her father is blinded by her superficial appearance. He is unable to recognize his daughter. He denies her; she creeps out of the castle, wandering through fields and meadows until she reaches the forest. Eliza enters the forest and discovers her inner-witch. Bathing in a forest lake fit for Artemis and her nymphs, Eliza becomes more beautiful than ever. Andersen emphasizes that her skin is now white again.

Eliza meets a "forest woman" who leads her to her brothers. She determines to free them from their curse. The swans carry Eliza to a magical land, where she moves into a mountain cave. Her youngest brother encourages her to incubate dreams.

Eliza prays to God but it is Fata Morgana who responds, offers solutions and instructions.

Fata Morgana explains that Eliza can remove the spell only by weaving eleven long-sleeved nettle shirts for her brothers. These can't be cultivated nettles but only wild ones growing near caves or in graveyards. Eliza must pick them by hand, crush the nettles underfoot, then plait and weave them. Furthermore, from the moment she embarks on her quest until it is complete, no matter how many years it takes, she must maintain utter silence, not only because speaking will counteract the spell but because the first word she utters will pierce her brothers' hearts like a deadly dagger.

Fata Morgana emphasizes that their lives hang on Eliza's tongue. Andersen highlights the physical suffering involved in the process: Eliza's hands blister and bleed and are no longer white and lady-like.

Eliza accepts the quest, living in a cave surrounded by nettles. A king discovers and falls in love with her. He brings her home to his kingdom, where the archbishop is convinced that Eliza is a powerful forest witch who has enchanted the king.

The king wants to make Eliza happy; he recreates an artificial forest-room for her, hung with green tapestries, to resemble the cave where she was found. Her supply of nettles is brought to her; by the seventh shirt, she is out of nettles.

Eliza creeps into the churchyard to gather more. There she discovers a circle of hideous, grotesque witches who undress as if they were about to bathe but instead open up fresh graves with their bare hands and devour corpse flesh. This scene ranks amongst the worst stereotyping of witches..

The archbishop, who has been spying on Eliza, witnesses her journey. He tells the king who doesn't believe him. Eliza miscalculated, gathering only enough nettles to last until the last shirt. She must gather more for the very last one. This time, the king is alerted; he follows her from a distance. When he gets to the graveyard and witnesses the hideous witches sitting on gravestones he imagines Eliza among them and is repulsed. He doesn't stop to observe further but allows Eliza to be charged with witchcraft and condemned to be burned.

Eliza is thrown into jail; her velvet and finery are taken away and she is given her nettles, as befitting a witch; ironically there is nothing she wants more. Andersen describes Eliza's journey to the pyre in harrowing detail. She's transported in an old wagon while crowds jeer her. She continues her attempt to complete the last shirt; the crowd notes that she carries no hymnal, only her *"ugly sorcery,"* which they attempt to wrest away from her.

The wild swans, who've located her at this very last moment, arrive and beat back the crowds with their wings. Just as the executioner seizes her, she throws the shirts over the swans and they instantly transform back into handsome princes—all except the youngest one, who still retains one swan wing because the final sleeve of the final shirt was incomplete. Eliza can now speak and explain herself. She and the husband who had been ready to burn her, live together happily ever after.

See **ANIMALS:** Frogs and Toads; **BOTANICALS:** Nettles, Opium Poppy; **DIVINE WITCH:** Morgan le Fay.

Jewish Fairy Tales

As elsewhere, Jewish magical and "supernatural" tales are considered the province of women. In Yiddish, these stories are called *Bubbe meises*, literally "Granny tales."

It is perhaps no coincidence that *"bubbe"* derives from the same roots as the Russian *"baba"* (see **DICTIONARY: Baba**). As elsewhere, some, though not all, fairy tales contain elements of ancient and now subversive spiritual traditions.

The heroines and heroes of Jewish fairy tales are midwives and miracle-working rabbis or *ba'al-shems*, respectively. The tradition of heroic midwives dates back to the biblical midwives of the Book of Exodus who outwitted Pharaoh. They are among the very few women named in the Bible. However the midwife as fairy-tale heroine is unusual because in European Christian folklore, midwives are stock villains, often in league with or equated with wicked witches. In Jewish folklore, midwives play a shamanic role, battling spirits (or specifically Lilith, see page 487) to rescue vulnerable women and newborns.

In Celtic tradition, fairies frequently steal midwives. The same theme occurs in Jewish folklore but with djinn, "demons" or vague "spirits," rather than fairies; however Jewish tales are told from the perspective of the midwife upon her successful return. These stories usually end happily for all including the demons, who are treated matter-of-factly as part of life. Lying beneath the surface of these fairy tales are instructions for safe, positive interaction with spirits.

Although the term "rabbi" is now almost exclusively identified with "clergy," technically it is a term of respect indicating "teacher." The rabbis of fairy tales play the roles of shamans, mediating with demons, exorcising vengeful ghosts and, especially, counteracting the effects of vicious witches and salacious wizards. These rabbis cast spells and create powerful amulets and counter-charms.

In the cosmology of Jewish folklore, there is no concept of Satan as the Creator's evil adversary. "Demons" are not Satan's servants but instead are volatile, dangerous spirits, best to avoid although, once in a while, they prove helpful. "Demon" may be understood as synonymous with "djinn."

Many of these stories are ambivalent: they celebrate what may technically (or officially) be forbidden and so are ambiguous. Narrators are ambivalent about the roles played by these rabbis: the spell-casting rabbi who performs the miracle is often humbled at the end of the story, frequently by his adversary the witch. (Never by male wizards, however, who are always vanquished.)

Although there are also plenty of Jewish stories featuring wicked, evil, grotesque witches, witches not infrequently get the last laugh or final triumph, perhaps indicating something about the sympathies of the narrator.

In one story, travelers have been mysteriously disappearing. A miracle-rabbi is hired to play detective. All missing parties were last seen at a certain roadhouse. The rabbi, investigating, realizes that the inn's owner is a witch who transforms her guests into donkeys who labor for her. The rabbi rescues the bewitched travelers, transforming them back. He then transforms the witch into a donkey and rides her back home. Unbeknownst to him, however, this witch has a sister-witch living in his very own hometown. Looking out her window, she sees the rabbi riding home and immediately recognizes that his donkey is her sister, whom she *instantly* transforms back into her true shape so that the formerly highly respectable rabbi suddenly finds himself publicly seated on a woman's back, highly compromising behavior in a sexually conservative community.

Lilith, Queen of Witches, dominates Jewish fairy tales. She is omnipresent, playing various roles from forest witch to Queen of Demons.

As Queen of Demons, she is sometimes married to the fallen angel Samael. They travel together in the guise of huge black dogs. Sometimes Lilith is married to the demon Asmodeus instead. Sometimes she has no male partner but preys on mortal men as the prototype of the succubus or vampire-witch.

Sometimes she leads a host of demons; sometimes she is the mother of a race of demons (the *Lilin*) who are conceived via men's nocturnal emissions. Her daughters are beautiful, seductive, vampiric succubi who prey on men, tempt and possess women, and hide inside mirrors waiting to cause mischief. Not all Lilith's daughters are spirits: she also serves as prototype for Jewish witches, sometimes called "Lilith's daughters."

Lilith is not always named: she is such an immediately recognizable figure that clues to her identity are frequently sufficient for identification. The foremost clue is her long, beautiful, wild, and disheveled hair: in the story *The Hair in the Milk*, Lilith leaves one single black hair as her calling-card, sufficient evidence for a heroic midwife to recognize her formidable opponent's true identity.

In fairy tales, Lilith is sometimes hag-like and grotesque but sometimes seductively beautiful. (And sometimes both, in the same story.) Although she preys on men and enjoys exposing them as lustful fools, her primary victims are women and newborn children.

These stories are ambivalent however: although she is feared, women in these stories also constantly interact with Lilith. It is dangerous to ignore her; stories reveal details on proper methods of appeasement and negotiation, indicating that she is more than just some baby-stealing bogie-woman.

> In fairy tales, Lilith often gets the better of men; her nefarious plots against babies and brides, however, are usually foiled by clever, intrepid midwives. Once in a while, the story ends happily for all.

In one variation of a popular tale, *The Demon in the Tree*, a young boy, a rabbi's son, playing hide-and-seek with a friend, sees a finger emanating from a tree in front of his house. Assuming the finger belongs to his friend, he plays a joke, sticking his ring on it and reciting the Jewish wedding vows three times—all that is required by Jewish law to be legally wed. Suddenly a strange woman with long disheveled hair appears from the tree and looks in his eyes. The boy faints. When he awakes he is alone but his ring is missing … He convinces himself not to believe what happened and tells no one.

Years later, a marriage is arranged for him. He is the rabbi's son, handsome, educated, and so considered a great catch. He is betrothed to an extremely wealthy, beautiful girl. Just as he is about to lead his new bride into his home, a tree branch from *that* tree slams into the bride's head, killing her. A new marriage is arranged, and then another. None of the marriages is ever consummated. None of the brides even gets into the house. Instead, each time, she is felled by the tree.

No one else ever actually witnesses the deaths; the boy's explanations about the branch sound suspicious, and people begin to wonder about him. After several brides have died, offers of marriage are no longer so forthcoming. Finally the only potential bride is an incredibly poor girl with no dowry; normally the rabbi's son would be out of her league. The girl decides to take her chances, although even she is told that she doesn't have to marry him.

Having heard the story of what happened to her predecessors, the girl ducks as she approaches her new home and avoids the tree branch. Inside, rather than consummating the marriage, she insists that her groom tell her *everything* he can about the tree. He finally, reluctantly, reveals his childhood prank.

This girl has heard a *bubbe meise* or two: she *immediately* goes straight to the tree with a plate of jam, favorite food of Jewish demons. Speaking respectfully and honestly, she explains that she now knows the story but didn't when she married the groom. She says she knows that the "demon" is Lilith who believes herself to be the true bride. Here they both are, married to the same man. The bride proposes a compromise: if Lilith agrees not to kill her or any of her future children, she will leave a plate of jam by the tree daily *and* send the groom to the tree once a week to fulfill his *"marital obligations."*

Suddenly the wild woman in the tree emerges; she says nothing but briefly looks the woman in the eye before disappearing. The next morning the plate of jam is empty except for a gold coin. The deal is on.

Every night the woman leaves the demon some jam. Every morning Lilith leaves her a gold coin. Once a week, the husband performs his marital obligations, whether he likes it or not. The "demon," posted in her tree, emerges as a somewhat reluctant family guardian.

This continues for seven years until one morning instead of the gold coin, the woman discovers her husband's old ring on the plate. He has been released from his vow. Although the deal has been honorably concluded, the story advises that Lilith continues to guard the woman and her children.

Further Reading: Lilith is so ever-present that it is virtually impossible to find a book of Jewish folklore without at least one Lilith story. Howard Schwartz's *Lilith's Cave* (Oxford University Press, 1988) is replete with tales of Lilith, as well as appearances by *ba'al shems* and shamanic midwives.

See **ANIMALS:** Cats, Dogs, Donkeys, Owls, Snakes; **BOTANICALS:** Trees; **DICTIONARY:** Ba'al, Djinn; **DIVINE WITCH:** Lilith; **WOMEN'S MYSTERIES:** Midwives.

Mother Goose

Silly old goose! That's the phrase most associated with geese today but it wasn't always the case. Fabulously territorial and aggressive, geese served as watchdogs in Europe: they were considered the guardians of ancient Rome.

Don't laugh. Geese are *big* birds. They hiss, honk, flap their wings aggressively, and they can peck *hard*. Observe small children at a pond tossing bits of bread to ducks versus geese. The smaller ducks usually wait for bread to be tossed; geese, on the other hand, often mob children as if they were trying to mug them of their bread.

Geese were kept as "guard dogs" in the Middle Ages. In Eastern Europe, they served as watchdogs for individual homes and families. Geese were the Celtic symbol of alertness, self-defensive aggression, and protection.

Geese were also considered sacred birds:

✹ *According to one of the many Egyptian creation myths, a cosmic egg was laid by the Nile Goose, known as the Great Cackler.*

✹ *Various female deities including Aphrodite, Juno, and Sequana are associated with geese or swans who, in artistic renderings at least, are not always easily distinguishable.*

✹ *In Greek terracottas of the sixth and fifth centuries* BCE, *Aphrodite is depicted standing, sitting or flying through the air on a goose like Mother Goose, or sometimes just accompanied by a trio of geese.*

✹ *A first-century* BCE *bronze statue of an unidentified Breton goddess sports a goose-crested helmet.*

✹ *Lilith is sometimes depicted with a goose's foot, as is the Queen of Sheba—sometimes considered among Lilith's avatars. (See* **DIVINE WITCH**: *Lilith.)*

✹ *Among the swan- or goose-footed goddesses is Herta, thus Mother Goose could be construed as Mother Earth. See* **DIVINE WITCH**: *Herta.*

In English-speaking countries, "Mother Goose" refers to a vast series of rhymes ostensibly told by Mother Goose to children. Sometimes Mother Goose is portrayed as a cozy old lady surrounded by children, but other depictions of Mother Goose feature her dressed in witch's garb, flying through the air on a goose or even on a broomstick with a goose occupying the spot at the back usually reserved for an animal familiar.

Who was Mother Goose?

The first references to Mother Goose seem to derive from France, where she is not associated with nursery rhymes but with fairy tales. In France, Mother Goose is the teller of tales, not rhymes.

The first known literary reference to Mother Goose as a teller of tales occurred in 1650 in Loret's *La Muse Historique*, which contains the line "Comme *un conte de la Mère Oye,*" meaning "*like a Mother Goose tale.*" In 1697, Charles Perrault (January 12, 1628-May 16, 1703) published a collection of fairy tales called *Les Contes de la Mère l'Oye* or *Tales of Mother Goose*. This collection of eight stories included versions of *Blue Beard, Sleeping Beauty, Cinderella, Little Red Riding Hood*, and *Puss in Boots*. The frontispiece of the first edition had an illustration of an old woman at a spinning wheel, surrounded by a girl, a man, a small boy, and a cat.

His collection included what are essentially French folktales. Perrault's primary source seems to have been his son's nursemaid. He rewrote these stories for a jaded audience of members of Louis XIV's court and so began the fashion for fairy tales.

Perrault described his "Mother Goose tales" as "*old wives' tales,*" told by governesses and grandmothers. In France, however, Mother Goose was traditionally associated with old Queen Bertha. In French, tall tales are described as told "*when good Queen Bertha spun …*" In France and Italy, the phrase "*when Queen Bertha was spinning*" is synonymous with "*once upon a time.*" Another name for "Queen Bertha" is "Goose Foot Bertha," traditionally depicted spinning and telling endless tales to hordes of attentive, listening children.

There are two possible historical Queen Bertha's, both of whom have associations with geese.

❊ Queen Bertha (d.783), wife of Pepin, King of the Franks (and Charlemagne's mother), allegedly had "goose feet," perhaps meaning that her toes were webbed. She was known as "Goose-foot Bertha" and is believed to be the mysterious La Reine Pédauque *or "Goose-foot Queen."*

❊ Bertha (c.962), wife of Robert II of France (Robert the Pious), is another possibility. King Robert fell in love with the widowed Bertha. Unfortunately she was his cousin and he was already her son's godfather; the Church felt that this relationship precluded marriage. When Robert married Bertha anyway, he was excommunicated and given seven years' penance. Rumors circulated that their forbidden marriage resulted in the birth of a goose-headed baby.

The first English translation of Perrault's *Mother Goose Tales* appeared in 1729. In English, however, Mother Goose is intrinsically connected to rhymes and verse. Many of these rhymes were ages-old; some had political or satirical roots, others were grounded in weather rituals, love spells and, some suspect, perhaps even old Druidic traditions.

Mother Goose's Melody, published in London by John Newberry in 1760, contained both rhymes and adult commentary. No known complete copy of this book exists today, however it did travel to Britain's North American colonies, where printer Isaiah Thomas recalled his childhood adoration of the book. When the Revolutionary War broke out, he took advantage of the situation, smuggling several copies of the book into the colonies and printing his own pirated versions.

There is also an American claim to Mother Goose: some believe that "Mother Goose" is really Elizabeth Foster Goose (also possibly Vergoose or Vertigoose, meaning "green goose").

Elizabeth Foster (April 5, 1665–c.1756) of Charleston married Isaac Goose of Boston and bore him six children. One daughter, also named Elizabeth Goose, married an English printer, Thomas Fleet, in 1715. Reverend Cotton Mather, a famed witch-hunter, officiated at their wedding. Elizabeth and Thomas had seven little Fleets whom Grandma Goose entertained with apparently endless stories. Thomas Fleet eventually published these stories, supposedly, as rumor had it, to embarrass his mother-in-law.

Allegedly the book, published in 1719, was entitled *Songs for the Nursery or Mother Goose's Melodies.* "Mother Goose" died around 1756 and was allegedly buried in the Old Granary Burial Ground, however no headstone exists. "Allegedly" is used so frequently because no such book or broadside has ever been discovered. Collectors continue to search for it like the Holy Grail. No record apparently exists; many now believe the book doesn't exist either!

An English tradition suggests that some Mother Goose counting rhymes may be relics of Druidic formulas for selecting sacrificial victims.

Among the less well-known Mother Goose rhymes are charms against witchcraft. Here are three of them:

St Francis and St Benedict
Bless this house from wicked wight
From nightmares and the goblin
That is old Goodfellow Robin
Keep it all from evil spirits,
Fairies, weasels, rats and ferrets
From curfew time to the next prime

Rowan tree and red thread
Bind the witches all in dread

Vervain and dill
Hinder witches of their will

Mother Goose rhymes also serve as spells. This one, which attempts to incubate prophetic dreams, is best performed at the New Moon.

1. Place a prayer book on your bed on the spot where you normally place your pillow.
2. Place the following atop the prayer book: a key, a ring, a flower blossom, a willow sprig, a heart-shaped cookie, a bread crust, and four playing cards: the Ace of Spades, the Ace of Diamonds, the Nine of Hearts and the Ten of Clubs.
3. Before going to sleep chant the following rhyme:

Luna, every woman's friend
To me your goodness please do send
Let this night in visions see
Emblems of my destiny

See **ANIMALS:** Ferrets (Polecats) and Weasels; **BOTANICALS:** Rowan, Vervain; **DIVINE WITCH:** Tante Arie.

Russian Fairy Tales

Russian folktales were not written down until the nineteenth century when many were collected by the pioneering ethnographer Aleksandr Afanas'ev (1826-1871), who published his versions between 1855 and 1864.

There was almost total illiteracy among Russian peasants (serfs) and so these stories truly encompass an *oral tradition*. Because of the Russian tradition of "double-faith," ancient Pagan elements in these stories remain fairly close to the surface.

> Double-faith is the name given the tenuous but simultaneous practice of Christianity *and* ancient Pagan traditions prevalent throughout rural Russia, despite opposition from the Church.

Baba Yaga casts a dominant shadow over Russian folklore (see **DIVINE WITCH:** Baba Yaga).

With the arrival of Christianity, Baba Yaga moved deep into the birch forest where she awaits visitors and inspired countless stories. In some, she is a wicked cannibal witch, in others she serves as spiritual guide and savior. She is always grouchy and unpredictable and must be handled with care.

Like Lilith in Jewish fairy tales (see page 487) Baba Yaga is so familiar and so intrinsically part of folk culture that she doesn't have to be named: references to the old woman in the birch forest are sufficient to identify her.

Baba Yaga, like Hulda, evolved into a bogie-woman, a tool used by parents to scare children into good behavior: don't play in the forest or Baba Yaga will get you and so forth. Many stories display ambivalence toward Baba Yaga, demonstrating both fear and tremendous respect and even love. At the ends of most stories, even those that seemingly end in Baba's demise, she has the last laugh.

There are two typical Baba Yaga story themes:

* Someone, usually a young girl, is sent to Baba Yaga, usually by a wicked stepmother, who anticipates that this will be a one-way trip as Baba Yaga is expected to eat the child.

* Someone, a young man or woman, in the midst of some impossible quest travels to Baba Yaga's hut for assistance that only she can provide. Baba Yaga insists they serve her. Some meet Baba Yaga's high standards and are rewarded; others are killed and consumed.

There are literally *endless* Baba Yaga stories, many simply titled *Baba Yaga*; one could spend an entire night telling nothing but Baba Yaga stories. These are merely a few.

Baba Yaga (1)

In a Russian variation of Grimms' *Mother Holle* (see page 477), two stepsisters take turns serving Baba Yaga. As befitting the respective deities, *Baba Yaga* is a harsher tale: one sister emerges empowered, transformed into a "fine lady"; the other's bones are carried home in a box.

Baba Yaga (2)

A stepmother wishes to be rid of her stepdaughter and so sends her to Baba Yaga on the pretext of borrowing a needle and thread but really because she expects the girl never to return. The stepmother doesn't explicitly say "Baba Yaga"; she tells the girl to get the needle and thread from "*Auntie in the woods.*"

The young girl is aware of *Auntie's* identity and understands her stepmother's true motivation quite well. Before embarking on her errand, she makes a pit-stop at her beloved real aunt's home to say goodbye forever. The aunt tells her not to be afraid. She then proceeds to give the girl such exceptionally detailed instructions that one suspects that the aunt herself has survived this journey:

* A birch will lash her face. She gives the girl a ribbon, advising her to tie up its branches. (This is reminiscent of the ribbons girls tie on the Rusalka's birch trees; see **FAIRIES**: Nature-spirit Fairies: Rusalka.)

* Baba Yaga's gates will creak and refuse to open; she gives the girl oil for the hinges.

* Baba Yaga's dog will try to eat the girl. The aunt gives her bread to propitiate the dog.

* Baba Yaga's cat will try to claw out her eyes. The aunt gives her meat to give the cat.

Notably the true aunt gives her everything but the needle and thread. She could give her a needle and thread and tell her not to go to Baba Yaga's hut but it is apparently crucial that the girl goes and that she passes this initiation. Everything the aunt advises comes to pass. By following her advice, the girl is able to make important spiritual alliances that, together with her own bravery, sharp wits, and honorable behavior, enable her to survive and return.

Most fairy-tale characters who survive Baba Yaga's initiations do so with the assistance of an older female relative or of animal allies.

Encyclopedia of Witchcraft

Prince Danila Govorila

A witch, who is not Baba Yaga, dislikes a princess and prince (sister and brother), although no reason is given. She plans a long-term trick intended to destroy them. The witch gives the children's mother a ring for her son the prince, advising that it will make him healthy and wealthy provided he never takes it off. When it's time for him to marry, he must only marry a girl whose finger fits the ring.

The ring works as promised and there are no problems—until he's old enough to marry. The ring won't fit *anyone* until, on a whim, his sister tries it on and it fits her perfectly.

The boy determines to marry her. She protests, begging him to *"think of the sin."* He doesn't care and, furthermore, he's in charge. The prince prepares the wedding. The sister grieves and mourns to no avail until just before the wedding some *"old women"* pass by. In the midst of her grief, she invites them in, offering hospitality which they accept. They ask why she's been weeping and she tells all. They tell her not to worry and offer a course of action. She must make four dolls, placing one in each corner of the honeymoon chamber. When the brother calls her to the wedding, she should go. When he calls her to the honeymoon chamber, she shouldn't hurry.

When the impatient brother demands that his sister enter the honeymoon chamber, the dolls suddenly begin to chant incantations. Earth opens up: the princess falls inside and is covered up. Finding herself in a subterranean realm, she begins to walk. Soon she sees a little hut on chicken legs … Luckily (and eventually it is!) she knows the proper charm to get inside the house: *"Little hut, Little hut, stand with your back to the forest and your front to me!"*

She enters and finds a beautiful girl embroidering towels with silver and gold thread. She is Baba Yaga's daughter; the two young women form an alliance. Baba Yaga's daughter teaches the girl how to embroider; when Mom is due home, Baba Yaga's daughter turns the princess into a needle and thrusts her into a birch broom in the corner to stay safe.

> The towels and napkins cited in Russian fairy tales are no mere household goods but ritual objects. Women once wove beautiful fabrics, painstakingly embroidered with age-old Pagan and goddess symbols. These served various functions:
>
> ✳ *As magical power objects*
>
> ✳ *As sacred offerings to deities like Bereginia or the Rusalka*
>
> ✳ *Incorporated into private ritual*
>
> In *Prince Danila Govorila*, Baba Yaga's daughter teaches the princess how to craft these towels; in other Baba Yaga stories, these towels are tickets to safety.

Eventually the princess completes her shamanic journey and departs safely in the company of Baba Yaga's daughter. They go home together where, amazingly, Prince Danila's ring fits the finger of Baba Yaga's daughter and all live happily ever after.

Vasilisa the Wise (Also called Vasilisa the Beautiful or Vasilisa the Brave)

"Not every question has a good answer; if you know too much, you will grow old too fast" warns Baba Yaga in this epic saga. It is the best known and most fully realized of the Baba Yaga tales.

The story begins like *Cinderella*: Vasilisa's mother has died and her father has remarried a woman with two daughters of her own. Eventually the father dies, too. The stepmother inherits his money and property and Vasilisa is left to her stepmother's mercy.

The stepmother is cruel and abusive to her, treating her like the household drudge. Vasilisa is good, kind, hard working, and exceptionally beautiful. She is not unaware of her situation but feels hopeless: she would run away if only she had somewhere to go.

Vasilisa does have a secret weapon. Before her mother died, she gave Vasilisa a small hand-crafted doll, advising her to keep it with her always as it will bring comfort and protection in time of need. The doll embodies Vasilisa's mother's love and blessings: it is a living doll. Although very plain (the story makes it clear that the stepsisters who possess fancy store-bought dolls would scorn the little doll), when Vasilisa is alone, the doll talks with her, offering comfort, encouragement, and advice. Vasilisa is wise as well as beautiful: she tells no one of her miraculous doll.

As the girls reach marriageable age, the step-mother becomes more anxious about Vasilisa, whose charm and beauty, she fears, threatens her own daughters' prospects. She decides to be rid of Vasilisa and hatches a plan. One night, she seats the three girls at a table lit by a single candle and gives them tasks. Vasilisa darns and mends while the stepsisters craft fine lace. Near midnight, the flame goes out and the house is plunged into darkness. The girls rush to light more candles but all attempts to light them fail. The story now reveals that the stepmother is a witch: she has cast a spell over the house so that no light can be lit within.

In *Vasilisa the Wise*, the heroine's dying mother gives her a miraculous doll that speaks, does household chores, and saves her from the witch Baba Yaga. Although the doll is usually interpreted as a fantasy device, it may, in fact, stem from the practice of the alraune. See **BOTANICALS: Mandrake.**

Instead she demands that Vasilisa journey across the forest to Baba Yaga's house and fetch them a light. Vasilisa goes to her room to pre-pare; the doll sensing her despair asks what's wrong. Vasilisa says she's been sent to Baba Yaga and is sure that she will never return. The doll tells her not to be afraid, to do as her step-mother says but to take the doll with her.

It's after midnight when Vasilisa begins her journey on foot across the forest, the doll safely and secretly in her pocket. She walks all night. As the night fades, a mysterious pale horseman on a white stallion rides directly across Vasilisa's path and disappears. She continues to walk.

At noon, suddenly a sunburnt horseman in scarlet armor riding a red stallion crosses her path and disappears. She continues to walk. Finally, as darkness falls, Vasilisa reaches Baba Yaga's little hut standing on chicken legs, surrounded by a fence of bleached human bones, a human skull with glowing eyes atop each fence-post. As Vasilisa hesitates, a black rider on a jet-black stallion crosses her path and disappears. She hears a rustling in the trees and Baba Yaga appears, riding in her mortar, a pestle in one hand, and a broom in the other.

Baba Yaga twitches her nose and announces that she knows someone is there. Whoever it is should step forward or else she'll come and get them. Vasilisa takes a deep breath and approaches, courteously greeting Baba Yaga, explaining that her stepmother sent her to fetch a light. Baba Yaga snorts, exclaiming that she's quite familiar with this stepmother and that Vasilisa is very welcome to a light—providing she earns it. Vasilisa is ordered to go inside the hut and work for Baba Yaga.

The house is full of mysterious things: disembodied hands, for instance, that materialize out of thin air and perform tasks. Baba Yaga sets Vasilisa to various household chores, warning her that if she fails, she's dinner.

For the next three days, Baba Yaga sets impossible tasks for Vasilisa to accomplish before leaving home riding in her mortar. As soon as Baba departs, the doll pops out of Vasilisa's pocket: it can do more than just talk. The doll performs miracles, literally finding needles lost in haystacks. All Vasilisa must do is cook. She labors in Baba's kitchen creating meals fit for a goddess. Meanwhile, like clockwork, the three riders continue to be seen outside.

Baba Yaga expects Vasilisa to fail but grudgingly acknowledges that all tasks are completed to perfection. Vasilisa is always gracious, respectful, and polite, never complaining, cringing or showing fear.

Finally, Baba issues a complaint: Vasilisa's cooking is wonderful but her conversation is dull. Ask me something, Baba demands. Vasilisa says there is one thing she is curious about: who are the three mysterious riders? Baba Yaga iden-

tifies them as her faithful knights, Dawn, Day, and Night.

Baba Yaga urges Vasilisa to ask more but Vasilisa politely declines. Baba Yaga's response: *"You're wise to ask only about what you see outside my house, not inside. I do not like to have my dirty linen washed in public and I eat the over-curious. Had you asked about what was in the house, I would have to eat you."*

Baba Yaga then announces that it's her turn to ask a question, and she asks Vasilisa point-blank how she accomplished the impossible tasks. Vasilisa doesn't want to expose the doll and so explains that she accomplished her assigned tasks with the help of the blessing of her mother. She says the magic words: Baba Yaga kicks her out the door, saying she wants no blessed ones in her house.

Vasilisa, relieved to be out of the house, begins to run away but Baba calls her back, asking if she isn't forgetting something. She pulls a skull with glowing eyes off her fence, sticks it on a post and hands it to Vasilisa, telling her to be sure to give it to her stepmother. The skull turns out to be useful: it's dark and the eyes light Vasilisa's path. During the day, the lights go out but reappear in darkness.

Five days have now passed since she left home and Vasilisa assumes the light is no longer needed. When she arrives home, she starts to leave the skull outside when suddenly it speaks to her, advising that Baba Yaga would be very angry if Vasilisa didn't follow her directions and give the light to her stepmother.

Vasilisa enters the house: the stepmother and sisters are sitting in pitch darkness. The stepmother's spell worked too well; they haven't had light since Vasilisa left, nor have they been able to leave. They are initially relieved to see Vasilisa when, suddenly, the glowing skull in her hand comes to life. The eyes seek out each step-relative in turn and, like a laser, burns each one to ashes. Then the light goes out.

This is just too much for Vasilisa: she runs out the door, empty-handed but for her doll. Having stayed with Baba Yaga, she is transformed: no longer afraid to run away, she walks until she finds a village where an old woman takes her in. Vasilisa weaves cloth that she gives the old woman to sell, but Vasilisa's work is so exceptionally fine that the old woman offers it to the Tsar instead. Even in the Tsar's palace, Vasilisa's exquisite work stands out: the Tsar's tailor insists that only the woman who wove the cloth can cut it. Vasilisa is summoned to the palace where the Tsar falls in love with her and all live happily ever after.

See Grimms' Fairy Tales: *Frau Trude*.

Further Reading: *Baba Yaga and Vasilisa the Brave* by Marianna Mayer (Morrow Junior Books, 1994) is a particularly evocative retelling of this story. Ernest Small combined various Baba Yaga themes to create his own *Baba Yaga* (Houghton Mifflin, 1966), in which Baba's skills as an herbalist are emphasized.

🐜 🐜 🐜

Baba Yaga's male counterpart is the sorcerer Koschei the Deathless. He is also a reoccurring character in Russian folklore, although not as frequently as Baba Yaga.

Koschei's name derives from Old Russian and Turkic tribal sources and literally indicates "Prisoner." Suave, sardonic, and sinister, but usually foiled, he is Baba Yaga's adversary in some tales, but her husband or ally in others.

Koschei and Baba Yaga both appear in the epic story of the warrior queen *Maria Moreevna*. In the opposite of a Bluebeard story, handsome Prince Ivan wins the hand of the beautiful, powerful, rich Maria Moreevna. She leaves him alone in her palace, handing him her keys but warning him not to open one door. Of course, like everyone else in these stories, he can't resist and discovers Koschei the Deathless hanging in the closet chained with twelve chains. Koschei pleads for a drink of water and good-hearted Ivan takes pity on him. The drink enables Koschei to regain his strength. He shakes his chains and they all snap. *"Thanks Prince Ivan,"* says Koschei. *"You'll never see Maria Moreevna again!"* Koschei disappears into a whirlwind, Moreevna with him.

Prince Ivan, feeling like an idiot, determines to get her back. He does, thrice, but each time is foiled because of Koschei's magical *táltos* horse, which comes straight from Baba Yaga's famed stables. Twice Koschei shows mercy because of Ivan's gift of water, but the third time he kills and dismembers him. Ivan's animal allies perform a shamanic resurrection. He comes back to life with the knowledge that there is only one thing now to be done—he has to get a horse from Baba Yaga too.

He finds her house surrounded by twelve stakes, eleven crowned with human heads but one ominously empty. He greets Baba Yaga politely, *"Good day, Grandmother!"* She responds in kind, knowing his identity immediately. Already a hero, she greets him with respect, *"Good day, Prince Ivan! Why are you here? From free will or need?"* He explains he's come to earn a horse. She says he can try. If he can tend her mares for three days, he can have his horse and depart but if he can't, she warns, *"don't hold it against me Ivan, but your head goes on that last stake."* (Ivan wins his horse, keeps his head and, with the horse, is able to regain the beautiful Maria Moreevna, too!)

Not every Russian witch is Baba Yaga. *The Sorceress* takes place *"in a certain kingdom"* ruled by a king whose daughter is the eponymous sorceress. At the same court is a priest with a ten-year-old son who takes lessons from *"a certain old woman."*

One day passing by the palace the boy looks in at the window (and although it's not explicitly stated that he's snooping or spying, it does just happen to be the sorceress-princess' bedroom.) He discovers that she has a novel way of preparing her coiffeur: she removes her head, shampoos, rinses, and combs out her hair, plaits it into beautiful braids and then puts her head back in place.

The boy goes home and tells everyone what he's witnessed. The princess suddenly falls ill and requests her father that, if she dies, he will ensure that the priest's son reads Psalms over her body for three consecutive nights. She dies and the king orders the priest to send for his son. The next day at his lessons, *"the old woman"* notices the boy looking glum. He explains that he must go to Church to read over the sorceress' body that night and he's sure he's doomed. The old woman gives him an iron knife and tells him to use it to cast a circle around himself in the Church and that no matter what happens to keep reading and never look around.

Alone in the church at night, he follows her advice. Indeed, at the stroke of midnight, the princess gets out of her coffin saying, *"Now I'll teach you what it means to spy on me and tell people what you saw."* She lunges at him but, because of his spell, is unsuccessful. At daybreak she jumps back into her coffin.

The same thing happens the second night. The next day he goes back to the old woman. She asks what he saw and warns that tonight will be worse. She gives him a hammer and four nails, advising him to drive one nail into each corner of the coffin and hold the hammer before him while reading. The old woman was right: the boy's experiences that night are truly horrific. In addition to rising from her coffin and attempting to kill him, the sorceress-princess surrounds the boy with terrifying illusions—for instance, the church appears to be on fire. However, the boy faithfully follows the old woman's instructions and resists the impulse to flee. He does not leave his circle of safety. At daybreak, the princess dives back into her coffin.

The king comes in. Finding the coffin open and the princess lying face down, he demands an explanation from the boy who tells all. The king orders an aspen spike thrust through his daughter's heart to prevent her from rising. The priest's son is rewarded with money and land.

This is a particularly subversive story: even though it occurs in Church (perhaps *particularly* because it occurs in Church) and the hero is a priest's son, solutions to his dilemma are Pagan ones. The boy doesn't go to his father, the priest (who is oblivious) for assistance but to an old Baba.

What do listeners learn from this story? Methods of surviving a vampire plus the underlying moral of the story: keep your mouth shut about magical people you observe.

See **BOTANICALS:** Birch; **CREATIVE ARTS:** Films: *Mask of Satan*; **DICTIONARY:** Táltos, Upir, Vampire; **DIVINE WITCH:** Baba Yaga, Hulda; **ERGOT:** Corn Mother: Baba Yaga; **FAIRIES:** Nature-spirit Fairies: Bereginy, Rusalka.

Witch-cats and Similar Transformation Tales

International fairy-tale witches are particularly associated with animal transformation. Although witches are identified with many animals (see **ANIMALS**), in fairy tales the animal is almost invariably a cat.

❋ *The cat may be a guise into which the witch transforms*

❋ *The cat may be the witch's alter ego*

❋ *The cat may be the witch's fetch (see* ***DICTIONARY****) or nahual (see* ***ANIMALS****)*

Often, in fairy tales, the secret witch's identity is revealed through the cat's fate:

❋ *The cat is killed; simultaneously the witch also dies*

❋ *The cat is killed but its body disappears; the witch's dead body appears in its place*

❋ *The cat is harmed, often via amputation of a paw; a previously unsuspected witch suddenly and mysteriously sports identical injuries or scars*

The classic example combining all the above motifs is *The Tale of Kowashi's Mother*, a Japanese story of magical identity-theft. Kowashi and his nice, normal mother live in a small village at the foot of a mountain. One day, all of a sudden, Kowashi notices that Mom's teeth are exceptionally long, sharp, and pointy. She has also suddenly developed a taste for fish heads and bones.

Their neighbor, a fisherman, comes home very late one night, carrying a basket of fish and is attacked by a pack of wild cats. The fisherman fights them off but the brazen cats refuse to retreat. One shouts, *"Get Old Lady Kowashi!"*

A huge raggedy gray cat appears. The fisherman whacks it on the head. As the sun comes up, the cats disappear. Kowashi wakes up to find Mom in the kitchen, her head all bandaged up, chewing on fish bones. He wonders …

Kowashi goes to school. When he returns home, his neighbor the fisherman is waiting for him and recounts his nocturnal adventure, including the part about *"Old Lady Kowashi."*

Kowashi enters his home where his mother, seeing him, arches her back and hisses. Kowashi decides that this cannot be his mother. A witch-cat must have killed her and stolen her image or so he reasons. He slices off her head with a sword. At his feet, lies a huge, ragged gray cat.

See **ANIMALS:** Cats, Transformation.

✪ Food and Drink

In Shakespeare's Macbeth, the Weird Sisters cluster around their cauldron. In *countless* Halloween postcards, decorations, and images witches stir cauldrons. Cauldrons are central to the myths of innumerable mythic witches from Medea to Cerridwen. With the exception of broomsticks (another kitchen tool) the cauldron is the tool most frequently associated with witchcraft.

Witch's brews, witch's potions: what's really cooking in that cauldron? Shakespeare envisioned an eerie, grotesque grocery list for his witches (*newt's eyes, frog's toes …*) corresponding to witch-hunt era stereotypes. Fairy tales and fiction reinforce that stereotype of witches' cauldrons filled with disgusting brews and horrific ingredients.

Yet, simultaneously, another counter-stereotype suggests that food from the witch's kitchen is the most satisfying food of all. In many cuisines, identifying a recipe with witches suggests that it is enchantingly seductive and guaranteed to please.

In reality, witchcraft is genuinely and profoundly associated with food, especially delicious, healing, charming food. To this day, the independent, solitary witch is often called a *"kitchen witch."*

One might also ask, *"What's in the chalice?"* The image of the witch proffering a cup is just slightly less popular than that of the witch atop a broomstick or stirring her cauldron. There is a theory, popular among some anthropologists, that the very origins of shamanism, witchcraft, and religion lie in so-called "beverage cults," including those that first developed beer and wine, both once considered sacred. The origins of many modern liqueurs do lie in old herbal formulas for healing and spell-casting.

✺ *Spells are cast with food, potions, elixirs, and brews.*

✺ *Witches heal, nourish, bless, curse, and seduce via food and potions.*

Many of the most popular and potent ritual tools of witchcraft now masquerade as common kitchen tools. Whether these tools, including brooms, sieves, cauldrons, mortars, and pestles began as kitchen tools and were adopted into witchcraft or vice versa, or whether cooking and witchcraft were once inseparable, is now unknown.

> If reversed, a long wooden spoon becomes a handy magic wand.

In fairy tales, witches have food when others do not. Hansel and Gretel's family was starving: allegedly there was a famine in the land, yet the witch's very house was edible. In other fairy tales, wise women offer heroines magical tablecloths that, whenever and wherever unfolded, produce incredibly delicious, luxurious meals. A witch's food is worth the price of a child, most notably in *Rapunzel* but also in numerous variations on that theme from Italy, France, and elsewhere. Apples are among the fairy-tale witch's primary tools and weapons.

Those stories reflected popular perceptions. Real-life witch-trial transcripts offer contradictory testimony regarding witch's food, too.

✸ *Witches were accused of concocting disgusting, murderous, sacrilegious potions from corpse flesh, aborted fetuses, assorted animal anatomical parts, and killer plants.*

✸ *Simultaneously, witch-hunters described witches' sabbats as sumptuous feasts with enormous*

quantities of food and drink, including fresh fruits out of season and luxuries like fresh roast ox.

There is tremendous emphasis on nourishment and especially on meat in both fairy tales and witchcraft accusations. At a time when few common people could afford to eat fresh meat with any frequency, witches were accused of having a consistent supply. During an era when asceticism was idealized, witches were accused of living lavishly, sensuously, and comfortably.

Theoretically, each and every food possesses magical uses. Just as every mineral, botanical or animal possesses specific magical gifts, so does food. Spells are cast by manipulating different foods to create a desired, intended effect.

Food spells are the simplest magic of all, cast by fine cooks all over Earth, most with no conscious knowledge or affiliation with witchcraft. All one needs to cast a spell with food is to imagine a meal as a means to an end. Plan a menu for seduction. It will likely be very different from a meal intended to humor a cranky child, appease an angry spouse, heal one's ailing self or ingratiate oneself to potential in-laws.

> Any recipe may be converted to a spell via the time-honored magical techniques of whispering and murmuring. Just before serving, secretly whisper your goals or intentions over the food or drink. The tradition of toasting derives from this type of spell. Spells may be cast over oneself too. Whisper affirmations over food or drink, then consume.

Every food has its magical uses; many extensive cookbooks devoted to magical recipes exist. The foods and beverages explored in this section are related to the general topic and history of witchcraft rather than to specific spells. Notably, in the light of the spiritual origins of witchcraft, a high percentage of them involve grain products, intoxicating beverages and sometimes both, as with barley-wine, beer, and kvass.

Absinthe

Absinthe is the Latin name for the herb wormwood (*Artemisia absinthium*) and for a controversial alcoholic beverage distilled from its leaves. In addition to wormwood, the distilled beverage is a sophisticated blend of other herbs including anise, dittany of Crete, fennel, and star anise.

Wormwood has long held a powerful magical reputation. It is mentioned in the Book of Revelation and is considered by some to be the original biblical bitter herb. Its Latin names, *Artemisia absinthium* and *Artemisia judaica*, indicate its affiliation with the lunar witchcraft goddess, Artemis.

> Wormwood is powerful: it possesses narcotic properties, contains the neurotoxic chemical constituent thujone and can potentially cause convulsions and brain damage. It can also cause intense uterine contractions, thus pregnant women or those actively attempting to conceive should avoid it.

Wormwood is traditionally believed to serve as a weapon against malevolent magic and so is identified as a witch's tool. Some perceive wormwood as a powerful and sacred plant; others consider it evil, and still others perceive that it guards *against* witchcraft.

These days, the "worm" in its name is believed to indicate its former use as a *vermifuge* or de-wormer, used to rid livestock of worms. In medieval Europe, however, "worm" was considered synonymous with "dragon" and especially that Old Dragon, Satan. In Christian Europe, wormwood was said to have first sprung up along the path the serpent took when it slithered out of Eden. Wormwood thus bore something of an ambivalent, ominous reputation.

That reputation transferred to the drink named after the herb. Herbal concoctions have been brewed from wormwood for millennia. Witches brewed healing and aphrodisiac potions with it. Wormwood allegedly enables one to communicate with the dead and potions were used for such purposes.

In classical Greece, wormwood leaves were infused in wine to create medicinal potions; Hippocrates recorded its virtues. In the Middle Ages, an English ale was brewed with wormwood. However, the beverage marketed as Absinthe that raised all the fuss and remains controversial did not exist until almost the end of the eighteenth century.

> Absinthe is an emerald-green color, which, combined with its aura of witchcraft, led to its nicknames—the Green Goddess or Green Fairy (*Fée Verte*).

Absinthe in its modern form was invented in either 1792 or 1797 by a Swiss country doctor, Dr Ordinaire. It developed a local reputation as a panacea. When Dr Ordinaire died, he willed the formula to his housekeeper, who gave it to her daughters who continued to bottle and sell it. Among those who purchased it was an army major who gave it as a wedding gift to his future son-in-law, Henri-Louis Pernod, who then purchased the formula from the sisters. He opened the first absinthe distillery in Switzerland. He then opened a larger one in France in 1805 and began manufacturing on a commercial scale.

Absinthe had an exceptionally high alcohol content, bottled between 120 and 160 percent proof. Because of its high alcohol content, it was hardly ever drunk undiluted but usually blended with water. Because of its bitter flavor, sugar was usually added. An absinthe-drinking ritual evolved with a lump of sugar on a special slotted absinthe spoon placed over the glass. Water was dripped over the sugar; as the water and sugar entered the glass, the drink's beautiful color shifted and evolved.

The *demi-monde* of Paris adopted absinthe as their personal potion. Many painters and artists swore by it, believing it stimulated creativity. Absinthe also maintained its reputation as an aphrodisiac.

> Among those associated with absinthe are painters Henri de Toulouse-Lautrec, Vincent Van Gogh, Paul Gauguin, Edgar Degas, and Edouard Manet, who painted *The Absinthe Drinker* in 1859; writers include Oscar Wilde, Arthur Rimbaud, Paul Verlaine, Charles Baudelaire, and Ernest Hemingway.

Among some circles, absinthe was considered provocative, modern, magical, and subversive in an appealing, positive way; in other circles, how-ever, it was considered counter-cultural and subversive in a malevolent, threatening way. Absinthe was associated with the degeneration of society; in 1905, when a very drunk Jean Lanfray murdered his wife, absinthe was fingered as the true culprit, although Lanfray had only consumed two glasses of the drink during a binge that included copious quantities of other alcoholic beverages as well. Calls to ban absinthe were at the vanguard of the Prohibition movement. Absinthe was banned in the United States on July 25, 1912. France followed suit in 1915.

It is now generally acknowledged that the dangers of absinthe derived largely from its exceptionally high alcohol content rather than its herbal ingredients. In addition, because of its trendy popularity, inferior cheaper bootleg absinthes were produced, which included toxic adulterations leading to increased health hazards like heavy metal poisoning.

The liqueur Pernod was developed and marketed as an alternative to the forbidden absinthe; its taste is somewhat similar. Many craft their own wormwood potions by infusing wormwood leaves in wine or Pernod, although these are not exact substitutes for the original, which was a distilled liqueur.

> Absinthe was made from the leaves of the wormwood plant; one must *never* substitute Essential Oil of Wormwood as the toxic ingredients are incredibly concentrated in the essential oil, which is poisonous to the point of fatality.

Anisette

Anisette is a liqueur distilled from the herb anise (*Pimpinella anisum*). It gained popularity following the ban of absinthe as its taste is somewhat similar, although its alcohol content is much lower. Anise has many magical uses; like wormwood, it is believed to guard against malevolent magic.

Anisette, however, was particularly beloved by spiritualists: because anisette is believed to be particularly appealing to dead souls it is a popular component of séances, necromantic summoning spells, and ancestral offerings. Anisette allegedly serves as an invitation, summoning ghosts and ancestors to visit.

Anisette, like absinthe, is often diluted with water. A glass of anisette, served neat or diluted, is often incorporated into séances, Dumb Suppers (see **CALENDAR:** Halloween) or ancestral altars. The formula known as *Spirit Water* is a further dilution: a tablespoon or splash of anisette is added to a glass of spring water and placed on an altar to beckon the spirits.

Anisette, like absinthe, was often identified as a woman's drink. True anisette is a distilled drink. Commercial anisettes are readily available; homemade infusions of anise are easily concocted.

Homemade Anisette Infusion

1. Place approximately one quart of spirits (vodka or similar) in an airtight jar.
2. Add approximately one ounce of bruised, crushed, green anise seeds.
3. Other seasonings may be also added to taste, for instance approximately one-half ounce crushed coriander seeds and/or a small quantity of cinnamon.
4. Seal the jar; allow it to infuse for a month in a cool, dark place, shaking it gently every so often.
5. Dissolve one pound of sugar in water and add to the container.
6. Filter out the solid material, bottle the liqueur and enjoy.

See **MAGICAL ARTS:** Necromancy.

Apples

Apples were once considered the fruits of life, symbols of love and happiness.

The *"golden apples of the sun"* were associated with glorious goddesses like Freya, Hera, Idunn, and (especially) Aphrodite. Apples had their very own deity, the apple-goddess Pomona. Slice an apple in half horizontally to see the pentacle hidden within.

Post-Christianity, apples were re-envisioned as the forbidden fruit of the Garden of Eden, emblems of sin and desire. Associations with goddesses evolved into associations with witches: poison apples are the fairy-tale witch's favorite tool. No recipes for poison apples are included here: fairy tales to the contrary, witchcraft favors apples for love, seduction, and divination, not for cursing.

Apples are primary ingredients of special Halloween recipes. Instructions and recipes are found on page 516 under Halloween Specialties.

Simple and popular apple spells include the following.

Apple Group Ritual for Good Luck

1. Distribute an apple to each person.
2. While everyone holds an apple, make a wish or blessing. (One person may preside over the ritual or every individual might make personal wishes.)
3. Wish the assembled company good fortune and together eat the apples.

Apple Love Spell

Among the simplest of spells is one from ancient Greece that involves tossing an apple into your intended's lap. If the apple was picked up and the person took a bite (and better yet, then offered you the next one) your feelings were mutual. If the person looked pained and attempted to return the apple or otherwise lose or dispose of it, well, it was clearly time to choose another intended or maybe, for the persistent, a stronger spell …

That spell may be intensified by whispering one's desires over the apple or via this spell:

1. Use a pin to scratch secret messages into the apple skin: explicitly write out your goals and desires or carve initials, images, runes, hearts or other personal symbols.
2. Using your fingers, rub honey over the apple while visualizing the spell's desired outcome.
3. Suck the honey off your fingers while visualizing success.
4. Deliver the apple to the spell's target; watch while they eat the apple. (Sharing the apple only increases the power of the spell.)

Boszorkányhab (Witch's Froth)

Once upon a time, and still sometimes today, people purchased spells from witches. This was the original take-out food; witches sold specially prepared meals or potions that would allegedly deliver the desired outcome when served. (A scene illustrating this is featured in the film *Haxan*: see **CREATIVE ARTS:** Films.)

Rumor had it, however, that witches kept their best, most potent recipes for their own private use. This Hungarian recipe is reputedly among them. Its name translates as "Witch's Froth" but it's also sometimes called "Witch's Snow." It has a reputation as a love spell. The ingredients are incredibly simple, nothing more than apples, sugar, and eggs are required and so was accessible to even the most modest kitchen witch.

Theoretically, the finished product is supposed to resemble clouds or snow. If this is desired, choose apples with very white flesh, otherwise the end result will have a pinkish hue. (If the pink color is preferred, adding tiny bits of red peel or the juice that emanates from the baked apples will enhance the effect.)

The quantity depends upon the size of the apples; four medium apples creates two generous servings.

Ingredients:

Four apples
One egg white*
Confectioner's (Powdered) Sugar to taste
Optional dashes of eau de vie, rum, Calvados or almond extract

1. Preheat the oven to 350°F / 180°C / Gas 4.
2. Wash four apples and bake them in the oven for approximately 45 minutes. (Prick the skins if you don't want them to burst although for this recipe it doesn't really matter.)
3. Remove the apples from the oven; when cool, remove the skins, core, and seeds.
4. With a fork or wire whisk beat the apple pulp until smooth.

5. Stir in the egg white and sugar and beat with a fork for an additional 10 minutes until a light, fluffy, frothy texture is achieved.
6. Add a touch of eau de vie, rum, Calvados or almond extract if desired.
7. Spoon into bowls. Serve immediately or refrigerate until served.

* This is an old-fashioned, traditional recipe and so a raw egg-white is incorporated. Many no longer consider consumption of raw eggs safe. The fluffy, cloud-like texture cannot be achieved without it, however if you are concerned, just eliminate the egg—the desert still tastes good.

See also Witch's Brew; **BOTANICALS:** Apples; **MAGICAL ARTS:** Charms.

Bean Divination

Magic beans lend themselves to divination. Although these are traditional Halloween recipes, they may be incorporated into New Year's festivities as well, or any meal devoted to divination.

Fortune-teller's Bean

This requires one bean but a lot of peapods.

Slit open *one* peapod very gently and push a single bean in, then close up the opening. Add this peapod to other peapods; steam, boil or otherwise prepare. Serve the peas in their pods or shell and serve with butter and salt. Whoever finds the bean is destined to find true love.

Another version suggests adding one single bean to an entire pot of peas. Cook them and serve. Now eat carefully! The person who finds the bean in her soup can look forward to a year of good fortune.

Bean Ritual for the Solitary Fortune-teller

Many divination dishes are intended for groups and parties. What if you'd just like to know your own fortune? This divination ritual is conducted privately and discreetly by the cook:

1. Mix a handful of peas into a large pot of beans.
2. Avert your eyes and stir the pot without looking.
3. Lift up a spoonful: if there's a pea amongst the beans, expect a year of good fortune ahead. (Other interpretations include true love, marriage or a baby within the year.)

See also Fava Beans, page 514.

Beer

Beer is a generic term encompassing all fermented malt beverages including ale. The word "beer" is believed to derive from an Old Norse word for barley, allegedly the oldest cultivated grain on Earth. The oldest historically documented cultivated grain (barley and emmer wheat) was discovered at Jericho at a pre-pottery Neolithic level dated *c*.8000 BCE. The earliest known brewery is dated to 3500 BCE in the Zagros Mountains of what is now Western Iran.

Large-scale grain cultivation began in Mesopotamia, in the region known as the Fertile Crescent. It was a dramatic development in human history. Western Civilization classes once taught that the desire for bread and similar carbohydrate foods stimulated this agricultural revolution; modern historians now suggest, based on more recent archeological discoveries, that the desire for fermented beverages like beer may actually have provided the initial stimulus.

> The close relationship between bread and beer may be witnessed in the aftermath of Prohibition legislation in the United States. When breweries were forced to close, many converted to bakeries instead.

> Ethno-botanist Dale Pendell suggests in his book *Pharmako/Poeia: Plant Powers, Poisons and Herbcraft* (Mercury House, 1995) that ancient Greek barley-potion rituals, including those of Demeter's Eleusinian Mysteries, resemble steps necessary to prepare psychoactive beverages from ergot-infested grain.

Beer was once brewed from more than just barley and hops. Brewing was a woman's art and an accomplished ancient Middle Eastern woman was expected to know *scores* of recipes for different types of beer using many different types of botanicals.

In ancient Sumeria, brewing was a sacred art. The Old Babylonian epic *Gilgamesh*, believed to be the oldest surviving written story on Earth (originally written on twelve clay tablets), recounts the adventures of a historical king (*c.*2750 BCE). Seeking the secret of eternal life, Gilgamesh journeys to the world's end, where the sacred barmaid Siduri owns a tavern on the road to the sea. Siduri suggests Gilgamesh turn back from his quest and offers him wise, sensible spiritual advice. When he rejects her advice, she provides him with shamanic directions to the realm of the dead.

Ale and beer were once identified with goddesses, women's arts, and magical potions:

❋ *The Latin word for beer,* cerevisia, *relates to the name of Ceres, the Corn Mother*

❋ *"Ale" derives from the Indo-European root word* alu, *related to magic, witchcraft, possession, and visions, cognate with "hallucinogen" and "hallucination."*

Wormwood was among the magical ingredients once included in fermented malt beverages. Henbane beers were particularly popular throughout Northern Europe and were the primary psychoactive substance in that region. The Bavarian Purity Act of 1516, sometimes described as the first modern anti-drug law, decreed that only barley, hops, and water could be used to brew beer; other ingredients were forbidden. Some historians believe this law, enacted during a conservative era coinciding with witch-hunts, was largely directed against henbane, a plant associated with witchcraft.

See also Absinthe, Barley-wine, Bread; **BOTANICALS:** Henbane; **DIVINE WITCH:** Kybele; **ERGOT:** Corn Mother: Demeter, Ergot.

Beltane Cake

Special cakes are traditionally part of Beltane rituals, usually featured at the conclusion of the celebration. Rituals and the style of cake depend on region and tradition. Sometimes one large cake is made and shared, sometimes smaller individual cakes are distributed.

The tradition emanates from the Scottish Highlands and the actual recipe for the cake, also known as a bannock, derives from Scottish cuisine. Usually made from oat and/or barley flour, milk, and eggs, cakes traditionally have a scalloped edge and are decorated with knobs, frequently nine knobs or multiples of nine. A thin batter made of beaten eggs, milk or cream, and a little oatmeal was often brushed over the top of the cake before baking. As Beltane is a solar feast, those Neo-Pagans who incorporate this ritual add spices associated with the sun to the cakes, for instance cinnamon, cloves, and saffron.

Various rituals and traditions involving these cakes exist:

At the close of Beltane festivities, the Master of Ceremonies or ritual officiant presided over the distribution of one single cake, large enough for a piece for every participant. One bit was previously marked, usually with charcoal (hence its name—"the blackened bit"). The cake was sliced and distributed; whoever received the blackened bit became the Beltane Carline. (See **HAG:** Beltane Carline.)

In a ritual traditionally combined with the creation and consumption of the Beltane Caudle (see next section) each participant was given an individual oat and/or barley cake decorated with nine raised square knobs. Each person faced the central fire, so that they stand in a circle. Together they break off knobs, one by one, throwing them over their shoulder without looking back. The throwing of each knob is accompanied by a different invocation.

The first invocations are dedicated to protective spirits; then propitiatory offerings are made to predatory ones. Descriptions of offerings to protective spirits are somewhat vague: written reports skirt exactly who is being thanked. However, offerings of propitiation are made directly to the presiding spirits of predatory animals. Thus:

❋ *"This I dedicate to you, preserve my horses."*

❋ *"This I dedicate to you, preserve my sheep."*

❋ *"This I give to you, Fox, spare my sheep!"*

❋ *"This I give to you, Hooded Crow, spare my chicks!"*

Following these offerings, each individual consumed the remainder of their cake and shared the Beltane Caudle.

This tradition originally derives from the Scottish Highlands where participants were primarily concerned about agriculture and livestock. By adjusting the invocations, however, it is easily adapted to suit participants with other concerns.

Sometimes Beltane cakes were intended for divination, not consumption. Participants rolled their individual cakes down a hill. Anthropologists suggest that this action mimics the sun's motion and/or recalls the ancient Druid tradition of rolling burning wicker wheels down hills. If the cake arrives at the bottom of the hill unbroken, the person to whom it belonged could anticipate a happy, fortunate year. If the cake broke en route, misfortune was predicted.

See **CALENDAR:** Beltane.

Beltane Caudle

The word "caudle" is related to "cauldron" and describes a concoction traditionally made from blending eggs and grain with ale or wine, brewed in a cauldron. This blending of beverages and grains was once quite popular.

The Beltane Caudle was incorporated into a Scottish Highland ritual also involving Beltane cakes (see page 506). Sir Walter Scott described the traditional ritual: a square trench was cut into the ground, leaving the turf in the middle. A wood fire was built for the cauldron, which was filled with eggs, butter, oats, and milk. Copious quantities of beer and wine were added: each participant was expected to contribute his share. (The suggestion is made that much beer and wine were also enjoyed independently prior to and during ritual preparations.)

The ritual began by spilling some of the caudle on the ground as a libation. Individual Beltane cakes were distributed; the ensemble then made various invocations to protective and dangerous spirits (see page 507). Once the invocations were complete, the caudle was consumed. The remainder of the Beltane cakes might be consumed or incorporated into different rituals.

See **ANIMALS:** Corvids; **CALENDAR:** Beltane.

Bock Beer

Bock Beer (or Bock Bier) is a strong lager with just enough hops to balance the malt. It was first brewed in Bavaria and allegedly named for its ability to make one caper like a goat. *Bock* is German for goat and many bock beers feature goats on their labels.

Exactly what was originally implied by the word "goat" is subject to conjecture. According to witch-hunters, bock beer was among the beverages reputedly featured at witches' sabbats presided over by the goat god.

See also Beer; **ANIMALS:** Goats; **CALENDAR:** Sabbats; **DICTIONARY:** Sabbat; **HORNED ONE**.

Bread

As they say, bread is the staff of life or perhaps, the magical staff. Cultivation of grain emerged amidst primal and profound spiritual traditions and magic rituals. (See **ERGOT**.) Thus, food created from grain products, especially bread, cakes, and ale, was considered especially magically powerful and spiritually potent.

That old cliché about pregnant women having "muffins in the oven" is even older than most realize. The earliest ovens were not square like modern stoves but resembled detached pregnant bellies. Placed on the ground outside, they looked like pregnant bellies emanating from Earth. This type of oven dates back at least as early as 5000 BCE and still survives in traditional cultures of Africa, Asia, and the Americas.

Bread at its most basic is, by definition, baked dough made from flour and water. Bread for ritual use is often intricately manipulated. Sometimes bread is intended to be eaten; sometimes, however, special breads are created to be preserved as amulets or talismans.

* *Chinese dried bread-dough Buddhas are hung on the wall with red thread to serve as protective, lucky talismans.*

* *In Russia, bread or pastry ladders were baked as part of funeral rituals. The bread symbolized the ladder to heaven: seven rungs for the seven heavens.*

* *Ritual bread was sometimes created from the last sheaf of the harvest (see **ERGOT**: Corn Mother; **HAG**: Cailleach).*

* *Pagan Germanic women once offered their long braids to their goddess. For most women, depending on rate of hair-growth, this ritual could only be replicated once or twice in a lifetime—and perhaps some simply preferred not to shear their hair.*

Eventually, braided loaves substituted for offerings of real hair. This bread was made with eggs and sometimes brushed with an egg glaze prior to baking so as to impart a golden glow reminiscent of fields of ripe grain as well as of blonde hair.

With the advent of Christianity, this last tradition was forbidden and abolished, but it still survives in the Jewish community as the weekly braided golden Challah offered to the Sabbath Queen. By at least the fifteenth century, this tradition of braided loaves was widely incorporated into German Jewish tradition.

Making bread is a woman's art, regardless of spiritual affiliation. Why this particular tradition survived among Jews, however, is subject to conjecture:

❉ *Pagan women seeking refuge joined the Jewish community, subtly incorporating their own traditions*

❉ *Jewish women were discreetly making offerings to Pagan goddesses; rituals survived even after its origins and original intent were forgotten*

❉ *The tradition appealed to Jewish women purely on aesthetic or culinary grounds and has nothing to do with spirituality*

❉ *Although the specific shape (braids) derives from European Paganism, the tradition is actually rooted in ancient Jewish ritual Cakes for the Queen of Heaven (see page 510).*

One clue to the past exists, however: although most Jews call the bread Challah, deriving from the Hebrew word for bride, German Jews name it *barches* instead, reminiscent of the Germanic goddess Perchta or Berchta.

Cakes

Cakes are more than just desert or a sweet conclusion to a meal. Since that old proverbial time immemorial, cakes have been incorporated into spiritual ritual and magic spells.

Cakes are among the most ancient offerings:

❉ *Dough formed into specific shapes (people, animal, objects) serves as ritual offerings and sacrifice*

❉ *During the ancient Greek Thesmophoria Festival, cakes dedicated to Demeter and Persephone were thrown into chasms inhabited by sacred snakes*

❉ *In Rome, women offered millet cakes to Ceres*

❉ *In ancient Egypt, pig- and other animal-shaped cakes were offered to Osiris*

❉ *Cakes are incorporated into Beltane, Yule, and Hecate Night rituals*

Cakes are also used to cast spells:

❉ *Dough is molded into the shape of humans or animals for purposes of image magic (see* **MAGICAL ARTS**: *Image Magic)*

❉ *Cakes are used for divination (see Halloween Specialties)*

❉ *Cakes are used to cast love and seduction spells: raw dough is held under the armpit to absorb perspiration, then shaped into a cake, baked, and served to one's heart's desire.*

The SATOR square, the renowned magic square, is incorporated into all kinds of spell-casting, particularly for healing and protection. An ancient Serbian spell uses cake to administer its effects; it was intended to prevent or heal various physical maladies including bites from rabid dogs in the days prior to rabies vaccinations.

1. Write the SATOR square onto a small cake:

S A T O R
A R E P O
T E N E T
O P E R A
R O T A S

2. Bake and eat the cake to obtain the square's magical protection.

Runes or sigils may be substituted for the SATOR square as desired.

See also Beltane Cake; Cakes and Ale; Cakes for the Queen of Heaven; Feast of Diana, Hecate Supper, Moon Cakes, Yule Cakes; **CALENDAR:** Beltane, Halloween, Hecate Night, Yule; **DICTIONARY:** Runes; **DIVINE WITCH:** Hecate; **ERGOT:** Corn Mother: Ceres, Demeter; **MAGICAL ARTS:** Divination, Runes, Sigils.

Cakes and Ale, Cakes and Wine

"Cakes and ale" or "cakes and wine" names food and drink, but they also name a Wiccan and Neo-Pagan sacrament. Many covens traditionally conclude circles and other rituals with the ritual of *cakes-and-wine* or *cakes-and-ale*. Food and beverages are blessed by the High Priestess or Priest and are considered sacramental offerings. Depending upon purpose, cakes and ale may also be incorporated at other points during the rite, not only the conclusion.

❋ *Cakes are often, but not always, formed in the shape of a crescent moon*

❋ *"Cakes" may include biscuits, cookies or bread as well as cake*

❋ *"Wine" or "ale" also includes beer, mead, and fresh fruit juices*

See **DIVINE WITCH:** Dionysus.

Cakes for the Queen of Heaven

Cake is among the most primeval traditional offerings made to female deities including Aphrodite, Artemis, Lady Asherah of the Sea, Astarte, Diana, Hecate, and Inanna-Ishtar. The blini offered to Baba Yaga may be understood to derive from this tradition. Specific ritual cakes were created for specific deities:

❋ *Triangle-shaped honey-cakes, representing female genitalia, were offered to Aphrodite*

❋ *Round cakes lit with miniature torches intended to represent the glowing moon were offered to Artemis and Diana*

In the grimoire *Aradia or the Gospel of the Witches*, the term "Cakes for the Queen of Heaven" is used to describe crescent-shaped cakes blessed in the name of Diana.

In the Middle East, archeologists have uncovered ancient cake molds used to create cakes in the shape of the goddess herself. These molds are similar to modern cake, chocolate or candle molds and could be used to form multiple cakes of uniform appearance. Anthropologists believe these molds were used to bake cakes for the Queen of Heaven.

The Queen of Heaven generally refers to the supreme Mesopotamian deity Inanna-Ishtar; in the Babylonian version of the Deluge, the rainbow that serves as the Creator's reminder not to cause another flood is really Inanna-Ishtar's necklace.

Offerings of cakes were incorporated into Inanna-Ishtar's rites. Ironically, the most lucid, detailed surviving information regarding ritual baking and offering of cakes derives from the biblical book of Jeremiah. Offering cakes to the Queen of Heaven was a family affair. In Jeremiah 7:18, the prophet reports that he heard the voice of God complain that *"the children gather wood, and the fathers kindle the fire and the women knead their dough to make cakes to the Queen of Heaven ..."*

Offering cakes seems to have been incorporated into ritual alongside burning incense and pouring libations. In Jeremiah 44, the prophet discovers a community of exiled Jews in Egypt, burning incense, pouring libations and offering cakes to the Queen of Heaven. He rebukes them, singling out the women.

Typically the Old Testament records complaints against those who deviate from extreme monotheism but fails to record opposing arguments. Unusually, in this case the Bible recounts the women's response to Jeremiah (44:16-19): they are not compliant. *"As for the word that thou hast spoken unto us in the name of the Lord, we will not hearken unto thee"* they say, explaining that when they offered to the Queen of Heaven *"... then had we plenty of victuals, and were well and saw no evil. But since we left off to burn incense to the Queen of Heaven ... we have wanted all things and have been consumed by the sword and by the famine."* The women also reject Jeremiah's attempts to identify this practice as a women's cult, pointing out *"... did we make her cakes to worship her ... without our men?"*

Unfortunately, the Bible is vague regarding exactly which spirit it describes as the Queen of Heaven—whether it is Inanna-Ishtar, Astarte (who may or may not be identical to Inanna-Ishtar), Anat (who may or may not be identical to Astarte) or Asherah (ditto).

See **CREATIVE ARTS:** Dance: Dance of the Seven Veils; **ERGOT:** Corn Mother: Anat.

Days of the Dead (Dias De Los Muertos)

Days of the Dead rituals are intrinsically associated with food: special foods are not only prepared for the dead but for the living, too. Foods specifically associated with the holiday are eagerly awaited year round. (Days of the Dead recipes courtesy of Angela Villalba, of the Mexican Sugar Skull Company.)

Mexican Sugar Skulls

Mexican Sugar Skulls are a traditional confection and folk art used to celebrate the Days of the Dead. Their name describes them exactly— packed, hardened sugar molded into the shape of skulls, then decorated with vividly colored icing, bright bits of colored foil, sequins, and/or colored sugar. The name of the loved one they are intended to honor is traditionally piped over the forehead with icing. Most sugar skulls are tiny although larger ones exist too.

Sugar skulls are sold as treats for children during the weeks leading up to the festival.

(Providing nothing inedible is used to ornament them, sugar skulls are edible but *very* sweet!) They are also used to decorate the home altars (*ofrendas*) that welcome the visiting souls of the dead. Sugar skulls are carried to the cemetery with flowers and other objects used to decorate tombs.

Mexican sugar skulls are not hard to make: requirements are sugar, meringue powder, water, and special skull molds. Blend one teaspoon of meringue powder into each cup of granulated sugar used. (Meringue powder is a must and *cannot* be omitted.) A little bit of water is then used to moisten the blended sugar so that it achieves the texture of beach sand. This is then added to the molds and allowed to dry for approximately eight hours, after which the skulls may be decorated as desired.

> Meringue powder and skull molds in various sizes are available from www.MexicanSugarSkull.com. Further information, ingredients (including the Royal Icing and colored sugar favored in Mexico), and beautiful images of Mexican sugar skulls and other traditional crafts may also be found at that website.

Molé Sauce

Among the discoveries made by the Spanish in Mexico was chocolate, indigenous to Meso-America, and previously unknown to Europeans. Chocolate was a sacred, ritual food associated with the deity Quetzalcoatl and usually served as a drink blended with ground chili peppers. (The concept of sweetened milk choco-

late was born in Europe.) Molé sauce reproduces the ancient formula, blending chili peppers and chocolate. Fine molé sauce is extremely time-consuming to make and so not traditionally an everyday food but one reserved for the most sacred of days.

In Oaxaca, Mexico molé is especially associated with the Days of the Dead. Turkey molé is a favorite of spirit and villager alike. Molé sauce is spooned over turkey and sesame seeds, which represent happiness in Oaxaca, are sprinkled on top of each dish. Plates of turkey molé are placed in the center of *ofrendas* to delight visiting spirits.

The original recipe, while varying slightly from village to village and household to household, generally has over 30 ingredients and takes days to make, but now many shortcuts to the traditional process of making molé exist. Oaxacan markets sell the ground chocolate/chili paste by the kilo, which is quickly fried with onion and tomato and thinned with broth. This paste is also sold in the Import section of many international gourmet markets.

Angela Villalba has further adapted the traditional Oaxacan molé recipe:

Ingredients:

One 30-ounce can red enchilada sauce
Two to four blocks Mexican hot chocolate mix
   (approximately 8 ounces or to taste)*
Three cloves of garlic, finely minced
One-quarter teaspoon ground oregano
Ground cinnamon to taste
Two cups chicken broth or consommé
Dried red chili flakes to taste
Toasted sesame seeds

1. Add the enchilada sauce to a large saucepan over medium heat.
2. Add the blocks of chocolate, garlic, oregano, and cinnamon.

3. When the chocolate has dissolved, add the chicken broth.
4. Stir and taste; then add the red chili flakes as desired.
5. Simmer for an hour, adding more broth if the mixture becomes dry.
6. Spoon the hot molé sauce over the main dish (traditionally turkey but it is also served over roasted chicken and Mexican dishes such as enchiladas and tamales) and sprinkle with toasted sesame seeds.

The sauce is best served the next day so that the flavors can meld.

* Mexican hot chocolate mix is sold in disks or blocks intended to dissolve in hot liquids and often incorporates ground cinnamon and almonds. (Villalba recommends *Mayordomo* brand.) If Mexican hot chocolate is unavailable, substitute dark, bitter chocolate, not sweetened chocolate.

Pan de Muerto

Pan de Muerto ('Bread of the Dead') celebrates the return of the spirits. Traditionally these breads are made by village bakers using lots of egg yolks and anise seeds. These round beautifully decorated breads are stacked on home *ofrendas* for the spirits to enjoy as well as being eaten by the living. Regional variations exist: in Oaxaca, loaves are sprinkled with sesame seeds representing happiness, while in Michoacan, pieces of dough are used to form skulls and bones to ornament the top of the round loaf, which are then dusted with colored sugar.
    Ingredients:

One-quarter cup lukewarm water
One tablespoon dry yeast

Four cups all-purpose flour
Three-quarter cup sugar
Two whole eggs plus five egg yolks
One-half cup melted butter
One teaspoon salt
One tablespoon anise seed
Two teaspoons nutmeg
Egg wash made from one egg white and one teaspoon melted butter
Sesame seeds (optional)
Sugar for decorating (colored sugar is most dramatic)

1. Proof yeast by dissolving in warm water.
2. Add ¼ cup of flour and blend with a spoon.
3. Allow the mixture to rest until it doubles in volume, approximately 30 minutes.
4. Place the rest of the flour in a large bowl, make a well in the center and add the sugar, eggs, egg yolks, melted butter, salt, anise, and nutmeg. Beat thoroughly.
5. Add the yeast mixture and blend.
6. Knead on a lightly floured board until the dough becomes elastic and not sticky, approximately 15 minutes.
7. Place the ball of dough into a greased bowl, cover with a cloth and allow to rise in a warm spot for approximately 2 hours or until the dough has doubled in volume. (Check by poking your fingers into the side of the dough; when your fingerprints stay in the dough, it's ready.) You may also raise it overnight, covered in the refrigerator.
8. Punch down the dough and knead five times. Do not add additional flour.
9. Cut one-third off the dough and set it aside.
10. Shape the remaining dough into a round loaf.
11. Pinch off a ball from the reserved dough and form a "skull" with it, placing it on top of the loaf.

12. Roll the rest of the reserved dough into a long rope. Pinch it off into approximately 3-inch long pieces and shape them into bones. These are traditionally placed onto the loaf like spokes on a wheel.

13. Cover the loaf and let it rise until doubled in size in a warm spot on a greased cookie sheet.

14. Brush it with the egg wash and sprinkle with sesame seeds, if desired.

15. Cover once again and let it rise once more.

16. Preheat the oven to 350°F/180°C/Gas 4.

17. Bake the Pan de Muerto on the center rack for approximately 45 minutes or until golden brown.

18. After the loaf has cooled on a rack, sprinkle the bread with colored sugar or decorate it with icing. Traditionally names of departed loved ones are inscribed on the bread.

See also Anisette, Bread; **CALENDAR:** Days of the Dead; **HAG:** Black Annis.

Fava Beans

Italian folklore is full of interesting magical references to beans:

✳ *Beans were spat in the directions of ghosts for purposes of exorcism*

✳ *Beans were believed to serve as containers for unborn human souls, thus serving as fertility symbols, and incorporated into fertility rituals*

✳ *Beans were also sometimes a tabooed food*

Beans thus were the seeds of life and death.

Although beans in general are perceived as a magical food by many traditions, these Italian traditions didn't just refer to any beans: many modern beans derive from the Western Hemisphere and, like tomatoes, were unknown in Europe pre-Columbus. The beans incorporated into Italian traditions are fava beans.

Fava beans (*Vica faba*) are traditionally associated with death and rebirth. Ancient Romans served them at funeral banquets. This tradition still survives in Italian witchcraft and spiritual practices. At midnight on October 31st, for instance, bowls of fava beans are placed outdoors for the spirits; they are then buried in Earth after sunrise on November 1st.

Fava beans were understood as a magically potent, potentially deadly food and for good reason: a condition known as "favism" is common throughout the Middle East and the Mediterranean. There is a genetic predisposition toward this condition, however it is triggered by the consumption of fava beans. Once upon a time, favism was considered to be an allergic reaction to fava beans. It is now known to be caused by a deficiency in an enzyme (glucose-6-phosphate dehydrogenase).

Favism is a type of anemia caused by hemolysis (destruction of healthy red blood cells). Victims are predominately male; almost all victims are of Middle Eastern and Mediterranean descent. Symptoms include intense fatigue, nausea, vertigo, and dark-orange colored urine. The condition is usually temporary but seasonal, corresponding to the sprouting of fava beans in the early spring. Thus favism is among the first signs of spring in that region. Favism can be fatal if an attack is sufficiently severe: approximately one in twelve cases proves fatal.

The oldest known fava beans were found in an archeological dig in Nazareth and date from *c.*6500 BCE but are believed to have been wild plants. Widespread cultivation of fava beans is believed to stem from the third-millennium BCE; they were widely cultivated throughout the

Middle East, Mediterranean, and North Africa.

Fava beans were a mixed blessing. Although they were potentially deadly to a sizable percentage of the population, they have also been found to protect against malaria, once among the primary causes of death in the region.

✴ *In ancient Rome, one single fava bean was baked within one of the ritual cakes of the Saturnalia. Whoever found it was crowned Lord of the Saturnalia. This tradition survives in the King Cakes of New Orleans' Mardi Gras, although instead of a fava bean, the token is a tiny baby doll.*

✴ *Italian immigrants to New Orleans brought other fava-bean traditions with them. On the Feast Day of St Joseph, dried, roasted fava beans are blessed, thus transforming into special St Joseph's Beans or Lucky Mojo Beans. Allegedly someone who carries one of these lucky beans will never want for money.*

The Romans spread fava bean rituals throughout their Empire; some continue to evolve. In France, the Feast of the Epiphany, also called the Feast of the Kings, is occasion for mass consumption of the *"galette of the kings"*—a flat, round pastry filled with almond paste baked with one trinket concealed inside. This lucky charm is called a *fève* (fava bean in French) because once that's what served as the trinket. Whoever finds the *fève* becomes king or queen for the day. (Galettes are sometimes sold with paper crowns.)

In the late nineteenth century, small porcelain figurines began to replace the traditional bean. *Fèves* are now collectors' items with the rarest commanding high prices. Some collect them for value or novelty but others for their magical aura as a charm. *Fèves* range from the traditional, like four-leafed clovers or horseshoes to the unusual—Harry Potter figurines or porcelain tiles depicting positions from the Kama Sutra.

Ovid and Petronius recommended a ham and bean soup to antidote effects of the *striges*, including loss of male sexual vigor. (See **DICTIONARY**: Strix.)

See also Bean Divination, Yule Cakes.

Festival of Diana

Diana's Roman feast day on August 13th traditionally incorporated feasting. Her celebratory meal included wine, roasted young goat, cakes served hot on plates of leaves, and apples still hanging in clusters on their boughs. Cakes in the shape of the moon, topped with lit candles—the original birthday cake—were a traditional offering.

See also Apples, Cake, Strega; **ANIMALS**: Goats; **BOTANICALS**: Apples; **DIVINE WITCH**: Diana.

Fox Spirit Tofu (Inari Sushi)

What do you serve a fox spirit? Well, they love fried tofu. If you wish to please or lure a fox spirit, a plate of fried tofu reputedly does the trick. *Aburage* is the Japanese name for thinly cut tofu, drained and fried in oil. Its association with fox spirits is so strong that it is also called *inariage*.

Inari is the Japanese spirit who presides over rice. Foxes are her/his sacred animal and messenger. There are approximately 40,000 Inari shrines throughout Japan.

The identification of fox spirits with fried tofu has inspired other dishes such as Fox spirit sushi or, in Japanese, *Inari sushi* (also sometimes spelled *Inarizushi*). Inari sushi is a simple, modest, and inexpensive type of sushi incorporating no fish. Despite the fox associations, this is a vegetarian dish: triangular, deep-fried tofu bags are filled with sushi rice (sticky, vinegared rice.) Inari sushi is sometimes placed under the paws of the stone foxes found in Inari shrines as an offering.

However, renegade fox spirits also crave this treat, as do those fox spirits affiliated with the sorcerers known as Fox Spirit Owners. Allegedly some fox spirits transform into human-shape just for easier access to Inari sushi.

Among the most renowned Inari shrines is the one in Fushimi, a saké production center near Kyoto. The shrine was established in 711 CE. Inari sushi is served at the many small restaurants along the shrine's hiking trail, as is another dish, *kitsune udon* ("Fox Udon"), a noodle soup topped with fried tofu.

See **ANIMALS**: Foxes.

Halloween Specialties

Outside the Pagan community, where it is a significant spiritual festival, modern Halloween is largely associated with juvenile trick or treating: children go door to door begging treats, which now usually consist of commercially manufactured candy. Once upon a time, however, Halloween (Samhain, November Eve) was an adult holiday dedicated to divination, romance, and feasting. Special dishes, both sweet and savory and often incorporating spell-casting and divination, were special features of this night.

Traditional Halloween tokens and their meanings include:

- *Anchor: stability*

- *Baby doll: a baby*

- *Button: mixed fortune, blessings and challenges*

- *Coin: wealth*

- *Dice: good luck*

- *Four-leafed Clover: luck, freedom from malevolent spells*

- *Horseshoe: luck, health*

- *Key: success, travel, solutions, adventures, luck in love, opportunity*

- *Ring: romance or marriage*

- *Thimble: professional success, steady income, independence (old-fashioned sources indicate "spinsterhood"; this once was considered the booby prize)*

- *Wheel: adventure*

- *Wishbone: your wish come true, your desires fulfilled*

Fortune-telling recipes often incorporate tokens to be added to the dish, then found during the meal and interpreted. One must eat carefully: tokens received indicate one's destined fortune in the coming year. If this is reminiscent of New Year's traditions, it should be: according to the ancient Celtic calendar, Samhain *was* New Year's Eve.

Special Halloween dishes include the following.

Apple Crowdie

Apple Crowdie is spiced apple sauce with whipped cream. The spice may be as simple as a dash of cinnamon; if serving adults, rather than children, a dollop of whiskey may be stirred in as well. Just prior to serving, tokens are added to the dish: each person takes one spoonful from a common pot. Eat carefully! If no token appears in the spoonful, then the jury is still out—your fortune cannot yet be foretold, or perhaps it's in your hands …

An alternative method is for each person to take a spoonful until they find a charm. This is a modern variation on the Scottish traditional desert Crowdie. (See below, Fortune-teller's Crowdie.)

Colcannon

Colcannon is a traditional Irish Halloween meal. Small tokens are hidden inside the meal for purposes of divination.

1. Boil potatoes, then drain and mash them.
2. While the potatoes are boiling, boil cabbage, too.
3. Stir chopped, cooked cabbage into the mashed potatoes.
4. Melt butter in a pan.
5. Chop onions and gently sauté them in the butter.
6. Mix the sautéed onions into the mashed potatoes and cabbage dish.
7. Add salt and white pepper to taste.
8. Carefully stir the tokens into the dish.
9. Serve the colcannon on individual plates. Make a well in the center of each mound of colcannon and place butter within.

Should someone not receive a token, this indicates that their destiny is unresolved or is in their own hands. Although any tokens may be incorporated, sometimes, particularly if serving children, coins are wrapped in wax paper and hidden as a treat instead.

Some prefer to substitute parsnips for the cabbage although both could easily be incorporated.

Fortune Cake

Fortune Cake (also known as "Halloween Cake") was once the centerpiece of Victorian Halloween parties. In addition to serving as desert, it was fortune-telling device. Trinkets and charms were baked into cake. (The safety conscious wrap each trinket individually in wax paper to lessen chances of accidental swallowing.) A modern variation substitutes ice cream or ice cream cake as it is so easy to insert the treats.

Fortune-teller's Crowdie

Fortune-teller's Crowdie is a very similar dish to Apple Crowdie (see above), except that it is made from oatmeal rather than apples. However the token ritual remains identical.

1. Add two tablespoons of lightly toasted oatmeal to a dish of whipped cream. (There must be sufficient cream to hide the charms.)
2. Stir in sugar to taste.
3. If desired, add a tablespoon of whiskey, rum or other spirits, stir and chill.
4. Just prior to serving, add tokens.

Participants take spoonfuls from the common dish until all the tokens have been claimed.

Lambswool

Lambswool is a traditional Irish Halloween drink. Various recipes exist. The basis of the potion are roasted, crushed apples, which are added to milk, hot spiced ale, cider, and/or wine. Sugar is added as desired. Bits of toast may be added to the drink, too.

The name "Lambswool" is believed to be a corruption of the Irish Gaelic *La Mas Nbhal* or "Feast of apple gathering." Pronounced "Lammas-ool," it eventually evolved into "lambs wool."

See also Beltane Caudle.

Mash of Nine Sorts

Mash of Nine Sorts is a traditional British Halloween Supper. Ingredients include potatoes, carrots, turnips, parsnips, leeks, and peas. These are boiled or otherwise cooked. Milk or cream is added and everything is mashed together and seasoned to taste with salt and pepper. If you dislike one ingredient, omit it but then incorporate something else as a substitution. It is crucial to maintain the lucky number of nine ingredients.

This dish was traditionally served to a group of unmarried people; only one token was hidden:

a wedding ring. Whoever found it was destined to be married first, however other tokens can also be substituted as desired.

Not all Halloween dishes are intended to be eaten; some serve purely for divination instead. One of the most famous Halloween rituals involves apple peels:

1. Begin to peel an apple; the peel must come off in one piece.
2. If and when the apple peel breaks, stop peeling and work with whatever you have.
3. Toss the apple peel over your left shoulder.

When the peel falls it will allegedly form the initial of your true love (or the one you're destined to marry—ideally one and the same).

To determine the future of a partnership or romantic relationship, carefully place two chestnuts on hot coals or within a burning fireplace. If the chestnuts sputter loudly, this is auspicious; if they jump apart, however, it's time to reconsider the relationship. (This ritual may also be performed with bay leaves instead of chestnuts.)

Hecate Supper

Ritual meals were among Hecate's traditional rites. Once upon a time, these dinners were consumed outside under the dark moon, ideally at a crossroads. One plate was reserved for Hecate; after her devotees dined, just before they departed, Hecate's plate was laid down at the crossroads. Traditionally whatever is given to Hecate cannot be reclaimed. Thus, do not break out your priceless set of china; lay the meal on the ground or use a serving dish that will be incorporated into the offering. Once the offering

Encyclopedia of Witchcraft

is laid down, depart without looking back. Hecate determines who picks up the offering. Once upon a time, observers scoffed at Hecate's rituals, commenting that offerings made to the goddess were consumed by homeless people or feral animals, however they misunderstood: this is among the ways Hecate accepts offerings.

A typical Hecate Supper menu included eggs, fish roe, goat and sheep's milk cheese, sprats, red mullet—a scavenger fish that was the subject of many taboos—garlic, mushrooms, and honey cake surrounded by blazing torches or cakes decorated with miniature imitation torches (candles).

Red mullet (also known as trigle) was tabooed at the Eleusinian Mysteries and at the shrine of Argive Hera. Poet and scholar of mythology and ancient history Robert Graves writes in *The White Goddess* that red foods were tabooed in ancient Greece, with the exception of feasts of the dead. (Hecate has many associations with Death.) These red foods included red mullet but also bacon, crayfish, crimson berries, and fruits, especially pomegranates.

See also Cakes, Cakes for the Queen of Heaven, Lunar Foods; **DIVINE WITCH:** Hecate.

Lunar Foods

For as long as can be remembered, the moon has been believed to rule magic, water, and women. Certain foods are identified as lunar foods; they transmit the effects of the moon and thus are believed able to impart great psychic power. Those wishing to further align themselves with the moon were encouraged to consume these foods.

Among these lunar foods are the following:

❋ *Cake, specifically round cakes with candles. The traditional round birthday cake derives from this ancient ritual practice. An alternative option is crescent- or horned-shaped bread or cakes, such as croissants.*

❋ *Cheese, not the legendary green cheese of which the moon is supposedly composed but round white cheeses, such as goat cheese or brie.*

❋ *Crabs and Crayfish; the creature assigned to the astrological sign Cancer, the only sign belonging to the moon, is the crab. Those born under the sign of Cancer are believed to resemble crabs, leading to many jokes about crabby personalities. In Mediterranean regions, crabs are intensely affiliated with the moon.*

Amphitrite, the Greek Queen of the Sea, wears a crown crafted of crab claws.

Older versions of the Tarot card The Moon traditionally feature a picture of a creature that, to modern eyes, resembles a lobster more than a crab. Many assume that the artists who created these images simply couldn't draw realistic crabs; modern versions of The Moon often feature more realistic depictions of crabs. However, many of these older versions are really depicting crayfish, hence the confusion.

In Central and Eastern Europe, especially in those areas whose magical traditions were heavily influenced by the Romany, the crayfish is the lunar animal par excellence. Crayfish are freshwater crustaceans: they are cooked in innumerable ways. Their shells are traditionally dried and preserved as amulets, particularly for fertility, long believed to be the moon's magical gift. (See **FAIRY-TALE WITCHES:** Grimms' Fairy Tales: *Hansel and Gretel*.)

May Wine

The traditional festive beverage of the May Eve/Beltane/Walpurgis celebration, May Wine is flavored and scented with the herb Sweet Woodruff (*Asperula odorata*). Sweet Woodruff's other folk names include Forest Queen, Forest Mother Herb, and Master (or Mistress) of the Woods. The earliest surviving recorded mention of May Wine occurred in 854 CE, when a Benedictine monk, Wandelbertus, referred to it.

In German, May Wine is called *Maitrank*. Traditionally any type of Rhine or Alsatian wine is used.

1. Place young, fresh woodruff shoots in a covered tureen.
2. Add a bottle of white wine. (Some now also add a few tablespoons of brandy.)
3. Cover the tureen and allow the wine to infuse for an hour
4. Dissolve sugar to taste in water and add to the infused wine, then serve.

As fresh woodruff is not always available, dried herbs may also be used. Sliced fresh strawberries are also frequently added just before serving.

See **CALENDAR:** Beltane, May Eve, Walpurgis.

Moon Cakes

The Chinese moon festival occurs annually on the fifteenth day of the eighth month of the Chinese lunar calendar. The day is dedicated to Lady Chang'o, the beautiful woman in the moon. Lady Chang'o lives alone on the moon in a beautiful cinnamon wood palace, her sole companion an alchemist rabbit who grinds out the potion of immortality with his mortar and pestle.

The moon festival corresponds with the night when the moon is at its brightest and nearest Earth. On that night, Lady Chang'o reputedly grants secret wishes to those people who address them to her. Moon cakes are eaten to honor Lady Chang'o, to commemorate the holiday but also as part of the magic ritual of asking for one's heart's desire.

Moon Cake Ritual

1. Take a private moment to commune with the Full Moon.
2. Holding your moon cake in your hands, silently address Lady Chang'o: make your wish or invocation.
3. Eat the moon cake in the moonlight.
4. Thank Lady Chang'o in advance, but be sure to keep this wish secret.

Moon cakes are round cakes, usually stuffed with some kind of filling. They are eaten and given as gifts during the moon festival. The simplest cake features an egg-yolk filling believed to resemble a bright full moon. Alternative fillings include nuts, red bean paste, white lotus paste, and Chinese ham. In Chinese tradition, foods are highly symbolic; thus moon-cake fillings are adjusted to reflect one's wishes. For instance, a watermelon seed filling indicates the wish to conceive.

Immediately preceding and during the moon festival, Chinese bakeries and specialty stores feature moon cakes, frequently beautifully packaged and intended as gifts.

See also Cakes, Lunar Foods.

Pancakes

Pancakes are thin battercakes fried in a pan. Essentially they are a quick, simple, homemade cake that lends itself to spontaneous preparation, unlike elaborate ritual cakes like the *Bûche de Noël* or the snake pasty of the *serpari*. Pancakes are now generally identified as a breakfast food (except in Holland where they are eaten all day), however they have a long history as a ritual food.

🕸 *In Britain, Shrove Tuesday (the day before Ash Wednesday) was once popularly known as "Pancake Tuesday." Ritually eating and making pancakes, as well as pancake-eating contests, were once part of celebrations. These pancakes were often used for divination: Lincolnshire farmers once threw pancakes to their roosters and observed the reaction. If the rooster ate the whole pancake, this was a bad omen; if the rooster summoned his hens to come share, good fortune for the entire family was believed assured.*

🕸 *In Brittany, pancakes and cider are brought to the cemetery as the traditional Day of the Dead offering.*

🕸 *The witch-goddess Perchta expects to find offerings of pancakes left for her on Twelfth Night or else dire consequences are threatened …*

🕸 *In traditional Macedonian ritual, the evil spirits believed buzzing about during the Twelve Nights of Yule are lured close with pancakes, then obliterated as the pancakes sizzle in the pan.*

🕸 *In Grimms' fairy tale* Hansel and Gretel, *the witch serves the children pancakes with apples, nuts, and sugar.*

See also Apples, Witch's Brew; **BOTANICALS:** Apples; **CALENDAR:** Days of the Dead, Festivals of the Dead, Twelve Nights of Yule; **DICTIONARY:** Ciaraula; **DIVINE WITCH:** Angitia, Perchta; **ERGOT:** Corn Mother: Perchta; **FAIRY-TALE WITCHES**: Grimms' Fairy Tales: *Hansel and Gretel.*

Pumpkins

Pumpkins are the food many people most associate with witchcraft. They are perceived as a magical food: it is no coincidence that Cinderella's coach was a transformed pumpkin.

Pumpkins are emblems of Halloween. Pumpkins, whether left whole or carved into jack o' lanterns symbolize Halloween for many; their image is incorporated into all sorts of Halloween memorabilia.

Pumpkins are the fruit of the Cucurbita gourd and are native to the Western Hemisphere. Although pumpkins may be boiled, baked, roasted or made into pie, 99 percent of all pumpkins sold are now used as jack o'lanterns. A jack o'lantern is a hollowed-out pumpkin that has been carved to resemble a face. Pulp and seeds are removed and may be cooked and eaten afterwards although many people do discard them, only desiring the pumpkin's shell. Most pumpkins are orange, however some are white. White ones have become popular recently and are used to create "ghostly" jack o'lanterns.

Jack o'lanterns are an Irish tradition and were first carved from turnips. However, Irish immigrants to the United States quickly realized that large round pumpkins were perfect for creating jack o'lanterns and turnips are now rarely used.

Pumpkins are also identified with African Diaspora spiritual and magical traditions. Enslaved Africans recognized the pumpkins they encountered in the West as a type of gourd, popularly used as containers and magic spell ingredients in Africa. Pumpkins were thus easily and naturally adapted.

Pumpkins are associated with Oshun, the Yoruba orisha of love, beauty, fertility, and magic. Orange is her sacred color; Oshun is said to cast her magic spells with pumpkins, and pumpkins are identified as her children. Oshun's devotees or those to whom she has rendered assistance are forbidden to eat pumpkins, especially the seeds. (The injunction also extends to yellow and orange squash.)

In Vodou and other traditions, pumpkins are often hollowed out to serve as magical lamps for divination and spell-casting. The pumpkin is treated as if similar to a cauldron. The hollowed pumpkins are filled with oil; cotton wicks are floated in the oil and lit.

See **DICTIONARY:** Orisha, Voudou.

Rapunzel

Also known as ramps and rampion (and in French, *raiponce*), rapunzel (*Campanula rapunculus*) grows wild in the fields but, as the story says, is easily cultivated in the garden. Roots are eaten raw or cooked like any other root vegetable; the leaves may be eaten raw as a salad or prepared like spinach.

See **FAIRY-TALE WITCHES:** Grimms' Fairy Tales: *Rapunzel*.

Salt

Salt's use as a natural preservative reveals its magical power. Salt's primary magical use is protection. The simplest protection spell of all consists of casting a circle with salt and sitting within it until all danger passes. Allegedly no evil power can transgress that salt circle. Salt is carried in amulet bags for protection.

Salt is also used for magical purification and cleansing rituals: the simplest personal cleansing spell involves bathing in water to which sea salt has been added.

It is considered among the lunar foods: most salt is white, and salt is extracted from water, whether from the sea or laboriously through the evaporation of brine water in salt mines.

Salt's associations with water enhanced its identification with lunar goddesses and with psychic, protective, magic power. The constant presence of the saltshaker on the table derives from its magical use: once upon a time, open saltcellars were preferred as this way salt emanates more power than when tightly enclosed.

It was once commonly believed that evil spirits wishing to take possession of a body or otherwise cause harm were likely to enter through the mouth together with food. Salt added to food allegedly foils these plans.

Many spirits allegedly *hate* salt, particularly djinn and sidhe (fairies), and will avoid it at all cost. They reject offerings made with salt; those cooking for these spirits are advised to omit salt *entirely*. Those wishing to prevent these spirits from partaking of a meal are conversely encouraged to use it. Some anthropologists believe that references to spirits' dislike of salt (usually accompanied by an equal hatred of iron) indicates references to aboriginal people without knowledge of iron or salt, and first introduced into their territory by invaders.

Not all spirits hate salt:

✴ *Ogun, West Africa's Spirit of Iron accepts bags of salt as a ritual offering*

✴ *Russia's horned spirits, the Leshii, accept offerings with salt*

✴ *An ancient Bavarian salt mine is named* Berchtesgaden *or Berchta's (Perchta's) Hall*

The notion that spirits despised salt carried over to Christian mythology of the devil. During the witch-hunt era, it was commonly believed that the devil hates salt. Witch-hunters claimed that salt was omitted during sabbat feasts. A legend developed that witches too despised salt; allegedly one way to identify a witch was merely to pay attention at table. The witch was the one complaining that the food was too salty. To cook without salt was thus to leave oneself vulnerable to accusations of witchcraft. Needless to say, many sought safety and protection by lavishly, ostentatiously, and publicly salting their food.

Salt is used to cast magic spells. Salt is an excellent conductor of energy and so is a primary tool of Russian whispering spells:

1. Murmur your desires over salt, then slip it into someone's drink, although it may be more discreetly added to food.
2. Feed this enchanted salt to your heart's desire as a seduction or romance charm.

See **CALENDAR**: Sabbats; **DICTIONARY**: Sabbat; **DIVINE WITCH**: Perchta; **FAIRIES**: Nature-spirit Fairies: Sidhe; **HORNED ONE**: Cain, The Devil, Leshii; **MAGICAL PROFESSIONS**: Metalworkers.

Snake Cake

In ancient Rome, traditional New Year's rituals included giving snake-shaped cakes as gifts for good luck. At the Thesmophoria, the festival dedicated to Demeter and Persephone, among the offerings ritually placed within Earth were cakes shaped like female genitalia and snakes.

Cakes shaped in the form of snakes were among the ritual foods offered to the witch-goddess Angitia. The ritual survives in the annual Festival of San Domenico that now incorporates many of Angitia's traditions. (See **DIVINE WITCH**: Angitia.) Although no recipes from Angitia and Demeter's ancient priestesses survive, the following is a modern variation based on the cakes carried in San Domenico processionals.

Snake Cake

Ingredients:

Two cups of all-purpose flour
One-half cup sugar
Scant teaspoon baking soda
Grated peel of an orange
Ground cinnamon to taste
Honey (at least one-quarter cup but to taste)
An espresso-sized cup of hot black coffee
One jigger chocolate or orange liqueur
Sour black cherry jam
Red and green candied fruit

1. Preheat oven to 350°F/180°C/Gas 4

2. Place the flour in a mixing bowl; add the sugar, baking soda, grated orange peel and cinnamon.

3. Warm the honey carefully until it is almost bubbling. (Be careful not to scorch it. Do not microwave; the best, safest way to warm honey is in a bain-marie or a bowl sitting in a pan of hot water.)

4. Remove the honey from heat. Immediately make a well in the middle of the blended flour and add the honey, hot cup of coffee and liqueur. Mix quickly.

5. Divide the dough in half.

6. Form one half into the shape of a long loaf.

7. Spread the jam down the center of this loaf, then fold or wrap the edges of the dough over the jam so that it is enclosed within.

8. Get creative: form a snake's head and tail.

9. Curl the snake and place it on a greased baking sheet.

10. Make green eyes from the green candy and trim the red candy into the form of a forked tongue. Insert into the snake's head. (Depending on the type of candy you are using, this may be done before or after baking.)

11. Repeat with the other half of the dough.

12. Place in the preheated oven for 20 minutes. Remove and allow the snakes to cool completely.

13. If desired, once cool the cakes may be decorated with pastry paint or a dark chocolate glaze. (Melt dark chocolate in a bain-marie and brush onto the snake using a pastry brush.)

See **ANIMALS:** Snakes; **DIVINE WITCH:** Angitia; **ERGOT:** Corn Mother: Demeter.

Strega Liquore

Strega means "witch" and so this is "Witch Liqueur." According to legend, this Italian liqueur is based on an ancient witchcraft potion. Its label and bottle feature witches: young witches dance around the famous tree of Benevento on the label, and the bottle also features a portrait of a snake-haired witch with her owl and broom.

Strega is a steam-distilled liqueur crafted from approximately seventy herbs, barks, roots, and spices. Its yellow color is obtained from saffron, which has an ancient reputation as a magical aphrodisiac.

There are two versions of Strega's origins:

✴ *Strega is genuinely based on a witch's love potion. Benevento, where Strega has been produced since 1860, is an area long associated with witchcraft traditions.*

✴ *The recipe originally belonged to local monks. Giuseppe Alberti, a liquor distributor, coaxed the recipe from them, marketing it as* Alberti Medical Elixir. *It didn't sell. So Alberti renamed it* Strega; *it became extremely popular and remains among Italy's best-selling liqueurs.*

Some suggest that both versions are true: Alberti received the formula from the monks but *they* received it from the witches!

Whether Strega was developed by witches or not, the liqueur has been incorporated into modern witchcraft traditions. It is an appropriate and popular offering to the Italian witch-goddess, Diana. It may be offered as a libation or in a glass, however Diana has a predilection for flame offerings:

1. Pour a small quantity of Strega into a flame-proof bowl and set it alight.

2. Toast Diana with your own glass while keeping an eye on the burning flames.

Don't be too generous with the Strega. Be sure to add only a little to the bowl—no higher than a quarter-full. As Strega is highly flammable there is a tendency for flames to shoot up.

See **DIVINE WITCH:** Diana; **PLACES:** Benevento.

Witch's Brew

In some parts of England, "Witch's Brew" is a nickname for cider with alcohol content, more commonly known in the United States as "hard cider" and in Britain as "Scrumpy."

See Apples, page 503.

Witch's Butter

Not all witch's food is edible, nor is it all really "food." It was once a popular belief in Sweden that witches sent their cats out to steal food from neighbors, especially butter. According to legend, these witches' cats once ate so much butter that they vomited it up on their way home. Thus the yellow bile that cats sometimes cough up is called "witch's butter."

See **ANIMALS:** Cats; **DIVINE WITCH:** Freya.

Witch's Egg

Although the individual kitchen witch's egg might be fried, boiled or scrambled, "witch's egg" is a nickname for several types of fungus.

Some types of mushroom have what is called a "universal veil," a tissue covering that serves to protect the immature mushroom, which makes it look something like an egg. The universal veil is, ultimately, ruptured by the expanding mushroom and either disappears altogether or leaves behind "warts" on the mushroom cap. Among the mushrooms displaying a universal veil are many amanitas and stinkhorns.

The following fungi bear the nickname "witch's egg":

❋ Amanita muscaria, *also known as Fly Agaric, is deadly poisonous and not to be played with. It is intrinsically linked to shamanism and witchcraft and is a symbol of good luck. Further information on this witch's egg is found in* **BOTANICALS:** Amanita muscaria.

❋ Elaphomyces granulatus, *also known as Deer Truffle, has long been considered an aphrodisiac. It is a component of love potions and burned as incense. The deer truffle, technically a "false truffle," matures underground and is not considered an edible delicacy, but is beloved by deer and wild boar. There is debate regarding whether it is poisonous. This witch's egg also has a reputation as a galactagogue, a substance that stimulates women's milk supply.*

❋ Phallus impudicus, *also known as Stinkhorn, is a member of the mushroom family whose Latin name indicates that they closely resemble penises. The tip of* phallus impudicus *is covered with a foul-smelling, spore-laden slime, hence the name "stinkhorn." Some consider them delicacies.* Phallus impudicus *(and other stinkhorns) emerge from Earth from what appears to be an egg. This witch's egg has traditionally been used in aphrodisiacs and love spells, and to induce abortions.*

Witches' Salt

Witches' Salt is another name for what is usually called "black salt." Black salt is either black or speckled black and white, unlike standard white salt. Black salt is usually table salt (sodium chloride) with additions although some simply dye salt black. It may or may not be edible but is usually used as a magical powder intended to either cast or antidote a malevolent spell.

Additions to the salt may include any of the following:

❋ *Scrapings from the bottom and sides of cast-iron pans or cauldrons*

❋ *Black pepper*

❋ *Charcoal*

❋ *Powdered, dried snakeskin*

Yule Cakes

The Saturnalia was the old Roman festival corresponding to the Winter Solstice. Many of its traditions have been incorporated into modern Christmas practices including giving gifts to children. The star of the Saturnalia, the Roman god Saturn, was a white-bearded old gentleman who bears a resemblance to the modern Santa Claus. Cakes were a part of Saturnalia rituals, and are now an important component of Christmas or Yule. Traditional Yule cakes include the following.

Bûche de Noël

Bûche de Noël means Christmas or Yule log in French. The Yule log, traditionally burned at Christmas time, derives from European Pagan traditions. Trees were sacred, the subject of the earliest spiritual traditions, especially those associated with goddesses like Frigga and Diana. In Gaul (ancient France) Diana was adored in the form of an oak log.

The bûche or log is generally made of a sheet of *Génoise* cake pasty, spread with various creams, usually a butter cream but maple cream has also recently become popular and extends the tree metaphor. This is an extremely sophisticated concoction: the cake is rolled into the shape of a log and decorated using a pastry bag with fluted nozzle and filled with some type of butter cream, often chocolate or coffee. *Bûche de Noël* are often beautiful, elaborately decorated cakes, ornamented with woodland motifs such as candied leaves.

Speculaas Poppen

The Dutch Yule cakes known as *Speculaas Poppen* ("spice cakes") were the focus of intense seventeenth- and eighteenth-century ecclesiastical opposition to the incorporation of Pagan practices into Christmas festivities.

Once upon a time, cakes and cookies baked in appropriate animal or human form replaced or substituted for Northern European Pagan blood sacrifices. Special wooden molds were used to create these cakes. These molds were preserved, used year after year and eventually developed an amuletic aura. Mold designs (and thus cake designs) included animals, horned spirits, and images of female and male shamans.

The tradition of creating speculaas poppen pre-dates Christianity, and the tradition was retained post-Christianity. Eventually these cakes were incorporated into Dutch Christmas traditions, however many explicitly Pagan motifs and designs remained. First Roman Catholic, then Protestant authorities passed ordinances forbidding the baking, selling, and eating of these cakes. The Church ordered more explicitly Pagan molds to be destroyed. The molds were banned; many were confiscated and burned.

> These cakes and cake molds also exist in German lands. Their German name is *lebkuchen*, with *leb* originally deriving from the Latin *libitum* or "offering."

Speculaas poppen cakes did not disappear: they remain popular today. Bakers merely adjusted the molds, favoring more neutral imagery or more discreet motifs although many are still very beautiful. Old Frisian cookie molds remain prized collectors' items. Many modern speculaas poppen, especially less expensive ones, simply favor geometric "cookie shapes" or are formed into people, similar to gingerbread cookies. More elaborate speculaas poppen are still made with old-fashioned carved wooden molds.

> Another popular Dutch Christmas tradition is that of offering gifts of chocolate initials. This derives from the Pagan tradition of small cakes shaped into the form of runes.

If an angry witch came to call, what would you offer her as refreshment? After all hungry, cranky witches are dangerous witches, liable to cast mean, destructive spells. This Italian dish is called The Witch's Supper and reputedly satisfies, pacifies, and pleases even the fussiest witch. Supposedly serving this dish to a witch (or perhaps anyone) disarms her, making her wish to do good things for you, not harm.

Luckily it is an extremely simple, quick, inexpensive (even cheap) dish to prepare featuring garlic (Hecate's favorite) and some magical beans—*Cicer arietinum*—currently the most widely consumed legume on Earth, known as garbanzo beans in Spanish-speaking countries, chickpeas in English and *cecci* in Italian.

Witch's supper

Two tablespoons of extra virgin olive oil
Peeled fresh garlic, finely chopped
One can of chickpeas
Chopped fresh mint
Salt and freshly ground black pepper to taste

1. Warm the olive oil in a cast-iron pan.
2. Carefully sauté the garlic in the olive oil.
3. When the garlic begins to brown, add the chickpeas to the pan (but not the liquid from the can*).
4. Add the chopped mint and sauté for fifteen minutes.
5. Season to taste with salt, pepper, and extra mint if desired.
6. Serve on pasta or on toast.

* If the mixture is too dry or if you prefer a saucier recipe add a little of the liquid.

※ ※ ※

the Hag

f hould you be flattered or insulted if someone calls you a witch? It all depends on how "witch" is defined. On the other hand, there's nothing ambiguous about being called an *"old hag."* It's clearly *not* intended as a compliment. Or is it?

In modern usage, hags are haggard, unattractive, harsh, ragged, often unhinged, and, especially, *old*. By definition, hags are old and they are female. In cultures that place inestimable value on youth, where female beauty and worth is often predicated on youthfulness, hags are ominous and scarily unattractive.

Dictionary definitions of "hag" include: *"female demon," "ugly, frightening spirit," "hobgoblin,"* and *"old woman"*—especially an *"ugly, slatternly evil-looking old woman."* Last but very much not least, among the dictionary definitions of hag is *"witch."*

Whether the word "witch" is solely identified with women depends on interpretation. Some are convinced that "witch" refers exclusively to female practitioners; others perceive "witch" as gender neutral and use it to indicate both men and women.

Hag, on the other hand, is intrinsically linked to the female gender. Men can certainly be old, harsh, ragged, and decrepit but they are *never*

hags. By definition, hags are women. Hag is much harsher than any equivalent term for men, such as *old codger*.

> If the same word applies to old women and witches, does this imply that, by definition, old women are witches? Historically, some have believed so.

Hags are not just any old women or witches but are envisioned as wild, volatile, ill tempered, and nasty. Hags flaunt common rules of politeness or civility, or perhaps don't consider that those rules apply to them.

Sweet, cuddly, wealthy, charming old ladies are never hags. Old grannies knit sweaters and bake cookies; hags mutter imprecations and deliver curses. It is not chronological age alone that defines the hag: they are *aged* women, those who bear the unmistakable signs of having been buffeted and scarred by life. Hags are visualized as dried-out *husks*, no longer juicy, pliant or fertile.

During the witch-hunt era, older women corresponding to this stereotype of the hag, whether or not they possessed *any* knowledge of magic or Paganism, were incredibly vulnerable to charges of witchcraft. Hags were perceived and feared as witches. So, on the one hand, hags would appear to be marginal people; on the other, witches are feared or revered as people with power and secret knowledge. Hags are witches, therefore hags, too, have their power.

> While not all hag-spirits look old, or at least not all the time, they are literally, genuinely *old*: hags rank among the most primordial, ancient spirits. Clichéd sayings describe extended longevity as being *"as old as the hills"* or *"as old as the rocks."* Significantly, many hags are mountain-trolls and rock-goddesses.

In Northern Europe, hags are not just old women or aged witches, they are also a type of female spirit: fierce, haggard, and often grotesque, legends describe hags as vicious, cannibal child-killers. Beneath this horror story folklore, however, vestigial evidence of powerful, grand, goddesses survives. Obscure, fragmentary myths featuring these hag-spirits offer their evidence: hags create and transform Earth's very landscape. And of course, why wouldn't displaced goddesses be hostile?

There are thus three possible kinds of hags:

❋ *A type of old woman*

❋ *A type of witch*

❋ *A type of female divinity*

The very word that names these spirits—*Hag*—is intrinsically tied to the very concept of witchcraft:

Both the English word *hag* (old woman, witch) and the German word *hexe* (witch) derive from *hae* meaning "hedgerow." The German and English words are inherently linked: German-English dictionaries suggest that English definitions of *hexe* include *"witch," "sybil," "prophetess,"* and *"hag."* Once upon a time, however, *hag* and *hexe* merely indicated "Lady of the Hedge."

"Hedge" derives from the Old English *haga*, meaning a fence or boundary formed from a dense row of bushes or low trees. Hedge, according to the dictionary, also indicates a means of protection or defense (as against financial loss—"hedging your bets").

What connects a natural phenomenon like hedges to words like "hag" or "hexe"?

Primal hedges weren't the neatly pruned shrubbery of modern suburbia: today, wilderness is endangered. Once upon a time, long ago, however, it was the other way around. Europe was covered by dense forest from the British Isles to Russia. Settlements were created by clearing away bits of the forest. In order to get to another settlement, one had to travel through the forest. The forest was all encompassing and all surrounding. Where it was cleared, a "hedge" developed. This hedge formed the threshold between wilderness and settlement, wild and tame, spirit and human.

> Hedgerows, according to modern dictionary definitions, are rows of trees or shrubbery enclosing or separating fields. Hedgerows create divisions. Where there are divisions, there are thresholds. Where there are thresholds, spirits hover. (See **PLACES:** Threshold.)

> Hedges may be understood as untamed nature; witches may be understood as untamed women.

Thresholds divide realms but they also serve as bridges between realms. Among the old Germanic synonyms for witch are "hedge-rider" and "hedge-sitter." *Hagezusse*, an Old High German word indicating "wise woman," is believed to have evolved over time into *hexe* or witch.

✷ Haegtessa, *from which the English "hag" derives, is the Anglo-Saxon equivalent of* Hagezusse

✷ Hagedisse, *meaning "witch" or "wise woman," is the Old Dutch equivalent;* hagedisse *also indicates a lizard, an animal traditionally associated with shamanism*

✷ *Linguists consider the archaic Norse word* tunritha, *"fence rider" or "witch," to be cognate as well.*

These Ladies of the Hedge, eventually known as hexen or hags, are those women who spent their time in the hedge, gaining spiritual knowledge and cultivating shamanic relationships. "Riding" on the hedge indicates that they are able to navigate the spiritual forces of the hedge; hexen or hags mediate between the realms of humans and spirits.

The ancient Norse word indicating "hedge" was also used to indicate "sacred grove." "Hags" or "hexen" thus might also be translated as "Women of the Grove": the Old Testament repeatedly complains of women who journey to sacred groves to engage in Pagan ritual.

Sacred groves are identified with the most ancient of Pagan traditions—veneration of sacred trees. (See **BOTANICALS:** Trees.) Sacred groves were intrinsic to indigenous Northern spiritual traditions. Many Celtic and Nordic deities preferred natural shrines to architectural ones. Groves served as temples and sacred precincts. When Christian missionaries first arrived in Northern Europe, their first actions typically included cutting down sacred trees and groves.

Tree-centered spirituality is relatively universal; hags, or the women who tend the grove, may be defined as "Priestesses of the Grove."

Associations of the etymological roots of *hag* with *holiness* are widespread and may originally derive from ancient non-Indo-European sources. Some believe the root word derives from or is related to the Egyptian *heka*, indicating sacred magic power. Other words possibly related to *hedge*, *hag*, and *hexe* include:

✷ Hagne *or "holy one" was among the titles of Cretan goddesses*

✷ Hagnos, *a Greek noun, indicates a hallowed, holy or sacred place or an undefiled person*

* Hagnidzo, *a Greek verb, indicates "to spiritually clean or purify"*

* Hagia Sophia, *"Holy Wisdom," names the sacred shrine in Istanbul*

* Hagiology *is the study of holiness or sacred subjects*

* Hagiography *technically indicates biographies of saints or blessed people*

Hagos, a Greek word deriving from the same roots, has dual meanings: it refers to religious awe or to a holy being but also indicates a curse signifying a "polluted person," "defiled place" or "abomination."

Among other archaic Norse words related to hag is *haggen*, meaning "to chop into pieces." Etymologists believe this word, related to words with sacred associations, described the treatment of sacrificial victims, whether human, animal or grain. (See **ERGOT:** Corn Mother.) It is also reminiscent of shamanic descriptions of spiritual initiations—often including metaphoric experiences of being chopped up. (See **FAIRY-TALE WITCHES.**) (*Haggen* also relates to the French *hachette*, which describes a culinary chopping technique, and the English *hash*, a dish often made from chopped meat.)

Hags were not conceived as being intrinsically evil, or at least not until advanced age became suspect. During the transition from Paganism to Christianity in Northern Europe, tribal elders were often stubborn hold-outs and leaders of organized resistance: where *elder* once held positive connotations, it became disparaged and discredited, as in *"old-fashioned old-wives' tales."*

Hags were powerful, influential, useful members of society. Hags were teachers, midwives, mediums, diviners, and healers. In mythology, hag-goddesses are guardians of the cauldron of birth, death, and rebirth and keepers of the Water of Life.

Although in what is now an intensely youth-centered world this can be difficult to envision, the face of authority was once that of an old lady: the face of the sacred was epitomized by fierce, wise old women.

Hag-spirits are sometimes understood as the personification of winter. In a reversal of the normal aging process, as the season turns to spring, hags become youthful and beautiful. This is reflected in folktales where the old hag is revealed really to be a stunningly beautiful woman: the two are different faces of one being.

Women are born, wax fertile, then wane. They die and disappear like the Dark Moon phase of the lunar cycle women were so identified with. But, if one believes in reincarnation, they reappear so that the cycle may continue. Each of the four phases (death was perceived as a life-stage rather than termination) possessed specific powers; the phases exist in continuum, no phase exists without the others.

The hag corresponded to the final stage of female existence. Many serve as psychopomps (those spirits who accompany and guide souls of the dead) or are otherwise associated with death or funeral rites. Once the notion of reincarnation disappears, however, then this sacred cycle no longer exists. If women are only valued for fertility, then there is no place in the pantheon for the sacred crone.

> Many goddesses not normally classified as hags sometimes temporarily manifest as one including Cerridwen, Demeter, Hecate, Hera, Isis, Lilith, and Maeve particularly when they are grieving, angry, seek justice or anonymity. Many divine witches possess a hag aspect. Even Oshun, the very personification of beauty, takes on hag-like characteristics in her guise as the swamp-witch, Oshun Ibu Kole.

By the Christian Era, hags were defined as ugly, scary, wicked female demons and monsters. Their tremendous power was retained but it was now perceived as evil not holy. Ambivalence to women's power, specifically that of older women, is reflected in the demonization and fear of hags.

Not necessarily the most sociable spirits to begin with, hag-goddesses, many of whom were mountain or cave spirits, retreated to remote areas. They did not fade away; instead their behavior became more volatile. Forgotten, disrespected but powerful goddesses evolved into angry, unfriendly goddesses.

Information regarding these spirits is sketchy, vague, obscure, and riddled with holes. Many use different names when manifesting in different forms or when demonstrating different aspects. Many don't use names but have titles instead; some of these titles are identical or virtually so. It is often impossible to definitively determine whether one is discussing distinct, independent deities or just different facets or legends of the same one.

❋ Hag *is the common British term*

❋ Cailleach *and* Carlin *(also spelled* Carline*) refers to the same concept in Celtic regions*

❋ *The* Jotuns *or Giants of Norse mythology are also identified with hag-spirits. Various other terms used to express the same concept include* troll-hag *and* ogress.

Renowned sacred hags and terms related to hags are explored on the following pages.

Angerboda

Also known as Angrboda, Aurboda.

This mysterious many-named, shape-shifting spirit manifests as a crow, a beautiful, golden goddess and a fierce iron hag. The name "Angerboda" (related to "foreboding") refers to her manifestation as a hag. It is the form that she prefers.

> Angerboda is also called "Hag of the Iron Wood" and "Hag of the East Winds." In folkloric retellings of Norse mythology, Angerboda is often called a "wicked witch." *Iron Wood* may refer to oak groves.

Modern culture so intensely prizes physical beauty that it may be surprising that Angerboda chooses to be a hag. However, in this manifestation she is the fierce, fearless ruler of her domain, whereas an early manifestation as a young, golden witch, Gulveig left her vulnerable to attempted murder.

> *Gulveig* means "power of gold." Gulveig is described as glistening like gold; she initially traveled to the Aesir gods seeking gold. Having been burned in the Aesir's forge three times, however, Gulveig emerged as Angerboda, the embodiment of the power of iron, the most magically powerful metal of all. (See **MAGICAL PROFESSIONS**: Metalworkers.)

Angerboda rules the Iron Wood. It is her home territory, where she raised her children. She prefers not to leave, perhaps recollecting past negative travel experiences. However intrepid people requiring her services may visit her, although she is fierce and not always welcoming.

Angerboda's children include Hella, Queen of Death, the Midgard Serpent, the Fenris Wolf and the wolves responsible for solar and lunar eclipses. Other sons are identified as werewolves. She is the grandmother of trolls.

Angerboda is a weather deity: in her guise as the Hag of the East Winds, her songs drive ships right into storms.

See also Hyrrokkin, Thokk; **ANIMALS**: Corvids, Wolves and Werewolves; **DICTIONARY**: Aesir, Trollkvinna; **DIVINE WITCH**: Angerboda, Hella; **FAIRIES**: Nature-spirit Fairies: Trolls.

Baba Yaga

Baba Yaga, the sacred (or demonic, depending upon perception) Russian forest witch might as well be a prototype for the Hag archetype: she is ancient and haggard, thin but voracious, solitary and all knowing. She is fierce, dangerous, unfriendly, and distinctly not interested in pleasing others. Her physical appearance inspires fear and is often described as grotesque. (She has huge iron teeth and sometimes sports protruding boars' tusks.) Like many other hags, she is allegedly a cannibal.

Baba Yaga is a death goddess: she wears a necklace of human skulls and lives in a bone house. Her myths place tremendous emphasis on her oven and cooking pots.

> Just as *hag* indicates both "witch" and "old woman," so the title *Baba* indicates "witch," but is also an affectionate (or pejorative) term for "grandmother."

Baba Yaga's kinship with Nordic hags serves as a reminder that *Russia* derives from the *Rus*, a tribe of invading Vikings whose traditions became intermingled with those of the people they conquered. More information about this ubiquitous, primordial witch is found in **DIVINE WITCH**: Baba Yaga; **ERGOT**: Corn Mother: Baba Yaga; **FAIRY-TALE WITCHES**: Russian Fairy-Tales. See also **DICTIONARY**: Baba.

Beltane Carline

Also known as the Beltane Hag.

Beltane Carline literally means *"Beltane Hag"* or *"Beltane Old Woman"* and is the person who, during Beltane rituals, received the blackened bit of Beltane Cake. *Carline* derives from Old Norse roots and indicates a woman, especially an old one and is a regional synonym for hag.

> Beltane is the ancient Celtic festival corresponding to May Eve and Walpurgis Night. See **CALENDAR:** Beltane for further details.

Special cakes were traditionally part of Beltane rituals in the Scottish Highlands. One single piece, the "black bit," was blackened with charcoal. Cakes were divided into portions, then randomly distributed or drawn by lot. The cake was distributed and eaten in company so there was no hiding or masking who had received the black bit. It was immediately apparent to all. That person automatically became the Beltane Carline with a role in the rituals that followed.

Anthropologists believe that once upon a time, similar to Shirley Jackson's classic 1948 short story *The Lottery*, the Beltane Carline involved genuine human sacrifice determined via lottery. Within historic memory, however, ritual symbolic miming of sacrifice has sufficed. Rituals include the following:

* *The Beltane Carline runs through the Beltane bonfires three times or jumps over them three times*

* *Sometimes a charade is made of tossing the Beltane Carline into the bonfires, often quite roughly.*

* *Sometimes the charade involves one group of men pretending to throw the Beltane Carline into the bonfires, while another group makes a great show of rescuing her. These attempts at sacrifice versus rescue might go back and forth several times.*

> Not all sacrificial pantomiming involved bonfires: in some communities, the Beltane Carline was laid flat on the ground. A show was made of drawing and quartering her before the crowd pelted the prone figure with broken eggshells.

Once the charade with the fire is over, the Beltane Carline was expected to play dead. For one full year until the following Beltane, when someone else assumed the role, the entire community treated and spoke of the Beltane Carline as if that person was dead. This was an intensive experience as this ritual typically occurred in small, often isolated, rural communities. For one year, you existed but were dead to the entire community.

In historic times, the part of the Beltane Carline has virtually always been played by a young man. Once upon a time, however, presumably the title *Beltane Carline* was accurate and so named an old woman. She may have personified the death of the Frost Queen that corresponded with the crowning of the May Queen. Another theory is that the Beltane Carline was a sacrificial offering to the deity known as the Carlin. Whether the sacrificial ritual was or wasn't always a charade is now unknown.

See also Cailleach Bheur, Carlin; **ANIMALS:** Chickens; **CALENDAR:** Beltane, Walpurgis; **FOOD AND DRINK:** Beltane Cake.

Black Annis

Also known as Black Agnes, Black Anna, Cat Anna, Gentle Annie.

Black Annis, Hag of the Dane Hills near Leicester, England, most frequently manifests as a blue-faced crone with long claws and yellow fangs but also as a cat demon.

Black Annis lives in a cave now known as Black Annis' Bower that she personally clawed out from the rocks. Some believe her cave marks an Iron Age shrine and that Black Annis, now a dread bogie-woman, was once a venerated goddess. Once upon a time, Black Annis liked to sit and observe her territory from within a giant oak near her cave, vestige of the vast forest that once covered this region. The oak was felled, however, and so she's now apparently moved permanently into the cave.

Some perceive that hidden behind Black Annis' mask is either of the ancient Celtic goddesses Anu or Danaan, although others perceive her as a distinct, independent spirit. See **FAIRIES**: Nature-spirit Fairies: Sidhe.

Black Annis allegedly eats children who stray into the Dane Hills after dark, or at least so their mothers have traditionally warned them. She skins then eats her victims, scattering the bones around the hills and hanging the skins from trees to dry. Allegedly, when she is hungry, Black Annis snatches lambs from pastures and climbs through windows to seize babies from inside houses—perhaps she is just blamed for missing children and livestock. Sometimes Black Annis is called Gentle Annie, although

this is generally perceived as an attempt at appeasement and supplication.

Also known as Cat Anna, Black Annis has powerful associations with cats, sometimes manifesting as a huge black forest cat. Until the eighteenth century a mock rabbit hunt was held annually, although "mock cat hunt" might be more accurate: a dead cat soaked in aniseed was dragged from Black Annis' Bower, her cave home, through Leicester's streets to the town mayor's door. Among aniseed's traditional magical uses are propitiation of spirits and protection against malevolent magic. Exactly what connection exists between Cat Anna and aniseed if any beyond the similarities of their names is now unknown.

Grendel, the monster in *Beowulf,* has a mother who is even fiercer and more powerful than he. She is identified as a *ketta* or cat spirit. Some perceive a resemblance between her and Cat Anna.

See **ANIMALS**: Cats; **FAIRIES**: Fairy Cats.

Caillagh Ny Gueshag / Caillagh Ny Groamach

Caillagh is the Manx variation of the Gaelic word *Cailleach* (see next section). Exactly where she originated is unclear but according to legend, Caillagh Ny Gueshag, the "Old Woman of Spells," was thrown into the Irish Sea for practicing witchcraft. On Imbolc, she was cast ashore on Manx shores and found herself transformed into Caillagh Ny Groamach, the "Old Women of Gloom."

She is a weather spirit. When she first landed on the Isle of Man, she gathered sticks to build a fire to dry and warm herself. It turned out to be a *very* wet spring: she didn't have enough sticks to stay warm for the whole season. (Apparently Caillagh Ny Groamach can *only* gather sticks on Imbolc.)

Since then, every year she attempts to gather enough sticks for the spring season. In a precursor to Hedgehog Day or Groundhog Day, Caillagh Ny Groamach's success determines the rest of the season's weather:

✱ *If Imbolc is fair, she'll gather enough sticks and so won't care if it rains all spring.*

✱ *If Imbolc is wet, she can't go out gathering and thus must ensure a dry season.*

See **CALENDAR:** Imbolc.

Cailleach

Cailleach (pronounced "coy-luk") is the Gaelic word corresponding to *Hag*. Cailleach literally means "old woman" but is usually translated into English as "hag," although in modern Gaelic dictionaries, Cailleach is also defined as "witch."

The Cailleach, like the hag, is by definition female but has various manifestations:

✱ *In Scottish and Irish folklore and mythology, Cailleach is a title for spirits corresponding to the archetype of the sacred hag.*

✱ *Cailleach may indicate an old woman and/or witch.*

✱ *Cailleach is also used to indicate a nun. This association is complex: nuns, like most hag-spirits, are celibate. Women whose lives do not revolve around men or children, nuns were perceived as holy or spiritually powerful women. Some believe that attempts were made to transfer the sacred connotations of the Pagan Cailleach to Christian holy women. In many communities, nuns (and priests) were traditionally respected but also feared, believed to possess secret magical knowledge similar to how many envisioned hags. Many Cailleach are described as veiled as, until recently, were nuns; taking vows as a nun was once described as "taking the veil." Some scholars believe the veil is the essential link between nuns and the Cailleach.*

✱ *Cailleach names the last sheaf of grain from the harvest. The Corn Mother is often believed incarnate in that last sheaf; many Corn Mothers also correspond to the archetype of the sacred hag. The Corn Mother is a hag at the harvest but emerges as a beautiful, fertile young bride in spring. (See **ERGOT:** Corn Mother.)*

How sacred and influential was the Cailleach? Caledonia, the ancient name for Scotland, may derive from Cailleach. Some historians translate Caledonia as "the Old Woman's country" or "the Hag's territory." In many myths, the Cailleach actually creates and shapes the very landscape. (An alternative theory proposes that Caledonia actually means "Hill of the Hazel Tree.")

In Scottish mythology, hags are the mothers of giants, corresponding to Norse *Jotuns* or Troll-Hags. Giants are mountain gods or personified spirits of mountains; mountains are frequently hags' sacred territory. Scottish hags are also weather witches: thundercloud hags who throw fireballs (lightning) or hailstones when angered.

Cailleach is a title ("*Old Woman*"), not a name. No complete, coherent mythology of the Cailleach exists; it is next to impossible to determine whether the various spirits bearing this title are identical or indistinct—whether there are one, many or several Cailleach. Spirits entitled Cailleach populate Scotland and Ireland. The Manx version is *Caillagh*.

> The Romans encountered the Cailleach in Britain and equated her with Juno.

Folklore sometimes describes *the* Cailleach. She is identified as a witch and as the primal mother, the Mother of All Existence. She is described as an old hag with bear's teeth and boar's tusks.

See also Cailleach Bhéara, Cailleach Bheur, Cailleach Mor, Hag Rune; **ANIMALS:** Bears, Pigs; **CALENDAR:** Lupercalia.

Cailleach Bhéara

Bhéara, also spelled Beara and Beare, is a region along the borders of Ireland's Counties Cork and Kerry.

There may be one, two or more Cailleach Bhéara. Her primary territory is southwest Ireland, where she is credited with shaping mountains and forming rivers, but she is also known throughout Ireland and the Scottish Highlands. Cairns are piles of stones fallen from her apron. Various specific geographical formations are identified with Cailleach Bhéara:

❈ *A cairn on top of a hill close to Slieve Gullion in County Armagh is called* Cailleach Bhéara's Chair. *Cailleach Bhéara allegedly now sleeps beneath it.*

❈ *Cailleach Bhéara is associated with the Beare Peninsula, near Cork, allegedly forming the peninsula herself. She was carrying stones in her apron when her apron strings broke: the stones fell out and formed the land.*

❈ *In Ireland's Dingle Peninsula numerous geographical formations are named in her honor.*

Cailleach Bhéara is a Corn Mother: she taught people the secrets of harvesting grain. She remains a prolific, rapid harvester of crops and enjoys challenging people to reaping contests they can never win.

She manifests as a rabbit in the grain fields. The person who reaps the last sheaf of grain in her territory is said to "*drive out the hare.*" Historians often point out that Ireland has no indigenous snakes, and so they could not have been banished by St Patrick. However according to ancient legends, Cailleach Bhéara sometimes manifests as a snake, and so perhaps *she* was what the saint banished.

According to a fourteenth-century manuscript, Cailleach Bhéara is also known as Búi. As Búi, she is one of the two wives of the Irish solar deity Lugh. Búi means "yellow" and may refer to the sun, or to the smith's fires.

Cailleach Bhéara's two sisters are the Cailleach Bolus and the Cailleach Corca Duibhne (see pages 538–9). Together they form a holy trinity or a triad of three queens.

See **ANIMALS:** Rabbits, Snakes; **CALENDAR:** Lughnasa; **ERGOT:** Corn Mother; **MAGICAL PROFESSIONS:** Metalworkers.

Cailleach Bheur

Also known as Cally Berry.

Cailleach Bheur, the Blue Hag of Winter, is a

weather spirit from the Scottish Highlands, traditionally described as a blue-faced hag wearing a plaid and carrying a heavy mallet. She wears a ripped apron filled with hailstones with which she blights crops. Ocean whirlpools serve as her washtubs and cauldrons.

Unlike some hags, Cailleach Bheur clearly retains her goddess qualities. She is the guardian spirit of cattle, boar, deer, goats, wolves, highland streams, and wells. Wild deer were once considered to be the equivalent of her cattle. They belong to her: she herds and protects them. Hunting them was the equivalent of poaching; in essence the Highlands are the Cailleach Bheur's personal animal reserve and she is the sacred warden. Her sacred plants include gorse and holly.

Cailleach Bheur is a Frost Queen. From Samhain to Beltane she is the personification of winter. She ushers in winter by striking the ground with her mallet to harden it. When she washes her clothes in her washtubs (ocean whirlpools) Cailleach Bheur raises winter storms.

From Samhain to Beltane, the dark half of the Celtic year, Cailleach Bheur dwells in a cave beneath the mountain Ben Nevis, where she keeps the Summer Maiden captive and has fun tormenting her. On Imbolc, one of Cailleach Bheur's kind sons (she has two) rescues the Summer Maiden and sets her free. Cailleach Bheur then unleashes the Wolf Storms to prevent and forestall the arrival of summer.

At Beltane, Cailleach Bheur transforms from the Blue Hag into a beautiful woman, a sea snake or a cat. Some years, however, Cailleach Bheur hibernates in the form of a standing stone until the arrival of Samhain when her cycle begins again.

When she's annoyed, Cailleach Bheur blights the harvest. One touch of her magic staff knocks all the leaves off the trees. In the spring she throws this staff under a holly bush, retrieving it at Samhain.

Cailleach Bheur's throne is at the summit of the hill named in her honor at Kilberry, Argyll. *Noblesse oblige*: she grants wishes to those who come to petition her there. Make a wish as you throw a stone as an offering onto the seat. Address her politely but do not call her by her name as it angers her.

There are also legends about what seems to be a different Cailleach Bheur. This one lived on the shores of Loch Ba on the Isle of Mull in Scotland's Inner Hebrides where, every hundred years or so, she immersed herself in the waters of the lake to renew her immortality. One year she waited until it was too late and died.

Another legend may be a variation of that one or may describe yet another Blue Hag. This Cailleach Bheur had charge of a well of flowing water on the summit of Ben Cruachan in Argyll. Every sundown it was her responsibility to cap the well with a large flat stone and then, in the morning, to roll away the stone, releasing the waters.

Once, absolutely exhausted from driving her deer and goats across the mountains, she fell asleep beside the well without capping it. The water flowed all night, creating Loch Awe but drowning people and animals in the process. When Cailleach Bheur awoke it was too late: she was so ashamed and horrified that she turned into a standing stone.

See **ANIMALS:** Cats, Goats, Snakes; **CALENDAR:** Beltane, Imbolc, Samhain.

Cailleach Bolus

Cailleach Bolus is one of Cailleach Bhéara's two sisters. She is associated with ancient standing stones, stone rings, menhirs, and dolmens. She manifests as an aged woman with a swollen belly and sometimes has antlers on her head.

See also Cailleach Bhéara, Cailleach Corca Duibhne; **HORNED ONE**.

See Cailleach Bhéara; **ANIMALS:** Snakes; **TOOLS:** Cauldron.

Cailleach Corca Duibhne

Cailleach Corca Duibhne, one of Cailleach Bhéara's sisters, is the Hag of the Black Cauldron. Like Cailleach Bhéara, her primary territory is southwestern Ireland.

She is also called the Black Veiled One; this allegedly refers to the long black hair that veils her face. According to myth, it was Cailleach Corca Duibhne's responsibility to tend the primordial Cauldron of Creation, containing the sacred Water of Life. Seven strands of her hair fell into the cauldron where they transformed into seven great snakes or dragons. When Cailleach Corca Duibhne left the cauldron briefly unattended, the snakes slithered out, in the process overturning the pot and allowing some of the Water of Life to spill.

The famished snakes went on a rampage, gnawing away huge portions of Earth. Eventually through spiritual intercession, the snakes were stopped and banished to the center of the Earth but the damage couldn't be undone. The parts gnawed away had filled with the Water of Life, becoming Earth's great rivers.

The myth describes the snakes as Cailleach Corca Duibhne's children: she was granted seven periods of youth and beauty as compensation for their loss, even though their rampage was technically her fault—had she been watching the cauldron, the snakes, her transformed hair, would not have escaped. Like her sister Cailleach Bhéara, Cailleach Corca Duibhne eventually married seven husbands, outliving them all. She fostered fifty children, teaching them the deepest, most primal secrets of the Universe. These children founded Earth's great nations.

Cailleach Mor

Her name literally indicates Great Hag but is also translated as "the large, old wife"—as in "old wives' tales." Cailleach Mor sends the dread south-westerly gales. She is also the keeper of deer, considered "fairy cattle" in Celtic regions. Some consider Cailleach Mor another name for Cailleach Bhéara (see page 537).

Cailleach Oidhche

This Scottish folk name for owl literally means "night hag" or "old woman of the night." Among the most ancient Neolithic statuettes are those depicting sacred owl goddesses. Ancient "Eye Goddesses" are also sometimes identified as owls. (These stark images emphasize large, staring, owl-like eyes and the exclusively female parts of the human anatomy.)

Owls are associated with death and rebirth. Hag-goddesses sometimes serve as psychopomps, those spirits who escort and guide dead souls to their next destination. In this role, hags sometimes manifest as owls.

See **ANIMALS:** Owls; **DICTIONARY:** Psychopomp.

Cailleach Uragaig

According to legend, this Frost Goddess from the Isle of Colonsay in Scotland keeps a young woman prisoner. When the young woman escapes in spring, Cailleach Uragaig transforms into the gray headlands above the sea until Samhain, when she captures that young woman again.

See also Beltane Carline, Cailleach Bheur; **CALENDAR:** Walpurgis.

Carlin

This Scottish word literally indicates "old woman" or "hag" but may have once been the name or title for the presiding spirit of Samhain, the Celtic festival corresponding with November Eve or Halloween. Some perceive this as the title for the witch-goddess Nicnevin in her Hag aspect.

The ancient Celtic calendar was divided into two halves, light and dark. Samhain marks the beginning of the dark half of the year, which ended six months later at Beltane. The Carlin, an aged Frost Queen, ruled this part of the year until she was superceded in the spring by the beautiful May Queen or Beltane Bride.

Traditionally, displaying the last reaped sheaf of grain (the *Carlin* or *Cailleach*) on Samhain indicated that the appropriate rituals had been followed. Displaying this sheaf kept a household safe from malicious spirits who might be out and about on that night.

See Beltane Carline, Gyre Carlin; **CALENDAR:** Beltane, Halloween, Samhain, Walpurgis; **DIVINE WITCH:** Befana, Mana, Nicnevin.

Demeter

Demeter, Greek goddess of fertility and cultivation, is usually described as a mature, beautiful woman whose golden hair resembles fields of ripe wheat, but when her beloved daughter Persephone was kidnapped, Demeter shed her beauty like a snake sheds its skin, transforming into a hag. In an instant, she aged, becoming gray, wrinkled, and bent over. The light disappeared from her eyes. She was emotionally bereft, burning with grief, rage, and a passionate desire for justice.

As Demeter transformed, she withdrew fertility from Earth: crops failed, people began to starve. In her hag aspect, however, the normally benevolent Demeter doesn't care: her own grief overwhelms her to the exclusion of anyone else's. To some extent, Demeter in her grieving stage is the prototype for the Hag.

> Like so many other hag-goddesses, Demeter's sacred animals are pigs and snakes. Like Demeter, many hags are Corn Mothers.

Her saga is often interpreted (as with so many other hags') as an allegory for the year's seasons. Demeter's hag phase corresponds with winter while her transformation back into a bountiful goddess with Persephone's annual return corresponds to spring. (Sometimes Persephone is understood as corresponding to spring, while Demeter symbolizes winter.) However, this tends to gloss over the emotional and spiritual aspects of her saga: Demeter doesn't just age and become an average old woman; she transforms into the epitome of a Hag specifically because of her intense grief, rage, and loss.

Demeter's saga, which ultimately became the central focus of the Eleusinian Mysteries, also recounts her healing process and recovery: Demeter rages and grieves, starving Earth and herself, until an aged (a crone but not a hag) female servant, Baubo, finally draws an involuntary laugh from Demeter.

Baubo accomplishes this, where others failed, through the mysterious act of *ana-suromai*, the name given the ritual act of exposing the vagina. This act, which also features in Egyptian mythology, is believed to represent the eternal life force, the unbeatable power of the Great Mother. The significance in Demeter's situation is that the ritual act is performed by an old woman for whom literal fertility is not possible. From the moment of her reviving laugh, according to the saga, Demeter channels her private grief into spiritual leadership.

Further information regarding ana-suromai and Demeter's saga may be found in Winifred Milius Lubell's *The Metamorphosis of Baubo: Myths of Women's Sexual Energy* (Vanderbilt University Press, 1994).

See also Beltane Carline, Skadi; **ANIMALS:** Pigs, Snakes; **DIVINE WITCH:** Proserpina; **ERGOT:** Corn Mother: Demeter.

The Devil's Grandmother

Powerful goddesses frequently had male consorts. Sometimes the consort is a horned male spirit, such as Diana and Virbius. Sometimes the goddess is envisioned as a beautiful, mature woman with a significantly younger male consort whom she initiates and tutors and, sometimes, ultimately kills. The goddess is eternal; her youthful consort can be replaced. Such myths are told of Kybele and Attis, Aphrodite and Adonis, Inanna-Ishtar and Tammuz. The story of Artemis and Actaeon, the hunter who is transformed into a deer and killed by his hunting hounds, may actually incorporate both these motifs.

Diana lived with Virbius, a horned stag spirit, in the sacred grove of Nemi, near Rome. He is clearly identified as *her* consort; he is subordinate to her. This image of the witch-goddess living in the forest with a horned man eventually emerged as the Christian prototype for the witch and devil, respectively—with one extremely significant difference. In the Christian version, the male devil is dominant; the female witches adore him. This is the opposite of the original Pagan perspective. The devil allegedly initiates and tutors women.

The Christian devil was popularly envisioned as a horned spirit, however, people may have remembered that once upon a time, the female half of this dyad was dominant and she did the initiating and tutoring. Throughout Russia, Northern, and Central Europe, the Devil's Grandmother emerged as a formidable force: she taught him everything he knows. Allegedly she retained some secrets and still knows a trick or two more than he does.

No longer the goddess in the form of a beautiful woman in her prime, the devil's grandmother corresponds instead to the once sacred image of the Hag. On the one hand, this old legend was intended to further diabolize old women; on the other, it recalls a time when women's wisdom was respected.

The devil's grandmother was frequently utilized as a bogie-woman to frighten children (*"be good or the devil's grandmother will get you!"*). She is also perceived as scarier and more dangerous than her son; if you can survive an encounter with the devil, you'll still have his mother to deal with, or so goes the theme of many folktales, similar perhaps to the monster Grendel and his even fiercer mother from the Anglo-Saxon epic *Beowulf.*

However, sometimes the goddess' essential benevolence shines through. In various somewhat subversive fairy tales, the devil's grandmother assists the hero to accomplish his goals.

See **FAIRY-TALE WITCHES:** Grimms' Fairy Tales: *The Devil With the Three Golden Hairs*; **HORNED ONE:** The Devil.

Giants

Norse hags are identified with the primordial spirits known as Giants; they are particularly fascinating because these spirits are observed as young, powerful women as well as old, gnarled hags. In all cases, however, they are fierce, powerful, warrior spirits.

Giants (Norse: *Jotuns*) play a significant but contradictory, confusing, and mysterious role in Norse mythology. The very first being in the cosmos was the giant Ymir, and giants emanated from parts of his body.

The first gods (Odin and his brothers) destroyed Ymir, grinding his corpse up in a mill and fashioning the universe from it. The giants are the enemies of the gods (and vice versa—Thor is always out battling giants) but they are also their parents, teachers, lovers, and spouses. Unlike the Aesir spirits, the Giants are permanent and eternal:

✳ *The very first being was a giant*

✳ *The universe was created from a giant's body*

✳ *The spirits destined to survive the Twilight of the Gods (Ragnarok) are sons of giantesses*

Norse mythology was not written down until the thirteenth century; its scribes were mainly Christian scholars who identified and empathized with the Aesir gods and so Norse mythology is told from their perspective. The giants were the enemies of the Aesir and they come off badly in myths: other names for giants include trolls and ogres. The stereotypical male giant is huge, ugly, fierce, harsh, and haggard, although many giantesses are very beautiful in a huge, wild, powerful kind of way.

Giants are wild, nocturnal beings, identified with ice, stone, and hailstones. Their home, *Jotunheim* (literally "Giant Home"), is a mountainous, freezing, harsh realm. Giants hurl boulders and hailstones as weapons. They are master shape-shifters: favored forms include eagles and wolves.

Female giants are also called troll-hags and ogresses, both words eventually synonyms for "witch." These giantesses correspond to Hags if one understands that the Hag is but one of the faces or manifestations of these potent spirits. Female giants manifest as fierce hags but also as beautiful warriors and nurturing mothers.

The cosmology of Giants is more complete than that of Hags or the Cailleach: some fairly lengthy narratives survive. Giantesses have personalities, lovers, husbands, and children, however they remain mysterious spirits:

✳ *Norse spirits tend to use different names to indicate different manifestations: it can be difficult to determine whether a name indicates an independent spirit or whether several different names just indicate different aspects of one spirit.*

✳ *Various giantesses appear in myths devoted to male heroes: although they are pivotal, significant characters, they are not the primary focus of the myth as conventionally told. Among those giantesses are Grid and Hyrrokkin (see pages 543 and 544).*

Angerboda may or may not be a giantess. Her husband Loki, identified as a giant, may or may not also be her brother. Hella, their daughter, is classified as a giant but whether this is based on paternal lineage alone or on both parents is unknown. See page 532, Angerboda.

See **ANIMALS:** Transformation, Wolves and Werewolves; **DIVINE WITCH:** Angerboda, Hella.

Grid

Also known as Hag Grid. Grid's name means "Peace." She is classified as a Hag or Frost Giant, however, unlike most giants she is friendly towards the gods. In her most famous story she rescues the thunder god Thor from certain doom.

Convinced to visit the hostile giant Geirrod without his magic hammer, belt, and iron gauntlets, Thor stops to spend the night at Grid's hall. She perceives his danger, although he does not. Grid instructs and cautions Thor, insisting he take her own pair of iron gloves and her unbreakable shield and girdle of might. Thor survives the encounter because of her.

Grid is the mother of Odin's son, Vidar, destined to avenge his father at Ragnarok. She made Vidar special shoes from the scraps of leather cobblers saved as they made all the other shoes on Earth. He wore these shoes at the battle of Ragnarok; allegedly the shoes enabled him to slay and survive the Fenris Wolf. Vidar is among the very few gods destined to survive this final battle and becomes one of the rulers of the new world.

See **DIVINE WITCH:** Odin.

Gyre Carlin

Gyre Carlin combines two words that may both be translated as Hag:

❋ *Gyre derives from the Norse* gyger *or* gjöger, *a giantess or troll-woman, also sometimes translated as ogress or Hag*

❋ *Carlin is the Scottish equivalent of Cailleach or Hag*

Folkloric studies usually classify the Gyre Carlin as a Scottish ogress and/or as a witch. She may be identical with the Carlin or an independent spirit. Either or both may be the hag aspect of the Scottish divine witch Nicnevin.

Gyre Carlin is also the name given to cakes created from the last sheaf of harvested grain.

See Beltane Carline, Carlin, Giants; **DIVINE WITCH:** Nicnevin.

Hag Rune

The ninth rune, Hagal or Hagalaz, is sometimes called the Hag Rune or the Mother Rune. On a metaphysical level, Hagalaz is considered the "root rune" that stands as the basis of this magical system.

Three is the sacred number of Norse cosmology: nine, as three times three, is the most intensely powerful number and reappears consistently throughout Nordic magic and spirituality. (The number is also sacred in many other traditions.) Hagalaz corresponds in sound with the letter "H."

Hagalaz literally means "hailstone." Water is the feminine element associated with creation; hail is frozen water in its dangerous or warrior aspect. Hagalaz is considered among the most potent binding runes and is invaluable in *Vardlokkur,* the

Norse tradition of protective "warding" magic. Hagalaz radiates feminine energy or polarity.

Hagalaz is associated with three deities:

❋ *Heimdall, watchman of the gods and son of the Nine Daughters of the Sea. He guards the Rainbow Bridge that connects and divides the realms of the living and the spirits.*

❋ *Mordgud, Hella's servant, the spirit who guards the Ice Bridge that connects and divides the realms of the living and the dead. Mordgud is among those deities associated with November Eve (Halloween, Samhain).*

❋ *Urd, most powerful of the Norns (Fates). The sacred Well of Urd was named in her honor. She is the Norn who looks backwards and possesses all knowledge of the past.*

See **DICTIONARY:** Rune, Ward, Warlock; **DIVINE WITCH:** Hella; **MAGICAL ARTS:** Runes; **WOMEN'S MYSTERIES:** Spinning Goddesses: The Norns.

Hag Stone

Hag stone is another name for a holed or holey stone. Hag stones are pebbles containing natural perforations. They are considered extremely magically powerful, bestowing protection and fertility and granting wishes. Hag stones cannot be created; boring a hole through a pebble is insufficient, they must be created by nature. Occultists consider hag stones valuable talismans. Usually they are strung on a cord and worn around the neck or hung on a wall or over a bed.

Hyrrokkin

When the Norse god Baldur died, a grand funeral was planned including a traditional boat burial. The boat built for the occasion was the largest ship in existence, so large that no one could launch it, not even Thor. The gods then sent for the giantess Hyrrokkin, who arrived on the shore riding a gigantic wolf and using snakes for her reins.

All it takes is one touch and she sends the vessel into the sea, but in the process the rollers catch fire. It's an ambiguous story: the gods either become angry with her or wish to sacrifice her. Berserkers, Odin's shaman warriors, kill her wolf; Thor threatens to kill Hyrrokkin with his hammer but is persuaded not to by the other gods.

Some scholars believe Hyrrokkin is yet another name for Angerboda.

See Angerboda, Giants, Thokk; **ANIMALS:** Bears, Snakes, Wolves and Werewolves; **DICTIONARY:** Valkyrie; **DIVINE WITCH:** Angerboda, Hella.

Leshovikha

The Russian forest spirits known as Leshii live in the woods in a society parallel to humans. There are male and female Leshii; they have children. Female Leshii are known as Leshovikha. They are not horned like male Leshii but, like their counterparts, they are master shape-shifters. The most common physical manifestation of the Leshovikha is as an old hag with long pendulous breasts. When they get in her way, she flings them over her shoulders. The Leshovikha also manifests as a beautiful naked woman and as a thin, spectral woman dressed in a white sarafan, the Russian national dress.

Wanderers in the forest sometimes witness the Leshovikha giving birth. When she is finished, it is recommended that the observer cover the baby with an item of one's own clothing if necessary; however do not offer Christian prayers or make the sign of the cross over the baby as this allegedly enrages its mother. If these actions are performed graciously, the Leshovikha will offer you a gift:

✸ *If you tell her that the opportunity to be of service is its own reward, your future will be filled with good fortune.*

✸ *If you request payment, however, she will give it you; it will materialize in your hands, however once you leave the forest, whatever cash or prize she gave will evaporate into dust and ashes.*

See **HORNED ONE:** Leshii.

Mala Liath

This Scottish hag's name indicates either "gray eyebrows" or "gray horse." She has dominion over pigs—her sacred animals—and so folklorists believe that she was an ancient sow goddess, perhaps similar to Cerridwen. Mala Liath may or may not be another aspect of Cailleach Bheur (see page 537).

See **ANIMALS:** Pigs; **DIVINE WITCH:** Cerridwen.

Muir Larteach

Muir Larteach, the Sea Hag, lives in an underwater realm. When she rises to the surface, this one-eyed bald hag with the bluish-gray face raises storms.

Muir Larteach is a trickster. She emerges from the water in the guise of a pathetic little old woman and hammers on doors of nearby homes begging for shelter. She looks harmless and so is ushered in. Once inside, however, she swells up like Alice in Wonderland in her growth phase and causes tremendous damage.

On the positive side, Muir Larteach carries a pot of balm that can heal any wound or illness. Moreover, by poking her finger in their mouth, she revives the dead.

Skadi

This Frost Giantess (Snow Queen) has dominion over winter, hunters, and skiers. She is a death goddess as well; her name indicates "Destruction." Skadi carries a quiver filled with arrows. She hunts bears and wolves; skiers and hunters who fail to come home are understood to have fallen to Skadi.

Skadi is the daughter of the Frost Giant Thiazzi who stole the apples of immortality from the gods. Eventually Loki the trickster stole the apples back and Thiazzi was killed. Skadi strapped on her snowshoes, armed and girded herself, then marched straight to Asgard seeking revenge. Her appearance terrified the gods including Odin. To placate her, they offered her *wergild* (reparations payments) for the loss of her father, including vast quantities of gold. She spurned this as she had plenty of her own.

The price she demanded was a husband from among the gods. They agreed but were terrified that she would demand handsome Baldur (indeed Skadi had him in mind). Odin insisted on a kind of beauty contest: Skadi could have any god as her husband but must choose him solely on the basis of his feet. Skadi agreed provided another condition was met: the gods must make her laugh—an impossible task because her heart was filled with rage and grief.

The male gods hid behind a screen with only their bare feet showing: Skadi chose the most beautiful pair of feet, assuming she was selecting Baldur. Instead it was the Vanir Sea god Njord, whose feet were worn smooth by the waves.

Skadi was bitterly disappointed and was even less likely to laugh, but Loki clowned around, playing circus tricks with Thor's goats, and eventually forced laughter from her.

Njord and Skadi married but it was an unhappy union as the two were unable to live together: Skadi hated sunshine and the seashore, Njord found her ice-palace painfully cold and oppressive. They live apart; Skadi spends her time among her snow-covered mountains.

When the gods ultimately turn on Loki, it is Skadi who personally places a poisonous snake over Loki's forcibly upturned face so that its venom drips on him, allegedly in revenge for her father's death.

See **ANIMALS:** Bears, Snakes, Wolves and Werewolves; **DIVINE WITCH:** Freya, Herta, Odin.

Sheela na Gig

Sheela na Gig names a specific image or architectural motif. The typical Sheela na Gig displays a wizened old hag: she is deathly skinny and completely naked. (The term names both the motif and the hag it portrays.) She may lack breasts or display scars on her chest. If she has breasts, they sag pendulously with age, clearly empty and dried out. She looks viewers directly in the eye; sometimes she grins but she always holds her enlarged vagina wide open with her hands as if it were a gateway. Some Sheela na Gigs have vaginas so disproportionately large that this gateway metaphor is no exaggeration.

The Sheela na Gig is extremely mysterious: she is most frequently found incorporated into church buildings in Celtic (or formerly Celtic) areas, although this is clearly *not* a Christian image. Scientific analysis suggests that Sheela na Gig carvings tend to be older than the rest of the church that incorporates them, as if they were brought from elsewhere.

The earliest identified Sheela na Gigs are found in late eleventh-century churches in southern France. She also appears in English and Irish churches dating from the twelfth to the sixteenth centuries. The name "Sheela na Gig" is Irish; its meaning is unknown although nineteenth-century folklorists who first began researching the Sheela na Gig motif were told by their sources that it meant an "immodest woman." Sheela na Gigs seem to have achieved their greatest popularity in Ireland where they also appear on secular buildings such as castles and mills.

The evocative image is extremely powerful; many find it shocking or disturbing.

※ *The Sheela na Gig may be a physical representation of the Cailleach or Sacred Hag*

※ *She may be a Death Goddess: her vagina is the gateway to the next realm in the same manner that a mother's genitalia is the gateway to Life*

※ *The Sheela na Gig is clearly* not *a fertility symbol; the artists who created her could not have made it plainer that she is a woman long past child-bearing*

Whatever her initial origins, the Sheela na Gig now represents the magically protective power of the female genitalia and the spiritual protection of the Great Mother. Nineteenth-century folklorists were advised by local people that the Sheela na Gig wards off evil in the same manner that images of female genitalia are used as magically protective devices throughout the world.

See also Demeter; **WORMWOOD:** Dangers of Witchcraft: Evil Eye.

Thokk

Upon Baldur's death, emissaries were sent to Hella begging for his release from her realm. She finally agreed, provided that every single living being in the universe mourned for Baldur. Frigga, Baldur's mother, journeyed through the various realms begging everyone to weep for her beloved son.

Everyone did until finally she reached the cave of the troll-hag Thokk ("Coal"). Thokk, a bitter, gloomy hag sat in the darkness of her cave and point blank refused to weep for Baldur, saying Hella could keep him, thus dooming all efforts at resurrection.

Thokk is generally believed to have been Loki in disguise. (Loki was responsible for Baldur's death.) Alternatively, some perceive Thokk as among Angerboda's seemingly endless manifestations. Angerboda was Loki's first wife and possibly his sister; Hella, Queen of the Dead, is their daughter.

See Angerboda, Hyrrokkin; **DIVINE WITCH:** Angerboda, Frigga, Hella.

Troll-Hags

The giants (*Jotuns*) of Norse mythology survive as the trolls and troll-hags of Norwegian folklore and fairy tales. Another name for them is *haugfolk* ("people of the mounds," similar to the *sidhe*). These spirits inhabit a hidden world, but most often reveal themselves to people in forests or on mountains, their preferred territory. In some regions, trolls own mountains, only permitting people access to them during the brief Northern summer.

Many troll-hags are beautiful although they are simultaneously large, fierce, wild, and potentially dangerous. Many also possess profound magical and botanical knowledge and the word "troll-hag" is also used to indicate "witch."

In the Norwegian fairy tale, *Polar Bear King Valemon*, a troll-hag bewitches the king, transforming him into a bear and forcing him to marry her. She is a powerful and independent entity, beholden to no one. In the 1991 Swedish film adaptation of the tale, *The Polar Bear King*, the troll-hag has become a beautiful but evil conventional fairy-tale witch and is explicitly identified as a liege of Satan.

See Giants, Gyre Carlin; **DICTIONARY:** Trollkvinna; **FAIRY-TALE WITCHES:** Nature-spirit Fairies: Sidhe; Trolls.

The Horned One and the Devil

In approximately 12,000 BCE, somebody ventured deep within Earth's caverns in what is now southern France to paint a picture of what appears to be a dancing man with various animal attributes, including an impressive rack of antlers. There are comparatively few cave paintings depicting humans; most are incredibly precise portrayals of animals and so this dancing human-like figure has attracted much scholarly attention:

❀ *Does it portray a sacred being or god?*

❀ *Does it portray a shaman, who have historically masqueraded as animals for assorted spiritual purposes (and still do)?*

The cavern in which this image appears is now named Les Trois Frères; the horned figure is popularly nicknamed *The Sorcerer* or *The Dancing Shaman.*

Whoever that horned man was, he didn't remain deep underground but surfaced, although he continued to be associated with caves. Ancient Greek artifacts frequently depict composite goat-men, typically combining a man's upper torso, face, and *very* erect phallus with a goat's lower quarters and horns. This image describes satyrs as well as the great god Pan.

When the Roman people first arrived in that region of Italy, they found a similar figure waiting for them. Faunus, their goat god, resembles Pan and the satyrs. According to legend, Faunus helped found the original city of Rome; the Lupercalia, a major festival whose vestiges survive in the modern Valentine's Day, was dedicated to him.

Another horned male spirit, this one with stag's antlers, is found all across Europe. Horned male spirits are found in Asia and Africa as well. These horned gods, some with goat or bull's horns, others with stag's antlers, are associated with fertility, sexual vigor, prosperity, survival, and wild nature. The cave painting's nickname is no accident: these horned gods are also identified with the earliest stages of shamanism and witchcraft.

In the Christian era, this same figure became identified as the devil, popularly envisioned as a composite goat-man including a man's perpetually erect phallus, and a goat's horns and hoofs.

Images of Pan can be virtually indistinguishable from those of the Christian devil, except that wings were eventually added to the devil's form, so as to combine the form of the horned god with that of a fallen angel. The horned god served as the prototype for the Christian devil.

The story doesn't end there: throughout Europe, as elsewhere, both before and after Christianization, men guised in the form of animals especially horned ones, perhaps ritually channeling horned spirits. Initially these were public communal rituals; however with the rise of Christianity, this practice was outlawed and so went underground, performed secretly in remote mountain clearings and caves.

We know that this occurred because of Christian descriptions and because similar practices still survive, albeit now usually considered "folkloric" rather than spiritual or magical. Photographs are available of Central European men, masked, costumed, and horned in the guise of *their* horned spirit, Krampus. Vestiges of masked, horned shamans also survive in modern figures like Santa Claus and his *"dark companions,"* as well as in what were once considered "lucky" chimney sweeps and hunchbacks.

During Europe's witch-hunt era, people, mainly but not exclusively women, were hysterically accused of assembling en masse and worshipping the devil, usually in the form of a goat or a composite goat-man. Many defined this worship of a goat-shaped devil as what constituted witchcraft.

✳ *Were these accusations based on fact or fantasy?*

✳ *Was this all hysteria, as some believe?*

✳ *Was the Inquisition attempting to stamp out surviving Pagan practices, as others think?*

It's impossible to determine: this was a period of religious fanaticism, not anthropology. The word "devil" was tossed around so broadly and loosely in relation to the horned ones that it's now impossible to determine when the word was intended to describe a spiritual entity and when a man. And of course, for many devout Christians, there was no distinction between the two.

An unknown number of people, mainly women but also children and men, were tortured and killed for allegedly venerating a horned god. The horned god was envisioned as presiding over witches' sabbats. Witches were accused of having sex with this figure, of receiving gifts from him in exchange for their immortal souls, and of offering him obscene obeisance. What the Inquisition described as the "witch's kiss of obeisance," or *"osculum obscenum,"* involved kissing the devil's anus, buttocks or genitals.

The story doesn't end there; the horned one never disappeared. His image remains potent, powerful, and virtually guaranteed to evoke some kind of reaction.

Today some perceive the horned one as sacred, not evil; a little rambunctious maybe but vital, powerful, and positive—the transmitter of Earth's blessings. Other people look at the very same image and see the devil.

What's so special about those horns?

Horns appear in the earliest manifestations of human religion, not only in the cave painting at Les Trois Frères but also in the temple complex at Çatal Hüyük and throughout the entire ancient world. Further information about the significance of horns may be found in **ELEMENTS OF WITCHCRAFT**, however, in short, horns indicate links between the moon, certain animals, men's genitals, and women's inner reproductive organs.

The Horned One and the Devil   549

* Horns indicate wisdom, magical power, and primal generative, reproductive energy (see **TOOLS**: Horns)

* Many horned spirits are lunar spirits

* Most, although not all, horned spirits are male

* Horns indicate protection and abundance: the cornucopia is the horn of plenty

Lunar goddesses like Artemis, Astarte, Diana, Inanna-Ishtar, and Isis often wear horns or horned headdresses. There was a Gaulish goat-goddess named Fenta. Many Celtic goddesses are profoundly identified with cattle. Some sacred hags sport antlers and boar's tusks. Celtic bronze statues portray antlered women, although whether they are divine or human is now unknown. During China's Chou dynasty (1050–256 BCE), female shamans danced wearing antlers.

Even goddesses who lack horns are frequently depicted in the company of horned animals. A famous Middle-Eastern image of a goddess variously identified as Inanna-Ishtar or Lady Asherah portrays her standing between two dancing ibexes (wild goats). Artemis is rarely without a stag at her side.

The male horned spirit is often the companion of a goddess; conversely he is a male divinity who is concerned with the welfare, prosperity, and fecundity of women. These male spirits are portrayed dancing, cavorting, and otherwise engaged with women.

Another name sometimes used for this horned man-spirit is the sacred Wild Man. The Horned Spirit/Wild Man presides over Earth's cyclical nature: birth, death, and rebirth. He is the personification of the male generative fertility needed to spark life. Many horned spirits are associated with the element of fire, identified as the "spark of life." Horned spirits proffer firebrands and, later, coal to their devotees. Conversely many horned spirits are associated with rainstorms that fertilize and were perceived as inseminating the feminine Earth.

The most obvious characteristic of horned deities are their horns. However there are also others:

* Horned spirits are often characterized by hoofs or a limp. Sometimes they have uneven feet (one foot, one hoof): this mysterious shuffling step is also associated with shamans.

* Horned spirits are often identified with specific tools: they carry birch switches, pitchforks, stangs, and sickles.

* Sometimes horns are omitted but other animal anatomy retained as a clue to their true identity, notably hairy legs or cloven hoofs. This tradition survives in the notion that even when the devil manifests as a human being, one cloven hoof is retained as identification.

When discussing horned spirits, exactly what are we talking about? Spirits who manifest as horned deities, or people in the guise of horned deities? Spiritual traditions involving horned spirits involved masquerading and possibly ritual possession similar to modern Vodouistes or Native American katchina dancers (see **MAGICAL ARTS**: Ritual Possession).

There was once a powerful, extensive spiritual tradition involving masquerading as animals which the Church worked tirelessly to eradicate, although it was a tradition that was *never* entirely destroyed:

In the 570s, the Council of Auxerre, France, forbade masquerading as a calf or stag and banned distribution of "devilish charms."

The seventh-century Liber Penitentialis *is the earliest collection of ecclesiastical disciplinary laws for England. One clause forbids anyone from dressing as a bull or stag during the Calends of January.*

In an early association of the horned one with the devil, the Liber Penitentialis *assigns three-years' penance to those who transform themselves into the appearance of wild animals since the practice is devilish.*

Hysteria regarding witches' sabbats presided over by goats may be understood as a response to these traditions. Because such a disproportionate number of women were killed as witches, the question is often posed: where were the male witches? Tremendous emphasis was placed on identifying witchcraft with women. Women, hence witches, were perceived as submissive; male practitioners, many apparently dressed in shamanic horned costume, were identified with the powerful devil, instead.

In the words of St Peter Chrysologus (405-450), "*All who have masqueraded in the likeness of animals ... have turned themselves into devils,*" and furthermore, "*The man who puts on the guise of an idol has no wish to be in the image and likeness of God. Who jests with the Devil cannot rejoice with Christ.*"

He urged Christians to convert those who "*have masqueraded in the likeness of animals, who have assumed the shape of herd animals, who have turned themselves into devils.*"

St Caesarius of Arles (470–542) wrote, "*Is there any sensible man who could ever believe that there are actually rational individuals willing to put on the appearance of a stag and to transform themselves into wild beasts? Some dress themselves in the skins of herd animals, others put on the heads of horned beasts ...*"

The tradition never completely died: dressing up as animals or masquerading in beast masks was incorporated into the medieval Feast of Fools and the Feast of the Ass. It eventually became associated with New Year's festivities; however it's quite likely that the practice also continued secretly in the forest and at remote, ancient sacred sites in the same manner that Vodouistes once put on shows for tourists but reserved true rituals for private, sacred occasions. Presumably these secret traditions were what the Inquisition was so anxious to root out and eradicate.

Nor did the horned spirit ever fade away even in the heart of the Church. An altar stone found at Notre Dame Cathedral, for instance, depicts a horned deity with torcs on his antlers similar to images of Cernunnos (see page 558).

There are *a lot* of horned spirits. The following is a selection of the most renowned, with a special focus on those historically associated with witchcraft.

See **CALENDAR:** Lupercalia, Sabbats; **CREATIVE ARTS:** Dance: Goat Dance, Maenad Dance.

Aatxe, Etsai

Aatxe, the name of this Basque deity, means "young bull." Another name for him, Aatxegorri, means "young red bull." Another Basque spirit named Etsai may or may not be identical with Aatxe. It is unclear whether there were originally two distinct spirits or whether Aatxe, having come to the attention of the Inquisition during their search for Basque witches, evolved into Etsai, a spelling more amenable to French and Spanish clerics.

Aatxe is a shape-shifter who can assume human form but most frequently manifests, as his name indicates, as a bull. (Other forms include dragon, goat, horse, and pig.) Like the Minotaur, Aatxe lives deep within Earth but reputedly leaves his cavern home on stormy nights (with the implication that Aatxe is responsible for the storms). Aatxe is among the spirits affiliated with the goddess Mari. Some believe that Aatxe is really among Mari's many manifestations.

Etsai is frequently described as an "evil spirit," although whether he has always been "evil" and dangerous or whether this reputation stems solely from Christian perceptions is now unknown. The name "Etsai" has become synonymous with "devil." Etsai allegedly teaches his devotees arts described by Christian sources as "diabolical." His classroom is a mountain cave. Allegedly, even his students fear him because he always forces one student to remain permanently with him following graduation, although exactly what happens to them when they stay is unclear. The intended implication is that staying with Etsai is similar to being trapped in Hell.

See also Akerbeltz, Devil, Minotaur; **DIVINE WITCH:** Mari.

Akerbeltz

Akerbeltz literally means "black he goat" in Basque, however "he" may really be "she" as some understand Akerbeltz to be a manifestation of the goddess Mari. Others perceive Aker-

beltz as Mari's companion or her alter ego, her twin soul; the nature of the close relationship between these two Basque spirits remains subject to debate.

Akerbeltz is ancient; Roman-era inscriptions refer to him. Akerbeltz dwells in mountain and underground caves, as does Mari. He protects flocks, especially from illness, raises storms, and leads a host of spirits. Akerbeltz reputedly presides over gatherings of witches every Monday, Wednesday, and Friday. Traditional Pagan offerings to Akerbeltz are modest, and include bread, eggs, and coins.

The Inquisition identified Akerbeltz as Satan and, in the sixteenth and seventeenth centuries, claimed that witches offered him more dramatic sacrifices, such as their immortal souls.

The name Inquisitors gave to Basque witches' sabbats was "Akelarre" or "Goat meadow." Goya's famed painting of that name depicts a witches' sabbat presided over by a mammoth upright goat.

See Boch de Biterna; **CREATIVE ARTS:** Visual Arts: Goya; **DICTIONARY:** Akelarre, Sabbat; **DIVINE WITCH**: Mari.

Almaqah

Information regarding pre-Islamic Arabian deities is sketchy. However, Almaqah seems to have been the pre-eminent deity of the South Arabian kingdom of Saba, now in modern Yemen. Almaqah was a lunar deity. He bears the title "Lord of the Horned Goats" and is sometimes depicted in the form of an ibex but more frequently as a bull, his primary sacred animal.

Almaqah's emblems are a cluster of lightning flashes and an "S"-shaped weapon. Sabeans referred to themselves as *"children of Almaqah."* The great temple of Marib in Yemen, now sometimes referred to as the Eighth Wonder of the World, seems to have been dedicated to him. (Conclusive archeological documentation is still pending.)

Ashmodai, Asmodeus

Asmodeus is the Greek version of the Hebrew name Ashmodai, which may or may not derive from the Iranian Aeshma Deva. There are two theories regarding Asmodeus' origins:

✴ *In dualist Iranian and Zoroastrian tradition, Aeshma Deva is an evil spirit, a* deva *(devil) who fights on the side of the Lord of Darkness. Aeshma means "Madness"; he is the third highest-ranking evil spirit. One theory is that Jews encountering Aeshma Deva during their Babylonian exile incorporated him into their own mythology.*

✴ *An opposing theory suggests that there are actually two dangerous spirits whose names merely sound similar. Although the names are similar, Ashmodai is an independent Jewish spirit. Occultist Samuel MacGregor Mathers subscribed to this notion, suggesting that the name derives from the Hebrew Asamod, "to destroy."*

In Jewish demonology, Ashmodai *is* the destroyer, a high-ranking avenging angel, the Prince of the Revengers of Evil. He visits Heaven daily to learn the destined fate of human beings and to receive his assigned orders. Alternately, he is the King of Demons or djinn.

According to Jewish tradition, Ashmodai is the son of Naamah, sister of Tubal-Cain, the first metalworker and a descendant of Cain. Naamah has her own reputation in Jewish folklore as a formidable demon, a sometime ally, sometime competitor of Lilith. Ashmodai is sometimes considered Lilith's husband.

Ashmodai was King Solomon's primary competitor. According to legend, Solomon enslaved Ashmodai, forcing him to help with Solomon's building projects including the Jerusalem Temple. Ashmodai paid him back by tricking Solomon into giving him his magic ring. Once Ashmodai possessed the ring, he sent Solomon into exile, assumed his form and ruled in his place, although Solomon eventually regained his throne.

In Christian demonology, Asmodeus is technically an extremely high-ranking demon or rebel angel, however his name is also sometimes used as a synonym for Satan. Asmodeus is traditionally envisioned as a horned, lame man or as a composite creature with three heads (bull, ram, ogre), a snake's tail, and goose feet, riding on a dragon.

See also Cain, Devil; **ANIMALS:** Snakes; **DIVINE WITCH:** Lilith; **FAIRY-TALE WITCHES:** Jewish Fairy Tales, Mother Goose; **MAGICAL PROFESSIONS:** Metalworkers; **HALL OF FAME:** Samuel MacGregor Mathers.

Attis

Attis was the young lover of the great goddess Kybele. Their relationship is the subject of a lengthy and very complex saga:

Zeus lusted after Kybele but she disdained him. He attempted to rape her. She escaped him by transforming herself into a rock. In the throes of passion, Zeus ejaculated onto the rock.

Even as a rock, Kybele is fertile. She conceived and bore a hermaphroditic child named Agdistis, who may or may not be an incarnation of Kybele herself.

Agdistis was immensely powerful and violent, perhaps expressing Kybele's rage. The gods, led by Dionysus, decide to eliminate him/her. Dionysus transformed a fresh water spring into wine; Agdistis, intending to drink deeply of water got drunk instead and fell into a stupor. Dionysus, meanwhile, had collected strands of Kybele's fallen hair and braided them into a rope, which he knotted into a noose and slipped over Agdistis' genitals.

Abruptly Dionysus or Pan let out a blood-curdling scream, jolting Agdistis awake. He/she jumped up, castrating her/himself. A river of blood poured forth from which a tree emerged, either an almond or pomegranate depending upon the version of the myth. (Sometimes the miraculous plant is also described as a red flower, perhaps a poppy.) A woman, passing by, picked the nut, flower or fruit. A virgin, she instantly conceived.

Her father, however, scoffed at the notion of virgin births and punished her by locking her in a tower, depriving her of food, attempting to induce miscarriage and starve her to death. Every night, however, Kybele slipped into her locked room, bearing apples and water as sustenance for the woman she had chosen to be her sacred vessel.

The young woman's magical child was born on December 25th. His grandfather rejected the baby and so the baby was brought to the river and placed in a basket to die among the reeds. An alternate version suggests the baby is abandoned on a mountaintop. There are two versions of what happens next: either a mother goat finds the baby and rescues him or a shepherd finds him and brings him home, nurturing the baby on the milk of a goat who has just given birth.

The baby is named Attis, derived from the Phrygian word for goat, *attagi*. Attis is the goat-god, although he is envisioned as the most handsome man on Earth.

That's just the beginning of this very complex saga, which eventually concludes with Attis' resurrection three days after his death, coinciding with the vernal equinox.

Attorney Pierre de Loyer, a contemporary of French witch-hunter Pierre de Lancre, suggested that the goat worshipped by witches was none other than Attis, the consort of Kybele. In his opinion, devotees of Kybele and Dionysus served as prototypes for the witches of his day.

See also Devil, Dionysus, Pan; **BOOKS:** Witch-hunters' Manuals: Pierre de Lancre; **BOTANICALS:** Apples, Opium Poppy; **DIVINE WITCH:** Dionysus, Kybele; **HAG:** The Devil's Grandmother.

Azazel

Azazel is a desert spirit worshipped by ancient Semites. He rules over a band of goat-spirits, the Se'irim. Azazel is famous for his part in Jewish Day of Atonement (Yom Kippur) rituals. As per instructions in Leviticus 16: 21-28, two goats were brought into the Jerusalem Temple. One was sacrificed to the Creator; the other dedicated to Azazel is the original *scapegoat*. The sins of the people were ritually transferred to this goat, which was then brought to the desert and set free as an offering to Azazel. Although this was a Jewish custom, its roots are believed to be pre-Judaic.

Azazel is also among the rebel angels. He taught the daughters of man the craft of metalworking and the sacred art of cosmetics. In Christian demonology, Azazel is considered a fallen angel and counted among Satan's host.

Perhaps because of his strong associations with goats, his name is also sometimes used as a synonym for Satan.

See The Devil, Se'irim; **MAGICAL PROFESSIONS:** Metalworkers.

Baphomet

In 1312, the Knights Templars, an organization of monastic knights, was accused of heresy and the order violently suppressed. Central to the accusations brought against the Knights Templars was that the knights adored an idol named Baphomet, incorporating his worship into various rituals including their initiation ceremonies.

Who was Baphomet? Did he or she exist? No one knows for sure. Accounts of Baphomet derive solely from the charges brought against the Templars and their trial testimony. Baphomet is not clearly identifiable as any other known spirit although, of course, this does not negate the possibility of his existence.

> It is unclear whether Baphomet ever existed (no idol was presented as evidence), whether the Knights Templars had adopted other spiritual traditions or whether more than one idol existed, leading to contradictory testimony.

Twelve of the 231 knights examined acknowledged existence of an idol. All confessions and testimony were obtained under severe torture. It is unknown whether any part of these confessions was genuine or whether confessions were just desperate attempts to end torture by agreeing to whatever their persecutors asked. The various accounts are contradictory and inconsistent. The men do not seem to be describing the same thing.

Their Inquisitors were not interested in the finer nuances of Pagan tradition; from their perspective the Knights Templars had gone from Christian warriors to devil-worshippers. They perceived Baphomet as Satan. The crucial point for their Inquisitors was that the Templars confessed to heresy; identifying Pagan spirits, if indeed Baphomet existed, was irrelevant. Inconsistent testimony remained unexplored and Baphomet remains mysterious.

If Baphomet existed, who was he? The facts may be impossible to determine.

Templar trial testimony described Baphomet as the following:

❋ *Baphomet was worshipped in the form of a head, either a skull, or a bearded head, or a head with two or three faces*

❋ *Baphomet was a black cat*

❋ *Baphomet had a goat's head and horns and a body combining features of a donkey, dog, and bull*

❋ *Baphomet was described as an actual human skull. Others said their idol was made from wood, others that it was metal.*

The Templar mystery continues to hold incredible fascination for people and various theories regarding Baphomet's name and existence have developed.

For years, the standard explanation was that *Baphomet* was a corruption of *Mahomet*, an archaic spelling of the Islamic Prophet Muhammad's name. The Knights Templars were in close daily contact with Muslims and so it was suggested that Baphomet represents attempts to syncretize Islam with Christianity. *However,* this explanation ignores the Islamic total abhorrence of idolatry. There is no "idol worship" or sacred imagery in Islam, quite the contrary. There are *no* depictions of Muhammad. No Islamic spiritual tradition resembles anything of which the Knights Templars were accused.

Nor were the Knights Templars accused of dabbling in Islam. They were accused of Christian heresy and of devil-worship, with the implication of witchcraft. Three possibilities exist:

✳ *Baphomet did not exist*

✳ *The Christian Templars were engaged in Christian devil-worship*

✳ *The Templars were engaging in Pagan-influenced practices possibly related to horned gods*

The image now most associated with Baphomet was drawn by the magus Eliphas Levi in 1854 and explicitly portrays a horned spirit. It does not necessarily correspond to Templar testimony but depicts what appears to be a masculine human body with woman's breasts topped by a crowned, horned goat's head. (Another suggestion is that the image depicts a masked female.) There is an upright pentacle on the figure's forehead.

The figure's right hand points up to a white crescent moon, while the left gestures down toward a black crescent moon shape, interpreted as indicating the metaphysical rule, *"As above, so below."* Baphomet's naked belly is scaly like that of a snake or dragon. Baphomet has black wings, although these are feathered birds' (angel) wings rather than the bat wings typically associated with the devil or demons.

An upright caduceus (Hermes' magic wand entwined by a pair of snakes) is placed phallically between Baphomet's legs, although it also obscures the figure's genitalia. The figure combines male and female anatomy, which may indicate perfect balance, the balance of complementary opposites. The black and white crescent moons are reminiscent of the Chinese yin-yang symbol.

Levi's image of Baphomet serves as the prototype for many Tarot depictions of The Devil.

> Aleister Crowley took the magical name Baphomet when he joined the Ordo Templi Orientalis.

See **ANIMALS:** Bats, Cats, Dogs, Donkeys, Goats, Snakes; **DICTIONARY:** Ordo Templi Orientalis; **MAGICAL ARTS:** Astrology; **HALL OF FAME:** Aleister Crowley, Eliphas Levi.

Boch de Biterna / Boch de Biterne

Boch translates as "he goat." This term first emerged on the French side of the Pyrenees in reference to Basque witches. It is possible that the term makes reference to Akerbeltz or to Mari. The Pyrenean ibex (*Capra pyrenaica*) is a unique type of ibex or *steinbock* (wild mountain goat) indigenous only to the Pyrenees. Goats make frequent appearances in Basque magical and spiritual traditions.

In 1458, Inquisitor Alfonso de Spina deplored *'perverse women … who come together by night in some deserted plain to adore a goat commonly called the boch de Biterne."* He claimed to have seen paintings in the chambers of the Toulouse Inquisition that depicted these women adoring their boch.

See also Akerbeltz; **DICTIONARY:** Akelarre; **DIVINE WITCH:** Mari; **WITCH-CRAZE!:** Basque.

Bossu

Bossu is a Vodou lwa usually depicted as a three-horned bull. He represents primal male vigor, similar to that other bull-spirit, the biblical Ba'al. Like Ba'al, Bossu is unpredictable and dangerous, manifesting the potential outcome of excess testosterone. He is the lwa of aggressive action, sometimes necessary if dangerous. Bossu is considered among the more volatile lwa and is among those identified as patrons of less ethical sorcerers, however he is also petitioned by women for enhanced personal fertility. His colors are red and black. Bossu's altars are decorated with horns.

See **DICTIONARY:** Bòkò, Lwa, Vodou.

Boujeloud

An annual festival similar to the ancient Lupercalia still occurs, although not in Italy. Instead it is held in the village of Jajouka, in the foothills of Morocco's Rif Mountains. There, Boujeloud, another horned male spirit, dances, sewn naked into the skin of a freshly slaughtered goat. The women that he flails with his oleander switches anticipate pregnancy within the year. According to the renowned Master Musicians of Jajouka, Boujeloud was the original source of their music. Like Pan, he is a music teacher.

Various recordings of the Master Musicians of Jajouka exist, including *Brian Jones Presents: The Pipes of Pan at Jajouka*, recorded in 1968 by Rolling Stone Jones.

See also Faunus; **CALENDAR:** Lupercalia.

Cain

God punished Cain by cursing him to a life of permanent wandering. Cain protests that this punishment is too great and fears that others will kill him. God relents, placing a magically protective mark on Cain. The Bible contains no description or identification of that mark, however many believe it was a set of horns. According to legend, Cain was eventually slain by his blind descendant Lamech, whose son Tubal-Cain saw Cain from afar. He thought he saw a horned animal and advised Lamech to let loose an arrow, which amazingly met its mark. Tubal-Cain is identified in the Bible as Earth's first metalworker.

A Jewish legend suggests that Cain was really Lilith's son by Adam, not the son of Eve. A Christian legend suggests that Cain was Eve's son but that his father was that old snake Samael, equated in Christian folklore with Satan.

In medieval Europe, Cain was among those believed to lead the Wild Hunt, sometimes called Cain's Hunt. Because he was identified as the ancestor of smiths, he was simultaneously associated with witchcraft, shamanism, and sorcery.

See **ANIMALS:** Corvids, Snakes; **DIVINE WITCH:** Lilith; **MAGICAL PROFESSIONS:** Metalworkers.

Cernunnos

Lord of Souls, Celtic Lord of the Underworld, the Dead, Healing, and Wealth, Cernunnos has dominion over nature, animals, and abundance. Cernunnos is traditionally depicted with a man's body and stag's horns, although this may be a shamanic guise.

Cernunnos is the Latin name given this mysterious Celtic deity. His original name is now unknown. Cernunnos is usually translated as "the horned one" and derives from an Indo-European root word *ker* meaning "growth" or "to become large and hard." It may be a name or it may be a title: the word appears on an altar found at Notre Dame that also depicts his image.

Images of this god appear throughout Celtic Europe. His worship seems to have been widespread throughout Celtic territory, from Ireland to Romania, and he remains beloved in the Neo-Pagan community.

Cernunnos appears on the Early Iron Age Gundestrup Cauldron, which was found in a peat bog in Denmark in 1891, as well as on over 30 surviving ancient depictions. On the Gundestrup Cauldron he sits cross-legged surrounded by forest animals, holding a ram-horned serpent in one hand and a torc in the other. In a relief found at Reims, France, Cernunnos sits cross-legged with a stag and bull at his feet. He has a large sack from which he distributes what appear to either be coins or grain.

Cernunnos' attributes include a huge sack of treasure and a torc, the Celtic sign of nobility and power.

See also Herne the Hunter; **ANIMALS:** Snakes; **TOOLS:** Cauldron.

Chimney Sweep

Throughout Europe but especially in Germany and Central Europe, chimney sweeps are considered auspicious harbingers of good luck, associated with New Year's festivities, the Yule season, and fertility.

It's considered incredibly lucky for a chimney sweep to be the first person one sees or the first person to cross one's threshold on New Year's morning. Chimney sweeps were once paid to make brief appearances immediately after midnight on New Year's Eve. However, to see a chimney sweep *any time* was considered lucky. Many would rush over and touch them for good luck. If a chimney sweep kissed a bride immediately after her marriage, she was believed blessed with luck, love, and fertility.

What the chimney sweep symbolizes and represents however, doesn't necessarily correspond to the chimney sweep's literal every day existence. As horned spirits like Krampus (see page 570) were suppressed and shamanism was forbidden, traditions associated with them were transferred to chimney sweeps. The Lucky Chimney Sweep thus is more than just a menial worker. He is a shaman in disguise; Krampus without his horns and hoofs.

This Lucky Chimney Sweep was a popular motif on early twentieth-century Central European Christmas and New Year's postcards, where his magical attributes are often on display. In these images, the Lucky Chimney Sweep brandishes Krampus' birch twig broom.

Dressed in black and red, similar to Krampus, the Lucky Chimney Sweep distributes money-bags, gold coins, and *Amanita muscaria* mushrooms. He brandishes lucky charms like four-leafed clovers and horseshoes. Horseshoes often symbolize the vulva: like Krampus, Lucky Chimney Sweeps are frequently depicted enjoying romantic encounters with beautiful ladies.

> Lucky Chimney Sweeps are intrinsically identified with coal, the gift (or punishment) that Santa and his horned helpers give disobedient children. Coal is the gift of warmth and life, similar to Prometheus' gift of fire. Another figure identified with this in Europe, and thus with good luck, was the professional charcoal burner.

The Lucky Chimney Sweep is almost always depicted as a very sweet, clean, rosy-cheeked child and so his image is far less overtly sexual and threatening than that of Krampus, whose phallus and lustful nature are often emphasized. Like Krampus, chimney sweeps are associated with coal, source of flame and heat.

Lucky Chimney Sweeps are associated with pigs: they ride them, herd them, carry them or train them to do circus tricks like jumping through hoops or horseshoes. Sometimes pigs pull the chimney sweep in a chariot, toboggan or sleigh similar to that of Santa Claus.

Chimney sweeps' natural associations with chimneys link them to Santa Claus, Easter witches, and shamans whose soul-journeys are sometimes described as *"trips up and down chimneys."* Chimney sweeps are often depicted wearing black backless slippers; in mythic imagery,

they frequently fall out of their shoes or seem to be missing one.

See Krampus, Santa Claus; **ANIMALS:** Pigs; **BOTANICALS:** *Amanita muscaria*, Birch; **CALENDAR:** Easter, Yule; **CREATIVE ARTS:** Dance: Step of Yu, Visual Arts: Halloween Postcards; **DICTIONARY:** Soul-journey.

The Devil

The devil is a complex topic with enough information to fill its own encyclopedia, thus what is included here is by necessity a brief overview, with the emphasis on the identification of Pagan horned spirits with the devil.

In a dualist Christian vision, the devil is the evil force that opposes Jesus Christ. His role is to tempt Christians and undermine Christianity. He is also, however, the ruler of Hell, the Christian realm where damned souls are eternally punished. The devil is a trickster who tempts people to perform acts for which he will later punish them.

This idea of the devil is a Christian concept; this devil did not exist prior to Christianity. The devil is a complex character, an amalgamation of many sources. It took centuries for him to evolve into the form that first became familiar during the Middle Ages and remains so today.

Although various names are now used for the devil as if they were synonymous (Lucifer, Satan, Beelzebub, and so forth) these names actually derive from different concepts and traditions and originally indicated different spirits. The Christian devil evolved from Jewish, Pagan, and Zoroastrian sources, however he is not identical with any of them. Because this modern conception of "the devil" is thus something of a pastiche, he is often a contradictory and elusive figure, perhaps befitting a trickster.

> *Devil* is related to the Indo-European root word *de* or divine. In pre-Zoroastrian Iran, a *deva* or *dev* was a divine being. The word still retains this meaning in Buddhism and Hinduism; Hindu devas are sacred and benevolent.

Christians were not the first to diabolize other people's gods. When Zoroastrianism came to prominence in Iran, the word "devil" came to indicate dangerous, evil spirits. Zoroastrianism is intensely dualist: the devas form the army of the Lord of Darkness, opponent of the Lord of Light.

Although the cosmology has changed, the Christian conception of the devil as an opposing and (almost) equal force derives from Zoroastrian tradition, as does this use of the word "devil."

Satan

Satan is a Hebrew word, however there is no Hebrew spirit named Satan. Rather it is a title: Satan means "Adversary" and in Jewish tradition; he is always described as *Ha-Satan* or "*the Satan.*" Similar to the ancient Egyptian conception of the judging of dead souls, Jewish tradition suggests that when one dies, a court of angels considers how one's time was spent on Earth, ultimately determining one's future destiny.

As in a modern court of law, there is a defense attorney (your guardian angel) and a prosecuting attorney, whose job it is to point out every single thing you ever did wrong. This adversary is *Ha-Satan* and obviously he was a feared, unpopular character. However, he is not innately evil—any more than a tax accountant is evil for determining what you owe. He is doing the job assigned to him by the Creator. It is unclear whether there is one Satan or whether different angels fill this role.

Satan appears very infrequently in Hebrew scriptures; he is not an especially significant figure in Jewish tradition. He is occasionally depicted as a tempter of humanity but more usually as an obedient servant of the Creator. In Jewish tradition, not all angels are envisioned as pleasant: *Ha-Satan* is an accusatorial, adversarial angel in the same manner as there are Angels of Death.

There is no concept of Satan as a force opposing the Creator in the Old Testament. The Creator is Creator of All, good and evil. According to Isaiah 45:7

> *I form the light and create the darkness.*
> *I make peace and create evil.*
> *I the Lord do all these things.*

The Hebrew *Ha-Satan* ("the Adversary") was eventually translated into Greek as *Diabolos* ("Accuser") This evolved into Diabolus (Latin), Diablo (Spanish), Diable (French), Djab (Kreyol), Diabolical (English), and Diavolo (Italian).

Lucifer

According to Jewish tradition, at the very beginning of time, some angels visiting Earth fell in love with the Daughters of Man (human women) causing them to betray their angelic vows. These angels taught women all kinds of secrets and various magical arts including metalworking. The Creator banished them from the heavenly host or, in some cases, inflicted severe punishment. Many of these rebel angels evolved into dangerous, volatile spirits, associated with witchcraft and the occult and are sometimes described as "demons." Many became allied with Lilith. These ex-angels include Azazel, Samael, and someone described as the beautiful "*Son of the Morning Star.*"

This notion of Fallen Angels entered Christian mythology and continued to evolve. In the Jewish story, the angels come to Earth and transgress once they're here: they rebel against rules; they yield to temptation.

In the Christian story, the angels are cast out of Heaven as punishment. Various reasons are given including their refusal to pay homage to Man. The most common reason however is that the Chief of the Rebel Angels believed himself equal or superior to God and thus challenged him, intending to take over the throne of Heaven. The rebellion failed and this angel with his celestial army of followers was thrown out of Heaven.

The devil is generally understood to be the chief of the fallen angels. Demons are children of fallen angels and human mothers, which relates back to the original story. Also related is the implication that women are more closely allied (or susceptible) to the devil's wiles and temptations than men. (See **BOOKS:** Witch-hunters' Manuals: Heinrich Kramer.) The name usually given this chief fallen angel is Lucifer.

"Lucifer" means "Light bringer" and it is an ancient epithet attached to many Italian divinities including Juno and Fauna, daughter and close ally of the horned spirit Faunus. It initially indicated glory, not evil. Lucifer is a beautiful devil; he is not a horned spirit. In the earliest Christian depictions of Lucifer, he is indistinguishable from other angels, except that he is consistently portrayed as falling. (Some translate Lucifer as an amalgamation of light, *luci* and iron, *fer*, interesting in light of the devil's associations with blacksmiths.)

🐜 🐜 🐜

The first animal to be associated by Christianity with Satan was the snake. The Book of Revelation, last book of the Christian Bible, first identifies Satan with the serpent in the Garden of Eden. Snakes and dragons (then understood as great snakes) were strongly identified with Pagan traditions, especially those associated with female divinity and power. Snakes were sacred in many traditions, and particularly associated with women's primal power and mysteries. Tales of devout Christian knights who slay dragons are metaphors for the destruction of Pagan spiritual traditions.

Devas, Ha-Satan, and Lucifer are pre-Christian concepts that eventually merged within Christianity. By the fourth century, when Christianity achieved political power, the concept of the devil as enemy of God and man was firmly entrenched into Christian belief. But it was a new vision of the devil that emerged, very different from the others. This devil physically resembled the male horned spirits, especially those spirits identified with goats.

Pagan worship and devotion to this male horned god was prevalent and deeply rooted throughout Europe and elsewhere; he was a major impediment to Christianity and perhaps to authority in general. It is no accident that these spirits so frequently take the form of goats: the horned god resembles a wild goat—he is rambunctious, anarchic, fun-loving, defiant, and uncontrollable. Some perceived the qualities associated with the horned gods as favorable; Christianity emphatically did not.

The horned gods celebrate the physical glories of Earth. They are *voraciously* hungry spirits who constantly crave sex, food, intoxicating substances, and comfort—in short, Earth's physical pleasures. Horned gods dance, sing, and make merry. They create musical instruments, teach people to play, invent wine, sponsor shamans, and proudly display their ever-erect phalluses.

> When the horned god manifests as a man (as he sometimes does) he appears as an archetypal Wild Man, resistant to rules, civilization, and all authority.

The horned spirits are mediating spirits: they negotiate the balance between people, animals, and plants. They are not dualist: they do not necessarily put the needs of people first. Their gift is fertility and abundance: they do not promise salvation or eternal life of the soul. (Some Pagan mystery traditions did, notably Demeter's Eleusinian Mysteries.) Instead they promise offspring, if you want them.

The Horned God is the Lord of Wild Nature, the powers of Earth. His domain eventually became the domain of the Christian devil.

The horned gods were particularly abhorrent to the early Christians; they perceived them as harmful, seductive devils. By the witch-hunt era, the image of Satan as a goat had superceded all others. Previously, if Satan was envisioned as having any form at all, it was that of an angel. The New Testament has no specific physical description of Satan.

To undermine widespread devotion to the horned spirits, Christianity labeled their worship as evil. Eventually the horned male god would become the prototype for the devil's physical manifestation. Many modern people will automatically identify an image of a horned spirit as the devil, whether it is a pre-Christian depiction of Pan or an early twentieth-century Krampus postcard.

From a dualist perspective, all spiritual entities must be on the side of good or the side of evil. By Christian definition, non-Christian spirits were perceived as subversive and evil. The official inclination was to banish and forbid all these spirits, eradicating them. *However*, many of these spirits had been worshipped for ages. Many were very beloved. Many of those who accepted Christianity were reluctant to completely abandon these spirits. In order to maintain these traditions in a safe (spiritually *and* legally) manner, many ancient Pagan spirits were identified as saints.

> The Christian devil is not restricted to the form of a goat or a horned, hoofed man. During witch-hunt era Europe, the devil was considered a master shape-shifter. His favorite manifestations, however, were usually black: black cats, dogs, goats, and men. If the devil is such a master shape-shifter, how can he be identified? Russian folk tradition suggests that loud laughter is a telltale sign of the devil, disguised demons, and witches.

The process of what is called "identification" or "syncretism" involves transferring the attributes of a now forbidden spirit to another acceptable one. In essence the forbidden spirit masquerades as the safe one. Because by necessity this practice demands secrecy, after a few generations it can become difficult to recall the original spirit. Frequently attributes of both spirits merge; they become as one. This process often occurred with the tacit cooperation of the Church as a way of bringing disbelievers and the ambivalent into the fold.

❋ *Some Pagan deities were identified by Christians as saints—Brigid, Walpurga*

* *Some Pagan deities were identified by Christians as fairies—Ainé, Maeve*

* *Some Pagan deities were identified by Christians as witches—Baba Yaga, Hulda*

* *Some Pagan deities were identified by Christians as devils—the irrepressible, disobedient, wild Horned God became identified as the Christian devil*

During the reign of Pope Gregory the Great (from September 3, 590 until March 12, 604), the devil assumed the form of a hunchbacked bearded goat-skinned man with cloven hooves, horns, and a stick. Gregory described Satan as a black man possessing goat's horns and hooves, an evil stench, and the power to control weather.

The devil's stick links him to the phallic sticks and staffs carried by horned spirits like Pan, Hermes, Dionysus, and Krampus. The horned spirit's stick is an emblem of phallic power: when he touches women with it, they conceive. When he bangs on a door with it, the household is filled with prosperity.

According to the Christian version, however, the devil's stick is used to punish and torture people and also as a crutch because he is lame. The rationale for his limp is that when cast out of heaven, he fell and permanently injured his foot. (Although of course the angel cast out of heaven originally looked *nothing* like a horned spirit.) This vision of a limping devil, however, links him to various lame gods and holy people lamed during initiations, including Hephaestus, Dionysus, Oedipus, Achilles, and Hermes with his one sandal and shepherd's crook. It also links him to the traditional shaman's dance.

Sometimes instead of an ordinary stick or staff, the devil carries a pitchfork. One theory suggests that the image of the pitchfork-wield-

ing horned devil is based on Shiva, the pre-Aryan deity from India. Shiva dances in the fire carrying a trident that resembles a pitchfork and leads a wild retinue of demons and witches. He may have been the original model for the Zoroastrian concept of the devil, eventually absorbed by Manicheism and Christianity. (See also Pashupati, Shiva; **DIVINE WITCH:** Shiva.)

Horned spirits like Hermes and Cernunnos often carry huge sacks from which they distribute largesse. The Christian devil also carries a large sack but in his case it is in which to carry away damned souls. That sack survives in modern Krampus and Santa Claus imagery.

Sometimes instead of being carried, the sack was envisioned as internalized, part of the Horned God/Wild Man's body: the hunchback's hump was perceived as this internal bag of treasure, hence the powerful association of hunchbacks with luck. Hunchbacks are also closely identified with Lucky Chimney Sweeps who also absorbed many of the characteristics of the horned spirits, as well as with cobblers, once closely associated with shamanism. See **DICTIONARY:** Bagatella.

The devil was no longer perceived as merely the head of a formerly angelic host; instead he led a fifth column of human devotees, identified by the Inquisition as witches. Eventually, for the Inquisition, worshipping the devil was what constituted witchcraft. For reasons discussed in **WITCHCRAZE!** it eventually became impossible to prove one wasn't a devil-worshipper once one was accused.

There are two different issues:

* *People were accused of worshipping the devil*

* *People worshipped deities that Christians perceived as the devil*

People worshipped horned spirits and other Pagan deities and many still do. However in these spiritual traditions, there is *no* devil. Horned spirits are not the devil.

> It is crucial to distinguish between what witches *really* believe versus what outsiders intrinsically opposed to witchcraft *say* that witches believe.

> Martin Luther described not believing in the devil as "un-Christian" because without the devil to tempt people into damnation, there is no need for a Christ to save them.

Other people did worship the Christian conception of Satan; this worship arose *within* Christianity as a reaction *against* Christianity. In its purest form "Satanism" simply reverses or opposes anything Christian. In order to genuinely worship the devil, one must subscribe to the Christian vision of the devil, as it is the only tradition in which he exists.

Christians have a unique relationship with the devil because Satan's primary role was envisioned as opposing Christianity. Satan was the relentless, tireless enemy of Christ and Christians. Satan consistently plots to undermine, ruin and seduce Christians. Satan and his host have nothing to do but oppose Christianity. In this dualist vision, Satan became the official opponent of Christ.

The devil's power was perceived as manifest in *any* form of resistance to Christianity. It was not necessarily to actively worship Satan to be a "Satanist": simply not accepting Christianity indicated alliance with Satan. Eventually a vast host of human beings found themselves associated with Satan including witches, Pagans (defined as anyone who wasn't Christian, Jewish or Muslim), Jews, Romany, and those Christians whose vision of Christianity did not correspond to official Church doctrine.

Witch-hunters accused witches of attending sabbats presided over by Satan usually in the form of a huge male goat or a Pan-like figure combining human and goat anatomy. In whatever shape the devil appears, what, according to witch-hunters, exactly does he do at these sabbats?

* *He presides over proceedings like a king, leading orgies and distributing gifts (food, cash, magical tools)*

* *He distributes malevolent materials and directs their use*

* *He distributes flying ointments so that his guests may return*

* *He rewards and punishes attendees as he deems fit*

* *He trades favors for immortal souls; people make compacts with the devil by signing his Black Book*

The first written reference to this Satanic pact emerged in the sixth-century *Tale of Theophilus*. By the tenth century, this story was very popular, widely distributed, and well known. First told in Greek, then translated into Latin and finally written in verse in the tenth century, *The Tale of Theophilus* recounts the story of a Greek priest, Theophilus, an ambitious cleric who believed he should be bishop. Instead he's dismissed from his office. Angry, Theophilus hires a sorcerer who arranges a meeting for him with Satan.

The devil offers Theophilus a written compact whose terms are that Theophilus must renounce Christ and pledge himself to Satan instead. If he does so, he'll be restored to his former post. Theophilus signs and indeed gets his position back. However, contemplating eternal damnation, he begins to have regrets and appreciates the magnitude of his sin. Finally the Virgin Mary personally intercedes, the contract is torn up, and Theophilus is saved.

Dionysus

In 1839, German historian Franz Josef Mone (1796–1871) was among the first to link European witchcraft with Pagan religion. (Mone was a devout Roman Catholic and *not* sympathetic to witches.) His theory: ancient Germans once lived by the Black Sea among devotees of Dionysus and Hecate. German slaves eventually fused German and Dionysian traditions into their own religion, characterized by devotion to a horned spirit, nocturnal gatherings, and the practice of magic. When the Germans headed west, slaves and lower classes brought this religion with them. The upper classes perceived it with contempt, eventually distorting Dionysus into the devil.

Dionysus is among those spirits classified as horned gods, however his myth is extensive and he transcends categories. Dionysus is a shape-shifter; among his favored forms is that of a bull, among his sacred animals. Dionysus is a close ally of Pan; they are often in each other's company. The satyrs are considered devotees of Dionysus.

For further information regarding Dionysus, see **DIVINE WITCH:** Dionysus. See also Minotaur, Pan, Satyrs; **CREATIVE ARTS:** Dance: Maenad Dances; **DICTIONARY:** Bacchanal, Conjurer, Maenad, Sabbat.

Eshu-Elegbara/Exu

The West African trickster spirit Eshu-Elegbara is Master of Roads. He determines whether someone's path is clear or blocked with obstacles. "Path" is meant literally but also metaphorically. Eshu determines how easy or challenging an individual's life will be. Devotion to Eshu-Elegbara was widespread; he is common to many West African pantheons. Because of this, Eshu-Elegbara exists in virtually all African-Diaspora traditions although, as befitting a trickster, his name, appearance, and personality is slightly different wherever he manifests. He is thus a lwa and an orisha.

In Brazil, Eshu-Elegbara evolved into Exu (pronounced "Eshu"), a special kind of spirit. The Exus are a category unto themselves: there are many Exus, or at least many individual aspects or manifestations of one Exu. He serves as a messenger and medium. This definition of Exu is common to Afro-Brazilian traditions but does not occur in other spiritual traditions such as Santeria, Vodou or Voodoo, where Eshu-Elegbara is known, respectively, as Elegba, Papa Legba, and Papa Labas.

Perceptions of Exu depend upon the spiritual convictions of the perceiver. Those with more purely African or Pagan orientations perceive

Exu as dangerous and volatile but not inherently evil. He performs valuable services for people including healing, and he provides opportunities and good fortune.

Many possessing a strong Christian orientation, however, perceive Exu as evil or even as the devil. In Brazil, Exu is closely identified with the Christian devil; the two are sometimes perceived as synonymous. Like the Christian devil, Exu signals his appearance with the scent of sulphur and carries a pitchfork. (In Africa and elsewhere, Eshu-Elegbara carries a shepherd's staff.) It can be impossible to distinguish statues of Exu from Satanic imagery.

Exu's sacred colors are red and black: he is depicted as a red devil or a black one. He is usually envisioned as a naked, horned man, sometimes with a little beard, always with a perpetually erect phallus. Sometimes he has one cloven hoof; sometimes he just limps. Like the Christian conception of the devil, Exu is a smooth-talking man who hangs around crossroads.

> In Brazil, Exu has a consort, Pomba Gira. She, too, is a road-opening spirit who shares many characteristics with Exu, including the sacred colors red and black. She is considered the matron saint of prostitutes, transvestites, the poverty-stricken, and the downtrodden. Pomba Gira is sometimes depicted as a beautiful, lascivious, horned woman. Like Exu, she sometimes also sports one cloven hoof.

Fauns

Fauns are Italian spirits who manifest as men with goats' legs and horns, similar to Pan and the satyrs. Fauns are among the spirits in the retinue of Faunus. Like the satyrs, they have a reputation for being lascivious, wild, and lustful.

See Faunus, Pan, Satyrs.

Faunus

Faunus is among the most ancient indigenous Italian spirits and is known as *"The Benefactor."* Faunus epitomizes Earth's irrepressible male generative force. He is a spirit of the forest and wild nature, representing the innate fertility of land and people, a surging force that cannot be contained.

Faunus manifests as a horned human male cloaked in a wolf-skin or with a human's upper torso and the lower body of a goat, similar to Pan and the satyrs.

Faunus uses different names:

* *As Lupercus, the wolf-god, Faunus arbitrates the balance between wolves and livestock.*

* *As Fatuus, Faunus gives oracles and bestows psychic ability. His devotees once slept in his sacred precincts, dressed in the skins of freshly sacrificed lambs, in hopes of receiving dreams from the god.*

* *As Innus, "He Who Makes Fruitful," Faunus increases herds.*

Faunus is a primordial spirit; he is so ancient that he cannot communicate as a human does but speaks through forest noises and nature sounds. His presence is often made manifest by nightmares even when he is bringing good news. Faunus is by nature a benevolent rather than a harmful spirit, however he is wild and uncontrollable. Once upon a time, his priests served as mediums, interpreting Faunus' oracles and communiqués.

Faunus' attributes include a goblet and a wreath. His sacred creatures are goats and wolves. His sacred day is February 14th. Faunus had a shrine on the Tiber Island. Rome's Church of St Stefano Rotondo sits on the site of a temple once dedicated to Faunus.

See also **ANIMALS**: Goats, Wolves and Were-wolves; **CALENDAR**: Lupercalia; **DIVINE WITCH**: Circe.

Goat God

Although this may be used as a generic term to refer to any horned male spirit, it usually indicates Pan (see page 576).

Hannya

Hannya are Japanese horned female spirits and they are dangerous. No iron club is necessary for the Hannya as it is for her male compatriots, the fierce, horned spirits known as Oni (see page 575)—she wields the power of a woman scorned and is fearsome indeed!

Hannya are frequently defined as female Japanese demons or as female Oni but, most famously, *Hannya* names a mask. The Hannya mask, perhaps the best known of Japanese Noh masks, has sharp fangs and horns and bears the name of the spirit it portrays. Hannya may originally have been snake spirits and are still sometimes described as "snake demons." Older Hannya masks appear more serpentine than modern ones, whose emphasis is on her horns.

The association between Oni and Hannya may derive from the tenuous alliance perceived between human women and Oni. When Oni wish to hide their identity, they transform into human women and so, in theory at least, the sweetest most innocuous woman might really be an Oni in disguise.

It's a one-way street, however: Oni transform into women but women don't transform into Oni. They can however transform into Hannya, although this is an involuntary and permanent transformation. Once a Hannya, there's no going back.

Women who die consumed with rage and jealousy transform into Hannya, vengeful, powerful spirits. In particular, those women spurned and scorned by lovers, especially if they then commit suicide, are believed potentially likely to become Hannya. The Hannya lingers on Earth, a malicious, destructive spirit, her anger overriding any residual human emotions or conscience. Hannya are perceived as negative, dreadful creatures; it is a terrible fate to become a Hannya and so the implicit message is that women must avoid, suppress and sublimate rage, anger, jealousy, and other dangerous emotions.

The most prominent feature of the Hannya mask is its horns. Horns, in Japanese cosmology, have strong associations with female anger. The Japanese gesture of two index fingers sticking up from a man's forehead traditionally indicates that his wife is angry with him or jealous. Although the Hannya is now typically portrayed in Noh drama as a (sometimes-tragic) villainess, she may have once been viewed with more ambivalence: the traditional Japanese bride was styled with her hair in a tall, vertical, structured hair-do, further enhanced by a large, tall, structured head-covering. This was intended to cover her horns and protect her privacy, just in case she was really a hannya. Why the Hannya was permitted, perhaps even encouraged, to keep these secrets remains mysterious.

See **ANIMALS**: Snakes.

Hathor

Hathor is the primordial Egyptian goddess; she was ever-present from the beginning. Many of her characteristics were eventually transferred to Isis but Hathor never lost her popularity.

Hathor has dominion over love, sex, reproduction, music, dance, intoxication, cosmetics, perfume, and all the joys and pleasures of life. Matron of women, Hathor is the guardian of females of all species. She embodies the female principle and grants fertility. She is also a warrior spirit, known as the *Eye of Ra*: when the supreme god Ra is in trouble, Hathor is his main line of defense. She was the guardian of pharaohs too.

Hathor is a shape-shifter and takes many forms (the cat goddess Bastet may or may not be Hathor's alter ego); however her primary and perhaps most ancient manifestation is as a horned cow.

🐾 *Hathor wears a horned headdress that combines lunar and bovine imagery*

🐾 *Hathor is the celestial cow; the Milky Way spills from her breasts*

🐾 *Hathor, one of the very few Egyptian deities commonly depicted full-face rather than in profile, has a special distinctive hair-do that resembles a "flip": the ends curl up sharply in imitation of horns*

🐾 *Hathor manifests as a cow. (You'll know it's her, not just any old cow; the clue to her identity is the impeccable eye makeup sported by the Hathor-cow.)*

Hathor is often portrayed as a gold cow. Some scholars believe that the biblical Golden Calf was either Hathor or her son. Hathor has dominion over the Sinai Peninsula where the events surrounding the Golden Calf are believed to have occurred.

Hathor embodies the powers implicit in horns. She is the Horn of Plenty providing devotees with all the bounties of life, but she also embodies the power of the horn as an aggressive weapon of self-defense.

See **ANIMALS**: Cats; **CREATIVE ARTS**: Music: Drum; **DIVINE WITCH**: Isis; **TOOLS**: Horns, Mirrors.

Hermes

Hermes is among those spirits classified as horned gods; however his myth is so extensive that he transcends such classification. That Hermes is considered a horned spirit might surprise many: the Hermes of Classical myth is invariably depicted as a man dressed in a uniform of traveler's hat and winged sandals. Originally, however, Hermes was a deity from rural Arcadia. He began his incarnation as a deity involved with human and agricultural fertility: he is the Lord of Flocks and is often depicted carrying a young lamb or kid, both horned animals.

Like many horned gods, Hermes carries a stick: in his case, it's the caduceus, a short staff entwined by two serpents, still the emblem of the medical profession. He often carries a large bag, too, from which he dispenses gifts and treasures. Hermes frequently limps and is sometimes described as missing one sandal.

Hermes is the father of the goat-god Pan. According to myth, Pan's mother was horrified by the goat-child she bore but Hermes was delighted and it was he who raised and protected his son. For further information, see **DIVINE WITCH:** Hermes; see also Pan, page 576.

Herne the Hunter

Herne the Hunter is an antlered man, swathed in deerskins. (It is unclear whether the antlers are his or whether it is a removable crown.) Sometimes Herne leads the Wild Hunt riding a fire-breathing stallion and accompanied by a pack of hounds.

Various legends surround Herne the Hunter:

❉ *He is the ghost of an English wizard who still haunts Windsor Great Park*

❉ *He was an innkeeper (and wizard) who was hung from an oak as punishment for his involvement with the occult*

❉ *Herne is a generic horned deity*

❉ *Herne is Lord of the Realm of the Dead, Leader of Dead Souls, and possibly Cernunnos in disguise*

❉ *The Christian Church identified Herne as the devil*

Herne is the ancient keeper of England's Windsor Park and allegedly may be found wandering around an old oak in the forest at night. (The tree is known as *Herne's Oak*.) He usually carries a firebrand, a musical instrument or a birch broom.

Reference is made to Herne in Shakespeare's *Merry Wives of Windsor*, where he is described as a hunter who hanged himself from an oak in Windsor Forest.

See also Cernunnos; **DICTIONARY:** Wild Hunt.

Juno Caprotina

Juno Caprotina is among the many paths or manifestations of the pre-eminent Roman goddess Juno. Juno Caprotina dresses in goatskins and drives a chariot pulled by goats. Enslaved women made up a large proportion of her devotees.

See **CALENDAR:** Lupercalia.

Khnum

The Egyptian deity Khnum manifests as a ram, the literal meaning of his name, or as a man with a ram's head. The Spirit of the Nile, it was at Khnum's command that the river rose in the annual life-giving flood.

Khnum fashions the bodies of children on his potter's wheel and places them into their mother's womb. In one Egyptian creation legend, Khnum creates all the Egyptian deities in this fashion. In parts of southern Egypt, Khnum was the supreme creator, shaping Earth and all its inhabitants from clay.

Khnum and his consort, the frog midwife goddess Heket, were present in the world from the beginning. Khnum is Lord of barley and wheat, flowers, fruit, birds, fish, and animals. In one creation legend, Khnum wearies of the labors of creating and maintaining life. Eventually he created a device to relieve him of the burden: by placing a replica of his potter's wheel into the womb of female creatures, he was able to transmit his creative power.

See **WOMEN'S MYSTERIES:** Midwife Goddesses: Heket.

Krampus

In Central European folklore and spiritual traditions, Krampus is most famous as the Yule-time companion of St Nicholas (Santa Claus). Good St Nick rewards children who have been good throughout the year with gifts; Krampus takes charge of bad, disobedient children. He rattles his chains at them, beats them with his birch-twig broom, gives them coal instead of toys and candy, and sometimes carries them off in a big sack or in a basket attached to his back.

Some perceive the Norse god Odin hiding under Santa Claus' mask. If so, then Krampus may be Odin's old sidekick and traveling companion, the trickster-spirit, Loki.

Krampus is a goat-man, usually corresponding *very* closely to the Christian conception of the devil. He is horned and hoofed, sometimes with one cloven hoof and one man's foot but sometimes with two goat's feet. Krampus carries or wears iron chains and shackles. When he punishes bad children by stealing them away, the implication is that he is taking them to Hell. Generations of Central European parents terrorized their children into good behavior by warning them that Krampus would "get" them otherwise.

Krampus, however, is a complex figure. One's understanding of him depends upon one's spiritual perceptions. If one sees the devil as a horned spirit (or vice versa) then Krampus perfectly corresponds to the image of the goat-shaped devil. He's wild, fierce, and scary.

However, if one examines Krampus with fresh eyes, without Christian context, a different image emerges. Krampus closely resembles ancient horned male spirits of fertility and abundance such as Faunus. Faunus *always* carries a small bundle of birch twigs. In Hungary, prime Krampus territory, this little broom has a specific name: *virgacs* (pronounced "veer-goch"). The virgacs is so identified with Krampus that in old postcard imagery, a picture of it is sufficient to indicate Krampus' presence. Ostensibly Krampus uses this little birch broom to keep children in line; in reality, he slaps women with it to increase their fertility, similar to the rites of Faunus in Rome and Boujeloud in Morocco.

Krampus' horned head and hoofed body further tie him to old horned gods. His iron shackles and chains indicate his kinship with ironworking shamans. Even the image of Krampus carrying children on his back like dolls can be read two ways: when Santa Claus carries toys on his back, one assumes that he intends to distribute them. Krampus may also be understood as carrying children in order to distribute them to those who desire them—future parents.

Krampus' predilection for "bad" children may also be reinterpreted. "Good" frequently really indicates "devout" and "obedient"; "bad" usually means "disobedient." Under the circumstances, why wouldn't a rambunctious, rebellious Pagan spirit favor rebellious children? Stealing them might be his way of rescuing them.

This isn't merely folklore, Christmas decorations, and speculations: on the Eve of the Feast of St Nicholas (December 5th), Salzburg, Austria hosts the annual winter festival known as the *Krampuslauf* or "the running of the Krampus." Hordes of young men, masked and dressed up as Krampus, are herded into town by a man dressed as St Nick, who then unleashes these Krampuses on the awaiting crowds.

December 5th is the feast day of St Nicholas but it also corresponds to an old Roman feast day dedicated to Faunus, the Faunalia.

Many Krampus costumes are homemade or family heirlooms. Krampus masks invariably include chamois, goat or ibex horns. Sometimes the Krampus wears mismatched shoes; alternately shoes are worn on the wrong feet so as to re-create the shaman's shuffling step. When fully costumed, some of these Krampuses tower over seven feet high. Krampuses run through the square like sacred clowns, rattling chains, clanging bells, and brandishing birch switches.

This tradition of masking, now considered rustic and folkloric, was once perceived as dangerously close to witchcraft and Paganism. Periodically these traditions were discouraged and suppressed. Many of Krampus' characteristics were transferred to Lucky Chimney Sweeps.

Krampus was a favorite subject of Central European Christmas and New Year's holiday postcards and greeting cards. Sometimes he is depicted as diabolical and conventionally Satanic; sometimes his complexities are portrayed. Krampus brings gold coins and flirts with women, sometimes very sexually explicitly.

Krampus rides a goat. Sometimes he is depicted riding a broomstick, indicating his affiliation with witches. Sometimes he drives a toboggan loaded with children, implying that he is driving them straight to Hell. (Sometimes this isn't implied but rendered explicitly with road signs spelling out their destination.)

In graphic depictions of Krampus, he almost always has an incredibly long, vividly red, protruding tongue. Scholars believe this tongue replaces what was once an ever-erect phallus, similar to Exu or the satyrs.

Krampus' sacred colors are red and black. Two artistic depictions of Krampus exist: he is either portrayed as a furry, black devil or as a classic red devil. Austrian postcards from the 1960s depict him as a little demon-child, albeit a lascivious one, usually accompanied by scantily clad pin-up girls. He looks like baby Pan.

Occasionally Krampus is depicted as a female; sometimes entire Krampus families are depicted, including husband, wife, and small Krampus children. In *any* form, Krampus inevitably has horns, at least one hoof, and his birch *virgacs*.

See also Boujeloud, Chimney Sweep, Devil, Exu, Faunus, Satyrs; **BOTANICALS:** Birch; **CALENDAR:** Lupercalia; **CREATIVE ARTS:** Films: *The Craft*, Visual Arts: Halloween Postcards; **FAIRY-TALE WITCHES:** Grimms' Fairy Tales: *Frau Trude*.

Leshii

Leshii means "Forest Lord." They are male Russian woodland spirits and protectors of the forest. They weep when trees are cut down.

Leshii are a category of spirits: there is more

than one Leshii under the dominion of Musail, the Forest Tsar. (Leshii is both singular and plural.) Different Leshii have dominion over different parts of the forest; each has his own territory so to speak. This explains the migrations of forest animals, especially unexpected ones: the Leshii gamble at cards with each other, wagering with animals as their stake. When one Leshii loses to another, animals are transferred from one part of the forest to another.

The Leshii are mischievous, sometimes dangerous trickster spirits. Woodcutters, in particular, earn their ire: the Leshii hide their axes or cause "accidents." The Leshii get people lost in the woods by using ventriloquism or mimicking familiar voices or sounds to lure "intruders" deeper into the forest.

The Leshii is a shape-shifter, manifesting in various ways. Leshii sometimes masquerade in the form of familiar people: this is one way he lures people deep into the forest. One assumes that one is following a known person, only for them to eventually disappear, transform into another shape or be revealed as the Leshii.

> The Leshii's most frequent manifestations include pigs, rabbits, ravens, roosters, wolves, burning fir trees, and even mushrooms, especially *Amanita muscaria* with which he has powerful associations.

Leshii also commonly manifest in specific forms:

✳ *The Leshii often appears with goat's horns and hooves, sometimes with black fur and wings.*

✳ *The Leshii manifests as a man. The clue to his identity is that something is wrong with his*

appearance: he lacks a belt, or his clothes are on backwards or his shoes are on the wrong feet. He usually carries a club.

✳ *Sometimes the Leshii appears as a person whose size dizzyingly shifts from dramatically small to large.*

The Leshii is usually found in the company of bears and wolves. His special companion is a huge white wolf. Wolves are his very favorite animals; in Slavic areas, wolves were once understood to be the rulers of the forest, the true local kings of beasts.

The Leshii, like Faunus, mediates between wolves and domestic herds. Like Faunus, the Leshii doesn't "speak" or at least not like a human. He makes forest noises instead, echoing the sounds of animals, birds or the rustling of trees. Sometimes the Leshii is described as "singing" although never with human words. There are many accounts of people encountering the Leshii or witnessing them in the forest. Those actually encountering the Leshii were often struck mute.

> One theory suggests that stories about the Leshii may reflect fugitives (vagabonds, escaped slaves, runaway soldiers) hiding in the forest. The many stories of Leshii approaching campgrounds and requesting food (with words) are used to bolster this theory.

People uttered protective spells when entering the forest hoping to avoid the Leshii or to be safe from him if they did encounter him. Sometimes the Leshii came out of the forest looking for people. The Leshii has a reputation for stealing children and (similar to fairy changelings), replacing them with less than brilliant Leshii children. (Presumably smart Leshii children aren't traded in.)

The Leshii also allegedly carries off (and marries) women, although notably he prefers unattached women or those trapped in unhappy unions. Sometimes women are stolen to serve as midwives or nannies for his children.

Similar to Persephone's saga, legends suggest that if those kidnapped by the Leshii refrain from eating his food, they can escape his domain. Those who escape are described as looking wild and distraught; some have lost powers of speech (others allegedly return having lost their minds). However still others exhibit new magical powers and knowledge, becoming exceptionally skilled shamans and magical practitioners.

Not all encounters with the Leshii are unhappy. Allegedly if you encounter him but get him to laugh, you'll be safe. Sometimes the Leshii befriends people; allegedly they must then make a pact to never wear a cross or take communion. Whether this is because the Leshii is the devil or whether this is because he is an exclusively Pagan spirit who reserves his favor for fellow-travelers is subject to interpretation. The Leshii sometimes offers spirit-familiars (animal allies) to those he favors.

Offerings may be left for the Leshii in order to earn his protection, patronage, and alliance. He traditionally prefers simple offerings of food, such as blinis, bread with salt (significant as so many spirits dislike salt), the Russian national dish *kasha* (buckwheat porridge), cookies or candy. Tree stumps and fallen logs serve as the Leshii's altar; leave offerings there or alternately, wrap the food in a clean cloth, tie it up with a red ribbon, and leave it at a forest crossroads.

The Leshii's domain extends beyond the forest.

* *He presides over hedges*

* *In meadows and fields, the Leshii plays a different mediation role: between people and rodents*

* *The Leshii has been known to turn up in urban taverns. However, the further away from the forest the Leshii gets, the more likely he is to manifest characteristics attributed to the Christian devil.*

Hunters allegedly make pacts with the Leshii that echo those that the Inquisition accused sorcerers of making with Satan. From the perspective of the Church, these are Satanic pacts; however from another perspective, the Leshii insists on allegiance to the Pagan world. Unlike spirits who don the masks of saints, the Leshii brooks no compromise. Allegedly hunters seeking his protection and gifts must remove their crosses, swear allegiance to the Leshii and no longer swallow the Communion Host but bring it to the Leshii as proof that it wasn't consumed.

In Northern Siberia, hunters allegedly earned the Leshii's alliance by offering him gifts of playing cards with the suit of clubs removed. Allegedly this is because clubs resemble crosses but it may be a reference to the club the Leshii always carries.

See The Devil, Faunus; **ANIMALS:** Pigs, Rabbits, Wolves and Werewolves; **DIVINE WITCH:** Simbi; **HAG:** Leshovikha.

Minotaur

This is the story: Poseidon, Greek Lord of the Sea, sent an amazingly beautiful white bull from out of the ocean to King Minos of Crete with instructions for Minos to sacrifice it to him. Minos had good intentions but that bull was so incredible he didn't have the heart to kill it and so substituted another, less magical, bull for the sacrifice.

Poseidon wasn't pleased. He punished Minos by causing Minos' wife, Pasiphae, to develop an overpowering lust for the bull. She persuaded the master inventor Daedalus to build her a life-size, hollow model of a cow in which she was able to hide and consummate the relationship. She conceived and bore a child with the head of a bull and the body of a boy. He was called Asterius, the Minotaur, which means the Bull of Minos. Minos was horrified and embarrassed.

In other Greek myths, unwanted sons are exposed in the wilderness or put out to sea in barrels, sometimes together with their sexually transgressing mothers. Not the Minotaur: Minos' solution was to build him his own underground domain, the *labyrinth.*

According to the Greek myth, the Minotaur lived within the labyrinth in total isolation and was never permitted to leave.

The labyrinth was a maze: the Minotaur who dwelled within knew it inside out but others who entered allegedly never came out. At some point, the Minotaur was placed on a diet of fresh meat. People were sacrificed to him: forced to enter the labyrinth where death awaited.

This sacrifice was locally unpopular; Minos found another solution. Following a dispute with Athens, the Athenians were forced to send seven young men and seven young women to Crete every nine years to serve as sacrificial offerings.

Theseus, son of the King of Athens, vowed to end the shipment of Athenians to Crete. He volunteered to be among the sacrificial youths. In Crete, he meets and seduces the Minotaur's beautiful sister, Ariadne, a high priestess. In love, she vows that Theseus will not die and with help from the inventor Daedalus who, in essence, was responsible for the Minotaur's conception, forms a plan that enables Theseus to battle with the Minotaur, kill him, and escape from the labyrinth.

The Minotaur is usually portrayed as diabolical and bloodthirsty; he is a consistent feature of books devoted to Classical "monsters." However, the story is an Athenian story, told from an Athenian perspective: the hero is the man who kills the Minotaur. It is, however, the only surviving story: accepting it at face value is akin to accepting stories about witches told from the perspective of the Inquisition.

Whether or not there was an actual living, breathing Minotaur in Crete, there was a labyrinth. Archeological remains survive in the palace of Knossos in Crete. The palace is a vestige of Minoan civilization, the pre-Hellenic people who once ruled Crete. Little is definitively known about them. Their writing remains undeciphered. Even their true name is unknown: historians named them Minoan after King Minos.

Much of what is known about the Minoans is gleaned from artwork and artifacts.

Bulls were a significant part of their culture: images exist of youthful acrobats joyfully vaulting over bull's horns. The Minotaur existed too, but apparently not as a scary monster: his image adorns Minoan coins. Minoan religion seems to have centered on a female divinity associated with snakes and a male divinity in the form of a bull. Clues that the Greek myth of the Minotaur is about spiritual conflict rather than merely killing a monster derive from the identity of the women in the tale, powers in their own right.

✺ *Pasiphae, the Minotaur's mother, is the sister of Circe, lending this tale of animal transformation a different aura.*

✺ *The name of Ariadne, his sister, indicates "Holy One." She is believed to have originally been a Minoan goddess and would eventually become the beloved wife of Dionysus, another deity identified with bulls.*

See **DIVINE WITCH**: Circe, Dionysus.

Oni

Horned spirits were demonized in places other than Europe. Often described as "Japanese demons," *Oni* are a class of Japanese spirits. They are shaggy, horned, and tusked with vivid red, blue or black skin.

"Oni" is also frequently translated into English as "devil" or "ogre." However unlike the European ogre, Oni are not stupid or slow but very smart and thus formidable opponents. Allegedly if an Oni loses a limb, it reconnects and heals *instantly*. They are now typically portrayed as vicious, malevolent, ominous demons up to no good.

Oni carry and wield the *kanabo*, a large spiked iron bar. The feared subject of horror stories, allegedly some Oni enjoy the taste of human flesh. This legend of the human-eating oni may derive from their origins as spirits of death. At least as far back as the second-century CE, Oni, then both male and female, served as supervisors in the Realm of Death. Although spirits of death are rarely popular, the Oni was perceived as fulfilling a spiritual function. Although dangerous, they were not evil and sometimes served as guardian spirits.

The Kamakura Period (*c.*1185–1333 CE) saw the rise of the new Samurai class and the concurrent demonization of Oni. The Oni evolved into enemies of the Samurai. A frequent subject of legends involves Samurai foiling evil Oni. Oni became increasingly masculine and malevolent. True female Oni became rare; the Hannya, a horned female spirit, became perceived as the Oni's female counterpart.

Oni and Hannya have something of the same nature; both are spiritual entities—some Hannya and Oni have always been spiritual entities but others are transformed humans, sort of vengeful angry ghosts possessing the extraordinary powers of demons.

✴ *Men who die in states of excess anger may be transformed into Oni after death*

✴ *Women who die in states of excess rage or jealousy may be transformed into Hannya*

Although Oni are now almost exclusively male spirits, their affiliation is with human women. When male Oni wish to travel incognito or disguise their true identity, they transform into the image of human women. The implication is that any woman might be an Oni in disguise.

Demonized in popular entertainment, among esoteric scholars Oni remain spirits of anger and justice; like Shiva they both destroy and protect. Oni guard the gates of the various Buddhist hells and Realms of Death.

See also Hannya, Shiva.

Oya

According to a Yoruba legend, Ogun, the sacred ironworker, witnessed a magnificently horned water buffalo emerge from the Niger River and transform into a beautiful woman. He surreptitiously followed this magical woman: she walked like a queen through the marketplace where she bargained intensely and successfully for fine cloth. Ogun was smitten; he approached her and begged to marry her. She first demurred but when he revealed that he knew her secret identity and threatened to expose her, Oya agreed—but only if he *never* told anyone about her true identity. He agreed and brought her home to his forest compound.

He loved her passionately but his other wives weren't delighted and sensed that there was something *different* about this woman. One night Ogun and Oya had an argument; he lost his temper and shouted out something regarding her true bovine identity. The other wives, eavesdropping by the door, heard all. Oya knew her secret was revealed; she didn't say another word but simply walked out of Ogun's home, never to return. She transformed back into her buffalo shape and entered the Niger River, over which she still presides.

That's one version of their divorce anyway; another suggests that Oya, the most intellectual of the orishas, was bored helping Ogun at the forge. When the opportunity arose, she eloped with his dashing brother, the warrior Chango, who made her his chief military advisor.

Oya is the woman warrior orisha of storms, winds, and hurricanes. She rules the marketplace, considered the magical domain of women. The cemetery is also under her domain; she is the only orisha willing to have contact with the dead. Oya presides over healing and necromantic divination.

Oya has become increasingly popular in the past few decades and is now among the most beloved of Santeria's orishas. Her horned aspect is not as emphasized in the Western Hemisphere as it is in Africa, where she is intensely associated with antelopes as well as water buffaloes. In African Diaspora traditions Oya is more popularly visualized as a beautiful, regal woman, but horns are traditionally placed on her altars and used to represent and summon her.

See **DICTIONARY:** Orisha, Santeria; **DIVINE WITCH:** Ogun; **MAGICAL ARTS:** Necromancy; **MAGICAL PROFESSIONS:** Metalworkers; **PLACES:** Burial Grounds, Marketplace.

Pan

O goat-foot god of Arcady!
The modern world hath need of thee!
(Oscar Wilde)

Pan is the most famous of the horned male spirits. Some suggest that other horned spirits, such as Faunus, Krampus or Virbius, are all derivatives, aspects or versions of Pan.

Pan's parentage is unclear: he may be the son of Zeus and Callisto, a bear spirit, who may or may not be a manifestation of Artemis. Or Pan may be the son of Hermes and Dryope, or Hermes and various other nymphs. If his parentage is mysterious, one thing is commonly acknowledged: Pan was born in Arcadia, a remote, mountainous region of Greece, as was Hermes.

Pan is half-man and half-goat. His lower half is goat-like; his upper half is human except for his goat's horns and ears. He's furry and shaggy. Sometimes he cavorts naked; sometimes he dresses in a deerskin. He carries a shepherd's crook and the Panpipes he invented. Pan offers his devotees music lessons. He often wears a pine bough wreath indicating his alliance with Dionysus and Kybele: the pine is sacred to both of them.

Pan dances, plays music, and has sex as frequently as possible—he is sexually vigorous and tireless. He is also omni-sexual, pursuing both women and men and perhaps goats as well.

Pan brings joy, panic, and fear. He is associated with overwhelmingly ecstatic emotions. He himself is described as moody and may perhaps be considered the deity of manic depression or bi-polar disorder. When Pan feels blue, he goes off by himself to a cave. Should he be disturbed, he emits a bone-chilling scream that causes "panic"—the emotion named in his honor.

On moonlit nights, Pan is usually in a happy mood. He likes to frolic in remote, wild places with nymphs and satyrs. He is the master of the satyrs, who physically resemble him. Pan dances with Maenads, too. He likes fun and sensual pleasures. Pan enjoys surprising and scaring unwary travelers in the forest who react with panic, much to his delight. Although often described as grotesque, many surviving images of Pan, particularly those from Pompeii, are graceful and beautiful.

> Pan's name may derive from a word for "herdsman," although the more popular explanation is that Pan means "all," indicating that he is Lord of All Nature.

Pan is the protector of the forest and flocks. He is the patron of hunters, fishermen, and shepherds and all those who, one way or another, depend upon animals for survival. Pan negotiates the balance between the lives and needs of animals and people.

Pan was no obscure deity but among the most widely worshipped divinities in ancient Greece, although he was never part of the Olympian pantheon. Eventually his cult extended over the Middle East and throughout southern Italy. The city of Panopolis, at the source of the Jordan River, was named in his honor, as was another city in Egypt (also known as Akhmim).

The Greek historian Plutarch (*c*.45–*c*.120 CE), a priest of Apollo at Delphi, wrote that during the reign of the Roman Emperor Tiberius (14–37 CE), an Egyptian sailor named Thamus, on his way to Italy, heard a spectral voice demanding, "*Thamus, are you there? When you reach Palodes, take care to proclaim that the great god Pan is dead.*"

Pan, however, was not dead: reports from a century after Plutarch's death indicate that Pan was actively worshipped in shrines found in mountain caves and grottoes.

Nevertheless, Thamus seems to have spread the news: this story was very popular among early Christians who suggested that it coincided with the day Christ was crucified. Allegedly, according to the story, all Pagan oracles ceased from that day forth, although that clearly isn't true, as Christians themselves forcibly closed many of these oracles centuries later. The story was interpreted as a parable of the death of Paganism in response to the resurrection of Christ.

> Robert Graves, author of *The Greek Myths*, doesn't dispute the truth of the story but suggested that Thamus misunderstood *Thamus Pan-megas Tethnece* or "the all-great Tammuz is dead"—a reference to Tammuz, Ishtar's consort, a dying god, who died annually only to be reborn each year.

During the later Hellenic period, Pan developed something of a disreputable aura. He was identified with rustic, county religion. Classical Greeks, with their emphasis on human beauty and perfection, considered gods who combined human and animal anatomy like those of the Egyptians to be vulgar.

Pan became more identified as a woodland creature than as a god. However, by the Victorian era, Pan returned to the forefront: he was believed to epitomize the vibrant, Earthy, authentic flavor of Paganism, hence Oscar Wilde's poem at the beginning of this section. Pan became extremely popular during the early Pagan renaissance and is the inspiration for

Dion Fortune's 1936 novel, *The Goat Foot God*. He remains an extremely significant and beloved deity among Neo-Pagans.

See also Satyrs; **CREATIVE ARTS:** Literature: *The Secrets of Dr Taverner*, Music: Flute; **DICTIONARY:** Pagan; **DIVINE WITCH:** Dionysus, Hecate, Hermes; **HALL OF FAME:** Dion Fortune.

Papa Bois

Papa Bois, French for "Father Forest," Caribbean guardian of the woods, is also known as *Maitre Bois* (Master of the Forest) and *Gran Bois*. He is a renowned shape-shifter:

🌿 *Papa Bois manifests as a stag*

🌿 *Papa Bois manifests as half-man/half-animal, usually a stag*

🌿 *Sometimes Papa Bois manifests as a tree with a human face and voice*

🌿 *Papa Bois manifests as an old man, usually dressed in old, raggedy clothes. He is usually very hairy; there may be leaves growing out of his beard. Although at first glance he may look like a man, a quick glance downward usually reveals at least one cloven hoof. (He allegedly doesn't like people staring at his feet and considers it rude.)*

Although usually manifesting as an aged man, Papa Bois is quite muscular and exceptionally strong. He lives in the heart of the forest with his lover, Trinidad's anaconda spirit Mama D'Lo, and is the guardian of forest animals and the custodian of trees.

Papa Bois roams the forests of Trinidad and Tobago. He carries a cow horn, which he sounds to warn animals of approaching hunters. Sometimes Papa Bois lures hunters deeper into the woods by assuming the shape of a deer; he then transforms back into human shape to scold them or issue stern warnings.

Papa Bois despises and does not tolerate wanton destruction of the forest. Nor does he tolerate wastefulness or cruelty, or killing merely for the sake of killing. He has been known to evict, trick, harm, and even kill hunters and woodcutters who incur his wrath.

The Wild Hunt rides in the Caribbean too and Papa Bois is its leader. Among those in his nocturnal troop are a band of reveling witches.

Although Papa Bois closely resembles European horned spirits, down to his associations with the Wild Hunt, scholars believe his roots lie in Africa. He is also among those spirits categorized as "Wild Men." Like Santa Claus, Papa Bois has been softened in recent years. Papa Bois, impersonated by a man, serves as ringmaster of Trinidad's famous annual Carnival. He is also more polite than he used to be: older versions were wilder, more ragged and anarchistic, close in spirit to Faunus than is generally now portrayed.

See Faunus, Santa Claus; **DICTIONARY:** Orisha, Wild Hunt.

Pashupati

An ancient depiction of a horned god has been found on a seal from Mohenjo-Daro in the Indus Valley, dated *c.*3000 BCE. Pashupati, Lord of the Beasts is portrayed sitting cross-legged in a yogic posture. He wears a high horned headdress. He is surrounded by animals including horned beasts like a bull, rhinoceros, and deer. The figure bears tremendous resemblance to that of Cernunnos on the Gundestrup Cauldron.

Devotion to Pashupati was never suppressed; he remains actively venerated and is recognized as a manifestation of Shiva. Once upon a time, Shiva became bored and frustrated with life and decided to go live with the animals in Slesmantak Forest in the Katmandu Valley, now modern Nepal. He lived there anonymously for a while but eventually the other gods (and his wife) came looking for him and his true identity was revealed. Shiva returned to his home and godlike responsibilities but still assumes the role of Pashupati when the desire hits him.

The region associated with Pashupati remains the holiest Hindu pilgrimage site in Nepal. A temple dedicated to Shiva existed at this site by 879 CE although the present temple was erected in 1697. The temple is filled with images of Shiva, especially numerous lingam, representing Shiva in his aspect of the divine phallus.

See also Shiva; **DIVINE WITCH:** Shiva.

Robin Goodfellow

This huge hairy goat-man, horned and hoofed holding a besom broom, was the star of the 1628 bestseller *The Mad Pranks and Merry Jests of Robin Goodfellow*. A medieval woodcut depicts a huge Robin presiding over a circle dance. He has donkey's ears and bull's horns and carries a broom in one hand, a lit candle in the other. Another horn is slung over his shoulder.

Robin is the son of a mortal woman and Oberon, the Fairy King, notorious wild man and shape-shifter. Robin is a trickster spirit. Together with Oberon and other spirits, he is responsible for human fertility and the maintenance of Earth's seasonal rhythms.

See **FAIRIES**.

Rod

Rod is considered the primordial deity of the Eastern Slavs. He usually manifests as a stag or male elk. Veneration of Rod dates back to prehistory. Rod and his wife and daughter, known as the Rozhanitsy (see next section) first appeared during the Neolithic era and are the earliest known Russian pantheon. They were actively venerated until the tenth century when other deities, including Mokosh, became increasingly popular.

"Rod" means "family line" or "lineage." He is Lord of Fertility, Birth, and Abundance. He is a solar deity; his holy days were the winter and summer solstices. Offerings to Rod included bread, curds, and mead.

See **WOMEN'S MYSTERIES:** Spinning Goddesses: Mokosh.

Rozhanitsy

The Rozhanitsy are a pair of deer spirits, mother and daughter. Some historians believe them to be part of the most ancient known pantheon of what is now Russia, dating back to Stone Age pre-agricultural hunter-gatherer times. They are deities of abundance and fertility.

Rozhanitsy names two distinct types of Russian female spirits. The horned Rozhanitsy are not the same as the Rozhanitsy Fate fairies who dwell in the Russian bathhouse. (See **PLACES:** Bathhouse.)

The Rozhanitsy manifest in various ways:

🕸 *As horned women*

🕸 *As women riding horned deer*

🕸 *As women riding horses but holding stag's antlers in their hands*

The mother Rozhanitsy was the daughter of a deer. Her consort, Rod, Lord of Growth and Prosperity, father of her daughter, usually took the form of a stag (see previous section).

Santa Claus

According to legend, witches fly through the night sky, sometimes on brooms but traditionally also sometimes on animals or in chariots drawn by animals. In some regions, among the times of year most associated with witches' flight is the period immediately following the Winter Solstice, corresponding to what the Norse called Yuletide. Witches traditionally fly up and down chimneys; in some areas, fires are kept burning all night to keep witches out (or in).

Santa Claus flies through the air during Yuletide, too, in a sleigh pulled by antlered reindeer. His assistants are elves. In parts of Europe, although not in America, Santa Claus is accompanied by a dark, threatening "helper" who often resembles a horned goat spirit. Santa Claus, too, goes up and down chimneys, although his arrival—unlike the witches'—is eagerly awaited.

The Yuletide night sky is a busy place: Santa Claus, his reindeer, and the witches aren't alone. The Wild Hunt flies through the night sky during Yuletide, too, often led by that white-bearded old spirit Odin. Good Christians were advised to avoid the Wild Hunt at all cost, to stay inside and hide until it had passed.

Once upon a time, night-riding witch-goddesses like Perchta visited homes during Yuletide, expecting to receive food offerings like pancakes or dumplings. Eventually during the witchcraze, households that left offerings to Perchta were charged with witchcraft, arrested, and destroyed.

On the other hand, to this very day, households make a ritual of leaving cookies and milk (or something stronger) for Santa Claus. Many consider this a charming, wholesome custom. What's going on here? Why is a saint lauded for behavior forbidden to witches? Who is Santa Claus anyway?

Santa Claus was unknown to early Christians. Incorporation of Santa Claus into Christmas festivals was considered disreputable, semi-Pagan and actively discouraged until the twentieth century. His association with Christmas remains controversial—fundamentalist Christians still reject him, recognizing that Santa Claus is clearly a Pagan importation. Fundamentalist Christian websites frequently point out that all one has to do is rearrange one letter to transform "Santa" into "Satan" or vice-versa.

> Modern Christmas celebrations incorporate many Pagan traditions including gift-giving, Christmas trees, the Yule log, mistletoe, and Santa Claus.

Ostensibly, Santa Claus is an affectionate nickname for St Nicholas, a beatified third-century bishop from what is now Myra, Turkey. He is among those saints now considered apocryphal by the Church. It is generally believed that beneath the mask of bearded St Nicholas lies the bearded Greek sea god, Poseidon. (Another suggestion is that St Nick was assigned dominion over what was once associated with Artemis/Diana of Ephesus.)

If St Nick is Poseidon, then who is Santa Claus? Various theories suggest who hides beneath the mask:

❈ *The horned god Hermes carries a sack in one hand, indicating that he is a deity who provides for his devotees, who brings them gifts. Santa Claus is the modern "deity" with a sack of gifts. Horned spirits survived within Christianity under the guise of Santa Claus. These days, Santa Claus no longer wears his horns on his head but remains closely identified with his herd of horned reindeer.*

❈ *Christmas corresponds in time with the Roman festival of the Saturnalia, characterized by feasting, happy celebrating, and giving gifts to children. The Saturnalia honored Saturn, an aged god who presided over a long-ago golden age. Saturn is a jolly old man with a long white beard who distributes gifts and presides over merriment.*

❈ *Odin flies through the air at Yuletide. He is a world traveler; once upon a time, his pet ravens covered the globe every day just like Santa Claus allegedly does at Christmas. Santa's associations with reindeer may recall Odin's sojourn with Saami shamans.*

❈ *Santa's role as leader of the elves however also indicates another Nordic spirit, Freyr, Lord of Fertility. Freyr is the Elven King; the elves work for him. Among Freyr's sacred attributes is the pine tree.*

❈ *Perhaps the reindeer are the key: reindeer are closely identified with the Saami people who live in the Arctic, close to the North Pole that is now so associated with Santa Claus. The Saami are traditionally nomadic reindeer herders. They were also renowned throughout Northern Europe for their powerful shamanic traditions. Saami shamans soul-journey, often utilizing chimneys.*

In parts of Europe, St Nicholas doesn't resemble red-suited, reindeer-driving Santa Claus. Instead men masquerade as St Nicholas by donning a bishop's traditional clothing and hat. This St Nick is dignified and devoutly Christian. Whether a child is deemed "good" often depends upon obedience and religious compliance. *However*, St Nicholas is inevitably accompanied by an assistant who is clearly Pagan and frequently horned. St Nicholas officially represents the Church; his partner stands in for Satan. The partner has charge of "bad" children and may beat them (literally), give them coal or take them away, ostensibly to Hell.

In Holland, Black Peter (*Zwarte Piet* in Dutch) is, similar to Krampus (see page 570), Santa's helper. He is now most frequently envisioned as a small black boy, dressed in ornate medieval clothing; he represents a Moor. White men masquerade as Black Peter in blackface. However, this was not the ancient original vision of Black Peter. Black Peter was once envisioned as a shaman. He dressed in rough, ragged clothes and wore a fur hat topped with horns. He carried a huge sack on his back that often has a pine tree sticking out, similar to the phallic pine logs once carried in Dionysian processions.

Black Peter is depicted carrying small human figures in his sack. However these weren't initially dolls for good little girls: they represented babies to be born in the New Year, given as gifts of fertility. "Black" Peter was covered with charcoal and soot, not because he was diabolical, but because black was recalled as the color of fertility, as it was for the ancient Egyptians.

If the original Black Peter was cleaned up, his soot removed, his horned hat traded in for a clean red hat but his big bag of gifts retained, he looks remarkably like Santa Claus.

Under Santa Claus' jolly demeanor may also lurk old Pagan frost gods like the Russian Morozko, also known as Father Frost, or perhaps the Nordic Holler, consort of the witch-goddess Hulda, also associated with Yule traditions and the Wild Hunt. (See **DIVINE WITCH:** Hulda.)

Modern American Santa Claus derives from the traditions of eighteenth- and nineteenth-century German immigrants to the United States. His costume hadn't yet been standardized; instead of his present red and white suit, he frequently dressed in animal skins or tattered rags. Yes, he carried a bag of treats, but he also carried a whip or a stick and a broom. He was soot-faced and carried jingle bells. This shamanic figure resembles those on Dutch Speculaas Poppen cookie molds (see **FOOD AND DRINK:** Yule Cakes).

Modern red-suited Santa Claus is a creation of the Coca-Cola Company. The figure spread worldwide in 1932 as part of an advertising campaign. (Some perceive that his bright red and white suit is a reference to *Amanita muscaria* mushrooms; although this may sound far-fetched, one does recall that the original Coca-Cola formula incorporated coca and kola, two botanicals associated with shamanic traditions, so who knows? *Amanita muscaria* spirits are reputedly red and white, as are the mushrooms.)

Further Reading: *When Santa Was a Shaman* by Tony van Renterghem (Llewellyn Publications, 1995) and *Santa, Last of the Wild Men* by Phyllis Siefker (McFarland and Company, 1997).

See also Chimney Sweep, Hermes, Krampus; **BOTANICALS:** *Amanita muscaria*; **CALENDAR:** Yule; **DIVINE WITCH:** Hermes, Odin.

Satyrs

Satyrs are ancient Greek wilderness spirits who physically resemble the goat-god Pan. Satyrs have the head and torso of man, horns and legs of a goat, and the tail of either a goat or a stallion. They make their home in forests and mountains but are part of the retinue of Dionysus and travel in his processionals.

Satyrs are wild, uncontrollable spirits associated with sex, dancing, and intoxication. They are *always* sexually aroused; an ancient Mediterranean aphrodisiac root charm called satyrion root allegedly bestowed the satyr's vaunted sexual prowess on human men.

Satyrs famously chase nymphs, the Greek female woodland spirits, frequently catching them, often to the nymphs' delight. Satyrs dance with Maenads, a popular motif in ancient Greek art. The satyrs' formalized traditional dance led to the origins of Greek drama, the tragic *goat-song*.

Satyrs are musicians: they play flutes, often the double vertical flutes rather than Panpipes. When Athena threw away the flute she invented, a satyr picked it up and preserved it.

See also Fauns, Pan, Se'irim; **BOTANICALS:** Roots; **CREATIVE ARTS:** Dance: Dance of the Maenads, Goat Dance, Music: Flute; **DICTIONARY:** Maenad; **DIVINE WITCH:** Dionysus; **PLACES:** Forest.

Se'irim

Se'irim (singular: se'ir) are goat-shaped Semitic spirits. Their name derives from *sai'ir* or "hairy" or "shaggy." In Leviticus 17: 7, Jews are forbidden to sacrifice to them, which of course indicates that some were following this practice, necessitating legislation against it.

It is possible that the medieval image of the devil goes back to the Se'irim. The word has come to mean "goat" but also "devil."

See also Azazel.

Shiva

Shiva is among the deities often classified as Horned Spirits however his myth is so extensive that he transcends categories. Shiva's many manifestations include the sacred bull, Nandi. He carries a trident that resembles a pitchfork.

Further information regarding Shiva may be found in **DIVINE WITCH:** Shiva. See also Pashupati.

Sylvanus

Sylvanus, horned spirit of forests, groves, and wild fields, presides over boundaries, thresholds, and hedges. Sylvanus is the protector of herds and cattle. He was worshipped in Northern Italy, perhaps as far as Pannonia, an ancient trans-Danubian nation now part of modern Hungary. What we know of Sylvanus derives from Roman writings and it is unknown whether they simply used a name that literally means "forest spirit" for what were originally independent deities.

The Romans associated Sylvanus with Faunus. He is also similar to Pan in that he too enjoys scaring lonely travelers. The first fruits of the season were offered to Sylvanus alongside meat and wine. These were exclusively male rituals; women were not permitted to witness sacrificial offerings made to Sylvanus. His attributes include a pruning knife and a pine bough.

See also Faunus, Pan.

Virbius

Virbius, a male woodland spirit, is Diana's chief companion at her shrine in the Forest of Nemi. Virbius is the patron of thieves and manifests as a man or a stag. Less emphasis is placed on chastity in Diana's cult than in that of Greek Artemis. Virbius is Diana's consort. Depending upon her aspect, their relationship may be platonic or not.

Statues of Diana that depict her standing beside a stag may indicate a literal stag, her sacred animal, or her consort in stag guise.

See **DIVINE WITCH**: Diana.

Magical Arts

What exactly do witches do? What are their special arts that help define them as witches? Witches around the world participate in all kinds of activities, ranging from healing to divination, from spell casting to spiritual guidance and leadership.

This section explores those magical arts historically identified with witchcraft. It is highly unlikely that any one witch practiced all these arts; individuals have specialties, preferences, areas of interest and expertise. However, all of the arts described below have at one time or another been associated with witchcraft, sometimes to the displeasure of their adherents. Snobbery and class-consciousness exists among the magical arts, too. It's no accident that certain types of magic are known as "High Ritual" or "Ceremonial" magic while others are known as kitchen witchery or "low magic."

For centuries, literacy and education was reserved for an elite male few: not all men were educated but an extremely high percentage of educated people were male. Women lacked formal schooling; during certain periods it was considered subversive for women to receive academic educations. Women were prohibited from entering many universities, guilds, and medical schools. Thus the magical arts closely identified with women were those that did not require literacy: divination, spell-casting, root-working, and necromancy, for instance.

The more intellectual, academically demanding arts—those that frequently demand literacy, such as alchemy, commanding and compelling, sigils, and astrology—have historically been identified with well-educated men, many of whom would be appalled to find themselves in the company of what were perceived as illiterate witches. This desire to disassociate themselves from witchcraft did not save them, however, from charges of witchcraft and the same punishments (usually burning at the stake) meted out to the humblest root-worker.

Many of these men were theologians who practiced occult arts secretly and probably genuinely perceived themselves as totally divorced from the women's art of witchcraft. A famous exception is the Swiss alchemist and pioneering physician Paracelsus, who advised others to throw away their medical texts saying he had learned everything he knew from wise women and Gypsies.

Brief descriptions of some of the most famous magical arts are listed alphabetically below; devotees would suggest that each is worthy of a lifetime's study.

Alchemy

Alchemy is the ancient art of transmutation: most people, if asked to describe alchemy, would say it was the art of transmuting (changing or transforming) base metals into more valuable, precious ones, particularly gold. The stereotype of the power-hungry sorcerer is largely based on negative perceptions of alchemy.

The birthplace of alchemy is hotly contested, however its primal roots lie in metalworking. The first metalworkers to develop alloys, the first ironworkers, and the first smith to forge steel might all be considered primordial alchemists. Marie Curie, in her compulsive attempts to extract, refine, and ultimately transform one element into another, actually changing its nature and molecular structure, might also be considered an alchemist.

> Famous alchemists include Dr John Dee and Edward Kelley, Dr Faust, Count Cagliostro, the Comte de Saint-Germain, Nicholas Flamel, and Paracelsus.

The English word "alchemy" derives from Arabic. "Alchemy" translates as either "the sci-ence of the black Earth" or as "the Egyptian science." The word derives from the Arabic *al* ("the") and *Khemeia* or *Kimia* ("Egyptian").

The name "Egypt" is actually of Greek derivation; ancient Egyptians called their country *Kemet* or "the black land." So alchemy is literally "the black art," a term now often used to indicate malevolent, diabolical practices. In ancient Egypt, however, black was considered the color of fertility, growth, abundance, eternal life, and resurrection: in short, a very positive color. *Red* was the color that indicated danger and malevolence to the Egyptians. Malevolent magic would thus have been considered "red magic."

> One theory suggests that the term "Black Arts" originated as a specific reference to alchemy. As alchemy became increasingly disreputable, "Black Arts" developed into a catch-all phrase for malevolent magic or occult practices in general.

Another suggestion is that the Arabic *al kimia* derives from the ancient Greek *chemeia* or *chymia*, which refers to working, fusing or casting metal.

Transmutation of metals may sound silly today but up until the conclusion of the medieval era it was generally believed that minerals were alive and that they grew in soil just like plants, except incredibly slowly. It was believed that metals progressed through stages. Base metals were very young metals; if metals were left alone in Earth to age, they would eventually transmute into other forms, becoming increasingly more valuable and "pure" with time, similar to the way fine wine improves with age. Gold, similar to a person's "golden years," was thus the natural outcome of any metal, although it might take millennia to achieve. Techniques of transmuting base metals into gold or silver were considered a method of speeding up a natural process.

Transmutation may be metaphoric as well as literal. Transmutation of metals is only one of the aims of classical alchemy. Ignorance can also be transmuted into enlightenment; the base human soul may be transmuted into the divine.

Alchemy expressed hope for the possibility of human renewal, the yearning of the soul for perfection and unification with the godhead. Just as base metals could be transformed into gold by removing impurities and imperfections, so a human could be transmuted into divinity. Alchemy is a method of perfecting what nature has left imperfect or unfinished. Alchemy transforms the raw into the cooked.

> Many traditional alchemical tools resemble those used for cooking and witchcraft: cauldrons, bottles, ovens, vessels, and stills.

Although obviously there were those who studied alchemy in pursuit of material gain, gold wasn't only desired for its material worth: gold was considered superior to lead (the base metal involved in many experiments) because gold contained the perfect balance of the four elements from which all matter derives.

These four elements (earth, water, fire, and air or ether) ultimately proceed from the *quintessence*, "the fifth essence" or Spirit which is what fills the universe with life.

An alchemical symbol illustrating this concept consists of a circle containing a cross. Each quarter of the circle (quadrant) represents one element. The point at the very center of the circle from which the lines emanate is the *quinta essential* or *quintessence*.

Other alchemical symbols include the ancient geometric shorthand for male and female primal power: an upward facing triangle indicates fire while the downward facing triangle indicates water. Conjoined together, they produce steam or the breath of life.

Alchemical formulas were frequently encrypted in secret codes, verbal but also frequently visual. Alchemy inspired beautiful, mysterious paintings whose symbols may be analyzed and interpreted in the search for alchemical clues. Formulas were encoded in these paintings; for instance antimony might be represented by a gray wolf. Those unfamiliar with alchemy merely saw beautiful, odd paintings; initiates saw a treasure map.

> Among the paintings believed to be influenced by alchemy are those of Hieronymus Bosch. Alchemists themselves eventually became popular subjects for paintings, especially between the seventeenth and nineteenth centuries.

Debate rages as to whether alchemy first emerged in China, Egypt, or Greece, or somewhere in the Middle East. Western alchemy, which is largely based on Alexandrian traditions, and Chinese alchemy seem to have developed independently, although as there were ancient trade routes between China, Egypt, and the Mediterranean, it's quite possible that they influenced each other and that there was communication between early alchemists. However, their paths diverged and are so different that they must be considered independently.

Western Alchemy

Wherever it originally came from, classical Western alchemy first flowered in Egypt, in Alexandria, in the first centuries of the Common Era. Alexandria possessed both a large community of cross-cultural occultists and a community of highly proficient metalworkers, many of whom specialized in copper and silver alloys resembling gold.

Alchemy is also known as *"the Hermetic Art"* and identified with Hermes Trismegistus, *"thrice-great Hermes,"* an ancient master of what was then considered the three primary occult arts: alchemy, astrology, and magic. (See **HALL OF FAME:** Hermes Trismegistus.)

Despite later stereotypes, from a very early stage, women were involved with all facets of alchemy, perhaps from its inception.

The first historically documented alchemist was a woman. Maria the Jewess, also called Maria the Prophetess, has been identified with the biblical Miriam, Moses' sister, (Moses was himself identified with Hermes Trismegistus), however she actually lived in Alexandria, Egypt in the early third-century BCE. The oldest existing description of a still comes from Maria and she is credited with inventing and designing several alchemical apparatuses, including ovens. Her most famous invention, the waterbath, remains named in her honor, the *balneum Mariae*, bain-marie or *Marienbad*.

Alchemy allegedly first emerged as an art via the text inscribed on the legendary Emerald Tablet (*Tabula Smaragdina*), allegedly written by Hermes Trismegistus. According to legend, the Emerald Tablet was discovered when the biblical matriarch Sarah, once a priestess of Inanna-Ishtar, found Hermes' cadaver in a cave in Hebron and removed the Emerald Tablet from his hands. The Emerald Tablet allegedly contained the first reference to the Philosopher's Stone.

The earliest documented reference to the Philosopher's Stone is from *c.*300 CE in the works of Zosimus whose writings are the oldest surviving alchemical texts. Zosimus was born in Panopolis, Egypt but lived in Alexandria. He was a prolific writer, composing at least 22 treatises independently plus a chemical encyclopedia incorporating 28 volumes written with his sister Eusebeia, of which only fragments now survive. Much of his writings incorporate quotes from earlier works, including those of Maria the Jewess, and so have been used to recreate alchemical history.

Even people who know nothing else about alchemy are often conversant with the Philosopher's Stone—the legendary substance that was the goal of so many obsessive quests over the centuries. Many understand alchemy to be nothing more than a means of acquiring this miraculous substance. Allegedly the Philosopher's Stone can:

✹ *Change base metals into gold (transmutation)*

✹ *Heal all ailments and illnesses*

✹ *Prolong life to the point of virtual immortality while simultaneously maintaining youth, health, and vigor*

Despite its name, the Philosopher's Stone was not usually envisioned as a rock but is generally believed to be a chemical or powder, or sometimes a wax or liquid.

In ancient Egypt, a black powder made from mercury was identified with the body of Osiris and the Philosopher's Stone is most frequently envisioned as a black powder. Fierce arguments have, however, raged regarding the appearance and true identity of the Philosopher's Stone. In addition to black, it has been described as vivid yellow, bright red or dark red. An Arabic scholar, perhaps trying to maintain peace, suggested that the Philosopher's Stone unites and contains all colors, hence the disagreements and differences in perception.

Other medieval names for the Philosopher's Stone include the "Powder of Projection," "The Elixir," and "The Tincture." New names still evolve: the first *Harry Potter* novel was published in the United Kingdom under the title *Harry Potter and the Philosopher's Stone*. Publishers, fearing that title would be intimidatingly erudite for American readers, renamed it *Harry Potter and the Sorcerer's Stone* when the book was published in the United States.

Alchemy's traditional secrecy is often blamed on the alchemists' selfish desires. They wish the Philosopher's Stone to be theirs exclusively. However historically there have been many other reasons why alchemists cloaked their work in secrecy, and alchemy has been perceived as dangerous and subversive by those in power:

❋ *If alchemists could produce sufficient quantities of precious metals this could cause dire economic consequences.*

❋ *If alchemists could cause spiritual transformations, then who needs priests, the Church or other religious authorities?*

Some rulers, for example Bohemia's Emperor Rudolph II, sponsored alchemists like Edward Kelley, setting up laboratories for them in the hope that they would eventually be able to produce gold; these alchemists were inevitably kept under close supervision. Other rulers imprisoned reputed alchemists, demanding that they produce gold, torturing and killing them if they were unable to deliver desired results.

Chinese Alchemy

Although "alchemy" is used to describe Chinese and Western traditions, their techniques and goals are not identical. Chinese alchemy places far greater emphasis on longevity and immortality than on the transmutation of metal and accumulation of wealth. Rather than acquisition of the Philosopher's Stone, the Chinese alchemical obsession has traditionally involved discovery of a potion, pill or magical technique that would produce immortality. Metal, considered a fifth element in Chinese metaphysics, is used to obtain these goals. Although people frequently died during alchemical experimentation, allegedly these experiments were sometimes successful.

In addition to metal, it was believed that manipulating and absorbing another person's magical power or life essence (see **DICTIONARY:** Chi) could also provide immortality, or at least extended longevity. Methods for absorbing another's life essence often involved sophisticated sexual techniques. Eastern Alchemists were, thus, sometimes identified with incubuses, vampires, and fox spirits. (See **ANIMALS:** Foxes.)

In China, alchemy was identified with Taoism, the indigenous Chinese spiritual philosophy that emerged from shamanism. Sometimes, particularly in older texts, "Taoist" is used as a euphemism for "alchemist." Alchemy was as disreputable in China as elsewhere; Buddhists and

Medieval alchemists were familiar with seven metals: they identified these with the seven known planets, the seven days of the week, and the zodiac signs. Each metal also had a symbol, based on astrological and planetary correspondences. Some planets are affiliated with two zodiac signs.

Metal	Planet	Day	Zodiac Sign	Symbol
Gold	Sun	Sunday	Leo	Sun
Silver	Moon	Monday	Cancer	Moon
Mercury	Mercury	Wednesday	Gemini/Virgo	Caduceus
Copper	Venus	Friday	Taurus/Libra	Beautiful woman
Iron	Mars	Tuesday	Aries/Scorpio	Shield and spear
Tin	Jupiter	Thursday	Sagittarius/Pisces	Lightning bolt
Lead	Saturn	Saturday	Capricorn/Aquarius	Old Man (Father Time)

Confucians often tried to associate it with Taoism specifically to discredit Taoist sages.

Even if discredited and controversial, Chinese alchemy remained an unbroken, if secret, tradition for millennia. This was not the case in the West.

In 290 CE, the Roman Emperor Diocletian decreed the destruction of all works regarding the alchemical arts. Diocletian specifically condemned *"old writings of the Egyptians which treat of the 'chemeia' of gold and silver."*

Virtually all Egyptian alchemical texts were destroyed following Diocletian's decree, thus the crucial significance of Zosimus' work. Among the other few exceptions are two third-century CE papyri discovered in a Theban gravesite. It is believed that because these papyri were buried, they escaped Diocletian's massacre of manuscripts. These papyri were written in Greek and are now named for the cities where they can be found:

* *Leyden Papyrus X includes formulas for making alloys and for making metals resemble gold, a process known as "tinging."*

* *The Stockholm Papyrus contains about 150 recipes, of which 9 deal with metals and alloys. The remaining formulas relate to color dyeing, the production of artificial gems and pearls, and techniques of whitening pearls.*

The study of alchemy in Alexandria centered in a building adjacent to the Temple of Serapis, which was destroyed in 391 CE on the orders of Theophilus, Archbishop of Alexandria. The study of alchemy went underground in Egypt. Persecuted scholars fled to Athens where some joined the academy of Proclus, the Thracian Neo-Platonist. However, this was only a short-lived solution as all Pagan traditions including alchemy were forbidden by the Emperor Justinian in 529.

Knowledge of alchemy survived in Arabia. Arabic scholars translated many ancient alchemical works, originally written mainly in Greek. Many ancient manuscripts survive only in Arabic translations. Alchemy officially reentered Europe when the Moors settled in Spain from the early eighth century onwards. (Jewish alchemists in Europe practiced discreetly; the strong identification of alchemy with Jews in medieval Europe enhanced its subversive aura for Christians.) Increased contact between Moors and Western Europeans beginning in the twelfth century eventually reintroduced alchemy to Christian Europe.

Chemistry (and modern science in general) is the daughter of alchemy, albeit an ungrateful one that usually tries to disparage and disavow its parent. Chemistry is the secular derivative of this once sacred art. Not that this would have been more respectable or less subversive during the witch-hunt era: many natural sciences were once also considered heretical by the Church.

The scientific laboratory is based on that of the alchemist, and many scientific procedures and instruments were first developed by alchemists. The word "experiment" was first used in the Middle Ages to refer to the practice of summoning spirits and is used in this context in medieval grimoires. Alchemists inspired the concept of the now clichéd "mad scientist." Moreover, many of the founding fathers of modern science were alchemists and occultists, as, for instance, Sir Isaac Newton.

Alchemy still exists; this is not an extinct art. There are still alchemists, however the emphasis is no longer so much on metallurgy as on its spiritual, transformational aspects.

See also **BOOKS:** Library of the Lost; **CREATIVE ARTS:** Literature: *Burn, Witch, Burn.*

Astrology

The words "astrology" and "astronomy" derive from the Greek root word *astron* or "star." Astrology is the science of the stars. Astrology's crucial key concept is encapsulated in one phrase, *"As above, so below"*; the theory at the heart of astrology is that a synchronicity exists between what happens on Earth (below) and what happens up above in the sky. By studying, interpreting, and analyzing celestial activity, one can better understand what happens on Earth, enabling one to make better decisions, understand situations, and (last but not least) foretell the future.

Astronomy is the modern science of the celestial realm. Once upon a time, no division existed between astrology and astronomy, once called *"natural astrology."* The ancient science of the stars was a holistic art: clinical observation of the planets, asteroids, and fixed stars (and anything else that might be floating around in the sky) was not distinct from magical and spiritual interpretation. Since the beginning of the Age of Science, however, astronomy has attempted to totally divorce itself from astrology. Astronomers frequently disparage the existence and validity of astrology. Many astrologers however remain keen observers of the heavens and are quite conversant with astronomy.

The word *astrology* is used here to encompass the sacred, holistic, mystical art; *astronomy* refers to clinical observations alone.

Astrology is a tool ideally used to improve one's existence. Like alchemy, Tarot or Kabalah, astrology is a vast topic worthy of a lifetime of study: there is always something new to learn. However, even a minimal knowledge of astrology can be very beneficial. Many practitioners of all sorts of different magical arts incorporate astrology to varying degrees.

Astrology was originally based on observations of the heavens. Seven planets could be seen with the naked eye and thus seven planets were incorporated into the art. However, with the emergence of modern technology has come awareness of planets, stars, and asteroids previously unknown. These have since been incorporated; modern astrologers eagerly await discovery of new planetary phenomena. Astrology is an exciting, vital, living, evolving art, not one stubbornly stuck in the past.

Most modern astrologers use computer programs to cast astrological charts, once exclusively done by hand. The modern astrologer may incorporate as many as 180 asteroids into an individual's chart. Instead of making astrology obsolete, modern technology has enhanced, refined, and improved it.

The zodiac is the wheel of the year. That wheel is divided into twelve segments, known as signs. Each sign corresponds to a constellation. A constellation is a cluster of stars that appear to make a picture; for example, *Ursa Major*, the Great Bear.

Virtually all cultures and traditions have perceived pictures in the sky; the concept of the constellation is universal. However how people traditionally interpreted these pictures is something of an ancient Rorschach (ink blot) test.

The ancient Greeks perceived Cancer as a crab; the ancient Egyptians saw it as a scarab beetle instead. Stories are often told about how these various constellations were formed or came to be in the Heavens. The ancient Greeks perceived the Milky Way as milk that sprayed from the goddess Hera's breast, hence the name; the ancient Syrians called it the River of the Snake, while in Teutonic cosmology the Milky Way was called Hulda's Road. (See **DIVINE WITCH:** Hulda.) Astrology takes these mythical and magical factors into account in addition to clinical observation.

Constellations have names, as do individual stars. Aldebaran is a star within the constellation Taurus the bull. Aldebaran is also called the Bull's Eye, which tells you something about where to locate it. The constellations do not move but the planets and asteroids do, each at its own pace and rhythm, in a sort of complex planetary dance. Astrology charts and interprets the movement of planets and asteroids through these fixed constellations.

Every sign is associated with a planetary ruler, a symbol, and an element. Aries thus is a fire sign; its planet is Mars; its symbol a ram. Earth and water signs are considered to radiate yin or feminine energy; fire and air signs radiate yang or masculine energy.

Every year the sun travels through these twelve signs, beginning at Aries and concluding with Pisces. When an astrologer says, *"we're in Pisces,"* what that means is that the sun is currently transiting through that sign.

Astrological signs may be understood as an annual, perpetual calendar. Each of the 12 signs has 30 degrees; each degree represents a 24-hour period. The following chart shows the signs of the zodiac in order alongside their symbols, ruling planets, and elements. Dates are approximate as the calendar begins anew every year in conjunction with the vernal equinox.

Magical Arts

Those signs and symbols correspond to the Western zodiac, the one most accessible in Europe, North America, and Australia, however there are many systems of astrology throughout the world, many actively in use. Every culture that has gazed at the stars has developed some sort of star-lore, however obviously some systems are more sophisticated than others.

The modern Western zodiac derives from Assyrian, Hindu, and Egyptian astrological systems and, most especially, from the Babylonian system. The Babylonians were extremely sophisticated astrologers; they created calendars sufficiently accurate and reliable to predict eclipses.

The basic elements of the Babylonian calendar are still in use: they pioneered the concept of months, weeks, days, and hours. The first documented use of a Babylonian astrological system incorporating twelve constellations dates back to the early fifth-century BCE. Earlier systems existed but these featured a lunar zodiac, incorporating eighteen constellations.

Babylonian astrology was absorbed into the Greco-Roman system, which is the direct ancestor of modern Western astrology. Ancient Egypt's astrological traditions also had tremendous influence on modern Western astrology.

Christianity has historically been ambivalent towards astrology. Because astrology pre-dates

Sign	Dates	Symbol	Planet	Element
Aries	March 21–April 20	Ram	Mars	Fire
Taurus	April 21–May 20	Bull	Venus	Earth
Gemini	May 21–June 20	Twins	Mercury	Air
Cancer	June 21–July 20	Crab	Moon	Water
Leo	July 21–August 20	Lion	Sun	Fire
Virgo	August 21–September 20	A beautiful woman holding a stalk of wheat	Mercury	Earth
Libra	September 21–October 20	Scales	Venus	Air
Scorpio	October 21–November 20	Scorpion	Mars/Pluto	Water
Sagittarius	November 21–December 20	Archer	Jupiter	Fire
Capricorn	December 21–January 20	Goat (sometimes a goat-mermaid)	Saturn	Earth
Aquarius	January 21–February 20	Water carrier	Uranus	Air
Pisces	February 21–March 20	A pair of fish	Jupiter/ Neptune	Water

Ten out of twelve signs of the Western zodiac derive from Babylonian ancestry; the remaining two, Aries and Leo, are of Egyptian derivation.

Christianity and was intrinsically identified with Paganism, it was initially damned as among the diabolical arts. On the other hand, Martin Luther suggested that signs in the sky should not be overlooked, as they are God's work.

Italian astrologer Cecco d'Ascoli was burned at the stake in 1327 for attempting to calculate Jesus Christ's horoscope.

Islam, Judaism, and Hinduism consider astrology a compatible art.

🕷 *Islamic astrology derives largely from the Sabeans of what is now Yemen but also incorporates Greek, Hindu, and Persian influences. Albumasar, a famous Islamic astrologer (died 886 CE) wrote a book called* The Flowers of Astrology, *which was translated into Latin and was among the first books printed by Gutenberg.*

🕷 *Jewish tradition venerates Abraham as a great astrologer, steeped in Chaldean tradition. Jewish astrology incorporates imagery associated with the twelve tribes of Israel, the emblems of Abraham's great-grandsons.*

🕷 *Hindu astrology is known as Vedic astrology or Jyotish, "the science of light." Vedic astrology uses a different system of calculation: Western astrology*

utilizes the tropical zodiac (planetary motion is measured against the position of the Sun on the vernal equinox); Vedic astrology uses the sidereal zodiac (planetary motion is measured against the fixed background of the stars). The most obvious effect is that a substantial percentage of planets in a Western chart move to the previous sign in a Vedic chart. Thus you might be a Cancer according to Western astrology; should one cast a Vedic chart, you might be classified as a Gemini instead.

Vedic astrology has developed independently for thousands of year. It is the predominate system in southern Asia. Many swear that it is the most accurate astrological system of all.

Chinese astrology is modeled after the cycle of Jupiter, which takes 12 years, rather than that of the sun, completed in one year. There are thus twelve Chinese astrological signs but each one lasts for one lunar year, therefore the year of one's birth is incredibly significant. The twelve signs of the Chinese zodiac are (in order): Rat, Ox, Tiger, Rabbit, Dragon, Snake, Horse, Goat, Monkey, Rooster, Dog, and Pig.

Vietnamese astrology substitutes the cat for the rabbit as the fourth sign of the zodiac, hence the name of the song "The Year of the Cat."

Chinese astrology is the oldest documented astrological system on Earth. It is among the crucial factors considered in feng shui. True Chinese astrology is more complex than merely determining one's year sign; this is also true of Western astrology. Each day, hour, minute and so forth is assigned an astrological correspondence. Every thing on Earth (objects, ethnic groups, plants, nations) also is assigned astrological and planetary correspondences and thus astrology can be incorporated into every aspect of life and every aspect of spell-casting or other magical art.

Although there is now a deep chasm between astrology and astronomy, this wasn't always the case. There is a tendency to "whitewash" biographies of respected scientific heroes to remove any enthusiasm and involvement with the occult. However, among the heroes of modern science who were also astrologers are the following:

✽ *Nicolaus Copernicus (February 19, 1473–May 24, 1543)*

✽ *Giordano Bruno (1548–February 17, 1600)*

✽ *Tycho Brahe (December 14, 1546–October 24, 1601)*

✽ *Galileo Galilei (February 15, 1564–January 8, 1642)*

✽ *Johannes Kepler (December 27, 1571–November 15, 1630)*

✽ *Sir Isaac Newton (December 25, 1642–March 20, 1727)*

Hippocrates (*c.* 460–380 BCE), widely acknowledged as the father of modern medicine, and author of the Hippocratic oath, still required of physicians, taught astrology to his students so that they could distinguish "critical days" in illness, treatment, and recovery. It was not an elective course, but a mandatory one. In the sixteenth century, master physician Paracelsus insisted that knowledge of astrology was *essential* for medical practitioners. Until the dawning of the Age of Science, physicians were expected to be well-versed in astrology.

With the coming of that Age, astrology became a neglected art, preserved only by occultists. Astrology's decline began to reverse in the latter half of the nineteenth century, however, in conjunction with increased mainstream interest in the occult. In the 1930s daily horoscopes gained massive popularity and became popular features in mass-market newspapers. Astrology is now considered among the most innocuous of the magical arts: there are people who perceive it as silly, invalid or untrue but, with the exception of intense religious fundamentalists, few perceive astrology as evil.

See also **ANIMALS:** Scorpions; **DIVINE WITCH:** Hulda, Isis.

Candle Magic

Candle magic, also known as "the philosophy of fire," ranks among the most beloved and popular magical arts. It is not an ancient art: wax candles were once rare and prohibitively expensive. Until the twentieth century candles were not readily accessible to the average person. With the development of paraffin wax, however, candle burning developed into one of the most prevalent arts. Many modern witches might not be able to conceive of casting a spell without the incorporation of candles.

Candle magic involves the use of candles in spell-casting. Candle magic spells can be extremely simple or incredibly complex. The simplest candle spell involves holding a candle in your hands while focusing intensely on your goals, desires, and aspirations, then lighting the candle.

A complex candle spell might incorporate several candles. Color and style of the candle might be dependent on various astrological, magical, and spiritual correspondences. Individual candles might be lit at a specific moment (not necessarily all at the same moment), left to burn for a specific period of time, then pinched out and lit again at specific intervals.

> Before wax, there was tallow. Comparatively inexpensive candles were crafted from animal fat. Tallow candles smoke heavily and have a strong aroma, however some prefer them for magical use. Tallow candles can be found in stores catering to Latin American magical practitioners.

Modern candle burning derives primarily from two sources. The first is the ancient art of the magic lamp. Before there were inexpensive candles, there were oil lamps. Cotton wicks were floated in small terracotta pots filled with oil. These wicks were lit, observed and interpreted. Magic lamps were popular throughout Asia and Africa; they retain their popularity in India and the Middle East. Magic lamps based on this concept also remain popular in the French Caribbean and in New Orleans Voodoo.

The second source is ecclesiastical use. For centuries, fine wax candles were reserved for church use. Among the first innovators of candle magic were theologians who secretly dabbled in magic. Other people stole candles from church in order to obtain supplies. This was very dangerous; if caught, they would be vulnerable to charges of heresy, witchcraft, and Satanism for daring to use church property for personal gain.

Candle burning is associated with many types of magic and many different traditions. It is now considered part of mainstream Western magic but for a long time was specifically associated with New Orleans Voodoo and Hoodoo, where candle magic is known as "setting lights." Thus someone will "set lights" to achieve health and happiness, for instance.

> A vast variety of candles are now available in different shapes and colors. Candles are chosen to suit the specific spell. That said, a white candle may always be used in any spell, as the equivalent of a magical blank slate.

Although there are many methods of candle magic, the following is a standard method based on Hoodoo tradition. Candles are crafted by charging, carving, and dressing them.

Charging the candle means magically transmitting one's goals and aspirations to the candle. This is done by holding the candle in both hands, closing your eyes, and focusing intently on your desires. This is deceptively simple: the key is to achieve a level of focus and intensity. Take as much time as you need.

Some charge the candle at the beginning of the spell, prior to carving, others when the candle is fully dressed, and others at both times and at various periods in between as inspiration hits.

Carving a candle means using a tool to write words, sigils, and symbols in the wax or to draw pictures or images. The goal is to personalize the candle. Thus a candle intended to provide distance healing might be carved with the spell target's name, birthday, astrological symbol, and perhaps a phrase encapsulating the spell's goal—something as basic as *"I am healthy now"* or *"I am cancer free."*

Magical arts in general, and candle magic in particular, are not compatible with multi-tasking. A spell cannot be effectively accomplished unless it has your completely undivided attention. So turn off the cell phone; shut off the television. Lock yourself in the bathroom, if that is the only place where you are assured privacy. The candles, oils, and herbs incorporated into candle magic are merely devices. The magic power that ultimately turns the key to success derives from within you.

Love spells frequently utilize a candle to represent each partner. Each candle would thus be carved (personalized) with that person's name, birthday, identifying information, and so forth.

The candle may now be **dressed**. Don't start crocheting little clothes; it's not necessary. Dressing usually indicates rubbing the candle with oil; however it may incorporate further embellishment such as rolling it in herbs or glitter or anything that can be safely burned.

Oils are selected to magically enhance the goal of the spell. Hoodoo has an elaborate science of what are known as *"condition oils"* (because they're intended to cure your condition). These once mass-marketed formulas have specific names and ideally are crafted from authentic materials. Commercial products are often little more than mineral oil and food coloring. It's best to craft one's own oils or only purchase from reputable practitioners and manufacturers.

The candle may now be charged again, if desired, and burned. The basic philosophy behind candle burning is that matter never entirely disappears. When candles burn they appear to disappear but (metaphysically speaking) in the process are actually transmitting the candle's goal (its "charge") to the powers that decide such matters.

Candles may be burned all at once or at intervals. Reaffirm the spell's goal each time you light the candle. It is considered bad metaphysical manners to ever blow out a candle. Pinch it out instead or smother the flames with a candlesnuffer or small fireproof plate placed over the flame until it goes out.

Professional magical practitioners and stores that sell occult and spiritual supplies make and sell candles to suit the needs of individual spell-casters. Some people prefer to have a professional craft their candles, although the advantage of doing it oneself is that one transmits one's own energy into the candle at every stage, thus enhancing its power. However, some professionals are expert candle-workers and may have access to a wider range of botanical and other materials. Should one purchase a candle crafted by another, the spell-caster should still personally charge it, as intensely as possible, for optimum chances of success.

Candle burning, as perhaps befitting its early church background, is an inherently spiritual art. Candles are often incorporated into spiritual petition. Candles are color-coordinated to match a saint or deity's sacred colors, thus candles for the orisha Oshun are customarily yellow.

Spirits and saints possess specific sacred colors; those heavily incorporating astrology into their craft might choose colors based on astrological correspondences. Beyond that, however, perceptions of colors are intensely personal. If green symbolizes romance for you, then incorporate that color into your romantic spells, even if that is not the conventional correspondence. Candle magic is a very personal magical art; the more vividly one personalizes any candle the more likely it is to achieve success.

That said, the following are traditional color correspondences:

✺ Black: fertility, healing, prosperity, protection. Black candles are burned in malevolent spells but also used in defensive magic to counteract another's negative intentions

✺ Blue: healing (especially emotional and psychic healing), protection, the power of the Sacred Mother; blue banishes malevolent spirits

✺ Brown: justice, stability, prosperity

✺ Gold: wealth, glory, victory, solar magic

✺ Green: growth, prosperity, fertility, financial success, healing especially for physical ailments including cancer and other serious maladies

✺ Pink: self-love, self-confidence, youthful romance, spells to benefit children

✺ Purple: personal power, self-confidence, sex

✺ Red: luck, protection, self-defense, prosperity, healing in terms of general vitality, love, sex and romance, menstrual magic, fertility

✺ Silver: lunar power, personal fertility, success, lunar deities

✺ White: creativity, initiating new projects, lunar magic. White candles can be used to substitute for any other color if necessary or desired

✺ Yellow: Love, romance

Once upon a time, you were lucky to get a plain wax candle versus the omnipresent tallow; today candles come in every imaginable form, some so beautiful it's impossible to burn them.

Candles are easily handcrafted as well. Wax molds are available to make sophisticated shapes in addition to the standard candle-crafting materials and tools. Sheets of beeswax can be rolled and folded to form beautiful, exceptionally fragrant candles.

Candles now come in an almost unimaginable variety; part of the fun of candle magic is searching for unique ones as well as letting the candles find you.

Charm Bags

This is among the simplest, most universal and most primal of magical arts. Charm bags go by countless names: amulet bag, mojo bag, mojo hand, medicine bag, tobie, gris-gris bag, huanga bag, gilly bag, and so forth. Virtually every language, magical tradition or culture has at least one name to describe this concept. In Romany, for instance, the charm is known as a *putzi* or pocket, which, in fact, is where they are frequently carried.

Charm bags involve a very simple concept: one or more magical ingredients are wrapped in fabric or placed in a container. This may then be carried on the person, pinned into clothing, slipped under a mattress or pillow or preserved in another private place. Sometimes they are openly hung on walls or doors as amulets and talismans.

It is an incredibly creative form of spell-casting; the possibilities are endless. There are innumerable ways of crafting a charm bag. The crucial point is to choose the ingredients and then choose the container.

Traditional ingredients include botanicals, bones, beads and other small amulets, crystals, lodestones, metal and minerals, and dirt, especially crossroads dirt or graveyard dust. Other popular ingredients include magical powders.

These ingredients may then be dressed with condition or other oils. (See page 594, Candle Magic.)

Traditional containers include cloth bags, especially those made of felt or silk. Leather bags may also be used. Sometimes a fabric bag is filled with ingredients and then placed inside another sturdier leather bag, particularly when the ingredients include loose powders that might easily spill out. The simplest charm bags consist of ingredients wrapped up in a handkerchief and knotted closed with a ribbon. Elaborate containers are made of precious metals, decorated with priceless jewels. In Latin America, old medical ampoules and vials are recycled and transformed into transparent charm vessels.

Although this tradition literally derives from everywhere on Earth, traditional African-derived charm bags are especially sophisticated, creative, and powerful.

Mojo refers to the power emanating from the container and its materials. Hoodoo mojo bags are traditionally made from fabric drawstring bags, usually red although they may be color-coordinated to suit the bag's purpose, thus someone creating a mojo bag to draw prosperity might choose a green bag.

Because mojo bags can be opened and closed, ingredients may be added or removed. Mojo bags are traditionally "dressed" or "fed" to empower them. This involves either sprinkling with a magical powder or perhaps adding a drop of wine or other alcoholic beverage, or a drop of a carefully chosen condition oil, once a week or on some regular schedule. Because the mojo is ultimately perceived as possessing a living, vibrant spirit (if not literally alive) then this feeding is necessary to maintain optimum power.

Mojo hands have nothing to do with anatomy. The hand refers to the power emanating from the charm, as in the hand of power or glory. *Hands* are enclosed packets, similar to a European sachet. Ingredients are placed between two pieces of fabric which are then sewn together completely enclosing the ingredients. A mojo hand will not be taken apart, nor will other materials be incorporated. It is complete as it is.

Mojo hands are traditionally made from red felt or other red fabric. They are square or rectangular and resemble a quilt patch. The practice of the closed hand may derive from African roots, such as the Paket Kongo (see below) or it may derive from European influence.

Traditional English charm bags bear tremendous resemblance to African-American mojo hands. They are also traditionally crafted from red fabric, often felt, but they may be cut into creative shapes, especially hearts for romantic magic. The fabric may be embellished with beads, lucky charms, embroidery or other fine needlework. Creating the bag is a spell unto itself; each stitch, each knot is accompanied by a blessing, wish or affirmation.

Gris-gris and mojo bags are sometimes now treated as synonymous, however originally they were not identical. Mojo bags are a simple, if powerful, folk tool. Gris-gris were originally elaborately constructed containers, similar to modern Pakets Kongo to which they are closely related. Many were formed in the shape of dolls and contained herbal or various magical ingredients. Enslaved Africans in the Western Hemisphere imported their tradition but were forced to create less elaborate gris-gris, and so southern American gris-gris have evolved into the equivalent of mojo bags.

The elaborate style and artistry survives in the Pakets Kongo, which are packets of Congolese origin usually intended for protective purposes and/or healing. Pakets Kongo are more solid and structural than the standard charm bag. Many feature a long-stemmed gourd or onion shape. Many also possess what appear to be arms.

The contents are wrapped in silk, then bound with ribbons, secured with pins, and ornamented with beads, sequins, metallic cloth, and feathers. Many Pakets Kongo are so beautiful people buy them as objets d'art without awareness of their real identity.

They may be topped with a cross, not because of Christian affiliation but because the cross-shape is significant to the indigenous Congolese concept of birth, life, death, and rebirth. Pakets Kongo are created under the aegis of the snake magician spirit, Simbi.

See **DICTIONARY:** Hoodoo, Mojo; **DIVINE WITCH:** Simbi.

Charms and Incantations

Charms, incantations, and enchantments are technically magic spells created via the power of the human voice. These are among the most ancient spells of all. On one hand, these are simple spells: no other ingredients are required. On the other, charms are among the most challenging, difficult spells of all because they rely entirely on your will, focus, and personal magic power.

Charms consist of two components: the voice and the words.

Charms are carefully crafted spells, not merely spontaneous expressions of desire and passion. Method of delivery is thus consciously chosen. Charms may be cast via the following vocal techniques:

❋ *Singing:* Charming *literally means "singing."* Once upon a time (and still in some traditions), spells were intended to be sung. A proficient magician was expected to possess a wide repertoire of magical songs. This was particularly true in Finnish, Saami, and other Finno-Ugric magical

traditions. Injunctions against women singing in churches and synagogues derived from fear that this left men vulnerable to women's spells. In many traditions, the Fates sing one's destiny. Everyone thus has a personal song that expresses his or her lifeline.

❋ *Chanting:* Incantation *and* Enchantment *refer to the power of the chant. Chanting involves rhythmic verbal expression, somewhere between singing and speaking. Among the dictionary definitions of "chant" is* "to recite in a monotonous repetitive tone." *That makes it sound boring but rhythmic chanting is used to induce trance. "Entrance" is sometimes used as a synonym for "bewitch." Chanting is a method of entrancing.*

❋ *Murmuring and muttering: Sometimes verbal expressions are not meant to be understood by other people. Some spells require that the caster murmur or mutter; the power of the word is transmitted without being directly understood or even clearly heard. This enables a spell-caster to maintain privacy even when casting a spell in public. Murmuring spells are often incorporated into healing; the healer murmurs over a wound, for instance, to hasten healing.*

❋ *Whispering: Whispering is more sibilant than murmuring. One metaphysical theory suggests that the power of the breath transmits magic power. Whispering is particularly incorporated into spells cast in the form of drinks or potions. (See* **FOOD AND DRINK.***) Whispering is also a synonym for witchcraft in Russia.*

❋ *Declaiming: Sometimes a magic spell demands that one boldly state one's intentions to the universe. Many commanding and compelling spells involve clear, loud articulation and careful pronunciation.*

The second component of charming involves choosing your words. Different magical philosophies choose words differently. Some systems suggest that you speak from your heart, carefully, concisely, and clearly. Express your desire in your own words, choosing them carefully to avoid ambiguity. This type of magic teaches you to clarify your desires and to be tremendously aware of the innate power of words.

Other systems suggest that only certain words expressed in certain ways possess optimum magic power. Thus certain words of power transmit magical energy even if no one understands any longer what the word means. These traditions suggest that words must be pronounced a specific way and delivered via specific rhythms.

Traditional charms are also incorporated: certain rhymes or magical poems have been handed down for generations. Others suggest repeating appropriate passages from the Book of Psalms, the Koran or other sacred texts. (See **BOOKS:** Magical Books of Power.)

Word charms are a particularly primal form of spell-casting. The ancient Egyptians suggested that this was the most primordial of all forms of magic. *Heka*, the Egyptian word indicating divine creative, magical energy, is often described as *"the art of the mouth."* Magic spells are conveyed via incantations, verbal spells, and word charms.

To this day, some people consider that all spells should contain a verbal component; this verbal component is the finishing touch that ultimately turns the trick.

The Egyptians believed that there was a secret rhythm that Thoth, Lord of Magic and inventor of language, had taught the earliest magicians, who then transmitted this magical art to others. Knowledge of this rhythm, together with knowledge of spirits' true names of power, was considered the crucial key to magical success. (See **DIVINE WITCH:** Thoth.)

Incantations are heavily incorporated into Commanding and Compelling rituals. Certain magical traditions, particularly Pow-Wow and traditional Russian magic, rely very heavily on word charms.

Commanding and Compelling

Commanding and Compelling is a style of High Ritual or Ceremonial Magic that involves summoning spirits, commanding and compelling them to do your bidding regardless of their own desires, and then sending them off.

This is the type of magic most frequently found in medieval grimoires. Anyone wishing to engage in this practice can obtain a grimoire and merely follow the specific directions. Because the spirits are not necessarily cooperative, nor are they necessarily pleased to work with you, it is crucial to follow all steps of spells and rituals exactly. The term "Commanding and Compelling" derives from the opening words incorporated in many chants, *"I command you, I compel you,"* and has become synonymous with this type of magic. *Commanding and Compelling* is the name given to condition oils that promise their users that others will do their bidding.

Commanding and Compelling derives from two related roots: magical systems popular in Alexandria during the first centuries of the Common Era, and Jewish systems of magic that evolved following the establishment of the Jewish monarchy.

The tradition of Commanding and Compelling derives largely from the legend of King Solomon who allegedly commanded a host of spirits. (See **HORNED ONE:** Asmodeus). Would-be commanders and compellers desire to emulate Solomon's power and magical feats.

Jewish tradition is ambivalent towards magic. The Bible forbids various types of magic, and coincident with the establishment of the Jewish monarchy, native shamanism and women's magical traditions were suppressed. (See **HALL OF FAME:** Witch of Endor.) Magic became a forbidden art, however, whenever magic is forbidden, would-be practitioners who don't wish to be *completely* defiant and disobedient try to find loopholes to the ban.

Rabbis discussed the situation and decided that although it was forbidden to practice magic, if an angel, demon or other spirit cast the spell or did the magical work for you, then technically *you* weren't engaged in magic. Commanding or interacting with spirits became the acceptable face of Jewish magic. It is also possible that a sophisticated system of demonology was also learned from Zoroastrians during the Babylonian Exile. (See **HORNED ONE:** The Devil.) This magical art eventually entered the Christian community where it continued to evolve and serve the different needs of new practitioners.

Commanding and Compelling has always been controversial because the system is easily used to disguise veneration of forbidden spirits. Christian Commanding and Compelling had more complex undercurrents than the traditional Jewish variant. Jewish magicians might summon potentially dangerous spirits who might cause harm, but the magician wasn't in any danger of eternal damnation.

In the Christian perspective, all spirits—with the exception of angels—were evil demons: Satan's host. Summoning spirits thus involved contact with demonic forces. The emphasis in Commanding and Compelling on abusive, disrespectful behavior toward spirits was intended to emphasize that no worship was going on, that one was neither engaged in Satanism nor in Pagan revivalism.

There is a significant difference between Commanding and Compelling and Spirit Working (see page 620). Spirit Working is ultimately a form of spiritual petition; one requests the spirit's cooperation, assistance, and blessings. Spirits cooperate or not as they choose. Although it is ideally a mutually beneficial relationship, spirits are perceived as sacred and are the dominant presence. Commanding and Compelling posits an inherently hostile relationship. If the spirits were so eager to do your bidding, then they wouldn't have to be commanded, would they?

Commanding and Compelling was particularly popular with Christian theologians. Like alchemy, it demands a certain educational background and orientation. One must be literate to read the grimoires, have access to ritual materials, and be familiar with names of angels and demons. Like rabbis centuries before, these theologians discussed and analyzed whether Commanding and Compelling was *really* forbidden or whether there were loopholes that permitted the practice. It was decided that if the human was clearly in the dominant position and if there wasn't an *ounce* of spiritual veneration involved, then Commanding and Compelling might be acceptable.

During the later Middle Ages, further various rationales and justifications of the practice emerged. For instance, the powers of evil must be harnessed in the service of good. Thus it's necessary to command them: demons won't voluntarily do any good. Another argument suggested that since the magician was ordering demons to do his bidding, demons were prevented from doing the devil's work instead.

Based on New Testament legends of the control Jesus exerted over demons, some magicians believed incorporating phrases from the Mass could imbue the magician with some of Christ's authority. Also, if the Roman Catholic exorcism ceremony forced demons *out*, perhaps the ritual could be adapted to obtain other results. (This belief is among the roots of the Black Mass.)

The Inquisition didn't particularly buy any of these rationales, particularly since popular purposes of Commanding magic included murdering enemies and procuring women, rather than forcing demons to deliver food to the poor.

Because demons are perceived as harmful, dangerous, and hostile, various precautions must be taken. Commanding rituals often include elaborate protective measures. Magic circles must be carefully and correctly drawn, in which the magician must stay until the whole ritual is complete. Various Hebrew or Latin chants are incorporated. As crucial as summoning and commanding is banishing: because the spirits are dangerous and unpredictable, they must be sent packing as soon as their task is complete. Until they are gone, the magician cannot safely leave the circle. A famous story involves a demon playing a trick on a magician; it appeared to leave but really didn't, invisibly hiding in a corner. (And of course, demons can materialize and disappear at will.) When the magician cautiously stepped from the circle, the demon swooped down and killed him.

Divination

Divination is the art of discovering the future right now in the present. It is the art of foretelling the unknown, whether in the past, present or future. Hidden secrets to which one is not usually privy are revealed via divination. One can thus understand the past, predict the future, and make better plans for the present.

Divination is ultimately a passive art. The diviner serves as a medium, as opposed to witchcraft, which is an active art that attempts to effect change. Many witches or other magical practitioners incorporate divination techniques; however many diviners do nothing more than examine and analyze events without attempting to cause change.

That said, fortune-tellers, prophets, and diviners have been traditionally lumped in with other practitioners of the magical arts; divination has frequently been forbidden, sometimes on pain of death.

Many psychics such as clairvoyants and clairaudients simply *know* the future or hidden information. They hear, see or dream the desired information; they may or may not have any control over the process. Divination, by definition, is a conscious attempt to obtain information based on specific techniques.

Countless techniques for divination exist, however most are based on specific systems:

✳ Scrying *involves gazing. Scrying techniques include reading a crystal ball or candle-gazing. The diviner fixes their gaze on the scrying object and waits patiently until visions appear, often in their peripheral vision. In some ways, this is a very accessible technique: one can scry into a fire, onto bare Earth or in a pan of water, a still lake or even one's polished thumbnail. No expense is required, no literacy, no materials or books. However, scrying can be difficult to accomplish. One must find just the correct gaze (focused but not too sharp) and state of mind (focused, but sometimes visions are revealed via the mind's wandering).*

* Synchronicity *is the name Jung gave to the theory that any two events that occur at the same moment are related. Methods of divination involving synchronicity usually incorporate tools like cards, dice, runes, coins or other objects. Objects are randomly scattered; the patterns created are interpreted and then related to the question at hand. Techniques using synchronicity are based on systems and rules (each rune has a specific meaning, for instance), however, intuition still plays a big role.*

* *Sometimes neither scrying nor synchronicity is required. The future may be revealed by interpretation of* signs. *Palm reading (chiromancy) for instance reveals the future via the interpretation of one's hand, particularly the lines but also features like shape, muscle tone, and skin texture. Other similar divination techniques involve interpreting the placement of moles on the body.*

* Psychic visions *and prophecies may also be induced via psychoactive substances, lucid dreaming, and various ecstatic techniques including music and dance.*

Divination is extremely popular worldwide. Among the most popular modern techniques are the I-Ching, Tarot and other cards, palm reading, and rune-casting.

The Greek suffix -mancy indicates prophecy or divination. Any word ending with that suffix (cartomancy, necromancy, aleuromancy, and so forth) indicates some type of divination technique. Astrology may also be considered a system of divination.

The successful, accomplished diviner often feels an energy surge during the process, similar to shamanic ecstasy. Diviners often describe it as being *"plugged into the sacred."* Those who love divination perceive it as a sacred and spiritual art.

Ancient oracles such as that of Delphi might be classified as shamanic divination. (Psychic visions were carefully induced using various substances and techniques.) Many modern games derive from divination techniques including cards and dice.

Many historians believe it was the need to record divination results for posterity that sparked the very birth of writing. Divination results were recorded on tortoise shells and the shoulder bones of sheep and cows.

Divination is an ancient practice, simultaneously perceived as crucial and dangerous. In the ancient world, important decisions were never made without consulting an experienced diviner. Rulers kept diviners on the payroll ready to interpret omens at any moment. Words like *auspice, harbinger, augur,* and *omen* all derive from ancient divination techniques. Diviners were crucial to early religion and spiritual practice too. Diviners determined when sacrifices should be offered and to whom. Sacrificial animals (and humans) were often treated as instruments of divination: among the most ancient forms of divination is the analysis and interpretation of the liver.

However, access to hidden or forbidden information has also been perceived as dangerous. Rulers, particularly the autocratic and dictatorial, prefer to keep this information to themselves. Diviners have historically found themselves imprisoned, endangered or expected to provide the prophecy the ruler wishes to hear *and* have it be accurate!

Divination has frequently been forbidden. Those who practice the art or consult practitioners have been threatened with dire punishment. The Roman jurist Paulus wrote in the early third-century CE, "… *if slaves consult about the life expectancy of their masters, they are to be subjected to the extreme penalty, that is, the cross. And any person consulted* [by them for this purpose], *if they give answers, shall be either condemned to the mines or banished to an island."*

Divination was equated with witchcraft during the witch-hunt era. It was believed that if proved accurate, then the information must have been provided by demons, hence it was a diabolical art. Divination remains outlawed in many places, although in Western regions this is because it is often perceived as fraud.

Healing

Some believe the origins of witchcraft lie in healing. Healers prescribed botanical cures, diagnosed causes of illness via divination and shamanic journey, and used various shamanic and magical techniques to safeguard the health of their communities.

Healing still remains an important magical art. Healing and magic are inextricably linked; healing and women are inextricably linked. Evidence suggests that Celtic women in Gaul followed many professions including that of medical doctor and this is true elsewhere. In many traditional communities, the face of the healer is that of a shaman or witch.

Although negative stereotypes suggest that witches are responsible for causing illness, witches are powerfully identified as healers. A Basque spell suggests, for instance, that should illness arise without obvious reason or cause, someone should bring a cauldron to a crossroads, place a comb inside the pot together with some stones, and turn the cauldron upside down. This serves as a signal to witches that healing action is required and allegedly assistance will soon arrive.

Many believe that the close identification of witches and healers sparked the European witch-craze. One theory suggests that witch-hunts resulted as a response to the medical revolution. According to this theory, medical advances contributed to witch-hunts and witchcraft hysteria.

As medicine became more sophisticated, more cures were found; understanding of the physical nature of illness expanded. Pagan traditions tend to view illness from a holistic standpoint: even illnesses derived from physical causes have a spiritual component, thus all cures tend to possess a spiritual component in addition to any other. Ancient healing rituals were thus conducted by shamans and witch doctors. Many of these rituals lingered among midwives and traditional female healers, even post-Christianity.

However with the advent of the new, exclusively male, university-trained physician, this situation changed. These physicians would not conduct traditional spiritual cures. Professional competition existed among traditional female healers and male medical practitioners. Some physicians believed that mysterious illnesses that resisted established cures were actually caused by witches specifically to create hurdles for the new medical doctors. If only a witch can cure an illness, then perhaps she caused it. The new university-trained physician notified the religious and secular authorities who pursued witchcraft charges.

An ancient theory, common around the world, suggests that "disease demons" cause ailments. These ailments were once diagnosed and treated via magical ritual. Post-Christianity, all magical ritual was perceived as diabolical and so people attempting to heal in this fashion were punished as witches.

This scenario inevitably leads to the conception of good witches versus bad witches. Bad witches cause illness; good witches heal them. "Witch" eventually became such a charged, dangerous word that no one wanted to be the "witch." Thus names like "wise woman" or "cunning man" were substituted, even though the techniques and practices might be identical.

There was a very good reason for the fear of the word "witch." During the witch-hunt era, healers were specifically targeted as witches. Those believed to cause illness were prosecuted as witches, but so were those who produced cures. The ability to heal, especially when an ailment had stymied a male physician, was considered evidence of witchcraft.

During the witch-hunt era, being requested to heal became a trap. If healing was accomplished, accusations of witchcraft might follow. At the same time, in the desperate face of illness, healers are desired at all cost. It is easy to see how community tension can arise: those who can heal or those believed able to heal refused to do so out of self-preservation, leading to anger, frustration, resentment, and further accusations. Healing was identified with witchcraft; refusal to heal became identified with witchcraft, too. It was a no-win situation.

Traditional healers were accused of causing illness and ailments so that they would then be requested to heal them, thus acquiring financial gain. In 1679, a witness was expressly asked during a Hungarian witch trial, *"What do you know of the enchantment and wisdom of Mrs Mihály Csonka, which she used to bewitch the health of others and then remedy again?"*

A very specific type of healing remains exclusively identified with magic.

In the indigenous traditions of the Americas and sub-Saharan Africa, malevolent witchcraft is practiced by introducing foreign objects into a victim's body. Among some indigenous American traditions, these objects are usually sharp things or are somehow associated with death, as the dead and anything associated with them are perceived as toxic, not just spiritually or psychically but physically as well. Any physical contact with the dead potentially leads to extremely debilitating, potentially fatal ailments, commonly called "ghost contamination sickness."

In the traditions of sub-Saharan Africa, "live things" are introduced into the body.

Hoodoo incorporates both traditions, describing these foreign substances as *"live things in the body."* Scientifically, they may not be literally alive, however because they are magically charged they generate malevolent energy.

Practitioners may introduce "live things" into the body by slipping them into food. "Live things" include frog or fungal spawn or similar eggs, as well as dried, powdered frogs, lizards, scorpions, and snakes. The results allegedly manifest as aches and pains, malaise, unnatural swelling, perpetual hunger that never abates regardless how much food is consumed, and gnawing sensations within. A strange tingling is experienced in the legs and arms. Women sometimes have the appearance of being pregnant although they are not.

In addition to introduction via food, in African tradition, harmful magical powders may be laid on the ground. When the target steps on or over the powder, the harmful substance is believed introduced into the body. Again, this may or may not have any scientific reality.

In Native American tradition, the sharp things are usually "shot" at a person, sometimes literally but sometimes only on a magical level. Although there is no exact European parallel tradition, it is similar to the Anglo-Saxon concept of elf-shot.

Malevolent Navajo witches use image magic to introduce sharp things into the target's body. Sand paintings of the spell's target are made using ashes. With a ritual bow, the witch shoots the figure with beans, beads or other objects. The essence of the object wings its way through the air, seeking out the correct victim and entering the body.

These are magical illnesses—hence they require magical solutions. Cures are effected by the medicine woman or man, healer or shaman, who usually sucks out or otherwise removes the source of trouble. This concept of extracting foreign substances, often perceived as living, is common to many magical and shamanic traditions, and this type of healing is not uncommon in many parts of the world. In South America, for instance, as in Siberia, "live things" or the equivalent are extracted via sucking, psychic surgery or via special magical tools and instruments.

Sometimes the shaman will display objects that allegedly have been removed from the victim's body. Sometimes this is literally the case but sometimes there is a performance aspect to the cure. Various shamanic theories suggest that it is crucial that the patient see the removed article even if it did not come directly out of their body, because the object produced by the shaman contains the essence of the harmful object. This is the kind of magical reasoning that frustrates and enrages the literal (rather than magical) minded and led to accusations of shamanism as fraudulent. What can be witnessed are the roots of theatrical conjuring, also originally a shamanic art. Sleight of hand is used as a healing technique.

Herbalism

Herbalism is the magical art of botanicals. Some believe that shamanism and witchcraft first emerged as a "botanical cult." Individuals studied plants, communicated with them and learned all about them, acquiring knowledge of physical healing, magical, and psychoactive effects. Witches and shamans were able to spiritually interact with plants (or at least with their presiding spirits, depending upon interpretation).

The ancient Greeks did not linguistically distinguish between herbal healers, poisoners, and witches: all three possessed the power of plants. (See **DICTIONARY:** Pharmakon.) Herbalism remains a beloved magical art. Botanicals are the primary component of magic spells from every tradition around the world.

Each individual plant is believed to radiate a specific magical power in addition to whatever healing or harmful physical effects it might also cause. Thus lavender is believed to sharpen the mind, while calamus root enhances your powers of command. Roses are favored in love spells; chrysanthemums are identified with death.

Different botanicals are identified as under the dominion of various spirits. Working with the botanicals is one way of attempting to contact spirits or avail yourself of their power. Cowslips—wild primroses—are identified with the Nordic goddess Freya. They are her favorite flower and are believed to transmit her grace and power. Washing one's face with a cowslip infusion is a method of petitioning Freya to share some of her beauty.

The simple act of gardening or tending the Earth becomes a spiritual interaction. A private garden is transformed into an outdoor altar. Magic spells are transmitted via gardens. A desire for personal fertility may be conveyed to the universe by crafting a garden filled with plants associated with fertility such as poppies, figs, and pomegranates.

A desire for protection might be signaled by planting cactuses, nettles, and poisonous plants like oleander or datura. Spirits may be summoned or fairies beckoned by planting inviting gardens filled with their favored botanicals.

Ancient priestesses of Kybele and Hecate were botanical experts. The tradition survives among Santeria's priestesses and priests, the Santera and Santero. A botanical education is a required part of initiation.

Every magical tradition also has a botanical tradition, some simple, others extremely elaborate and complex. This remains very accessible magic; many fine herbal books are available, as are academies devoted to the botanical arts including aromatherapy and flower essences in addition to traditional herbalism.

Image Magic

Many consider "Voodoo Dolls" to be the height of harmful magic. The Voodoo doll is envisioned as a figure crafted to resemble a specific human target. The target's fingernail parings or strands of his hair may be imbedded in the doll to further personalize it. Pins are then plunged into the doll, according to this stereotype. The part of the target's body corresponding to that part of the doll pierced by the pin is subject to sharp pains. A pin through the heart or throat might be fatal. This stereotype is unfortunate as it has served to demonize Voodoo and Vodoun, sophisticated magical and spiritual systems with relatively little to do with what might be better called image magic.

Image magic is an ancient practice, common to every corner of Earth.

The wizard or witch
Sits in the shade of the wall
Sits making spells against me
Fashioning images of me

That poem or charm may sound current but it was composed during the later Babylonian Empire and is featured amongst the *Maklu* or "Burning" Babylonian magical tablets. The *Maklu* consists of eight tablets giving directions for protective spells and incantations to be used against malevolent witches and wizards. The chant describes the harmful witch or wizard fashioning images for malicious purposes, but protective instructions also incorporate image magic, instructing the bewitched person to make figures of their enemies, and then to ritually destroy these figures accompanied by prayer and spiritual petition.

Image magic is among the most primordial magical arts. Various creation tales including the one in the Bible suggest that people were first created via image magic. In the Bible, God creates people from Earth. The Egyptians posited a similar scenario: Khnum the ram-headed god created the first people out of clay on his potter's wheel. His wife, frog-goddess Heket breathed life into the forms he created.

A Chinese myth suggests that a female spirit created people also via image magic. Lonely Nu Kua the Dragon Goddess was playing alone on the beach with wet sand, when she started molding human figures to amuse her and keep her company. She crafted the first people this way, breathing life into them: eventually she grew tired and bored. When Nu Kua realized how much work it would be to fill the entire Earth with individual human beings, she invented sexual intercourse so people could reproduce independently.

Most people are only familiar with the sensational, harmful aspects of witchcraft such as malevolent killing spells. Image magic has traditional been used to cast malevolent spells but it is just as frequently used for beneficial magic, including healing, love, success, and fertility spells.

Figures may be crafted from clay, wax, cloth, wood, or bone—just about any material that exists. Photographs are now also incorporated into modern image spells; paintings and other visual images have been used in similar fashion for centuries.

It is unfair to ascribe harmful image magic to Voodoo or any other modern magical or spiritual tradition for that matter. The concept of causing harm by piercing an image of a specific target dates back *at least* to ancient Egypt and Mesopotamia.

Piercing was not always intended to cause harm, illness or physical pain. In Alexandria, wax figures were pierced with pins to induce the pangs of love. Pierced doll magic was incorporated into a less-than-romantic love spell. The image was personalized as the person the spell-caster wished to seduce. Pins were introduced into various parts of the image along with the appropriate incantation: as the pin pierces an eye, for instance, the spell-caster croons "You see only me" or "Your eyes burn with desire for me" or something similar. Ancient magic wasn't shy and tends to be sexually graphic, and so the spell-caster would describe in detail exactly what effects those pins were expected to cause.

Image magic was used for all sorts of goals and purposes. An Egyptian story dates back to *c.*3830 BCE: a man suspects his wife of betraying him so he crafts a small, wax crocodile image. He chants spells over it and commands the crocodile to catch his wife's lover. The wax crocodile comes to life and proceeds to capture (and punish) the lover. The guilty wife is punished by the king. The story views the magic spell as perfectly appropriate; the wax image is not an object of dread and horror but an avenue toward justice and truth.

> According to legend at least, wax images are a favorite tool of those who conspire against royalty: in 968 CE, his enemies allegedly used a wax image to try to kill King Duffus of Scotland. The perpetrators were caught and identified as witches. The king survived the spell; those accused of witchcraft were burned. In 1479, allegedly one dozen Edinburgh witches participated in the burning of a wax image of Scotland's King James III.

Although harmful image magic exists, *many* methods of causing magical harm exist. It is not the only one. In sub-Saharan African practices, from whence the roots of Vodoun derive, magical harm is more traditionally caused via direct application, not indirect image magic. Topical poisons or inserting foreign objects into the body are more common. In Africa, image magic is more closely identified with acquisition of fertility than with harmful spells.

> Image magic might also be called Doll Magic. The word "doll" derives from the same roots as "idol." The first dolls were crafted for spiritual and magical use as well as to entertain children. See **TOOLS**: Dolls.

Image magic for whatever reason is created by first crafting an image that resembles the target of the spell. Love spells involving a couple require two images, one to represent each person. A Chinese spell intended to stimulate family harmony and protection requires an image to represent each member of the family.

> Candles, formed from wax, may be understood as the direct descendant or even just another branch of Image Magic.

The Scottish magical image is known in Gaelic as the *Corp Creadh*. Traditionally, a clay figure is formed in the image of the spell's target, and then pierced with pins to cause pain. The piercing is not done haphazardly but deliberately; each pin is accompanied by a verbal curse. Similar images were formed in Ireland, too, but the figure was created from twisted sheaves of wheat.

> Marie de Medici, widow of France's King Henry IV, together with her friend Leonora Galigai Concini, was accused of trying to kill Marie's son Louis XIII using a clay statuette baptized in his name and stabbed with a needle. Marie was exiled; Leonora was burned as a witch in July 1617.

Image magic was particularly feared in Christian Europe; it became exclusively identified in the popular imagination with negative, harmful practices. Because all magic was forbidden, it was impossible to discuss the various beneficial techniques to which image magic may be put—for instance distance healing or protection spells.

Although most images are small, the Golem is a dramatically large magical image, larger than life, so to speak. The golem may be the single most dramatic manifestation of image magic. A golem is an artificial man created from Earth and brought to life by various techniques, including mastery of names of power. In folklore, the golem often acts as a servant who eventually grows more powerful than its master and creator. It can't be controlled so it must be destroyed. Legends of the Golem inspired Mary Shelley to write her novel *Frankenstein*.

> Eliezer of Worms (now Wûrzburg) recorded a formula for creating a Golem:
>
> 1. Craft an image from virgin soil obtained from a mountainous place where no one has ever previously dug.
> 2. Chant the incantation comprising *"the alphabets of the 221 gates"* over every single organ individually.
> 3. Incise either the name of God on the image's forehead or the Hebrew word *EMET* or "truth."
> 4. The golem may be destroyed by erasing the first letter of *EMET*, creating the word *MET* or "death." Conversely the entire creative combination may be reversed so that it becomes a destructive combination.

Golem is a Hebrew word indicating "formless" or "lifeless matter." It also means an embryo, something not fully formed or complete. The Latin name for this concept is *homunculus*. Alchemists like Dr Faust were suspected of trying to create artificial people; herein lie the origins of the archetypal mad scientist and perhaps of modern cloning.

Solomon ibn Gabirol (*c.*1021–1058) allegedly created a rare female golem from wood. Rabbi Samuel, a twelfth-century French Kabalist, allegedly created a golem that was able to accompany him on his travels and serve him, but was unable to speak.

The most famous golem of all was the one created by Rabbi Judah Löwe ben Bezalel. Its remains are allegedly among the debris in the attic of the Prague synagogue the *Altneuschule*.

Kabalah

Kabalah (also spelled Kabala or Kabbalah) literally means "that which is received," implying "tradition," but also refers to what was originally an oral tradition, transmitted directly from teacher to student and restricted to a small circle of devotees. Among its other definitions is "received love."

Kabalah is a broad term encompassing various spiritual and magical traditions.

Although it has recently become popular, it was once a secret tradition, open only to initiates and perceived as dangerous to those unprepared for its wisdom. For centuries, in traditional Jewish mysticism, only married men over the age of forty were officially permitted to study Kabalah. Only they were believed stable, grounded, and sensible enough to withstand its profound spiritual dangers.

Kabalah was controversial and somewhat disreputable (and to some extent remains so) in the conventional Jewish community, heavily influenced by rationalist philosophies such as those of Moses Maimonides. In the Christian community, Kabalah was simply synonymous with magic.

Where does Kabalah come from? According to one legend, when Moses received the Ten Commandments on Mount Sinai he also received additional knowledge that he was instructed to keep secret. ("Occult" is a synonym for "secret" and so this secret knowledge is the basis for occult wisdom.) (See **BOOKS:** Grimoires: *Eighth, Ninth and Tenth Books of Moses, Sixth and Seventh Books of Moses.*)

Among Kabalah's most prominent leaders were Moses Cordovero, Isaac Luria, and Chaim Vital who was also a skilled alchemist.

There is not one single book known as the Kabalah. Instead various sacred texts are used, including:

❋ Sefer Yetzirah *(Book of Creation): Traditional wisdom suggests that the* Sefer Yetzirah *was divinely revealed. Another version suggests that it was composed between the third and sixth centuries* CE *in Palestine. Among its themes is that the Creator formed the universe via the twenty-two letters of the Hebrew alphabet and the ten sephirot of the Tree of Life, thus the world has thirty-two secret (occult) paths to wisdom.*

❋ Sefer Habahir *(Book of Brightness): This text emerged in the Jewish community of Provence between 1150 and 1200* CE.

❋ The Zohar *(Book of Splendor): In approximately 1280, Moses de Leon (1238–1305), a Spanish Jew, began circulating booklets in Aramaic among his fellow Kabalists. De Leon claimed that he had transcribed them from an ancient book composed in the second-century* CE *in the academy of Rabbi Simon bar Yochai. These booklets gradually formed* The Zohar.

According to *The Zohar*, the Creator initially taught the Kabalah to angels who then shared them with people. They taught Adam, who passed it on to Noah, who passed it on to his descendants. Abraham brought the teachings to Egypt. Moses, King David, and Solomon were all initiated into the Kabalah's secrets so these male patriarchs and heroes were all simultaneously occult masters and spiritual adepts. The information was transmitted orally. No one wrote it down until Simon Bar Yochai.

Sephirot are the ten paths or rungs of Kabalah's Tree of Life. The Sephirot may be diagrammed as a tree or in the form of a candelabrum. The ten sephirot are:

1. Keter (Crown)
2. Chochma (Wisdom)
3. Bina (Understanding)
4. Hesed (Love)
5. Geburah/Gvura (Power)
6. Tiferet (Beauty)
7. Netzach (Endurance, Eternity, Victory)
8. Hod (Glory, Splendor)
9. Yesod (Foundation)
10. Malkuth (The World)

In popular terminology Kabalah has become a catch-all name for any kind of Jewish or Jewish-derived magic. (There was even once a type of mass-marketed witch board sold under the name *Kabalah*.) These may have nothing to do with Kabalah in its pure form. Within the Jewish magical and mystical communities, distinctions are drawn between "theoretical Kabalah" (Kabalah in its pure form) and "practical Kabalah," which includes various and sundry magical practices.

During the Renaissance, Kabalists developed reputations as powerful sorcerers and magicians. The traditional image of the robed, bearded wizard with a peaked hat and big book is based on the stereotype of a Kabalah master.

Christian practitioners also began to adopt Kabalah for their own spiritual purposes and magical purposes. (See below, Cabala.) During a time of tremendous cultural segregation, metaphysicians were the exceptions to the rule. Christian spiritual and magical seekers including the great Cornelius Agrippa ventured into Jewish ghettoes (Jews were often not permitted to leave) to study and trade secrets with the Kabalists.

Since the fifteenth century, Kabalah has exerted a tremendous influence over mainstream European magical practices, especially Ceremonial Magic and High Ritual Magic. In the sixteenth century it began to be associated with witchcraft and took on a disreputable air.

Kabalah has since evolved into a general term for Jewish mysticism: via techniques such as fasting and the recitation of hymns, prayers, and names of power uttered either in a state of trance or of complete, *total* focus, the devotee attempts to progress up the ten paths, intelligences, or rungs of the ladder of the Sephirot or Tree of Life. Among those greatly influenced by Kabalah were Eliphas Levi, Samuel MacGregor Mathers, and Aleister Crowley.

Cabala

The Christian derivative of Kabalah is spelled with a "c" to distinguish it from its ancestor. Kabalah posed a dilemma for some medieval Christian spiritual seekers. They were fascinated with its traditions and sought to understand and master them; yet for many, its clear and unavoidable associations with Judaism were troubling. In response, Christian Cabala developed based on the teachings of Kabalah but consciously attempting to incorporate a Christian overlay. (This may also have been necessary for practitioners' safety.) Cabala first developed in Spain during the Golden Age when Christians, Jews, and Muslims mingled in the academies of mysticism in Toledo.

Qabala

This metaphysical system is based on Kabalah but also incorporates other mystical traditions including Hermeticism, Buddhism, Christianity, and Sufi wisdom.

Necromancy

"Necromancer" is sometimes used as a synonym for "sorcerer" with the added implication of "evil sorcerer." Necromancy is frequently used as a synonym for malevolent, harmful witchcraft. Often, those who realize that necromancy has something to do with death interpret the word to mean "corpse desecration." None of these definitions are correct.

Technically, necromancy indicates divination using the dead as a tool in the same manner that cartomancy indicates divination via cards. There are many techniques of divination; most do not involve a trip to the cemetery or any contact with a corpse although a few methods do.

Necromancy is most frequently practiced via various divination techniques included scrying, dream incubation, séances and the use of witchboards. Botanical techniques are also incorporated: in Virgil's *Aeneid*, the golden bough (mistletoe) is the passport to the realm of the dead.

Of course, necromancy is not just any form of divination. People have always been fascinated with mysteries of life and death: necromancy is, at its finest expression, a sacred, spiritual art that attempts to bridge the realms of the living and the dead.

Necromancy is rooted in shamanic techniques for journeying between realms. There are several beliefs at the heart of necromancy:

* *Certain secrets can only be discovered in the realm of the dead*

* *When the living die, time stops for them and they are able thus to see the past and future equally well*

* *Because dead souls were once living people, they can communicate with people more clearly than spirits, who sometimes have difficulty expressing themselves to people in a lucid, understandable fashion. (See* **HORNED ONE:** *Faunus, Leshii.)*

* *Ancestral spirits are genuinely interested in your welfare: there are no ancestors without descendants. Their well-being depends on yours. Therefore, ancestral spirits in particular may be contacted for assistance and information.*

Most necromantic systems believe that dead souls can communicate with the living no matter how long they've been dead—hence the practice of attempting to contact historic figures, sometimes long gone, at séances. Ancient Greek shamans, however, disagreed. They perceived that the longer someone was dead, the further away from the living they traveled. The longer a person was dead, the less likely it would be that they could communicate lucidly with the living or even understand the living person's concerns—hence the need for actual contact with a fresh corpse or a recently buried one. Classical Greek and Roman authors describe witches digging in the cemetery with horror but this was the true spiritual basis of the practice, however by then shamanic traditions had fallen from fashion.

> Legendary necromancers include Circe and the Witch of Endor. In Assyria, a special name existed for this type of practitioner: "Raiser of the Departed Spirit."

In Book XI of Homer's *Odyssey*, composed in the ninth-century BCE but based on earlier sources, the goddess Circe advises Odysseus that he must obtain council from the dead prophet Tiresias. There is only one way to accomplish this: under Circe's tutelage, Odysseus engages in necromancy. He enters the realm of the dead via shamanic rituals including a blood sacrifice. Homer indicates no revulsion or sense of wrongdoing. By Plato's time however, in the fourth-century BCE, necromancy was viewed with revulsion.

Witches have traditionally been accused of defiling gravesites and corpses. However, most necromantic practices do not require either.

Séances

Séances remain a popular modern form of necromancy. Séance literally indicates a "session" or "seating." Traditionally at least one of the participants possesses some mediumistic skill. Professional mediums sometimes hold séances attended by people who are otherwise strangers. The purpose of the séance is generally to establish communication with dead souls for various reasons, however some people also conduct séances for fun, sensationalism or just to see what will transpire. Purposeless séances are to be discouraged as they tend to invite the presence of malevolent or low-level spirits.

Ironically perhaps, those who play with necromancy, treating it as a joke, tend to have worse experiences than those who treat it seriously. Proper magical and spiritual safeguards should be taken to ward off malevolent entities who might attempt to use a séance as a portal. (See **CREATIVE ARTS:** Comics: *Black Widow*.) A proper séance takes spiritual precautions to ensure that only invited guests show up.

References to rituals similar to séances have been recorded as far back as the third century. In 1848, however, the Fox Sisters of upstate New York inaugurated the modern phenomenon of spiritualism. It became a craze. Although séances are traditionally conducted to contact the dead, eventually many stopped treating it as necromancy and considered séances as venues for experiencing paranormal phenomena.

Séances became increasingly dramatic. Outsiders or those new to the occult expecting sensational results are frequently disappointed: real psychic phenomena are rarely as physically dramatic as the fantasy magic of television, literature or fairy tales.

Mediums began displaying ectoplasm, a subtle substance that allegedly exudes from the bodies of some mediums. Spectral photographs were produced as well as the sound of trumpets or other discarnate noises. Dramatic expectations led to abuse and fraud. Sensational effects are easier to fake then genuine psychic ability. (And, truth be told, sensation seekers desired dramatic effects often more than they wanted genuine psychic experience.)

The phenomenon known as table turning was apparently first recorded in Europe. When two or more people sat at the séance table, holding their hands and legs in certain ways, the table began to tilt, turn or even levitate. By 1854, the practice of table turning was widespread. This evolved into table tapping. Once the table began to tip, signaling the appearance of the spirit, participants ask the spirit questions. The spirit answers by tapping, one tap indicating "yes" for instance, with two taps for "no."

Modern séances still exist and are an important feature of the Spiritualist movement. Special effects are no longer as emphasized; spiritual aspects of the séance are considered most crucial. Séances are usually conducted by sitting around a round table. Some traditions initiate the séance by singing hymns or other songs to set the mood.

Witch Boards

Witch boards, also known as Egyptian luck-boards, spirit boards and talking boards, are probably the most accessible and popular modern necromantic technique. The most famous of these boards are ouija boards, however the category also includes planchettes and any other similar devices.

Witch boards serve as party games, oracles, and conduits to the realm of ghosts and spirits. They have gone from serious occult tools to teen (or younger) party games, and are currently experiencing something of a renaissance. Artists and/or occultists are creating beautiful new forms based on this ancient concept.

Although these are modern devices, witch boards have ancient roots. Witch boards may derive from devices like Central African oracle boards, such as those used by the Zande nation. These "rubbing boards" consist of a small portable table with a board that covers it. Liquid is poured onto the table and then the board is rubbed over it. Affirmative or negative answers are determined by whether the board sticks to the table or not.

Before there was the ouija board, there was the planchette, which derives from the personal system of spirit writing or automatic writing. A pencil was attached to a small basket. The medium touches the basket; contact is made with the spirit who takes over, using the medium's hand to write messages. This is similar to ritual possession but using the hand instead of the voice.

> Chinese oracles using a sand table and a writing implement to produce spirit writing have existed for centuries.

This evolved into the formalized planchette. Planchette means "little plank" and was first invented in France in 1853. A planchette is a small board or table on rolling wheels with an attached pencil that writes on sheets of paper placed underneath. Messages are produced by moving the planchette over the paper. The planchette may be used by one person but is large enough for two people to rest their fingers on.

The advantage of the planchette over the traditional séance was that it was portable and could be accomplished by one person alone; the planchette introduced the concept that any individual could independently be a medium. However it was unwieldy. Ultimately they were unnecessary and were replaced by automatic writing, which simply utilized a pen and paper to produce messages from other realms.

Witch boards combine the planchette with séance table turning techniques. Instead of the rolling planchette, letters were printed directly onto a board together with words like "yes," "no," and "goodbye." (Sophisticated modern witch boards include messages like "ask again later" or even "no comment.")

In Europe, early witch boards were improvised using a shot glass or tumbler and individual letters. (Letters were created on small squares of paper or game board pieces such as Scrabble© may be used.) Two people sit with their fingers placed gently on an upside-down drinking glass placed within a circle of letters. Letters touched by the glass's movement allegedly spell out messages.

By the late nineteenth century, several different witch boards were sold through Sears Roebuck and other catalogs. From approximately 1890 until 1950, dozens of manufacturers created and marketed different witch boards. The most successful of these boards was marketed as *"Ouija, the Mystifying Oracle Talking Board."*

The origins of the ouija board are steeped in mystery. It was allegedly patented on July 19, 1892 by a Baltimore customs inspector, William Fuld. However, a patent filed in 1890 and granted in 1891 for the ouija board lists Elijah J. Bond of Baltimore as the inventor and assigns marketing rights to Charles W. Kennard and William H. A. Maupin. The Kennard Novelty Company produced the first commercial line of ouija boards. Sales steadily increased; eventually William Fuld took over the helm of the company. He reinvented the history of the board and claimed to have invented the first board together with his brother Isaac in his home workshop.

Despite the spelling, ouija is pronounced "wee-jee."

Why is it called "ouija" board? Various reasons are given.

❋ *Fuld claimed that he asked the board what to call it and it spelled out O-U-I-J-A. Fuld suggested that this was an Egyptian word for good luck. Egyptologists remain unfamiliar with it, however this is allegedly the explanation given by the board.*

❋ *The name may derive from the Moroccan city Oujda (also spelled Oujida or Oudjda), or the West African city of Whydah.*

❋ *The board may be named in honor of popular author Maria Louise de Ramée (1839–1908) who signed her novels with the nom de plume Ouidah. Two of her novels,* Under Two Flags *and* Moths *were bestsellers in the United States during the Civil War.*

❋ *Ouija may combine the French* (oui) *and German* (ja) *words for "yes."*

William Fuld died in February 1927 after falling from the roof of his factory while supervising the replacement of a flagpole. His children took over the business until they retired in 1966. On February 23, 1966, Parker Brothers, the leading American manufacturer of board games, bought out William Fuld's trademark. They currently own all trademarks and patents.

Early ouija boards were beautiful, evocative, and well constructed. In the 21st century, evocative, handcrafted, often magically-themed witch boards are again available. Modern witch-board masters include Kipling West and the Brothers

Johnson of Portals to the Beyond.

Since the board's earliest inception, mainstream Christian religions have cautioned against its use, some actually describing ouija boards as diabolical and tools of Satan. At best, they are considered dabbling with Satanism. The very accessibility of these boards (ouija boards are sold in toy stores amongst board games) makes them a threat.

Because many kids perceive ouija boards as a party game, they sometimes invite Satan or demons (by name) as a prank or show of machismo. Occultists caution that spirit summoning is not for the inexperienced or unprepared. Those who are ambivalent about spirits, not sure whether they believe in them but if they do exist, then they must be evil demons, sometimes have unpleasant or frightening experiences.

The reaction of occultists towards ouija boards is more ambivalent: some perceive them as wholly benevolent devices while others caution that they genuinely can serve as a portal and thus are not for the inexperienced.

Further information regarding witch boards may be found at the online Museum of Talking Boards (www.museumoftalkingboards.com).

Ritual Possession

General occult wisdom suggests that although spirits are incredibly powerful, they often must accomplish their work through people. People are the magical tools belonging to spirits. Ritual possession is a shamanic art where a person is temporarily possessed by a spirit. Spirits are described as "coming down" and entering or "mounting" the person. In Vodoun terminology, the lwa are described as riding the person, who is described as their "horse."

This is a sophisticated, powerful technique that is usually incorporated into a system of spiritual devotion. It is not for the uninitiated or the inexperienced and is always performed under the supervision of a priestess, shaman or other spiritual leader. Ritual possession is common to shamanism around the world.

Why is this magical art practiced? Via ritual possession, spirits can perform healing and divination. It is also a sacred rite of communion with spirits. Spiritual rituals intended to induce ritual possession include dance, ecstatic music especially drumming, and masquerading.

The crucial difference between ritual possession and what is described as demonic possession is one of cooperation. Demonic possession is involuntary; ritual possession is welcomed and invited. Spirits are beckoned with their favorite foods and offerings and with music specifically believed to serve as an invitation.

Practitioners learn various shamanic techniques for temporarily accepting spirits into their bodies. Spirits do not as a rule possess those who are unprepared, however once in a while this is their way of signaling that they wish this person to become initiated into their tradition. Even in a case like this, however, possession will occur when an experienced person can observe, understand, interpret, and supervise. The spirit intends no harm and will depart.

The person who has been possessed is empowered and blessed by the spirit's presence. (The person's own nature is envisioned as being present but pushed down and temporarily suppressed, so that the spirit can ride them like a horse.) In shamanic trance, the person *is* the spirit. The spirit is present in their body. The person temporarily possesses the personal attributes of the spirit and can thus perform healing, divination, and magical feats. True possession is sometimes demonstrated by plunging one's hand into a boiling cauldron or walking over glowing coals and displaying no pain or injury—impossible in a normal state.

Of course this vision of ritual possession depends upon whether one believes that temporary, voluntary, *beneficial* spiritual possession is possible. In traditional Christian belief, all spiritual possession is demonic possession. Voluntary ritual possession is, from this perspective, Satanism: one voluntarily becomes a tool of demons. And although someone from another spiritual perspective wouldn't perceive these spirits as evil demons, fundamentalist Christians assuredly do.

Most traditional cultures do not perceive voluntary, trained, ritual possession as evil or malevolent but as a natural spiritual technique. According to Acts 16:16, a female slave in Philippi was subject to possession by a prophetic spirit. Her owners put her to work as a prophetess, pocketing the substantial income she earned. When St Paul exorcised her spirit, they sued him for loss of income.

The concept of ritual possession leads to interesting speculation when one considers Europe's witchcraze and the sabbats witches were accused of attending. If people were indeed secretly worshipping a Pagan horned spirit, were shamans or priests ritually channeling him? Accounts of costumes, music, dance, intoxicating beverages, and food designed to attract the spirit might indicate that ritual possession did occur or was part of the rite.

See also **DICTIONARY:** Lwa, Vodou, Zar.

Runes

Runes are a Nordic magical and spiritual system incorporating what is frequently described as an "alphabet," although that is not exactly accurate and only begins to suggest the power of the runes.

Runes are a system of sacred symbols. Runic alphabets are known as a *futhark*. The oldest-known full futhark is the Elder Futhark or the Common Germanic Futhark and consists of 24 runic characters in a specific order, in the manner that an alphabet has letters arranged in specific order.

The Runes of the Elder Futhark

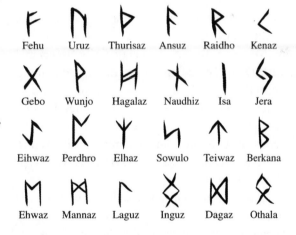

Fehu	Uruz	Thurisaz	Ansuz	Raidho	Kenaz
Gebo	Wunjo	Hagalaz	Naudhiz	Isa	Jera
Eihwaz	Perdhro	Elhaz	Sowulo	Teiwaz	Berkana
Ehwaz	Mannaz	Laguz	Inguz	Dagaz	Othala

Every rune contains three elements or aspects:

* An audible, phonetic sound (this aspect of a rune is similar to a letter of an alphabet; runes are used to compose words). In some traditions each rune is also a song.

* A geometric shape or form (sometimes called a "stave").

* A mystical meaning, radiant energy or "mystery": each rune may be interpreted and has literal, magical and spiritual meanings. Each rune is affiliated with at least one spirit and expresses their power and energy.

In addition to its other meanings rune literally means "lot" and they are used for divination. Runes are placed in a bag and either individually drawn or randomly cast and then interpreted.

The Roman historian Tacitus, writing about the Germani living in what is now modern Copenhagen in the last decade of the first-century CE, describes their system of divination using what are recognizably runes. Sigils were carved onto strips of wood cut from nut-bearing trees. These sigils were randomly distributed over a white cloth and then interpreted.

The word "alphabet" derives from the first two letters of the Greek alphabet (*alpha*, *beta*), in turn derived from the ancient Semitic alphabet (*aleph*, *bet*). Likewise "futhark" derives by spelling out the first six rune characters.

Runes are almost exclusively identified with Nordic tradition today. However, they may once have been more widespread. Historic events were, for example, recorded by Pagan Hungarian priests in what are described as "runic writings." During the eleventh century these texts were completely destroyed by the Church.

Runes are used for divination, spell-casting, meditation, and to contact and communicate with spirits. Runes are particularly associated with Odin: according to his myth, Odin hung himself on the World Tree for nine nights in order to acquire knowledge of the runes. Legend also has it that he acquired knowledge of the runes or of the shamanic techniques required to use them from Freya. (See **DIVINE WITCH:** Freya, Odin.)

"Rune" is also closely associated with words indicating witches and witchcraft. The Old German *runa* indicates a "whisperer" and is believed to refer to wise women or witches. The word *alruna* or *alraune* is also cognate with rune. (See **BOTANICALS:** Mandrake; **DICTIONARY:** Alraune.)

Runes are also incorporated into magic spells. Each rune is identified with one or more Nordic deities. Each radiates a specific power and may be used for various magical purposes. Runes are considered especially beneficial for protective magic. Runes are often used to empower ritual tools and objects. They are easily incorporated into candle magic spells.

The Elder Futhark is the most popular runic alphabet, however there are also others including the Younger Futhark and Gothic and medieval interpretations. Modern rune systems are sometimes sold with a blank rune, however this does not correspond to traditional systems and remains a controversial practice subject to disapproval by traditional rune scholars.

> *Bind-runes* are two or more runes combined to form a sigil. The last rune drawn is the binding agent.
>
> *Wend-runes* are runes written from right to left with magical intentions.
>
> *Svartrunir* (literally *black runes*) are runes that may be used to communicate with the dead.

Beautiful runes are sold crafted from minerals, glass, and other fine materials, however many believe that one should always handcraft runes. They are traditionally made from strips of bark although small pieces of leather are also used.

Sigils

Sigils are also known as seals. They are specific geometric or visual designs usually enclosed in a circle and are used for various magical and spiritual purposes.

Commanding and Compelling makes much use of sigils: each spirit, whether angel or demon, is believed to possess a specific sigil. Allegedly if the sigil is created perfectly, the spirit must answer its summons.

Traditions similar to sigils exist round the world. Although the designs are unique, purposes and concepts are closely related.

In Vodou, each lwa possesses a veve, which may be used to beckon (although *never* command; this is a far more respectful tradition) their presence. Veve designs may be carved onto candles similarly to sigils or used for meditation, however they are most frequently drawn on the

ground by sprinkling corn meal or other powder.

Sigils are also used for various magical purposes. Seals are incorporated into candle magic and are used to create protective talismans. Sigils can also be used to create personal defensive shields.

Pennsylvania Dutch hex signs are another form of sigil. Hex signs are often considered nothing more than Pennsylvania Dutch folk art, however they are actually magical signs and sigils. They are most commonly found painted onto building façades or gable ends of barns. Designs have historically also been included on furniture, documents, tombstones, pottery and ceramics, and written amulets.

> Hex sign literally means "witch sign." Hex signs are also known as *hexafoos* or "witch foot."

Their origins are mysterious. Jakob Grimm and other scholars recognized the geometric patterns as deriving from pre-Christian spiritual and magical traditions. They were first used in medieval Germany and Switzerland and may be based on runes. Another school of thought, however, insists that hex signs are nothing more than aesthetically pleasing adornment.

Hex signs consist of simple and colorful geometric designs that require relatively little artistry. If you can draw a straight line, you can draw a simple hex sign, although perhaps not the most elaborate ones. Different hex signs have different names, meanings and powers—for instance to keep lightning or hail from striking or to prevent animals from becoming *ferhexed* (bewitched). Explanations dating back to the 1920s, especially those geared to tourists, suggest that hex signs are decorations intended to ward off malevolent witchcraft or evil influences including the devil—in other words, they are sigils.

Spell-casting

Although witches practice many arts, the one most associated with them is spell-casting: the casting of magic spells. Popular fiction, movies, and television programs suggest witches cast spells by wiggling their noses or repeating stock phrases like *"Hocus Pocus!"* or *"Abracadabra!"* Real magic is more complex.

The most basic theory of the magic spell depends on the concept of magical energy. This concept suggests that everything that occurs naturally radiates some sort of magic power. Different things radiate different powers of varying potencies. Plants radiate power, as do animals, minerals, metals, people, and *you.*

A magic spell is a formalized, conscious attempt on the part of the spell-caster to harness and manipulate this power for the purpose of achieving a goal. Every culture on Earth possesses some sort of magical tradition incorporating spells. Magic spells come in an endless variety of styles and forms. The simplest spell may involve nothing more than standing under the light of a full moon and making a silent wish, vow or affirmation; complex spells may take weeks to accomplish and require a battery of priceless ingredients.

Spells may be cast for any purpose. Among the most popular types of spell-casting are candle magic, image magic (see page 607), and spirit working (see below).

Spirit Working/Spirit Summoning

Spirit working is the art of communicating with spirits for spiritual and magical purposes. The difference between spirit working and ritual possession is that no possession is involved. Communication is between the spirit and the person; the person doing the summoning doesn't become the venue from which the spirit communicates.

Spirit working is often accomplished via construction of altars: tableaux designed to attract the attention of a specific spirit. Thus an altar designed to honor the orisha Yemaya or attract her favor or attention would incorporate her sacred colors (blue and white), her sacred number (seven), and objects identified with her. Yemaya is an ocean spirit. A glass of salt water might be placed on the altar alongside seashells, sea glass or other gifts of the sea. Seven blue and white candles might be lit to call Yemaya, who might be symbolized on the altar by the image of a mermaid. Special foods or drink that the spirit allegedly favors would be placed on the altar as well.

Spirit working is among the most common forms of magic; it is very traditional magic.

The Inquisition regarded *"spirit worship"* (devotion to spirits) as especially dangerous because it encouraged the rise of *"heretical sects."*

> According to the Talmud, the reason spirits are usually invisible is that if we saw them all swarming through the air we'd probably die of terror.

There are an innumerable number of spirits. Every thing on Earth, every animal, creature, plant or object has at least one affiliated spirit, and so spirit working may be used to accomplish any purpose.

Tarot

Tarot are cards used primarily for divination although they may also be used for meditation, spiritual contemplation, and magic spells. They may also be used for card games, particularly the Italian game *tarocchi*. A complete Tarot deck consists of 78 cards, and is actually a fusion of two decks incorporated together:

❋ *The Major Arcana or Greater Secrets consists of 22 cards*

❋ *The Minor Arcana or Lesser Secrets consists of 56 cards*

Although traditionally Major and Minor cards are integrated together some prefer to use only one deck, usually the Major Arcana, which are generally believed to contain greater mysteries and spiritual depth.

The Minor Arcana is recognizable as the ancestor or close relation of modern playing cards. The Minor Arcana is divided into four suits: cups (chalices), pentacles (coins, discs), wands (staves), and swords. These correspond to the Western playing-card suits of hearts, diamonds, clubs, and spades. Playing cards from Spain utilize the same suits as the Tarot.

Each Tarot suit consists of cards numbered from one to ten plus four court cards. Regular playing cards have a jack, queen, and king corresponding to the Tarot's page, queen, and king. However Tarot cards also feature a knight. One theory suggests that playing cards no longer contain knights because of the destruction of the Knights Templars; another theory suggests that Tarot cards do have knights specifically to indicate that the Knights Templars survive, albeit incognito and underground.

The sole member of the Major Arcana to appear in a regular deck of cards is the one unnumbered card, The Fool, who materializes as The Joker.

Paper playing cards originally came from China, India or Korea where they were also used for divination, spell-casting, and fun. Cartomancy was established in France, Germany, and Italy by the late fourteenth century.

The origins of the Tarot cards are mysterious; the images are powerful and evocative and so many theories of their origins exist. The origins of the Tarot have been attributed to the Romany and the Knights Templars.

Others suggest that they are of Egyptian origin and are perhaps remnants of the ancient Book of Thoth, the magic book authored by the god. (See **DIVINE WITCH:** Thoth.) The book was redesigned as cards, which are portable and easily and discreetly stored for reasons of safety. French theologian Antoine Court de Gebelin, author of one of the earliest works on Tarot, published in Paris between 1775 and 1784, suggests that the Major Arcana comes from the Egyptian Book of Thoth saved from the ruins of a burning temple. The book was rescued and brought to Europe by traveling Gypsies.

Other theories suggest:

❋ *Tarot, especially the Major Arcana, was devised as a secret method of preserving ideologies forbidden by the Church. Tarot was not only a divination system but also a repository for sacred but now forbidden lore and symbols.*

✷ *A convention of occultists met in Morocco c.1200 CE to develop a way to preserve metaphysical wisdom as they foresaw dark times ahead. Among their solutions were Tarot cards.*

✷ *The magus, Eliphas Levi (1810–1875) integrated the Major Arcana with the twenty-two letters of the Hebrew alphabet. Levi, who despite his name was a devout if conflicted French Catholic, suggested that the origins of the Tarot lie in ancient Israel. Various ancient divination systems were practiced in the Jerusalem Temple; when it was destroyed, "certain wise Kabalists" preserved and recorded its mysteries, first on ivory, then on parchment, gilt or "silvered leather," and finally on simple card stock.*

✷ *The Hindu deity Ardhanari holds a cup, scepter, sword, and ring. These four attributes correspond to the four Tarot suits. Some suggest that the origins of Tarot lie in India and were carried through the world during the Romany migration.*

✷ *The most mundane origin of the Tarot suggests that it was invented between 1410 and 1424 in Northern Italy and is nothing more than a deck of playing cards!*

In 1392, King Charles VI of France paid artist Jacquemin Gringonneur for three decks of cards, although it is unclear whether these were Tarot decks, playing cards or something else all together. These cards have not yet been found, if they still exist. The oldest surviving decks seem to be from fifteenth-century Italy. The Bibliothèque Nationale in Paris has seventeen cards in its collection, sixteen of which are recognizable as Tarot cards. These were once thought to have been the Gringonneur cards but are now acknowledged as Venetian and dating from c.1470.

Tarot cards are traditionally read by shuffling them, then drawing individual cards at random. Cards are also arranged in specific patterns, known as "spreads," some very simple, others extremely sophisticated and utilizing the entire deck. Patterns made by the cards, and the placement of individual cards within the spread, are interpreted.

The simple three-card spread involves laying three cards face down. Cards are read from left to right: the first card represents the past, the second the present, and the third the future.

Literally thousands of decks are now available: some are genuine divination tools; others qualify as works of art. Salvador Dali, for instance, illustrated a Tarot deck. The most significant modern decks are the Rider-Waite-Smith deck, designed by Arthur Waite and executed by Pamela Colman-Smith, and the Crowley Deck (or the Deck of Thoth) designed by Aleister Crowley, with artwork executed by Lady Frieda Harris.

Magical Professions

Although anyone may cast a spell and, historically, people from *all* walks of life have been accused or suspected of witchcraft, certain professions have, over the centuries, accrued a magical reputation. Belonging to one of these professions bestowed an aura of mystery and power, although sometimes, depending on mainstream societal orientation, that aura was considered sinister.

Midwifery is also a profession intrinsically identified with witchcraft. During the witch-hunt era, for various reasons, midwives were among those most vulnerable to accusations of witchcraft. Connections between midwifery and witchcraft are deeply rooted in women's ancient spiritual rites, and midwives are discussed in **WOMEN'S MYSTERIES.**

In general, those practicing the magical professions were skilled people: not just anyone could operate a mill or create fine swords. These professions were also renowned for maintaining professional secrets. However these were not obscure professions but somewhat common-place, necessary, every-day, even superficially mundane ones, particularly in agricultural societies: there was no bread without a miller; no agricultural tools without a smith.

It is crucial to appreciate that all or even most individual millers, smiths and metalworkers and stonemasons have *nothing* to do with occult sciences and many, although not all, tremendously resent these associations. It is the *profession* itself that is traditionally identified with sorcery and witchcraft.

With the exception of the coachman who is a special case (see page 625), what these professions have in common is *transformation*. Like the stage magician producing a rabbit from that seemingly empty hat, the miller transforms grain into flour; the mason transforms solid rock into sacred architecture, and the metalworker transforms lumps of metal into practical, sacred, beautiful, and valuable objects.

For the modern rationalist mind this is impressive, although, in a world that denies magic, it is hardly magical. Ancient minds, however, perceived stone, grain, and lumps of metal very differently and so these transformations were powerfully magical indeed. Millers, and *especially* smiths, were cut from the same cloth as alchemists: spiritual masters of transformation and transmutation—except that millers and smiths demonstrated their expertise and magical mastery daily for the greater good.

Magic, at its most primal, ultimately derives from mysteries of creation. The act of sexual intercourse, which produces new life where once it didn't exist, may be understood as the first magic spell and the one that still remains most powerful and mysterious. (And of course, in addition to the philosopher's stone, alchemists like Dr Faust strove to create artificial but living people, the *homunculus*.)

With the exception of the coachman, associated with mysteries of death rather than birth, the other magical professions are all involved with acts of creation.

Millers, masons, and smiths transform the fruits of Mother Earth's body (grain, stone, and metal) into new, crucial, and sacred forms.

One other factor to keep in mind when considering the magical aspects of these professions: two of the magical professions have historically been dominated by women, fortune-telling and midwifery. During the witch-hunt era, both were intrinsically identified with witchcraft; both professions were subsequently decimated. Even after the witch-hunts, both professions retained a disreputable air, identified with poverty and superstition. Fortune-telling remains illegal in many places; midwifery often has so many legal restrictions placed upon it as to make its practice virtually impossible. In the twenty-first century, both professions still bear the scars of the witch-hunts.

The other professions, however, are almost exclusively identified with men (although, as we will see, women associated with these professionals—ironworkers' wives, millers' daughters—were also traditionally considered magically empowered). Because victims of the witch-hunts were overwhelmingly female, many often ask, where were the male witches? At the time, witch-hunters claimed the preponderance of women accused of witchcraft indicated women's special relationship with Satan and their general moral weakness, however many historians now suggest that men were simply not as frequently labeled "witches."

Skilled professional men went to work daily, grinding grain and crafting metal. These professions, rooted in shamanism and Pagan priesthoods, were utterly necessary for the everyday maintenance and continuation of society. Society would have ground to a halt without millers and metalworkers. Therefore they did not become official targets of witch-hunters even if concurrent legends suggested that it was impossible to be a successful miller without a Satanic pact, that masons were in the forefront of the devil's army, and that the devil himself was a smith when he wasn't moonlighting as a coachman.

These professions retained their magical aura; rumors regarding individual professionals were quietly but insistently whispered and legends regarding these professions still survive. However, their ancient shamanic associations were often publicly ignored—as they were not with midwives and healers. (See **MAGICAL ARTS:** Healing.)

Coachmen

Spectral coachmen, demonic coachmen, headless coachmen, coachmen with glowing eyes … Phantom coachmen are the subjects of *many* ghost and horror stories. The seemingly innocuous appearance of a coachman in a fairy or folk-tale signals an ominous note to those familiar with the tradition. Throughout Central Europe and beyond, coachmen were often identified as powerful sorcerers, sometimes even as the devil and not just in fairy tales: the very last woman executed for witchcraft in the Germanic lands, Anna Maria Schwaegel, beheaded in 1775, told the court that the devil tempted her in the form of a coachman. (See **WITCHCRAZE!:** Germany.)

Why? What's so significant about a coachman? It seems like a fairly straightforward profession. Before the invention of automobiles, if you wanted to get somewhere that was too far to walk, you either got on a horse or hired a coach, the equivalent of a horse-drawn taxi. The coachman is the driver. People wealthy enough to own a coach and horses kept one or more coachmen on staff as personal chauffeurs, so they could go wherever they wanted, whenever they wanted.

So what's so significant, powerful or threatening about what was theoretically nothing more than a skilled but relatively menial profession? Once upon a time, after all, back before automobiles, trains, and airplanes, coachmen were pretty crucial: if you wanted to get somewhere, you *needed* one. One should be glad to have a coachman; the alternative was an incredibly long walk or a trip not taken. So then, why are coachmen often depicted as so malevolent?

The coachman is the exception among professions associated with sorcery and witchcraft. In general, the magical professions involve the ability to transform one substance into another. Coachmen play a different role.

What precisely does the coachman do? A coachman ferries people from one spot to another; he shuttles people from one destination to another, back and forth if needed. He makes sure they arrive safely at their destination; he is familiar with routes and shepherds them safely back home, too, ideally as painlessly as possible.

Who else plays a role similar to this? A shaman—someone who soul-journeys from realm to realm. And, more especially, a shaman responsible for ferrying others from realm to realm.

A metaphysical theory suggests that certain types of illness, particularly comas, catatonia or some emotional disorders, are caused by "*soul loss.*" Usually caused by intense fear or emotional trauma, a piece or an aspect of the soul (in extreme cases, sometimes the entire soul) is lost. Shamanic healing involves locating, then returning the lost soul.

Sometime dead souls (ghosts) are believed stuck in the realm of the living, whether inadvertently or because for one reason or another they've refused to depart for the Realm of Death. A skilled shaman serves as a coachman, transporting—by force, if need be—the dead soul to the realm where it now belongs.

"Coachman," thus, can be a euphemism for "shaman." Many shamans were also priests or high-ranking practitioners of ancient Pagan faiths; following the rise of Christianity, these traditions—and shamanism in general—were forbidden and diabolized. Shamanism developed a notorious reputation, and the position of coachman was tainted by association. (Of course, although many shamans could be considered coachmen, not all coachmen were shamans.)

However, uneasy associations with coachmen may pre-date Christianity. After all, what is the most frequent destination of the shamanic coachman? What mythological figures play a similar role?

Charon, the ancient Greek ferryman, shuttles dead souls from the Realm of the Living to Hades' Realm of Death. Charon is among the sons of Nyx (see **DIVINE WITCH:** Nox/Nyx). He *only* ferries those who have been given spiritually correct funeral rites including payment for his services (the source of the practice of placing coins in a corpse's mouth or over its eyes.) Others are left stranded. Like a skilled, professional coachman, Charon must be paid or his services are withheld.

Theoretically, Charon only ferries souls in one direction but legends recall shamans, notably Psyche, who know the right tricks and techniques to persuade Charon to make it a round-trip, returning them to the Land of the Living again.

Charon may originally have been an angel-of-death-like figure who did more than just chauffeur: the name of the Etruscan spirit of death is usually spelled *Charun* in English to distinguish between them, although Charon and Charun are most likely the same deity. Charun wields a hammer while accompanying his friend Mars, Lord of War, onto battlefields, the better to finish off victims before carrying them off to his realm. The connection with coachmen is even more explicit with Charos, an angel-of-death-like figure of modern Greek folklore, who rides a horse to ferry dead souls to their next home.

On the other hand, maybe Hades, ancient Greek Lord of Death, is the prototype for the supernal coachman: a coachman himself, he drives a coach pulled by black stallions. When Demeter received a description of the vehicle in which her kidnapped daughter Persephone was last seen, the identity of the kidnapper was immediately apparent.

The association of vehicles with death survived. The devil was often envisioned as a coachman transporting damned souls. Krampus, Santa Claus' diabolical sidekick, is often portrayed carrying crying children off to Hell, sometimes in a car and sometimes driving a sled down a torturous, slippery slope. Of course, Krampus' friend Santa has his own sled, famously pulled by reindeer, the animal intimately identified with Saami shamans. (See **HORNED ONE:** Krampus, Santa Claus.)

In many cultures, deities are envisioned driving a chariot pulled by various animals; the type of animal that pulls their chariot reveals much about the nature of the spirit. Aphrodite's chariot is pulled by doves; Freya's by cats. Thor drives a chariot pulled by goats while Hecate's chariot is pulled by dragons. The ability to command animals' cooperation and assistance was perceived as magical and a sign of tremendous spiritual and shamanic power.

Once upon a time, emblems representing deities were transported in wagons during sacred processionals—as is still done with saints on their feast days. This occurred through much of the world, especially in Germanic areas—a region with particularly intense associations between coachmen and wizards. The wagon driver fulfilled the function of the coachman but was usually the deity's trusted priest.

Associations between wagons and shamanism survived for centuries, even after the introduction of Christianity, among the Nordic siedkona. (See **DICTIONARY:** Seidh, Siedkona.) The siedkona was a traveling shaman and diviner, going from community to community in her wagon. Although it might not be the primary listing on her résumé, she—or whoever drove her—was also a skilled and competent coachman, shamanically and also literally.

The invention of the automobile made the occupation of coachman obsolete. Most people can learn to drive a car sufficiently well to get from one destination to another. Although perhaps most people can learn to ride a horse sufficiently well to get from one place to another, not everyone can drive a team of horses attached to a coach, especially because the nobility preferred having *their* coaches pulled by beautiful, powerful but high-strung and frequently temperamental stallions, not nice tame, old, slow donkeys. The coachman who could drive the most difficult team of horses, those horses who couldn't be driven by just anyone, was the most prized, valued coachman of all.

Driving a team of horses is not the same as beating circus animals into submission so that they'll perform simple, repetitive tricks. To be an accomplished coachman implied the ability to communicate with horses.

The Hungarian táltos is strongly identified with coachmen. During the witch-hunt era, being a táltos was forbidden on pain of death. Rumor had it that individual táltos sought safety and the ability to discreetly maintain their craft by becoming coachmen. Although not all coachmen were táltos, many táltos became coachmen. Those who required their services thus knew where to find them.

In Europe, alongside ravens, bears, and wolves, horses are the animals most identified with shamanism. Horses were once considered exceptionally sacred, and vestiges of this tradition survive in the magical, talking horses that populate fairy tales. In Hungary, not only a human can be a *táltos*, the indigenous powerful shaman, certain animals can too—most notably horses. (See **DICTIONARY:** Táltos.)

The coachman who commands horses, simultaneously maintaining a good relationship with them—*crucial* to long-term success at the occupation—is intrinsically tied to shamanic horse-whispering, the gift of communicating with horses. This coachman can harness the horses to take him on magical journeys as well as on mundane.

Although the professional coachman is now largely obsolete, the coachman remains identified with wizardry and magical powers, especially in creative works but also in legend, although few recollect *why*:

❧ *In Bram Stoker's 1897 novel* Dracula, *the count's coachman commands wolves (and presumably werewolves!)*

❧ *In the MGM musical* The Wizard of Oz, *actor Frank Morgan portrayed the wizard, the conjurer Professor Marvel, and the coachman of Oz.*

Theologian and folklorist Harry Middleton Hyatt amassed a *massive* folkloric archive, personally interviewing over 1600 people, with special focus on African-American and German-American folk traditions. During the later 1930s, one German-American informant from Quincy, Illinois identified a whip-cracking coachman as a witch.

Masons

Mention the word "mason" and what automatically springs to mind for many is secret societies. "Mason" is indeed an abbreviation for Freemasonry, the controversial and mysterious fraternal organization. For the past few hundred years, the very notoriety of Masons (whom some still suspect of plotting world domination) has obscured what was so special and mysterious about masons in the first place. After all, Freemasonry's name evokes the mysterious mystical reputation of the stonemason, not the other way around.

> Although there may be Masons who are masons, masons are not necessarily Masons. In the context of these pages, "Mason" with a capital "M" refers to Freemasons; "mason" with a lower-case "m" refers to the professional artisanal craft.

The relationship between Masons and masons is no coincidence, however. As the historical witchcraze died down, hysteria over Freemasonry increased and has never entirely abated. Because Freemasons were initially identified as a small but elite and powerful group (some might also say because Freemasonry was originally exclusively male), the hysteria it engendered never reached witchcraze proportions, however at one time to be a Freemason was a crime punishable by death in many regions. The magus Alessandro Cagliostro, for instance, died in jail, sentenced to life imprisonment in particularly brutal solitary confinement, not for practicing alchemy, the magical arts or fraud (all of which he did indeed perform) but for promulgating Freemasonry.

Freemasons could have called themselves anything but chose the term *Freemason* because they claimed to be the spiritual descendants of ancient master masons who bore a potent reputation for possessing secret magical and spiritual traditions. The master mason wasn't just associated with general magical arts but with crucial and significant magical secrets. Master masons were identified as powerful, elite, educated wizards.

For a moment, let's forget Freemasons and focus on stonemasons. What exactly do masons do? They build architectural structures. Masons are builders but not just *any* builders. Once upon a time, masons rarely built common, everyday homes, for instance, although as house architecture became more sophisticated, this was no longer necessarily the case. Average people didn't hire masons, who were fine craftsmen with expectations of proper compensation.

Royalty and nobility who lived in estates, palaces, and castles would hire (or commandeer) masons but, in general, the first professional masons were involved with building places of worship: the massive stone temple structures of Egypt, the Mediterranean, East Asia, and the Middle East. (Similar traditions also existed among the Aztec, Inca, and Maya.)

> Like metalworkers and millers, the mason is also a master of transformation:
>
> ✸ *He transforms raw stone into buildings*
>
> ✸ *He transforms mere edifices into sacred territory*

These masons knew architectural secrets: they built arches and vaults. However masons knew spiritual and magical secrets too.

Beyond the required technical expertise, sacred buildings couldn't just be thrown together like some rustic barn-raising. Simply building a beautiful building wasn't sufficient to create *sacred* space. Shrines and temples were dwelling-places for deities; the shrine was intended as the deity's home.

Centuries before the concept of "Commanding and Compelling" emerged, these supreme deities could not be commanded or compelled to live in homes so carefully built for them. (See **MAGICAL ARTS:** Commanding and Compelling.) "Inviting" them or summoning them wasn't sufficient either. Instead the edifice had to be transformed into a dwelling place *worthy* of the deity. Construction of shrines and temples thus entailed spiritual and magical rituals. Careful attention must be paid to taboos: nothing could offend the deity.

Different deities required different rituals and different types of edifices. Usually some type of sacrifice was incorporated, quite often, once upon a time, blood sacrifice. If an animal was sacrificed, it had to be sacrificed according to specific ritual. Different deities expect different types of animals and different rituals. The wrong ritual or ritual done incorrectly can evoke rage, rather than favor. And, of course, sometimes, once upon a time, animals were considered insufficient: some deities apparently expected human sacrifice.

People were walled up within structures or their blood carefully and ritually spilled. The nature of sacrifice is very tenuous. What is intended to please may enrage instead, as demonstrated in the Greek myth of Tantalus and Pelops. Tantalus thought to please the Olympian gods by offering them his most precious possession, his son Pelops. Perhaps once this would have been acceptable but Tantalus was out of date and behind the times: the Olympian gods now considered human sacrifice passé and reprehensible and so punished Tantalus *severely* while returning Pelops to life. (It's believed that the myth exists to remind people of the current unacceptability of human sacrifice and to describe the transition. Notably, one deity is shown accepting Tantalus' sacrifice: the Corn Mother Demeter.)

Where human sacrifice were once permitted but later forbidden, rituals became especially complex. Substitutions had to be carefully and correctly made to avoid evoking the deity's displeasure.

The mason needed to know *exactly* what type of sacrifice was expected and acceptable because as buildings became larger and more impressive they were both more expensive to build and could potentially cause more damage if they fell. The collapse of a thatched cottage does less damage than the collapse of a huge stone structure filled with people—a collapse understood as the displeasure or vengeance of the god.

The Code of Hammurabi decreed the death penalty for builders and masons whose building collapsed onto inhabitants. (Hammurabi himself had trained as a stonemason.) Moreover, important buildings weren't believed to *just* collapse: among Merlin's first feats was explaining to the Saxon overlord Vortigern *why* the watchtower Vortigern had commissioned would *never* stand but would continually topple, no matter how well it was rebuilt. (The tower was built over a nest of dragon's eggs.)

Master masons were the spiritual craftsmen in charge of these rituals and sacrifices. Many practices were secret; master masons were the ones who *knew*.

These Pagan masons built the Parthenon, the Serapeum, the Pyramids of Egypt, the Temple of Isis at Philae, and so many other ancient, sacred structures. One brotherhood of skilled masons was reputedly initiates of a Dionysian Mystery tradition. Most significantly in terms of their later reputation and their association with witchcraft, ancient master masons built King Solomon's Jerusalem Temple under the supervision of Solomon, himself a master magician; among his wives was a pharaoh's daughter. Solomon had access to magical secrets from all over the ancient world and perhaps beyond.

King Solomon is renowned as the first "Commander and Compeller." Among the many legends told about Solomon is that he harnessed the power of spirits (djinn) to build the Jerusalem Temple. Asmodeus himself served as master mason and may have passed some professional secrets along to human masons, as well. (See **HORNED ONE:** Asmodeus.)

Alternative legends, based more closely on biblical accounts, suggest that Solomon hired master craftsmen from many lands. No comparable building had ever been built in the Jewish kingdom and thus Solomon hired experienced craftsmen from elsewhere. History indicates that the Jerusalem Temple was similar in architectural style to Semitic Pagan shrines.

According to legend, among those master craftsmen were those Dionysian initiates. These masons would eventually become associated with the Knights Templars, who set up base on the site of what was once Solomon's Temple, hence their name.

Legend had it that the Knights Templars did some excavation and exploration. What they learned remained secret, privy only to the inner-most circles of their fraternal order. No longer just monastic knights, the Knights Templars also transformed, at least according to this legend, into an elite, secret mystical society. (See **HORNED ONE:** Baphomet.

The Jerusalem Temple was eventually destroyed, subsequently rebuilt, and destroyed once again, as eventually were most Pagan temples and shrines. Christianity's rise to political power was accompanied by a strenuous campaign to close and destroy Pagan shrines. (See **DIVINE WITCH:** Kybele.)

The professional masons who built those shrines and supervised their maintenance survived, however, as did their artisanal skills. Regardless of spiritual orientation or mystic secrets possessed, their professional builder's secrets were invaluable and irreplaceable. Master masons were soon hard at work supervising the building of cathedrals. Perhaps because their professional expertise was so crucial, former Pagan affiliations were overlooked. From the beginning, masons, not average builders or stonecutters, but elite *master* masons, carried an aura of magical power and bore a spiritually subversive reputation that never entirely dissipated.

Although master masons were intrinsically associated with the rise and glory of Christianity, they never entirely shook that old reputation of being secret, subversive, magical adepts. Based on the inclusion of Pagan motifs like Sheela na Gigs, gargoyles, and horned deities (sacred or diabolical, take your pick) into sacred Christian architecture, that reputation may not have been undeserved.

Images that later appear on Tarot cards were carved onto church façades. Some believe this indicates that Tarot cards are nothing more than a game, deriving from common, everyday medieval life; the cards thus were inspired by sacred architecture. Others interpret this appearance as indicating that some masons were privy to ancient Egyptian mysteries and that the cards and architectural motifs both derive from the same Pagan source.

> Modern European stonemasons' guilds first appeared in approximately 1000 CE. In order to work as a mason, one was required to join a guild. Other masons had to accept you. Upon acceptance, one went through levels of apprenticeship, after which one rose to the rank of journeyman. Finally, after *many* years and much training, one might earn the status of master. Although many professions had guilds, masons were unusual for their time: they did not sell products but instead sold their labor and expertise, their knowledge.

Many Christian cathedrals are built over the sites of ancient Pagan holy places. It was suspected that master masons were secret guardians of these Pagan sites who maintained authority by infiltrating Christianity. Master masons are also associated with the mysterious Black Madonnas who may or may not be Isis or Mary Magdalen in disguise, as well as with the Grail mysteries of the Priory of Sion, as described in Dan Brown's bestselling novel *The Da Vinci Code.*

Various explanations for these rumors were offered, the most popular being that master masons, who pass on their secrets from one to another, generation after generation, were descended from survivors of Pagan Mystery Schools—Dionysian and others. Following the destruction of Paganism, these survivors even-

tually discreetly joined together in exile. They continued to ply their trade but secretly maintained and preserved Pagan traditions. Some suggested that these masons, like witches, were an insidious fifth column just waiting their opportunity to take over the world—a fear eventually transferred to Freemasons.

Another theory regarding the secret masonic Pagan traditions ties directly into the legendary origins of Freemasonry. When the victorious crusaders, the Knights Templars, settled into their Jerusalem headquarters, they unearthed old metaphysical secrets, many beyond their understanding. In their attempt to comprehend, according to this legend, they made contact with people who possessed ancient Pagan masons' secrets or somehow became initiated into the secrets of this mystery tradition.

When the order of the Knights Templars was later suppressed, many knights were arrested and executed but some escaped and survived. Some of these surviving knights allegedly traveled to Scotland, where they hid incognito before emerging among Scottish stonemasons' guilds. These Scottish craftsmen's guilds, secretly infiltrated by Templars and others possessing ancient masons' mystical and spiritual secrets, were the seed that sprouted the international fraternal organization known as the Freemasons.

Whether or not this is true, legends purported to stem from the building of the Jerusalem Temple are central to the mythic origins of Freemasonry.

Freemasonry derives its origins from the legendary mason *Hiram Abiff, Son of the Widow,* who was murdered during the building process, although some suggest this "murder" actually refers to human sacrifice. Freemasonry, like alchemy, has historically employed codes to transmit information and so it is unknown how literally this story should be taken. It is not the story as told in the Bible, which does discuss the building of Solomon's Temple.

The first book of Kings (7:13-15) describes how Solomon sent for Hiram of Tyre, son of a widow of the tribe of Naphtali, although his father was a Tyrian. Some understand Hiram to be the name of an individual however others interpret the phrase as referring to "*the* Hiram of Tyre." Tyre, now located in modern Lebanon, was then an important city-state; its rulers may have been known as "*Hirams*" just as Egyptian rulers were "*pharaohs.*" Whether Hiram was common man or king doesn't preclude his being a magical adept. According to scriptures, however, Hiram did not die but lived to see the completion of the project. Furthermore he was not a stonemason but that most magical of artisans, a metalworker, a man who crafted bronze and brass (see below, Metalworkers).

Metalworkers

Metalworkers or smiths are primal magicians, shamans, and alchemists. The most primeval forms of magic are menstrual magic, shamanic spirit-working, and botanical (herbal) magic; modern magic was born with the advent of the Iron Age. The history of the modern magical practitioner is intertwined with the history of smithcraft.

Smiths, the original alchemists, evolved the art of transmutation, transforming one substance into another via the elemental powers of fire and water. The smith's art was kept secret for centuries: those who possessed its secrets were able to craft weapons and tools by which they could *completely* dominate their neighbors—world domination indeed. These secrets were invaluable; people died maintaining them or attempting to obtain or steal them.

Metalworkers existed before the Iron Age. Metalworkers created beautiful sacred ritual objects of gold and silver; they crafted alloys of brass and bronze, and both remain sacred amongst many traditional cultures. *However*, iron was special and not just because it could be used to forge steel and create incredibly sturdy, powerful tools and weapons.

Iron derives from two sources: the purest iron on Earth comes from outer space, in the form of meteorites, thus it was metal from heaven, a gift of the gods. And yes, the ancients recognized where these meteorites came from, perhaps witnessing them fall. We know because some meteorites were extensively described, and were considered holy objects sacred to various powerful goddesses, most notably Artemis of Ephesus and Kybele. (See **DIVINE WITCH:** Artemis, Kybele.) The black stone that is the center of veneration at Mecca's Kaaba is a similar meteorite; prior to Islam, the shrine was associated with a mother goddess.

Iron from the sky was affiliated with sacred deified mothers; the other source of iron is iron ore from within Earth. That, too, has primordial associations with primal female power, the power of the Great Earth Mother.

The magical art of metalworking didn't emerge from thin air as an independent art. It was a continuation, a *transformation*, of an earlier magical art, the most ancient magic of all: women's lunar, menstrual mysteries. This is a type of magic obviously restricted to women alone. Ironworking enabled men to participate too.

Menstrual blood was considered the most magical charged substance on Earth (and in many magical traditions it is still considered so). What could possibly be more powerful than an individual woman's menstrual power? The Earth Mother's own menstrual secretions—iron. In the right hands, this was regarded as potentially the single most powerful object on Earth.

Central Asia's Turkic tribes had another perception of iron ore: they perceived raw metals as Earth's waste products. If left alone, for a sufficient amount of time, they would eventually develop into finished metal. This *"sufficient amount of time"* might, however, be thousands of years—too long for any individual to wait. Smithcraft was a method of hurrying up the process. (This is the seed from which alchemy grows.)

Of course, not only is no other substance as magical, powerful, and potentially dangerous as menstrual blood, no other substance is subject to so many taboos and restrictions. Mining, shaping, and working iron were thus fraught with danger. Digging around in Earth was once considered akin to rape; it could not be done safely without the guidance and protection of Earth's guardian spirits, especially snake spirits, powerfully affiliated with both women's lunar mysteries and magical ironworking. (See **ANIMALS:** Snakes.)

By virtue of their contact with this magic material and their mastery over the substance and its spiritual mysteries, smiths were more than just artisans. They were the original master magicians, priestesses, and priests of the Earth's mysteries. Although some smiths might also perform shamanic functions, smiths became the first professional magicians, requested to perform rituals and spell-casting on behalf of other individuals.

No wonder iron and steel swords were so much more powerful and efficient than older bronze weapons! Traditional menstrual magic is often used for defensive, protective reasons; ironworking puts the power of the Earth Mother's blood into the hands of warriors.

The ironworker is traditionally more than just a metalworker, however. Like the professional witch and midwife, the ironworker is usually a multi-tasker, serving as healer, herbal practitioner, dentist, barber, body artist, and often the only person in the community authorized to perform circumcisions. (To this day, there are Bedouin communities who will await the arrival of a nomadic smith to perform all needed circumcisions, even if it takes years for one to turn up.) The smith carves amulets and musical instruments, performs cures, devises and leads rituals, and communes with the spirits. Metalworking (and associated spiritual and magical) secrets were closely guarded.

Smiths were simultaneously respected and needed, feared and persecuted. Rulers needed master smiths to create weapons and tools for them, so that they could maintain their authority. Others wishing to topple that authority would approach the smith as well, hoping for assistance. Because smiths were master diviners, theoretically they would know which side to back. Smiths thus held a pivotal position of power and an uneasy association with authority.

Smiths' spiritual associations led to other concerns:

❋ *Because he is in daily contact with Earth's ultimate power substance and is able to bend it to his will, the smith is perceived as having greater magical power than the average person. That magical power is continually replenished and reinvigorated by his proximity to iron.*

✳ *However, iron, as Earth's menstrual blood, is not only powerful but dangerous, subject to taboos and spiritual restrictions, especially in the hands of a man. The ironworker who handles it openly and constantly is obviously powerful but also commonly perceived by outsiders as somehow "tainted" or unclean.*

Historically, both women and men have been ironworkers. Various myths suggest that women first discovered smithcraft or, conversely, that its mysteries were uncovered by a married couple: forged metal is created from fire and water, the most intensely male and intensely female elements.

Traditional smithcraft often involves a man and woman working together—the man wielding the hammer, the woman working the bellows. This dyad is reproduced in the marriages of sacred smiths: Athena and Hephaestus, Oya and Ogun. Notably, neither marriage worked out happily, perhaps reflecting that professional smithcraft, dependent on physical strength, eventually became a male-dominated profession.

A professional class of magical practitioners was born. Outsiders' ambivalence toward magic was born, too. Smithcraft evolved into clans in order to keep precious magical secrets in the family. (And also because outsiders liked the smith's services but often preferred keeping them at arm's length when not needed.) The smith's wife, who often worked alongside him, became a power in her own right: many ironworkers' wives were healers, midwifes, and fortune-tellers. In the Middle East, spiritual and magical use of henna, a botanical substitute for menstrual magic, was strongly associated with djinn and with ironworkers' wives.

Iron is the one material that consistently repels harmful spells and malicious spirits. Fairies and djinn allegedly fear iron, although djinn, like dwarfs, are also simultaneously considered master metalworkers. A piece of iron or steel, iron's derivative, placed under the pillow keeps the spiritual dangers of the night away. Iron is considered so powerful common magical wisdom suggests that if you don't have any, just saying the word *"iron"* offers spiritual protection.

Many smiths evolve into nomads: the most famous are the Romany whose traditional lifestyle epitomized ironworking clans. Clans travel together and marry within their group. Men work as smiths and musicians; women as healers, shamans, and diviners.

Unlike masons and millers, but like fortune-tellers and spell-casters, in many traditional societies, ironsmiths are explicitly identified with magic. Many engage in divination and spell-casting themselves. This type of ironworker still exists in communities in Africa and Asia.

In Christian Europe, ironworking became identified with the devil. The devil was envisioned hard at work in a forge, hammer in hand, frequently wearing the leather apron that is the smith's uniform and which derives from women's ancient magical costumes.

Sacred smiths exist too. Like ancient smiths, smith gods are both male and female. Female smith spirits are in touch with their martial side; male smith spirits have intense relationships with women, and often demonstrate complex relationships with their mothers. Male smith spirits tend to be intensely macho, testosterone-driven deities, however the magical art of smithcraft is *never* entirely divorced from women's mysteries.

> The traditional history of ironworking to a great extent parallels that of magic working. People need and desire smiths. Their services are crucial, yet people are also afraid to get close to them and will often not allow them to live as fully integrated members of society.

Among the spirits identified with metalworking are the following.

Athena

The Goddess of Crafts: in addition to dominion over spinning, weaving, and war craft, Athena is credited with inventing metal craft.

Few spirits have gone through as many permutations as Athena. She originated in North Africa as a deity presiding over women's mysteries. Centuries later, she would emerge as the staunchest defender of Greek patriarchy, the sponsor of such heroic quests as killing Gorgon Medusa, once her alter ego. In her guise as Matron of Smithcraft, Athena was once wed to Hephaestus, sacred Greek metalworker (see page 636). Their son, a snake, was the founder of Athens and progenitor of the Athenian ruling family.

Athena eventually became powerfully associated with literal, physical virginity; her ancient relationship with Hephaestus and ironworking was subsequently downplayed. Athena wears the aegis, a power apron, possibly related to the smith's leather apron (or vice versa). Her sacred animals include crows, dogs, goats, horses, owls, rams, spiders, wolves, and snakes.

Brigid

Brigid, whose epithets include "The Fiery Arrow," "The Ash-less Flame," and "Moon Crowned Lady of the Undying Flame," is the Celtic goddess of healing, music, poetry, and smithcraft. Sometimes depicted with a serpent wreathed around her head, she may also manifest as a column of fire. Alternately, a pillar of flame emerges from her head. Her attributes include a cauldron, a spinning wheel, and smith's tools. Brigid was venerated throughout Celtic Europe and incorporated into the Christian pantheon as St Brigid.

Dactyls

"Dactyls" means "fingers." These mysterious Anatolian spirits were considered Earth's first metallurgists. They discovered iron and the art of forging metal. There may be three dactyls or ten; they may be female, male or count both genders among their roster. According to one legend, when the Earth Mother was in the throes of labor, she plunged her fingers into Earth. These fingers took on a life of their own as the Dactyls. The Dactyls travel in Kybele's retinue, dancing and clashing their cymbals.

Dwarfs

Dwarfs are the master smiths of Nordic mythology. They helped forge the World Mill from which Earth was created. (See page 639, Millers.) Dwarfs, also known as dark elves, are ultimately under the dominion of Freyr, the Elven King.

Like Snow White's seven dwarfs, dwarfs are traditionally miners: they are involved in every aspect of metalworking, from extraction to the crafting of exquisite jewelry and weapons. Unlike Snow White's dwarfs, however, sacred mythological dwarfs don't live in little houses but deep within Earth, inside mountain caverns.

Hephaestus

Hephaestus is the Greek sacred smith. Like Brigid, he is a fire spirit, in his case Lord of the Forge's Eternal Flame. Hephaestus' own forge was believed located within Mt Aetna.

Hephaestus was unique for a Greek god, who are typically described as perfect physical specimens. Hephaestus was described as misshapen and ugly. Some stories suggest that his mother, Hera, was so appalled when she saw her deformed child that she flung him from Mt Olympus; another version of the story suggests that it was Zeus who did the flinging, enraged when Hephaestus sided with his mother during a quarrel.

Like a fallen angel, Hephaestus fell for nine days and nights, landing in the sea where beautiful water spirits rescued and raised him, teaching him the art of smithcraft.

His first projects involved creating beautiful jeweled ornaments for these mermaids. He eventually constructed a palace and forge under a volcano on the island of Lemnos. Eventually, the gods discovered what marvelous, magical crafts Hephaestus could create and subsequently welcomed him back to Olympus.

Hephaestus was usually depicted as a large, lame, bearded man bent over his anvil. He walks with the shaman's limp. Homer described him as walking with a stick or cane. According to another myth, Hephaestus was unable to walk unassisted so he created the first robots: a pair of incredibly beautiful, naked, life-size mechanized women crafted from gold. One walked on either side of him.

The agora (marketplace) of Athens was dominated by the Hephaistheum: a temple dedicated to Hephaestus and Athena. Snakes are Hephaestus' sacred animals.

Inari

Inari, the Shinto fox spirit, is most often associated with rice but also has dominion over smithcraft. Inari is invoked for abundance, prosperity, longevity, and love. (See **ANIMALS: Foxes.**)

Ogun

Ogun, West Africa's Lord of Iron, is not just the spirit of ironworking—he is iron itself. No need to "offer" Ogun a blood sacrifice; he is present in the very knife that draws blood, thus the Yoruba proverb that Ogun always eats first. His presence may be invoked by crossing two pieces of iron and anointing them with red palm oil.

Ogun cut the first paths through Earth's primordial wilderness. He creates tools for hunting, protection, war, healing, and magic. Ogun is among the few deities common to the various West African pantheons: under the names Gu, Gun, and Ogou, Ogun remains as constant and reliable as iron. Devotion to and awareness of Ogun is also shared by the various spiritual traditions of the African Diaspora including Candomblé, Santeria, and Vodou. Devotees of Palo know him by the name Zarabanda. Ogun sponsors all those who work with metal: soldiers, police officers, hunters, body artists and circumcisers, surgeons, and taxi and truck drivers. Ogun both protects against car accidents and causes them.

Although Ogun is considered an exceedingly macho deity, and the occupations he sponsors were traditionally almost exclusively associated with men, the connection between iron and women's mysteries is never forgotten. Ogun's most sacred attribute is an iron cauldron. Devotees maintain his cauldrons with tremendous care and reverence, placing offerings to Ogun within them. Also within them, one will usually discover carefully cultivated red rust as a reminder that traditional ironworking magic stems from Earth's menstrual mysteries and never strays very far from those roots.

Attitudes towards Ogun parallel ambivalence toward iron. Santeria tends to view Ogun with caution: he is volatile and potentially dangerous and so should be handled with utmost care. Without iron weapons, Earth would be a much safer place; wars could not be as devastating or as violent. The implication is that it is the nature of iron itself to be bloodthirsty.

In Haitian Vodou, however, Ogun is a heroic figure. The Haitian war for independence began as a slave rebellion, inaugurated at a ritual honoring Ogun. In Vodou, Ogun is syncretized to the Archangel Michael, Protector of Humanity, depicted with his flaming sword in hand, always vigilant to defend those who request his help. Ogun is also syncretized to the ever-victorious warrior, St James the Greater.

In African cosmology, Ogun lives deep within the forest, amongst a band of brothers: orishas like trickster spirit Eshu-Elegbara, master hunters Ochossi and Erinle, and herbalist Osain. (See **DIVINE WITCH:** Ochossi; **HORNED ONE:** Exu; **PLACES:** Forest: Osain, Swamps: Abatan.) Ogun may be a king but he lives simply and works *constantly*. He was once married to the warrior orisha Oya who worked the bellows for him. Ogun subsequently had a happier relationship with Oshun, crafting the copper, brass, and bronze with which she is closely identified.

Ogun's sacred creatures are dogs and snakes. (See **DICTIONARY:** Orisha, Palo, Santeria, Vodou; **DIVINE WITCH:** Orisha Oko, Oshun, Yemaya.)

Svarog

Svarog, ruler of the sun and spirit of fire, once headed the Slavic pantheon. Svarog is a divine smith and patron of human smiths. He forged the sun. His sacred territory is the hearth; he is present in hearth fire and forge fire. Hearth fire was once called "Svarog's son."

He is literally a patriarch, considered the father of other Slavic deities. He invented the concept of marriage. Svarog is a shape-shifter; he can assume any form, sometimes appearing with three heads. Favorite manifestations include his sacred animals: a bull, a horse, a gray wolf or, especially, a falcon.

Post-Christianity, he was demoted to a fire demon or sometimes equated with Satan. Some of his old functions were assigned to St George.

Tubal-Cain

Tubal-Cain is identified in the Bible as the first worker in bronze and iron. A direct descendant of Cain, he is sometimes considered responsible for his ancestor's death. (See **HORNED ONE:** Cain.) Tubal-Cain's brother was the first musician. Masons reputedly venerate Tubal-Cain; a piece of Masonic jewelry allegedly makes sly punning reference to Tubal-Cain and to the fertility power with which smithcraft is associated. A lapel pin or tie stickpin is crafted in the form of a phallic-shaped cane with a ball on either side (*Tubal-Cain, Two-ball Cane* …).

Magical Professions

Wayland the Smith

Wayland the Smith is also known as Weyland, Woland and Völund, depending on region. The legend of Wayland, Saxon Lord of Smithcraft, appears throughout Teutonic territories, most famously in an Icelandic saga but also in Anglo-Saxon, Frankish, Germanic, and Nordic sources.

Wayland learned smithcraft from the dwarves. In his very earliest incarnations, Wayland is an Elven King and the creator of many magical objects. In his most famous tale, Wayland encounters a swan maiden (Valkyrie) bathing in a lake. He steals her feather cloak and she is obliged to remain with him. He falls deeply in love with her and they live happily together for a while—in some versions for as long as seven years. Eventually however, for reasons unknown, the Valkyrie flies away.

Wayland pines for her but remains faithful. He waits, living by her sacred lake, working in his forge, making beautiful things he intends to give his beloved on her return, especially magical, golden rings.

King Nidud of the Swedes and his sons discover Wayland and lust for his gold. They steal his treasures and kidnap him, keeping him imprisoned on a small island complete with smithy. Nidud orders Wayland to produce treasure for him, and he has the sacred blacksmith lamed to prevent his escape and to compel Wayland to serve.

The power of the metalworker trumps all; Wayland begins his process of revenge. He lures Nidud's two sons to his island with promises of wealth. He kills them and converts their skulls into spectacular jeweled drinking cups.

Ironworking magic is intensely intertwined with sexual capacity and fertility, and metalworkers are traditionally identified with sorcery and spell-craft. Wayland causes the king to lose sexual prowess and vitality; because of this,

Nidud stops sleeping with his wife. The queen secretly visits Wayland, and begs him, as a sorcerer, to give her a spell to regain her husband's affections. He agrees but tells her the price is one night of love: she must spend the night in Wayland's bed. He assures her that in return she will be the mother of a king.

> **Further Reading:** Various works detail the spiritual and magical traditions surrounding iron and metalworking. Sandra Barnes' *Africa's Ogun* (Indiana University Press, 1997) and Patrick R. McNaughton's *The Mande Blacksmiths* (Indiana University Press, 1993) detail the still vibrant traditions of Africa. Nor Hall's *Irons in the Fire* (Station Hill, 2002) explores the worldwide poetry and mysteries associated with ironworking.

The next day he gives her the two skull cups, telling her to serve the king wine within them. She does. The king, having drunk deeply, hears the supernal voices of his sons and realizes he has violated a major taboo, akin to cannibalism, by drinking from their skulls. He commits suicide. In the meantime, Wayland has constructed wings for himself and flies away to freedom. The queen discovers she is pregnant with Wayland's child. She sees him flying away and reproaches him bitterly: he assures her that he is an accurate prophet and that all he has told her is true. In fact, the son she bears does become the next king. Wayland's son, unlike the previous king, turns out to be a caring, ethical, responsible ruler.

Wayland makes cameos in various myths and sagas including *Beowulf*, where he forges tools for the hero. Eventually, smiths would be diabolized rather than deified and Wayland's name would become a synonym for Satan. He may or may not appear, in this guise, in Mikhail Bulgakov's novel, *The Master and Margarita*. (See **CREATIVE ARTS:** Literature.)

Millers

Millers or references to millers appear in an amazing number of fairy tales. The most famous are *Rumpelstiltskin* and *Puss in Boots*.

In *Rumpelstiltskin*, a miller boasts to the king that his daughter can spin straw into gold. The king takes him at his word and orders the girl to come to the palace, where she is placed in a room filled with straw, given a spinning wheel and told to get started. If she can complete her task, she'll marry the king; if not, she'll be killed. Eventually, through the intercession of the dwarf, goblin, spirit or whatever he is named Rumpelstiltskin, the girl is able to accomplish her tasks and become queen.

In *Puss in Boots*, a miller dies, leaving three sons behind. The eldest son inherits the mill and the second inherits his donkey. There is nothing left for the youngest son to inherit but the miller's cat. The boy prepares to eat the cat when the cat suddenly speaks, saying that if the boy will only get the cat a pair of boots, the cat will provide for him forever. In the face of a miracle—a talking cat!—the boy does as requested and spends his last pennies having a pair of boots crafted for the cat's paws. The cat promptly begins scheming: by the end of the tale the poor miller's son has been transformed into the fictitious Marquis of Carabas. The cat has killed a giant, given the boy the giant's castle, and arranged for the boy to be married to a princess.

These stories remain among the most beloved fairy tales but are generally considered silly, nonsense stories. Of course, there's no reason to consider them otherwise, unless one appreciates the magical reputation millers once possessed.

Milling may seem like commonplace work: what does a miller do after all but grind grain into flour? But that's a superficial, modern, rationalist view. What does the miller *really* do? The miller *transforms*: he takes the harvested grain and through the process of milling, traditionally involving a millstone and millpond, transforms it from botanical material into food.

Milling may be understood as the further continuation, post-harvest, of the mysteries of the Corn Mother. The miller may be understood as the Corn Mother's priest; a role he undoubtedly played at one time very long ago. (See **ERGOT** for further details.)

Stonemasons were associated with elite spiritual mysteries. Metalworkers might be sorcerers but theirs was a private craft and always slightly distant from the community. The miller, on the other hand, might be considered the magician next door. Extensive mythology and folklore detail the miller's magical connections.

Let's take another look at those two fairy tales:

Both father and king in *Rumpelstiltskin* are usually portrayed as fools. Dad is a braggart: if he hadn't boasted of his daughter's ability to spin straw into gold, she would never have gotten into the predicament. The king is gullible: how can he possibly believe that a mere girl could perform such feats? But of course, the average reader no longer understands the central point of the story. There's a reason why the father's occupation is named; it isn't just extraneous detail. The girl isn't just a mere girl; she's explicitly identified as a *miller*'s daughter. Once upon a time, that had a magical resonance, now forgotten. Odds are, the king wouldn't believe that any old girl could perform magical transmutations—essentially the equivalent of alchemy. But a miller's daughter? That's a different matter.

The father (the miller) may be perceived as doing one of two things: he is bragging, but what he's bragging about is his own magical prowess, so powerful that it has rubbed off on his child or is transmitted genetically. He may also be understood as setting up his child's future. Like the cat in *Puss in Boots*, he is manipulating a royal future for his charge. He has faith that she will rise to the challenge, and indeed she does.

It is no accident that Rumpelstiltskin shows up. The girl was never expected to literally turn straw into gold by herself: the king realizes that a human can't do that. However, millers are traditionally identified with spirit working and *spirits* can perform miracles, which indeed is exactly what happens in the story.

The girl is expected to tap into her shamanic skills and contact a spirit who will help her. Ultimately she successfully does this. The part of *Rumpelstiltskin* that is most vague is *why* the little dwarf shows up—specifically what prompts him. Spirit-summoning techniques are millers' secrets and the story does not expose (or know) them.

Rumpelstiltskin performs transmutations for the girl: his ultimate price, her first-born child if she can't identify his name, marks the contest between them. Which of the two will command the other? If she gives up her child, she is making him an offering and pledging obeisance to the spirit; on the other hand, according to tenets of spirit-working going back to tales of Isis and Lilith, one can only have complete power over a spirit, the ability to command, if one knows the spirit's real name. (See **DIVINE WITCH**: Isis, Lilith.) By the end of the story,

the miller's daughter is queen and a full-fledged spirit-commanding shaman.

In *Puss in Boots*, the superficial interpretation (shared by the brothers in the tale who apparently haven't been privy to their father's secrets) is that the youngest son has received the least valuable inheritance. From an economic standpoint, that's true. The eldest son inherited real estate; the second son inherited livestock. The youngest son has inherited only a small pet animal and a disreputable, apparently useless animal at that. This tale was first told during the witch-hunt era when cats were still closely identified with demons and witchcraft. The cat was presumably the guardian of the granary, protecting it from vermin; it's a useless animal unless one possesses a barn.

But that's the point: the story demonstrates that the miller's most precious inheritance is not wealth but his magical traditions. Notably the cat requests footwear: the item of clothing most identified with shamanism. He needs those boots to activate his power.

The stories may also be understood as muffled protests. In both stories, the protagonists, millers' children, are poor, ignorant, out of touch with their innate magic power, and in trouble. Milling was once a sacred task. Grinding up the Corn Mother's botanical children into food for her human children was magical work, fraught with spiritual injunctions. Post-Christianity it evolved into menial labor but by the conclusion of those fairy tales, the millers' children have regained their psychic power (the daughter can summon and command powerful spirits; the son can communicate with the magical cat) and earned positions as rulers.

Millers once rivaled Masons for secret power: in Scotland, an organization or brotherhood called The Miller's Word was formed in the eighteenth century, inspired by an earlier Freemason group, The Mason's Word. The Miller's Word was based upon a system of local groups with initiations and professional secrets. They held nocturnal meetings. Rumors spread that its members acquired magical power via mill equipment.

Millers assert a strong presence in Central, Eastern, and Northern European folklore although the association of millers with magic power was once common throughout Europe. Millers were perceived as ordinary professionals during the daytime; at night, however, they were skilled sorcerers and shamans, commanding spirits that were sometimes believed to erect mills and grind grain for the miller.

The animals closely associated with millers were cats, which protected grain from vermin, and donkeys, traditionally hitched to millstones. Both species developed disreputable reputations in Europe, as did millers. (See **ANIMALS:** Cats, Donkeys.) In devoutly Christian areas, millers became identified with Satan. Successful millers were frequently rumored to have sold their souls.

The role millers often play in fairy tales (when they're not standing in for the devil, as they sometimes do) is that of a shamanic guardian or initiator. Millers save heroes or give them little tips that enable the hero to complete his impossible task.

Millers' associations with shamanism make sense when one realizes that the miller was the last defense against ergot poisoning (see

ERGOT). Although, theoretically, ergot-infested grain should not be included in the harvest, millers were the final inspectors, particularly in communities where the secrets of ergot had been suppressed or forgotten. A miller could not be ignorant of the effects of ergot; presumably these were among the secrets passed from one miller to another. One of the more recent cases of ergot poisoning in Europe occurred when a local miller accepted and ground contaminated grain that had earlier been earmarked for destruction.

In Slavic and Teutonic traditions, mills are believed to be the favored haunts of malevolent spirits (or at least spirits described by Christian sources as "evil.")

✳ *In Karelia, all millers were once reputed to be wizards*

✳ *In Russia, millers were traditionally believed able to shape-shift into animals*

✳ *In Russia, millers were perceived as sorcerers because of their (alleged) relationship with the Vodianoi.*

The Vodianoi is a much-feared Russian water spirit who usually manifests as a very white, naked, old man. He's bloated, wrinkled, and his skin has the blue tinge of someone who's spent way too much time in the water. He has green hair and is covered in slime and swamp moss. Sometimes the Vodianoi has scales like a fish, horns, and eyes that glow in the dark. Sometimes he manifests as a fish; sometimes like a scary merman. The Vodianoi lives underwater in a *magnificent*, luminescent, crystal palace. He *never* comes completely out of the water. The furthest he ventures out are riverbanks, although his favorite haunts are millponds.

The Vodianoi is feared because he drowns people (either as sacrifice or as pay-back for rude, disrespectful behavior). Not only does he kill people, he often refuses to return their bodies to loved ones until he has been propitiated with offerings.

There is only one kind of person on Earth the Vodianoi likes and that's a miller. It was once popularly believed that it wasn't possible to be a successful miller without a spiritual alliance (compact) with the Vodianoi. When new mills were constructed, black roosters were traditionally offered at the threshold. (Offering black roosters to a spirit in Christian Russia was heresy.) Other rumors were less savory: allegedly, at the construction of new mills—or even just periodically on a regular basis—millers drowned drunks as offerings to the Vodianoi. Because these men were intoxicated, they appeared to have merely fallen into the water; no one suspected that they were really pushed in.

In Hungary, the miller's magical skills include the ability to order rats about. Various Hungarian legends regarding millers feature the following details:

✳ *Millers enlist the aid of spirits they keep enclosed in small boxes*

✳ *Millers fly through the air on broomsticks*

✳ *Millers can magically make the mill stop and start working*

✳ *Millers can recall, by magic power, details regarding any object that has ever been stolen from them.*

Everyday offerings were allegedly less dramatic: millers reputedly offered the Vodianoi offerings of bread, salt, and vodka. Legends tell of millers invited to dine with the Vodianoi in his underwater palace; notably, the millers return to tell the tale. These tales may be understood as fairy-tale legends, fantasy stories or tall tales, or they may be understood as descriptions of shamanic soul-journeying.

According to a famous Norwegian legend, a mill burned to the ground twice, each time on Whitsun Eve. Witchcraft was suspected. The third year, a watch was set: a traveling tailor, new to the area, offers to sit watch all night. He engages in a little Christian witchcraft: casting a circle with chalk, he writes the Lord's Prayer around it and sits within.

At midnight, a gang of cats creep in carrying a cauldron filled with pitch. They hang it up in the hearth and light a fire beneath it. Soon the pitch boils and the cats start swinging the cauldron back and forth to overturn it. The tailor, within his protective circle, orders the cats to stop. The leader of the cats tries to drag him from the circle but the tailor cuts off its paw. All the cats run off howling. In the morning, the mill is still standing but the miller's wife is in bed nursing her amputated hand.

Mills appear in mythology: alongside the now more famous World Tree, Norse mythology also has a World Mill. Nine giantesses vigorously turn the mill wheel. (See **HAG:** Giants.) These millstones grind so loudly, they drown out the sound of even the most violent storms. This mill was used to create Earth out of the body of the giant Ymir.

The *Kalevala* is Finland's national epic. It, too, features a magical mill created to suit a witch's specifications. Elias Lönnrot (April 9, 1802–March 19,1884), folklorist and country physician, traveled the length and breadth of Finland—as far south as Estonia, as far north as

Lapland and as far east as Russian Karelia—to search for surviving ancient sung poetry or "*runot*"—Finnish magical songs. (See **MAGICAL ARTS:** Charms, Runes.) *Runot* (singular *runo*) had remained alive in the Eastern Orthodox regions of Finland although they had been long banned and suppressed in Lutheran areas.

Like fairy tales, women were major sources for the *Kalevala*. Lönnrot organized the material he had gathered into a unified body of work. He selected favored variants of stories, writing connecting passages for them and creating a unified, coherent mythic saga. The first phase of the *Kalevala* was completed on February 28, 1835, which to this day is celebrated as Kalevala Day in Finland.

Central to the saga contained in the Kalevala is the construction of something called the Magic Sampo. The Sampo remains mysterious; its identity has never been completely established but it is generally believed to be a mill.

❋ *On one side the Sampo mills corn*

❋ *On one side it mills salt*

❋ *On one side it mills coins*

The Sampo effectively grinds out comfort, stability, and prosperity. Louhi, Mistress of the North (see **DIVINE WITCH:** Louhi), orders a hero to construct the Sampo for her according to her specifications. She offers to pay for it with her daughter's hand in marriage. The Sampo is forged and Louhi is satisfied and content. She locks the Sampo behind nine locks and roots it in Earth via magic. All seems to be going well except that her daughter, the Maid of the North, doesn't want to be married and Louhi, respecting her wishes, won't force her. In response, three heroes decide to steal the Sampo from Louhi.

Vainamoinen, divine shaman and wizard, lulls Louhi to sleep with magical music played on his *kantele* (a harp-like instrument). Ilmarinen, the divine smith who actually crafted the Sampo, smears the nine locks with butter to open them. The third hero, a lover-boy Don Juan figure, Leminkainen, attempts to pull the Sampo out of the Earth; the roots are too strong so he "borrows" Louhi's oxen, hitches them to a plough and cuts right through the roots to steal the Sampo.

As the three comrades escape with their prize, Leminkainen can't resist singing his victory song, which finally wakens Louhi who is enraged. A witch-war between Louhi and Vainamoinen is waged: each trying to outdo the other with magic. Eventually, Louhi transforms herself into a fantastical bird and reaches the heroes' ship, where she settles on the mast. A little late, Vainamoinen tries to negotiate: "*Oh, Mistress of the North,*" he asks, "*won't you share your Sampo with us?*" Louhi refuses and demands the return of her Sampo. Vainamoinen strikes her with an oar, knocking her off the mast.

Louhi falls into the sea but grabs the Sampo, taking it down with her. The Sampo falls to pieces. The corn mill and money mill are smashed up. Only the salt mill continues to grind out salt on the bottom of the sea.

Places: A Witch's Travel Guide

Witchcraft ultimately has but one requirement: human needs and desire. Witchcraft occurs wherever there are people, and so witchcraft is at home all over Earth.

That said, for one reason or another, certain places have powerful associations with witchcraft. Although some locales may be physically remote or difficult for the average person to access, that doesn't mean these are rare locations. Quite the contrary. *Many* places are associated with witchcraft. These places fall into two categories:

❋ *Generic places identified with witchcraft practices. Thus bathhouses, forests, and crossroads, in general, are by their very nature, "witchcraft places" and may be considered witchcraft's "power places"*

❋ *Specific locations that for various historic reasons are identified with witchcraft*

During Europe's witch-hunt era, witch-hunters identified and named specific locations as the haunts of witches. Sometimes they posted scouts and spies to see who was traveling to and lingering in these areas. In many cases these were places that had ancient associations with Pagan religions or were by their nature (caves, mountain peaks) places that would be conducive to witchcraft practices.

In addition to places specifically associated with witchcraft, there are also many places around the world favored by contemporary witches, Wiccans, and Neo-Pagans including many ancient Pagan shrines—especially those associated with ancient Egypt, standing stones and stone circles, and places identified with the Arthurian saga. Many modern witches would consider Carnac, Glastonbury, and Stonehenge sacred sites for instance.

What is described below is but the tip of the iceberg: there were allegedly no less than 800 known locations specifically identified as witches' rendezvous places in Lorraine *alone* during the height of its witchcraze (approximately 1580–1630). There are two ways of looking at this statistic: witchcraft, rooted in ancient Pagan traditions, was banned but never disappeared. The sheer number of places associated with witchcraft serves as proof of survival. Conversely (and not only in Europe!) the sheer number of places associated with witchcraft may reveal more about witchcraft-hysteria than about witchcraft itself.

Take your pick. Let's take a tour!

Bathhouse

Pagan shrines were very frequently situated by natural springs (see also Wells, page 681). From a *very* early era, fresh water springs, whether hot or cold, still or sparkling, were considered among Earth's most sacred places. Natural springs radiated magical energy: they were sources of healing and spiritual cleansing. In fact, many mineral springs demonstrate healing powers. To this day, many travel to therapeutic spas built over mineral springs to "take the waters" or "the vapors." Modern spiritual shrines feature sacred springs too, most famously the shrine at Lourdes, France.

Spas, shrines, *thermes*: if there is a structure near or over a natural spring and if that structure has facilities so that people can bathe while inside that structure, then whatever else you may call it, that structure is, in very plain English, a *bathhouse*.

☀ *Bathhouses were among the earliest shrines and temples constructed: taking the baths was a spiritual, sacred act. (Ancient rites of baptism derive from these primordial traditions or vice versa.)*

☀ *In many spiritual traditions, even the simplest, most ramshackle, dilapidated bathhouse retains these sacred, magical, spiritually powerful connotations.*

☀ *Where bathhouses are considered places of power, bathhouses are also considered places for witchcraft. Whether this is meant positively or negatively depends upon how one defines and perceives witches.*

Before there was readily available piped water, springs were a magnet: every living being in the area, human or animal, would eventually come to a spring to drink or bathe. Spirits are drawn to springs as well. Djinn, for instance, are known to linger at springs. In addition, each individual spring is believed to have its own presiding spirit who is its guardian and shares its essence.

Water is a feminine element, aligned with the moon. Many springs were identified with sacred and powerful female deities, particularly those with lunar affiliations, such as Artemis, Diana, and Oshun.

Spirits like the Vila, Rusalka, and Bereginy congregate near springs as well. Often elaborate rules for springs associated with spirits developed: one could only bathe or do laundry on certain days of the week, for instance. The other days, the spring was reserved for the spirits' use. (See **FAIRIES**: Nature-Spirit Fairies: Bereginy, Rusalka, Vila.)

> Springs are a double threshold: not only places where Earth meets water but also places where humans and spirits mingle. (See page 680, Thresholds.)

There is much current amusement mixed with disapproval regarding medieval European aversion to bathing. Water (and thus bathing) was considered dangerous and detrimental to health: during the witch-hunt era, many bathed but once or twice a year, particularly very devout Christians.

However, once upon a time, Pagan Europeans bathed frequently incorporating physical pleasure and bodily hygiene with spiritual and magical rituals. In perhaps the ultimate example of *"throwing the baby out with the bath water,"* once these spiritual and magical traditions were forbidden and diabolized, bathing was forbidden too. The simplest way of guaranteeing that people weren't participating in these practices was to discourage them from bathing.

People were warned that bathing was dangerous and it was indeed: too much time bathing and you might be suspected and accused of having Pagan leanings or even of being a witch! In some regions, witches, like Pagan spirits, reputedly liked frolicking in water.

❋ *Among the ancient Egyptian shrines dedicated to the primordial goddess Hathor, some served as therapeutic temples (ancient hospitals), featuring a form of hydrotherapy. Her shrine at Dendera was the ancient world's equivalent of Lourdes. (See* **HORNED ONE:** *Hathor.)*

❋ *Among his many other feats, master inventor Daedalus was renowned for his ability to provide patrons with indoor plumbing including private baths with hot and cold running water. (See* **HORNED ONE:** *Minotaur.)*

❋ *Greeks and Romans of the classical era adored bathing. Public baths were ubiquitous. Not content with a mere tub of lukewarm water, a variety of baths to make a modern spa proud existed: hot air, hot water and cold plunge.*

❋ *The Romans, in particular, created monumental bathhouses, veritable temples of bathing. Roman emperors built thermal bath complexes as monuments to their glory. The baths of Emperor Diocletian (245–313 CE), for instance, held a maximum capacity of six thousand bathers. The earlier baths of Caracalla (186–217 CE), could only accommodate 1,600 people at a time but covered 27 acres; the complex included meeting rooms, gymnasia, walkways, gardens, at least two libraries and a public stadium as well as bathing facilities.*

Then as now, bathhouses may be spiritual shrines but they were also dens of iniquity: in late antiquity, public baths were also frequently centers of promiscuity and vice. Public baths were associated with male and female prostitution, thus baths frequently came under civil and ecclesiastical regulation.

Early Christians suspected that bathhouses, in addition to encouraging immorality, were also haunted by demons. This was actually in accordance with Pagan belief, although they would phrase it differently: bathhouses are the residences of spirits. If you wish to meet and greet spirits, the bathhouse is frequently the place to do it.

So, what do witches do in bathhouses?

❋ *They commune with spirits*

❋ *They practice divination and hold séances*

❋ *The atmosphere in the bathhouse has traditionally been conducive to soul-journeying*

❋ *The bathhouse is the ideal place for spiritual and magical cleansing rituals*

❋ *Various spiritual rituals are held in the bathhouse, particularly those having to do with threshold experiences, like birth, marriage, and death*

✸ Spiritual initiations are held in bathhouses

✸ Magic spells are cast in the bathhouse; power places are often considered conducive to spell-casting because the spell absorbs power from the surroundings

✸ Bathhouses rejuvenate, revive, reinvigorate, and empower bathers. Witches, like so many others, have fun in the bathhouse!

Basically two types of bathhouses exist. They may feature cold or hot pools, or there may be steam baths. Bathhouses associated with witchcraft more frequently feature what are now called steam baths, saunas or Turkish baths.

> In steam bathhouses, water meets fire to produce healing, cleansing steam. From a metaphysical perspective, the steam bathhouse reproduces the act of creation: male (fire) meets female (water) to create new life (steam or air).

Steam bathhouses were once common to many traditions; wherever they exist, they are associated with spirits and are typically considered magically powerful. Native American sweat lodges remain a vital spiritual tradition. There were once comparable Irish and Norse sweat bathhouses as well. Although the tradition didn't survive past the nineteenth century, the *teach an alais* (sweathouse) was once common in Ireland and perhaps elsewhere in the Celtic world. These bathhouses consisted of beehive-shaped huts constructed from stone covered in clay and turf. Many had stone seats within. Frequently located near springs or rivers, they were used for the alleviation of physical conditions, including rheumatism, but also for healing fairy-related sickness.

Among the traditional bathhouses especially associated with witchcraft are the following:

Bania

Nowhere is the bathhouse more associated with witchcraft than in Russia. Historically, most Russian villages featured at least one bathhouse or *bania*, usually a log shack set at a distance from residences, ideally very near or over a source of water. Officially the reason for maintaining a distance between residences and the bania was fire safety—the bathhouse being very fire-prone—but spiritual issues were also a significant, if sometimes unspoken, reason.

Banias tended to be fairly dilapidated buildings. It is usually a small, one-room cabin similar in style to a Finnish sauna; there's an outer area for dressing and an inner sanctum for the actual steam bath. An open hearth, usually constructed from cobblestones, is in the corner of the room. A bathhouse attendant builds a fire in order to heat the stones. When sufficiently hot, the smoke is vented and bathers may enter. Dry heat may be used but traditionally water is thrown onto the stones to produce steam. Aromatic herbs may also be strewn onto the stones for medicinal and other effect. Benches are set at different heights for sweating or washing.

The bania is more than just a place to clean one's body. It is a place of tremendous spiritual and magical power, descended from ancient Slavic water shrines. In Russia, bathhouses were also temples, a threshold space where fire and water merge and where spirits may be approached.

The bania is the traditional meeting place for revenants (ghosts), spirits, and witches. Russian village bathhouses are only heated during hours of conventional use. Thus anyone attending at unusual hours is assumed to be there for less than conventional reasons. Being seen entering or leaving the bathhouse during unconventional hours was considered a telltale sign of witchcraft. Entering the bathhouse during magically significant days like St John's Eve, Yule or New Year was considered even more of a telltale sign.

> Banias were also sometimes built underground or semi-underground, in which case they were called *laznya*, from the Russian *lazit* "to creep" or "to crawl." Entering or leaving the *laznya* was like entering or emerging from the womb.

Rumor had it, Russian magicians and witches congregated in the bathhouse while others attended Church. (This also recalls that baths were once sacred territory, too.) The safe, proper time for respectable Christians to use the bathhouse was between dawn and midday. Bathing was done in company as it wasn't considered safe to enter the bania alone. (It was certainly *not* safe for one's reputation as entering alone fostered rumors regarding Pagan predilections or witchcraft activity.) Any time after midday was considered less conventional and "safe."

Between midnight and dawn, the bania belongs to the spirits. A high percentage of Russian divination techniques, magic spells, and rituals involve a trip to the bathhouse at midnight. Typical Russian magic spell instructions start *"Enter the bathhouse at midnight."* Initiation rituals took place in the bathhouse at midnight, too.

It was generally acknowledged that Christianity's authority stopped at the threshold of the bania. No icons were hung in the bathhouse, and bathers removed amulets, crosses, and icons. Technically this is for convenience and because intense, prolonged steam may damage these items, particularly painted icons, but in addition the bania is tacitly acknowledged as a place where old ancestral traditions reign.

The ruler of the bathhouse is the *bannik* and his wife, the *bainikha, bannaia* or even *bannaia babushka* if one wished to take an affectionate, respectful tone with her. Bannik literally means "bathhouse spirit."

The bannik is usually visualized as a little old one-eyed man. He is usually naked but lack of clothing is appropriate to the bathhouse environment. Banniks are a race of spirits; each bania has a resident bannik who may or may not have a wife and/or children, too. Devout Christians identified these spirits as evil demons; those with other spiritual orientations describe the bannik as volatile, temperamental, and grouchy but potentially helpful.

The bania is the prescribed location for threshold experiences. Magical traditions involving birth, death, and marriage took place in the bania:

❋ *Brides prepared for their nuptials in the bania*

❋ *Corpses were laid out, cleansed, and prepared for interment in the bania*

❋ *Babies were born in the bathhouse, and the bannik is believed to personally welcome babies to Earth.*

The bannik, like most spirits, generally maintains invisibility. Allegedly if one wished to actually see the bannik or make personal contact with him, one must go to the bathhouse after dark, preferably at midnight. One must then step halfway into the bathhouse by hovering over the threshold and placing only the right foot inside. Meanwhile, remove the cross from around your neck, put it on the ground outside the bathhouse and place your left heel over it.

There are two ways to interpret this ritual. The standard explanation identifies the bannik with the devil and suggests that contact is diabolical and anti-Christian. The action of stepping or indeed stamping, if done with passion, is the equivalent of religious desecration. In more devoutly Christian regions, the bannik was explicitly identified with the devil and so going to see him was akin to the classical diabolical pact. (See **HORNED ONE:** The Devil.)

The alternative explanation suggests that the bannik is a pre-Christian spirit whose rites have been neglected and forbidden since the rise of Christianity. People continue to frequent bathhouses but offerings given are half-hearted and not up to pre-Christian standards. In order to inaugurate a new relationship, the bannik needs a commitment and needs to know where you stand.

Corresponding to the tenets of Russian double-faith, some might profess Christianity in the daytime but at night venture to the bathhouse to engage in older ancestral rituals: removing emblems of Christianity identifies these ritualists to the bannik.

The bannik is not the only spirit to consider the bania home. The Rozhanitsy, Russian fate goddesses or fairies, live in the bathhouse, too, not to be confused with that other set of goddesses also known as Rozhanitsy. (See **HORNED ONE:** Rozhanitsy.)

The word *rozhanitsy* derives from the Russian *rodit*, "to give birth." In many traditions, birth fairies travel to the baby's home to proclaim the baby's destiny. For the rozhanitsy, however, an offering table is set up in the bania where babies were traditionally born. The rozhanitsy are present and attend the birth. Images of these rozhanitsy squatting like a laboring woman, arms flung open wide, were once popularly embroidered onto Russian women's sacred embroideries and napkins. (See **FAIRY-TALE WITCHES:** Russian Fairy Tales.)

> Similar bathhouse traditions may once have extended throughout Slavic regions. Goddess Pirta Mate, "Mother of the Bathhouse," for instance, is the presiding spirit of the Latvian bathhouse. Similar to the bania, in pre-Christian Latvia the bathhouse was where babies were born and the scene for rituals associated with birth, marriage, and death.

Temescal

The temescal is the traditional Aztec sweat bathhouse, also called *temazcal* or *temazcalli*. The word derives from the Nahuatl (Aztec) language: *tema*, "to bathe," and *calli*, "a house." The temescal is a complete bath facility incorporating areas for bathing, dressing, and relaxation. Direct heat derives from a stone fireplace, many traditionally lined with potshards set in mortar. The temescal is a permanent structure and is not to be confused with the now more familiar Native American sweat lodge.

Temescal-style bathhouses were standard features of Meso-American cities. The temescal simultaneously played (and plays) various roles: offering hygienic, magical, spiritual, rejuvenating, relaxation, and therapeutic services to bathers. Healing rituals *were* spiritual rituals; in a holistic system, the two are not distinct and cannot be separated.

Sweat lodges are a vital, popular Native American spiritual tradition. The sweat lodge is a sacred place, considered akin to a church. In general, they are small structures, often temporary and constructed as needed. People sit inside the tent-, womb- or cave-like structure; heated stones are bought within. Water is splashed onto the stones creating steam. Because the sweat lodge is smaller than bania or sauna, the physical experience can be particularly intense.

Information regarding the traditional temescal derives largely from Spanish records and sources. In 1567, Brother Duran, in the first written history of Mexico, described the temescal as a small hut heated with fire into which at most ten people will fit, although it was not high enough for the people to stand. (It was a womb-like structure into which people had to crawl in and out.)

An oven stood in the far corner. Baths were hot and dry, intended to make the bather sweat. This sweat bath was followed by a cold, water bath. Bathers were beaten with botanical switches, identifiably related to modern *barrida* cleansings of Mexican curanderas, which involve massaging the body with similar botanical switches. (See also **BOTANICALS**: Birch; **DICTIONARY**: Curandera.)

The Spanish did not approve of bathing, let alone spiritual rites connected with bathhouses, very clearly reminiscent of Pagan practices left at home. A sixteenth-century Spanish priest described temescal rituals:

✳ *The temescal's attendant was simultaneously a healer, spiritual practitioner, and leader.*

✳ *Ailing people offered copal incense to the "idol" within the temescal complex.*

✳ *Both men and women frequented the temescal and were naked within the sweat house.*

Those who enter the temescal come into direct contact with various spiritual beings, but most especially Tlazolteotl. Tlazolteotl, a witch goddess and the deity responsible for cleansing Earth and all her inhabitants, is credited with inventing the temescal. She is Matron of Midwives and Female Healers. The sweatbath was crucial for midwives and their clients. Babies were traditionally born in the temescal; pregnant, laboring, and recently delivered women frequented the temescal, too.

The temescal attendant, known today as a *temescalera*, was also traditionally a curandera skilled in herbal and spiritual therapies. Various herbal treatments were available, administered internally and externally. Those seeking to conceive but unable might request her assistance; the temescal was also considered beneficial for infertility.

According to one Codex, temescals were also dedicated to the Lord of Magic, the deity Tezcatlipoca.

The temescal tradition was almost entirely suppressed. Maintenance of the temescal or partaking of its services was equated with witchcraft and subject to the criminal penalties associated with witchcraft. Because the temescal is a permanent structure intended to serve a community it isn't easily hidden, however the tradition was secretly and surreptitiously kept alive in remote locations.

Since the late twentieth century, there has been a revival of indigenous traditions and a subsequent revival of the temescal.

Burial Grounds

The most controversial place associated with witchcraft is the cemetery. Among the worst stereotypes propagated against witches is that they desecrate graves. The Classical Roman era equivalent of horror fiction depicted witches (*striges*) digging up, dismembering and sometimes consuming corpses for assorted reasons, all nefarious. That stereotype survived through the centuries and continues to plague modern witches. However it is nothing more than a stereotype and a false one at that. Witchcraft has *nothing* whatsoever to do with grave desecration.

And yet, much to the discomfort and embarrassment of many, including some witches, burial grounds *have* historically been associated with witchcraft. One must explore attitudes towards death and the afterlife to appreciate witchcraft's associations with burial grounds.

Spiritual traditions aligned with witchcraft tend to see the world as filled with spiritual entities. Although these spirits are usually invisible, they are ever-present.

✳ *Birth is the gateway into the Realm of the Living*

✳ *Death is the gateway into the Realm of the Dead*

✳ *The cemetery is the threshold or crossroads where the Realms of Life and Death meet, intersect, and collide.*

In terms of magical energy, thresholds and crossroads are the most powerful places of all.

The cemetery is a place of exponentially charged magic power:

✳ *The cemetery is where one can access, absorb, and manipulate this magical energy*

✳ *The cemetery is where one may contemplate mysteries of death and existence*

✳ *The cemetery is where one can encounter ghosts and perform necromantic rituals (see **MAGICAL ARTS**: Necromancy)*

✳ *The cemetery is where one can commune with spirits, especially those who are guardians of this special crossroads*

Just like human magical practitioners, it is believed that many spirits also seek to access the profound magical energy associated with burial grounds. Many types of spirits, such as djinn, are believed to reside in cemeteries. Other spirits, like sidhe, trolls, and barrow-wights are believed to make their home inside ancient burial mounds.

These magical traditions hew very closely to mysteries of death and the afterlife, a topic many find disconcerting, historically as well as now. For this reason and others (the topic also borders closely on intensely *sacred* mysteries), these are not aspects of witchcraft and magic that are commonly or openly discussed. There is not even a simple term that defines this type of place: "cemetery" is limited and inadequate, as is "burial ground" which implies interment in Earth. Because death is such a profound threshold, *any* physical space or location intrinsically identified with it potentially possesses this threshold quality, and potentially generates exponential quantities of magical energy.

These places include cemeteries but also cremation grounds, barrow mounds, mausoleums, groves where the dead are buried, or where once upon a time corpses were hung from trees. Ruins or disaster zones where many people have died, especially violently or abruptly, are also classified among these places. Coffin factories that make traditional wooden coffins as well as funeral parlors and crematoria also generate this type of magical energy.

Trees historically associated with death, including alder, beech, cedar, cypress, elder, elm, hemlock, juniper, pine, willow, and yew, sometimes generate this type of power, particularly if there is a grove of these trees. (Groves of these types of trees sometimes indicate ancient and perhaps forgotten burial grounds. These trees were perceived as portals between realms of death and life and so particularly conducive towards easy transitions between them.)

The modern wooden coffin evolved from ancient spiritual devotion to trees. In some traditions, the dead were simply hung in trees but Neolithic hollowed-out tree trunks in which the dead were laid as in a wooden cradle have been discovered. This practice is reminiscent of the ancient myth of Osiris, whose coffin floated from Egypt to Syria, where it was grounded on tree roots. The tree enveloped and enclosed the coffin. Isis, searching desperately for her beloved's body finally located it cradled within a cypress tree. (See **DIVINE WITCH:** Isis.)

Although there are certainly witches as squeamish as anyone, in general, because of affiliated spiritual philosophies, many witches do not find the topic of death distasteful. The cemetery is not a scary place but the place where one celebrates life and the links between those who reside in different realms. Many witches find burial grounds to be places of magical energy: witches venture to cemeteries, not to desecrate graves but to dance, hold rituals, perform divination, and cast spells.

A technique once common to Celtic and Germanic shamanism involved lying down on a tomb, either merely to rest meditatively or to actually sleep, in order to receive spiritual revelations and messages from beyond.

This identification of witches with burial grounds exists not only in Europe but also in Africa, Asia, and the Americas. (In many, although not all, Native North American traditions, the dead are *not* viewed as benevolent but as possessing an energy that can contaminate and poison the living. Those who spend time in burial grounds thus are considered with suspicion, as only harmful, malevolent energy is available to be harnessed. See **MAGICAL ARTS:** Healing.)

Among those spirits who live in the cemetery are Kali and Shiva. Shiva, the Cosmic Dancer, is envisioned leading a nocturnal parade of ghosts, spirits, and witches through cremation grounds. See **DIVINE WITCH:** Kali, Shiva.

Many traditions envision witches convening in cemeteries at night to dance, sing, cast spells, and make merry. Many traditions involve sharing meals with loved ones who have passed onto the next realm. Picnics are enjoyed graveside. These traditions survive in annual festivals of the dead. (See **CALENDAR:** Days of the Dead.) In these traditions, witches tend not to have negative associations with cemeteries, nor with darkness.

In contrast, from the earliest days of Christian Europe, to be observed in the graveyard, particularly after dark, was to be branded a witch (see **FAIRY-TALE WITCHES:** Hans Christian Andersen: *The Wild Swans*). St Basil (*c.*329-January 1, 379) denounced *"shameless women"* who rendezvoused in graveyards for nightly revels. They sang, danced, and according to Basil, attracted *"a swarm of young men to watch them."* (It's also possible, although Basil doesn't suggest it, that the young men were participating in rituals themselves and were not merely spectators.)

Everything that occurs naturally on Earth is believed to radiate some sort of magical energy, including Earth herself. Dirt is a common ingredient of magic spells in many traditions. Different kinds of dirt, dirt from different places, possess different magical energies. Among the most magically charged dirt of all is that within the cemetery.

Graveyard dirt, also called *graveyard dust,* is a common spell ingredient used for all kinds of purposes, both malevolent and benevolent. Graveyard dirt is a component of protection spells, fertility spells, good fortune and employment spells, as well as hexes. Exactly what constitutes graveyard dirt depends on personal perception:

✻ *Some consider any dirt from within the confines of a burial ground to be effective, magical graveyard dust*

✻ *Some believe it must actually be dug out from a grave*

✻ *Some perceive that there are different "grades" of graveyard dust. Thus any dirt from the cemetery counts as graveyard dust, however* maximum strength *graveyard dirt comes from within a grave—ideally as close as possible to the heart of the person buried in there.*

Graveyard dirt is not just there for the taking, especially the closer one gets to an actual grave. Payment is usually offered to the spiritual guardians of the cemetery. Dirt taken from an actual grave belongs to the person buried there. One must pay or barter for it. Typical payment includes small cash payments (coins) or libations poured onto the grave, especially alcoholic beverages but basically anything that the deceased would favor.

See **BOTANICALS:** Alder, Elder, Elm, Juniper, Willow; **CREATIVE ARTS:** Dance: Dance of Death, Danse Macabre; **DICTIONARY:** Orisha; **FAIRIES:** Nature-spirit Fairies: Sidhe, Trolls.

Crossroads

Folk tales and blues songs recount journeys to crossroads. For those with a magical orientation, crossroads are the locations believed most conducive for successful spell-casting. Those of other orientations identify crossroads as the devil's territory.

Exactly what are crossroads and what's so special about them?

Despite all the legend and lore, superficially at least, crossroads are just intersecting roads. The most common varieties are three-way and four-way crossroads, although once in a while a five-way crossroad presents itself, as well as those offering even more roads to choose from. The "ways" of a crossroad indicate the possible number of available paths or choices: a three-way crossroad usually forms the shape of a "T" or "Y" while a four-way crossroad forms an "X" shape.

Magically speaking, of course, a "path" or "road" is more than just a cleared, paved street. Your "road" or "path" is also your destiny; literally and metaphorically, crossroads offer choices, change, opportunity and the ability to determine (or at least try to determine) one's own future.

From a magical perspective, all energies converge and diverge at the crossroads.

Every type of spirit eventually passes the crossroads too, thus, if one has a little patience, it is the most likely place to encounter them. Journeying to a crossroads almost inevitably empowers magic spells and personal magical energy.

True magic involves manipulation of natural magical energy and power; the point where two lines intersect is considered especially powerfully charged, absolutely radiant with magical energy. After all, as they teach in elementary geometry, a line *radiates* from a point. The concept of the magically powerful crossroads exists virtually worldwide. It is common to a tremendous number of magical traditions.

Crossroads are prime arenas for casting magic spells. Crossroads are also associated with the safe and effective disposal of magically charged items. Spells often leave remnants, the equivalent of leftovers or garbage or, from an energy perspective, nuclear waste: these items include bits of candle wax, left-over food or fabric, the contents of now obsolete charm bags, and so forth. The spell isn't complete until these items have been carefully and safely laid to rest.

Crossroads are the appropriate place to dispose of these items, whether by burying, dispersing them into the air or placing in a trash can, so that their energy safely dissipates or, conversely, so that their energy finds the correct path to accomplish its goal.

> In many Latin American magical traditions, crossroads are the place to leave spiritually contaminated objects or objects that radiate dangerous magical energy, such as those associated with illness.

A literal crossroads is a conjunction of two roads. Midnight is a metaphoric crossroads in time. It's where day meets night and is considered a very magically powerful moment. Time and space can converge to create one of the most powerful magical places of all: a crossroads at midnight, especially on a special magic night, say Halloween or Midsummer's Eve. Journey to the crossroads during this time and tradition suggests that one will encounter ghosts and spirits. Expect the Wild Hunt and Fairy Host to troop past.

Witches and other magical practitioners desiring either to avail themselves of the natural radiant power or to dance with the spirits, linger at crossroads too, especially on those magically charged nights.

Witches weave their spells at crossroads, sometimes literally. In Slavic tradition, witches bring their looms and spindles to crossroads during the Full Moon, where they simultaneously spin thread, weave tapestries, and/or weave spells. These witches require privacy although they are not inherently harmful: anyone interrupting or accidentally witnessing them will find themselves bewitched to sleep. They'll wake in the morning when the witches have gone.

Crossroads are understood to be populated by hosts of divergent spirits. However certain spirits are especially identified with crossroads and are often classified as "Crossroads Spirits" or "Gatekeepers." Sometimes they're called "Road Openers" too.

In magical parlance, these spirits *"own the roads"*; in plain English this means that these spirits provide and prevent opportunities and success. Those spirits who own roads permit or even encourage Opportunity to arrive at your door. Conversely, if displeased or in the mood for tricks, these spirits keep Opportunity far away, dooming one to stagnation at best, failure at worst.

Among the most famous road-owning spirits are Eshu-Elegbara, Hecate, Hermes, and Pomba Gira. (See **DIVINE WITCH:** Hecate, Hermes; **HORNED ONE:** Exu.) In general, three-way crossroads are associated with female spirits; four-way crossroads with male.

Once upon a time, back in ancient Greece, in order to contact Hermes one erected a cairn of stones at one of his crossroads. These cairns eventually evolved into monuments known as "herms." The traditional herm was a monolith, a solid block of stone featuring a man's head at the top and an erect phallus sticking out. (The oldest, simplest herms didn't even bother with the head.) Traditional herms were very simple; eventually they incorporated artistic touches and were personalized to indicate the god whose power was embodied. Many herms are crowned by Hermes' characteristic traveler's hat, for instance. (Herms, as their name indicates, almost always portray Hermes; a few however depict Dionysus instead.)

Herms were the ancient equivalent of modern roadside shrines. Those who wished to beseech Hermes' favor made offerings there. Women seeking personal fertility, which Hermes allegedly bestows, ornamented herms with floral garlands and wreathes as part of spiritual petition.

In ancient geometric symbolism, a T-shape reproduces the potent, sacred unification of male and female energies: the long vertical bar represents male genitalia, the horizontal bar, female. (The Y-shape is perhaps even more explicit: the vertical bar represents the phallus, the downward pointed "v" at the top is the vulva.)

In indigenous traditions of Meso-America, crossroads were considered dangerous places haunted by volatile and sometimes malicious spirits, notably the Aztec female warrior spirits, the *Cihuateteo.* The Cihuateteo are spirits of women who died in childbirth, understood as the equivalent of dying valiantly in battle. The Aztec afterlife was fairly dismal for most dead souls, but the valiant Cihuateteo were given the glorious role of escorting the sun on its downward passage through the sky. When not busy with these celestial chores, the Cihuateteo allegedly haunted crossroads where they were suspected of stealing children, seducing gullible men and then punishing them, and last but not least, causing seizures and madness. Shrines to appease and propitiate the Cihuateteo were often placed at major crossroads.

Once upon a time, crossroads were commonly accepted as places of magical and spiritual power. Although perhaps witches always had business to conduct there, crossroads were not originally identified solely as witchcraft places. This changed with Christianity's rise to power. Appreciation of the crossroad's volatile energy was retained, but crossroads were now considered sinister, threatening places where Pagan or anti-Christian forces held sway.

* *Herms were toppled and replaced with large crosses*

* *Gallows were erected at crossroads; crossroads became venues for public hangings*

* *Suicides or others forbidden church burial were buried at the crossroads, with the implication that crossroads were unhallowed ground*

* *To be observed lingering (loitering) at a crossroads, especially after dark, was frequently considered a telltale sign of witchcraft and grounds for accusation*

* *In witch-hunt era Europe, crossroads became defined specifically as witches' territory*

* *Witches were accused of attending sabbats held at crossroads*

Crossroads were always the place to meet spirits; post-Christianity, they became identified as the place to meet the devil. Various rituals for meeting the devil or selling one's soul to him involved journeying to the crossroads after dark. Allegedly the devil offered violin lessons at the crossroads. He held all-night parties at crossroads, where witches allegedly danced with demons, familiars, and damned souls.

The most famous modern legend regarding the devil and crossroads involves Delta bluesman Robert Johnson (died August 16, 1938), who allegedly sold his soul in exchange for musical power and talent at the intersection of US Highways 61 and 49 in Clarksdale, Mississippi. Other locations in Mississippi also claim to be the spot. In the twenty-first century this has evolved into a point of pride and humor but

once upon a time, many people took this very seriously: people hurried past crossroads, fearful for their very souls.

Ancient Pagan crossroads spirits by nature tended to be affiliated with witchcraft and shamanism. In addition to opening those roads to opportunity, many of these spirits also cleared the way for spiritual and/or necromantic communication.

In many African-Diaspora traditions, Eshu-Elegbara must be approached before one can communicate with any other spirit: he is the doorkeeper to spiritual interaction. Hecate, on the other hand, reputedly patrols the borders between Life and Death, determining who passes and who doesn't. Shamans traveling to the Realm of Death but expecting to return to Life would do well to court her favor and avoid her displeasure.

Post-Christianity, these spirits became particularly diabolized:

* *Hecate was considered a dread spirit rather than the grand goddess she had been previously.*

* *Pomba Gira, the Afro-Brazilian spirit, seems to derive from a confluence of Iberian, Romany and Central African roots. (Pomba Gira is the crossroad where those three traditions meet.) Sometimes depicted as a she-devil complete with pitchfork, horns, and cloven hooves, she is often vilified and described as an evil, sexually deviant spirit.*

* *The devil himself took on characteristics of male spirits like Hermes and Eshu. People reported encountering Satan at the crossroads, describing him as a suave bantering musician who walked with a limp or hobbled on a cane.*

Despite efforts at denigration, crossroad magic remains a powerful, vital magical tradition, one never abandoned or forgotten. A particularly

Encyclopedia of Witchcraft

simple magical spell intended to dissipate personal stagnation and encourage the arrival of opportunity and good fortune suggests that one go to a crossroad (ideally not a busy traffic intersection but a nice, old-fashioned country crossroad) and just linger, allowing negative energy to disperse and positive energy to attach itself to you.

See **BOTANICALS:** Mandrake; **CALENDAR:** Halloween, Midsummer's Eve, Time of Day; **CREATIVE ARTS:** Dance: Step of Wu; Films: *Alraune*; Music: Violin; **DICTIONARY:** Alraune; **DIVINE WITCH:** Dionysus; **HORNED ONE:** The Devil, Dionysus, Eshu-Elegbara, Hermes.

Forest

Once upon a time, vast primordial, dense forests covered much of Earth. Human settlements were but small clearings within forests; in order to reach another settlement, one had to pass through forests. The forest was not something rare, as it is today, but ever-present and familiar.

Many consider the forest to be witchcraft's birthplace. It is certainly the place where the craft was nurtured. Dedicated solitary practitioners and spiritual seekers lived alone in the forest, discovering the powers of botanicals and mushrooms, learning to negotiate with animal powers and navigate the world of Spirits. These practitioners, among Earth's first shamans, witches, and healers, shared their skills and knowledge with those who ventured into the forest. For these practitioners, the forest was home, shrine, and medicine cabinet all in one. But other visions of the forest exist, too.

In fact, there are various different visions of the forest. Here's one: the forest is a wild place not under human control. This forest is a mysterious, uncontrollable realm where wild nature holds sway. Animals, trees, and spirits reign supreme, not people. The only way for people to control this forest is to destroy it.

That vision fills some with dread and others with awe. Many people, in the past and now at present, consider the forest a holy place, hallowed ground. Deep forests were and remain sacred shrines, places where people venture to pay obeisance to the Spirit World. Some consider the eradication of Europe's forests to be a form of spiritual warfare, the equivalent of destroying temples, churches or shrines.

The hedge divides the forest from human settlements. The hedge is the realm of witches who mediate between domesticity and wilderness, the human realm and those others not under human control. (See **HAG.**)

Here's another vision of the forest, one commonly found in fairy tales: the forest is a dangerous place filled with ravenous beasts, evil, malicious spirits, and wild, dangerous people. Murderers, thieves, and outlaws live in the forest; chief among these dangerous folk are witches.

Folktale forests are inhabited by ravenous, cannibal witches. Some initially seem innocuous and even helpful but that's just part of their trap: the witch in the Brothers Grimm story *Hansel and Gretel* epitomizes *this* witch. (See **FAIRYTALE WITCHES:** Grimms' Fairy Tales: *Hansel and Gretel*.) In addition to the potential dangers of getting hopelessly lost or being attacked by wild animals, you can't even trust humans encountered in the wood. In fairy tales, benign little old ladies transform into evil killer witches lurking deep in the woods.

Here's yet *another* vision of the forest: maybe Hansel and Gretel feared they'd wander lost in the woods for ever but historically people have valued the forest precisely because they could get lost in it. Sometimes *"lost"* is the safest place to be. Despite tales of Baba Yaga and other cannibal witches lurking in the woods, the forest has traditionally been a place of refuge. Many people have preferred taking their chances with the dangers *in* the forest rather than those dangers outside it.

Over the centuries many have entered the forest in hopes of evading human persecution. Sometimes they had no choice: in the Pagan Nordic legal tradition, those decreed "outlaws" were forbidden to live among people. Anyone was free to kill them.

Where else were they to go? Many found refuge in the woods, some living solitary lives, others creating outlaw communities, à la Robin Hood. Similarly, lepers once lived in colonies in European woods, forbidden to come out.

🌿 *The forest is not under human control: laws, just or unjust, are often ignored*

🌿 *The forest is a great equalizer: inside the forest, rank matters less than survival skills*

If the forest presents dangers to some, it has traditionally offered protection to others. Because after all, although living in the forest presents obvious challenges and dangers, sometimes so does living *outside* the forest. The most famous people to take refuge in a forest are Robin Hood and his band of merry men (merry women, too!) who found fun and safety in Sherwood Forest, but there are many others too, many much more recently:

🌿 *The Maroons of the Caribbean and southern United States were escaped African slaves who established free communities in wild, remote, wooded places. (Maroon derives from the Spanish Cimarron and indicates "wild," "unbroken," "untamed.")*

🌿 *The Netotsi ("Men of the Woods") are escaped Romany slaves who found refuge and safety in a Carpathian maze of rocks and forests. (Romany were enslaved in Hungary and Transylvania as early as the fifteenth century, but the most brutal area of persecution was Moldavia and Walachia, now modern Romania, where two hundred thousand enslaved Romany were freed in 1855, just five years prior to the American Civil War.)*

🌿 *In 1941, when the Nazis began mass executions of Polish Jews, some fled to the Naliboki Forest to form combined refugee and resistance communities, eventually numbering over one thousand people including women and children. Other partisans of World War II also found safety and shelter in Europe's forests.*

While some suggest that the destruction of forests is akin to spiritual desecration, others suggest that it is a method of population control: without forests, where would people hide and resist persecution?

Going back several centuries, among those seeking refuge in forests were those who refused to accept the then-new Christian faith. Some rejected its spiritual precepts, preferring ancient ancestral traditions: priestesses, priests, and other devotees retreated into the woods. Others resisted new authority and rules: when Christianity banished spell-casting and magical traditions, some practitioners sought privacy and independence in the woods.

These people eventually came to be called witches and are among those dangerous people that fairy tales describe as populating the woods.

Forests have *always* been associated with witch-craft, whether witches live there or just visit. Forests were where botanical supplies were gathered and where one communed with wild forest spirits. Many spirits make their home in the forest, the most famous being witch-goddesses like Artemis, Diana, Faunus, Kybele, and Baba Yaga. (See **DIVINE WITCH:** Artemis, Baba Yaga, Diana, Kybele; **HORNED ONE:** Faunus.)

The forest is sometimes called the mother of witchcraft: according to one legend, the great goddess Kybele herself invented witchcraft in the forest. According to this myth, Kybele was born an unwanted female child, left abandoned and exposed to die in the Anatolian woods. Rather than kill her, the leopards that discovered the crying baby raised her and nurtured her, feeding her on their own milk. Kybele, the original Catwoman, grew up in the forest, away from all human contact, finally emerging as a strong, smart, competent, independent, magically empowered woman.

She discovered all the necessary components of witchcraft in the forest: botanicals, especially trees and roots, animals, and spirits. Kybele became a healer, a musician (inventing the flute and percussion instruments), a shaman, and the first witch. She was finally motivated to leave the forest (temporarily!) in order to teach other women her newfound skills.

Other spirits associated with forest include:

Arduinna

Arduinna, Mistress of the Forest, rides through the woods on a wild boar. The Romans equated this Gaulish (Celtic) lunar deity with Diana. The Ardennes, an extensively forested region primarily in Belgium and Luxembourg but also extending within France and Germany, is named in her honor. There is a powerful history of ironworking in the Ardennes region, and the Ardennes Forest was for a long time considered a bastion of Pagan tradition.

Meza Mate

Meza Mate, Latvian "Mother of the Forest," has dominion over wilderness and the animals that reside within. She also asserts dominion over those humans who make their living from the forest, presiding over the balance between the forest, animals, hunters, and woodcutters.

Ogun

Ogun, West Africa's sacred smith, is also Lord of the Forest where he maintains his forge. Ogun lives in a forest-compound together with a band of male spirits (collectively known as the "Warriors.") These spirits include Elegba, Ochossi, and Osain, Lord of Botanicals. (See **DIVINE WITCH:** Ochossi; **MAGICAL PRO-FESSIONS:** Metalworkers.)

Osain

Osain is a powerful sorcerer who knows all of Earth's botanical secrets. He is described as having one eye and one arm. He hops around like a bird on his one leg. He does have two ears: one is huge but the other is tiny and shriveled up. The huge ear is deaf but the little one is so acute it can hear the sound of a single flower crying.

Osain sponsors botanists, herbalists, healers, pharmacists, and chemists. His sacred creatures include parrots, roosters, turtles, and goats. His sacred color is green. Osain expects offerings such as coins and tobacco from those who harvest forest botanicals.

Other forest spirits include Papa Bois, "Father Forest," woodland guardian spirit from Trinidad and Tobago. See **HORNED ONE**: Papa Bois.

Osain, Ogun, and Arduinna are individual spirits; the forest is also home to various bands of roving spirits including Leshii, Rusalka, and Vila. Many of these wild nature spirits are among those classified as Fairies.

In general, these spirits are identified with the balance of nature and traditionally mediated between the needs of people and the needs of forest animals, trees, and other botanicals. They regulate hunters, woodcutters, and those who harvest wild plants. Once upon a time (and still today for some) these actions were not performed without accompanying spiritual ritual.

Perhaps it is understandable that those who no longer maintained those traditions perceived these spirits as threatening. Why would those spirits look upon them with favor?

However, those maintaining those old traditions, who respected the spirits and continued to venerate the forest as holy territory had no reason to fear. If some legends tell of people killed or pursued by Vila, other legends describe Vila dancing with devotees in moonlit glades, performing miracle cures, and offering shamanic lessons.

Similar spirits closely identified with forests include the *Skogsfruar* (Swedish: "forest wives"). These are described as manifesting in the form of beautiful, naked women who mysteriously appear in the forest, often joining men at campgrounds, luring them deeper into the woods, from whence they never return. (Because they've met with foul play or because they're too happy to leave is unknown.) "Forest wife" is also sometimes a euphemism for "witch" and it is not entirely clear if all these Skogsfruar are spirits or whether some are human forest dwellers.

Yakshas also take the form of beautiful women but they are spirits inhabiting the forests of India. They protect hidden forest treasure, especially that concealed beneath tree roots. Yakshas distract treasure hunters as well as other intruders in the woods. Men pursue them deeper into the forest where the Yakshas suddenly transform into trees, leaving the men hopelessly— and fatally—lost.

Sometimes specific forests are identified with witchcraft:

The *Iarnvid* (Iron Wood) is the legendary forest of Teutonic mythology, a deep, dark forest of iron trees at the very edge of the world, home of a witch clan feared by deities and mortals alike presided over by their matriarch, witch-goddess Angerboda. Wolves and witches make their home in the Iron Wood. (*Iron* Wood may be meant literally and/or mythically. Iron has profound associations with witchcraft, and in Northern Europe, iron trees also indicate strong, powerful oaks.) See **DIVINE WITCH**: Angerboda; **HAG**: Angerboda.

The New Forest in Hampshire, England was created by William the Conqueror in 1079 as a royal deer-hunting preserve. His son, William Rufus, was killed in a suspicious accident while hunting there. Rufus is among those that witchcraft scholar Margaret Murray identifies as sacred, sacrificed kings. (See **HALL OF FAME**: Margaret Murray.)

The New Forest figures prominently in the history of modern witchcraft and Wicca. Similar to the tale of Robin Hood in Sherwood Forest (also a royal preserve), the New Forest was a refuge for smugglers, outlaws, and especially witches. Various covens allegedly made their home in the woods. Gerald Gardner, father of modern Wicca, claimed to have been initiated into one of these New Forest covens in 1939 by Old Dorothy Clutterbuck.

> The word "forest" now indicates a deeply wooded region. Forest in the medieval English sense of that word, however, originally indicated a hunting reserve: a legally defined area, subject to special laws, where "beasts of the chase" were protected and *reserved* for royal pleasure. (*Beasts of the chase* usually means deer and boar, both once present in the New Forest.) Although most of the New Forest is forested in the conventional sense of being a thickly wooded region, a substantial percentage also includes bogs and open heath.

In addition to witches, the New Forest was also home for various Romany bands; there had long been interaction between the two communities. The most famous witch associated with the New Forest is Sybil Leek, who lived within in the forest with the Romany, studying many of their traditions. Leek grew up in the area, became High Priestess of a New Forest coven, and claimed that the forest was home to four covens surviving since the days of William Rufus. (See also Grove; **HALL OF FAME:** Gerald Gardner, Sybil Leek; **WITCHCRAZE!:** England: Pendle Forest Witches.)

Grotto

A natural grotto is a small cave, usually located near water (ocean or spring) and subject to flooding or liable to flood at high tide. A grotto may be a real cave or an artificial recess or structure created to resemble one. Although some grottoes are very small, others are the size of a good-sized room and can accommodate a small throng (at least at low tide!).

The English word "grotto" derives from an Italian word (*grotta*), which in turn derives from the Latin *crypta* meaning "cavern" or "crypt." Caves in general are associated with uterine imagery but natural grottos—wet, fluid-filled caves—are even more intensely identified with Earth's womb, resembling a pregnant womb filled with amniotic fluids. Tidal patterns of water flowing in and out of grottoes are equally reminiscent of women's lunar, menstrual mysteries. It's no wonder that grottoes were considered sacred, power-charged places, identified with mermaids and other spirits. Dionysus was born in a grotto.

Grottoes thus had natural affiliation with witchcraft and various female spiritual traditions. Many were believed under the protection of powerful female spirits; this tradition survived post-Christianity. No doubt the pirates and smugglers who favored grottoes for caching their treasures made sure those legends stayed alive to discourage trespassers.

Ancient people transformed natural grottoes into sacred shrines and chapels. Some contained mineral springs and may be understood as primordial bathhouses. (See page 645, Bathhouse.) Although many are naturally very beautiful, grottoes were also ornamented with altars, statues, and paintings. Italian grottoes, in particular, were decorated with images of intertwining vines, floral garlands, and fanciful creatures.

Not all grottoes occurred naturally, although the first ones did. Creating artificial grottoes was a popular fad during the French and Italian Renaissance, between the fifteenth and seventeenth centuries. Ancient ornamented Italian grotto-shrines had been unearthed and served as inspiration.

These artificial grottoes were recreations of Pagan shrines. The outside was usually designed to resemble a rocky cave: the inside was decorated with a combination of natural and mythic features. Ceramic stalactites and stalagmites enhanced the natural cave ambience: walls might be covered with seashells, both real and crafted from ceramics. Images of mermaids, spirits of the classical age and herms decorated the interior. Many contained fountains, intended to resemble sacred springs. Some of these grottoes served as conventional baths or chapels but others were rumored used for secret Pagan and witchcraft rites.

This type of architecture and interior design associated with grottoes was called "grotesque." Grotesque is now most frequently understood to mean hideous but that was a reaction to changing styles. Originally grotesque merely indicated this type of painted, ornamented cave characterized by fanciful human and animal forms typically interwoven with foliage.

From the start, witches were associated with grottoes, both natural and artificial, and the grotesque style, especially Circe, the beautiful island-dwelling sorceress, and the Sibyls, who prophesized from within caves. Mountain witches Sibilla and Tante Arie might also be considered grotto-goddesses. (See **DIVINE WITCH:** Circe, Sibilla, Tante Arie.)

Eventually grottoes, their Pagan associations and grotesque style fell from fashion, but the word "grotesque" remained attached to witches while developing other, very negative connotations. When people heard witches described as grotesque they misunderstood and envisioned them as physically hideous,

when literally what it indicates are witches festooned with garlands, seashells, and perhaps a mermaid's tail or two.

Natural grottoes remain identified with witchcraft, for example, the *Gruta das Bruxas* ("Witches' Grotto") found near the village of Sao Thome das Letras, in the state of Minas Gerais, Brazil. The village is now a popular New Age travel destination, particularly for those fascinated by UFOs. Another nearby feature is the *Cachoeira das Bruxas* or "Witches' Waterfall."

Grove

The notion of the "sacred grove" is familiar to many people, if only because of the many complaints about them in the Bible. Groves are clusters of sacred trees: they may stand alone as an isolated group of trees, or sometimes as a designated cluster of trees within a larger, encompassing forest. Some groves might consist of no more than a small clump of trees; others, like the one dedicated to the oracular spirit Daphne in what is now Turkey, were large, imposing complexes and might be understood as a small forest. Sacred groves were once also located near lake shrines, such as that dedicated to the goddess Angitia. (See **DIVINE WITCH:** Angitia.)

The crucial difference between "grove" and "forest" isn't size; historically some groves were quite extensive. Forests, however, are theoretically wild, untouched, natural places filled with magical energy; grove implies that the area has been consecrated.

Tree-centered spirituality is among the most primordial forms of religion. Among the earliest sacred images was that of a tree entwined by a snake or the combined features of a tree and woman. Some of the most ancient goddesses, like Artemis, Lady Asherah, and Hathor, were worshipped in the forms of trees. These fertile tree-goddesses were the original trees of life. (See **BOTANICALS**: Trees; **DIVINE WITCH**: Artemis; **HORNED ONE**: Hathor.)

Groves were associated with Pagan spiritual traditions in general and women's spiritual traditions specifically. The Bible repeatedly complains of women journeying to *"high places"* to worship Asherah in her groves.

Sacred groves existed throughout Europe and the British Isles, and also in the Middle East, Anatolia, North Africa, throughout India, the Himalayas, the Caucasus Mountains, Indonesia, and East and West Africa. The city of Vienna arose around a sacred grove.

Groves were a very specific group of trees and so were extremely vulnerable to being cut down. Powerfully associated with Paganism, many were destroyed in the often-violent transition between Paganism and Christianity. The Roman Emperor Theodosius II (April 401–July 28, 450) issued an edict directing that all surviving groves be cut down except those already appropriated for purposes compatible with Christianity. (A few became monastery gardens and churchyards.)

The Grove of Aricia

Groves were dedicated to those deities now known as Queens of Witches: the Grove of Aricia within the Forest of Nemi was dedicated to Diana and is located approximately 16 miles east of Rome in the Alban Hills. The name Nemi derives from the Latin *nemus* or "sacred grove."

The grove overlooks Lake Nemi, a circular, volcanic crater. The lake was known as *Diana's Mirror*. Once upon a time, her temple stood amidst the sacred grove. The reflection of the full moon in the mirror-still lake could clearly be observed from the Temple.

Diana's shrine combined various locations associated with magical power: forest, grove, hill—and a grotto, too. A stream flowed into the lake from a sacred grotto near Diana's Temple. The entire Forest of Nemi was under Diana's dominion. Diana had broad powers: she was a lunar, fire, and water goddess with dominion over magic, witchcraft, women and children, fertility, hunting, and wild animals. In addition, Diana was a Matron of Slaves and Outlaws; many sought and found refuge in her forest.

The shrine was the equivalent of Diana's home: she lived in the shrine together with her male consort, the horned spirit Virbius, and her friend, the mermaid Egeria.

Rügen Island

Very little is now known about ancient Teutonic goddess traditions; the Teutonic tribes left no writing and descriptions. What little is known derives from writings by outsiders to their culture—Pagan Romans and Christian missionaries.

Among the little that is known (mainly from Roman sources) involves the grove of the goddess Herta on Rügen Island. (See **DIVINE WITCH**: Herta.) Rügen Island, the largest of the German islands, is located in the Baltic Sea, off the northwest coast of Pomerania. It was once covered with beech forests.

A deep black lake on Rügen Island was surrounded by woods. Herta's sacred grove was allegedly by the lakeside. Although she has not been actively worshipped for centuries, Herta's association with Rügen Island, her stronghold where Odin once came courting her, remains powerful. The lake is still called Hertha Lake. Ruins of a castle ("Hertha Castle") are located nearby, not far from the *Stubbenkammer* (Slavonic for "rock steps"), a sheer chalk cliff. Some believe that these remnants are what is left of the goddess' sacred shrine. The area remains wooded.

According to reports, the statue of the goddess Herta was ritually removed from the shrine and bathed in the lake several times a year. Herta's rites were secret and little else is known. (Whether they were always secret or whether secrecy increased under Roman threat is also unknown.) Allegedly most ritual attendants were drowned following fulfillment of their tasks, although whether as sacrifices to Herta or whether to maintain secrecy (to make sure they'll never reveal her secrets) is also now unknown.

Although no longer actively worshipped, Herta has apparently not abandoned her old hometown. According to local lore, on Full Moon nights, a beautiful woman emerges from the woods and bathes in the lake accompanied by female attendants. Once in the water, sometimes they become invisible but still can be heard splashing about. These specters eventually reappear, emerge from the water and disappear into the woods. The bathers do not welcome company and it is considered dangerous to observe them: allegedly observers feel magnetically drawn to enter the deep lake where they then drown. (Local rumor suggests that at least one person drowns annually.)

Rügen, populated since at least 4000 BCE, was an important center of the ancient amber trade and as such was highly desirable real estate. (Among other stories related to Rügen Island is that it is Apollo's original birthplace; Greek mythology sometimes describes him as coming from "the North." The theory is that the Greeks encountered Apollo via amber

trade routes.) It changed ownership many times over the centuries.

The Teutonic tribes were eventually displaced by Slavs, who considered the entire island to be sacred territory, and the groves in particular to be sacred to their war deity, Svantovit, revered by Balts and Slavs alike. (The name *Rügen* derives from the Slavic tribe, the *Rugieris*.) The island was also sacred to another Slavic deity, the seven-headed, sword-wielding war god Rugeviet, whose name literally means "Master of Rügen." He had a sacred grove of rowan trees, his sacred tree.

Rügen remained among the very last bastions of European Paganism. Active Pagan worship continued openly throughout the twelfth century before it was violently suppressed.

Saterland is a region now within North West Germany close to the Dutch border. It contained an alder grove on an island deep in the Frisian moors that served as a witches' dance ground and was allegedly a popular destination for witches and wizards from all over Europe throughout the Middle Ages.

Not all sacred groves are ancient history: some are living, vital traditions. In the 1950s, Austrian architect, painter and sculptor Suzanne Wenger arrived in Oshogbo (Osogbo), Nigeria. She married a traditional drummer and became deeply involved in the indigenous spiritual traditions of the region, eventually becoming a priestess of the orishas Obatala and Oshun.

When Wenger arrived, Oshun's shrine and grove were in disrepair. Nigeria is now equally split between Christianity and Islam and indigenous sacred sites, for a variety of reasons, were neglected. Wenger and the local community set about re-building and revitalizing the shrine. Gates, walls, and Wenger's sacred sculptures were installed. An annual festival honoring Oshun, attracting thousands from worldwide, is held every August in her Sacred Grove. Festivities last for nine days, the ninth day featuring a mass pilgrimage to the Oshun river. Although the grove is sacred to devotees and served by priestesses, it has also become a primary tourist attraction in the region.

Magical Places

Various places on Earth have developed reputations as being particularly associated with witchcraft. Ancient Greeks associated Thessaly, Thrace, and Etruria as lands of magic. Lucius, hero of the second-century CE novel *The Golden Ass*, opens his adventures by explaining that he is in the very heart of Thessaly, which he describes as *"world-famous as the birthplace of incantations."*

Some places remain associated with magic and witchcraft.

Benevento

Benevento, Italy is known as the *City of the Witches*. In some circles, Benevento's very name is synonymous with witchcraft.

Midway between Rome and Naples, Benevento is located in the Sabato Valley, a natural basin beneath Italy's Apennine Mountains. In antiquity, Benevento was an important, significant city. The Romans named it *Beneventum* (literally "Good" or "Happy Event" but implying "Good Omen") in 275 BCE following a military victory here, the first of several.

Benevento has been the capital of southern Lombardy and an enclave of the Papal State. It joined the Italian Republic in 1860. From its earliest history Benevento has been identified with witchcraft. Local legend suggests that not only did Benevento harbor a community of powerful witches, other witches traveled from far away to join in rituals and celebrations.

The "Walnut Witches" of Benevento allegedly conducted rituals and held their sabbats beneath a huge walnut tree near the town. Allegedly witches have gathered about the walnut trees of Benevento since that old time immemorial: one particular tree, however, *the* Walnut Tree of Benevento, was particularly ancient and allegedly *always* in full leaf. Its walnuts were auspiciously shaped and served as amulets. It was the largest tree in the valley and witches rendezvoused under it. Rituals dedicated to Diana, Nyx, and Proserpina were conducted in the darkness that resulted from the old tree's deep shade.

Benevento allegedly remained a Pagan stronghold long after Christianity's rise to power.

In 662 CE, St Barbato, a local Christian, converted the ruling Duke of Benevento to Christianity. Previously the Duke had been a Pagan and allegedly joined in rituals beneath the walnut tree himself.

Barbato convinced him to cut the witches' tree down. Various stories recount what happened next: one version says a church was built on the site, another that the tree replanted itself and grew back so quickly that it was considered an omen and left alone. The most popular version of events says that the witches replanted the tree from one of its own nuts but in another secret location. Allegedly they danced around it during the witch-hunt era and dance around it still.

* *In* Aradia or the Gospel of the Witches *(see* **BOOKS: Grimoires***), the name* Benevento *is synonymous with witches' sabbat.*

* *Folklorist Charles G. Leland, an authority on Italian witchcraft and compiler (or author) of* Aradia, *describes the Benevento witches as* "good witches" *renowned for healing the sick and providing for the poor.*

* *According to the records of the Spanish Inquisition, Sicilian fairy-witches claimed to fly, at least in spirit, to witches' sabbats held under the walnut tree of Benevento.*

* *The witches' liqueur* Strega *was invented here. The label features a picture of Benevento's dancing Walnut Witches.*

Chiloé Island

Chiloé Island, located 500 miles south of Santiago off Chile's Pacific coast, is culturally very different from the rest of Chile and perhaps from anywhere else on Earth. A unique culture has developed on this small archipelago of islands at the world's end, accessible by an approximately 45-minute ferry crossing from the mainland. The seas around Chiloé are stormy, rough, and dangerous, thus until recently the trip was avoided unless necessary.

Chiloé, known as the "Enchanted Island," is famed for its old wooden churches and because legend claimed that it was once inhabited and ruled by witches. People used to avoid Chiloé for fear of witchcraft; now its magical aura is a draw for tourists.

Originally inhabited by the Mapuche, an indigenous people of Chile and Argentina, the Spanish landed here in 1553 and occupied the island until 1567. Jesuits built the wooden churches around the island's perimeter so that missionaries from Peru could "*visit.*" This was optimistic: in fact, priests rarely visited Chiloé due to a combination of political turmoil, armed resistance from the Mapuche, reluctance to navigate the stormy seas, and, not least, Chiloé's location at what seems the end of Earth.

A Spanish population was settled on the island and left to "civilize" the Mapuche. After a violent earthquake in 1646, these settlers begged permission to leave the island, but their request was denied by the Jesuit authorities who insisted they stay among the Mapuche.

The Spanish and Mapuche populations were left together in isolation; to the fascination of scholars, historians, and anthropologists, the Chilotes, as the local population is called, developed a very unique occult folklore. It is unclear how much of this folklore is indigenous to the island, how much was imported by the Spanish settlers, and how much is the result of a merger of the two cultures.

Old, persistent rumors suggest that Chiloé is ruled by a secret cabal of powerful witches. Attitudes toward the witches are somewhat ambiguous; on the one hand, there is an ancient indigenous goddess tradition on Chiloé. Witches serve as priestesses of this ocean goddess, Pincoya, and mediate with her to provide safety and prosperity for islanders. Allegedly, merchants who make contracts with the witches prosper, too. However, much of Chiloé's witch lore is exceedingly negative and would not be out of place amongst the fantasies of Europe's most virulent witch-hunters. Legends depict local witches as grotesque in the absolute most negative sense of that word. (See page 661, Grotto.)

Chiloé's witches fly and shape-shift. They can raise or lower the sea level at will. They control the tides. Witches plot and scheme and cause death, disaster, illness and assorted mayhem, mischief, and mishaps.

Chiloé is allegedly home to a unique type of witch known locally as *La Voladora* or "the flying woman." No broomsticks for La Voladora; instead she transforms into a bird. In order to fly, La Voladora must lighten her body so that it functions like a bird's: to accomplish this, she vomits up her intestines into a *zapa*, a wooden pan, which is then hidden in the forest. (Alternately she vomits into an empty mollusk shell.) She then transforms into a bird and takes flight.

The witch's flight must be concluded by dawn. La Voladora *must* return to her intestines and swallow them again before the first rays of sunrise if she ever hopes to regain her human nature. Should she be unable to reach her intestines in time, or should someone hide them, La Voladora must fly ceaselessly for a year and then die.

Another version of the legend of La Voladora suggests that she doesn't *really* fly: the witch merely lies on the ground while making flying motions. No, it's not a shamanic soul-journey: instead, while she's going through the motions, the devil flies in her place. (An even less pleasant alternative suggests that witches create special jackets from the flayed skins of virgins, enabling them to fly.)

The witches' other methods of travel may be preferable:

✻ Caballo Marino *(the sea horse) is a horse with a golden mane. It is so large that it can comfortably carry 13 witches at a time. All a witch has to do is whistle for it and Caballo Marino comes; slap it on the rear and it departs.*

✻ *The witches also possess a ghost ship, which rides over or under water like a magical submarine.*

The witches' headquarters are maintained in a cave, rumored to be in Quecavi, a village on the eastern side of the island. (Other legends suggest that rumors of witches' caves kept nosy neighbors from exploring smugglers' stashes.) The cave is guarded by the Imbauche or Invunche, the witches' sentry. Witches allegedly kidnap babies, preferably first-born males, whom they then deform hideously, breaking the baby's right foot and then binding it to the left shoulder so that the baby can never escape. (This mimics the way witches were often bound during European witch-trial ordeals.) The Imbauche is entirely dependent on the witches for sustenance; in exchange, he is forced to guard their caves.

Salem

Salem, Massachusetts, is called the "Witch City" and for good reason. Based on Hollywood movies and popular literature versions of witchcraft, one would think *every* witch came from Salem or had an ancestor that was burned there. One might even think that witchcraft hysteria began and ended in Salem, which is absolutely not true. In the scope of hundreds of years of witch hunting, Salem was not even unique: more people were killed in longer panics elsewhere. Nor was it uncommon for young girls claiming to be bewitched to accuse others of witchcraft both in Europe and elsewhere in the American colonies, just as occurred in Salem.

Be that as it may, the witchcraft panic in Salem has gripped the public imagination like no other witch panic. It is extensively taught in American schools, and is the subject of countless books and movies and an award-winning play—see **CREATIVE ARTS:** Literature: *The Crucible.*

Those who journey to Salem will discover that its witchcraft history is not ignored but is a crucial part of the local economy; many sites, both historical and entertainment-oriented, are devoted to various visions of witchcraft.

The first thing one must realize is that there are two Salems: Salem Village and Salem Town. The historical center of witchcraft hysteria was in Salem Village, a parish of Salem Town. Following the notoriety (and subsequent embarrassment) of the witch trials, Salem Village, changed its name to Danvers. Thus most of the surviving historical sites associated with the hysteria are really located in Danvers, approximately 17 miles north of Boston.

The Salem Village Historic District of Danvers has several properties related to the witch trials that are accessible to the public, including the home and burial place of Rebecca Nurse (who was among those executed) and of Ann Putnam (one of the "bewitched girls"), as well as the Salem Village Parsonage, where Salem's witchcraft hysteria began. (This was home for Reverend Samuel Parris' family and his slave Tituba, the first person in Salem to confess to witchcraft. Also living here at an earlier time was Reverend George Burroughs, Parris' predecessor, who was convicted of witchcraft and hanged.)

Other sites of interest in Danvers include:

❋ *The Witchcraft Victims' Memorial, dedicated in 1992 to commemorate those who died during the witchcraft hysteria. It sits opposite the site of the old Salem Village Meeting House, scene of many of the witchcraft examinations. The monument includes the names of those who died as well as final statements of eight of those executed.*

❋ *The Ellerton J. Brehaut Witchcraft Collection, housed at the Danvers Archival Center, a department of the Peabody Institute Library of Danvers. This is a collection of printed materials, including many original documents, devoted to the Salem witch trials. The collection includes the signature mark of Giles Corey, pressed to death for refusing to enter a plea and stand trial.*

Most people associate the township of Salem with the historic events that occurred at Salem Village. In addition, popular media used the name "Salem" in all kinds of explorations and exploitations of witchcraft, so that many people assumed that Salem remained a city filled with witches. Over the years, people flocked there for a variety of disparate, contradictory reasons including historical research, thrills, and pilgrimages. A substantial and growing Wiccan population is now also based in Salem.

Although historic sites are found in Danvers, locations geared for students and tourists are mainly in Salem, including the Salem Witch Museum, the Witch Dungeon Museum, featuring a reenactment of a witch trial based on actual trial transcripts and a guided tour of a recreated dungeon, and the Witch History Museum, offering a guided tour of fifteen scenes recreating the panic of 1692. In addition, the Salem Witch Village offers a guided tour on the subject of witchcraft. Created in conjunction with contemporary witches, the Village hosts ongoing programs and events relating to themes magic, Paganism, and witchcraft that are open for public participation.

Halloween/Samhain in Salem is now a major tourist destination; hotels are reserved months in advance. Salem is filled with special seasonal activities:

❋ Haunted Happenings *is an annual three-week Halloween festival featuring many family-oriented activities (see www.hauntedhappenings.org).*

❋ *The annual* Festival of the Dead, *founded by Salem witch elders Shawn Poirier and Christian Day, explores death's mysteries through haunting events that investigate both the favored and forbidden ways in which cultures have revered, celebrated, and secretly divined the meaning of life's inevitable destination. Events include a dumb* supper, séances, psychic fair and witches' exposition, and, for children, Ms. Firefly's School of Spirit Conjuration (*www.festivalofthedead.com*).

Further information regarding the Witch City may be found at www.hauntedsalem.com.

> Adjacent to Salem's Old Burying Point is the Witch Trials Memorial erected in memory of those who suffered in Salem in 1692; it's open to the public.

Siquijor Island

Siquijor Island is located between the large Visayan Islands of Mindanao and Negros in the Philippines and may be reached via ferry. Siquijor, described as the "Island of Sorcerers," is feared by many Filipinos as a source of malevolent, evil magic.

Two opposing viewpoints exist regarding Siquijor Island, depending upon one's spiritual perspective. Either it is home to a sophisticated, magical system deeply rooted in indigenous pre-Colonial traditions, or it is the home of evil practices and malevolent magic.

Attitudes toward the magical traditions of Siquijor and its practitioners are comparable to attitudes toward Hoodoo and New Orleans Voodoo in the United States. However, many Siquijor witchcraft activities are reminiscent of Sweden's Easter witches and Russian witchcraft.

Similar to Swedish Easter witches, the primary witchcraft activity on Siquijor occurs on the Eve of Good Friday. Healers, practitioners, shamans, and witches allegedly gather botanicals during Holy Week before converging on San Antonio Mountain, the highest peak on the island on Good Friday Eve. The *mananambals* (indigenous shamans and healers) craft their brews on their sacred mountain on Good Friday Eve: ingredients are added to a large cauldron or *kawa*. While it brews, the night is devoted to spiritual and magical rituals; then the brew is apportioned to the various practitioners.

Holy Week evolves into an unofficial "Witches' Festival" during which practitioners and healers from various parts of the Phillipines and elsewhere converge on Siquijor Island. Russian witches travel to Bald Mountain to gather herbs on Midsummer's Eve: allegedly botanicals picked at this time in this place possess maximum magical power. Likewise, practitioners journey to Siquijor during this time to gather botanicals, especially healing medicinal plants. (Allegedly some plants are *only* available on Siquijor.)

Powerful shamanic and botanical healing traditions survive in Siquijor. Botanical potions are bottled in oil, reminiscent of Hoodoo preparations, themselves reminiscent of magical concoctions from ancient Egypt. For instance, *haplos*, a healing ointment, is crafted from over 100 herbs steeped in coconut oil in large empty liquor bottles.

Siquijor witches allegedly cast hexes and turn tricks, not dissimilar in style from those of the Southern United States. Malevolent spells are cast using intimate items belonging to the spell's target (pieces of clothing, hair, fingernail clippings, and the like). The concept of "live things" introduced into a victim's body by a malevolent practitioner also exists, although the techniques used are allegedly different. (See **MAGICAL ARTS:** Healing.)

Some villagers boast of the island's witches and perceive its reputation for witchcraft as beneficial, crediting Siquijor's low crime rate to fear of witches; others deny their existence, claiming these stories are all innuendo and superstition.

Others acknowledge that historically there were witches but all have since been killed. (An elderly couple was killed in the 1960s when their house was dynamited. Allegedly neighbors feared the couple's relationship with spirits.) Still others suggest that the witches still exist, living quietly and discreetly in mountain caves.

Marketplace

Envision a time and place with no shopping malls, no department stores, and no main streets lined with stores. Envision a time and place with no mail-order catalogs and no online shopping. Now, in that context, envision the magic of the traditional marketplace, another place intrinsically associated with witchcraft.

The marketplaces traditionally associated with witchcraft aren't modern shopping malls or strip malls; instead they are traditional markets where merchants brought their wares to sell and trade. This type of market might be considered a crossroads: it is where different people's lives intersected. (And in fact, historically many markets were held at crossroads. These markets didn't have fixed locations: vendors converged on schedule at a particular location, essentially bringing the market with them. The easiest, most convenient place to meet was frequently a crossroads.)

Once upon a time, and still in some places, the marketplace was a realm where women held sway. This remains true in rural West Africa. Women man the marketplace, buying, selling, and trading.

Services are also commonly found in the traditional marketplace: healers, diviners, body artists (tattoo and henna artists as well as piercers), story-tellers, and entertainers also offer their services, as do craftsmen like ironsmiths and other artisans who do repair-work and commissions as well as sell goods. This type of traditional market survives amongst the souks of North Africa and the Middle East as well as elsewhere, but once existed around the world.

The marketplace is identified with witchcraft for two reasons:

* *The more obvious reason is that for centuries, the marketplace was where one could obtain the services of a witch, magical healer or fortune-teller. It was where stories and information was circulated; instruction in various traditions could also be obtained.*

* *It was also where witches and other practitioners obtained supplies. (The marketplace thus is the replacement for the forest.) The marketplace is the location where practitioners could meet, socialize, and trade techniques and secrets.*

* *The less obvious reason has to do with the magical energy generated by the marketplace. The marketplace is the equivalent of a crossroads: anything can theoretically happen in the marketplace, it is a world of possibility and opportunities, either to be won or lost. Fortunes may also be won or lost. The excitement of the marketplace, the high emotions and interaction between so many people generates a powerful magical energy that spirits love and upon which they thrive. Spirits hover at the marketplace and thus witches and magical practitioners do too.*

Many traditional cultures believe witches deliberately linger in the marketplace, absorbing the magical energy generated by impassioned trading and bargaining to enhance their own power.

Just as human women are believed to rule the physical marketplace, its spiritual rulership is overseen by powerful female spirits:

✻ *Ferronia, Italy's ancient shamanic goddess now wanders through traditional markets in the guise of a shabby old hag. Don't be fooled by her humble appearance: she remains the spiritual queen of the marketplace.*

✻ *Oya, the orisha of storm winds and cemeteries exerts authority over the marketplace too. Shopkeepers wishing to improve business and profits are advised to petition this powerful orisha and leave her offerings every Thursday.*

There are also markets specifically devoted to witchcraft. These witchcraft markets are where practitioners obtain botanical and other supplies. (They are also popular with tourists.) Among the most world-famous witchcraft markets are the Witchcraft Market (*Mercado de Hechiceria*) in Mexico City, and the Witches' Market (*Mercado de Brujas*) of La Paz, Bolivia.

See **DICTIONARY:** Orisha; **DIVINE WITCH:** Feronia; **HORNED ONE:** Oya.

Mountains

Witches revel. But where do they revel? According to widespread European folklore, witches hold their parties and perform sacred rituals atop hills and mountains.

This actually makes sense if one considers witchcraft's ancient origins: in days of yore, before maps, sat-nav and road signs (and sometimes even roads), the easiest places to rendezvous were those characterized by obvious geographic features—crossroads for instance. Once upon a time, roads often only intersected in only one place and so a crossroads couldn't be missed. All you had to do was keep walking until you arrived. Other popular meeting points including standing stones, large barrow mounds or similar unique monuments and, of course, the highest point in the area.

The highest point in the area is a vantage point: it has an obvious advantage.

Those already in attendance can see exactly who's approaching, crucial during the witch-hunt era when festivities, rites, and revelry were forbidden and threatened by legal persecution. Many of the mountains associated with witchcraft combine features: they are also forested and dotted with caves. If the wrong people crashed the party, devotees might have the opportunity to find safety within these caves and forests.

Mountains and hills are more than that, however: they are also sacred places, the places on Earth closest to the Heavens. The Bible continually complains of people traveling to "high places" to worship "foreign gods." The practice has never ended.

There are a tremendous number of these places. Some (Bald Mountain, The Brocken) are very famous: allegedly witches flew from all over the world to attend the massive festivities held there. Others are only of local repute. The ones listed here are but the tip of the iceberg.

Bald Mountain

Bald Mountain is perhaps the most famous "witches' peak" on Earth. The name is sometimes used generically to indicate *any* mountain associated with witchcraft, however, the original Bald Mountain is in the Ukraine.

Bald Mountain is a nickname for Mount Triglav near Kiev, also called Bare Mountain. Russian, Belorussian, and Ukrainian witches, plus those from much further afield, allegedly applied ointment to their bodies and rode broomsticks, pitchforks or chimney pokers up chimneys to journey to Bald Mountain, especially on Midsummer's Eve, known in Russia as the Feast of Ivan Kupalo.

Bald Mountain is more than just a place to hold a party, however: Bald Mountain was a pilgrimage point for collecting magical supplies. Witches and others journeyed to Bald Mountain on Midsummer's Eve because that was the sole time and place where one could collect Earth's most magical plants. The fact that they were collected at the magical conjunction of Bald Mountain and Midsummer's Eve (space and time) was what gave these plants their immense power.

Bald Mountain is crucial to the concept of the Russian magical plant. According to the tenets of Russian botanical magic, it isn't sufficient for a plant to be of a magical species. For instance, in other parts of Europe rowan or elder is innately powerful: *any* rowan twig possesses incredible power. Obviously it can be enhanced through ritual and spell-casting, however the plant itself is inherently powerful.

Not so with Russian magical plants. It is not the species alone that creates power. For maximum power, a botanical must be picked at a specific place and time, and often specific rituals and incantations must be incorporated for magical activation. Rituals and incantations may vary but *the* best place and time is invariably Bald Mountain on Midsummer's Eve. This is true for witches but also for anyone wishing to obtain such a plant: one must go and gather among the witches, a civilian amongst priestesses.

Bald Mountain has historically served as an artistic muse, inspiring Russian composer Modest Mussorgsky to create "A Night on Bald Mountain." Mussorgsky claimed to have been inspired by the confession of a witch who was burned at the stake in the 1660s as well as by Nikolai Gogol's novella *St John's Eve*. The piece did not meet with immediate critical success, originally rejected as too "raw." Five years after Mussorgsky's death, Nikolai Rimsky-Korsakov completed his own orchestration of the work. It is among the works featured in Disney's *Fantasia*.

> Another Bald Mountain is also identified with witches' revelry: *Kopasz Tetö* (literally "Bald Head"), is a peak in the Hungarian Tokay hills, in the shade of the Carpathian Mountains. Tokay is famous for its wine, which once held a reputation almost as magical as absinthe. Presumably it was on the menu at the witches' sabbats allegedly held there.

See **BOTANICALS:** Elder, Rowan; **CALENDAR:** Ivan Kupalo, Midsummer's Eve; **CREATIVE ARTS:** Films: Disney Witches, Literature: *The Master and Margarita*.

Blokula, Blockula, Blakulla or Blokulla

Sweden had a brief but brutal witchcraze. According to confessions extracted, witches flew off to sabbats presided over by Satan at a mountain called Blockula. Where exactly is Blockula? Who knows? It is unclear exactly where Blockula was or whether in fact it ever really existed. According to confessions, extracted under torture, witches allegedly flew tremendous distances on broomsticks with assistance from flying ointments.

Blockula has developed a famous name and is frequently sited in fictional depictions of witchcraft; however, it's unclear whether or not it even exists. If it does, these are likely suspects:

✻ *The most popular explanation is that Blockula is another name for The Brocken (see below), the German mountain also known as the Blocksberg. The Brocken is profoundly associated with Freya and hence it would make sense that Swedish witches, if indeed there were witches, might join German compatriots at The Brocken.*

✻ *Another suggestion is that the Blockula is not a mountain at all but a rocky island in the Baltic Sea, located between Öland and Småland, a still heavily forested region of Sweden characterized by extensive marshes and lakes.*

Blockula is intrinsic to the legend of Sweden's Easter witches who still allegedly fly to the Blockula on Maundy Thursday, returning home on Saturday just in time to be present for Easter.

See **CALENDAR:** Easter; **DIVINE WITCH:** Freya; **WITCHCRAZE!:** Sweden.

The Brocken

At 3,747 feet, the Brockenberg, more popularly known as The Brocken, is the highest peak of Germany's Harz Mountains and a fabled haunt of witches. (Older maps identify The Brocken as the Blockberg or the Blocksberg) Alongside Bald Mountain, it is the location in Europe most associated with witchcraft and witches.

Prior to Christian influence, The Brocken was a sacred area. Rübezahl the dwarf lives on the peaks but the deity most identified with The Brocken is Freya. Allegedly, following the acceptance of Christianity, Freya didn't disappear: instead she retreated to her old stronghold, The Brocken. Her priestesses sought refuge there too; those who wished to honor or petition her sought her in The Brocken.

Allegedly witches flew from all over Europe to dance atop The Brocken on Walpurgis Night (May Eve). Local lore reported that witches danced with such fervor and gusto they wore out their shoes by morning. Boys traditionally dressed up as werewolves to scare and drive off the enemies of approaching summer in re-enactments of Pagan rituals.

The region was closely identified with witches: medieval maps illustrate the area with images of witches riding broomsticks. In 1589, the ecclesiastical authorities of Quedlinburg, in The Brocken's shadow, burned 133 women accused of being witches to death in one day.

✻ *A mass of huge granite blocks at The Brocken's summit is known as* "The Witch's Altar," *or alternatively* "The Sorcerer's Chair" *or* "Devil's Pulpit."

✻ *A nearby spring is called the* "Magic Fountain."

✻ *A local anemone (wind-flower) is known as* "The Sorcerer's Flower."

It isn't only The Brocken's height that earned its reputation as a magical, holy place. The Brocken is also home to a unique meteorological phenomenon known as the *Brockengespenst* (Specter of the Brocken). Given the right atmospheric conditions, this specter, technically an optical illusion also known as the *anti-corona* or *glory*, causes a person's shadow cast from a ridge to appear magnified. Although really only a shadow, it appears that a specter walks alongside you. Rainbow-like bands or rings may surround the shadow.

Witches still really do meet at The Brocken on Walpurgis Eve. Walpurgis Eve (May Eve) is exactly opposite Halloween (November Eve) on the calendar. Now Halloween may be the witches' night in North America, Ireland, and elsewhere but in Germany and Central Europe, April 30th is their special night. Beginning in the 1930s, a special steam train brought Walpurgis Night revelers up The Brocken, children and adults, many costumed as witches, especially red witches, although whether these disguises serve as masquerade or as ritual clothing are the secrets of individual revelers.

See **ANIMALS:** Wolves and Werewolves; **CALENDAR:** Halloween, May Eve, Walpurgis Night; **DIVINE WITCH:** Freya, Rübezahl.

Gellért Hill

Once upon a time, Gellért Hill was where Budapest's witches celebrated nocturnal rituals and festivities. These days, it's prime real estate: the hill offers beautiful panoramic vistas of Budapest and the Danube River. At least one dozen thermal springs gush from the hill; the source for Budapest's fabled thermal baths and spas and the reason for its status as sacred Pagan territory.

Gellért Hill is now covered by shops, residences, and hotels: it's hard for modern observers to visualize Gellért Hill as a natural slope and sacred site.

The hill was named in honor of Gellért, the eleventh-century Venetian bishop, missionary, and martyr who, under the reign of King Stephen (now St Stephen), converted Hungary to Christianity. After Stephen's death, the Hungarians revolted and captured Gellért. They stuck him in a wooden barrel, hammered spikes through it and rolled Gellért down the hill into the Danube. After Christianity was reinstated, the hill was renamed in his honor (a statue of him stands there today), but according to witchcraft

trial records, centuries later Hungarian witches continued to mount the hill to dance on moonlit nights. (See **WITCHCRAZE!:** Hungary.)

Horselberg

The Horselberg, also known as the Venusberg or Mountain of Venus, lies in Thuringia, between Eisenach and Gotha in Germany. Witches from Eisenach accused of venerating Hulda allegedly celebrated sabbats here, but the Horselberg is now most famous as the location associated with the legendary German knight Tannhäuser.

The story of Tannhäuser describes his visit to a deity called *"Frau Venus"*; it's unclear whether this deity was a euphemism for Hulda or Freya or even whether the story was inspired by tales of Sibilla and just transposed to Germany from Italy. (See **DIVINE WITCH:** Freya, Hulda, Sibilla.)

A cavern near the summit is known as the *Horselloch* or Venus' Cave. Sounds resembling subterranean waters emanate from this cave so that it is reminiscent of a grotto. The Horselloch is allegedly an entrance to Frau Venus' palace.

Tannhäuser was a celebrated *minnesinger*, a German minstrel knight, similar to the French troubadours of the twelfth to fourteenth centuries. The minnesingers were among those who composed tales of the Grail Knights but they specialized in romantic sagas like those of Tristan and Isolt. They composed elaborate, flowery love songs, although whether these were inspired by individual women or by the Goddess remains subject to speculation. During their own time, minnesingers were frequently accused of having Pagan sympathies and eventually fell from favor.

According to the legend, Tannhäuser was riding past the Horselberg at twilight when an incredibly beautiful woman mysteriously appeared and beckoned to him. He left his horse, joined her and discovered that she was none other than "Frau Venus." He accepted her invitation to enter her palace in the very heart of the mountain. Before he knew it, seven years of pleasure and happiness had passed.

For whatever reason, after these seven years, Tannhäuser was suddenly stricken with pangs of homesickness and remorse. He longed to see sunlight. In some versions of the story, Tannhäuser just bids farewell to Frau Venus and leaves. In others, he prays to the Virgin Mary who releases him from Frau Venus' spell. Tannhäuser immediately went to a church seeking absolution. After hearing his tale, the local village priest doesn't know what to do with him and sends him to a superior who does the same. Tannhäuser goes from priest to priest, bishop to bishop, confessing to all: none grant him absolution until finally he goes to the Pope. He begs for absolution but the Pope rebukes him, telling him that guilt such as his is unforgivable. The pope declares that his almond wood staff will flower before Tannhäuser's sins will ever be forgiven.

Tannhäuser, despairing, returns to the one place that will welcome him with open arms: the Venusberg. Three days after his departure, the Pope discovered that his staff had budded and flowered. He realized that he was wrong to reject Tannhäuser's repentance and sent messengers after him. But it was too late: observers described seeing Tannhäuser reach, ascend and enter the mountain.

Several other mountains in Germany had reputations as "witches' mountains", including:

❦ *Heuberg Mountain, near Balingen in the district of Baden-Wurttemberg*

❦ *Huiberg Mountain, near Halberstadt, Saxony-Anhalt*

❦ *Koterberg, in Westphalia*

Monte della Sibilla, The Sibyl's Mountain in Norcia

According to legend, the Cumaean Sibyl took refuge in a mountain cave where she transformed into the witch-goddess Sibilla. (See **BOOKS:** Library of the Lost: Sibylline Books; **DIVINE WITCH:** Sibilla.) That cave may allegedly be found on Mt Sibilla in the Sibillini Mountains, part of Italy's Apennine mountain chain, now a National Park.

Her cave is near the summit, which is wrapped by rocks resembling a crown. Archeological evidence indicates that whether or not the Sibyl herself lived there, the cave served as a shrine to a prehistoric goddess.

Another feature of the Sibillini Mountains is now called Lake Pilato, named after Pontius Pilate, the Roman procurator responsible for the crucifixion of Jesus Christ. According to legend, he was later condemned to death and was drowned in the lake. (Rumors suggest that Lake Pilato is the gateway to Hell.)

The lake was renowned long before the Crucifixion however; it has a mirror-smooth surface but periodically during the year, its waters turn red. Christian myth suggested this was because of the devil's influence. Modern science reveals that Lake Pilato is the home of a unique shellfish, similar to the Phoenician mollusks that produced wonderful vivid red and purple dyes. One may only imagine how ancient Pagan goddess-worshippers envisioned this periodically red lake.

Lake Pilato and Mt Sibilla were famous all over Europe. Documents dating to the fifteenth century indicate that sorcerers and wizards traveled from great distances to consecrate their grimoires here, despite the gallows erected at the entrance to the valley by a local bishop to serve as a warning to visitors.

Mount Hekla

Mount Hekla, an active volcano in southern Iceland, was allegedly the favorite haunt of Danish witches who flew there to attend sabbats. Mount Hekla is among Earth's most active volcanoes and was believed to be among the entrances to Hella's realm. A nearby town is named Hella. Some have suggested that the mountain shares its name with the goddess, although others protest that *Hekla* means "slab" or "covering," which would still make it cognate with Hella as that is what her name means, too. Another suggestion is that the name Hekla is linguistically related to *hexe* or "witch."

See **DICTIONARY:** Hexe; **DIVINE WITCH**: Hella.

Old Woman's Mountain

The Old Woman's Mountain or Grandmother's Mountain, allegedly once favored by witches and wise women, is found in the Tatra Mountains, part of the Carpathian range between Poland and Slovakia. Called *Babia Gora* in Polish, Old Woman's Mountain is now a National Park. Its highest peak is called *Diablak* (Devil).

Pendle Hill

On August 20, 1612, ten women and men were convicted of charges of witchcraft and hanged at Lancaster Castle in England. These ten are known as the Pendle Witches. Pendle Hill, located in northeastern Lancashire, part of the Pennine chain of hills, dominates Pendle Forest.

Pendle Hill combines the characteristics of sacred hill, forest, and burial ground: a Bronze Age burial site is located at the hill's summit. Pendle Hill remains powerfully identified with witchcraft and is a popular destination on Halloween. (See **WITCHCRAZE!:** England.)

Puy de Dôme

Puy de Dôme is a mountain in the Auvergne region of French, near Clermont. For at least two thousand years the thermal waters of the spa town of Royat have been considered healing and beneficial. The area is filled with thermal springs, caves, and grottoes.

The Celts considered Puy de Dôme sacred to the solar deity Lugh. The Romans worshipped Mercury here, building him a temple at the summit of this 5,000-foot peak during the first century of the Common Era. By medieval times the mountain was famous as the setting for witches' sabbats.

Information about sabbats comes primarily from the confessions of a woman, Jeanne Boisdeau, tried as a witch in 1594 and subsequently burned at the stake. According to her confession, which, as with virtually all confessions of witchcraft, may be assumed to have been made under torture and so is questionable, witches journeyed from all over France, from as far away as Languedoc to rendezvous at Puy de Dôme on Midsummer's Eve.

Witches mounted broomsticks and let the winds carry them to Puy de Dôme. Jeanne told her Inquisitors that witches worshipped Satan there in the form of a goat. Witches greeted him by kissing his posterior; the Devil said Mass using a radish as a sacrament. (Those familiar only with little round red radishes may be unaware of the phallic nature of many more rustic radishes.) The devil distributed charms to his devotees that served as amulets, providing safety from fire, animals, and assorted dangers. He allegedly breathed on witches to bestow oracular power on them.

During sabbats, allegedly during a Satanic Mass, a gigantic black hen appeared at *La Cratère du Nid de la Poule* (Crater of the Hen's Nest) where it laid three black eggs before disappearing in flames. (This may be intended to recall the phoenix or to indicate Hellfire.)

The witches broke the eggs open: Satan's instructions for the following year were found within. They then had a picnic of bread, wine, and cheese followed by dancing. Witches, demons, and the devil did a back-to-back circle dance going in a widdershins direction. The eldest person present held the goat's tail while others held hands. (See **ANIMALS:** Chickens; **DICTIONARY:** Widdershins.)

It is unknown how much, if any, of Jeanne's confession was true.

Witches' Caves of Zugarramurdi

Cuevas de las Brujas or the Caves of the Witches are an extended, natural tunnel, running some 100 meters within the mountain in the Pyrenees, which is also dotted with smaller galleries of caves known as *Sorgin Leze* in Basque or "Witches' Galleries." A stream flowing within the Witches' Caves beneath a large natural arch is called "Hell's Stream."

These caves and mountains are among the many powerfully identified with the Basque goddess Mari (see **DIVINE WITCH:** Mari). The cavern was believed to be a rendezvous point for Basque witches. Akelarres were allegedly held beneath the cavern's arch (see **DICTIONARY:** Akelarre).

Legends strongly advise that one should never enter Mari's homes without an invitation or without conducting proper ritual. One should *never* damage anything in her homes and never, ever, ever take anything away from her homes. Allegedly, her punishment of those who infringe these rules is swift and sure.

Mari's homes are largely subterranean. Many caves in the Pyrenees are identified with Mari and hence with witches. The Inquisition spent several months stationed in Zugarramurdi, and twelve people convicted of witchcraft by the Inquisition were condemned to die by burning in November 1610. (Five were burned in effigy only as they had already died in prison prior to the verdict.) Others were punished by imprisonment and loss of property.

The caves still bear associations with witchcraft. An annual "Witches Festival" is celebrated here every July. Other mountain caves associated with Mari include Amboto, Azcondo, Aizkorri, and Muru.

Museums of Witchcraft

Although many occultists have famed personal collections, notably Raymond Buckland, the following museums are open to the public:

Castle Halloween

Castle Halloween in Benwood, West Virginia houses the collection of the Halloween Queen, Pamela E. Apkarian-Russell, author and renowned authority on Halloween. The collection consists of over 15,000 items of Halloween and related memorabilia from the 1860s until the present. Among the exhibits are over one thousand Halloween costumes, a fortune-telling display, a Harry Potter exhibit and a section devoted to the Salem Witch Trials. Apkarian-Russell's extensive Halloween postcard collection is also on display as well as many games, toys, and paintings. Website: http://www.castlehalloween.com. Telephone: 304 233 1031.

Hexenmuseum Schweiz

Located in Auenstein, approximately 30 miles from Zurich, the Museum of Witchcraft Switzerland opened in April 2009 and features an extensive collection of books, artifacts, and art. This region suffered among the earliest and most severe witch hunts. The museum features an archive devoted to the Swiss witchcraze. Its mission is to dispel fear of witches and witchcraft. Guided tours in English are available, if booked in advance. Website: www.hexenmuseum.ch/Englisch.htm.

Museum of Icelandic Sorcery and Witchcraft

The Museum of Icelandic Sorcery and Witchcraft in Hólmavík, Iceland, is open between June 1st and September 15th and at other times by special appointment. Hólmavík is 273 miles north of Reykjavík in the region of Strandir. The museum is devoted to traditional Icelandic sorcery and witchcraft as well as the history of Iceland's seventeenth-century witch-hunts. Website: http://www.galdrasyning.is/.

Museum of Witchcraft

The Museum of Witchcraft in Boscastle, Cornwall, has for fifty years housed the world's largest collection of witchcraft-related artifacts and regalia.

Originally opened by Cecil Williamson in 1951 on the Isle of Man, it coincided with the repeal of the Witchcraft Act; Gerald Gardner was briefly employed as "resident witch". (See **HALL OF FAME:** Gerald Gardner, Cecil Williamson.) After several moves—local communities were, to say the least, less than welcoming to Williamson and his extensive witchcraft collection—he relocated finally to Boscastle, where the museum has been since 1960. Williamson ran the museum personally until he sold it in 1996 just shortly before his death aged 90.

Graham King, the present owner, bought the museum from Cecil Williamson at midnight on Samhain/Halloween 1996. His mission statement is *"to educate and entertain."* Website: www.museumofwitchcraft.com. Telephone: 01840 250111.

Several museums devoted to witchcraft in general or the Salem Witch Trials specifically are located in the towns of Salem and Danvers in Massachusetts. Please see Magical Places, page 665 for further details.

Swamps

Swamps may be considered to include bogs, fens, and marshes. The bogs of Northern Europe were once repositories for sacrifices: treasures have since been uncovered and brought to the surface. Bodies of human sacrifices have been dredged up too.

Swamps are thresholds between land and water, spirits and humans, danger and safety. Mangrove swamps are uniquely powerful thresholds where salt water and fresh water meet and mingle.

Swamps, like forests, are wild territory; swamps can't be cultivated or not at least without draining and destroying the swamp. In the days prior to modern technology, that was virtually an impossible task.

"Swamp" is an ominous word: when one is in trouble or overwhelmed, one is "swamped." This is based on reality: swamps can be ominous, overwhelming places.

Venomous or dangerous creatures live in the swamp: alligators or cottonmouth snakes for instance. Mosquitoes breed in swamps: swamps were the cauldron where malaria brewed. Alders, bleeding trees, are swamp specialties, as are weeping willows and mangrove trees whose roots lie treacherously above ground ready to trip and catch the unwary. (See **BOTANICALS:** Alder, Willow.) Swamps sometimes feature *will o' the wisps*, those glowing lights that lead travelers dangerously astray. Now it's known that will o' the wisps are phosphorus gas; once upon a time, they were understood as malevolent trickster specters.

Most people find swamps unfriendly, unwelcoming places: swamp witches are the exceptions. Legends say that swamp witches live in isolated shacks in the marshy depths of swamps. They are entirely self-sufficient, navigating the swamps by boat, gathering herbs, roots, and supplies as needed. Swamp animals (predatory birds, crocodilians, turtles, frogs, and snakes) are their allies and familiars.

Isis is the prototype of the swamp witch: her saga explains why witches appreciate the swamp. Isis and her beloved brother/husband Osiris were ancient Egypt's sacred couple: while Osiris traveled Earth teaching the sacred arts of civilization (cultivation of grain and wine), Isis spent her time studying magic and becoming the most powerful sorceress on Earth. Her prime competition was her other brother Set, also a skilled master magician. (See **DIVINE WITCH:** Isis, Set.)

Isis and Osiris' perfect life ended when Set murdered Osiris. Isis put her magic to practical use: temporarily resurrecting Osiris in order to conceive the son she was destined to bear, and who was destined to avenge his father. Her plan was not unbeknownst to Set: Lord of Miscarriage and Abortion, he pursued her, hoping to foil her plans. Isis took refuge in the Nile swamps, letting them protect her. The swamp offered her secrecy and privacy as it would for so many other witches.

The most famous swamp witches are those of the American South. When Voodooists were chased from New Orleans in the nineteenth century many found peace and refuge in the swamps of Louisiana. Here Marie Laveau led St John's Eve rituals on the banks of the Bayou St John, where she danced with her snake.

In addition to Isis, swamp spirits include the following:

Abátàn, or Abàtá

Abátàn/Abàtá is the Yoruba orisha of marshlands. Abàtá literally means "swamp" and that is where offerings and petitions to this orisha are traditionally brought. Abàtá is identified with accumulation of wealth. Her colors are coral, gold, green, pink, and yellow. Santeria identified her as the female compatriot of the hunter orisha Erinle, who has dominion over regions where salt and fresh waters meet, as they do in mangrove swamps.

Bolotnyi

Bolotnyi is a Slavic female swamp or bog spirit. In Russia, swamps are considered the special abode of mischievous, troublesome spirits. Post-Christianity, they've been reclassified as demons who usually live in Hell, but should they ever feel like residing on Earth, they make their homes in deep forests, lakes, springs, and *especially* in swamps. As long as they stay in these places, they do no harm, unless of course someone approaches them … Should they venture out to raise Hell, these spirits must be charmed back to the swamps where they belong.

Yemaya and Oshun

The Yoruba orishas Yemaya and Oshun (mother and daughter respectively or, depending on legend, sisters) usually manifest as grand, beautiful, beneficent goddesses. Yemaya is orisha of the sea and Oshun is orisha of sweet water: streams, rivers, waterfalls, lakes, and springs. They have other manifestations as well: in their guise as powerful witches, Oshun and Yemaya take to the swamps to become fierce, tough, haggard but still resplendent and magnificent swamp witches. (See **DIVINE WITCH:** Oshun, Yemaya.)

Thresholds

Magical energies radiate from everything (and everyone) that occurs naturally on Earth, although to varying degrees. Thresholds are border areas where one force, power or element encounters another. Thresholds are divisions and boundaries where two forces simultaneously meet, separate, and diverge. These meeting places are potentially the most magically charged areas of all.

Thresholds exist *everywhere*! The most obvious are seashores or riverbanks where water meets land, but there are many, many others.

"Thresholds" may be literal areas (the threshold of a door, for instance) but thresholds are also a crucial magical concept intrinsic to witchcraft. The most obvious thresholds are geographical locations but there are metaphoric thresholds too.

✳ *There are thresholds in time: midnight divides one date from the next. Midnight divides night from day. Twilight and dawn divide light from darkness.*

✳ *There are architectural thresholds: doors and windows separate outside from within.*

✳ *There are life-cycle thresholds: birth and death are thresholds between realms. Birth transforms someone into a parent. Before your first child, you were not a parent; at the moment of birth, you suddenly become one.*

✱ Transformative rituals are, by definition, thresholds. A magic spell is a threshold between unfulfilled need or desire and successful acquisition.

✱ Witches have traditionally served as thresholds (mediums) between the general population and the world of spirits. This is an ancient metaphoric observation: the words hag *and* hex *derive from a root word meaning "hedge"—the boundary between the wild and tame. (See* **HAG.***)*

✱ The hedge is the threshold between wilderness and civilization.

> The Indo-European cultures of Northern Europe, including Celtic, Germanic, and Slavic peoples, possessed a mythic concept of the *Haga:* the all-enclosing World Hedge, which separates the world under human dominion from wilderness. This *Haga* is a thorny boundary that keeps the wild forces of chaos at bay.

The hedge serves as the boundary but the hedge is also a force of nature: if not cut back periodically it expands. Hedges threaten order and civilization: left alone, hedges inevitably overtake cultivated vegetation. Without vigilant pruning and maintenance, the Earth Mother inevitably reclaims her land.

The hedge marked the threshold and boundary of human dominion. The shyest birds and animals live deep within the forest but others, curious threshold animals, those with less fear of people or who wish to interact with people, often make their home in the hedge. Predatory animals, those who might prey on humans or their livestock, linger in the hedge, too.

The hedge was the threshold where humans could commune with wild nature, with spirits, birds, animals, and other realms and planes of existence. Many shamanic plants (psychotropic plants) thrive in the hedge. The hedge is the birthplace of shamanism.

Perhaps because witches are concerned with magical energy, most of the locations closely associated with witchcraft are thresholds: forests, caves, mountains, grottoes, crossroads, and cemeteries.

La Hendaye Beach in the French Basque country exemplifies a geographical threshold associated with witchcraft: here land meets the ocean in the vicinity of mountain in this frontier, seaside town on the Spanish border. According to French witch-hunter Pierre de Lancre, more than 12,000 witches once attended sabbats here; rumor has it it's still a favored spot.

Wells

From a literal standpoint, wells are sources of fresh water. Once upon a time, unless a community was situated directly near a source of fresh water, wells were required to support the community. If a well went dry a community might be forced to relocate.

> Jac Ffynnon Elian (John Evans), hereditary guardian of the well of Ffynnon, was imprisoned twice in the early nineteenth century for reopening the sacred well after it was sealed by a local Christian priest. The well at Llanelian yn Rhos, near Abergele, Denbigh, Wales, stood in a field, surrounded by a grove and was destroyed in January 1829.

From a magical standpoint, wells are portals to other realms and fonts of fertility. The inherent moisture as well as the shape of the well is reminiscent of the vaginal canal. Many fairy tales involve heroines and heroes forced to journey up and down wells: their adventures metaphorically reproduce the birth process.

Wells were sacred sites identified with healing, renewal, divination, good fortune, love, and fertility magic. The concept of "wishing wells" derives from these old magical traditions. Wells were either portals to spirits who heard your pleas or they were portals to the heart of the Earth Mother herself. Sometimes wells were understood as portals to the Realm of Death.

Wells are identified with sacred spirits like Brigid, Asherah, Hulda, and the djinn. Lilith occasionally makes her home at the bottom of a well. Once upon a time, priestesses affiliated with these spirits sat in vigil beside wells, attending their spirits. If one wished advice, healing, magical information or assistance, one could find the priestess or prophetess seated by the well. The Norns, Nordic fate goddesses, live by the Well of Urd. (See **DICTIONARY:** Djinn; **DIVINE WITCH:** Hulda, Lilith; **WOMEN'S MYSTERIES:** Spinning Goddesses: The Norns.)

Wells are also often associated with sacred tree traditions. Many ancient wells are located near trees that were once venerated or associated with spirits. Sometimes the well survives long after the demise of the tree.

The tradition of "dressing" wells derives from Pagan spiritual traditions. Those wishing to make a spiritual vow or petition travel to a sacred well. Rituals may be performed there, frequently including circumambulations (circling) of the well. The visit is marked by tying a rag or cloth around the well or sometimes around trees beside the well. This practice is common to Europe, Asia, and North Africa. The rags are left to hang as testaments. Eventually the surfaces of some wells are entirely covered in fabric offerings.

Among the most famous sacred wells is the Chalice Well of Glastonbury in Somerset, England. The Chalice Well is among the oldest continuously used holy wells in Britain. Archeological evidence indicates the spring was used in prehistoric times; historical evidence for its use dates back two thousand years.

Sacred sites weren't chosen arbitrarily; water from the Chalice Well is unique as it is red. The scientific explanation is that the color is caused by red iron oxide minerals in the local soil. This wouldn't have been disputed by ancient Pagans: iron and iron oxides were once identified as the Earth Mother's amazingly magical, powerful, solidified menstrual blood. Before it was known as the Chalice Well it was known as the Blood Well.

The red waters of Glastonbury were identified as sacred to the Earth Mother and/or to the Goddess. Sacred associations spread to Christianity: according to one tradition, Joseph of Arimathea brought the Holy Grail, the chalice that caught Christ's blood during the crucifixion to England. Fearing thieves, he safeguarded the grail cup by burying it deep within the Glastonbury hillside. A miraculous healing spring welled up at this precise point: because it runs through the Grail before reaching the surface it is stained red with Christ's eternal blood. (The story doesn't take into account that Glastonbury was sacred much earlier than Christianity, however theoretically, if Joseph did have the grail-cup in his possession, what better place to secrete it than somewhere too sacred to search?) The area around Glastonbury has powerful associations with King Arthur and/or the Grail; water from the Chalice Well is prized by many from very different traditions.

See **CALENDAR:** Imbolc; **FAIRY-TALE WITCHES:** Grimms' Fairy Tales: *Mother Holle*; **MAGICAL PROFESSIONS:** Metalworkers.

☽ Tools of Witchcraft

Different traditions and different practitioners require and desire different tools. It is unlikely that any one witch will own or use every tool listed here. The witch who is afraid of fire doesn't need candles; the witch who works purely with verbal charms doesn't require a mortar and pestle.

> If a witch or practitioner uses *any* tool consistently in her magical work, it is, by definition, a magical tool.

Some tools, like the bolline, cauldron or mortar and pestle serve entirely functional uses, but in addition to practicality, witches' tools are also magical tools—tools that are perceived as radiating their own magic power. Different tools radiate different energies. Individual tools express specific elemental energies that empower and enhance spells and rituals, for instance candles radiate the power of fire.

Among the ways of determining what type of power a tool radiates is to consider what kind of materials are used in its creation. Thus a wooden magic wand places the power of trees into the hands of its wielder. Sometimes this is obvious; sometimes the radiant energy is more subtle. The concept of gazing into a crystal ball derived from gazing into the moon. A crystal ball essentially brings the moon inside and enables you to access lunar magic anytime not just during the Full Moon. The moon is identified with water and women. These associations have passed on to the crystal ball, which is perceived as radiating feminine, watery energy.

Female and male energies, yin and yang, are considered the most powerful radiant energies on Earth. Unifying these male and female forces provides the spark for creation, and what is a magic spell after all but an act of creation? Instead of a new baby, ideally new possibilities, solutions, hopes, and outcomes are born from each magic spell.

A high percentage of magical tools radiate male or female powers. Many tools metaphorically represent the unification of these forces. Earth's most ancient religions venerated the sacred nature of the human genitalia, representing male and female generative power.

Sacred spiritual emblems evolved into tools of witchcraft. Many magical tools now hide in the kitchen disguised as ordinary kitchen utensils including sieves, pots and cauldrons, cups and chalices, mortars and pestles, knives, dinner bells, and most famously, brooms. To some extent this parallels the hidden history of women: once worshipped or at least respected as goddesses, priestesses, and community leaders, for centuries (and still in some circles) women were perceived as the weaker, less intelligent, meek gender, fit for little other than preparing meals. Women's old tools of power lurked in the kitchen with them. In recent years, however, witches and their tools have emerged from their broom-closets to reveal their long suppressed powers.

In fact many tools serve dual uses: few ancient people had the variety or quantity of possessions that many take for granted today. The average kitchen witch of not that long ago made magic with whatever was at hand. She didn't have a catalog of wares to choose from. Rare, precious items were treasured but, by definition, these were accessible to only a very few.

Never permit the lack of a specific tool to stall a magical goal. Among the key ingredients of magical practice is inventiveness. The one and only tool that *is* a requirement is the spell-caster herself, her full and entire focus and commitment to a spell. According to French master mage Eliphas Levi (see **HALL OF FAME**) there are four requirements of successful magic: Knowledge, Daring, Will and Silence.

One cauldron served a family's purposes: from creating nutritious soup to concocting healing brews to crafting magic potions. The mortar and pestle ground up botanical materials for whatever purpose was currently needed: healing, magic or cooking. In a holistic world, purposes may not have been considered distinct in any case. This holistic tradition still survives in Traditional Chinese Medicine (TCM) where medicinals are sometimes administered via food. Edible, medicinal ingredients are prescribed for the patient: the meal *is* the prescription and may contain magical protective elements as well.

Athamé

Also sometimes spelled *Athalmé*, the athamé (pronounce *a-tham-ay* or *ath-may*) is a ritual knife. The origin of the name is unknown. It is usually, although not exclusively, black-handled with a double-edged steel blade. Whether it is sharp or dull is irrelevant as the athamé is not used as a cutting tool and is *never* used to draw blood. Symbols, such as runes or sigils, may be engraved or painted onto the handle.

The athamé, as with other metal blades, radiates male energy. Some identify swords and knives with the air element, others with fire. (The process of forging metal is complex and involves *all* the elements.)

Although the use of ritual knives, daggers or swords is common to very many traditions, the name *athamé* is almost exclusively Wiccan or Wiccan-influenced. It is among the standard tools of Wicca.

✳ *The athamé is used to cast ritual circles*

✳ *The athamé is used to direct magical energy*

* *Some traditions incorporate an athamé into the creation of Holy Water*

* *Athamés are used for invocations and banishing rituals*

Some traditions magnetize the blade by repeatedly, rhythmically stroking the blade from base to tip with a lodestone or magnet.

Black-handled knives have a long magical history. Their modern use derives from Celtic tradition but is reinforced by Ceremonial Magic. The athamé probably derives from the black-handled knives of Irish fairy-lore. In the eleventh century, the scholar Rashi (1040–1105) stated that a black-handled knife is required when invoking the *"Princes of the Thumbnail,"* the divinatory spirits evoked by scrying.

See also Bolline.

Bells

Bells are common in various traditions. Generally smaller hand bells, free standing bells with a handle, are used.

* *Bells are used for summoning and banishing spirits*

* *Bells are used to vanquish and remove the Evil Eye*

* *The sound of a bell ringing, especially a metal bell, is believed to exert a purifying influence and so bells are used for cleansing spells*

* *Bells are protective devices: malicious spirits allegedly flee from their sound*

* *Bells are used in fertility spells*

* *Bells are a tool for magical healing: ringing bells facilitates healing, and sometimes healing potions are drunk from magical bells in the belief that the "cup" adds potency to the brew*

Bells derive from ancient sacred images of human genitalia. The bell's body represents the vulva while the clapper represents the penis. An alternative vision suggests that the bell's body represents the womb while the clapper represents the child within.

Unlike other images deriving from sacred genitalia, the bell's two components cannot be separated. (The horseshoe and nails is a similar emblem: the horseshoe represents the vulva, the nail hammered into it is the penis. However, horseshoes and iron nails are independently powerful: a bell is not a functional bell unless the clapper is retained within the bell.)

The fertility imagery is sometimes enhanced by crafting the body of the bell to resemble a woman. The handle is crafted to resemble her head and torso while the round bell is her skirt.

Bells are also hung from chains or incorporated into mobiles to serve as amulets or the equivalent of a magical guard dog. If strategically hung, allegedly the bells will spontaneously ring as needed. Devices from Pompeii and elsewhere in the Roman Empire combined bells with phallic imagery.

Bells were attached to the ritual clothing of the priests who served the Jerusalem Temple. Bells are still attached to clothing around the world to serve as protective devices to repel mean spirits and the Evil Eye.

It was a common European belief during the witch-hunt era that the sound of church bells ringing repelled witches and caused them to fall off their brooms if flying through the sky.

✳ *Grease scraped from church bells is a common component of* Goofer Dust, *the Hoodoo magical powder whose primary ingredient is graveyard dust*

✳ *Slavic witches have traditionally used church bell grease to make similar concoctions*

✳ *Grease scraped from church bells is allegedly a primary component of the flying ointment favored by Sweden's Easter witches*

Bolline

The bolline is a knife used as a cutting tool in Wiccan spell-casting and spiritual rituals. The bolline is traditionally a white-handled knife with a double-edged blade.

An athamé traditionally has a black handle while the bolline's handle is white. The athamé is the ritual knife; the bolline is the practical knife. Beyond metaphysical and spiritual significance, by color-coding the handles, the two knives are easily and immediately distinguishable, thus lessening the chances of accidentally desecrating the athamé.

The bolline was originally used to harvest herbs and is believed to derive from the sickle. Older bollines often had a sickle-shaped blade although most modern bollines are standard knives. Among the uses of the bolline are carving and inscribing candles and wax tablets, chopping herbs, and cutting cord, thread or fabric.

See also Athamé.

Brooms

Brooms represent the perfect union of male and female energies: the stick represents the male force plunged into and attached to the female straw. Himalayan shrines display sacred images of the phallus and vulva crafted from stone, usually designed so that the phallus fits snugly into the vulva without falling off or rolling out. They may be separated or unified by attaching and detaching. Some, the most sacred, are natural rock formations but others were created by talented artisans.

The broom may be understood as a similar symbol but one that may be spontaneously crafted by *anyone*. All you have to do is attach straw to a branch or stick. The primitive broom is an incredibly simple device, child's play; no artisan is required to craft that kind of broom although modern artisans, wood-carvers, do create beautiful ritual brooms for witches that qualify as works of art.

According to Rhiannon Ryall, author of *West Country Wicca* (Phoenix Publishing, 1989), her journal of pre-Gardnerian Wicca, "*broom*" was old English country slang for women's genitals. "*Riding the broom*" thus was slang for intercourse, and "*Riding the* witch's *broom*" a reference to ritual copulation.

Although brooms are now associated with housecleaning, they may originally have been invented for magical and spiritual rites. The act of sweeping was a ritual act: the chore remained after the spiritual aspects were suppressed or forgotten. Depending on direction, sweeping over a threshold manipulates energy in or out, inviting or repelling.

In ancient Greece and Anatolia, brooms were the professional emblem of midwifery, similar to modern pawnbrokers' balls. Midwives once did more than just deliver the baby; they were expected to magically supervise the birthing chamber, keeping it free from malevolent spirits and negative spiritual debris. The midwife was expected to provide protection to mother and child: magical protection rituals often incorporated sweeping, especially sweeping over the vulnerable thresholds.

> The broom was among the sacred attributes of Hecate, Matron of Midwives and Witches. In recent years, the broom has evolved into an emblem of witchcraft. They are displayed as a badge of pride as well as a device to memorialize the Burning Times. As a bumper sticker proclaims, *"My other car is a broomstick!"*

Brooms were also used in agricultural fertility rites: women danced on brooms, men on pitchforks.

Brooms are men's tools, too, although generally without the long broomstick. Herne, Faunus, and other horned gods carry short brooms, usually switches or whisks made from branches, especially birch branches. Whether this broom was intended to represent male or female genitalia is subject to debate. In Europe, Santa Claus' dark helpers, like Krampus, usually carry this type of switch or broom. (Older images of Santa Claus sometimes depict him wielding a whip.)

This birch whisk remains a popular tool in the sauna and Russian bathhouse and may also derive from shamanic roots.

Of course, the most famous thing witches do with brooms is ride them. Another theory regarding the origin of brooms is that they are a shamanic tool for soul-journeying. The witch's broom may have originated as a shamanic spirit horse. A hobbyhorse is essentially a broomstick with a horse's head instead of a broom head.

In many witchcraft traditions, a broom alone is insufficient for flight: incantations and especially flying ointments may also be necessary components. The connection of the broom with soul-journeying may not be merely metaphoric. It is widely believed that the broomstick was a traditional tool used for topical applications of witches' flying ointments. (See page 693, Flying Ointments.)

In Mexico and Central America, brooms and the act of sweeping are symbolic of ritual purification. Central Mexican codices display grass brooms placed beside crossroads, the traditional place for depositing spiritually dangerous or potentially contaminating items.

> The broom is the emblem of the Aztec midwife-witch goddess Tlazolteotl as surely as it is that of her Eurasian counterpart, Hecate.

Purification and protection are closely linked: brooms are also used for protective magic. The footprints one leaves behind are believed particularly vulnerable to malevolent magic; someone who wishes you harm can do so via your footprints. An old spell suggests dragging a broom behind you to sweep away your traces; this way, no enemies can work on your footprints. (And indeed, the broom will sweep away footprints and without prints, no malevolent foot-track magic can be worked either.)

Baba Yaga performs similar actions: she flies in a mortar and steers with her pestle, but she uses a broom to sweep away her traces. (Russia had a strong tradition of foot-track magic.)

In Spanish witchcraft, brooms are used in love spells, sometimes dressed up as women. (There are legends of witches who could make these brooms dance!) A similar living witch's broom entertains an elderly woman in Chris van Allsburg's illustrated children's book *The Widow's Broom* (Houghton Mifflin, 1992).

Jumping the broomstick once indicated a marriage unsanctioned by the Church. It was a British folk custom and used by Romany. Slaves in the former British colonies were married by jumping the broomstick. The tradition has regained popularity among African-Americans as well as in Wiccan and Neo-Pagan handfastings.

It is considered unlucky to step over a broom. (The antidote is to step back over it backwards, as if rewinding a video.) Other traditions suggest that a broom leaned against or across a door keeps enemies away. They will be unable to cross your threshold and enter. A broom placed across a doorway at night allegedly keeps witches, ghosts, and spirits away.

See also **BOTANICALS:** Birch; **CALENDAR:** Easter; **DIVINE WITCH:** Hecate, Tlazolteotl; **HORNED ONE:** Herne, Krampus, Santa Claus; **PLACES:** Bathhouse.

Candles

Candles rank among the most popular of all magical tools in very, very many traditions. For further information please see **MAGICAL ARTS:** Candle Magic.

Cards

Cards are used for divination and for spell-casting. Cards (including Tarot cards) are also used for playing games. It is impossible to tell by the existence of cards alone the purposes for which they were used. Perhaps for this reason, the Puritans called playing cards *"the devil's picture book"* and considered it a sin to even keep a deck of cards in one's home. In the fifteenth century both secular and religious authorities inveighed against playing cards.

Cards were invented in East Asia; scholars debate as to whether their origins are in China or Korea. The earliest deck of European playing cards dates to fourteenth-century Italy. Before the invention of the printing press, cards were hand crafted. Many still craft their own cards for personal magical use.

With the exception of one card, The Fool, the cards in a Tarot deck are numbered. Card number one is The Magician. Older decks sometimes call him The Mountebank. The magician is traditionally portrayed standing at a table laid with his magical tools, which correspond to the Tarot suits: pentacle, wand/staff/stave, chalice, and sword (dagger/knife/athamé). The earliest surviving depiction of this image is found within the fifteenth-century Visconti-Sforza Italian Tarot deck.

Cards are most commonly expected to provide an oracle but are also incorporated into spell-casting and used as meditation tools and amulets. In Roman Catholic folk tradition, Holy Cards depicting the Holy Family and saints are used for protection and luck as well as spiritual and meditative purposes. Roman Catholic Holy Cards are also incorporated into magical practice, although this is not sanctioned by the Church.

Tarot cards remain the most popular magical cards; however a regular pack of playing cards has profound magical uses too, as do traditional "Gypsy Fortune-Telling Cards." Various special decks have been published over recent years specifically for divination, meditation or other magical and spiritual use. (See **HALL OF FAME:** Aleister Crowley, Marie Lenormand.)

Cauldrons

The word cauldron is related to words indicating heat or to warm up. The English word is believed to derive from the Latin *caldarium*, "hot bath."

Cauldrons metaphorically represent the female generative organs, the womb, uterus, and vagina. In old Egyptian hieroglyphics, the sign indicating "woman" was a pot.

Cauldrons and pots signify the universal womb.

Cauldrons are mythically identified with birth and resurrection. In an old Welsh poem, "The Spoils of Annwn," King Arthur visits the Next World to bring back a magical cauldron of regeneration that will return the dead to life. Like a womb, the cauldron reproduces the birth process.

According to Roman writers, cauldrons were used in Teutonic human sacrifice. (As with the Druids, whom the Romans also accused of conducting human sacrifice, this may or may not be true: they were not necessarily impartial observers.)

Cauldrons are consistent motifs in Celtic mythology:

✻ *The Cauldron of Bran the Blessed is the cauldron of resurrection and rebirth*

✻ *The Cauldron of Cerridwen brews the potion that confers all wisdom*

✻ *The Cauldron of the Dagda leaves no one unsatisfied*

✻ *The Cauldron of Diwrnach will not serve a coward*

Various spirits and witches are closely identified with cauldrons:

✻ *Bran is the Lord of the Dead: ravens are his sacred bird. Bran resurrects the dead in his cauldron. Shamans are "cooked" in Bran's cauldron, too. (Cooking may be understood as transforming raw material)*

✻ *Branwen is Bran's sister and the star of her own mythic saga. The Cauldron of Resurrection is her marriage dowry*

✻ *Cerridwen brews the potion of wisdom within her cauldron. A cauldron serves as her primary attribute. Her name may derive from a word for cauldron. (See DIVINE WITCH: Cerridwen)*

✻ *Medea rejuvenates an old ram in her cauldron; she then converts the cauldron into a murder weapon (See HALL OF FAME: Medea)*

✻ *Ogun has among his primary attributes an iron cauldron (See MAGICAL PROFESSIONS: Metalworkers)*

✻ *Teutates, an ancient Celtic (Gaulish) deity, drowned humans in his cauldron in the alder groves. Some believe he masquerades as the Grail legend's Fisher King*

Cauldrons were common grave goods throughout Europe and Asia. Hun graves, for instance, are often identified by their characteristic tall, slim bronze cauldrons.

Cauldrons were also spiritual offerings. Bronze and iron cauldrons were deliberately cast into lakes as votive offerings in the British Isles as well as throughout the European continent. Archeological evidence exists for the ritual depositing of cauldrons in lakes and marshes throughout the last millennium before the Common Era.

A great bronze cauldron filled with over two hundred pieces of bronze jewelry was discovered in Duchcov, Bohemia, now the Czech Republic. The cauldron and its contents, presumed to be an offering to a water-deity, were placed in the Giant's Springs—a natural spring that was the focus of much ritual activity during the third-century BCE.

The most famous cauldron is the gilded silver Gundestrup Cauldron, so called because it was discovered in a peat bog in Gundestrup, Denmark, in 1891. It had been placed on a dry spot within the bog sometime during the first-century BCE. The Gundestrup Cauldron is now housed in the National Museum of Copenhagen.

This ceremonial vessel measures three feet in diameter and is constructed from 13 plates, each one bearing repoussé images of deities or mythological scenes. The images include an antlered male deity, deities wearing torcs, and a ram-horned snake.

It is unknown where the cauldron was crafted; scholars suggest that it contains combined Thracian and Celtic elements, perhaps the result of interaction between silversmiths. Some believe it was taken from somewhere in Central Europe and brought to Denmark as war booty.

Cauldrons are used for spell-casting. Ancient spells frequently assumed that one had access to a hearth or similar open fire. This is rarely the case nowadays and cauldrons provide the safest substitute.

A Greek spell to conjure up a lover (whether a lost love or a brand new one) suggests that one wreathe a cast iron cauldron with red wool during a waxing moon. Add dried bay laurel leaves and barley grains and burn them within.

Cauldrons rejuvenate: Mullo are Romany vampire-ghosts who return and hover around the living. They may assist their relatives or torment them, however they feel inclined. Among the most feared mullo are those who were stillborn infants.

Once a mullo, always a mullo. A mullo is eternal. Baby mullos are boiled in a cauldron every year on what would have been their birthday by compatriot mullo. This invigorates and rejuvenates them.

Cauldrons are used to cook brews and potions but are also used to contain fire. A fire may be built within an iron cauldron. Conversely candles may be burned within. Should one wish to burn candles within a cauldron, it is advisable to spread a layer of clean sand, rock salt or similar within the cauldron beneath the candles for fire-safety and easier clean-up. A lidded cauldron enables you to smother the flames within easily.

See also Tripod.

Chalice

A chalice, sometimes known as a goblet, is a sacred or ritual cup or similar drinking vessel. Chalices are one of the four Tarot suits, also known as Cups. This suit represents the element water and corresponds to the playing card suit, Hearts.

The chalice is one of Wicca's four elemental tools. The chalice represents the feminine element of water. It may also be understood to represent the Womb of the Goddess.

> The Grail is sometimes envisioned as a chalice. One traditional explanation was that this was the cup of the Last Supper brought to Britain by Joseph of Arimathea, in which he had caught Christ's blood during the Passion.

The chalice represents the goddess or the eternal, universal, sacred feminine. During some traditions the Great Rite is celebrated by plunging an athamé into a chalice. The chalice represents the Goddess, Lady or female principle; the athamé the God, Lord or male principle.

In some traditions, a chalice holds wine during rituals. This is passed between ritual participants and shared. Usually a libation or offerings are also poured out to the Goddess.

Chalices are identified with Circe as she used a potion to transform Odysseus' crew into animals. Circe is commonly portrayed proffering a chalice, ostensibly to Odysseus. However she is often painted full-face looking straight at the viewer, her arm holding the chalice outstretched as if offering it to *you.*

Cord

Cords serve a variety of magical purposes. Smaller cords are used in knot spells, which are virtually universal, common to a multitude of magical traditions. Knot spells are among the most primordial types of spells. The underlying concept is that, as one pulls the knot tight, one's wish, desire or command is activated within the knot. Knot spells are most commonly used for healing, love, sex, and protection spells as well as, most notoriously, for hexing.

Knotting is inexpensive, highly accessible magic, only requiring a piece of string or cord and human will or desire. Knotting is, however, amongst the most difficult types of spells to master: unless one is consumed with emotion, it can be difficult to summon up the intense focus and will necessary for success.

Long cords are used in Wiccan ritual. The Wiccan cord is frequently titled a "cingulam." The standard cingulam is a nine-foot-long silk cord. (Other natural fabrics such as cotton or wool may also be used.) Style and color vary. It may be a single red or green braided cord or three cords braided together, traditional colors being black, red, and white. The cingulam is used in a variety of binding rituals and may be used to measure the circumference of a coven circle. The cingulam also enables a solitary witch to easily cast a circle:

1. Hold the end of the cingulam in what will be the center of the circle.
2. Mark the center by placing a large crystal or rock atop that end of the cingulam.
3. Rotate the cingulam's other end in a circle; mark the cardinal points with additional crystals or, alternately, sprinkle salt or powder to denote the physical boundaries of the circle.

The power of the cingulam is stored within its knots. Typically a series of nine knots are made, which may be tied and untied as desired to release or sustain power, reminiscent of ancient weather magic spells.

The Witch's Ladder names a knot spell, once strongly associated with hexes and so very feared. However it is also used for blessing and protective spells.

1. Three cords of equal length and nine feathers are required. Hen's feathers were traditional, perhaps because they were most accessible; adjust as desired.
2. Braid the cords together while focused on your desired intent.
3. Knot a feather into the bottom, where the braid begins.
4. Continue braiding and adding feathers: the nine feathers are knotted into the cord at equal intervals, evenly spaced from bottom to top.
5. Reserve the cord in a safe, secret place. Should you change your mind, undo the knots.

In some Wiccan traditions, the cingulam is knotted at Initiation. It may be used to fasten a robe around the waist. When not worn or in ritual use, the cingulam may be maintained on an altar; alternatively, it is stored by wrapping it around a staff or ritual broom.

Crystal Balls

Nineteenth- and early twentieth-century images of witches and fortune-tellers often portrayed them gazing into a crystal ball. The image has somewhat fallen out of fashion but crystal balls remain potent magical tools.

They are used for divination (scrying), for spirit-summoning and for shamanic communication with other realms. A crystal ball is exactly what it sounds like: a round globe formed from crystal. The crystal ball of the stereotype is a clear ball; however crystal balls also come in colors. The crucial element is that it is a smooth surface into which the user may scry: i.e., one gazes into the crystal ball until one sees images, whether in the ball itself or one's mind's eye.

Crystal balls derive from the ancient tradition of lunar gazing, either gazing directly at the moon or into a basin of water into which the moon reflects. Thus they are associated with the feminine, lunar element of water.

Crystal balls are less popular than Tarot cards or runes for two reasons: a fine crystal ball is an investment. They are not cheap and so inaccessible to many. Crystal balls can also be more difficult to master than cards or runes and hence more frustrating: scrying is an entirely intuitive, shamanic process. A beginner can read Tarot cards, instructional guidebook in hand. This is not the case with a crystal ball. One may gaze into a crystal ball for weeks, months or even years before images dependably appear.

Traditionally, crystal balls are kept covered when not in use. They are cleansed using incense smoke or by careful cleansing with magical washes, usually herb-infused spring water or spring water to which flower essences have been added.

Dolls

The archaic word used is "poppet" but that obscures the identity of what are plainly dolls. "Poppet" is related to "puppet." In English that implies that a puppet-master manipulates the puppet. (The French word for "doll" is *poupée*.) Puppetry derives from sacred ritual and is still used so in traditional Indonesia. In Japan, as elsewhere in East Asia, dolls serve as oracles; legends describe some very special ones that actually literally communicate prophecies.

Traditionally dolls are handmade, however commercially manufactured dolls may be embellished for magical purposes. Dolls are crafted from bone, clay, cloth, wax, wood or any other possible substance.

> Among the evidence brought against Bridget Bishop at the Salem Witch Trials was that several rag poppets were discovered in her former residence pierced with hogs' bristles and headless pins.

The most famous dolls are those made for harmful magic but that's partly because people like discussing the titillating, scandalous aspect of magic. Doll magic is also used for healing, romantic spells, protective spells, and especially fertility spells. Dolls were once used to stimulate pregnancy virtually around the world including indigenous North American traditions, Italy, and China. The tradition remains vital in sub-Saharan Africa. The most famous African fertility doll is the Ashanti *Akua'ba*, so prominent it has been featured on Ghana's postage stamps although it has now somewhat devolved into a tourist's souvenir.

Flying Ointments

Flying ointments, although still occasionally used by some, are not a common magical tool nor is it known whether they were ever common. However they are so commonly *discussed* during the history of witchcraft, especially during the Burning Times, that, even if they were rarely, if ever, used, they cannot be ignored.

Flying ointments are exactly what they sound like: ointments or unguents that allegedly enable people to fly, whether literally or shamanically (see **DICTIONARY:** Soul-journey).

The very earliest mention of a flying ointment may occur in Greek mythology. In the *Iliad*, Hera is described as anointing herself with fine oil before flying from Mount Olympus to Zeus on Mount Ida. Similarly, the hero in the second-century CE Roman novel *The Golden Ass* secretly observes a Thessalian witch transform into a bird and fly away after applying an ointment to her naked body.

During the witch-hunts, witch-hunters accused witches of literally using these ointments. Very often accused witches were tortured until they confessed that these ointments were gifts from Satan.

Various formulas for flying ointments survive from the witch-hunt era. No recorded surviving formulas come directly from witches or shamans: all known formulas were recorded by clerics, witch-hunters, and early physicians. It is unknown where these formulas truly originated or whether they were even used. They cannot be verified. In general, they contain combinations of potentially psychoactive but definitely poisonous botanicals like henbane, belladonna, opium, and water hemlock.

Recent scientific studies indicate that some of these herbal formulas may indeed stimulate hallucinations, visions, and sensations of flying and transportation, *if* they don't kill you first. Allegedly the highly poisonous combination of wolfsbane and belladonna produces a sensation of flight, for instance. If these ointments were indeed produced and used as described, this indicates that European shamanic traditions, replete with profound botanical knowledge, secretly existed well into the witch-hunt era.

Despite witch-hunters' allegations, records indicate that these ointments were associated with shamanic, rather than literal flight, even back then:

✹ *The Dominican Inquisitor Johann Nider, writing c.1435, described a peasant woman who offered to demonstrate to Dominican observers how she flew with Diana. He wrote that she sat inside a basket, anointed herself with balm, uttered magic words and fell into such a deep trance that she failed to awaken even when she fell from the basket to the floor. When she awoke, she told her observers that she had been with Diana and refused to believe otherwise.*

✹ *In 1545, the Duke of Lorraine lay ill; a married couple was arrested and charged with casting a spell on him to which they confessed. Their home was searched and a jug containing a salve was found. Renowned Spanish physician Andrés de Laguna (1499–1560) analyzed its contents and suggested that it was a green poplar salve base containing belladonna, water hemlock* (Cicuta virosa), *and other botanicals. He tested it on the local hangman's wife who lay comatose for three days and was annoyed when awakened because she had enjoyed her dreams and erotic adventures.*

The connection between brooms and flying ointment isn't arbitrary. It's believed that *if* these ointments were used, then certain parts of the body lend themselves to most effective application, notably sensitive, highly absorbent vaginal tissue. Some scholars perceived the broom as the applicator tool for the ointment. The ointment was secret; the broom became symbolic for witches' flight.

One theory suggests that following the increase in witch persecutions, fewer ventured out to literally dance on mountaintops or forests. Instead shamanic flight to witches' balls was substituted.

Traditional Swedish Easter witches usually fly brooms but are sometimes depicted riding vacuum cleaners or flying machines instead. These machines don't fly by themselves. Easter witches must prepare their brooms or flying vehicles with a special flying ointment, which is rubbed onto the broom rather than on their bodies. On their way to Blakulla or wherever they ramble, they gather in church towers to rest and socialize. The desire to stop in church towers isn't just the joy of sacrilege as some might imagine but because it's a necessary refueling stop. Ingredients in their flying ointment include grease scraped from church bells and bits of metal scraped off the bells. Their ointment is stored in hollow horns.

Encyclopedia of Witchcraft

In witch-hunt era Europe, similar ointments with similar ingredients also allegedly provided werewolf transformations, too. As with flying ointments, information regarding European werewolf-transformation ointment derives solely from witch-hunters' records, however similar traditions survived in Haiti.

The Haitian *loup-garou* is usually translated as "werewolf" but may be more accurately understood as "transformed sorcerers in flight." The concept of the *loup-garou* originated in Brittany, from whence it traveled to France's American colonies. These wolf shamans merged in Haiti with various Dahomean traditions involving secret magical societies.

The European werewolf was almost exclusively male; the *loup-garou* is frequently female. She anoints her wrists, ankles, and neck with herbal preparations enabling her to transform into animal shape and fly. Her most common form is a wolf; others include black cats, black pigs, crocodiles, horses, leopards, and owls. Botanical ointments aren't sufficient, however; transformative ability is ultimately bestowed by the deity presiding over *loups-garoux*, the lwa Ogou-ge-Rouge, Red Eyed Ogun, a sorcerer aspect of the Spirit of Iron. (See **ANIMALS:** Wolves and Werewolves; **DIVINE WITCH:** Ogun; **MAGICAL PROFESSIONS:** Metalworkers.)

Horns

The primeval admiration and awe for horns has not been forgotten but remains vital. Horns and their derivatives, cornucopias, still serve as ritual tools: they are placed on altars and are especially used for summoning spells for ghosts and/or spirits.

✳ *Horns are filled with candy as Day of the Dead treats for child-ghosts*

✳ *They are traditionally stuffed with grapes to summon Dionysus*

✳ *Some Wiccan traditions, Seax-Wica for instance, substitute a drinking horn for a chalice during rituals*

✳ *Horned helmets or caps are sometimes worn during Neo-Pagan or Wiccan rituals, especially when a High Priest is impersonating a horned god*

✳ *Among modern Masons, the cornucopia remains symbolic of joy, peace, and plenty*

✳ *Easter witches carry flying ointment in horns in the same way that African witches carry hyena butter in gourds (see* **ANIMALS:** *Hyenas)*

✳ *In sub-Saharan Africa, horns are frequently stuffed with botanical and other magical material to create amulets and talismans*

✳ *In Italian and many North African traditions, small horns or replicas of horns made from various natural and synthetic materials are popular amulets. They are used for many purposes but the most common are protection of male fertility and libido and destruction of the Evil Eye*

The cornucopia, ancient emblem of abundance, is a large hollow horn from which fruits and other botanicals overflow. Deities who carry it implicitly promise peace and prosperity. If one considers the numerous images of female deities displaying the cornucopia, then the number of goddesses associated with horns increases exponentially. These deities include Demeter, Persephone, Fortuna (Rome's Lady Luck), Fauna, and Flora. Epona, the Celtic horse goddess of fertility and abundance, holds a cornucopia, too.

Cornucopias are still used today, often as festive table centerpieces, but they are rarely if ever made from real horns now. Paper or wicker cornucopias are far more common, thus many perceive it as an abstract, crescent shape and forget the associations with horns. However these associations are explicitly stated in the symbol's name: "cornucopia" derives from the Latin *cornu* ("horn") and *copiae* ("abundance," "plenty"). By definition, the cornucopia is the horn of plenty.

> Allegedly, the very first cornucopia was the horn of Amaltheia, the goat that suckled Zeus; he placed it in the sky as a constellation in honor of his wet-nurse.

Labrys

The labrys is a double-headed ax used for agricultural, military, ritual, and magical use. It is a primeval symbol found in Paleolithic cave paintings but now most often identified with the Amazons and with Minoan women's mystery traditions.

The labrys is associated with the labyrinth, the famous maze-like structure of the Palace of Knossos in Crete that allegedly once housed the Minotaur. (See **HORNED ONE:** Minotaur.) The labrys was the emblem placed on the door of the labyrinth.

The labrys is a mysterious symbol, ubiquitous in the ancient Mediterranean from tiny ornamental replicas to powerful battleaxes. A nine-foot tall labrys is believed to have stood beside an altar of Athena.

In Mediterranean regions, the labrys was intensely identified with women. As a weapon, it was identified with the Amazons (and, further north, with the Valkyries). The use of the term *"old battle-ax"* to describe a powerful, sharp-tongued older woman may derive from the labrys. In ancient Greek art, the labrys was almost exclusively depicted as a woman's weapon; men rarely if ever wield it, with one crucial exception: according to Greek mythology, Athena was born fully-formed from Zeus' head after he swallowed her pregnant mother, Metis. Hephaestus performed the equivalent of a cranial caesarian section by cleaving Zeus' skull open with a labrys so Athena could emerge. The labrys remains among Athena's sacred attributes. It is also identified with Ariadne and with Demeter, who used a labrys as her scepter or magic wand.

Various origins and symbolism are attributed to the labrys, none mutually exclusive:

❉ *The labrys derives its shape and name from the labia, the vaginal lips; the handle of the ax might represent the phallus or the vaginal canal*

❉ *Archeologist Marija Gimbutas suggested that the labrys derives its shape from that of the butterfly, itself symbolic of the human soul, reincarnation, and rebirth*

❉ *The two heads of the labrys represent the waxing and waning moon*

❉ *In ancient times, the labrys was sometimes mounted between bull's horns, intensifying all three of the symbols and meanings listed*

In the ancient Mediterranean, Anatolia, and Middle East, the labrys was a woman's tool. However, the double-headed ax is also associated with Thor (Northern Europe) and Chango (West Africa, African Diaspora)—both intensely masculine thunder-gods whose myths feature episodes of cross-dressing.

In the twenty-first century, the labrys has emerged as a feminist and lesbian symbol of pride. The labrys is also incorporated into various witchcraft and Neo-Pagan women's spiritual and magical rituals. Some believe the labrys is the ancestor of the magic wand and that when deities like Circe are described as holding a "wand" what is really meant is a labrys. (See page 703, Wands.)

Masks

Masks serve so many spiritual and magical functions that a thousand pages could easily be devoted to them alone. The invention of the mask is so primordial as to be unknown and unknowable. How old are masks? Masks are as old as art, religion, spirituality, and magic. They appear all over Earth and are common, in one form or another, to virtually every human culture.

❊ *A cave painting in Lascaux in southwest France (dated to c.17000–12000 BCE) depicts a bird-headed man, generally assumed to be a shaman wearing a bird mask. He is depicted near a bird-crowned staff, similar to modern African magical and spiritual staffs*

❊ *The oldest known surviving mask is estimated to be about ten thousand years old. It depicts Coyote and was found in what is now Mexico. (See* **ANIMALS:** *Coyotes)*

Masks are crafted from and embellished with wood, metal, fabric, leather, hemp, clay, quartz and other crystals, feathers, seashells, papier mâché, stone, beads, and animal hair and horns.

Masks are shamanic tools; they are portals to other realms and existences; they enable spiritual possession. Putting on the mask enables a person to enter the realm of the sacred, to become another person or another being.

They are ceremonial objects. Some masks are believed to possess or radiate their own personal power as, for instance, Balinese barong masks. Masks are power items. They are the receptacle of divine force or the manifestation of normally invisible divine forces. For centuries, masks were the most precious, valuable possessions of many spiritual traditions around the globe.

Masks are created for countless purposes:

❊ *Masks are used in religious ceremonies*

❊ *They serve as talismanic shields; some are believed to deflect malevolent spirits*

❊ *Masks have served as votive offerings*

❊ *Masks were used to cover faces of the dead; death masks cast from corpses but preserved by the living may have served as oracles or in necromantic rituals*

❊ *Masks are components of various magic spells, especially those for healing*

Masks are also used for protection and privacy. During the witch-hunt era, many witches wore full- or half-masks when attending gatherings or dances in order to maintain anonymity and prevent identification. Many wealthy nobles allegedly wore masks while attending witches' balls, whether as participants or observers (it was the medieval equivalent of slumming) to protect their privacy and prevent blackmail. The concept of the masked ball is believed rooted in witches' balls.

❊ *Horned shamanic masks continued to exist in Europe until the twentieth century when most* finally ended up as children's toys (see **HORNED ONE**: Krampus).

✳ The Schemenlaufen Festival is Austria's most famous masked festival. "Witch masks" are worn. In medieval times, masked figures chased malevolent spirits away to ensure a good harvest. The festival is still held every three years in the town of Imst.

✳ Ancient pre-Christian Central and South American masks are now worn during Christian festivals; many of these festivals, however, are rooted in indigenous traditions. Sixteenth-century Spanish priests disapproved of masks representing ancestors and spirits. Horns were added to the masks, which were then renamed "devils."

✳ In Russia, masks were traditionally associated with Pagan ritual, especially with mid-winter festivities. Tsar Ivan the Terrible was accused of dancing in masks as an example of his alleged sorcery.

✳ The Hekataion is a carved wooden image of Hecate. The earliest may have been a pole or post hung with masks, perhaps facing in three directions, placed where three roads met.

✳ In Italy and Sparta, masks were associated with Artemis. Clay masks discovered in the Temple of Artemis Orthia in Sparta, dating from the seventh and early sixth centuries BCE, were made in imitation of wooden masks used in rituals and performances dedicated to Artemis

The most famous modern Western masks are those associated with Halloween costumes and with Carnival/Mardi Gras traditions. Both derive from ancient shamanism. Halloween masks are now largely mass-produced. Fine Carnival masks are still handcrafted from beads, sequins, and (especially) feathers.

Mirrors

Modern mirrors are commonly crafted from glass but ancient mirrors were usually created from smooth metal, usually copper, highly polished to be reflective.

Magic mirrors are popular in many traditions including ancient Egyptian, Chinese, Western Ceremonial, Aztec, and Italian folk magic. They are used for the following purposes:

✳ Divination and scrying

✳ Love magic

✳ Lunar magic

✳ Protective spells

✳ Spirit-summoning

Mirrors are frequently found among the remains of Scythian priestesses and/or queens. (We don't really know exactly *who* they were, only that they were people of importance based on their grave goods. No writings or explanations survive.) Mirrors were also found among the grave goods of women at Çatal Hüyük.

Mirrors are identified with specific deities:

Hathor, among the most primordial of Egyptian deities, presides over beauty, love, sex, fertility, romance, cosmetics, magic, and copper, the material from which ancient Egyptian mirrors were crafted. She and copper share the same essence: to hold a mirror in your hand is to hold Hathor. This was made explicit in ancient Egyptian mirrors, which very frequently incorporated an image of Hathor's face and characteristic flip hair-do into the mirror's handle. To hold a Hathor mirror and gaze into it is to absorb a little of the goddess' own beauty, power, and essence.

Tezcatlipoca is known as the Lord of the Smoking Mirror. The omniscient, all-knowing Aztec Lord of Sorcery, Tezcatlipoca observes *everything* in his obsidian mirror. He is the equivalent of the All-Seeing Eye, similar to *The Lord of the Ring*'s Sauron. Tezcatlipoca was the sponsor of Aztec shamans and sorcerers. We know that pre-European-conquest Aztec wizards used magic mirrors for divination and spiritual communication; the practice remains popular in Mexico and Central America. The most famous of the Aztec obsidian mirrors belonged to Dr John Dee and is now in the collection of the British Museum.

Magic mirrors remain popular with witches, spiritualists, and Pow-Wow artists.

Because magic mirrors derive from the tradition of scrying in water, they are associated with feminine, lunar mysteries and energy. Ancient mirrors were most commonly crafted from copper, traditionally considered a feminine metal. Copper is identified with the planet Venus and with powerful goddesses of love and beauty like Aphrodite, Hathor, and Oshun, but this feminine identification applies strongly to modern glass mirrors as well which bear even stronger resemblance to the moon or to a body of water like a lake.

Mirrors frequently serve as protective amulets as they are believed to repel the Evil Eye. Small mirrors are sewn on to clothing and furnishings. They are hung from the rear view mirrors of automobiles. Mirrors repel the malevolent forces that Feng Shui terms "poison arrows"; the *ba gua* is an octagonal mirror placed outside the house to repel these dangerous forces and provide safety, security, and stability for the inhabitants.

See **DIVINE WITCH:** Oshun, Tezcatlipoca; **HORNED ONE:** Hathor; **PLACES:** Groves: Nemi.

Mortar and Pestle

Mortars and pestles are ancient, primal tools used for grinding. The modern mortar and pestle is now most commonly used to grind herbs, whether for cooking, healing or spell-casting, but it was once also used to prepare flax for spinning.

More sophisticated grinding tools such as food processors have largely replaced the mortar and pestle for the purposes of cooking, but for magical purposes the mortar and pestle is irreplaceable for two reasons:

✻ *The manual act of grinding puts one literally in touch with the spell-casting materials: by simultaneously concentrating on one's desired goal, visualizing its accomplishment, one is able to insert one's intentions and desires into a spell in a way that merely pressing a button will not afford you.*

✻ *The act of grinding with the mortar and pestle metaphorically reproduces sexual intercourse. What is a magic spell after all but an act of magical creation, the birth of a new reality or new outcome? Mimicking the literal, physical process further empowers the spell as well as imbuing it with sacred male and female energies.*

If one lacks a mortar and pestle, it is preferable to substitute manual methods for grinding materials rather than automated ones. Place the material between folded wax paper and use a rolling pin or hammer as a pulverizing tool.

Mortars and pestles come in all sizes, from huge to miniscule, and are crafted from various materials: stone, terracotta, glass, brass, and marble. The *molcajete*, the traditional Mexican variant on the mortar and pestle, is created from volcanic rock.

Mortars and pestles were once visualized as witches' transportation devices, perhaps a subtle reference to the use of psychoactive herbs in witches' flying ointments.

The ointments would likely have been prepared using mortars and pestles.

✺ *Baba Yaga flies in a mortar and uses the pestle as her steering device.*

✺ *Witches and goddesses, according to various legends, convert mortars into boats and travel across the sea in them.*

✺ *Witches were sometimes envisioned riding pestles like others ride brooms.*

Pentacle (Pentagram)

"Pentacle" and "pentagram" are now frequently used synonymously but technically a five-pointed star is a pentagram: a pentacle is a small flat disc on which a pentagram has been engraved or inscribed. So the pentagram is the geometric shape and a pentacle is a round amulet or magical tool that displays a pentagram. Many people use the words interchangeably, however, and do not distinguish between the two.

Pentacles can be formed from clay, wax, bone, and wood; most frequently they are made from metal. A practitioner on a low budget could cut a round pentacle from construction paper and inscribe it with a pentagram. Pentagrams may be drawn in the air, with an athamé or other ritual knife, in each of the four directional points to consecrate a magic circle.

Over the centuries, pentagrams, five-pointed stars, have been used to represent witches and to protect others against them. The pentagram has been used to symbolize Jesus Christ and also to represent Satan. Talk about contradictions!

A German folk name for pentagram is *drudenfusz*, "witch's foot." German folk tradition indicates the use of pentagrams as protective talismans against evil spirits. During the Middle Ages and the Renaissance, pentagrams were painted on homes or mounted within them to protect against evil spirits and witches.

The Pennsylvania Dutch *hexafoos* also indicates "witch's foot" and is sometimes used as a synonym for hex signs. It also names a specific architectural motif involving an arch or decoration painted beneath a barn window that was expected to protect against witches. (See **DICTIONARY: Drude**.)

Pentacles are traditionally a protective talisman. In much of the ancient world, especially the Middle East and North Africa, the number five radiates protective energy and is the number most associated with protective spells. The pentagram may, thus, be understood as related to five-fingered hand-shaped amulets like the Hand of Fatima or the Hamsa, which symbolizes the all-protecting Five Fingers of God.

Master magus Cornelius Agrippa explains that every pentagram reveals the ideal qualities represented by the number five: it demonstrates five triangles, five obtuse angles, and five acute angles and is an excellent symbol for counteracting demons or malicious spirits.

Pentacles are one of the Tarot suits where they are also called coins. They correspond with the playing card suit of Diamonds and represent the feminine element Earth. Pentacles represent Earth's bounty, abundance, and protective energies. A parallel image would be the cornucopia, the horn overflowing with fruit and wealth. (See page 695, Horns.)

> The pentacle is one of Wicca's elemental tools, representing Earth, usually serving as a protective talisman. It has evolved into the religious emblem of Wicca in the manner of the cross for Christians and the hexagram (Star of David) for Jews.

Pentacles are *ancient*; earliest surviving images date back to over four thousand years before the Common Era. The pentagram within a circle appears on rings worn by members of the Pythagorean brotherhood. Pentagrams, both with and without surrounding circles, appear in Kabalistic writings, and they are among the sacred, magical images associated with Onmyoji, the wizards of Japan.

The pentacle may be interpreted in various ways:

✳ *The pentacle may represent a human figure*

✳ *The pentacle may represent a parturient (birthing) woman*

✳ *The pentacle's solitary point may represent spirit while the others indicate the four elements (air, earth, fire, water)*

✳ *Magus Eliphas Levi suggested that the pentacle represented the triumph of the human will over the power of the four elements*

✳ *East Asian cosmology perceives five elements (air, earth, fire, water, metal) not four, and so the pentacle may represent the eternal interplay of the elements.*

The solitary point may be considered the pentacle's head. A pentacle may be positioned head up, down or sideways. Satanists have adopted the inverted pentagram but not because of any witchcraft associations. Many historians suggest that Satanists adopted the inverted pentacle as their emblem because early Christians used the pentacle as a symbol of Christ with the uppermost point indicating his head. Thus turning the pentacle upside down was perceived as a hostile, desecrating act.

Sieve

Among the magical tools hiding in the kitchen disguised as mundane kitchen utensils are sieves. The term refers not only to the modern metal strainer but to any type of sifter including grain winnows, which may have been the first sieves. The sieve may derive originally from agricultural rites associated with the Corn Mother.

According to legend, when her beloved Osiris was murdered, Isis collected the dismembered parts of his body together in a sieve. Her act was ritually re-enacted during the annual harvest festivals that commemorated Osiris the Grain God's death.

Sieves for culinary use are now mainly identified with sifting water from a pot. One removes pasta from boiling water, for instance, by pouring the contents of the pot into the sieve: the food remains while the water drains through the multitude of holes. However, herbalists also use sieves to sift botanical materials. Henna in particular must be very finely sifted in order to create henna paste, a natural dye used to ornament and magically empower the body, the equivalent of a temporary sacred tattoo. (To understand how finely henna needs to be sifted—and the effort required—an appropriate makeshift henna sifter can be concocted by stretching panty hose over a bowl and sifting the botanical powder through the exceedingly fine mesh.)

Sieves are crafted from all kinds of materials; North African and Middle Eastern frame drums, women's magical, musical, and practical tools, are sometimes riddled with tiny holes so that they served as sifters too.

Sieves are used in divination and various spells, especially for fertility, healing, and weather magic. Witches were once popularly envisioned using sieves as a travel device, by converting them to boats.

Bulgarian witches were rumored to cause lunar eclipses by drawing the moon from the sky using a magical sieve. (Why would they wish to do this? Not merely to terrorize people. Allegedly they were able to temporarily transform the moon into a cow and milk her before letting her transform back and return to the sky. Presumably this was very powerful, magical milk.)

See **CREATIVE ARTS:** Music: Drums.

Staff

The distinction between staffs and wands often comes down to size. The staff is longer, thicker, and often doubles as a walking stick. A staff should be long and sturdy enough to lean on comfortably. (Thus a tall person requires a longer staff than a shorter person.)

Staffs are now identified primarily as wizards' tools. The most famous modern image derives from J.R.R. Tolkien's *Lord of the Rings* cycle, whose wizards Gandalf and Saruman do battle with their staffs. Staffs are also closely identified with the biblical Moses and his opponents, powerful Egyptian magicians.

Deities identified with staffs include Odin and Eshu-Elegbara. When Hermes isn't carrying his caduceus (see Wand), he substitutes a shepherd's staff instead.

> Like most magical tools, staffs have other uses besides magic, being associated with walking sticks and shepherds' staffs.

The staff is not a subtle tool: it's a *big* piece of wood. When walking sticks (and perhaps walking in general) fell from fashion, so did the magical staff. Its niche has somewhat been filled by the smaller, and thus more subtle and versatile, magic wand.

Magic staffs are now most profoundly identified with Obeah, the African-derived magical and spiritual traditions of the British West Indies. The Obeah or Obi Stick is a carved wooden staff, frequently ornamented with a serpentine motif. The Staff of Moses is a more elaborate staff that usually features a carving of a snake encircling the staff from top to bottom.

Staffs were once also powerfully identified with Nordic spiritual and magical traditions. Staffs were engraved with powerful runes to further empower and direct their inherent energies. Many traditions recommend hollowing out a staff and filling it with botanicals, amulets or other magically empowered materials.

Staffs radiate male magical energy; they are the direct descendants of sacred phallic poles, especially those carried in Dionysian processions. Wooden staffs radiate the power of the type of tree they were crafted from.

Staffs, also called staves, are among the Tarot's four suits, corresponding to the playing card suit of Clubs.

See also Wands; **ANIMALS:** Snakes; **DICTIONARY:** Obeah; **DIVINE WITCH:** Hermes, Odin; **HORNED ONE:** Eshu-Elegbara, Hermes.

Swords

Magic swords have historically played a role in Chinese, Japanese, Jewish, and Persian magical traditions. They remain popular in East Asian magic, High Ceremonial Magic, and modern Wicca.

Magic swords may be actual functional swords complete with sharp blades or ceremonial replicas. Swords invoke primal metal magic although wooden swords also exist, particularly in East Asia. Swords are powerfully associated with the primordial magical traditions of metalworking (see **MAGICAL PROFESSIONS:** Metalworkers).

Swords radiate masculine energy; the scabbard is its feminine partner. Swords are most commonly associated with the element air, however this is controversial; some also identify swords with fire. Swords do not fit neatly into elemental categories being the product of all elements. The raw material for swords is dug from Earth and the process of crafting a sword involves the interplay of air, fire, and water.

Crafting swords was a secret, magical operation. Spell-casting and spiritual invocation was once involved in the creation of powerful magic sword (and in some cases it still is). Rumors periodically circulated that blood sacrifice, including human sacrifice, was required to forge magic swords. Vestiges of these legends survive in Japanese mythology.

Swords may be engraved with runes, sigils, Names of Power, Kabalistic inscriptions or other magical embellishments. They are used for casting circles and for various magical practices including protection spells, exorcisms, spirit-summoning, and banishing spells.

Swords are among the four Tarot suits, corresponding to the playing card suit of Spades.

Tripod

No, not a camera tripod: this tripod is based on ritual equipment from the Oracle of Delphi. The Pythoness at Delphi sat atop a tripod, a high three-legged stool, overlooking a steaming chasm that allegedly inspired psychic vision in order to deliver her prophesies. The key to the tripod is the three legs.

Early Greek altars were sometimes placed on a tripod. The most common modern tripod is essentially a cauldron standing on three legs (see Cauldron).

Wands

Harry Potter to the contrary, it is crucial to recall that a magic wand is but a tool. Magic power ultimately derives from the person who wields that tool. The wand serves to enhance and direct that power but never substitutes for it.

Wands rival brooms for the title of tool most associated with magic and witchcraft. It is important to note that, as with brooms, not every practitioner uses a wand. They are not a requirement of magical practice, merely among one of its most popular tools.

Wands represent male phallic power but are used by both male and female practitioners. Wizards use wands but so does the sorceress-goddess Circe. Female fairies are commonly depicted employing wands. The Maenads brandished Dionysus' sacred wand, the thyrsus. The wand may put masculine power in the hands of a woman in the same manner that a broom or birch switch places feminine power in the hands of a man.

The wand may be understood as deriving from ancient sacred phallic images and is closely related to the staff. It may also be understood as deriving from the ancient feminine mysteries of the labrys (see page 696).

The wand may be understood as tapping into the power of trees. Different types of wood are believed to radiate different energies and thus suit different magical purposes.

A magic wand carved from apple wood, for instance, is believed especially beneficial for love magic, while a wand carved from yew, oleander or hemlock, poisonous plants all, enables necromancy. Some practitioners only use one wand; others collect different wands, using each for specific purposes.

> Although less common than wooden wands, wands are also crafted from metal.

Wands specifically direct the power of humans: there's a crucial reason why most children are taught early on that it's rude to point. Pointing is a potent magical gesture, quite often used in spontaneous, hostile magic: the curse that just slips out of someone's mouth is usually accompanied by a pointing finger directing hostile words in their intended direction. The wand may be understood as an extension and enhancement of that finger of power.

Wands may be ornamented with crystals, feathers, and amulets. They may be engraved with sigils, runes, hieroglyphs, Names of Power or magical inscriptions. As described in the *Harry Potter* novels, wands may be hollowed out and filled with a reed or some other material, however due to limitations of size, obviously less material can be placed within a wand than inside a staff.

> In the German mythic epic *The Song of the Nibelungs (Die Nibelungenlied)*, the dragon's treasure hoard includes a tiny gold wand that enables its possessor to rule the world.

Don't have a magic wand? Not to worry. Substitutions are easily made: an umbrella serves as a magic wand as does a cane, folding fan or flute. (And when in need, one's finger really can substitute!) The crucial thing is to recall that once the instrument has been designated as a magic tool it must be treated as such: an umbrella magic wand is potentially no less sacred than a more conventional wand. If one expects it to behave magically, it must be treated with the respect and care due any magical tool.

Witchcraft Hall of Fame

Within these pages you will find a variety of witches, sorcerers, magicians, alchemists, and spiritual leaders. Some embrace the title "witch"; others would be appalled to be associated with witchcraft. Some are names you would expect to find here; others may be shocking in their inclusion.

Are the following portraits representative of the history of witchcraft? No.

There are a disproportionate number of men. The history of male magicians, particularly astrologers, alchemists, and High Ceremonial magicians is very well documented: their names, histories, and achievements are well known. Female practitioners, especially folk magicians, herbalists, and healers have typically labored in obscurity. Often their very names are unknown.

Witchcraft, along with its related arts, has largely been forbidden for the past two thousand years. The few who practiced relatively publicly tended to be male, well educated and either wealthy or under the protection of powerful and prominent people. The vast majority who practiced discreetly has no left record of their actions. Those who embrace a more theatrical vision of witchcraft (Aleister Crowley, for instance) have far more recognition than their peers who hewed to discretion (for example, Franz Bardon).

When Gerald Gardner published *Witchcraft Today* in 1954, he initiated a new phenomenon: the witch or practitioner as author and teacher. Since then, *thousands* of books have been published, delineating all facets of witchcraft, Wicca, the magical arts, and Neo-Paganism.

Now, in the first decades of the twenty-first century, for the first time, many, particularly solitary practitioners, learn arts and traditions from books. This is history in the making; space precludes closer examination. The following list includes but a few of many prominent, influential authors:

Margot Adler	Dorothy Morrison
Freya Aswynn	Christopher Penczak
Stephanie Rose Bird	Elizabeth Pepper
Laurie Cabot	Silver RavenWolf
Stewart and Janet Farrar	Lexa Rosean
Anna Franklin	Starhawk
Raven Grimassi	Patricia Telesco

Abei no Seimei (c.921–1005 CE)

Abei no Seimei, renowned magician, exorcist, astrologer, and diviner of Japan's Heian Era (c.794–1192 CE), is the subject of countless stories and legends. He is sometimes described as the Japanese Merlin although documented historical records for Abei no Seimei do exist, dating to 960. There is no doubt he existed. There are, however, as many tales of Abei no Seimei as there are of Merlin and these remain very popular in Japan.

His birth name was Hauraki Abei. His birthplace is generally acknowledged as Abeno-ku in Osaka, although different towns compete for the honor. He lived much of his life in Kyoto.

According to legend, Abei no Seimei was the son of a fox spirit (see **ANIMALS:** Foxes): his mother reputed to be a white fox rescued from hunters by Abei's father. Abei's extraordinary powers manifested in childhood: he could see spirits, converse with birds and visited a dragon's palace. Abei no Seimei served six emperors. His specialty was lifting curses.

Abei no Seimei, is considered the ultimate master of Onmyo-Do, which literally means "the way of Onmyo." (See **DICTIONARY:** Onmyoji.)

Demonstrating the difference in attitudes toward magicians in Japan and in contemporaneous Europe, after his death Abei no Seimei was considered a saint and divine soul. He still continues to help others at his shrines in Kyoto and Osaka. Two years after his death, the Japanese Emperor built the Seimei Jinjya shrine in his honor at Abeno-ku, Osaka. Every September an annual festival honors Abei no Seimei there.

Some Onmyoji (practitioners of Onmyo-Do) remain dedicated to Abei no Seimei's teachings. Abei's other shrine is the Seimei Shrine on Horikawa Avenue in Kyoto, where Onmyoji are available for consultations and exorcisms.

> *Onmyoji*, directed by Yojiro Takita, was Japan's box-office king in 2001. It recounts some of the adventures of Abei no Seimei, as does its follow-up, *Onmyoji II* (2004). Enough legends of Abei no Seimei exist to fill many more sequels.

Agrippa von Nettesheim, Henricus Cornelius (September 14, 1486–1535)

Cornelius Agrippa was the leading occultist of the sixteenth century and among the most influential magicians of all time. His influence is felt over High Ceremonial magic as it is over folk magic. His *Three Books of Occult Philosophy* is the cornerstone of Western occult tradition.

Agrippa was legendary in his own time and continues to be: many believe him to be the prototype for legends of Dr Faust. He lived at a time when it was deathly dangerous to be an occultist, and he spent most of his life just one step ahead of witch-hunters.

Henricus Cornelius Agrippa von Nettesheim was born of noble parentage in Cologne. His family, the von Nettesheims, had served the royal house of Austria for generations. However, in his writings Agrippa almost exclusively referred to himself only as *"Cornelius Agrippa"* and he is most commonly known that way today—or even as just plain Agrippa.

In 1499, he entered the University of Cologne where he read Plato and Plotinus. His interest in the occult manifested at an early age, perhaps inspired by Albertus Magnus, reputedly another master magician, whose work Agrippa studied and who is buried in Cologne. From the start, Agrippa was independently minded with an incorrigible thirst for knowledge.

He spent time in Italy studying Hermeticism and Kabalah with Jewish masters (and acknowledged them!) at a time when the Church suggested Kabalah was diabolical. He was among the founding fathers of Cabalah, the Christian variation of the Jewish mystical tradition.

Agrippa consorted and traveled with Romany. He studied with Abbot Trithemius of Sponheim with whom he shared an interest in contacting planetary spirits. Shortly after staying with Trithemius in *c.*1509, Agrippa composed his first book *De Occulta Philosophia*, though it would not be published for another 20 years.

In his early twenties, Agrippa was sent on a mission to France by Emperor Maximilian I. In Paris he fell in with a group of free-thinking dissident scholars who formed a secret society dedicated to world reform. Agrippa fought for a time with peasants dispossessed of their lands.

Agrippa became professor of Hebrew at the University of Dole, France. A Franciscan monk accused him of heresy (the first of many such accusations) and he quickly left town, beginning a life of wandering. Sometimes he won the patronage of aristocrats who supported him. Other times, he was jailed for debt or for insulting the powerful. He had a sharp tongue and offended many, as when he suggested that nunneries often served as private brothels and that houses of prostitution tended to be located suspiciously close to monasteries.

As a part-time lecturer at a Dutch university, Agrippa expounded on the superiority of the female sex and the wisdom of the Jewish Kabalah. He landed in trouble with Dutch clerics who once again sent him packing.

* *Agrippa went to London where he worked as an astrologer and taught Hebrew.*

* *He went to Pavia where he lectured on Hermes Trismegistus. Once again, he fell foul of the clergy and had to leave town quickly.*

* *He went to Metz where he was appointed Public Advocate.*

Nicholas Savini, Dominican Inquisitor of the Faith at Metz, arrested a peasant girl whose mother had been condemned as a witch. Agrippa as Public Advocate protested that this was irregular procedure as heredity was insufficient evidence for accusation. Despite his efforts, Agrippa was unable to prevent the girl from being tortured; however he was able to secure her acquittal. The result of her acquittal was that those who had initially accused her of witchcraft were fined and Agrippa, in turn, was accused of being a witch.

He got out of town fast, fleeing home to Cologne where he found the Inquisition a little too uncomfortable. He left Cologne and went to Geneva, then to Chambrai, Fribourg, and Lyons supporting himself by practicing medicine. Although not technically a physician, he was extremely knowledgeable and apparently a very skilled healer. During various episodes of the plague, licensed physicians reputedly fled but Agrippa stayed, ministering to the ill, although his primary instruction for others on how to avoid and survive plague was to leave the area *immediately*. Practicing medicine was the skill that enabled Agrippa to support himself and his family for most of his life.

Agrippa developed a reputation as a sorcerer, magician, and alchemist. He allegedly dabbled in necromancy and divined via crystal balls and magic mirrors. He evolved into something of a bogeyman figure. Mothers would frighten children into obedience by warning that otherwise Agrippa would "get" them.

> Margaret of Austria invited Agrippa to the Netherlands; in order to accept, he was obligated to obtain a passport. Upon seeing his request, the Duke of Vendôme tore it up rather than sign it, refusing to sign passports for conjurors.

Many legends sprang up about him. Agrippa was allegedly *always* accompanied by his big black poodle, Monsieur. Some said he was just crazy about his dog; some suggested Monsieur was his familiar; still others insisted the dog was a disguised demon. According to legend, following Agrippa's death, the dog jumped into the Saône River and either died or disappeared. Other legends suggested that Agrippa could be in two places at once and that he paid for lodg-

ings with money that later transformed into seashells after Agrippa had left town.

The most famous legend regarding Agrippa involves a visitor who persuaded Agrippa's wife to let him enter his laboratory while the master was away from home. The visitor, the classic sorcerer's apprentice, started playing with Agrippa's books and tools and managed to conjure up a demon who demanded to know why he'd been summoned. The demon was in no mood for amateurs and when Agrippa returned, he discovered the young man dead. Fearing he'd be charged with murder, Agrippa himself summoned the murderous spirit and had the spirit temporarily revive the young man, who was then taken to the marketplace so that he would be witnessed walking around there. He collapsed and finally died for good there in the market.

> Considering the era in which he lived, Agrippa himself displayed amazing tolerance for others' spiritual beliefs, writing that *"the rites and ceremonies of religion vary with different times and places and each religion has something good."* His personal motto was *"Let no man who might belong to himself belong to another."*

De Occulta Philosophia was published in Antwerp in 1533, despite the Inquisition's attempts to halt publication. *De Occulta Philosophia* suggests that the universe is a living being with a soul as well as a carnal body composed of four elements: air, earth, fire, and water. The knowledge of the elemental composition of an object reveals its powers (or, in the language of Agrippa's time, its "*virtues*").

Shortly after his death in Grenoble, a fourth

volume was attributed to Agrippa. This book deals mainly with demons and is apparently partly derived from the *Lemegeton* (see **BOOKS:** Grimoires). Johann Weyer, Agrippa's closest follower, denounced this book as a fraud and it is now generally acknowledged that Agrippa did not write that fourth book, or at least not all of it. (When the grimoire *The Magus* was published in 1801, its compiler and editor Francis Barrett was accused of plagiarizing the *Fourth Book of Agrippa*.)

> Further Reading: Although English translations of Agrippa first appeared in 1651, his work was largely available only in fragments. *Finally*, in 2003, an eminently readable, clear, lucid translation of Agrippa's *Three Books of Occult Philosophy* was published under the Llewellyn Sourcebook Series, with translations by James Freake and edited and annotated by occult scholar Donald Tyson.

Albertus Magnus (c.1193– November 15, 1280)

Albertus Magnus, Count of Bollstädt, Dominican bishop, alchemist, astrologer, philosopher, scholar, saint, and alleged master magus was born in Lauingen, Swabia to a wealthy family. His date of birth is unknown; various birth years are suggested, as early as 1193 to as late as 1206. (*Albertus Magnus* indicates *Albert the Great*. He is also known as *Albertus of Cologne*.)

Albertus joined the Dominicans, which some

perceive as lending him safety in an era when others who shared his reputation and activities were persecuted. He taught at various German universities and went to Paris in 1245 where he attained a great reputation as a scholar. He studied Arabic, Aristotelian, Jewish, and Neo-Platonic philosophy, as well as botany, medicine, and zoology. He was appointed Bishop of Ratisbon in 1260. In 1262, he taught at the University of Cologne, lecturing on Aristotle and Plato (Pagan philosophers, somewhat racy at the time).

Rumors of his magical activities may be why it took so long for him to be made a saint: canonized in 1932, the Vatican initially denied that Albertus had any interest in alchemy and suggested that alchemical treatises attributed to him were forgeries. However, since then, based on analysis of various manuscripts written in what is conclusively his hand, it is now generally acknowledged that he was at least an alchemist, if not also a master magician too.

> Words of wisdom from Albertus Magnus include, *"The alchemist must be silent and discreet. To no one should he reveal the results of his operations"* and *"Avoid all contact with princes and rulers."*

Albertus publicly asserted that he did not believe knowledge of magic was harmful. (This was an embarrassment to later writers.) He is acknowledged as the founder of what is now called "planetary magic." Albertus considered astrology to be the basis for all divination and was a firm believer in the power of engraved gems, crafted to astrological specifications.

Five alchemical treatises and two grimoires (*Le Grand Albert* and *Le Petit Albert*) are attributed to him (see **BOOKS:** Grimoires). These were published in the sixteenth century and deal with alchemy, astrology, and the properties of minerals and plants.

The Alraunas

Julius Caesar and Tacitus agreed that all the German tribes they encountered firmly believed in the prophetic powers of women. These prophetesses, the Alraunas, were considered sacred and sometimes divine. The most acclaimed were celebrities of their era; little is known of them, but some names still survive.

❋ *Ganna, the "Seer of Semnones," went to Rome in 91 CE with King Masyas, where they were honored by the Emperor Domitian. (Her name may be related to the Old Germanic* gandno, *"magic.")*

❋ *Veleda sang the Germans into battle during Vespasian's reign (69–79 CE). She lived near a shrine by the River Lippe and accurately prophesied Germanic victories. Her name, also spelled Weleda, may be related to the root word for "wisdom" and "witch" and may actually be a title. She is described as a member of the Bructeri tribe; after a military defeat, she was captured and taken to Rome in 78 CE, where she was treated with surprising respect, and was housed with the Vestal Virgins. Allegedly, during her tenure in Rome, she served as a translator and negotiator between the Romans and various Germanic tribes. She apparently died in Rome c.80.*

❋ *Waluberg traveled to Egypt with Germanic troops in the second-century CE. (*Walus *is an Old German term for a magical staff.)*

Bardon, Franz (December 1, 1909–July 10, 1958)

Franz Bardon, a highly influential author and occultist, was born near Opava, now in the Czech Republic, the oldest and only son of thirteen children. His father, Viktor Bardon, was a devout Christian mystic. Allegedly when Franz was 14, his father performed a ritual whereby the soul of a Hermetic adept entered Franz's body.

Bardon is well known among magical adepts, although largely unknown to the general public. Partly this is a result of his nature: Bardon was a modest, private man. His four books, published in the 1950s, focus on magic rather than on the magician who wrote them.

Bardon's books teach a complete magical system, described as deriving from Holy Egyptian Mysteries once reserved for the elite few, and taught by Christ to his disciples. All his books have been translated from their original German into English.

Bardon places emphasis on the tangible results of magic as well as on magical theory. Among the influences he cites are Alexandra David-Neel's work on Tibetan magic and mysticism. Other powerful influences included traditional Jewish Kabalah and the works of Eliphas Levi. He did not cite Aleister Crowley as an influence although Bardon's motto, *"Love is the law but love under a strong will,"* obviously compares with Crowley's (see page 720).

During the 1920s and 1930s, Bardon worked as a stage magician in Germany, using the name *Frabato*, while pursuing his occult interests. Following the ascension to power of the Nazis in 1933, Masonic and occult organizations were closed and persecuted (although individual occultists were sometimes cultivated by the Third Reich).

According to Bardon's legend, he was arrested sometime in late 1941 or early 1942 and tortured. When he and a compatriot demonstrated true occult ability, the compatriot was executed but Bardon was offered a position within the Third Reich, which he refused. After the war ended, he returned to what was then Czechoslovakia and worked as a mechanic, naturopath, and graphologist.

Bardon is a classic example of the archetypal "wounded healer." He was allegedly able to heal cancer patients using his own botanical/alchemical formulas, although he had severe health problems of his own which he was unable to cure, including pancreatic disorders and periods of debilitating overweight.

He fell foul of local medical authorities who felt that he was usurping their positions and cutting in to their income. After his books were published in 1956 foreign visitors, especially from Germany, flocked to see him. He was arrested in Opava early in 1958, although exactly *why* is unclear. The following are among reasons offered:

❋ *Competing physicians accused Bardon of being a Western spy.*

❋ *He was accused of illegal production of pharmaceuticals (his healing potions).*

❋ *He was accused of failing to pay taxes on alcohol purchased for herbal extraction.*

❋ *He was arrested specifically because he was an occultist; scientists wished to experiment on him to determine whether he, in fact, did have special powers.*

Bardon, imprisoned in Brno on March 26, 1958, died in jail of unexplained causes. He is buried in Opava. His personal possessions, including many occult articles, were confiscated at his arrest and were never returned to his family.

Blavatsky, Helena Petrovna (August 12, 1831–May 8, 1891)

Author, visionary, occultist, philosopher, Helena Blavatsky was the founder of the Theosophical Movement and often described as the "Mother of the New Age." Together with Henry Steel Olcott (August 2, 1832–February 17, 1907), she founded the Theosophical Society, responsible for introducing Eastern ideas of reincarnation and karma to Western occultism. She also played a crucial role in disseminating occult and spiritual concepts at the dawning of the twentieth century.

Popularly known as Madame Blavatsky or by her initials, HPB, Helena Petrovna von Hahn was born in Russia to a prominent and wealthy family. Her father was descended from German nobility; her mother, Helena Andreyevna, was a highly regarded novelist, unusual at a time when few women were published. She wrote under the pen name Zenaide R. and was called "the Russian George Sand." Her grandmother was a Russian princess and noted botanist.

Little Helena spent much time with household servants who taught her Russian folkloric and magical traditions. She was fascinated by magic and ancient spiritual traditions from an early age. Voices spoke to her as a child including those of the stuffed, mounted animals in her grandfather's private museum.

The countryside where they lived was allegedly shared with Rusalka (see **FAIRIES**: Nature-spirit Fairies: Rusalka). When not pleased with adult authority, little Helena would threaten to have the Rusalka tickle the offending adult to death.

A local fourteen-year-old boy once annoyed the four-year-old Helena as she was walking beside a riverbank with a nurse. She screamed that the Rusalka would get him so loudly that the boy ran away. He disappeared for several weeks until fishermen discovered his dead body. The official story was that he had been trapped in a whirlpool but local peasants believed that the Rusalka had followed through on Helena's orders. Even at that early age, she was developing a reputation for magic power that never abated.

She married General Nikephore Blavatsky when she was seventeen; reports of his age range anywhere from 40 to 80; in any case he was much older than her. Three months later, she ran away for reasons unknown but subject to all sorts of speculation. She spent the next years traversing the globe: her activities between 1848 and 1858 are mysterious and fabled—she worked as a concert pianist in Serbia and a bareback rider in a Turkish circus. She worked as a lady's companion and a spirit medium. In 1856, she was allegedly in India from whence she traveled to Tibet, among the first Europeans to do so. She may or may not have lived in Tibet for seven years.

She traveled back to Russia for a time, where she may or may not have had a son who died in young childhood. Many of her writings are contradictory as are reports allegedly told to other people. She cultivated an aura of mystery and, despite her superficial flamboyance, may have been an intensely private person.

Blavatsky may have fought with Garibaldi in Italy in 1867; she claimed to have been wounded by bullets and sabers. She may also have studied with Kabalists in Egypt and with Voodooists in New Orleans.

In 1873, Blavatsky boarded a boat for New York with just enough money to pay her passage. Arriving completely destitute, she moved into a residence for working women, laboring in a sweatshop sewing purses and pen wipers. Spiritualism was then very popular: Blavatsky had conducted séances in Russia and France and she began working as a spirit medium in the United States.

She was an unusual medium, commanding and summoning spirits rather than just channeling or receiving them. Her cast of characters included family members, two Russian servants, a Kurdish warrior and an Iranian merchant. Through Spiritualist circles, she met Henry Olcott, author, attorney, philosopher, and Freemason, on October 14, 1874. They became compatriots, allies and close friends.

On September 13, 1875, Blavatsky and Olcott formalized the Theosophical Society in her home at 302 West 47th Street in New York City. Olcott was President of the Society while Blavatsky was Corresponding Secretary.

Blavatsky's home, birthplace of Theosophy, was dubbed *The Lamasery*. She held on-going salons there where adepts and occultists from all walks of life mingled, women as well as men, blacks, whites and Asians, Hindus, Jews and Christians.

Theosophy is a philosophical/spiritual organization dedicated to universal brotherhood and which emphasizes the study of ancient philosophies, religions, sciences, and spiritual traditions. The objectives of the Theosophical Society were:

* *To form a universal brotherhood of humanity without distinction of caste, color, creed, gender, race or religion*

* *To encourage study of comparative religion, philosophy, and science*

* *To investigate unexplained laws of nature and mysterious powers latent in people*

"Theosophy" indicates sacred science or divine wisdom, deriving from *Theos* (god) and *Sophia* (wisdom) and was founded on the theory that all religion emanates from identical roots of lost wisdom.

Blavatsky's extremely influential two-volume work *Isis Unveiled*, published in 1877, is Theosophy's manifesto, attempting to unify various strands of mystical philosophy into a cohesive, coherent spiritual world-view. It draws heavily on Egyptian Mysteries and Kabalah, however Blavatsky gave primacy to India in the diffusion of the original root religious system. She described the old Pagan deities as necessary personifications of natural forces, and Christ as merely one adept of that ancient "true" religion.

Controversially, Blavatsky did not give credit to human mentors or teachers but claimed that the information in *Isis Unveiled* was given to her by direct revelation from superior beings, the immortals who had first given the universal religion to Atlantis. She described these beings as the *"Mahatmas,"* the *"Ascended Masters of the Hidden Brotherhood"* or *"The Great White Brotherhood of Masters."*

She defined these beings as those whose esoteric training and absolute purity have resulted in supernatural powers. They were literally immortal: the Masters inhabit bodies (material or semi-material) at will. The Masters communicate with each other telepathically, forming a link between humans and the ruling divine hierarchy. Home base for all Ascended Masters is a secluded Tibetan valley.

The Brotherhood of Masters includes all great spiritual leaders and occult teachers of the past including Abraham, Cagliostro, Confucius, Jesus, King Solomon, Lao Tzu, Mesmer, Moses, and Plato. The Brotherhood usually remains hidden from all but a very few because when they have attempted to transmit information to humanity through human agents, those agents were too often met by disbelief or worse: persecution by humans under the influence of malign powers called *"The Dark Forces."* The crucifixion of Jesus is but the most obvious example of this persecution.

If talk of "Ascended Masters" and "The Dark Forces" reminds you of *Star Wars*, then you have some idea of how far Blavatsky's ideas and influence has traveled, although she is rarely credited in mainstream sources, perhaps because of the aura of controversy that still surrounds her. Many theories of the lost lands of Atlantis and Lemuria are also based on Blavatsky's writings.

According to Blavatsky, all history has a hidden esoteric meaning: history recounts the secret struggle between powers of light and dark. The Brotherhood works in secret to direct, preserve, and protect Earth's destiny.

She claimed *Isis Unveiled* was written under the influence of spirits who held ancient books filed with Gnostic and Kabalistic instruction open before her while she smoked hashish and wrote down information as fast as she could.

Other information was channeled, while other pages, she claimed, simply appeared. She would leave an empty desk but would return to discover pages of the manuscript waiting for her, a writing technique that very many authors, including this one, would absolutely love to emulate if only they could.

Isis Unveiled was also written as a challenge to Darwinism, which she accused of narrowing the notion of science so that it applied *only* to the Material Universe, disregarding the existence of all else. She suggested Buddhism as a doctrine that could reconcile modern science and religion.

Isis Unveiled was a *huge* bestseller. Among those who claimed to be influenced by the work were Mohandas Gandhi and Thomas Edison. (One stated purpose of the early phonograph was to speak to the spirit world.) Others influenced by Blavatsky included philosophers Krishnamurti and Rudolf Steiner and artists Vasili Kandinsky and Piet Mondrian. Among her personal students was W.B. Yeats, prior to his entry into the Golden Dawn (see **DICTIONARY:** Golden Dawn).

On December 17, 1878 Blavatsky and Olcott left New York to go live in the native quarter of Bombay, India. She continued to be dogged with controversy. She was accused of fraudulence; although never proven, she was never able to live down the stigma of the accusation. Others simply treated her as a joke.

Blavatsky evoked powerful reactions from people, both negative and positive. She was an independent, earthy, stubborn, frank-speaking, bohemian, rather authoritarian, Russian woman who had traveled the globe by herself, *sans* chaperone. She was not considered a "respectable woman." She was accused of being a sexual libertine; a generation before Aleister Crowley, many perceived Blavatsky to be a *"wicked woman."*

Her allegiance to India and the Himalayas as the ultimate home of spiritual truths also offended Western occultists, particularly those with a Christian orientation such as Dion Fortune (see page 732). Various Western mystical organizations, including those founded by Fortune and the Christian occultist Anna Kingsford (see page 744), were stimulated by a reaction against Blavatsky's internationalist orientation with its emphasis on cultural diversity.

Blavatsky was a complex, contradictory person: although she was allegedly a powerful medium herself, she despised other mediums. She despised High Ritual Magic and Darwinism equally. She met MacGregor Mathers (see page 749) in Paris and was impressed with him but allegedly felt he was wasting his gifts with Ceremonial Magic.

Buckland, Raymond (August 31, 1934–)

Raymond Buckland is a prolific author, spiritual leader, authority on witchcraft, magic and the occult, and the person responsible for introducing Gardnerian Wicca to the United States.

Buckland describes his father as a *"full-blood Romany"* and a freelance writer who encouraged his son to write. At age twelve, Buckland was introduced to Spiritualism by a paternal uncle, beginning his life-long interest in all aspects of the occult.

In the late 1950s, having read Gerald Gardner's *Witchcraft Today* he began a correspondence with Gardner and later with Gardner's High Priestess, Monique Wilson (Lady Olwen). When Buckland emigrated to the United States in February 1962, he became Gardner's spokesman there. At the end of 1963, during a trip to Perth, Scotland, Buckland was initiated by Lady Olwen and was able to meet Gardner, shortly before Gardner died.

Inspired by Gerald Gardner's witchcraft collection, Buckland amassed his own vast collection, which became the first Museum of Witchcraft and Magic in the United States. The collection remains in Buckland's possession.

Buckland has been instrumental in introducing two more Wiccan traditions to the States:

❋ *Seax-Wica was founded by Buckland in 1973. Buckland, despite introducing Gardnerian Wicca to the US, became frustrated and disappointed by some of the evolutions of this tradition. Therefore he founded Seax-Wica, intended to be a more open, democratically organized branch of Wicca.*

❋ *PectiWita is based on Pictish traditions of Scotland. It is a solitary witchcraft practice with strong emphasis on shamanic rather than ceremonial aspects of witchcraft. The emphasis is on folk magic, divination, and magical healing. The father of the PectiWita tradition is considered to be Highlander Aidan Breac (1897–1989), whose foremother was burned at the stake as a witch in 1661.*

Buckland has also written screenplays, fiction and is an accomplished ragtime musician. He served as technical advisor for Orson Welles' film, *Necromancy*.

Budapest, Z. (January 30, 1940-)

Magical practitioner, author, and founding mother of Dianic Wicca—an important, influential feminist witchcraft tradition—Z. Budapest was born Zsuzsanna Emese Mokcsay in Budapest. Her mother, Masika Szilagyi, was a ceramics artist and medium, palm reader, and psychic. Through her mother, Budapest derives from a long line of herbalist witches.

She left Hungary following the 1956 Hungarian Revolution, eventually immigrating to the United States in 1959. In the US Budapest studied improvisational theater with the Second City theatrical school in Chicago for two years. When her marriage broke up in 1970, she moved to California.

In 1970, she discovered the Women's Liberation Movement; she writes that she then became a *"conscious woman."* She connected witchcraft with feminism: on the Winter Solstice of 1971, Budapest formed the Susan B. Anthony Coven in Los Angeles in honor of the suffragist leader. She opened a store "The Feminist Wicca" in the Venice area of Los Angeles, where she was arrested in 1975 by an undercover policewoman for violation of laws against "fortune telling for a fee." Budapest was arrested for reading Tarot cards. She was put on trial and lost; the law would be repealed nine years later.

Dianic Wicca or *Wimmin's Religion* is a feminist religious and spiritual tradition. Women's rights and rites are combined in celebration of the Goddess. Most covens are exclusively female. The focus is on female divinity, especially Diana, hence the name *Dianic*. Dianic Wicca may be considered similar in essence to women's ancient mystery traditions such as that of Rome's Bona Dea.

Also in 1975, Budapest self-published *The Feminist Book of Light and Shadows*, a collection of rituals and spells that became the basic text of Dianic Wicca; it was subsequently republished as *The Holy Book of Women's Mysteries: Feminist Witchcraft, Goddess Rituals, Spellcasting and Other Womanly Arts* (Wingbow Press, 1980, revised 1989).

In the early 1980s, Budapest moved to Oakland, California, where she hosted a radio show serving the San Francisco Bay area and became director of the Women's Spirituality Forum in Oakland, a nonprofit organization sponsoring a monthly lecture series about the Goddess, spirituality retreats, and annual spiral dances on Halloween.

Buzzard, Dr

Dr Buzzard is the name of a famous conjure man and root-worker from St Helena Island, near Beaufort, South Carolina. He performed physical healings as well as a wide variety of magical services.

Buzzards allegedly served as his familiars, hence his name. Clients traveling to the doctor's home were allegedly rowed across the river by a pair of buzzards.

Dr Buzzard's true identity is somewhat mysterious, perhaps because more than one conjurer may have operated under that name. This was for centuries not an uncommon metaphysical tradition, particularly during eras when magical practice was illegal or discouraged: if a name had power, people would use it, for a variety of reasons. At a time when there was little or no media, people frequently had few expectations as to someone's appearance and so this was not a difficult practice.

Dr Buzzard's prime specialty was court cases. Clients paid him to win their cases. He would dust the courtroom with magical powders and

attend trial daily, sitting prominently in the courtroom, chewing on Court Case Root (Laos or galangal root, so-called because it reputedly provides courtroom success). He did not hide but was a highly visible presence wearing his trademark purple sunglasses that he never removed in public. The sheer intimidation factor of having him in the courtroom cannot be overlooked. (He also allegedly once made a buzzard fly around the courthouse.)

Dr Buzzard achieved financial success through root-working. He owned his home on St Helena Island, drove an expensive car, and financed the building of two churches.

There are references to Dr Buzzard in Harry Middleton Hyatt's five-volume compilation of Hoodoo and Conjuration lore. J. Edward McTeer, High Sheriff of Beaufort County from 1926 until 1963, recounted his experiences with Dr Buzzard in two books, *High Sheriff of the Low Country* (1970) and *Fifty Years as a Low Country Witch Doctor* (1978) (McTeer was also a magical practitioner).

McTeer's Dr Buzzard, who is generally acknowledged as the *real* one, is Stepney Robinson, a tall dark-skinned man who wore expensive black suits and purple sunglasses and whose father may have been an African-born conjurer. He was born in the latter half of the nineteenth century and died in 1947. His practice (and name) was inherited by a son-in-law, who died in 1997.

Cagliostro, Count Alessandro di (June 2, 1743–August 6, 1795)

Casanova was jealous of Cagliostro; Goethe loathed him. Pope Pius VI accused Cagliostro of threatening the very survival of the Roman Catholic Church. He inspired Johann Strauss' operetta, *Cagliostro in Vienna* and served as the prototype for the character of the magician Sarastro in Mozart's *The Magic Flute*. He has inspired at least half a dozen films (so far), with Orson Welles playing him in Gregory Ratoff's 1949 film *Black Magic*, based on a novel by Alexander Dumas.

Not bad for a poor boy from the slums of Palermo.

Alchemist, magician, charlatan, thug, philanthropist, Cagliostro embodies *all* the multifaceted contradictions of the Tarot card The Magician.

He was a mountebank in both the positive and negative senses of that word. A traveling magician, he picked up occult secrets wherever he wandered. His skills included alchemy, astrology, clairvoyance, and healing. He was a master of what today would be called aromatherapy. He was a practitioner of High Ritual Magic but was also adept at what some consider "low magic"—he concocted and sold love potions and was not averse to revenge magic.

He learned shamanic techniques whilst staying in the poor quarters of St Petersburg, where he did *not* get a warm reception from Catherine the Great (she wrote a lampoon of him). Instead he spent his time at marketplace crossroads among the poor whom he healed and fed at his own expense.

He could be very generous to the poor when so inclined. He ran soup kitchens, paid for out of his own pocket, when the concept of feeding the poor barely existed. He was also a pimp, thief, fraud, con artist, and illusionist.

Giuseppe Balsamo was born in Palermo, Sicily of Moorish-Sicilian ancestry. He was raised in Palermo's old Arab quarter. His father was a jeweler who died bankrupt only a few months after Giuseppe's birth. Giuseppe, his mother and older sister lived in a two-room apartment on a poor street in the poorest quarter of Palermo, the *Albergheria*, amongst Arab, Jewish, and Turkish immigrants.

As a boy, Giuseppe led a street gang, more than occasionally brawling with police, however he *was* educated, home-schooled by a private tutor until aged 10, after which he was enrolled for several years at a seminary for orphan children.

He also had private lessons from an art master, becoming an excellent copyist and draftsman. He could draw very well—well enough to reproduce maps, documents, and other people's handwriting. He forged theater tickets and possibly legal documents.

Balsamo spent several years as a novice monk at the Monastery of the Fatabenefratelli healing order. At Fatabenefratelli, he learned basic rites of exorcism plus Hermetic traditions. Under Sicily's two centuries of Moorish rule, the Catholic orders had become copyists and keepers of Arabic manuscripts including those devoted to alchemy and magic forbidden elsewhere. In the monastery, Balsamo learned the basics of alchemy, astrology, and *gematria*, Kabalah's sacred numerology.

In 1764, Balsamo fled Sicily. For about a year, no documentation of his whereabouts exists. He may have visited Rhodes and become involved with a scam for an "alchemical procedure" turning hemp into silk. He may have gone to Egypt. He used different names in different places and so is not easily traced.

He next appears in Malta in 1765. Malta was the headquarters of the Knights of St John, competitors of the Templars. Balsamo sold elixirs and beauty creams before establishing a friendship with Grand Master Emanuel Pinto of the Order of the Knights of St John.

Grand Master Pinto was the longest-serving Grand Master (1741–1773). He set up a laboratory where Balsamo/Cagliostro worked as an alchemist, chemist, and pharmacist. The two men searched for the Philosopher's Stone together.

In 1767, Cagliostro traveled to Naples, and then to Rome where he got work as a secretary for Cardinal Orsini but sold love potions on the side. In Rome, he met the love of his life, Lorenza Seraphina Feliciani, aged 14. Beautiful, blonde, and blue-eyed, she was the daughter of an illiterate brass worker from Trastevere. Lorenza and Cagliostro were married on April 20, 1768. He insisted she call herself by her more evocative middle name.

He loved her passionately, considering her his soul mate. However he allegedly sometimes beat her. When cash was short, he prostituted her in order to raise funds and used her beauty to attract and seduce wealthy patrons.

Cagliostro and Seraphina's first appearance in history together occurred in 1769 when they met Casanova, a compulsive diarist, in a café. Casanova, a consummate conman himself, was peeved when he realized that Cagliostro had conned him instead: Cagliostro allegedly forged Casanova's signature on a check.

Some, admiring Cagliostro's grand metaphysical work but appalled by his criminal record reconcile his contradictions by insisting there were really two individuals, and that Giuseppe Balsamo of Sicily could not possibly be the adept Cagliostro of Paris.

Seraphina and Cagliostro traveled for years, sometimes wealthy, sometimes utterly impoverished. He studied genuine magic and occult tra-

ditions, supplementing his income with illusions and fraud as needed.

He used at least two *noms de plumes* consistently, switching between them as convenient: *Count Cagliostro* (the name, but not the title, borrowed from an uncle) and *Colonel Pellegrini* of the Brandenburg Army.

In July 1776, Giuseppe and Seraphina arrived in London for the second time where he described himself as an *"occult scientist."* They rented a house at 4 Whitcomb Street in Leicester Square, complete with an alchemical laboratory, but wound up several times in the debtor's section of both King's Bench and Newgate jails.

Cagliostro became a Freemason in London, simultaneously initiated into the first three grades of Strict Observance Freemasonry. After these initiations, he discovered a treatise on the Egyptian origins of Freemasonry on a bookseller's stall. According to this treatise, all contemporary Masonic rites were corrupt to varying degrees. Pure unadulterated Masonry was rooted in ancient Egypt amongst the pyramid builders; the founder of this ancient tradition an Egyptian high priest known as the Great Copt.

Cagliostro was inspired to establish what he called Egyptian Freemasonry lodges, initiating both men and women. (Admission of women is still controversial amongst some Freemasons.) Cagliostro as the Grand Master took the title the Grand Copt; Seraphina was Grand Mistress of the Order. Freemasonry was a secret organization; the flamboyant Cagliostro to some extent became its public face.

For his time, Cagliostro was a visionary man of tolerance, insisting that Egyptian Masonry be open to all sincere spiritual people including Jews and Muslims and supporting membership for women. The only requirements were belief in a Supreme Being and in the immortality of the soul. (On the other hand, he laid a public curse on

82-year-old Countess Constanze von Korff because she publicly called him a charlatan.)

He was a bit of a Robin Hood figure, scamming the rich but giving to the poor. He distributed remedies for free for those in financial need. Running free clinics for the poor may sound commendable today but at that time it landed Cagliostro in trouble with powerful local physicians who resented this competition. Perhaps inspired by his memories of himself as a poor boy in Palermo, he ran what were essentially soup kitchens for the urban poor.

He was controversial amongst Masons too and not only because of his insistence on women's inclusion. Masons in Latvia were appalled to hear Cagliostro boast that he could concoct potions that would make women lust for men.

Cagliostro eventually became the rage in Paris where wild stories were told about him: not only could he transmute base metals into gold, silver, *and* diamonds, he could also double existing diamonds and precious gems so that they were twice their size and value.

🕷 *It was rumored that he had personally spoken with Christ on the shores of Galilee*

🕷 *It was rumored that Cagliostro was the legendary Wandering Jew himself*

🕷 *It was rumored that he had entered into a conspiracy against Queen Marie Antoinette*

Many who know nothing else about Cagliostro know his name because of his involvement in the notorious *Affair of the Queen's Necklace*. In 1784, Cagliostro was a key figure and accused as a co-conspirator of stealing a priceless diamond necklace under the forged signature of the queen as well as forging steamy love-letters signed in the queen's name (and not addressed to the king).

Although Cagliostro was acquitted unconditionally, he was banished from Paris the day after acquittal. Ordered to leave France within three weeks, he went back to London on June 20, 1786.

Seraphina was tired of wandering and perhaps tired of her husband. She wished to return to Rome and persuaded Cagliostro to do so. Returning to Rome was like entering fire. The Inquisition hunted Freemasons like witches. Pope Clement XII had condemned Freemasonry in 1738; Catholics were forbidden from joining on pain of excommunication.

Once in Italy, Seraphina, who may have been unable to conceive of any other way of terminating their relationship, denounced Cagliostro to the Inquisition apparently in the hope of being free of her husband. Pope Pius VI personally issued the order to the Governor of Tome to seize Cagliostro and search his premises. Captured by the Inquisition on September 27, 1789, Cagliostro was taken to the prison of Sant'Angelo while Seraphina was escorted to the convent of Santa Apollonia "for her own protection."

Seraphina, also a Freemason and magical adept, had long served as Cagliostro's assistant. She was allegedly promised immunity in return for testimony against her husband. She apparently hoped to begin life anew in Italy among her family. However, to her bitter disappointment, Seraphina was confined for life in the Convent of Santa Apollonia where she died in 1794. For his part, Cagliostro allegedly never entirely believed his beloved Seraphina had turned him in.

Cagliostro endured 43 interrogations over 15 months, the Pope himself attending several of these interrogations. He was condemned to life imprisonment in the fortress of San Leo, described by Machiavelli as the strongest fortress in all of Europe.

He was a defiant prisoner, continually attempting to break free. Eventually he was chained in a tiny cell, forbidden to converse or communicate with *anyone* either in or out of jail—truly a terrible punishment for a man born under the sign of Gemini, the zodiac sign ruling communication.

He suffered two strokes in his cell, dying aged 52. Jailers were so suspicious of their prisoner that lighted rushes were held to Cagliostro's bare feet to make sure he was really dead. As an unrepentant heretic, he was buried in an unmarked pit.

Crowley, Aleister (October 12, 1875–December 1, 1947)

Despite his notoriety, Aleister Crowley was a master magus wielding tremendous influence over contemporary spiritual and magical traditions. He was involved in all facets of magical practice with the exception of folk magic, which didn't interest him (and perhaps would have forced him to work with female practitioners as equals). Briefly a member of the Golden Dawn, Crowley also worked with Gerald Gardner in the formational stages of Gardnerian Wicca.

In many ways he was not an admirable person; there are certainly many aspects of his personal life that are easily criticized (he was emotionally, financially, and physically abusive to women, he failed to support his children, he demonstrated cruelty to animals, he had Fascist leanings, and, despite his wealth, sponged off others—and that's for starters), *however*, ironically, many in the magical community who condemn Crowley have been influenced by him. Few who condemn him (and few who laud him too!) have actually read his work, which is dense and intended for adepts or almost-adepts. He was extremely influential, a prolific author and, in many ways, a visionary occultist.

Edward Alexander Crowley was brought up a strict member of the ultra-conservative Plymouth Brethren, so conservative they perceived themselves as the only true Christians in existence. His father was a wealthy brewer and preacher for the Brethren. Crowley was taught that God was all-powerful and that sins of the flesh (sins in general!) would be punished in eternal hell-fire. His father died when Crowley was 11, leaving his son a large inheritance that would be his at maturity.

As a child, Crowley preached with his father but at the age of 12, he said, he went over "*to Satan's side.*" In his early teens, his mother caught him masturbating and denounced him as "*the Great Beast*"—as in the one from the Book of Revelation. Crowley took great pride in being called the Beast and adopted the nickname as his identity, also identifying with the number 666.

Despite his reputation, he was *not* a Satanist or at least not by his standards. Satanism requires a certain interplay with Christianity: the devil is worshipped because he is the enemy of Christ. Satanic rites invert and desecrate Christian rituals.

Crowley wasn't interested in Christianity or Satanism; his goal was the creation of a new spiritual tradition that would ultimately replace previous ones, making them irrelevant—although from the perspective of fundamentalist Christians that vision would certainly be considered diabolical.

> Crowley developed his own theology based on personal communication with spirits. His motto, known as the Law of Thelema, was *"Do what thou will shall be the whole of the law."* He published this law before Gerald Gardner published the Wiccan Rede, *"An it harm none, do what you will."*

Crowley had great emotional investment in being considered *"the wickedest man alive"* as he was described. He reveled in his reputation and put great effort into enhancing it. He was a trickster and it can be difficult to determine what was authentic in his behavior, what was illusion, and what was meant to inflame.

He enrolled at Trinity College, Cambridge in 1895 reading moral science. When the trust fund from his father matured, he was no longer dependent on his family for financial support. A wealthy young man, he mingled with top society. During this period, he read and was very influenced by Arthur Waite's *The Book of Black Magic and Pacts*. In Cambridge, he wrote poetry, much of it erotic or pornographic and took up mountaineering. He dropped out of university in 1898 and got in touch with the metaphysical organization, the Golden Dawn.

Crowley was initiated into the Golden Dawn on November 18, 1899 taking the magical name *Frater Perdurabo* (Latin for "I will endure"). He was not a diplomatic, charming person although he was allegedly very charismatic. W.B. Yeats, another Golden Dawn member, described him as *"an unspeakable mad person."* Crowley was either expelled from the Golden Dawn or quit after two years following bitter conflict with its leader MacGregor Mathers (see page 749).

Crowley bought Boleskin House, a manor located on the shores of Loch Ness, in 1900, and devoted the next six months to the techniques of *The Sacred Magic of Abramelin*. The house was rumored to have been built on the site of a church that had been razed to the ground with the congregation still within and already had a reputation as a haunted house where odd phenomenon occurred.

He married Rose Kelly, the sister of his friend the artist Sir Gerald Kelly, in 1903 and the two traveled widely together. During a visit to an Egyptian museum, Rose was drawn to an exhibit numbered 666 that depicted the Egyptian deities Hadit and Ra-Hoor-Khuit. Shortly after, she was possessed by a spirit who called itself *Aiwass*. Aiwass dictated *The Book of the Law*, the basis for Crowley's new spiritual philosophies, to Crowley through Rose Kelly's mouth over three days in April 1904.

> Rose Kelly played the role Edward Kelley played for Dr Dee. She spoke while Crowley wrote. She is now largely considered to have been clairvoyant, however she had never previously had a similar psychic episode. Following her experiences in Egypt, her psychic experiences continued and she was Crowley's first "high priestess" or "Scarlet Woman."

While in Egypt, Rose discovered she was pregnant. She gave birth to a daughter on July 28, 1904, named Nuit Ma Ahathoor Hecate Sappho Jezebel Lilith. Crowley would eventually abandon them both. Nuit died of typhoid before she reached the age of two in a hospital in Rangoon. Crowley claimed the cause was an improperly sterilized bottle nipple for which he blamed Rose and her increasing alcoholism. A second daughter, Lola Zaza, survived. Crowley divorced Rose in 1909; she was eventually institutionalized, her brother assuming financial support for Lola.

In 1907, Crowley began the Order of the Silver Star (*Argentinum Astrum*; AA for short), heavily influenced by the Golden Dawn. In 1909, he founded the magazine *Equinox* in which, from 1909 to 1913, he published some of the Golden Dawn's sworn secrets much to their displeasure. MacGregor Mathers went to court to stop him but to no avail.

Among Crowley's primary magical influences were Abramelin, Madame Blavatsky, and Eliphas Levi. Crowley was born on the day Eliphas Levi died and claimed to be the reincarnation of Levi. He also claimed Pope Alexander VI (Rodrigo Borgia), Edward Kelley and Count Cagliostro as previous incarnations. He was influenced by Buddhism and Tantra and was among the first to combine Western and Eastern mystical traditions into a coherent magical system.

In 1912 Crowley visited Germany and met with Theodor Reuss, head of the ten-year-old Ordo Templi Orientis, heavily influenced by erotic magic and the teachings of magus Paschal Beverly Randolph (see page 760). Crowley was appointed the head of the British OTO, assuming the grandiose title "*Supreme and Holy King of Ireland, Iona and all other Britons within the Sanctuary of the Gnosis*" (see **DICTIONARY:** Ordo Templi Orientis). In 1913, Crowley spent time

in Moscow promoting a dance troupe, *The Ragged Ragtime Girls*, who played violins and danced seductively in scanty clothing. Among the Ragtime Girls was violinist Leila Waddell (1880–1932), a prominent occultist in her own right, and among the most influential of Crowley's Scarlet Women.

Crowley defined a magician as one with mastery of the science and art of causing change to occur in conformity with the will. Magic was the science of self-understanding and the art of putting knowledge towards practical action.

In 1915 he moved to New York and spent the following years of World War I writing anti-British propaganda for the Germans; the British press would soon dub him "*The Wickedest Man in the World*." Crowley later claimed that this was subterfuge and some evidence suggests that he was secretly in the employ of Britain's MI5, although this, too, remains controversial. He lived in New York until 1919. It is believed that Crowley met or corresponded with German author Hanns Heinz Ewers in New York at this time. (See **CREATIVE ARTS:** Film: *Alraune*.)

Crowley envisioned that his magical work required a female partner, the equivalent of a high priestess, whom he dubbed a "Scarlet Woman." The concept derives from references in the Book of Revelation to the Whore of Babylon.

Crowley intended to return the Scarlet Woman to her former glory. He spent a tremendous amount of time searching for the right Scarlet Woman with whom he would conceive a "*magickal child*." It's believed the closest he came was with Leah Hirsig, whom he met in New York in 1919 and with whom he would have a long, passionate relationship.

In 1920, Crowley and Leah Hirsig moved to Cefalu in Sicily, purchasing an old farmhouse, which they named Thelema and which became the center of his new spiritual tradition. He would be accused of conducting orgies, animal sacrifices and all kinds of diabolical magic there, as well as luring others into drug abuse, addiction, and sexual perversions.

French author François Rabelais' (1494–1553) fictional utopia the *Abbey of Thelema* inspired Crowley to create his own version in the early twentieth century. *Thelema* means "will" or "free will" in Greek and was the name Crowley gave his new religion. Thelema, said Crowley, would represent the New Age and would release humanity from its obsessions with fear and sin. Crowley claimed each individual was the center of their own world.

One of Crowley's disciples, 23-year-old Raoul Loveday died at Thelema on February 11, 1923. Loveday's wife, Betty May, who was not a disciple but who had accompanied her husband, fled back to England and sold her detailed, sordid story to the press. She accused Crowley of poisoning Loveday to death by making him drink cat's blood. (According to the attending physician, the cause of death was enteric fever.)

In April 1923, Benito Mussolini had Crowley deported from Italy. He wandered through France, Germany, and North Africa. Scarlet Women came and went. He married Maria Ferrari de Miramar (born 1894) in Leipzig in 1929 so she could gain entry to England. Ferrari, born in Nicaragua of Italian and French ancestry, was described by Crowley as a Voodoo High Priestess. He would eventually abandon her too; she ended up destitute, institutionalized in the same facility as Rose Kelly. Crowley never divorced Maria for fear that she might be entitled, as a lawfully wedded wife, to some of his dwindling property.

In 1934, Crowley was declared bankrupt after losing a court case in which he sued an old friend, artist Nina Hamnett, for defamation for describing him as a *"Black Magician"* in her autobiography. Life became increasingly difficult as he battled a debilitating 25-year heroin addiction he was never able to shake.

In 1945, he moved into a boarding house in Hastings on the southern coast of England, where he corresponded with Gerald Gardner among others. Gardner visited Crowley during the last year of his life. Crowley presented Gardner a charter to start a branch of the OTO on the Isle of Man. (Gardner never used the charter but eventually placed it in his museum collection.)

How much Crowley contributed to the Gardnerian Book of Shadows remains subject to bitter debate. He was clearly an occultist and magician and not a Wiccan (Gardner said Crowley perceived Wicca as *"too tame"*). Many would prefer to think that he had little to do with it. He was, however, a prolific writer and some believe that he originally contributed a great deal to the Book of Shadows, although Doreen Valiente later removed and revised most of his contributions.

He was cremated four days after his death in December 1947 from a combination of myocardial degeneration and severe bronchitis.

Crowley wrote dozens of books including *Gems from the Equinox, The General Principles of Astrology, Magick, Enochian World of Aleister Crowley: Enochian Sex Magick, Eight Lectures on Yoga*, and *The Diary of a Drug Fiend: Magick in Theory and Practice*.

Crowley's fame and notoriety only continues to grow. He has developed a bit of a rock star reputation, which no doubt he would have enjoyed: Crowley's is among the faces on the cover of the Beatles' *Sgt. Pepper's Lonely Hearts Club Band* album.

Cunningham, Scott (June 27, 1956–March 28, 1993)

Scott Cunningham was a prolific writer who authored over 15 books, some considered magical classics. He was a key individual in facilitating solitary Wiccan practice. His book, *Wicca: A Guide for the Solitary Practitioner* (1988) was controversial as some Wiccans felt (and feel) that only coven initiations and group ritual were valid.

Cunningham moved to San Diego, California in early childhood where, at the age of 15, he became fascinated by witchcraft. One evening he watched the film *Burn, Witch, Burn!* on television (see **CREATIVE ARTS:** Films). The following day at school, Cunningham met a fellow student, Dorothy Jones, who told him that she had been initiated as a witch two years earlier. Her craft name was Morgan. Cunningham described her as a "Moon Priestess": she was to become Cunningham's magical teacher and would initiate him into her Wiccan tradition.

Cunningham was fascinated by herbs and became an authority on them. His book *A Witch's Herbal* was rejected by many publishers before its publication in 1982 under the title *Magical Herbalism*. It quickly became a favorite and was followed by many others.

He contracted cryptococcal meningitis in 1990 from which he never fully recovered. There were many more books he wished to write; those that he did include: *Earth Power* (1983), *Cunningham's Encyclopedia of Magical Herbs* (1985), *The Truth About Witchcraft* (1987), *Cunningham's Encyclopedia of Crystal, Gem and Metal Magic* (1987), *The Magic of Incense, Oils and Brews* (1989), *The Magic in Food* (1991), *Living Wicca* (1993), *Spell Crafts* (1993), *Hawaiian Religion and Magic* (published posthumously, 1994)

David-Neel, Alexandra (October 28, 1868–September 8, 1969)

Alexandra David-Neel was an adventurer, mystic, Spiritualist, anarchist, metaphysical adept, and scholar, and the first European woman to explore the then-forbidden Tibetan holy city of Lhasa. She lived in Tibet for 14 years, living among the shamans of Tibet and Sikkim, another Himalayan kingdom, which was annexed by India in 1975.

She was instrumental in preserving Tibet's spiritual legacy. After leaving Tibet in 1924, she traveled, returning to France in 1946. She authored over 30 books including *Magic and Mystery in Tibet* (1932), *Initiations and Initiates in Tibet* (1931), and *Love Magic and Black Magic: Scenes from Unknown Tibet* (1938).

Louise Eugenie Alexandrine Marie David was born in Paris and showed early interest in metaphysical study. By the age of 18, she had joined Blavatsky's Theosophical Society, which led to an interest in Himalayan traditions. She traveled through India in 1890/91 stopping only when she ran out of funds. She married Phillippe Neel on August 4, 1904. Her husband was tolerant of her travels.

She returned to India in 1911 where she became a Tantric adept and was soon given an invitation to travel to the remote kingdom of Sikkim, where she visited Buddhist shrines, studied with shamans and learned to speak Tibetan. She studied shamanic arts of telepathy and attempted to master "tumo" breathing, the Tibetan art of generating body heat in freezing conditions.

For two years, she lived in a cave in Sikkim near the Tibetan border, with the Tibetan monk Aphur Yongden, who became her life-long friend and companion. (She eventually adopted him.) They were eventually expelled from Sikkim for several times crossing the Tibetan border, which was then forbidden.

After leaving the Himalayas, she continued to be a global traveler, first going to East Asia where, in Mongolia, she managed to create a "tulpa"—a phantom generated by intense mental focus and constant repetition of specific ritual over a period of months. She created a fat, phantom monk who was visible to others and who traveled with her. However, he gradually began to transform into a thin, sinister being who resisted her control. It took David-Neel six months to dissolve the tulpa, who clung desperately to his existence.

On February 21, 1924 David-Neel and Yongden, having returned to the Himalayas, abandoned all they owned and disguised as beggars sneaked over the Tibetan border, where they lived quietly for several years. David-Neel died in France aged 100, having just recently renewed her passport.

Dee, Dr John (July 13, 1527-March 26, 1609)

Dr John Dee, renowned as Queen Elizabeth's astrologer was also an alchemist, magician, scholar, and author of 79 books, although only a few were published in his lifetime. Dee is one of the founders of Enochian Magic and considered a brilliant occultist, although in his lifetime, as with Cornelius Agrippa, he was always just one step ahead of the witch-trials.

John Dee was born in London of Welsh ancestry, the son of a servant at the court of Henry VIII. Dee entered Cambridge University aged 15 to study science and mathematics.

Despite his youth he had already developed a reputation as an occultist. This reputation eventually reached the ears of university officials and Dee was asked to leave. He transferred to the University of Louvain where he met people who had known Agrippa in whose work he was very interested.

In 1551, at age 24, he returned to England where, in 1552, he met a magician called Jerome Cardan, who inspired him to begin conjuring spirits.

> According to Dr Dee, the ideal day was sixteen hours dedicated to the study of the magical arts, two hours spent eating, and any time left spent sleeping.

Dee rendered an unknown but seemingly important service to the court of Edward VI for which he was granted an annuity of £100. This "service" has been the subject of speculation ever since. It is generally believed to be of a magical nature as the reason for the annuity was never made public. (Alternatively he is believed to have served as a spy.)

Following Edward's death, Dee then worked for Edward's sister, Mary, who had ascended the throne, telling her fortune daily and casting her horoscope. Dee also became friendly with Mary's half-sister Elizabeth who allegedly asked him to astrologically calculate Mary's death. (Now of course, as a master astrologer, he would know which sister to bet on.)

Mary found out and Dee was thrown in jail on charges of witchcraft, heresy, killing children via magic, and plotting to kill the queen also via magical means. According to Dee, Mary accused him of being " *a companion of hellhounds and a caller and conjurer of wicked and damned spirits."*

His relationship with Princess Elizabeth was investigated by the authorities and Dee was imprisoned from 1553 until 1555, when he was able to persuade Archbishop Bonner that he was orthodox in religious matters and set free. He was acquitted and released but was for ever identified as a sorcerer. His acquittal was perceived by many as proof of Dee's magic power. The Archbishop was extremely conservative, even bigoted; Dee's ability to persuade him of his innocence was perceived by some as evidence of witchcraft.

Mary died in 1558 and Elizabeth assumed the throne. Dee became her spiritual advisor, also advising her on medical matters. Allegedly he also served as her spy and informer, reporting what others said of her. He also worked as a cartographer and geographer and was a great friend of the Flemish cartographer Mercator (as in the Mercator Scale). Dee began an extensive collection of books on magic and the occult, which eventually numbered several thousand works.

Elizabeth trusted Dr Dee to choose the date for her coronation. He chose January 14, 1559 with Jupiter in Aquarius to signal universality and Mars in Scorpio for victory and endurance. Her long, glorious reign may be considered testimony to his astrological skill. Queen Elizabeth even visited him at his home in Mortlake.

Dee longed to communicate with angels and attempted to do so via scrying. His scrying tools included an Aztec obsidian mirror and a pink crystal, a gift from an angel. According to his diary, Dee saw spirits on May 25, 1581, however he had some difficulty and so began hiring professional scryers (crystal-gazers) to work with him—the first of which there is record is Barnabas Saul. In his diary entry of October 9, 1581, Dee wrote that Saul raised a spirit around midnight. Saul scryed for him through the rest of 1581.

Dee then met Edward Talbot, aka Edward Kelley or Kelly, beginning a pivotal collaboration. Dee and Kelley worked together for seven years: Kelley contacted the spirits while Dee recorded their communication. (See page 742, Kelley.)

In 1582, Kelley began to receive messages in a new angelic language called Enochian. The angels taught him the "language of Enoch," which had been spoken by Adam while in Paradise. The language has a 21-letter alphabet with consistent grammar and syntax. Letters are related to elements, numbers, and planetary forces.

Although Queen Elizabeth was Dee's ally, he had powerful enemies at court as well, and he was always under the threat of charges of sorcery. Bishop Jessel, preaching before the queen, suggested that her proximity to magicians was a threat to her majesty.

Dee, Kelley, their wives and families left England in 1583 and traveled with Prince Albert Laski to his estate in Poland where he had promised to set them up in an alchemical laboratory. In his absence, a mob sacked Dee's house at Mortlake, stealing books and objects, when rumors spread that he was a witch.

Laski however didn't have as much money as they'd hoped and Kelley, Dee and their respective families began a life of wandering throughout Central and Eastern Europe, always in search of wealthy patrons who would sponsor their alchemical experiments.

After leaving Laski they traveled to the court of Emperor Rudolph II in Prague. Rudolph, who was fascinated by the occult, reputedly maintained a staff of alchemists, diviners, and magicians but the Papal Nuncio sent him a message saying that the Pope didn't approve of the presence of English heretics and magicians at his court. Kelley and Dee hit the road quickly, traveling to King Stephen of Poland's court in Krakow. Once again, the reaction was not favorable.

Encyclopedia of Witchcraft

Wandering magicians, completely broke, they continued to search for patrons through Central Europe giving demonstrations of their alchemical aptitude. Dee wanted to work with the spirits but Kelley wished to focus on alchemy. Allegedly he had had success in England and had even extracted the Philosopher's Stone, but running an alchemical laboratory was expensive and he needed a patron.

> Dee and Kelley sent Queen Elizabeth an ordinary metal warming pan from which they had cut a piece, which they transformed into gold and then stuck back in place. Was this real or legerdemain?

In 1586, Tsar Boris Godunov offered Dee £200 a year, a fabulous salary, to enter his service as an alchemist. Kelley wished to go but Dee was not enthusiastic about alchemy, perceiving that it was a dangerous trap in which they would be commanded and exploited by rulers.

In 1587, Kelley insisted on returning to his work as an alchemist. Dee attempted to replace Kelley with his son Arthur but with no success.

Two years later Dee resolved to return to England following six years abroad. Kelley stayed in Europe to continue his alchemical work. Upon his return to England Dee was immediately given an audience with Queen Elizabeth; she ordered that he be allowed to conduct alchemical and other experiments without hindrance. He complained of the pillaging of his home and was able to secure the return of some books and tools.

Within a year of his return, Dee felt obligated to publish a tract refuting allegations that he was a conjuror. In 1596, Dee was appointed warden of the Collegiate Chapter in Manchester, probably as a means of removing him from London, but he was unpopular because of his lack of Protestant orthodoxy and magical reputation. Only Elizabeth still favored him; when she died in 1603, his position became perilous. Witchcraft trials were becomingly increasingly common.

> Dr Arthur Dee was an alchemist, too. In 1587, when Edward Kelley left his father's employ, Arthur was delegated to take his place as seer, but with no success. Arthur went to Moscow where he had a successful career as a royal physician. While there, he wrote his treatise *Arcana Arcanorum*. He returned to England where he continued to work as a physician.

Dee petitioned Elizabeth's successor James I to be cleared of slanderous accusations that he was an *"invocator of devils."* He wanted James to publicly declare that Dee had never been a magician but rather a scholar, mathematician, and scientist. James declined but never persecuted him.

Dee retired to Mortlake in poverty and attempted to earn his living as an astrologer. He died of natural causes in 1608 and is buried at Mortlake. His book collection and some tools now belong to the British Museum.

> Prospero, the magician in Shakespeare's *The Tempest*, is believed at least partially to be based on Dr Dee.

Dye, Aunt Caroline

Aunt Caroline Dye was a renowned African-American Hoodoo doctor from Newport, Arkansas. Her birth date is unknown: suggested dates are as early as 1810 and as late as 1855. She apparently died sometime between 1918 and 1944, depending upon one's source. Part of the problem regarding her identity is the age-old tradition for practitioners to borrow (or pay tribute, depending how you look at it) other more successful practitioners' names. Thus more than one person may have used the name Caroline Dye.

Caroline Dye was a healer, spiritualist, and root-worker who served a black and white clientele. References to her and descriptions of her work are found in Harry Middleton Hyatt's five-volume collection, *Hoodoo-Conjuration-Witchcraft-Rootwork*, compiled mainly between 1935 and 1939. She served as inspiration for various blues songs, most famously the 1929 recording by Will Shade and the Memphis Jug Band *Aunt Caroline Dyer Blues.*

Endor, The Witch of

The biblical shaman popularly known as "the Witch of Endor" appears in the First Book of Samuel, 28:7-25. Although shamans appear elsewhere in the Bible—Saul, her royal client, himself has shamanic power—the Witch of Endor is the only biblical figure explicitly identified in English as a "witch." She is often used as an example of biblical disapproval of witchcraft, however the text of the Bible itself is, at worst, neutral toward the Witch of Endor.

On ascending the throne, King Saul forbids witchcraft, divination, and shamanism on pain of death. However, when he later runs into scary political turmoil and other licit forms of divination, including his own dreams, fail him, Saul, apparently appreciating that forbidden professionals have merely gone underground, orders his minions to find him a female practitioner.

The minions bring Saul to a woman in Endor who performs necromantic rituals, bringing up the shade of the Prophet Samuel who talks with Saul and informs him that not only will he lose the next pivotal battle with the Philistines, by this time tomorrow Saul and his sons will be with Samuel. The woman of Endor comforts Saul and feeds him—hardly a "wicked witch."

Whether or not the original text of the Old Testament actually called her a "witch" is subject to debate and subject to one's definition of witchcraft. "Witch" is an English word; the Hebrew words originally used to identify her are *Baalat ob,* literally "Mistress of the Ob." This term frustrated later translators as they were unable to translate *"ob."* Different words in different languages are used to identify the profession of the conjuring woman from Endor.

❋ *The Septuagint (the original Greek translation of the Bible) translates it as* engastrimuthos *or* "belly-speaker"

❋ *The first Latin translation was "*Woman possessing an oracular spirit*"*

❋ *The King James English translation uses* "witch"

❋ *More contemporary English translations of the Bible, aware of negative connotations associated with the word "witch" now frequently describe the woman of Endor as a "Mistress of a Talisman" or "Mistress of a Divining Spirit."*

So, what exactly is an *ob*? Unfortunately, no one is completely sure; Jewish shamanic traditions were almost entirely suppressed. Interpretations are elusive. It seems to have been some sort of container used in divination or necromancy, perhaps a bottle, jug, oil lamp, charm bag, wine or water-skin.

It is believed that the *Baalat ob* used some sort of ritual vessel, perhaps as a container for the familiar spirit with which one could contact other realms, maybe something like the gourds used to house oracular spirits in many African traditions.

Faust, Dr Johannes

Dr Faust was the most famous mage of the medieval era and the inspiration for countless artistic masterpieces; he has been immortalized in works by Marlowe, Goethe, Berlioz, Gounod, Thomas Mann, and Klaus Mann. (For information on his legend, see **CREATIVE ARTS:** Literature: Faust.)

Was there really a Faust or was the legend inspired by a fictionalized version of Cornelius Agrippa (see page 706)? Was Faust based on a real person? Possible candidates include:

✻ *Johann Fust (1400–1466), a printer*

✻ *Georgius Sabellicu Faustus, a sixteenth-century German itinerant alchemist and fortune-teller*

✻ *Johann Faust, an early sixteenth-century German theologian*

It is also possible Dr Faust is a pseudonym for someone else, other than Agrippa. It was once a tradition for magicians to use each other's names partly as tribute and partly, as witchcraft was illegal, because no one wished to reveal their own true name. In any case, *someone* named Faust (Latinized as Faustus) seems to have lived *somewhere* in what is now southwestern Germany in the early sixteenth century.

The earliest known evidence for Faust's existence comes in a reference from the scholar Abbot Trithemius, who wrote a letter in 1507 saying that Faust, whom he described as a "*blasphemer*" and "*charlatan,*" had stayed with him the previous year. Trithemius wrote that Faust had held a teaching position in Kreuznach, which he was forced to resign because of allegations of lewd behavior with young male students. Evidence also comes from Protestant pastor Johann Gast, who preached a sermon about Faust's powers after dining with him at Basel in 1548.

Johann Weyer, Agrippa's disciple, also knew Faust and described him as a drunk who invented the story about his pact with Satan to add to his reputation.

Was there a Satanic pact? Faust himself allegedly said that, through ignorance, he failed to protect himself with correct magical ritual and symbols and was thus at the mercy of the spirit Asteroth, who manifested in the guise of a "*gray monk.*"

According to the Archives of the University of Heidelberg a student named Johannes Faust received a Baccalaureate on January 15, 1509 with a degree in Theology. He was placed first among his class of sixteen. He allegedly went on to lecture on Homer and mythology at the University of Erfurt, complete with a show-and-tell program realistic enough to terrify his students.

Faust became a prominent astrologer. On February 12, 1520 he allegedly was paid ten florins to cast a horoscope for prince bishop Georg III Schenk von Limburg. In 1525, Civic authorities in Wittenberg ordered Faust's arrest. He fled to Ingolstadt, from which he was banished on June 17, 1528.

In 1530, Faust was allegedly in Prague where competitive astrologers at Emperor Rudolf's court prevented him from gaining a permanent position. In 1532, he tried to settle in Nuremburg but, according to the city records, he was refused permission by the authorities on the grounds of being a necromancer and sodomite.

There are many legends regarding Faust:

✻ *He invited the Prince of Anhalt to dine with him at his castle, which had magically and suddenly materialized. As soon as the meal was over, the castle disappeared.*

✻ *Faust allegedly conjured up Alexander the Great for Emperor Charles V who wished to speak with him.*

✻ *Faust allegedly transported himself, while invisible, to the Vatican where he (still invisible) slapped the Pope across the face with a dead fish and stole his dinner.*

Claiming to be Faust's hometown is Knittlingen, approximately 30 miles northwest of Stuttgart, Germany on the edge of the Black Forest. A bronze statue of Faust has been erected near the City Hall. *This* Faust, ostensibly the illegitimate son of a wealthy farmer, allegedly studied astrology, chemistry, magic, and medicine at the University of Krakow, a school with a reputation for educating sorcerers, followed by further studies at German universities. He lived on a bequest from a wealthy uncle rather than gifts of Satan. (See **WITCH-CRAZE!**: Germany.)

Ficino, Marsilio (October 19, 1433–October 1, 1499)

Marsilio Ficino was a Renaissance magician, physician, and priest who developed a system of "natural magic" intended to draw down and utilize the natural powers of the cosmos, especially of the planets. The leading philosopher of the Italian Renaissance, Ficino, a physician's son, was an authority on classical Greek and Latin. Cosimo de Medici sponsored Ficino to translate Greek manuscripts for him.

Ficino received a copy of an ancient collection of writings called the *Hermetica* and became convinced that the *Hermetica* was the source of Plato's knowledge. Ficino believed it to be the work of Hermes Trismegistus, a contemporary of Moses, and implied that Moses might actually be Hermes Trismegistus. Ficino believed that Moses received the Kabalah on Mount Sinai alongside the Ten Commandments and that he was the custodian of secret wisdom as well as the giver of the law.

(Many modern scholars disagree, dating the Hermetic Collection to *c.*200 CE, after Plato's time. Those occultists who ascribe the Hermetic to the legendary Hermes Trismegistus of course agree with Ficino.)

From the *Hermetica*, Ficino learned that all life, including human life, is connected with the seven visible planets. Images may be used to attract the influence of these planets. This became the basis for his system of magic. In his writings, Ficino emphasized that magic was fully compatible with orthodox Christianity. He claimed his system intended to utilize planetary forces (natural, impersonal powers), *not* summon demons.

Some historians (even in his own time) suspected that Ficino really believed that spiritual beings conveyed these planetary influences but that this was too dangerous for him to publicly admit. Because of written disclaimers and political connections, Ficino was never persecuted.

Ficino composed his masterwork, *Three Books About Life*, between 1482 and 1489, a comprehensive guide to the health of body and soul—a work of holistic medicine, essentially. He established a magical academy in Florence and served as private tutor for Cosimo de Medici's grandson and heir, Lorenzo the Magnificent. Among those influenced by Ficino are Cornelius Agrippa and Paracelsus.

> The artist Botticelli, also suspected of having Pagan sympathies, was among Ficino's devotees. Some believe Botticelli's famous painting *Primavera* was originally intended as a magical image designed to attract the spiritual influence of Venus.

Flamel, Nicholas (c.1330-?)

The French alchemist Nicholas Flamel allegedly found the secret of the Philosopher's Stone, gaining immortality and wealth. Although some suggest he died in 1418, others claim to have met him long after and for all we know Flamel may be sitting in some café reading this description of himself even now.

Flamel labored as a scribe; one day while shopping at a bookstall, an unusual volume caught his eye and he purchased it for two florins. The gilded manuscript had 21 pages made from bark, not paper or parchment as was customary. It had a copper cover. Every seventh page lacked writing but was inscribed with, respectively:

❋ *A serpent swallowing rods*

❋ *A serpent crucified on a cross*

❋ *A vast, arid desert*

Written on the first leaf in gilded letters was "*Abraham the Jew, Prince, Priest, Levite, Astrologer and Philosopher to the Nation of the Jews Scattered by the Wrath of God in the Gaules* [France], *Salvation D.1,*" followed by various curses and imprecations against those who, unauthorized, attempted to use the book. Many believe this manuscript to be an early reference to the system of Abramelin magic found in the grimoire *Abramelin* and so influential on the work of the Golden Dawn and Aleister Crowley. (See **BOOKS:** Grimoires.)

Flamel believed the book to have been a confiscated magical text that had ended up on the bookstall; the bookseller offered no further information. According to the text, a full study of Kabalah was required for comprehension.

He recognized the work as an encoded alchemical text but was unable to decipher it. Flamel fell under the book's spell and was obsessed with it, spending 21 years trying to crack its code to no avail. Finally his wife Perenelle suggested he go to Toledo to consult with the rabbis there. They spent two years in Toledo. When he returned he was able to transmute mercury into silver and gold.

There are two versions (at least!) of his life:

❋ *Flamel did not create the Elixir of Life but lived to be 116 years old, dying in 1417 and distributing his considerable wealth to various churches and hospitals. His will provided for the construction of 14 hospitals, 7 churches, and 3 chapels. His wealth and extreme longevity led to rumors of his alchemical career.*

❋ *Flamel did discover the Philosopher's Stone and, together with his beloved Perenelle, still walks the Earth. An eighteenth-century Turkish dervish, for one, described meeting Flamel in Uzbekistan.*

Fortune, Dion (December 6, 1890–January 8, 1946)

Dion Fortune was an important British occultist and author whose works continue to influence modern Wicca, witchcraft and Neo-Paganism.

She was born Violet Mary Firth to a wealthy family in the steel business. She later adapted the family motto, "*Deo, non Fortuna,*" ("God, not fortune") for her magical name. Her mother was a Christian Scientist and from an early age, Violet was exposed to mystical concepts. She also began experiencing visions as a child, including one of her past incarnation as a priestess in Atlantis.

She was briefly involved with Blavatsky's Theosophical Society in London. She was initiated into the Golden Dawn in 1919 but allegedly disliked mingling Eastern and British occult traditions. A staunch British nationalist with an intensely Western orientation, she reacted against Eastern influences in Theosophy. She turned instead to mystical Christianity and especially British mythology regarding King Arthur and the Holy Grail.

Fortune was a student of occultist Theodore Moriarty who taught that the Christ Principle was first propounded in Atlantis and manifested through Horus, Mithras, Quetzalcoatl, and Buddha as well as Jesus. Fortune was also influenced by Carl Jung's ideas, especially his concept of the anima and animus. She studied both Freud and Jung, preferring Jung, but felt both lacked an adequate spiritual element.

Beginning in 1926, she published books on magical cosmology, Kabalah, practical magic and several novels with an occult theme. Fortune wrote before the repeal of the Witchcraft Act and it is thought that, for legal reasons, she obscured instructional material by writing it as fiction. Rituals in her novels have since been incorporated into modern Wiccan and Neo-Pagan rituals.

She left the Hermetic Order of the Golden Dawn in 1927 to found the Fraternity of Inner Light. Fortune died of leukemia at the age of 56.

The Society of the Inner Light continues to teach Western Esoteric traditions. The Society emphasizes that they are not associated with witchcraft in any way and that Fortune was neither a witch nor a member of a coven.

More information on her novels is found in **CREATIVE ARTS:** Literature. Other books include *Applied Magic* (1922), *Sane Occultism* (1926), *The Training and Work of an Initiate* (1930), *Psychic Self-Defence* (1930), and *The Mystical Qabbalah* (1936).

Gardner, Gerald Brosseau (June 13, 1884–February 12, 1964)

Author and scholar Gerald Gardner is the founder of modern Wicca, sometimes called Gardnerian Wicca both to honor him and to distinguish his tradition from earlier, less formalized ones.

Gardner was born near Liverpool, England into a prosperous family of Scottish descent. His ancestors included Vice Admiral Alan Gardner, Commander in Chief of the Channel Fleet against Napoleon and Grizel Gairdner, burned as a witch in 1610 in Newburgh, Scotland.

Gardner spent much of his life as a globetrotter and despite severe asthma was an inveterate and hardy traveler. In his youth, he was influenced by the books of the Spiritualist Florence Marryat. He developed a firm belief in the immortality of the soul and began studying occult and spiritual practices of the many places he visited around the world, discovering correspondences between many of them.

Gardner went to work at age 16 on a Ceylon tea plantation. He spent time in the jungle with local tribespeople. In 1908, he went to Borneo where he spent time with the Dyak people. He continued on to Malaysia where he entered government service. In 1923, he served as inspector of rubber plantations and then later as a customs officer. He eventually made a fortune as a rubber planter in Malaya and also served for a time as an inspector of opium establishments.

Wherever he traveled, he studied local magical customs as well as anthropology and archeology. He was an authority on the art and lore of knives and accumulated a vast collection. His first book *Keris and Other Malay Weapons* (1936) is considered an authoritative text on the magical weapons of Malaya and Indonesia. He received an honorary doctorate from the University of Singapore.

When he retired in January 1936 and returned to England, Gardner became involved with English witchcraft. He had originally wished to retire in Malaya but his English wife, whom he married in 1927, wished to return home. (Because of his asthma, Gardner still annually wintered outside England.)

The winter after his return, he visited Cyprus, Aphrodite's holy island. While there, he had various spiritual experiences that resulted in his wish to establish a temple of Aphrodite. He purchased land that already included the ruins of a temple, but the local authorities disapproved and Gardner was forced to leave and return to England.

He retired to the New Forest region of Hampshire where he made contact with local occultists. He met people who were members of establish covens and who held secret sabbats in the New Forest. Gardner became a devotee and claimed to be initiated by "Old Dorothy" Clutterbuck in 1939.

In 1939, Gardner published his first novel, *A Goddess Arrives*, which focused on devotions to Aphrodite in 1450 CE.

Gardner, along with Dorothy Clutterbuck and Dion Fortune, was involved in "Operation Cone of Power" on Lammas Day, 1940. British witches coordinated massive major rituals against Germany's threatened invasion of Britain.

In 1946, Gardner was introduced to Aleister Crowley by a mutual acquaintance, stage magician, puppet-master, occult scholar, and author Arnold Crowther. Their meeting is the crossroads where Ceremonial Magic met coven-based witchcraft. In the year before Crowley's death, the two renewed the relationship.

Gardnerian Wicca is the oldest formal Wiccan tradition and is based on the teachings of Gerald Gardner. The Gardnerian Book of Shadows, which he co-authored with High Priestess Doreen Valiente, is the standard text and liturgy for Gardnerian Wiccans. It was based on one belonging to the New Forest Coven he had joined but was heavily modified by him. He included contributions from Aleister Crowley, Charles Godfrey Leland, and Rudyard Kipling. Doreen Valiente edited and revised this Book of Shadows, contributing much of her own poetry.

Gardner started his own coven in Bricketts Wood, St Albans in 1947; they convened in a cottage on the grounds of a nudist colony where

Gardner was a member. He moved to the Isle of Man one year later, first living with Cecil Williamson (see page 769) who had earlier established the Witchcraft Research Centre there.

The last law against witchcraft was repealed in Britain in 1951. Prior to the 1951 repeal of the Witchcraft Act of 1604, books advocating the practice of witchcraft could not be published in the United Kingdom. Gardner had initially sidestepped the law, as had others before him (notably Dion Fortune), by publishing *High Magic's Aid* in 1949 as a novel or work of fiction. He was now free to publish *Witchcraft Today* in 1954—*a* factual work published under his own name. A companion volume, *The Meaning of Witchcraft*, was published in 1959. The books established Gardner as a spokesman for witchcraft and garnered him fame.

Gardner continued to travel, journeying to New Orleans to study Voodoo. He made two trips to West Africa, in 1951 and in 1952.

Gardner died at sea while returning to England on a cruise ship from Lebanon. He was taken ashore and buried in Tunis. He bequeathed his museum to his High Priestess Lady Olwen (Monique Wilson).

Hanussen, Erik Jan (June 2, 1889–March 25, 1933)

Prophet, clairvoyant, hypnotist, publisher, charlatan, and illusionist, Erik Jan Hanussen was, like Cagliostro, a conjurer in every sense of the word. Like Cagliostro he met a sad end; like Cagliostro, Hanussen was a celebrity. Once renowned, he is now largely forgotten, mainly because few wished to remember him: a Jewish man, sometimes described as the "Nazi Rasputin," Hitler was allegedly among his clients before Hanussen's fall from grace. Hanussen's former Nazi clients wished to forget that they had been scammed, while Jews and many occultists resent his involvement with the early Nazis.

Herschmann-Chaim Steinschneider, the future Jan Erik Hanussen, was born in a Vienna jail cell. His unwed mother, Julie Cohen, from an Orthodox Jewish family, had eloped with an actor Siegfried Steinschneider. She was nine months' pregnant when her enraged father had them arrested on phony charges of property theft.

It was standard practice for Austrian birth certificates to list the baby's religion and so Julie's son was classified as a "Hebrew male." That document would be his eventual downfall.

He displayed powerful clairvoyant skills by age three. On his father's side, he claimed descent from miracle-rabbis, celebrated for magical and healing skill. It is theorized that the name *Steinschneider* ("stone-cutter") derives from the practice of crafting amulets with engraved stone blocks.

At age 14, he ran away to join the circus, spending his adolescence mastering tricks, legerdemain, and confidence scams. He worked in a lion-taming act and as a fire-eater, a knife thrower, and he sometimes did a fake strongman act, snapping cardboard chains.

At the time, a popular form of entertainment involved demonstration of psychic skills to assembled crowds. The alleged clairvoyant would stand before a packed lecture-hall and proceed to reveal information about the supposed strangers assembled there. Obviously it was a system highly conducive to fraud. The clairvoyant would have secret assistants planted in the audience. Hanussen achieved tremendous acclaim in this way, sometimes via illusion and tricks but not always.

Hanussen possessed authentic clairvoyant skills. Sometimes he went into trance and offered genuine, honest, and not always popular prophesies, shocking even himself with his skills. A cynical man, he had a hard time believing in his own skills; however they are documented by various psychic incidents. He was also clairsentient: able to obtain information about objects by touching them.

An accomplished Tarot card reader and master hypnotist, Hanussen may have studied tricks and frauds but he also traveled through Egypt, the Middle East, Turkey, and Ethiopia, studying with genuine occult masters.

Harry was conscripted into the Austro-Hungarian army at the beginning of World War I. While conscripted he was offered the opportunity to present his telepathic act in Vienna on April 30, 1918. It was a golden opportunity but he knew he was unlikely to receive permission from his superiors, nor could he just openly perform without incurring severe punishment from the army. Therefore Harry Steinschneider disappeared off the face of the Earth; *"Eric Jan Hanussen, Danish clairvoyant"* was born in his place. The show was a success and Hanussen became a star.

Hanussen became a prominent occultist, consulted by law enforcement agencies in various sensational crimes. He appeared in a film and began a publishing empire, specializing in occult magazines. He became wealthy and famous, a fixture of Weimar Germany's decadent nightlife. His parties were scandalous; he allegedly hypnotized people who, while entranced, performed in ways they would later prefer not to remember.

Among those in his social circle were authors Thomas Mann and Hanns Heinz Ewers, and actor Peter Lorre. Aleister Crowley and Franz Bardon also traveled in these circles; although there is no documentation, it's likely they met.

On March 25, 1932, Hanussen predicted Hitler's electoral victory and success in his publication. This brought him to the attention of Hitler and other Nazis who allegedly began consulting him. It also brought him attention from those who opposed the Nazis; by the fall of 1932, rumors of Hanussen's ethnic origins were circulating—his past identity was an open secret. He made little pretense of being Danish and socialized with people from his past who knew him under many names.

In 1933, Hanussen leased a dilapidated mansion in Berlin; on February 26, 1933, the Palace of the Occult had its grand opening. It allegedly resembled a Pagan temple; Hanussen offered consultations and lectures, notably predicting the subsequent fire in the Reichstag. (His prediction was *too* good; as with William Lilly (see page 747) he was suspected of collusion.)

The Palace was lush and luxurious; Hanussen threw lavish parties attended by important members of the Nazi party but also simultaneously by occultists and entertainers, in particular Jewish occultists and entertainers. Whether he genuinely thought he could create some sort of integrated balance, whether he liked to live dangerously or was just self-destructive is subject to conjecture.

He was certainly courting danger by the end of his life; there were lots of illicit drugs and sex at his parties. He allegedly provided orgies for his new friends, which he secretly filmed, capturing important people in embarrassing moments. Rumors of these films, which have never surfaced, also circulated and may have contributed to his murder. Various highly placed Nazis were also allegedly indebted to him for great sums of money.

Hanussen was reckless: he bragged about his sessions with Hitler, whom he allegedly described as resembling an *"unemployed hairdresser."* Hanussen published an updated horoscope for Hitler; although predicting initial success, it also detailed (accurately) eventual, violent failure. Allegedly Hitler was furious, adjusting his birth time on future horoscopes by two hours so that similar results would not be obtained.

By the summer of 1932, Hanussen had advised friends that his days were numbered. He paid last goodbyes to several people. He never attempted to flee, however; instead at some point in February 1933, he simultaneously converted to Roman Catholicism and joined the Nazi Party.

At some point during this time, journalists located his original birth certificate and revealed his true ethnic origins. On March 24, 1933, he was arrested and charged with submitting a fraudulent Aryan certificate to gain admittance to the Nazi party. A squad of Nazi officers searched and looted his apartment and safe, demanding Hanussen surrender all loan receipts from Nazi debtors, which he did.

Hanussen was brought to Nazi headquarters, interrogated for two hours and released. Early next morning three men in Nazi uniforms broke into his apartment. He was taken to Gestapo headquarters where he was shot; his body was dumped in a field. His apartments and the Palace of the Occult were systematically searched and looted, his villa, yacht, jewelry and valuables confiscated.

Further information about Hanussen's life and adventures may be found in Mel Gordon's *Erik Jan Hanussen: Hitler's Jewish Clairvoyant* (Feral House, 2001).

By personal order of Josef Goebbels, Hitler's Chief of Propaganda, no word of Hanussen's murder was published in German newspapers although he was a very public figure. There was no investigation. He was eventually buried in a pauper's grave.

Hermes Trismegistus

Hermes Trismegistus was a legendary Egyptian master magician whose name means "Thrice Great Hermes." He allegedly composed the works now known as the *Hermetica*, laying the foundation for alchemy and Ceremonial Magic. He was the first to coin the term *"As above, so below,"* which is the cornerstone of astrology. He is credited with writing thousands of texts allegedly once contained in the Egyptian Temple of Neith in Sais, whose library supposedly contained works dating back nine thousand years. (See **WOMEN'S MYSTERIES:** Spinning Goddesses.)

"Hermeticism" is the term used to describe beliefs and practices deriving from a set of Greek writings known as the Hermetic Texts or *Hermetica*. Most modern historians date these texts to Alexandria between the first and third-centuries CE, although some suggest they're much older. These writings include teachings attributed to Hermes Trismegistus. See also Ficino.

Some believe the Tarot card called The Magician is intended to represent Hermes Trismegistus. Trismegistus may have been a man, a deity or a deified man. An alternative theory suggests he was the son of a deity and a human mother.

Among those identified as Hermes Trismegistus are:

🌟 *the Egyptian deity Thoth*

🌟 *the Greek deity Hermes*

🌟 *an otherwise anonymous Egyptian High Priest of Thoth*

🌟 *the biblical prophet Moses*

Some theorize that some or all of the above may in fact be identical.

Jesus (c.1–33)

A controversial legend, long discouraged and suppressed by the Church, is that Jesus was a magician. Count Cagliostro, for instance, described Jesus as *"the first and greatest magician who ever lived."*

The Church did not take that statement as a compliment. At the time of Jesus' life, Egypt, the Middle East, and the Mediterranean were filled with traveling magicians, many of whom specialized in healing and exorcisms. A few even claimed to have performed resurrections. (And Jesus does not perform the first or only resurrection in the Bible. The prophet Elisha earlier revives someone from the dead.)

Jesus was a contemporary of these magicians; he first came to attention as a miracle healer. His cures were what first made him famous. A recurrent theme and issue of the Gospels is that Jesus is divine, the Son of God, and not just another magician.

Was Jesus a magician or did his enemies just accuse him of being one in an attempt to deny the divine origin of his miracles? Part of the problem about attempting to answer that question is that virtually everything now known about Jesus was written by his devotees.

What did those who were not devotees say? Many, if not most ancient writings are now lost. In 396 CE, Emperor Constantine ordered books of *"heretics"* hunted down and eliminated. A series of decrees issued by Constantine and his successors ordered the discovery and destruction of written works that contradicted official teachings.

How do we now know anything about these writings and what they contained? Fragments of a few survive as do lists of lost books, and official refutations of their content survive. This is how we know that among the accusations early Christians were eager to refute were suggestions that Jesus was a magician. (Not everyone who perceived him as a magician presumably refuted his divinity. Simon Magus (see page 767) was openly acknowledged as a great magician but also worshipped by some as a god.)

A list of titles of lost books about Jesus attributed to Pope Gelasius (492–496 CE) ends: *"We declare that these and similar works which Simon Magus ... and all heretics and disciples or heretics or schismatics have taught or written ... are not only repudiated but indeed purged."*

Justin Martyr, writing in Rome between 150 and 165 CE, complained that Jews were describing Jesus as *"a Galilean magician."* (Among Jews, Galilee bore a reputation of retaining Pagan and/or less conventional Jewish traditions.)

Sometime near the end of the second century or the beginning of the third, a Platonist named

Celsus made a study of Christianity, writing a treatise attacking it. The treatise itself no longer exits. Following the political triumph of Christianity, all copies of the treatise were destroyed, but earlier, *c.*247, the Christian Origen (185–254) wrote a reply, *Against Celsus*, quoting from the original text, and *this* refutation survives.

Apparently Celsus began his attack by describing Jesus as a conjuror of miracles. Because Christians know that other conjurers will also claim to perform miracles by the power of God, they will not permit the presence of other conjurers. Celsus wrote that Jesus grew up in Galilee, went to Egypt as a hired laborer and returned home as a magical practitioner.

This theory suggests that what are described as miracles ascribed to Jesus were actually performed by controlling spirits, a forerunner of High Ceremonial Magic and Commanding and Compelling. King Solomon too allegedly commanded spirits and a powerful tradition of angelic magic already existed.

Although the most common legend is that Jesus allegedly learned magic in Egypt, an alternative theory suggests that he studied with master magicians in Babylonia. He reputedly performed miracles and resurrections (including his own) via the magical use of the Ineffable Name, the greatest of all spells.

> According to these legends, Jesus was allegedly tattooed with magical spells or symbols, known as *"the Egyptian marks."*

In the Roman world, Jews were renowned for exorcism skills and spirit-summoning magic in the same manner that the Greeks viewed Thessalians as powerful magicians or the Nordic people viewed Saami shamans as exceptionally powerful.

The Mandaeans of southern Iraq claim descent from devotees of John the Baptist. According to Mandaean tradition, Jesus was a magician in contact with Samaritan practitioners similar to Simon Magus.

In the Gospel of Matthew 27:62 some translations suggest that the Chief Priests tell Pilate, *"that deceiver said, while yet alive ..."* Other translations substitute the word *"magician"* for *"deceiver."* Similarly, the Gospel of John 18:30, in some translations, has the Chief Priests describing Jesus to Pilate as a *"malefactor"*—a word that during certain eras (notably the Burning Times) had powerful magical implications; the quote has been interpreted as indicating that Jesus is charged before Pilate with practicing magic.

Furthermore, among the crimes punishable by crucifixion are political sedition, rebellion against the empire, rebellions by slaves against masters, rabble rousing, *and* the practice of magic and witchcraft.

It is possible that, like Simon Magus, some early worshippers of Jesus, particularly Gnostic devotees, adored him as a sacred magician. It is also possible that the earliest Christians were not as vehemently anti-magic as they would eventually become, and that after Christianity gained official status, previous magical aspects of the religion were suppressed.

Early Christians used the fish or ChiRo as emblems of their faith rather than the cross. According to historian Morton Smith, author of *Jesus the Magician*, two of the three oldest representations of the crucifixion are engraved on magical gems while the third also probably refers to Christian magical beliefs. A fourth-century gold glass plate in the Vatican Library depicts Jesus as a magician complete with wand in the process of raising Lazarus from the dead.

It is not a malicious depiction. The image may be found on the cover of the 1978 paperback edition of Morton Smith's book.

Within Jesus' own lifetime, magicians began to use his name in spells as a Name of Power, although whether they considered themselves Christians is unknown. Acts 19:13 describes Jewish magicians and exorcists using Christ's name, and in the Magical Papyri and Greek curse tablets of the first and second centuries, Jesus' name is among those used to conjure and control spirits as well as perform exorcisms in Pagan as well as Christian spells.

> Further Reading: Morton Smith's *Jesus the Magician* (Harper & Row, 1978).

Joan of Arc (January 6, 1412–May 30, 1431)

The story of Joan of Arc, the illiterate French peasant girl who crowned a king, is well known. Joan emerged from the French countryside to lead French troops to victory. She was successful but was captured and placed on trial. Notably, the French king she had crowned made little if any attempt to rescue or ransom her, preferring to distance himself from her instead, although he did reward others in her entourage. Joan was eventually burned at the stake; five hundred years later she was canonized. Her story continues to elicit admiration and fascination. A question guaranteed to raise hackles and passions, then as now, is whether Joan was or wasn't a witch or a devotee of the Fairy Faith.

Joan was born in Domrémy, France. When Joan was 13, she heard a voice that she described as from God. During the next five years she heard sacred voices several times weekly. They identified themselves to her as those of the Archangel Michael and saints Catherine and Margaret.

According to the twelfth-century historian and chronicler Geoffrey of Monmouth, Merlin prophesied that *"a marvelous maid will come from the Nemus Cenutum for the healing of nations."* During Joan's time this mysterious *Nemus Cenutum* came to be identified with the Bois Chenue forest near Domrémy where a Fairy Tree was situated.

Among the accusations made against her was that Joan was in the habit of attending Friday-night witches' sabbats at a fountain near this oak.

The opposing English forces certainly perceived her as a witch. Both sides perceived her as possessing or having access to supernatural powers.

> Shakespeare's play *Henry VI* Part 1 expresses the contemporary English view that Joan was a witch: *"Bring forth the sorceress condemned to burn."*

Joan was captured at Compiègne on May 23, 1430 and charged with heresy and witchcraft. The bishop before whom she was brought was intent on proving her a witch. If it could be proved that Charles VII had gained the crown of France via witchcraft, the English could challenge his divine right to rule.

On what grounds was she charged with witchcraft? Her enemies charged that she spoke with evil spirits (demons) not saints or angels. They claimed that Joan had induced the voices by chewing on a mandrake root she carried tucked into her bosom. (During her trial she was asked whether she possessed a mandrake root; Joan denied this, although she admitted hearing of the practice—see **BOTANICALS:** Mandrake.)

The whole concept of a young girl leading an army was strange and radical; however Joan's brief campaign had been punctuated with odd occurrences that could be interpreted as signs of magical activity:

❋ *A man on horseback once swore at Joan, who despised foul language. She retorted,* "In God's name, why do you swear and you so near your death?" *An hour later, the rider fell from his horse into a moat and drowned. Clairvoyance? Divine revelation? Or witchcraft?*

❋ *Joan waited two days at Chinon before being granted a royal audience. She was shown into a grand hall where Charles played a trick on her. He was hidden among approximately 300 bystanders while someone else was dressed in royal garb. Joan, who had never seen Charles before, went straight to the true dauphin, saying,* "The King of Heaven sends words by me that you will be anointed and crowned …"

Other aspects could be interpreted as signs of witchcraft or Pagan faith if so desired. Joan first heard her voices at the Fairy Tree near Domrémy. The tree was situated by a healing well linked to the fairies. Allegedly fairies and witches danced around the tree together. When Joan was a child, she too had sung and danced around the tree with other village children. She hung garlands from it but claimed this was done to honor Our Lady of Domrémy. Joan denied all dealings with Fairies.

There are three ways of considering these actions:

❋ *Joan genuinely hung the garlands in honor of the Virgin Mary, although hanging garlands from trees is not exactly orthodox Christian practice.*

❋ *For whatever reason Joan refused to admit to having partaken of Fairy traditions.*

❋ *Through the process of Identification, traditions once associated with a Fairy Queen or Goddess were now performed in honor of Our Lady of Domrémy. Whether local peasants in Joan's time were aware of the history of the practice is unknown.*

Joan's power to heal was also considered by some as evidence of witchcraft. Her title, *La Pucelle* or "the Maid," could be interpreted as having witchcraft significance. In some covens, Maid or Maiden is a title for a high-ranking individual.

Joan refused to say the Lord's Prayer; years later this would be considered the equivalent of a confession of witchcraft. She was reputedly the friend or even lover of King Rene d'Anjou of Provence, who narrowly escaped charges of heresy himself. Joan also chose Gilles de Rais to serve as her patron and protector. Nine years later, he too was charged with witchcraft and executed.

Joan was imprisoned in a dungeon for one year and one week, often chained to a wooden block with chains securing her neck, arms, and feet. At her formal ecclesiastical trial before 37 clerical judges, Joan faced 70 charges including being a witch, diviner, sorceress, false prophetess, conjurer, and invoker of evil spirits, in addition to various charges involving heresy. She was accused of being *"given to the arts of magic."*

She represented herself and held her own with this powerful group of educated men. Most of the charges could not be substantiated and were dropped.

The Inquisitors continued with 12 charges, including the ability to see visions, heresy in refusing to submit to the authority of the Church, her insistence that she was responsible only to God and not the Church, and the one for which she was finally convicted and condemned to death: wearing men's clothing.

During the trial evidence favorable to Joan was deleted from the official record. The court scribe, Guillaume Mauchon, later claimed that when proceedings recorded in French were translated into Latin, the judges ordered him to change meanings and language.

On May 30, 1431, Joan was publicly burned at the stake. The authorities wished to destroy her mystique and prevent any rumors of last-minute supernatural rescue as had been circulating. When her clothes were burned off, the executioner was instructed to reduce the flames so that the crowd could see *all the secrets which can or should be in a woman.*

After her death, her remains were thrown in the river so that no sacred relics could be taken, although the crowd did collect ashes. According to tradition, a dove flew from her lips at the moment of her death. How one interprets this depends upon spiritual orientation. As a sign of the Holy Ghost? Or as a visible wandering double or fetch?

Joan became an unofficial saint immediately. Peasants set up shrines to her and carried votive images. Just as she had healed the sick while alive, Joan allegedly performed miracles of healing following her death. It took five hundred years of popular pressure, however, before Joan was eventually canonized on May 16, 1920.

Long before that though, she had been legally vindicated: in June 1456, Joan was declared a martyr in France; her oppressors were in turn described as heretics engaging in a political vendetta. One theory for her retrial is that after twenty years on the throne, Charles VII was annoyed by the rumors and innuendo that he had been placed there by a witch, and so he ordered a retrial.

Margaret Murray interpreted Joan of Arc's title *La Pucelle* to indicate her position as Maiden of a coven. Murray postulated that Joan was a "divine victim" who served as a substitute for a royal victim. Gerald Gardner claimed that questions of heresy would have been very easy to prove without need of questions regarding Fairies and witchcraft.

John, Dr (c.1801–August 23, 1885)

Dr John is the most famous of the male New Orleans Voodoo doctors. He worked closely with Marie Laveau, possibly serving as her teacher and mentor. His name retains renown because of its adoption by the New Orleans musician Mac Rebennack.

His birth name is unknown but Dr John was also known as Bayou John, Jean Bayou, John Montaigne, John Montanet, John Monet, Jean Racine (Racine means root), Jean Gris-Gris, Jean Macaque, Hoodoo John, and Voodoo John. He was a practitioner in New Orleans from the 1820s to the 1880s but flourished especially in the 1840s. He sold amulets and charms and was an accomplished astrologer. In his time, he was described as the *"black Cagliostro."*

He was born a prince in Senegal. His face displayed medicine scars (cicatrisation) from his native Africa believed to indicate Bambara heritage and royal status. Kidnapped by Spanish slavers, he eventually wound up in Cuba where he learned to be a chef. Allegedly his master was very fond of him and granted John's freedom in his will.

John took to sea; serving as a ship's cook, he traveled the world including trips back to Africa. When he got tired of traveling, he got off the ship in New Orleans where he lived for the rest of his life. He first worked as a cotton-roller, eventually attaining the status of overseer on the docks, and began to establish his magical practice. He allegedly practiced divination by interpreting marks on bales of cotton. Both black and white people began to consult him.

He is described as a large, charismatic man and an extremely effective healer. He became wealthy enough to retire from his day job and buy land on the Bayou Road, then a swamp, where he constructed a home. Eventually he owned substantial real-estate holdings on Bayou Road between Prieur and Roman Streets.

John Montanet appears in the United Census of 1850, 1860, 1870, and 1880. His address is given as 232 Prieur Street. In 1880, his age was given as 79. According to the 1880 census his household included five of his sons and daughters, the youngest only one year old.

Dr John served as a healer, magician, amulet-maker, and fortune-teller. He is described as divining via shells, perhaps the same or similar as the Yoruba cowrie shell divination system, *dilogun*.

Dr John unifies various spiritual, herbal, and magical traditions: it is unknown how old he was when he left Africa and what training he brought to the West but in Cuba he must have been familiar with Santeria and/or Palo, based on Yoruba and Congolese traditions respectively. New Orleans Voodoo, which he mastered and helped formulate is based on Dahomean spirituality combined with Congolese, Native American, and European traditions.

He was controversial. Although some adored him, he *enraged* others. He lived well, like the prince he was born. Dr John allegedly had a harem of some 15 women, white as well as black. His white wife especially aggravated some.

Like Cagliostro, Dr John maintained the equivalent of soup kitchens: the former chef himself cooked gumbo and jambalaya for the poor and hungry. At the end of his life he was in financial distress; he was not educated in finances and had been cheated of his real-estate holdings. He spent the end of his life living with a daughter. He died of Bright's disease on August 23, 1885. Folklorist Lafcadio Hearn eulogized him in an article published in *Harper's Weekly* on November 7, 1885, called "The Last of the Voodoos."

In *The New Orleans Voodoo Tarot*, by Louis Martinié and Sallie Ann Glassman (Destiny Books, 1992) Dr John plays the role of the Magician.

Kelley, Edward (August 1, 1555–1597)

Edward Kelley, also known as Edward Talbot or Edward Kelly, was an alchemist, spirit medium, and necromancer. However, he is most famous as the most successful scryer employed by Dr John Dee (see page 725). Together they created the system of Enochian Magic.

Kelley was apparently from Worcestershire. There is much conjecture about his history prior to his work with Dr Dee. He apparently studied law and Old English with the intention of entering the legal profession. He may or may not have studied at the University of Oxford under the name Talbot. He was fluent in Latin and proficient in Greek. He was adept at deciphering old scripts and documents and was a good copyist. Perhaps too good: Kelley always wore a tight black skullcap pulled down low over his ears, allegedly to conceal that they were missing. (Although this is frequently stated as fact, there is no evidence one way or the other.) His ears had allegedly been cropped as punishment for forgery or counterfeiting. Rumor had it he had been pilloried in Lancaster as punishment, too.

Kelley is usually described as being *"of ill repute"* and many believe he was a scam artist who conned the gullible Dee. (And for those who are ambivalent about magic, Dee can be a "good" magician, if Kelley is the fraud.)

Kelley and Dee met in 1581. Dee was passionately interested in contacting angels but needed a scryer (a crystal-gazer) to assist him. Kelley became Dee's scryer at a salary of £50 a year. Kelley saw and communicated with the spirits while Dee kept records. Kelley gazed within a crystal ball or magic mirror until he received visions or was able to make contact with spirits and angels. He spoke while Dee recorded his descriptions and conversation.

Dee was so enthusiastic about Kelley's scrying skills that Kelley complained of being kept a virtual prisoner at Dee's estate at Mortlake. Kelley periodically threatened to quit unless he received more money. Some interpret this as Kelley exploiting Dee, although one could argue that many skilled technicians frequently ask for raises without being accused of exploitation, and that Kelley never particularly wanted to scry; he was more interested in alchemy and necromancy. In any case, inevitably Dee gave in to his requests; they worked closely together for seven years.

Dee and Kelley's work together produced the occult tradition, Enochian Magic. In a trance, Kelley dictated *The Book of Enoch* to Dr Dee, which revealed mysteries of creation.

In 1583, Kelley and Dee traveled to Europe, together with their families, seeking patrons for their alchemical work. They gave public demonstrations of their alchemical gifts as they traveled. They also simultaneously continued their angelic communications.

Kelley allegedly was able to extract the Philosopher's Stone. His sister claimed that he made gold and silver and showed it to visitors in England. Arthur Dee, Dr Dee's son, claimed to have seen Kelley make gold. In April 1587, Kelley insisted on concentrating on alchemy and refused to scry for Dee any longer.

Kelley convinced Dee that the angels wanted them to share all things including their wives. Jane Dee was reluctant but Dr Dee agreed. It didn't work out: the two women had violent arguments. Their dire financial situation and the constant threat of legal persecution didn't help either. In 1589 Dee decided to go back to England. They never saw each other again.

Kelley continued to travel in Europe, looking for patrons and supplementing his income via fortune-telling. He was arrested at least once on charges of heresy and witchcraft.

Emperor Rudolf II of Bohemia ultimately became Kelley's patron, knighting him in 1593. He set him up in laboratory, expecting him to produce gold. Kelley was paid handsomely and temporarily enjoyed a lavish lifestyle. Rudolf grew tired of waiting for the gold, however, and periodically imprisoned Kelley, allegedly to stimulate him to produce gold faster. In 1597, Kelley was once again imprisoned, this time in the Castle of Hnevin where he died. According to legend, he tried to escape by lowering himself from the tower with a rope but the rope was too short and he fell, broke his leg and eventually died from his injuries (Whether or not he was chained in a dungeon when he died is subject to debate.)

Kingsford, Anna Bonus (September 16, 1846–February 22, 1888)

Anna Kingsford, a Christian occultist/spiritualist, established Theosophy in Britain and served as mentor to the magus Samuel MacGregor Mathers. Kingsford was among the first British women to become a physician; she obtained her medical degree in Paris as no British university would accept her as she was a woman.

Kingsford had had visions since early childhood. She was a passionate women's rights activist, an anti-vivisectionist, vegetarian, and animal rights activist. She believed herself to be the reincarnation of Mary Magdalen.

In 1882, Kingsford became president of the London Lodge of the Theosophical Society, although she was among Madame Blavatsky's rivals and critics. She once accused Blavatsky of attempting to cast a spell over her. Blavatsky dismissed Kingsford, describing her as a *"medium."* (Yes, Blavatsky was a medium, too …)

Kingsford's followers broke away from the Theosophical Society to form the Hermetic Society on April 22, 1884. (MacGregor Mathers was also a member.) Kingsford described the conflict in terms of Oriental Occultists (Blavatsky) versus Occidental Mystics (herself). She perceived Occultists as further down the spiritual evolutionary scale.

Kingsford died of chronic lung disease. Her revelations, received in trance and while asleep, were published posthumously in the book *Clothed With the Sun* (1889).

Laveau, Marie

Marie Laveau was a Voodoo priestess, medium, diviner, and spell-caster. She is credited with formalizing and establishing the tradition of New Orleans Voodoo. She has been called the Queen of Conjure; she proclaimed herself the Pope of Voodoo and few would disagree with her.

Marie's life is somewhat mysterious. She was born a free woman of color in New Orleans. Her date of birth is variously given as 1783, 1794, and 1801. She was of mixed African, European, and Native American ancestry, born to a family allegedly well versed in Hoodoo and Voodoo.

A "free person of color" was a legal classification of status in French colonial North America. French law distinguished between enslaved and free people of color. A free person of color was forced to carry papers proving their status so as not to be pressed into service as escaped slaves, as no doubt many were.

In 1819, Marie married Jacques Paris, a free man of color from Saint-Domingue, now modern Haiti, but Paris disappears from history within a few years. There is no known record of his death but Marie became known as the Widow Paris. She then entered into a relationship with Louis Christophe Dominic Duminy de Glapion until his death in 1855.

Legend had it that he too was a free man of color from Saint-Domingue, but historian Carolyn Morris Long, author of *Spiritual Merchants* (University of Tennessee Press, 2001) claims that based on death certificate and property succession records he was born in Louisiana, the legitimate son of white parents. He was allegedly related to the Haitian ruler Henri Christophe via his paternal grandfather, the French nobleman Chevalier Christophe de Glapion, Seigneur du Mesnil-Gauche.

Marie Laveau worked as a hairdresser, a position of tremendous power for a magical practitioner and not just because she was privy to intimate gossip, as has been suggested, but because she had access to *hair*. This is a powerful component in a vast variety of magic spells.

By approximately 1850, Marie Laveau was recognized as the leader of the New Orleans Voodoo community. She worked from her home, offering personal consultations and leading rituals. The Glapion-Laveau family lived at 152 St Ann Street. Marie's cottage was demolished in 1903. The site is now 1020–1022 St Ann Street.

Interviews with those who knew her describe her home as filled with lit candles. She had a statue of St Anthony turned upside down to make him "work" more efficiently and images of St Peter (Elegba?) and St Marron, an unofficial Louisiana saint. She also maintained an altar in the back of her house that featured statues of a bear, lion, tiger, and wolf.

Marie presided over annual St John's Eve (Midsummer's Eve) ritual celebrations on Lake Pontchartrain where she famously danced with her snake, the Grand Zombi. (Not *zombi* like the living dead; *zombi* as in a corruption of the Vodou magician lwa, Simbi. See **DIVINE WITCH**.)

A famous legend of Marie Laveau suggests that when she was elderly, she entered the lake, submerged and re-emerged as if she were decades younger. Devotees considered this proof of her power; skeptics believe this was how she retired and passed power to her daughter, also named Marie. Some believe Marie Laveau died on June 15, 1881. Others believe she never died

but kept regenerating herself and her power.

Marie's grave is in New Orleans' oldest cemetery, St Louis Cemetery Number One. It is visited annually by thousands who come to pay tribute to Mamzelle Marie Laveau, as she is known, and to beg for the favors she allegedly grants from beyond the grave. (There are also rumors suggesting that the Marie in the grave attributed to Marie Laveau is really High Priestess Marie Comtesse, a Voodoo Queen in late nineteenth-century New Orleans, known as La Comtesse.)

Leek, Sybil (February 22, 1922–October 26, 1982)

Astrologer, author, lecturer, witch, ghost-hunter, and radio and television personality, Sybil Leek was born at a crossroads where three rivers meet in what she described as a "witch-ridden" part of Staffordshire.

She claimed to be a hereditary witch of Russian and Irish descent. She traced her maternal Irish lineage back to 1134. On her father's side, she was descended from occultists affiliated with the royal court in Russia. She grew up in the New Forest region of England, one of the country's oldest surviving forests, and was largely home-schooled until age 11. Beginning in childhood, she studied astrology, occultism, witchcraft, the Kabalah and the Bible, and Eastern religions and philosophies.

Aleister Crowley was a family friend during her childhood and predicted great things for her. H.G. Wells was another friend of the family. In her twenties she moved into the New Forest where she lived among Romany horse-traders for a year, studying their herbal traditions.

She eventually became High Priestess of a New Forest coven. According to Leek, the New

Forest supported four distinct covens living in different sections of the wood. There were thirteen people per coven, six men and six women plus a High Priestess. Leek was the High Priestess of the Horsa Coven. She described the phenomenon of "religious" people who feared witches coming to the forest to seek healing from them anyway.

Leek ran an antique store in Burley. Her familiars included Mr Hotfoot Jackson, her jackdaw and Miss Sashima, a boa constrictor. She attracted too much notoriety, and some neighbors encouraged her to leave. Leek moved to the United States where she became an astrologer, which she described as her *first love.* Her 1969 autobiography, *Diary of a Witch*, was followed by dozens of other books.

Lenormand, Marie (May 27, 1772–June 25, 1843)

Marie Anne Adelaide Lenormand, an astrologer and fortune-teller, was known as "The Sibyl of the Faubourg Saint-Germain." She was born in Alençon, France. She left for Paris at age 21 where she started a salon with a partner, Madame Gilbert. She achieved great popularity and was consulted by thousands.

Among those who consulted her were French revolutionaries Marat, Robespierre, and St Just, whose deaths she allegedly predicted, but she is most famous for her relationship with Josephine de Beauharnais, Napoleon's future bride. Josephine, from Martinique, reputedly knew a thing or two about magic herself and was also a card-reader. Lenormand predicted her divorce from Napoleon, as well as Napoleon's own rise and fall. Lenormand read Napoleon's astrological chart for him.

When she correctly foretold Napoleon's intention to divorce Josephine, Napoleon had Lenormand imprisoned until the divorce was finalized. When she predicted the downfall of his Empire, he banished her from Paris.

Lenormand designed her own 36-card fortune-telling system. Neither Tarot nor playing cards but an original system, Lenormand decks, once obscure, underwent a sudden jolt in popularity in the second decade of the 21st century.

Lenormand was also a skilled palm-reader and studied numerology and Kabalah. Her grave in Paris' famed Père Lachaise Cemetery has evolved into a pilgrimage point for card readers.

Levi, Eliphas (c.1810–October 12, 1875)

French occultist Eliphas Levi exerted tremendous influence over contemporary metaphysical traditions. He was born Alphonse Louis Constant in Paris, a shoemaker's son. He was educated at Roman Catholic schools and at the seminary of St Sulpice, and was eventually ordained as a deacon in 1835. He had an early fascination with the occult, especially the works of Cornelius Agrippa and Francis Barrett's grimoire *The Magus*. He studied the *Sacred Magic of Abramelin the Mage* and pursued studies in advanced Kabalah.

He was eventually expelled from St Sulpice; exactly why is unclear. Various reasons have been offered: either he taught doctrines contrary to the Church, had radical political values, difficulty maintaining his vow of celibacy, or all or some of the above. He eventually adopted the magical name Eliphas Levi.

His first book, *The Dogma and Ritual of High Magic*, was published in 1861 and linked Tarot to the Kabalah and the 22 letters of the Hebrew alphabet. He connected the four suits of cards to the four natural elements and the four letters of the Tetragrammaton.

Levi was a powerful influence on the Golden Dawn, who incorporated Levi's rituals, and also on Aleister Crowley who, born on the day Levi died, believed himself to be a reincarnation of Levi.

Levi committed his life to metaphysical study and practice. He suffered tremendous financial hardship—at one point he was virtually homeless. However, Adolphe Desbarolles, a successful palm-reader, came to his assistance, giving him a room in a lovely house at 19, Avenue de Maine in Paris, where Levi began attracting students. He taught various occult arts until his death.

His works include *Doctrine of Transcendental Magic*, *History of Magic*, *The Key of the Grand Mysteries*, and *Fables and Symbols*.

Lilly, William (May 1, 1602–June 9, 1681)

William Lilly was an astrologer, prophet, publisher of almanacs, and treasure hunter. He was known as the "English Merlin."

He came from a family of yeoman farmers but young William had no interest or aptitude for farming. Lilly learned astrology from a Mr Evans, a well-known necromancer of the time, who had allegedly been consulted by Lord Bothwell, Mary Queen of Scots' third husband.

In 1636, Lilly bought a house at Hersham, near Walton-on-Thames, Surrey where he carried out his studies and consultations. In 1644, he published the *Prophetical Almanack*, which brought him prominence and renown. He continued to write and publish this almanac until his death as well as writing a number of books devoted to astrology.

Allegedly Lilly had over 2,000 occult consultations each year between 1645 and 1660. Lilly's predictions had a high reputation for accuracy. Among those who frequently consulted with him was King Charles I. Lilly foretold the Great Fire of London in 1666 so accurately that he was arrested on charges of arson. He was later proven innocent.

Lilly managed to stay in the good graces of Charles *and* Charles' opponents. He was consulted as to where Charles should retire when he escaped from Hampton Court. Lilly's advice was allegedly not followed. Also, allegedly, Lilly provided the saw and acid with which Charles nearly removed the bars of a window during an attempt to escape from Carisbrooke Castle, the fortress on the Isle of Wight where he was imprisoned prior to his execution.

Lilly exerted great influence during the English Civil War. His prophesies in *Merlinus Anglicanus* were used by leaders on both sides. In 1649, Lilly received a pension amounting to £100 a year from the Council of State.

Mathers, Moina (February 28, 1865–July 25, 1928)

Moina Mathers was a High Priestess, occultist, and a founding member of the Golden Dawn. Born Mina Bergson in Geneva, Switzerland, she was the fourth of seven children. One brother would become the renowned French philosopher Henri Bergson.

The family on her father's side were reputedly Kabalah scholars, although as Kabalah was traditionally not taught to women (at least not publicly), it's unknown whether Mina learned any of this tradition at home.

The family moved incessantly across Europe as her father attempted to support his family via a musical career. Eventually they settled in London where Mina, an accomplished artist, attended the Slade School of Art where she became good friends with Anne Horniman, a tea heiress, who later would become the main financial supporter of the Golden Dawn.

In November 1887, Mina was sketching in the Egyptian hall of the British Museum when she met Samuel MacGregor Mathers. Although her parents disapproved, they were married on June 16, 1890 in the library of the Horniman Museum. Mina changed her name to the more Celtic Moina so as to give it a more *"Highland ring"* in keeping with Mathers' predilections. Her motto was *Vestiga Nulla Retrorsum*, "I never retrace my steps."

Moina referred to Mathers as her teacher, husband, and friend. They agreed from the outset of their relationship to abstain from sexual intercourse although exactly why is unknown. They were extremely devoted to each other. Moina had an excellent command of Hebrew and there is some speculation that she actually did much of the Hebrew translation credited to Mathers. Certainly it is safe to say that she contributed to his work, although always without official credit. She was also clairvoyant and served as a medium.

In 1892, the Mathers moved to Paris where they lived in abject poverty. In 1894, they established the Ahathoor Temple there. Moina adored Mathers and allowed him the limelight but she worked alongside him until he died.

Her magical and metaphysical contributions are often overlooked in favor of the scandals with which she was involved. Dion Fortune, with whom Moina feuded, claimed that Moina had subjected Fortune to psychic attack and was responsible for the magical murder of Fortune's friend Netta Fornario, although Moina had died eighteen months before Fornario.

After MacGregor Mathers' death, Moina returned to London in 1919 where she directed the Alpha et Omega Lodge for nine years. She was in desperate financial straits in London. Her health began to fail. Eventually she stopped eating although, as with her abstention from sex, exactly *why* is unknown. She died at St Mary Abbott's Hospital on July 25, 1928.

Further Reading: Rare information about Moina Mathers and the other women so crucial to the development of the Golden Dawn is found in Mary K. Greer's *Women of the Golden Dawn: Rebels and Priestesses* (Park Street Press, 1995).

Mathers, Samuel L. MacGregor (January 8, 1854–November 20, 1918)

Samuel L. "MacGregor" Mathers was perhaps the most important member of the Golden Dawn, responsible for the creation of most of their rituals. He was the first to translate various occult texts into English.

Samuel Liddel Mathers was born in London; he claimed to be of Highland Scottish ancestry, a member of Clan MacGregor, and hence his eventual adoption of that name. He is most popularly called MacGregor Mathers. He was very devoted to his Scottish heritage and frequently dressed in Highland garb complete with kilt. (He liked to dress as an Egyptian priest too.)

He was a fervid vegetarian and anti-vivisectionist, a non-smoker at a time when it was customary for men to smoke. He was a strong believer in women's rights and equality and insisted that women be equal partners and participants in all facets of the Golden Dawn.

Mathers insisted that the order respect the truths of all religions. He created a flexible system of magic that could be used in various ways. He was a self-taught scholar with a sound knowledge of French, Greek, and Latin as well as some Coptic, Gaelic, and Hebrew.

Mathers' major intent and goal was the translation and publication of key magical documents that might otherwise languish in obscurity in museum and library archives. He dedicated his life to the study of the Western Mystery Tradition.

He was initiated into Masonry in 1877. Within 18 months he became a Master Mason although he later resigned in order to devote himself to the new order, The Golden Dawn.

Mathers made the first English translation of Christian Knorr von Rosenroth's, *Kabbalah Unveiled* in 1887. His mentor was Anna Kingsford (see page 744) to whom he dedicated the work. In 1892, Mathers moved to Paris with his wife, Moina (see page 748), where he began translating the classical grimoires into English, including *The Sacred Magic of Abramelin the Mage*.

He was Chief of the Second Order of the Golden Dawn and author of almost all the Golden Dawn documents and teachings. Mathers introduced the Egyptian pantheon into the Golden Dawn.

He returned to London in 1910 to engage in litigation with Aleister Crowley over Golden Dawn secrets that Crowley had published in his magazine *Equinox*. Mathers was unsuccessful, however, and returned to Paris in 1912.

Moina Mathers felt her husband eventually died of exhaustion caused by the accumulated effects of his profound metaphysical work. Dion Fortune stated that he died of Spanish Influenza but no cause of death is listed on his death certificate. It is unknown where he is buried.

Among his many works are *The Tarot: A Short Treatise on Reading Cards, Egyptian Symbolism, The Grimoire of Armadel, The Tarot, Its Occult Significance and Methods of Play, The Key of Solomon the King: Clavicula Solomonis, The Sacred Magic of Abramelin the Mage,* and *Astral Projection, Ritual Magic and Alchemy.*

Medea

High Priestess of Hecate, Circe's niece, herbalist supreme, potions-mistress and spell-caster,

Medea is among those serving as prototypes of the witch.

Medea's name is related to *metis* or "wisdom" and is usually translated as "the cunning one." She was the daughter of the King of Colchis, now part of modern Georgia. Her mother is variously described as an "ocean spirit" or even as Hecate herself. (Whether this was meant literally or whether Hecate should be considered her spiritual mother is subject to interpretation.) Medea is Hecate's priestess and acolyte. She may channel and embody the goddess.

Circe, Medea's aunt, is plainly a spirit; Homer uses the word *"goddess"* to describe her. Medea may or may not be a human being. It has been suggested that she is a pre-Olympian deity whose murders reflect past human sacrifices.

Medea was the central figure in at least ten Greek and Roman plays, of which only two survive in more than fragmentary form. From what does survive, she seems to have usually been portrayed as a foreigner witch. (Whether anything survives—or existed—in her Georgian homeland is unknown.)

She is the hero who accomplishes the task Jason is given credit for, obtaining the Golden Fleece.

In order to gain his throne, Jason, a disenfranchised prince of Iolchus in Thessaly, must obtain the Golden Fleece, which hangs on a branch in a grove in Colchis on the shores of the Black Sea. Jason was a student of the centaur Chiron and under the protection of the goddess Hera. The Argonauts include the shaman Orpheus, the sons of the North Wind, and even, for a while, Heracles.

Aeëtes, King of Colchis, son of Helios the Sun and brother of Circe, wishes to retain the Golden Fleece. He sets a task for Jason that should result in certain death, which would please both himself and the king of Iolchus and maintain the status quo. The appointed task, to be accomplished between sunrise and sunset, was to harness Aeëtes' fire-breathing bulls, plough up a field and sow it with dragon's teeth. If Jason is successful, he gets the Golden Fleece. If he fails, Aeëtes will snip out the tongues and lop off the hands of Jason and the Argonauts.

However Jason has Hera on his side. Hera asks Aphrodite to tell Eros to shoot Medea with an arrow of love. She falls madly in love with Jason. Without being asked, Medea concocts a salve for him that renders him safe from fire or iron for 24 hours. She requests that Jason meet her at the Temple of Hecate where she tells him she loves him enough to betray her father and gives him the salve. Jason says he loves her too and swears by all the gods to make her his queen and love her for ever, much to the delight of Hera, Aphrodite, and Eros.

Although Jason fulfills the task, Aeëtes has no intention of giving him the Fleece. He orders his men to seize the Argo and kill the foreigners at daybreak. Medea warns Jason, telling him to take the Golden Fleece and run.

At night, she leads him to the grove where the Fleece is guarded by a sleepless dragon. Medea bewitches it via incantations so that it does fall asleep. (Notably she does not kill the dragon, Hecate's sacred creature.) Jason and Medea grab the Fleece and escape.

When the king's men go to attack the Argo at dawn, it's gone, as is the Fleece and the king's daughter. Ships are sent in pursuit. A faster ship, steered by one of Aeëtes' sons, overtakes the Argo. Medea again saves Jason: she arranges an ambush for her brother on a nearby island, having tricked him into meeting her. Jason kills Medea's brother, and her father has to stop the pursuit in order to give his son immediate funeral rites.

After various adventures Jason and Medea finally arrive at Iolchus, Jason having been gone now for years. Jason is warned that Pelias the king knows he's back and intends to kill him. Once again, Medea saves him. Disguised as a humble old crone witch peddling magical herbs that will rejuvenate the old, Medea tricks Pelias' daughters into boiling their father to death.

The throne now belongs to Jason. He is welcomed home as a hero but the people don't trust Medea, perceiving her as a foreigner witch. They refuse to accept her as queen and so another king is chosen in Jason's place. Jason and Medea flee to Corinth.

Jason doesn't love Medea anymore. He asks her to leave so that he can marry the Princess of Corinth and inherit her father's kingdom. Medea sends a magic robe to his bride-to-be. It's irresistibly beautiful, but as soon as the bride tries it on, it goes up in flames, as does her entire palace. Medea escapes in a chariot drawn by two dragons, sent for her by Hecate. (Other versions of the myth have her escaping in a chariot sent by her grandfather Helios, the Sun god.)

What happens to Medea then? Again there are different versions:

🜏 *In her youth, Medea rejected Zeus' advances, thereby earning Hera's eternal devotion. Although she dies (she commits suicide), she is sent to the Isles of the Blessed, the Greek paradise, where she is happily married to Achilles*

🜏 *Now (or always) a goddess, she travels to Italy where she assumes the name Angitia*

🜏 *She married King Aegeus of Athens and tried but failed to poison Theseus*

🜏 *She went to Asia where the Medes were named in her honor*

Merlin

Merlin's very name has become a synonym for wizardry. He was a poet, prophet, magician, hermit, teacher, and wizard. A Welsh origin is most commonly attributed although claims are also made by Brittany, Ireland, and Scotland. One version suggests he was born off the coast of Brittany, on an island associated with witchcraft during the Roman era.

There are *countless* legends featuring Merlin. Many are contradictory; they may not all be of the same person. In most versions, Merlin's mother is a princess. His father is a mystery.

One story suggests that Merlin's mother lost her way home and slept beneath a tree in the woods where a Wild Forest Man discovered her. Merlin inherited his prophetic ability from his father and was periodically seized by fits of wildness that drive him into the woods to live like a wild man. He finally arranges his own capture so that his prophetic ability will be of service to others. Disguised as a stag, he reveals how to capture a wild man (himself) who is the only one able to interpret the King's ominous dreams.

Legends once suggested that Merlin was responsible for Stonehenge. One of the Welsh Triads suggests that Britain was once called *Clas Myrddin* (Merlin's Enclosure) in his honor. Merlin may originally have been a deity or a deified ancestor. Some suggest he was worshipped at Stonehenge.

Merlin either fought with or against King Gwenddolau, a British king believed to have Druid connections, at the Battle of Arfderydd in

573 CE. Merlin and his brothers fought; all the brothers except Merlin were killed. In grief, Merlin escaped to the forest of Celidon in the Scottish Lowlands where he lived as a wild man (*Merlin Wyllt*) together with his sister Gwenddydd, living on berries, writing prophesies and consorting with spirits. He eventually emerged from the forest to become the sage Merlin Emrys.

In a later legend, the devil (or a demon) is Merlin's father: Merlin was intended by Satan to be the Anti-Christ but his mother's confessor had the foresight to baptize baby Merlin at birth so that he turns out to be benign not evil.

> Merlin has powerful associations with women: in early legends, Merlin is closely identified with his sister, a female magician. Some legends suggest that Gwenddydd taught Merlin all he knew. In later Arthurian legends, Merlin is the *"good"* male magician as opposed to *"wicked"* female magicians, especially Morgan le Fay.

Merlin allegedly orchestrated the birth of King Arthur and supervised his upbringing until he could assume his throne. Merlin served as Arthur's advisor and protector; it isn't until Merlin eventually disappears that Arthur's kingdom and the Society of Knights of the Round Table began their final deterioration.

Merlin's disappearance involves his love life. One version suggests that Merlin fell in love with Nimue, the Lady of the Lake, but the feeling wasn't mutual. She feels threatened by him, justifiably, as he creates a spell to bind her to him. She begs him to teach her magical arts. He agrees and takes her to a lakeside grotto where she casts a spell on Merlin that he himself taught her. Merlin now sleeps in that cave for eternity.

According to another version, Merlin met the fairy Vivien in the Forest of Broceliande in Brittany. He fell in love with her and allowed himself to be enchanted. Merlin was resting beside a spring in the forest when Vivien appeared and asked what he was doing. Merlin gave her a magical demonstration: he traced sigils in the grass and a castle complete with knights and ladies appeared.

Vivien is charmed and asks to keep the castle grounds, named the "Joyous Garden" after Merlin dismisses the vision. The pair promise to rendezvous a year later on Midsummer's Eve. Merlin goes to England for Arthur and Guinevere's wedding but then returns to Broceliande where he is enchanted by Vivien.

He tells her how to perform a binding spell and then goes to sleep. She circumambulates him nine times chanting incantations. Some depict her action as treacherous but the romantic might perceive that having found bliss, Merlin wished to retain it forever and that he and Vivien lived (and live) happily ever after. Some identify Vivien as the Lady of the Lake.

> There are also other versions of what happened to Merlin:
>
> ❋ He transformed himself into an oak following Vivien's rejection
>
> ❋ He fled in the face of Christianity accompanied by a party of nine including bards to Bardsey Island off the Lleyn Peninsula, taking with him Britain's Thirteen Treasures

The first fully developed written account of Merlin was Geoffrey of Monmouth's *The Little Book of Merlin* or *Merlin's Prophesies*, written *c.*1135. Nennius' ninth-century *History of the Britons* told the tale of a fatherless boy and red and white dragons battling beneath the foundations of a tower. Geoffrey identified the boy as Merlin although this may have been based on oral tradition.

Geoffrey of Monmouth was also the first to turn Arthur from a Pagan warrior into a romantic (and Christian) hero. He wrote *History of the Kings of Britain c.*1160, combining legend and invention. How much was true? How much based on oral tradition, how much pure literary invention or embellishment? Who knows? Geoffrey was fluent in Welsh and Latin and he refers to an earlier book written in Welsh as his source of information. However this book has not yet been located.

Murray, Margaret (July 13, 1863–November 13, 1963)

Margaret Alice Murray, British author, archeologist, anthropologist, and Egyptologist, is perceived by some to be the mother of contemporary witchcraft.

Her work evokes passionate reactions in many; some venerate Murray; others openly despise her. Many who disagree with her theories are quite disrespectful toward her. She is frequently described as a "crackpot." Many fellow anthropologists and historians are quite dismissive toward her, beyond professional criticism. Whether one agrees with her theories or not, Margaret Murray was an eminently educated woman and was once considered an authority in her field.

Born in Calcutta, she studied archeology at Cambridge University, joining its faculty in 1899 at a time when very few women served in such positions. She studied Egyptian hieroglyphics, holding the position of Assistant Professor of Egyptology until 1935. She went on various archeological digs in the United Kingdom, Middle East, Egypt and the Mediterranean, including Sir Flinders Petrie's excavations at the Egyptian holy city of Abydos.

Having studied Sir James Frazer's *The Golden Bough* and Charles Leland's *Aradia, or the Gospel of the Witches*, Murray developed an interest in witchcraft, theorizing that it was a pre-Christian Pagan religion. She began studying witch-trial records.

In 1921, Murray published *The Witch Cult in Western Europe*, which stated that victims of the witch-hunts were practitioners of surviving Pagan religions. The controversial theories described within were embraced by Gerald Gardner but disputed by other scholars. Her theories would be a major influence on Gardnerian Wicca.

Among the issues regarding her work is that she based her theories on witch-trial testimony (particularly from Scotland) obtained under torture. Murray cited the consistency of many concessions. Was this consistency proof of witchcraft, as she surmised, or proof of the witch-hunters' obsessive need for consistency?

Another argument against her theories is that she virtually ignored trial records from outside Western Europe. Her information derives heavily from the British Isles and France with little emphasis on Germany, which had a *massive* witch-hunt, or Central and Eastern Europe.

According to her (very hostile) critics, Murray was guilty of selective editing: she was accused of inventing or slanting evidence and lost scholarly credibility. She quoted witch-trial defendants extensively but deleted what she seems to have perceived as "fairy tale" parts such as shape-shifting, riding through the air and other magical elements. Murray was interested in the religious and spiritual aspects of witchcraft, not necessarily any magical or shamanic parts. Thus she emphasized what she perceived as spiritual aspects of Paganism but eliminated the shamanic. Her work is actually quite reflective of the tension between the two camps—magic/shamanic vs spiritual—that still resounds today.

Ironically, Murray has been somewhat rehabilitated in recent years by witchcraft historians like Carlo Ginzburg who have explored genuine shamanic elements emerging from witch-trial records, the Benandanti for instance, and who suggest that even if all of Murray's theories are not correct, she was a pioneer to recognize the existence of European Pagan vestiges.

Murray was not the first to postulate that witches represented pre-Christian traditions, although she was the first to do so in English. In 1749, Girolamo Tartarotti published a book in Italian, *Del Congresso Nottorno delle Lammie*, stating that witchcraft derives from rites of Diana.

The person frequently credited as the first to put forward the idea that witches represented pre-Christian traditions was Karl-Ernst Jarcke, Professor of Criminal law at the University of Berlin. In 1828, he edited seventeenth-century German witch-trial records for a legal journal, adding his own commentary. He argued that witchcraft was a survival of the nature religion of pre-Christian Germans. According to Jarcke, the Church condemned this surviving nature religion, identifying it with devil worship so intensely that over time even witchcraft's own devotees subscribed to the Church's notion.

Jarcke was a devote Roman Catholic and *not* sympathetic to witches. Margaret Murray's radicalism may have been in being the first to publicly express empathy and sympathy for witches, and there are those who believe that this is what actually created the controversy that still surrounds her work.

Margaret Murray's other books include:

✳ The God of the Witches *(1933), which focused on the horned god and the Paleolithic origins of witchcraft*

✳ The Divine King *in England (1954), which argued that all English kings from the eleventh to the early seventeenth centuries secretly practiced witchcraft and died ritual deaths, similar to those described in Frazer's* The Golden Bough. *The general response to The Divine King was mockery. Branded a crackpot, many simply dismissed* all *Murray's work*

Nostradamus, Michel De (December 14, 1503– July 2, 1566)

The most famous prophet perhaps of all time, Nostradamus was also an astrologer, *"celestial scientist,"* herbalist, healer, and formulator of prized cosmetics and fruit preserves: his recipe for quince jelly won acclaim from the Papal Legate of Avignon.

Michel de Nostredame was born in Provence of Jewish ancestry. His maternal grandfather, Jean de Saint Remy was the astrologer/physician for Rene d'Anjou, Ruler of Provence. Under Rene d'Anjou, Provence was a haven for Jews; following the death of his heir, however, Provence reverted to the less-tolerant French crown; an Edict of September 26, 1501 gave Provençal Jews three months to convert or leave. The family converted before the birth of Nostradamus and his two brothers.

Michel was raised and schooled by his grandfathers, who taught him Greek, Hebrew, Latin, astrology, and Kabalah. At age 14, he studied liberal arts at the University of Avignon where his fellow students dubbed him *"the little astrologer."*

Indeed, Michel wished to become an astrologer but his family feared that metaphysical interests combined with Jewish ancestry would make him a target for the Inquisition and advised a more circumspect career. So instead, Michel studied medicine at the acclaimed University of Montpelier.

Nostradamus earned tremendous renown as a healer, allegedly exhibiting great courage in the face of the Plague as well as creativity and resourcefulness, i.e., he was an unorthodox healer. His unconventional medical practices eventually brought him into conflict with the local medical authorities. Nostradamus *resolutely* opposed bleeding patients, then standard medical practice, and instead emphasized hygiene and cleanliness, which was then very controversial.

A fresh wave of the Bubonic Plague struck; although he saved many patients, his wife and children died. This was the beginning of a turbulent time for him. He had conflicts with patrons and many patients abandoned him after he was unable to save his own family; his deceased wife's family went to court to try to recover her dowry.

A few years earlier, in 1534, he had sarcastically told a workman casting a bronze Madonna that the workman was casting devils instead. Several years later when, having lost his patrons, clients, and much income, Nostradamus was perceived as vulnerable, the workman alerted authorities of the remark, which, *at best*, reeked of Protestantism. (Nostradamus did not deny the statement but claimed it referred to the mediocrity of the art.) In 1538, he was ordered to appear before the Inquisitor of Toulouse. Instead he hit the road.

For the greater part of a decade, he wandered. Little record of him exists for the next six years but it's known that he traveled through Lorraine, Venice, and Sicily where he studied with Sufi mystics. He visited alchemists, astrologers, healers, Kabalists, diviners, and magicians and studied the works of Paracelsus and Agrippa.

He eventually returned to Provence where, on November 11, 1547, he married a rich widow with whom he had six children, three daughters and three sons. He settled in Salon-de-Provence, living there for the rest of his life. The street where he lived, in his time Rue du Moulin-d'Isnard, has been renamed Rue Nostradamus; his home has been restored and is now a museum.

Nostradamus owned treasured copies of the *Key of Solomon* as well as various Kabalistic works but wrote that he burned them when the Inquisition got too close. (See **BOOKS**: Grimoires: *Key of Solomon*; **MAGICAL ARTS**: Kabalah.)

He converted the upper floor of his home to a metaphysical laboratory. As far as is known, Nostradamus did not engage in prophesy until his return to Provence. His prophecies were derived via a combination of astrology and scrying. (See **MAGICAL ARTS**: Astrology, Divination.)

Inspired by the prophetic pythonesses of Delphi, Nostradamus sat atop a high tripod, whose legs were angled at the same degree as the Egyptian pyramids, and gazed down into a brass bowl filled with steaming water to which essential oils were added, placed atop another tripod. (See **TOOLS**: Tripod.) He saw visions of the future and then recorded them, believing his psychic vision was a divine gift.

In 1550, he published his first almanac, containing his predictions as well as weather, astrology, and standard almanac information. His almanac was a success and he published an annual almanac for the rest of his life.

His first prophecies were cautious; they were not written as straightforward predictions but as quatrains (four-line poems). Each almanac contains twelve quatrains, one prophecy for each month of the year.

He began a more ambitious series of books, titled the *Centuries*: ten volumes each containing 100 quatrains, totaling one thousand predictions. It is these predictions published in the *Centuries* that have earned Nostradamus the renown that makes his very name a synonym for prophesy.

The verses are not easy to read. Writing prophecies and practicing divination was dangerous and controversial and thus, for his own protection, the verses are mysterious and obtuse, written in anagrams and riddles in a mixture of Greek, Italian, Latin, and Provençal. They must be interpreted. From first publication until today, people have argued and debated about the meaning, accuracy, and veracity of Nostradamus' predictions. Prophecies extend until at least 3797 CE and so these debates are in no danger of dissipation.

The project was initiated on Good Friday, 1554. Four volumes were published in Lyons in 1555 to tremendous interest and success. They were bestsellers of the time and Nostradamus developed a huge following among the nobility and the upper classes. However, others described him as a tool of Satan. Medical colleagues were embarrassed by his forays into prophecy and the occult and repudiated him.

In 1556, Nostradamus was summoned to the court of French Queen Catherine de Medici (April 13, 1519–January 5, 1589), who was deeply involved with the occult and maintained a staff of astrologers, diviners, and magicians, most brought from her native Italy. Although superficially a devout Catholic, Catherine allegedly practiced Pagan rites in private, keeping a staff of priestesses devoted to Pagan deities. She had a wide collection of occult books and was a skilled mirror reader in her own right.

Nostradamus arrived in Paris and promptly became a celebrity. According to legend, the strenuous journey to Paris took a month. When he finally arrived, he was stricken with an attack of gout and laid up in bed for ten days. A steady stream of people came to visit, consult, and pay court to him, at a time when he really wished peace and quiet. Nostradamus, exasperated at a persistent knocking on his door, called through the door, *"What's the matter, page? This is a lot of noise over a lost dog. Look on the road to Orleans; you'll find the dog on a leash."* Indeed, the boy outside his door was a young page, employed by a renowned family, desperately seeking the valuable, lost dog entrusted to him. He followed Nostradamus' directions and discovered another servant who had located the dog bringing it home on a leash. The story circulated and further cemented Nostradamus' reputation.

Nostradamus had published a prediction that Catherine's husband, King Henri II, would either become a second Charlemagne and heal the breach between French Catholics and Protestants *or* be killed in a jousting accident. Months earlier, apparently unbeknownst to Nostradamus, Catherine's astrologer Luc Gauric had made a similar prediction, advising the king to avoid jousting, although Gauric's prediction lacked the specific, poetic detail of Nostradamus':

The young lion will overcome the older one
On the field of combat in single battle
He will pierce his eyes through a golden cage
Two wounds made one, then he dies a cruel death

(Century 1, Quatrain 35)

Catherine interviewed Nostradamus in depth and was very impressed with him. She consulted with him for the rest of his life. She had Nostradamus cast the horoscopes of the royal children, all of whom were doomed to sad fates. Nostradamus was not only a prophet but a diplomat, managing to deliver his prophecies delicately. He did not fall from favor with Catherine nor did she ever claim his prophecies were inaccurate. (He told her all her sons would be kings, which was true, if only because of their early deaths and the death of their father.)

Catherine took Nostradamus' predictions seriously but Henri did not. He was killed in a joust with the Captain of his Scottish Guards, Count de Montgomery. A splinter from Montgomery's lance pierced the king's golden visor and entered his eye, simultaneously blinding him and penetrating his brain. Henri II died after ten days of excruciating suffering.

When their prophecies ultimately proved true, Gauric and Nostradamus were blamed. Crowds burned Nostradamus (the more famous of the two) in effigy. Rumors spread that the Inquisition was looking for him and he headed home.

Nostradamus remained famous for the rest of his life, variously admired or vilified. The local nobility flocked to have their horoscopes cast and buy the cosmetics he formulated. (The term "aromatherapy" hadn't been coined yet; however Nostradamus may be understood to have been the equivalent of an aromatherapist.) He was always controversial, however, and was periodically accused of Satanism, of being a secret Jew, and/or of practicing witchcraft, although his association with Catherine de Medici ultimately protected him.

Books appeared accusing him of heresy, witchcraft, and fraud. His house was frequently stoned by young local fundamentalist Catholics. The threats were so extreme that for a while he sought safety for himself and his family in the local jail. Some perceived him as engaged in evil arts; others perceived his prophecies as threats, not predictions.

Among the events Nostradamus allegedly predicted were the execution of the English king Charles I, the Great Fire of London, the French Revolution and the subsequent executions of the royal family, Napoleon's rise and fall, World War II, the emergence of the United States, Communism, the stock market crash, the Apollo Moon Landing, the assassinations of the Kennedy brothers and the Space Shuttle *Challenger* disaster.

Among his predictions was his own death and a secret joke: Nostradamus' final request was to be buried upright within a wall inside the Church of the Cordeliers of Salon so that no one could ever tread on his grave. In 1700, officials decided to exhume his body and move his remains to a safer, more prominent wall in the church. Nostradamus had anticipated the move: a medallion discovered around the skeleton's neck and buried with him when he died was engraved with the year 1700.

Paracelsus (1493–September 1541)

Philippus Aureolus Theophrastus Bombastus von Hohenheim called himself Paracelsus, probably to indicate that he believed himself superior to Celsus, the first-century Roman medical authority. He inevitably is identified solely by his nickname today, perhaps because his true name is such a mouthful.

Magus, alchemist, astrologer, philosopher, and physician, he was a controversial figure in his own time and aroused passionate opposition especially from other physicians and apothecaries.

Born in Switzerland, he spent his childhood in Carinthia, a province of Austria.

He is believed to have studied medicine under his father, a physician. He received his doctorate from the medical school at the University of Ferrara *c.*1515. He traveled to Rome, Naples, Spain, Portugal, Paris, London, Moscow, Constantinople, and Greece.

He was the first researcher to describe zinc and to use chemical compounds in medical practice. In 1526, he was appointed Professor of Medicine at Basel University and City Physician. He began by publicly burning the works of Avicenna and Galen.

Paracelsus was so foul-mouthed that Thomas Thompson, Scottish historian of chemistry, was incapable of completing a translation of his work. After only 11 months, he was obliged to resign his chair at Basel and spent the rest of his life wandering through Europe as an itinerant physician, mainly in Austria and Germany.

His specialty was bronchial illnesses. He developed the first comprehensive treatment for syphilis. He was fascinated by potential links between weather and illness and wrote extensively on the connections between astrology and medicine.

Paracelsus regarded illness as a form of imbalance. His theories would now be described as "holistic"; he insisted that body and soul must be simultaneously addressed in order to bring about a true cure.

> *"Everywhere I enquired diligently and gathered experience of the medical art, not alone from doctors, but also from barbers, women, sorcerers, alchemists."* (Paracelsus)

He believed in the existence of natural magic powers, and allegedly kept a spirit named Azoth imprisoned in the crystal pommel of his sword.

In 1541, utterly impoverished, he settled in Salzburg under the protection of Archbishop Duke Ernst of Bavaria. He died there, allegedly thrown off a precipice by his enemies.

Pickingill, "Old George" (1816–1909)

"Old George" Pickingill, an influential figure in modern witchcraft, claimed to be a hereditary witch. His roots allegedly stretched back to his ancestor Julia, the Witch of Brandon in Norfolk. According to a family legend, Julia was hired in 1071 to chant incantations to inspire Hereward the Wake's soldiers when they battled the Normans and to confuse the Normans. Unfortunately, the Normans burned Julia's village with her in it.

Pickingill worked as a farmer in Canewdon, Essex. Suspicious neighbors accused him of magical intimidation, alleging that they feared to argue with him lest he cast spells over them. Neighbors claimed Pickingill relaxed by his hedge while a host of imps did his heavy labor for him.

Pickingill openly advocated the demise of Christianity and suggested that witches form alliances with Satanists in order to further that vision.

He established covens in Essex, Hampshire, Hertfordshire, Norfolk, and Sussex.

Pickingill formed the Nine Covens with hereditary witches serving as leaders. Tremendously proud of his hereditary witchcraft lineage, he placed great emphasis on "witch blood." Men and women were accepted into the coven but only women were permitted to conduct rituals. Pickingill also reputedly led an all-female coven as well, the Seven Witches of Canewdon.

He was reputed to have initiated both Aleister Crowley and Gerald Gardner into the Nine Covens.

Pythagoras (c.569 BCE–c.475 BCE)

Mathematician, musician, and sage, Pythagoras allegedly coined the word "philosopher" meaning "lover of wisdom." He is most famous for his mathematical "Pythagorean theorem," however he was a tremendously influential spiritual teacher and occultist as well.

The son of a wealthy jeweler, Pythagoras was born on the island of Samos and consecrated to Apollo before he was born. At one year old, his mother took him to an Israelite High Priest who blessed the baby.

Mathematics was his first passion, followed by music. He may have learned sacred geometry in Egypt. He devised the theory of the "music of the spheres" and healed through specially prepared musical compositions.

> The Pythagoreans believed that everything in existence possesses a voice with which to sing praises of the Creator.

Pythagoras studied magic and spirituality in Egypt, Babylonia, and India and possibly with Druids in Europe. He allegedly studied in Egypt for 22 years. He underwent circumcision in Egypt, common to Egyptian spiritual traditions but not to Greek.

Pythagoras also studied with Thessalian witches from whom he learned a divination technique of holding a polished metal mirror up to the moon, then reading messages within. He also possessed a wheel with which he divined. He was a firm believer in divination via astrology, augury, dreams, and entrails.

Pythagoras calculated that Earth was spherical and a satellite of the sun (although these ideas may have been learned in Egypt). Around 518 BCE Pythagoras moved to the Greek city of Crotona in southern Italy where he founded his school of philosophy. His followers were known as *mathematikoi* and obeyed a code of secrecy.

Pythagoras allegedly never came out in daylight; he only ventured outside at night. He appeared in a long white garment; he had a long flowing beard and wore a garland around his head. He allegedly encouraged his acolytes to consider him an avatar of Apollo who had assumed human form the better to teach them. He could allegedly call eagles from the sky and converse with animals.

Various miracles were attributed to him:

His thigh was made from pure gold

He was seen in two places simultaneously

He was allegedly the reincarnation of King Midas

A river called out "Hail Pythagoras!" to him as he passed by

He lived to almost 100, marrying one of his students when he was 60. They had seven children. He taught that the human soul can achieve union with the divine, mathematics is related to all aspects of reality, and philosophy is a vehicle of spiritual purification. He also taught the necessity of a pure and simple life including vegetarianism.

His students were divided into two classes:

Neophytes, who received a general education

Initiates, who were admitted to the inner teachings. To become an initiate one had to donate one's property to the school and live within its community

Students were not permitted to argue with the teacher. They had to endure long periods (years) of silence. Pythagoras taught beginner students from behind a curtain—perhaps the inspiration for the Wizard of Oz.

If students were discovered deficient in any area—including intellectual aptitude (and Pythagoras had high standards)—they were summarily expelled from the community.

Whatever property they had donated was doubled in value and returned to them. Funerary headstones and monuments were erected in their memory in the communal meeting hall. They were as if dead. Should they meet other members later, their past would not be acknowledged and they would be treated as strangers.

The beginning of Pythagoras' end came when a prominent man called Cylon, perhaps the Prince of Crotona, enrolled in the academy. He was *very* rich and influential. He spent three years in probation, five years in complete silence, and was then found intellectually wanting and expelled.

Cylon described Pythagoras as an intolerable despot and set about a campaign against him. Assassins were hired to torch the academy and kill Pythagoras. The college was set afire by a mob and 40 students were killed, although Pythagoras and two followers were either not present or just barely escaped. Other Pythagorean communities were also destroyed. Pythagoras took refuge in the Temple of the Muses where he died after a 40-day siege.

Pythagoras spread the idea of political liberty throughout the Greek communities of Italy. He left nothing in writing; whatever is known about him derives from the writings of disciples and others. Most of his mathematical secrets were never committed to paper and died with him.

Randolph, Paschal Beverly (October 8, 1825–July 29, 1875)

Paschal Beverly Randolph, a prominent nineteenth-century spiritualist, occultist, and prolific author was perhaps the primary exponent of magic mirrors and sex-magic. His theories influenced Helena Blavatsky and Aleister Crowley among others.

Randolph was a brilliant metaphysician: a High Ritual adept, Rosicrucian, Spiritualist, *and* Hoodoo doctor. He traveled in the circles of elite French and English occultists but also sold something called the "New Orleans Magnetic Pillow" via magazine ads. (He studied with

Voodooists in New Orleans although later publicly criticized them.) Randolph founded various metaphysical societies including the Hermetic Brotherhood of Luxor and the Brotherhood of Eulis.

Randolph was born at 70 Canal Street in New York City's notorious Five Points slum. Five Points was that rare phenomena, a five-way crossroads. He identified his father, to whom his mother may or may not have been married, as a member of the prominent Randolph family of Virginia and, through him, claimed descent from Pocahontas. Randolph's mother, Flora, was of African descent. He described her as being psychically gifted and believed he inherited his intuitive skills from her.

Randolph eventually became a sailor, then a barber. By 1853, he was listed in the New York City directory as *"Dr. Paschal Beverly Randolph, clairvoyant physician and psycho-phrenologist."*

Although he used the title "Doctor," Randolph was not a medical doctor but a *"clairvoyant physician"* who used powers of clairvoyance, sometimes while entranced, to diagnosis illness and prescribe treatment. The medical field was more eclectic at that time; by 1854, Randolph was working for two physicians in New York, seeing fifty patients a day.

He became involved with Spiritualism and was a gifted trance medium. Among those he channeled were Benjamin Franklin, Zoroaster, Napoleon, and his mother who chided him for allowing himself to be susceptible to so many spirits. He became entranced easily and suddenly (some said at the drop of a hat); a handsome, charismatic man, he was a popular lecturer as it was never sure whether he would deliver the advertised lecture or suddenly begin to channel some spirit.

He traveled through Europe, Turkey, the Middle East, and North Africa, spending time with the Dervishes and various occultists, and becoming proficient in various languages including Arabic and Turkish. In Paris, he may have met Eliphas Levi, who may or may not have initiated Randolph into the societies to which Levi belonged. Returning to the United States, Randolph became an importer and publisher, founding the Randolph Publishing House. He wrote many works, although usually under pseudonyms like *Le Rosicrucien.*

By 1860, Randolph was the foremost advocate of the magic mirror in the United States and was using it to teach a system of true, conscious clairvoyance. He authored books teaching these techniques and was also the primary distributor of magic mirrors.

Previously mirror-gazing was a passive activity; the medium merely received messages from the device. Randolph created a system of active magic using specially designed mirrors. The mirrors he advocated usually consisted of two pieces of glass or metal, one convex and one concave, fitted together in a frame leaving a narrow cavity that could be filled with various substances, such as ink, hashish, and/or assorted sexual fluids.

Randolph also became the foremost scholar and theorist of sex magic. Randolph's sex magic is unusual: most systems of sexual magic involve relationships between the practitioner and discarnate entities. Randolph's theories actually involve sex between men and women. Equally unusually, especially for his time, he placed tremendous emphasis on women's sexual happiness.

Randolph taught that human vitality is dependent upon *mutual* sexual fulfillment. The moment of mutual, simultaneous orgasm is the point of supreme magic power. The vital energy that flows during correct sexual intercourse supports clairvoyance and mediumship and ultimately links the human soul with those of the celestial spheres.

The key word is "correct" sexual intercourse; Randolph believed that in order to achieve this state, men and women must find their soulmates, their "correct" compatible partner. Much of his life was devoted to finding that partner; he had a stormy love life, marrying at least three times. With the correct partner, it would theoretically be possible to conceive a magical child. (Randolph believed this was accomplished with the birth of his son, Osiris Budh, on March 29, 1874.) It is theorized that many of Aleister Crowley's later obsessions with Scarlet Women and magickal children are rooted in Randolph's work (see Crowley, page 720).

This sexual vitality, which he envisioned as a type of fluid, similar to lymphatic fluid, is intrinsic to human well being and magical power. In addition to sex, vitality may be bolstered and enhanced through certain foods, as well as through various herbal elixirs that Randolph formulated and sold via mail order, their primary ingredient hashish. He made various, presumably potent, concoctions of hashish, opium, henbane, and belladonna.

Randolph became very bitter at the end of his life; he was in severe financial straits and was perhaps drinking. He felt he was not given the respect due to him by other occultists, blaming it, with much justification, on prevalent race prejudice.

On July 29, 1875, Randolph committed suicide by shooting himself with a pistol in Toledo, Ohio. Just a few months later, Helena Blavatsky and Henry Olcott formed the Theosophical Society, many of whose early theories were closely related to Randolph's. Randolph and Olcott corresponded with each other, and it's known that Olcott admired Randolph's books. Various rumors exist, none substantiated, regarding Randolph's relationship, if any, with Blavatsky:

❧ Some suggest they knew each other in Paris before Blavatsky came to the US

❧ Some suggest they belonged to the same secret societies and that Randolph was privy to Blavatsky's Ascended Masters

❧ Some suggest that Blavatsky and Randolph feuded, possibly fatally. One story suggested that Randolph had attempted to hex Blavatsky but the spell rebounded, causing him to kill himself. (In all fairness, this story derives from those who wished to paint Blavatsky as a powerful but malevolent witch.)

Further Reading: An extensively detailed, long-overdue biography, *Paschal Beverly Randolph: A Nineteenth-Century Black American Spiritualist, Rosicrucian and Sex Magician,* by John Patrick Deveney (State University of New York Press, 1997) also includes two of Randolph's most famous works, *The Ansairetic Mystery: A New Revelation Concerning Sex!* and *The Mysteries of Eulis.*

Rucker, "Black" Herman (1892–April 1934)

Herman Rucker was an African-American author, conjurer, illusionist (stage-magician), occultist, Freemason, fortune-teller, and herbalist. Like the old Italian mountebanks, he offered a combination of entertainment, occult, and healing services at his medicine shows. He possessed a rare combination of personal charisma and financial acuity to be one of the few occultists to achieve lasting financial success and stability.

He dubbed himself *"Black Herman"* to make his ancestry very clear. He wished to avoid trouble and cancellations in the Jim Crow South. Magicians would be hired and would travel at their own expense to distant locations where, when it was discovered that they were of African ancestry, they would be refused work and reimbursement for their expenses, or worse. Other African-American magicians (or anyone remotely dark-skinned) took to wearing turbans and pretending to be Hindu magicians from India, which at that time was very stylish. Rucker took a different, direct, and very brave approach.

Benjamin Rucker was born in Amherst, Virginia. In his youth, he met a traveling magician, Prince Herman, also an African-American, who sold health tonics and did card tricks. Young Benjamin was fascinated with the tricks and asked to become a student. The two became friends. On Benjamin's 16th birthday, Prince Herman offered him a position as his apprentice.

Benjamin hit the road with Prince Herman serving as chauffeur, valet, ticket seller, and general all-around assistant. He learned the tricks of the trade and the tricks of the stage. Rucker learned the art of concocting the health tonics sold at medicine shows as *"Herman's Wonderful Body Tonic."*

Brewing the tonic was part of the show: a cauldron was set up over a bonfire and the potion brewed on the spot. He himself was an excellent testimonial for his brew: tall, handsome, charismatic, and expensively dressed. He encouraged spectators to toss silver dimes into the pot for extra power and luck.

Prince Herman died in 1909. Apparently at that time, Rucker assumed the name *"Black Herman."* He became a solo act and moved to Harlem, then in the midst of what is now known as the "Harlem Renaissance." When not on the road, Rucker held salons in his home.

His repertoire included divination and faith healing rooted in Christianity but also incorporating various occult traditions. Illusionist tricks were incorporated including classics like the Sword Cabinet or sawing a pretty lady in half. Rucker also wrote various books that were sold at his shows. The greatest demand was for fortune-telling and so eventually that was emphasized. Rucker got around anti-fortune-telling laws by not charging for them. Readings were included as a free bonus with purchase of the health tonic.

Because Rucker was also an illusionist, the assumption now tends to be that his occult and divination interests and skills were fraudulent or also an illusion, however he was a knowledgeable and skillful occultist.

He bought a three-storey townhouse at 119 West 136th Street. It was expensively furnished with a telephone on each floor, a comparative rarity at that time. He conducted his fortune-telling business from his home where he offered private consultations. He was sufficiently in demand to employ two secretaries to handle his scheduling and appointments.

One room in his home served as an altar room, painted black and hung with African masks. The altar is described as *"Voodoo-inspired"* although which tradition, whether Haitian or New Orleans or other, is unclear. A human skull was surrounded by candles, and African drums were rigged to play by themselves.

A garden behind the house supplied the ingredients for his tonics and spells as well as the beauty products his family also marketed. It was a family business with his wife and brother overseeing various aspects.

A fairly high percentage of his business focused on selecting numbers for local lottery games. Rucker had a reputation for selecting winning numbers for people. He was arrested in New York on charges of fortune-telling and was incarcerated briefly in Sing Sing prison in Ossining New York.

By 1923, Rucker had incorporated the stunt, "Woman Buried Alive" into his repertoire. He would first hypnotize a woman, then bury her alive (six feet under) for almost six hours. In 1933, searching for a new angle, he adapted this stunt and began burying himself. Eventually he himself began to star in "Buried Alive."

Rucker would pretend to be dead. The audience was invited to feel his wrist for a pulse and find none. (His trick involved a balled-up handkerchief in his armpit to artificially stop his pulse.) The coffin was nailed shut and buried. The crowd would then come back days later for a resurrection. Rucker's trick involved a secret passage by which he could leave the coffin and travel disguised to another town. Eventually he'd return and slip back into the coffin to emerge triumphantly alive.

In April 1934, while performing in Louisville, Kentucky, Rucker collapsed. A doctor in the house was unable to revive him. (Cause of death was listed as "acute indigestion.") The audience, however, used to his tricks, expected a resurrection. His body was brought to a local funeral parlor. People still believed it was a trick. Finally Herman's assistant Washington Reeves began charging people for the opportunity to view the body because, in his words, it was what Herman would have done. Herman, genuinely dead, was shipped home by train and was buried, for good, in Woodlawn Cemetery in the Bronx.

Various other illusionists continued to use his name for years including his assistant, Washington Reeves, who performed under the name "*The Original Black Herman.*"

Sanders, Alex (1926–April 30, 1988)

Alex Sanders, once known as the "King of the Witches," founded a Wiccan tradition and was once considered Gerald Gardner's primary competitor.

Born in Manchester, Sanders stated that age seven he accidentally stumbled onto his Welsh Grandma Bibby naked in the kitchen in the midst of a ritual. Those who stumble onto rituals must be initiated and so he was sworn to secrecy.

Grandma Bibby initiated Alex and advised him that now he was one of "*us.*" She explains that she (and he, through her) derived from a long line of witches stretching back to the fourteenth-century Welsh chieftain Owen Glendower who preserved Celtic traditions.

Alex and Grandma became very close. She taught him magic, how to create charms, potions and write a Book of Shadows. Grandma Bibby died in 1942. Sanders burned her Book of Shadows but retained many of her ritual tools including a magic sword.

Sanders said he initially engaged in magic for personal financial and sexual gratification, apparently quite successfully, but then resolved to continue his grandmother's work and began initiating covens in the Manchester area.

Sanders met Maxine Morris (1946–), convent-educated and raised a devout Roman Catholic. She had had visions since her childhood and Sanders recognized her as a natural witch. They married in 1967 and moved to London, establishing a new coven together. They became celebrities of a kind: Maxine was very beautiful and the couple made various radio and television appearances.

Maxine and Sanders separated in 1973. Maxine began a new lower-key coven and

Sanders, semi-retired, moved to Sussex where he died of lung cancer in 1988.

Scot, Sir Michael (c.1214–c.1291)

Sir Michael Scot was a renowned Scottish sorcerer. He allegedly learned the magical arts in the renowned occult academies of Toledo, Spain. He himself lectured at the University of Padua on judicial astrology and spent several years teaching in Salamanca and Toledo. He practiced divination at the court of Emperor Frederick II to whom he dedicated a book on natural history.

He is interred in either Melrose Abbey or Holme-Cultram in Cumberland, his magical books allegedly buried with him.

Dante placed Michael Scot in the Fourth Level of Hell, the part of the inferno where sorcerers are sent.

Sendivogius, Michael (–1646)

Michael Sendivogius was a famed Moravian alchemist. Alchemists were allegedly calling themselves Rosicrucians during the sixteenth century; Michael Sendivogius' Society of the Unknown Philosophers is considered among the precursors to the Rosicrucians.

Sendivogius rescued the alchemist Alexander Seton (see below) and used Seton's powder to make gold, apparently creating several genuine transformations. When the powder was gone, he bluffed for a while based on his previous success but was eventually reduced to poverty.

Sendivogius married Seton's widow whose dowry included an alchemical manuscript left by Seton. Sendivogius published this manuscript under his own name in Gdansk in 1604, titled, *Twelve Treatises on the Philosopher's Stone.*

Seton, Alexander (–1603)

Alexander Seton was a Scots alchemist who reputedly mastered the art of transmuting lead into gold by means of a mysterious black powder. Seton traveled to Holland, Italy, Switzerland, and Germany giving demonstrations of his ability to create high-quality true gold from base metals.

Sometime during the very early seventeenth century, c.1602, in Cologne, Seton allegedly produced 6 ounces of gold, which stood up to testing. His experiments were well publicized and news of this miracle reached the ears of Christian II, Elector of Saxony, who summoned Seton to his court and demanded his alchemical secrets. Seton refused. When bribes and threats didn't work, he was brutally tortured.

Moravian alchemist Michael Sendivogius (see above) rescued Seton but demanded the formula for the black powder as his reward. Seton explained that he was unable to reveal the secret to the uninitiated but gave him the remaining powder; Seton then died from the injuries he'd incurred during torture.

Seven Sisters

The notion of seven spiritually powerful sisters seems universal. China has Seven Weaving Maidens; the Bible has the Seven Midianite Sisters, daughters of the shaman-priest Jethro. Even the sky has the Seven Pleiades, popularly believed to represent "Seven Sisters." "Seven Sisters" is also a popular name for Hoodoo practitioners, regardless of whether there are really seven or only one.

✳ *Seven Sisters was the magical name of Ida Carter, a celebrated Hoodoo doctor from Hogansville, Alabama*

✳ *The Seven Sisters of New Orleans, renowned conjure women, were the inspiration for the 1931 blues song by J.T. "Funny Paper" Smith. According to the song, the names of the sisters are Sarah, Minnie, Bertha, Holly, Dolly, Betty, and Jane.*

Shipton, Mother (1488–1558)

Mother Shipton was a renowned English witch and prophetess. Details of her life are hazy, and alternative birth and death dates are suggested (1448 and 1518 respectively). Her maiden name is usually given as Ursula Southeil or Sonthiel.

One legend suggests she was born in a cave near the River Nidd in Yorkshire. The cave is now a memorial for Mother Shipton. Her mother was reputed to be a witch. Some said her father was the devil. Shipton was apparently orphaned at birth, her mother dying during childbirth. Her mother could allegedly heal, hex, foretell the future, and raise storms. Her daughter, raised by a local woman, seems to have inherited the powers.

Mother Shipton's reputation as a witch began in childhood. She could allegedly move things without touching them. Strange phenomenon occurred: women found themselves dancing in circles, unable to stop because when they tried an imp in the form of a monkey pinched them.

She had a reputation as being "ugly" and is sometimes described as "deformed" although few details are offered. She allegedly cast spells over those who mocked her appearance. Her familiar was a black dog who accompanied her everywhere.

She married Toby Shipton, a carpenter, in 1512. It was rumored that she had bewitched him with a love potion because of her lack of looks. By the time of her marriage, she was already famous for her prophecies. They lived in the village of Skipton in North Yorkshire.

Although she was feared, she was also very much in demand because of the accuracy of her prophecies. People traveled from great distances to consult with her and request her advice.

According to legend, Mother Shipton was summoned to court for taking revenge on prying neighbors. She had bewitched them at a breakfast party; the guests fell into fits of hysterical, uncontrollable laughter. They ran out of the house pursued by what were described as goblins. Mother Shipton allegedly threatened the court that she'd do worse if prosecuted. She allegedly then said, *"Up draxi, call Stygician Helleuei."* A dragon appeared and she soared off on its back.

The most famous legend regarding Mother Shipton is that she predicted Cardinal Wolsey, Henry VIII's Lord Chancellor, would never reach York. The cardinal had sent three lords incognito to check up on Mother Shipton. She knew them for who they were immediately and told them to deliver a message to Wolsey: he would see but never arrive in York. Their response was that when Wolsey reached York, he'd see Mother Shipton burned as a witch. Shipton tossed her handkerchief into the fire, saying that if it burned so would she. Allegedly the handkerchief did not burn.

Her prophecy regarding Wolsey proved accurate. He arrived at Cawood, eight miles from York, close enough to view York from the top of the castle tower. While there, he received a message saying that the king wished to see him immediately. Wolsey turned back towards London but became sick and died in Leicester.

Mother Shipton gave her prophesies in rhyme. She predicted the automobile (*"Carriages without horses shall go"*) and e-mail and the Internet (*"Around the world thoughts shall fly, in the twinkling of an eye"*) and the California Gold Rush (*"Gold shall be found and found, In a land that is not known"*). Not all her prophesies were accurate, however—she predicted the world would end in 1881.

In 1684, Richard Head wrote a book detailing her life and prophesies.

Simon Magus

Simon Magus, or Simon the Magician, was a magician and spiritual leader from Samaria. It is unknown whether he was an ethnic Samaritan or a Jew originally from Caesarea. A magician named Simon lived in Caesarea *c.*40 CE; this is sometimes acknowledged to be Simon Magus. Justin Martyr however claims Simon was born in Gitta, a Samaritan village.

Simon was baptized a Christian by the Apostle Philip and is described by Bishop Irenaeus of Lyons as the man *"from whom all the heresies take their origin."* Simon Magus became the Christian symbol of arrogance and pride.

Simon is recalled in the word "simony," the practice of buying positions of power within the Church. In the Book of Acts, Simon is portrayed as a wandering magician who has converted to Christianity. He observes Peter laying on hands. He wished to acquire this skill too and so offers to pay Peter for it and is sharply rebuked for assuming these were powers that could be bought.

Simon may have been a disciple of John the Baptist. He achieved tremendous success as a magician and spiritual leader in Samaria and Rome.

He is credited as the founder of the school of Simonian Gnosticism. Its doctrine suggested that the world was created by a female power who then became lost in her own creation. God exists but the Cosmos was not created directly by God but by a female emanation of God, the Ennoia (Thought). She created the angels who then rebelled against her. The battle was so vicious that Ennoia lost herself in her Creation and forgot her identity. She wandered through various incarnations, one after another, becoming ever more confused.

In the meantime, the angels tried to rule the world but fought amongst themselves. The world filled with suffering, which was not God's original intention. God finally decided to rescue Ennoia and save humankind, so he came to Earth in the form of Simon Magus. God, in the form of Simon Magus, found Ennoia in the form of a prostitute named Helena in the Phoenician city of Tyre, the cradle of sacred prostitution. Thanks to Simon, Helena regained her memory.

Simon taught that anyone who recognized him as God was saved. Once saved, there was no need for conventional rules of morality, because these rules were originally created by the angels in order to enslave people.

Knowledge of Simon comes from Christians who opposed him and perceived him as a competitor of Jesus Christ. It was said that he conjured spirits, concocted potions, and encouraged free sex (as told by people who perceived these as dreadful things). Simon was identified as the Anti-Christ, and some early Christians accused Simon Magus of accomplishing his miracles via control of the spirit of a murdered boy via necromantic rituals.

Simon allegedly died during a magical duel with Peter when he flew off the top of the Roman Forum. Alternatively he buried himself for three days but did not resurrect. After his death, he was buried in Aricia, near Rome.

Simon Magus was worshipped in Rome. A community of devotees built temples to him featuring statues of Simon and Helena. After his death, leadership of Simon's sect was assumed by his disciple Menander. Simonian Gnosticism survived alongside Christianity in the Roman Empire for over 150 years. However, by the early third century, Origen claimed there were less than 30 Simonians left.

All writings of Simon's School were destroyed.

Valiente, Doreen (1922–September 1, 1999)

Doreen Valiente is the Founding Mother of modern Wicca and the author of many of its most beloved rituals. She served as one of Gerald Gardner's High Priestesses and with him co-authored what is now known as the Gardnerian Book of Shadows, the book of rituals that has become the standard text and liturgy of Wicca.

Doreen Dominy was born in London and educated at a convent school. Her clairvoyant skills manifested in her youth. She studied various occult traditions and Theosophy. (See Blavatsky, page 711.)

In 1944, Doreen married Casimiro Valiente, who disapproved of his wife's occult interests and psychic skills. However, Doreen began corresponding with Cecil Williamson (see page 769); from him she learned of covens in the New Forest and eventually met Gerald Gardner, who had been initiated into one of those covens. In 1953, Gardner initiated Valiente into his own new coven.

Together with Gardner, Valiente revised his liturgy, deleting much of Aleister Crowley's contributions (which she found offensive) and incorporating her own poetry instead, including "The Charge of the Goddess" and "The Witches' Rune."

Valiente had read and admired Charles Leland's work prior to meeting Gardner and modeled "Charge of the Goddess" after his *Aradia*. She labored over the *Book of Shadows* from 1954 until 1957 before she and Gardner were completely satisfied with the results. In 1957, Valiente left Gardner's coven to form her own.

Doreen Valiente died of cancer in 1991. Her books include *Natural Magic*, *An ABC of Witchcraft Past and Present*, and *Witchcraft for Tomorrow*.

Virgil (70–19 BCE)

Publius Vergilius Maro is now most famous as the Roman poet Virgil, however he was also a legendary magician. Born near Mantua, he is buried in Naples, which legend says he founded and still protects via his magical arts.

Virgil was the son of a Roman senator and allegedly a graduate (with honors!) of a Moorish magical college of Toledo. In addition to being a magician, he was an escape artist and esteemed worker in metals for magical purposes (copper, gold, and iron). The implication is that he was an alchemist.

Virgil allegedly founded a school for sorcerers in Naples and taught there himself.

> According to one legend Virgil was once jailed; he sketched a ship on the prison wall, climbed aboard and escaped by sailing away through the air.

He allegedly constructed magical, healing thermal baths. Jealous physicians in Salerno, who had an investment in people's illnesses, destroyed them as the baths were destroying their business.

Virgil used magic to protect Naples:

✱ *He created a bronze frog-sized fly and set it atop a city gate to ward off other flies*

✱ *He created a golden leech to free the city from a plague of leeches*

✱ *A horse made from copper chased thieves who ignored the city curfew, trampling them underfoot*

✱ *A huge iron horse cured horse diseases. (It was eventually melted down by jealous farriers, whose responsibilities then included veterinary work, and used to craft church bells.)*

✱ *In days before outdoor lighting, he prepared a glass lamp that was never extinguished*

While digging in a vineyard, according to one story, Virgil unearthed a corked bottle containing not one genie but twelve demons. They demanded to be released. He negotiated: the demons would teach him magic in exchange for popping the cork.

On his deathbed, he decided to carry out a magical rejuvenation ritual, requesting help from a faithful servant. He told the servant to kill him and chop him into little pieces. His head was to be quartered and salted. The various pieces were to be placed in a barrel in the cellar in a very specific order under a magic oil lamp that Virgil had prepared, arranged so as to leak into the barrel and onto his body parts. The lamp was to be kept burning for nine days and nights after which time Virgil said he'd be revivified. The servant initially protested and refused to do it but Virgil was very persistent and the man finally agreed, killed him and followed directions.

The Emperor missed Virgil and came looking for him. He forced his way into the house, which was searched. Virgil's dismembered body was found. The Emperor refused to believe the story about the magical resurrection and killed the servant before the operation was completed. After the servant's death, the Emperor saw an apparition of a naked child run three times around the barrel and say to the Emperor, *"Cursed be the time you came here!"* The child disappeared, never to be seen again, nor was Virgil resurrected.

He was buried in Naples.

Williamson, Cecil (September 18, 1909–1996)

Cecil Williamson was a life-long student of witchcraft and the founder of the Witchcraft Museum in Boscastle, Cornwall.

He was born in Paignton, Devon. His father was a naval officer; he and Cecil's mother traveled extensively. Cecil was sent to boarding schools and spent holidays with various relatives.

At age 7, Williamson was bullied mercilessly at school by another boy, to the point where Williamson would hide in hedgerows to escape him. One day, he met an elderly woman who taught him to cast a spell to rid himself of his tormentor. It worked; the other boy suffered an accident and left off tormenting Williamson. Not long after, he discovered a bunch of drunken men attempting to strip the same old lady of her clothing. The boy made a fuss and the men explained she was a witch and they were looking for her *"devil's tit."* Cecil, although still a young child, attempted to protect her. The ruckus attracted his uncle's attention and the men retreated. The woman later began teaching Cecil magic.

Williamson's grandmother, who lived in France, was a well-known astrologer. Through her he met Aleister Crowley, Margaret Murray, and the vampirologist Montague Summers. His parents lived for a time in the New Forest where Cecil met many witches including Gardner's Dorothy Clutterbuck. He began researching witchcraft in 1930 and continued to do so for the rest of his life.

During World War II, Williamson worked for MI6, the British intelligence service. As an occultist, he researched Nazi involvement with the occult.

Margaret Murray introduced Williamson to Gerald Gardner in 1947. In 1949, Williamson opened the Witchcraft Research Centre in the old Witches' Mill in Castletown, Isle of Man. He had originally wished to house his collection in Stratford-on-Avon and had been offered a building, but local disapproval of a museum devoted to witchcraft was so intense that he went to the Isle of Man instead.

Gardner joined Williamson and became (temporarily) the museum's "official witch." He stayed with Williamson for three moths before a financial dispute caused him to purchase his own cottage near the museum. The two had a falling out but when Williamson decided to return to England, Gardner purchased the building from him (although not the collection). Williamson tried various places to house his collection until arriving in Boscastle, Cornwall, where the Museum of Witchcraft remains.

Yah-Yah, Dr

Dr Yah-Yah was a renowned Hoodoo Doctor and an African-American slave on a plantation near New Orleans. On the plantation where he labored he was called Washington but his professional name was Dr Yah-Yah. Also known as Dr Yah, he emerged as a renowned practitioner in New Orleans during the late 1850s.

Among his potions was a concoction of honey, jimsonweed (datura) and sulfur sipped from a glass that had been rubbed against a black cat. That formula is recorded because that's the formula that got Dr Yah-Yah into trouble.

In 1861, Dr Yah-Yah was arrested. An Italian client had given a sample of Dr Yah-Yah's potion to his physician, who in turn called the police. Dr Yah-Yah's owner was ordered to pay a fine of $15, and Dr Yah-Yah was punished by being transferred to the backbreaking work of a field hand and forbidden to practice his craft.

Witchcraze! Persecution of Witches

Magical practitioners and shamans historically have to varying degrees been looked upon with suspicion by outsiders to their craft. This is perhaps natural, considering that secrets and mysteries are intrinsic to magical arts as well as the reality that those who can heal can also harm.

If an individual has the capacity to bless others with good fortune, for instance, then that individual also possesses the capacity to withhold that blessing ... or worse.

This is true not only of witches, however, but of any specialist. Although it's a rare occurrence, every once in a while one does hear of a physician who has forsaken the Hippocratic Oath to do no harm but instead emerges as a secret, malevolent Angel of Death. However, those rare occurrences have *not* caused prejudice against physicians amongst the general public, nor have they caused "physician hysteria": the panic-stricken fear that *every* physician is secretly committed to causing only harm.

Likewise, in many traditional societies, it's recognized that although the occasional witch or shaman may become corrupt, the majority are responsible, ethical professionals. Most traditional societies have age-old legal mechanisms

(not necessarily fair or "nice" ones) in place for magical practitioners perceived as malefactors, but this does not reflect negatively on the greater community of magical practitioners, nor does this constitute a "witch panic."

A witch panic is characterized by an absolutely hysterical, irrational, fear of witchcraft and witches. A witch doesn't have to cause harm for others to fear and persecute her. In fact, she may not have to be a witch at all: the key word in *"witch hysteria"* or *"witch panic"* is not the first but the second. Witch panics are characterized by a crazed terror that there is a secret conspiracy of witches, a fifth column that seeks to undermine society and cause harm to individuals. No need to wait for the witches to prove they mean harm; in a witchcraze, authorities search out any possible link to witchcraft and attempt to terminate it mercilessly.

Although witch panics existed earlier and still exist today, in some parts of Earth, the term

"Witchcraze" historically refers to a specific era of European history, also called the "Burning Times."

> ✴ *Witch-hunt indicates a concerted, active search for witches in order to prosecute or eliminate them*
>
> ✴ *Witch panic refers to hysterical fear of witches, leading to extensive witch-hunts. Witch panics have historically occurred in waves: hysteria rises to fever pitch, sometimes for years, then abates only to rise again, sometimes years later*
>
> ✴ *Witchcraze refers to the peak fever pitch of hysterical witch panics; in some communities, a witchcraze was sustained for years*
>
> ✴ *The Burning Times refers to the centuries-long European witch-hunts and witchcraze. In most regions, although not all, those convicted of witchcraft were condemned to death by burning, hence the name. It is to some extent more accurate than "witch-hunt" or "witch panic" because not all or even perhaps most of those convicted of witchcraft were genuinely witches, although many were.*

Although the European Witchcraze lasted hundreds of years, covering most of the continent as well as colonies in the Western Hemisphere and claimed as victims, *at a minimum*, thousands of people, until recently it was a relatively obscure historical subject; it is still generally treated as a footnote or aberration of history.

Many studies of the Witchcraze have, however, been published in the last two decades; in general, their focus is on perpetrators rather than on victims. All sorts of rationales are offered as to why "normal" people went so witch-crazy. Various books posit all kinds of different solutions for that dilemma, from physical causes (ergot poisoning, for instances) to cultural (virulent sexism—victims were, in most regions, overwhelmingly female), and all points in between.

However, to paraphrase author and physician M. Scott Peck, nothing of significance has but one root cause. There is a tendency to study the vast, sprawling topic of the European witch-hunts as an isolated subject, rather than in historical context. It is not really possible to fully understand them without also considering other concurrent historical events:

> ✴ *The persecution of landless minorities in Europe: Jews, Romany, and Saami*
>
> ✴ *Continued efforts to eradicate all vestiges of Pagan tradition*
>
> ✴ *Unresolved issues stemming from, often forced, conversion to Christianity*
>
> ✴ *The emotional and psychological impact of the Black Death and other deadly plagues*
>
> ✴ *The imposition of feudalism in some parts of Europe and the development of a professional class in others*
>
> ✴ *The denigration and demonization of an entire gender (see **BOOKS**: Witch-hunters' Manuals: Sprenger).*

How many people died in the Witchcraze? *There's* the million-dollar question! Figures offered range from as low as the tens of thousands to as many as nine million. The answer to the question, *"How many people were killed during the Burning Times?"* often reveals more about the orientation of the person quoting the figure than it does about the witch-hunts themselves.

So how many people were killed? Who knows? That's the honest answer. The records are a mess and often unreliable. Records are missing, truncated, and edited. For instance, a 1412 decree from Aneu, Spain makes references to previous witchcraft trials for which no records and thus no information exist. And documents from those privy to witchcraft trials demonstrate that existing records aren't necessarily accurate or trustworthy. (See page 800, Germany.)

Many scholars offer documented but conflicting numbers of victims of the Burning Times. Their totals may all be correct; they're not necessarily using the same numbers. When considering total numbers of those killed, one must consider various factors:

❋ *Who is being counted as a victim?*

❋ *What years are being considered?*

❋ *What regions are considered in the total count?*

Those victims who died during the interrogation process may or may not be counted alongside those who perished during documented executions. Not all executions were documented. Sometimes records of convictions of witchcraft exist with no further information regarding eventual punishment: do you assume that the convicted witch was executed or do you reserve judgment and not count that person among the total number?

When considering total numbers of victims, what years are included to arrive at a total?

Some consider only the fifteenth and sixteenth centuries, the absolute fever peak of the Witchcraze, to be worthy of consideration. Others begin counting much earlier, in the twelfth or thirteenth centuries for instance. Some consider early Pagan martyrs accused of witchcraft to be among the victims of the Burning Times, although others consider this a whole different historical body count.

When did the Witchcraze end? With the last government-authorized execution of witches in Western Europe, or in the whole continent of Europe? Legal executions of witches in Europe did not end until close to the end of the eighteenth century, although by then there were comparatively many fewer of them. Some stop counting once the fever pitch cooled. Repeal of laws against witchcraft was often unpopular with the masses; after the laws were repealed, sometimes fatal vigilante justice took its place (see page 786, England). Are those deaths counted amongst the Witchcraze numbers or not?

And what regions are considered? Witch-panics were overwhelming in some regions (the German lands, Scotland) and lighter in others (Finland, Ireland), however virtually no part of Europe was completely untouched. There were witch-trials and executions in Croatia, Estonia, and Transylvania as well as in France, Italy, and England; are *all* territories being incorporated into totals or just a few? Some regions have maintained serviceable records; some have hardly any. Lack of records does not indicate lack of witch-trials; it merely indicates lack of documentation, that's all.

And who exactly do we count in the totals? Many people were charged with multiple crimes: heresy *and* witchcraft. Do we automatically include anyone with a charge of witchcraft in the totals of victims killed during the Burning Times or is the count more selective? And what of those Jews, Romany, and Saami who were accused of witchcraft or sorcery, although others in their community were killed simply because of their cultural identity with no added charges? Where do you count *them*?

These are all factors one must consider when meditating on the huge disparity between the totals offered for numbers killed during the Burning Times. In general, those coming up with larger numbers aren't intentionally exaggerating for political purposes as they are so often accused; they are merely counting a broader spectrum of victims.

The largest number bandied about, nine million, is often criticized as a "feminist exaggeration"; however the first person to quote that number seems to have been Cecil Williamson (see **HALL OF FAME**). The number was derived by looking at a broad spectrum of historical persecution of witches rather than a narrower one.

Witch panics possessed regional characteristics:

✷ *In Russia, there was no "witch-hunt" per se; however those attending at court were frequently accused of using witchcraft for political purposes or to harm the royal family*

✷ *In Transylvania, wives and female relatives of political competitors were targeted*

✷ *In Hungary, practitioners of shamanism were targeted*

✷ *In German lands, wealthy people were particularly vulnerable to charges of witchcraft as if convicted land and assets were confiscated by witch-hunters*

✷ *In France, a series of highly publicized cases involved demonic possession of nuns within convents, usually with a priest charged as perpetrator*

Included in these pages is but a brief overview of witchcraft persecutions including but not limited to the Burning Times. For reasons of space, the areas that now constitute modern Germany and Italy are considered together although there were no unified nations known as Germany or Italy during that time. Instead, there were independent states, which did not all have the same laws or leaders; hence witchcraft persecutions were worse in one region of what is now one country than in another.

The scope of the entire witchcraze is beyond these pages. What you see here is only representative, not a total. Witches were burned in the Isle of Man as well as in Scotland; Austria had a particularly virulent witchcraze; the Alpine region in general is often considered the geographic nucleus of the Burning Times.

As a rule, regions that placed greater emphasis on torture as a device for uncovering witches discovered greater numbers of witches than those regions that placed less emphasis on torture. Among the primary lessons of the witch-hunts is that if people are tortured, most will confess and tell their torturers *whatever* they wish to hear. Thus virtually all confessions recorded during the witch trials are suspect and may reveal more about the manias and obsessions of the torturers than about anything regarding the victims, heresy or witchcraft.

Some things to bear in mind: there is a tremendously sexual aspect to the witch trials that is often ignored or glossed over. Women were the majority of the victims; men were, almost without exception, in positions of authority and judgment during this time. Women may have testified against other women but they were not in positions of authority. Sometimes women were hired to examine arrested women; however these hired women were consistently supervised by men. They did not work independently or unsupervised.

Female prisoners, frequently naked, were routinely left alone in rooms with one or more men. Women were undressed, their bodies examined *minutely*. Their interrogation often involved explicitly sexual subjects: orgies, sex with Satan, demons and imps. Imagine yourself shaved, bound, examined, and asked tremendously embarrassing, humiliating questions by those who hold your life in their hands.

There is a pornographic quality to many trial transcripts. Men accused women of participating in sexual acts; women routinely denied these accusations and then were tortured, often in sexual ways, until they confessed and elaborated on their torturers' fantasies.

Although trial transcripts often quite explicitly describe the torture of victims, which subsequently cannot be denied, reports of sexual abuse are less forthcoming, perhaps because many (although not all) of those in authority were clerics who had taken vows of celibacy. Women were routinely raped. When reading trial testimony, this can never be forgotten or overlooked, even when not explicitly stated. The history of the witch trials is as much about men behaving abusively toward women as it is about abuses of religious authority. Even when there was not rape, there was *constant* sexual humiliation and the threat of rape.

Witch-burning evolved into an industry. Some people made fine livings killing others convicted of witchcraft. Many torture weapons still in use were invented during the Burning Times. Ovens were not first used as murder weapons to kill Jews during World War II; they were used in German lands to roast convicted witches 300 years before. It wasn't fantasy when Gretel burned the witch in the oven in the Grimms' fairy tale *Hansel and Gretel*; the candy house in the middle of the forest may have been make-believe but killing witches in ovens was pure reality.

Were any of the victims actually practitioners of witchcraft? Apparently yes, many were, again depending upon definitions of witchcraft. Some were practitioners of magical arts and shamanism. Others held stubbornly to Pagan faiths or traditions. The witch-hunters eventual obsession with Christian-derived demonolatry obscures these practices, and because of the standard use of torture it may be impossible to determine definitively, but within trial transcripts there are occasional hints, pieces, and vestiges of ancient witchcraft, magical, Pagan, shamanic, and Fairy traditions.

Africa

Prior to colonial rule, in general, individuals were accused of being magical malefactors and dealt with on an individual basis. European-style witch-hunts began during colonial rule and still continue. Whether this change of attitude derives from enforced colonialism and/or exposure to Christianity is subject to debate.

Although hysterical witch-hunts and trials are now considered an aberration elsewhere, a relic of history, they are on the rise in sub-Saharan Africa. Witches are accused of transforming into bats and night birds, transforming people into *zombis* or committing murder via lightning or poison. Witchcraft is also blamed for AIDS.

✳ *In 1992, over 300 people in Kenya were lynched as witches*

✳ *From April 1994 to February 1995, 97 women and 46 men accused of witchcraft in South Africa were killed by mob violence*

✳ *Between January and June 1998, South Africa's Northern Province reported 386 crimes against suspected witches including assault, property damage, and murder*

✳ *Thousands of children throughout sub-Saharan Africa have been the targets of witchcraft hysteria. Children have been tortured, abandoned, and killed. Many have suffered brutal exorcisms of the demons they are assumed to house*

The Ministry of Safety and Security of South Africa's Northern Transvaal Province established a *Commission of Inquiry into Witchcraft, Violence and Ritual Killings*. A report published in May 1996 stated that thousands accused of witchcraft had been driven from their homes, losing all their property.

Bacchanalia

Hysterical witch-hunting is older than Christianity; Roman persecution of the Bacchanalia is sometimes called the very first "witch-hunt."

The Bacchanalia was the Latin name for the Dionysian mystery traditions of the Maenads or, as they were known in Italy, the *Bacchanals*. (See **DICTIONARY:** Bacchanal, Conjure, Maenad.) Initially held in Etruria, these traditions traveled to Southern Italy and thence to Rome. Rituals were initially restricted to women and conducted secretly three days a year in the Grove of Stimula near the Aventine Hill.

> **Stimula or Simula is the Roman name for Semele, Dionysus' mother, goddess of women's passions, venerated by the Bacchanals.**

Men were eventually admitted to the rites, which increased to five days a month. However the majority of the initiates were female. Initially the Bacchanalia was identified with slaves and immigrant women from Greece, the Balkans, and elsewhere but it eventually attracted respectable Roman matrons who assumed leadership roles.

The Bacchanalia became increasingly controversial; it developed a malevolent, mysterious reputation amongst conventional society and was accused of fomenting political conspiracies. The Bacchanals were accused of poisoning, ritual murder, sexual deviance, and treason. The Roman senate issued a decree, the *Senatus consultum de Bacchanalibus* in 186 BCE, forbidding the Bacchanalia throughout Italy except where the Senate itself reserved the right to permit the rites. (The decree was inscribed on a bronze tablet discovered in Calabria in 1640 and now housed in Vienna.)

According to the Roman historian Livy (*c.*64 BCE–17 CE), the Bacchanals were charged with holding secret nocturnal meetings, allegedly featuring dancing, music, feasting, orgies, homosexuality, and ritual murder. But for the absence of Satan, it sounds remarkably like a European witch-hunters' sabbat of over a millennium later.

The charges that detonated these witch-hunts allegedly began with a family dispute: a young Roman patrician, Aebutius was asked to leave home by his mother. She later claimed it was because her husband, Aebutius' stepfather, was strapped for money; Aebutius claimed he was thrown out because he refused to be initiated into the Bacchanalia as his mother desired.

Aebutius said his concubine Hispala, a freedwoman, had previously attended the Bacchanalia and warned him that it was depraved. Aebutius went to his late father's sister who advised him to make a formal complaint to the Consul, which he did. Essentially he denounced his mother as a Bacchanal.

Hispala was called in and questioned for details regarding what the Bacchanals were *really* doing at their secret nighttime revels. She allegedly initially refused to testify but was advised that she herself would be prosecuted unless she provided authorities with information. Hispala first claimed that she only attended the Bacchanalia as a child and so had limited information; after further questioning however she gave more details, describing torch-lit oracular rites by the Tiber River and naming the current leader of the Bacchanalia as Paculla Annia, a High Priestess from Campania.

The Consul held a public assembly where he accused the Bacchanals, now called the *Conjurari* ("conspirators"), of a criminal conspiracy intended to undermine Roman society. The Senate ordered an immediate extraordinary investigation permitting torture and denying defendants' rights of appeal. A zero-tolerance policy was instituted in the form of a massive witch-hunt for members of the secret society, followed by mass executions.

❋ *An edict outlawed initiates of the Mysteries from convening*

❋ *The Senate offered a reward to anyone denouncing participants in the Bacchanalia*

❋ *Officials were ordered to seek out ritual leaders*

❋ *Roman men were ordered to reject participating members of their family (Aebutius was held up as a role model)*

The Senate simultaneously enacted legislation against diviners and foreign magicians.

Panic swept first Rome, then all of Italy. There were rumored to be over seven thousand *conjurari*. Recent initiates were merely imprisoned but thousands were condemned to death. The state allowed men to punish their female relatives in the privacy of their home (to safeguard the men's privacy, not that of the female prisoners) but if no one was available to execute them privately, it was done publicly. Heads of households thus personally executed wives, daughters, sisters, and slaves or ran the risk of disgracing the family via public executions.

What happened to Paculla, the priestess, is unknown, but her sons were arrested as leaders, tortured to denounce others, and executed. Those they denounced were also tortured until *they* denounced still others.

Known initiates, both female and male, committed suicide rather than face arrest. Some however escaped, including some who had been denounced but whom the authorities were then unable to locate. These Bacchanals are believed to have escaped into forests and mountains. Many believe these escaped Bacchanals are the prototype for Europe's future witches.

Even after the Bacchanalia-panic receded in Rome, the hunt for surviving Bacchanals continued throughout Apulia and other parts of the Italian countryside through 185–184 BCE. What happened to Aebutius' mother is unknown but the Senate rewarded Aebutius and Hispala out of the public treasury and promoted Hispala to a higher social rank so that the couple could be legally wed.

Basque Region

The Basque region spreads over the western edge of the Pyrenees Mountains that divide France from Spain overlooking the Bay of Biscay. There are seven Basque provinces, four in Spain and three in France. The Basque people have lived there since that old proverbial time immemorial; they are believed to have occupied a geographical territory longer than any other European ethnic group.

Their origins are mysterious and continue to confound anthropologists. They are apparently unrelated to any other ethnic group. The Basque language (known in Basque as *Euskara*) is apparently unrelated to any known language. Some suggest it is the original indigenous, Paleolithic European language. The Basques were comparatively late converts to Christianity, and ancestral traditions including ritual dances and offerings to the dead survived conversion.

There were no Basque witch-hunts *per se*; instead French witch-hunters and the Spanish Inquisition took turns entering Basque territory to hunt down and execute witches, and the Basque territory was the scene of extensive witch-hunting in the sixteenth and seventeenth centuries: the Spanish Inquisition targeted Basque witches in the sixteenth century; French witch-hunters targeted Basque witches in the seventeenth.

The ethnic aspect of these witch-trials cannot be forgotten. Basque women were interrogated by French and Spanish men, most of whom could not speak their language and who thus relied on local translators and paid witchfinders.

Traditional Basque society was very different from that the witch-hunters left behind in Spain and France: Basque women were exceptionally independent for their time. Although men wintered at home, a high percentage of Basque men were fishermen who spent the entire summer fishing in Newfoundland. Adult women were, thus, left "unsupervised."

Spanish and French witch-hunters simultaneously disapproved and were titillated by these women. Witch-hunter Pierre de Lancre, in particular, reveals more about his own sexual fantasies in his memoirs than he does of any witchcraft practices (see **BOOKS**: Witch-hunters' Manuals: Pierre de Lancre).

Spain conducted an intensive witch-hunt in Basque territory beginning in 1507. In 1507, over 30 women were burned as witches in Calahorra. In 1527, a craze began when two little girls, aged 9 and 11, claimed to belong to a coven. They told officials that if they were granted immunity, they would identify other witches for the witch-hunters. They claimed they could recognize witches by gazing into their left eyes: in witches, the sign of a frog's foot appeared above the pupil.

Officials took the girls, guarded by 50 horsemen, to various towns so that they could identify witches. Upon arriving in a village, the guards arrested all the women. Each child was placed in a separate house and women were sent in one by one to have their eyes inspected. If the girls pronounced a woman a witch, she was arrested. Over 150 were imprisoned and charged with witchcraft based on the testimony of these two children.

Rumors of thousands of Basque witches engaged in Satanic activity spread through France and Pierre de Lancre, an especially aggressive witch-hunter, was sent in his capacity as the French king's councilor to lead a ferocious witch-hunt through French Basque territory. De Lancre confirmed these rumors: according to him, La Hendaye Beach in French Basque territory had sabbats attended by no less than 12,000 witches.

De Lancre indicted so many witches that the jails literally couldn't hold them all. He reported executing 600 Basque witches, burned alive at the stake, during four months in 1609.

De Lancre despised and hated Basque people, and *especially* independent Basque women who were used to acting as heads of their households. De Lancre was particularly aggravated that women acted as sacristans in church.

He suggested that the Basque witches were part of an international conspiracy with other European witches in order to eradicate Roman Catholicism and Christianity. De Lancre went too far when he began executing priests accused of being or supporting witches: for instance Basque priest Pierre Bocal, accused of wearing a goat mask and presiding over both Christian and Pagan rites and subsequently burned alive. The French public lost its taste for the witch-hunts at that point, and de Lancre fell from public favor.

Official records of the French Basque witch trials were destroyed in a fire in 1710. The best surviving source is de Lancre's own rambling memoirs. To this day, de Lancre's text provides major source material for most discussions of Basque witchcraft. De Lancre did not understand the Basque language; all interrogations were done via interpreters. The witches' confessions, offered in Basque, were recorded by de Lancre in French.

British North American Colonies

Witch-hunting did not start in 1690 at Salem Village. Salem was the site of neither the first nor the last executions for witchcraft in British North America. At least 100 British settlers were charged with or convicted of witchcraft before 1690. Those convicted of witchcraft in the British colonies were, like those convicted in England, typically executed by hanging.

✳ *1628: A Puritan militia in Quincy, Massachusetts suppresses May Day celebrations including dancing, drinking, and a May Pole.*

> Witchcraft was against the law in each of the original thirteen colonies. Crimes included astrology, fortune-telling and what are described as *"magick arts."*

✳ *1642: First Connecticut laws against witchcraft are passed.*

✳ *May 1647: Alice Young is hanged as a witch in Connecticut, the first person executed for witchcraft in British North America.*

✳ *1648: Margaret Jones, midwife, healer, and the first person executed for witchcraft in the Massachusetts Bay Colony, was hanged in Boston on June 15th.*

✳ *1662: Witches are executed in Providence, Rhode Island.*

✳ *1662: Ann Cole of Connecticut claims to be possessed by demons. During a fit, she accuses two women of witchcraft. One of them, Rebecca Greensmith, confesses to belonging to a coven and consorting with Satan. She is executed, as is her husband although he protested his innocence until the end. Following Rebecca's death, at least nine other people are arrested, suspected of belonging to her alleged coven. Most of these people were executed by hanging: trial records are unclear about exactly how many died. However, witch trials and executions continue in Connecticut until 1697.*

The Goodwin Witch Trials

The Goodwin witch trials of Boston in 1688, like the Salem witch trials, also involved bewitched children but have failed to grip the public imagination in the same manner as the Salem Village trials.

There are two versions of what precipitated the Goodwin crisis. According to one, the family accused a Mrs Glover, their Irish washerwoman, of stealing their linens; she denied their accusations, responding with a curse. Alternatively, the eldest Goodwin child, a 13-year-old girl, *asked* the laundress about some missing linens and the laundress retorted with what is described as *"very bad language."*

This daughter began to have fits, quickly followed by her sister and two brothers. The children were struck deaf, dumb, and blind, alternately; their tongues were thrust dramatically out and then pulled back with a snap, like a retractable cord. Physicians were called in but to no avail.

Mr Goodwin requested that the town clergy fast and pray for his family. Cotton Mather the witch-hunter was called in to observe. His observations were published as *Memorable Providences Related to Witchcraft* in Boston, 1689, influencing the Salem witch-trial judges. Most of what is known about the case derives from Mather's writings. He was not sympathetic to the laundress, describing her as the *"daughter of a scandalous Irishwoman."*

The washerwoman was arrested and brought to trial where she claimed that although she understood English well enough, she was unable to speak anything but Gaelic, her native tongue. (Mather claimed her spoken English was previously perfectly functional.) She then claimed that *another* witch had placed a spell on her to prevent her from communicating. (This other witch apparently counting on the court not to obtain an interpreter.)

It was a moot point; there was no need to talk: the laundress was made to touch one of the Goodwin children in court and the child immediately fell into a fit, tantamount during that era to proof of witchcraft.

The laundress' residence was then searched and rag poppets discovered. She then confessed to bewitching the Goodwin children via those dolls. The judges interviewed her for hours and ordered the self-professed Roman Catholic to recite the *Pater Noster* in Latin, which she did except for one or two clauses. She was found guilty of witchcraft; physicians decided she was not insane and she was condemned to hang. Cotton Mather personally accompanied her to the gallows.

Grace Sherwood

Although New England is most closely associated with witchcraft trials, they occurred elsewhere in the colonies too. The most famous American witch trial not occurring in New England was the case of Grace Sherwood of Virginia, in 1689.

When accused of witchcraft, *not* filing suit for slander was tantamount to confessing guilt. James Sherwood, a carpenter, and his wife Grace brought suits for slander and defamation against two different neighboring families. Two charges were filed, £100 requested per count, roughly equivalent to $2,000 dollars today. One neighbor had accused Grace of using witchcraft to blight their small cotton crop; the other claimed that Grace had appeared at their farm in the form of a black cat, in which shape she jumped on Elizabeth Barnes, whipped her, and drove her *"like a horse,"* finally departing through the keyhole not the door.

Both charges of slander and defamation were dismissed; the Sherwoods were fined court costs including those incurred by the entertainment of nine witnesses over four days.

In 1704, Grace, now widowed, reappeared in court charging that another neighbor, Elizabeth Hill, had beaten her. Hill did not deny the charges, claiming she was acting in self-defense as Grace had bewitched her. Grace was awarded £1 in damages but Hill and her husband then charged her with witchcraft in court.

On March 7, 1706, a jury of women was directed to physically search Grace for witches' marks. The forewoman of this jury was Elizabeth Barnes who, years earlier, had been the woman to claim Grace had ridden her in the form of a black cat. Perhaps not surprisingly, several witch marks were quickly found; Grace was convicted of witchcraft.

There was no precedent for witchcraft trials in Virginia. Grace Sherwood was the first conviction. There were various debates as to who had jurisdiction with no one overly eager to assume responsibility. The Attorney General of the Virginia Colony announced that accusations against Grace had been too vague. Her case was turned over to the Sheriff of Princess Anne County, who ordered Grace's home searched for evidence and Grace to be subjected to a water ordeal: a witch ducking. Grace was formally ducked in a local lake on July 10, 1706; she managed to stay afloat, which was considered a sure sign of witchcraft. Had she sunk like a stone and drowned, she might have been judged innocent. (The spot where she was thrown into the water is still called Witch Duck Point.)

Grace was brought back to shore; once again she was bodily searched by five elderly women. Grace was ordered to be chained and imprisoned, awaiting further trial. There are no records indicating this trial was ever held. In 1740, her three sons presented the court with their mother's will and proof of her demise. Her estate included 145 acres of land inherited by her eldest son.

Salem Village Witch Trials

The Salem Village Witch Trials of 1690–1692 are the most written about incident of the entire Burning Times.

Many believe the Salem witch trials to be the only witch trials that occurred in the British Colonies. Others believe them to have been the only trials stimulated by accusations from children. (They were not; there was tremendous precedent for children as witnesses throughout the Burning Times and especially in England. The judges of the Salem witch trials were well aware of this.)

Only one thing is very unique and unusual about the Salem witch trials and that is that not long after the trials had concluded, judges, accusers, and the community repented of their actions, many publicly. Judge Samuel Sewall (1652–1730) so repented of his role in the death of the 19 "Salem Witches" that for the rest of his life he wore coarse penitential sackcloth against his skin, beneath his outer garments. Many later appreciated that participation in the witch trials (as accusers and judges) was something of which to be ashamed or embarrassed; hence even the records of these trials demonstrate some gaps. It is believed that families later edited documents to minimize records of involvement.

The name "Salem" means Peace and was derived from "Jerusalem." The Puritan founders had set themselves a high standard for creating an outpost of God in the wilderness surrounded by Paganism. They lived in absolute fear of the surrounding forest, where witches were believed to make pacts with the devil in the form of Native Americans, especially the local Abenaki who had mounted an aggressive campaign to force the Europeans from their ancestral territory. Many of those involved with the witchcraft trials and accusations had first-hand knowledge of Indian attacks on English settlements. It was a community with a high percentage of people suffering from what would now be considered repressed post-traumatic syndrome.

The epicenter of the Salem witch crisis was the parish home of Reverend Samuel Parris, whose household included his ailing wife, his daughter Betty, two slaves—Tituba and her husband John Indian—and an 11-year-old relative named Abigail Williams, usually described as his niece.

The settlers had an extremely conservative vision of Christianity. No fun was permitted nor leisure time, especially for girls. During the cold winter, Tituba entertained her charges and other young girls with stories while sitting in the kitchen, the one warm spot in the home. Exactly what stories she told them is unknown: the oft-repeated speculation that she told them *"voodoo tales"* is just that: speculation.

The girls allegedly experimented with household divination: floating egg whites on water to reveal information about future husbands. Betty suddenly began to develop odd symptoms. Reverend Parris consulted physician William Griggs, who was unable to discover any physical cause for Betty's condition. Griggs suggested the possibility of bewitchment. Betty began to suffer convulsions and fits; she and Abigail accused Tituba, their slave, of bewitching them. Tituba was beaten; she eventually confessed to witchcraft. Two other women, Sarah Good and Sarah Osborne, were also accused of tormenting the girls. The circle of bewitched girls grew larger and accusations of witchcraft soon flew against various members of the Salem Village community as well as those from other towns.

Details of the trials are complex; many books from many perspectives examine the crisis in Salem. Stories of the victims are famous: only a few can be briefly told here.

On June 2, 1692 Bridget Bishop was the first to stand trial. Bridget was a tavern keeper,

owning two taverns: one in Salem Village and another at Salem Town. Among the accusations against her was maintaining her youthful appearance despite her years. Various upstanding married men of the community testified that she sent her *"shape"* or apparition to torment them in their dreams.

She was accused of attending witches' sabbats and giving suck to a familiar in the form of a snake. She was stripped and carefully searched; a *"witch's tit"* (an extra nipple) was allegedly found between her anus and pudendum.

Martha Corey was arrested in March 1692, followed by her husband Giles in April. She was sentenced to death on September 10th. Giles stood trial several days later. Eighty-year-old Giles Corey knew that by English law, refusing to plead, whether innocent or guilty, would stall the legal procedure. If he never entered a plea, the authorities would be unable to confiscate his property and assets, which would instead be inherited by his heirs as normal.

Giles Corey refused to plead. He was never convicted of witchcraft, although he is perhaps the most famous victim of the Salem witch trials. Giles Corey was *pressed* to force him to either confess or plead innocent. The procedure involved lying a person flat on their back with their limbs extended outwards as far as possible so as not to provide any buffering. Stones and heavy iron weights were then gradually piled atop the body: the person must plead or die.

Pressing occurred only once in American history; Giles Corey is the only victim to this date. Technically, it was illegal under law established in England in 1641; the procedure should not have been administered to Corey. As each weight was added, the victim was asked if he would now like to plead. Giles Corey's only response during the process (and his last words) was the demand *"More weight!"*

Reverend George Burroughs, a Harvard

Encyclopedia of Witchcraft

graduate, was the former pastor of Salem Village. Twelve-year-old Anne Putnam accused him of appearing to her in the form of an apparition, torturing her, and demanding that she sign his book, which she refused. Putnam claimed Burroughs' first two wives appeared to her in sheets with napkins about their heads and told her Burroughs murdered them. Others then came forward and accused Burroughs of being *"the devil of a witches' coven."*

Burroughs was eating dinner with his family in Boston when a marshal arrived with an arrest warrant for *"suspicion of confederacy with the devil."* Burroughs, who once held the same position as Reverend Parris did then, was brought back to Salem to face trial as the alleged coven leader. He was convicted. Standing on the gallows, just before his execution, Reverend Burroughs recited the Lord's Prayer *perfectly*, which, according to then-popular belief, should have been impossible: it was believed that those in league with Satan could not say the Lord's Prayer correctly and in full. His recital received an instant reaction: many among the crowd of observers demanded Burroughs be freed. However, Cotton Mather stepped forward and personally convinced those in positions of power that the hanging should proceed; Burroughs was executed.

Sarah Good denied the charges against her to the bitter end. Her very last words, when encouraged to confess by one of her accusers, Reverend Noyes, were to tell him: *"I am no more a witch than you are a wizard and if you take away my life, God will give you blood to drink."* Sarah was executed; Noyes died in 1717 choking on his own blood as a result of internal hemorrhaging.

The youngest accused witch was Sarah's daughter, Dorcas Good, aged four, charged with *"suspicion of acts of witchcraft."* While jailed, little Dorcas confessed to owning a snake, a present from her mother, which sucked on her index finger, and displayed a red spot on that finger. Those words condemned her to imprisonment while awaiting trial. Special miniature child-sized chains were crafted for her. Dorcas Good remained in jail until December 1692 when Samuel Ray of Salem posted a £50 bail bond for her release. No records indicate whether she was ever brought to trial.

A group of Salem Village girls eventually leveled charges resulting in 150 witch accusations, 141 arrests, 31 convictions, and 19 executions. The accusers were young girls, not politicians; they did not know whom it was safe to accuse. When they accused Lady Phips, wife of the governor, and the pregnant wife of the prominent Reverend John Hale of witchcraft, Hale, for one, began to oppose the whole prosecution, publicly confessing that his previous strong support for the proceedings had been wrong. A number of ministers and other prominent men came to his support and the court recessed.

Between June 10th and September 22nd, 1692, the following 19 people were hanged in Salem Village:

Bridget Bishop	Alice Parker
George Burroughs	Mary Parke
Martha Carrier	John Proctor
Martha Corey	Ann Pudeator
Mary Esty	Wilmot Reed
Sarah Good	Margaret Scott
Elizabeth How	Samuel Wardwell
George Jacobs	Sarah Wilds
Susanna Martin	John Willard
Rebecca Nurse	

The final straw occurred when several people accused of witchcraft in nearby Andover responded by bringing a defamation suit against their accusers demanding heavy financial damages. The Salem witchcraze promptly ended.

In May 1693, Governor Phips ordered all those awaiting trial on witchcraft charges be released from prison, once their legal fees were paid. Excommunications were erased.

Canon Episcopi

The *Canon Episcopi*, one of the first official documents of the Roman Catholic Church regarding witchcraft, was attributed to the Council of Ancyra in 314 CE, however no known document appears prior to the tenth century. Many modern scholars think Bishop Regino, who presented it in 906, actually wrote it himself but ascribed it to earlier sources for credibility.

According to the Canon, no such thing as "witchcraft" exists because only God can possibly have power over humans. Anyone claiming to be a witch or of seeing or experiencing witchcraft is deluded. Furthermore, anyone believing in witchcraft is by definition practicing Paganism and can be prosecuted for heresy.

In early Christian Europe, witchcraft was officially considered an illusion. Those who believed in the possibility of witches were ordered to do penance. The whole concept of witches was described as a Satanic delusion. At that point in history, it may have been perceived as important to deny the reality of witches because they were linked to Pagan female deities like Abondia, Diana, Freya, Herodias, and Hulda: hence denying the witches' power was inherently denying the power of their deities.

The *Canon Episcopi* was incorporated into Church law in the twelfth century. It was gener-

ally understood that night flight and transformations didn't occur on the literal level.

> By the fifteenth century, witches were accused of worshipping Satan and witchcraft was no longer considered an illusion. Among the most influential voices against the *Canon Episcopi* was Thomas Aquinas, who wrote that magicians perform miracles through personal contact with demons.

The *Canon Episcopi* was the official teaching of the Roman Catholic Church regarding sabbats until, in December 1484 Pope Innocent VIII issued a papal bull *Desiring With Supreme Ardor*, stating that witch hunts were a necessity and emphasizing the realities of witchcraft. The *Malleus Maleficarum* was published in 1486 at which point, witchcraft, the witch-hunters' version anyway, was officially perceived as real.

Rather than saying the *Canon Episcopi* was wrong, Church officials explained that Satan had exploited the document to encourage proliferation of witchcraft: a new army of witches had arisen, more powerful and dangerous than ever before, and so new, drastic measures were necessary.

Christianity

As demonstrated by the Bacchanalia, witch hysteria existed prior to Christianity. However, the European Witchcraze was almost entirely Church sponsored; legislation against witches was written into official Church documents. The

Witchcraze was largely (and officially) based on the premise that an international conspiracy of witches was working tirelessly to overthrow Christian civilization.

In the fifth century, St Augustine wrote that at the very beginning of time, God divided Creation into two contrasting realms: the City of God inhabited by angels and good people (i.e., true Christians), and the City of the Devil inhabited by demons and their Pagan allies.

The two domains battle continually; history records their struggle. Demons (and by extension Pagans, which Augustine once was) are agents of the Devil. Their efforts to corrupt Christian souls never cease. Among their primary weapons of seduction are magic and witchcraft. Even healing charms and protective amulets are demonic.

The following are but some of the official decrees contributing to the persecution of witches (depending, of course, upon one's definition of witchcraft) and creating the social climate that would ultimately culminate in the Burning Times:

❋ In 313, Emperor Constantine makes Christianity the official religion of the Roman Empire. That year Pagan religions are proclaimed demonic; Constantine decrees that Pagan shrines be demolished or converted to Christian sites

❋ In 314, Constantine defends Christian massacres of Pagans in Egypt and Palestine

❋ In 314, the Synod of Ancyra decrees five-years' penance for fortune-telling and for healing illness via occult means

❋ In 319, Constantine passes a law exempting Christian clergy from taxes or military service

❋ In 335, Constantine decrees death by crucifixion for magicians and diviners in Asia Minor and Palestine

❋ In 356, Emperor Constantius decrees the death penalty for all forms of worship involving "idolatry" or sacrifice

❋ In 357, Constantius bans all forms of divination, except for astrology

❋ In 375, the Synod of Laodicaea forbids wearing amulets on pain of execution

❋ In 389, Emperor Theodosius bans all non-Christian calendars

❋ In 391, Theodosius prohibits visiting Pagan shrines; even looking at Pagan statues is now a criminal offence

❋ In 395, Theodosius decrees that Paganism is a criminal offence; all Pagan events including the Olympic Games are banned

❋ In 396, Emperor Flavius Arcadias decrees that Paganism is the equivalent of high treason. Remaining Pagan priests in the Roman Empire are ordered imprisoned

❋ In 506, a Visigothic Synod in Languedoc decrees excommunication for anyone practicing divination, whether clergy or layperson

- *In 511, 533, 541, 573 and 603, Frankish Synods in Orleans and Auxerre decree excommunication for fortune-tellers; based on the need for repetition, legislation was apparently not very effective*

- *In 528, Emperor Justinianus orders execution of diviners via crucifixion, fire or rending by iron nails or wild beasts*

- *In 743, the Synod of Rome outlawed offerings and sacrifices to Pagan deities*

- *In 829, the Synod of Paris issued a decree advocating that magicians, sorcerers, and witches be put to death*

- *Although the Inquisition was originally created to combat heresy, circa 1326, Pope John XXII also authorizes it to proceed against sorcerers. John defines any deliberate contact with "demons" to be heresy, thus the Inquisition is empowered to act against ritual magicians*

Having broadened the definition of witchcraft as a crime, the Church was overwhelmed and unable to handle the flood of cases. The Church now encouraged secular authorities to become involved with all phases of witch-hunting and prosecution. The first secular witch trial is held in Paris in 1390, followed by thousands more in Catholic and Protestant regions alike.

- *In September 1409, new pope Alexander V issues a papal bull complaining that many Christians and Jews practice witchcraft, divination, invocations to the devil, magical spells, superstition, and*

"forbidden and pernicious arts, with which they pervert and corrupt many true Christians"

- *Pope Eugenius IV (reigns 1431–47) orders the Inquisition to act against all magicians and witches, emphasizing their diabolical associations*

- *In 1484, Pope Innocent VIII issued a papal bull sanctioning witch-hunting. This was reprinted as an introductory foreword to the witch-hunters' manual the* Malleus Maleficarum. *This essentially gave the entire manuscript the papal seal of approval and many believed the* Malleus Maleficarum *to be an official papal document, thus making the book tremendously influential. (See* **BOOKS**: *Witch-hunters' Manuals: Kramer.)*

Protestants emulate the Roman Catholic Church in only one thing: witch-hunts:

- *Lutheran preachers bring the witchcraze to Denmark*

- *Calvinist missionaries bring the witchcraze to Transylvania*

- *Lutheran preachers lead witchcrazes in Baden, Bavaria, Brandenburg, Mecklenburg, and Württemberg during the 1560s*

England

Witchcraft was prosecuted very differently in England than on the Continent or in neighboring Scotland. During the thirteenth and fourteenth centuries, witchcraft itself was not a crime *per se* in England. The only witches prosecuted were those using magic to cause physical harm to another person or their property, including animals. Anyone convicted of causing harm via malicious magic was punished in the same manner as someone who caused similar harm in a non-magical way: fines, incarceration, and/or public humiliation such as the pillory or stocks. During the fifteenth century some began demanding a more stringent approach.

English witchcraft trial records are comparatively complete; *many* fascinating witchcraft trials occurred in England. The following are but a few of the most famous:

Eleanor Cobham

In 1441 Eleanor Cobham, wife of Humphrey, Duke of Gloucester, was accused of conspiring to kill the king via wax image magic. Two priests, Roger Bolingbroke and Thomas Southwell, were charged as her accomplices as well as Margery Jourdemayne, known as the Witch of Eye because she lived in Eye-next-Westminster.

Jourdemayne had allegedly helped Eleanor wed Gloucester via charms and love spells. In 1430, she was imprisoned for sorcery but released two years later. She then disappears from documents until charged alongside Eleanor.

Eleanor was accused of practicing malevolent magic in order to obtain political power for her husband. The accusations were corroborated by occult scholar Roger Bolingbroke, who was charged alongside Eleanor. Tortured, Bolingbroke confessed that he was a master sorcerer who taught Eleanor everything she knew including wax image magic. He confessed to performing divination at her request.

The childless Eleanor confessed that she made a wax poppet to increase her fertility not to injure or control the king or anyone else. The figure however was judged to be the likeness of the king. Of course, every judge queried was allied with Eleanor's husband's enemies.

Father Thomas Southwell was accused of performing a mass over Bolingbroke's necromantic instruments, seized when Bolingbroke was arrested. None of the accused denied practicing magic but all *vociferously* denied treason or attempts on the king's life.

Thomas Southwell died in prison before sentencing. Margery Jourdemayne, the Witch of Eye, was burned at the stake. Bolingbroke was made to stand on a high scaffold in London wearing magician's robes and surrounded by his ritual tools including the wax figure allegedly made of the king. He was then hanged, drawn, and quartered. His severed head was displayed on London Bridge. His limbs were exhibited, one each in Cambridge, Hereford, Oxford, and York.

Eleanor was convicted and condemned to do public penance on three occasions. She was made to walk barefoot and bareheaded through the streets of London carrying a two-pound candle. She was imprisoned for the rest of her life, first at Chester, then at Peel Castle on the Isle of Man, where she died in mysterious circumstances in 1447.

Anne Boleyn

Anne Boleyn (*c.*1507–1536) is the perfect example of political, cynical use of witchcraft accusations. When Henry VIII was in love with Anne, many critics suggested that she had bewitched the king in order to become queen. When Anne first gave birth to a daughter (the future Elizabeth I), then a still-born son, Henry described it as God's punishment on him for consorting with a witch. He ordered her arrest for treason. (The charge was based on accusations of infidelity.) She was convicted and beheaded in 1536.

* * *

During the sixteenth century, witchcraft laws were made more severe. In 1542 a law was passed decreeing mandatory strict sentences—but not death—for conviction of maleficia (see **DICTIONARY**). In 1562 Queen Elizabeth I passes the Witchcraft Act. A first offense was punishable by being pilloried; the death sentence was only permitted after three separate convictions. Execution is mandated for cases of maleficia involving murder. In 1581 severe physical punishment is mandated for maleficia even if it does not result in murder. (Merely practicing folk magic, however, was not a crime.)

The number of witchcraft accusations rose, as did the number of sensational trials that gripped the public imagination such as the Burton Boy and the Chelmsford Witches.

Witch persecutions were disproportionately strong in Essex and Lancashire; historians suggest that this was in response to religious tension between Roman Catholics and Puritan evangelists.

Chelmsford Witch Trials

Chelmsford, Essex, was racked with witch trials in 1566, 1579, 1589, and 1645.

In 1566 three women were charged as witches in Chelmsford during a two-day trial. Charges included consorting with the devil and harming others via magic (maleficia).

Elizabeth Francis confessed that her grandmother, Mother Eve, had instructed her in witchcraft, teaching her to renounce God and give her blood to the devil. She also confessed to bewitching a baby who then "became decrepit." She had a white spotted cat named Sathan who was her familiar and obtained goods and sheep for her. Sathan, who could speak English (this ability was not demonstrated at the trial), stole 18 black and white sheep for Elizabeth.

Sathan also helped her obtain a lover; when the lover wouldn't marry Elizabeth, the cat killed him via witchcraft. On the cat's advice she became pregnant by Christopher Francis, whom she later married, but the marriage was unhappy. Elizabeth testified that she requested that Sathan kill her child, which he did. She later wanted her husband lamed, which the cat accomplished by transforming into a toad and hiding in Christopher Francis' shoe. The cat also allegedly killed a neighbor's cattle.

After 15 or 16 years of service, Elizabeth Francis said she had enough of Sathan the cat and gave him to her impoverished neighbor, 65-year-old Mother Agnes Waterhouse, instructing her to call him "Sathan" and feed him bread, milk, and her own blood.

Agnes Waterhouse confessed to the murder by witchcraft of William Fyness and sending Sathan to destroy a neighbor's cattle and geese. She also had a toad familiar whom she kept in a pot. She also testified that she tried to get Sathan to kill a local tailor, Mr Wardol, with whom she had a dispute, but Wardol was too strong in his faith.

Joan Waterhouse, her daughter, aged 18, was charged with bewitching 12-year-old Agnes Brown. Both older women confessed but Joan did not, begging for mercy instead, which she received.

Elizabeth Francis was sentenced to a year in prison. Agnes Waterhouse was condemned and hanged on July 29, 1566. Joan Waterhouse, Agnes' daughter, was found innocent.

In 1579 four women were charged with witchcraft in Chelmsford including Elizabeth Francis who had served one year in jail after being convicted of witchcraft in 1566. Charges included two cases of bewitchment resulting in a person's death and one charge each of bewitching a cow and a gelding to death. Elizabeth Francis, Ellen Smith, and Alice Stokes were executed by hanging. Margaret Stanton was released for lack of evidence.

In 1589 ten people were accused of witchcraft in Chelmsford. Records show that four were hung and three were found innocent. It is uncertain what happened to the last three defendants.

The Windsor Witches

This 1579 trial was stimulated by the discovery of three female wax images, pierced with bristles and found buried in a dung heap. Four elderly, impoverished women (Mother Devell, Mother Dutten, Mother Margaret, and Elizabeth Stile) were accused of witchcraft. They denied the charges until they were told that leniency would be shown if they confessed. They confessed and were promptly convicted and hanged.

St Osyth Trial

There were approximately 14 defendants in this 1582 trial. Ten were charged with committing murder via witchcraft. (Margaret Murray reported 13 defendants, however many historians believe she manipulated numbers to support her theory of 13-member covens. Trial transcripts allegedly indicate 14 witches.)

The central figure was Ursula Kemp, a professional healer who included folk magic in her practice: it is unclear whether she was tortured. The person who first accused her of maleficia was a former patient who had refused to pay a bill and claimed Kemp had retaliated by worsening the illness.

Kemp's eight-year-old son was coerced into offering detailed testimony about witchcraft practiced in their home. After her son's testi-

mony, Ursula confessed to being a witch and named four other women as witches. Ursula claimed to be a solitary witch but said the other women were part of two covens in the area. The four women were arrested and charged; they in turn confessed and named others as witches. Two women, Ursula Kemp and Elizabeth Bennet, were hanged on February 18, 1582. Four others were acquitted. Two women were released prior to the trial's conclusion for lack of evidence and the rest were incarcerated.

Following Ursula's death, her body was dipped in tar and displayed, hanging from a gibbet, for almost a month. She was refused a Christian burial and was buried in wasteland. Her remains were discovered during a 1921 excavation just outside the Priory of St Osyth. Metal spikes had been driven through her wrists, knees, and ankles—presumably so she wouldn't rise again. Her body was displayed before being buried once more under a heap of rubble. Cecil Williamson purchased her remains in the 1940s for £100. (See **HALL OF FAME:** Margaret Murray, Cecil Williamson.)

The Warboys Witches

The trial of the Warboys Witches in 1593 was a sensational case; it is sometimes cited as a major factor in the passage of the 1604 Witchcraft Act. The Warboys Witches were Alice Samuel, aged 76, her husband John, and her daughter Agnes.

In 1589, Alice was visiting her neighbor Robert Throckmorton in Warboys when his 10-year-old daughter Jane suffered some sort of seizure, for which Jane blamed Alice. Soon other girls in the Throckmorton family, aged 9 to 15, were having fits too and blaming Alice Samuel.

Their parents doubted witchcraft was the cause. Wealthy and well-educated, they consulted the finest physicians possible who could find no physical cause. The fits increased in frequency and in violence. Other women in the household (the girls' aunt, female servants) started having fits too. At first there was no pattern to these fits but after a while they *only* occurred in Alice Samuel's presence. (Alice was frequently summoned to the Throckmorton estate as part of the process of determining what was wrong with the girls. She had no choice but to appear.)

Eventually Throckmorton asked Alice to live in his house, reasoning that the girls couldn't sustain their fits 24 hours a day. He was right: the fits became intermittent, but instead the girls now began to see demons. A visitor, Lady Cromwell, experimented by burning a little of Alice's hair in the belief that this could lessen her power. The girls were no better and Lady Cromwell later claimed that Alice appeared in her dreams that night and attacked her. Lady Cromwell developed a long illness and died one year later. Alice Samuel was blamed for her death.

Three years later in 1592, the Throckmorton girls were still pitching fits, still seeing demons, still in misery, and still blaming Alice Samuel. Alice apparently finally had enough: she lost her temper and ordered the girls to stop their nonsense—they did!

The fits stopped. Unfortunately for Alice, this was taken as incontrovertible proof of witchcraft. Alice herself began to wonder if she possessed some kind of power, confiding her fears to a local clergyman. He shared her concerns with others: a formal investigation was opened.

Alice Samuel soon confessed to witchcraft. She was placed on trial for bewitching the ladies of the Throckmorton household and the magical murder of Lady Cromwell.

During that era it was commonly believed that if someone practiced witchcraft, others sharing her household must be practitioners, too, especially daughters. Alice's husband and her daughter were charged with witchcraft too, although both protested their innocence. The Samuel family was convicted and hanged in August 1593, after which all signs of bewitchment in the Throckmorton household ceased.

the Pendle Forest Witches

The trial of the Pendle Forest witches in 1612 was one of the largest and most complex of the English witch trials. Twenty defendants from two families were charged. The trial was the subject of a 1613 book by the court clerk, Thomas Potts—*The Wonderful Discovery of Witches in the County of Lancaster*.

Elizabeth Sowthern, also known as Old Mother Demdike, and Anne Whittle, also known as Old Chattox, worked together for a while selling magic potions. Each lived with her large extended family in Lancashire's Pendle Forest. Eventually rivalry developed between the two families and a feud developed, each family accusing the other of malevolent witchcraft. Accusations were lobbed against each other: magical baby killing, murder via familiar (spotted dog), Satanic pacts, and so forth.

Authorities eventually arrested the two matriarchs and nine of their relatives; officials later learned that about twenty members of the two families that hadn't been arrested were conspiring to spring the accused from jail. Nine were caught and jailed for this conspiracy, but were also charged with witchcraft. The new defendants were accused of using magic to murder 16 people as well as assorted cows and horses.

Nine-year-old Jennet Device was the prosecution's star witness, offering damning testimony against her grandmother (Sowthern/Demdike), her mother Elizabeth Device, her sister Alison, and her brother James. She testified that her mother used witchcraft to kill three people and had a familiar in the shape of a brown dog named Bell.

Mother Demdike, aged 80, confessed that she became a witch 50 years earlier when she was initiated by a boy wearing parti-colored clothing whom she met near a stone pit in Pendle Forest. She had since dedicated herself, her children, and her grandchildren to Satan. (Whether this was code for hereditary witchcraft remains subject to debate.) Her granddaughter Alison testified that Demdike had initiated her into the family coven with the gift of a big black dog.

Mother Demdike was allegedly the leader of one group of witches; her rival Anne Whittle (Chattox) was accused of killing John Device (Mother Demdike's son-in-law) via witchcraft because he didn't pay Chattox the annual tax he promised her for not harming him or his family.

The magistrate ordered Demdike and three others be arrested and taken to Lancaster Castle where Mother Demdike died in jail. Ten people were hanged in August 1612 including Anne Chattox and her daughter as well as Elizabeth, Alison and James Device. Young Jennet Device, who was left without immediate family, largely because of her own testimony, was herself hanged as a witch 20 years later.

The Burton Boy

Thomas Darling (c.1582–?) was from Burton-on-Trent and so was called "the Burton Boy." At age 14, Thomas experienced a brief illness; he began having convulsions and reported seeing visions of demons. Physicians were consulted; most diagnosed bewitchment. (One diagnosed worms.) Thomas was asked who was responsible; he named 66-year-old Alice Gooderidge, with whom he had quarreled in the forest. She was tracked down and tortured to extract her confession. Alice denied being a witch but was unable to recite the Lord's Prayer, then considered proof of witchcraft. She was tortured until she began to give details of her "crimes."

Alice said Satan visited her in the form of a dog she had received from her mother, Elizabeth Wright. No record exists of what happened to Wright; Gooderidge died in prison while serving a one-year sentence for witchcraft.

In the meantime, famed exorcist John Darrell cast out Darling's demons. He suffered no more convulsions. Three years later, Thomas Darling admitted faking convulsions, possessions, and exorcism in order to achieve celebrity and fame. (Some believe Darrell was also involved in the deception.)

In 1604, King James I passed the Witchcraft Act. Death by hanging is decreed for *all* cases of maleficia, even first offenses not involving murder. It becomes a crime to consort with the devil, concoct potions, and practice divination. Rural practitioners of folk magic were reclassified as devil-worshiping witches.

Elizabethan law had preserved distinctions between "good" and "bad" witches. Reginald Scot's 1584 book *Discoverie of Witchcraft* became increasingly influential (see **BOOKS:** Witchhunters' Manuals: Scot). Trial judges more and more found accused witches innocent or even refuse to try them. James changed the law because, in his words, he *"found a defect in the statute … by which none died for witchcraft but only who by that means had killed so that such were executed rather as murderers"* than as witches.

Following the 1604 Act, professional witch-finders begin to appear, most notoriously Matthew Hopkins. Because English law did not permit brutal torture as in parts of the Continent, English witch-finders devised their own techniques. (What constituted torture was subjective; although "torture" as practiced in Germany and Scotland was forbidden in England, starving, exhausting or otherwise creating *"discomfort"* was permissible.)

Accused witches were kept awake for days, made to walk continuously, and refused food and water. When exhausted, they were more easily bullied, coerced or tricked into confessions.

Witchcraft was also proven by water ordeal, known as *"swimming the witch"* or *"being swum."* The accused was tied up and tossed into deep water. Most people at that time could not swim. If the person floated, she was guilty. Many panicked and confessed. This ordeal was banned by Parliament in 1645, although it remained commonly practiced.

Matthew Hopkins

Between 1645 and 1646 Matthew Hopkins was responsible for the executions of over two hundred accused witches. Hopkins (*c.*1621–*c.*1647), a professional witch-finder, appointed himself *Witch Finder General.* He received a fee of 40 shillings for each charge and investigation and a bonus per conviction. His profit per "job" ranged from £4 to £26. He traveled through the countryside offering his services.

Hopkins' family came from East Anglia. He was a Puritan and lived in the village of Manningtree in Essex; very little else is known of his early life. He had been a struggling lawyer but in 1645 began advertising his services as a witch-hunter. Essex was his preferred territory but he extended his efforts throughout East Anglia.

Hopkins placed emphasis on imps, familiars, and witch's marks rather than on the sabbats popular among witchcraft accusations elsewhere. An accused person was searched for a devil's or witch's mark, which was almost inevitably found. Searching wasn't limited to visual examination: long pins were stuck all over the accused's body in search of a witch's mark, which might be visible or merely a spot on the body perceived as being insensitive to pain. If the person didn't cry out in pain then the witch's mark had been found. After the mark was discovered, the accused was strapped naked onto a stool or table and left with observers to await the arrival of an imp, familiar, demon or devil. Any appearance was considered sufficient: an ant, a fly, a mouse …

Hopkins had two assistants. John Stearne, a Puritan, searched men, and Mary Phillips, a midwife, searched female suspects for marks, under the supervision of Hopkins.

The first witch Hopkins investigated was old, one-legged Elizabeth Clarke whose neighbors in Chelmsford disliked her. Clarke was tortured and named five others. All were executed. From that very first trial, people were disconcerted by Hopkins' fees and by the financial incentive he had in discovering and proving witchcraft.

The public became increasingly uneasy about Hopkins' methods. Opposition to him grew. A 1646 publication, *Select Cases of Conscience Touching Witches and Witchcraft* by John Gaule, a clergyman in Huntingdonshire, wrote against the cruelties of witch-hunting in general and attacked Hopkins' procedures in particular. After publication of Gaule's book, Hopkins' business began to taper off.

In 1647, Hopkins self-published a pamphlet, *The Discovery of Witches: in Answer to Severall Queries lately Delivered to the Judges of Assize for*

Norfolk County, that defended his actions and claimed that the sincere desire to eliminate evil (not financial motivation) stimulated his career as a witch-finder.

Hopkins then disappeared. What happened to him? Who knows? Some suggest that Hopkins was himself accused of witchcraft and executed. Others suggest that relatives of a witch he caused to be executed killed him or that a mob seized him and dunked him in the village pond until he drowned (Hopkins was particularly fond of swimming witches). This may be wishful thinking: Stearne, his old assistant, suggested that Hopkins died of tuberculosis.

The Somerset Witch Trials

In 1664, 16 women and 9 men are tried in what became known as the Somerset Witch Trials. They allegedly belonged to two covens, both under the alleged personal supervision of Satan, who appeared to them as a mysterious man named "Robin." The witches confessed to the charges; they claimed they'd been given devil's marks and that they had used ointments and incantations to fly off to sabbats. The court, however, didn't believe their confessions and dismissed the case.

Margaret Murray relied heavily on trial transcripts from the Somerset Witch Trials for her books and theories of witchcraft. See **HALL OF FAME: Margaret Murray.**

Exeter Witch Trials

In 1682 three impoverished elderly defendants were arrested in Exeter—Susanna Edwards, Mary Trembles, and Temperance Lloyd. Lloyd, who had twice previously been unsuccessfully tried for witchcraft, was accused of leading a coven that included the other two women. It is not clear whether the women were tortured but all three confessed to being witches and consorting with the devil. This was one of the last English witchcraft trials. The judge, convinced that the confessions stemmed from the defendants mental and physical infirmities, wished to acquit the women. The public massed outside the courtroom however roared for conviction and execution, and the judge, fearing public's reaction, ordered their execution. The three women were hanged in August.

In 1684 Alice Molland was hanged as a witch in Exeter. She was the last person executed for witchcraft by an English court of law.

The last official trial for witchcraft in England occurred in Leicester in 1717. Twenty-five neighbors accused Mother Norton and her daughter of practicing witchcraft. The two women were subjected to swimming and were publicly stripped naked and pricked. However, in court, the presiding judge, Justice Parker, and the Grand Jury found no substance to the charges and released both women.

The Witchcraft Act of 1736, enacted under George II, sharply reduced penalties for practicing witchcraft. The gist was that witchcraft doesn't exist, therefore no one should in the future be prosecuted for it, *but* anyone pretending to be a witch or to practice witchcraft should be prosecuted as an impostor.

A substantial segment of the populace disapproved of the Act as being too lenient towards witches, permitting them to get away with their crimes. Thus instead of charging people with witchcraft, mob violence became more customary when witchcraft was suspected. As late as the early twentieth century, stories of mobs attacking suspected witches were not uncommon.

In 1751 John and Ruth Osborne were killed by a mob that suspected the elderly couple of witchcraft. The Osbornes had long been unpopular in their Hertfordshire community; they are described as holding differing political views from their neighbors. A dairy farmer named Butterfield apparently refused Ruth Osborne some free buttermilk; shortly afterwards his cows died. With no cows, he sold his farm and opened a tavern instead. Butterfield then began to have convulsions for which he blamed Ruth, as he had the cows' demise. Butterfield grumbled to his tavern customers who spread the gossip. A *"rumor"* spread that on April 22, 1751, the Osbornes would be swum to determine if they were witches. Local authorities hid the Osbornes for their own safety but a mob, led by chimney sweep Thomas Colley, found them on the appointed day. They were stripped naked, tied up, and tossed into a stream.

Ruth Osborne did not sink and so Colley pushed her under with a stick until she nearly died. The crowd then dragged her from the water and beat her to death. Her husband was dragged out as well and beaten; he died several days later.

In 1875 80-year-old Anne Tennant was fatally wounded with a pitchfork wielded by James Haywood, a local farmhand, in the village of Long Compton, Warwickshire. She was pinned to the ground with a pitchfork through her throat; a cross was carved over her breast with a billhook. *"I meant to do it!"* Haywood said when arrested. Haywood, terrified of witches since childhood, believed there were at least 15

in the area and intended to eliminate them. A jury declared him insane.

The 1944 trial of Helen Duncan (born in 1898) is cited as the reason for the repeal of Great Britain's 1736 Witchcraft Act. Duncan was a medium. In 1941, she claimed to have spoken with the spirit of a recently drowned sailor. However, the event in which he had drowned had been classified as a military secret; no one outside a very limited military circle was aware of the drowning. The media picked up the story and the government was forced to admit the truth. There was speculation as to what other secrets Duncan might reveal and so she was placed on trial under the 1736 Witchcraft Act as plans for the Allied invasion of Normandy were being finalized.

During her trial, the government argued that Duncan was a life-long fraud and charlatan. However, dozens of witnesses, Duncan's satisfied clients, testified to the contrary. Helen Duncan was convicted and spent nine months in prison, despite public protest against her incarceration.

In 1945 Charles Walton (1871–February 14, 1945) was discovered murdered. He had been pinned to the ground with a pitchfork through his throat. A cross had been slashed onto his body using a billhook, which was then thrust into his torso. The case became known as the *"Witchcraft Murder"*; Walton may have been killed because he was assumed to be a witch. A laborer who lived with a niece, he had a reputation as a cunning man with clairvoyant skills. Walton had taken his billhook and gone to trim hedgerows for a local farmer. He was seen at work at midday but never returned home. His niece and the farmer searched for him, discovering his body under a tree.

Scotland Yard was never able to solve the crime despite taking over four thousand statements. Villagers were not forthcoming: Walton was not well-liked. There was much speculation regarding his witchcraft practices and whether he was personally responsible for poor crops in the area. The murder remains unsolved to this day.

Does the murder sound familiar? It occurred but two miles from where Anne Tennant had been similarly killed as a witch in 1875 (see page 794).

In 1951 all British anti-witchcraft laws were repealed. Up until then, books perceived as advocating witchcraft practices and rituals, such as this one, could not be published in the UK.

France

The earliest French penalties against witchcraft consisted mainly of heavy fines: the fifth-century Salic Law established various levels. A fine of 72 sous and a half golden coin, for instance, was levied upon those who fashioned a witch's knot and launched mortal curses, but also upon those who defamed a man as a wizard. In other words, one couldn't make false accusations without penalty, a situation that would change during the Burning Times.

In 589, the Council of Narbonne decrees that diviners be whipped and sold as slaves. Those who consult with them are excommunicated and fined six ounces of gold. The Church designates secular rulers as the recipients of these fines, thus encouraging their cooperation.

Charlemagne (*c.*742–January 28, 814), ruler of the Frankish lands, was crowned Holy Roman Emperor by the Pope during a mass on Christmas Day, 800. Charlemagne was no longer merely the leader of a nation; he was the leader of Western Christendom and eligible to lead crusades, his army was now an arm of the Roman Catholic Church. In essence, *any* war conducted by Charlemagne was potentially a "Holy War," *especially* if his opponents were Pagan, even if it was conducted for increased territory.

Charlemagne's territories eventually spanned Europe from the Pyrenees to the Danube. At the Church's bidding, he attempted to stamp out all traces of Paganism within his territory: not just "*idolatry*" but anything remotely occult or magical. Magical practitioners were aggressively persecuted during Charlemagne's reign. Laws demanded that fortune-tellers, diviners, sorcerers, and witches be handed over to the Church for punishment or, alternatively, used as slaves. First offenders were to have their heads shaved and be paraded through town on a donkey (see **ANIMALS:** Donkeys). Those convicted of a second offense were liable to have noses and tongues lopped off, while three-time offenders were liable to be executed.

In 873, Charles the Bald decreed, "*It is the duty of Kings to slay the wicked, not to suffer witches and poisoners to live …*" He also condemned those who consulted or consorted with witches.

The earliest French witch-hunts were heresy-trials conducted by fourteenth-century Inquisitors. The first French secular witch trial occurred in 1390. As secular courts became more involved in witch-prosecution, the French government strengthened its anti-witchcraft laws to increase likelihood of conviction and execution.

France now saw the rise of the celebrity witch-hunter. Nicholas Remy (*c.*1530–1612), for instance, judge, attorney, and author of the 1595 witch-hunters' guide *Demonolatry* (see **BOOKS: Witch-hunters' Manuals: Remy**), demanded execution of all witches as well as automatic punishment for their children, an unusual point but one subsequently adopted by many witch-trial judges. As a witch-hunter, Remy was responsible for the execution of over 900 accused witches, personally supervising the torture of over twice that number.

Remy believed his eldest son had been magically murdered in 1582 by a beggar-woman witch after the son had refused to give her alms. From that day forth, Remy was merciless towards witches, conducting a personal vendetta.

In *Demonolatry*, Nicholas Remy boasted, *"so good is my justice that last year there were no less than sixteen killed themselves rather than pass through my hands."* He described children of condemned witches being *"stripped and beaten with rods round the place where their parents were being burned alive."* Remy found this insufficient, however: *"out of consideration for the public safety, such children ought in addition to be banished or exiled ... for experience has shown that they who have fallen into the power of the Demon can rarely be rescued except by death."*

In 1275, the Toulouse Inquisition executes Angèle de Labarthe (or Labara) after she is convicted of eating babies and having sex with the Devil. According to trial testimony, Angèle claimed to have conceived a son by the devil; eye-witnesses testified that the boy had a wolf's head and a snake's tail. He was fed on a diet of dead babies and lived until age 15, but died before her trial and so could not be presented to the court. Angèle is frequently cited as the first woman burned at the stake for having sex with Satan.

The Paris Witch Trial is France's first secular witch trial, held in 1390. Jehan de Ruilly's wife Macette fell in love with a handsome young curate; Macette hired Jehenne de Brigue la Cordière ("the rope maker") a 34-year-old fortune-teller, to cast a spell to cool her husband's ardor. The incantations made Jehan ill. La Cordière felt sorry for him and removed the spell. The two women were arrested and charged with witchcraft.

At first la Cordière denied everything, but she was tortured and confessed to casting spells invoking the Holy Trinity and neglecting her prayers. This wasn't sufficient for the court; tortured again, she recalled that her aunt taught her to summon a demon named Haussibut. She confessed to casting spells via wax dolls and a frog familiar.

Her trial continued throughout the winter and spring, with periodic recesses. She was sentenced to burn but was granted a reprieve because she thought she might be pregnant. Macette initially denied the charges but was tortured on the rack and confessed.

La Cordière's sentence was reinstated but she appealed to the Parliament of Paris, the highest tribunal in the land. A new set of judges reviewed her case. Both verdicts were confirmed; on August 19, 1391 the two women were taken to the Pig Market and burned alive at the stake.

Between 1428 and 1447 a witchcraze in the Dauphiné region resulted in 110 women and 57 men being burned alive at the stake. In another witchcraze in Lorraine, between 1580 and 1595 over 900 people are burned alive during this period in this one region alone.

In 1579, the death penalty was mandated for divination: the Church Council at Melun declared, *"Every charlatan and diviner and others who practice necromancy, pyromancy, chiromancy, hydromancy, will be punished by death."*

Father Louis Gaufridi, a 34-year-old priest, was accused of bewitching several nuns at the Ursuline convent in Aix-en-Provence in 1610, and of forcing them to consort with the devil.

In December 1610, Father Gaufridi was interrogated by the Inquisition and tortured for approximately three weeks until he confessed to signing a pact in his own blood with Satan and bewitching the nuns. He confessed that a late uncle left him a collection of books including a magical text rendered in French verse. When, from curiosity, he repeated a conjuration, a demon appeared and made a pact with Gaufridi: his body and soul in exchange for honor, worldly success, and luck with women. He confessed to engaging in orgies at sabbats and presiding over services mocking those of the Church.

Gaufridi retracted his confession but on April 18, 1611 was found guilty of sorcery and sen-tenced to death. Before his sentence was carried out, however, he was tortured yet again to extract the names of accomplices. On April 30, 1611, Father Gaufridi was tied to the stake, strangled, and then burned. The next day Madeleine was fine but Louise continued to have visions of demons and witches. Other nuns continued to exhibit signs of possession and so finally, they were imprisoned.

The Loudon Witch Trials

The Loudon Witch Trials of 1634 featured the demonic possession of nuns at the Ursuline Convent in Loudon where the defendant, Father Urbain Grandier, had served as priest since 1617. He was a ladies man who reputedly had many mistresses among prominent local women. In 1630, a secular court found Grandier responsible of fathering the local prosecutor's daughter's illegitimate child. Only the intervention of the Archbishop of Bordeaux kept Grandier from jail although the prosecutor subsequently held a grudge against the priest. He was not the most dangerous of Grandier's enemy's however: Grandier was an outspoken critic of Cardinal Richelieu, chief minister to Louis XIII. Historians believe this to have been his ultimate undoing.

In 1633, Sister Jeanne des Anges, the Mother Superior of the Ursuline Convent, and several of the nuns began demonstrating "classical symptoms" of demonic possession. Grandier was blamed for their condition. Two other priests, enemies of Grandier, were summoned to conduct exorcisms. Sister Jeanne blamed Father Grandier along with a host of impressive demons including Asmodeus and Ashtaroth for tormenting her with demons and sending her depraved dreams. The Archbishop of Bordeaux intervened, sending physicians to examine the nuns. The physicians found nothing amiss and the exorcisms were halted.

Richelieu then intervened, arranging for new public exorcisms and appointing a special investigator. During the public investigation, Grandier's former mistresses came forward with racy tales of sexual escapades.

Grandier was arrested as a witch. A search was made for devil's marks, which were found although his supporters present at the search claimed there were none. These supporters were then threatened with charges of witchcraft themselves unless they stopped protesting. Some of the nuns began recanting their previous accusations. Richelieu offered to pay the nuns a pension in exchange for their testimony.

At Grandier's trial, a document purported to be a pact signed in blood by Grandier and countersigned by Lucifer, Satan, Beelzebub, and other "demons" including Leviathan (who knew this legendary sea creature could write?) was presented as evidence. This rare demonic document was perceived as highly damaging evidence.

> Further reading: Aldous Huxley's *The Devils of Loudon* (Carroll & Graf Publishers, 1952) is devoted to the trial of Urbain Grandier. *The Devils* (1971), a film loosely based on the case, was directed by Ken Russell, and starred Oliver Reed as Grandier.

In August 1634, Grandier was found guilty and sentenced to be burned alive. He was then tortured so that he'd confess and name accomplices. Despite the brutality of torture (his bones were crushed), Grandier neither confessed nor named names. At his execution, Grandier attempted to make a public statement but several priests doused him with Holy Water and made noise so that his voice could not be heard.

After Grandier's death, some nuns continued to display signs of demonic possession. Richelieu cut off their pensions and the fits promptly stopped. Sister Jeanne became a healer and prophetess, displaying signs of the stigmata. She died in 1665.

Although some French monarchs brutally suppressed any trace of witchcraft; others displayed more tolerance. Some, like Catherine de Medici, were whispered to be witches themselves. In 1670, 525 people were convicted of witchcraft at Rouen, but their death penalties were commuted to banishment by order of Louis XIV. During Louis' reign a thriving community of fortune-tellers and spell-casters existed in Paris; some may also have provided illicit "pharmacological" services, including abortion and poisons. Many among the upper classes and nobility utilized these services.

In 1676, Marie-Madeleine D'Aubray, the Marquise de Brinvilliers, tried to poison her husband; he had been tipped off, however, and possessed an antidote. The authorities were summoned, and potions were found among the Marquise's belongings. She was accused of causing the deaths of her father and two brothers. An attempt to kill a sister had allegedly failed. She was arrested, tortured confessed to witchcraft and was beheaded. Under interrogation, the Marquise claimed other high-society people dabbled in witchcraft too. Paris Chief of Police Nicholas de la Reynie began searching for them.

It was then very fashionable among high society to have fortunes told, especially via cards. In 1678, an attorney named Perrin went to a party at the salon of Madame Vigoreux where they were entertained by a card-reader,

Marie Bosse, known as La Veuve, "the widow." She jokingly said that she could retire after only three more poisonings. Perrin later explained that he saw "*something*" in her face as she joked and he determined to investigate. He contacted the officers who had arrested the Marquise de Brinvilliers. They sent a police officer's wife to La Veuve to have her fortune told. In what might be perceived as a set-up, the wife complained bitterly of her husband. After her second visit, she went home with a vial of poison.

La Veuve and Madame Vigoreux were arrested, as were those of their acquaintances who shared their professions (charm-sellers, fortune-tellers). Tortured, the women confessed to selling poison and revealed their clients who were subsequently arrested and tortured too. They revealed further sources of poison and more fortune-tellers, who were now linked in the eyes of the law.

Eventually the alleged leader of the "poison ring" was discovered: Catherine Monvoisin, known as La Voisin, an astrologer who read palms and cards. The elite consulted her in her Paris home on Rue Beauregard. She also allegedly sold aphrodisiacs and performed abortions.

> In 1664, La Voisin allegedly held her own when invited to the Sorbonne to engage in debate with its male scholars regarding the validity of astrology.

La Voisin was arrested on church steps while leaving Sunday Mass. She was tortured mercilessly for three days but continued to proclaim her innocence. Eventually she allegedly confessed to performing over 2,500 abortions. Her home allegedly contained an abortion clinic and a chapel in which corrupt priests conducted Black Masses. Under interrogation, she revealed names of her clients, some *very* close to the crown.

In response, in January 1679, Louis XIV created the *Chambre Ardente* to investigate charges of abortion, infanticide, and poisoning operating under cover of occult services. The *Chambre Ardente* ("Burning Chamber") was a secret court that investigated "witchcraft crimes" of the rich and powerful closely connected to the throne. The name didn't refer to burning people but to describe the room brilliantly lit with burning candles and flambeaux.

Some nobles fled, allegedly helped by the king, but others were implicated including the king's mistress, Madame de Montespan, mother of six of his illegitimate children. The *Chambre Ardente* arrested 319 people. Their fates varied: 36 were killed, others were exiled, incarcerated or enslaved on galley ships, although those of noble blood (including the king's mistress) were set free. (She quietly retired to the convent of St Joseph in Paris in 1691 where she died in 1707.)

La Voisin was burned at the stake on February 20, 1680. Louis banned fortune-tellers and limited the sales of poisons. In 1709, he terminated the *Chambre Ardente* and ordered that all evidence of its existence be destroyed. On July 13, 1709, the king allegedly burned certain documents personally.

Father Louis Debaraz is usually cited as the last person executed for witchcraft in France, in 1745. He was accused of performing Black Masses in hopes of locating hidden treasure. After a lengthy trial, he was burned alive.

Witchcraft was struck from the French law code in 1791.

Germany

The worst atrocities of the Witchcraze occurred in German lands between the fifteenth and eighteenth centuries. Some suggest that at least half of all witch-trial related deaths occurred in German lands.

The German witch-hunts operated on a particularly broad scale; at its peak almost no one was truly safe. The stereotypical image of the witch-hunt victim is an elderly impoverished woman; these women were certainly killed during the German witch-hunts but the wealthy were targeted too, as were the socially prominent.

> Magic and traditional witchcraft were among the duties of the ancient Pagan Germanic housewife. Sagas describe ordinary women routinely practicing magical healing and divination and casting protective spells for the benefit of their families.

In the twelfth and thirteenth centuries most witch-trials in German lands were tried by Papal Inquisition, not by civil courts. Witches were usually hanged or imprisoned, although they were often dragged out of prison by local townsfolk and burned alive in public lynchings. By the fifteenth century, the customary means of execution for witches in German lands was burning alive, unlike other regions where convicted witches were traditionally strangled before burning.

Local German courts exercised tremendous autonomy over witch trials in their regions. German Inquisitors and witch-hunters developed torture into a fine art. All torture instruments were blessed by a priest before use, and witches were tortured so severely, confession was virtually guaranteed.

* *Victims were force-fed salted herrings to induce thirst and then denied water*

* *Victims were stripped naked and frequently raped, sometimes gang-raped, before being led to torture chambers*

* *Children of convicted witches were typically treated identically to their parents under the theory that, as acorns don't fall far from oaks, witchcraft ran in families and the children would inevitably become witches eventually. Children were tortured to provide information about parents and relatives and to provide greater lists of suspects.*

In 1563, 63 women were executed in the small Lutheran territory of Weisensteig, and in 1572 the Law Code of Saxony decreed that even "good" witches must be burned.

The region around the city then known as Treves (now Trier) was beset by natural disasters in 1580, including storms and plagues of grasshoppers and mice. Witchcraft was blamed; a witch panic ensued. Trials were begun in both ecclesiastical and civil courts. A series of convictions eliminated two entire villages. No one was left. Only two members of the female population of a third village were left alive.

Among the last victims was Dietrich Flade (?–1589), Chief Civil Magistrate of Trier, arrested in 1588 and charged with witchcraft and with showing leniency to witches in his courtroom. Could the judge himself be a witch?

A boy swore he witnessed Flade at a sabbat. A woman about to be killed testified that Flade was a witch in exchange for the mercy of strangling before burning. Flade, brutally tortured, confessed to plotting against the Archbishop of

Trier and of throwing dirt into the air, which transformed into crop-eating slugs. He was convicted, strangled, and burned.

※ *1589: In Quedlinburg, Saxony, 133 women are burned as witches in one day*

※ *1590: 32 are burned as witches at Nordlingen*

※ *1590: A witness writes that in Wolfenbüttel "the place of execution looked like a small forest from the number of stakes"*

※ *1590–1: Forty-nine out of a population of 4,700 are burned as witches at Werdenfels in Bavaria*

Between 1590 and 1640 Eichstadt was the site of a series of witch-hunts. Conservative estimates of numbers killed range from between 1,500 and 2,000 people. The first wave occurred in 1590, followed by continuous witch panics between 1603 and 1630, slowly tapering off after that.

The Pappenheimers were an impoverished Bavarian family; they worked seasonally as privy-cleaners, supplementing their income with begging. In 1600 the family was arrested in the middle of the night, literally pulled from their beds in a rooming house, and charged with witchcraft. The youngest son, 10-year-old Hansel, was left behind but the next day, their landlord brought the child to the prison where his parents were incarcerated, giving him to the authorities.

The family was tortured mercilessly, including strappado, squassation, and torture by fire (see page 827, Torture). Hansel was caned. Although all initially pleaded innocent, eventually they confessed to anything put to them. The adults confessed to virtually every unsolved crime of the past decade in that region as well consorting with Satan. They implicated over 400 other people.

It was decided that examples would be made of the Pappenheimers and so their public execution was particularly brutal. Ten-year-old Hansel was forced to watch from the crowd; the Sheriff of Munich was stationed beside him to observe the child's reactions and to force him to watch the torture and murder of his parents and brothers.

Sixty-year-old Anna Pappenheimer's breasts were torn off via a torture instrument known as "the spider." Her severed breasts were first stuffed into her own mouth, then into the mouths of two of her sons who were concurrently being tortured.

Using red-hot pincers, flesh was ripped from the bodies of the male victims. Paulus Pappenheimer, the father, was broken on the wheel. Following the execution, the sheriff brought Hansel back to jail. On November 26, 1600, Hansel Pappenheimer was burned at the stake.

Witchcrazes continued in German lands throughout the seventeenth century:

※ *Between 1603 and 1606 Balthasar Ross, Judge of the town of Fulda, orders the execution of 300 witches. He later boasts that because of his activities over 700 people had been executed. He himself is later hanged for embezzling state funds.*

※ *1609–1623: A witch panic begins in Bamberg that only continues to escalate. At least 400 people are recorded as executed from 1609 until the ascension to power of a new ruler in 1623, Prince-Bishop Gottfried Johann Georg II Fuchs von Dornheim, whereupon things take a turn for the worse.*

Although witch-hunting was well established in Bamberg before his ascension to power, Prince-Bishop von Dornheim streamlined the process by which the accused were interrogated, tried, and executed. From first accusation until execution could now take less than three weeks.

Von Dornheim became known as the "*Witch Bishop*." He established a professional witch-hunters' organization with expert torturers and executioners. Attorneys were hired with express orders to convict. He built a new prison solely to house accused witches. The *Hexenhaus* ("Witches' House") was constructed specifically for the interrogation (torture) of accused witches. Suffragan Bishop Friedrich Förner presided over what was essentially an extended torture chamber.

Trials were short and speedy and closed to the public. Defendants were not permitted lawyers. Testimony on behalf of the accused was virtually impossible and a guilty verdict was pretty much a sure thing. Those who criticized procedures, verdicts or the witch-hunters' organization usually found themselves quickly accused of witchcraft themselves.

Von Dornheim directed that all accused witches be tortured before *and* after confession. Tortures included dunking suspects in boiling water mixed with caustic lime, forcing suspect to kneel on spikes, and having their armpits set afire, as well as standard tortures like thumbscrews and bone-crushing. Convicted witches often had their right hands cut off before execution.

In general, most defendants in Bamberg were wealthy. Witch-hunters targeted the wealthy, because those found guilty (and once targeted, virtually everyone was condemned) were required to surrender all their property and possessions to the head of the witch-hunting organization, Bishop Förner, who then distributed the funds, rewarding witch-hunters according to the wealth each had collected.

Witnesses were typically paid informants. All accusations were kept secret until after the suspected witch was arrested, eliminating the possibilities of escape and revenge.

Affluent citizens began abandoning Bamberg in fear for their lives. From exile, some petitioned Ferdinand I, Emperor of Germany, to end the Bamberg witch-hunt. The Emperor eventually issued mandates in 1630 and again in 1631 requiring all accusations of witchcraft be made public. The procedure of seizing a convicted witch's property was ended. Von Dornheim died in 1632 and the witchcraze tapered off.

Johannes Junius, Burgomaster of Bamberg (*c.*1573–1628) is the sole victim of the *entire* Witchcraze to speak to us in his own voice without the filter of torturers. A literate, articulate man, he took tremendous effort to write a farewell letter to his daughter, which was smuggled from prison by a jailor and eventually published.

Junius was accused of witchcraft, as, ultimately, were all the burgomasters of Bamberg. On June 28, 1628, he protested his innocence but witnesses testified they saw Junius at a sabbat and at a witches' dance on the Haupstmoor where a communion wafer was desecrated. Junius still denied the charges and was given 48 hours in jail to think about them. He *still* asserted his innocence on June 30th and so was put to thumbscrews and boots. He was stripped and searched for a witch's mark, which was allegedly found. The strappado was administered and finally, on July 5th, he confessed to consorting with Satan since 1624.

The authorities paraded Junius down the streets of Bamberg, ordering him to name other witches. He did but in insufficient numbers; he was tortured again to name more and was then condemned to burn at the stake in late July. Before his death, Junius wrote a letter to his daughter Veronica, which was smuggled out by a jailor and delivered. This is an excerpt of the lengthy letter:

Many hundred thousand goodnights, dearly beloved daughter Veronica. Innocent have I come into prison, innocent have I been tortured, innocent I must die. For whoever comes into the witch prison must become a witch or be tortured until he invents something out of his head ... the executioner ... put the thumbscrews on me, both hands bound together, so that the blood ran out at the nails and everywhere, so that for four weeks I could not use my hands, as you can see from the writing ... Thereafter they first stripped me, bound my hands behind me and drew me up in the torture [strappado; see page 829, Torture]. Then I thought heaven and earth were at an end, eight times did they draw me up and let me fall again, so that I suffered terrible agony ... When at last the executioner led me back into the prison he said to me, "Sir, I beg of you, for God's sake confess something, whether it be true or not. Invent something, for you cannot endure the torture which you will be put to; and even if you bear it all, yet you will not escape, not even if you were an earl but one torture will follow another until you say you are a witch" ... And so I made my confession ... but it was all a lie ...

Dear child, keep this letter secret so that people do not find it, else I shall be tortured most piteously and the jailers will be beheaded ... I have taken several days to write this; my hands are both lame ...

Goodnight, for your father Johannes Junius will never see you no more. July 24, 1628.

He added a postscript to the margin: *"Dear child, six have confessed against me ... all false, through compulsion, as they have all told me and begged my forgiveness in God's name before they were executed ... They were forced to say it, just as I myself was ..."*

❋ ❋ ❋

At the same time as the Bamberg witchcraze, between 1623 and 1632 approximately 900 people including 300 children were tortured and executed at Würzburg, ruled by Prince-Bishop Phillipp Adolf von Ehrenberg, cousin of Prince-Bishop von Dornheim of Bamberg.

A contemporary chronicler wrote:

A third of the city is surely implicated. The richest, most attractive, most prominent of the clergy are already executed. A week ago, a girl of 19 was burned, said everywhere to be the fairest in the whole city ... there are 300 children of 3 or 4 years who are said to have intercourse with the devil. I have seen children of seven put to death, and brave little scholars of ten, twelve, fourteen ...

Among the victims was Ernest von Ehrenberg, the Prince-Bishop's sole heir. A guard who permitted some prisoners to escape was executed, as were travelers who had the misfortune to be passing through the region.

In 1630, three women were killed when mandrakes were found in their home in Hamburg (see **BOTANICALS:** Mandrake), and Rheinbach, near Bonn, was the site of two major witch panics, one in 1631 and another in 1636.

The panics in Rheinbach were documented by Law Court Official Hermann Löher, who estimated that every other family in Rheinbach lost at least one member to the witch-hunts. Löher wrote that what he learned is that those tortured will confess to anything. He urged local German princes to terminate the practice of torture. His opposition to the witch trials put him and his family in jeopardy. He sold his property and fled to Amsterdam in 1636.

Franz Buirmann, who presided over the Rheinbach trials, was authorized by the Prince-Archbishop of Cologne to discover witches and confiscate their property and so wealthy citizens were particularly vulnerable. In 1631, town leaders offered to pay Buirmann to go away, abandon his hunt, and move elsewhere. He took the bribe but returned in 1636 for a new series of trials.

> Forty years later, Löher published a description of the panic in Rheinbach, *Most Pressing Humble Complaint of the Pious Innocents,* in which he described how one judge conducted a witch trial. The judge addressed the cowering defendant, *"Confess your sins of witchery; reveal the names of your accomplices! You filthy whore, you devil's wanton, you sackcloth-maker, you dumb toad! ... Tell who it was that taught you witchcraft and who you saw and recognized at the witches' sabbat."*

Even by the standards of his time, Buirmann was brutal, condemning those few who refused to confess despite torture to death anyway, against standard procedure. Instead of the usual stakes, living victims were placed inside dried straw huts, which were then set ablaze. Buirmann held power to override any objections of the civil authorities and had his opponents tried and executed.

It's estimated that the Rheinbach witch trials of 1631 and 1636 led to the executions of 150 people from the 300 families living in the region. However, many died before reaching trial, during the torture and interrogation process. Their numbers are unknown. The Mayor of Rheinbach, Dr Schultheis Schweigel, charged with witchcraft, died after seven hours of continuous torture.

❋ ❋ ❋

Friedrich von Spee was the leading Jesuit official at Würzburg. His duties included hearing the last confessions of condemned prisoners prior to their executions. In the process he came to the conclusion that virtually all those accused of demonic practices were completely innocent. He wrote, *"Grief has turned my hair white, grief for the witches I have accompanied to the stake."*

In 1631, Spee anonymously published a revolutionary book, *Cautio Criminalis* (*Precautions for Prosecutors*—see **BOOKS:** Witch-hunters' Manuals: Spee), in which he denounced torture, and called for rational trial proceedings with fair use of evidence and permitting defendants legal representation. Spee wrote, *"Previously, I never thought of doubting that there were many witches in the world. Now however when I examine the public record, I find myself believing that there are hardly any."* He wrote further, *"There is nobody in our day ... who is safe, if he have but an enemy and slanderer to bring him into suspicion of witchcraft"* and *"Often I have thought that the only reason why we are not all wizards is due to the fact that we have not all been tortured."*

Spee claimed that, under the existing system, confessions were inevitable, writing, *"If she confesses, her guilt is clear: she is executed; if she does not confess, the torture is repeated—twice, thrice, four times. She can never clear herself; the investigating body would feel disgraced if it acquitted a woman; once arrested and in chains, she has to be guilty, by fair means or foul."*

In *Cautio Criminalis* Spee exposed what he saw as the true incentive of the German witch-hunts: Inquisitors received payment for each person burned. Assets of the condemned were confiscated. He denounced claims that some confessions were secured without torture, explaining that trial records indicating *"no torture"* really indicate that *"light"* torture was used rather than the most severe.

After publication, many Jesuits denounced Spee's book and attempts were made to suppress it; however it was eventually translated into 16 languages and widely read throughout Europe. Although it was initially published anonymously, his fellow Jesuits suspected Spee's identity and were hostile towards him. Shortly after publication, his superiors transferred Spee to serve as a confessor for plague victims. He contracted the plague and died in 1635 at age 44.

Benedict Carpzov (1595–1666) published *Practica Rerum Criminalum* in response to *Cautio Criminalis* in 1635, which justifies aggressive pursuit and persecution of witches: witches deserve fewer rights during trials than other criminal defendants, he writes, because of the danger they pose to society and to judges and jurors. Torture is required in order to extract confessions. Carpzov, Chief Witchcraft Prosecutor of Saxony, personally signed no fewer than 20,000 death warrants.

✸ *1651: The executioner in Neisse built an oven in which to roast witches. That first year, he roasted, according to records, at least 42 women and children, including little girls as young as two years old. Over the next nine years, the same executioner roasted at least 1,000 people.*

✸ *1676: Chaterina Blanckenstein (1610–1679) of Saxony served a child some of her homemade jam. When the child died four days later, the 66-year-old widow was arrested for murder via witchcraft. During her trial, others came forward to blame her for various crimes (she magically overturned a cart, for instance). Despite torture, including thumbscrews and ropes around her neck, Blanckenstein refused to confess. No devil's mark could be found. The judge decided the case couldn't be proved and released Chaterina once she paid the cost of her imprisonment, trial, and torture. Neighbors shunned her when she returned home and she eventually relocated. Her daughter, whose name is only given as L. in trial transcripts, remained in town however. L. was arrested on charges of murder by witchcraft in May 1689. A local baby had died unexpectedly. During the investigation into the death it was discovered that the baby's father owed L. money. Because of the family's reputation, it was quickly decided that L. was responsible for the baby's death and arrested. At first sight of the instruments of torture, she confessed. Jailed, L. tried to hang herself two days later, but was discovered and revived so that she could be burned alive.*

Anna Maria Schwaegel was the last woman executed for witchcraft in Germany, in 1775. She was a servant in a wealthy household in Lachen. She fell in love with the household coachman who promised to marry her but instead married another. Anna Maria took this very badly, running away to become a homeless, vagabond beggar. Discovered starving, her clothing in rags, she was taken to a church asylum for the deranged where she told the Mother Superior that the devil had seduced her in the form of a coachman. He had brought her to sabbats and encouraged her to commit unspeakable acts. The Mother Superior reported the case to the magistrate of nearby Kempten, Bavaria. Anna Maria was arrested and placed on trial: she repeated her story and was convicted of witchcraft and beheaded.

Iceland

Iceland had a comparatively brief witchcraze from 1625 until 1683, to some extent imported from Europe by a ruling class of semi-nobles largely educated in Denmark and Northern Germany.

Iceland was unusual because, unlike almost everywhere else during the witch-hunt era, the accused witches were predominately male. Of approximately 170 people accused of witchcraft, less than 10 percent were female. Twenty-one people are recorded burned as witches; only one was a woman. (Iceland's population at that time was approximately 50,000.)

There is no evidence that physical torture was used in Iceland. One-quarter of those accused were acquitted. Approximately 15 percent of those accused evaded arrest, and records do not indicate what happened to approximately another 15 percent of those accused. Most of those convicted were punished by severe whipping.

In 1639 using runes was defined as witchcraft and the practice was banned. It was decreed that people found with runes in their possession would be condemned to death by burning. In 1681 Arni Pétursson was burned alive in the presence of the Althing, the Icelandic Parliament, for using runes to achieve success at backgammon.

The Inquisition

The Inquisition was a crucial part of the witch-hunts. Although many now joke about the Inquisition, few truly understand its dynamics. The Inquisition was a formal court of inquiry first officially established by Pope Gregory IX in 1233 to deal with heresy in Toulouse, France. It takes its name from *"Inquisitorial Procedure"* and was based on old Roman legal procedures. Witch-hunting in turn was largely based on Inquisitorial procedure.

The Inquisition was a Holy Office, an arm of the Church. It was administered by Dominican friars who reported *only* to the Pope, no matter where they were, regardless of region, territory or country.

The Inquisition was created in response to perceived threats to the Church from Christians who protested or deviated from official Vatican practices. It was the responsibility of the Dominicans to identify and eliminate any trace of heresy before it could take root, spread and infect the faithful.

Pope Lucius III authorized the very first Inquisition in 1185 in response to the growth of independent, unorthodox versions of Christianity in Europe. In 1199, Pope Innocent III proclaimed that all property and assets of convicted heretics should be confiscated; they were often shared with local secular governments to encourage their cooperation. In 1233, Pope Gregory IX centralized and formalized the Inquisition. He placed the Dominicans in charge and decreed that no one might interfere with their work.

The Inquisition was based on an accusatorial procedure; it was dependent on denunciations. In other words, somebody had to initiate the process with an accusation that must then be proved or a confession of guilt obtained.

Confession was *required* from the accused and torture was used to extract it. Torture was perceived as necessary for completing the Inquisitorial process as it was believed no one would confess completely without it. Even those who voluntarily confessed were likely holding something back that they would not voluntarily reveal without torture.

It was permissible to imprison the accused indefinitely on a diet of bread and water both before and after interrogations, scheduled at the pleasure of Inquisitors. If the person never confessed, despite torture (unusual, as torture was unlimited), the accused could be imprisoned for life. There was never a point where the accused was required to be released.

If the accused did confess, that confession *had to* be reaffirmed three days later. The person *had to* explicitly attest that they confessed of their free will and not because of torture or fear of torture, whether or not this was true.

If one confessed and denounced others, one could theoretically be *"reconciled"* with the Church. The person would be spared execution and assigned punishment instead, usually fasting, penance, public humiliation (stocks, pillory), and/or pilgrimage. One might be obligated to wear a special uniform for the rest of one's life, usually a yellow felt cross sewn onto the back and chest of one's clothing. In Portugal and Spain, these were customary punishments for confessed witches; very few were executed in Portugal and in Spain proper. (The Spanish Inquisition did, however, kill witches in the Basque regions.)

> Unlike the old *Accusatorial* process that was the legal standard before the Inquisition, *Inquisitorial* proceedings were typically secret, as were the accusations. Previously, accusations were often public; the accuser had to face the accused.

The Inquisition was responsible for collecting information from the public that could lead to the discovery of crimes or identification of criminals. The Inquisition, at its simplest, was a mechanism for social control. Informers were welcomed and frequently paid or otherwise favored.

Under the Inquisition, the accused was seldom, if ever, allowed an attorney. Women, children, and slaves were permitted to testify for the prosecution but were forbidden to testify for the defense. Ecclesiastical courts were empowered to seize the personal property and assets of anyone found guilty of *any* charges brought by the Inquisition.

The Inquisition *never* killed or burned a witch. Following conviction, heretics and/or witches were handed over to the secular authorities for punishment. Any official refusing to administer the Inquisition's decreed punishment was charged with heresy.

The Inquisition was finally restrained in the nineteenth century. The Inquisition survives today but since December 7, 1965 it has been known as the *"Congregation for the Doctrine of the Faith."*

Ireland

Ireland is frequently cited as the place where witch-burning began and ended. Some date the Burning Times from the burning of Petronilla of Meath in 1324, and ending with the burning of Bridget Cleary in 1895. However, the last legal European witch execution occurred in Poland in 1793 (see page 813). Bridget Cleary was never formally charged with witchcraft; nor was she tried or executed in legal proceedings. Her husband burned her in their home, on his own volition, in what he claimed was an attempt to exorcise a demon, changeling or witch (see **FAIRIES:** Fairy Witch).

Despite the notoriety of the Alice Kyteler case, the witchcraze in Ireland was comparatively mild. There were fewer than 10 significant witch trials, the bulk of which were carried out by Protestant (English and Scots) settlers.

The Kilkenny Witch Trials

Beginning in approximately 1320, Richard de Ledrede, Bishop of Ossory, a Franciscan of English descent, aggressively investigated heresies in his diocese under the personal commission of Pope John XXII, in the process discovering, he claimed, the existence of many sorcerers and witches. Chief among them was Lady Alice Kyteler of Kilkenny, also known as Dame Alice Kyteler.

Lady Alice lived in Kilkenny with her fourth husband Sir John le Poer. She was independently wealthy, having inherited the wealth of her previous, deceased husbands. She was descended from a noble Anglo-Norman family who had lived in Kilkenny, a city within the diocese of Ossory, for generations. The ultimate point of the accusations against her was that she had no right to her wealth as it had been obtained by witchcraft and diabolical means.

The adult children of Lady Alice's previous husbands accused her of killing their fathers to obtain their property. (They were hoping that the property she had inherited would instead pass to them.) They accused Lady Alice of attempting to kill her present husband who at the time was ill with a *"wasting disease."*

A maid-servant warned him of the rumors: his children from a previous marriage suspected Lady Alice was poisoning him in order to inherit the estate. Suspicious, Sir John forcibly took Lady Alice's keys to her private chests and boxes where he allegedly discovered witchcraft tools including magic flying ointment and a sacramental wafer with the devil's name stamped upon it. Two friars were summoned to carry these to Bishop Ledrede.

Sir John and his children accused Lady Alice and her son from a previous marriage, William Outlawe, of killing her first three husbands with witchcraft and attempting to do the same to

John. William Outlawe was a banker and money-lender; documents indicate that many local nobles were heavily in his debt.

> Lady Alice's alleged accomplices, popularly known as the "Kilkenny Witches" included her son, William Outlawe, her maidservant, Petronilla de Meath and Petronilla's daughter, Sarah, Robert de Bristol, John, Helena and Sysok Galrussyn, William Payn of Body, Alice, the wife of Henry the Smith, Annota Lange, and Eva de Brounstoun.

Alice's first husband William Outlawe, also a wealthy banker, was the brother of Roger Outlawe, Lord Chancellor of Ireland and chief of the Irish branch of the Order of the Knights of St John. (Husbands two and three were Adam le Blond and Richard de Valle, respectively.)

Bishop Ledrede charged that Lady Alice and company didn't attend church but had renounced Christianity to sacrifice roosters and peacocks at crossroads to a spirit named variously "Robin" or "Robert Artisson" or "Filius Artis." This shape-shifting spirit was allegedly Lady Alice's familiar, sometimes appearing as a cat or a large, shaggy black dog or sometimes as a huge black man accompanied by two tall dark companions carrying iron rods. Robin is described in records as *"Aethiopis"* or *"negro."* Charges suggested that the only reason Lady Alice was rich, fortunate, and privileged was because of this spirit's patronage.

The Kilkenny Witches were further accused of holding nocturnal meetings in churches, making *"infernal candles,"* ointments, powders, and unguents from dead men's nails, botanicals, scorpions, snakes, spiders, and worms. Allegedly these concoctions were brewed in a cauldron made from a decapitated thief's skull.

> Among other allegations against her, Lady Alice was accused of walking the streets of Kilkenny armed with a broom, sweeping toward the house of her son William Outlawe while chanting, *"To the house of William my son, Hie all the wealth of Kilkenny town."* Whether or not Lady Alice actually cast this spell, it is authentic, genuine folk-magic.

In essence, Bishop Ledrede was a precursor, a witch-hunt pioneer; as a disciple of Pope John XXII, he was on the cutting edge of witch-hunting. He attempted to bring Alpine-style witch-hunting to Ireland; some of the resistance of the local clergy toward him was because of their unfamiliarity with this type of demonolatry.

The Bishop wished to try the case personally but sorcery cases were still considered secular crimes and the Church had no jurisdiction. He was forced to ask the Lord Chancellor of Ireland to issue a writ for the arrest of the accused. The Lord Chancellor, of course, happened to be Roger Outlawe, Alice's old brother-in-law and William Outlawe's uncle.

The Bishop then sent a representative to William Outlawe's house where Lady Alice was now living, demanding that she appear before the Court of the Bishopric. Lady Alice refused, stating quite correctly that the Ecclesiastical Court was not empowered to judge her, or anyone else for that matter, on a case of this kind. Bishop Ledrede responded by excommunicating her and charged William with *"harboring and concealing his mother in defiance of the Church."*

Lady Alice fled to Dublin where she called upon influential and powerful contacts.

Arnald de Poer, Government Seneschal of Kilkenny and a distant relative of Alice's present husband, sided with William and Alice instead of his blood relations. He attempted to have Ledrede reduce the charges against Alice and William but Ledrede refused.

De Poer in turn had the bishop seized and held captive in Kilkenny Castle. Bishop Ledrede was jailed for 17 days until *after* the date William was supposed to appear in court. (The bishop's supporters accused William of bribing officers of the law to arrest and detain the bishop.)

Upon his release, the bishop attempted to speak at the secular court but was ejected by the Seneschal. The bishop tried several times to have Lady Alice arrested on charges of sorcery but was unsuccessful.

Finally, Bishop Ledrede publicly named those accused of sorcery and demanded that the secular court give the accused up to the Church. Lady Alice had the bishop indicted in the secular court for slander and defamation of character. In turn, William Outlawe scoured criminal records, discovering an old deed of accusation claiming that the bishop defrauded a widow of her husband's inheritance. Local ecclesiastical authorities were also unsympathetic to the bishop, describing him as a *"truant monk from England"* with excessive zeal in carrying out Papal Bulls they had never heard of before, and defaming Ireland by accusing her of harboring heretics.

Lady Alice escaped to England where she lived for the rest of her life. She was denounced in Kilkenny as a magician, sorceress, witch, and heretic. Some suggest Sarah de Meath was brought to England with her.

William Outlawe eventually showed up in court, after much delay, bringing a posse of well-armed supporters with him. Charges were read out; he was held for nine weeks although sources differ as to whether he was formally arrested. William ultimately begged for reconciliation with the authorities, confessing and renouncing his crimes. In exchange for publicly renouncing his heresies, he received a Church pardon. As penance, he was required to pay for the Cathedral's new lead roof and fast every Tuesday until a special pilgrimage to Canterbury was completed.

After the case, Bishop Ledrede accused Arnald de Poer of heresy. He was excommunicated and sent to the Dublin Castle dungeons, where he died during the investigation.

In England, the still wealthy and well connected, if excommunicated, Lady Alice continued to exert pressure against Bishop Ledrede, who was also eventually accused of heresy. He was sent to the Vatican for further investigation; while he was gone, his lands were seized.

The fates of accused members of Lady Alice's Kilkenny coven differed: some were burned at the stake, some *solemnly whipped* through the town and marketplace; some were banished while others fled and disappeared. In the words of Bishop Ledrede, *"by the special grace of God, that most foul brood was scattered and destroyed."*

Petronilla de Meath did not escape. She was flogged six times before she publicly confessed to charges of witchcraft and orgies involving Lady Alice. Petronilla claimed to be Lady Alice's go-between. She claimed that Lady Alice, the most powerful witch in the world, had taught her sorcery and witchcraft. She said she saw Lady Alice's demon manifest as not one, but three black men, who each had sex with Lady Alice. Petronilla acknowledged that she herself cleaned the bed.

Like William Outlawe, Petronilla confessed; unlike William, she was not pardoned. (Whether this was because she was female and neither wealthy nor noble, or because the court genuinely believed her to be a witch is subject to speculation.) Descriptions of her suggest that she did not repent and expressed pride in her sorcery. Speculation remains as to whether Petronilla was a spiritual witch or Pagan, as she allegedly refused Christian last rites before her execution.

Although Lady Alice is described as the first person tried for witchcraft and heresy in Ireland, and although it is her name that is most commonly cited, it was her maid, Petronilla de Meath, who ultimately paid the price and was the first woman burned as a witch in Ireland. Many mark the beginning of the Burning Times with the death of Petronilla, burned at the stake before a crowd on Saturday, November 3, 1324.

Other trials followed:

✻ *1544: An entry in a table from the Red Council Book of Ireland refers to "a witch" sent to the Lord Deputy for examination. However, unfortunately, only the table survived, not the Red Council Book or other records; no further information is currently available.*

✻ *1578: A witch trial occurred in Kilkenny. Beyond the fact that 36 were executed, few details are preserved*

Anti-witchcraft statutes were passed by the Parliament of Ireland in 1586: *"Death as a felon"* was decreed for anyone convicted of murder via witchcraft, enchantment, charm or sorcery. *"Death as a felon"* was accomplished by hanging, drawing, and quartering for men or strangulation followed by burning for women.

First-time offenders convicted of practicing witchcraft resulting in destruction or impairment of goods or property were sentenced to

Encyclopedia of Witchcraft

imprisonment for one year. In addition, they had to stand in the town square pillory once every quarter year for six hours and confess their sins. Second-time offenders were subject to a mandatory death sentence.

The Island Magee Witch Trial

The Island Magee Witch Trial was the last significant Irish witch trial. In 1710, the home of Mr and Mrs James Haltridge of Island Magee, near Carrickfergus in County Antrim, allegedly began to be plagued by poltergeist-like activity. The Haltridge family perceived it as symptomatic of psychic attack and witchcraft: although the identity was unknown, *someone* was attacking them. The death during this time of Haltridge's mother, who lived in the house, was popularly attributed to witchcraft.

On approximately February 27, 1711 18-year-old Mary Dunbar was hired to live in the house as a companion for Mrs Haltridge following the death of her mother-in-law. On her first night in the house, Mary allegedly retired intending to sleep but was shocked to discover that some of her clothing had been removed from her trunk and scattered through the house. While searching for her missing clothes, Mary discovered an apron that had been rolled up tightly and tied with, depending on the version, either five or nine "strange knots." Mary untied the knots, discovering a flannel cap belonging to the deceased Mrs Haltridge tied up within.

That night, Mary Dunbar was seized with fits: she claimed a knife was run through her thigh and that three women, whom she could vividly describe but not name, afflicted her. At midnight, she was seized with more fits: she had a vision of seven or eight women talking together. During their conversation, which Mary overheard in her vision, they revealed their names. Upon emerging from her fit, Mary identified those names: Janet Carson, Elizabeth Cellor, Janet Liston, Kate M'Calmont, Janet Mean, Latimer and Mrs Ann. Mary was able to provide such vivid descriptions that the women were quickly picked up from various local districts: Janet Mean of Braid Island, Jane Latimer of the Irish quarter of Carrickfergus, Margaret Mitchell of Kilroot, and Catherine M'Calmont, Janet Liston, Elizabeth Sellar, and Janet Carson, all of Island Magee.

The accused were brought to trial on March 31st. Testimony included descriptions of Mary's fits. Various Presbyterian ministers testified against the accused. (All the accused women were Presbyterian.) No medical evidence was offered nor did the prisoners have an attorney. All denied charges of witchcraft but a jury returned guilty verdicts.

They were sentenced to one year in prison during which time each had to stand in the local pillory on four separate occasions. These pillory sessions attracted mobs who pelted them with eggs and cabbage stalks so aggressively that one of the convicted witches had an eye knocked out.

In August 1807, Alexander Montgomery of Carmoney feared his cow was bewitched. Although she gave plenty of milk, none could be churned into butter. Mr and Mrs Montgomery hired Mary Butters, local herbalist and spellcaster, now known as the "Carmoney Witch."

Mary Butters instructed Mr Montgomery and a young man named Carnaghan to put their coats on inside out and stay in the barn near the cow's head until she called them. In the meantime, she prepared a hex-breaking spell in the Montgomery's kitchen in the presence of Mrs Montgomery, the Montgomerys' son and an elderly woman named Margaret Lee. Butters' curse-breaking spell involved boiling nails, needles and pins in a cauldron containing the afflicted cow's milk and perhaps some other ingredients. Windows and doors were tightly closed; the chimney was sealed up.

Montgomery and Carnaghan waited in that barn for *hours*. Finally, at dawn, they returned to the house where they discovered everyone passed out on the floor. Mrs Montgomery and her son were already dead. Lee died shortly afterwards. Only Mary Butters survived.

On August 19, an inquest was held and the court determined that death was caused by smoke inhalation and *"noxious ingredients."* Mary Butters, however, claimed that a black man carrying a big club appeared during the spell and clubbed everyone present. She was scheduled to stand trial in Carrickfergus in March 1808 but the charges were withdrawn.

In 1821 the Witchcraft Act of 1586 was repealed. Despite this, in 1865 Biddy Early was charged with witchcraft; local Church leaders denounced her as a witch but the charges were dismissed. (See **FAIRIES:** Fairy Doctor: Early.) Incomplete trial records suggest another witch trial was held at Dungannon 1890.

Italy

Witch-hunting was comparatively mild in Italy. Although there were executions by burning, most of those convicted of witchcraft suffered incarceration, flogging, penances, and banishment.

In 1181 the Doge of Venice passed laws forbidding sorcery. Trials and executions of witches in Como were held *c.*1360. Over 300 were eventually executed.

In 1384 Sibillia, wife of Lombardo de Fraguliati, appeared before Friar Ruggiero da Casale, Inquisitor of Upper Lombardy, accused of *"dreadful crimes."* She was punished with various penances but in 1390 she was again accused and sentenced to die by a new Inquisitor.

Fragments of the records survive: Sibillia confessed that for years, every Thursday evening she journeyed to pay homage to a sacred being called *"Madame Oriente."* Inquisitors identify Madame Oriente in trial records as *"Diana, called Herodias."*

Pierina, wife of Pietro de Bripio also appeared before Friar Casale in the same year, and was also assigned penances for heresy. Just like Sibillia, in 1390 a new local Inquisitor, Friar Beltramino da Cernuscullo, sentenced her to death for backsliding.

Pierina told the Inquisition that she had attended Madame Oriente's Society every Thursday since she was 16. She described Madame Oriente as *"Mistress of the Society"* in the same fashion that Christ is *"Master of Earth."*

The Society roamed through various houses, feasting and drinking. Madame Oriente blessed them and taught them herbal remedies, spell-breaking techniques, and how to locate lost and missing items. Pierina told the Inquisition that Madame Oriente could resurrect dead animals, but not humans. Devotees sometimes slaughtered oxen and ate them. The oxen's bones were saved and placed atop the animal's hide. Madame Oriente struck the hide with her wand and the oxen returned to life but could no longer be used for labor.

Later in the trial transcript, possibly after torture, Pierina confessed to giving herself to a spirit named Lucibello and signing a compact in her blood. At this point, she explains that Lucibello led her to the Society, a point not made previously but more in line with the witch-hunters' vision of diabolical witchcraft.

In 1428 Matteuccia di Francesco of Ripa Bianca near Deuta was charged with witchcraft, accused of casting spells to prevent pregnancy, cause impotence and ease pain, as well as journeying to sabbats in Benevento by covering herself with ointment made from dead babies, vultures' fat, and bat's blood. Allegedly Matteuccia invoked Lucibello who manifested as a goat and carried her on his back through the air to Benevento. She was burned at the stake on March 20, 1428. (See **PLACES:** Benevento; **TOOLS:** Flying Ointments.)

🕷 *1484: Forty-one people were burned at the stake at Como*

🕷 *1510: In Valcanonica, the Inquisition allegedly investigated over 5,000 witches; 70 were burned*

🕷 *1514: A further 300 people were burned at the stake in Como*

In 1520, the Venetian government complained about the number of deaths resulting from witch-hunts. Pope Leo X's response was to voice his support for the Inquisition.

Information regarding the Benandanti, "those who walk well," derives from Inquisitorial archives in the Venetian province of Friuli, a crossroads area where Italian, Slavic, Germanic, and other influences meet. (See **DICTIONARY:** Benandanti.)

The Inquisition first learned of the Benandanti in 1575 when a priest heard reports of a man, Paolo Gasparutto, who healed the bewitched and was said to roam at night in the company of witches and spirits. Summoned, Gasparutto acknowledged his activities and the Inquisition was called in. Trials and interrogations were conducted from 1575 to 1644.

The Inquisition tried to get the Benandanti to confess to witchcraft and consorting with the devil—the usual set of accusations—but the Benandanti resisted. They didn't deny their activities but insisted that they acted in God's service and protected people from witches. By 1623, however, some Benandanti had confessed to attending sabbats, making diabolical pacts, desecrating crosses, and vampirism.

The Church was not overly enthusiastic about the Benandanti trials, which were not pursued as aggressively as some others. Punishment tended to be banishment or prison. The last major trial took place in 1644 although a few scattered efforts continued until the end of the century.

Poland

For centuries, Poland was a bastion of European liberalism and tolerance. A rich herbal and magical tradition was preserved in the country. Russians once viewed Polish magicians with the same awe with which ancient Greeks viewed Thessaly. Alchemists flocked to Polish courts, hoping for patronage and protection. The University of Krakow developed a reputation as a school for sorcery.

However, when Poland came under Russian and, especially, Swedish control, this era of tolerance ended. Poland, too, suffered witch panics. Witch trials were abolished in Poland in 1787 although witches were still burned. Poland is significant in the history of the Burning Times as the case of two women burned in Posen in 1793 is frequently cited as the last legal European witch-burning.

Procedure

Treatment of those accused of witchcraft during the Burning Times was not random or arbitrary. Legal procedures dictated the entire process from accusation to punishment.

Typically a judge, Inquisitor or witch-finder arrived in town and posted a general summons on public buildings demanding that *everyone* report *any* knowledge or suspicion of witchcraft. Everyone was welcome to tattle or settle scores: criminals, children, those bearing grudges. In general, however, no one was punished if accusations didn't pan out or were later discovered to be false.

The Inquisitor would preach a sermon against heresy and witchcraft, explicitly describing what sort of activities should be immediately reported. All local heretics were invited to present themselves as if they voluntarily confessed, they would usually receive penances and/or fines rather than death, although this was not guaranteed.

Once someone was accused, an order was given for immediate arrest. Generally the accused witch was immediately jailed. Their residence was searched for signs or instruments of witchcraft. Friends, servants or anyone who happened to be present in the home might be seized too. Anyone accused was interrogated; no one was above suspicion.

The accused was presumed guilty. She was not asked *"if"* she had committed her "crime" but *"why"* she committed it.

Many Inquisitors, witch-hunters, and judges feared witches and were cautioned to wear bags of consecrated salt as protection. An accused witch was typically led into interrogations backwards as it was believed if she entered face-first and made immediate eye contact with her interrogators, she could cast a spell over them that would cause them to be merciful.

Any hair on the accused witch's body (including eyebrows and sometimes eyelashes) was often immediately removed, not only to facilitate the search for witches' marks but also to lessen her power. *"Bleeding the witch"* (letting small amounts of blood, usually from the face) was also believed to weaken her power and enable a successful prosecution of witchcraft.

Accused witches had fewer legal rights than other defendants, whether in secular or ecclesiastical court, allegedly because it was believed they already had a powerful advantage over judge and jury: they had witchcraft, magic, and the devil on their side! The only perceived way, so witch-hunters claimed, to level the playing field was to deprive witches of all rights. Witches were typically denied attorneys and the right to call witnesses. Witnesses against them were granted anonymity, so no discussion of possible motivation was possible.

Prosecutors could call as many witnesses as desired; these witnesses could also be tortured or intimidated. Children were frequently called as witnesses because they were considered innocent and thus more likely to be truthful than adults.

A suspect's inability to cry on command was considered an incriminating sign of witchcraft as witches were believed incapable of shedding tears. Some still hold this belief; it is among the themes of the romantic comedy film *Bell, Book and Candle*. Of course, being able to cry on command didn't prove that you weren't a witch.

When a witch was arrested, it was recommended that she be taken away in a basket or atop a plank so that she was unable to touch the ground. It was believed that her power was weakened by loss of contact with Earth.

In general, witches could not be condemned unless they had "freely confessed."

So they were tortured to confess but then they had to confess again without torture; they had to affirm that they would have confessed without torture before they could be killed.

The accused witch might be promised mercy, which usually meant life imprisonment. However, sometimes judges who promised mercy in exchange for confessions or extra information then turned the witch over to another judge who, having made no such promise, sentenced her to death.

Witch-hunters' manuals offered guidelines for the administration of torture and appropriate punishments. Questions used to interrogate witches eventually became so standardized that court clerks often designated them by number in official transcripts rather than writing the entire question out. In other words, if the clerk designated "*Question 4*," for instance, other witch-hunt professionals would understand the reference.

Witches were killed by burning because it was believed that this was the only way to rid the world of the "*witch's evil.*" From the late fourteenth century to the early eighteenth, burning was the most popular form of execution for convicted witches. In the late fourteenth and early fifteenth centuries, burning took the form of cremation. Witches were executed first, usually by strangling or hanging, and then burned.

In the latter part of the fifteenth century in continental Europe, Scotland, and Ireland (but not England) killing the witch prior to burning became more unusual. Witches were more typically burned alive, usually tied to a stake in the public square.

There was also a spiritual aspect to burning a witch: she was effectively denied Christian burial rites.

In England and her North American colonies, burning witches alive was *not* legal procedure, no matter how many movies tell you otherwise. Witches were typically executed by hanging. In England, witches were burned alive only if also convicted of treasonous murder or attempted treasonous murder. Treasonous murder was defined as either a man or woman attacking the monarch or women killing their husbands. Punishment by burning for this crime continued as late as the eighteenth century.

If a witch confessed, she was usually strangled first (by hanging or garroting) then burned after death. Once someone was convinced of their eventual doom, this was a tremendous incentive to confess. Uncooperative witches—those who either protested their innocence or recanted confessions—were burned alive, frequently on pyres laid with green wood to prolong their agony. The incentive for *not* confessing was that theoretically one's property might not be forfeited.

Death was rarely private. Witch burnings were considered local entertainment. Crowds were encouraged to come out and witness the deaths. Those who avoided these scenes or expressed sympathy or compassion for the witch increased their own vulnerability to charges of witchcraft.

Witches were usually transported to their execution sites in wagons. They might be bound or chained and were usually placed backwards, to decrease their magic power. Crowds were encouraged to throw things at the witch and insult her. They were encouraged to look upon the witch in horror: indeed by the time they saw her on the way to her death, having been starved, beaten, tortured, and raped, terrified and denuded of all her hair, odds are she was genuinely a frightening sight.

The witch might be brought to the execution site naked or in special clothing. In Northern Europe, this uniform was frequently made from nettles, which destroyed the age-old tradition of nettle fabric as it became associated with a convicted witch's garb. If dressed, the convicted witch's clothing might be stripped off before the crowd before execution. Among those forced to appear naked during their execution was the fiercely modest Joan of Arc.

Russia

There is no witchcraze in Russia comparable to that of Western and Central Europe. Some were accused of witchcraft, and some were executed as witches, but there was no concept of an Inquisitor who would actively go from village to village searching out witches. There was relatively little interest among the authorities in the activities of the Russian serfs provided they accomplished their assigned work, hence the survival of many Russian Pagan traditions.

The concept of witches magically transporting themselves to distant sabbats, demonic pacts, and destructive malefic witches existed in Russia as elsewhere in Europe, but witchcraft and magic were generally recognized as relating to Paganism. Almost all references in Russian ecclesiastic texts prior to the eighteenth century that address anything that might be construed as "magical" condemn the practices as demonic and Pagan.

The role of female witches in rural Russia was to maintain the vestiges of Pagan traditions and devotion to female divinities, as well as providing healing and divination services, preparing feasts for the dead and invoking fertility for barren women, animals and Earth. Knowledge, wisdom, and traditions were preserved via sto-

ries. These rural magical and spiritual practitioners were rarely charged with the crime of witchcraft in Russia.

Malevolent witches existed in the countryside too, but many were vampire-witches—those who had already died. Suicides or those who died as a result of alcohol or violence were often believed to transform into vampire-witches. Magical protection against them was required; legal action was impossible. How do you torture and execute someone who is already dead?

As late as the fifteenth century, Pagans were still living in remote areas of Russia. It wasn't until the sixteenth century that Tsar Ivan the Terrible created the Stoglav Council to eliminate Pagan elements from the population.

So who was legally charged with the crime of witchcraft in Russia? The nobility and those who served them, clergymen, and, following introduction of a military law condemning witchcraft, soldiers. (In 1721, allegedly a great number of grimoires and magical texts circulated through military ranks.)

Instead of witchcrazes, Russia had political witch-hunts. An effective method for getting rid of political rivals was to tar them with associations of witchcraft, which were almost impossible to refute. Political witchcraft, those accused of using maleficia against the royal family and the nobility, wasn't mere witchcraft: it was treason, an attack on the state.

❋ *Between 1462 and 1505, three women were arrested for possessing herbs while visiting the wife* of Tsar Ivan III. *(The implication being that they plotted magic against her.)* They were punished by being pushed through a hole in the ice of the frozen Moscow River, then not an unusual punishment for common criminals.

❋ *In 1635, the Tsarina's servant dropped a handkerchief that was found to contain a root. Interrogated, she confessed that it was a charm intended to ensure her husband's love. She was tortured and exiled as punishment.*

❋ *In 1638, a court seamstress was accused of throwing ashes and sand over the Tsarina's footsteps, a type of spell. Tortured, she confessed that in addition to her magical attack on the Tsarina, she used enchanted salt and soap to encourage her husband's love for her.*

❋ *In 1671, Marfa Timofeevna, a servant of the Tsarina, was accused of stealing salt and mushrooms that had been prepared for the Tsarina. She confessed to theft, saying she had just stolen them to eat them. Even after torture with the strappado and fire (see Torture, page 829), she confessed to nothing else although her interrogators sought to prove that her plans really included poison, treason, and/or witchcraft.*

From the time of Peter the Great, possession of explicitly magical texts was made illegal. If discovered, they (together with other magical items) were supposed to be burned. Possession of herbs and roots was frequently used as evidence against those accused of witchcraft in the seventeenth and eighteenth centuries.

Many Russian witch-trial transcripts feature genuine magical practices, as opposed to the absurd diabolical obscenities of many Western trials; however they still may not be authentic. Torture was used to extract confessions. Although the magical practices may genuinely have existed, the purpose of a specific trial may have been political.

Various tsars and their wives were rumored to be magical adepts or to employ witches: Ivan the Terrible, for instance, was allegedly conceived with the help of witches summoned by his father. Ivan allegedly employed witches himself. He was both a practitioner and a persecutor of magical practices.

In the sixteenth and seventeenth centuries, the Russian government department with authority over criminal cases was also given jurisdiction over cases involving sorcery and malevolent magic, as well as blasphemy, false interpretations of scripture, sodomy, and assorted crimes against the Church. Punishment if convicted was for men to be burned alive and women to be beheaded.

In 1715, Peter the Great introduced severe punishment for magic and witchcraft in the military law code: death by burning was decreed as standard punishment for magicians who had caused harm or had dealings with the devil. Punishment of those who had not caused harm or interacted with the devil depended on the specific offense and included house arrest, wearing irons, and being made to run a gauntlet. Those hiring magicians or encouraging others to do so were punished similarly.

In 1753, a group of peasants were arrested for trying to kill their estate's landowner with magic, a previous attempt with arsenic having failed. They offered one ruble to a local magician, Maksim Markov, so that he would concoct a fatal spell for them. Markov allegedly enchanted some wax for them by reading spells over it in front of an icon and then doing a somersault over a knife stuck in the floor (see **ANIMALS:** Wolves and Werewolves).

Markov told the conspirators that the wax had to be rubbed on the victim's shoes, his bed and door thresholds. While attempting to follow his directions, the conspirators were discovered, arrested, and sent to Moscow for trial. Tortured, they confessed. They were condemned to death by burning but the sentence was commuted to 70 blows, slitting their nostrils and hard labor in the dockyards for life.

In the 1850s, a tailor in Siberia was almost beaten to death by a mob who believed him to be a magician responsible for a cholera outbreak. Evidence included casting his fishing line from the left and throwing his beer dregs to the left.

Scotland

Scotland suffered a particularly bad witchcraze, second only perhaps to the Germanic and Alpine regions. Prior to the sixteenth century, however, there were relatively few witch trials. Scottish law made it difficult to prosecute witchcraft: evidence was required for conviction of murders via charms, potions or other magical means.

In 1563, however, new laws enacted by Mary, Queen of Scots (December 8, 1542–February 8, 1587) broadened criteria for witchcraft crimes. Practice of *any* kind of magic, beneficial as well as malefic, became subject for trial, not just magic resulting in murder. All witches, as well as those who consult with them, were to be punished by death. The number of witchcraft trials and subsequent executions increased dramatically.

Gerald Gardner quotes Mackay's *History of Extraordinary Popular Delusions* statement that from the passing of the 1563 Act until the accession of Mary's son James VI (June 19, 1566–March 27, 1625) to the throne of England 39 years later, the average number of executions for witchcraft in Scotland was 200 annually, or upwards of 17,000 altogether.

James VI took witchcraft personally, believing that as God's anointed, *he* was the primary target of witchcraft. Witchcraft was thus not only heresy but also treason.

Witches in Scotland were generally burned although some were hanged. When the court wished to show mercy, it permitted witches to be strangled after they were tied to the stake but before burning, so that effectively burning was cremation not execution. At the opposite extreme, however, when the court wished to display no mercy, witches were thrust into the fire, pulled out, and thrust back in again repeatedly.

In 1479 the Earl of Mar, together with twelve women and several men, was burned at Edinburgh for roasting a wax image of the king. In 1537, Lady Glamis was burned as a witch for working magic against King James V.

In 1576, Bessie Dunlop of Ayr was burned alive for healing via witchcraft. (No harm had been caused; she was convicted for *healing*.) Dunlop, described as a "wise woman," was charged on November 8th. She allegedly claimed her healing powers and clairvoyance ("second sight") were gifts from the Queen of Elfhame. (See **FAIRIES:** Nature-spirit Fairies: Elves.)

On May 28, 1588, Alesoun Piersoun (also spelled Alison Pearson) of Byrehill was charged with witchcraft and of consorting with fairies for seven years. Her cousin, William Simpson, six years older, the son of the king's smith, had allegedly been educated in Egypt by a giant. Will had returned from his travels and discovered that Alison was ailing *"powerless in hand and foot"* and *"afflicted by many diseases."* He healed her, then allegedly took her to Fairy Land where he introduced her to some good witches he had known for years.

The Fairy Folk were abusive toward Alison. She claimed never to be free from various associates who came to initiate her into knowledge, whether she wished it or not. It is unclear whether she meant witches or fairies, or whether the terms are interchangeable. These associates showed Alison how to gather herbs and how to make salves. In short they initiated her as a Fairy Doctor. (In many traditional cultures, it is customary for someone who is healed to be obliged to become a healer.)

Alison developed a reputation as a healer. Even the Bishop of St Andrews requested her help. She prescribed a meal of spiced claret and boiled capon and a Fairy salve for topical application. This prescription worked but the bishop refused to pay her bill and charged her with witchcraft. Tortured, she named prominent people, claiming she saw them at Fairy balls. Alison was strangled and burned.

the North Berwick Witch Trials

The North Berwick Trials of 1590–1592, perceived as an attack on the king, fueled witchcraft hysteria. Approximately 70 people were accused of witchcraft.

This trial convinced King James that he was the target of witchcraft and motivated him to become an "authority" on the subject. James' fascination with witchcraft grew. He wanted his subjects to appreciate the reality of witchcraft and the dangers it posed. The king published *The Daemonologie* to counter Reginald Scot's book disputing the reality of witchcraft. He ordered existing copies of Scot's book burned. James' book was often quoted by witch-hunters.

In 1590, Geillis Duncan (aka Gilly Duncan), who worked as a servant for Deputy Bailie David Seaton of Tranent, a small town near Edinburgh, suddenly began exhibiting healer's skills. In demand for these skills, she began going out at night. This aroused her employer's curiosity: he suspected she was now in the devil's employ.

Seaton first tortured Geillis personally using ropes and thumbscrews. She did not confess. Her body was searched and a witch's mark, a blemish, was discovered on her throat. Her fingers were then crushed and Geillis confessed to witchcraft and began to identify other witches. She named dozens, including schoolmaster John Fian (aka John Cunningham), midwife Agnes Sampson, Barbara Napier, Agnes Tompson, and Euphemia Macalzean (also given as Euphemia Maclean), the daughter of Lord Cliftonhall, Senator of the College of Justice. Those implicated were arrested and tortured. Sampson already had a reputation as a *"wise-woman"* but the others were described as *"respectable citizens."*

Agnes Sampson was well educated and known as the *"wisewyff"* of Keith. Her head was repeatedly jerked by ropes. The inside of her mouth was punctured with sharp implements. She was kept forcibly awake beyond her endurance. Despite this torture, Agnes continued to maintain her innocence.

All the hair on her body was then shaved; examiners found a devil's mark on her genitals and Agnes finally confessed. She confirmed whatever her interrogators asked and thus implicated everyone already named by Gilly

Duncan. She confessed to 53 charges of witch-craft, most of which involved diagnosis and treatment of illness via magical means. She allegedly placed powdered dead men's bones under Euphemia's pillow during labor so that she delivered safely, created magical powders, and kept a familiar, a dog named Elva.

Agnes was brought before King James. She told him tales of witchcraft. On Halloween, she and 200 other witches set out to sea in sieves, drinking wine as if they were on a cruise ship until they reached the church at North Berwick, where they disembarked, made merry, and kissed the devil's rear.

Their company took over the church as if it was a dance hall. They danced and sang with the devil; Gilly Duncan played a dance tune on the Jew's harp. The king requested that Gilly be summoned to play for him, which she did, according to trial records, *"to his great pleasure and amazement."*

Agnes Sampson told King James that on Halloween in North Berwick, the devil in the form of a man spoke against the king. (Some believed that the Earl of Bothwell, next in line to the throne and implicated in the case, was really the one who spoke against the king, whether in the devil's guise or not.)

Agnes described two sabbats held within the church at North Berwick, one attended by 200 guests, the other by only 100. At the smaller one, she said, the witches paid homage to the devil by kissing his anus. They danced widder-shins around the church several times, then John Fian blew the church doors open, like the big bad wolf huffing and puffing the three little pigs' houses down. Within the church, they lit black candles. Satan mounted the pulpit and preached a sermon, exhorting his faithful to eat, drink, be merry, and *"not spare to do evil."* He promised to *"raise them all up gloriously at the last day."* The devil then took the coven members out to the churchyard and showed them how to transform corpses into magical charms.

During the winter of 1589/90 King James and his wife Anne of Denmark had experienced storms at sea. Agnes confessed to raising these storms because the devil commanded them to kill James, the devil's very worst enemy on Earth.

Sounds as if she's attempting to flatter the king, doesn't it? James thought so too and initially didn't buy her story. Agnes Sampson, however, proved her powers to him by telling him something (it's unknown what; it was private between the two of them and is not included in testimony) that James had said to his wife when they were alone on their wedding night. James then became convinced Agnes was a witch and that her confession was true in its entirety. *Why* she convinced him is among the mysteries of the witch trials.

Agnes Sampson now testified that she was part of a conspiracy to kill James. In fact, the whole Halloween coven meeting had been focused on the king's demise. Agnes described making figures, wrapped in linen, which she gave to the devil at the coven. He chanted incantations over them and returned them to her. The figure was passed back and forth among coven members with everyone uttering the devil's incantation, *"This is King James the Sixth, ordered to be consumed at the instance of a noble man, Francis Earl Bothwell."*

Agnes confirmed Geillis Duncan's confession, saying she saw Gilly dancing with the devil at the Sabbat. Both women testified that John Fian was their coven leader.

On December 26, 1590, John Fian, Master of a school at Saltpans in Lothian, and referred to in trial records as *"Secretar and Register to the Devil,"* was arraigned for witchcraft and high treason. Twenty counts were brought; conviction of one was sufficient for burning.

He was brutally tortured, but no confession was forthcoming. Other witches suggested that his tongue be searched. Two pins were allegedly discovered thrust in as far as their heads, preventing him from confessing. The pins were pulled out, and Fian was brought before the king where he confessed to whatever was demanded. He confessed to leading a coven in North Berwick but said he abjured the devil and had returned to Christianity. He was returned to jail and placed in solitary confinement.

The night after his confession, someone helped John escape from jail. (There is speculation that Lord Bothwell orchestrated the escape. Another suggestion is that he somehow obtained the keys and released himself.) Eventually recaptured, he recanted his confession, insisting on his innocence. Having recanted, he was re-tortured, this time even worse than before. His fingernails were removed and needles jammed into their places. His legs were completely crushed in the "boots." He was periodically brought before the king but refused to confess again.

Many came forward to accuse Fian of witchcraft, devil worship, and grave robbing for purposes of obtaining components for potions. There were so many accusations that Fian was deemed guilty even though he never again confessed. Lack of confession despite torture was interpreted as proof of the devil's protection.

Agnes Sampson and John Fian were strangled and their bodies burned.

Another alleged conspirator, Euphemia Macalzean (aka Maclean), daughter of Lord Cliftonhall, was the wife of wealthy, prominent Patrick Moscrop. A Roman Catholic and a friend of Lord Bothwell, she did not confess despite torture. She hired attorneys to fight her conviction but was executed for witchcraft on July 25, 1591. (Other witches died as early as January 1591.) Euphemia was burned alive and not strangled first, unlike other North Berwick witches including Sampson and John Fian.

Another alleged conspirator, Barbara Napier, wife of an Edinburgh burgess and the Laird of Carschoggil's sister-in-law, was accused of consorting with Agnes Sampson and consulting Richard Grahame, a necromancer. Her crimes were considered petty witchcraft crimes: for instance she requested assistance from a witch to ease the morning sickness of her friend and patron Dame Jeane Lyon, Lady Angus.

Barbara was arrested but acquitted. King James, however, wrote a letter demanding that she be strangled and burned at the stake and that all her goods be forfeit to him. Barbara responded that she was pregnant and so received a stay of execution. Exactly what happened to her is unclear; some sources state that having given birth she was burned while others suggest that with the passage of time, her case was overlooked and she was eventually released. Richard Grahame, however, the alleged necromancer with whom Barbara Napier consulted, was burned at the Cross of Edinburgh on the last day of February 1592.

Margaret Thompson, another alleged conspirator, died while being tortured.

James chose to personally supervise the torture and interrogation of the accused, taking special interest in demonic sexual practices. He promoted the concept that demonic witchcraft was actively and aggressively practiced and a threat to society. His statute of 1604 was the legal basis of witchcraft prosecutions in Great Britain and her Colonies until 1736.

The king's cousin, Francis Stewart, Earl of Bothwell, could have succeeded James to the throne were James to die childless. In the wake of the trials, he fled to Naples where, impoverished, he wrote letters denouncing Christianity, and urged Christians to deny Christ and their baptism.

In June 1596, John Stuart, Master of Orkney, was accused of consulting with a witch, Margaret Balfour, in attempts to poison his brother the Earl of Orkney and assume his position. In order to elicit her confession, which had not been forthcoming, Margaret's 81-year-old husband, her son (age unknown) and her 7-year-old daughter were tortured before her eyes. Margaret confessed but recanted later when her family was no longer being tortured. She was burned on December 16, 1596.

The Aberdeen Witch Trials

The Aberdeen Witch Trials of 1597 were among the largest in Scotland. Most of those accused of witchcraft during this panic were elderly women, the majority of whom were accused when a condemned witch seeking leniency claimed to have attended a gathering of over 2,000 witches and named several of her neighbors as attendees.

Several women confessed to making herbal cures, love charms, raising storms, stimulating nightmares, and dancing with demons. A few of the accused committed suicide prior to trial or execution. Twenty-three women and two men were burned in Aberdeen for crimes of witchcraft and magic. Five people were set free because the court lacked sufficient evidence for conviction. However because suspicion of witchcraft remained, they were branded on the face

with hot irons and commanded to leave Aberdeen forever.

> Following trials and executions, families of the dead were held liable for all costs incurred. The bill for Aberdeen witches, dated February 1596, charged their families for the cost of the coal, peat and tar used to set the fire that incinerated them, as well as the cost of stakes, ropes, and the executioner's salary and labor for carrying the supplies to the hill where the women were burned.

Isobel Gowdie

Isobel Gowdie is among the most famous witches of the Burning Times although her case is very mysterious and there are many gaps in the account, not least what eventually befell her.

She allegedly volunteered a confession of witchcraft in Auldearn, Morayshire, triggering a series of witch trials when she claimed to be part of a local coven consisting of thirteen members, whom she named to authorities.

Very little is known about Isobel Gowdie other than she confessed to witchcraft on four occasions during April and May 1662. It is unknown *why* she confessed or even whether her confession was truly voluntary. She was described as an attractive, red-haired, childless woman, married to a farmer and living on a remote farm in Morayshire.

In April 1662, Isobel confessed, saying, *"I do not deserve to be seated here at ease and unharmed, but rather to be stretched on an iron rack; nor can my crimes be atoned for, were I to be drawn asunder by wild horses."*

She said the witches of Auldearn were divided into companies called covens. Each coven was commanded by two officers, one of whom was called *"The Maiden."*

Isobel began her confession by discussing fairies. She said that she had visited the Queen of Fairy for years and that the Queen provided her with meat. Isobel also used her magic for positive, healing purposes. Based on surviving testimony, neither fairies nor beneficial magic particularly interested her interrogators. They encouraged her to speak of the devil and malicious magic instead.

Isobel told the court that in August 1659, she and the coven disguised themselves in the forms of cats, crows, and hares and rampaged through the countryside, eating, drinking, and generally ruining their neighbors' property. They got into the dye-works at Auldearn and played such pranks that ever after it would only dye one color, black, *"the colour of the Devil."*

According to Isobel's testimony, her life was boring, her husband was boring, and so she became involved with Satan in 1647, first encountering him in the form of a man in gray. She promised to meet him at the local church where the devil stood in the pulpit with his Black Book and insisted she renounce Jesus. He sucked her blood in the church, and then baptized her with her own blood. He renamed her Janet and left a mark on her shoulder, which authorities reported finding. Isobel described the devil as a big, hairy, black man who visited her a few days later when they had sex. She also had sex with a demon while lying in bed beside her oblivious husband. While she was away, Isobel said she put a broomstick in the bed to fool her husband into thinking she was present. He apparently never knew different.

She told her interrogators that the devil had a huge scaly penis and ice-cold semen. Penetra-tion was excruciatingly painful she said, but still the best sex she'd ever had. Sex with the devil, her interrogators recorded, was more pleasurable than any she'd experienced with a mortal man, which may in fact be saying something of Isobel's experiences.

She described witches' sabbats attended by covens consisting of thirteen witches each. Witches flew to sabbats on beanstalks and corn straws, which they charmed by shouting *"Horse and Hattock, in the Devil's Name!"*

Isobel claimed that she transformed herself into a hare by saying three times:

> *I shall go into a hare,*
> *With sorrow and sighing and little care*
> *And I shall go in the Devil's name*
> *Until I come home again*

When she wished to transform back, she said:

> *Hare, hare, God send thee care*
> *I am in a hare's likeness now*
> *But I shall be a woman soon*
> *Hare, hare, God sent thee care!*

Isobel confessed that her coven caused all the male children of the local landowner, the Laird of Parkis, to die via clay image magic. She was unable to demonstrate her powers, claiming that they deserted her when she confessed.

Isobel's confession was confirmed by Janet Braidhead, whom Isobel had implicated. No record exists as to what befell either of them although one suspects it was not good.

June 1722 saw the last Scottish witch trial: two Highland women, a mother and daughter, were charged with witchcraft and consorting with the devil. The mother was accused of using her daughter as *"horse and hattock."* Her daughter had been "*shod*" by Satan. (The daughter was allegedly lame and unable to use her hands.) The daughter was found innocent but the mother, Janet Horne, was burned alive.

In 1736 statutes against witchcraft were repealed.

Spain

The Spanish Inquisition was established by Pope Sixtus IV in 1478, at the request of their Most Catholic Majesties, Ferdinand and Isabella, who were exceedingly distressed by the tolerance of faith and diversity then existing in Spain.

The Spanish Inquisition was a separate organization from the regular Inquisition (see page 806), which reported directly and only to the Pope. Although the Spanish Inquisition was created by papal order, ultimate control lay with a royal council (the *Suprema*) appointed by the reigning monarch, as were all officials of the Spanish Inquisition. The Spanish Inquisition would periodically descend on a town or village and conduct inquiries into the religious correctness of its citizens.

The Spanish Inquisition's obsession was with uncovering secret Jews and so it paid comparatively little attention to witches. Providing witchcraft was not aimed directly at the Roman Catholic Church (not in an abstract way, as elsewhere in Europe) it was treated as simple heresy. Following repentance and penance, the witch or wizard was received back into the faith.

The worst witch-hunts occurred in Catalonia and the Basque region. Elsewhere, witches tended to be punished rather than killed. Punishments included the imposition of religious penances, confiscation of property, public flogging, imprisonment, fines or exile.

In the late fifteenth century, Grand Inquisitor Don Alfonso Manriquez issued an edict ordering good Christians to report any instances of fellow citizens practicing magic. The list of crimes to be reported includes:

* *Invoking spirits for purposes of divination*

* *Reading or possessing grimoires or other magical manuscripts*

* *Creation of mirrors, glass vials or other vessels for purposes of spirit communication*

* *Astrology, geomancy, hydromancy, pyromancy, divining by dice or lots, palm reading, dream interpretation, necromancy, divining by smoke or ash, or "any other magic craft"*

Gracia la Valle, the first woman burned to death as a witch by the Spanish Inquisition, was killed in Zaragoza in 1498, and in 1582 the Spanish Inquisition forbade the University of Salamanca from teaching astrology, as this was fortunetelling and therefore heresy. Astrology books were added to the official Index of Forbidden Books.

In 1781 Maria Dolores Lopez, the last person killed as a witch by the Spanish Inquisition, was burned for laying eggs with Kabalistic designs.

The Spanish Colonies (New Spain)

New Spain was a vast territory, including what is now the southwestern United States, Mexico, Central America, parts of the Caribbean, Peru, and the Phillipines.

Papal bulls of 1521 and 1522 initially established the Inquisition in New Spain. In 1571,

King Philip II formally established the Spanish Inquisition in Mexico and Peru.

During its initial years, the primary focus was on *conversos* (converted Jews and their descendants, always suspected of backsliding) and on suspected Protestants. The majority of Inquisition cases involved not witchcraft but priests who had broken their vows, Jewish conversos who had allegedly become Judaized again, Spanish heretics, and blasphemers. This was not that different from Spain. A new factor did exist in the Americas, however: indigenous American spiritual traditions and magical practices.

In 1571, those Indians newly converted to Christianity were exempt from the Inquisition, but a parallel institution was created just for them, the *Proviserato*.

> Women traditionally held positions of prominence in indigenous spirituality, healing, and magical practices. Spanish Inquisition documents as well as other colonial-era documents use the term *mujeres de mal vivir* ("women who live evil lives") to identify witches, enchantresses, healers, and spiritual leaders. Sometimes variations such as *mujer-sillas de mal vivir* ("worthless women who live evil lives") were substituted.

In the 1600s the Spanish Inquisition targeted Andean Aymara and Quechua women who sought to maintain indigenous religions. The women are described as "witches" who challenge the authority of Church and state.

Both men and women worshipped the Corn Mother, Saramama, but women felt especially close to her and served as her priestesses. The Saramamas (a genre of deity rather than one exclusive Corn Mother) were the center of women's spiritual activities.

In the early seventeenth century Bernardo de Noboa was sent by the Archbishop of Lima into the surrounding countryside to root out and terminate Pagan traditions. Noboa brought charges including witchcraft against five women. Isabel Yalpey, Francisca Quispe Tanta, Francisca Quillay Tanta, Francisca Nauim Carhua, and Maria Chaupis Tanta, a priestess of Saramama, were charged with witchcraft, leading and instructing women in idolatrous practices, and teaching ancestral traditions.

Maria Chaupis Tanta, the woman identified as a priestess and described in trial transcripts as a *"witch confessor,"* was convicted of exhorting Indian women not to adore Christ but their ancestral spirits instead. Her hair was shorn in punishment and she was forced to go out in the manner of a penitent with a rope around her throat, holding a cross in her hands. She was seated astride a llama and paraded through public streets while a town crier denounced her crimes, and she was given 100 lashes. She was then sent to the Church of Acas for ten years to serve at the disposition of its priest.

The other women were given similar sentences. All were sentenced to serve in the same church but were specifically forbidden to meet together in public or private. Directions were given for each woman to be isolated.

By the seventeenth century in the District of Peru, indigenous women were confessing to pacts with Satan and having sex with Satan. Ironically during witch-trial confession transcripts, indigenous women claim the devil appeared to them in the guise of a Spaniard. In Peru, the commonest punishment meted out to women accused of witchcraft was exile to the *obrajes*, sweatshops where women were forced to spin and weave.

In Guatemala, the *maestras* (female teachers and masters of magic) were accused of corrupting the masses. Colonial officials expressed less concern for men's witchcraft societies, which also existed. Women were perceived as the cancerous force. The Inquisition aggressively pursued renowned *maestras* (or notorious *mujeres de mal vivir*) as an example and warning to other women. By the 1690s the Head of Guatemala's Inquisition complained that they lacked sufficient jails to imprison all the *mujeres de mal vivir*.

Further Reading: Martha Few's *Women Who Live Evil Lives* (University of Texas Press, 2002) and Irene Silverblatt's *Moon, Sun and Witches* (Princeton University Press, 1987).

Sweden

Between 1520 and 1699, over 1,000 people were accused of witchcraft and sorcery in Sweden. This is only an estimate as the true number is unknown as some court records were destroyed by fire.

The most famous and best-documented witch panic in Sweden occurred between 1668 and 1670 in the villages of Mohra and Elfdale. Children testified that multitudes of witches brought them to sabbats at a place called Blakulla, where they were placed in the service of the devil.

The citizens of Mohra drafted a petition to Charles XI, the 14-year-old king. He responded by sending two commissions to Mohra with the power to examine witnesses and proceed with legal action. Records of these witch trials were preserved in an official report.

Witnesses claimed that somewhere between 100 and 300 children were carried away to Blakulla. When they returned, they were witches. The children were never physically missing: during the time these witchy revels allegedly occurred, the children were typically at home, asleep, supervised by parents. However, parents noted (and testified) that their children behaved oddly in their sleep: they were restless, unnaturally cold, and difficult to wake up. When they finally awakened, they gave long, detailed descriptions of their journeys.

Three thousand people ultimately testified before the Commission. The confessions of the children uniformly state that they journeyed to Blakulla.

The standard story was that they traveled to a gravel pit near a crossroads and danced around it, then ran to the crossroads and called the devil three times: once softly, once more loudly, and then finally really loudly. They called, *"Come Antecessor, carry us to Blakolla!"* And immediately he did. The devil is described as having a red beard and sporting a brightly colored wardrobe, favoring the colors red and blue.

Antecessor brings animals for the witches to ride to the sabbat and also gives them flying ointment. Other witches traveled on posts, rails, and sticks with children mounted behind. Secrecy was enforced: if anyone mentioned the name of another witch, except at the sabbats, they were beaten to the point of fatality. At the sabbat, they danced while the devil played the harp.

Seventy people were accused of witchcraft; twenty-three confessed. They were beheaded and their bodies burned. Fifteen children were executed. Thirty-six others, ranging in age from 9 to 16, were sentenced to run a gauntlet and then be caned once a week for one year. Twenty infants were punished otherwise (details unknown); presumably these infants were too young to run a gauntlet.

In another witch panic between 1675 and 1676, at least 157 people were accused of witchcraft; 41 were executed. The death penalty for witchcraft was abolished in 1779 by King Gustavus III.

Switzerland

There were sporadic outbreaks of witch panics in Switzerland from the late fourteenth century to the sixteenth:

❋ *1392–1406: Peter von Greyerz of Bern, Governor of the Simme Valley, conducts major witch-hunts*

❋ *1428: There is a witchcraze in the Canton of Valais region led by the Bishop of Sion, who declared that anyone accused of witchcraft by more than two people should be arrested and forced to confess so that they may be burned; allegedly over 100 are burned*

❋ *1480: Two women of the Alpine region of Valtellina, Domenega and Contessia, are denounced as "wicked" and condemned to time in the pillory followed by three-years banishment for worshipping the "Mistress of the Grove"*

❋ *1513: 500 accused witches are executed in Geneva*

The last legal execution of a witch in Switzerland occurred in 1782. A physician accused Anna Göldi of casting a spell over his young, ailing son. She was executed by hanging at Glarus.

Torture

If you were tortured to name names, who would you name? In the desire to protect those you love, whose names would you divulge? "Standard" tortures during the Witchcraze included:

❋ *Burning*

❋ *Dipping in boiling oil*

❋ *Flaying of skin*

❋ *Flogging*

❋ *Garroting*

❋ *Impaling on stakes or spikes*

❋ *Inducing thirst by force-feeding salty food or liquids*

❋ *Rape*

❋ *Scalding the body with boiling and/or caustic liquids*

❋ *Scalding liquids poured down throats*

❋ *Sleep deprivation*

❋ *Stretching limbs until bones broke and muscles ripped*

❋ *Vises or other instruments to break or crush bones*

❋ *Whipping*

Witch-hunters' manuals offered guidelines for the administration of torture. Some sort of torture occurred to varying degrees wherever there were witch-hunts; although certain regions are described as lacking torture, what constitutes torture is subjective. Certainly the threat of death was constant. Also, when historians consider torture, they often think in terms of "torture devices" or formalized techniques like the strappado (see page 829), but sometimes overlook rape, sexual humiliation, and intimidation, which were constant.

> In regions where torture was comparatively mild, there were many, many fewer convictions and less witch panic.

The worst, most sadistic torture occurred in German regions—also the regions with highest rates of confessions and convictions. Victims in these lands included pregnant women and children as young as two. German witch-hunters tortured accused witches until they confessed or died. Resistance to torture, refusal to confess or perhaps higher tolerance levels to pain was perceived as the devil's protection and a proof of magic powers.

When a victim died under torture, it was commonly claimed that the devil had killed her either to protect her from further harm (and foil the witch-hunters) or to prevent her from talking and exposing secrets and other witches.

In 1257, Pope Innocent IV authorized torture as a means of extracting confessions.

Many torture procedures still in use today were invented by the Inquisition.

The *Malleus Maleficarum* insisted that only confessions obtained under brutal torture could be considered valid.

French witch-hunter Jean Bodin advocated the harshest, most brutal torture possible for all witches. (Of course, this was a man who regretted that the experience of burning alive didn't last long enough.) Bodin advocated torturing children just as brutally as adults so that they would testify against parents, relatives, and other adults. Bodin was proud that, as a judge, he had ordered children and adults burned with hot irons until they confessed to every charge. His success rate was a point of pride for him.

> Friedrich von Spee's publication *Cautio Criminalis* offers meditations on the nature of torture: Spee noted that any sign of "goodness" in an accused witch was perceived by her Inquisitors as a trick or falsehood. Refusal to confess under torture was not understood as innocence but as proof of connivance with Satan. Spee revealed that in his experience, most official documents stating that an accused witch had voluntarily confessed were fraudulent: some sort of torture was almost always used.

Near the end of the witch-hunt era, perhaps in response to Spee, the use of torture to extract confessions had become controversial, disreputable, and unpopular with the general public as well as many prominent authorities.

Torturers responded to public opinion: they recorded, in official trial transcripts, that suspects had confessed *without* torture so that confessions would appear voluntary when, in fact, torture was used. This was especially done in cases presented before judges with a reputation for "leniency" toward witches. These falsifications are a further reason why records are unreliable.

Further, action taken during "preparatory examinations" didn't count as torture. Torture only "officially" began when proceedings "officially" began. Being arrested and searched didn't count. The accused were customarily stripped of their clothing, roughly handled, and raped: this wasn't recorded and so didn't count as torture.

The following are a list of "specialized tortures" used during the Burning Times.

❋ *Black Virgin: this was a German invention and used mainly in German regions; the victim was placed within a hinged, life-sized iron form with spikes within so that she was pierced when the form was closed around her. Also known as the* Iron Maiden.

❋ *Boots: also known as the* Spanish Boots, *in honor of the Spanish Inquisition. There were various kinds of boots, the standard was a kind of special leg-ware intended to break legs and crush bones; this torture device encased both legs from the knees to the ankles and was then tightened until bones cracked. A torturer could also intensify torture by hammering wedges between the victim's knees. Other boots were large metal devices containing the feet and legs into which boiling oil or water could be poured.*

❋ *Creative torture was encouraged: for instance, in sixteenth-century Holland, victims were bound in a prone position and dormice were placed on their abdomens. A bowl was placed over the trapped dormice and a fire lit on top of the bowl. In their efforts to escape the heat and fire, the dormice dug into the victim's stomach.*

❋ *Pear: a vise-like device used to pry an orifice open to excruciatingly painful degrees. Mouth, anal, and vaginal pears existed.*

❋ *The Rack: the victim was placed on a board so that their wrists were tied to one end and their ankles tied to the other end. Rollers at each end of the board (the rack) were turned so that the victim's body was simultaneously wrenched in two opposing directions.*

❋ *Sexual torture: red-hot iron instruments were inserted into vaginas and rectums. Burning feathers coated with sulfur were applied to genitalia.*

❋ *The Spider: a claw-like iron device typically heated in fire until red-hot and then used to gouge flesh, often breasts, from the victim's body.*

❋ *Squassation: this is essentially the strappado (see below) taken to the maximum degree; the victim was tied up then fitted with weights, potentially as heavy as 600 pounds. The person was repeatedly jerked up to the ceiling, and then abruptly dropped to the floor. Squassation was used sparingly as typically as few as three repetitions were sufficient to kill the prisoner.*

❋ *Strappado: the victim's arms were tied behind the back; weights were attached to her feet. She was then repeatedly and violently hoisted to hang from the ceiling and then let fall abruptly so that, among other damage, shoulders and assorted arm joints dislocate.* Strappado *derives from* strappare *(Latin: "to pull") and was known as* Garrucha *in Spain.*

❋ *Swimming the witch: the suspected witch's wrists were tied to her ankles and then she was tossed into water, usually a stream or river. Traditionally, her left thumb was tied to her right big toe and the right thumb tied to the left big toe. If she floated, her status as a witch was confirmed. If she sank, she had been vindicated and was deemed innocent, although this might be posthumous. Theoretically, she was supposed to be pulled out, however frequently standard procedure involved leaving her in long enough to be* sure *she was really innocent. Swimming the witch was widely practiced throughout England. It was not considered torture but an ordeal intended to prove witchcraft.*

*   *Thumbscrew: the victim's thumbs and/or toes were placed in a device resembling a press. By turning a screw, the device was lowered onto thumbs or toes, crushing them at the base of the nail.*

*   *The Wheel: the victim was stretched and bound across the spokes and hub of a large wheel. The torturer then used a heavy instrument to break her arms and legs. The wheel might be horizontal but also could be propped upright so that it was vertical in order to provide a better view for an onlooking crowd.*

*   *Witch's Bridle or Witch's Bit: a hoop was passed over the head, forcing a piece of iron with four prongs or points into the mouth. Two prongs were directed towards the tongue or palate, the other two pointed outwards towards each cheek. The bridle was secured with a padlock. A ring was fixed to the back of the collar so that it could be attached to a cell wall.*

Witch's Mark, or Devil's Mark

A witch's mark is ostensibly a bodily mark allegedly identifying someone as a witch. Locating the witch's mark was highly subjective, as was exactly what constituted the mark. However, most witch-hunters agreed that a witch's mark was secret; a pimple smack in the center of your nose was not likely to be a witch's mark. Favored places included genitals, armpits, beneath the breasts, within folds of skins, beneath eyelids or behind ears and knees.

Among the various things that passed for a witch's mark were birthmarks, scars, especially scaly pitches that wouldn't bleed easily if pricked with a pin, also calluses, scars or other hardened patches of skin. Some witch-hunters included moles, pimples, age or liver spots, even hemorrhoids. Withered or extra fingers or any other unique aspects of anatomy were also considered evidence of witchcraft.

Witch-hunters searched for this mark, which allegedly proved that someone had made a pact with Satan. In order to locate the witch's mark, victims were stripped, shaved, and minutely searched, sometimes in public.

At the height of the Burning Times, some witch-finders claimed witch's marks were so secret they were invisible, making allowances for when they were not located.

Witch's Tit

A witch's tit was believed to be the most definitive form of witch's mark. Unlike vague witch's marks, witch's tits or teats are clearly defined. The witch's tit is a supernumerary nipple, an extra nipple beyond the standard two, interpreted as intended for the devil or imps to use for sucking blood. It was allegedly a sign of initiation, created by the devil by branding, beating, touching, clawing or licking the witch. The witch's tit, sometimes classified among witch's marks, was considered irrefutable evidence of the existence of an imp or familiar.

✪ Women's Mysteries

*R*ecognition of magic power was born from recognition and awe at the mysteries of the universe.

In order to even begin to comprehend this, one must attempt to look at the world with fresh eyes, like a child approaching something brand new and unexplored. Look around and appreciate the magic of the natural world. Look around and see how all these different magic powers interrelate with each other.

Go outside on a dark night and look at the beautiful moon as it rules the night sky. Go out on different nights and watch the moon change: the moon shifts continually and rhythmically, simultaneously unique and consistent.

Look at the tides: they move in harmony with the lunar phases. Temporarily, throw out all your scientific knowledge; think about the moon and tides and access your pre-scientific mind. Now ask yourself, "How does that happen?" The simple answer is, "By magic!" That answer remains true in addition to the scientific explanations now accepted. Scientific explanations don't negate the mysterious magic of the process. They only enhance it.

Now, look at women.

Suddenly, in adolescence, women begin to bleed on schedule with the moon and tides. These days, menstruation is popularly perceived as, if not a curse, then at least a bother. Once upon a time, it was considered amazing.

Women bled from no wound, often with no pain, *on schedule!*

Women bled, for days at a time, without death as the end result.

Instead of death, women bring forth new life, as if by magic, just like Earth brings forth plants. Women were connected to the moon because of their cycles, but their fertility connected them to Earth.

Ancient ovens intended to bake loaves from grain were built in the form of women's pregnant bellies. Mysteries of fertility stimulate the birth of magic and spirituality; these mysteries are never forgotten, even among the most sophisticated of alchemists.

The alchemist's laboratory may be understood as the precursor to the modern infertility laboratory. Alchemical masters didn't only want to produce the Philosopher's Stone; they wanted to create the Homunculus too—a living being created not in a test tube but in an alchemist's vessel, a vessel that was formed in the shape of a woman's body. Female bodies inspired the creation of alchemical ovens, beakers, and other vessels.

Before these labs however, there were women's mysteries: places where women congregated alone and shared the secrets of these mysteries to which only they were privy. (Don't feel left out guys. Men had societies, too! Just think of all those werewolf cults.)

Women originally were not banished to red tents and menstrual huts, although as the balance of power shifted, eventually they would be. At first, based on mythology and artifacts, they seem to have gone willingly to these places, with joy and awe.

Spiritual traditions, women's mystery religions, were based on these practices. When the spiritual traditions were banished, these mysteries lingered openly in but a few places—in birthing chambers and in spinning rooms. (Islamic women also had the haven of the hammam.)

Birthing chambers and spinning rooms, of course, are places where women openly congregated together: women's attendance in these places was, in fact, often mandatory. However, other women's meetings that focused on women's mysteries were forbidden on pain of death, and thus held secretly in forests, caves, and on mountaintops.

Witches, as survivors and descendants of lunar priestesses, have the skill, ability and knowledge to access lunar power. The moon is believed able to control the reproductive capacity of humans, animals, and crops, as well as the tides, the sea's harvest (fishing), weather conditions, and the human body—especially human sexuality and mental stability. It is no coincidence that lunacy derives from word for moon.

Lunar animals include bats, cats, owls, and nightjars, all animals associated with witchcraft.

Midwives

The labor room was one of the few areas considered feminine territory. All sorts of taboos were associated with birth. Men, for centuries, were excluded from birthing rooms except in medical emergencies.

Midwife literally means "mediating woman." The midwife is the equivalent of a medium.

✻ *In Russia, the word or honorific for midwife* (Baba) *is synonymous with "Witch"*

✻ *The French word for midwife is* sage-femme, *literally "wise woman"*

Once upon a time, the midwife's services were broader than childbirth alone. Beyond pregnancy and birth, the midwife served as professional consultant for all "female issues" including menstrual difficulties, irregular cycles, lactation, infertility, menopause, and venereal diseases. The midwife supervised spiritual and magical rites for mother and child as well as for menopausal women and girls just beginning to menstruate. She was a priestess who initiated women into the lunar mysteries of blood, birth, and magic power.

Midwives were responsible for anything to do with reproduction or with the female aspects of the anatomy. They nurtured pregnancies and delivered babies, but they also provided contraceptives and terminated pregnancies.

Some understand the witchcraze as an attack on midwives, although this is a gross over-simplification: many, if not most, of those accused and killed as witches were *not* midwives. *How-*

ever, a high percentage of midwives were subject to accusations of witchcraft. Among the results of the Witchcraze was that the duties of the midwife narrowed considerably, and much of her ancient lore and wisdom was suppressed.

> Once upon a time, there were midwives for death as well as birth. Midwives assisted the dying, easing transition and supervising proper funeral rites. The German *Leichenwäscherin*, literally "corpse washerwoman," was considered a kind of midwife. This tradition of death midwifery has been revived in the 21st century.

Hardening feelings toward abortion were partially responsible for negative feelings towards midwives and their associations with witches. Plato accused midwives of causing abortions via drugs and incantations. In the ancient world, herbal abortifacients were the rule, rather than surgical procedures. Thus the Greek *pharmakos* may be a witch, poisoner, healer, or abortionist.

> Roman laws of the third-century CE ordered exile for women who attempted abortion against the father's wishes. Not because abortion was wrong, per se but because this was a deprivation of paternal privilege. The *paterfamilias* (father of the family) could force an abortion on his wife or female slaves, regardless of their personal wishes.

Midwives were repositories of fertility magic and women's mysteries, maintaining pre-Christian birthing traditions, even while veiling them as Christian, into the Middle Ages.

Shamans sometimes must guide a dead soul to the Realm of Death; midwives were shamans who guided the new soul to the Earthly Realm of the Living.

In the traditional cultural perspective of the Andes, women who help other women give birth are considered blessed and imbued with sacred power. Fertility was a sacred power; giving birth a sacred act, thus the one who facilitates presides over holiness.

Midwifery was a sacred profession. Traditional Andean midwives were (are) expected to undergo various rituals to attain their position, not only functional professional rituals but also spiritual ones. Ceremonies, ritual fasts, and sacrifices were required.

In Andean tradition, women are spiritually called to become midwives. Some receive the summons in their dreams. Giving birth to twins was considered such a summons too.

Midwife Goddesses

Midwives were demonized and yet there are midwife goddesses, too. These goddesses protect midwives but are also perceived as being midwives. Midwives are the heroines of the Jewish Bible (the prophetess Miriam and also Shifra and Puah are among the very few biblical women named for their own accomplishments).

Birth was considered sacred and magical but also a dangerous experience. Midwives in ancient times were affiliated with shrines and temples in Egypt, Sumeria, and elsewhere in Asia and Africa as well as among the Aztecs and Incas.

Midwife goddesses include the following:

✳ *Artemis is the sacred Greek midwife. Her first act upon being born was to help her mother give birth to Artemis' twin, Apollo. Artemis was the Greek deity responsible for determining which women died in childbirth and which survived. (See **DIVINE WITCH**: Artemis.)*

✳ *Brigid protects and sponsors midwives. Veneration of Brigid once extended throughout the Celtic world. Brigid's associations with birth were so powerful that eventually a Christian myth would suggest that Brigid had traveled all the way to Nazareth to serve as the Virgin Mary's midwife.*

In the West Highlands, newborn babies were traditionally passed over a fire three times then carried around it deasil (in a sun-wise direction) three times before receiving the *"midwife's baptism"* of water accompanied by an invocation of Brigid.

✳ *Hecate is the goddess with dominion over the borders between Life and Death. Her priestesses were midwives who assisted human souls' transition over those portals. Their sacred emblem was the broom with which they purified the birthing chamber.*

✳ *Heket may be the oldest Egyptian spirit of all. She is a spirit of childbirth and the protector of the dead and the newly born. She is associated with the tomb, birth, and resurrection and all the transitions between them. She helps place the child in the womb. Heket prevents miscarriage and stillbirth. She has dominion over contraceptives.*

Heket, a frog goddess, may or may not derive from the same roots as Hecate, who considers frogs and toads among her holy animals.

✳ *Pachamama is the Andean Spirit of Earth. Peruvian midwives were understood to have a special relationship with her, to serve as her priestesses.*

Midwife Magic

Ancient and medieval midwives paid attention to signs and symbols as birth drew near. As the midwife approached the birthing chamber, she observed what animals crossed her path, what people she met, even the weather. She read the atmosphere like a fortune-teller reads cards. The atmosphere advised of the circumstances of the upcoming birth, both physical and spiritual.

The midwife stayed with the mother after the birth to greet, appease, and/or thank the birth fairies and spirits. She supervised a new mother's attempts at nursing and, if necessary, taught her how.

The magic role of midwives survived early Christianity. This verbal charm from Ulster was once spoken by midwives before entering the homes of laboring women:

> *There are four corners to her bed,*
> *There are four angels at her head,*
> *Matthew, Mark, Luke and John*
> *God bless the bed that she lies on!*
> *New moon, new moon, God bless me!*
> *God bless this house and family!*

A Christian charm from fifteenth-century Austria was written on paper and laid over the laboring woman's stomach or attached to her clothing:

> From a man, a man
> From a virgin, a virgin
> The Lion of Judah triumphs!
> Mary bore Jesus
> Elizabeth, though sterile, bore John the Baptist
> I adjure the Infant, by Father, Son and Holy Ghost!
> Whether male or female that you issue forth from
> your mother's womb
> Be empty! Be empty!

Midwife Persecution

"Midwives, who surpass all others in wickedness ..." (*Malleus Maleficarum*)

The *Malleus Maleficarum*, the witch-hunter's manual, devoted not one but two chapters to midwives. (See **BOOKS**: Witch-hunters' Manuals: Sprenger.) They were accused of attempting to prevent babies from being baptized: killing the newborn or presenting it to devils deprived the baby of salvation. Witchcraft and midwifery became linked.

The *Malleus Maleficarum* and its contemporaries considered witches' crimes to be seven-fold:

1. Practicing fornication and adultery
2. Obstructing the generative act by rendering men impotent
3. Performing castrations and sterilizations
4. Engaging in bestiality and homosexuality
5. Destroying women's generative power
6. Procuring and providing abortions
7. Offering children to devils

In 1580, Jean Bodin, French philosopher, rationalist, and demonologist declared these charges true and valid. All of these charges are *somehow* related to reproduction, at least tangentially. Many are related to contraception. Most are explicitly related to sex and sexuality.

> Witchcraft became considered a woman's crime, like abortion, prostitution, and infanticide. In Luxembourg, words indicating "witch" were associated with those for "whore."

In Genesis 3:16, God condemns Eve to labor with pain and difficulty. This led to Christian suspicions of easy births: is Satan responsible? Midwives, trained to ease labor pains and speed birth became regarded by some as apostles of Satan.

The politics of childbirth changed. Women were encouraged to complain about birth and focus on its pain and difficulty. Midwives who were accused of witchcraft were consistently accused of *easing* labor pains; this was considered a sin.

The Church developed a hardening stance toward reproductive issues:

❋ *If sex is only for procreation, then there's no point to contraception*

❋ *God determines the outcome of sexual liaisons, thus aphrodisiacs, many of which are also fertility enhancers, are wrong*

❋ *Abortifacients are wrong to the point of heresy because, beyond any other issues, their use implies that* you *have autonomy, not God*

The entire art and science of midwifery was called into question; the herbal science of childbirth would effectively be eradicated.

Reproductive (or any) herbalism is a complex art and science, not for amateurs. Not all parts of a plant have the same effect; not all preparations and routes of administration have the same effect. The skilled herbalist is an expert on all these details and often an intuitive healer.

Dosage and determining the correct frequency of administration is crucial. Depending on the plant, there can be a very narrow margin between medicine and poison: the healing dose versus the fatal dose. As an example, a small dose of tansy infusion may have no effect on a pregnancy. A larger one can cause miscarriage and an even larger one can be potentially fatal.

Instead of appreciating the traditional midwife's artistry and knowledge, she was eliminated. It was well recognized that midwives were stubborn repositories of women's mystery traditions:

✳ *In some Teutonic regions (and elsewhere), medicinal law and Church prohibitions decreed that a priest must be present at each birth to prevent midwives from practicing superstitious and heathen customs.*

✳ *In 1494, a priest in Breslau wrote that* "In childbirth the midwives are busy with a thousand devilish things as well as with the women in travail."

The medical profession was changing; the birthing room was no longer exclusively female territory, nor was a woman necessarily in charge. Physicians were by legal requirement university trained. Women were not permitted to enter these universities and thus could not become physicians.

Physicians replaced midwives in the labor-room but they did not reproduce their role; the physician's art was devoted to healing disease, ailments, and injury, not reproductive issues. Practical reproductive knowledge remained in the hands of midwives, wise women, old wives, *sage-femmes*, and witches, however these became fewer and fewer.

Midwives became associated with the poor, ignorant, and uneducated as well as those with Pagan leanings or those who were less than devout Christians. They became low-status professionals. Upscale women began to go to hospitals or have physicians attend them. Because of their low status, relatively little written information about midwifery exists. The exception is when midwives ran afoul of the law: *that* was recorded in detail. This offers a skewed picture.

Midwifery became a risky profession:

By the latter half of the fifteenth century, midwives throughout much of Europe were pressured to submit to licensing procedures involving an oath that they would not practice in secret. In one 1588 oath, the midwife promises *"not in any wise use or exercise any manner of witchcraft."* The Paris Oath of 1560 states, *"I will not use any superstition or illegal means, either in words or signs, nor any other way …"*

In 1624, an English law put the onus on women to prove that an infant's death was natural. If unable to do so, the woman might be accused of homicide and hanged. Collaborative evidence was necessary from male professionals like physicians, surgeons, and apothecaries when female midwives testified regarding the viability of premature babies. Male midwives were permitted to provide collaborative evidence.

In the late sixteenth century, Nuremburg issued an ordinance prohibiting midwives from burying fetuses or dead children without informing the city council. When an infant was buried, the midwife was expected to have several *"unsuspected female persons"* as witnesses of the procedure. The witchcraze was raging in

German lands during the sixteenth century; "unsuspected" females were not easy to find.

In 1711, an edict issued in Brandenburg forbade midwives from selling or giving away fetuses, placentas or umbilical cords. In Würzburg, they were required to dispose of these in running water.

Spiritual conflicts ensued as well. Traditional midwives wished to perform rituals and magical acts intended to safeguard births. Pious, devout Christian mothers, midwives, and observers objected to these practices. Some objected to them sincerely, others for fear of Pagan associations and vulnerability to suspicions of witchcraft.

Henri Boguet's *Examen of Witches*, written in the 1580s, observes that many witches are midwives. *"These midwives and wise women who are witches are in the habit of offering to Satan the little children which they deliver and then of killing them ... they do even worse; for they kill them while they are yet in their mother's wombs. This practice is common to all witches."*

In other words, Boguet is suggesting that all witches are abortionists.

Midwife Witch Trials

Identification of midwives with witches was more powerful in some areas than others. Between 1627 and 1630, at least one third of all those executed as witches in Cologne were midwives. (Statistics indicate at least one in three; because many did not have occupations listed it may have been more but not less.)

Of the nearly 200 people accused of witchcraft at Salem Village in 1692, 22 were identified as midwives and/or healers. (The occupation of many remains unknown; it's impossible to achieve an accurate statistic.)

On the other hand, midwives also turned in witches and testified against them at trials.

By necessity, information regarding witch trials is fragmentary. All that survives are pieces of stories. For further information on Witch Trial Records, see **WITCHCRAZE!**

On September 20, 1587, Walpurga Hausmannin, a licensed midwife practicing in Dillingen in Augsburg in southern Germany, was burned at the stake as a witch. She had confessed to a long list of crimes, most having to do with her professional career.

In 1632, Alie Nisbet, a Scottish midwife, was arrested as a witch and accused of using charms and incantations to remove a woman's labor pains. Alie denied the charges but admitted that she might have bathed the woman's legs with warm water that she had charmed so that it would have beneficial healing properties by sticking her fingers in it while running three times around the bed widdershins. The woman's labor pains were immediately relieved but entered another woman who died 24 hours later. Nisbet was charged with committing murder by sorcery and burned to death.

In pre-conquest Andes, midwives were perceived as sacred. Spanish chroniclers acknowledged that the indigenous Andeans viewed midwives as "special." However for the Spanish Inquisition, midwives, traditional curers, doctors, and healers were all considered sorcerers and witches.

In 1660, two husbands in colonial Guatemala denounced a midwife, Marta de la Figueroa, an Indian woman married to a former government official, for using malicious sorcery during their wives' pregnancies. She was charged with witchcraft. (Her trial transcripts suggest that Marta may have been caught in a political conflict—at least her husband thought so.)

In order to extract a confession, Marta was hung up in public and exposed to the smoke of burning chili peppers. Her face and body were covered with the pepper until she confessed.

Both men who accused Marta had wives who died during pregnancy. Marta was accused of causing the death of one via magical means because the two women had argued. Marta had allegedly asked to be the midwife for the second woman but she had already hired one and, based on the trial record, may not have been too polite in turning Marta away. From that moment the woman became incurably ill and began having recurrent dreams that Marta wished to smother her. Other men came forward, charging Marta with magically causing death and disease.

Marta was convicted of sorcery and superstition. She was punished with 100 lashes administered in the public streets.

Margaret Jones of Charleston, Massachusetts, midwife, cunning woman, and alleged fortune-teller was accused of witchcraft, convicted and executed on June 15, 1648.

In 1680, the neighbors of Elizabeth Morse of Colonial New England complained that she was a witch. Elizabeth stood trial in Boston. She was found guilty in May 1680 and sentenced to die although she was later reprieved. One neighbor described Elizabeth as a "healing and destroying witch."

Spinning

Technically, spinning is the art of transforming loose fibers into thread but spinning is more than just the art of spinning thread. Spinning is the magical art of transformation. Spinning connects every woman to the sacred actions of the Goddess.

Spinning was associated with the entire cycle of life—with birth, nurturing, and death, symbolized by the weaving of one's burial shroud. It is a metaphor for providing order and structure. It regulates fertility and controls cyclical occurrences like the moon, tide, and seasons, and thus the weather.

Many spinning goddesses are associated with water, especially wells. The Norse Norns live by the Well of Urd. In the fairy tale *Mother Holle*, a spindle enables the girls to reach Hulda's realm at the bottom of a well.

Spinning and weaving metaphorically suggests creating something powerful and beautiful from one's own essence and substance, like a spider.

Spinning is like cooking: it transforms the raw material into the useable. It provides the action of completion and fulfillment. There is a fertility aspect to spinning. One creates something from raw material in the way that raw material is transformed into a living, vital baby within the womb.

Spinning in many parts of Earth was a woman's art; the spinning room was female territory. In colder climates during the winter, when agricultural work was not possible, women joined together at night to spin together.

An older woman might be delegated to "entertain" the spinners with old stories. Mother Goose is frequently depicted in the company of a spindle. In some communities, professional story-tellers were hired to preside over the spinning room: they may be understood as priestesses or as repositories of ancient lore.

Children ran in and out of the spinning room; an exciting or entertaining story kept restless children well behaved.

Hungarian preachers complained that the common people found greater pleasure listening to the old wives' tales told in the spinning room than in sermons told in Church.

> Flax, hemp, and nettles, the plants that can be "spun" into fabric, were once sacred to goddesses (Freya, Frigga, Hulda, assorted fairies) but were later demonized as "witch plants." Some believe the negative passions aroused by the hemp plant are derived from its associations with witchcraft, shamanism, and women's magical traditions.

Spinster is now a negative word indicating an unmarried woman but it literally means "one who spins" or "woman who spins." Spinsters were independent women able to support themselves via spinning thread or spinning tales.

Divination

Spinning was once associated with divination. A method of scrying involves gazing into a moving spinning wheel (literally a *wheel of fortune*). In ancient Greece, *sphondulomantis* involved "divination via spindle." Bobbing spindle wheels and the monotony of spinning may induce prophetic trances.

Embroidery and Fine Needlework

Spinning and weaving aren't the only sacred arts associated with fabric. Embroidery was often a safe repository for sacred but now forbidden symbols, akin to Tarot or tattooing.

In much of Europe, embroidering for the Goddesses included ritual towels, aprons, and embroidered bread covers for the loaf placed on the domestic altar for ancestors.

These ornamented fabrics were incorporated into women's spiritual and magical rituals.

> Examples of these embroideries have been collected by Mary B. Kelly and published in *Goddess Embroideries of Eastern Europe* (Northland Press, 1996) and *Goddess Embroideries of the Balkan Lands and the Greek Islands* (Studiobooks, 1999).

Spinning Goddesses

The Spinning Goddess spins the thread of life. Spinning goddesses are Fate goddesses and spider goddesses. The Spinning Goddess sees and knows all.

As evidenced by rock art and pottery going as far back as the Neolithic period, "Bird goddesses" and owls were associated with spinning.

Among the many spinning goddesses are the following:

Amaterasu

Amaterasu is the glorious, beautiful Japanese solar goddess; her occupation is spinning and weaving. Amaterasu gave humans the sacred gift of spinning hemp and silk. Every twenty years, Amaterasu's shrine at Ise is renewed; during the ritual she is given a miniature sacred loom as well as spindles and thread boxes.

Athena

Athena, the artisanal goddess, created many crafts, not least among them spinning. In one of the most famous of all Greek myths, Athena challenges a mortal woman, Arachne, to a spinning contest (see **ANIMALS:** Spiders for more information). She presided over all women's arts. Young Athenian women once offered Athena sacrifices of their own hair curled around spindle whorls.

Athena and the Egyptian goddess Neith (see page 841) are believed linked although the connections between them are not fully understood. Both originally derive from Libya, among the ancient strongholds of women's mystery traditions. Some believe Neith, an incredibly primeval deity, crossed the Mediterranean and transformed into Athena. Another suggestion is that Neith and Athena once formed part of a trinity of goddesses; the third goddess, in this case, was Medusa.

Circe

The Witch Circe sits in her island palazzo spinning and weaving; she is understood as magically weaving destiny as well as crafting tapestries. She is often portrayed at her loom and so spinning became explicitly associated with witchcraft.

Frigga

Frigga knows everyone's fate although she will not or cannot reveal it. In Pagan Scandinavia, the constellation now known as *Orion's Belt* was considered *Frigga's Distaff.*

Habetrot (Habitrot, Habtrot)

Habetrot is a Scottish spinning wheel fairy and Fairy-matron of spinsters and spinning. She manifests as an aged woman whose lips are deformed from excessive spinning. She has been known to assist women with little skill at spinning or weaving. Her sacred creature is the spider. Habetrot lives beneath a huge stone in a grassy knoll with her sisters.

Hulda

Hulda, according to legend, introduced flax to the world. Spinning and weaving are among her sacred arts and rituals. In the story *Mother Holle*, Hulda's realm is accessed by throwing a spindle down a well. (See **FAIRY-TALE WITCHES:** Grimms' Fairy Tales: *Mother Holle*.)

Ix Chel

Ix Chel is the Mayan spirit with dominion over fertility, sexual relations, childbirth, healing, creativity, and weaving. In her benevolent aspect, Ix Chel represents the waters of life, whether it is the ocean or the amniotic fluids. In her negative aspect, Ix Chel represents destruction through water. She is the personification of torrential rains and hurricanes.

Ix Chel manifests in all phases of womanhood: as a young girl, a fertile woman, and an old crone. Ix Chel often wears a skirt embroidered with crossbones. She wears a snake as a headband. In Mayan script, she is represented by a uterine symbol. Ix Chel has dominion over lunar cycles and thus also over menstrual cycles. She is often depicted with a loom and is credited with inventing weaving.

Keshalyi

The Keshalyi are Romany fairies whose name apparently derives from *kachli* ("spindle"). Linguists suggest these Romany words (*kachli*, *keshalyi*) derive from the Middle Eastern root word *kesh*, whose other derivatives are explicitly related to magic:

✳ *In Akkadian,* kashshapu *indicated a magician, sorcerer or wizard*

✳ *In Hebrew,* kesem *is magic*

An invocation of the Keshalyi allegedly enhances personal fertility: *"Keshalyi lisperesn!"* or *"Fairies spin!"*

Mari

Mari is often encountered spinning in the moonlight, often outside one of the mountain caves she calls home. The Basque witches who adored her once brought their spinning tools outside too; spinning at night under the moonlight, especially by a well, sacred tree or at a crossroads, was considered an unmistakable sign of witchcraft.

The Moirae

The Moirae (also the Moires) are the three Greek Fates. They represent the waxing, full, and waning moons: creation, existence, and destruction. In Greek, *moira* indicated a "portion," "lot" or "share." The Moirae determined one's allotted portion or fate. Their emblems include a spindle, scroll, and scales. The Moirae are eternal and were considered even more powerful than the gods. One of their number, Klotho, is also a goddess of spinning.

✳ *Klotho the Spinner puts the wool around the spindle*

✳ *Lachesis the Sustainer or Caster of Lots, Caster of Fate, spins the wool. Alternatively, she measures the thread*

✳ *Atropos the Cutter snips the thread. She is also known as "The Inevitable"*

Mokosh

Mokosh, "Mother Moist Earth," is the Russian deity of spinning, weaving, fertility, divination, and occult knowledge. She protects Earth's moisture including amniotic fluids and semen. Mokosh was, just prior to Christianity's ascendancy, the most significant Russian goddess. Post-Christianity, she may or may not have donned the mask of St Paraskeva (see page 843).

Neith

Neith is the ancient Egyptian goddess of weaving, witchcraft, and warfare. She is the Oldest One. In one Egyptian creation myth, Neith brought forth Ra the sun. Then she picked up a shuttle, put the sky on her loom and wove the world into existence. Neith invented weaving in the same way that Thoth invented magic: it doesn't exist without her.

The Norns

The Norns are the Nordic Fate Goddesses. These three sisters live at the Well of Urd and are sometimes envisioned as mermaids. The Norns gather at the Well of Urd to water and care for Yggdrassil, the World Tree. The Norns are responsible for maintaining it and watering its roots. The tree is the spindle on which they weave destiny. The fate of the world is in their hands. The Norns' sacred creature is the spider.

The Norns are the most powerful of all beings, even more powerful than the gods. They determine the fate and destiny of all living beings:

❋ *Urd (also sometimes spelled Urdh), "Past," is the eldest sister. She wraps the wool around the spindle*

❋ *Verdandi spins the wool and rules the present*

❋ *Skuld, "Shall Be," is the youngest of the Norns. She cuts the thread, terminating existence. Skuld has been known to change the benevolent fates bestowed by Urd and Verdandi.*

Another perspective suggests that Urd, Verdandi, and Skuld represent Past, Present, and Future. Alternatively, Urd spins the thread of existence, Verdandi weaves it into existence (the Web of Urd), and Skuld rips it apart.

The Parcae

The Parcae are the Roman Fate goddesses. Their name derives from the Latin root, *parere*,

"to bear or give birth." Originally there were only two Parcae, the Roman deities Decuma and Nona. Later, to match the prototype of the Greek Moirae, they became a triad with the addition of death, Morta.

❋ *Nona, the goddess of birth, rules the nine months of pregnancy*

❋ *Decuma rules birth*

❋ *Morta rules death*

Perchta

Twelfth Night is Perchta's sacred day; in her honor, women are supposed to stop working. According to one legend, a hard-working woman kept working on Twelfth Night. Perchta looked in the window, saw her, gave her two gold bobbins and told them to fill them within the hour. The woman did the best she could, and then threw the bobbins into a running stream in order to reach Perchta.

Saule

Saule is the Baltic solar goddess of spinning and weaving. She spins rays of sunshine.

Spider Grandmother

Spider Grandmother is the primary deity of various Native American spiritual traditions. Spider Grandmother brings fire to people and trains and initiates the heroes who lead people to victory against a host of spiritual, magical, and physical dangers.

Spider Woman

Spider Woman is the direct, simple name given to spinning goddesses in many cultures around the world.

St Paraskeva

St Paraskeva is venerated in Russia as well as in Greece and the Balkans. She is depicted as a tall, thin woman with long, flowing hair carrying a spindle. Paraskeva is associated with growing and spinning flax but she transcends the role of *"botanical spirit"*.

Among Paraskeva's epithets are "The Flaxen One," "The Muddy One," and "The Dirty One." Paraskeva is described as black as fertile Earth.

St Paraskeva literally means *"St Friday"* and Friday is her holy day. Her ritual consists of 12 Fridays spread throughout the year when her devotees cannot work.

Those who keep her 12 fasts from work are said to be guaranteed abundance, happiness, and prosperity. On those days men are forbidden to work the soil. It is a day of respite for Earth: hunting, fishing, and gathering berries are forbidden, as is cooking and washing. One may only do what revitalizes: dance, sing, and have sex. Women (but not men) may perform acts of healing. Paraskeva's Fridays are considered very auspicious days on which to get married and give birth.

Paraskeva's origins are obscure. The official story is that St Paraskeva was a virgin-martyr during the Diocletian persecution of Christians. Her name Friday indicates her devotion to the day of Christ's Passion.

It is generally believed that she was a Pagan deity of such importance and popularity that the Church was obligated to incorporate her as a saint. Beneath the mask of the saint lies a Slavic deity protector of women and their sacred arts. Her official feast day, October 20, lies amid the period traditionally dedicated to spinning and considered favorable for marriage.

The sixteenth-century Stoglav Council complained that Paraskeva's festivals featured men and women, old and young, all naked with loose, unbound hair, engaged in jumping and shaking. Devotees claimed Paraskeva ordered them to honor her feast days with dancing. However, in 1589, the Patriarch of Constantinople banned her cult.

> St Paraskeva sometimes appears with two other saints, St Sreda (Wednesday) and St Nedelia (Saturday). They fulfill the concept of a triplicity of spinning goddesses.

Tante Arie

Tante Arie is the fairy-witch goddess of the Jura Mountains and Franche Comte. She spins Fate in her mountain sanctuary. Tante Arie is a goddess of spinning. Singing and spinning lure her from her caverns.

Tante Arie manifests as a woman with goose-feet or as a snake. She rewards those who are industrious and protects pregnant and laboring women. She is sometimes represented as an old woman, half fairy, half witch, who comes down from a mountain on Christmas Eve, riding a donkey.

A children's legend suggests that Tante Arie invisibly shakes fruit trees so that the fruit falls for good children. She brings nuts and cakes at Yule time. Another legend suggests that Tante

Arie brings gifts for good children but birch rods or dunce caps (witches hats) for the naughty ones.

Uttu

Uttu was the Sumerian spider goddess of weaving and cloth.

The Weird Sisters

The Weird Sisters or Wyrd Sisters are the Germanic variant of the Norns. Urd, the Norn of the Past, is etymologically related to the Old German *wurt* and Anglo-Saxon *wyrd*, both indicating "destiny" but also magic, power, and prophetic knowledge. *Wyrd* eventually evolved into the English "weird"—"strange" or "eerie."

> *Wyrd* is the eternal and all-powerful thread of destiny that shapes existence. It may be visualized as a web *(The Web of Wyrd)*. All of life is magically interconnected via this web.

The Fate goddesses evolved into Fairies, known as *Fatas* in Italian. (See **FAIRIES**.) These weren't merely fairy tales: in twelfth-century Denmark it was customary for Pagans to consult a trinity of goddesses regarding children's future. Three seated priestesses served as the Oracle for these Fates.

Spinning Tools

In an Inca belief, the moon controls the tools of female labor. The moon is the ultimate controlling force over anything female or related to women. It was feared that spindles and looms would transform into bears, jaguars, and snakes during lunar eclipses.

Witches in trance sent their doubles to battle with each other armed with agricultural tools as well as spinning tools like distaffs and shuttles.

Anthropologists suggest that the practice of spinning fibers into thread and yarn has existed for over ten thousand years with very few changes in technology during that time. The distaff, spindle, and spindle whorl remain the constant tools of spinning from pre-history until almost the eighteenth century. (The spinning wheel was invented in the fourteenth century but did not gain general usage until the eighteenth.)

> Miniature spinning wheels, spindles, and gold bobbins are often the sole items of baggage carried by fairy-tale heroines. Similar items were buried with queens during the Middle Ages.

These tools are no longer familiar to most of us, but not too long ago they were women's constant companions.

Distaff

The distaff is a long staff to which fibers were tied to keep them untangled. Distaffs feature frequently in paintings and engravings of witches, including those by Dürer. They served as an emblem or attribute of witchcraft. Witches are frequently depicted flying on distaffs.

The distaff, of course, was a tool found in virtually every home and used for spinning yarn. What does this imply? That every woman is at least potentially a witch? That the distaff served as a tool of divination too? That witches have the ability to influence and control life and death similar to the Fates?

The simplest distaffs were forked sticks; more elaborate ones consisted of a stick with a fork or comb on the top intended to hold the fibers during the spinning process.

Mary B. Kelly, author of *Goddess Embroideries of Eastern Europe*, writes of women who bring their distaffs to the riverside annually and hang them in trees so that the Bereginy (nature spirits) can spin their own clothing. Distaffs were considered to be incarnations of the goddess who supervised spinning, similar to Hathor's mirror or sistrum in ancient Egypt.

Some Russian spinning distaffs are created in the form of a woman or are ornamented with goddess imagery painted on them.

Loom

Just spinning thread isn't sufficient. Once spun, the thread must be woven into cloth. A loom is a frame for interlacing two or more sets of threads to form cloth.

Fabric, tapestries and carpets are woven on looms. Among some nomadic tribes, their very homes, their tents, were woven on large looms. All clothing, all fabrics, from the most mundane to the most holy and sacred, were woven on looms.

Looms, thus, were not luxury items; they were basic, everyday tools necessary for survival. In many cultures, from the Middle East to the Maya, women were not deemed ready for marriage until they were proficient weavers.

> According to legend, instead of broomsticks, Bulgarian witches traditionally flew on weaving looms.

Depending on culture and need, a wide variety of looms exist, although all are recognizable as looms:

❋ *There are heavy, massive free-standing looms complete with complex foot pedals*

❋ *Light, mobile back-strap looms can be carried anywhere*

❋ *Tiny bead looms facilitate the creation of intricately beaded bands*

If spinning thread was envisioned as birthing and cutting thread as terminating life, then weaving is the metaphor for living. That old cliché about weaving the "tapestry of life" still survives.

> In some indigenous American cultures, spinning is perceived as akin to pregnancy; weaving represents birth and life. This becomes a metaphor for infertility: a woman who spins but never weaves. Some Mayans also believe this to be among the telltale signs of malevolent witchcraft: witches are believed to spin but never weave.

Weaving is not only a practical and aesthetic art but a spiritual and magical art too; weaving may be understood as a direct descendant and link to primordial tree religions. Metaphorically, the loom is the tree while the shuttle (see below), weaving in and out amidst the threads, represents the serpent. (See **ANIMALS:** Snakes; **BOTANICALS:** Trees.) Many fairies and fate goddesses spin thread and weave webs while seated by the World Tree.

Through the use of the loom, *any* tree is potentially, metaphorically transformed into the World Tree: traditionally, large freestanding looms used logs as frames, and while one end of the Mayan back-strap loom loops around the weaver, the other traditionally loops around a tree, as if one weaves destiny on the sacred World Tree.

Although details are mysterious, the Old Testament records women weaving *"houses"* for the Asherah, a sacred wooden pole believed to represent the Hebrew goddess Lady Asherah and/or the sacred tree of life, periodically a fixture of King Solomon's Temple. The woven houses are believed to be some sort of garment.

Weaving may also be perceived as an act of specifically female resistance; women wove their equivalent of history books and reference works: woven tapestries, carpets and sacred fabrics were repositories for the symbols and images of women's ancient spiritual and magical traditions. These motifs dominate traditional Oriental carpets, and still ornament modern ones.

Shuttle

A shuttle is the weaving device used for passing the thread of the weft between the threads of the warp on the loom. A skilled weaver manipulates the shuttle in a consistent, sure rhythm. "Shuttle" thus also refers to this back and forth, hyp-notically repetitive, rhythmic motion: in modern usage, a train or plane continually traveling between two points at regular, consistent intervals is called a shuttle. Shuttle also names a spindle-shaped device that holds the thread in tatting, knotting, and lace or net making.

The shuttle is also called *"the woman's voice"*; Sophocles described the Athenian heroine Philomela as the *"voice of the shuttle."* Philomela's tale is retold in Ovid's *Metamorphoses*:

Tereus, King of Thrace, married Procne of Athens; her younger sister Philomela traveled to Thrace with Procne. Tereus developed an illicit passion for the virgin, Philomela; he raped her then tore out her tongue so that she couldn't reveal the crime. He secretly imprisoned Philomela, telling Procne her sister was dead.

Left alone with a shuttle and loom, Philomela wove her story into a tapestry, which she gave to a serving woman to deliver to her sister. Procne, able to read the tapestry like a letter, immediately understood the situation and is able to liberate Philomela.

Spindle

The spindle is a short shaft weighted with a spindle whorl (see page 847), The spindle, like the distaff, symbolized women and served as a magical tool.

Spindles, although women's tools, represent phallic energy; they are sharp and are frequently described as doubling as weapons. In essence, the spindle puts phallic energy in the hands of a woman, in the manner that the birch switches identified with horned gods places feminine power in the hands of men.

Spindle Whorls

The spindle whorl is the weight attached to the spindle, which provides momentum and the downward pull of gravity. The simplest, most ancient spindle whorl was a rock. Ancient spindle whorls were ornamented to resemble owls, spiders, and women.

Spindle whorls seem to have served as progenitors of *milagros* (ex-votos). Spindle whorls were used as votive offerings, inscribed with the maker's name, a deity's name and a vow or contract that bound them. Figurines, plaques, and vessels were similarly fashioned.

A high percentage of pilgrims to Romano-Celtic healing sanctuaries appear to be female based on the offerings that have been recovered: spindle whorls as well as anatomically shaped *milagros* (especially breasts) and hairpins.

Hoards of spindle whorls have been uncovered in Neolithic, Chalcolithic, Minoan, Mycenaean, and Greek caves and sanctuaries as well as in Eastern and Central Europe and the Balkans.

Spinning Wheels

Spinning wheels were developed in the late fourteenth century but because the first wheels were large, awkward, inefficient, and expensive, the simple hand-held spindle remained in common use until the eighteenth century. It is believed spinning wheels were first developed in Asia, perhaps in China or Persia.

In George MacDonald's fairy-tale novel *The Princess and the Goblin* (first published in 1872), Princess Irene discovers her mysterious, goddess-like great-grandmother spinning alone in a turret room. Unlike the lone spinner of *Sleeping Beauty*, Irene's great-grandmother spins the thread of life, not death, creating an invisible but unbreakable thread for Irene that always leads her safely home. MacDonald describes the sound of the spinning wheel as the "*hum of a very happy bee that had found a rich well of honey.*"

Wormwood and Garlic: Dangers and Protection

Despite all the romance, revelry and fun of witchcraft, the reality is that many people are deathly afraid of witches. They consider witchcraft terrifying and witches dangerous.

What exactly is it that they fear? That answer varies; as usual, much depends upon how one defines witches and witchcraft. Some are genuinely afraid of *all* aspects of occultism or Paganism. For these people, fear of witchcraft may border on hysteria. The witches don't actually have to *do* anything to incite fear: their very existence is perceived as dangerous. Others are fearful of specific aspects of the magical arts— what are perceived as potentially hazardous practices. And then, of course, there can be a fine line between respect and fear: if witches do have access to greater knowledge and/or power, then they should indeed be respected and perhaps handled with care.

The flip side of the power to heal and bless is the power to harm and curse. This has always been a crucial dilemma for many when considering witchcraft. Much depends upon whether someone perceives witches as inherently good, neutral, or evil. If they are good or neutral, then even if they can cause harm, most likely they will not, in the same manner that although physicians and attorneys certainly have the knowledge to create damage and mischief, most rarely do so. However, if you believe, as many do, that witches are inherently evil and malicious and exist solely for the pleasure of creating havoc and harm, then there is no way to consider them without tremendous fear and anxiety. Because these fears and anxieties have existed for *ever*, various protective measures have developed over the ages as well.

Dangers of Witchcraft

Curses

"Stick and stones can break my bones, but words can never hurt me." If that old adage was really true, no one would ever have to worry about curses.

A curse is the opposite of a blessing. It is impossible to truly understand curses without

848

an appreciation of the power of blessings. The words "blessing" and "curse" are now often used very loosely, casually, and thoughtlessly—blessings are mechanically offered whenever someone sneezes; "cursing" may be considered synonymous with using profanities. "*I cursed him out,*" now most often just means that someone directed harsh language at another person.

These words however originally referred to something exceptionally powerful and specific: magical energy transfers from one person toward someone or something else with the intention of affecting the destiny of the target, either positively (blessing) or adversely (curse).

According to traditional belief, some people, for one reason or another (heredity, skill, knowledge, innate ability or otherwise), possess so much power that, if they so choose, they can consciously transmit good fortune or specific miraculous occurrences (healing, fertility, prosperity, safety, and so on) to other people. Although *any* blessing is valuable, some blessings—those from powerful people who are in touch with sacred forces—are believed to be especially potent.

A curse is the antithesis of a blessing. Conventional occult wisdom suggests that anyone possessing enough power to create good fortune also possesses the power to block, repeal or remove it as well. Blessings bring health, happiness, and success and enable your dreams to come true; curses bring the opposite.

Intrinsic to this original concept of blessing and cursing is the notion that spoken words possess the power to create reality. Blessings and curses may be accompanied and reinforced by hexes, spells or various other magical practices. A true curse is not some vague utterance, nor is it casual use of profanity. Neither is it merely angry emotions randomly directed toward someone.

A curse is a lucidly articulated wish for harm directed toward another. When you casually tell someone to "drop dead" you have just cursed him, although you may not have really intended to do so. Now if there was no intent and you are not a person of exceptional power, that curse may not be strong enough to take effect. However, if you *are* an exceptionally powerful person …

Curses were once taken very seriously. There was an art to cursing. People prided themselves on their creative and unusual curses and boasted of their efficacy. People competed to create more inventive curses. It was a crime associated with witchcraft during the Burning Times.

Not all curses are equal. Traditional wisdom suggests that just as some people's blessings are more valuable than others, some people's curses are especially dangerous:

❋ *Witches, shamans, and other magical practitioners are believed to deliver powerful curses, as do smiths and metalworkers, who often double as sorcerers and shamans in traditional cultures.*

❋ *Menstruating women are often traditionally believed capable of delivering* really *lethal curses, one reason why they were often isolated from society.*

❋ *Curses cast by dying people are believed to be exceptionally powerful and almost impossible to repeal. This counts for any words said during the dying process, however "last words" constitute the most potent curse (or blessing) of all.*

Witches executed during the Burning Times were frequently prevented from uttering public "last words" for fear that this offered them an opportunity to irrevocably curse their persecutors. A witch's curse, delivered when she was alive and well, was considered a fearsome thing; a witch's curse cast as she was dying was once feared as the most potent curse of all. Many local legends recall curses cast by murdered witches and impossible to lift.

The Evil Eye

The Evil Eye may be transmitted with a glance; however it really has little to do with eyes. A substantial percentage of traditional witchcraft and magical practice involves attempts to boost creative, generative, fertility power. Certain magical powers are believed capable of generating this positive creative energy; the Evil Eye can be understood as producing a force that is the antithesis of this generative magic power. Rather than growth and well-being, the Evil Eye stimulates desolation, stagnation, and sterility.

Who casts this Evil Eye or how is it cast? This pertinent question has never been conclusively resolved. Different cultures, traditions, and individuals offer different explanations:

✷ *The Evil Eye may be a random universal force that is mechanically attracted to certain targets in the manner of a heat-seeking missile.*

✷ *The Evil Eye may emerge from individual people. No consensus exists as to whether it is cast deliberately. Some believe that the Evil Eye stems from resentment and jealousy and that* anyone *has the capacity to cast it when frustrated or angry. Other schools of thought believe that the Evil Eye is cast deliberately, and that* some people *are more likely to cast it than others.*

Witches (surprise, surprise) are traditionally at the top of the list of dangerous people. (Other suspects include childless women, metalworkers, priests, and certain ethnic groups—inevitably minorities within a culture. Sometimes unusual physical traits are also associated with casting the Evil Eye: blue eyes in places where dark eyes predominate, dark people in largely fair-skinned societies, red-haired people almost everywhere.) Some fear witches specifically because they believe that witches maliciously enjoy casting the Evil Eye.

This association with the Evil Eye is simultaneously a terrible insult and an acknowledgement of perceived power. The person believed capable of casting the Evil Eye is not considered weak and helpless but instead as a person of extraordinary individual power. (This, however, has never stopped persecution of those believed to possess the Evil Eye.)

Although anyone may fall victim to the Evil Eye, some are believed more vulnerable than others: babies and children; brides, pregnant women, young mothers; horses and cattle; and anything new, shiny, and valuable, especially if it's rare.

Men are not believed especially vulnerable to the Evil Eye, except for their reproductive capacities including basic sexual function.

Luckily there are many effective techniques for preventing, blocking, and removing the effects of the Evil Eye.

The Evil Eye creates a withering effect. The counter-attack often involves the concept of moisture, sometimes symbolically, sometimes literally. Spitting is a common quick-fix remedy to perceived casting of the Evil Eye.

In addition to saliva, the magically protective powers of the human body are often summoned to provide protection from the Eye. Magical replicas of moisture-producing parts of the anatomy are often used to repel and remove the effects of the Eye, such as eyes and genitals.

The gesture known as the *"fig hand"* repels the Evil Eye. The fig hand depicts a human fist, with the thumb thrust between the first two fingers. The gesture mimics the sexual act and is considered powerfully life-affirming, thus overriding the Evil Eye. ("Fig" literally names the fleshy, lushly seeded fruit but is also ancient Italian slang for "vulva.") The fig hand amulet is believed to have originated in Italy; it remains popular throughout the Mediterranean as well as in Brazil.

Other protective measures include bells, particularly those cast from metal. Mirrors reflect the Eye back on itself, creating a boomerang effect. The color red repels the Eye and creates an aura of protection: this may be understood as drawing upon women's primal menstrual power.

Hexes

Technically, *"hex"* derives from the German word for *"witch"* (*hexe*), however it is commonly used in the English language to indicate a malevolent spell. The linguistic implication is that hexes are the common province of the *hexe*.

Thus in English, a hex is a malicious, harmful spell. A curse relies on the power of the individual who casts it; a hex follows the format of a spell. Although *anyone* can cast a hexing spell, many believe that hexes cast by a witch are more powerful than those cast by a layperson:

✳ *Witches possess secret knowledge and thus know of more lethal spells.*

✳ *Witches are professional spell-casters and thus have greater access to "professional secrets."*

✳ *Witches possess greater experience with hexes and, as that old saying goes, "practice makes perfect."*

✳ *Witches are allied with potent spiritual entities who may be invoked to assist and reinforce their spells.*

✳ *Those who define witches as possessing supernatural power believe that, by their very nature, witches can cast more powerful spells than the average human.*

None of these reasons are necessarily true, although all are commonly believed. Intent is the key with hexes: identical material and techniques may be used to cast or break a hex. Identical spells may be used to cast a malicious hex or to create loving magic: tossing graveyard dirt at someone may be intended to stimulate disaster or to create an aura of protection. Actions and materials may be *identical*; the sole difference is the focus and intent of the spell-caster. That focus and intent is sufficient to produce the desired outcome.

Menstrual Power

What's that old gender stereotype? Women are the frail, gentle species; men are the stronger sex? Well, there may be an even more ancient, primordial stereotype that turns the tables on that cliché: physical power isn't the strongest force on Earth. Women were once considered to be the more magically potent gender, as demonstrated by their spiritual alliance with powerful natural phenomena like the moon, tides, and Earth herself. The following were considered to demonstrate proof of women's magic power:

✳ *Women's ability to bring forth life from their own bodies*

✳ *Women's ability to miraculously provide food from their own bodies*

✳ *Menstruation, the monthly flow of blood that indicates the potential for fertility and the promise of life rather than death*

Women were initially revered, respected, and worshipped because of this power. It is no accident that the earliest sacred images took the form of females.

No material on Earth, *nothing*, is traditionally considered more magically powerful than menstrual blood; no practitioner is as powerful as a menstruating woman—with the exception of a menopausal woman. This isn't a contradiction; women weren't perceived as losing power as they aged but gaining it.

The respect, reverence, and fear of menstrual power are fairly universal and are commonly perceived by anthropologists to be extraordinarily primordial beliefs.

❋ *Traditional metaphysical wisdom suggests that menstrual blood creates a solid wall of magical protection: it can break and prevent curses, hexes, and the Evil Eye. It can counteract virtually every other power, ward or spell. (See DICTIONARY: Ward.)*

❋ *Consumption of as little as a single drop of a woman's menstrual blood is believed to stimulate undying love and devotion for her. Should you consume a woman's menstrual blood, knowingly or unknowingly, it is believed that she will for ever command your heart.*

❋ *Once upon a time, very long ago, many historians, scholars, and anthropologists suggest that menstrual blood provided the very first blood sacrifices: no one was killed, no one got hurt. However, only women— and women of a certain age—were capable of making these offerings. It thus offered a certain segment of the population monopoly on spiritual power.*

However, anything so potent is also potentially dangerous. There is a theory that the real reason behind the tradition of isolating menstruating women is not because they were temporarily "unclean" but because they were temporarily too powerful and dangerous to be left unsupervised. (In many traditional cultures, as in offices where women work very closely together, menstrual cycles tend to become synchronized, therefore all the women in one com-munity might menstruate simultaneously, creating a formidable magical army.)

What else can menstrual blood magically do? Because menstrual blood is such an intensely yin (female) power, it may counteract or deactivate yang (male) energy. It can deactivate men's amulets; it may be able to deactivate men and their magic as well. Admonitions to avoid sexual contact with menstruating women may have been initially intended to preserve male power.

❋ *In traditional Romany culture, a curse delivered by a menstruating woman, particularly if she flaps her skirts in your direction, is believed to be virtually irremovable.*

❋ *In ancient Hawaii, a menstrual rag carried as a flag created an aura of protection around a party traveling through dangerous territory; it was the equivalent of a white flag of safety.*

Menstruation came to embody the most shameful, sinful aspects of the female gender. However ancient legends and awareness of its power never entirely disappeared from the general population. Witches still reveled in the moonlight and gathered lunar plants like mugwort, among whose primary uses is aligning one's personal cycle with the moon.

If the witch is understood as embodying this primordial potent female power, then this is a crucial reason why she became so feared and why she is perceived as *potentially* dangerous and capable of being destructive. Her curses and hexes are especially potent because of her ability and willingness to access this power.

Over the millennia, substitutes have evolved that echo and closely approximate that power: *anyone* regardless of age or gender can learn to use them, although in general they are affiliated with women's magic and power. While not as innately powerful as the real thing, they come pretty close, and in the hands of an expert practitioner they may be extremely effective. Furthermore, even those with access to true menstrual blood may not find it convenient or socially acceptable to use and so the following substitutes are very popular magic spell ingredients: henna; iron, iron oxide powder, and ground hematite; vermillion powder, red ochre or red brick dust; red botanical material like bloodroot, dragon's blood resin or red sandalwood powder; dried ground scarlet flower petals like carnations, roses or poppies; and red witch candles.

See also **BOTANICALS:** Mugwort, Opium Poppy; **MAGICAL PROFESSIONS:** Metalworkers; **PLACES:** Bathhouse; **WOMEN'S MYSTERIES**.

Protective Measures

All these dangers and hazards; what can a person do? Because witchcraft is so ancient, various solutions, remedies and obstacles to its perceived dangers have evolved over the millennia.

When considering protective measures against witchcraft, it's crucial to consider how the term "witchcraft" is being defined. Some consider witchcraft to be dangerous in general. However many discussions of the "dangers of witchcraft" are actually about the dangers of malevolent spell-casting. It isn't *all* witchcraft that's perceived as dangerous; witchcraft itself isn't the problem. Instead protective measures are needed to ward off only malevolent magic. Many solutions have been devised by witches and utilize the tools of the witchcraft trade.

Botanical Solutions

Certain botanicals are believed to protect against malevolent magic. Many are used in protective spells and are incorporated into rituals to remove hexes and curses. If planted on one's property they keep the area safe from magical harm. Among the most popular are:

Agrimony (*Agrimonia eupatoria*)
Aloe vera (*Aloe barbadensis, A. vera*)
Angelica (*Angelica* spp.)
Bamboo (*Bambusa* spp.)
Benzoin (*Styrax benzoin*)
Betony (*Betonica officinalis*)
Black Cohosh (*Cimicifuga serpentaria*)
Blackthorn (Sloe) (*Prunus spinosa*)
Cinquefoil (Five-finger grass) (*Potentilla reptans*)
Devil's Pod (Ling Nut) (*Trapa bicornis*)
Eupatorium (*Eupatorium odorata*)
Frankincense (*Boswellia carterii*)
Galangal (Laos root) (*Alpinia galanga*)
Garlic (*Allium sativum*)
Hydrangea (*Hydrangea arborescens*)
Juniper (*Juniperus communis*)
Mucura (*Petiveria alliacea*)
Mugwort (*Artemisia vulgaris*)
Mullein (*Verbascum thapsus*)
Rose of Jericho (*Anastatica hierochuntina*)
Rosemary (*Rosmarinus officinalis*)
Rowan (*Sorbus aucuparia*)
Rue (*Ruta graveolens*)
Saint John's Wort (*Hypericum perforatum*)
Syrian Rue (Harmal) (*Peganum harmala*)
Ti Plant (*Cordyline terminalis*)
Wisteria (*Wisteria* spp.)
Wormwood (*Artemisia absinthium*)
Yarrow (*Achillea millefolium*)

The Cross and Christian Power

Among the earliest promises of Christianity was that believers would be safe from all malevolent magic. The early Christian writer Athanasius wrote in *c.356*, "*Where the sign of the cross appears magic loses its power and witchcraft is ineffective.*" (So then, who needs witch trials?)

Many believe that Christian prayers and symbols will protect against witchcraft. Whether they will only serve true believers or whether their inherent power is so great that they automatically repel witchcraft and other malevolent powers like vampires remains subject to vociferous debate.

First and foremost among these Christian symbols is The Cross, and crosses are a common motif in protective magic around the world. (Missionaries who've discovered crosses used in similar fashion in non-Christian areas have historically understood this phenomenon to be a spiritual testament.) However, crosses (two crossed lines) are a very simple geometric shape, and their use as a sacred symbol pre-dates Christianity by millennia. Because Christianity has been such a powerful modern influence, many automatically assume that any cross must indicate Christianity. This is not the case:

✳ *Crosses were sacred to Aphrodite long before the birth of Christ.*

✳ *Crosses were important symbols in the indigenous traditions of Africa and the Americas, long before contact with Christians.*

✳ *Crosses may indicate that magical energy is able to travel in all directions, thus the shape is beneficial for protective spells. No area is left unprotected and vulnerable.*

✳ *In Congolese tradition, crosses represent the eternal human cycle of birth and rebirth.*

Stores that sell "spiritual supplies" or "religious goods" may sell small wax candles in the shape of a cross. These candles represent "crossed conditions"—the heavy cross some seem cursed to bear. Burning the cross effectively removes the crossed condition and these candles are thus used in magical spells to remove hexes, tricks, and curses.

A novena is a nine-day prayer ritual, and may be held for any desired goal. This one allegedly protects against witchcraft, the devil, dogs, and disease: accompany a nine-day regimen of blessed bread and holy water with daily recitations of three *Pater Nosters* and three *Ave Maria*'s in honor of the Trinity and St Herbert.

The concept of the novena pre-dates Christianity and so the ritual is easily adapted for those possessing other spiritual orientations.

1. Burn a new candle each evening for nine consecutive evenings.
2. Murmur over the candles, recite blessings and sacred verses, direct appeals to sympathetic higher powers.
3. Each morning throw the wax remnants from the candle as far away from your house as possible.

Protection against witchcraft isn't limited to Christian spiritual traditions. Certain deities and spiritual entities are believed capable of providing protection and remedying all magically derived harm. Among the most powerful are the archangels Michael and Gabriel, Kapo, Elegba, the Seven African Powers, Medusa, Durga, Kali, and Kwan Yin.

Certain sacred texts are believed to possess the power to remove and repel magical harm. Constant repetition and meditation on these texts turns the key to safety. Among the most popular of these texts are the biblical Book of Job and the Book of Psalms, most especially the 91st Psalm.

Power of the Witch

Among the many ironies associated with witchcraft is that many, if not most of the materials allegedly used to combat witchcraft are actually primary tools of the trade.

This may be understood as fighting fire with fire; magical practices used to protect against harmful witchcraft include charms, spells, and amulets. Among the most powerful protective devices are salt, iron, and menstrual blood, important components of many magic spells and part of the witch's own arsenal. Body imagery is also considered especially effective against harmful magic as it is against the Evil Eye: replicas of hands, eyes, and genitals magically preserve and protect.

Where this begins to get strange is when certain practices or symbols are reputed to banish or deactivate witches themselves. For instance, elder and rowan wood, known as witch trees, allegedly guard against witchcraft and keep its practitioners far away. The dilemma is that these very materials are favored by the witches themselves. Thus while some believe that mullein, for instance, keeps witches far away, no one seems to have bothered to inform the witches. Instead they keep using these same materials in their own spells.

Part of the confusion derives from language. When people describe the *dangers of witchcraft*, they often don't mean *all* magical practice, merely the harmful ones. What they're trying to say is that these materials ward off all malevolent magic. However in societies where all magical practice has officially been condemned and where practitioners fear for their lives, such precise language may be impossible. And after all, how can one categorize rowan twigs wrapped in scarlet ribbons as anything but a spell? It will only be authorized and safe to use if one describes it as intended to combat witchcraft. Describing something as being anti-witchcraft often permitted specific magical practices to continue in safety. What was really being prevented was harm, not witchcraft per se.

Real witchcraft practices are often cloaked in what are described as measures protecting against witchcraft itself. For instance, the following allegedly protect against witchcraft:

🕷 *Horseshoes nailed over doors*

🕷 *Brooms placed across doors*

🕷 *Silver in the form of bullets or charms*

Silver coins, if truly made from silver, allegedly alert you to the presence of malevolent witchcraft. Silver coins were worn on chains around the neck or placed inside one's shoe: should one encounter malevolent forces, allegedly the coin will suddenly, dramatically blacken or tarnish.

Silver, horseshoes, and (especially) brooms are all magical symbols and tools of witches themselves: each one evokes primal female magical power. How could they then be used to banish witches and prevent them from accessing their power? They don't; however they will prevent malevolent magic, as they have allegedly done for ages, whether in the hands of witches or others. Anti-witchcraft language permitted these tools of witchcraft to continue to be accessible to witches during times when witchcraft was dangerous to practice.

See **BOTANICALS:** Alder, Elder, Mullein, Rowan; **TOOLS:** Brooms.

Bibliography

Aaland, Mikkel *Sweat* (Santa Barbara, Calif: Capra Press, 1978)

Achtemeleier, Paul J. *HarperCollins Bible Dictionary* (New York: HarperSanFrancisco, 1996)

Afanas'ev, Aleksandr *Russian Fairy Tales* (New York: Pantheon Books, 1973)

Albion Press Ltd *The Complete Fairy Tales of Charles Perrault* (New York: Clarion Books, 1993)

Ancient Egypt: Myth and History (New Lanark, Scotland: Geddes & Grosset Ltd, 1997)

Anderson, Karen *Chain Her by One Foot* (New York: Routledge, 1993)

Ann, Martha, and Dorothy Myers Imel *Goddesses in World Mythology* (New York: Oxford University Press, 1993)

Ann, Martha, et al. *The Great Goddess* (Boulder, Colo: Our Many Names, 1993)

Arkins, Diane C. *Halloween* (Gretna, La: Pelican Publishing Company, 2000)

Asbjornsen, Peter Christen, and Jorgen Moe *Norwegian Fairy Tales* (New York: Viking Press, 1960)

Asbury, Herbert *The French Quarter* (New York: Capricorn Books, 1936)

Ashley, Leonard R.N. *The Complete Book of Devils and Demons* (New York: Barricade Books, 1996)

Aswynn, Freya *Northern Mysteries and Magick* (St. Paul, Minn: Llewellyn Publications, 2002)

Atkins, Stuart *Johann Wolfgang von Goethe: Faust I & II* (Cambridge, Mass: Suhrkamp/Insel Publishers, 1984)

Aveni, Anthony *Behind the Crystal Ball* (New York: Times Books, 1996)

Aymar, Brandt *Treasury of Snake Lore* (New York: Greenburg Publishers, 1956)

Badger, David *Frogs* (Stillwater, Minn: Voyageur Press, 2000)

Bannatyne, Lesley Pratt *Halloween* (New York: Facts on File, 1990)

Baring-Gould, William, and Ceil Baring-Gould *The Annotated Mother Goose* (New York: Bramhall House, 1962)

Barnes, Sandra T. *Africa's Ogun* (Bloomington, Ind: Indiana University Press, 1997)

Barstow, Anne Llewellyn *Witchcraze* (San Francisco: Pandora, 1994)

Bartel, Pauline *Spellcasters* (Dallas, Tex: Taylor Trade Publishing, 2000)

Bazin, Andre *Orson Welles* (Los Angeles: Acrobat Books, 1991)

Beauchamp, Monte *The Devil in Design* (Seattle, Wash: Fantagraphics Books, 2004)

Bilu, Yoram *Without Bounds* (Detroit, Mich: Wayne State University Press, 2000)

Boddy, Janice *Wombs and Alien Spirits* (Madison, Wisc: The University of Wisconsin Press, 1989)

Bonnerjea, Biren *A Dictionary of Superstitions and Mythology* (London: Folk Press Ltd, 1927)

Bord, Janet, and Colin Bord *Sacred Waters* (London: Granada, 1985)

Botermans, Jack, et al. *The World of Games* (New York: Facts on File, 1989)

Bourke, Angela *The Burning of Bridget Cleary* (New York: Viking, 1999)

Breslaw, Elaine G. *Tituba, Reluctant Witch of Salem* (New York: State University of New York Press, 1996)

Briggs, Katharine M. *Nine Lives: The Folklore of Cats* (New York: Pantheon Books, 1980)

Brooke, Elisabeth *Medicine Women* (Wheaton, Ill.: Quest Books, 1997)

Buckland, Raymond *The Witch Book* (Detroit, Mich: Visible Ink, 2002)

Budapest, Zsuzsanna *The Holy Book of Women's Mysteries* (Berkeley, Calif: Wingbow Press, 1989)

Buffalo Horn Man, Gary, and Sherry Firedancer *Animal Energies* (Spokane, Wash: Dancing Otter Publishing, 1992)

Bulgakov, Mikhail *The Master and Margarita* (New York: Vintage, 1995)

Burland, Cottie, and Werner Forman *The Aztecs* (New York: Galahad Books, 1980)

Burnie, David, and Don E. Wilson *Animal* (London: Dorling Kindersley, 2001)

Burr, George Lincoln *Narratives of the New England Witchcraft Cases* (Mineola, N.Y: Dover Publications, 2002)

Burriss, Eli Edward *Taboo, Magic, Spirits* (New York: Macmillan Company, 1931)

Busch, Robert T. *The Wolf Almanac* (New York: Lyons and Burford, 1995)

Bushnaq, Inea *Arab Folktales* (New York: Pantheon Books, 1986)

Byock, Jesse L. *The Saga of the Volsungs* (Berkeley, Calif: University of California Press, 1990)

Cahill, Robert Ellis *New England's Witches and Wizards* (Peabody, Mass: Chandler-Smith Publishing, 1983)

Calamari, Barbara, and Sandra DiPasqua *Holy Cards* (New York: Harry N. Abrams, Inc., 2004)

Callow, Simon *Orson Welles: The Road to Xanadu* (New York: Viking, 1996)

Calvino, Italo *Italian Folktales* (New York: Harcourt Brace Jovanovich, 1980)

Capstick, Peter H. *Death in the Long Grass* (New York: St Martin's Press, 1977)

Caro Baroja, Julio *The World of the Witches* (London: Phoenix Press, 2001)

Cavendish, Richard *The Black Arts* (New York: Perigee Books, 1967)

Cervantes, Fernando *The Devil in the New World* (New Haven, Conn: Yale University Press, 1997)

Cheever, Susan *My Name is Bill* (New York: Simon & Schuster, 2004)

Chesnutt, Charles W. *Conjure Tales* (New York: E.P. Dutton & Company, 1973)

Chesnutt, Charles W. *The Conjure Woman and Other Conjure Tales* (Durham, N.C: Duke University Press, 1993)

Christensen, Shane, et al. *Frommer's Argentina and Chile* (New York: Wiley Publishing, 2003)

Christiansen, Reidar *Folktales of Norway* (Chicago: University of Chicago Press, 1964)

Clebert, Jean-Paul *The Gypsies* (London: Penguin Books, 1969)

Cohn, Norman *Europe's Inner Demons* (New York: Basic Books, 1975)

Condren, Mary *The Serpent and the Goddess* (New York: Harper & Row, 1989)

Conrad, Jack Randolph *The Horn and the Sword* (London: MacGibbon and Kee, 1959)

Crompton, John *The Spider* (New York: Nick Lyons Books, 1950)

Curran, Bob *The Creatures of Celtic Myth* (London: Cassell & Co., 2001)

Dale-Green, Patricia *Cult of the Cat* (New York: Weathervane Books, 1963)

Daly, Kathleen N. *Norse Mythology A to Z* (New York: Facts on File, 1991)

Dance Perspectives Foundation, Inc. *International Encyclopedia of Dance* (New York: Oxford University Press, 1998)

Danielou, Alain *Gods of Love and Ecstasy* (Rochester, Vt: Inner Traditions, 1992)

Daraul, Arkon *Witches and Sorcerers* (New York: The Citadel Press, 1969)

D'Aulaire, Ingri, and Edgar D'Aulaire *Book of Greek Myths* (New York: Doubleday, 1962)

Davis, Wade *The Serpent and the Rainbow* (New York: Simon & Schuster, 1985)

Day, David *The Search for King Arthur* (New York: Facts on File, 1995)

DC Comics *Justice League of America: Zatanna's Search* (New York: DC Comics, 2004)

De Givry, Emile Grillot *Witchcraft, Magic and Alchemy* (New Hyde Park, N.Y: University Books, 1958)

Degh, Linda *Folktales of Hungary* (London: Routledge & Kegan Paul, 1965)

Deveney, John Patrick *Paschal Beverly Randolph* (Albany, N.Y: State University of New York Press, 1997)

Dixon, Laurinda S. *Perilous Chastity* (Ithaca, N.Y: Cornell University Press, 1995)

Dorson, Richard M. *Folk Legends of Japan* (Rutland, Vt: Charles E. Tuttle & Company, 1962)

Drury, Nevill *Magic and Witchcraft* (London: Thames & Hudson, 2003)

Dunn, Jane *Elizabeth and Mary* (New York: Alfred A. Knopf, 2004)

Earl, Amanda, and Danielle Sensier *Traditions around the World: Masks* (New York: Thomson Learning, 1995)

Ehrenreich, Barbara, and Deirdre English *Witches, Midwives and Nurses* (Old Westbury, N.Y: The Feminist Press, 1973)

Ellis, Bill *Lucifer Ascending* (Lexington, Ky: The University Press of Kentucky, 2004)

Ellis, Bill *Raising the Devil* (Lexington, Ky: The University Press of Kentucky, 2000)

Fenton, M. Brock *Bats* (New York: Facts on File, 1992)

Few, Martha *Women Who Live Evil Lives* (Austin, Tex: University of Texas Press, 2002)

Fleming, Fergus, and Alan Lothian *The Way to Eternity: Egyptian Myth* (London: Duncan Baird Publishers, 1997)

Fox, Levi *The Shakespeare Handbook* (Boston, Mass: G.K Hall & Company, 1987)

Fricke, John, et al. *The Wizard of Oz: The Official 50th Anniversary Pictorial History* (New York: Warner Books, 1989)

Fyfe, Andy *When the Levee Breaks* (Chicago: A Cappella Books, 2003)

Gadon, Elinor W. *The Once and Future Goddess* (New York: Harper & Row, 1989)

Galeano, Eduardo *Memory of Fire: 1. Genesis* (New York: Pantheon Books, 1985)

Gandee, Lee R. *Strange Experience: The Secrets of a Hexenmeister* (Englewood Cliffs, N.J: Prentice Hall, 1971)

Gardner, G.B. *The Meaning of Witchcraft* (New York: Samuel Weiser, Inc., 1959)

George, Leonard *Crimes of Perception* (New York: Paragon House, 1995)

Gettings, Fred *The Secret Lore of the Cat* (New York: Carol Publishing Group, 1989)

Gettings, Fred *Secret Symbolism in Occult Art* (New York: Harmony Books, 1987)

Gilbert, Bil *The Weasels* (New York: Pantheon Books, 1970)

Gilbert, Steve *Tattoo History: A Source Book* (New York: Juno Books, 2000)

Gimbutas, Marija *The Goddesses and Gods of Old Europe* (London: Thames & Hudson, 1982)

Ginzburg, Carlo *Ecstasies: Deciphering the Witches' Sabbath* (New York: Penguin Books, 1999)

Glass-Coffin, Bonnie *The Gift of Life* (Albuquerque, N.Mex: University of New Mexico Press, 1998)

Godwin, Joscelyn *Mystery Religions in the Ancient World* (San Francisco: Harper & Row, 1981)

Golden, Christopher, and Nancy Holder *Buffy the Vampire Slayer: The Watcher's Guide* (New York: Pocket Books, 1998)

Gordon, Mel *Erik Jan Hanussen* (Los Angeles: Feral House, 2001)

Grant, Michael *Eros in Pompeii* (New York: William Morrow & Company, 1975)

Graves, Robert *The Golden Ass* (New York: Farrar, Straus and Giroux, 1951)

Graves, Robert, and Raphael Patai *Hebrew Myths* (Garden City, N.Y: Doubleday & Company, 1964)

Green, Miranda *Celtic Goddesses* (New York: George Braziller, 1996)

Green, Miranda *The World of the Druids* (London: Thames & Hudson Ltd, 1997)

Greenwood, Susan *The Encyclopedia of Magic and Witchcraft* (London: Lorenz Books, 2001)

Greer, Mary K. *Women of the Golden Dawn* (Rochester, Vt: Park Street Press, 1995)

Gregor, Arthur S. *Witchcraft and Magic* (New York: Charles Scribner's Sons, 1972)

Grimassi, Raven *Encyclopedia of Wicca and Witchcraft* (St. Paul, Minn: Llewellyn Publications, 2000)

Guiley, Rosemary Ellen *The Encyclopedia of Witches and Witchcraft* (New York: Checkmark Books, 1999)

Haining, Peter *Ghouls* (New York: Stein and Day, 1971)

Haining, Peter *An Illustrated History of Witchcraft* (New York: Pyramid Books, 1975)

Hall, David D. *Witch-Hunting in Seventeenth-Century New England* (Boston, Mass: Northeastern University Press, 1999)

Hall, Jamie *Half Human, Half Animal* (Bloomington, Ind: 1st Books, 2003)

Hall, Manly P. *Paracelsus* (Los Angeles: The Philosophical Research Society, 1964)

Hanson, Jeanne K. *The Beastly Book* (New York: Prentice Hall General Reference, 1993)

Harmetz, Aljean *The Making of the Wizard of Oz* (New York: Hyperion, 1998)

Harrison, Colin, and Alan Greensmith *Birds of the World* (London: Dorling Kindersley, 1993)

Haskins, Jim, and Kathleen Benson *Conjure Times: Black Magicians in America* (New York: Walker & Company, 2001)

Hausman, Gerald, and Loretta Hausman *The Mythology of Cats* (New York: St. Martin's Press, 1998)

Hecht, Ann *The Art of the Loom* (New York: Rizzoli, 1989)

Hirschfelder, Arlene B, and Paulette Molin *Encyclopedia of Native American Religions, Updated Edition* (New York: Facts on File, 2000)

Hoff, Joan, and Marian Yeates *The Cooper's Wife is Missing* (New York: Basic Books, 2000)

Hofmann, Werner *Goya: "To Every Story There Belongs Another"* (London: Thames & Hudson, 2003)

Hole, Christina *Witchcraft in England* (London: Charles Scribner's Sons, 1947)

Hook, Brian (ed.) *The Cambridge Encyclopaedia of China* (Cambridge: Cambridge University Press, 1991)

Hopman, Ellen Evert *A Druid's Herbal for the Sacred Earth Year* (Rochester, Vt: Destiny Books, 1995)

Howie, M. Oldfield *The Cat in Magic and Myth* (Mineola, N.Y: Dover Publications, 2003)

Hoyt, Olga *Witches* (London: Abelard-Schuman, 1969)

Hubbs, Joanna *Mother Russia: The Feminine Myth in Russian Culture* (Bloomington, Ind: Indiana University Press, 1993)

Hughes, Robert *Goya* (New York: Alfred A. Knopf, 2003)

Hutton, Ronald *The Triumph of the Moon* (Oxford: Oxford University Press, 1999)

Huxley, Aldous *The Devils of Loudun* (New York: Carroll & Graf Publishers, 1952)

Huxley, Elspeth *With Forks and Hope* (New York: William Morrow & Company, 1964)

Illes, Judika *Earth Mother Magic: Ancient Spells for Modern Belles* (Gloucester, Mass: Fair Winds Press, 2001)

Illes, Judika *The Element Encyclopedia of 5000 Spells* (London: Element, 2004)

Illes, Judika "Frogs and Pomegranates" (unpublished manuscript)

Ingle, Annie *Robin Hood* (New York: Random House, 1991)

Ivanitz, Linda J. *Russian Folk Belief* (London: M.E. Sharpe, 1989)

Jackson, Nigel *Compleat Vampyre* (Milverton, Somerset: Capall Bann Publishing, 1995)

Johns, Andreas *Baba Yaga* (New York: Peter Lang Publishing, 2004)

Johnson, Buffie *Lady of the Beasts* (New York: HarperSanFrancisco, 1988)

Johnson, Tom, and Tim Miller *The Sauna Book* (New York: Harper & Row, 1977)

Johnston, Ollie, and Frank Thomas *The Disney Villains* (New York: Hyperion, 1993)

Jones, Prudence, and Nigel Pennick *A History of Pagan Europe* (London: Routledge, 1995)

Jong, Erica *Witches* (New York: Harry N. Abrams, Inc., 1981)

Karlsen, Carol F. *The Devil in the Shape of a Woman* (New York: W.W. Norton & Company, 1987)

Katz, Brian P. *Deities and Demons of the Far East* (New York: MetroBooks, 1995)

Kelley, Ruth Edna *The Book of Hallowe'en* (Boston, Mass: Lothrop, Lee and Shepard, 1919)

Kelly, Mary B. *Goddess Embroideries of Eastern Europe* (McLean, N.Y: Studiobooks, 1996)

Kelly, Sean, and Rosemary Rogers *Who in Hell…* (New York: Villard, 1996)

Kenrick, Donald, and Grattan Puxon *The Destiny of Europe's Gypsies* (New York: Basic Books, 1972)

Kieckhefer, Richard *Forbidden Rites* (University Park, Penn: The Pennsylvania State University Press, 1998)

King, Francis *Modern Ritual Magic* (Bridport, Dorset: Prism Press, 1989)

Koltuv, Barbara Black, Ph.D. *The Book of Lilith* (York Beach, Maine: Nicolas-Hays, 1986)

Koltuv, Barbara Black, Ph.D. *Weaving Woman* (York Beach, Maine: Nicolas-Hays, 1990)

Kors, Alan Charles, and Edward Peters *Witchcraft in Europe 400–1700* (Philadelphia: University of Pennsylvania Press, 2001)

Krull, Kathleen *They Saw the Future* (New York: Atheneum Books, 1999)

Kruuk, Hans *The Spotted Hyena* (Chicago: The University of Chicago Press, 1972)

Kummer, Hans *In Quest of the Sacred Baboon* (Princeton, N.J: Princeton University Press, 1995)

Lake, Veronica, with Donald Bain *Veronica: The Autobiography of Veronica Lake* (New York: Bantam Books, 1972)

LaPlante, Eve *American Jezebel* (New York: HarperSanFrancisco, 2004)

Lea, Henry Charles *The Inquisition of the Middle Ages*, abridged Margaret Nicholson (New York: The Macmillan Company, 1961)

Leakey, Louis B. *The Wild Realm: Animals of East Africa* (Washington, D.C: National Geographic Society, 1969)

Lecouteux, Claude *Witches, Werewolves, and Fairies* (Rochester, Vt: Inner Traditions, 2003)

Lee, Patrick Jasper *We Borrow the Earth* (London: Thorsons, 2000)

Leek, Sybil *Diary of a Witch* (Englewood Cliffs, N.J: Prentice-Hall, 1968)

Leiber, Fritz *Conjure Wife* (New York: Ace Books, 1981)

Leifur Eiriksson Publishing *The Sagas of Icelanders* (New York: Viking, 1997)

Leland, Charles G. *Aradia, or the Gospel of the Witches* (Blaine, Wash: Phoenix Publishing, 1999)

Leland, Charles G. *Etruscan Roman Remains* (Blaine, Wash: Phoenix Publishing, n.d., first published 1892)

Leon, Vicki *Uppity Women of Ancient Times* (New York: MJF Books, 1995)

Leoni, Edgar *Nostradamus and his Prophecies* (Mineola, N.Y: Dover Publications, 2000)

Lesko, Barbara S. *The Great Goddesses of Egypt* (Norman, Okla: University of Oklahoma Press, 1999)

Lewis, Arthur H. *Hex* (New York: Trident Press, 1969)

Lewis, Matthew *The Monk* (London: Penguin Books, 1998)

Linton, E. Lynn *Witch Stories* (London: Chapman and Hall, 1861, facsimile reprint Harper & Row, 1974)

Linton, Ralph, and Adelin Linton *Halloween through Twenty Centuries* (New York: Henry Schuman, 1950)

Llorente, Juan Antonio *A Critical History of the Inquisition of Spain* (Williamstown, Mass: The John Lilburne Company, 1967)

Long, Carolyn Morrow *Spiritual Merchants* (Knoxville, Tenn: The University of Tennessee Press, 2001)

Lubell, Winifred Milius *The Metamorphosis of Baubo* (Nashville, Tenn: Vanderbilt University Press, 1994)

Lurker, Manfred *The Dictionary of Gods and Goddesses, Devils and Demons* (London: Routledge, 1987)

McCalman, Iain *The Last Alchemist* (New York: HarperCollins, 2003)

McGowan, Tom *The Black Death* (New York: Franklin Watts, 1995)

McHargue, Georgess *Meet the Werewolf* (Philadelphia: J.B. Lippincott and Company, 1976)

Mackenzie, Donald A. *German Myths and Legends* (New York: Avenel Books, 1985)

McNaughton, Patrick R. *The Mande Blacksmiths* (Bloomington, Ind: Indiana University Press, 1993)

McNulty, Karsten D. *Romanian Folk Art* (Farmington, Conn: Aid to Artisans, 1999)

Maltin, Leonard *The Disney Films* (New York: Hyperion Books, 1995)

Manheim, Ralph *Grimms' Tales for Young and Old* (New York: Anchor Books, 1977)

Mann, Thomas *Doctor Faustus* (New York: Vintage Books, 1992)

Markale, Jean *The Pagan Mysteries of Halloween* (Rochester, Vt: Inner Traditions, 2001)

Marlowe, Christopher *Dr. Faustus* (Mineola, N.Y: Dover Publications, 1994)

Marshall, Richard *Witchcraft: The History and Mythology* (New York: Barnes and Noble, 1998)

Marwick, Max *Witchcraft and Sorcery* (London: Penguin Books, 1970)

Matthews, Caitlin, and John Matthews *The Encyclopaedia of Celtic Wisdom* (Shaftesbury, Dorset: Element Books, 1994)

Mezlekia, Nega *Notes from the Hyena's Belly* (New York: Picador, 2000)

Michelet, Jules *Witchcraft, Sorcery, and Superstition* (Secaucus, N.J: Citadel Press, 1997)

Midelfort, Erik H.C. *Witch-Hunting in Southwestern Germany 1562–1684* (Palo Alto, Calif: Stanford University Press, 1972)

Miller, Mary, and Karl Taube *The Gods and Symbols of Ancient Mexico and the Maya* (London: Thames & Hudson, 1993)

Montagne, Prosper *Larousse Gastronomique* (New York: Crown Publishers 1971)

Morrison, Phylis *Spiders' Games* (Seattle, Wash: University of Washington Press, 1979)

Morton, Lisa *The Halloween Encyclopedia* (Jefferson, N.C: McFarland & Company, 2003)

Moura, Ann *Grimoire for the Green Witch* (St. Paul, Minn: Llewellyn Worldwide, Ltd, 2003)

Müller-Ebeling, Claudia, Christian Ratsch and Wolf-Dieter Storl *Witchcraft Medicine* (Rochester, Vt: Inner Traditions, 2003)

Murphy, Joseph M. and Mei-Mei Sanford *Osun across the Waters* (Bloomington, Ind: Indiana University Press, 2001)

Murray, Margaret *The Witch-Cult in Western Europe* (Oxford: Oxford University Press, 1963)

Muten, Burleigh *Goddesses: A World of Myth and Magic* (Cambridge, Mass: Barefoot Books, 2003)

Nardo, Don *Women of Ancient Rome* (Farmington Hills, Mich: Lucent Books, 2003)

Néret, Gilles *Devils* (Köln: Taschen Books, 2003)

Netzley, Patricia D. *The Greenwood Encyclopedia of Witchcraft* (San Diego, Calif: Greenhaven Press, Inc., 2002)

Newall, Venetia *The Encyclopedia of Witchcraft & Magic* (New York: A & W Visual Library, 1974)

Newall, Venetia *The Witch Figure* (London: Routledge & Kegan Paul, 1973)

Nicholson, Irene *Mexican and Central American Mythology* (London: Paul Hamlyn, 1975)

Norton, Mary Beth *In the Devil's Snare* (New York: Alfred A. Knopf, 2002)

Obeyesekere, Gananath *Medusa's Hair* (Chicago: The University of Chicago Press, 1981)

Olson, Arielle North, and Howard Schwartz *Ask the Bones* (New York: Viking, 1999)

Pagels, Elaine *Adam, Eve, and the Serpent* (New York: Random House, 1988)

Patai, Raphael *The Jewish Alchemists* (Princeton, N.J: Princeton University Press, 1994)

Pelton, Robert *Voodoo Charms and Talismans* (Plainview, N.Y: Original Publications, 1997)

Pendell, Dale *Pharmakodynamis* (San Francisco: Mercury House, 2002)

Pendell, Dale *Pharmako/Poeia* (San Francisco: Mercury House, 1995)

Pennick, Nigel *The Complete Illustrated Guide to Runes* (Shaftesbury, Dorset: Element Books, 1999)

Pepper, Elizabeth *Witches All* (Tiverton, R.I: The Witches' Almanac, Ltd, 2003)

Pepper, Elizabeth, and Barbara Stacy *Magical Creatures* (Middletown, R.I: The Witches' Almanac, Ltd, 2000)

Pepper, Elizabeth and John Wilcock *Magical and Mystical Sites* (New York: Harper & Row, 1977)

Pereira, Filomena Maria *Lilith: The Edge of Forever* (Las Colinas, Tex: Ide House, 1998)

Perry, Mary Elizabeth, and Anne J. Cruz *Cultural Encounters: The Impact of the Inquisition in Spain and the New World* (Berkeley, Calif: University of California Press, 1991)

Peters, Edward *The Magician, The Witch, and the Law* (Philadelphia: University of Pennsylvania Press, 1978)

Phelps, Ethel Johnston *The Maid of the North* (New York: Henry Holt and Company, 1981)

Philip, Neil *Odin's Family* (New York: Orchard Books, 1996)

Pilato, Herbie J. *Bewitched Forever* (Irving, Tex: Tapestry Press, 2001)

Pocs, Eva *Between the Living and the Dead* (Budapest: Central European University Press, 2000)

Quaife, G.R. *Godly Zeal and Furious Rage* (New York: St. Martin's Press, 1987)

Rabinowitz, Jacob *The Rotting Goddess* (Brooklyn, N.Y: Autonomedia, 1998)

Rainieri, Caelum, and Ivory Andersen *The Nahualli Animal Oracle* (Rochester, Vt: Bear & Company, 2003)

Regensteiner, Else *The Art of Weaving* (New York: Van Nostrand Reinhold Company, 1970)

Ricciuti, Edward R. *The Devil's Garden* (New York: Walker and Company, 1978)

Riddle, John M. *Contraception and Abortion from the Ancient World to the Renaissance* (Cambridge, Mass: Harvard University Press, 1992)

Riddle, John M. *Eve's Herbs* (Cambridge, Mass: Harvard University Press, 1997)

Riland, George *The New Steinerbooks Dictionary of the Paranormal* (New York: Warner Books, 1980)

Roberts, David *The Pueblo Revolt* (New York: Simon & Schuster, 2004)

Rojas, Fernando de *The Celestina* (Berkeley, Calif: University of California Press, 1955)

Rose, Carol *Spirits, Fairies, Leprechauns and Goblins: An Encyclopedia* (New York: W.W. Norton & Company, 1998)

Ross, Anne *Druids, Gods, and Heroes from Celtic Mythology* (New York: Peter Bedrick Books, 1986)

Ruckenstein, Lelia, and James A. O'Malley *Everything Irish* (New York: Ballantine Books, 2003)

Russell, Jeffrey B. *A History of Witchcraft* (London: Thames & Hudson, 1980)

Ryall, Rhiannon *West Country Wicca* (Custer, Wash: Phoenix Publishing, 1989)

Ryan, W. F. *The Bathhouse at Midnight* (University Park, Penn: The Pennsylvania State University Press, 1999)

Sadoul, Jacques *Alchemists and Gold* (New York: G.P. Putnam and Sons, 1972)

Salamon, Hagar *The Hyena People* (Berkeley, Calif: University of California Press, 1999)

Salinas, Bobbi *Indo-Hispanic Folk Art Traditions II* (Auburn Hills, Mich: Piñata Publications, 1994)

Santino, Jack *Halloween and Other Festivals of Death and Life* (Knoxville, Tenn: The University of Tennessee Press, 1994)

Saunders, Nicholas J. *People of the Jaguar* (London: Souvenir Press, 1989)

Savage, Candace *Witch: The Wild Ride from Wicked to Wicca* (Vancouver: Greystone Books, 2000)

Sceurman, Mark, and Mark Moran *Weird N.J.* (New York: Barnes & Noble Books, 2003)

Schafer, Edward H. *The Divine Woman: Dragon Ladies and Rain Maidens* (San Francisco: North Point Press, 1980)

Scheffler, Lilian *Magia y Brujeria en Mexico* (Mexico City: Panorama, 1984)

Schneider, Steven Jay (ed.) *1001 Movies You Must See Before You Die* (London: Quintet Publishing, 2003)

Schneider, Stuart *Halloween in America* (Atglen, Penn: Schiffer Publishing, 1995)

Schober, Wilfried, and Eckard Grimmberger *The Bats of Europe and North America*, trans. William Charlton (Neptune City, N.J: T.F.H. Publications, 1997)

Schodt, Frederik L. *Manga! Manga! The World of Japanese Comics* (Tokyo: Kodansha International, 1988)

Schwartz, Howard *Lilith's Cave* (New York: Oxford University Press, 1988)

Scot, Reginald *The Discoverie of Witchcraft* (Mineola, N.Y: Dover Publications, 1972)

Seymour, St John D. *Irish Witchcraft and Demonology* (London: Portman Books, 1989, first published 1913)

Shakespeare, William *Macbeth* (New York: Washington Square Press, 1964)

Shuker, Dr. Karl *Dragons: A Natural History* (New York: Simon & Schuster, 1995)

Siefker, Phyllis *Santa Claus, Last of the Wild Men* (London: McFarland & Co., 1997)

Silverblatt, Irene *Moon, Sun and Witches* (Princeton, N.J: Princeton University Press, 1987)

Simmons, Marc *Witches in the Southwest* (Lincoln, Nebr: University of Nebraska Press, 1980)

Smith, Morton *Jesus the Magician* (San Francisco: Harper & Row, 1981)

Smith, Page, and Charles Daniel *The Chicken Book* (Athens, Ga: University of Georgia Press, 2000)

Snyder, James *Northern Renaissance Art* (New York: Harry N. Abrams, Inc., 1985)

Sorell, Walter *The Other Face: The Mask in the Arts* (Indianapolis, Ind: The Bobbs-Merrill Company, 1973)

Spariosu, Mihai I., and Dezso Benedek *Ghosts, Vampires and Werewolves: Eerie Tales from Transylvania* (New York: Orchard Books, 1994)

Sparks, John, and Tony Soper *Owls* (New York: Facts on File, 1989)

Spence, Lewis *The Magic and Mysteries of Mexico* (North Hollywood, Calif: Newcastle Books, 1994)

Stafford, Nikki *Bite Me! Sarah Michelle Gellar: Buffy the Vampire Slayer* (Toronto: ECW Press, 1998)

Stephens, Walter *Demon Lovers: Witchcraft, Sex and the Crisis of Belief* (Chicago: The University of Chicago Press, 2002)

Stewart, Iris J. *Sacred Women, Sacred Dance* (Rochester, Vt: Inner Traditions, 2000)

Stone, Peter F. *Tribal and Village Rugs* (New York: Thames & Hudson, 2004)

Strom, Yale *The Book of Klezmer* (Chicago: A Cappella Press, 2002)

Summers, Montague *Geography of Witchcraft* (New Hyde Park, N.Y: University Books, 1965)

Summers, Montague *The History of Witchcraft* (New York: Barnes & Noble Books, 1993)

Summers, Montague *The Malleus Maleficarum of Heinrich Kramer and James Sprenger* (Mineola, N.Y: Dover Publications, 1971)

Sutin, Lawrence *Do What Thou Wilt: A Life of Aleister Crowley* (New York: St. Martin's Griffin, 2000)

Tabori, Lena, and Natasha Tabori Fried *The Little Big Book of Chills and Thrills* (New York: Welcome Books, 2001)

Tatar, Maria *The Classic Fairy Tales* (New York: W. W. Norton & Company, 1999)

Tatar, Maria *The Hard Facts of the Grimms' Fairy Tales* (Princeton, N.J: Princeton University Press, 2003)

The Video Hound and All-Movie Guide Stargazer (Detroit, Mich: Visible Ink, 1996)

Thompson, C.J.S. *The Mystic Mandrake* (New Hyde Park, N.Y: University Books, 1968)

Thompson, Reginald Campbell *Semitic Magic* (London: Luzac & Company, 1908, Elibron Replica Edition)

Tokyo Pop *Tokyo Babylon* (Tokyo: Clamp, 1991)

Trachtenberg, Joshua *Jewish Magic and Superstition* (New York: Atheneum, 1970)

Tresidder, Jack *Dictionary of Symbols* (San Francisco: Chronicle Books, 1997)

Treuherz, Julian, Elizabeth Prettejohn and Edwin Becker *Dante Gabriel Rossetti* (London: Thames & Hudson, 2003)

Van Renterghem, Tony *When Santa was a Shaman* (St. Paul, Minn: Llewellyn Publications, 1995)

Vana, Zdenek *The World of the Ancient Slavs* Detroit, Mich: Wayne State University Press, 1983)

Waite, Arthur Edward *The Book of Ceremonial Magic* (Maple Shade, N.J: Lethe Press, 2002, first published 1913)

Walker, Barbara G. *The Woman's Encyclopedia of Myths and Secrets* (San Francisco: Harper & Row, 1983)

Walsh, Michael *An Illustrated History of the Popes* (New York: Bonanza Books, 1980)

Washington, Peter *Madame Blavatsky's Baboon* (New York: Schocken Books, 1995)

Webster, Reverend Wentworth *Basque Legends* (London: Griffith and Farran, 1879)

Webster's Seventh New Collegiate Dictionary (Springfield, Mass: G. & C. Merriam Company, 1965)

White, T.H. *The Sword in the Stone* (New York: G.P. Putnam and Sons, 1939)

Wilkinson, Richard H. *The Complete Gods and Goddesses of Ancient Egypt* (New York: Thames & Hudson, 2003)

Williams, Selma R., and Pamela Williams Adelman *Riding the Nightmare* (New York: HarperCollins, 1978)

Wilson, Colin *The Occult: A History* (New York: Random House, 1971)

Witches and Witchcraft (Alexandria, Va: Time-Life Books, 1990)

Wullschlager, Jackie *Hans Christian Andersen* (New York: Borzoi Books, 2000)

Yalom, Marilyn *Birth of the Chess Queen* (New York: HarperCollins, 2004)

Yarnall, Judith *Transformations of Circe: The History of an Enchantress* (Urbana and Chicago: University of Illinois Press, 1994)

Yeats, William Butler *Irish Fairy and Folk Tales* (New York: The Modern Library, 1994)

Yoder, Don, and Thomas E. Graves *Hex Signs* (New York: E.P. Dutton 1989)

Yolen, Jane *Mother Goose Songbook* (Honesdale, Penn: Boyds Mills Press, 1992)

Yronwode, Catherine *Hoodoo Herb and Root Magic* (Forestville, Calif: Lucky Mojo Curio Company, 2002)

Internet Sources

American Psychological Association www.apa.org 2004

Artmetal and Tom Joyce www.artmetal.com 1998–1999

Bat Conservation International www.batcon.org 1997

Bufoland www.mitologiachilota.cl 2001

Cornelius www.redflame93.com

Daly, Perla P. www.babaylan.com 2003

Dashu, Max www.suppressedhistories.net 2000

El Tigre Journeys www.biopark.org 1997–2012

Glamorous Pig Ranch Productions, Inc. www.porkopolis.org 2004

Harapan Media Tech www.harapan.co.jp 1999

Hermetic Order of the Morning Star, Inc. www.golden-dawn.org 1995–2004

Institute for Cultural Memory www.cimec.ro 1996–2004

Khandro.Net www.khandro.net 1998–2004

Knight, K. www.newadvent.org 2003

Knowne Whorl Spinners and Heather McCloy www.kws.atlantia.sca.org 2001

Markstein, Donald D. www.toonopedia.com 1999–2004

Murphy, Todd www.whydah.com 2002

The Museum of Talking Boards www.museumoftalkingboards.com 1996–2004

Skott, Frederik *"Easter Witches in Sweden"* www.hi.is/~terry/turku/papers.htm

Telesterion www.telesterion.com 1999–2004

Theatana, Kathryn Price www.bandia.net 1998, 2004

Trees for Life www.treesforlife.org.uk 2003

Weare, Robin M. www.liberalmafia.org 2001–2004

Index

Main entries are indicated in **bold**

weasel–witchcraft
association 59
Askhe-tanne-mat 94
Asklepios 55, 90, 92, 174, 329
Asmodeus 55, 116, 400, 487,
553, 630, 797
Astarte 163, 510, 511, 550
Asteria 387
Asteroth 729
astrologers *see* Albertus
Magnus; Cagliostro; Dee,
John; Lilly, William;
Faust, Johannes; Hermes
Trismegistus; Leek,
Sybil; Lenormand,
Marie; Nostradamus;
Paracelsus
astrology 86, 109, 347, 584,
590–4, 603
Babylonian 217, 592, 593
astronomy 590, 594
athamé **684–5**, 686
Athanasius 854
Athena 80, 93, 304, 354, 382,
582, 634, 635, 696
and metalworking **635**
and spinning **840**
atropine 155
Attis 541, **553–4**
August Herbs 209
Augustine, St 32, 785
Augustus Caesar 137
Aunt Caroline Dyer Blues
728
*Aunt Sally's Policy Players
Dream Book and Wheel of
Fortune* 113–14
Australia 43, 592
Austria 188, 223, 734, 758,
835
Corn Mother **423**
Dragon Cave 42
Krampuslauf 570–1
Perchtennacht 245
postcards 320
Schemenlaufen Festival 698
witchcraze 774
Autolykos 102
autumn equinox 210
Aventinus 323
ayahuasca 75
Ayida Wedo 91
Aymara people 65
Azazel 68, **554–5**, 561
Aztec codices **135–6**
Aztec deities *see* Tezcatlipoca;
Tlazolteotl
Aztec spirits *see* Cihuateteo
Aztecs 628, 833
frogs and fertility 65
hemerologies 110
jaguars 75
nahual ritual 78
obsidian mirrors 699

"owl-men" 80
sweathouses *see* temescal
terracotta dog burial 54
understanding of death 191

Baal 25, 62, 188, 324, 422
Ba'al/Ba'alat **324**, 557
ba'al shem 324
Baalat ob 324
Baal-Zebub 62
Baalzebub 324
baba **324**
Baba Yaga 17, 156, 174, 196,
206, 270, 274, 296,
375–7, 395, 411, 424,
465, 510, 563, 658, 659,
688, 700
Corn Mother **422**, 439
hag aspect **533**
Baba Yaga stories 10–11, 461,
466, 491–2
Baba Yaga (1) **492**
Baba Yaga (2) **492**
Prince Danila Govorila **493**
Vasilisa the Wise 473–4,
475–6, **494–6**
Babalu-Aye 55
babaylan **324**
Babi (Baba) 38
baboons **36–9**
Babylonia 340, 420, 738,
759
astrology 217, 592, 593
Deluge 511
Maklu 607
Babylonian deities *see* Gula
Bau
Bacchanalia **324**, 57, 80,
329
persecution **776–7**
Bacchanals **324**, 382, 776–7
Bacchus *see* Dionysus
Badbh 51, 52
Bagatella **325**
Bahram I of Persia 31
BaKongo people 97
Balaam 56
balazar 324, 365
Balch, Anthony 262
Bald Mountain 212, 216, 293,
669, **671–2**
Baldur/Balder 19, 162, 169,
385, 406, 544, 546, 547
Balent, Jim 232–3
Balfour, Margaret 822
Balkan spirits *see* Vila
Balkans 256, 461, 843, 847
fairy doctors 447
"fairy societies" 451, 462
goat dance 242
Saint Helen 460
vampire–werewolf–witch
link 40, 216, 357, 358
werewolf flower 103

Baltic deities *see* Ragana;
Rugiu Boba; Saule;
Svantovit
Baltic tradition
Lauma **438**
snake reverence 92
transformation 96
Bamana/Bambara 76, 403
Bandai Entertainment 299
bane 148
banias **647–9**
Banneker, Benjamin 110
banniks **648–9**
banshee **325**, 434, 441–2
Bantu 69, 346
baobhan sith **434**
Baphomet 57, **555–6**
baraka **325**
Barbara, St 351
Barbato, St 665
Bardon, Franz 705, **710–11**,
735
Barnes, Elizabeth 780, 781
Barrett, Francis 126, 709, 746
barrows 325, 440, 441
Basil, St 653
Basque deities *see* Aatxe/Etsai;
Akerbeltz; Boch de
Biterna; Mari
Basque region
sorguiñe **353**
witch-summoning spell 604
witchcraze 67, 144, 317,
556–7, 677, **777–9**
xorguina **364**
xorguinería **364**
see also akelarres; La Hendaye
Beach; Witches' Caves of
Zugarramurdi
Bastet 45–6, 245, 568
bathhouses 270, **645–51**, 661
bats **39–41**
Bau 55
Baubo 284, 541
Baum, L. Frank 272, 273, 295,
296, 297
Bautista, Fray Juan 78
Bava, Mario 266
Bavaria 508, 523
Bavarian Purity Act (1516)
506
Bayou St John 213, 247,
679
bean divination **505**
bears **41–3**, 82, 248, 350
Beauty and the Beast 8
Beelzebub 62
beer **505–6**
Befana la Strega/Befana la
Vecchia 223, **377–8**
Bekker, Balthasar 138, **139**
Bel (Belenus) 25, 188
Bell, Book and Candle 3, **253–4**,
260, 263, 310, 814

belladonna 149, 154–5, 694
Bellona 155
bells **685–6**
Belorussia 206, 358
Beltane **187–9**, 205, 208, 217,
509, 534, 538
Beltane cake **506–7**, 534
Beltane Carline 507, **534**
Beltane Caudle **507–8**
Benandanti 245, 311, **325–6**,
334, 341, 356, 430, 754,
813
Benevento 181, 238, 459, 524,
665–6, 813
Beowulf 535, 542, 639
Berach, St 333
Berbers 331m
Bereginy **434–5**, 645, 845
Berendt, John 267
Bergman, Ingmar 242, 265,
269, 274
Bergson, Henri 748
berserkers 42–3, 430, 544
Bertha, wife of Pepin 490
Bertha, wife of Robert II 490
Bes 301
Beta Israel 72
Bewitched 3, 10, 260, 308,
309–10, 312, 313
Bibby, Grandma 764
Bible 8–9, 27, 88–90, 139, 110,
176, 181, 322, 324, 449,
463, 449, 463, 465, 557,
601, 607, 637, 662, 663,
671, 728, 737, 766, 833
binding **326**
birch **156**
birth-spirit fairies **433–4**
Bishop, Bridget 693, 782
Black Annis 47, **535**
Black Death (Bubonic Plague)
174, 241, 242, 247, 249,
269, 389, 755, 772
Black Dogs 432
Black Herman's Secrets of Magic
132
Black Macbeth (*The Voodoo
Macbeth*) 264
Black Madonnas 394, 423, 631
Black Magic 717
Black Mass 145, **326–7**, 602
Black Peter 222, 406–7, 581–2
Black Pullet **120**, 127
Black Widow, The **226–7**
Black Widow spiders 94
Blair Witch Project, The **254–5**,
274
Blanckenstein, Chaterina
805
Blavatsky, Helena Petrova
711–14, 306, 722, 744,
760, 762
blessings 848–9
Blodeuwedd 80

Graymalkin 338
miller association 641
Pyewacket 254
see also fairy cats; witch-cat
tales
cattle and fertility 26–7
Catwoman 233
caul **328**, 354, 471
cauldrons 499, **689–91**
Cautio Criminalis (Spee) **146**,
804–5, 828
cave bears 42
Celestina, La (de Rojas) 225,
277–8
Celsus 737–8
Celtic calendar 540
Celtic deities *see* Badbh;
Brigid; Cernunnos; Lugh;
Maeve; Morgan le Fay
Celtic fairies *see* sidhe
Celtic festivals *see* Beltane;
Imbolc; Lughnasa;
Mabon; Samhain
Celtic hags *see* Beltane
Carline; Cailleach; Carlin;
Sheela na Gig
Celtic shamanism 652
Celtic tradition 184, 219, 433
antlered women 550
black-handled knives 685
cat goddesses 47
cat's eye gazing 446
cauldrons 689
crow/raven trickster heroes
52
fairies stealing midwives 486
goats 68
horned snakes 88
mistletoe 169
rowan dye 176
royal frogs 66
sacred groves 530
sacred pigs 81
willows in graveyards 183
wolfhound breeding 100
see also Druids
Celts 529, 676
cemeteries *see* burial grounds
Central Africa 247, 339
oracle boards 614
Central America 190
brooms 687
devil masks 698
jaguars 74
magic mirrors 699
moon–rabbit association 85
slit-drums 303
spirit-dogs 54
transformation 96–7
"vampiric" spirits 40
Central Asia 76
Turkic tribes 357, 633
Central Europe 443, 726, 727,
753, 847

coachmen 625
Devil's Grandmother 541
ergotism 427
fairy magicians 448
frog traditions and
fertility/as children's
souls 67
juniper–witchcraft
association 163
lucky chimney sweeps 558
lunar crayfish 519–20
millers 641
vampire–werewolf–witch
links 40, 357
Walpurgis Night 674
see also Krampus
Cerberus 55, 184, 387
Ceremonial Magic *see* High
Ceremonial/Ritual Magic
Ceres 200, 409, 410, **422–3**,
506, 509
identification with Demeter
83
Cernunhos 17, 218–19, 551,
558, 563, 578
Cerridwen 84, **378**, 499, 532,
689
chalice **691**
Chalice Well, Glastonbury
682
Challah 509
changelings 438, 444–6,
454–5
Chango 25, 351, 576, 696–7
Chang'o, Lady 520
Channel Islands 383
chanting 599
Chaos 404
Charlemagne, Emperor 100,
385, 795
Charles I of England 58, 747
Charles V, Emperor 729
Charles VI of France 622
Charles VII of France 739,
740, 741
Charles IX of France 139
Charles XI of Sweden 826
Charles the Bald 795
charm **328**
charm bags **597–9**
Charmed **311–12**
charmer **328**
charms and incantations
599–600
Charon 300, 626
Charos 626
Charovnik **328**
Chartres cathedral 333
Charun 626
Chatwin, Bruce 76
Chelmsford witch trials **788–9**
chemistry 590
chervioburgium **329**
Chesnutt, Charles W. 468

Chi, Qi **329**
chickens **50–1**, 677
Chile 666
Chiloé Island **666–7**
chimney sweeps 558–9
China 31, 108, 110, 158, 183,
184, 346, 688, 698, 713,
766, 847
black cats 49
bread-dough Buddhas 508
creation myths 607
erotic texts 304
female shamans 20, 550
fertility dolls 693
five-bat design 40
five elements 347
fox spirits 63, 64–5
frogs as yin 65
image magic 609
magpie bridge 77
moon cakes **520–1**
moon rabbit 85
Nu Kua 90, 607
playing cards 621
sand table oracles 614
scorpion symbolism 87
snakes and childbirth 88
spider myths 94
Step of Yu **248**
winning number spells 113
Chinese alchemy 586, **588–9**
Chinese astrology 593–4
Chiron 169, 750
Chocolat (Harris) **278**
chocolate 512
chovihano/chovihani **329**
Christ Principle 732
Christensen, Benjamin 261–2
Christian Cabala **611–12**, 707
Christian II, Elector of
Saxony 765
Christian demonology 553,
554
Christian II, Elector of
Saxony 765
Christianity 97, 130, 141, 152,
213, 264, 279, 380, 438,
469, 612, 658, 664, 665,
673, 674, 730, 732, 759,
768, 775, 782, 821, 822
animal masquerades banned
550–1
and apples 154
and astrology 592–3
and banniks 649
Basque conversion 778
Celsus' attack 737–8
Commanding and
Compelling 601
control in Ireland 449
cross 330, 854
and crossroads 655–6
dancing disapproved 236–7,
241

devil conception 541, 566,
559–60 562, 563–4 570
"double-faith" 491, 649
dream-books discouraged
113
and Druidry 332–3
and elder trees 159–60
Ember Days 333
Etruscan culture suppressed
135
fairy doctors condemned 447
fallen angels 440, 561
forced conversion 772
Freemasonry opposed 336
Glastonbury sacred 682
Gnostic influence 30–1
irrelevance to Wicca 326
and Jesus as magician 737
and Lake Pilato 676
Magi 377
and Manicheism 31, 32
midwives as villains 486
and music 301
and ouija boards 616
and Pagan deities 6, 47, 158,
368, 381, 383, 384, 390,
392, 398–9, 404, 409, 410,
413, 548–9, 551, 552, 561,
562–3, 568, 573, 637, 656,
680, 843
and Pagan festivals 56, 188,
190, 206, 208, 212, 218,
220, 222, 388
Pagan groves destroyed 663
Pagan oracles closed 577
Pagan shrines destroyed 375,
630
pig denigration 82
pork eating 81
and Pow-Wow 121
protective power 854
and reproductive issues 835
and ritual possession 617
rue blessed 377
runic texts destroyed 618
Satan–black association
473
Satan–crow association 52
Satan–miller identification
641
Satan–snake identification
90, 561
and Satanism 720
shamanism suppressed 345,
355, 625
"simony" 767
speculaas poppen banned
526
and Spiritism 353
theurgy suppressed 356
and tree devotion 182
violin disliked 305
and warlocks 361
and Wild Hunt 363

Encyclopedia of Witchcraft

Francis, Elizabeth 788–9
Frankenstein (Shelley) 261, 609
Franklin, William 110
Franks 329, 381
Frau Trude (Grimm) **472–4**
Frazer, James 169, 188, 381,
 753
Frederick II, Emperor 765
Freemasonry 213, **335–6**, 339,
 348, 359, 628, 631–2, 695,
 719, 749
 see also Egyptian Masonry
French Caribbean
 loups-garoux 104
 magic lamps 595
French colonial North
 America 744
French postmodernism 9–10
Freud, Sigmund 732
Freya 45, 47, 68, 84, 98, 169,
 195, 221, 223, 391, 352,
 357, 362, 363, 367, 368,
 369, 370, 371, **384–5**,
 405, 406, 503, 607, 618,
 626, 673, 674, 784, 839
Freyr 181, 223, 369, 371, 384,
 391, 437, 581, 635
Frigg 169, 219, 223
Frigga 367, **385–6**, 392, 405,
 473, 526, 547, 839
 and spinning **840**
Frizzly Rooster, The 50
Frog Prince, The 470
frogmouths **43–4**
frogs **65–7**
fruitful earth **23–8**
Fuld, William 615
*Funk and Wagnall's Standard
 Dictionary of Folklore,
 Mythology and Legend* 2, 8

Gabriel, Archangel 854
Gaia 68, 404
Gaiman, Neil 227, 230, 231
Gairdner, Grizel 732
Galanthis 62
Galeen, Henrik 253
Galileo Galilei 594
Gamache, Henri 126
Gandhi, Mohandas 714
Ganna 710
garaboncias **336**
Garden of Eden 89, 154, 181,
 400, 503
Gardner, Alan 732
Gardner, Gerald 109, 111,
 112, 113, 118, 194, 288,
 361, 660–1, 678, 705, 714,
 715, 720, 721, 723, **732–4,**
 741, 753, 759, 764, 768,
 770, 818
Garibaldi 712
Garnier, Gilles 104–5
Gasparutto, Paolo 813

Gast, Johann 729
Gaufridi, Louis 797
Gaule, John 792
Gaulish deities *see* Arduinna;
 Teutates
Gaulish tradition 208, 218,
 526, 550, 604
Gauric, Luc 756, 757
Gebelin, Antoine Court de
 621
Gelasius, Pope 737
Gellért Hill **674**
Gent, P. F. 283
Geoffrey of Monmouth 403,
 739, 753
George II 793
George, St 92, 257, 637
Gerard, John 164
German–American tradition
 121, 222, 582, 627
German–Jewish tradition 509
Germanic spirits *see* Rübezahl;
 Nixie; White Women
Germanic calendar 206–7, 221
Germanic deities *see* Herta;
 Hulda; Ostara; Perchta;
 Weird Sisters
Germanic shamanism 652
Germanic tradition 94, 159,
 219, 638
 alraune 166–7, 252, 276, 323
 braid/braided loaf offerings
 508–9
 henbane 162
 Eve of St Lucy's 195
 goat-tallow spell 68
 lebkuchen 526
 mistletoe 169
 Mother's Night 222
 snake guardian Unke 90
 wagon processions 626
 Wild Hunt 363
 wolf–witch association 101
Germany 171, 192, 284, 293,
 385, 710, 723, 729, 730,
 735, 758, 765
 "corpse washerwoman" 833
 cartomancy 621
 chromolithography 320
 elder "palms" 160
 ergot 427, 429
 folk magic 121, 123, 327
 fairy tales 463
 Freya revival 47
 Geisterwegen 452
 hex signs 619
 hexe (nightjars) 44
 hexensessel 152
 Hulda processionals 392
 kraut **341**
 krauthexen **341**
 lucky chimney sweeps 558
 Maitrank (May Wine) 520
 pentagram talismans 700

Perchtennacht 245
pig-sty dream incubation 84
Rye Wolf 429
*Sixth and Seventh Books of
 Moses* 130–1
toad–witchcraft association
 66
witch/witchcraft synonyms
 323, 339, 346, 357
witch craze 11, 49, 139, 140,
 141, 143, 146, 316, 350,
 474, 625, 753, 754, 773,
 774, 775, **800–5**, 828,
 836–7,
 Yule celebrations 223
 see also Brocken; Horselberg;
 Walpurgis
Ghana 346, 693
giants 536, **542–3**
Gifford, George **141**
Gilgamesh 397, 506
Gilles de Rais 740
Gimbutas, Marija 17, 382,
 425, 696
ginseng 175
Ginzburg, Carlo 754
Ginzburg, Louis 168
Giselle 444
Glamis, Lady 818
glamour, glamoury **336**, 349
Glapion, Louis Christophe
 Dominic Duminy de
 744–5
Glastonbury 644, 682
Glendower, Owen 764
Glover, Mrs 780
Gnosticism 9, 30, 89, 738
 Simonian 767, 768
goat dance **242–3**
Goat Foot God, The (Fortune)
 452, 578
goat god **567**
goats **67–8**, 210, 323, 508,
 556, 561, 626
 devil association 44, 68, 242,
 548–9, 560
goddesses and gods 367–416
Goebbels, Josef 736
goes/goetes **336–7**
Goethe, Johann Wolfgang von
 283, 284, 292, 293, 716
goetia, goeteia **337**
goetic magic **337**
Gogol, Nikolai 266, 672
Golden Ass, The (Lucius
 Apuleius) 57, 61, 80, **285**,
 355, 665, 693
Golden Bough, The (Frazer)
 169, 188, 381, 753
Golden Dawn 114, 122, **337**,
 714, 720, 721, 731, 732,
 747, 748, 749
Golden Fleece 750
Göldi, Anna 827

Golem 225, 609–10
Golem, The **260–1**
Good Friday Eve 669
good people 337
Good, Dorcas 783
Good, Sarah 782, 783
Gooderidge, Alice 791
goodfellow **337**
Goodwin witch trials **779–80**
Goofer Dust 685
Goophered Grapevine, The
 (Chesnutt) 468, 469
Goose, Elizabeth Foster 490
Gorgons 387
Gospel of John 738
Gospel of Mark 239, 390
Gospel of Matthew 239, 360,
 738
Goths 338
Gowdie, Isobel 86, 217, 460,
 822–3
Goya 68, 314, **317–18**, 323,
 552
 Black Paintings 318
 Caprices **317–18**
 Witchcraft Paintings **318**
grabancijas **336**
Gradlon, King of Cornwall
 379, 380
Grahame, Richard 821
Grand Grimoire **122–3**, 124,
 127–8, 131
Grand Zombi 247, 745
Grandier, Urbain 797–80
Graves, Robert 519, 577
graveyard dirt 653
Gray Wolf's Ha'nt, The
 (Chesnutt) 468–9
Great Albert, The **123**, 710
Great Mother *see* Earth
 Mother
Great Rite 186, 218, **337–8**,
 691
Greece 165, 843
 goat dance 242
 love spell 690
 red Easter eggs 193
Greek mythology 19, 61, 90,
 230, 284, 300, 304, 463,
 574, 629, 664, 693, 696,
Green Man 382, 472
Greenland 359, 385
Greensmith, Rebecca 779
Gregory IX, Pope 49, 806
Gregory of Tours 381
Gregory the Great, Pope 563
Grendel 535, 542
Grenier, Jean 105–6
Greyerz, Peter von 827
Grid 542
Grien, Hans Baldung 314, 316
Grierson, Isobel 49
Griffin, Maurice 448
Griggs, William 782

Encyclopedia of Witchcraft

witchcraze 807, **813**
Polanski, Roman **264**, 268
Polar Bear King, The 407, 547
Polar Bear King Valemon 547
Poludnica **425**
Pomba Gira 566, 655, 656
Pomona 202–3, 503
Pontius Pilate 675, 738
Ponty, Jean-Luc 262
Poor Richard's Almanac 110
"popular art" 314
popular songs **307**
Portugal 97, 122
  witchcraze 806
Poseidon 573–4, 581
Potocki, Jean 106
Potts, Thomas 790
power doctors **349**
Pow-Wow 121, 130–1, 339,
  349–50, 600
  hexenmeister **339**
Pre-Raphaelites 318–20
Prince Danila Govorila **493**
Princess and the Goblin, The
  (MacDonald) 847
printing press 108, 116, 314
Priory of Sion 631
processions **245–6**
Proclus 356, 589
Proctor, John and Elizabeth
  282
Proserpina 108, 384, **409–10**,
  423, 665; *see also*
  Persephone
protective measures **853–5**
Protestantism 141, 336, 347,
  755
Protestants 139, 322, 527,
  786
Psyche 626
psychic visions 603
psychopomps 325, **350**, 389,
  433, 531–2, 539
Ptah 15
Ptolemy II 133
Pueblo Indians 63, 97, 98
Puerto Rico 65
Pullman, Philip 20, 287
pumpkins **521–2**
Punic War 50
Punt 38
Puritans 144, 222, 282, 688,
  781, 788, 792
Puss in Boots 639, 640
Putnam, Anne 668, 783
Puy de Dôme 208, **676–7**
pysanky 193
Pythagoras **759–60**

Qabala **612**
qosem **350**
Queen of Heaven 511
Queen of Sheba 399, 489
Quetzalcoatl 91, 414, 512

Quine, Richard 253

Ra 38, 394, 415, 568, 841
rabbits **85–6**
Rabelais, François 723
Rabenalt, Arthur Maria 253
Rachel 165
Ràcz, Erzsébet 460
Ragana **410**, 438
Randolph, Paschal Beverly
  347, 721, **760–2**
rapunzel (rampion) **522**
Rashi 685
Rategno, Bernado 372
Ratherius, Bishop of Verona
  390
Ratoff, Gregory 717
ravens 51–2, **376**
Raziel, Angel 107, 116
Read, Donna 256
Rebennack, Mac 741
Red Dragon, The **127–8**
Red Shoes, The 482
Reeves, Michael 257
Reeves, Washington 764
Regino of Prüm 381
Regino, Bishop 784
rhizotomoki **350**
rhythm and blues **307–8**
Rice Mother 425
Rice, Ann 289
Richelieu, Cardinal 797, 798
Rigaud, Milo 414
Rimsky-Korsakov, Nikolai 672
ring dance **238**
ring forts *see* fairy forts
Ring of the Nibelungs, The 391
ritual possession **616–17**
Robin Goodfellow **579**
Robin Hood 658
Robinson, Stepney 716
Rod **579**, 580
Rolling Stones, The 293
Roman Catholicism 123, 126,
  190, 268, 293, 347, 348,
  357, 411, 717, 736, 779
  and Black Mass 326
  Canon Episcopi **784**
  communion wafers 424
  exorcism 455, 457, 602
  Holy Cards 688
  Jews/witches 351
  and Manicheism 31
  saints syncretized 205, 351,
    359, 371, 405
  and Santeria 351–2

werewolf beliefs 103–4
  and witchcraze 785–6, 795,
    797, 824
  see also Inquisition; Spanish
    Inquisition
Roman Catholic festivals *see*
  All Hallows Eve; All
  Saint's Day; Candlemas
Roman Catholics 780, 788,
  821
Roman Empire 57, 371, 515,
  685, 768
  Christianity official 785
Romania 84, 242, 305, 354,
  382, 391, 451, 558, 658
  fairy magicians 451
  goat dance 242
Romany people 484, 520, 707,
  772, 773–4
  ironworking clans 634
  love of violins 305
  Netotsi 658
  New Forest 661, 745
  San Cipriano 122
  Satan association 564
  tarantism 249
  Tarot origins 621, 622
Romany fairies *see* Keshalyi
Romany tradition 121, 232,
  339, 433
  banshees 325
  black cats 49
  chovihano/chovihani **329**
  datura 158
  drabarni **331**
  drabengro **331**
  drum divination 302
  jumping the broomstick 688
  magic elm wands 161
  menstrual curse 852
  mullo 690
  orchid root gathering 168
  pig-sty dream incubation 84
  putzi (charm bags) 597
  violin music 306
  wolf–witch association 101
Romulus and Remus 101, 200,
  209, 210
Roosevelt, Franklin 264
root doctor, root woman, root-
  worker **350** *see also*
  Buzzard, Dr
roots 175–6
Rosemary's Baby 266, **268**
Rosenberg, Ethel and Julius
  281
Rosicrucians 765
Rosmerta 91
Ross, Balthasar 801
round dance **238**
rowan **176–7**, 855
rowan 855
Rowling, J. K. 14, 94, 261, 286,
  444

Rozhanitsy (fate fairies) 649
Rozhanitsy (horned) **579–80**
Rübezahl **410–11**, 673
Rübezahl's Wedding 411
Rucker, "Black" Herman 132,
  336, **762–4**
Rudolph II, Emperor 726,
  729, 743
Rudolph II of Bohemia 588
rue **177–8**, 326
Rügen Island 391, **663–4**
Rugeviet 664
Rugiu Boba **425**
Rumpelstiltskin 639–40
rune-caster **351**
runes 176, **350–1**, 510,
  617–19
  banned in Iceland 806
  see also Hag Rune
Rural (Lesser) Dionysia 222
Rus 533
Rusalka 415, 431, 435, 436,
  439–40, 483, 492, 645,
  659, 711–12
Russia 123, 150, 157, 212, 273,
  529, 711, 712, 745, 843
  banias (bathhouses) **647–9**
  birch bark "paper" 156
  botanical magic 672
  bread ladders 508
  Charovnik **328**
  chernobyl (mugwort) 169
  Christmas celebrations
    222
  dark half of the year 218
  Devil's Grandmother 541
  "double-faith" 491, 649
  ergotism 426
  foot-track magic 688
  Herod's Daughters 391
  Ivan Kupalo **205–6**
  magic word charms 600
  magpie-witches 77
  masks 698
  mushroom spirits 153–4
  ovinnik (cat spirit) 49
  story-telling condemned 464
  transformation 96, 98
  whispering spells 523
  witch synonyms 8, 341, 358,
    832
  witchcraze 774, **816–18**
Russian spirits *see* banniks;
  Leshii; Leshovhika;
  Rusalka; Vodianoi
Russia deities *see* Baba Yaga;
  Mokosh; Poludnica;
  Rod
Russian fairy tales 461, 463,
  473–4, **491–7**
Ryall, Rhiannon 452, 686
Rye Mother 426, 427, 429,
  430
Rye Wolf **429–30**

Vanir, Vana **358**, 369, 370–1, 384, 391
vardlokkur 361
Vasilisa the Wise 473, 475–6, **494–6**
Vatican 143, 268, 336, 424, 709, 730
Vatican Library 123, 135, 138, 738
Vavra, Otakar 271–2
ved'ma, ved'mak, ved'mar **358**, 361
Veleda 710
veneficia, venefica **358**
Venerable Bede 222
Venus of Willendorf 16
vernal equinox 85, 192, 213, 363, 371
Vertigo Comics 227, 228, 230, 231, 234
Vertumnus 202–3
vervain **182**
Vestal Virgins 201
vetulae **358**
Vidar 543
Vietnam 52
Vietnamese astrology 593
View of the Duplicity of the Messengers of Evil, A (de Lancre) **144**
Vigoreux, Madame 798–9
Vij, The (Gogol) 266
Vila, Wila, Veles, Veela, Vily 415, 433, 434, 435, **443–4**, 451, 645, 659
violins **305–7**
Virbius 381, 541, **583**, 663
Virgil 386, 612, **768–9**
visual arts **313–21**
Vital, Chaim 610
vitki 361
Vivien 752
vjestica **358**, 361
Vodianoi 641–2
Vodo **359**
Vodou, Vodoun 130, 336, 347, **359–60**, 365, 407, 550, 565, 607, 679
  Masonic components 213
  paket kongo **348**
  parade of spirits 245
  pumpkins 522
  ritual possession 616
  veves 619
volkhv/volkva **358**
Volsung Saga 92
Voluspa, The 359
völva **359**, 371, 384
von Dornheim, Gottfried Johann Georg II Fuchs 801–2
von Ehrenberg, Phillipp Adolf 803
Voodoo 121, **360**, 565

"Voodoo dolls" 607
Vortigern 629
vucodlak **360**
Vulcan 636
Vulgate Cycle 402

Wadjet 91
Wagner, Richard 391
Waite, Arthur E. 122, 129, 131, 337, 622, 720
Wajda, Andrzej 269
Wales 188, 207–8
  owl hooting 81
  rowan trees 177
  Three Spirit Nights **219**
  see also Druids: Cerridwen
"Walnut Witches" 665
Walpurga 220, 562
Walpurga, St 220
Walpurgis 151, 152, 192, **220–1**, 284, 385, 673–4
Walton, Charles 794–5
Waluberg 710
Wandering Jew 413, 719
wands 182, 697, **703–4**; *see also* thyrsus
wanga **360**
Warboys Witches **789–90**
ward, warding **360**
warlock 254, 311, **360–1**
Warren Magazines 233
Waterhouse, Agnes 788
Waterhouse, Joan 788
Waterhouse, John William 319
Waters, Muddy 307
Watkins, Alfred 451–2
Wayland the Smith 248, **638–9**
weasels **59–62**
Webster's Seventh New Collegiate Dictionary 1
Wegener, Paul 260, 261
Weiditz II, Hans 317
Weird Sisters 260, **843**
Weird Woman 267, **271**
Well of Urd 682, 838, 842
Welles, Orson 251, **264–5**, 310, 715, 717
wells **681–2**
Wells, H. G. 745
Welsh deities *see* Cerridwen
Welsh Romany lore 325
Welsh spirits *see* Tylwyth Teg
Wends 425
Wendy the Good Little Witch **233–4**
Wenger, Suzanne 664–5
werewolf panic 102, 104, 1 45
werewolf-transformation ointment 695
werewolves 95, **102–6**, 381, 429–30; *see also* vucodlak

West Africa 247, 338, 339, 359, 407, 663, 670, 734
West African deities *see* Eshu-Elegbara; Ogun
West Country Wicca (Ryall) 452
West, Kipling 73
Western alchemy **586–8**
Western Asia 53, 162–3, 386, 393
Western Europe 272, 427, 438
  ergotism 427
Weyer, Johann 125, 140, **146**, 709, 729
Wheel of the Year 217, 351
whispering 354, **361**, 500, 523, 599
White Goddess, The (Graves) 519
White Women **415**
Whittle, Anne (Old Chattox) 790, 791
Wicca 2, 112, 187, 226, 287, 299, 310, 312, 319, 326, 348, **361–2**, 686, 723, 732, 764
  cakes-and-ale ritual 510
  definition 13
  Dianic 715–16
  esbat 194
  Gardnerian 13, 118, 258, 288, 714, 720, 732, 733, 753, 768
  handfasting 688
  horned helmets 695
  New Forest 660
  PectiWicca 715
  sacred sites 644
  Seax-Wicca 695
  solitary 724
  widdershins 362
Wiccan Books of Shadows 111–13
Wiccan Rede 721
Wiccan sabbats 214, **217–18**, 351 *see also* Beltane; Imbolc; Lammas, Litha, Lughnasa; Mabon; Ostara; Yule
Wiccan tools *see* athamé; bolline; chalice; cingulam; pentacle; swords
wicca/wicce, definition 13
Wiccan, definition 13
Wiccans 111, 311, 386
  in Salem 668
Wicked: The Life and Times of the Wicked Witch of the North (Maguire) **295**
widdershins **362**
Widow's Broom, The (Allsburg) 688
Wilcock, John 110

Wild Hunt 54, 195, 201, 219, 220, 223, 244–5, 246, **362–3**, 390, 391, 392, 404, 406, 409, 568, 578, 580, 654
Wild Swans, The 172, **484–5**
Wilde, Oscar 469, 576, 577
will o' the wisps 679
William Rufus 660
William the Conqueror 660
Williams, Abigail 282, 782
Williamson, Cecil 678, 734, 768, **769–70**, 774, 789
Willibrord 181
willow **182–3**, 679
Wilson, Monique (Lady Olwen) 714, 715, 734
Windsor witches **789**
winter solstice 103, 175, 204, 217, 221, 362, 526, 580, 715
witch
  archetypal 3
  definitions 1–2, 13
  as insult 6
  meanings 2–5
  power of **855**
  telltale clues 12
Witch, The (Middleton) 292
Witch: The Wild Ride from Wicked to Wicca 4
witch boards **614–16**
witch-cat tales **498**
Witch Hammer (film) **271–2**
Witch Hammer (Kaplicky) **295–6**
Witch Hunter Robin 299
Witch's Brew **525**
witch's butter **525**
witch's egg **525**
Witch's Ladder 692
witch's mark **830**
witch's supper **527**
witch's tit **830**
Witchcraft Act, England
  (1562) 788
  (1604) 789, 791, 821
  (1736) 793–4
  repeal (1951) 109, 294, 678, 732, 734, 794, 795
Witchcraft Act, Ireland
  (1586) 810
  repealed (1821) 812
Witchcraft Act, Scotland
  (1563) 818
witchcraft
  author's perceptions 10–11
  definitions 5, 13
  elements of 14–33
  and fun 9
  and healing 7, 605
  and knowledge 8–9
  and magic 5
  and misogyny 6–7

Encyclopedia of Witchcraft

ENCYCLOPEDIA
OF 5,000
SPELLS

the ultimate reference book
for the magical arts

Judika Illes

ENTER THE WORLD OF FOLKLORE, MYTH, AND MAGIC

Spanning five thousand years of magical history from Earth's every corner, this book is the definitive magic reference book for all devotees of the magical arts.

Since the dawning of human history, the goal of magic has always been the improved quality of life. The *Encyclopedia of 5,000 Spells* is a comprehensive treasure trove of spells and rituals rooted in magical and spiritual traditions from all over the world. It contains unusual information for the skilled practitioner, clear instructions for the newcomer, as well as a wealth of fascinating information for the curious. This master spell book has a place in our collective imaginations.

Discover binding spells and banishing spells, spells for love, luck, wealth, power, better sex, spiritual protection, physical healing, enhanced fertility, and much much more.

Encyclopedia of 5,000 Spells
— the ultimate reference book for the magical arts.
ISBN 978–0–06–171123–7